New Jersey Pennsylvania

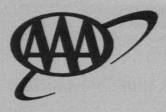

Published by:

AAA Publishing
1000 AAA Drive
Heathrow, FL 32746-5063

Valid through April 1999

The publisher is not responsible for changes that occur after publication. Published for the exclusive use of members. Not for sale.

Send Written Comments To:

AAA Member Comments
Box 61, 1000 AAA Drive
Heathrow, FL 32746-5063

Advertising Rate and Circulation Information
Call: (407) 444-8280

Printed in the USA
by Quebecor Printing, Buffalo, NY

Cover: *Morristown National Historical Park, NJ*
© Jeff Gnass

Stock #4617

Introduction

Tell us what you think 5
How the book is organized 5
What the color bars mean 5

About Attractions

Schedules and prices 7
Reading the listings 7
Maps 7
Admission discounts 8
Golden passports 8

Attractions

■ NEW JERSEY 11
Fast Facts 12
For Your Information 13
Index to Starred Attractions 15
Recreation Areas Chart 16
Points of Interest 18
  Atlantic City and Vicinity 19

■ PENNSYLVANIA 52
Fast Facts 53
For Your Information 54
Recreation Areas Chart 56
Index to Starred Attractions 58
Points of Interest 62
  Pennsylvania Dutch Country 99
  Philadelphia and Vicinity............. 106
  Pittsburgh and Vicinity................ 133
  Pocono Mountains Area 146

About Lodgings & Restaurants

Using lodging listings 163
What the SAVE means 163
What the ⊕ or ⊛ means 163
Rate options and discounts 164

Maps 164
Making reservations 165
Lodging Reservation and Deposit
  Definitions 165
Guest safety 166
Hotel/Motel fire safety 166
Access for disabled 167
The 🔷 Diamonds 168
Lodging Classifications 169
Sample Lodging Listing 170
Lodging Evaluation Criteria 170

Lodgings & Restaurants

▧ NEW JERSEY 171
  Atlantic City 171

▧ PENNSYLVANIA 254
  Pennsylvania Dutch Country 330
  Philadelphia & Vicinity 352
  Pittsburgh & Vicinity 395
  Pocono Mountains Area 417

Maps

New Jersey Orientation 15
Atlantic City 21
Pennsylvania Orientation 58
Gettysburg National Military Park 81
Harrisburg 83
Hershey 86
Pennsylvania Dutch Country 100
Philadelphia Downtown 109
Pittsburgh 135

Accommodations:
Atlantic City 172
New Jersey Metro Area 206
Newark to Paramus 210
Harrisburg 292
Pennsylvania Dutch Country 330
Philadelphia Downtown 354
Philadelphia and Vicinity 368
Pittsburgh Downtown 396
Pittsburgh & Vicinity 401
Pocono Mountains Area and
  Vicinity 418

For Your Information

🔷 Offices 452
Temperature Chart 454
Driving Distances 455

AAA SUPERNUMBER®
1-800-AAA-HELP

For 24-hour road service when away from home and unable to find AAA or CAA in the phone book. 1-800-955-4TDD for hearing impaired. 3

Indexes

Points of Interest 457
🔳 Attraction Admission Discount
  Index 472
Bed & Breakfast Lodgings 473
Country Inns 474
Historical Lodgings &
  Restaurants 474
Resorts 475

What's your MPG? Find out in four easy steps:

Step 1: Fill your tank completely and write down your odometer reading.

Step 2: When it's time to refuel, again fill your tank completely and write down your odometer reading. Also write down how many gallons of fuel your tank took.

Step 3: Subtract your first odometer reading from your second odometer reading.

Step 4: Divide the result of Step 3 by how many gallons your tank took during your second refueling. This result is your MPG – miles per gallon.

When traveling away from home...

SUPERNUMBER®
1-800-AAA-HELP

a 24-hour, toll-free, Emergency Road Service information system.

It's easy to use:

Look in the white pages of the telephone book for a listing under "AAA" in the United States or "CAA" in Canada, since road service is dispatched by the local club in many communities.

If there is no listing, have your membership card handy and call:

SUPERNUMBER®, 1-800-AAA-HELP, for the nearest road service facility.

SUPERNUMBER®, is available in the United States and Canada 24 hours a day, but **only** for Emergency Road Service and **only** when traveling outside the area served by your home club. Contact the nearest club office regarding other services you may require.

Introduction

*W*E'RE glad you selected the AAA TourBook to help you plan your trip. You can trust AAA to give you objective information; no attraction, lodging or restaurant pays for a listing. Each is listed on the basis of merit alone after being carefully evaluated by a AAA/CAA inspector or designated representative. An establishment's decision to advertise has no bearing on its inspection, evaluation or rating. Advertising for services or products does not imply AAA endorsement.

We work hard to give you the most accurate information available. All information in this TourBook was reviewed before publication for accuracy at press time; however, changes often occur between annual editions. We've included phone numbers in the listings so that you can confirm prices and schedules.

Tell us what you think

We encourage you to tell us what we need to improve and what we have done well. We reply to thousands of letters from members every year, and your good ideas are reflected in our products and services.

Please report both pleasant and unpleasant experiences to your local AAA/CAA club, or write directly to AAA Member Comments, 1000 AAA Dr., Box 61, Heathrow, FL 32746-5063.

How the book is organized

The AAA TourBook contains two sections: attractions, and lodgings and restaurants. Both sections list towns or designated places in alphabetical order, and the attractions or facilities are then listed in alphabetical order under the appropriate town. Attractions and AAA RATED® lodgings and restaurants are listed in this book under the name of the city or town in which they physically are located or in some circumstances under the nearest recognized city or town. Use AAA/CAA maps in conjunction with this book when planning a trip.

Major metropolitan areas are organized in separate sections and have expanded treatments. A description of the primary city is presented first, followed by a listing of communities in the vicinity. These AAA/CAA Defined Metro Areas were modeled on U.S. and Canadian government definitions based on economic and social interaction among residents of the core city and surrounding communities. Cities and towns grouped under a

metropolitan area's vicinity heading will have cross references where they would typically be alphabetized in the Attractions and Lodgings & Restaurants sections.

Destination areas also have been identified for regions with broad tourist appeal. Towns in these geographic areas are organized alphabetically under the destination area's title. Towns grouped under destination areas have appropriate cross-references inserted where they would normally be alphabetized in the Attractions and Lodgings & Restaurant sections.

Maps created specifically for this book have precise purposes and should be used in *conjunction* with the more complete sheet maps and Triptik maps provided by your AAA/CAA travel counselor. To ensure your complete satisfaction, use book maps as *supplementary* guides only.

What the color bars mean

In TourBooks that contain more than one state or province, you will notice the presence of bars of color along the page edges. The purpose of these bars is to color code corresponding state or province sections. For example, the New Jersey At-

tractions section will contain the same color bar code as the New Jersey Lodgings & Restaurants section. This coding allows the reader to conveniently flip back and forth between the pertinent sections of the state.

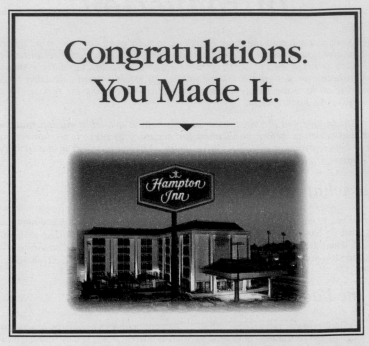
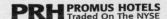

About Attractions

The Attractions section of your TourBook serves as a guide to selected places rather than as a commercial, geographic or promotional encyclopedia. Communities or areas included offer something for you to do or see that sets them apart from others in the area or nation. We call these "points of interest."

Schedules and prices

All information was reviewed before publication for accuracy at press time. However, changes often occur between annual editions. We regret any inconvenience resulting from such instances, but they are beyond our control. Please use the phone numbers in the listings if you wish to confirm prices. Prices pertaining to attractions in the United States are quoted in U.S. dollars; Canadian province and territory attraction prices are quoted in Canadian dollars.

Reading the listings

Any attraction with a separate heading has been approved by a AAA/CAA field inspector or designated AAA/CAA representative. An attraction's quality is reflected in the length and scope of its general description. We have placed a star (★) before attractions of exceptional interest and quality. An index to starred attractions appears with the orientation map. *(See Maps, below.)* Stand alone casino gambling operations—those establishments that are not contained within hotels—are not inspected and are presented for informational purposes only.

In most cases, distances given are computed from the center of town, unless otherwise specified, using the following highway designations: I (interstate highway), US (federal highway), Hwy. (Canadian highway), SR (state route), CR (county road), FM (farm to market road), FR (forest road), MM (mile marker).

Descriptive information about the attraction follows the location description. Next come the days, hours and seasons the attraction is *open*. These may be preceded by a suggested minimum visiting time. Following are admission prices quoted *without* sales tax; children under the lowest age specified are admitted free when accompanied by an adult. Days, months and age groups written with a hyphen are *inclusive*.

Credit cards accepted for admissions or fares may be indicated at the end of the listing as follows: AE, American Express; CB, Carte Blanche; DI, Diners Club; DS, Discover; JCB, Japanese Credit Bureau; MC, MasterCard; VI, VISA. Minimum amounts that may be charged appear in parentheses when applicable.

Maps

State, province or territory orientation maps appear before the Points of Interest listings in the Attractions section. Their purpose is to illustrate the relative positions of towns, recreation facilities and starred points of interest listed in TourBooks. Only major road networks are portrayed on these maps.

Coordinates (for example: A-3) following the place or city names in the Points of Interest listings refer to this map; stars next to town names on the maps indicate the presence of highly recommended attractions. An index to starred attractions appears with or adjacent to each orientation map.

City maps show metropolitan areas where numerous attractions are concentrated. While reading an attraction description, refer to this map to see where it is located in relation to major roads, parks, airports, etc.

Walking or Self-Guiding tour maps provide an exceptional level of detail, showing specific routes corresponding to text in the TourBooks. Well-known buildings are often outlined for easier identification. Routes are well-marked with beginning and ending points as well as directional arrows.

National park maps familiarize drivers with the area in and around the park. The main features depicted are mountains, streams, hiking trails, canyons, ice fields, etc. Some of the campground sites and lodges spotted on the maps do not meet AAA/CAA criteria, but have been listed as a service to members who wish to stay at these facilities.

Admission discounts

Your AAA/CAA membership card is the key to reduced prices at many attractions because they value your patronage and respect the AAA/CAA name. A [SAVE] icon appearing in an attraction listing indicates that a discount is offered to holders of a AAA/CAA membership card, AAA MasterCard, AAA VISA or international Show Your Card & Save discount card. The discount must be at least 10% and must be offered to all age groups. **Note:** If only a senior discount is offered, the attraction will not receive the [SAVE] icon. Senior citizen rates are already listed in the normal attraction rate structure.

Whether or not a listing shows the icon, present your valid AAA or CAA membership card when purchasing tickets; some attractions not formally enrolled in the program may still give members a discount. A full list of participating attractions appears in the Indexes section of this book. Discounts are offered for the validity period noted on the title page of this book. The discount may not apply if any other price reduction is offered or if tickets are purchased through an outlet other than the attraction's ticket office. In addition, discounts may not apply during special events or particular days or seasons; phone ahead to confirm.

Some AAA/CAA clubs sell tickets for area attractions; phone the local club to confirm.

Golden passports

Citizens or permanent residents of the United States who are 62 and older can obtain Golden Age Passports for a one-time $10 fee. Golden Access Passports are free to citizens or permanent residents of the United States (regardless of age) who are medically blind or permanently disabled. Both cover entrance fees for the holder and accompanying private party to all national parks and historic sites, monuments and battlefields within the U.S. national park system, plus half off camping and other fees. Apply in person at most federally operated areas.

The Golden Eagle Passport is available to everyone, despite country of origin. It costs $50 annually and covers entrance fees for the holder and accompanying private party to all federally operated areas. Obtain the pass in person at any national park or regional office of the U.S. Park Service or Forest Service.

Now AAA can help you shop overseas without any exchanges.

 ## With delivery of foreign cash to your door.

Whether you're going for the shopping, the culture, the cuisine, or to see the sights, the last place you want to end up on your vacation is waiting in line, wasting precious vacation time exchanging your dollars and worrying about the fees. That's why AAA and American Express® are offering this exciting new service. With just a phone call, you can now order all the foreign cash and American Express® Foreign Currency Travelers Cheques you need to take on your trip, and have it conveniently delivered to your home or office before you go.

That way, all you're exchanging is a lot of hassle for more time enjoying the vacation experience of a lifetime. To order foreign cash or American Express® Foreign Currency Travelers Cheques for your next trip, call your local AAA, today.

Travel with someone you trust.®

Travelers Cheques

West Point

major balloon festivals

280 historical sites

extraordinary inns

4,000 lakes

winter olympic training facility

historical ports

trophy fresh and salt water fishing

unforgettable foliage

6.5 million wilderness acres

world-class golf courses

fun parks

64 performing arts centers

world-class wineries

WHAT DID YOU EXPECT.

THIS IS NEW YORK.

exciting alpine and nordic ski areas

mountain biking

dude ranches

I ♥ NY.

CALL 1-800-I LOVE NY EXT. 254

http://iloveny.state.ny.us

George E. Pataki, Governor, State of New York

Charles A. Gargano, Chairman, Empire State Development

whitewater rafting

Lady Liberty

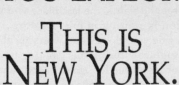

Princeton University

New Jersey

An introduction to the state's history, geography, economy and recreation

NEW JERSEY IS A STUDY IN CONTRASTS. ONLY FOUR STATES ARE SMALLER IN LAND AREA; FEWER THAN 10 HAVE A LARGER POPULATION. A TRANSPORTATION SYSTEM THAT IS AMONG THE NATION'S BUSIEST SNAKES THROUGH STRETCHES OF PINE FOREST AND THE ROLLING GREEN HILLS OF HORSE COUNTRY. KNOWN AS THE GARDEN STATE, NEW JERSEY ALSO IS ONE OF THE COUNTRY'S MOST URBANIZED AREAS. WHILE BEDROOM COMMUNITIES AND HISTORIC TOWNS FORM INTERLOCKING WEBS OF BUSINESS AND COMMERCE, ATLANTIC CITY OFFERS A GLITTERING GETAWAY.

HISTORY

In 1524 only the shorebirds and the Lenape Indians knew the New Jersey coast, and Giovanni de Verrazano's brief appearance in that year did not interfere with their dominion. In 1609 Henry Hudson claimed the area for the Dutch. By 1623 the land was called New Netherland, and busy trading settlements had sprung up along the Hudson and Delaware rivers. New Sweden was established along the Delaware River for several decades in the mid-1600s before the Dutch captured the rival colony.

When England assumed control of New Netherland in 1664, New Jersey was part of the area deeded by King Charles II to his brother James, Duke of York. The duke granted the region between the two rivers to John Berkeley, Baron of Stratton, and to Sir George Carteret. Carteret, former governor and defender of the Isle of Jersey, named the colony.

In 1676 Berkeley sold his portion of the land to English Quakers who formed a business called the Board of Proprietors of West Jersey. Carteret was bought out by the East Jersey Board of Proprietors in 1682. In 1702 the boards relinquished the right to govern the colony to the Crown, which was then responsible for appointing a royal governor.

Anti-British sentiment grew, fueled by commercial limitations imposed by England and the constant conflict among the proprietors, the popular assemblies and the royal governors.

The first provincial congress met in New Brunswick in 1774 to appoint delegates to the proposed Continental Congress at Philadelphia. By mid-1776 the last royal governor was deposed; on July 2 the provincial congress adopted a combined state constitution and declaration of independence.

Four times during the Revolutionary War the Continental Army crossed the state; Washington made his headquarters at Morristown during two harsh winters and at Camp Middlebrook near Somerville during the mild winter of 1778-79. Among the more than 100 battles fought on New Jersey soil were the engagements of Trenton, Princeton and Monmouth. Twice New Jersey claimed the nation's capital: Congress met at Princeton in 1783 and at Trenton in 1784.

On Dec. 18, 1787, New Jersey ratified the Constitution. Earlier the state had left its mark on that document by advocating equal state representation in the Senate. Trenton was designated the state capital in 1790.

Diversified industrial development began early, aided by ample water power, excellent harbors and the construction of canals and railroads. The machinery for the *Savannah*, the first steamship to cross the Atlantic, was built near Morristown. The first industrial city—later called Paterson—grew up around a textile-printing establishment on the Passaic River.

New Jersey, though suffering the same internal dissension as the other states, fought fiercely for the Union during the Civil War. Growing distrust of the corporate giants resulted in the antitrust laws of 1913, popularized by Gov. Woodrow Wilson. In response to the needs of World Wars I

Fast Facts

POPULATION: 7,988,000.

AREA: 7,836 square miles; ranks 46th.

CAPITAL: Trenton.

HIGHEST POINT: 1,803 ft., High Point.

LOWEST POINT: Sea level, Atlantic Ocean.

TIME ZONE: Eastern. DST.

MINIMUM AGE FOR DRIVERS: 17.

MINIMUM AGE FOR GAMBLING: 21.

SEAT BELT/CHILD RESTRAINT LAWS: Seat belts required for driver and front-seat passengers; child restraints required for under 5.

HELMETS FOR MOTORCYCLISTS: Required.

RADAR DETECTORS: Permitted.

FIREARMS LAWS: Contact the New Jersey State Police Division Headquarters, Firearms Investigation Unit, P.O. Box 7068, West Trenton, NJ 08628-0068; phone (609) 882-2000, ext. 2663-2667 or 2316.

HOLIDAYS: Jan. 1; Martin Luther King Jr.'s Birthday, Jan. (3rd Mon.); Presidents Day, Feb. (3rd Mon.); Memorial Day, May (last Mon.); July 4; Labor Day, Sept. (1st Mon.); Columbus Day, Oct. (2nd Mon.); Election Day, Nov. (1st Tues.); Veterans Day, Nov. 11; Thanksgiving; Dec. 25.

TAXES: New Jersey's statewide sales tax is 6 percent. Localities may impose an Occupancy Tax of up to 6 percent. Atlantic City has a 3-percent alcoholic beverage tax and a 9-percent lodgings and related services tax; combined state and city taxes may not exceed 13 percent.

STATE INFORMATION CENTERS: Welcome centers that provide details about state attractions, accommodations, historic sites, parks and events are at about 8 locations throughout the state, including many state parks, forests, recreation areas and marinas as well as service areas along the New Jersey Turnpike, the Garden State Parkway and the Atlantic City Expressway. Hours vary according to the site; phone (609) 292-2470.

and II, the mammoth industrial concerns produced avalanches of goods for the war efforts.

New Jersey was a key player in industry by the early 1900s. Thousands of people emigrated from Europe to seek their fortunes in the state's factories. The state's populace, which grew to include people from many religious, ethnic and economic backgrounds, led to complex feuds in the political arena, as well as in mainstream society. Race riots that erupted in Newark in 1967 resulted in 26 deaths.

Despite these conflicts, New Jersey's business leaders did not give up. They persevered to maintain the state's viability with the development of Newark as an important airport and seaport. Their hopes were again bolstered with the completion of the Hackensack Meadowlands, a $300 million sports complex.

GEOGRAPHY

Far from its stereotype of an undistinguished flatland overrun by pavement, New Jersey displays a billion years of geologic evolution in its varied terrain. From mountain building through flood and uplift, glaciation and subsequent erosion, the history of the land can be read in its terracelike descent from the Kittatinny Ridge of the Appalachians to the broad outwash of the coastal plain.

Rocky and wooded, the folded roots of the Appalachian Mountains form the northwestern part of the state. These drop to a narrow highland belt that gives way to the rolling Piedmont. Throughout this area ribs of traprock are interspersed with countless lakes; both are the legacy of the last ice age.

Scraping southward, the glaciers plowed the softer rock from between the hard ridges and dumped it, pulverized, in a line of moraines that straggles southwest from Staten Island into Pennsylvania. The three-fifths of the state south of this zone is the level coastal plain, marked by sandy soil and the extensive Pine Barrens.

The Pine Barrens are unique. Once encompassing nearly one-fourth of the state, the "Pines" are now 1,000 square miles of virtually uninhabited marsh and woods centering around Chatsworth. Hardly less fragile than the ecosystem of the area is the timeless lifestyle of the "Pineys," those few individualistic residents who live on the seasonal gifts of their forest and wouldn't live anywhere else.

Except for the 48-mile boundary with New York, New Jersey is bordered by water. The Delaware River forms the western boundary of the state, separating it from Pennsylvania and Delaware; on the east the Hudson River and New York Bay divide it from New York. Between the Atlantic and the deeply serrated mainland coast lies a strip of long, narrow barrier beaches that is a major vacation area.

ECONOMY

Although New Jersey is one of the most industrialized states in the nation, tourism and farming also are important to the economy. New Jersey manufactures a greater variety of commodities than any other state. Pharmaceuticals, chemicals, textiles and clothing, foodstuffs, machinery, transportation equipment, primary and fabricated metal goods, rubber products, leather and refined oil are produced in staggering quantities.

The greatest industrial concentration adjoins New York City: It extends from Paterson and Hackensack through Hoboken, Jersey City, Newark, Bayonne and Elizabeth to Perth Amboy and New Brunswick. A second complex, focusing on the Philadelphia marketing center, includes Trenton and Camden. High-tech and service industries, however, began replacing the traditional "smokestack" industries in the 1970s.

In Mauricetown high-grade silica sand is prepared for shipment to glass manufacturers and steel foundries throughout the country. The glassmaking industry is important in such southern cities as Bridgeton and Millville. Illuminite, used in the manufacture of paints, is mined in the southern part of the state.

The crops of New Jersey are as diversified as the industrial products of the state. Cranberries, blueberries, peaches, tomatoes, asparagus, sweet corn, lettuce, cucumbers, bell peppers and spinach are primary; beets, beans, potatoes, onions, eggplants, apples and grapes also are grown. Nursery and greenhouse products are the state's leading cash crops.

In the livestock category, dairying is the leader in the nine northern counties, followed by egg production: More than 500 million eggs are sent to market each year. New Jersey is one of the leading commercial fishing states in the nation. Commercial fishing centers profit from the shellfish taken from the Atlantic coast and Delaware Bay; Atlantic mackerel, cod, sea bass, croaker, flounder and bluefish also are caught. Most of the harvest is processed locally.

RECREATION

The beaches and the state parks and forests are New Jersey's largest recreation centers. The state has more than 127 miles of beaches. More than 305,000 acres are state park and forest land; the largest is the 109,328-acre Wharton State Forest in southern New Jersey. The state parks and forests provide many recreational opportunities such as **hiking, swimming, picnicking, nature study** and **camping.**

New Jersey's beaches protect the interconnected bays and channels behind them, providing excellent **boating.** Water transportation is as common in the seaside towns as the automobile. Float trips range from **canoeing** along the state's inland waterways

to **white-water rafting** within the Delaware Water Gap National Recreation Area.

Saltwater fishing along the coast yields marlin, tuna and sea bass; Atlantic City, Belmar, Cape May and the Wildwoods in particular have numerous boat charters for **deep-sea fishing.** Many good fishing spots exist among the islands south of Great Bay near Pleasantville. The state's inland lakes, rivers and streams offer good fishing for trout, shad, bass, perch, bluegill, northern pike and pickerel. A license is required for **freshwater fishing.**

Hunting in the Pine Barrens of the southern part of the state and in the mountains of the northwest yields deer, squirrels, rabbits and raccoons. Migratory waterfowls flock to the marshy bays; Brigantine National Wildlife Refuge offers selective hunting during specified seasons. State forests, some parks and the state fish and game management areas also permit hunting. A license is required.

In the winter, sports traffic turns inland. Vernon Valley/Great Gorge on Hamburg Mountain in Vernon offers **downhill skiing** early December to mid-April, depending on conditions, on more than 50 slopes. Other ski areas in northern New Jersey are Hidden Valley in Vernon, Craigmeur in Newfoundland and Campgaw in Mahwah.

Cross-country skiing, tobogganing, snowmobiling, ice skating and **snowshoeing** are permitted in many of the state parks and forests.

The Appalachian Trail runs through High Point and Wawayanda state parks, Abram Hewitt, Stokes and Worthington state forests and the Delaware Water Gap National Recreation Area. Several offshoots of this trail tour the Kittatinny Mountains and the New Jersey Highlands. The Batona Trail, which runs through Lebanon, Wharton and Bass River state forests, explores the Pine Barrens.

The New Jersey Coastal Heritage Trail winds from Perth Amboy to Deepwater. The focus of the 275-mile vehicular touring route is the state's association with the ocean.

Many parks and forests charge entrance or parking fees daily from Memorial Day through Labor Day. Fees also are levied on such facilities as cabins and campsites. Reservations must be made through the individual park office at least 5 days in advance; contact the New Jersey Division of Parks and Forestry (see For Your Information box) for addresses. For complete information about camping see the AAA Mideastern CampBook.

Throughout the TourBook, you may notice a Recreational Activities heading with bulleted listings of recreation-oriented establishments listed underneath. Since normal AAA inspection criteria cannot be applied, these establishments are presented for information only. Age, height and weight restrictions may apply. Reservations are often recommended and sometimes required. Visitors should phone or write the attraction for additional information, and the address and phone number are provided for this purpose.

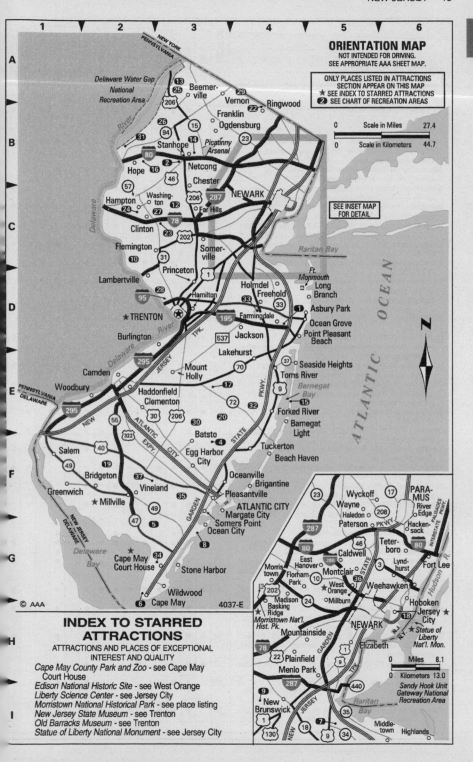

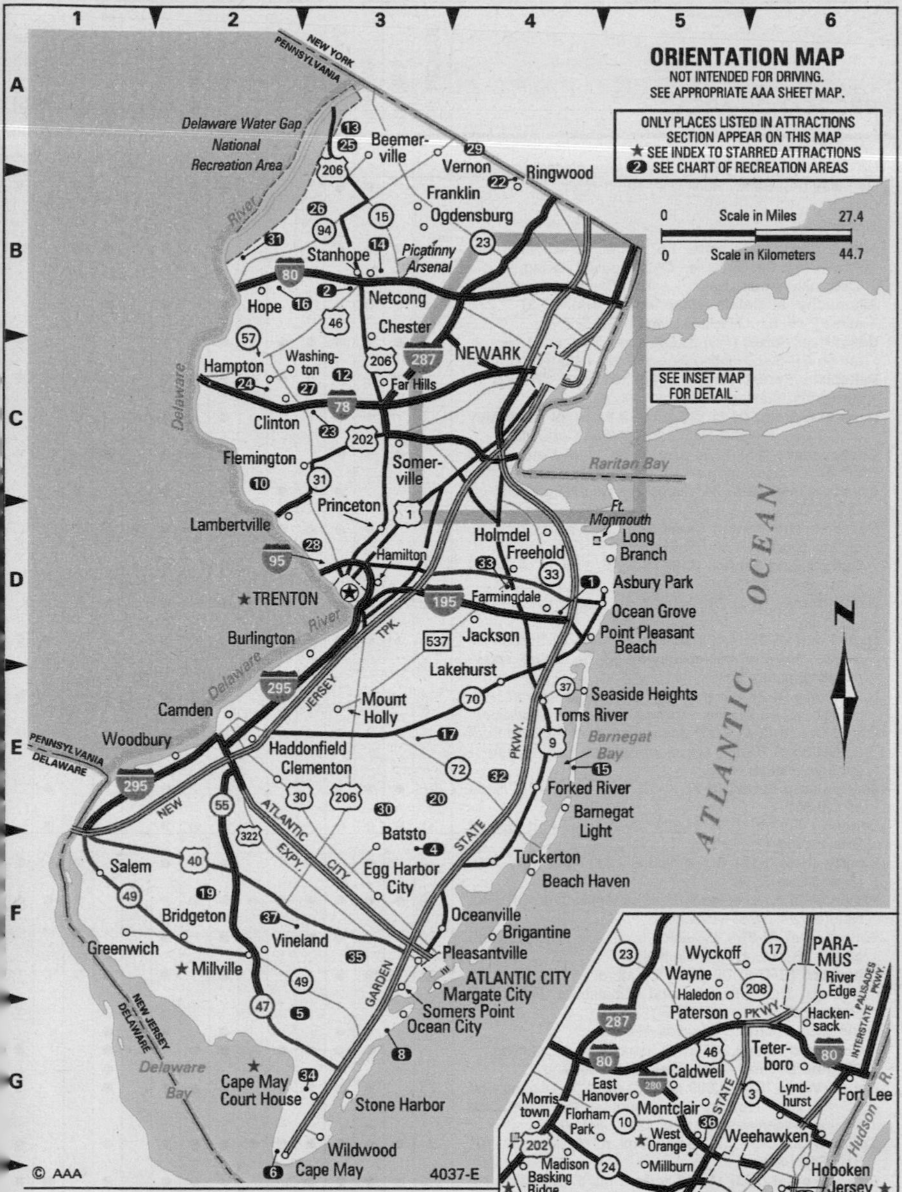
ORIENTATION MAP
NOT INTENDED FOR DRIVING.
SEE APPROPRIATE AAA SHEET MAP.
ONLY PLACES LISTED IN ATTRACTIONS SECTION APPEAR ON THIS MAP
★ SEE INDEX TO STARRED ATTRACTIONS
2 SEE CHART OF RECREATION AREAS
0 Scale in Miles 27.4
0 Scale in Kilometers 44.7
SEE INSET MAP FOR DETAIL
NEW YORK
PENNSYLVANIA
Delaware Water Gap National Recreation Area
Beemerville
Vernon
Ringwood
Franklin
Ogdensburg
Stanhope
Picatinny Arsenal
Netcong
Hope
Chester
NEWARK
Hampton
Washington
Far Hills
Clinton
Flemington
Somerville
Princeton
Lambertville
Raritan Bay
Ft. Monmouth
Holmdel
Long Branch
Freehold
Hamilton
★ TRENTON
Asbury Park
Farmingdale
Ocean Grove
Burlington
Jackson
Point Pleasant Beach
Lakehurst
Seaside Heights
Camden
Mount Holly
Toms River
Woodbury
Barnegat Bay
PENNSYLVANIA
DELAWARE
Haddonfield
Clementon
Forked River
Barnegat Light
Batsto
Salem
Egg Harbor City
Tuckerton
Beach Haven
Bridgeton
Oceanville
Brigantine
Greenwich
Vineland
Pleasantville
★ Millville
ATLANTIC CITY
Margate City
Somers Point
Ocean City
NEW JERSEY
DELAWARE
Delaware Bay
Cape May Court House
Stone Harbor
Wildwood
Cape May
ATLANTIC OCEAN
NEW JERSEY TPK.
ATLANTIC CITY EXPY.
GARDEN STATE PKWY.
Delaware River
N
© AAA
4037-E

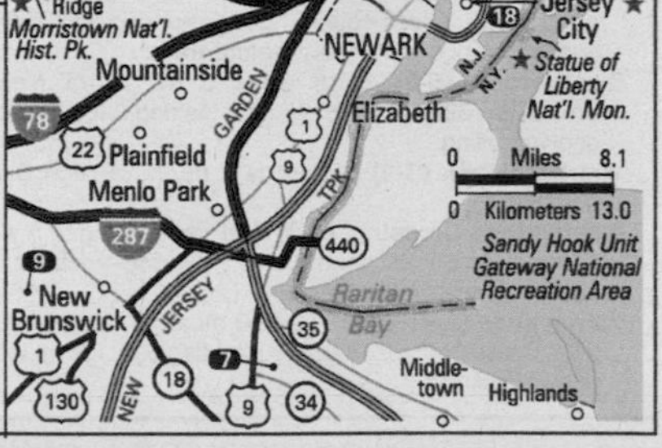
Wyckoff
PARAMUS
Wayne
River Edge
Haledon
Paterson
PKWY.
Hackensack
PALISADES PKWY.
INTERSTATE
Teterboro
Caldwell
Fort Lee
East Hanover
Lyndhurst
Morristown
Montclair
Florham Park
West Orange
Weehawken
Hudson R.
Madison
Millburn
Hoboken
Basking Ridge
Jersey City
Morristown Nat'l. Hist. Pk.
NEWARK
Statue of Liberty Nat'l. Mon.
N.J.
N.Y.
Mountainside
Elizabeth
Plainfield
Menlo Park
0 Miles 8.1
0 Kilometers 13.0
Sandy Hook Unit Gateway National Recreation Area
Raritan Bay
New Brunswick
Middletown
Highlands
GARDEN STATE
NEW JERSEY TPK.

INDEX TO STARRED ATTRACTIONS

ATTRACTIONS AND PLACES OF EXCEPTIONAL INTEREST AND QUALITY

Cape May County Park and Zoo - see Cape May Court House
Edison National Historic Site - see West Orange
Liberty Science Center - see Jersey City
Morristown National Historical Park - see place listing
New Jersey State Museum - see Trenton
Old Barracks Museum - see Trenton
Statue of Liberty National Monument - see Jersey City

RECREATION AREAS

RECREATION AREAS	MAP LOCATION	CAMPING	PICNICKING	HIKING TRAILS	BOATING	BOAT RAMP	BOAT RENTAL	FISHING	SWIMMING	PETS ON LEASH	BICYCLE TRAILS	WINTER SPORTS	VISITOR CENTER	LODGE/CABINS	FOOD SERVICE
NATIONAL RECREATION AREAS *(See place listings)*															
Gateway (I-6) Sandy Hook Unit; 1,600 acres.			•	•				•	•	•			•		•
STATE															
Allaire (D-4) 3,062 acres 1.5 mi. w. of Garden State Pkwy. exit 98. Historic. Cross-country skiing; bridle trails, nature trails, nature center. *(See Farmingdale)*	1	•	•	•				•		•		•	•		•
Allamuchy Mountain (Stephen's Park) (B-3) 7,276 acres 2 mi. n. of Hackettstown on CR 517.	2	•	•	•				•		•			•		•
Bass River Forest (F-3) 23,585 acres 3 mi. w. of Tuckerton on CR 592. Hunting; horse rental, nature programs.	4	•	•	•	•	•	•	•	•	•				•	•
Belleplain Forest (G-2) 12,165 acres on CR 550 at Belleplain. Hunting.	5	•	•	•	•	•	•	•	•	•					
Cape May Point (H-2) 190 acres 2 mi. w. of Cape May on CR 606. Historic. Nature trails. *(See Cape May)*	6		•	•				•		•			•		•
Cheesequake (I-5) 1,284 acres 3 mi. w. of Matawan on SR 34. Cross-country skiing; nature trails.	7	•	•	•					•	•			•		•
Corson's Inlet (G-3) 341 acres just n. of Strathmere on Ocean Dr.	8		•	•	•	•		•		•					
Delaware and Raritan Canal (I-4) 3,723 acres 7 mi. w. of New Brunswick on CR 514.	9		•	•	•	•	•	•		•	•	•	•		
Bull's Island Section (C-2) 79 acres 3 mi. n. of Stockton on SR 29.	10	•	•	•				•		•					
Hacklebarney (C-3) 892 acres 3 mi. s.w. of Chester via US 206.	12		•	•				•		•			•		
High Point (A-3) 14,193 acres 8 mi. n.w. of Sussex on SR 23. Scenic. Cross-country skiing, ice fishing, snowmobiling; nature trails.	13	•	•	•	•		•	•	•	•		•	•	•	•
Hopatcong (B-3) 113 acres 2 mi. n. of Landing off I-80. Ice fishing, ice skating, snowmobiling. *(See Stanhope)*	14		•	•				•	•	•					•
Island Beach (E-4) 3,002 acres 3 mi. s. of Seaside Park on SR 35. A 10-mile strip from Seaside Park to Barnegat Inlet. Nature trails.	15		•	•				•	•	•			•		
Jenny Jump Forest (B-2) 1,387 acres 3 mi. e. of Hope off CR 519.	16	•	•	•				•		•			•		
Lebanon Forest (E-3) 31,879 acres s. of Fort Dix off SRs 70 and 72. Hunting.	17	•	•	•				•	•	•				•	
Liberty (H-6) 1,114 acres off the N.J. Tpke. exit 14B. *(See Jersey City)*	18		•	•				•		•			•		•
Parvin (F-2) 1,125 acres 6 mi. w. of Vineland on CR 540. Nature trails. *(See Vineland)*	19	•	•	•	•	•	•	•	•	•			•	•	•
Penn Forest (E-3) 3,366 acres 5 mi. s.e. of Chatsworth off CR 563. Hunting; bridle trails.	20	•	•	•				•		•					
Ringwood (B-4) 6,199 acres 2.5 mi. n. of Ringwood via Skyland Dr., CR 511 and Sloatsburg Rd. *(See Ringwood)*	22		•	•				•		•			•		
Ringwood Manor 895 acres. Historic.			•	•				•		•			•		
Shephard Lake 1,220 acres. Ice fishing, ice skating.			•	•	•	•	•	•	•	•			•		•
Skyland Section 4,084 acres. Snowmobiling.				•						•		•			
Round Valley (C-3) 3,639 acres 2 mi. s. of Lebanon off US 22. Cross-country skiing, hunting, ice fishing, ice skating, wilderness camping. *(See Clinton)*	23	•	•	•	•		•	•	•	•					
Spruce Run (C-2) 1,961 acres 3 mi. n. of Clinton on SR 31. *(See Clinton)*	24	•	•	•	•	•	•	•	•	•					•
Stokes Forest (A-3) 15,482 acres 3 mi. n. of Branchville on US 206. Cross-country skiing, hunting, ice skating, snowmobiling; bridle trails, nature trails.	25	•	•	•				•	•	•			•	•	•
Swartswood (B-3) 1,718 acres 5 mi. w. of Newton on CRs 622 and 619. Ice fishing, ice skating, snowmobiling.	26	•	•	•	•	•	•	•	•	•			•		•
Voorhees Park (C-3) 613 acres 2 mi. n. of High Bridge on CR 513.	27	•	•	•						•			•		
Washington Crossing (D-3) 841 acres 8 mi. n.w. of Trenton on SR 29, then n.e. on CR 546. Historic. Nature programs. *(See Trenton)*	28		•	•						•			•	•		•
Wawayanda (A-4) 11,332 acres 3 mi. e. of Vernon on CR 94. Cross-country skiing, ice fishing, ice skating, snowmobiling.	29	•	•	•	•	•	•	•	•	•			•		

RECREATION AREAS	MAP LOCATION	CAMPING	PICNICKING	HIKING TRAILS	BOATING	BOAT RAMP	BOAT RENTAL	FISHING	SWIMMING	PETS ON LEASH	BICYCLE TRAILS	WINTER SPORTS	VISITOR CENTER	LODGE/CABINS	FOOD SERVICE
Wharton Forest (E-3) 109,328 acres 35 mi. s. of Trenton off US 206. Canoeing, hunting, ice fishing, ice skating; bridle trails, nature programs. *(See Batsto)*	30	•	•	•	•	•	•	•	•	•			•	•	•
Worthington Forest (B-2) 5,770 acres 16 mi. n.e. of Blairstown on Millbrook Rd. Cross-country skiing, hunting, snowmobiling.	31	•	•	•	•	•		•		•			•		
OTHER															
Cape May County (G-3) 120 acres 2 mi. n. of Cape May Court House on SR 9. Nature trails. *(See Cape May Court House)*	34		•	•				•				•	•		•
Estell Manor County Park (F-3) 1,700 acres 3 mi. s. of Mays Landing on SR 50.	35		•	•				•		•	•	•	•		
Lake Lenape Park (F-2) 1,900 acres on Old Harding Hwy. in Mays Landing.	37	•	•	•	•	•		•		•					
Ocean County (E-4) 325 acres in Lakewood on SR 88. Golf, tennis; nature trails.	32		•	•				•	•	•	•	•			
South Mountain Reservation (G-5) 2,047 acres off I-280 exit 7, then 2 mi. s. on Pleasant Valley Way in West Orange. Indoor ice skating; bridle trails.	36		•	•				•		•		•			
Turkey Swamp County Park (D-4) 498 acres 4.5 mi. s. of Freehold via US 9, CR 524 and Georgia Rd. Ice skating; archery range, nature trails. *(See Freehold)*	33	•	•	•	•			•		•		•			

IN CASE OF AN EMERGENCY, THE AMERICAN RED CROSS ADVISES:

✓ *Check* the scene for safety.

Check an injured person for consciousness, breathing, pulse and bleeding.

 Call 9-1-1 or the local emergency number for an ambulance.

♥ *Care* for conditions you find.

Not breathing:	Open the airway and give rescue breathing.
No pulse:	Find correct* hand position on the breastbone and give CPR.
Bleeding:	Apply pressure to wound with a clean cloth. Avoid contact with blood.
Burns:	Stop the burning. Cool the burn with large amounts of cool water. Cover with dry, clean dressings.
Injuries to bones, muscles, and joints:	Keep the injured part from moving. Apply ice to the injury site.

To find hand position, find the notch where the lower ribs meet the breastbone. Place the heel of your hand on the breastbone, next to your index finger. Place your other hand on top of the first. Use the heel of your bottom hand to apply pressure on the breastbone.

Points of Interest

ASBURY PARK (D-5) pop. 16,800, elev. 23′

Asbury Park was established in 1871 as a summering spot for temperance advocates so that the nearby camp meeting center of Ocean Grove *(see place listing p. 42)* would have no unseemly neighbors. During the late 1930s and 1940s Asbury Park's mile-long Boardwalk and its centerpiece, the restored Convention Hall, made the city a premier shore resort.

The city declined during the 1960s as newly constructed shopping centers drew people away. It gained new life, however, as a music center. Local blue-collar bars began nurturing their own brand of home-grown rock 'n' roll, which soon was made famous by such performers as Bruce Springsteen and Southside Johnny.

Greater Asbury Park Chamber of Commerce: 100 Lake Ave., P.O. Box 649, Asbury Park, NJ 07712; phone (732) 775-7676.

Atlantic City
and Vicinity

Casino gambling has stimulated development in
city whose halcyon days were further back than
most citizens cared to remember. Since 1978 nearly
dozen casino-hotels have opened, primarily situ-
ted along the Boardwalk area. The marina area,
which opens onto the Absecon Inlet northwest of
the Boardwalk and casino-hotel strip, also has felt
the effects of the city's revitalization.

What was to become a leading East Coast re-
ort during the late 1800s began as a fishing vil-
ge at the north end of Absecon Island, a swath
of sand separated
om the mainland by
maze of bays, in-
ts and salt marshes.
probably would
ave remained so
ad not someone
ted that the con-
guration of the
ast spared the is-
nd some heavy
orms, and that the
arness of the Gulf
ream tempered its
imate.

The Camden &
lantic Railroad si-
ultaneously began

Boardwalk / Image Copyright © 1995 PhotoDisc, Inc.

lay track and promote the area. When the first
in arrived in 1854, Atlantic City was incorpo-
ed, the railroad's land company was selling
s and a hotel had been established. By the
80s two rail lines were carrying streams of
ssengers to the many hotels of a town that had
sumed the shape and character it was to exhibit
til the casino law was passed.

In 1870 the first 8-foot-wide lane of planks
s laid directly on the sand to keep hotel lob-
s and railroad cars free from sand. Since then
Boardwalk has been the city's best-known at-
ction. Four-and-one-eighth miles long (6 miles
g if you include the adjacent towns' footage)
d 60 feet wide, the current steel and concrete
ucture is surfaced with planks arranged in a
gonal pattern. It is a foundation for stores,
usements, concessions and thousands of
venture-seeking visitors.

The Boardwalk's success spawned such now
iliar forms of entertainment and promotion as
picture postcard and the rolling chair, which
still a popular mode of transportation. Prob-
y the best known innovation, however, was
amusement pier, the first of which was built
1882.

Applying the same principle as the skyscraper
but in a horizontal direction, each pier occupied
as little space on the Boardwalk as possible, yet
packed as much entertainment as would fit behind its entrance.

Atlantic City's reign declined as the automobile's increasing popularity and the introduction
of air transportation freed people to travel farther
from home. Age and neglect took their toll on
the city until the arrival of the casinos, which became the successors to the entertainment piers.
The casinos have
built on—and in some
ways surpassed—their
predecessors' tradition
of opulent entertain-
ment.

While some of the
Boardwalk's new pal-
aces reflect the gra-
cious past, others,
such as the $1 billion
Trump Taj Mahal,
have razed several
city blocks and
erected dramatically
modern commercial
castles. Saltwater
taffy, palm readers
and rolling chairs are a few threads of continuity
that have remained during this transition from
frayed resort to glossy playground.

Approaches
By Car

The city's principal gateway is the Atlantic
City Expressway, a superhighway that connects
with nearly all major mid-Atlantic highways. In
the Philadelphia-Camden metropolitan area the
expressway collects I-76 traffic from central
Pennsylvania; I-95 from the Washington, D.C.-
Baltimore-Wilmington corridor to the southwest
and Newark-New York City to the northeast; I-
295 between Wilmington and Trenton; and the
New Jersey Turnpike.

A few miles west of Atlantic City the expressway intersects with the Garden State Parkway, a
major coastal route linking Newark to the north
and, via the Cape May-Lewes ferry, Delaware
and southern Maryland to the south. US 30 and
US 40/322 also enter Atlantic City, arriving via
Absecon Boulevard and Albany Avenue respectively. The Atlantic City Expressway is the preferred route.

Getting Around
Street System

As neatly gridlike as the Monopoly board on which some of its street names are perpetuated, Atlantic City's basic plan is easy to comprehend. Avenues parallel to the ocean are named for oceans or seas: Arctic, Mediterranean and Baltic. Some of these change names near the inlet or "downbeach"; for example, Baltic becomes Madison at its north end and Winchester at its south.

With a few exceptions, streets perpendicular to the ocean bear the names of states in an order roughly approximating the state's geographic position. New Hampshire and Vermont are at the northeast end of the island; Indiana and Illinois are about in the middle. Why Iowa Avenue is farther south than Texas and California avenues remains a mystery.

Numbers are in blocks of 100, increasing as they progress southward from Maine Avenue and inland from the Boardwalk. The few diagonal streets are mostly extensions of the roads that lead into the city.

Parking

Most businesses provide parking space near their premises, and most casino-hotels charge a state-mandated $2 fee for parking. That fee is valid at all Atlantic City casino-hotels for on day, with the proceeds earmarked for the revita ization of Atlantic City.

Public parking lots are many and scattere throughout the city, and the Atlantic City Conver tion Center at Mississippi Avenue and Boardwal offers indoor parking. Daily rates—sometimes ap plied to any part of a 12-hour period—at private owned lots range from $3 to $5 on weekdays an from $4 to $12 on weekends.

What To See

ATLANTIC CITY ART CENTER AND HISTOR CAL MUSEUM, on the boardwalk at New Jerse Ave., consists of two facilities. The museum col tains exhibits depicting Atlantic City's reign as vacation playground, Miss America memorabil and a display saluting the Steel Pier's celebrate diving horse. The art center contains three galle ies that feature rotating displays. Allow 1 ho minimum. Daily 10-4; closed major holiday Free. Phone (609) 347-5837.

What To Do
Gambling

Gambling in Atlantic City is confined to tl casino-hotels. To qualify for a casino operation, hotel must have a minimum of 500 rooms an

---

The Informed Traveler

CITY POPULATION: 36,600   **ELEVATION:** 21 ft.

Whom To Call

Emergency: 911

Police (non-emergency): (609) 347-5780

Time: (609) 976-1616 in N.J.

Temperature: (609) 976-1212 in N.J.

Hospitals: Atlantic City Medical Center, (609) 344-4081.

Where to Look

Newspapers

The Press is published daily. Check the events section for a list of current entertainment offerings.

Radio and TV

Atlantic City radio station WOND (1400 AM) is an all-news/weather station; WHYY (90.1 FM) is a member of National Public Radio.

The major TV channels are 3 (CBS), 6 (ABC), 10 and 40 (NBC), 12 and 23 (PBS) and

29 (FOX). For a complete list of radio and television programs, consult the daily newspaper.

Visitor Information

The Greater Atlantic City Convention & Visitors Bureau, 2314 Pacific Ave., Atlantic City, NJ 08401, provides information about entertainment, transportation and city tours; phone (609) 348-7100. The free weekly papers Whoot and At The Shore provide information about cultural activities.

What to Wear

The ocean and its breezes have a moderating effect on Atlantic City's weather, delaying the onset of the warmest weather by a few weeks and maintaining mild temperatures into late autumn. High temperatures average in the mid-80s in July and August and in the low 40s in January and February. Average low temperatures range from the mid- to upper 60s in summer to the mid-20s in winter. The annual precipitation of 45 inches is fairly evenly distributed throughout the year. Snowfall averages 16 inches annually.

neet architectural requirements, not the least of which is approval of the design by the Atlantic City Planning Board and the New Jersey Casino Control Commission. Casinos are open daily 24 hours. The minimum age for participation is 21.

Baccarat, minibaccarat, big six wheel, black-ack, craps, poker, red dog, pai gow, sic bo, rou-ette, slots and keno are available, making the visitor who resists the temptation to gamble a arity. It is recommended that those who accept he challenge to gamble first pick up one of the eadily obtainable "how-to" books about gam-ling. While knowing something about the game von't alter the odds, which ultimately favor the ouse, it will increase the chances of breaking even or provide some understanding of why the et was lost.

Some casinos will provide literature about the ames; others even give classes for novice pa-rons. For first-time visitors, credit will be tight r non-existent. Once credit has been established vith further visits, it will be as easy to obtain 1,000 as $10.

Sightseeing
Boardwalk Tours

Atlantic City's highlight is its Boardwalk, which can be explored on foot or by bicycle. Another way of seeing the Boardwalk is in the legendary rolling chair, which resembles a huge wicker chair on wheels. Pushed by an attendant, the chairs seat up to three people. The Atlantic City Famous Rolling Chair Co. can be found at 1601 Boardwalk, near Kentucky Avenue. The chairs operate Sun.-Thurs. 10 a.m.-2 a.m., Fri.-Sat. 10 a.m.-5 a.m., Memorial Day to mid-Sept.; Sun.-Thurs. 10-10, Fri.-Sat. 10 a.m.-2 a.m., Feb. 1-day before Memorial Day and mid-Sept. to mid-Dec.; Sun.-Thurs. 10-10, Fri.-Sat. 10 a.m.-midnight, rest of year (10 a.m.-6 a.m. on Dec. 31).

The fare is $5 for 6 blocks and fewer, $10 for 7-14 blocks, $20 per half-hour and $35 per hour for two people. Phone (609) 347-7148.

Sports and Recreation

Before gambling came to this resort, it was the sun, ocean breezes and breakers washing the

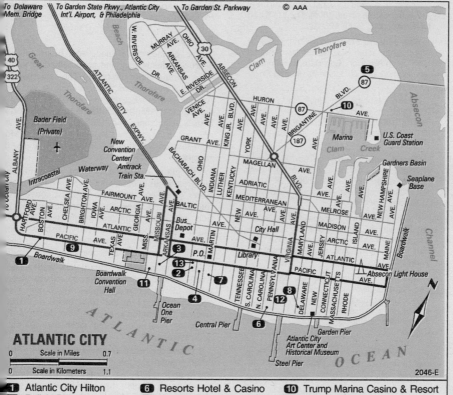

ATLANTIC CITY

Scale in Miles	0 — 0.7
Scale in Kilometers	0 — 1.1

2046-E

1. Atlantic City Hilton
2. Bally's Park Place
3. Caesars Atlantic City
4. Claridge Casino Hotel
5. Harrah's Casino Hotel
6. Resorts Hotel & Casino
7. Sands Hotel & Casino
8. Showboat Hotel & Casino
9. Tropicana Casino & Entertainment Resort
10. Trump Marina Casino & Resort
11. Trump Plaza
12. Trump Taj Mahal Casino & Resort
13. Bally's Wild Wild West Casino

wide sand beach that made Atlantic City a leading playground. Popular as early as the 19th century, the beach is still a major attraction. Because
there is less undertow than at other beach areas,
swimming is particularly good. **Surfing** is permitted dawn to dusk, except at Delaware and Ra-
leigh avenues. The beaches at South Carolina
and Albany avenues have facilities that are accessible to the physically impaired. Lifeguards
are on duty from about Memorial Day through
Sept. 30.

Fishing is as close as the ocean or inlet. Surf
or pier fishing brings in striped bass, flounder,
tautog, kingfish and snapper blues; the inlet also
yields croakers and crabs. Farther out, such fight-
ers as marlin, tuna and bonito can be caught. In
general, the summer months see the heaviest
runs of most species.

Transportation

Air travel: The International Airport in
Pomona is served by Continental Airlines,
(800) 525-0280; Spirit, (800) 772-7117 and
USAir Express, (800) 428-4322.

Rail service: New Jersey Transit, (800)
582-5946 in south N.J., travels from the rail
terminal to Absecon, Egg Harbor, Hammonton, Atco, Lindenwold, Cherry Hill and Philadelphia.

Buses: Greyhound Lines Inc., (800)
231-2222 in south N.J. and New Jersey
Transit, (800) 582-5946 in south N.J., run
from the terminal at Arctic and Arkansas
avenues.

Rental cars: Hertz, at the airport in
Pomona, offers discounts to AAA members;
phone (609) 646-7733 or (800) 654-3131.
For listings of other agencies check the
telephone directory.

Public transport: The buses of New Jersey Transit operate along Atlantic and Ventnor avenues as far south as Longport. The
fare is $1 each way. Minibuses (jitneys) op-
erate 24 hours a day.

Jitneys with a pink sign stay on Pacific
and Ventnor avenues; those with a blue
sign run from Jackson to Pennsylvania avenues, then to Harrah's Casino Hotel and
Trump Marina Casino & Resort. Those with
a green sign run from Caspian to Arkansas
avenues, with stops at the bus terminal and
within two blocks of the rail terminal, then to
the marina casinos. The jitney fare is $1.50.

Taxis: Cab companies include City, (609)
345-3244, and Yellow, (609) 344-1221.
Base fare is $1.45, plus 30c per one-tenth
mile. Base fare rises 30c for each additional
passenger.

Boating can be for fun as well as for fishing;
the Thorofares—the network of waterways that
separates Absecon and other islets from the
mainland—provide a different perspective from
which to view the city. Rental crafts ranging
from one-person day sailers to six-person power
boats are available.

Bicycling is a popular pastime, particularly
along the Boardwalk. Bicycle rentals, available
about 6 a.m. to 10 p.m., can be found along the
length of the Great Wood Way.

Some large hotels provide facilities for racquetball, squash or **tennis**. The Showboat Hotel
has an ultramodern 60-lane **bowling** center
equipped with electronic scoring. Public tennis
courts are at N. Jerome and Amherst in Margate
City and at S. Suffolk and Atlantic avenues in
Ventnor.

Horse racing takes place at the Atlantic City
Race Course, 14 miles west at the junction of US
40/322. Post time is daily at 7:35 p.m., early
June through late August; phone (609) 641-2190.

Note: Policies concerning admittance of children to pari-mutuel betting facilities vary. Phone
for information.

Shopping

The casinos have made the Boardwalk the
heart of Atlantic City and have helped to revital-
ize shopping along the beach. The centerpiece of
this revival is Ocean One, a mall at Arkansas
Avenue and the Boardwalk. Built on the site of
the legendary Million Dollar Pier, this emporium
houses restaurants and 150 shops featuring everything from designer clothes to T-shirts. More
high-fashion boutiques can be found in the
casinos.

The glitter of the casinos has not diminished
the Boardwalk's older charms: A wide range of
stores offers everything from plastic souvenirs to
fine jewelry. Between these extremes visitors can
find nearly anything they might want or need.
Toys, fudge and saltwater taffy, T-shirts embla-
zoned while you wait, swimwear and other beach
supplies are a sampling of available merchandise.

In addition to the Boardwalk and Atlantic
Avenue, Pennsylvania Avenue to Albany Avenue
is considered the main downtown shopping section. A highlight in the 1000 block of Atlantic
Avenue is Gordon's Alley—New Jersey's first
shopping mall—containing more than 30 shops
and restaurants.

Beyond the beach and Atlantic City are several
other popular shopping areas, including the Central Square Shopping Center on US 9 in Lakewood, with more than 70 specialty stores;
Hamilton Mall in Mays Landing next to the Atlantic City Race Course; the New Shore Mall on
the Black Horse Pike in Pleasantville; and the
Towne of Historic Smithville, which offers
Colonial-style crafts.

Special Events

Shortly after Labor Day the Miss America pageant commences with Pageant Week, during which preliminary competitions and a parade take place. The selection of a new queen from the array of contenders remains the hub around which the local calendar revolves. The pageant has been considered synonymous with the community since the first competition in 1921.

In addition to the Miss America Pageant, many other shows and events take place in the Atlantic City Convention Center. Shows include the Antique and Classic Car Auction and Flea Market and the Atlantic City Boat Show in February, and the Antiques and Collectibles Exposition in mid-March. The Archery Classic is held late April. Three arts and crafts shows are held Brighton Park: one in mid-May, one in early ly and one in early September.

Other special events in Atlantic City include the New Jersey Fresh Seafood Festival, which takes place at Gardner's Basin Maritime Park, and the National Boardwalk Professional Art Show, both held in June.

Harborfest, which includes the World Championship Ocean Marathon Swim around Absecon Island, occurs in August. The Labor Day Weekend Festival features arts, crafts, antiques and collectibles in Brighton Park. The Indian Summer Art Show is held on the Boardwalk in September, and the Atlantic City Christmas Parade takes place in December.

The Atlantic City Vicinity

BRIGANTINE (F-4) pop. 11,400

MARINE MAMMAL STRANDING CENTER, just of the lighthouse at 3625 Brigantine Blvd., is devoted to the rescue and rehabilitation of stranded or distressed marine mammals that come ashore along the New Jersey coast. Whales, dolphins, seals and sea turtles are among the mammals the center has assisted. Displays are offered at the Sea Life Educational Center, and rescued sea animals may be viewed in observation tanks.

Allow 30 minutes minimum. Daily 11-5, Memorial Day-Labor Day; Sat.-Sun. noon-4, rest of year. Donations. Phone (609) 266-0538.

EGG HARBOR CITY (F-3) pop. 4,600

The hallmark of Egg Harbor City is neither eggs nor a harbor, but acres of vineyards. The 1858 discovery that the soil was conducive to growing wine grapes brought German vintners to the area, and the town prospered. A second boom ensued as Italian growers arrived after the Civil War. Some of the vineyards are operated by the original families.

Egg Harbor City Chamber of Commerce: P.O. Box 129, Egg Harbor City, NJ 08215; phone (609) 965-3751.

WINERIES

- **Historic Renault Winery** is n. of US 30 on Bremen Ave. Mon.-Sat. 10-4, Sun. 11-4; closed Jan. 1 and Dec. 25. Phone (609) 965-2111.

MARGATE CITY (G-4) pop. 8,400

LUCY THE MARGATE ELEPHANT, 9200 Atlantic Ave., is a building in the shape of an elephant, complete with a canopied seat called a howdah. Six stories high and built of wood and tin, it was constructed in 1881 by real estate developer James V. Lafferty to draw prospective buyers to his holdings. It has served as a real estate office, a residence and a tavern.

Lucy can be toured daily 10-8, June 15-Labor Day; Sat.-Sun. 10-4:30, Apr. 1-June 14 and day after Labor Day-Oct. 31. Admission $3; under 12, $1. Phone (609) 823-6473.

OCEANVILLE (F-4)

EDWIN B. FORSYTHE NATIONAL WILDLIFE REFUGE, 1 mi. e. of US 9 on Great Creek Rd., covers more than 24,000 acres on the Atlantic

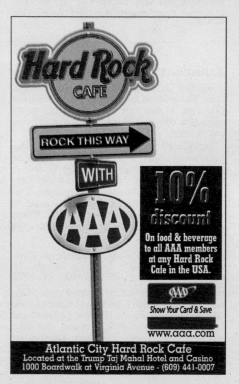

coast. More than 275 species of waterfowls and other birds have been sighted at the refuge's bays, channels and tidal marshes. The best seasons for wildlife observation are spring and fall. There is an 8-mile drive through wetland and upland areas as well as two short nature trails. Daily dawn-dusk. Admission $4 per private vehicle. Phone (609) 652-1665.

SAVE THE NOYES MUSEUM OF ART, off SR 9 on Lily Lake Rd., exhibits permanent collections of paintings, mid-Atlantic folk art, sculpture and works on paper by contemporary American artists. The museum also features a gallery of bird and animal decoys. Rotating fine arts and crafts exhibits are displayed. Allow 30 minutes minimum. Wed.-Sun. 11-4; closed major holidays. Admission $3, over 65 and students with ID $2, under18 free. Phone (609) 652-8848.

PLEASANTVILLE (F-4) pop. 16,000, elev. 20'

STORYBOOK LAND, 2 mi. w. of the Garden State Pkwy. on US 40/322, features rides, animals and more than 50 buildings and displays depicting storybook characters and scenes.

Daily 10-5:30, mid-June to mid-Sept.; Mon.-Fri. 10-3, Sat.-Sun. 11-5, May 1 to mid-June; Mon.-Fri. 4:30-9, Sat.-Sun. 2-9, day after Thanksgiving-Dec. 30; Thurs.-Fri. 10-3, Sat.-Sun. 11-5, mid-Sept. through Oct. 31; Sat.-Sun. 11-5, mid-Mar. through Apr. 30. Closed Dec.

24-25. Admission $10.95; over 65, $7.95; unde 1 free. Phone (609) 641-7847.

SOMERS POINT (G-4) pop. 11,200

ATLANTIC COUNTY HISTORICAL SOCIETY L BRARY AND MUSEUM, just n. of the traff circle at 907 Shore Rd. (CR 585), has a 20,00(item collection of artifacts ranging from a con nental dollar to an 1870 bed. Shipbuilding, or of the county's major 19th-century industries, represented by boat models, paintings and tool Other items include American Indian stor implements, weapons, furniture and turn-of-th 20th-century clothing.

The historical society's library is open to t public for genealogical research. Allow 30 mi utes minimum. Guided tours of the museum a available Wed.-Sat. 10-3:30; closed holiday Museum free; $5 fee for library research. Pho (609) 927-5218.

SOMERS MANSION, adjacent to the traffic circ at 1000 Shore Rd. (CR 585), was built arou 1725 by Richard Somers, son of an early ar settler. The three-story brick dwelling, the olde house in Atlantic County, contains 18th-centu furnishings. An interesting architectural detail the interior woodwork decorated with hea shaped perforations. A textile collection includ locally fashioned quilts, coverlets and samplers

Allow 30 minutes minimum. Wed.-Sat. l noon and 1-4, Sun. 1-4; closed winter holiday Free. Phone (609) 927-2212.

BARNEGAT LIGHT (E-4) pop. 700

Barnegat Light, the northernmost community on Long Beach Island, was settled by Scandinavian fishermen; whalers first came to the isle in the early 18th century. Fishing, particularly for tuna, and summertime diversions sustain the town.

Because the area around Loveladies Harbor has a scenic appeal likened to that of Cape Cod, the town, named for an 18th-century landowner, has become a well-known art colony. Long Beach Island is an 18-mile-long segment of the barrier isles that outline the New Jersey coast. Its width ranges from about three blocks to 1 mile. A long causeway carries SR 72 across Barnegat Bay to Ship Bottom.

Southern Ocean County Chamber of Commerce: 265 W. Ninth St., Ship Bottom, NJ 08008; phone (609) 494-7211 or (800) 292-6372.

BARNEGAT LIGHTHOUSE STATE PARK, on the n. tip of Long Beach Island, is 32 acres of parkland surrounding historic Barnegat Lighthouse. A forest nature trail; fishing, crabbing and bird-watching opportunities; and picnic facilities are available. Daily 8 a.m.-10 p.m., Memorial Day-Labor Day. Free. Fires are not permitted. Phone (609) 494-2016.

Barnegat Lighthouse, known as the "Grand C Champion of the Tides," was rebuilt 1857-58 Gen. George G. Meade after the original str ture, built in 1834, toppled into the water. T lighthouse rises 172 feet above the tides a marks Barnegat Shoals, the scene of more th 200 shipwrecks. A fine view is available fr the top of the lighthouse, 217 steps above base. Daily 9 a.m.-9:30 p.m., Memorial D Labor Day; Wed.-Sun. 9-4:30, May 1-day bef Memorial Day and day after Labor Day-Oct. Admission $1, under 12 free.

BASKING RIDGE (H-4) elev. 357'

Animals coming from the surrounding swar land to sun themselves on a hillside inspired name Basking Ridge. More than 10,000 ye ago most of the area to the east was part of L Passaic, created when the terminal accumulat of earth and stone carried by the Wisconsin C cier blocked the Passaic River. The remain portion of the former lake—now a wetland— known as the "Great Swamp" of New Jersey.

GREAT SWAMP NATIONAL WILDLIFE REFU is e. from N. Maple Ave. on Madisonville Rd Long Hill Rd. The 7,500-acre refuge, rescued

esidents from being turned into an airport, pre-
erves the marsh and swamp woodland habitat of
muskrats, foxes, fish, wildfowls and 223 bird
species. A wildlife observation center features a
boardwalk trail into the swamp; interpretive displays and blinds are available. The swamp's
habitats contain more than 8 miles of hiking
ails. Center open Mon.-Fri. 8-4:30. Trails open
aily dawn-dusk. Free. Phone (973) 425-1222.

OMERSET COUNTY PARK COMMISSION'S
NVIRONMENTAL EDUCATION CENTER is in
ord Stirling Park, 3 mi. s. from I-287 on S.
laple Ave., then 1 mi. e. to 190 Lord Stirling
d. The center is on a 427-acre tract that is part
f the Great Swamp Basin. The interpretive
uilding, said to be the country's first public
uilding heated and cooled by solar power, offers
library, exhibit areas and science programs. A
ermanent exhibit, "Secrets of the Great
wamp," spotlights the outdoor experience.

Native wildlife can be seen from nature trails
d boardwalks. Observation towers, blinds and a
ecial-use trail are available. Allow 2 hours mini-
um. Center open daily 9-5; closed holidays.
ails open daily dawn-dusk. Free. Phone (908)
6-2489.

ATSTO—*see Philadelphia and Vicinity in
ennsylvania p. 130.*

EACH HAVEN (F-4) pop. 1,500

ONG BEACH ISLAND HISTORICAL MUSEUM,
each and Engleside aves., features displays that
cus primarily on the area's tie to the water—

swimsuits, surfboards, marine life and storm
photographs. The museum also schedules guided
tours of 24 Victorian homes on the island. Mon.,
Wed.-Thurs. and Sat.-Sun. 2-4 and 7-9, Tues. and
Fri. 10-noon, June 25-Labor Day; Sat.-Sun. 2-4,
late May-June 24 and day after Labor Day-late
Sept. Admission $1.50; under 13, 25c. Phone
(609) 492-0700.

BEEMERVILLE (A-3) elev. 760'

SPACE FARMS ZOO AND MUSEUM is just n. on
CR 519, w. of Sussex. The 100-acre preserve is
home to bears, bobcats, otters and many other
species of North American wildlife; exotic animals, birds and reptiles also can be seen. The
museum displays such Americana as antique automobiles and horse-drawn vehicles. Picnic facilities are available. Daily 9-5, May-Oct.
Admission $8; ages 3-12, $3.50. Phone (973)
875-5800.

BRIDGETON (F-2) pop. 18,900, elev. 60'

Bridgeton mingles its New England atmosphere and the architecture of past centuries with
the advancements and automation of the present.
Quakers settled this area in the late 1600s and
within 50 years constructed the bridge across Cohansey Creek that would lend the town its name.

The 19th century saw the growth of Bridgeton,
by then the seat of Cumberland County, and the
establishment of a woolen mill, a nail factory

The Pine Barrens

If most people don't know about New Jersey's Pine Barrens, it could be because the 450,000
year-round residents of this national reserve that overlies more than a million acres of the state's
bottom half, prefer to keep a good thing to themselves. Wedged between the roar of traffic along
the New Jersey Turnpike and the Garden State Parkway, this quiet wilderness shows little evidence
of the human settlement and enterprise that have occurred. Yet the Pines are far from barren.

The area's heart is a tapestry of impenetrable scrub and pitch pine, rivers, swamps and bogs
where rebelling Colonials mined iron to make cannonballs. Villages, foundries and glassworks
churned out the region's products until the late 1800s, after which the forest resumed full reign. Local residents, affectionately called the "Pineys," learned to "work the woods" by selling its seasonal
gifts and tending its cranberry and blueberry crops. Cranberries have been commercially raised in
the Pine Barrens since about 1835, while the first commercial blueberry planting was made in 1916.
The Pine Barrens account for approximately 25 percent of the state's agricultural income.

Many recreational opportunities exist in the Pine Barrens. Boating, canoeing, swimming, fishing
and hunting are popular activities. Hikers can enjoy the Batona Trail, a marked wilderness trail that
traverses the Pine Barrens, or explore old abandoned towns and the restored Batsto Village. More
than 1,000 known sites in the vicinity show that man lived in this area as early as 10,000 B.C.

Left undisturbed are the woodland's wonders: a confusing tangle of sand roads cut during Colonial times, 12,000 acres of stunted pygmy pines in an area called the Plains, insectivorous plants,
exotic orchids, ventriloquist tree frogs found almost nowhere else and a legendary winged creature
known as the "Jersey Devil."

The muck soil in the Pine Barrens produces monobactum, a microorganism expected to revolutionize the antibiotics industry. An aquifer inside the Pine's deep sand beds holds 17 trillion gallons
of water with the purity of glacial ice. The water in this shallow aquifer usually is at or near the surface, producing bogs, marshes and swamps. A maze of serpentine streams fed by the aquifer,
stained the color of tea by cedar sap, rises within the low dome of land on which the Pines exist.
With development encroaching on all sides, the Pines' uniqueness becomes more apparent each
year—except to local residents, who have always known it.

and an ironworks. As the residents prospered, they constructed the many Colonial, Federal and Victorian buildings that remain. Reminders of early Bridgeton still crowd its historic district, which has more than 2,200 period homes and commercial buildings.

Bridgeton Chamber of Commerce: 57 E. Commerce St., Bridgeton, NJ 08302; phone (609) 455-1312.

Self-guiding tours: Brochures outlining self-guiding tours past period homes on Bridgeton's historic east and west sides are available at the Bridgeton/Cumberland Tourist Center, 50 E. Broad St., Bridgeton, NJ 08302; phone (609) 451-4802. Audiocassettes that complement the brochures are available for a small fee.

Shopping areas: Cohansey Crossing on W. Commerce Street is a row of restored Victorian buildings containing a variety of shops. Dutch Neck Village, an enclave of antique and craft shops 1 mile southwest of town, also evokes the past.

BRIDGETON CITY PARK, W. Commerce St. and Mayor Aitken Dr., encompasses 1,100 acres and has recreational facilities as well as a zoo. Also on the grounds is Nail Mill Museum, a diverse collection of memorabilia and items related to local history. The New Sweden Farmstead Museum is a reproduction of 17th-century buildings typical of the area's early Swedish settlement. Park open daily dawn-dusk. Free. Phone (609) 451-9208 or 455-9785 for the farmstead museum.

Cohanzick Zoo focuses on wildlife native to New Jersey and also contains primate and feline groups.Daily 9-4. Free.

WOODRUFF INDIAN MUSEUM, in Bridgeton City Library at 150 E. Commerce St., includes 20,000 American Indian relics collected within a 30-mile radius of Bridgeton. Many of the stone and organic implements, though found locally, were brought to the area during tribal meetings, migrations or warfare. Arrowheads, gravers and knives date from 10,000 to 8000 B.C.; more recent artifacts, such as the Lenni Lenape Indians' ceramic pipes, date from A.D. 700 to 1800. Mon.-Sat. 1-4, Sept.-May; Mon.-Fri. 1-4, Sat. 10-3, rest of year. Free. Phone (609) 451-2620.

BRIGANTINE—*see Atlantic City and Vicinity p. 23.*

BURLINGTON—*see Philadelphia and Vicinity in Pennsylvania p. 130.*

CALDWELL (G-5) pop. 7,500, elev. 411'

GROVER CLEVELAND BIRTHPLACE STATE HISTORIC SITE, 207 Bloomfield Ave., is the house in which the 22nd and 24th president of the United States was born in 1837. He lived in the house until 1841. Restored by the state, contains many of his possessions. Allow 2 hou minimum. Wed.-Sat. 9-noon and 1-5, Sun. 1- closed holidays and periodically without notic Free. Phone (973) 226-1810.

CAMDEN—*see Philadelphia and Vicinity in Pennsylvania p. 131.*

CAPE MAY (G-2) pop. 4,700, elev. 16'

Explorer Cornelius Jacobsen Mey, sent by t Dutch East India Company to explore the coa found the climate "charming" and lent his nam to the shore area. The gingerbread of Victori architecture is a recurrent theme in Cape Ma the prevalence of well-preserved late 19t century structures resulted in the community b ing designated a national historic landmark 1976.

Representative of this architectural style is t Emlen Physick Estate, 1048 Washington St., d signed in 1879 by noted architect Frank Furne The Pink House on Perry Street typifies the c nate "wedding cake" style.

At the southeasternmost tip of the state, Ca May is one of the oldest seashore resorts on t Atlantic Coast. During the first half of the 1! century it rivaled Newport as a favored summ retreat for Philadelphia and New York socialit Presidents Buchanan, Grant, Harrison and Pie were among the luminaries who vacationed the resort. An earlier, less extolled visitor was rate Captain Kidd, who filled his water ca near Lily Pond.

In addition to the pleasures of the beach a the amusements of the promenade, Cape May fers good boating and fishing. Various craft c be rented for fishing in the ocean or in Delaw Bay. Rockhounds pursue their interest also; tide-worn quartz pebbles known as "Cape M Diamonds" can be found on the beach at nea Cape May Point and along the lower Delaw Bay.

t Cape May Point State Park (*see Recreat Chart*), a mile southwest of Sunset Boulev (SR 606), is the historic Cape May Point Lig house, erected in 1859. Visitors can climb spiral staircase to the watchroom for a panorar view of the ocean and bay. The state park is c of three places adjacent to Cape May Bird (servatory in nearby Cape May Point that off prime bird watching areas. Higbee's Beach W life Management Area and Cape May Migrat Bird Refuge also provide observation points.

Cape May can be explored on several tours fered daily spring through fall and on a redu schedule the rest of the year. Trolley tours of historic district depart from the Washing Street Mall information booth; for sched phone (609) 884-5404.

Carriage tours and guided walking tours start at the Washington Street Mall informa booth. Tickets for evening house tours can be bought at the Physick Estate. For tour information contact the Mid-Atlantic Center for the Arts, P.O. Box 340, 1048 Washington St., Cape May, NJ 08204; phone (609) 884-5404 or (800) 275-4278. The Cape May County Art League is in the Washington Street Mall and offers exhibits, classes and workshops; phone (609) 884-8628.

The Cape May-Lewes ferry runs daily between Cape May and Lewes, Del. Its terminal is on US 9, 3 miles west of the southern terminus of the Garden State Parkway. The 17-mile trip takes 70 minutes. Reservations may be made at least 1 day in advance by calling (800) 643-3779 daily 7 a.m.-8 p.m. For schedule information write P.O. Box 827, North Cape May, NJ 08204. Phone (800) 643-3779.

Cape May Welcome Center: 405 Lafayette St., Cape May, NJ 08225; phone (609) 884-9562.

Self-guiding tours: The Washington Street Mall information booth provides brochures outlining a walking tour of Cape May's historic sites.

HISTORIC COLD SPRING VILLAGE, 720 US 9, is an open-air, living-history museum that portrays the lifestyles, trades, crafts and architecture of an 1800s southern New Jersey rural community. The village consists of more than 20 restored buildings on a 22-acre wooded site. Craftspersons and interpreters demonstrate such trades and crafts as basketry, printing and spinning. Narrated horse and buggy tours are available for a fee.

Allow 3 hours minimum. Daily 10-4:30, mid-June through Labor Day; Sat.-Sun. 10-4:30, day after Labor Day-Sept. 30 and Memorial Day to mid-June. Admission $5; over 62, $4; ages 5-14, 2. Phone (609) 898-2300.

THE SCHOONER *YANKEE*, 1 mi. e. on CR 621 (Ocean Dr.) from s. terminus of Garden State Pkwy. to Ocean Hwy. Dock, offers 2-, 2.5- and 3-hour harbor, Intracoastal Waterway and ocean cruises aboard an 80-foot tall ship schooner. The 3-hour afternoon cruise allows visitors to assist

in setting sails and manning the helm or to simply relax and enjoy the ocean breezes. Sightings of dolphins or whales are possible. Refreshments are included.

Cruises depart daily at 2 and 6, Memorial Day-Sept. 20. Fare $26.50; under 11, $18. Reservations are recommended. MC, VI. Phone (609) 884-1919 or 886-9003.

CAPE MAY COURT HOUSE (G-2)
pop. 3,600, elev. 18'

The county seat, Cape May Court House is a good place to begin a tour of the Victorian and historic homes throughout Cape May County.

Cape May County Chamber of Commerce and Visitor Information Center: Crest Haven Road and Garden State Parkway, P.O. Box 74, Cape May Court House, NJ 08210; phone (609) 465-7181.

★**CAPE MAY COUNTY PARK AND ZOO,** 707 SR 9N, houses nearly 250 species of animals including bobcats, black bucks, deer, exotic birds, foxes, giraffes, leopards, lions, monkeys, oryxes, prairie dogs, reptiles, tigers and zebras. Many of the creatures on display, such as the golden lion tamarin from Brazil, are members of rare or endangered species. An 800-foot boardwalk leads to a 35-acre African savannah. Picnicking is permitted. Food is available. Park daily 9-dusk. Zoo daily 10-4:45. Closed Dec. 25. Donations. Phone (609) 465-5271. *See Recreation Chart.*

HISTORICAL MUSEUM, .7 mi. n. on US 9, is in the John Holmes House. Its collections of local American Indian artifacts, whaling implements, glass, costumes, ship models and other antiquities provide a survey of life in early Cape May County. Allow 1 hour minimum. Tues.-Sat. 9-4, Apr.-Nov.; Sat. 9-4, rest of year. Last admission 45 minutes before closing. Ninety-minute tours are given at 10:30 and 2. Closed holidays. Admission $3; under 12, 50c. Phone (609) 465-3535.

LEAMING'S RUN GARDENS AND COLONIAL FARM, Garden State Pkwy. exit 13, then 1 mi. n. on US 9, offers 25 gardens, each with its own

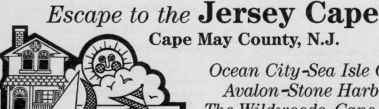

theme, as well as a reconstructed Colonial farm. A winding path leads visitors through 20 acres of seasonal gardens. The farm's one-room log cabin depicts 17th-century life and the animals and crops it supported. Allow 2 hours minimum. Daily 9:30-5, May 15-Oct. 20. Admission $4.50; ages 6-12, $1. Phone (609) 465-5871.

CHESTER (B-3) pop. 1,200, elev. 860'

COOPER GRISTMILL is on SR 24 in Black River Park, 1 mi. w. of jct. US 206. The mill, used for grinding flour in the 1760s, served as a gristmill until closing in 1913; the present building dates to 1826. The restored mill represents a typical gristmill of the 1880s. Four sets of grinding stones once produced 1,600 pounds of whole wheat flour and corn meal per hour. Two sets of millstones continue to operate.

Tours are conducted on a continuous basis Fri.-Tues. 10-5, July-Aug.; Sat.-Sun. 10-5, May-Oct. Last tour begins 1 hour before closing. Admission $3; senior citizens $2; ages 6-16, $1. Phone (908) 879-5463.

CLEMENTON—see Philadelphia and Vicinity in Pennsylvania p. 131.

CLINTON (C-2) pop. 2,100, elev. 184'

Clinton, a prominent milling town and stagecoach stop in the mid-1800s, presents a pleasing picture with its dam, waterfall and mill structures. Nearby Spruce Run and Round Valley state parks offer recreation.

HUNTERDON ART CENTER is on the south branch of the Raritan River at 7 Lower Center St. Housed in a restored grain mill, the center exhibits works by established and emerging contemporary artists. Educational programs and guided tours also are offered. Allow 1 hour, 30 minutes minimum. Wed.-Sun. 11-5; closed major holidays. Donations. Phone (908) 735-8415.

HUNTERDON HISTORICAL MUSEUM is .5 mi. n.w. off I-78 Clinton-Pittstown exit at 56 Main St. The 10-acre site is highlighted by the Old Red Mill, built around 1810. Its four floors of displays depict early regional life, agriculture and industries. Other buildings include a blacksmith shop, a quarry office, a general store, a log cabin and a one-room schoolhouse.

Recalling the area's former limestone quarrying industry that converted limestone from the surrounding cliffs into fertilizer are a stone crusher/sorter, old lime kilns and machinery sheds. Allow 1 hour minimum. Tues.-Sat. 10-4, Sun. noon-5, Apr.-Oct. Admission $4; over 65, $3; ages 6-16, $1. Phone (908) 735-4101.

DELAWARE WATER GAP NATIONAL RECREATION AREA—

see Pocono Mountains in Pennsylvania p. 147.

EAST HANOVER (G-4) pop. 9,900

IMAGINE THAT!!!, 2 mi. w. of Livingston Cir. on SR 10, is a discovery center designed to edu-

cate and entertain. More than 35 hands-on activities let children dabble in such pursuits as computers, art, music, drama and science. Food is available. Allow 1 hour, 30 minutes minimum. Sun.-Thurs. 10-6, Fri.-Sat. 10-8; closed Thanksgiving and Dec. 25. Admission $7.99; over 18, $2; under 1 free. AE, MC, VI. Phone (973) 952-0022.

EGG HARBOR CITY—

see Atlantic City and Vicinity p. 23.

ELIZABETH (H-5) pop. 110,000, elev. 29'

As part of the great industrial, densely populated urban area associated with New York City, Elizabeth and the adjoining sections of Union County are home to more than 1,500 manufacturing concerns. The city's marine terminal is one of the largest container ports in the world. It was here that John Philip Holland assembled the first successful submarine, later purchased by the U.S. Navy. The school that ultimately would become Princeton University was founded here by Jonathan Dickinson in 1746 as the College of New Jersey.

Elizabeth was the home of Alexander Hamilton and Aaron Burr, both of whom attended the old academy on the site now occupied by the First Presbyterian Church parish house. Other historic figures from Elizabeth include James Caldwell, the fiery "Fighting Parson" of the Revolution; William Livingston, who as governor of New Jersey 1776-90, lived at Liberty Hall, now known as Ursino; and Gen. Winfield Scott, the 1852 Whig presidential candidate.

Although the city suffered many attacks and skirmishes during the Revolution, nearly two dozen pre-Revolutionary buildings remain. Identified by plaques, several of these are in the 1000 and 1100 blocks of E. Jersey Street; the Bonnell House, at 1045, dates from about 1682 and is one of the oldest structures in Elizabeth.

Several parks offer respite from business. One of the largest is Warinanco Park at the west edge of town on Rahway Avenue. In addition to recreation, it offers a stadium and the Chatfield Memorial Garden, adorned by flowering trees, shrubs and other seasonal displays.

Union County Chamber of Commerce: 135 Jefferson Ave., P.O. Box 300, Elizabeth, NJ 07207-0300; phone (908) 352-0900.

BOXWOOD HALL STATE HISTORIC SITE is at 1073 E. Jersey St. The house, also known as Boudinot Mansion, was built in the 1750s. A noted resident was Elias Boudinot, president of the Continental Congress and signer of the Treaty of Peace with Great Britain. George Washington was entertained in the mansion on April 23, 1789, en route to his presidential inauguration in New York City. Wed.-Sat. 10-noon and 1-6, Sun. 1-6; closed major holidays. Free. Phone (973) 648-4540.

FAR HILLS (C-3) pop. 700, elev. 166'

On the western fringe of the northeastern New Jersey metropolitan complex, Far Hills developed as the center of a rolling region of grand estates where the wealthy engaged in farming and fox hunting. Recent years have seen a number of these estates converted into institutions and corporate headquarters.

GOLF HOUSE—U.S. GOLF ASSOCIATION, 2 mi. e. of US 202 on CR 512, has a library and museum with paintings, memorabilia and exhibits tracing the history of golf. The house is a three-story Georgian mansion that was the heart of the 50-acre W.J. Sloane estate. Allow 1 hour minimum. Mon.-Fri. 9-5, Sat.-Sun. 10-4; closed Jan. 1, Easter, Thanksgiving and Dec. 25. Free. Phone (908) 234-2300.

LEONARD J. BUCK GARDEN is at 11 Layton Rd., 1 mi. s.e. of US 202 via Liberty Corner Rd. This 33-acre garden contains wooded trails that connect gardens blended with natural rock outcroppings. Each area presents selections of alpine and woodland plants. Highlights include extensive collections of ferns and wildflowers; the peak blooming season is mid-April to mid-June. Allow 1 hour minimum. Mon.-Fri. 10-4, Sat. 10-5, Sun. noon-5, Mar.-Nov.; Mon.-Fri. 10-4, rest of year. Closed holidays Dec.-Feb. Admission $1. Pets and picnicking are not permitted. Phone (908) 234-2677.

FARMINGDALE (D-4) pop. 1,500, elev. 72'

ALLAIRE STATE PARK is 1.5 mi. w. of Garden State Pkwy. exit 98. Within the 3,062-acre park is the historic Howell Works, the site of a bog ore furnace and forge where iron was smelted in the early 1800s. The furnace was constructed and operated by industrialist and inventor James P. Allaire. Allaire Village, built 1822-37, comprises carpenter shop, a smithy, a general store, an enameling furnace, a carriage house, a bakery, a church and houses. A visitor center provides maps. Pine Creek Railroad displays antique steam trains, two of which offer 20-minute rides.

Allow a full day. Park open daily 8-dusk. Visitor center open Wed.-Sun. 10-5, Memorial Day-Labor Day; Sat.-Sun. 10-4, day after Labor Day-Oct. 31. Buildings open Sat.-Sun. 10-4, May-Oct. Train rides daily noon-4:30, July-Aug.; Sat.-Sun. noon-4, May-June and Sept.-Oct. Park and village free. Train, including Christmas train, $2.50. Parking $3 Sat.-Sun. and holidays, Memorial Day-Labor Day. Phone (732) 938-2371. *See Recreation Chart and Freehold in the AAA Mid-Eastern CampBook.*

FLEMINGTON (C-2) pop. 4,000, elev. 183'

Already a prosperous distribution point for the region's agricultural products, Flemington became widely known in the early 20th century for the manufacture of pottery and cut glass. A different kind of notoriety came to town in 1935 when the much-publicized Lindbergh kidnapping trial was held in the county courthouse.

One of the area's highlights is the seven-story Vollendam Windmill, about 21 miles northwest via SR 12 and CR 519 to Adamic Hill Road in Milford. With sail arms spanning 68 feet from tip to tip, this operating Holland-style windmill is an unusual sight. The first three floors of the windmill can be toured May through October.

Shopping areas: Liberty Village features specialty shops and outlet stores housed in Colonial-style buildings on the site of an old railroad turntable.

THE BLACK RIVER & WESTERN RAILROAD departs from Black River Station in Liberty Village/Feed Mill Plaza on Stangal Rd. off SR 12W in Flemington, and from the Ringoes Station on CR 579. Steam and vintage diesel locomotives provide the power for 11-mile round trips. Departures every 90 minutes from Flemington Sat.-Sun. and holidays 11:30-4, from Ringoes 10:45-3:15, mid-Mar. through Dec. 31 (also Thurs.-Fri. from Flemington 11:30-2:30, from Ringoes 10:45-1:45, July-Aug.). Round-trip fare $7; military with ID and ages 3-12, $3.50. Phone (908) 782-9600.

FLORHAM PARK (G-4) pop. 8,500

The name Florham Park was derived from the first names of millionaire Hamilton Twombly and his wife, Florence; the "Park" was added in honor of Dr. Leslie D. Ward's estate, Brooklake Park.

The College of St. Elizabeth, a Catholic liberal arts college founded in 1899, is said to be the oldest women's college in the state. The 420-acre campus is partially in the town of Convent Station. Shared by the town of Madison, the Florham-Madison campus of Fairleigh Dickinson University occupies 187 acres on the site of the former Twombly estate. Tours of the campus are available by appointment; phone (973) 593-8900.

The Little Red Schoolhouse, Ridgedale Avenue and Columbia Turnpike, was built in 1866 and used as a school until 1914. The schoolhouse is now a museum operated by the Florham Park Historical Society. The Twombly Mansion, begun in 1893 and completed in 1896, serves as an administration building at Fairleigh Dickinson University. The 100-room manor house is a replica of one wing of Hampton Court in England.

Florham Park provides the summer training grounds for the New York Giants professional football team. The practice sessions, held at Fairleigh Dickinson University, are open to the public; parking is available at the Park Avenue lot. The Hamilton Park Conference Center, 175 Park Ave., is the home of the New Jersey Stars, a professional tennis team; phone (973) 377-2424.

FORKED RIVER (E-4) pop. 4,200, elev. 13'

POPCORN PARK ZOO, on Lacey Rd. 7 mi. w. of Garden State Pkwy. exit 74, provides a haven for more than 200 wild, domestic and exotic animals no longer able to exist in their natural habitats. Visitors are greeted by friendly geese, goats and deer who often serve as escorts through the zoo. A Bengal tiger, bull elephant, lions, black bears, foxes, bulls and a macaw live in comfortable compounds. Many animals roam freely.

Picnicking is permitted. Allow 1 hour, 30 minutes minimum. Daily 11-5. Admission $3.25; over 65 and under 1, $2.25. Phone (609) 693-1900.

FORT LEE (G-6) pop. 32,000, elev. 141'

In one of her endless succession of perils, Pauline clings to the sheer cliff above the river; the Sheik perpetrates an incendiary love scene in a silken tent. These great moments on the silver screen were filmed not in Hollywood but in Fort Lee, movie capital from 1907 until the mid-1920s. At the peak of activity before World War I, seven studios and 21 companies produced the silent films that revolutionized entertainment around the world.

The convenient and dramatic location on the Hudson River palisades that made Fort Lee the first movie capital had some 130 years earlier made it a critical point in Gen. George Washington's unsuccessful attempt to stem the tide of British forces.

Fort Lee has matured into a residential suburb of New York City, to which it is connected by the George Washington Bridge. The bridge also serves as the southern terminus of the Palisades Interstate Parkway, a scenic section of highway that skirts the Hudson River and continues north into New York.

Greater Fort Lee Chamber of Commerce: 2357 Lemoine Ave., Fort Lee, NJ 07024; phone (201) 944-7575.

FORT LEE HISTORIC PARK is on Hudson Terr. s. of the George Washington Bridge in Palisades Interstate Park. Fort Lee was built in 1776 by Washington's troops as a link in fortifications defending New York and the Hudson River against British warships. Gen. Charles Cornwallis and more than 5,000 soldiers, however, crossed the river 5 miles north of the fort. To avoid capture Washington led his demoralized army on a hasty retreat during the winter of 1776-77. These were the days later described by Thomas Paine as the "times that try men's souls."

Reconstructed cannon batteries, a rifle parapet and a firing step overlook the river and the Manhattan skyline beyond. A visitor center offers a 12-minute film hourly; lighted displays depict the campaign. Exhibits include models, miniature scenes and pictures accompanied by descriptive text. Wed.-Sun. 10-5, Mar.-Dec. Free. Parking $4, Apr.-Oct. Phone (201) 461-1776.

FORT MONMOUTH (D-5)

Fort Monmouth began in 1917 as the Signal Corps Camp—a cluster of tents on a small portion of the present installation. The camp has evolved into the home of the U.S. Army Communications and Electronics Command headquarters, one of the largest military and technological centers devoted to developing, supplying and overseeing command, control, communications, computers, intelligence, electronic, sensor and warfare systems used by U.S. troops worldwide.

U.S. ARMY COMMUNICATIONS-ELECTRONICS MUSEUM, in Kaplan Hall near the Avenue of Memories, displays communication systems used by the U.S. Army, from the earliest developments to current technology. Included are exhibits about the Army Pigeon Service from World War I, radios developed by early radio pioneer Edwin Armstrong, heliographs, battlefield sensors and radar and satellite dishes. Mon.-Fri. noon-4. Free. Phone (732) 532-4390.

FRANKLIN (B-3) pop. 5,000, elev. 554'

Rockhounds swarming over the old mine dumps at Franklin often are rewarded amply; nearly 300 minerals are found in the town. Zinc was the reason for Franklin's development. For nearly a century, until the ore body was depleted in the 1950s, New Jersey Zinc Co. mined 00,000 tons of ore annually.

FRANKLIN MINERAL MUSEUM, on Evans St., 5 mi. n.w. of jct. SR 23 and Franklin Ave., has samples of the minerals mined from the area. Ores and minerals are displayed under ultraviolet light in the Fluorescent Room, producing brilliant colors. An adjacent mine replica demonstrates zinc mining. Dinosaur footprints and fossils from around the world also are on display. Visitors can prospect at a nearby site that operates during museum hours.

Allow 1 hour minimum. Mon.-Sat. 10-4, Sun. 12:30-4:30, Mar. 1-Dec. 1; closed Easter and Thanksgiving. Museum $4, students $2. Prospecting $4, students $2. Combination rate for museum and prospecting $7, students $3. MC, VI. Phone (973) 827-3481.

FREEHOLD (D-4) pop. 10,700, elev. 180'

The Battle of Monmouth occurred in Freehold on June 28, 1778, when Gen. George Washington's army overtook Sir Henry Clinton's army as it retreated from Philadelphia. During this battle Molly Pitcher—so called because she brought water to the battlefield for the soldiers—helped keep her husband's cannon in action when he was overcome by the 100-degree heat.

Just before the battle Clinton used the home of farmer William Covenhoven as his headquarters; the house, at 150 W. Main St., dates from the early 1750s and contains period furnishings; phone (732) 462-1466.

Outdoor recreation is available at nearby Turkey Swamp County Park (see Recreation Chart). Entertainment includes harness racing at the Freehold Raceway, US 9 and SR 33, during most of the year.

Note: Policies concerning admittance of children to pari-mutuel betting facilities vary. Phone for information.

Western Monmouth Chamber of Commerce: 36 W. Main St., Freehold, NJ 07728; phone (732) 462-3030.

MONMOUTH BATTLEFIELD STATE PARK, 3 mi. w. on SR 33, was the scene of one of the largest Revolutionary battles, fought on June 28, 1778. British troops under Sir Henry Clinton stopped at Freehold before proceeding to Sandy Hook, where ships were waiting to carry them to New York. Before they could leave, Gen. George Washington led his troops from Valley Forge into a head-on collision with the British. The American troops, trained by Maj. Gen. Friedrich Von Steuben, matched British regulars in pitched battles for the first time.

The visitor center features displays that trace the troops' movements during the battle. On the grounds is the Craig House, built in 1710 and restored to its 18th-century appearance. The British used the house as a field hospital. Owl Haven, on CR 522, is a New Jersey Audubon Society facility. Park open daily 8-8, Memorial Day-Labor Day; 8-6 day after Labor Day-Sept. 30; 8-4:30, rest of year. Visitor center open daily 9-4. Owl Haven open Tues.-Sat. noon-5, Sun. 1:30-5:30. Free. Phone (732) 462-9616 for the park, or (732) 780-7007 for Owl Haven nature center.

MONMOUTH COUNTY HISTORICAL ASSOCIATION MUSEUM AND LIBRARY is at 70 Court St. Collections of furniture, paintings and decorative arts, most of which were owned or made in New Jersey, occupy two floors. Highlights include English and Chinese ceramics, folk art and toys. A research library houses genealogical materials. Museum open Tues.-Sat. 10-4, Sun. 1-4. Library open Wed.-Sat. 10-4. Both closed Jan. 1, July 4, Thanksgiving and Dec. 24-25. Admission $2; senior citizens $1.50; ages 6-18, $1. Phone (732) 462-1466.

GATEWAY NATIONAL RECREATION AREA (I-6)

Gateway National Recreation Area, so named because it is at the entrance to the great New York-New Jersey estuary, consists of the Breezy Point, Jamaica Bay and Staten Island units in New York and the Sandy Hook Unit in New Jersey. The recreation area was created by Congress in 1972 to reclaim the parkland's ocean beaches, dunes, wooded uplands and bays from the effects of urbanization, which had decimated the region's bird, fish and animal populations.

Among the numbers of replenished wildlife are more than 300 species of birds that frequent the Jamaica Bay Wildlife Refuge and Sandy Hook Unit along the Atlantic flyway.

SANDY HOOK UNIT, entered by bridge from SR 36 at Highlands, is a barrier beach peninsula extending into the mouth of New York Harbor. First sighted by the crew of Henry Hudson's *Half Moon* in 1609, the hook was a favorite fishing and clamming ground of the Lenni Lenape Indians. It was later the estate of Richard Hartshorne, an English Quaker. During the Revolution the site was occupied by British troops as part of their defense of New York City.

Fort Hancock, established in 1895, is still largely intact, as are the gun emplacements that defended the entrance to New York Harbor during the Spanish-American War and World Wars I and II. Also present are the remains of the Sandy Hook Proving Ground, where new U.S. Army ammunition and weapons were tested 1874-1919.

The Sandy Hook Lighthouse, one of the oldest in the nation, has operated since 1764. Because many shipwrecks occurred despite New Jersey's lighthouses, the first station of the U.S. Life Saving Service was established at Sandy Hook in 1849.

Sandy Hook presents a variety of natural environments unusual in so compact an area. A forest of large holly trees, a dune area supporting some of the beach plums sought by the American Indians, a salt marsh, mudflats and the seashore— each with its individual ecosystem—are available for exploration.

The peninsula's ocean beaches provide opportunities for swimming and surf fishing. A visitor center at Spermaceti Cove is open daily 10-5. The Sandy Hook ranger station is staffed 24 hours a day. The Sandy Hook Unit charges a $4 parking fee Mon.-Fri., $5 Sat.-Sun. and holidays, Memorial Day weekend-Labor Day. *See Recreation Chart.*

Fort Hancock Museum is housed in an 1899 building that served as the post guardhouse, or jail. The museum features original jail cells, photographs that depict the history of Fort Hancock and dioramas of the fort's buildings. Daily 1-5, July-Aug.; Sat.-Sun. 1-5, rest of year. Free. Phone (732) 872-5970.

GREENWICH (F-1) pop. 900

GIBBON HOUSE, on Ye Greate St., was built in 1730 by wealthy merchant Nicholas Gibbon and is patterned after a London townhouse. The house is furnished with 18th- and 19th-century items, including locally made rush-seated "Ware" chairs. Tues.-Sat. noon-4, Sun. 2-5, Apr. 1-Dec. 15. Donations. Phone (609) 451-8454.

HACKENSACK (G-6) pop. 37,000, elev. 11'

Remembering where their journeys had begun the Manhattan Dutchmen who crossed the Hudson to establish a trading post on a lesser rive about 4 miles west called their site New Barbados. For 274 years the name, as well as the architecture of some buildings and institutions retained the Dutch stamp. Not until 1921, in an act that traded euphony for a city charter, did New Barbados become Hackensack, an American Indian term meaning "place of sharp ground."

Due to its location on the road that linked Manhattan and its bastion at Fort Lee *(see place listing p. 30)* with the Passaic River, the village was a strategic point during the Revolution. Gen George Washington and his troops stopped in the village after evacuating Fort Lee. Intrigue and skirmishes were common throughout the war; in 1780 a plundering party of Hessians and Britons burned the New Barbados courthouse.

The Green at the south end of Main Street was the core of New Barbados. It contained in one small area the courthouse for government and justice, the pillories for punishment and the Church on the Green for absolution. Built at the Green's northeast corner in 1696 and reconstructed several times since, the church is one of the oldest in the state. Its Dutch Colonial architecture served as a prototype for several churches in the area.

A major 20th-century project in the vicinity was the draining of the tidal marshes known as the Meadowlands south of Hackensack in nearby East Rutherford.

The resulting Meadowlands Sports Complex includes Giants Stadium, home of both the Giants and Jets of the National Football League Continental Airlines Arena, home court of the National Basketball Association's New Jersey Nets; and Meadowlands Racetrack, which features both thoroughbred and harness racing. The complex is at the intersection of exit 16W of the New Jersey Turnpike and SR 3; phone (201) 935-8500 for general information or (201) 935-3900 for the box office.

Hackensack Chamber of Commerce: 140 Main St., Hackensack, NJ 07601; phone (201) 489-3700.

SAVE SUBMARINE USS *LING* NEW JERSEY NAVAL MUSEUM, 150 River St. at Court St., is a memorial to those who served aboard U.S. submarines during World War II. The museum includes pictorial history of the development of the submarine from 1900 to the nuclear age, uniforms medals, a two-man periscope and models Navy vessels and aircraft. Allow 1 hour minimum. Tours Wed.-Sun. 10:15-4. Admission $5 ages 3-12, $2.50. Phone (201) 342-3268.

HADDONFIELD—*see Philadelphia and Vicinity in Pennsylvania p. 132.*

HALEDON (F-5) pop. 7,000

During the 1913 Paterson Silk strike, Haledon achieved a certain notoriety when its socialist mayor allowed strikers to meet in co-worker Pietro Botto's home. Thousands gathered, unmolested by the Paterson authorities, to hear labor organizer William "Big Bill" Haywood and writers John Reed and Upton Sinclair. Although the workers' demands were not immediately met, the Paterson Silk strike was a major turning point in the history of unionized labor.

AMERICAN LABOR MUSEUM/BOTTO HOUSE NATIONAL LANDMARK, 83 Norwood St., occupies the 1908 Botto House, which was the home of an Italian immigrant silk mill worker. Featured are period rooms and changing exhibits that illustrate the history of the labor movement in the United States and the lifestyle of immigrant workers and their families. An exhibit about the Paterson Silk strike in 1913 is in the library. Allow 1 hour, 30 minutes minimum. Wed.-Sat. 1-4; other times by appointment. Closed holidays except Labor Day. Admission $1.50, under 12 free. Phone (973) 595-7953.

HAMILTON (D-3) pop. 86,600, elev. 191′

Hamilton, in the southern part of Mercer County, is next to the Trenton metropolitan area. Dedicated to area residents who served in the U.S. Armed Forces, Veterans' Park covers 320 acres.

GROUNDS FOR SCULPTURE, off I-295 exit 63, .5 mi. w. on SR 33, .3 mi. n. on Ward Ave. Extension, then .1 mi. e. to 18 Fairgrounds Rd., is a 22-acre sculpture park and museum on the site of the former New Jersey State Fairgrounds. It features changing exhibits and contemporary sculpture by American and international artists. Food available. Allow 1 hour minimum. Fri.-Sun. 10-4, Tues.-Thurs. by appointment only; closed holidays. Free. Phone (609) 586-0616.

KUSER FARM MANSION AND PARK, with entrances at 390 Newkirk Ave. and Kuser Rd., is the restored 22-acre estate of prominent businessman Fred Kuser. The Kuser family was instrumental in forming Fox Film Corp., later to become 20th Century Fox. A private projection and viewing room is among the 17 rooms open in the mansion. Built in 1892 by German craftsmen, the house is furnished with original and period pieces. The family also manufactured the Mercer Motor Car in Hamilton; Mercer-related items are displayed.

A self-guiding walking tour visits the formal garden, tennis house, windmill, gazebo and other outbuildings. Picnic and playground facilities are available. Allow 1 hour minimum. Thurs.-Sun. 11-3, May-Nov.; Sat.-Sun. 11-3, Feb.-Apr. Last tour begins 30 minutes before closing. Free. Phone (609) 890-3630.

HAMPTON (C-2) pop. 1,500

TOWNSHIP OF LEBANON MUSEUM is 7 mi. n. of I-78 off SR 31 at 57 Musconetcong River Rd. This Greek Revival structure was built in 1823 as a one-room schoolhouse; a second story was added in the 1870s. The first floor is a re-created schoolroom with period furnishings, and the second floor displays changing exhibits. Tues. and Thurs. 9:30-5, Sat. 1-5; closed holidays. Free. Phone (908) 537-6464.

HIGHLANDS (I-6) pop. 4,800

Summer vacationers and anglers are the backbone of the economy of Highlands, connected by bridge to the Sandy Hook Unit of the Gateway National Recreation Area (see place listing p. 32). With neighboring Highlands Beach and Atlantic Highlands, the town takes its name from the hills that rise abruptly from the shore.

Nearby 266-foot Mount Mitchill is one of the first points of land sighted by ships bound for New York Harbor. Ocean Boulevard, a scenic drive off SR 36, connects Highlands to Atlantic Highlands. The Highlands hills provided the setting for James Fenimore Cooper's 1831 book "The Water Witch." The title of the novel refers to the hero's vessel that hid among the coves of Sandy Hook.

Eastern Monmouth Chamber of Commerce: 170 Broad St., Red Bank, NJ 07701; phone (732) 741-0055.

TWIN LIGHTS STATE HISTORIC SITE, Lighthouse Rd. off Highland Ave., is a twin-tower 1862 lighthouse that replaced a structure built in 1828. An important site in lighthouse technology, the tower once was the primary light source for New York harbor. A museum contains exhibits about the history of the lighthouse. Visitors can climb the north tower. Allow 2 hours minimum. Grounds open daily 9-dusk. North tower and museum open Wed.-Sun. 10-5. Closed Jan. 1, Thanksgiving and Dec. 25. Free. Phone (732) 872-1814.

HOBOKEN (H-6) pop. 33,400, elev. 7′

Squeezed into little more than a square mile of land between the Hudson River and North Bergen, Hoboken is a major railroad terminal and seaport across the river from New York City. West of the Hudson River is Stevens Institute of Technology, founded in 1870 as an engineering academy. The college has expanded from its original location at Castle Point to include centers for science, research, management and engineering.

Pleasure and art, rather than business, were the foundation of Hoboken's early reputation. While beer gardens, fireworks and assorted cheery charlatans attracted throngs to the city's River Walk, the scenic countryside drew such literary, artistic and society figures as John Jacob Astor, Washington Irving and William Cullen Bryant. A prominent Hoboken native was John Stevens, who built the country's first steam locomotive in 1824.

Numerous shops, restaurants and nightclubs exist, making Hoboken an alternative to nearby New York City for nightlife.

HOLMDEL (D-4) pop. 11,500, elev. 101'

The tree-shaded village of Holmdel is one of the oldest communities in Monmouth County, having been settled by the Holmes family in the mid-1600s. The Holmes-Henrickson House, built by William Holmes about 1754, still stands at Longstreet and Roberts roads and is a fine example of local Dutch building traditions. Visitors can tour the house from May through October; phone (732) 462-1466.

HOPE (B-2) pop. 1,700, elev. 415'

"Jenny, jump!" Apparently the little girl did, foiling the American Indians whom her father had spotted sneaking up on her. No one knows the true story, but the warning cry is commemorated in the name of the mountain that rises above Hope. The village was founded in 1774 by Moravians from Bethlehem, Pa. They built a sturdy, self-sustaining community, with homes, a church, a public inn, mills, a brewery and a distillery.

Several of the structures remain, their stone walls contrasting with newer concrete buildings. The Moravians' position as conscientious objectors during the Revolution did not endear them to the Patriot forces, but they won respect by their care for sick or wounded soldiers. The colony—or the few who had survived a smallpox epidemic—returned to Pennsylvania in 1808.

Self-guiding tours: Brochures outlining a walking tour past Hope's Moravian architecture can be obtained at stores and banks throughout town and at the Municipal Building Clerk's Office a 407 Great Meadows Road (CR 611), Mon.-Fri 8-4; phone (908) 459-5011.

LAND OF MAKE BELIEVE, .7 mi. s. on CR 611 off I-80 exit 12, is a family amusement and water park oriented to children under 13 that offers rides, shows and attractions in addition to play areas and water activities. Features include Pirates Cove, a life-size pirate ship with slides; Black Beards River; Middle Earth Theater; an 1862 train; Pirates Peak tube slides; hayrides; roller coaster; and "Old McDonald's Farm." Picnic facilities are available.

Daily 10-6, mid-June through Labor Day; Sat. Sun. 10-6, Memorial Day weekend to mid-Jun and first weekend after Labor Day. Ages 2-18 $14.50; ages 19-62, $11.50; over 62, $10. Phone (908) 459-9000. *See ad.*

JACKSON (D-4) pop. 33,200

A township at the northern fringes of the Pine Barrens, Jackson contains several campgrounds and parks. The Jackson Forest Nursery is off CR 527-528. Prospertown Lake, a wildlife management area west on CR 537, offers hunting and fishing. Canoeing is available on the Upper Toms River.

Jackson Chamber of Commerce: 19 N. County Line Rd., P.O. Box AC, Jackson, NJ 08527; phone (732) 363-1080.

SIX FLAGS GREAT ADVENTURE is about 1 mi. s. of I-195 off CR 537. It features approximately 100 rides, shows and attractions in areas such as Fantasy Forest, Boardwalk, Frontier Adventures and Movietown. Other highlights include Adventure Rivers, a water ride section; and Bugs Bunny Land, which offers rides and activities for youngsters under 54 inches tall. Visitors can drive their own vehicle or take a guided bus tour through adjacent Six Flags Wild Safari Animal Park, which consists of 350 acres fit for more than 1,200 animals from six continents.

Allow a full day. Theme park opens daily at 10, mid-May through Labor Day; otherwise varies. Closing times vary between 6 and 11 p.m. Six Flags Wild Safari Animal Park open daily -4, mid-May through Labor Day; otherwise varies. Theme park $35; under 54 inches tall $25;

over age 55, $18.02; under age 3 free. Six Flags Wild Safari Animal Park $15. Two-park ticket $38.02; under 54 inches tall $28.02; over age 55, $20.99. Parking $7. DS, MC, VI. Phone (732) 928-1821. *See color ad p. 35.*

JERSEY CITY (H-6) pop. 228,500, elev. 180'

Jersey City is a major manufacturing and transportation center on a peninsula in the Hudson River west of Manhattan Island. Each year more than $1.3 billion in steel, chemicals, soaps, perfumes, elevators and a myriad of other products pour from approximately 600 industrial plants. Completion of the Hudson River railroad tunnels in 1910 cemented the city's position as the transportation and distribution heart of the New York-New Jersey megalopolis.

The peninsula, Paulus Hook, first was settled by the Dutch about 1630, but less-than-friendly relations with the American Indians postponed the establishment of the first permanent settlement at Bergen until 1660. Gradually the hook became a strategic link between New York and cities to the west and south. As such it played an important role in the American Revolution; it was the 1779 site of the Battle of Paulus Hook.

Urban revitalization has rescued such architectural treasures as the brownstone houses in which the city's rich and powerful lived during the late 19th and early 20th centuries. The Hamilton Park area boasts a number of these restored homes.

Hudson County Chamber of Commerce: 574 Summit Ave. #404, Jersey City, NJ 07306; phone (201) 653-7400.

COLGATE CLOCK, 105 Hudson St., faces the bay and is best seen from the water. The dial is 50 feet in diameter; the minute hand weighs 2,200 pounds and moves 23 inches every minute.

[SAVE] ★ **LIBERTY SCIENCE CENTER,** 251 Phillip St. in Liberty State Park, presents hundreds of interactive exhibits, theater shows and displays on four levels. An 11-ton geodesic dome houses one of the nation's largest IMAX® theaters, and a tower capped with a glass observation deck provides views of the Manhattan skyline. Exhibits are divided into three categories—Environment, Health and Invention—each with its own floor.

The Environment floor features salt marsh displays and Bug Zoo. On the Health level, visitors can navigate a darkened 100-foot Touch Tunnel using their tactile sense. The Invention floor provides opportunities to create your own animation or build structures with the aid of a 10-foot-tall electromagnetic crane. Scientific demonstrations are presented throughout the day. Food is available.

Allow 3 hours minimum. Daily 9:30-5:30, Apr. 1-Labor Day; Tues.-Sun. 9:30-5:30, rest of year. Closed Thanksgiving and Dec. 25. IMAX® shows begin on the hour.

Exhibit admission $9.50; over 62 and ages 13-17, $8.50; ages 2-12, $6. IMAX® $7; over 62 and ages 13-17, $6; under 12, $5. Laser show $2. Combination ticket $13.50; over 62 and ages 13-17, $11.50; ages 2-12, $9.50. Parking $5. Under 12 must be with an adult. AE, DS, MC, VI Phone (201) 200-1000.

LIBERTY STATE PARK, off exit 14B of the New Jersey Tpke. Extention, is a 1,114-acre urban based park facing Liberty Island, site of the Statue of Liberty and Ellis Island, the nation' immigration center for several decades. The park which has a view of the New York City skyline has a picnic area and playground. The historic Central Railroad of New Jersey Terminal, from which early settlers departed, also is in the park.

The toll ferry *Miss Freedom* makes daily trips to the Statue of Liberty and Ellis Island. Park open daily 6 a.m.-10 p.m.; closed Dec. 25. Ferry operates daily 9-5, Memorial Day-Labor Day 9:30-3:30, rest of year. Closed Dec. 25. Park free. Ferry $7; senior citizens $6; ages 3-17, $3. Parking $5. Phone (201) 915-3400 or 915-3401. *See Recreation Chart.*

SANDY HOOK LADY, exit 14B off New Jersey turnpike, following signs to Liberty Landing Marina. The authentic 85-foot paddlewheeler sail along the Shrewsbury and Navesink river Lunch, dinner and Sunday brunch cruises are available. Sightseeing, theme and holiday cruise are offered. Three-hour dinner cruises depart Wed. and Fri.-Sat. at 7, Sun. at 6:30, May-Oct. Dinner cruise $35 Wed., Fri. and Sun.; $40 Sat. Reservations are recommended. Fares for other cruises vary. MC, VI. Phone (732) 291-4354.

★ **STATUE OF LIBERTY NATIONAL MONUMENT** is in Upper New York Bay on Liberty Island. The statue was presented to the United States by France in 1884 in commemoration of the two countries' alliance during the American Revolution. Measuring 151 feet high on a 154-foot-high pedestal, it is the tallest statue of modern times. The American Museum of Immigration in the base traces the history of immigration into the United States; also presented is a exhibit about the history of the statue. Nearby Ellis Island in N.Y. was the main point of entry into the United States for immigrants 1892-192

Visitors should arrive early during the summer to ensure access to the crown viewing area. On peak visitation days the wait and the climb can take more than 3 hours. Food is available. Picnicking is not permitted.

Allow 2 hours minimum. Ferry service from Battery Park in Lower Manhattan to Liberty Island is available daily 9:30-3:30 (also 3:30-4:30 in the summer). Return trips every 30 minutes phone for schedule. Tickets sold daily 8:30-3:30 (also 3:30-4:30 in the summer). Ferry service from Liberty State Park in Jersey City, N.J., runs every 45 minutes Mon.-Fri. 9:30-3:40, Sat.-Sun.

9:15-4:15, Memorial Day-Labor Day; daily 9:30-3:30, rest of year. Hours may vary; phone ahead. Closed Dec. 25. Statue free. Ferry $7; over 61, $6; ages 3-17, $3. Phone (212) 363-3200 for the monument, (212) 915-3200 for Liberty State Park or (212) 269-5755 for the ferry.

LAKEHURST (E-4) pop. 3,100, elev. 72′

Surrounded by fish and wildlife management areas, Lakehurst is best known for its role in aviation history. The community served as the American terminal for the huge, transatlantic lighter-than-air craft during the 1920s and 1930s. The naval air station at Lakehurst was home to the German dirigibles Graf Zeppelin and Hindenburg. In 1937 the Hindenburg burned in the air while landing, resulting in the loss of 36 lives. Hangar #1 is a reminder of that era.

The event is commemorated by a small monument on the Naval Air Engineering Station grounds. An area is outlined that approximates the size of the gondola of the airship. Self-guiding tours of the area outside the hangar are available; phone (732) 323-2620 for information.

LAMBERTVILLE (D-2) pop. 3,900

HOWELL LIVING HISTORY FARM, 2 mi. s. via SR 29 and 2 mi. e. on Valley Rd. to 101 Hunter Rd., is a restoration of an early 1900s farm. This 126-acre homestead presents a portrait of the period, with farmhands tilling the fields and tending livestock just as their ancestors did. A self-guiding tour brochure is available at the visitor center. Tues.-Sat. 10-4, Sun. noon-4, Feb. 1-Dec. 6. Free. Phone (609) 737-3299.

LONG BRANCH (D-5) pop. 28,700, elev. 28′

One of America's first seashore resorts, Long Branch rivaled Saratoga, N.Y., in popularity during its heyday. Founded upon stiff Philadelphia moral codes in the late 18th century, the resort required that a female beachgoer be escorted to the water by a male companion. Preferring to choose their own partners, the wealthy socialites fostered a lucrative business for available young men, an enterprise that lasted until the Gay '90s.

Having relaxed its mores, Long Branch boomed with coed beaches, gambling and other adult amusements introduced and perpetuated by the rich and famous. Such colorful personalities as Diamond Jim Brady and Lily Langtry frequented the town. Long Branch also was the preferred summer home of Presidents Ulysses S. Grant, Rutherford B. Hayes, James A. Garfield, Chester A. Arthur, Benjamin Harrison, William McKinley and Woodrow Wilson.

Long Branch offers a 2-mile boardwalk and 5 miles of oceanfront with good swimming, sunbathing and surf fishing. Seven Presidents Park, (732) 229-0924, has 33 acres along the oceanfront. Monmouth Park, just inland in Oceanport,

offers horse racing early June through early September.

Note: Policies concerning admittance of children to pari-mutuel betting facilities vary. Phone for information.

Greater Long Branch Chamber of Commerce: P.O. Box 628, Long Branch, NJ 07740; phone (732) 222-0400.

LYNDHURST (G-6) pop. 18,300, elev. 39′

MEDIEVAL TIMES DINNER AND TOURNAMENT is off New Jersey Tpke. exit 16W, w. on SR 3, then s. on SR 17 to 149 Polito Ave. In a building resembling an old European castle, visitors are treated as guests of a royal family. Serfs and wenches serve dinner during an arena performance of knights on horseback catching flags, piercing rings, throwing javelins and fighting with swords.

Allow 3 hours minimum. Wed.-Thurs. at 7:30 p.m., Fri.-Sat. at 8 p.m., Sun. at 4:30. Admission $36.95; under 12, $26.95. Reservations are suggested. AE, DS, MC, VI. Phone (201) 933-2220 or (800) 828-2945.

MADISON (G-4) pop. 15,900, elev. 248′

Madison, settled about 1685, was known as Bottle Hill after a local tavern that existed in Colonial days. It was renamed for President James Madison in 1834. Tours of the Drew University and Fairleigh Dickinson University campuses can be arranged; phone (973) 408-3739 for Drew University or (973) 593-8900 for Fairleigh Dickinson University. The New Jersey Shakespeare Festival, in residence at Drew University, presents Shakespearean works as well as classical and modern plays.

Madison Chamber of Commerce: P.O. Box 152, Madison, NJ 07940; phone (973) 377-7830.

MUSEUM OF EARLY TRADES AND CRAFTS, Main St. and Green Village Rd., explains the tools and techniques of trades and crafts from the late 1600s to 1850. The museum displays implements used by cobblers, coopers, tinsmiths, wheelwrights, leather workers and others whose trades have either disappeared or been mechanized. Changing exhibits also are presented throughout the year.

Arranged in such settings as a schoolroom, Colonial kitchen and workshop, many of these tools and other items evoke the lifestyles of early New Jersey settlers. Tues.-Sat. 10-4, Sun. 2-5; closed Jan. 1, July 4, Thanksgiving and Dec. 25. Admission $3.50; under 13, $2. Phone (973) 377-2982.

MARGATE CITY—
see Atlantic City and Vicinity p. 23.

MENLO PARK (H-4) elev. 78′

A suburb at the fringe of the industrial metropolis, Menlo Park was less congested when

Thomas Alva Edison moved to the area in 1876. For the next decade the "Wizard of Menlo Park" astonished his neighbors by conducting field experiments on an electric railway and by creating the first Christmas holiday light display in the area; he amazed the world with such innovations as the dynamo, phonograph, automatic telegraph and incandescent light bulb *(see Edison National Historic Site in West Orange p. 50).*

THOMAS A. EDISON MEMORIAL TOWER AND MUSEUM is .6 mi. w. of Garden State Pkwy. exit 131 to Christie St. On the site of Edison's laboratory is Edison Memorial Tower, designed to incorporate the devices pioneered by the inventor. A 13-foot replica of the first incandescent bulb tops the edifice. The museum contains some of Edison's early inventions and memorabilia. Allow 1 hour minimum. Wed.-Fri. 12:30-4 (also Tues. 12:30-4, Memorial Day-Labor Day), Sat.-Sun. 12:30-4:30. Donations. Phone (732) 549-3299.

MIDDLETOWN (I-5) pop. 68,200, elev. 111'

On Raritan Bay, Middletown is the largest township in Monmouth county. A Colonial atmosphere prevails along some of the city's residential streets, where ancient shade trees tower over large old homes. Some 17th-century structures remain. Marlpit Hall, currently closed for renovation, is a Dutch cottage that contains furnishings from the mid-18th century; phone (732) 462-1466.

Northern Monmouth Chamber of Commerce: 500 Union Square Commons, SR 35, P.O. Box 424, Middletown, NJ 07748; phone (732) 747-9630.

MILLBURN (G-5) pop. 18,600

Millburn, settled in the 1720s, evolved from a 1664 land grant by Charles II. Having acquired more than 1,500 acres in Millburn in 1877, Stewart Hartshorn, inventor of the window shade, designed a village called Short Hills. Although it probably cut into sales of his invention, Hartshorn's meandering street plan called for the preservation of as many trees as possible.

The success of Millburn's many lumber, paper, fulling, cloth and hat mills became assured with the arrival of the Morris and Essex Railroad, later called the Erie-Lackawanna Railroad. The tracks linked the town with Newark and New York City and the coal industry to the northwest.

A former mill on Brookside Drive is now the home of the Paper Mill Playhouse, New Jersey's designated state theater; phone (973) 376-4343.

Millburn-Short Hills Chamber of Commerce: 56 Main St., P.O. Box 651, Millburn, NJ 07041; phone (973) 379-1198.

MILLVILLE (F-2) pop. 26,000, elev. 35'

At the head of tidewater on the Maurice (MOR-ris) River, Millville began as a river port, but with the discovery of silica sand the town soon became a glass-making center. By the end of the 19th century the only American city to produce more glassware than Millville was Pittsburgh. Glass remains among the city's diversified industries.

The region also is noted for having been the home of hunter and woodsman "Stretch" Garrison, whose alleged feats included riding sharks and porpoises up the Maurice River and raising a rooster so tall that it ate from the porch roof. Although it is suspected that his nickname resulted from what he might have done to the truth, "Stretch" remains a local folk hero.

Millville Chamber of Commerce: 25 E. Main St., P.O. Box 831, Millville, NJ 08332; phone (609) 825-2600.

★ **WHEATON VILLAGE,** off Wade Blvd. following signs to 1501 Glasstown Rd., is a 60-acre re-creation of a glassmaking community. Glassmaking demonstrations are given daily in the working 1888 glass factory; a narrator provides a description of the glassmaking process. On the grounds are the Museum of American Glass, a lake, a playground, the Folk-Life Center, a stained-glass studio, an 1876 one-room schoolhouse, the 1897 Palermo train station, a general store, a train ride and picnic facilities.

Food is available. Allow 3 hours minimum. Daily 10-5, Apr.-Dec.; Wed.-Sun. 10-5, rest of year. Closed Jan. 1, Easter, Thanksgiving and Dec. 25. Admission $6.50; over 62, $5.50; ages 6-18, $3.50. Phone (609) 825-6800 or (800) 998-4552.

Museum of American Glass is the highlight of the village. Displays include more than 7,500 objects, from paperweights and Mason jars to Tiffany art glass and one of the largest bottles in the world. Forty-five-minute guided tours of the museum are given daily at 2:30.

MONTCLAIR (G-5) pop. 37,700, elev. 241'

Because West Bloomfield wanted a rail link to New York City and Bloomfield did not, the former separated from the latter in 1868, renamed itself Montclair and built the railroad. The result is a prosperous suburban business center, of which little could be purchased with the original price paid the American Indians for the region—"two guns, three coats and 13 cans of rum."

For a backdrop Montclair has First Mountain, from which the British were denied entry to the upper Passaic River Valley during the Revolution. Mountainside Park on Upper Mountain Avenue in neighboring Upper Montclair includes the Presby Iris Gardens, which usually bloom in May.

Montclair Chamber of Commerce: 50 Church St., Montclair, NJ 07042; phone (973) 744-7660.

MONTCLAIR ART MUSEUM, Bloomfield and S. Mountain aves., houses permanent collections of

American and American Indian paintings. Included are paintings, works on paper, sculpture and costumes. Gallery talks, recitals and special programs also are offered. Allow 1 hour minimum. Tues.-Wed. and Fri.-Sat. 11-5, Thurs. and Sun. 1-5, Sept.-May; Wed.-Sun. 1-5, rest of year. Closed major holidays. Admission $5, senior citizens and college students with ID $4, under 12 free. Phone (973) 746-5555.

MORRISTOWN (G-4) pop. 16,200, elev. 404'

The Revolutionary War demanded iron, and iron it got, processed at the furnaces and forges of Morristown. Much of the powder used by the Continental Army was made at Jacob Ford's powder mill. These operations were attractive targets for the British, who made several attempts to take the town.

It was this defensibility that led Gen. George Washington to select Morristown for his army's winter quarters in 1777 and again 1779-80 (see *Morristown National Historical Park p. 40*). Elaborate Victorian homes remain in some of the oldest neighborhoods.

Dogs seen trotting along Morristown's streets are not average canines, but highly trained students of the Seeing Eye Headquarters on Washington Valley Road. Started in 1929 in Nashville, the school was moved to Morristown in 1965. Tours are offered by appointment; phone (973) 539-4425.

Historic Morris Visitors Center: 6 Court St., Morristown, NJ 07960; phone (973) 631-5151.

FOSTERFIELDS LIVING HISTORICAL FARM is off I-287 exit 35, then w. on SR 24 (Madison Ave.) to Kahdena Rd. The farm, which represents the years 1880-1910, was purchased in 1852 by the grandson of Paul Revere. Joseph Warren Revere built The Willows, a 19th-century Gothic Revival house with a two-story veranda, steeply pitched roofs and decorative arched pillars. Visitors can explore the farm on a self-guiding tour, view exhibits, watch an introductory film and see demonstrations of late 19th-century farming practices.

Allow 1 hour, 30 minutes minimum. Grounds open Wed.-Sat. 10-5, Sun. noon-5, Apr.-Oct. House open Thurs.-Sun. 1-4, Apr.-Oct. Grounds $4 Sat.-Sun.; over 64 and ages 6-16, $2; donations Wed.-Fri. House $4 Sat.-Sun. (includes grounds admission), $3 Thurs.-Fri.; over 64 and ages 6-16, $3 Sat.-Sun. (includes grounds admission), $2 Thurs.-Fri. Phone (973) 326-7645.

FRELINGHUYSEN ARBORETUM is 3 mi. e. on Morris Ave., then n. on Ridgedale Ave. and e. to 53 E. Hanover Ave., opposite Morris County Library. Contrasts between field and woodland, naturalized plantings and formal gardens characterize the 127-acre preserve, which surrounds a historic Colonial Revival mansion that is the headquarters for the Morris County Park Commission.

Trees and shrubs are labeled. Two self-guiding trails and a braille nature trail are available; a guide book is available for $2. An education center features exhibits. Allow 1 hour, 30 minutes minimum. Visitor center Mon.-Sat. 9-4:30, Sun. noon-4:30. Grounds daily 8-dusk. Mansion closed major holidays. Donations. Pets are not permitted. Phone (973) 326-7600.

HISTORIC SPEEDWELL, 333 Speedwell Ave., preserves part of the Speedwell Iron Works built by Stephen Vail in the early 1800s. It contains the home and factory of Vail, who in 1818 made the engine for the *Savannah,* the first steamship to cross the Atlantic. In 1837 Samuel F.B. Morse and Stephen's son Alfred conducted the first successful public demonstration of the telegraph at this location.

There are patterns for early engine parts and other items relating to the ironworks. A collection of early communications equipment traces the history of the electromagnetic telegraph. Five farm buildings and three historic homes are on the grounds. Thurs.-Fri. noon-4, Sat.-Sun. 1-5, May-Sept.; Sat.-Sun. 1-5 in Oct. Last admission 1 hour before closing. Admission $3; senior citizens $2; ages 6-16, $1. Phone (973) 540-0211.

THE MORRIS MUSEUM, 2.5 mi. e. on CR 510 at Normandy Heights and Columbia rds., features galleries that include minerals, fossils and mounted and live small animals. The museum also has exhibits about North American Indians, Colonial life and decorative and fine arts as well as a 5,000-square-foot gallery that houses changing exhibits. The Five Senses Gallery is designed for those under age 6. Allow 2 hours minimum. Mon.-Sat. 10-5 (also Thurs. 5-8), Sun. 1-5; closed major holidays. Admission $5; over 60 and under 3, $3. Phone (973) 538-0454.

★MORRISTOWN NATIONAL HISTORICAL PARK (H-4)

Morristown National Historical Park consists of three units: Washington's Headquarters and the Historical Museum and Library, Fort Nonsense and Jockey Hollow. Two units are in Morristown, and the last is about 5 miles southwest. Gen. George Washington selected this easily defensible site for his military headquarters and the main encampment of his Continental Army in the winter and spring of 1777 and again during the bitter winter of 1779-80.

Despite starvation, disease and mutiny, he reorganized his weary and depleted forces almost within sight of strong British lines in N.Y. For a time this village was the U.S. military capital. Most park buildings are open daily 9-5; closed Jan. 1, Thanksgiving and Dec. 25. Admission, paid at the Historical Museum and Library, $2, over 61 and under 17 free. Phone (973) 539-2085.

FORT NONSENSE, accessible from Washington St., is the site of an earthen fort built at Washington's order in 1777 as a defense for supplies stored in the village. Built on a hill adjoining Morristown, the fort had cannons to protect the town below and the main roads leading north and south. Legend has it that the fort's name derives from the intent of Washington to keep his troops busy, thus preventing idleness and desertion. Allow 1 hour minimum. Daily 9-6. Free.

HISTORICAL MUSEUM AND LIBRARY are at the rear of Washington's Headquarters. The museum displays material relating to the 1779-80 encampment, historical objects, documents and military weapons. The library houses some 40,000 manuscripts and more than 20,000 printed works dealing with both the Colonial and Revolutionary eras. A 20-minute film is shown every half-hour. Park headquarters are on the premises.

Allow 2 hours minimum. Museum and library daily 9-5. Guided tours are given on the hour 10-4. Phone (973) 539-2016.

JOCKEY HOLLOW, 5 mi. s.w. of Morristown, contains most of the sites occupied by the Continental Army 1779-80. That "Hard Winter" proved to be one of the harshest of the 18th century. The army used the abundant timber in the area to construct log huts and provide the firewood necessary to withstand the winter. Five reconstructed soldiers' huts can be seen. The area is a wildlife sanctuary with wooded hills, streams and a variety of flowers. Several hiking trails wind through this section. A visitor center offers displays and a short film.

Allow 1 hour minimum. Grounds open daily 8-5. Visitor center and Wick House open daily 9-5, Apr.-Nov.; Wed.-Sun. 9-5, rest of year. Call to verify winter hours. Free. Phone (973) 543-4030.

Soldier Huts are reconstructions of lodgings on the site occupied by Continental Army troops during the 1779-80 encampment.

Wick House is a restored 18th-century farmhouse that was occupied by Maj. Gen. Arthur St. Clair 1779-80. The house, with its garden and buildings, reflects the life of a relatively prosperous farmer during the Revolutionary period.

WASHINGTON'S HEADQUARTERS (FORD MANSION), Washington Pl., was built 1772-74 for Col. Jacob Ford Jr. A Colonial house furnished in period, it has many original 18th-century pieces. During the winter of 1779-80 it was the home of Gen. and Mrs. George Washington. Allow 1 hour, 30 minutes minimum. Admittance is by guided tour, leaving from the historical museum daily on the hour 10-4. Free. Phone (973) 539-2085.

MOUNTAINSIDE (H-4) pop. 6,700

TRAILSIDE NATURE AND SCIENCE CENTER is n. off US 22 New Providence Rd. exit, n. on Ackerman Ave., then n. on Coles Ave. in the Watchung Reservation. The 2,000-acre preserve has a visitor center with changing exhibits about human and natural history as well as a collection of live reptiles. A museum contains taxidermy displays, fossils and a hands-on discovery room for preschoolers. The planetarium offers star and laser shows.

Park open daily dawn-dusk. Visitor center open daily 1-5. Museum open daily 1-5, Apr.-Nov.; Sat.-Sun. 1-5, rest of year. Star shows Sun. at 2 and 3:30. Visitor center and museum closed Jan. 1, Easter, July 4, Thanksgiving, day after Thanksgiving and Dec. 25. Donations. Planetarium shows $3, senior citizens $2.55. Phone (908) 789-3670.

MOUNT HOLLY—see Philadelphia and Vicinity in Pennsylvania p. 132.

NETCONG (B-3) pop. 3,300, elev. 882'

WILD WEST CITY, .5 mi. e. of jct. US 206 and CR 607 (Lackawanna Rd.), re-creates the Old West. Visitors can experience a stagecoach ride complete with a hold-up by masked bandits; see Pony Express riders race into town; witness gunslingers in action; and view a re-enactment of the

Gunfight at the O.K. Corral. Train and pony rides, a petting zoo, live entertainment and panning for gold also are available. Picnicking is permitted. Food is available.

Allow 3 hours minimum. Daily 10:30-6, mid-June through Labor Day; Sat.-Sun. and holidays 10:30-6, May 1 to mid-June and day after Labor Day through Columbus Day. Admission $6.75; ages 2-12, $6.25. Stagecoach, pony and train rides are additional. AE, DS, MC, VI. Phone (973) 347-8900.

NEWARK (H-5) pop. 275,200, elev. 225′

From two streets laid out by Puritans from Connecticut in 1666, Newark has become New Jersey's largest city and a major land, sea and air transportation center. Although manufacturing is important, Newark is increasingly concerned with commerce, government and education. Newark is the headquarters for several leading insurance, banking, retail and commercial businesses as well as many federal and state agencies.

The city's midtown college complex is the home of five institutions: Rutgers University at Newark, Seton Hall Law School, the University of Medicine and Dentistry of New Jersey, the New Jersey Institute of Technology and Essex County College. The Rutgers Institute of Jazz Studies maintains an extensive collection of jazz recordings. A gallery in Rutgers' Paul Robeson Center displays changing art exhibits.

Statuary in Military Park includes the monumental "Wars of America" by Mount Rushmore sculptor Gutzon Borglum and a bust of President John F. Kennedy by Jacques Lipchitz. Eight hundred acres of county and municipal parks include Branch Brook Park.

The Newark City Hall, 920 Broad St., is a fine example of Beaux Arts architecture. Dedicated in 1906, the building features a grand central staircase and a skylight. Also of interest is the section known as James Street Commons. Next to the business section and Washington Park, this 20-block area has a number of well-preserved Victorian rowhouses. Symphony Hall, 1020 Broad St., is home of the New Jersey Symphony, (800) 255-3476, and the New Jersey State Opera, (973) 623-5757.

Metro Newark Chamber of Commerce: 1 Newark Center, 22nd Floor, Newark, NJ 07102-5265; phone (973) 242-6237.

CATHOLIC CATHEDRAL OF THE SACRED HEART is at Clifton and Park aves. The French Gothic cathedral, comparable in size to Westminster Abbey, resembles the basilica at Rheims. Among its features are hand-carved reredos, more than 200 stained-glass windows, bronze doors and 14 bells cast in Italy. The towers are 232 feet high. Mon.-Sat. 9-9, Sun. 1-5. Donations. Phone (973) 484-4600.

NEWARK MUSEUM, 49 Washington St., is a four-building structure with 60,000 square feet of exhibit space. The museum has American paintings and sculpture, decorative arts including glass and ceramics, American Indian and African articles, ancient glass, a sculpture garden, a miniature zoo and a planetarium. An Asian display includes an extensive collection of Tibetan art and objects. The museum garden contains a firehouse and schoolhouse.

Allow 1 hour, 30 minutes minimum. Wed.-Sun. noon-5; closed Jan. 1, July 4, Thanksgiving and Dec. 25. Free. Phone (973) 596-6550 or (800) 768-7386.

Ballantine House was the mansion of brewer John H. Ballantine. The restored 1885 Victorian house contains paintings and other objects from the museum's collections and many original furnishings.

NEWARK PUBLIC LIBRARY, 5 Washington St. opposite Washington Park, is one of the largest public libraries in the state and a major resource center. It has large collections about the history of the city and state, fine arts, business and current affairs. Also housed in the 1901 library are more than 1 million books, pictures and periodicals. Changing exhibits are presented. Allow 1 hour minimum. Mon.-Sat. 9-5:30 (also Tue.-Thurs. 5:30-8:30); closed state and federal holidays. Free. Phone (973) 733-7800 or 733-7784.

NEW JERSEY HISTORICAL SOCIETY, 230 Broadway at Taylor St., was established in 1845. The Georgian-style building houses historical collections, which include original land grants, prints and decorative arts, furniture and changing exhibits relating to New Jersey themes. Permanent exhibits include KIDS, an educational center for children that encourages interaction, and Life in Early New Jersey. The reference and research library contains historic publications.

Allow 1 hour minimum. Wed.-Fri. and first and third Sat. of the month 10-4. Museum and library $3, senior citizens $2. Library $1. Phone (973) 483-3939.

NEW BRUNSWICK (I-4) pop. 41,700, elev. 47′

Diversified industry and higher education support the busy city of New Brunswick, which originated in 1686 as a ferry crossing in a settled area known as Prigmore's Swamp. The good port and water power afforded by the Raritan River made the city one of New Jersey's major shipping and milling depots by the 1750s.

A 1770 charter resulted in the opening of Queen's College the following year in a tavern. After years of shifting locations and monetary struggles, the college took form in 1766 and now occupies several campuses in the city. It was renamed Rutgers in 1825.

Buccleuch Park, a 78-acre park at the north end of College Avenue, overlooks the Raritan River. In addition to recreational facilities, it contains a house built in 1729 by a British officer.

The birthplace of Alfred Joyce Kilmer, best known for his poem "Trees," is at 17 Joyce Kilmer Ave.

Middlesex County Regional Chamber of Commerce: 1 Distribution Way, Monmouth Junction, NJ 08852; phone (732) 821-1700.

NEW JERSEY MUSEUM OF AGRICULTURE is off US 1 on College Farm Rd., at the entrance to the Cook College campus at Rutgers University. The museum depicts 300 years of Garden State heritage through displays that include early farm equipment, household technology, innovative harvesting machines and historical photographs. Allow 1 hour minimum. Tues.-Sat. 10-5, Sun. noon-5; closed holidays. Admission $3; over 61, $2; ages 5-11, $1. Phone (732) 249-2077.

RUTGERS UNIVERSITY is comprised of four campuses: Busch and Livingston campuses, n. off SR 18; College Avenue Campus in downtown; and Cook/Douglas Campus, s. off SR 18, n.w. of US 1. In addition to its Colonial background, the school claims origins as a land-grant college and the status of a state university. The first formal collegiate football game was held in 1869, when Rutgers beat Princeton six goals to four.

Old Queens, a three-story 1809 brownstone building that originally held all the facilities now serves as the administrative center of the university; phone (732) 932-1766. Tours of William L. Hutcheson Memorial Forest, a 65-acre primeval tract preserved as a living forest laboratory, are offered on selected Sundays; phone (732) 445-2075.

Geology Museum, College Ave. and Somerset St. on the College Avenue Campus, displays minerals, vertebrate fossils, American Indian artifacts and an Egyptian mummy. Tues.-Fri. 9-noon, Mon. 1-4,; closed holidays and Dec. 25-Jan. 2. Free. Phone (732) 932-7243.

The Jane Voorhees Zimmerli Art Museum, at George and Hamilton sts. on the College Avenue Campus, contains a permanent collection of more than 50,000 works from varied media. Of particular note is the display devoted to printmaking. Also presented are children's literature exhibits, the Dodge Collection of Soviet Art and the Riabov Russian Art Collection. Changing exhibits also are featured. Tues.-Fri. 10-4:30, Sat.-Sun. noon-5; closed holidays and Dec. 25-Jan. 2. Free. Phone (732) 932-7237.

Rutgers Display Gardens and Helyar Woods are entered via Ryders Ln. just e. of US 1 and s. of SR 18. The 50-acre gardens feature a diverse series of plant collections arranged in garden settings. The peak season for annuals is mid-June through September; most flowering shrubs bloom from late April to June. Perennials bloom throughout the spring, summer and fall, and many trees and shrubs display fall color September through October. Helyar Woods is a 41-acre

old-growth forest with a marked trail. Daily dawn-dusk. Donations. Phone (732) 932-8451.

NORTH WILDWOOD—*see Wildwood p. 50.*

OCEAN CITY (G-3) pop. 15,500, elev. 10'

When the Lake brothers, ministers all, established Ocean City as a proper Christian summer resort in 1879, they decreed that no liquor would be sold. Still in effect, this injunction might account in part for the town's long-standing popularity with families. The other reasons that the area is a favorite vacation spot are obvious: the 8-mile-long beach, the equable climate, excellent sport fishing and all the standard pleasures of a well-mannered seashore vacation community.

At the north end of an island between the Atlantic Ocean and Great Egg Harbor, Ocean City offers easy access to the ocean and inland waterways, making it a favorite summer port with yachtsmen. Its many recreational facilities include the boardwalk, which contains shops and amusements. Marinas accommodate visiting craft as well as charter boats for sightseeing and fishing.

The Music Pier is the primary entertainment center in summer when band concerts regularly take place. Wonderland Pier and Playland have amusement parks, which operate during the summer. Ocean City Arts Center presents monthly art exhibits.

Ocean City Chamber of Commerce: P.O. Box 157, Ocean City, NJ 08226; phone (609) 399-6344 or (800) 232-2465.

OCEAN CITY HISTORICAL MUSEUM, 17th and Simpson Ave., depicts life in the region during the late 19th century. Exhibits include period room settings, fashions, dolls and a maritime room dedicated to the *Sindia,* which ran aground on the island in a gale in 1901. Mon.-Fri. 10-4, Sat. 1-4, Memorial Day-Dec. 31; otherwise varies. Closed holidays. Free. Phone (609) 399-1801.

OCEAN GROVE (D-5) elev. 20'

Ocean Grove, a family-oriented seaside resort, has been under the leadership of the Camp Meeting Association since 1869. Musical performances featuring well-known pop and symphony concert artists as well as entertainers, cultural events and religious services and programs are held throughout the summer at the 6,500-seat Great Auditorium. Organ concerts are given Wednesday and Saturday on a 1908 Hope-Jones pipe organ.

Of historical interest is the Victorian architecture typical of many of the community's homes. Centennial Cottage, a restored 1874 vacation home at Central Avenue and McClintock Street, is open to visitors. Also of interest is the tent colony surrounding the auditorium. A tabernacle, chapel, pavilions, parks, the boardwalk and the beach complete Ocean Grove's chautauqua setting.

Ocean Grove Chamber of Commerce: P.O. Box 415, Ocean Grove, NJ 07756; phone (800) 388-4768.

OCEANVILLE—
see Atlantic City and Vicinity p. 23.

OGDENSBURG (B-4) pop. 2,700, elev. 629'

SAVE STERLING HILL MINE & MUSEUM is .5 mi. s. on CR 517, .2 mi. w. on Brooks Flat Rd., then .5 mi. n. to 30 Plant St., following signs. Visitors can learn about the mining process during a guided 1.5- to 2-hour walking tour through the last underground mine to operate in the state. A museum displays minerals and mining equipment.

Allow 1 hour, 30 minutes minimum. Daily 10-5, Apr.-Nov.; Sat.-Sun. 10-5 in Mar. and Dec. Tours are given at 1 and 3. Fee $8; over 64, $7; under 17, $5. Tour is not recommended for preschoolers. Phone (973) 209-7212.

PARAMUS (F-6) pop. 25,100

BERGEN MUSEUM OF ART AND SCIENCE, Ridgewood and Fairview aves., features the Hackensack mastodon skeleton as the centerpiece of its science and art collections. The museum also offers a variety of changing exhibits, workshops and events throughout the year, including a children's program on Saturday mornings. Tues.-Sat. 10-5, Sun. 1-5. Donations. Phone (201) 265-1248.

NEW JERSEY CHILDREN'S MUSEUM, 599 Industrial Ave., is an interactive learning and play center designed for children 8 and under. Each of the museum's 30 rooms has its own theme. In Aviation youngsters can climb inside a real helicopter and use an authentic flight simulator. They can operate cash registers in the Grocery and Pizzeria and watch themselves on television in the T.V. Studio.

Allow 2 hours, 30 minutes minimum. Mon.-Fri. 9-5, Sat.-Sun. 10-6, Oct.-Apr.; Mon.-Fri. 9-5, Sat.-Sun. 10-5, rest of year. Closed Oct. 31, Thanksgiving and Dec. 24-25. Admission $7, under 1 free. MC, VI. Phone (201) 262-5151.

PATERSON (G-5) pop. 140,900, elev. 118'

The potential power of the Great Falls of the Passaic River, which can be viewed at McBride Avenue and Spruce Street, inspired Alexander Hamilton to organize the Society for Establishing Useful Manufactures (S.U.M.) and to plan Paterson as America's first industrial city.

Pierre L'Enfant, planner of Washington, D.C., submitted the original design for a raceway to harness the falls and supply water power to the industrial mills. His design was deemed too expansive and time consuming. Investors wanted an earlier return on their investment, so Peter Colt completed the design for a shortened workable recovery system to supply water to the mills.

The restored upper raceway parallels a section of Spruce Street, the site of such early mill complexes as the Rogers Locomotive Erecting Shop, which produced the "General" and other historic engines. In the Old Gun Mill, at Van Houten and Mill streets, Samuel Colt made the first successful repeating revolvers, and John Ryle launched the silk industry for which the city was to become well-known.

Paterson, still an important center of diversified manufacturing, is striving to infuse new life into parts of the old industrial area while preserving it as the Great Falls/S.U.M. Historic District. Restorations on Mill and Van Houten streets are forerunners of the program of adaptive re-use of the old mills.

Greater Paterson Chamber of Commerce: 100 Hamilton Plaza, Paterson, NJ 07505; phone (973) 881-7300.

Self-guiding tours: A brochure outlining a walking and/or driving tour as well as information and appointments for guided walking tours can be obtained Mon.-Fri. 9-4, Sun. noon-4, Apr.-Sept. at Great Falls Visitor Center, 65 McBride Ave., Paterson, NJ 07501; phone (973) 279-9587.

ROGERS MILL (PATERSON MUSEUM), 2 Market St., has American Indian artifacts; mineralogy collections; archeological, historical and geological exhibits; and a display about the silk industry. The museum is host to a gallery of photographs and paintings by local artists inspired by Great Falls. Of note are the hulls of the first two submarines, invented and constructed by J.P. Holland of Paterson. Tues.-Fri. 10-4, Sat.-Sun. 12:30-4:30; closed holidays. Admission $2, under 18 free. Phone (973) 881-3874.

PICATINNY ARSENAL (B-3)

ARDEC MUSEUM, off I-80 exit 34, then 1 mi. n. on SR 15, contains exhibits outlining the history

of munitions from World War II to the present. In addition to displays of bullets and cartridges, the museum also presents a history of explosives. Allow 30 minutes minimum. Tues.-Thurs. 9-3; closed Dec. 25-Jan. 1. Free. Phone (973) 724-2797.

PLAINFIELD (H-4) pop. 46,600, elev. 102'

At the south end of the Watchung Mountains, Plainfield has become one of the many suburbs that radiate from the Elizabeth *(see place listing p. 144)* and Newark *(see place listing p. 41)* metropolitan areas. A few reminders of the Revolutionary period remain.

While planning the Battle for the Watchungs, Gen. George Washington often stayed at the Plainfield home of a friend, the Rev. Nathaniel Drake; the 1746 house is headquarters for the local historical society. Another 18th-century building still in use is the 1788 Friends Meeting House on Dover-Chester Rd.; phone (973) 361-9427.

Central Jersey Chamber of Commerce: 120 W. 7th St. #217, Plainfield, NJ 07060; phone (908) 754-7250.

PLEASANTVILLE—
see Atlantic City and Vicinity p. 24.

POINT PLEASANT BEACH (D-5) pop. 5,100

The Unami Indians spent spring and summer collecting shells and fish along the coast of what is now Point Pleasant Beach. This ritual ended in the 1700s with the arrival of the first European settlers. Farming and boat building were common occupations until the mid-1800s when the area began developing as a seaside community. Rail service and the completion of the Garden State Parkway turned Point Pleasant Beach into one of New Jersey's leading summer resorts.

A mile-long boardwalk offers family-style amusements. Point Pleasant Beach borders Manasquan Inlet, providing access to the ocean and opportunities for boat watching.

Point Pleasant Area Chamber of Commerce: 517A Arnold Ave., Point Pleasant Beach, NJ 08742; phone (732) 899-2424.

JENKINSON'S AQUARIUM, n. of jct. Arnold and Ocean aves., features a touch tank, a live coral reef, exotic birds, seals, sharks, alligators and penguins. Food is available. Allow 1 hour minimum. Daily 10-10, June-Aug.; Mon.-Fri. 9:30-5, Sat.-Sun. 10-5, rest of year. Closed Jan. 1 and Dec. 25. Admission $6.50; over 61 and ages 3-12, $4. Parking $4-$7, Memorial Day to mid-September. AE, MC, VI. Phone (732) 899-1212.

PRINCETON (D-3) pop. 12,000, elev. 213'

The key to Princeton's future was turned in 1756 when the College of New Jersey, founded in Elizabeth by royal charter in 1746, was moved to the town; it was not officially renamed Princeton University until 1896. In its Nassau Hall another pivotal event occurred, the 1776 meeting of the first New Jersey State Legislature at which William Livingston was inaugurated as governor.

Shortly thereafter Gen. Charles Cornwallis' troops occupied Nassau Hall as they pushed Gen. George Washington's army westward. Early the next year Washington followed up his victory at Trenton by surprising and defeating the British in the Battle of Princeton. A monument at Mercer, Nassau and Stockton streets commemorates the battle.

In 1783 the Continental Congress met in Nassau Hall when mutinous American soldiers drove its members from Philadelphia. During this time the members received the news of the treaty of peace with Great Britain.

The life of the community has melded with that of the university and the other institutions of higher education. Albert Einstein spent his last years at the Institute for Advanced Study.

The Historical Society of Princeton offers a 2-hour guided walking tour of historic Princeton every Sunday at 2 for $5; phone (609) 921-6748.

Chamber of Commerce of the Princeton Area: 216 Rockingham Row, Princeton Forrestal Village, Princeton, NJ 08540; phone (609) 520-1776.

Self-guiding tours: The Historical Society of Princeton has brochures outlining walking tours with such topics as 18th-century houses and architecture. These brochures can be obtained at the society's museum shop in the Bainbridge House *(see attraction listing).*

BAINBRIDGE HOUSE, 158 Nassau St., was the birthplace of William Bainbridge, commander of the USS *Constitution* during the War of 1812. The restored 1766 residence serves as a museum with changing exhibitions, a library, photographic archives and a museum shop; the house also is the headquarters of the Historical Society of Princeton. Tues.-Sun. noon-4. Free. Phone (609) 921-6748.

PRINCETON UNIVERSITY encompasses more than 1,660 acres with many buildings representing a wide variety of architecture. The campus's original 1756 building, Nassau Hall, served as a barracks and hospital during the Revolutionary War and was the temporary home of the Continental Congress. Sculpture from the John B. Putnam Jr. Memorial Collection, including works by Alexander Calder, Jacques Lipchitz, Henry Moore, Louise Nevelson and Pablo Picasso, are displayed on the campus.

Visitors may contact the Maclean House, 73 Nassau St., Princeton, NJ 08540. Tours of the campus, including Nassau Hall and the University Chapel, are available Mon.-Sat. at 10, 11, 1:30 and 3:30, Sun. at 1:30 and 3:30; closed holidays and mid-Dec. to early Jan. Free. Phone (609) 258-3000 for general campus information, or (609) 258-3603 for tours.

The Art Museum, in McCormick Hall on campus, contains outstanding paintings and sculpture spanning ancient and modern times. Noteworthy are Chinese paintings and bronzes and examples of pre-Columbian and African art. Tues.-Sat. 10-5, Sun. 1-5. Admission $3. Phone (609) 258-3787.

Natural History Museum, in Guyot Hall, is dedicated to evolution and geology. Displays pertain to marine and land inhabitants ranging from prehistoric to modern species. Mon.-Fri. 9-5. Free. Phone (609) 258-4101.

The University Chapel, near Firestone Library, is one of the world's largest university chapels. The pulpit and lectern, which date from the mid-16th century, were brought from France. Of interest are the chapel's stained-glass windows and pews. Sun.-Fri. 8 a.m.-11 p.m., Sat. 8-6:30, third Sun. in Sept.-second Sun. in June; daily 8-4:30, rest of year. Free. Phone (609) 258-3050.

ROCKINGHAM STATE HISTORIC SITE, 5 mi. n. on CR 518 e. of Rocky Hill in Franklin Township, was Washington's headquarters Aug.-Nov. 1783 while the Continental Congress was in session in Princeton. He wrote his "Farewell Orders to the Armies" at this site. The restored house contains period furnishings. Wed.-Sat. 10-noon and 1-4, Sun. 1-4; closed Jan. 1, Thanksgiving and Dec. 25. Free. Phone (609) 921-8835.

THE THOMAS CLARKE HOUSE, 1.5 mi. s.w. on Mercer Rd., is in Princeton Battlefield State Park, where Gen. George Washington led his forces to victory in 1777. Gen. Hugh Mercer, a Patriot, died in the house from wounds suffered in the battle. Thomas Clarke, a Quaker farmer, built the Georgian-style home about 1772 and lived in it until his death in 1802.

The house, furnished in the Revolutionary style, is being developed as a working Colonial farm. Weapons, paintings and maps highlighting the battle are some of the items exhibited. Guided tours Wed.-Sat. 10-noon and 1-4, Sun. 1-4. Closed Jan. 1, Thanksgiving and Dec. 25. Free. Phone (609) 921-0074.

RINGWOOD (B-4) pop. 12,600, elev. 339'

Claiming a colorful past as an iron-mining and forging center, Ringwood has been described as "more a company than a town, and more a tradition than a company." The iron-rich Ramapo Mountains first gained attention in the early 1700s; the first forge was built in 1739. By 1771 the forge had been sold twice and had become the lucrative London-based American Iron Co. Vast tracts of land became the homes of wealthy mine and forge owners.

When the Revolutionary War erupted, ironmaster Robert Erskine sided with the Colonies

and became the surveyor general for the Continental Armies. Meanwhile his forges worked overtime turning out munitions, cannons and most of the huge chain that was stretched across the Hudson to prevent British ships from reaching West Point. The Ringwood iron mine produced steadily until 1931, when it succumbed to competition from Western iron ranges.

Ringwood Chamber of Commerce: P.O. Box 62, Ringwood, NJ 07456; phone (973) 962-7916.

RINGWOOD STATE PARK, 2.5 mi. n. via Skyland Dr., CR 511 and Sloatsburg Rd., consists of three units totaling 6,199 acres. The Shephard Lake section, which offers water sports, is 14 miles north of Pompton Lakes. The Ringwood Manor and Skylands sections boast mansions and gardens. Shephard Lake open daily 8-8, Memorial Day-Labor Day. Admission $7 Sat.-Sun., $5 Mon.-Fri. Phone (973) 962-7031. *See Recreation Chart.*

New Jersey State Botanical Gardens surround the 44-room Tudor Skyland Manor. The 300 acres of gardens contain flowering trees from around the world; annuals and perennials bloom from spring through the first frost. Marked trails traverse the gardens. Guided tours are available on Sun. at 2, May-Oct. Gardens open daily 8-8. Mansion open selected Sun., Mar.-Dec.; phone for schedule. Admission $3 Sat.-Sun., Memorial Day-Labor Day; otherwise free, rest of year.

Ringwood Manor is the grand former home of Gen. Robert Erskine; Peter Cooper, founder of the Cooper Union in New York; and Abraham S. Hewitt, a leading ironmaster of the 19th century. Twenty-one of the mansion's 78 rooms have been restored. Woodlands and formal gardens are on the grounds. Picnicking is permitted. Wed.-Sun. 10-4, May-Oct. Admission $3 Sat.-Sun., otherwise free.

RIVER EDGE (F-6) pop. 10,600, elev. 90'

STEUBEN HOUSE STATE HISTORIC SITE (ACKERMAN-ZABRISKIE-STEUBEN HOUSE) is at 1209 Main St., n. of SR 4 on the Hackensack River. The house was Gen. George Washington's headquarters in 1780. Presented to Maj. Gen. Friedrich von Steuben by the state in gratitude for his services to the Continental Army, the 1713 house now displays the collection of the Bergen County Historical Society and 1650-1850 Jersey Dutch furnishings. Wed.-Sat. 10-noon and 1-5, Sun. 2-5; closed Jan. 1, Thanksgiving and Dec. 25. Free. Phone (201) 487-1739.

SALEM—*see Philadelphia and Vicinity in Pennsylvania p. 132.*

SEASIDE HEIGHTS (E-5) pop. 2,400

Established in 1913, Seaside Heights lies between the Atlantic Ocean and Barnegat Bay. The town features a mile of boardwalk that has two amusement piers, an antique Dentzel/Looff carrousel, games of chance, fishing, arcades, nightclubs and Wednesday night fireworks. The ocean and bay beaches as well as most establishments are open daily Memorial Day through Labor Day. The boardwalk is open year-round.

CASINO PIER AND WATER WORKS, 800 Ocean Terr., is an amusement park with a variety of rides. The highlight is the water park, with slides, river rides and an activity pool. Complex open daily, Memorial Day-Labor Day; amusement park also open Sat.-Sun., Easter-day before Memorial Day. Hours vary; phone for schedule. Water park $12 for 2 hours. Amusement park free; rides priced individually. Phone (732) 793-6488.

SOMERS POINT—
see Atlantic City and Vicinity p. 24.

SOMERVILLE (C-3) pop. 11,600, elev. 91'

Somerville's occupation with commerce, county government and industry exemplifies its position in the transitional zone between city and country. The area was first settled by American Indians who later negotiated with European settlers for a peaceful withdrawal. Later, soldiers of the Continental Army frequented the area, then called Raritan, while Gen. George Washington stayed at the Wallace House. Somerville began to take shape with the construction of a courthouse in 1787.

Somerset County Chamber of Commerce: 64 W. End Ave., P.O. Box 833, Somerville, NJ 08876; phone (908) 725-1552.

DUKE GARDENS, 1.7 mi. s. of Somerville Cir. on US 206S, has 11 glass-enclosed gardens, each representing the theme and climatic conditions of a country. Guided walking tours daily noon-4, Oct.-May; closed Jan. 1, Thanksgiving and Dec. 25. Admission $5; over 61 and ages 6-12, $2.50. Reservations are required. Phone (908) 722-3700 Mon.-Fri. 9-4.

OLD DUTCH PARSONAGE STATE HISTORIC SITE, 65 Washington Pl., was built in 1751 and was the 1758-81 home of Rev. Jacob Hardenbergh, founder of Queens College in New Brunswick. The college later became Rutgers University. The site is furnished as it may have appeared in 1780. Wed.-Sat. 10-noon and 1-4, Sun. 1-4; closed holidays. Donations. Phone (908) 725-1015.

WALLACE HOUSE STATE HISTORIC SITE, 38 Washington Pl., was used as a headquarters by Gen. George Washington during the winter of 1778-79 while his Continental Army stayed at Camp Middlebrook. The house contains period furnishings. Wed.-Sat. 10-noon and 1-4, Sun. 1-4; closed holidays. Donations. Phone (908) 725-1015.

STANHOPE (B-3) pop. 3,400, elev. 873'

Stanhope serves the needs of local farmers as well as visitors to Hopatcong State Park *(see Recreation Chart)* on nearby Lake Hopatcong. The town dates from Revolutionary times when the Sussex Iron Works was a major industry; a few ironworkers' cottages resembling French peasant bungalows remain. The nation's first anthracite furnace was built in town about 1821.

Stanhope is the eastern terminus for a scenic stretch of I-80 that runs 28 miles to the Delaware Water Gap and continues into Pennsylvania.

WATERLOO VILLAGE is off I-80 exit 25. The village's beginnings in the 1740s revolved around the Andover Forge, a major supplier of armaments for the Continental Army. The village is preserved as a living-history museum. Costumed guides and artisans explain 18th- and 19th-century life in 14 historic buildings, including an inn, a general store, a church, a gristmill and a smithy. The Lenape/Delaware way of life is depicted at Winakung, a life-size reconstruction of a Minisink Indian village. Picnicking is permitted. Food is available.

Wed.-Sun. 10-6, mid-Apr. through Sept. 30; 10-5, Oct. 1 to mid-Nov. Closed Easter. Schedule may vary; phone ahead. Admission $9; over 65, $8; ages 6-15, $7. Additional fees may be charged during concerts or special events. Phone (973) 347-0900.

STONE HARBOR (G-3) pop. 1,000, elev. 7'

THE WETLANDS INSTITUTE, 3 mi. s.e. of Garden State Pkwy. exit 10 on CR 657, is dedicated to providing education and research on coastal ecosystems. The education center houses saltwater aquariums, exhibits depicting life in the local saltwater marshes, a touch tank, a children's discovery room and an observation deck. A self-guiding salt marsh trail, observation tower and marsh boardwalk also are featured.

Allow 1 hour minimum. Mon.-Sat. 9:30-4:30, Sun. 10-4, May 15-Oct. 15; Tues.-Sat. 9:30-4:30, rest of year. Admission $5; ages 3-11, $2. Phone (609) 368-1211.

TETERBORO (G-6)

AVIATION HALL OF FAME & MUSEUM OF NEW JERSEY is off SR 17 following signs in two locations at Teterboro Airport—the museum is at 400 Fred Wehran Dr., and an educational center is on the e. side of the airport. The museum contains aviation memorabilia and historic aircraft equipment and depicts the roles played in aviation history by New Jerseyans. A short film is shown in an auditorium, and visitors can listen to radio transmissions between air-traffic controllers in the tower and pilots.

Tues.-Sun. 10-4; closed Jan. 1, Easter, July 4, Thanksgiving and Dec. 24-25 and 31. Admission $5; over 65 and under 12, $3. Phone (201) 288-6344.

TOMS RIVER (E-4) pop. 7,500, elev. 33′

Founded in the early 18th century, the village of Toms River in Dover Township was a haven from which privateers wreaked havoc on British shipping early in the Revolutionary War. It rose to brief post-Revolutionary prominence in 1782 when Tories tried to seize the highly prized local saltworks and warehouses by burning the blockhouse, killing its defenders and hanging its commander, Capt. Joshua Huddy. Huddy Park and a replica of the original blockhouse, both near the waterfront in downtown Toms River, commemorate this event.

Linked to the sea and bay, the town primarily relied upon whaling, shipping and seafood industries. The first tourists, adventurous harbingers of a thriving modern industry, reputedly arrived aboard seafood carts that were empty after the morning's deliveries to Philadelphia. The revitalized downtown area contains shops, restaurants and coffee houses.

Winding River Park, north on Main Street to SR 37 then 1 mile west, straddles the Toms River. The park offers facilities for canoeing, hiking, bicycling, horseback riding and ice skating.

Toms River-Ocean County Chamber of Commerce: 1200 Hooper Ave., Toms River, NJ 08753; phone (732) 349-0220.

CATTUS ISLAND COUNTY PARK, 1170 Cattus Island Blvd., is really a peninsula jutting into Barnegat Bay. The 500-acre park is the quintessential transition zone between land and sea, with salt marsh blending into pine-oak uplands. The Cooper Environmental Center presents exhibits that relate to the area. Trails wind through the preserve, and boat and van tours are offered in July and August. Park daily dawn-dusk. Environmental center daily 10-4. Free. Phone (732) 270-6960.

RIVER LADY CRUISE AND DINNER BOAT, .5 mi. e. of Garden State Pkwy. exit 81, just e. of SR 166 (Main St.) overlooking the Toms River, offers dinner, dance, lunch and sightseeing cruises along Barnegat Bay and the Toms River aboard a reproduction of a paddle-wheel riverboat. The historical sightseeing cruise provides narration about area history. Cruises vary in length from 2 to 4.5 hours.

Sightseeing cruises depart Tues. and Thurs. at 11:30, Sat. at 12:30, May-Sept. Fare $10-$45, depending upon type of trip. Tickets must be purchased in advance. MC, VI. Phone (732) 349-8664.

SAVE **ROBERT J. NOVINS PLANETARIUM,** on College Dr. off Hooper Ave. on the campus of Ocean County Community College, presents a variety of star shows. Tues.-Wed. at 2, Thurs. at 2 and 8, Fri. at 1, 2 and 8, July-Aug.; Fri. at 8, Sat. at 1, 2, 3:15 and 8, Sun. at 2 and 3:15, Sept.-May. Shows at 1 are for ages 4-6. Admission $5; under 13, $3.50. Phone (732) 255-0342.

TRENTON (D-2) pop. 88,700, elev. 42′

Capital of the state, Trenton was settled about 1680 with the building of a mill at the falls of the Delaware River. The site's potential for industry, trade and shipping was recognized by Philadelphia merchant William Trent, who purchased the original mill in 1714. By 1719, with Trent's vision and financial support, the village had developed to such an extent that its name was changed from The Falls to Trenton.

In 1776 the Hessians occupied the city while pursuing Gen. George Washington and his troops across New Jersey and into Pennsylvania. On Dec. 26, 1776, after crossing the Delaware 8 miles upstream, Washington surprised the Hessian garrison, taking about 1,000 prisoners.

Trenton became the state capital in 1790. The world's first fully operative steamboat, perfected by a Trentonian named John Fitch, plied the Delaware River daily between Philadelphia and Trenton. Industry expanded and the city's name traveled around the world on rubber products, steel cable and pottery. Porcelain from Boehm and Cybis are now among Trenton's major products.

Trenton's historic districts preserve many key Colonial buildings and sites. The Mill Hill Historic District between Mercer and Jackson streets has brick sidewalks, gaslights and restored Victorian homes. The State House Historic District, W. State Street between Willow and Calhoun streets, is an architecturally eclectic residential area where Trenton's prominent families lived during the late 19th century.

Trenton Convention and Visitors Bureau: Lafayette at Barrack, Trenton, NJ 08608; phone (609) 777-1771.

CADWALADER PARK, W. State St. and Parkside Ave., honors Dr. Thomas Cadwalader, the community's first chief burgess and a pioneer in the use of preventive inoculation. He vaccinated the populace of Trenton for smallpox in the late

1740s. Laid out in 1891 by Frederick Law Olmsted, one of America's foremost landscape designers, the park includes a deer paddock, a stream, a small lake, hundreds of trees and an arm of the historic Delaware-Raritan Canal. Daily dawn-dusk. Free.

Ellarslie—The Trenton City Museum contains art galleries with changing displays as well as Trenton ceramics exhibits and a period room. Allow 30 minutes minimum. Tues.-Sat. 11-3, Sun. 2-4. Donations. Phone (609) 989-3632.

★NEW JERSEY STATE MUSEUM, 205 W. State St., is in the State House Historic District. Allow 1 hour minimum. Tues.-Sat. 9-4:45, Sun. noon-5; closed state holidays. Free. Phone (609) 292-6464 for recorded information.

The Main Museum has three floors of exhibits dealing with archeology, fine arts, cultural history and natural science. Highlights include American Indian artifacts, mastodon skeletons, a full-size model of a dinosaur and a mine replica with fluorescent minerals. Changing art exhibits also are presented. The auditorium offers films, concerts and lectures. Museum free. Fees are charged for special exhibits and programs.

The Planetarium offers changing programs emphasizing the solar system and the night sky. Laser concerts also are presented. Programs Sat.-Sun. at 1, 2 and 3. Admission $1. Under 4 are not permitted at the 2 p.m. show. Phone (609) 292-6303.

★OLD BARRACKS MUSEUM, Barrack St., is the only surviving British colonial barracks in the United States. Constructed in 1758, it was occupied at various times by British, Hessian and Continental troops and by Tory refugees. Gen. George Washington and his troops crossed the Delaware to reach the barracks in the Battle of Trenton.

A cultural history museum includes a restored officers' quarters with 18th-century furnishings and permanent and changing exhibits. Costumed guides portray New Jerseyans of the Revolutionary era. Daily 10-5; closed Jan. 1, Easter, Thanksgiving and Dec. 24-25. Admission $2; senior citizens and students with ID $1; under 13, 50c. Phone (609) 396-1776.

STATE HOUSE, W. State St., has collections of art as well as period rooms. A gold dome, cur-

rently under restoration, crowns the 1792 building, which has undergone many changes since its construction. Visitors can view the rotunda, legislative chambers, caucus rooms and the governor's reception room, all of which have noteworthy decorative treatments. Guided tours are offered on the hour Tues.-Wed. and Fri. 10-3, Sat. noon-3. Free. Phone (609) 633-2709.

WASHINGTON CROSSING STATE PARK is 8 mi. n.w. on SR 29, then n.e. on CR 546 to the entrance. The park is the site of the historic Delaware River crossing by Gen. George Washington and the Continental Army before the Battle of Trenton. Continental Lane, over which the Colonial troops marched on Christmas night in 1776, extends nearly the length of the park.

Historical tours can be arranged at the visitor center/museum, which contains a large collection of Revolutionary War artifacts. An interpretive center contains exhibits; nature tours, offered by appointment, depart from the center.

The Nelson House, across SR 29 near the river bank, is a small museum that has historical exhibits. The George Washington Memorial Arboretum holds an assortment of native trees and shrubs. An Open Air Theatre sponsors performances in the summer.

Park open daily 8-8, Memorial Day weekend-Labor Day; 8-4:30, rest of year. Visitor center/museum open Wed.-Sun. 9-4. Interpretive center open Wed.-Sat. 9-4, Sun. 1-4. Free. Parking $3 Sat.-Sun. and holidays, Memorial Day-Labor Day. Phone (609) 737-0623 for the park, 737-0609 for the interpretive center, 737-9303 for the visitor center/museum or 737-1826 for a schedule of performances for the theater. *See Recreation Chart.*

The Ferry House, at the s. end of Continental Ln., has been restored as a Dutch farmhouse; a taproom, a kitchen and a bedroom contain period furnishings. Wed.-Sat. 10-noon and 1-4, Sun. 1-4. Free. Phone (609) 737-2515.

SAVE **THE WILLIAM TRENT HOUSE,** 15 Market St., is said to be Trenton's oldest remaining house. Built in 1719 by William Trent, it was subsequently the home of a number of prominent men, including the first Colonial governor of New Jersey, Lewis Morris. Notable among the period furnishings are the curtains and copies of

old fabrics. Allow 1 hour minimum. Daily 12:30-4; closed major holidays. Admission $2.50; senior citizens and students with ID $2; under 12, $1. Phone (609) 989-3027.

TUCKERTON (F-4) pop. 3,000, elev. 23'

BARNEGAT BAY DECOY AND BAYMEN'S MUSEUM is on US 9 at the entrance to Ocean County Tip Seaman Park. The museum contains a large collection of decoys, in addition to tools of a bayman's trade, such as rakes, snapper canes and a sneakbox. Also featured are approximately 4,500 antique photographs and a wax figure of legendary decoy carver Harry V. Shourds. Allow 30 minutes minimum. Wed.-Sun. 10-4:30; closed Jan. 1, Easter, Thanksgiving and Dec. 25. Admission $2, under 12 free. MC, VI. Phone (609) 296-8868.

VERNON (A-4) pop. 2,200

 RECREATIONAL ACTIVITIES

Skiing

- **Vernon Valley Great Gorge** is 5 mi. n. of SR 23 on SR 94. Write P.O. Box 391, Rte. 94, Vernon, NJ 07462. Daily 9 a.m.-10 p.m., mid-Dec. to mid-Mar. Phone (973) 827-2000.

VINELAND (F-2) pop. 54,800, elev. 115'

Plenty of room to grow is the hallmark of 69-square-mile Vineland, geographically the largest city in the state. The primary marketing and distributing point in southern New Jersey, Vineland also is an industrial city. The city has many specialty glass, food-processing and clothing factories as well as numerous transportation concerns and retail and factory outlets.

As its name implies, Vineland was intended to be the focus of a wine-producing region. In 1861 promoter Charles K. Landis attracted to the area farmers from the mid-Atlantic states and Italian immigrants familiar with vineyards. For the town, Landis platted a 1-square-mile grid with equally spaced streets, houses and trees. While this plan remains evident as the nucleus of present-day Vineland, the vineyards did not last.

After a quarter-century of growth, disease struck the vines, and most of the wine-grape industry was abandoned. All was not lost, however: An enterprising dentist developed a nonfermentative method of preserving grape juice, one that permanently associated the product with his name—Thomas Welch.

In 1868 the women of Vineland staged one of the earliest women's suffrage demonstrations in the country. Unwilling to allow their opinions to go unheard during that presidential election, 172 women defiantly cast their token votes, a number of whom supported Elizabeth Cady Stanton for president.

Recreational facilities are provided in Landis, Magnolia, Gittone and Giampetro parks. Six miles west of town via CR 540 is Parvin State Park *(see Recreation Chart and the AAA Mideastern CampBook).*

Greater Vineland Chamber of Commerce: City Hall #106, 7th & Wood streets, P.O. Box 489, Vineland, NJ 08360-0489; phone (609) 691-7400.

VINELAND HISTORICAL AND ANTIQUARIAN SOCIETY, 108 S. 7th St., has material relating to Vineland and its surroundings, including items belonging to town founder Charles K. Landis and his family; locally crafted glassware; military memorabilia; a music room; old firefighting equipment; American Indian relics; and period furniture and clothing. Archives are available for genealogical research. Tues.-Sat. 1-4; closed major holidays. Tours are given on Sat. Museum free. Library fee $2-$5. Phone (609) 691-1111.

WASHINGTON (C-3) pop. 5,400, elev. 490'

THE BLUE ARMY SHRINE OF THE IMMACULATE HEART OF MARY is off SR 31, 1 mi. w. on CR 632, 1 mi. n. on Cemetery Hill Rd., then .2 mi. w. on Mountain View Rd., following "Blue Army Shrine" signs. Featured are the shrine; Blessed Sacrament Chapel; Capelinha, a replica of the chapel at Fatima, Portugal; Rosary Garden; Outdoor Way of the Cross; Holy House U.S.A., a replica of the Holy House of Loreto, Italy; and Angel Pond. Daily 10-4:30. Mass is celebrated daily at 11:30. Free. Modest dress is required. Phone (908) 689-1700.

WAYNE (F-5) pop. 47,000

The Wayne area is familiar to dog fanciers as the setting for Albert Payson Terhune's "Lad, A Dog" and other books about the collies he raised until his death in 1942. Sunnybank, Terhune's estate, is 4 miles north of Wayne on US 202; it is now Terhune Memorial Park, featuring gardens and a picnic ground.

Tri County Chamber of Commerce: 2055 Hamburg Tpke., Wayne, NJ 07470; phone (973) 831-7788.

Shopping areas: Wayne Town Center, at the junction of SRs 46E and 23S, has a JCPenney. Across the street is Willow Brook, which offers Macy's, Sears and Sterns among its stores.

DEY MANSION, 199 Totowa Rd. in Preakness Valley Park, is a brick and brownstone Georgian house built in the 1740s by Dirck Dey, the father of the commander of the Bergen County militia, Col. Theunis Dey. At Dey's invitation, Gen. George Washington used the mansion for his headquarters in July, October and November 1780. That fall the home was supposedly offered to Washington as a haven after a British plot to kidnap him was discovered.

The detached kitchen and the main house display antiques and items from the 18th century. Picnic facilities are available. Guided tours Wed.-Fri. 1-4, Sat.-Sun. 10-noon and 1-4; closed Jan. 1, Easter, Thanksgiving and Dec. 25. Last tour begins 30 minutes before closing. Admission $1, under 10 free. Phone (973) 696-1776.

WEEHAWKEN (G-6) pop. 12,400, elev. 189′

SPIRIT OF NEW JERSEY, 2 blks. e. of Lincoln Tunnel entrance at Lincoln Harbor Marina, offers sightseeing cruises of the New York City harbor. The Statue of Liberty, Empire State Building, World Trade Center, Ellis Island and Brooklyn Bridge are landmarks that can be seen on the 2- and 3-hour lunch and dinner cruises. Weekend moonlight cruises also are available. Music and entertainment are provided.

Lunch cruises depart Mon.-Fri. at noon, Sat.-Sun. at 11:30. Dinner cruises depart Mon.-Thurs. at 7:30, Fri.-Sat. at 8:30, Sun. at 6. Boarding for all cruises is 30 minutes prior to departure. Lunch cruise $27.95-$33.95; ages 3-11, $13.80-$21.95. Sunday lunch cruise $36.50; ages 3-11, $21.30. Dinner cruise $52.95-$69.95. Reservations are required. AE, DI, MC, VI. Phone (201) 867-5518.

WEST ORANGE (G-5) pop. 39,100

With its sister municipalities—Orange, South Orange, East Orange and Maplewood—the city of West Orange is a primarily residential section of the Newark suburbs. An overlook in Eagle Rock Reservation, west on Eagle Rock Avenue, affords a view of much of the densely populated metropolitan area. West Orange is probably best known for its association with Thomas Edison.

★EDISON NATIONAL HISTORIC SITE, Main St. and Lakeside Ave., consists of the preserved laboratory complex and Glenmont, the home of inventor Thomas Alva Edison and his wife, Mina Miller Edison. The visitor center features exhibits and films; access beyond the visitor center is by guided tour only. Passes must be obtained at the visitor center.

Allow 2 hours, 30 minutes minimum. Visitor center open daily 9-5. Glenmont tours depart on the hour Wed.-Sun. 11-4. Closed Jan. 1, Thanksgiving and Dec. 25. Laboratory complex tours depart from the visitor center on the half hour daily 10:30-3:30. Video cameras and strollers are not allowed on the tours. Admission (includes both sites) $2, under 17 free. Phone (973) 736-5050 or 736-0550.

Glenmont, in Llewellyn Park, was Edison's home from 1886 until his death in 1931. The 23-room Queen Anne-style mansion sits on a 15.5-acre estate and contains its original furnishings. Of special interest is the living room on the second floor, where, seated at his "thought bench," Edison conceived many of his inventions. The

graves of Mr. and Mrs. Edison are behind the house.

Laboratory Complex, built in 1887, includes chemical, physics and metallurgical laboratories, a machine shop, a stockroom and Edison's library/office. Many original inventions are on display. A full-size reproduction of the Black Maria, the world's first motion picture studio, is in the complex.

TURTLE BACK ZOO, in South Mountain Reservation at 560 Northfield Ave. (CR 508) between Cherry Ln. and Prospect Ave., houses a variety of animals in paddock enclosures and an animal nursery. An 1850 miniature train offers a free, scenic 1-mile ride around the grounds. All zoo exhibits are outdoors. Picnicking is permitted. Food is available.

Allow 2 hours minimum. Mon.-Sat. 10-5, Sun. and major holidays 10-6, Apr.-Oct.; daily 10-4:30 in Nov.; Sat.-Sun. 10-4:30, rest of year. Closed Jan. 1, Thanksgiving and Dec. 24-25 and 31. Admission Apr.-Oct., $7; over 61 and ages 2-12, $2.50. Admission rest of year, $6; over 61 and ages 2-12, $2. Phone (973) 731-5800 to verify schedule.

WILDWOOD (G-3) pop. 4,500, elev. 8′

Rarely are the three communities that constitute this popular shore resort referred to in other than the plural. Although the Wildwoods—Wildwood, Wildwood Crest and North Wildwood—are separate entities, their boundaries are indistinguishable. Together they occupy the southernmost isle just north of Cape May.

Because the surf line lies as far as 1,000 feet from shore, the Wildwoods' beach is one of the safest in the state. The 2.5-mile-long boardwalk includes five amusement piers and a variety of shops. North Wildwood's 1873 lighthouse at First and Central avenues is open in the summer.

Greater Wildwood Chamber of Commerce: Schellenger Avenue and the Boardwalk, P.O. Box 823, Wildwood, NJ 08260; phone (609) 729-4000.

Shopping areas: Downtown on Pacific Avenue, Holly Beach Station is an open-air mall with shops, restaurants and nightclubs.

CAPE MAY COUNTY DINNER CRUISE, departing from 6006 Park Blvd., offers dinner cruises of the inner harbor and Intracoastal Waterway. Passengers can enjoy a seafood buffet and live entertainment as they watch the setting sun. Dolphins also may be seen. Allow 3 hours minimum. Cruise departs daily at 6 p.m., Apr. 1-day before Labor Day; at 5:30, Labor Day-Dec. 31. Fare $26; children's rates available by request. Reservations are required 24 hours in advance. DS, MC, VI. Phone (609) 523-8989 or (800) 942-5373.

CAPTAIN SCHUMANN'S BOAT RIDES, 2.7 mi. s.e. on SR 47 from Garden State Pkwy. exit 4B to Park Blvd., then 3.5 blks. n. to 4500 Park Blvd., are aboard *Big Blue,* a converted World War II PT boat. Schumann shares his knowledge of wildlife, ecology and the local fishing industry during 2.5-hour cruises along the Wildwood and Cape May coasts. Morning, afternoon and sunset cruises are available—spotting dolphins and whales is most likely on the afternoon cruise. Food is available.

Cruises depart daily at 10:30, 2 and 7, July 1-Labor Day. Fare for departure at 2, $12; departures at 10:30 and 7, $10; under 6 free. Phone (609) 522-2919.

CAPTAIN SINN'S SIGHTSEEING CENTER, 6006 Park Blvd. in Wildwood Crest, is the departure point for sightseeing and whale- and dolphin-watching cruises. The sightseeing cruise sails in the inner harbor and along the coasts of Wildwood and Cape May.

Allow 3 hours minimum. Sightseeing cruise departs daily at 10:30 and 7 p.m., May-Sept.; Sat.-Sun. at 10:30, in Apr. and Oct. Whale- and dolphin-watching cruises depart daily at 1, May-Sept.; Sat.-Sun. at 1 in Apr. and Nov. Fare $12. Under 6 free with adult. Phone (609) 522-3934.

DELTA LADY SIGHTSEEING CRUISES sail from the Wildwood Marina at the foot of the bridge at Rio Grande and Susquehanna aves. aboard an 1850s replica stern-wheeler. Passengers are introduced to local wildlife, the U.S. Coast Guard Base, commercial fishing fleets and other sights on a 2-hour narrated cruise on the Intracoastal Waterway. A banjo player and sing-alongs are featured on the 7 p.m. cruise.

Cruises depart daily at 10:30, 2 and 7 p.m., July-Aug.; schedule varies, May-June and Sept. 1 to mid-Oct. Fare $10.95; ages 2-11, $5.95. Fare for dinner cruise $23.95; ages 2-11, $14.95. MC, VI. Phone (609) 522-1919.

GEORGE F. BOYER HISTORICAL MUSEUM, Garden State Pkwy. exit 4, 3 mi. s. on SR 47, then .5 mi. n. to 3907 Pacific Ave., contains local antiques, photographs and memorabilia from the late 1800s and early 1900s. A postcard collection and displays about the beach patrol and fire and police departments offer glimpses into the past of a beachside town.

Allow 1 hour minimum. Mon.-Fri. 9:30-2:30, Sat.-Sun. 10:30-2:30, May 1-Oct. 1; Thurs.-Sun. 10:30-2:30, rest of year. Donations. Phone (609) 523-0277.

HEREFORD INLET LIGHTHOUSE, First and Central aves. in North Wildwood, began operation in 1874 when the area was known as the fishing village of Anglesea. The restored Victorian lighthouse is notable for its five chimneys and T-shaped design. It is surrounded by flower and herb gardens and a gazebo; paths lead to the nearby shore. Allow 30 minutes minimum. Daily 9-5, May 1-Oct. 15; Sat.-Sun. 9-5, Oct. 16-Dec. 30 and Feb.-Apr. Donations. Phone (609) 522-4520 or (800) 882-7787.

MARINER'S LANDING AND RAGING WATERS WATER THEME PARK is s. on SR 47, then n. on Ocean Ave. to Schellenger Ave. Overlooking the Jersey shore, the amusement center has more than 100 rides, including carrousels, roller coasters and a Ferris wheel. Food is available. Mon.-Fri. 12:30-12:30, Sat.-Sun. noon-12:30 a.m., mid-June through Aug. 31; days and hours vary Apr. 1 to mid-June and Sept. 1 to mid-Oct. Admission $20-$50. Phone (609) 522-3900.

Raging Waters is a water recreation park with raft rides, slides, a 900-foot activity pool, a children's play area and an adult spa. Food and locker facilities are available. Daily 9-7:30, Memorial Day-Labor Day. Admission $13.95-$15.95, under 48 inches tall $9.95-$11.95. DS, MC, VI.

SILVER BULLET SPEEDBOAT, at the foot of the bridge at Rio Grande and Susquehanna aves. at Wildwood Marina, offers 90-minute sightseeing trips through the Intracoastal Waterway and along the Wildwood coast. Birds, dolphins, seals and whales may be seen. Trips depart daily at 9:30, noon and 2:30, May-Sept. Ticket office open 8 a.m.-10 p.m. Fare $16; ages 2-11, $10. Reservations are recommended. MC, VI. Phone (609) 522-6060.

WILDWOOD CREST—*see Wildwood p. 50.*

WOODBURY—*see Philadelphia and Vicinity in Pennsylvania p. 132.*

WYCKOFF (F-5) pop. 15,400

JAMES A. McFAUL ENVIRONMENTAL CENTER OF BERGEN COUNTY, on Crescent Ave., is an 81-acre wildlife sanctuary. A nature trail, a waterfowl pond, native birds, an herb garden and flowering displays are on the grounds. An indoor exhibit hall contains natural history displays, live animals and monthly art exhibits. Picnic facilities are available. Sanctuary grounds open daily 8-dusk. Exhibit hall open Mon.-Fri. 8-4:45, Sat.-Sun. 1-4:45. Donations. Phone (201) 891-5571.

City Island, across from downtown Harrisburg

Pennsylvania

An introduction to the state's history, geography, economy and recreation

IN THE KEYSTONE POSITION AMONG THE 13 COLONIES, PENNSYLVANIA ALSO HAS BEEN THE KEYSTONE IN THE DEVELOPMENT OF THE NATION. DEMOCRACY WAS BORN OF WILLIAM PENN'S "GREAT LAW," AND HIS PHILADELPHIA BECAME ITS CRADLE. THE NATION FOUND ITS STRENGTH AT VALLEY FORGE, CHOSE ITS COURSE AT GETTYSBURG, AND DEFENDED ITS FREEDOM FROM THE STEEL MILLS OF PITTSBURGH AND THE SHIPYARDS OF PHILADELPHIA. IF AMERICA IS THE FLAG, THEN PENNSYLVANIA IS THE POLE.

HISTORY

Pennsylvania was occupied by Delaware, Shawnee, Susquehanna and Iroquois Indians before the first Europeans arrived. In 1609 English explorer Henry Hudson charted the coasts along the Delaware River, and in 1643 New Sweden governor Johan Printz established a colony north of the Wilmington, Del., area on Tinicum Island near Chester. The settlement fell into Dutch hands in 1655 and was claimed by the English in 1664.

In 1681 King Charles II availed himself of the opportunity to be rid of a troublesome young Quaker named William Penn while also making good on a £16,000 debt owed Penn's father. He granted Penn a huge tract of land—between 40 and 43 degrees longitude and up to 5 degrees west of the Delaware River—to be called Penn's Woodlands, or Pennsylvania. The 37-year-old Penn immediately set out to establish his "city of brotherly love" at the confluence of the Delaware and Schuylkill rivers.

Religious freedom became the purpose to which the new colony would be dedicated. Penn's "Holy Experiment"—an exercise in social idealism—was soon delineated in his "Great Law of Pennsylvania," guaranteeing freedom of conscience, judicial restraint, voting rights, fair taxation, education and gainful employment. Penn's tenets gradually evolved into his Charter of Privileges of 1701, which made Pennsylvania's government the soundest in the land.

Pennsylvania attracted increasing numbers of European immigrants in the 1700s. Joining the English, Welsh and Dutch Quakers were Rhineland Germans representing several religious sects. These Amish, Dunkers, Mennonites, Moravians and Schwenkfelders—who gained the collective misnomer Pennsylvania Dutch—settled in the fertile farming region northwest of Philadelphia. A third major group braved the frontier; the trail for the hardy Scottish and Irish settlers led past the English and German settlements into western Pennsylvania.

Penn's scrupulous dealings with the American Indians helped to forestall the conflict, but by 1750 the natives had grown weary of increasing encroachment into their lands. The French, too, were concerned; their claim to the Ohio Valley, an essential trade route, was at stake. The French-Indian alliance was established, and the British were intent on gaining the frontier for themselves.

In December 1753, George Washington, a 21-year-old major in the Virginia Militia, led an expedition to French Fort LeBoeuf south of Lake Erie. He was politely but firmly rebuffed and soon retreated home. Washington's return the following spring was both historic and inauspicious. After defeating a French detachment east of present-day Uniontown, he was soon besieged by a large French force at hastily constructed Fort Necessity. The first real battle of the French and Indian War began and ended there on July 3, 1754.

The tide began to turn for the British in 1758 with a series of important victories, among them the capture of Fort Duquesne by British general John Forbes. Rebuilt and renamed Fort Pitt, the outpost not only hastened the departure of the

Fast Facts

POPULATION: 12,100,000.

AREA: 45,308 square miles; ranks 33rd.

CAPITAL: Harrisburg.

HIGHEST POINT: 3,213 ft., Mount Davis.

LOWEST POINT: Sea level, Delaware River.

TIME ZONE Eastern. DST.

MINIMUM AGE FOR DRIVERS: 16.

SEAT BELT/CHILD RESTRAINT LAWS: Seat belts required for driver and front-seat passengers; child restraints required for under 4.

HELMETS FOR MOTORCYCLISTS: Required.

RADAR DETECTORS: Permitted.

FIREARMS LAWS: Vary by state and/or county. Contact Pennsylvania State Police Headquarters, 1800 Elmerton Ave., Harrisburg, PA 17110; phone (717) 783-5504.

HOLIDAYS: Jan. 1; Martin Luther King Jr.'s Birthday, Jan. (3rd Mon.); Presidents Day, Feb. (3rd Mon.); Memorial Day, May (last Mon.); July 4; Labor Day, Sept. (1st Mon.); Columbus Day, Oct. (2nd Mon.); Veterans Day, Nov. 11; Thanksgiving; Dec. 25.

TAXES: Pennsylvania's statewide sales tax is 6 percent; individual counties can levy additional increments. Pittsburgh levies a 10-percent amusements tax. Local options allow certain lodgings taxes of up to 6 percent.

STATE WELCOME CENTERS: Three centers are on the Pennsylvania Turnpike: one near Sideling Hill, one eastbound between exits 2 and 3 and one westbound between exits 28 and 29. Others are on I-79S at Edinboro; I-80E at the Ohio line; I-70W at the Maryland line; I-83N at the Maryland line; I-81N near Newville; I-95N at the Delaware line; I-78W at the New Jersey line; and I-81S south of Lenox. Centers are open daily 8-6, May-Sept.; 8-5, rest of year. Centers are closed Jan. 1, Martin Luther King Jr.'s Birthday, Presidents Day, Easter, Thanksgiving and Dec. 25.

French, but also opened the region to new settlement. France relinquished all claims to North America in 1763, but the British toll was high. War debts and unwieldy new growth so weakened the empire that within a decade they were vulnerable to a new threat—by the colonists.

By 1774 Pennsylvania had become the military, economic and political center of the colonies. The First Continental Congress convened in Philadelphia in 1774 and the Second Continental Congress 1775-76, where the Declaration of Independence was drafted and approved on July 4, 1776. When the Articles of Confederation were endorsed in York in 1777, the 13 Colonies effectively became one nation. On Dec. 12, 1787, Pennsylvania became the second colony to ratify the U.S. Constitution—drafted at the Pennsylvania State House in Philadelphia—thus becoming the nation's second state. Philadelphia was the national capital 1790-1800.

Pennsylvania also was a major battleground during the American Revolution. George Washington, now a general and commander in chief of the American forces, earned a pivotal early victory at Trenton, N.J., after leading his troops across the Delaware River on Christmas night 1776. After suffering a serious setback at Brandywine Creek in September 1777, Washington's forces regained some success at Germantown before quartering for that legendary winter at Valley Forge.

The 19th century brought tremendous growth and development to Pennsylvania. An intricate network of roads, bridges and canals hastened an already rapid westward expansion; between 1794 and 1832 the original Philadelphia-Lancaster Turnpike had grown to include some 3,000 miles of roadway. With the arrival of the railroad in the mid-1800s came the ability to fully exploit Pennsylvania's extensive coal, oil, iron and lumber resources, making the state among the nation's richest.

Pennsylvania was staunchly pro-Union during the Civil War. The state had guaranteed the end of slavery with the Pennsylvania Emancipation Act of 1781, and the Mason-Dixon Line, established as the state's southern boundary in 1769, became the official dividing line between North and South. Pennsylvania lent nearly 340,000 soldiers and all its industrial might to the Union cause. So critical were Pennsylvania's supply routes that in the summer of 1863 they brought Confederate general Robert E. Lee and some 70,000 seasoned troops into the Cumberland Valley.

The 3-day battle at Gettysburg resulted in more than 51,000 casualties—nearly equal to America's toll in all of the Vietnam War—and marked the beginning of the end for the Confederacy. President Abraham Lincoln's dedication of the national cemetery there on Nov. 19, 1863, was the occasion of his simple but brilliant summation of America's purpose known as the Gettysburg Address.

At the end of the war, Pennsylvania found itself at the forefront of the Industrial Revolution. It was home to the three largest steel mills in the country, and by 1870 Pittsburgh's mills alone were producing two-thirds of the national total. Such industrial magnates as Andrew Carnegie, Henry Clay Frick and J. P. Morgan forever changed the face of American business and commerce, and Ohioan John D. Rockefeller built his refining empire on Pennsylvania crude. Also from Pennsylvania's industrial boom came the labor movement, whose influence is still felt today.

A series of extensive public works programs kept Pennsylvanians busy during the Great Depression, and they regained their industrial and military prominence with the onset of World War II. Though some undesirable effects of the waning industrial age remain in Pennsylvania, the sort of modern pioneering that brought the nation the first commercial radio station and the first digital computer today makes the state a leader in the fields of science, medicine and technology.

GEOGRAPHY

The most prominent feature of this rectangular state is the arc of rocky, nearly unbroken parallel ridges and narrow valleys that curves from southwest to northeast. East of the Appalachian ridges and the Susquehanna River, the southeastern lowlands roll gradually down to a strip of the

Atlantic Coastal Plain along the lower Delaware River.

West and north of the mountains lies the Appalachian Plateau. The highest section, called the Laurel Highlands, abuts Maryland east of Uniontown. The northern section of the plateau is Pennsylvania's wooded wilderness; its main feature is Pine Creek Gorge, about 50 miles long and 1,000 feet deep. The Pocono Mountains in the northeastern part of Pennsylvania also are part of the Appalachian Plateau.

The Susquehanna and Delaware river systems drain the central and eastern part of the state. Most of the west is within the Ohio River watershed, to which Pennsylvania contributes the Allegheny and Monongahela rivers. A narrow plain borders Lake Erie.

The hard Appalachian ridges diverted the ice sheet that planed and enriched northern New Jersey and most of Ohio. Thus, much of Pennsylvania's soil is shallow sandstone and shale. The limestones of the southeast lowlands and the Great Valley, as well as some river bottom soils, are the most productive. Short summers and harsh winters prevail in the Appalachians and northern Allegheny Plateau; the rest of the state has the hot, humid summers and fairly mild winters associated with the mid-Atlantic region.

ECONOMY

Pennsylvania was at the forefront of America's Industrial Revolution. The world's first oil well was drilled in Titusville in 1859, marking the birth of the petroleum industry, and it was in Pennsylvania that Andrew Carnegie established the forerunner of the U.S. Steel Corp. By the start of the 20th century, Pennsylvania had emerged as an industrial giant, out-producing not only the rest of the country but the world.

In recent years Pennsylvania's economy has diversified, and it is no longer dependent on heavy manufacturing. The state blended its manufacturing and industrial strengths with high-technology. New market opportunities have emerged to complement the state's traditional industries, particularly in the specialized manufacturing and high-growth area of biotechnology.

Tourism is Pennsylvania's second largest industry, surpassed only by agriculture. Popular destinations for vacationers include the Pocono Mountains, Gettysburg, Lancaster and the Pennsylvania Dutch Country, the Laurel Highlands, Philadelphia and Pittsburgh. Still others find themselves drawn to Hershey—Chocolate Town U.S.A.—and Reading, which calls itself the "Outlet Capital of the World."

From trim farms come corn, buckwheat, potatoes, tobacco, oats and other grains. The mountain valleys of the south central counties and the far northwest grow apples, peaches, cherries, berries and grapes. Pennsylvania is the leading producer of mushrooms in the nation; mushroom farms lend their fusty scent to the countryside surrounding Kennett Square near Longwood.

Through extensive reforestation, a significant lumber industry has emerged in Pennsylvania; the state has the nation's largest supply of hardwood resources. Also significant is the production of Christmas trees—the town of Indiana is reputedly the "Christmas Tree Capital of the World."

Basic to Pennsylvania is coal, and due largely to a coal mining industry that produces more than 87 million tons annually, Pennsylvania is the nation's second leading producer of electricity. The only anthracite deposit in the eastern United States underlies the northeast section of the state. In the west the reserves of bituminous coal are at the northern end of the vast Appalachian coalfields.

RECREATION

Wooded mountains provide the setting for most outdoor recreation. The main vacation areas are the Poconos, Allegheny National Forest and the Laurel Highlands. Resorts with complete social and recreational programs dot the Poconos, which encompass the picturesque Delaware Gap and numerous waterfalls. The Allegheny National Forest remains mostly natural, with miles of fishing streams and forested hills for hiking.

Water sports are popular at the Allegheny Reservoir east of Warren, in the Laurel Highlands at Somerset and Ligonier, at Lake Wallenpaupack in the Poconos, at Pine Creek Gorge and at Conneaut Lake and Pymatuning Reservoir in western Pennsylvania. White-water rafting is popular on several of the state's rivers, most notably the Youghiogheny River at Ohiopyle State Park and the Lehigh River in Lehigh Gorge State Park.

Fishing is a rewarding sport throughout Pennsylvania. Anglers find the lakes and streams stocked with bass, bluegill, crappie, muskellunge, perch and trout. Hunting is most profitable in the forested regions of the state. Hunters find bears, deer, grouse, pheasants, quails, rabbits, squirrels, wild turkeys and woodcocks in the Allegheny National Forest and in several Appalachian areas.

Horseback riding also is popular throughout Pennsylvania. One trail, the Horse-Shoe Trail, extends some 130 miles west from Valley Forge where it joins the Appalachian Trail. A detailed guidebook is available for $6. For more information contact the Horse-Shoe Trail Club, Warwick County Park, RD 2, Pottstown, PA 19464; phone (215) 469-9461.

The National Heritage Tour Route is a series of 60 trails throughout Pennsylvania providing hiking opportunities along the routes of early railroads and canals. A guidebook is available that provides descriptions, maps, historical background and photographs of the more than 700 miles of trails. For information phone (800) 898-3636.

Winter sports flourish in this mountainous state. **Snowmobiling, downhill skiing** and **cross-country skiing** are possible at numerous state parks. Resort areas in the Poconos and the Laurel Highlands have facilities that cater to both the beginner and to the more advanced skier. Other areas popular for snow sports are near Gettysburg, Scranton and York.

Camping season usually runs mid-April to mid-October, though some parks offer extended seasons. Hiking and **backpacking** trails are in most state parks. The parks are open daily 8 a.m.-dusk, all year. Although no entrance fees are charged, user fees are charged for some facilities. Pets are not permitted in camping or swimming areas. For more information or to make a reservation at one of Pennsylvania's state parks, phone the Bureau of State Parks at (888) 727-2757. For information about camping in Pennsylvania *see the AAA Mideastern CampBook.*

Throughout the TourBook, you may notice a Recreational Activities heading with bulleted listings of recreation-oriented establishments listed underneath. Since normal AAA inspection criteria cannot be applied, these establishments are presented for information only. Age, height and weight restrictions may apply. Reservations are often recommended and sometimes required. Visitors should phone or write the attraction for additional information, and the address and phone number are provided for this purpose.

RECREATION AREAS	MAP LOCATION	CAMPING	PICNICKING	HIKING TRAILS	BOATING	BOAT RAMP	BOAT RENTAL	FISHING	SWIMMING	PETS ON LEASH	BICYCLE TRAILS	WINTER SPORTS	VISITOR CENTER	LODGE/CABINS	FOOD SERVICE
NATIONAL FOREST (See place listing) **Allegheny** 516,000 acres. Northwestern Pennsylvania.		•	•	•	•	•	•	•	•	•	•	•	•		•
NATIONAL RECREATION AREA **Delaware Water Gap (E-12)** 70,000 acres. Hunting.		•	•	•	•	•		•	•	•		•	•		
ARMY CORPS OF ENGINEERS **Cowanesque Lake (C-7)** 3,200 acres 3 mi. w. of Lawrenceville off SR 15. Hunting, water skiing.	87	•	•	•	•	•	•	•	•	•					•
Raystown Lake (G-6) 29,300 acres s.w. of Huntingdon off SR 26. Water skiing.	84	•	•	•	•	•	•	•	•	•				•	•
Tioga-Hammond Lakes (D-7) 6,700 acres 12 mi. n. of Mansfield on US 15. Hunting, water skiing.	89	•	•	•	•	•	•	•	•	•					
STATE **Bald Eagle (F-7)** 5,900 acres off SR 26 at Howard. Tobogganing.	1	•	•	•	•	•	•	•	•			•			•
Beltzville (F-10) 2,972 acres 6 mi. e. of Lehighton off US 209. Cross-country skiing, tobogganing.	2		•	•	•	•	•	•	•	•					•
Bendigo (E-5) 100 acres 3 mi. n.e. of Johnsonburg off US 219. Tobogganing.	3		•					•	•	•		•			•
Black Moshannon (F-6) 3,481 acres 9 mi. e. of Philipsburg on SR 504. Cross-country skiing.	5	•	•	•	•	•	•	•	•	•		•	•	•	•
Blue Knob (H-5) 5,600 acres 5 mi. n.w. of Pavia off SR 869. Cross-country and downhill skiing, snowmobiling.	6	•	•	•				•	•	•		•			•
Caledonia (I-7) 1,130 acres 4 mi. e. of Fayetteville on US 30. Historic. Cross-country skiing. (See Fayetteville)	7	•	•	•				•	•	•		•			•
Canoe Creek (G-5) 959 acres 7 mi. e. of Hollidaysburg off US 22. Cross-country skiing, tobogganing; horse rental.	8	•	•	•	•	•	•	•	•	•		•			•
Chapman (D-4) 805 acres 5 mi. w. of Clarendon off US 6. Cross-country skiing, snowmobiling, tobogganing.	9	•	•	•	•	•	•	•	•	•		•			
Cherry Springs (D-6) 48 acres 4 mi. e. of Coudersport on US 6, then 11 mi. s.e. on SR 44. Hunting, snowmobiling.	91	•	•							•		•			
Clear Creek (E-4) 1,209 acres 4 mi. n. of Sigel off SR 949. Cross-country skiing.	10	•	•	•	•	•	•	•	•	•		•	•	•	
Codorus (I-8) 3,320 acres 2 mi. e. of Hanover off SR 216. Snowmobiling, tobogganing.	11	•	•	•	•	•	•	•	•	•		•			•
Colonel Denning (H-7) 273 acres 9 mi. n. of Newville off SR 233. Cross-country skiing, tobogganing.	12	•	•	•				•	•	•		•	•		•
Colton Point (D-7) 368 acres 5 mi. s. of Ansonia off US 6. Cross-country skiing, snowmobiling. (See Wellsboro)	13	•	•	•				•				•			•

RECREATION AREAS	MAP LOCATION	CAMPING	PICNICKING	HIKING TRAILS	BOATING	BOAT RAMP	BOAT RENTAL	FISHING	SWIMMING	PETS ON LEASH	BICYCLE TRAILS	WINTER SPORTS	VISITOR CENTER	LODGE/CABINS	FOOD SERVICE
Cook Forest (E-3) 6,422 acres 1 mi. n. of Cooksburg off SR 36. Cross-country skiing, sledding, snowmobiling; horse rental.	14	•	•	•	•	•	•	•	•	•		•	•	•	•
Cowans Gap (I-6) 1,085 acres n. of Fort Loudon off SR 75. Cross-country skiing.	15	•	•	•	•	•	•	•	•	•		•	•	•	•
Delaware Canal (G-11) 60-mile area along SR 32; headquarters is in Upper Black Eddy. Cross-country skiing, sledding.	103		•	•	•			•	•	•		•	•		•
Elk (D-5) 3,192 acres 9 mi. e. of Wilcox.	17		•	•	•	•			•	•			•		
Evansburg (H-11) 3,349 acres 2 mi. e. of Collegeville on US 422. Golf (18 holes).	92		•	•				•		•		•			
Fort Washington (H-11) 493 acres at 500 Bethlehem Pike in Fort Washington. Cross-country skiing, sledding.	93		•	•				•		•		•			
Fowlers Hollow (H-7) 104 acres 4 mi. s. of New Germantown off SR 274 on Upper Buck Ridge Rd. Cross-country skiing, snowmobiling.	94	•	•	•				•		•					
Frances Slocum (E-10) 1,035 acres 4 mi. e. of Dallas off SR 309. Cross-country skiing, sledding.	18	•	•	•	•	•	•	•	•	•		•	•		
French Creek (H-10) 7,339 acres 6 mi. n.e. of Pennsylvania Tpke. exit 22 on SR 345.	19	•	•	•	•	•	•	•	•	•		•		•	•
Gifford Pinchot (H-8) 2,338 acres 2 mi. e. of Rossville off SR 74. Cross-country skiing.	21	•	•	•	•	•	•	•	•	•		•	•		
Gouldsboro (E-11) 3,050 acres s. of Gouldsboro.	22		•	•	•	•	•	•	•	•		•			
Greenwood Furnace (G-6) 406 acres 5 mi. n.w. of Belleville on SR 305. Snowmobiling.	23	•	•	•				•	•	•		•			
Hickory Run (F-10) 15,500 acres 5 mi. s.e. of White Haven on SR 534. Cross-country skiing, snowmobiling.	24	•	•	•				•	•	•		•	•		
Hills Creek (D-7) 407 acres 7 mi. n.e. of Wellsboro off SR 6. Tobogganing.	25	•	•	•	•	•	•	•	•	•		•			
Hyner Run (E-6) 180 acres 7 mi. e. of Renovo off SR 120. Snowmobiling.	26	•	•	•				•	•	•		•			
Kettle Creek (E-6) 1,626 acres 8 mi. n.w. of Westport off SR 120. Sledding, snowmobiling; horse rental.	27	•	•	•	•	•	•	•	•	•		•			
Keystone (H-3) 1,190 acres 3 mi. s.e. of New Alexandria on SR 981. Snowmobiling; horse rental.	28	•	•	•	•	•	•	•	•	•		•	•	•	•
Kooser (H-3) 170 acres 10 mi. w. of Somerset on SR 31. Cross-country skiing.	29	•	•	•				•	•	•		•		•	
Lackawanna (D-10) 1,373 acres 3 mi. n. of Waverly on SR 407. Tobogganing.	30	•	•	•	•	•	•	•	•	•		•			
Laurel Hill (I-3) 3,935 acres 10 mi. w. of Somerset off SR 31 near Trent. Snowmobiling.	31	•	•	•	•	•	•	•	•	•		•			
Leonard Harrison (D-7) 585 acres 10 mi. s.w. of Wellsboro off SR 660. *(See Wellsboro)*	33	•	•	•				•		•			•		
Linn Run (H-3) 565 acres 10 mi. s.e. of Ligonier off SR 711. Snowmobiling.	34	•	•	•				•		•		•		•	
Little Buffalo (G-7) 830 acres 4 mi. s.w. of Newport off SR 34. Cross-country skiing, tobogganing.	35		•	•	•	•	•	•	•	•		•			
Little Pine (E-7) 2,158 acres 3 mi. n. of Waterville off SR 44. Cross-country skiing, ice fishing, ice skating, sledding, snowmobiling.	36	•	•	•	•	•	•	•	•	•		•			
Locust Lake (F-9) 1,144 acres 3 mi. s. of Mahanoy City off I-81 exit 37.	37	•		•	•	•	•	•	•	•		•	•		
Lyman Run (D-6) 595 acres 8 mi. s.w. of Galeton off US 6. Snowmobiling.	38	•	•	•	•	•	•	•	•	•			•		•
Marsh Creek (H-10) 1,705 acres 5 mi. n.w. of Downingtown off SR 282. Iceboating, ice fishing, ice skating, sledding; horse rental.	39		•	•	•	•	•	•	•	•			•		•
Maurice K. Goddard (E-2) 1,417 acres 14 mi. w. of Franklin on US 62.	40		•	•	•	•	•	•		•			•		•
McConnells Mill (F-2) 2,534 acres 8 mi. s.e. of New Castle off US 422.	41	•	•					•		•		•	•		
Memorial Lake (G-8) 230 acres 5 mi. n.e. of Grantville off US 22 and I-81. Cross-country skiing.	42		•	•	•	•	•	•		•		•			
Milton (F-8) 77 acres on the island between Milton and West Milton.	96		•	•	•			•		•					
Moraine (F-2) 15,838 acres 8 mi. n.w. of Butler off US 422. Cross-country skiing, hunting, iceboating, ice fishing, snowmobiling, tobogganing.	44		•	•	•	•	•	•		•		•	•	•	•

INDEX TO STARRED ATTRACTIONS

ATTRACTIONS AND PLACES OF
EXCEPTIONALINTEREST AND QUALITY

Brandywine River Museum - see Chadds Ford
The Carnegie - see Pittsburgh
The Carnegie Museum of Natural History -
   see Pittsburgh
Carnegie Science Center - see Pittsburgh
Cathedral of Learning - see Pittsburgh
Christ Church - see Philadelphia
Clayton - see Pittsburgh
Congress Hall - see Philadelphia
Devil's Den - see Gettysburg National Military Park
Dorney Park and Wildwater Kingdom - see Allentown
Drake Well Museum - see Titusville
Eisenhower National Historic Site - see Gettysburg
Eternal Light Peace Memorial -
   see Gettysburg National Military Park
Fairmount Park - see Philadelphia
Fallingwater - see Ohiopyle
Fort Necessity National Battlefield - see place listing
Fort Pitt Museum - see Pittsburgh
Franklin Institute Science Museum - see Philadelphia
Gateway Clipper Fleet - see Pittsburgh
Gettysburg National Cemetery -
   see Gettysburg National Military Park

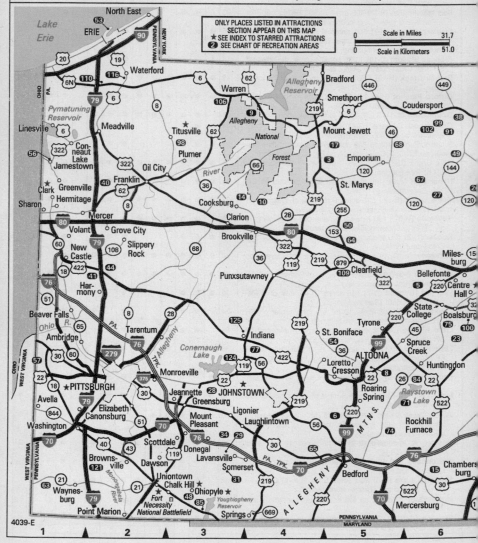

Gettysburg National Military Park -
    see place listing
Golden Plough Tavern, General Horatio Gates
    House and Bobb Log House - see York
Hartwood - see Pittsburgh
Hershey Museum - see Hershey
Hersheypark - see Hershey
Hershey's Chocolate World - see Hershey
Historical Society of York County - see York
Independence Hall - see Philadelphia
Independence National Historical Park -
    see Philadelphia
Johnstown Flood Museum - see Johnstown
Kentuck Knob - see Chalk Hill
Landis Valley Museum - see Lancaster
Liberty Bell Pavilion - see Philadelphia
Longwood Gardens - see Kennett Square
Masonic Temple - see Philadelphia
National Park Visitor Center -
    see Gettysburg National Military Park

Penn's Cave - see Centre Hall
Philadelphia Museum of Art - see Philadelphia
Phipps Conservatory - see Pittsburgh
Pittsburgh Zoo - see Pittsburgh
Point State Park - see Pittsburgh
Quiet Valley Living Historical Farm - see Stroudsburg
Second Bank of United States - see Philadelphia
State Capitol - see Harrisburg
State Museum of Pennsylvania - see Harrisburg
Tara - see Clark
The University of Pennsylvania Museum of
    Archaeology and Anthropology - see Philadelphia
Valley Forge National Historical Park -
    see place listing
Washington Crossing Historic Park -
    see place listing
Watch and Clock Museum of the National
    Association of Watch and Clock
    Collectors Inc. - see Columbia
Wheatland - see Lancaster

© AAA

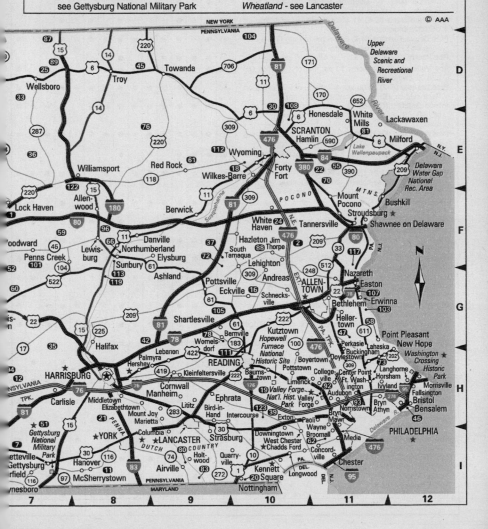

RECREATION AREAS	MAP LOCATION	CAMPING	PICNICKING	HIKING TRAILS	BOATING	BOAT RAMP	BOAT RENTAL	FISHING	SWIMMING	PETS ON LEASH	BICYCLE TRAILS	WINTER SPORTS	VISITOR CENTER	LODGE/CABINS	FOOD SERVICE
Mount Pisgah (D-8) 1,302 acres 10 mi. n.w. of Troy off US 6. Cross-country skiing, ice fishing, ice skating, sledding, snowmobiling.	45	•	•	•	•	•	•	•	•	•			•		•
Neshaminy (H-12) 330 acres near Croydon off SR 132.	46		•		•	•		•	•	•					
Nockamixon (G-11) 5,283 acres 5 mi. e. of Quakertown off CRs 513 and 563. Tobogganing; horse rental.	47		•	•	•	•	•	•	•	•	•	•	•		
Ohiopyle (I-3) 18,719 acres 14 mi. e. of Uniontown on SR 381. Cross-country skiing, snowmobiling.	48	•	•	•				•		•	•	•	•		•
Oil Creek (E-3) 7,007 acres 4 mi. n. of Oil City on SR 8 via signs. Cross-country skiing.	98		•	•				•		•	•		•		
Ole Bull (E-6) 117 acres 3 mi. s.w. of Oleona off SR 144.	49	•	•	•				•	•	•					
Parker Dam (F-5) 968 acres 4 mi. e. of Penfield off SR 153. Cross-country skiing, snowmobiling.	50	•	•	•	•	•	•	•	•	•		•	•		•
Patterson (D-6) 10 acres off SR 44 between Cherry Springs and Sweden Valley.	99	•	•	•											
Penn Roosevelt (G-6) 41 acres 10 mi. w. of Milroy off US 322. Snowmobiling.	100	•	•	•				•		•		•			
Pine Grove Furnace (H-7) 696 acres at Pine Grove Furnace on SR 233. Cross-country skiing.	51	•	•	•	•		•	•	•	•	•	•	•		•
Poe Paddy (F-7) 10 acres n.e. of Milroy off US 322.	101	•	•	•		•		•		•					
Poe Valley (F-7) 620 acres 10 mi. n.e. of Milroy off US 322. Snowmobiling.	52	•	•	•	•	•		•	•	•					
Presque Isle (C-2) 3,200 acres 7 mi. n. of I-90 exit 5 on Peninsula Dr. (SR 832). Historic. *(See Erie)*	53		•	•	•	•		•	•	•	•	•	•		•
Prince Gallitzin (G-5) 6,249 acres 16 mi. n.w. of Altoona off SR 53. Cross-country skiing, tobogganing; horse rental.	54	•	•	•	•	•	•	•	•	•		•	•		•
Promised Land (E-11) 2,971 acres 10 mi. n. of Canadensis on SR 390. Cross-country skiing, snowmobiling.	55	•	•	•	•	•	•	•	•	•		•	•	•	•
Prouty Place (D-6) 5 acres 8 mi. s. on unmarked route off SR 44 between Cherry Springs and Sweden Valley.	102	•	•	•				•							
Pymatuning (E-1) 21,122 acres 4 mi. n. of Jamestown off US 322. Cross-country skiing, iceboating, ice fishing, ice skating, snowmobiling. *(See Linesville)*	56	•	•		•	•	•	•		•			•	•	•
Raccoon Creek (G-1) 7,323 acres 2 mi. n. of Frankfort Springs on SR 18. Cross-country skiing.	57	•	•	•	•	•	•	•	•	•		•	•	•	•
Ralph Stover (G-11) 45 acres 9 mi. n.w. of New Hope on SR 32. Tobogganing.	58		•	•				•		•					
Raymond B. Winter (F-7) 695 acres 20 mi. w. of Lewisburg on SR 192.	59	•	•	•				•	•	•		•	•		
Reeds Gap (G-7) 220 acres 13 mi. n.e. of Lewistown off US 322. Tobogganing.	60		•	•				•	•	•					
Ricketts Glen (E-9) 13,050 acres 4 mi. n. of Red Rock on SR 487. Cross-country skiing, snowmobiling. *(See Red Rock)*	61	•	•	•	•	•	•	•	•	•			•	•	•
Ridley Creek (H-11) 2,600 acres 7 mi. e. of West Chester via SRs 3 or 352.	62		•	•				•		•	•		•		
Ryerson Station (I-1) 1,164 acres 1 mi. s. of Wind Ridge off SR 21. Tobogganing.	63	•	•	•	•	•	•	•	•	•		•	•		
Salt Springs (D-10) 400 acres 1 mi. w. of Franklin Forks off SR 29. Primitive.	104	•	•					•		•					
S.B. Elliott (F-5) 318 acres 9 mi. w. of Clearfield on SR 153. Snowmobiling.	64	•	•	•				•		•		•		•	
Shawnee (H-4) 3,983 acres 9 mi. w. of Bedford off US 30. Cross-country skiing, snowmobiling.	65	•	•	•	•	•	•	•	•	•		•	•		•
Shikellamy (F-8) 125 acres 1 mi. n. of Shamokin Dam off SR 11.	66		•		•	•	•	•		•			•		•
Sinnemahoning (E-6) 1,910 acres 10 mi. n. of Sinnemahoning on SR 872. Snowmobiling.	67	•	•	•	•	•		•		•		•		•	
Sizerville (E-5) 386 acres at Sizerville off SR 155. Cross-country skiing, snowmobiling.	68	•	•	•				•	•	•	•	•	•		
Tobyhanna (E-11) 5,440 acres 2 mi. e. of Tobyhanna on SR 423. Snowmobiling.	70	•	•	•	•	•	•	•	•	•		•			
Trough Creek (H-6) 541 acres 3 mi. n. of Entriken off SR 994. Snowmobiling.	71	•	•	•				•		•		•	•		
Tuscarora (F-9) 1,716 acres 5 mi. n.w. of Tamaqua off SR 309. Tobogganing.	72		•		•	•	•	•	•	•		•			•

RECREATION AREAS	MAP LOCATION	CAMPING	PICNICKING	HIKING TRAILS	BOATING	BOAT RAMP	BOAT RENTAL	FISHING	SWIMMING	PETS ON LEASH	BICYCLE TRAILS	WINTER SPORTS	VISITOR CENTER	LODGE/CABINS	FOOD SERVICE
Tyler (H-11) 1,711 acres 1.5 mi. w. of Newtown off SR 413. Cross-country skiing, sledding; horse trails.	73		•	•	•		•	•		•	•	•			•
Warriors Path (H-5) 334 acres 1 mi. s. of Saxton on SR 26.	74	•	•					•		•		•			
Whipple Dam (G-6) 256 acres 12 mi. s. of State College off SR 26. Snowmobiling.	75	•	•	•	•	•		•	•	•		•			•
Worlds End (E-8) 780 acres 7 mi. n.w. of Laporte on SR 154. Snowmobiling.	76	•	•	•				•	•	•		•		•	•
Yellow Creek (G-4) 2,981 acres 18 mi. n.w. of Ebensburg on US 422. Cross-country skiing, sledding, snowmobiling.	77		•	•	•	•	•	•	•	•		•			
OTHER															
Auburn Dam (G-9) 187 acres 1 mi. from Landingville on LR 53075.	105		•		•	•		•		•					
Blue Marsh Lake (G-9) 6,276 acres 8 mi. n. of Reading on SR 183. Ice fishing, ice skating, sledding, water skiing.	78		•	•	•	•		•	•	•		•			
Blue Spruce Park (G-3) 420 acres 6 mi. n. of Indiana on SR 110.	125		•	•	•			•		•					
Buckaloons Access Area (D-3) 5 mi. w. of Warren at jct. US 6 and US 62.	106	•	•	•	•	•		•		•	•	•	•		
Chapman Lake (D-10) 98 acres near Montdale.	108	•	•		•	•		•	•	•					•
Conemaugh River Lake (G-3) 7,609 acres 8 mi. n. of New Alexandria off SR 981.	124	•	•	•	•	•		•		•			•		•
Curwensville Lake (F-5) 362 acres 3 mi. s. of Curwensville on SR 453. Cross-country skiing.	109	•	•	•	•	•		•	•	•		•			
Edinboro Lake (D-1) 240 acres on SR 99 in Edinboro.	110	•		•	•	•		•	•	•				•	•
Felix Dam (H-9) 3.5-mile area n. of Reading at Tuckerton, via Tuckerton Rd. to Stoudts Ferry Bridge Rd. Water skiing.	111		•		•	•		•		•					
Harveys Lake (E-9) 658 acres near Harveys Lake.	112	•	•		•	•	•	•		•		•			•
Hibernia Park (H-10) 800 acres 6 mi. n. of Coatesville on SR 82, then w. on Cedar Knoll Rd.	123	•	•	•				•		•		•			
Hugh Moore Park (G-11) 260 acres on SR 611 in Easton.	107		•	•	•			•		•		•			
Lake Aldred (I-9) 5,000 acres 25 mi. s.e. of York on SR 425.	80	•	•	•	•	•		•	•	•					
Lake Augusta (G-8) 3,000 acres near Sunbury.	113	•	•		•	•	•	•	•	•					
Lake LeBoeuf (D-2) 70 acres 2 blks. s. on Hazel St. in Waterford.	116	•	•		•	•	•	•	•	•					
Lake Wallenpaupack (E-11) 5,700 acres 10 mi. e. of Hamlin off SR 590. Horse rental.	81	•	•	•	•	•	•	•	•	•		•	•	•	•
Leaser Lake (G-10) 396 acres on SR 143 in Jacksonville. Bridle trails.	16		•	•	•	•		•		•		•			
Martins Creek (G-11) 225 acres 3 mi. n. of Martins Creek via SR 611N to LR 48025.	117		•	•	•	•		•		•		•			
Mauch Chunk Lake (F-10) 2,445 acres 4 mi. w. of Jim Thorpe. Cross-country skiing.	88	•	•	•	•	•	•	•	•	•		•	•		•
Muddy Run (I-9) 700 acres 4 mi. w. of Buck on SR 372.	83	•	•	•	•	•		•		•		•	•		•
Nottingham (I-10) 651 acres .25 mi. s. of Nottingham at 150 Park Rd. Birdwatching, cross-country skiing.	20	•	•	•				•		•		•	•		
Susquehanna Access Area (G-8) 10-mile area near Selinsgrove.	119		•		•	•		•							
Susquehanna Park (E-7) 20 acres on Susquehanna River in Williamsport.	122		•		•	•		•		•					
Ten Mile Creek Access Area (I-2) two sites: 3-mile area at Prosperity and an 11-mile area at Marianna.	121		•		•	•		•							
Youghiogheny Reservoir (I-3) 4,034 acres 20 mi. s.e. of Uniontown on US 40.	85	•	•		•	•		•	•	•			•		

If a tire blows, ease your foot off the accelerator, maintain a firm grip on the steering wheel and do not step on the brake until you have the car under complete control.

Points of Interest

AIRVILLE (I-9)

On the grounds of the Indian Steps Museum is a giant holly tree that is more than 350 years old. Each year a small branch of the tree is broken off and presented to the Pennsylvania Power and Light Co. as payment of rent for the land occupied by the museum.

INDIAN STEPS MUSEUM, 4.5 mi. n.e. on SR 425, then .7 mi. s.e. on Indian Steps Rd., houses American Indian relics. Animal and Indian patterns from 1500 B.C. through the Colonial period are imbedded in the walls. A nature trail winds through 26 acres of wooded hillsides; an arboretum contains 60 identified tree species. Allow 30 minutes minimum. Thurs.-Fri. 10-4, Sat.-Sun. and holidays 10-5, Apr. 15-Oct. 15. Donations. Phone (717) 862-3948.

ALLEGHENY NATIONAL FOREST

Elevations in the forest range from 1,071 ft. at Baker Island near Tionesta to 2,044 ft. at Jake's Rocks. Refer to AAA maps for additional elevation information.

Allegheny National Forest, the only national forest in Pennsylvania, extends 40 miles south from the New York-Pennsylvania border through the counties of Warren, Forest, Elk and McKean. Its 516,000 acres include 500 miles of fishing streams, 226 miles of hiking and cross-country ski trails, 297 miles of snowmobile trails and 106 miles of trailbike and ATV routes.

Six boat launches and a full-service marina provide access to the 12,000-acre Allegheny Reservoir, impounded by the Kinzua Dam. Water skiing is popular, and 10 of the forest's 16 campgrounds are on or near the shore. Five of these can be reached only by boat or on foot. Rimrock and Jake's Rocks overlooks offer picnicking and views of the dam and reservoir as well as spectacular displays of Pennsylvania's state flower, the mountain laurel, in June. Seven other picnic areas are available throughout the forest—four with unsupervised swimming facilities.

Other recreational activities include fishing; hunting for deer, bears, grouse and small game; ATV riding; and cross-country skiing. Canoeing is popular on the Allegheny Wild and Scenic River, the Clarion River and, in the early spring, Tionesta Creek. Heart's Content, a 122-acre primeval tract of 300- to 400-year-old hemlock and beech trees, is 15 miles south of Warren.

The 8,570-acre Hickory Creek Wilderness provides opportunities for primitive camping, hiking, hunting, fishing and wildlife watching. Allegheny Islands Wilderness, comprised of seven islands totalling 368 acres in the Allegheny River, holds the distinction of being the smallest federally designated wilderness in the United States.

For more information contact the Forest Supervisor, Allegheny National Forest, P.O. Box 847, Warren, PA 16365. Phone (814) 723-5150, or TDD (814) 726-2710. *See Recreation Chart and the AAA Mideastern CampBook.*

ALLENTOWN (G-11) pop. 105,100, elev. 304'

The business hub for a rich agricultural area, Allentown was originally incorporated as Northamptontown. The city later adopted the name of its founder, Pennsylvania Chief Justice William Allen. German settlers played a key role in the development of the fledgling community.

Allentown contributed to several aspects of early American history. After the Battle of Brandywine in 1777, George Washington had no hope of saving Philadelphia from the British. The Liberty Bell and the bells of Christ Church were secretly removed by wagon to Allentown and hidden in Zion's Church for safekeeping.

The Lehigh County Historical Society operates several historic sites in the area which are open June through October weekends. The sites include the 1756 Troxell-Steckel House, 4229 Reliance St. in Egypt; the 1768 George Taylor House, Lehigh and Poplar streets in Catasauqua; and the 1893 Frank Buchman House, 117 N. 11th St. in Allentown.

The 1893 Claussville School at 2917 SR 100 north of Fogelsville was the last one-room schoolhouse in the county; it now functions as a museum. The Haines Mill Museum, 3600 Dorney Park Rd., is an operating gristmill built in 1760 and restored in 1909. The Lock Ridge Furnace Museum at 525 Franklin St. in Alburtis chronicles the growth of the iron industry in the 19th century. The Saylor Cement Museum, 245 N. 2nd St. in Coplay, features nine Schoefer cement kilns. These four buildings are open weekends, May through September.

The Old-Fashioned Rose Garden, Parkway Boulevard and 27th Street, contains more than 100 varieties of roses as well as water plants in lagoons and many other flowers. The peak bloom seasons are in the spring and fall.

Nearby Trexlertown boasts the Lehigh Valley Velodrome, one of only about a dozen outdoor bicycle tracks in the country. National and international bicycling events are held at the track every Friday night, June through August. The track also is open to the public for leisure riding when races are not taking place; phone (610) 967-7587.

An end-of-summer tradition, the Great Allentown Fair provides all the customary diversions associated with such events—sideshows, 4-H livestock judging, cake-baking contests, Ferris wheels and other rides, crafts—and, of course, the traditional foods that go along with such funfests. The fair is held from the Tuesday before Labor Day through Labor Day itself.

Lehigh Valley Convention and Visitors Bureau: 2200 Ave. A, Bethlehem, PA 18017; phone (610) 882-9200 or (800) 747-0561.

Self-guiding tours: Brochures describing self-guiding driving tours of the area's covered bridges and winery trail are available at the convention and visitors bureau. A brochure for a self-guiding walking tour of downtown Allentown is available from the Allentown Downtown Improvement District Authority, 805 Hamilton Mall, Allentown, PA 18101; phone (610) 776-7117.

Shopping areas: A series of malls and shopping centers form a local shopping center cluster. Among these are Lehigh Valley Mall, N. MacArthur Road and US 22, which includes JCPenney, Macy's and Strawbridges; Whitehall Mall, MacArthur Road and Grape Street, containing Sears and Woolworth's; and Whitehall Square Mall, also on MacArthur Road, featuring Bradlees.

ALLENTOWN ART MUSEUM is at 5th and Court sts. Permanent exhibitions range from 14th-17th-century European paintings and sculptures to the architecture of Frank Lloyd Wright, and 200 years of American art. Also featured are decorative arts from the American Arts and Crafts Movement, textiles and the 350-piece Fuller Gem Collection. Food is available.

Allow 1 hour minimum. Tues.-Sat. 11-5, Sun. noon-5; closed major holidays. Admission $3.50; over 61, $3; full-time students with ID $2; under 12 free; free to all Sun. noon-1. MC, VI ($10). Phone (610) 432-4333.

★**DORNEY PARK AND WILDWATER KINGDOM,** I-78 w. to exit 16B, then e. on Hamilton Blvd., or e. on SR 22 and s. on Cedar Crest Blvd., following signs, is a 200-acre entertainment complex with more than 100 rides and attractions as well as a water park.

Included in the amusement park are four roller coasters—two vintage wooden coasters, a looping roller coaster and Steel Force, a 200-ft.-high roller coaster traveling up to 75 miles-per-hour; Thunder Canyon, a white-water rafting ride; a 1921 Dentzel carrousel; a sky ride; and a splashdown ride. Wildwater Kingdom has a wave pool, 11 water slides, two river rides and several family activity areas.

Also featured are rides just for children and Berenstain Bear Country, a children's activity area based on the children's book series. The area contains a variety of play areas and interactive attractions. Live entertainment is provided daily. Food is available. Picnic facilities are located adjacent to the park.

Allow a full day. Both parks open daily at 10; closing times vary. Dorney Park open daily Memorial Day weekend-Labor Day; Sat.-Sun. early May-day before Memorial Day weekend and day after Labor Day-early Oct. Wildwater Kingdom open daily late May-Labor Day; Sat.-Sun. day after Labor Day to mid-Sept.

Admission (includes both parks and all rides and attractions) $28, over 59 and under 48 inches tall $5.95, under age 4 free. Admission varies during spring and some weekends. Parking $5. DS, MC, VI. Phone (610) 398-7955 or (800) 386-8463.

LEHIGH COUNTY HISTORICAL SOCIETY, 501 Hamilton St., is in the Old Courthouse. Displays depict Pennsylvania German heritage and the development of the area's industries. American Indian artifacts also are featured. Mon.-Sat. 10-4, Sun. 1-4. Free. Phone (610) 435-4664.

LIBERTY BELL SHRINE MUSEUM, in Zion's Reformed United Church of Christ at 620 Hamilton St., houses a replica of the Liberty Bell on the spot where the original was hidden during the Revolutionary War. A mural incorporates sound and light to describe the Liberty Bell. Mon.-Sat. noon-4; closed Jan. 1, July 4, Thanksgiving and Dec. 25. Free. Phone (610) 435-4232.

LIL'LE'HI TROUT NURSERY, off Little Lehigh Pkwy. on Fish Hatchery Rd., contains 65,000 brook, brown and rainbow trout. Fish food can be purchased; exact change is required in winter. Daily 9-dusk. Free. Phone (610) 437-7656.

TROUT HALL, 4th and Walnut sts., was built in 1770 by James Allen, son of William Allen, city founder and Pennsylvania chief justice. Furnished in period style, the building is Allentown's oldest home. Tues.-Sat. noon-3, Sun. 1-4, Apr.-Nov.; closed holidays. Free. Phone (610) 435-4664.

WINERIES

• **Clover Hill Vineyards & Winery,** 2.7 mi. w. of SR 100 via Schantz Rd., then e. on Newtown Rd. Tastings Mon.-Sat. 11-5, Sun. noon-5. Tours Fri. at 2, Sat. at 1 and 3, May 1-last week in Sept. Closed major holidays. Phone (610) 395-2468.

ALLENWOOD (F-8) elev. 481'

CLYDE PEELING'S REPTILAND, 6 mi. n. of I-80 exit 30B on US 15, provides close-up views of turtles, tortoises, frogs, lizards, alligators and snakes, displayed in a year-round herpetarium. Picnic facilities are available.

Allow 1 hour, 30 minutes minimum. Daily 9-7, Memorial Day-Labor Day; 10-6, Apr. 1-day before Memorial Day and day after Labor Day-Oct. 30; 10-5, rest of year. Closed Jan. 1, Thanksgiving and Dec. 25. Shows are given daily at 10:30, noon, 1:30, 3 and 4:30. Admission $7; ages 4-11, $5. AE, DS, MC, VI. Phone (717) 538-1869.

ALTOONA (G-5) pop. 52,000, elev. 1,171'

The Pennsylvania Railroad, now Conrail, founded Altoona in 1849 during construction of the first railroad over the Alleghenies. For years the town's economy depended on railroad building and repair shops; other industries have since developed. Popular events in Altoona include Hoss's Keystone Country Festival in early September.

Blair County Convention Bureau: Logan Valley Mall, Rte. 220, Goods Lane, Altoona, PA 16602; phone (814) 943-4183.

Shopping areas: The major local shopping center is Logan Valley Mall, US 220 and Goods Lane. It features JCPenney, Kaufmann's and Sears.

ALTOONA RAILROADERS MEMORIAL MUSEUM, 1300 9th Ave., adjacent to the Station Mall complex, traces the development of the Pennsylvania Railroad and its impact on local and national history. Exhibited are the "Loretto," the private railroad car of steel baron Charles M. Schwab; and "Nancy," a locomotive built in 1918.

Allow 2 hours minimum. Daily 10-6, Apr. 5-Oct. 25; Tues.-Sun. 10-5, rest of year. Closed holidays. Last admission 1 hour before closing. Admission $8.50; over 62, $7.75; ages 3-12, $5. MC, VI. Phone (814) 946-0834 or (888) 425-8666.

BAKER MANSION, 1 mi. w. of US 220 via Logan Blvd., was the Greek Revival home of ironmaster Elias Baker. The 1844 mansion has carved oak pieces he imported from Belgium, as well as American Indian and railroad artifacts and material about Abraham Lincoln. Guided tours are available. Christmas tours are given the first 2 weekends in December.

Allow 1 hour minimum. Tues.-Sun. 1-4:30, Memorial Day weekend-Labor Day; Sat.-Sun. 1-4:30, mid-Apr. through day before Memorial Day weekend and day after Labor Day-Oct. 31. Closed major holidays. Last tour begins 1 hour before closing. Admission $3; over 65 and ages 13-18, $2.50; ages 4-12, $1.50. Phone (814) 942-3916.

BENZEL'S PRETZEL FACTORY, 5200 Sixth Ave., offers self-guiding tours that illustrate the pretzel making process. Visitors can view workers through windows and monitors. A 7-minute videotape presentation also is featured. Freshly baked pretzels are provided at the end of the tour. Allow 30 minutes minimum. Mon.-Fri. 9-5, Sat. 9-1; closed major holidays. Free. Phone (814) 942-5062 or (800) 344-4438.

FORT ROBERDEAU, in Sinking Valley, 9 mi. n.e. via I-99 Bellwood exit, is a reconstructed log fort on the original site of a Revolutionary War fort established to mine lead for the army. Facilities include enlisted men's barracks, officers' quarters, a lead miner's hut, a blacksmith shop and lead smelters. An adjacent nature area has marked trails and a rock and mineral museum; picnic facilities are available.

Allow 1 hour minimum. Tues.-Sat. 11-5, Sun.-Mon. 1-5, May-Oct. Admission $3; senior citizens $2.50; under 13, $1. Phone (814) 946-0048.

HORSESHOE CURVE NATIONAL HISTORIC LANDMARK, 6 mi. w., showcases the Horseshoe Curve, which opened in 1854 and revolutionized rail travel. The two sides of the arc are almost parallel, an engineering masterpiece in conquering the Alleghenies. The entire curve is visible from the trackside observation area which is reached by a short funicular ride or by climbing 194 stairs. Food is available.

Visitor center open daily 10-6, Apr. 5-Oct. 25; Tues.-Sun. 10-3:30, rest of year. Last admission 1 hour before closing. Admission $3.50; over 62, $3; ages 3-12, $1.75. Phone (814) 941-7960.

LAKEMONT PARK, 700 Park Ave., is an amusement park with more than 30 rides and attractions. Food is available. Daily 11-9, June 9-Aug. 21; Sat.-Sun. noon-8, May 2-June 8 and Aug. 22-Sept. 13. Free. All-day ride pass $7.95. Phone (814) 949-7275.

WOPSONONOCK TABLELAND, 6 mi. n.w., rises to an elevation of 2,580 feet and affords a panoramic view of the city and six surrounding counties.

AMBRIDGE—
see Pittsburgh and Vicinity p. 143.

ANDREAS (G-10) elev. 587'

JEM CLASSIC CAR MUSEUM, 5 mi. e. of SR 309 on SR 443, displays about 40 vintage automobiles, including a 1902 Curved Dash Oldsmobile, a 1929 Stutz Blackhawk and a 1931 Cadillac Cabriolet. The 1929 Graham-Paige is thought to be one of only two remaining in the country. Also displayed are collections of antique motorcycles and collectible dolls.

Allow 30 minutes minimum. Mon.-Fri. 10-4, Sat.-Sun. and holidays noon-4, Memorial Day weekend-Oct. 31. Admission $4; over 60, $3.50; ages 5-12, $2.50. Phone (717) 386-3554.

ASHLAND (G-9) pop. 3,900, elev. 885'

[SAVE] MUSEUM OF ANTHRACITE MINING is .2 mi. off SR 61 at 17th and Pine sts., next to the Pioneer Tunnel Coal Mine. Tools, machinery, models, photographs and graphic displays explain the mining and processing of anthracite.

Allow 30 minutes minimum. Mon.-Sat. 10-6, Sun. noon-6, May-Oct.; Tues.-Sat. 9-5, Sun. noon-5, rest of year. Closed Jan. 1, Easter, Thanksgiving and Dec. 25. Admission $3.50; over 60, $2.50; ages 6-12, $1.50; family rate $8.50. Admission $2.50 with ticket stub from Pioneer Tunnel Coal Mine or steam train ride. Phone (717) 875-4708.

PIONEER TUNNEL COAL MINE AND STEAM TRAIN RIDE, 4 blks. off SR 61, following signs, offers a tour through a coal mine on battery-powered mine cars. Experienced miners act as guides and explain the operation. Mine temperatures range from 48 to 52 degrees Fahrenheit; a sweater or light jacket is advised. On another tour, a 1920s steam train powers mine cars three-fourths of a mile around a mountainside to an abandoned strip mine and bootleg coal hole. Picnicking is permitted.

Allow 1 hour, 30 minutes minimum. Mine tours and train rides daily 10-6, Memorial Day-Labor Day; Sat.-Sun. 10-6, May 1-day before Memorial Day and day after Labor Day-Oct. 31. Mine tours only Mon.-Fri. at 11, 12:30 and 2, Apr. 1-day before Memorial Day and day after Labor Day-Oct. 31. Mine tour $6; under 12, $3.50. Train ride $3.50; under 12, $2. Phone (717) 875-3850 or 875-3301.

AUDUBON—
see Philadelphia and Vicinity p. 122.

AVELLA (H-1)

[SAVE] MEADOWCROFT MUSEUM OF RURAL LIFE, 3 mi. w. on SR 50, following signs, is a 19th-century rural community; buildings from other locations have been rebuilt on the site. Allow 2 hours minimum. Wed.-Sun. noon-5, Memorial Day-Labor Day; Sat.-Sun. noon-5, May 1-day before Memorial Day and day after Labor Day-Oct. 31; otherwise by appointment. Admission $6.50; over 60, $5.50; ages 6-16, $3.50. DS, MC, VI. Phone (724) 587-3412.

BAUMSTOWN (H-10)

[SAVE] DANIEL BOONE HOMESTEAD, 1 mi. n. off US 422 on Daniel Boone Rd., was the birthplace of the famous frontiersman. The 579-acre restored Boone Homestead incorporates the original 10-room stone house built 1730-79 by the Boones. The home is furnished with mid-18th-century Pennsylvania furniture.

Included on the site are a restored blacksmith shop, sawmill and barn, the 1730 Bertolet log house, picnicking and hiking areas and a visitor center. Allow 1 hour minimum. Tues.-Sat. 9-5, Sun. noon-5; closed holidays. Admission $4; over 59, $3.50; ages 6-12, $2. Phone (610) 582-4900.

BEAVER FALLS—
see Pittsburgh and Vicinity p. 144.

BEDFORD (I-5) pop. 3,100, elev. 1,060'

The Allegheny mountain area of Bedford was first settled in 1751 by Robert Ray, after whom Fort Raystown was named when it was built in 1758. Eventually, the community was renamed in honor of the Duke of Bedford.

Several historic buildings have been preserved in downtown Bedford, including the Espy House, which served as President Washington's headquarters in 1794 when he led Federal troops into western Pennsylvania to quell the Whiskey Rebellion. Also, the Anderson House, 137 E. Pitt St., was built 1814-15 and housed what is believed to be the first bank west of the Allegheny Mountains. The original bank vault can still be seen.

During the French and Indian War historic Forbes Road (US 30) was used by Gen. John Forbes on his way to capture Fort Duquesne, which is now known as the city of Pittsburgh. The road winds through the farmlands and valleys of Bedford County and over more than 14 covered bridges. Schellsburg Church, built in 1806, also is along Forbes Road.

The Great Bedford County Fair is held in August, and the Fall Foliage Festival in early October features an antique car parade.

Bedford County Conference and Visitors Bureau: 141 S. Juliana St., Bedford, PA 15522; phone (814) 623-1771 or (800) 765-3331.

Self-guiding tours: Brochures for self-guiding walking, driving and bicycle tours are available at the conference and visitors bureau.

SAVE **FORT BEDFORD MUSEUM,** N. Juliana St., is housed in a reproduction of an early blockhouse. The museum displays a scale model of the original fort. Daily 10-5, June-Aug.; Wed.-Mon. 10-5, Apr.-May and Sept.-Oct. Admission $3; over 60, $2.50; ages 6-18, $1.50; family rate (two adults, four children) $7. Phone (814) 623-8891.

OLD BEDFORD VILLAGE, 1 mi. n. on US 220, .7 mi. s. of Pennsylvania Tpke. exit 11, is a 40-building reproduction of a village from the 1750-1850 period. Many of the log cabins, one-room schoolhouses and other buildings were brought from their original locations and reassembled. Among the crafts demonstrated are gunmaking, tinsmithing, broom making, leather making, quilting, spinning, weaving and woodworking.

Allow 1 hour, 30 minutes minimum. Daily 9-5, early May-Aug. 31; Mon.-Sat. 9-4, Sun. 11-5, Sept.-Oct. Admission $6.95; over 60, $5.95; ages 6-12, $4.45. MC, VI. Phone (814) 623-1156 or (800) 238-4347.

REYNOLDSDALE FISH CULTURAL STATION, 12 mi. n.w. on SR 56, is a modern plant operated by the Pennsylvania Fish and Boat Commission for the propagation of mountain trout. Daily 8-3:30. Free. Phone (814) 839-2211.

BELLEFONTE (F-6) pop. 6,300, elev. 747'

Built on several hills at the base of Bald Eagle Mountain, Bellefonte was named for its "beautiful fountain," the spring that furnishes the town's water supply. Many of Bellefonte's homes are fine examples of early Georgian architecture. Known as the "Home of Governors," seven of the town's residents have become governors of Pennsylvania and other states.

Centre County Convention & Visitors Bureau: 1402 S. Atherton St., State College, PA 16801; phone (814) 231-1400 or (800) 358-5466.

Self-guiding tours: A walking-tour brochure can be obtained Monday through Friday from the Bellefonte Area Chamber of Commerce, Train Station, 320 W. High St., Bellefonte, PA 16823; phone (814) 355-2917.

BIG SPRING, on SR 150, maintains a temperature of 50 degrees Fahrenheit all year. It flows at the rate of 11,500,000 gallons daily; its overflow forms part of Spring Creek. Free.

FISHERMAN'S PARADISE, 3 mi. s.w. on Spring Creek, offers supervised fly fishing along 1 mile of the stream. A state fishing license is required, and fish must be released. A fish hatchery also is featured. Picnicking is permitted. Fly fishing daily dawn-dusk; hatchery 8-3. Free. Phone (814) 355-4159.

BENSALEM—
see Philadelphia and Vicinity p. 122.

BERNVILLE (G-9) pop. 800, elev. 317'

KOZIAR'S CHRISTMAS VILLAGE is 1 mi. s.w. via SR 183; follow signs to Christmas Village Rd. One of the largest Christmas displays in the country, the village uses half a million colored lights, tinsel and replicas of storybook characters to portray various Christmas themes. The village is a converted farm; a dozen buildings house displays that depict different facets of Christmas, including a miniature train display. Children can visit with Santa Claus.

Allow 1 hour minimum. Mon.-Fri. 6-9 p.m., Sat.-Sun. 5-9:30 p.m., Thanksgiving-Jan. 1; Fri.-Sun. 5:30-9:30 p.m., Nov. 1-day before Thanksgiving; Sat.-Sun. 7:30-9:30 p.m., in Oct. Admission $5.50; over 65 and ages 5-12, $4.50. Phone (610) 488-1110.

BERWICK (F-9) pop. 11,000, elev. 505'

Berwick was founded as a religious refuge in 1786 by the Quaker Evan Owen, who named his community after Berwick-upon-Tweed, an English town on the Scottish border. Berwick is an industrial community that produces clothing, boxes, decorative ribbons, containers, snack foods, manufactured housing and metal parts.

Berwick Area Chamber of Commerce: 206 Mulberry St., Berwick, PA 18603; phone (717) 752-3601.

SUSQUEHANNA ENERGY INFORMATION CENTER AND RIVERLANDS, 5 mi. n. on US 11, or 12.5 mi. n. of I-80 exit 36N, has displays explaining nuclear energy, as well as a nature center exhibit. Forty-five-minute perimeter bus tours of the Susquehanna Steam Electric Station and a 2.5-hour plant tour are available by advance arrangement.

Next to the center is Riverlands, a 1,400-acre recreation and nature area that offers picnicking, fishing, canoeing, boating (electric motors only), cross-country skiing and nature trails.

Energy information center open Mon.-Sat. and holidays 8-5, Sun. noon-4:30, Apr.-Oct.; Mon.-Fri. and holidays 8-5, Sat. 11-4, Sun. noon-4, rest of year. Riverlands open daily 8 a.m.-dusk. Both closed Jan. 1, Easter, Thanksgiving and Dec. 24-25. Free. Phone (717) 542-2131 or 759-2281.

BETHLEHEM (G-11) pop. 71,400, elev. 236'

In 1741 a group of Moravian missionaries from Europe arrived in what is now Bethlehem and established a communal church-village. They christened their settlement during their traditional Vigils on Christmas Eve with their patron, Count von Zinzendorf, who was visiting from Europe. Many of the large stone buildings constructed by the Moravians are still in use; the structures are considered among the finest examples of pre-Revolutionary German architecture in the country.

Burnside Plantation, an 18th-century farm, was built by James Burnside, an Irish immigrant who joined the Moravian church in 1745. Since all Moravians lived communally by age, sex and marital status, the farm is notable since it was the first privately owned Moravian residence in Bethlehem. The crops raised on the farm provided food for the residents of the town. The 6.5-acre plantation, much smaller now than in the 1700s, is being restored. Guided tours of the house are by reservation only; the grounds can be seen on a self-guiding tour. Phone (610) 691-0603.

The Bach Festival is a development of the Moravians' love of music. Orchestras accompany a choir of local singers and guest soloists in this nationally known event held the second and third weekends in May; phone (610) 866-4382. For 9 days beginning the second Saturday in August, Musikfest sees 300 musical groups ranging from classical to funk, presenting more than 650 concerts on 17 stages; phone (610) 861-0678.

The last weekend in September, colorful tartans blossom as the leaves fade during the Celtic Classic Highland Games and Festival. This 3-day event includes dance and bagpipe competitions, Highland games, music and crafts; phone (610) 868-9599.

The town's Yuletide observance includes a large lighted Star of Bethlehem on South Mountain, hundreds of lighted trees and other decorations and a Moravian Christmas manger. Additional highlights include a live Christmas pageant and nightly bus tours with costumed guides.

Bethlehem is the home of three institutions of higher education: Lehigh University, Moravian College and Northampton Community College. Moravian, established in 1742, is one of American's oldest colleges, and Lehigh is a major research university with facilities that include the Iacocca Institute, spearheaded by alumnus Lee Iacocca.

Bethlehem Visitors Center: 52 W. Broad St., Bethlehem, PA 18018; phone (610) 868-1513 or (800) 360-8687.

Self-guiding tours: Brochures detailing self-guiding walking tours of the town's historic district are available from the visitors center which is open daily except on Dec. 25. Guided tours of the historic district also can be arranged.

EIGHTEENTH-CENTURY INDUSTRIAL AREA, along Monocacy Creek at 459 Old York Rd. (access via Union Blvd.), features the restored 1761 tannery, 1869 Luchenbach Mill and the 1762 waterworks—the first pumped municipal water system in the Colonies. Open Mon.-Fri. 8:30-5; closed major holidays. Hours may vary; phone ahead. Admission $6; under 12, $3. Phone (610) 691-0603.

John Sebastian Goundie House, 501 Main St., was built in 1810 and is considered to be the first Federal-style brick residence in Bethlehem.

THE KEMERER MUSEUM OF DECORATIVE ARTS, 427 N. New St., uses period rooms, galleries and changing exhibitions to present more than 250 years of folk art, furnishings, paintings and historical fine arts. Collections of cast-iron toys, maps and prints and textiles provide insight into daily life in the past. Allow 1 hour minimum. Tues.-Sun. noon-5; closed major holidays. Admission $3; over 55, $2; under 13, $1; family rate $7. Phone (610) 868-6868.

MORAVIAN MUSEUM OF BETHLEHEM, 66 W. Church St., is in the 1741 Gemeinhaus (community house), the oldest building in Bethlehem. Twelve exhibit areas interpret the ideals, art and culture of the early Moravians, members of a protestant church. Tues.-Sat. 1-4. Admission $5, students $3. Phone (610) 867-0173.

SUN INN, 564 Main St., was established in 1758 as a way-station for such Colonial statesmen as George Washington, the Marquis de Lafayette and John Adams. It is fully restored and furnished in period. Food is available. Allow 1 hour minimum. Guided tours Mon.-Sat. 11:30-8. Admission $2; ages 6-12, $1. Christmas tours $3; refreshments additional. Phone (610) 866-1758.

BIRD-IN-HAND—
see Pennsylvania Dutch Country p. 99.

BOALSBURG (G-6)

An early stagecoach stop founded in 1808, Boalsburg has retained much of its original architecture and street layout. The nation's first Memorial Day was celebrated in the village cemetery in 1864, a tradition Boalsburg continues with an annual Memorial Day Festival drawing more than 25,000 people.

Centre County Convention & Visitors Bureau: 1402 S. Atherton St., State College, PA 16801; phone (814) 231-1400 or (800) 358-5466.

Shopping areas: The Village of Boalsburg offers taverns and quaint shops filled with antiques, art, flowers, crafts, gifts and collectibles. Many of the shops are housed in historic homes.

COLUMBUS CHAPEL AND BOAL MANSION MUSEUM are on US 322 Bus. Rte. The Columbus Chapel once belonged to the family of Christopher Columbus and was brought to the estate in 1909. The chapel features a desk once owned by Columbus, family heirlooms dating to the 1400s, Renaissance and baroque art and religious relics. The Boal Mansion contains original furnishings. The grounds include a 1789 stone frontier cabin.

Allow 1 hour minimum. Tues.-Sun. 10-5, June 15-Sept. 15; 1:30-5, May 1-June 14 and Sept. 16-Oct. 31. Admission $5; over 59, $4; ages 7-16, $3. Phone (814) 466-6210.

[SAVE] **PENNSYLVANIA MILITARY MUSEUM,** on US 322, honors Pennsylvania's soldiers from Benjamin Franklin's first volunteer unit in the Revolutionary War through Operation Desert Storm. Displays include a full-scale World War I trench scene, cannon, infantry weapons, uniforms, memorabilia, military equipment and vehicles. The 66-acre park also features monuments and memorials commemorating the sacrifices of generations of Pennsylvania patriots.

Allow 1 hour minimum. Tues.-Sat. 9-5, Sun. noon-5; closed Jan. 1, Thanksgiving, day after Thanksgiving and Dec. 25. Hours may vary Nov.-Mar.; phone ahead. Admission $3.50; over 59, $3; ages 6-12, $1.50; family rate $8.50. Phone (814) 466-6263.

BOYERTOWN (H-11) pop. 3,800, elev. 386'

Known to the Pennsylvania Dutch who settled here as Boyer's Eck or Boyer's Corner, this community prospered because of the craftsmen employed in the manufacturing of caskets and vehicles, and in its foundries. Today its orchard covered hills, antiques shops and farmers market attract visitors.

[SAVE] **BOYERTOWN MUSEUM OF HISTORIC VE-HICLES,** from SR 100 to jct. SRs 73 and 562, then 2 blks. s. to 28 Warwick St., displays southeastern Pennsylvania vehicles from the 18th, 19th and 20th centuries. Sleighs, carriages, wagons and bicycles are exhibited as well as electric-, steam- and gas-powered vehicles and the tools used to assemble them. A collection of early and contemporary electric vehicles also is displayed.

Allow 1 hour minimum. Tues.-Sun. 9:30-4; closed major holidays. Admission $4; over 60, $3.50; ages 6-18, $2. Phone (610) 367-2090.

BRADFORD (D-5) pop. 9,600, elev. 1,437'

Bradford began as a sparse community on the Tunungwant Creek in 1843. In 1871 oil was discovered, and the price of land soared from 6.25 cents to $1,000 an acre. The city boomed as residents sank wells everywhere. Bradford also has become a leader in manufacturing: Lumber products, cutlery, electronic parts and boxes are produced locally.

One mile north of Bolivar Drive on the Seaward Avenue extension is Crook Farm, a collection of restored buildings that includes a farmhouse, barn, carpenter shop, one-room schoolhouse and nature trails.

Bradford Chamber of Commerce: 10 Main St., Bradford, PA 16701; phone (814) 368-7115.

PENN-BRAD OIL MUSEUM, 3 mi. s. on US 219, features a 72-foot-tall wooden standard drilling rig used in developing the first billion dollar oil field. A museum displays local artifacts from the town's oil-producing days. Allow 1 hour minimum. Mon.-Sat. 10-4, Sun. noon-5, Memorial Day-Labor Day; otherwise by appointment. Admission $4; over 65, $3.50; under 12 free with adult admission. Phone (814) 362-1955, or 368-5574 for appointment.

BRISTOL—
see Philadelphia and Vicinity p. 122.

BROOKVILLE (F-3) pop. 4,200, elev. 1230'

Brookville was settled in 1796 at the confluence of Sandy Lick and Mill creeks by Samuel Scott and Joseph and Andrew Barnett. Growth was slow, but in 1830 the town was named the county seat and settlement began in earnest. By the early 19th century Brookville had a thriving lumber industry and supplied all the lumber markets in Pittsburgh. The arrival of the railroad in 1873 augmented industrial and commercial development.

A 90-acre historic district features more than 300 buildings dating from the 19th century. The Jefferson County Courthouse, Main and Pickering streets, is a three-story Italianate structure built in 1867. The Marlin Opera House is a 900-seat hall built in 1883 by Civil War veteran Col. Silas Marlin.

Brookville Chamber of Commerce: 70 Pickering St., Brookville, PA 15825; phone (814) 849-8448.

Self-guiding tours: Maps detailing a self-guiding walking tour of the town's historic district are available at the chamber of commerce and the local AAA office.

JEFFERSON COUNTY HISTORICAL AND GENEALOGICAL SOCIETY, 232 Jefferson St., is in the Brady Craig House. The home, built in the late 1830s or early '40s, displays Victorian furniture, maps, diaries and photographs. A genealogical library offers a newspaper collection and periodical references. Allow 1 hour minimum. Tues.-Sun. 2-5; closed major holidays. Free. A fee is charged for research. Phone (814) 849-0077.

BROOMALL—
see Philadelphia and Vicinity p. 122.

BROWNSVILLE (H-2) pop. 3,200, elev. 380'

NEMACOLIN CASTLE, Brashear and Front sts., was built in 1789. The stately brick home features 22 rooms furnished in various manners. A frontier trading post is represented as well as a formal Victorian style. Allow 1 hour minimum. Tues.-Sun. 11-5, June-Aug.; Sat.-Sun. 11-5, Easter-May 31 and Sept. 1 to mid-Oct. Candlelight tours daily 4-9, late Nov.-early Dec. Admission $5; senior citizens $4; under 13, $2. Phone (724) 785-6882.

BRYN ATHYN—
see Philadelphia and Vicinity p. 122.

BRYN MAWR—
see Philadelphia and Vicinity p. 122.

BUCKINGHAM—
see Philadelphia and Vicinity p. 122.

BUCKS COUNTY—
see Philadelphia and Vicinity p. 123.

BUSHKILL—
see Pocono Mountains Area p. 146.

CANONSBURG—
see Pittsburgh and Vicinity p. 144.

CARLISLE (H-7) pop. 18,400, elev. 469'

Founded in 1751, Carlisle was the home of James Wilson and George Ross, two of the signers of the Declaration of Independence. The First Presbyterian Church, facing the main square of town, was built in 1757. In this church the citizens of Carlisle chose Wilson and Ross to represent them at the Continental Congress. Mary L. Hays, the famous Molly Pitcher of the Battle of Monmouth *(see Freehold, N.J., p. 31),* also lived in Carlisle. A life-size memorial in a cemetery on E. South Street marks her grave.

During the Confederate invasion in 1863, Gen. A.G. Jenkins and about 500 cavalry fresh from victory at Chambersburg took Carlisle without resistance. They were followed by Gen. Richard S. Ewell's corps, some of whom camped on the grounds of Dickinson College. The occupation lasted 3 days. After their departure, Union troops occupied Carlisle. The retreating Confederates then shelled the town.

Carlisle Indian School, the first non-reservation school for American Indians, was established in 1879 at Carlisle Barracks, which is now the site of the U.S. Army War College. During its 39 years of existence the Indian school attained an enrollment of 6,000 students representing all tribes in the United States. Jim

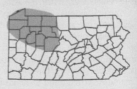

Thorpe, winner of the pentathlon and the decathlon in the 1912 Olympic Games, attended the school. Monuments at the courthouse square, High and Hanover streets, honor Thorpe and Cumberland County's Civil War dead.

Wednesday through Sunday in nearby Boiling Springs, the Allenberry Playhouse offers nine contemporary and classic Broadway musical and comedy productions from early April through early November. For schedule and ticket information phone (717) 258-3211; for reservations phone (717) 258-6120.

Harrisburg-Hershey-Carlisle Tourism Agency: 4211 Trindle Rd., Camp Hill, PA 17011; phone (717) 975-8161 or (800) 995-0969.

CARLISLE BARRACKS is 1 mi. n. on US 11. One of the oldest Army posts in the United States, it was the site of a Revolutionary War forge. The Hessian Powder Magazine Museum is in a magazine built by Hessian soldiers in 1777. Also on the grounds is the Omar N. Bradley Museum, which displays personal items and military memorabilia of the five-star general who was chairman of the joint chiefs of staff 1949-53.

Allow 30 minutes minimum for each museum. Site open Mon.-Fri. 8-4:30. Hessian Powder Magazine Museum open daily 10-1, late May-early Sept. Closed federal holidays. Free. Phone (717) 245-3152.

CUMBERLAND COUNTY HISTORICAL SOCIETY LIBRARY AND MUSEUM, 21 N. Pitt St., exhibits one of the oldest American printing presses, woodcarvings, early mechanical banks, 18th-century iron-furnace products, memorabilia of the Carlisle Indian School and products made by Cumberland County artisans and manufacturers. The library contains books, monographs, newspapers, manuscripts and other materials relating to local history. Tues.-Fri. 10-4, Sat. 10-1, Mon. 7-9 p.m. Library $4. Museum donations. Phone (717) 249-7610.

TROUT ART GALLERY, on W. High St., is in the Emil R. Weiss Center for the Arts on the Dickinson College campus. The gallery's upper level houses changing exhibits, while the lower level displays the college's permanent pieces, which compose one of the nation's oldest collegiate collections. Begun in 1836, it boasts works dating from classical Greece through the 20th century and includes African and Oriental art.

Guided tours are available by prior arrangement. Allow 30 minutes minimum. Tues.-Sat. 10-4, mid-Jan. to late June and early Sept. to mid-Dec. Free. Phone (717) 245-1711.

CENTER POINT—
see Philadelphia and Vicinity p. 123.

CENTRE HALL (F-6) pop. 1,200, elev. 1,187′

★**PENN'S CAVE,** 5 mi. e. on SR 192, is America's only all-water cavern and wildlife sanctuary.

A 1-hour cavern tour includes a motorboat trip in the cavern and a ride on Lake Nitanee. During the interpretative cavern tour many colorful limestone speleothems, or cave formations, can be seen.

Also offered is a guided 90-minute tour of Penn's Cave Farms and Wildlife Sanctuary, featuring white-tailed deer, elk, mountain lions, wild turkeys, mustangs, longhorn cattle and wolves housed in a natural setting. A 15-minute plane ride offers a view of nearby Amish farms and Pennsylvania's scenic ridge and valley area.

Cavern tours depart on the half-hour daily 9-7, June-Aug.; on the hour 9-5, mid-Feb. through May 31 and Sept.-Dec. Farm and wildlife sanctuary tours available daily Apr.-Nov. Plane ride daily June-Aug. (weather permitting). Closed Thanksgiving and Dec. 25. Cave tour $9; over 65, $8; ages 2-12, $4.25. Farm and sanctuary tour $10; over 65, $9; ages 2-12, $5. Plane fare $17, under 2 free. Combined cavern, farm and sanctuary tour and flight $30; ages 2-12, $22.25. Under 1 year are not permitted on cave tours. DS, MC, VI. Phone (814) 364-1664.

CHADDS FORD—
see Philadelphia and Vicinity p. 123.

CHALK HILL (I-3) pop. 400, elev. 2,000′

★**KENTUCK KNOB,** just e. on US 40, then 6 mi. n. on Chalk Hill-Ohiopyle Rd., was built in 1953 by renowned architect Frank Lloyd Wright. Constructed entirely of tidewater red cypress and native fieldstone, the house seems part of the mountainous western Pennsylvania terrain. The home is built on a hexagonal grid with an open floor plan and expanses of glass that bring the outdoor and indoor spaces together. A sculpture park and woodland trail are on the grounds. Special in-depth tours are available by reservation. Food is available.

Allow 1 hour, 30 minutes minimum. Guided tours are given Tues.-Sun. and Mon. holidays 10-4, Apr. 1-Dec. 1; Sat.-Sun. 10-4 or by appointment, rest of year. Closed Jan. 1, Thanksgiving and Dec. 25. Admission Tues.-Sat. $10; Fri.-Sat. and holidays $15. Under 9 are not permitted. Reservations are suggested. MC, VI. Phone (724) 329-1901.

CHAMBERSBURG (I-6) pop. 16,600, elev. 613′

Nestled in the historic Cumberland Valley, Chambersburg was occupied by Confederate forces three times during the Civil War. The last time ended in 1864 with the burning of the city upon its refusal to pay an indemnity. The house on the northeast corner of Lincoln Way West and Garber Street has stars on it marking where Confederate artillery penetrated its outer wall on July 30, 1864. Downtown in Memorial Square is the five-tier Memorial Fountain and its statue of a

Union soldier; the memorial was rededicated in 1995 to honor American soldiers of all wars.

In 1859 Chambersburg served as a base of operations for John Brown prior to his raid on Harper's Ferry, W. Va.; he stayed in what was then Mary Ritner's boarding house, at 225 E. King St. Another structure of interest downtown is the Presbyterian Church of the Falling Spring at 221 N. Main St.; the church was founded in 1734. Behind the church is the grave site of Col. Benjamin Chambers, the town's founder.

Cumberland Valley Visitor Station: 1235 Lincoln Way East, Chambersburg, PA 17201; phone (717) 261-1200.

Self-guiding tours: The visitor station offers self-guiding walking and driving tour brochures for Chambersburg and other communities in the Cumberland Valley. This full-service center also has a nature walk and picnic area.

THE OLD JAIL, 175 E. King St., was built in 1818 and was one of the few buildings that survived the burning of Chambersburg by Confederate forces in 1864. The building houses the Kittochtinny Historical Society, which features an early drugstore, a pioneer kitchen, gun collection and genealogical library. Fri.-Sat. 9:30-4, May 1-Oct. 15; closed holidays. Library hours vary; phone ahead. Donations. Phone (717) 264-1667.

CHESTER—
see Philadelphia and Vicinity p. 124.

CLARION (E-3) pop. 6,500, elev. 1,500′

SUTTON-DITZ HOUSE MUSEUM & LIBRARY is off I-80 exit 9, then n. on SR 68, or just s. of US 322 at 18 Grant St. Built in 1850 by attorney Thomas Sutton, the two-story home has been remodeled to reflect the 1910 late Victorian period. A library houses information about local history. Allow 30 minutes minimum. Tues.-Sat. 10-4; closed holidays. Admission $1.50; over 60, $1; students with ID 50c. Phone (814) 226-4450.

CLARK (E-1) pop. 600, elev. 774′

★**TARA,** I-80 exit 1N, then 7 mi. n. on SR 18 to SR 258, is a country inn recalling "Gone With the Wind." Spacious lawns dotted with blossoming flowers in the summer and a long veranda with white wicker furniture help enhance the Southern atmosphere of the Greek Revival mansion, built in 1854. Each room is named after a character from "Gone With the Wind" and is decorated accordingly with antiques, period furnishings and original works of art.

Opulent chandeliers, luxurious Oriental rugs and a large collection of art and antiques create an atmosphere of Southern elegance. Tours are conducted by guides in Civil War era costumes. Food is available. Allow 1 hour minimum. Tours depart on the hour daily 10-3. Admission $5. Phone (724) 962-3535 or (800) 782-2803.

CLEARFIELD (F-5) pop. 6,400, elev. 1,100′

GRICE CLEARFIELD COMMUNITY MUSEUM, 119 N. 4th St., houses collections of classic cars and mounted wild game and fish. Allow 30 minutes minimum. Mon.-Sat. 10-4, Sun. noon-4, June-Aug. Admission Wed.-Mon. $5, under 12 free. Admission $3 Tues. Phone (814) 768-7332.

COLLEGEVILLE—
see Philadelphia and Vicinity p. 124.

COLUMBIA—
see Pennsylvania Dutch Country p. 100.

CONCORDVILLE—
see Philadelphia and Vicinity p. 124.

CONNEAUT LAKE (E-1) pop. 700

The largest natural lake wholly within the state, Conneaut Lake is 3 miles long and 1.5 miles across at its widest point. For the outdoor enthusiast, Conneaut Lake Deck Hockey, 12810 Foust Rd., offers volleyball courts, softball and baseball fields and walking trails; phone (814) 382-2267.

Crawford County Convention and Visitors Bureau: 242½ Chestnut St., Meadville, PA 16314; phone (814) 333-1258 or (800) 332-2338.

 WINERIES

• **Conneaut Cellars Winery,** .5 mi. e. on US 322. Daily 10-6, Apr.-Dec.; Tues.-Sun. 10-6, rest of year. Phone (814) 382-3999.

COOKSBURG (E-3)

Cook Forest State Park *(see color ad p. 69),* is 1 mile north of Cooksburg off SR 36. The park comprises nearly 6,500 acres of scenic drives and hiking trails set against the backdrop of the winding Clarion River. The area is noteworthy for its abundance of deer. River activities—canoeing, tubing, and watersliding—are popular, as is horseback riding. Mountain streams and reservoirs in the vicinity offer good trout fishing. *See Recreation Chart and the AAA Mideastern CampBook.*

CORNWALL (H-9) pop. 3,200

The Cornwall Ore Banks, on the knobs of South Mountain, Grassy Hill, Middle Hill and Big Hill, contain one of the most valuable deposits of iron ore in the East. The mines operated 1735-1972.

CORNWALL IRON FURNACE is off US 322, following markers, on SR 419. The furnace, built by Peter Grubb in 1742, operated until 1883. Structures on the grounds include the original furnace stack; the blast machinery; blowing tubs; wagon and blacksmith shops; the open-pit mine;

the ironmaster's mansion; and the Charcoal House, which is now a visitor center with displays depicting mining operations, charcoal making and iron making. Guided tours are available. Allow 1 hour minimum. Tues.-Sat. 9-5 (also Memorial Day and Labor Day), Sun. noon-5; closed Jan. 1, Thanksgiving and Dec. 25. Hours may vary; phone ahead. Last tour begins 1 hour before closing. Admission $3.50; over 60, $3; ages 6-12, $2; family rate $8.50. Phone (717) 272-9711.

COUDERSPORT (D-6) pop. 2,800, elev. 1,650'

Coudersport was founded by John Keating, an Irish mercenary who managed the Ceres Land Co., which owned most of the county. Keating gave 50 acres to each of the first 50 settlers and named the community after Jean Samuel Couderc, a Dutch banker.

Coudersport is a light manufacturing community on the banks of the Allegheny River. A monument to David Zeisberger, a Moravian missionary who camped nearby in October 1767, is in the county courthouse square at Second and Main streets.

Coudersport Chamber of Commerce: P.O. Box 261, Coudersport, PA 16915; phone (814) 274-8165.

[SAVE] PENNSYLVANIA LUMBER MUSEUM, 10 mi. e. on US 6, preserves the colorful heritage of the state's prosperous lumber era—more than a century ago when white pine and hemlock were the wealth of the nation. More than 3,000 objects, from everyday tools to a logging locomotive, are displayed. A tour of the museum includes a walk among the weathered wooden buildings of a logging camp and sawmill. Allow 1 hour minimum. Daily 9-5, Apr.-Nov. Admission $3.50; over 60, $3; ages 6-12, $1.50. Phone (814) 435-2652.

CRESSON (H-4) pop. 1,800, elev. 2,022'

ALLEGHENY PORTAGE RAILROAD NATIONAL HISTORIC SITE is 3 mi. e. on US 22; take Gallitzen exit, following signs. The historic site preserves traces of the first railroad crossing of the Allegheny Mountains. Built in the early 1830s, this railroad used 11 levels and 10 inclined planes to connect the eastern and western divisions of the Pennsylvania Mainline Canal. Carrying passengers, freight and sectional canal boats, the railroad provided a critical link for travel and trade between Pittsburgh and Philadelphia. It was eventually abandoned in 1857 upon completion of the Pennsylvania Railroad.

Remnants of the Allegheny Portage Railroad, including the Skew Arch Bridge, Incline Plane No. 6, stone railroad ties, and stone quarry can be seen. The visitor center has a 20-minute slide and film presentation, models, exhibits and artifacts that depict the history of the railroad and

the canal. The Engine House 6 Interpretive Shelter offers exhibits about stationary steam engines. Tours are given of the Lemon House, built in the 1830s as a tavern.

A picnic area and hiking trails are available. Ranger-conducted programs and stone-cutting and log-hewing demonstrations are held during the summer. For additional information contact the Superintendent, Allegheny Portage Railroad National Historic Site, P.O. Box 189, Cresson, PA 16630; phone (814) 886-6150. Allow 1 hour minimum. Daily 9-6, Memorial Day-Labor Day; 9-5, rest of year. Closed Dec. 25. Admission $2. Phone (814) 886-6100.

DANVILLE (F-9) pop. 5,200, elev. 456'

MONTOUR PRESERVE, 5 mi. w. of I-80 exit 33 on SR 54, then 4.5 mi. n.e., following signs, is a nature preserve and recreation area centering on 165-acre Lake Chillisquaque. Visitors enjoy boating, hiking, picnicking and fishing in summer and cross-country skiing and ice fishing in winter. There are four marked nature trails and a visitor center displaying nature, wildlife and history exhibits. Special programs are held throughout the year.

Allow 1 hour minimum. Visitor center open daily 9-4, May-Sept; Mon.-Fri. 9-4, rest of year. Closed major holidays. Trails open daily dawn-dusk. Free. Phone (717) 437-3131.

DAWSON (I-2) pop. 500, elev. 850'

The Linden Hall Mansion, off SR 819 on Linden Hall Road, is a 35-room English Tudor mansion built in 1913; phone (724) 529-7543 or 461-2424.

DELAWARE WATER GAP NATIONAL RECREATION AREA—

see Pocono Mountains Area p. 147.

DONEGAL (H-3) pop. 200

Just off I-76 west of Somerset, the small community of Donegal is surrounded by the Laurel Mountains and is convenient for such outdoor recreation as hiking on the Laurel Highlands Trail, which traverses several nearby state parks. One of the area's historical landmarks is a restored 1850s farmhouse on Mountain View Road, once part of an 18th-century land grant witnessed by Benjamin Franklin. It is now the Mountain View Bed and Breakfast; visitors can tour the house and see its period furnishings and antiques.

DOWNINGTON—

see Philadelphia and Vicinity p. 124.

DOYLESTOWN—

see Philadelphia and Vicinity p. 124.

EASTON (G-11) pop. 26,300, elev. 211'

Rich in history, Easton served as a focal point of the Revolutionary War. The first public reading of the Declaration of Independence in the

Colonies occurred on the steps of Northampton County Courthouse when it was located in Centre Square. Easton also was the home of George Taylor, a signer of the Declaration of Independence. The Parson-Taylor House, a stone house built in 1757, still stands on S. 4th Street.

During the 19th century, Easton became one of America's earliest industrial centers due to its strategic location at the confluence of the Delaware and Lehigh rivers, the Morris Canal and five major railroads. It was during the height of the canal era that many of Easton's fine examples of American architecture were built.

Easton's industrial prosperity was reflected in the founding of Lafayette College in 1832. Daniel Chester French's heroic bronze statue of Lafayette, the French aristocrat who fought with the American Colonists against the British, stands above the city on the Lafayette College campus.

Walking tours of Historic Easton are available through the Easton Heritage Alliance; phone (610) 258-1612.

Two Rivers Area Chamber of Commerce: 1 S. Third St., P.O. Box 637, Easton, PA 18044; phone (610) 253-4211.

Shopping areas: The downtown area surrounding Two Rivers Landing consists of coffee houses, art galleries, antique shops, restaurants, stores and historic architecture.

CANAL BOAT RIDES are offered in Hugh Moore Park, 2.5 mi. from I-78 or 2 mi. s. off US 22, 25th St. exit, following signs. The mule-drawn canal boat *Josiah White II* operates on a section of the Lehigh Canal; a costumed interpreter provides narration. An 1890s locktender's house, now a museum, is in the park. Boat rentals are available; picnicking is permitted.

Allow 1 hour, 30 minutes minimum. Trips depart Mon.-Sat. 10:30-4:30, Sun. and Labor Day 1-4:30, day after Memorial Day-Labor Day; Tues.-Sat. 9:30-3:30, Sun. and Memorial Day 1-4:30, early May-Memorial Day; Sat.-Sun. 1-4:30, day after Labor Day-late Sept. Fare (including locktender's house) $5; over 64, $4.50; ages 3-15, $3. MC, VI. Phone (610) 515-8000.

SOLDIERS AND SAILORS MONUMENT is on the square in the business district. On this site stood Northampton County's first courthouse, built in 1765 on a tract presented by the Penn family at an annual rent of one red rose.

TWO RIVERS LANDING AND THE DELAWARE AND LEHIGH NATIONAL HERITAGE CORRIDOR VISITOR CENTER is downtown off S. Third St. at 30 Centre Square. The Delaware and Lehigh National Heritage Corridor Visitor Center, on the first floor of Two Rivers Landing, has exhibits and a 7-minute audiovisual presentation depicting the history of Easton and the Lehigh Valley. Also part of the visitor center are displays about the area's immigrant ethnic groups, canals and the industries that have been the community's mainstays. Food is available.

Allow 30 minutes minimum. Mon.-Sat. 9-6, Sun. 11-6, Memorial Day-Labor Day; Tues.-Sat. and Mon. holidays 9:30-5, Sun. noon-5, rest of year. Closed Jan. 1, Easter, Thanksgiving and Dec. 24-25. Free. Phone (610) 515-8000.

The Crayola Factory, on the second floor of Two Rivers Landing, allows children to learn while having fun with interactive exhibits and craft stations. Visitors are shown how markers are produced and how crayons are molded, labeled and packed, while a timeline traces colorful moments in Crayola history. Children of all ages can color on giant glass walls and create with Crayola products and computers.

Allow 1 hour, 30 minutes minimum. Mon.-Sat. 9-6, Sun. 11-6, Memorial Day-Labor Day; Tues.-Sat. and Monday holidays 9:30-5, Sun. noon-5, rest of year. Closed Jan. 1, Easter, Thanksgiving and Dec. 24-25. Admission is limited based on building capacity; early arrival is recommended. Last admission 90 minutes before closing. Admission (includes The National Canal Museum) $7; over 64, $6; under 3 free. MC, VI. Phone (610) 515-8000.

The National Canal Museum, on the third floor of Two Rivers Landing, contains exhibits about the history and technology of America's 19th-century canals and inland waterways. Interactive exhibits allow visitors to operate an incline plane model and pilot a boat through a lock.

Allow 30 minutes minimum. Mon.-Sat. 9-6, Sun. 11-6, Memorial Day-Labor Day; Tues.-Sat. and Mon. holidays 9:30-5, Sun. noon-5, rest of year. Closed Jan. 1, Easter, Thanksgiving and Dec. 24-25. Admission may be limited based on the building's capacity. Last admission 90 minutes before closing. Admission (includes The Crayola Factory) $7; over 64, $6; under 3 free. MC, VI. Phone (610) 515-8000.

WELLER CENTER FOR HEALTH EDUCATION, 2009 Lehigh St., presents lectures, exhibits and audiovisual programs designed to promote healthful living. Though especially designed for school group tours, the center is open for others on a walk-in basis. Allow 30 minutes minimum. Mon.-Fri. 9-4, Labor Day to mid-June; 9-2, rest of year. Admission $4; ages 3-18, $3. Phone (610) 258-8500.

ECKVILLE (G-10)

HAWK MOUNTAIN SANCTUARY, 2 mi. e. of SR 895 to 1700 Hawk Mountain Rd. on Blue Mountain, is primarily for migrating birds of prey. The area covers about 2,400 acres of forested Appalachian mountaintop with bold rock promontories as well as 8 miles of hiking trails. The visitor center contains birds of prey exhibits and a museum. The chief attraction is the hawk and eagle migration from late August to late November. Pets are not permitted.

Allow 2 hours minimum. Daily 8-5, day after Labor Day-Thanksgiving; 9-5, rest of year. Admission Sat.-Sun., Sept.-Nov. $6; senior citizens $4; ages 6-12, $3. Admission Mon.-Fri., Sept.-Nov. and rest of year $4; senior citizens $3; ages 6-12, $2. MC, VI. Phone (610) 756-6961.

ELIZABETH—
see Pittsburgh and Vicinity p. 144.

ELIZABETHTOWN—
see Pennsylvania Dutch Country p. 100.

ELYSBURG (F-9) •
KNOEBELS AMUSEMENT RESORT, 2 mi. n. on SR 487, has more than 40 rides, games, entertainment, miniature golf, waterslides, a swimming pool and camping facilities. Picnicking is permitted. Allow 6 hours minimum. Daily 11-10, Memorial Day weekend-Labor Day; Sat.-Sun. hours vary, May 1-day before Memorial Day weekend and day after Labor Day-Sept. 30. Park admission free. Rides 40c-$1.50, children's rides 40c-$1. All-day ride pass available Mon.-Fri. after mid-June. Phone (717) 672-2572 or (800) 487-4386.

EMPORIUM (E-5) pop. 2,500, elev. 1,040'
BUCKTAIL STATE PARK, 23,013 acres on SR 120 between Emporium and Lock Haven, provides a scenic drive through a narrow valley called the Bucktail Trail. The trail commemorates the Civil War regiment of area woodsmen known as the Bucktail Regiment because of their bucktail insignia. The trail also is known as the Sinnemahoning Trail, used by American Indians to travel between the Susquehanna and Allegheny rivers. Daily dawn-dusk. Free. Phone (814) 486-3365.

EPHRATA—
see Pennsylvania Dutch Country p. 100.

ERIE (C-2) pop. 108,700, elev. 710'
Pennsylvania's only port on the Great Lakes, Erie is a city of widely diversified industry and commerce and has complete facilities for overseas shipping.

Erie's first known inhabitants were the Eriez Indians, for whom the lake and city were named.

In 1753 a French military expedition built Fort Presque Isle on the site of Erie and Fort LeBoeuf on the site of Waterford *(see place listing p. 158).* A small village of French and Indians grew up around Fort Presque Isle. The French abandoned their forts in 1759, and the next year the English took possession and rebuilt them.

Three years later the English were driven out by Indians led by Chief Pontiac, who destroyed both forts. The region remained deserted by white men until 1795, when a permanent settlement was laid out. During the War of 1812 ships built at Erie under the command of Commodore Oliver Hazard Perry were instrumental in eliminating British naval control of Lake Erie.

Nearby Girard was the 1850s-1875 winter home of Dan Rice's circus. Although he was best known as the prototype for Uncle Sam, it was Rice who commissioned the first memorial to the Civil War dead; the 1865 obelisk is on Girard's Main Street. The importance of the railroad to neighboring Lake City is today evidenced only in the few commercial establishments which inhabit a depot and caboose. The downtowns of both communities reflect the 19th century with their gaslights and flower- and tree-lined pathways.

Baseball fans can watch the Erie SeaWolves of the New York-Penn League play at Jerry Uht Park from mid-June to mid-September. The Erie Otters hockey club plays at the Erie Civic Center from late September to mid-March. Forty-five-minute sightseeing boat trips depart from the East Public Dock at the foot of State Street, Memorial Day through Labor Day; charter service specializing in coho salmon fishing is available May through October.

Erie Area Chamber of Commerce: 1006 State St., Erie, PA 16501; phone (814) 454-7191.

Shopping areas: The major shopping center in Erie is Millcreek Mall, US 19 and Interchange Road, featuring JCPenney, Kaufmann's, Lazarus and Sears. Blair Warehouse, outside Millcreek Mall, is a major warehouse clothing outlet. Keystone Center includes Kohl's.

ERIE ART MUSEUM, 411 State St., is in a Greek Revival-style brick and marble building built in 1839. The galleries display changing exhibits of

---

PLAN AHEAD FOR ECONOMY

- Select the optimum route in terms of distance and type of highway. A AAA Travel Counselor can assist you.
- Travel light and avoid using a car-top rack. The less weight and wind resistance, the better the gas mileage.
- Combine short trips, such as visits, errands and shopping.

paintings, drawings, photography, sculpture, ceramics and other media. Allow 30 minutes minimum. Tues.-Sat. 11-5, Sun. 1-5; closed holidays. Admission $1.50; senior citizens and students with ID 75c; under 12, 50c; free to all Wed. MC, VI. Phone (814) 459-5477.

ERIE HISTORICAL MUSEUM, 356 W. 6th St., is in a 24-room mansion built about 1890. The museum highlights local history and contains art and changing exhibits. Allow 1 hour minimum. Tues.-Sun. 1-5, Sept.-May; Tues.-Fri. 10-5, rest of year. Closed holidays. Admission $2; ages 2-12, $1. Phone (814) 871-5790.

Erie Planetarium creates images of the sun, moon, planets and stars and their movements. Allow 1 hour minimum. Shows Sun. at 2 and 3; closed holidays. Admission $2; ages 2-12, $1. Phone (814) 871-5790.

ERIE HISTORY CENTER, 417 State St., is in an 1840 building. Exhibits highlight local industry and architecture. The complex includes the 1839 Cashiers House and the Greek Revival residence of the chief officer of the United States Bank, located next door. Walking and driving tours also are available. Allow 30 minutes minimum. Center open Tues.-Sat. 9-5. Cashiers House open Tues.-Sat. 1-4. Donations. Phone (814) 454-1813.

ERIE ZOO is 3 mi. n. of I-90 exit 7. The main zoo contains more than 300 animals on 15 acres. Next to the zoo is the GMC Ice Arena. Food is available. Allow 1 hour minimum. Open daily 10-5; closed Jan. 1 and Dec. 25. Children's zoo open May-Sept. GMC Ice Arena open Sept.-Mar. Admission, including park and main zoo, $4.75; over 62, $4.25; ages 3-11, $2.75. Train ride $1. Ice arena $4; over 62 and ages 3-11, $3.50. DS, MC, VI. Phone (814) 864-4091 or (814) 868-3651 for the ice arena.

EXPERIENCE CHILDREN'S MUSEUM is downtown at 420 French St. The museum's two floors of science and humanities exhibits offer hands-on expERIEnces for children. Young visitors learn about energy, force and motion, light, weather safety, recycling, fossils, paper making and nutritional meal planning. Face painting, costumes for dressing up and a mini-market also are available.
Allow 1 hour, 30 minutes minimum. Tues.-Sat. 10-4, Sun. 1-4, July-Aug.; Wed.-Sat. 10-4, Sun. 1-4, rest of year. Closed holidays. Admission $3.50, under 2 free. MC, VI. Phone (814) 453-3743.

PRESQUE ISLE STATE PARK, 3,200 acres, is 7 mi. n. of I-90 exit 5 on Peninsula Dr. (SR 832). The park is a wildlife refuge and conservation area with miles of beaches. Nature trails, swimming, boating, fishing, birdwatching and picnicking are available. An interpretive center contains ecological and nature exhibits. Presque Isle has no overnight accommodations. Daily 5 a.m.-dusk; beaches open Memorial Day weekend-Labor Day. Phone (814) 833-7424. *See Recreation Chart.*

SAVE A RECONSTRUCTION OF THE US BRIG NIAGARA, 150 E. Front St., was the flagship of the fleet that Commodore Oliver Hazard Perry used against the British to win the Battle of Lake Erie in 1813. Nautical equipment, including a bilge pump, rigging and a movable block and tackle are displayed. Phone to verify that the ship is in port.
Allow 1 hour minimum. Mon.-Sat. 9-5, Sun. noon-5, Memorial Day weekend-Sept. 30. Admission $4; over 60, $3.50; ages 6-12, $2; family rate $10. MC, VI. Phone (814) 871-4596.

WALDAMEER PARK & WATER WORLD, 5 mi. n. of I-90 exit 5 on Peninsula Dr. (SR 832) at the entrance to Presque Isle State Park, is an amusement and water park complex. The amusement park contains rides, puppet shows, midway games and a video arcade. The water park features 16 slides, a lazy river ride and children's play areas. Picnicking is permitted. Food is available.
Waldameer Park open Tues.-Sun. and Mon. holidays 1-10 (weather permitting), Memorial Day-Labor Day. Water World open Tues.-Sun. and Mon. holidays 11-7:30 (weather permitting), Memorial Day-Labor Day. Waldameer Park free. Individual ride tickets 75c. Unlimited ride pass $11.50, under 42 inches tall $7.50. Water World $10, under 42 inches tall $7.50. Combination unlimited Waldameer Park and Water World ride pass $14.95, under 42 inches tall $9.75. Rates are $1.50 less in the evening. DS, MC, VI. Phone (814) 838-3591.

ERWINNA (G-11) pop. 100

WINERIES

• **Sand Castle Winery,** .5 mi. s. on SR 32. Mon.-Sat. 10-6, Sun. 11-6. Phone (610) 294-9181 or (800) 722-9463.

EXTON—
see Philadelphia and Vicinity p. 125.

FAIRFIELD (I-7) pop. 500, elev. 531′
STRAWBERRY HILL NATURE CENTER AND PRESERVE is at 1537 Mt. Hope Rd.; from SR 116 go 3.5 mi. n.w. on Bullfrog Rd., which becomes Mt. Hope Rd. This 588-acre preserve in the Blue Ridge mountains offers bird and animal spotting opportunities, hiking trails, cross-country ski trails and natural history displays in its nature center. Nature center open Mon.-Sat. 9-5; closed holidays. Donations. Phone (717) 642-5840.

FALLSINGTON—
see Philadelphia and Vicinity p. 125.

FAYETTEVILLE (I-7) elev. 792'

Totem Pole Playhouse in Caledonia State Park *(see Recreation Chart and the AAA Mideastern CampBook)* is a 450-seat theater that presents summer stock productions featuring nationally known actors, directors and designers. Performances are held early June to early September. The box office opens March 1. For more information phone (717) 352-2164.

Also of interest in the park are artifacts and displays in the reconstructed Thaddeus Stevens' Blacksmith Shop. Recreational facilities include an Olympic-size swimming pool, 18-hole golf course, nature trails and cross-country ski trails.

★ FORT NECESSITY NATIONAL BATTLEFIELD (I-2)

Fort Necessity National Battlefield, 11 miles east of Uniontown on US 40, surrounds a reconstruction of the fort built by George Washington in 1754. The Battle of Fort Necessity, in which Washington led Virginia militiamen and South Carolina regulars against a strong force of French and American Indians, occurred at the site on July 3, 1754. This was Washington's first campaign and the marked beginning of the French and Indian War.

Reconstructions of the fort, entrenchments and earthworks have been erected on their original sites. Picnic facilities are available. Allow 30 minutes minimum. A visitor center features exhibits and a 10-minute audiovisual presentation.

Mount Washington Tavern, on US 40 near the fort, is a restored 19th-century stagecoach inn. Refurnished period rooms include the barroom, parlor, kitchen and bedrooms. The dining room has exhibits pertaining to the National Road. Allow 30 minutes minimum.

A mile west on US 40 is the grave of Gen. Edward Braddock. During the Battle of the Monongahela, Braddock was fatally wounded; his aide-de-camp, George Washington, had two horses shot out from under him. The troops carried Braddock back as far as the site of the Old Orchard Camp, where he died. He was buried in the road, and wagons were driven over his grave to prevent the Indians from finding the body and desecrating it. In 1804 remains said to be those of Braddock were moved to the present gravesite, which is marked by a monument.

Jumonville Glen, 7.5 miles from Fort Necessity, is reached via Jumonville Road (LR 26115), 2.5 miles north of US 40 at Mount Summit. It was the site of a 15-minute skirmish between French and British forces that led to the battle of Fort Necessity, which also is said to have been the spark that ignited the French and Indian War. For more information write the Superintendent, Fort Necessity National Battlefield, 1 Washington Pkwy., Farmington, PA 15437.

Park open daily dawn-dusk. Visitor center daily 8:30-6:30, Memorial Day-Labor Day; 8:30-5, rest of year. Closed Dec. 25. Mount Washington Tavern daily 8:30-5; closed Dec. 25. Admission $2, under 17 free. The general entrance fee, which covers the fort, tavern, visitor center, Jumonville Glen, Braddock's grave and the park grounds, is payable at the visitor center. Phone (724) 329-5512.

FORT WASHINGTON—

see Philadelphia and Vicinity p. 125.

FORTY FORT (E-10) pop. 5,000, elev. 554'

Built in 1790, the Nathan Denison House is 1 mile north of town via Wyoming Avenue at 35 Denison St. The home was built by Nathan Denison, a Revolutionary War colonel and later a Luzerne County judge. His 1717 ancestral homestead is in Mystic, Conn.

Col. Denison was among the first 40 settlers, for whom the Forty Fort settlement was named. Dennison's property is considered to be the oldest frame dwelling in the Wyoming Valley. The restored home is mostly furnished with authentic 18th-century pieces. Special events and programs of historical interest are presented throughout the year, concluding with an afternoon of Colonial hospitality in December. Costumed interpreters are available Sunday afternoons, May through August, and by appointment. Phone (717) 288-5531 or 287-7055 for appointments or events information.

FRANKLIN (E-2) pop. 4,100, elev. 1,017'

Franklin's history dates back to the French Fort Machault, built in 1753 near the confluence of French Creek and the Allegheny River. In 1760 the British built Fort Venango, which fell to the American Indians during Pontiac's War in 1763. According to local legend, the American Indians often played ball near the fort, and the British would allow them entry if the ball went over the fort's wall. On the day of the raid many more Indians than usual were playing. The ball went into the fort, and the British opened the gate to disaster.

The county of Venango was established in 1800 with Franklin as the county seat. The town retained its rural atmosphere until the start of the oil boom in 1859. Drilling began in Franklin shortly after Edwin Drake's successful well came in near Titusville *(see place listing p. 156).* Refineries were started, and Franklin's population more than tripled in the 1860s; three railroads came into the community, new businesses flourished, hotels were built and Franklin became a city in 1868.

The Venango County Historical Society is at 301 S. Park St. in the Hoge-Osmer House, a circa 1865 building; displays about local history are featured. The Venango County Courthouse at 12th and Liberty streets has an interesting architectural design and features a collection of prehistoric artifacts. The Pioneer Cemetery at Otter and 15th streets dates from 1795. A farmers' market is held on 12th Street on Wednesday and Saturday.

Franklin marks the fall season with the Applefest Celebration the first full weekend in October. Recreation, in the form of walking and bicycling, can be enjoyed on the Allegheny River Trail and the Samuel Justis Trail, both in the city.

Franklin Area Chamber of Commerce: 1259 Liberty St., Franklin, PA 16323; phone (814) 432-5823.

Self-guiding tours: Booklets outlining a walking tour of historic Franklin can be obtained at the chamber of commerce for $1.

DeBENCE'S ANTIQUE MUSIC WORLD is n.e. via SR 8 at 1261 Liberty St. A collection of more than 100 automated music machines ranges from small music boxes to large carnival organs such as the nickelodeon, calliope and orchestrion. Historical facts and demonstrations of each machine are provided. A potpourri of other antiques also is on view.

Allow 1 hour minimum. Tues.-Sat. 10-5, Sun. 12:30-5. Hours may vary; phone ahead. Last tour begins one hour before closing. Admission $6; senior citizens $5; ages 3-12, $3. Phone (814) 432-5668 or (888) 547-2377.

GETTYSBURG (I-7) pop. 7,000, elev. 520′

Marsh Creek Settlement was founded between two low ridges just north of the Mason-Dixon Line in the 1780s. Renamed Gettysburg in honor of Gen. James Gettys, the town grew quickly after being incorporated in 1806. Its square, at the crossroads of four major highways and several secondary roads, was a stopping point for travelers. This strategic location led to the town's involvement in one of the bloodiest battles of the Civil War *(see Gettysburg National Military Park p. 80)*.

Gettysburg Convention and Visitors Bureau: 35 Carlisle St., Gettysburg, PA 17325; phone (717) 334-6274. *See ad p. 285.*

Self-guiding tours: Area sightseeing excursions include a 14-block walking tour past 90 restored buildings in downtown Gettysburg and a 36-mile driving tour of the surrounding valley. A 40-mile driving tour includes East Cavalry Field, Victorian New Oxford and Early American East Berlin. Free brochures describing these tours are available from the convention and visitors bureau daily 9-5; closed Jan. 1 and Dec. 25.

CONFEDERATE STATES ARMORY AND MUSEUM, 529 Baltimore St., displays a variety of Confederate and Union Civil War memorabilia including small arms and swords. Allow 30 minutes minimum. Fri.-Mon. noon-7, mid-Apr. through May 31 and Sept.-Nov.; Wed.-Mon. 12:30-7:30, June-Aug. Hours may vary; phone ahead. Admission $1.50, under 7 free. Phone (717) 337-2340.

"THE CONFLICT", .3 mi. s. on US 15, is a theater featuring "Gettysburg: A Study in Valor," a definitive study of the famous battle; "Adventure at Gettysburg," which explains the battle to ages 8-14; "The War Within," which chronicles the entire Civil War; and a four-program documentary that offers a more complete account of the war and its battles (summer only).

Allow 1 hour minimum per program. Daily 9-9, Memorial Day-Labor Day; Mon.-Sat. 10-7, Apr. 1-day before Memorial Day and day after Labor Day-Nov. 30; otherwise varies. Individual programs $5, over 60 and students with ID $4. Reduced rate for 2 or more programs. AE, DS, MC, VI. Phone (717) 334-8003.

"Mr. Lincoln Returns to Gettysburg", at "The Conflict," is a live one-man performance that traces Abraham Lincoln's life from his boyhood in Kentucky to the nation's capital, giving special emphasis to Gettysburg. Allow 1 hour minimum. Mon.-Fri. at 8 p.m., June 15-Labor Day; phone for weekend schedule. Admission $6; ages 6-12, $5. Reservations are suggested. Phone (717) 334-6049 or 334-8003.

★**EISENHOWER NATIONAL HISTORIC SITE** is accessible by a shuttle bus that departs from the National Park Service Visitor Center on SR 134. The 231-acre Eisenhower farm was the only home ever owned by President Dwight D. Eisenhower and his wife Mamie. The house, grounds and buildings are carefully preserved. Displayed are the Eisenhower's formal living room, sun porch, original furniture and photographs, as well as many of the president's paintings, gifts and other items. Visitors also can see a video presentation and exhibits about the president's life.

Among the dignitaries who visited the estate were Nikita Khrushchev, Charles DeGaulle and Winston Churchill. Self-guiding walking tours of the cattle barns and grounds are available. Park rangers conduct tours of the grounds April through October.

Allow 1 hour minimum. Shuttle departs at regular intervals daily 9-4, Apr.-Oct.; Wed.-Sun. 9-4, Nov. 1-early Jan. and early Feb.-Mar. 31. Closed Jan. 1, Thanksgiving and Dec. 25. Hours and days of operation may vary; phone before visiting. Tickets are sold at the National Park Service Visitor Center daily 8-5. Admission $5.25; ages 13-16, $3.25; ages 6-12, $2.25. AE, DS, MC, VI. Phone (717) 338-9114, or 334-4474 to purchase tickets in advance.

GETTYSBURG BATTLEFIELD TOURS depart from 778 Baltimore St. On this 2-hour tour of the Gettysburg Battlefield passengers listen to an audiotape dramatized narration. Daily 9-9, June-Aug.; 9-7, Apr.-May and Sept.-Nov.; 9-5, rest of year. Fare $12.95; ages 6-11, $9.50. AE, DS, MC, VI. Phone (717) 334-6296.

GETTYSBURG BATTLE THEATRE, 571 Steinwehr Ave., offers a Battle of Gettysburg orientation program, presented via electronic map and a film featuring multimedia battle re-enactments.

Allow 1 hour minimum. Daily 9-9, June-Aug.; 9-7, Apr.-May and Sept.-Oct.; 9-5 in Mar. and Nov. Admission $5.25; ages 6-11, $3.25. DS, MC, VI. Phone (717) 334-6100.

HALL OF PRESIDENTS, 789 Baltimore St., displays life-size, wax reproductions of the United States presidents. Allow 1 hour minimum. Daily 9-9, June-Aug.; 9-7, Apr.-May and Sept.-Oct.; 9-5 in Mar. and Nov. Admission $5.25; ages 6-11, $3.25. DS, MC, VI. Phone (717) 334-5717.

JENNIE WADE HOUSE AND OLDE TOWN, 547 Baltimore St., offers a guided tour of the house in which the only civilian killed in the Battle of Gettysburg died. Olde Town features life-size depictions of merchants and craftsmen in their roles in the aftermath of the battle. Allow 1 hour minimum. Daily 9-9, June-Aug.; 9-7, Apr.-May and Sept.-Oct.; 9-5 in Mar. and Nov. Admission $5.25; ages 6-11, $3.25. DS, MC, VI. Phone (717) 334-4100.

SAVE LAND OF LITTLE HORSES, 3 mi. w. off US 30, features performing Falabella miniature horses and other farm animals. Also available are a barn display, a carriage museum, nature trails and a petting farm. A Christmas extravaganza is held four weekends following Thanksgiving. Shows are offered daily 10-5, June-Aug.; Sat.-Sun. 10-5, Apr.-May and Sept.-Oct. Admission $6.50; ages 2-12, $4.50. DS, MC, VI. Phone (717) 334-7259.

LEE'S HEADQUARTERS AND MUSEUM is .7 mi. w. on US 30. On July 1, 1863, Gen. Robert E. Lee established his personal headquarters in this old stone house, which dates from the 1700s. Displays include Union and Confederate military equipment and Civil War artifacts and documents. Allow 1 hour minimum. Daily 9-9, mid-Apr. to mid-Oct.; 9-5, mid-Mar. to mid-Apr. and mid-Oct. through Nov. 30. Admission $2. Phone (717) 334-3141.

SAVE LINCOLN ROOM MUSEUM, in the Wills House on the square at US 15 Bus. Rte. and US 30, is where Abraham Lincoln stayed in 1863 and completed his Gettysburg Address. The furnishings are original. Visitors can have their photograph taken with a life-size bronze sculpture of Lincoln created by J. Seward Johnson. Allow 30 minutes minimum. Daily 9-7, Memorial Day weekend-Labor Day; otherwise varies. Admission $4; over 62, $3.75; ages 9-18, $2.50. AE, DS, MC, VI. Phone (717) 334-8188.

Sightseeing is your thing?
Check the Points of Interest Index for attraction categories of special appeal to you.

THE LINCOLN TRAIN MUSEUM, 425 Steinwehr Ave., contains more than 1,000 toy trains. Visitors take a simulated trip aboard the train which took President Lincoln to Gettysburg in 1863, see the Civil War countryside and overhear conversations which might have occurred on that trip. Allow 1 hour minimum. Daily 9-9, June-Aug.; 9-7, Apr.-May and Sept.-Oct.; 9-5 in Mar. and Nov. Admission $5.25; ages 6-11, $3.25. DS, MC, VI. Phone (717) 334-5678.

SAVE MAGIC TOWN OF GETTYSBURG, 49 Steinwehr Ave., is a miniature American neighborhood created by artist Michael Garman. Holograms, mirrors, lights, sound effects and grand illusions make the city come alive. Allow 30 minutes minimum. Daily 10-9 (also Fri.-Sat. 9-11 p.m.), June-Aug.; daily noon-8, Mar. 15-May 31 and Sept.-Dec.; Fri.-Sun. 11-8, rest of year. Closed Jan. 1 and Dec. 25. Admission $2.75. Phone (717) 337-0442 or (800) 878-4276.

SAVE NATIONAL CIVIL WAR WAX MUSEUM, 1 mi. s. on US 15 Bus. Rte. at 297 Steinwehr Ave., presents an audiovisual account of the Civil War. Tableaux comprising more than 200 life-size wax figures delineate the causes and effects of the conflict. A scene re-creating the climactic Battle of Gettysburg is in the Battle room.

Allow 1 hour minimum. Daily 9-9, mid-June through Labor Day; daily 9-7, mid-Apr. to mid-June; daily 9-5, day after Labor Day-Dec. 31 and Mar. 1 to mid-Apr.; Sat.-Sun. 9-5, rest of year. Closed Jan. 1, Thanksgiving and Dec. 25. Admission $4.50; ages 13-17, $2.50; ages 6-12, $1.75. Phone (717) 334-6245.

SAVE NATIONAL TOWER, .5 mi. s. on SR 97 or SR 134, across from the National Park Visitor Center, is a 307-foot observation tower offering views from enclosed and open decks. A 12-minute audio program describing the battle is presented. Allow 1 hour minimum. Daily 9-6:30, June-Aug.; 9-5, Apr.-May and Sept.-Oct.; Fri.-Sun. 10-4, in Nov. Admission $5; over 62, $4.50; ages 6-12, $3. Phone (717) 334-6754.

SAMUEL COLT HERITAGE MUSEUM, 241 Steinwehr Ave., exhibits firearms dating from the early 1700s to the present. A tribute to gun manufacturer Samuel Colt, the museum contains rare and historic guns including the Flintlock, cap and ball, the Gatling, automatics and machine guns. Many guns are fully engraved and inlaid. Allow 1 hour minimum. Daily 9-8, May-Aug.; 10-6, Mar.-Apr. and Sept.-Oct. Closed Thanksgiving. Admission $5; ages 6-16, $3. AE, DS, MC, VI. Phone (717) 334-6852.

SOLDIERS NATIONAL MUSEUM, 777 Baltimore St., displays Civil War artifacts, many dealing with weaponry. Forty dioramas depict major battles of the war. Daily 9-9, June-Aug.; 9-7, Apr.-May and Sept.-Oct.; 9-5 in Mar. and Nov. Admission $5.25; ages 6-11, $3.25. DS, MC, VI. Phone (717) 334-4890.

★GETTYSBURG NATIONAL MILITARY PARK (I-7)

Gettysburg National Military Park virtually surrounds the city of Gettysburg; the main entrance is at the National Park Visitor Center on SR 134. The park comprises the Gettysburg battlefield, where one of the most important and hotly contested battles of the Civil War was waged on July 1, 2 and 3, 1863. Resulting in 51,000 casualties, it also was the bloodiest battle of the war.

The Federal Army of the Potomac, with some 92,000 men under Gen. George Meade, met the Confederate Army of Northern Virginia, with about 70,000 men under Gen. Robert E. Lee. The battlefield covers 25 square miles. About 5,900 acres are in Gettysburg National Military Park, and 21 acres are in Gettysburg National Cemetery.

After his victory at Chancellorsville, Va., Lee invaded Pennsylvania, hoping to destroy the Union Army on its own soil. On the morning of July 1, a Confederate division attacked Gen. John Buford's cavalry. Fierce fighting followed, and the Union forces were driven to the heights south of town, known as Cemetery Hill, Cemetery Ridge and Culp's Hill. That night the armies moved into battle position. Confederate assaults on both Union flanks gained some ground late the next day.

On the third day, after a heavy 2-hour artillery barrage, a Confederate force advanced on the center of the Union line in the face of deadly fire that shattered their ranks and spelled disaster. They retreated on the evening of July 4, ending the last major offensive of Lee's army and presaging the war's outcome.

On Nov. 19, 1863, President Lincoln dedicated Gettysburg National Cemetery on the battlefield, delivering his most famous speech, the Gettysburg Address.

There are now more than 1,300 monuments, statues and markers, three observation towers and 31 miles of marked avenues. The park roads are open daily 6 a.m.-10 p.m.

Monuments and historical points are scattered throughout the park. On Cemetery Ridge, Meade, commander of the Union forces, is depicted on his horse. His headquarters on Taneytown Road is preserved. In the summer there are interpretive walks to the High Water Mark, where there is a monument to the bravery of both armies, and to the National Cemetery.

Many states have erected monuments in the park. The Virginia memorial is surmounted by a statue of Lee, and the North Carolina memorial was designed and carved by Gutzon Borglum, sculptor of Mount Rushmore.

CCINC. AUTO TAPE TOURS describe historical points of interest in the park. The Civil War battle is presented with voice, music and sound effects and is explained with reference to the specific battle sites. The tape can be purchased for $12.95 at the National Civil War Wax Museum *(see attraction listing in Gettysburg)*, or by sending $14.95 (includes postage) to CCInc., P.O. Box 227, Allendale, NJ 07401. Phone (201) 236-1666.

★**DEVIL'S DEN,** off Warren Ave., is a group of huge boulders from which Union troops were driven in Gen. James Longstreet's attack of July 2, 1863. A barricade used by Confederate sharpshooters who fired on Little Round Top can still be seen.

★**EISENHOWER NATIONAL HISTORIC SITE—** *see Gettysburg p. 77.*

★**ETERNAL LIGHT PEACE MEMORIAL** is on Oak Hill, scene of some of the first day's fighting in the Battle of Gettysburg. It was dedicated by President Franklin D. Roosevelt on the 75th anniversary of the battle. A perpetual flame lights the top of the monument, and an inscription reads, "Peace Eternal in a Nation United."

★**GETTYSBURG NATIONAL CEMETERY,** off Baltimore Pike, consists of 21 acres and contains the graves of 3,706 Civil War dead, 1,664 of them unknown. The Soldiers' National Monument stands near the spot where President Lincoln delivered his immortal dedication address on Nov. 19, 1863. Interpretive walks are given during the summer.

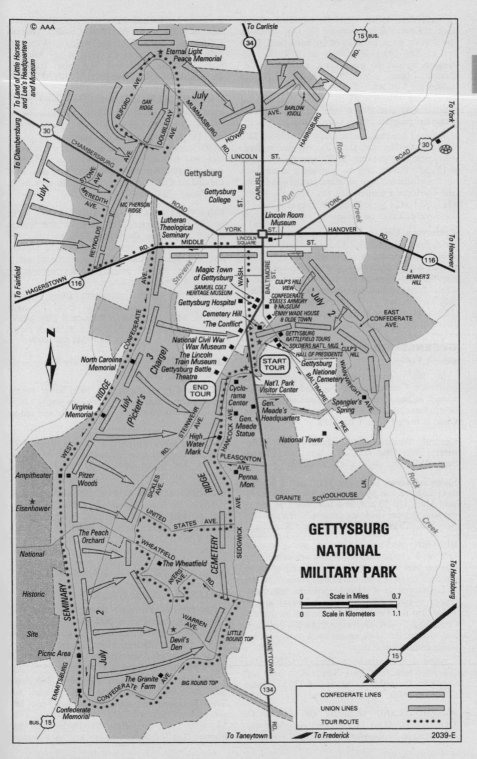

© AAA

To Carlisle

To Land of Little Horses and Lee's Headquarters and Museum

34

15 BUS.

RD.

★ Eternal Light Peace Memorial

July 1

OAK RIDGE

BUFORD AVE.

DOUBLEDAY AVE.

MUMMASBURG RD.

HOWARD AVE.

BARLOW KNOLL

To Chambersburg

30

July 1

CHAMBERSBURG AVE.

STONE AVE.

MEREDITH AVE.

REYNOLDS AVE.

MC PHERSON RIDGE

Gettysburg

Gettysburg College

HARRISBURG

LINCOLN ST.

York Run

YORK

ROAD

30

To York

Lutheran Theological Seminary

ROAD

MIDDLE

YORK ST.

CARLISLE ST.

LINCOLN ST.

Lincoln Room Museum

HANOVER ST.

ROAD

To Hagerstown

116

To Fairfield

Stevens AVE.

Magic Town of Gettysburg

SAMUEL COLT HERITAGE MUSEUM

Gettysburg Hospital

Cemetery Hill "The Conflict"

National Civil War Wax Museum

The Lincoln Train Museum

Gettysburg Battle Theatre

WASH. ST.

BALTIMORE ST.

CONFEDERATE STATES ARMORY & MUSEUM

JENNY WADE HOUSE & OLDE TOWN

CULP'S HILL VIEW

July 2

116

To Hanover

BENNER'S HILL

North Carolina Memorial

CONFEDERATE AVE.

3 July (Pickett's Charge)

RIDGE

START TOUR

GETTYSBURG BATTLEFIELD TOURS

SOLDIERS NAT'L. MUS.

HALL OF PRESIDENTS

Gettysburg National Cemetery

CULP'S HILL

EAST CONFEDERATE AVE.

WAINWRIGHT AVE.

Virginia Memorial

END TOUR

Cyclorama Center

Nat'l. Park Visitor Center

Gen. Meade's Headquarters

Spangler's Spring

PIKE

Pitzer Woods

WEST

STEINWEHR AVE.

High Water Mark

Gen. Meade Statue

HANCOCK AVE.

BALTIMORE

Ampitheater

★ Eisenhower

RD.

SICKLES AVE.

PLEASONTON AVE.

Penna. Mon.

National Tower

LN.

Rock

National

The Peach Orchard

WHEATFIELD

UNITED STATES AVE.

RIDGE

SEDGWICK AVE.

GRANITE

SCHOOLHOUSE

Creek

Historic

SEMINARY

2 July

The Wheatfield

AYERS AVE.

CEMETERY RD.

GETTYSBURG

NATIONAL

MILITARY PARK

Site

Picnic Area

WARREN AVE.

Devil's Den

LITTLE ROUND TOP

0 Scale in Miles 0.7

0 Scale in Kilometers 1.1

To Harrisburg

BUS. 15

EMMITSBURG

CONFEDERATE AVE.

The Granite Farm

BIG ROUND TOP

TANEYTOWN RD.

15

Confederate Memorial

134

To Taneytown

To Frederick

CONFEDERATE LINES	
UNION LINES	
TOUR ROUTE	• • • • • •

2039-E

★**NATIONAL PARK VISITOR CENTER,** across from the national cemetery on SR 134, serves as the starting point for tours of the battlefield. Both self-guiding and guided tours are available. Arrangements can be made for a personally conducted 2-hour tour with licensed battlefield guides for $30. Also in the visitor center are the Gettysburg Museum of the Civil War and an electric map that uses colored lights to demonstrate the progress of the 3-day battle.

Allow 1 hour minimum. Daily 8-5; closed Jan. 1, Thanksgiving and Dec. 25. Admission free. Electronic map program $2.50; over 61, $2; ages 6-15, $1. Tickets may be purchased in advance for the electronic map program, battlefield guides and Cyclorama Center. AE, DS, MC, VI. Phone (717) 334-1124 for park information or 334-4474 for advance ticket purchases.

Cyclorama Center features the famous cyclorama painting "Pickett's Charge." Completed by Paul Philippoteaux in 1884, this painting is displayed with a dramatic sound-and-light program. Exhibits and films in the building tell the story of the battle. Allow 30 minutes minimum. Daily 9-5; closed Jan. 1, Thanksgiving and Dec. 25. Admission free; sound-and-light program $2.50; over 61, $2; ages 6-15, $1. AE, DS, MC, VI.

GREENSBURG (H-2) pop. 16,300, elev. 1,114'

In the western Pennsylvania bituminous coalfields, Greensburg was founded in 1787 and named in honor of Gen. Nathanael Greene. Another Revolutionary War general, Arthur St. Clair, is buried in St. Clair Park.

Central Westmoreland Chamber of Commerce: Toll Gate Hill, P.O. Box 240, Greensburg, PA 15601; phone (724) 834-2900.

Shopping areas: Greengate Mall, on US 30, features Lazarus and Montgomery Ward. Westmoreland Mall, US 30 and Donohoe Road, is one of the largest local shopping centers. It features The Bon-Ton, JCPenney, Kaufmann's and Sears.

HISTORIC HANNA'S TOWN, 3 mi. n. via US 119, is a reconstruction of the settlement that was the first county seat west of the Alleghenies. On their original sites are Robert Hanna's house, which served as a residence, tavern and courthouse; a one-room jail; and a storage house. There also is a German log cabin and an original Conestoga wagon. Guides describe the buildings and, during the summer, interpret extensive ongoing archeological digs.

Allow 1 hour minimum. Tues.-Sat. 10-4, Sun. 1-4, June-Aug.; Sat. 10-4, Sun. 1-4, in May and Sept.-Oct. Guided tours $2; ages 6-12, $1. Phone (724) 836-1800.

WESTMORELAND MUSEUM OF AMERICAN ART, 221 N. Main St., features American and southwestern Pennsylvanian paintings, sculpture,

drawings, prints and decorative arts. The collection includes works by Mary Cassatt, Thomas Eakins, Benjamin West and Andrew Wyeth. A reference library is in the west wing. Allow 1 hour minimum. Wed.-Sun. 11-5 (also Thurs. 5-9); closed holidays. Free. Phone (724) 837-1500.

GREENVILLE (E-1) pop. 6,700, elev. 945'

THE CANAL MUSEUM, Lock 22, Alan Ave., chronicles the history of the Erie Extension Canal. Displays include a full-size replica of an 1840s canal boat, a working model of a canal lock and historic artifacts. Tues.-Sun. 1-5, Memorial Day-Labor Day; Sat.-Sun. 1-5, day after Labor Day-Oct. 31. Admission $1.50; ages 6-18, $1. Phone (724) 588-7540.

GREENVILLE RAILROAD MUSEUM, 314 Main St., features Engine #604—one of the largest switch engines in the world. Built in 1936, the engine hauled iron ore on the Duluth, Mesabi and Iron Range Railroad. Also displayed are a coal tender, hopper car, a 1913 Empire touring car and a 1952 caboose.

Allow 30 minutes minimum. Daily noon-5, Memorial Day weekend-Labor Day; Fri.-Sun. noon-5, May 1-day before Memorial Day weekend and day after Labor Day-Oct. 31; other times by appointment. Free. Phone (724) 588-4009.

GROVE CITY (F-2) pop. 8,200, elev. 1,245'

Grove City celebrates its local crop during Grove City Strawberry Days in early June complete with strawberry treats, crafts and entertainment.

Shopping areas: Grove City Factory Shops, I-79 exit 31, contains more than 150 outlet stores including Ann Taylor, Bass, Bugle Boy, Jockey and Royal Doulton.

WENDELL AUGUST FORGE, 620 Madison Ave., is one of the few remaining forges in the country that produce forged aluminum, bronze, pewter and sterling silver items by hand. Visitors can take a self-guiding tour through the work area and watch craftsmen at work. Tours are available Mon.-Sat. 9-4 (workload permitting). Free. Phone (724) 458-8360 or (800) 923-4438.

HALIFAX (G-8) pop. 9,000

LAKE TOBIAS WILDLIFE PARK, 760 Tobias Dr., offers safari tours in a 200-acre wildlife park. Hundreds of animals are featured, including alligators, bears, buffaloes, emus, llamas and monkeys. Also offered are animal and reptile shows and a petting zoo. Food is available.

Allow 3 hours minimum. Mon.-Fri. 10-6, Sat.-Sun. 11-7, June-Aug.; Sat.-Sun. 11-7 in May and Sept.; Sat.-Sun. 11-6, in Oct. Last safari tour begins 1 hour before closing. Admission $1. Tour $4; ages 2-12, $3. Show $1. Petting zoo $1. Phone (717) 362-9126.

HAMLIN—

see Pocono Mountains Area p. 148.

HANOVER (I-8) pop. 14,400, elev. 599'

Founded by Col. Richard McAllister, Hanover was known as both "McAllister's Town," for its founder, and "Rogue's Roost," for the many outlaws who migrated to the area due to the lack of law enforcement that resulted from the Pennsylvania-Maryland boundary dispute.

On June 30, 1863, the first Civil War battle north of the Mason-Dixon Line was fought nearby when Union generals Hugh Kilpatrick and George Custer defeated Confederate general J.E.B. Stuart and prevented him from reaching Gettysburg until the day after that major battle.

Hanover is the base for several industries which produce such goods as yarns, furniture and textiles. The city's most famous product, however, is horses. Just south on SR 194 is Hanover Shoe Farms, one of the largest Standardbred horse breeders in the world. The 4,000-acre farm, founded in 1926, is home to some 1,800 horses, many of which are record-breaking trotters and pacers. The grounds and buildings are open for self-guiding tours.

Two miles east of town is Codorus State Park *(see Recreation Chart)*, which offers a 1,275-acre lake with 26 miles of shoreline, swimming, boating, fishing, camping and picnic facilities. Also in the area are nature trails and snowmobiling and tobogganing facilities.

Hanover Area Chamber of Commerce: 146 Carlisle St., Hanover, PA 17331; phone (717) 637-6130.

BASILICA OF THE SACRED HEART OF JESUS—*see McSherrystown p. 94.*

UTZ POTATO CHIPS, 900 High St., allows visitors to observe the potato chip production process from an elevated, glass-enclosed observation gallery in their 500,000-square-foot plant. Allow 1 hour minimum. Mon.-Thurs. 8-4. Free. Phone (717) 637-6644.

HARMONY—

see Pittsburgh and Vicinity p. 144.

HARRISBURG (H-7) pop. 52,400, elev. 358'

Around 1710 John Harris established a trading post in the area that is now Harrisburg; in 1733 he obtained a grant of 800 acres of land. His son, John Harris Jr., began operating a ferry across the river in 1753 and had William Maclay, Pennsylvania's first U.S. senator, plat the town in 1785. A few years later he refused to sell land to the legislature until the name of the town was changed from Louisburg, for Louis XVI, to Harrisburg.

Incorporated as a borough in 1791, Harrisburg was chosen as the site of the state capital in 1812, and within several years the removal of the capital from Lancaster was accomplished. Today's downtown Capitol Complex includes the ornate capitol building, the State Museum of Pennsylvania, plazas and fountains, and landscaped areas open to the public.

Paxton Presbyterian Church, at Paxtang Boulevard and Sharon Street, is one of the oldest Presbyterian churches still in use in the United States. The present structure dates from 1740. In the sanctuary are the baptismal font and pulpit light holder that have been in use for more than 200 years. The archives contains a pewter communion set that was used as early as 1734.

The adjacent cemetery, which dates from the early 1700s, contains the graves of John Harris Jr.; Rev. John Elder, the "fighting parson" of the Revolution; and William Maclay. A brochure describing a self-guiding tour of the graveyard is available.

The Fire Museum, at 1820 N. 4th St., houses major exhibits of antique firefighting gear and artifacts. For sports enthusiasts, the Harrisburg Heat, an NPSL indoor soccer league franchise, entertains fans; phone (717) 783-3071 for more information.

City Island is located in the middle of the Susquehanna River across from downtown. Owned

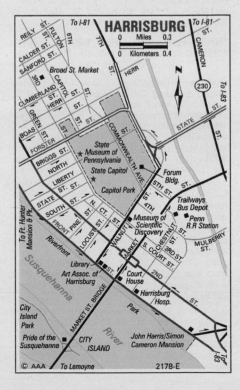

and operated by the Parks and Recreation Department of the City of Harrisburg, this natural park setting offers nature trails, a swimming beach and a playground. Also in the park are commercial amusement and recreational facilities, including games by a AA league baseball team, the Harrisburg Senators, an affiliate of the Montréal Expos. The island also is the site of special events.

The Capital Area Greenbelt, a 20-mile parkway used for bicycling, jogging, walking and nature studies, loops around the city and passes through many of the city's scenic parks. Reservoir Park, 21st and Walnut streets, has art galleries, gardens, plazas, fountains, playgrounds, basketball courts and other facilities. Riverfront Park *(see attraction listing)*, along a 5-mile stretch of scenic waterfront, features sunken gardens, public art and various memorials. Other recreational facilities are in Italian Lake Park, 3rd and Division streets. Phone (717) 255-3020 for more information.

The Pennsylvania Farm Show Building covers 14 acres at Cameron and Maclay street. Among the many events held are the Pennsylvania Farm Show and the Auto Show in January, the Eastern Sportsman Show in February, the Zembo Shrine Circus in April and the Pennsylvania National Horse Show in October.

Center City, City Island and City-Wide Sites brochures are available free by calling or writing the Mayor's Office, 10 N. 2nd St., Harrisburg, PA 17101; phone (717) 255-3040.

Harrisburg-Hershey-Carlisle Tourism Agency: 4211 Trindle Rd., Camp Hill, PA 17011; phone (717) 975-8161 or (800) 995-0969.

Shopping areas: Shopping areas include Kline Village Shopping Center, in the 100 block of S. 25th Street, which houses more than 45 stores. Downtown's Strawberry Square, N. 3rd and Walnut streets, offers more than 85 shops, restaurants and galleries. The other 200 shops, restaurants and galleries in downtown Harrisburg provide retail diversity. Uptown Plaza, N. 7th and Division streets, features more than 35 specialty stores.

Two local malls are Colonial Park, US 22 and Colonial Road, and Harrisburg East at I-83 and Paxton Street. The former has more than 70 stores, including The Bon Ton, Boscov's and Sears; the latter offers more than 90 stores, among them Hecht's, JCPenney and Lord & Taylor. Nearby Camp Hill has two other major malls: Camp Hill Mall at 32nd Street and Trindle Road with Boscov's and Wards, and Capital City at the Highland Park exit off US 15 with Hecht's and Sears.

For those seeking an escape from the present, The Broad Street Market is open Thursday and Friday 7-5, Saturday 7-4. This farmer's market, which sells fresh produce, meat, poultry, confections and food, has been operating since the Civil War and is housed in two buildings dating from 1863 and the 1880s. The market is one-half mile north of the Capitol Complex, on Verbeke Street between Third and Sixth streets.

ART ASSOCIATION OF HARRISBURG, 21 N. Front St. across from Riverfront Park, is housed in the Italianate Gov. Findlay Mansion. Five galleries present works by various regional and national artists in all styles and media artists. Mon.-Thurs. 9-8, Fri. 9-4, Sat. 10-4, Sun. noon-3; closed major holidays. Free. Phone (717) 236-1432.

FORT HUNTER MANSION AND PARK is 6 mi. n. on Front St. overlooking the Susquehanna River Valley. Built in 1787 on the site of old Fort Hunter and enlarged in 1814, the stone home is decorated with 19th-century items including pewter, pitchers, furniture, costumes, toys and the original fireplace. A 35-acre park surrounds the mansion and includes other historic buildings, playgrounds, picnic facilities and nature trails.

Allow 1 hour minimum. Tues.-Sat. 10-4:30, Sun. noon-4:30, May-Nov.; Tues.-Sun. noon-7, Dec. 1-23. Admission $4; over 60, $3; ages 6-17, $2. Phone (717) 599-5751.

JOHN HARRIS/SIMON CAMERON MANSION, between Mary and Washington sts. at 219 S. Front St., was built by the city's founder in 1766 and enlarged in 1863 by Simon Cameron, a former U.S. senator and President Lincoln's first Secretary of War. Exhibits highlight local history and art. Guided 1-hour tours are available Tues.-Sat. 10-4; closed Thanksgiving and Dec. 25-Jan. 1. Library open Mon.-Fri. 1-4; archives open Mon.-Thurs. 1-4. Admission $7; senior citizens, $6; ages 6-15, $4. Reservations are recommended. Phone (717) 233-3462.

MUSEUM OF SCIENTIFIC DISCOVERY, 3rd and Walnut sts. in Strawberry Square, is a hands-on science center with more than 100 exhibits covering a wide range of scientific topics. The museum also offers themed areas, special programs and demonstrations. Allow 2 hours minimum. Tues.-Fri. 9-5, Sat. 10-5, Sun. noon-5; closed most holidays. Admission $5; over 60 and ages 3-17, $4. Under 12 must be accompanied by an adult. AE, DS, MC, VI. Phone (717) 233-7969.

PRIDE OF THE SUSQUEHANNA, Market St. Bridge to City Island, offers a cruise of the Susquehanna River on an authentic paddlewheeler. A history of the city and island is given on the 40-minute narrated cruise. Dinner and special event cruises also are available. Departures Tues.-Sun. on the hour noon-3; schedule varies in May and day after Labor Day-Oct. 31. Fare $4.95; ages 3-12, $3. Wed. fare $4.25; ages 3-12, $2.50. Reservations are required for dinner and special event cruises. Phone (717) 234-6500.

RIVERFRONT PARK, on the Capital Area Greenbelt, extends 5 mi. along the e. bank of the Susquehanna River, bordering Front St. The area contains war memorials and a sunken flower garden. At the foot of a bank on the riverside is a promenade where "Harrisburg's front steps" descend to the water's edge.

★ **STATE CAPITOL** is on Capitol Hill. A magnificent building in a 13-acre park, the Capitol covers 2 acres and contains more than 600 rooms. The 272-foot dome, bronze doors, statuary, mural paintings and stained-glass windows are notable features. The marble grand staircase is designed after the one in the Paris Grand Opera House. Flanking the central entrance are two groups of statuary by the Pennsylvania-born sculptor George Grey Barnard. The Welcome Center, in the East Wing of the Capitol, offers 18 exhibits.

Thirty-minute guided tours are offered every half-hour Mon.-Fri. 8:30-4, on the hour Sat.-Sun. and holidays 9-11 and 1-4. Welcome Center open Mon.-Fri. 8:30-4:30; closed holidays. Free. Phone (717) 787-6810 or (800) 868-7672.

★ **STATE MUSEUM OF PENNSYLVANIA,** on Third St. between North and Forster sts., chronicles Pennsylvania's history from the Earth's beginning to the present. Exhibits relate to Earth science, dinosaurs, natural science, archeology, military and political history, industry, technology and fine art. "The Battle of Gettysburg: Pickett's Charge" is displayed; the painting is said to be one of the world's largest. A planetarium also is available.

Allow 2 hours minimum. Tues.-Sat. 9-5, Sun. noon-5; phone for holiday schedule. Planetarium shows Sat.-Sun. at 1 and 2:30. Museum free. Planetarium $2, over 60 and children $1.50. Phone (717) 787-4978.

HAZLETON (F-10) pop. 24,700, elev. 1,624'

According to local legend, a deer pawing the earth uncovered the rich veins of anthracite coal on Spring Mountain in 1818. By 1837 Hazleton was founded, as more and more miners migrated to the area. After the Civil War mining was resumed on an even larger scale, until finally both the demand and supply waned. With an eye to the future, a community industrial development group known as "Can Do" formed in 1956; since then more than 30 industries have moved to the area.

Just northeast of town on SR 940 is the Sacred Heart Shrine, with depictions of the life of Christ on landscaped grounds; picnicking is permitted. The Greater Hazleton Historical Society Museum, 55 N. Wyoming St., contains exhibits relating to American Indians, the mining and railroad industries, sports, the military and the life of actor and Hazleton-area native Jack Palance.

Greater Hazleton Chamber of Commerce: 1 S. Church St., Hazleton, PA 18201; phone (717) 455-1508.

[SAVE] **ECKLEY MINERS' VILLAGE** is 9 mi. e. off SR 940, following signs. This living-history museum is a 19th-century anthracite mining village with 50 buildings. Exhibits, pictures and slide shows in the visitor center depict the lives of miners and their families. Some houses not open to the public are occupied by retired miners. Guided walking tours are available.

Allow 2 hours minimum. Mon.-Sat. 9-5, Sun. noon-5; closed holidays, except Memorial Day, July 4 and Labor Day. Guided walking tours offered several times daily, Memorial Day weekend-Labor Day. Admission $3.50; over 60, $3; ages 6-12, $1.50; family rate $8.50. Phone (717) 636-2070.

HELLERTOWN (G-11) pop. 5,700, elev. 278'

LOST RIVER CAVERNS AND THE GILMAN MUSEUM are .5 mi. e. of SR 412. The limestone cavern contains five chambers of crystal formations. One chamber, the Crystal Chapel, is used for weddings and baptisms. The formations include stalagmites, stalactites, flowstone and dripstone. Displays include a tropical garden, lapidary shop, museum of natural history, rocks, minerals, gems and antique weapons. Picnicking is permitted.

Allow 1 hour minimum. Daily 9-6, Memorial Day weekend-Labor Day; 9-5, rest of year. Closed Jan. 1, Thanksgiving and Dec. 25. Admission $7.50; ages 3-12, $3.75. MC, VI. Phone (610) 838-8767.

HERMITAGE (E-1) pop. 15,300

THE AVENUE OF 444 FLAGS is in Hillcrest Memorial Park at 2619 E. State St. A paved avenue is lined with 444 American flags, one for each day that 53 American hostages were held captive in Iran under the reign of the Ayatollah Khomeini. The flags fly 24 hours a day as a symbol of hope and freedom. A monument and eternal flame are dedicated to the eight U.S. servicemen who died trying to rescue the hostages in April 1980.

American Freedom Museum, at the visitor center directly across from the Avenue of 444 Flags, offers a photojournalistic review of the events occurring between Nov. 4, 1979, and Jan. 20, 1981. A videotape presentation documents this time of patriotic resurgence. Guided tours are available. Allow 30 minutes minimum. Daily 10-5, May-Dec. Donations. Phone (724) 346-0444.

KRAYNAK'S SANTA'S CHRISTMASLAND AND EASTER BUNNY LANE are on SR 18, then left .5 mi. at jct. with US 62 Bus. Rte. Santa's Christmasland has more than 60 decorated trees. Animated figures depict religious themes, traditional Christmas scenes and favorite childhood characters. Easter Bunny Lane features trees blooming with blossoms and mini-lights. Animated figures, bunnies and chicks accent the Easter scenes.

Allow 30 minutes minimum. Santa's Christmasland open Mon.-Sat. 9-9, Sun. 10-6, day after

Labor Day-Dec. 24; Easter Bunny Lane open Mon.-Sat. 9-9, Sun. 10-6, mid-Feb. through mid-Apr. Closed Easter. Free. Phone (724) 347-4511.

HERSHEY (H-8) pop. 7,400

The aroma of chocolate pervades Hershey, a name synonymous with the confection. In the rich Lebanon Valley, the town was founded in 1903 by Milton S. Hershey, who planned and built an attractive industrial community. The Hershey Foods Corp. factory is one of the largest chocolate and cocoa plants in the world.

Pennsylvania State University's Milton S. Hershey Medical Center, just off US 322 at 500 University Dr., is on a 550-acre campus that includes the hospital, a medical sciences building, a biomedical research building, outpatient physicians center, animal research farm, fitness center, a women's and community health center, and magnetic resonance imaging building. Pennsylvania State University's College of Medicine also is at this location.

Of interest in the area is the State Police Academy, 1 mile northeast on SR 743, which offers tours by appointment.

Harrisburg-Hershey-Carlisle Tourism and Convention Bureau: 4211 Trindle Rd., Camp Hill, PA 17011; phone (717) 975-8161 or (800) 995-0969.

CHIMNEYS GALLERY 444, LTD., 575 E. Chocolate Ave., features works by local artist Bruce Johnson. Works include his well-known "Statements," humorous depictions of the human condition. Mon.-Sat. 10-5, Sun. noon-5. Free. Phone (717) 533-0444.

FOUNDERS HALL, 1.25 mi. e. of jct. SR 743 and US 322, is a tribute to Milton Hershey and his wife, Catherine, founders of the Milton Hershey School. The building includes a banquet hall, chapel/auditorium and rotunda. A 22-minute film about the founding of the school is shown daily. Self-guiding tours are available. Allow 1 hour minimum. Daily 10-4, mid-Mar. through Dec. 31; 10-3, rest of year. Closed most holidays. Free. Phone (717) 520-2000.

SAVE HERSHEY GARDENS, across from Hotel Hershey, is a 23-acre botanical garden with seasonal floral displays May through October. Featured are more than 7,000 roses of 275 different varieties, which bloom June through September. Several theme gardens include a Japanese garden, a garden of ornamental grasses and a collection of hollies and dwarf conifers. Seasonal displays feature spring flowering bulbs, annuals and chrysanthemums.

Allow 1 hour minimum. Daily 9-6, mid-May through Oct. 31 (also Fri.-Sat. 6-8 p.m., Memorial Day-Labor Day). Admission $5; over 62, $4.25; ages 3-15, $2.50; family rate $13.50. Phone (717) 534-3492.

SAVE ★ HERSHEY MUSEUM, next to Hersheypark Arena, highlights the life of philanthropist Milton S. Hershey, the development of his chocolate empire and local history. Other exhibits chronicle the settlement and growth of south central Pennsylvania by the Pennsylvania Dutch. The hands-on Discovery Room allows the younger set to explore everyday life in the 1800s.

Allow 1 hour minimum. Daily 10-6, Memorial Day-Labor Day; 10-5, rest of year. Closed Jan. 1, Thanksgiving and Dec. 25. Admission $5; over 62, $4.50; ages 3-15, $2.50. Phone (717) 534-3439.

★ HERSHEYPARK, just off SR 743 and US 422, has more than 50 rides, including six roller coasters, six water rides, and more than 24 children's rides. Great Bear is an inverted steel looping roller coaster, while Wildcat is a twisting, turning wooden roller coaster that crosses over and under itself 20 times. Daily live entertainment includes a marine mammal presentation, numerous song and dance reviews, and top-name entertainers.

Hersheypark Arena seats 7,300 spectators for hockey, concerts, ice shows and other events. Public skating is available in season; phone (717) 534-3911.

Allow 4 hours minimum. Open daily at 10, mid-May through Labor Day; Sat.-Sun. at 10, selected weekends in May and Sept. Closing hours vary. All-inclusive admission, including Zooamerica, $29.95; over 54 and ages 3-8, $16.95. Evening rates available. AE, DS, MC, VI. Phone (800) 437-7439.

Zooamerica North American Wildlife Park, on Park Ave. opposite Hersheypark, is an 11-acre zoo depicting regions of North America and the plants and animals native to each. Indoor and

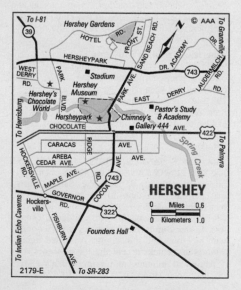

outdoor exhibits house more than 200 animals of 75 species. Picnicking is permitted.

Allow 1 hour minimum. Daily 10-8, mid-June through Labor Day; 10-5, rest of year. Closed Jan. 1, Thanksgiving and Dec. 25. Included in Hersheypark admission when entering by park's front gate, or separately $5; over 54, $4.50; ages 3-12, $3.75. AE, DS, MC, VI. Phone (717) 534-3860.

★ HERSHEY'S CHOCOLATE WORLD, Park Blvd., is the official visitor center of the Hershey Foods Corp. and the information center for the Hershey area. A 12-minute automated tour ride explains the chocolate-making process from harvesting the cocoa bean to packaging the finished product. There also are indoor tropical gardens and shops. Food is available.

Allow 30 minutes minimum. Daily 9-5; closed Dec. 25. Hours vary; phone ahead. Free. Free parking is available at the Park Blvd. entrance. Phone (717) 534-4900.

INDIAN ECHO CAVERNS, off US 322, 3 mi. w., offers a 45-minute guided, narrated tour amid the natural beauty of stalagmites, stalactites, columns, flowstone and lakes. The caverns are electronically lighted, contain level pathways and maintain a constant temperature of 52 degrees Fahrenheit. Visitors may pan for gemstones at Gem Mill Junction or ride in a horse-drawn carriage. Food is available.

Daily 9-6, Memorial Day-Labor Day; 10-4, rest of year. Closed Jan. 1, Thanksgiving and Dec. 25. Admission $8; over 62, $7; ages 3-11, $4. DS, MC, VI. Phone (717) 566-8131.

PASTOR'S STUDY AND ACADEMY, 248 E. Derry Rd. at Derry Presbyterian Church, is one of Hershey's most historic buildings. Erected in 1724, it has been enclosed in glass and can only be viewed from the outside.

HOLTWOOD—
see Pennsylvania Dutch Country p. 100.

HONESDALE—
see Pocono Mountains Area p. 148.

HOPEWELL FURNACE NATIONAL HISTORIC SITE (H-10)

One of the finest examples of an early American 18th- and 19th-century iron-making community is the 848-acre Hopewell Furnace National Historic Site, about 5 miles south of Birdsboro on SR 345. The site also is accessible via the Morgantown exit off the Pennsylvania Turnpike, using SRs 23 and 345.

Englishman William Bird was prominent in the early iron industry in Pennsylvania. His son Mark built Hopewell Furnace on French Creek in 1771. Around the furnace developed a small industrial settlement where many of the employees lived in tenant houses. A resident manager lived on the site in the ironmaster's mansion.

The furnace cast pig iron, hollowware, stoves and many other items; during the Revolutionary War it produced cannon and shot. The furnace operated until 1883, when more advanced technology made it unprofitable.

Many of the structures have been restored and refurnished. The water wheel, blast machinery, bridge house, cooling shed, barn, store, ironmaster's mansion and tenant houses can be seen. The ruin of an 1853 anthracite furnace has been uncovered and stabilized.

A visitor center features an audiovisual program and an exhibit area with original iron castings produced at Hopewell Furnace and tools associated with the operation of 18th- and 19th-century cold-blast charcoal furnaces. Allow 2 hours minimum. Daily 9-5; closed Jan. 1, Martin Luther King Jr.'s Birthday, President's Day, Veterans Day, Thanksgiving and Dec. 25. Admission $4, under 17 free, family rate $10. An additional fee may be charged for some programs and special events. Phone (610) 582-8773 or 582-2093.

HORSHAM—
see Philadelphia and Vicinity p. 125.

HUNTINGDON (G-6) pop. 6,800, elev. 630'

Near Huntingdon is Raystown Lake (see Recreation Chart), the largest lake wholly within

Pennsylvania. Recreation available at the lake includes hunting, boating, camping, swimming and fishing, especially for small- and large-mouth bass, striped bass and lake trout. Wildlife inhabiting the area includes deer, turkeys, grouse and squirrels.

Raystown Country Visitors Bureau: 241 Mifflin St., Huntingdon, PA 16652; phone (814) 643-3577 or (888) 729-7869. *See color ad.*

JUNIATA COLLEGE, n. edge of town, was founded in 1876. The L.A. Beeghly Library has an extensive collection of Pennsylvania-German printing and publications. The Shoemaker Galleries offer regular exhibits of paintings, prints and photographs; the Cloister exemplifies the Pennsylvania-German style of architecture.

Galleries open Mon.-Fri. 9-5, Sat.-Sun. by appointment. Library open Mon.-Thurs. 8 a.m.-midnight, Fri. 8-8, Sat. 10-10, Sun. noon-midnight, during school sessions. Free. Phone (814) 643-4310.

SAVE LINCOLN CAVERNS, 3 mi. w. on US 22, offers 1-hour interpretive tours through two crystal caverns that display a variety of formations. Gem panning is available, and nature trails are on the grounds. Picnicking is permitted. Guided haunted cavern tours are offered the last four weekends in October.

Allow 1 hour minimum. Guided tours daily 9-7, July 1-Labor Day; daily 9-6, Memorial Day weekend-June 30; daily 9-5, Apr. 1-day before Memorial Day weekend and Sept.-Oct.; daily 9-4 in Mar. and Nov.; Sat.-Sun. 9-4, in Dec. Fee $8; over 65, $7; ages 4-14, $4.50. DS, MC, VI. Phone (814) 643-0268.

SEVEN POINTS CRUISES, Seven Points Marina on Raystown Lake, offers 90-minute sightseeing cruises with music and historical narration aboard the *Raystown Belle* and *Raystown Queen.* Dinner cruises also are available July through August. Departures Mon.-Fri. at 2, Sat.-Sun. at 1, 2:30 and 4, June 22-Aug. 31; Sat.-Sun. and holidays at 2, May 1-June 21; Sat.-Sun. at 2 with a minimum of 10 persons, Sept.-Oct. Reservations are required. Fare $7; over 65, $6; under 12, $3. Phone (814) 658-3074.

SAVE SWIGART MUSEUM, 4 mi. e. on US 22, contains restored antique automobiles, including a 1909 Model T Ford touring car, a 1920 Carroll and a 1930 Model J Duesenberg. Displays include U.S. and foreign license plates, more than 2,000 radiator emblems and collections of horns, lights and other accessories. Allow 1 hour minimum. Daily 9-5, Memorial Day-Oct. 31; by appointment rest of year. Admission $4; over 65, $3.50; ages 6-12, $2. Phone (814) 643-0285.

INDIANA (G-3) pop. 15,200, elev. 1,310′

Indiana was founded in 1805 when George Clymer of Philadelphia, a signer of the Declaration of Independence, donated 250 acres of land for county buildings. Later, before the Civil War Indiana became an important station on the underground railroad. In more recent history, the town was the birthplace and childhood home of actor Jimmy Stewart. A bronze statue of the actor, unveiled for his 75th birthday, stands on the lawn of the Indiana County Courthouse on Philadelphia Street.

Northern Indiana County is Amish country. Horse-drawn buggies are a common sight, especially in nearby Smicksburg.

Two historic buildings can be seen on the campus of Indiana University of Pennsylvania. John Sutton Hall, built in 1875, now houses administrative and faculty offices. Breezedale, a recently restored mansion, serves as the alumni center. The University Museum in John Sutton Hall has changing art exhibits and displays; phone (724) 357-6495.

Known for its Christmas tree production, the county exports more than a million trees each year. Recreational opportunities include the Ghost Town Trail, which offers 16 miles of hiking and bicycling. The area also presents many opportunities for hunting, fishing and boating. For information about game areas phone the Pennsylvania Game Commission regional office at (724) 238-9523, or (800) 243-8519 in Pa. For fishing information and boating regulations phone the Pennsylvania Fish and Boat Commission regional office at (814) 445-8974.

Indiana County Tourist Bureau: 1019 Philadelphia St., Indiana, PA 15701; phone (724) 463-7505.

THE JIMMY STEWART MUSEUM, on the third floor of the Indiana Free Library at 845 Philadelphia St., is dedicated to the life and career of film, radio and television star Jimmy Stewart. Displays include original movie posters; family photographs; mementos from his personal life, military duty and career; and various citations and awards, including the Oscar for his role in "The Philadelphia Story." Visitors can view some of Stewart's film clips and documentaries in a 1930s-style vintage theater.

Allow 2 hours minimum. Mon.-Sat. 10-5, Sun. noon-5; closed Easter, Thanksgiving, Dec. 24-25 and 30-31. Admission $5; over 62 and military and students with ID, $4; ages 7-17, $3. MC, VI. Phone (724) 349-6112 or (800) 835-4669. *See ad p. 308.*

INTERCOURSE—
see Pennsylvania Dutch Country p. 100.

IVYLAND—
see Philadelphia and Vicinity p. 125.

JAMESTOWN (E-1) pop. 800, elev. 990′
PYMATUNING DEER PARK, .5 mi. e. of US 322 on SR 58, is an animal park containing bears, camels, donkeys, llamas, mountain lions, monkeys, ostriches, tigers and six species of deer. A highlight is the petting zoo. Visitors can purchase food and feed the animals. Pony and train rides also are available. Allow 30 minutes minimum. Mon.-Fri. 10-5, Sat.-Sun. and holidays 10-6, Memorial Day weekend-Labor Day; phone for weekend fall hours. Admission $4; over 65, $3.50; children $3. Phone (724) 932-3200.

JEANNETTE—
see Pittsburgh and Vicinity p. 144.

JIM THORPE—
see Pocono Mountains Area p. 148.

JOHNSTOWN (H-4) pop. 28,100, elev. 1,178′

Four times disastrous floods have claimed Johnstown, which is in a deep, irregular valley formed by Stony Creek and the Little Conemaugh and Conemaugh rivers. The first two floods, in 1862 and 1889, were a result of the collapse of the South Fork Dam, about 12 miles east on the Conemaugh. Some of the older buildings still show high water marks of the 1889 disaster, one of the country's worst peacetime catastrophes. Debris held behind a stone bridge in the downtown area caught fire and added to the losses.

In 1936 a third flood caused a great deal of damage to the city and its environs. A fourth flood occurred in July 1977, when heavy rains caused rivers and streams to overflow throughout the Conemaugh Valley. Once again damage was severe.

Conemaugh Gap, a gorge cut by the Conemaugh River as it passes through Laurel Hill Ridge Mountain, extends 7 miles and is about 1,700 feet deep.

Culturally speaking, the Pasquerilla Performing Arts Center at the University of Pittsburgh Johnstown Campus stages plays, dance performances and concerts as well as productions especially for children. The Johnstown Symphony Orchestra also provides musical entertainment; their 1,000-seat theater is at the performing arts center.

The Johnstown FolkFest is a 3-day heritage festival held Labor Day weekend; the working-class neighborhood the festival is held in was the first home for many immigrants who came to the city in the 19th and early 20th centuries to work in the coal mines and steel mills. Guided tours of historic churches are offered, and music of all types, ethnic food and children's programs are featured. Another popular event is the Arts Festival, held the Saturday and Sunday of Labor Day weekend. The festival highlight is the diversity of crafts displayed by 130 traditional craftsmen.

Greater Johnstown-Cambria Convention and Visitors Bureau: 111 Market St., Johnstown, PA 15901; phone (814) 536-7993 or (800) 237-8590. *See ad.*

Shopping areas: The Johnstown Galleria, SR 219, has more than 100 specialty stores, including Bon Ton, Boscov, JCPenney and Sears. In addition, numerous shops line Scalp Avenue.

GRANDVIEW CEMETERY contains the Unknown Plot, where 777 unidentified victims of the 1889 flood are buried. Daily 8-dusk. Free.

INCLINED PLANE, SR 56 and Johns St., is 996 feet long with a grade of 71 percent, making it one of the steepest passenger inclined planes in the country. It connects the central part of Johnstown with a residential suburb on a plateau 502 feet above the city. Both cars and pedestrians are carried. An observation platform at the top overlooks the city. Food is available.

Allow 30 minutes minimum. Mon.-Thurs. 6:30 a.m.-10 p.m., Fri.-Sat. 7:30 a.m.-midnight, Sun. and holidays 9 a.m.-10 p.m., Memorial Day weekend-Labor Day; daily 6:30 a.m.-10 p.m., rest of year. Closed Jan. 1 and Dec. 25. Round-trip fare $3; ages 6-12, $1.75. Cars, vans and trucks $5 (includes driver; occupants' fares additional); motorcycles $3 (plus riders' fare). Over 65 with ID ride free 9-3:30 and 6:30 to closing. Phone (814) 536-1816. *See ad.*

SAVE ★ JOHNSTOWN FLOOD MUSEUM, 304 Washington St. at Walnut St., features the 26-minute, 1989 Academy Award-winning documentary film "The Johnstown Flood" shown hourly. Other multimedia exhibits depict the cause of and the course of events prior to, during and after the devastating flood of May 31, 1889. A 24-foot, 3-D relief map with sound effects and fiber-optic animation shows the path of the 40-foot wall of water which traveled through the Conemaugh Valley, destroying everything in its path.

Allow 1 hour, 30 minutes minimum. Sun.-Thurs. 10-5, Fri.-Sat. 10-7, May-Oct.; daily 10-5, rest of year. Closed Jan. 1, Thanksgiving and Dec. 25. Admission $4; over 65, $3.25; ages

6-18, $2.50. DS, MC, VI. Phone (814) 539-1889. *See ad p. 89.*

JOHNSTOWN FLOOD NATIONAL MEMORIAL, 10 mi. n. via US 219, then 1.5 mi. e. on SR 869 and 1.5 mi. n. on Lake Rd., following signs, is on the site of the former South Fork Dam. When the dam broke and sent a 40-foot wall of water crashing through the Conemaugh Valley in 1889, Johnstown was devastated and more than 2,200 people died in about 10 minutes.

The visitor center presents a 35-minute film entitled "Black Friday" and contains a model of the dam as well as exhibits about local geography and events leading up to the flood. Ranger-conducted programs are held in summer. The dam site has a picnic area and walking trails.

Allow 1 hour minimum. Daily 9-6, Memorial Day weekend-Labor Day; 9-5, rest of year. Closed Dec. 25. Admission $2. Phone (814) 495-4643. *See ad p. 89.*

KENNETT SQUARE—

see Philadelphia and Vicinity p. 125.

KLEINFELTERSVILLE (H-9) pop. 300

MIDDLE CREEK WILDLIFE MANAGEMENT AREA, 2 mi. s. on Hopeland Rd., is administered by the Pennsylvania Game Commission. The 6,254-acre area, which includes a visitor center, provides a habitat for waterfowls and wildlife. Nature trails also are available. Visitor center open Tues.-Sat. 8-4, Sun. noon-5, Mar.-Nov. Free. Phone (717) 733-1512.

KUTZTOWN (G-10) pop. 4,700

Kutztown was settled in 1771 by Pennsylvania Germans and named for founder George Kutz. An 1892 schoolhouse at White Oak and Normal avenues portrays a classroom and library of the era. It is open by appointment; phone (610) 683-7697. Also in town is Kutztown State University.

In late June and early July the town celebrates its German heritage during the Pennsylvania German Festival, complete with food, crafts and demonstrations.

Shopping areas: Renningers Antique & Farmers Market, 740 Noble St., is open weekends. Antique and collectors' shows with more than 1,200 dealers from 42 states take place the last Thursday-Saturday in April, June and September; phone (717) 385-0104 Mon.-Thurs. or (610) 683-6848 Fri.-Sat.

CRYSTAL CAVE, 2 mi. n. off US 222, following signs, is named for the crystalline formations found in the cavern. Also on the grounds are a Pennsylvania Dutch food center, ice cream parlor, miniature golf course, theater, museum, rock shop and nature trail. Picnic facilities are available.

Allow 1 hour, 30 minutes minimum. Mon.-Fri. 9-6, Sat.-Sun. 9-7, Memorial Day-Labor Day; Mon.-Fri. 9-5, Sat.-Sun. 9-6, day after Labor Day-Sept. 30; daily 9-5, Mar. 1-day before Memorial Day and Oct.-Nov. Admission $8; ages 4-11, $4.75. Miniature golf $2.75. MC, VI. Phone (610) 683-6765.

LACKAWAXEN—
see Pocono Mountains Area p. 149.

LAHASKA—
see Philadelphia and Vicinity p. 126.

LANCASTER—
see Pennsylvania Dutch Country p. 101.

LANGHORNE—
see Philadelphia and Vicinity p. 126.

LAUGHLINTOWN (H-4)

SAVE **THE COMPASS INN MUSEUM,** on US 30, is a restored 1799 stagecoach stop. A reconstructed barn displays a Conestoga wagon, stagecoach and tools. A blacksmith shop and cookhouse contain implements of the time. Costumed docents conduct tours of the complex. Allow 1 hour, 30 minutes minimum. Tues.-Sat. 11-4, Sun. noon-4, May-Oct. Candlelight tours Sat.-Sun. 2-5, in Nov.; Sat.-Sun. 2-8, Dec. 1 to mid-Dec. Admission $4; ages 6-16, $2. Phone (724) 238-4983.

THE LAUREL HIGHLANDS

The Laurel Highlands encompasses a five-county area in the Allegheny foothills of southwestern Pennsylvania. The region that once hid the exclusive resorts of wealthy Pittsburgh industrialists now yields to the modern vacationer a wide range of activities and experiences.

Excellent white-water rafting is possible on the Youghiogheny River, which runs southeastward from McKeesport to the Maryland border *(see Ohiopyle p. 96);* boating on Conemaugh Lake and Youghiogheny Reservoir also are popular. The Laurel and Chestnut ridges of the Allegheny Mountains provide for good mountain-stream fishing and hunting in season and downhill and cross-country skiing in winter. The

region also offers more than 25 hiking, bicycling and bridle trails and about 30 golf courses.

The Laurel Highlands is especially scenic in the spring and fall. Wildflowers are in bloom mid-April to mid-May; mountain laurel blooms at higher elevations for about 3 weeks in June. The fall foliage fireworks explode mid- to late October. Viewing is best in Forbes State Forest in the central highlands and from Mount Davis, the state's highest point, north of Springs. The scenic Pennsylvania Turnpike (I-70/76) traverses the region from east to west.

Places and towns in the Laurel Highlands listed individually are Brownsville, Cresson, Dawson, Donegal, Fort Necessity National Battlefield, Greensburg, Jeannette, Johnstown, Laughlintown, Ligonier, Loretto, Mount Pleasant, Ohiopyle, Point Marion, St. Boniface, Scottdale, Somerset, Springs, Uniontown and Waynesburg.

Laurel Highlands Visitors Bureau: 120 E. Main St., Ligonier, PA 15658; phone (724) 238-5661 or (800) 925-7669.

LAVANSVILLE (H-3) pop. 200

 WINERIES

- **Glades Pike Winery,** 1 mi. w. on SR 31 at 2706 Glades Pike Rd. Tours and tastings daily noon-6, June-Dec.; Thurs.-Mon. noon-6, rest of year. Closed major holidays. Phone (814) 445-3753.

LEBANON (H-9) pop. 24,800, elev. 466′

A community of German agricultural and English industrial origins, Lebanon was founded in 1750 and named after the "White Mountain" of Biblical times.

Lebanon's historic churches include the 1760 Tabor United Church of Christ at 10th and Walnut streets and the 1760 Salem Lutheran Church at 8th and Willow streets. Both churches are open for tours by appointment.

North of Lebanon off SR 72 at Tunnel Hill Road is Union Canal Tunnel, one of the oldest tunnels in the United States. At the time it was completed, the tunneling through 729 feet of solid rock was considered an engineering marvel. The feat completed the canal between Harrisburg and Reading.

Lebanon Valley Chamber of Commerce: 252 N. 8th St., P.O. Box 899, Lebanon, PA 17042; phone (717) 273-3727.

STOY MUSEUM AND HAUCK MEMORIAL LIBRARY, 924 Cumberland St., contains such reconstructed rooms as a drugstore, doctor's office, one-room schoolhouse, toy shop and general store, as well as exhibits about early local industries and crafts. The front part of the building, constructed in 1773 as a home, was later used as the county courthouse, where James Buchanan, the 15th U.S. president, practiced law as a young attorney. Guided tours are available.

Allow 1 hour, 30 minutes minimum. Museum and library open Tues.-Wed. and Fri. 12:30-4:30, Thurs. 10-4:30, Sun. 1-4:30, Mon. 1-8; closed holidays and Sun.-Mon. of holiday weekends. Last tour begins 1 hour, 30 minutes before closing. Admission $3; over 65, $2; ages 5-18, $1. Phone (717) 272-1473.

LEHIGHTON—
see Pocono Mountains Area p. 149.

LEWISBURG (F-8) pop. 5,800, elev. 460'

Lewisburg, on the West Branch of the Susquehanna River, is noted for its late Federal and Victorian architecture. Lewisburg also is a college town: Bucknell University is a private liberal arts college.

Lewisburg is the home of White Deer Station, headquarters for the Central Pennsylvania Chapter of the National Railway Historical Society. The station has information about and relics from the railroad era of the central Susquehanna Valley.

Union County Chamber of Commerce: 219D Hafer Rd., Lewisburg, PA 17837; phone (717) 524-2815.

Self-guiding tours: Brochures describing a walking tour are available from the chamber of commerce.

Shopping areas: An interesting local shopping center is Country Cupboard, 3 miles north of town on SR 15. It offers crafts, gifts, Christmas items and specialty foods. Another unusual collection of shops is Brookpark Farm, 1 mile west of SR 15 on SR 45, offering furniture, rugs, gourmet foods, crafts, antiques, collectibles and Christmas items. Roller Mills Marketplace, 517 St. Mary St., and Roller Mills East, on N. Water St., feature more than 400 antique dealers. Two miles south on SR 15 the handcrafted wares of almost 60 artisans are displayed.

CENTER GALLERY, jct. Moore Ave. and S. 7th St. on the third floor of the Elaine Langone Center on the Bucknell University campus, presents permanent and changing exhibitions. The permanent collections include Renaissance paintings, Oriental pieces and musical instruments from around the world. Allow 30 minutes minimum. Mon.-Fri. 11-5, Sat.-Sun. 1-4; closed holidays. Free. Phone (717) 524-3792.

PACKWOOD HOUSE MUSEUM, 15 N. Water St., built 1796-99, is one of the oldest log structures of its kind in Pennsylvania. The building has evolved into a three-story edifice with 27 rooms that contain a collection of 18th- through 20th-century Americana, especially central Pennsylvanian artifacts. Included in the collection are quilts, coverlets, guns, deeds, painted furniture, paintings, glass and ceramics. The house and

special exhibitions are visited by guided tour only. Tours start at the adjacent Tour Center.

Allow 1 hour minimum. Museum and Tour Center open Tues.-Sat. 10-5, Sun. 1-5; closed holidays. Last tour departs 1 hour before closing. Fee $4; over 62, $3.25; students with ID $1.75; under 6 free. Phone (717) 524-0323

SLIFER HOUSE MUSEUM, 1 mi. n. on US 15, was built 1860-62 and is an excellent example of Victorian architecture. Designed by architect Samuel Sloan, the mansion was built for Eli Slifer, Secretary of Pennsylvania during the Civil War. Victorian furnishings and decorative arts are displayed. Allow 1 hour minimum. Guided tours Tues.-Sun. 1-4, Apr.-Dec.; Tues.-Fri. 1-4, rest of year. Fee $4; over 60, $3.50; ages 10-16, $2. Phone (717) 524-2245.

LEWISTOWN (G-7) pop. 9,300, elev. 495'

Lewistown lies in a scenic region: To the east is Lewistown Narrows, a 6-mile gorge through which the Juniata River flows to meet the Susquehanna. The Stone Arch Bridge, curiously constructed without a keystone, is on the east side of US 22 at the south entrance to town. North of Lewistown is the Seven Mountain District, known for good hunting and fishing. Kishacoquillas Valley, site of an Amish community, is 6 miles north.

The Pennsylvania Fire School is in Lewistown. Firefighters from Pennsylvania and other states attend classes throughout the year.

The original county courthouse, built in the 1800s, is at Monument Square. Near the courthouse at 17 N. Main St. is the McCoy House the 1874 birthplace and home of soldier-statesman Gen. Frank Ross McCoy. The courthouse and McCoy House are home to the Mifflin County Historical Society Museum and Library.

Juniata Valley Area Chamber of Commerce: Monument Sq., Lewistown, PA 17044; phone (717) 248-6713.

LIGONIER (H-4) pop. 1,600

THE COMPASS INN MUSEUM—
see Laughlintown p. 91.

FORBES ROAD GUN MUSEUM, 2.25 mi. n. on SR 711, then 1 mi. e., exhibits firearms dating from 1450 to the present. War relics, mounted animal heads, Indian arrowheads and a butterfly collection also are shown. Guide service is available. Allow 1 hour minimum. Daily 9-5. Admission $1.50; over 62, $1.25; ages 13-16, 75c; ages 6-12, 50c. Phone (724) 238-9544.

FORT LIGONIER, US 30 and SR 711, is a reconstruction of the English fort built in 1758. The fort was abandoned in 1766 after serving as a major English stronghold during the French and Indian War. The museum contains interpretive exhibits from the site, two period rooms and collections of decorative arts. Allow 1 hour minimum. Mon.-Sat. 10-4:30, Sun. noon-4:30, Apr.-Oct. Admission $5; over 62, $4.50; ages 6-14, $2.25. Phone (724) 238-9701.

IDLEWILD PARK, 2.5 mi. w. on US 30, offers amusement rides, miniature golf, waterslides, a swimming pool, live entertainment and picnicking. Gates open Tues.-Sun. at 10, May 30-Aug. 30 (also during Memorial and Labor Day weekends); closing times vary. All-inclusive admission $14.95; over 55, $7.50; under 3 free. Phone (724) 238-3666.

Hootin' Holler is a re-created mining town featuring live entertainment, train rides and Confusion Hill.

Jumpin' Jungle has a pool of balls through which visitors can swim, as well as a treehouse, rope climb, slides, Tarzan swing and raft ride.

Mister Rogers' Neighborhood of Make-Believe takes youngsters on a trolley ride to see life-size puppets, "X" the Owl, Henrietta Pussycat, Lady Elaine Fairchilde and King Friday XIII. There also is the Museum-Go-Round, Royal Castle and Daniel's Clock.

Story Book Forest is a walk-through theme park where live characters depict many familiar nursery rhymes.

LIMERICK—
see Philadelphia and Vicinity p. 126.

LINESVILLE (D-1) pop. 1,200, elev. 1,034'

Pymatuning Reservoir arcs through Crawford County for 16 miles, its south end near Jamestown on US 322 and its northern apex near Linesville on US 6. Its western shore curves into Ohio. Pymatuning State Park *(see Recreation Chart and Jamestown in the AAA Mideastern CampBook)* surrounds the Pennsylvania shoreline.

At the spillway in the park visitors can buy bread to feed the fish and ducks; the site is known as "the place where the ducks walk on the fishes' backs," since the fish are said to be so numerous that the ducks use them as stepping stones to walk across the water. The lake is stocked with bass, bluegill, crappie, muskellunge, perch and walleye. Recreational activities include hunting and fishing.

The upper part of the reservoir near Linesville is a state waterfowl sanctuary. A number of islands mark this part of the reservoir. Events in Linesville include the Ducks Unlimited Festival the third weekend in September.

Shopping areas: Desiderata Farm Mall, off SR 198 on Maples Rd., is a former dairy farm converted into a shopping mall featuring crafts and antiques.

PYMATUNING VISITOR CENTER, 2 mi. s. on Hartstown Rd., features more than 250 mounted birds and animals. The center overlooks Pymatuning Lake and two bald eagle nests. A .25-mile nature trail has labeled exhibits. Allow 1 hour minimum. Mon.-Fri. 8-4, Sat.-Sun. 9-5, Mar.-Oct. Free. Phone (814) 683-5545.

LITITZ—
see Pennsylvania Dutch Country p. 103.

LOCK HAVEN (F-7) pop. 9,200, elev. 563'

Lock Haven was laid out at the site of Fort Reed, which had once protected frontier settlers from the American Indians. The 1778 evacuation of the fort during a fierce Indian raid became known as the "great runaway." During the 19th century Lock Haven was a major lumbering center and an important port on the Pennsylvania Canal.

Clinton County Chamber of Commerce: 151 Susquehanna Ave., Lock Haven, PA 17745; phone (717) 748-5782.

Self-guiding tours: Audio cassettes describing a walking tour of Water Street can be borrowed from the Ross Library on Main Street. The tour takes at least an hour. Tapes are available Mon.-Sat. 9-5 (also Mon. and Thurs. 5-8); phone (717) 748-3321.

Be cautious when driving
in mountainous areas –
there may be sharp curves
or sudden gusts of wind.

HEISEY MUSEUM, 362 E. Water St., is in a restored two-story Victorian house that contains period rooms and furnishings as well as local memorabilia. Allow 30 minutes minimum. Tues.-Fri. 10-4; other times by appointment. Donations. Phone (717) 748-7254.

LONGWOOD—
see Philadelphia and Vicinity p. 126.

LORETTO (G-5) pop. 1,200
SOUTHERN ALLEGHENIES MUSEUM OF ART, on the campus of St. Francis College, displays a fine survey of American art with emphasis on 19th- and 20th-century painting and graphics. Regional and national artists are represented in the permanent collection and changing exhibits. Allow 30 minutes minimum. Mon.-Fri. 10-4, Sat.-Sun. 1:30-4:30. Free. Phone (814) 472-3920.

MANHEIM—
see Pennsylvania Dutch Country p. 104.

MARIETTA—
see Pennsylvania Dutch Country p. 104.

McSHERRYSTOWN (I-8) pop. 2,800
BASILICA OF THE SACRED HEART OF JESUS is 2 mi. n. on Second St. from SR 116. The original 1741 log chapel was replaced in 1787 by the present stone structure. Made a minor basilica in 1962, it contains frescoes, statues and paintings. Allow 30 minutes minimum. Daily dawn-dusk. Free. Phone (717) 637-2721.

MEADVILLE (D-2) pop. 14,300, elev. 1,078′
The invention of the hookless fastener by Whitcomb L. Judson in Chicago came to the attention of Meadville's Col. Lewis Walker in 1893. Impressed by the new idea, Walker persuaded Judson to build a machine to produce the fastener. When Judson lost interest after several years of failure, Walker moved the enterprise to Meadville. Then Gideon Sundback invented the fastener as it is currently known, as well as the machinery to produce it economically.

The fastener did not become a commercial success, however, until 1923, when the B.F. Goodrich Co. decided to put it on a new line of galoshes. The popular new galoshes were called "Zippers," a name that has evolved to mean the fastener itself.

Of interest in Meadville's historic downtown is the Unitarian Church in Diamond Park. Built in 1835, the church is a fine example of Greek Revival architecture. The Market House on Market Street has been used as an open-air marketplace since its founding about 1870 and is the cultural hub of the community. The Meadville Council on the Arts occupies the second floor.

Twelve miles northeast of Meadville via SR 77 and LR 20118S in New Richmond is the John Brown Tannery, operated by the abolitionist 1825-35. All that remains of the tannery are its 8-foot stone walls; nearby are the graves of Brown's first wife and two of their sons.

Western Crawford County Chamber of Commerce: 211 Chestnut St., Meadville, PA 16335; phone (814) 337-8030.

ALLEGHENY COLLEGE, 520 N. Main St., was founded in 1815 and is one of the oldest colleges west of the Allegheny Mountains. The college has a number of buildings constructed in the early 19th century, including Bentley Hall, a fine example of Federal architecture. Pelletier Library contains a notable collection of Lincoln memorabilia. Phone (814) 332-3100.

BALDWIN-REYNOLDS HOUSE, 639 Terrace St., was built 1841-43 for Supreme Court Justice Henry Baldwin. The building, furnished in period, houses tools, costumes and other artifacts. Adjacent is a 19th-century doctor's office. Ninety-minute tours depart every 30 minutes Wed.-Sun. 1-5, Memorial Day-Labor Day. Last tour departs 1 hour, 30 minutes before closing. Admission $3; under 16, $1.50. Under age 16 must be with an adult. Phone (814) 724-6080.

MEDIA—*see Philadelphia and Vicinity p. 127.*

MERCER (E-2) pop. 1,100, elev. 1,006′
Founded on the banks of the Neshannock Creek in 1803, Mercer was named for Brig. Gen. Hugh Mercer, a Scottish physician who moved to America and fought in the Revolutionary War. The city is a light industrial center in a farming region. Recreation is available at nearby Maurice K. Goddard and Pymatuning state parks *(see Recreation Chart).*

Mercer Chamber of Commerce: P.O. Box 473, Mercer, PA 16137; phone (724) 662-4185.

MERCER COUNTY HISTORICAL MUSEUM, 119 S. Pitt St., chronicles the history and development of Mercer County. Exhibits include clothing, dolls, furniture, photographs and toys. Primitive farm tools and machinery and a collection of American Indian arrowheads also are displayed. A reference library is available. Allow 30 minutes minimum. Tues.-Fri. 10-4:30, Sat. 10-3; closed holidays. Free. Phone (724) 662-3490.

MERCERSBURG (I-6) pop. 1,600, elev. 581′
BUCHANAN'S BIRTHPLACE STATE PARK, 18 acres 1 mi. n.w. off SR 16, is run by Cowans Gap State Park *(see Recreation Chart).* Activities include fishing and picnicking. A stone monument marks the birthplace of James Buchanan, the only Pennsylvanian to become a U.S. president. Open daily dawn-dusk. Free. Phone (717) 485-3948.

MERCERSBURG ACADEMY, 1 mi. e. on SR 16, is an independent co-educational secondary school and the site of President James Buchanan's 1791 log cabin birthplace, which was moved from its original location. Also on campus is the McFadden Railroad Museum, containing Lionel trains and accessories, including 148 engines and more than 500 cars. The academy chapel houses a 43-bell carillon.

Allow 1 hour minimum. Recitals are performed Sun. at 3. Recitals are not given and the museum is closed when school is not in session. Museum open Sun. 1-4. Free. Phone (717) 328-2173 for academy or 328-3511 for museum.

MIDDLETOWN (H-8) pop. 9,300

Due to its key position at the confluence of Swatara Creek and the Susquehanna River, midway between Lancaster and Carlisle, Middletown was the first town laid out in Dauphin County. The town boomed after the opening of the Pennsylvania and Union canals in the early 1800s.

THREE MILE ISLAND VISITORS CENTER is 3 mi. s. on SR 441. Exhibits, videotapes and staff explain nuclear energy and the TMI plant. Center open Thurs.-Sun. noon-4:30, June-Aug.; Thurs.-Sat. noon-4:30, Sept.-Dec. and Mar.-May. Closed major holidays. Free. Phone (717) 948-8829.

MILESBURG (F-6) pop. 1,100

CURTIN VILLAGE is 3 mi. n.e. of I-80 exit 23 on SR 150. The 1830 Federal-style mansion is restored and furnished in period. Pleasant Furnace was added in 1848. Curtin's 30,000 acres provided food for the entire community, and Curtin Village became largely self-sufficient until the ironworks closed in 1921. Guided tours are available. Train rides from Bellefonte to Curtin Village are available through Bellefonte Historic Railroad; phone (814) 355-0311.

Allow 1 hour minimum. Wed.-Sat. 10-4, Sun. 1-5, Memorial Day weekend-Labor Day; Sat. 10-4, Sun. 1-5, day after Labor Day to mid-Oct. Admission $4; ages 6-12, $1. Phone (814) 355-1982.

MILFORD—
see Pocono Mountains Area p. 149.

MONROEVILLE—
see Pittsburgh and Vicinity p. 144.

MORRISVILLE—
see Philadelphia and Vicinity p. 127.

MOUNT JEWETT (D-5) pop. 1,000, elev. 2,195'

KINZUA BRIDGE STATE PARK, 3.5 mi. n.e. off US 6, covers 316 acres. The 2,053-foot bridge crosses 300 feet above Kinzua Creek. The original bridge was built to carry trains of the Erie Railroad into the Alleghenies of northern Pennsylvania. The highest railroad viaduct in the world when completed in 1882, it was advertised as the eighth wonder of the world. Sunday excursions brought sightseers from as far away as Buffalo and Pittsburgh. The bridge offers pedestrians an unusual view of the scenic Kinzua Valley.

The Knox Kane Railroad excursion train now utilizes the tracks. An information kiosk is on the grounds; picnicking, fishing and hiking are permitted. Daily dawn-dusk. Free. Phone (814) 965-2646.

MOUNT JOY—
see Pennsylvania Dutch Country p. 104.

MOUNT PLEASANT (H-3) pop. 4,100, elev. 1,105'

L.E. SMITH GLASS CO. is e. via SR 31 to Liberty St. Visitors can observe glass artisans ply their craft. Allow 30 minutes minimum. Tours Mon.-Fri. 9:30-3; closed holidays. Free. Under age 6 are not permitted. Phone (724) 547-3544.

MOUNT POCONO—
see Pocono Mountains Area p. 149.

NAZARETH (G-11) pop. 5,700, elev. 530'

The area was originally part of a 5,000-acre tract of land owned as a feudal estate by the William Penn family. In 1740 evangelist George Whitefield purchased the land. He employed Peter Boehler and a small band of Moravians, a group of Protestants from Germany, to oversee the construction of what is now called the Whitfield House, located at 214 E. Center St. The house now contains the Moravian Historical Society's Museum and Research Library. The following year the Moravians bought the property and Nazareth remained exclusively a Moravian settlement for more than a century. Nazareth Hall, built in 1755, was a boys school 1759-1929.

Nearby Jacobsburg Environmental Education Center, 435 Belfast Rd., encompasses the remains of the 18th-century village of Jacobsburg and the site of the second Henry Gun Factory.

The Nazareth Speedway, SR 191, is the site of NASCAR and Indy racing in the spring. For race ticket information phone (610) 759-8800.

Nazareth Area Chamber of Commerce: 201 N. Main St., P.O. Box 173, Nazareth, PA 18064; phone (610) 759-9188 or (888) 629-7223.

MARTIN GUITAR COMPANY, 510 Sycamore St., offers a one-hour guided tour through the guitar factory. The tour includes a demonstration of each step in the production process, from planing the wood to manufacturing the strings. A museum displays unusual and vintage Martin guitars and memorabilia dating back to the company's founding in 1833. Allow 1 hour, 30 minutes minimum. Guided tours Mon.-Fri. at 1:15. Museum open Mon.-Fri. 9-5; closed holidays. Free. Phone (610) 759-2837.

NEW CASTLE (F-1) pop. 28,300, elev. 806′

HOYT INSTITUTE OF FINE ARTS, 124 E. Leasure Ave., occupies two restored 25-room mansions built in the early 1900s; it now contains art galleries, art and dance studios and exhibitions. Classes, performances, concerts, lectures and workshops are offered. Four acres of landscaped grounds surround the institute. Self-guiding tours of the Alex Crawford Hoyt Mansion are available. Allow 1 hour minimum. Tues.-Sat. 9-4. Art institute by donations. Mansion tours $2. Phone (724) 652-2882.

LIVING TREASURES ANIMAL PARK, I-79 exit 29, then 4 mi. w. on US 422, features more than 120 species of animals in a wooded setting. Included are monkeys, bears, African antelopes, elk, reindeer, kangaroos, zebras, camels and miniature horses. Visitors can feed pygmy goats, miniature sheep and llamas in a petting area. Food is available.

Allow 1 hour minimum. Daily 10-8, Memorial Day weekend-Labor Day; Sat.-Sun. 10-6, May 1-day before Memorial Day weekend and day after Labor Day-Oct. 31. Admission $5.50; over 62, $5; ages 3-11, $4.50. Phone (724) 924-9571.

NEW HOPE—
see Philadelphia and Vicinity p. 127.

NORRISTOWN—
see Philadelphia and Vicinity p. 127.

NORTH EAST (C-2) pop. 4,600, elev. 803′

With the help of Lake Erie's moderating effect on the climate and proper soil conditions, the area surrounding North East has developed into a prosperous winemaking area. The first vines were planted in 1850 and today there are four thriving wineries, thousands of acres of vineyards, and a large Welch's processing plant. The fertile soil, distinctive microclimate and a location on the shores of Lake Erie have combined to create an economy based upon tourism, recreation, industry and retail sales.

Of interest is the Lake Shore Railway Museum at Wall and Robinson streets. The museum is an 1889 passenger train station containing railroading relics.

North East Area Chamber of Commerce: 21 S. Lake St., North East, PA 16428; phone (814) 725-4262.

NORTHUMBERLAND (F-8) pop. 3,900, elev. 452′

[SAVE] **JOSEPH PRIESTLEY HOUSE,** 472 Priestley Ave., contains the laboratory and books of Dr. Joseph Priestley, the Unitarian theologian who discovered oxygen. The house contains period furnishings. A visitor center depicts the life of Dr. Priestley, who emigrated from England in 1794. Allow 1 hour minimum. Tues.-Sat. 9-5, Sun. noon-5; closed holidays except Memorial Day, July 4 and Labor Day. Admission $3.50 over 60, $3; ages 6-17, $1.50. Phone (717) 473-9474.

NOTTINGHAM—
see Philadelphia and Vicinity p. 127.

OHIOPYLE (I-3) pop. 100, elev. 1,221′

Once a hunting area for the Delaware, Shawnee and Iroquois, Ohiopyle was named "Ohio pehhle" by the American Indians for the "white frothy water" of the Youghiogheny River. George Washington had hoped to use the river as a water route to Fort Duquesne (now Pittsburgh) but he abandoned the idea after discovering the falls at Ohiopyle. The falls are within Ohiopyle State Park (see Recreation Chart and the AAA Mideastern CampBook); a day-use area provides overlook platforms.

Ohiopyle is best known as a popular starting point for white-water rafting on the "Yough."

Trips can be arranged through several outfitters in town.

Laurel Highlands Visitors Bureau: 120 E. Main St., Ligonier, PA 15658; phone (724) 238-5661 or (800) 925-7669.

BEAR RUN NATURE RESERVE, on SR 381 next to Fallingwater, has more than 20 miles of trails traversing a variety of habitats, ranging from dense oak and hemlock forests to the spectacular Youghiogheny River gorge overlook and the sparkling waters of Bear Run and Laurel Run. The 4,000-acre reserve is open all year for hiking, photography, backpack camping and cross-country skiing. Free. Phone (724) 329-8501.

FALLINGWATER, on SR 381, was a weekend home designed by Frank Lloyd Wright in 1936. Constructed of reinforced concrete and native stone, the house is dramatically cantilevered over a waterfall. This famous house blends so well with the mountainous terrain that it seems to grow out of its site. Self-guiding ground tours and tours for children also are available.

Allow 1 hour minimum. Tues.-Sun. 10-4, Apr. to mid-Nov.; Sat.-Sun. 10-4, mid-Nov. through Jan. 1 and in Mar. In-depth tours Tues.-Sun. at 8:30 a.m. Children under 9 can be left at the child care center; a nominal fee is charged. Admission Tues.-Fri. $8, Sat.-Sun. $12. Reservations are required for guided, in-depth and children's tours. Phone (724) 329-8501.

 RECREATIONAL ACTIVITIES

White-water Rafting

- **Laurel Highlands River Tours,** on SR 381. Write P.O. Box 107, Ohiopyle, PA 15470. Trips depart daily, Mar.-Oct. Phone (724) 329-8531 or (800) 472-3846. *See color ad.*

- **Mountain Streams & Trails Outfitters,** on SR 381. Write P.O. Box 106, Ohiopyle, PA 15470. Trips depart daily, Apr.-Oct. Phone (724) 329-8810 or (800) 723-8669. *See color ad.*

- **White Water Adventurers Inc.,** Whitewater St. Write P.O. Box 31, Ohiopyle, PA 15470. Other activities are offered. Middle and Lower Youghiogheny trips depart daily, Mar. 15-Oct. 15. Upper Youghiogheny trips depart Mon.-Fri., Mar. 15-Oct. 15. Cheat River trips depart daily, Mar.-June. Phone (724) 329-8850 for information or (800) 992-7238 for reservations. *See color ad p. 96.*

- **Wilderness Voyageurs,** on SR 381. Write P.O. Box 97, Ohiopyle, PA 15470. Raft trips depart daily, Apr. 1 to mid-Oct. Phone (800) 272-4141.

OIL CITY (E-2) pop. 12,000, elev. 1,028'

The discovery of oil in 1860 precipitated the almost overnight settlement of Oil City. The narrow ravine of Oil Creek became the busiest valley on the continent and in a short time was covered with derricks from Oil City to Titusville. From 1860 to 1870, 17 million barrels of oil were shipped from this region to Pittsburgh. McClintock Well No. 1, drilled in 1861, is still producing.

The Oil Creek and Titusville Railroad which offers train trips between Titusville and Oil City in restored 1930s passenger cars, has a boarding stop at Rynd Farm, 4 miles north of Oil City on SR 8 *(see Titusville p. 156).*

Oil City Area Chamber of Commerce: 102 Center St., Oil City, PA 16301; phone (814) 676-8521.

VENANGO MUSEUM OF ART, SCIENCE AND INDUSTRY, 270 Seneca St., has displays about early oil exploration, discovery and production in the surrounding area. SCIENTRIFIC offers hands-on exhibits with a physical science theme. Allow 30 minutes minimum. Tues.-Sat. 10-4, Sun. 1-4. Admission $2; senior citizens and students with ID $1; under 12, 75c. Phone (814) 676-2007.

PALMYRA (H-9) pop. 6,900, elev. 450'

Founded by John Palm in the late 1700s, Palmyra bases its economy on food manufactur-ing and farming. Of interest 3 miles north o Main and Railroad streets is the 1803 Bindnagle Evangelical Lutheran Church, a two-story brick structure with round arch windows and doors The grave of John Palm is in the churchyard.

SELTZER'S LEBANON BOLOGNA CO. INC. is blks. n. of US 422 at 230 N. College St. A vid eotape tour of the production process is avail able. Allow 30 minutes minimum. Mon.-Fri. 8-4 Free. Phone (800) 282-6336.

PAOLI—
see Philadelphia and Vicinity p. 128.

PENNS CREEK (F-7)

Named for the stream that flows nearby, Penn Creek is surrounded by the rich, rolling farmlan of Snyder County. Just east at US 11 and US 1 is the site where the Penns Creek Massacre oc curred on Oct. 16, 1755, when American Indian killed or captured 26 settlers.

WALNUT ACRES ORGANIC FARMS is .5 mi. of SR 104 on Walnut Acres Rd. Established i 1946, Walnut Acres was one of the first organi farms in the country; its chemical-free foods ar sold world-wide. Guided tours through the can nery, bakery and mill are conducted. Food an picnic tables are available. Allow 30 minute minimum. Tours Mon.-Fri. at 9:30, 11 and closed holidays. Free. Phone (800) 433-3998 fc events information.

Pennsylvania Dutch Country

The rich farmland of the Pennsylvania Dutch Country was settled in the Colonial years by several religious groups, primarily of German descent, seeking freedom of worship. The Pennsylvania Dutch have retained the convictions and customs of their ancestors. These beliefs are reflected in their dress, their work and the ways in which they spend their leisure time. The Plain People, as they are known to many, include some members of the Amish, Mennonite and Brethren faiths.

Simplicity is the keynote of the Pennsylvania Dutch, but each sect manifests it differently. Some eschew any motive power except the horse; others do not use electricity or modern plumbing. Most dress in plain colors and clothing. But all exhibit singular speech characteristics, and all are noted for excellent foods that originated in the old countries. Souse, shoofly pie, schnitz, cup cheese, various sausages and the famous pretzels can all be sampled.

The bounty on their tables indicates the bounty of their land; few farms are as productive as these. Other regional features are hex signs—colorful radial

Lancaster County / © J. Irwin / H. Armstrong Roberts

designs painted on barns—and decorative stenciled motifs applied to furniture, tiles and household items.

Broadly, the Pennsylvania Dutch Country encompasses an area bordered by the State of Maryland, the Schuylkill and Susquehanna rivers and I-78. At the heart of this country is Lancaster.

BIRD-IN-HAND (H-9) elev. 360'

As did many early Lancaster County settlements, Bird-in-Hand took its name from a tavern sign, which pictured a bird resting in a hand. Taverns of the period chose pictures over words because it was immediately recognizable to travelers, many of whom could not read. Four hotels have since stood on the site of the original Bird-in-Hand, which was built to serve travelers on the Philadelphia Turnpike.

ABE'S BUGGY RIDES, 2596 Old Philadelphia Pike, offers 20-minute rides through Amish country in a horse-drawn Amish family carriage.

Mon.-Sat. 8-7, June-Aug.; 8-dusk, rest of year. Fare $10; ages 3-12, $5. Phone (717) 392-1794.

OLD VILLAGE STORE, on SR 340, remains much as it was in 1890, with checkerboards and a potbellied stove. It is one of the oldest hardware stores in the country. Allow 30 minutes minimum. Mon.-Sat. 9-5:30, May-Oct.; 9-5, rest of year. Free. Phone (717) 397-1291.

PLAIN AND FANCY FARM 1 mi. e. on SR 340, is a shopping village featuring buggy rides and craft and gift shops. Food is available. Open daily. Phone (717) 768-4400.

Amish Country Homestead is furnished to reflect the Amish way of life. Guided tours are available. Allow 30 minutes minimum. Mon.Sat. 9:30-6:45, Sun. 10-4:45, July-Oct.; daily 10-4:45, Apr.-June and in Nov.; Sat.-Sun. 9:30-4:30, rest of year. Closed Thanksgiving and Dec. 25. Admission $5; ages 4-11, $3.25. MC, VI. Phone (717) 768-3600, ext. 10.

The Amish Experience Theatre is at 3121 Old Philadelphia Pike. This experiential theater offers a high-tech, 30-minute presentation about a teenager who must choose between remaining in the modern, outside world or joining the Amish church and adopting the Amish lifestyle. Events from Amish history are re-created using special effects.

Presentations are given on the hour Mon.-Sat. 9-8, Sun 10-6, July-Oct.; Mon.-Sat. 9-5, Sun. 10-5, Apr.-June; daily 10-5, rest of year. Admission $6.50; ages 4-11, $3.75. MC, VI. Phone (717) 768-3600, ext. 10.

WEAVERTOWN ONE-ROOM SCHOOLHOUSE is .7 mi. e. on SR 340. Animated wax figures depict a typical day in a Pennsylvania Dutch school. The bell, desks and blackboards are original. The school held classes for almost a century, until 1969. Daily 9-5, Memorial Day-Labor Day; 10-5, Apr. 1-day before Memorial Day and day after Labor Day-Oct. 31; Sat.-Sun. 10-5 in Mar. and Nov. Admission $2.75; senior citizens $2.25; ages 5-11, $2. Phone (717) 768-3976 or 291-1888. *See ad p. 338.*

COLUMBIA (I-9) pop. 10,700, elev. 252'

Founded in the early 1700s, Columbia is in the Susquehanna River Valley, a location that encouraged the development of the town's livelihood as a transportation and commercial center.

Columbia Chamber of Commerce: 445 Linden St., P.O. Box 510, Columbia, PA 17512; phone (717) 684-5249.

★ WATCH AND CLOCK MUSEUM OF THE NATIONAL ASSOCIATION OF WATCH AND CLOCK COLLECTORS INC., off US 30 and SR 441 at 5th and Poplar sts., contains more than 8,000 horological items from around the world, including clocks, watches, movements, tools and machinery. Changing exhibits trace the history of timekeeping from the 1600s through the present. There are examples of various styles and technological developments, from the earliest mechanical to the futuristic "atomic clock."

The museum displays Stephen D. Engle's "Monumental Clock," an 1877 timepiece with 48 moving figures and two organ movements. A reference library is available. Allow 1 hour minimum. Tues.-Sat. 9-4, Sun. noon-4, May-Sept.; Tues.-Sat. 9-4, rest of year. Closed major holidays. Admission $3; over 59, $2.50; ages 6-17, $1. Phone (717) 684-8261. *See ad p. 340.*

WRIGHT'S FERRY MANSION, 2nd and Cherry sts., was the Colonial home of Susanna Wright, a literary Quaker. The restored 1738 English-style stone house contains a collection of early 18th-century Philadelphia furniture and reflects life in a Pennsylvania Quaker household prior to 1750. Allow 1 hour minimum. Guided tours are offered Tues.-Wed. and Fri.-Sat. 10-3, May-Oct.; closed July 4. Last tour begins at 3. Admission $5; ages 6-18, $2.50. Phone (717) 684-4325.

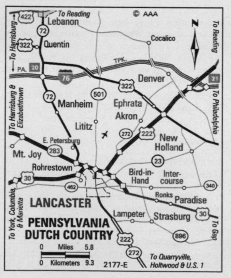

ELIZABETHTOWN (H-8) pop. 10,000, elev. 462'

THE MASONIC HOMES of the Grand Lodge of Free and Accepted Masons of Pennsylvania are on 1,400 acres on the s.w. edge of town on SR 241. The Masonic Homes serve as a retirement residence and Masonic health care facility for Masons and their relatives. A 6.5-acre garden is on the grounds. Guided tours are available. Daily 8-noon and 12:30-4. Free. Phone (717) 367-1121.

EPHRATA (H-9) pop. 12,100, elev. 381'

The Ephrata-Denver area has a number of factories that maintain retail outlets. The Green Dragon Auction Market offers almost everything from live animals to hardware at its indoor and outdoor stands.

Ephrata Chamber of Commerce: 77 Park Ave., Suite 1, Ephrata, PA 17522; phone (717) 738-9010.

SAVE EPHRATA CLOISTER, 632 W. Main St., was one of America's earliest communal societies. Occupying a distinctive group of medieval-style buildings, this community of religious celibates practiced an austere lifestyle, emphasizing spiritual goals rather than material ones. The Ephrata Cloister also was an early center for publishing and printing in Pennsylvania. Ten of the original buildings have been restored and furnished to recreate the atmosphere of the 18th-century communal village.

Allow 1 hour minimum. Mon.-Sat. 9-5, Sun. noon-5; closed holidays. Tours are offered on the hour Mon.-Sat. 10-4, Sun. 1-4. Admission $5; over 60, $4.50; ages 6-12, $3. Phone (717) 733-6600.

HOLTWOOD (I-9)

MUDDY RUN INFORMATION CENTER, 172 Bethesda Church Rd. W., offers exhibits that highlight resource conservation and information about wildlife, nuclear waste management and power generation. Audiovisual and nature programs also are presented. The center is part of a 700-acre recreation area. Picnicking is permitted. Allow 1 hour minimum. Tues.-Sat. 10-4, Apr.-Oct. Free. Phone (717) 284-2538, or 284-4325 for camping and boating information.

INTERCOURSE (H-10)

In the heart of Pennsylvania Dutch Country, Intercourse was founded in 1754. First called Cross Keys after a local tavern, the town was renamed in 1814. Its name is believed to have evolved from either the entrance to the old racecourse (the "Entercourse") just outside of town or from the joining, or intercourse, of the Old Kings Highway and the Wilmington-Erie Road.

Amish and Mennonite craftwares, including such items as quilts, toys and tablecloths, can be found at the Old Country Store on Main Street. Cross Keys Village is a converted warehouse with a tourist information center; stores offering Amish and other handmade items, antiques and Victoriana; foodstuffs; and a pretzel factory whose products include stuffed pretzels.

THE PEOPLE'S PLACE, 3513 Main St., is Lancaster County's center for Amish and Mennonite arts and crafts. It also interprets the story of the Amish, Mennonite and Hutterite people. "Who Are the Amish?" is a three-screen documentary slide show with music and narration.

The Amish World Museum presents an inside look at the spirit and faith of the Amish. There also are special features for children. "Hazel's People," is a feature film dealing with a Mennonite family's clash of cultures.

Slide show shown every 30 minutes 9:30-6:45, Memorial Day-Labor Day; 9:30-4:30, rest of year. Museum open Mon.-Sat. 9:30-8, Memorial Day-Labor Day; 9:30-5, rest of year. Film shown at 7:30, Memorial Day-Labor Day. Closed Jan. 1 and Dec. 25. Museum $4; ages 5-11, $2. Slide show $4; ages 5-11, $2. Various combination tickets are available. MC, VI. Phone (717) 768-7171. *See ad.*

The People's Place Quilt Museum across the street on the second floor of the Old Country Store, displays a collection of antique Amish quilts. The museum is closed for renovations and is scheduled to reopen March 1998. Phone ahead for hours. Admission $4; ages 4-12, $2. MC, VI. Phone (717) 768-7101. *See ad.*

LANCASTER (I-9) pop. 55,600, elev. 377'

During the Revolutionary War, Lancaster was the largest inland city in the Colonies. It was capital of the nation for 1 day, Sept. 27, 1777, when Congress stopped in Lancaster as it fled Philadelphia after the Battle of Brandywine *(see Chadds Ford in Philadelphia and Vicinity p. 123).* Lancaster was the state capital 1799-1812.

The city is in the heart of Lancaster County, known for its Amish and Mennonite population, its picturesque and productive farms and its heaping platters of Pennsylvania Dutch food. The Visitor Information Center, on US 30 at the Greenfield Road exit, presents a brief orientation to the area through exhibits, a multi-image program, brochures and maps.

Pennsylvania Dutch Convention and Visitors Bureau: 501 Greenfield Rd., Lancaster, PA 17601; phone (717) 299-8901 or (800) 723-8824.

Shopping areas: Lancaster boasts a large number of factory outlets, including the Charles Chips Outlet Store at 1098 Ivy Dr.; Dansk Factory Outlet on SR 30; Hamilton Watch and Clock Shoppe at 2450 Lincoln Hwy. E.; MillStream Designer Factory Shops at 311 Outlet Dr.; and

Totes Factory Store, offering umbrellas and rainwear at 220 Centerville Rd. Rockvale Square Factory Outlet Village, at SR 30E and SR 896, is another large center, containing more than 120 factory outlets.

AMISH COUNTRY TOURS, 5 mi. e. of SR 30 on SR 340 at 3121 Old Philadelphia Pike (grounds of the Plain and Fancy Restaurant), offers narrated minibus tours of Amish farmlands and the Pennsylvania Dutch Country. Tours of historic Philadelphia also are available.

Two-hour tour departs Mon.-Sat. at 10:30 and 2, Sun. at 11:30, Apr.-Oct.; daily at 11:30 in Nov.; Sat.-Sun. at 11:30, rest of year. Nine-hour Philadelphia tour departs Wed. at 8:30, May-Oct. Two-hour tour $17.95; ages 4-11, $10.95. Nine-hour tour $34.95; ages 4-11, $29.95. Reservations are recommended. MC, VI. Phone (717) 768-3600, ext. 10.

THE AMISH FARM AND HOUSE is 5 mi. e. on US 30. A 45-minute lecture tour explaining the Plain People's way of life is given through the 1805 house. Major local crops, barns and farm animals can be seen on the grounds. Food is available April through October. Allow 1 hour, 30 minutes minimum. Daily 8:30-6, June-Aug.; 8:30-5, Apr.-May and Sept.-Oct.; 8:30-4, rest of year. Closed Dec. 25. Fee $5.75; senior citizens $5.25; ages 5-11, $3.25. AE, DS, MC, VI. Phone (717) 394-6185. *See ad p. 338.*

ANDERSON BAKERY COMPANY, .5 mi. e. of jct. SR 340 and US 30 at 2060 Old Philadelphia Pike, offers self-guiding tours of one of the world's largest pretzel bakeries. The tour, which chronicles the history of the Anderson family and the bakery, winds through the facility and illustrates all phases of production. Free pretzels can be sampled at the end of the tour. Allow 30 minutes minimum. Mon.-Fri. 8:30-4; closed holidays and Good Friday. Free. Phone (717) 299-1616.

CCINC. AUTO TAPE TOURS offers a 3-hour taped tour of the Lancaster area and Pennsylvania Dutch Country, including information about the customs, culture and lifestyles of the Amish people. The audiotapes include music and sound effects; a map is provided. The tapes can be purchased for $12.95 at The Amish Farm and House, Dutch Wonderland Family Fun Park and Wax Museum of Lancaster County History *(see attraction listings),* or the tape can be purchased in advance by sending $14.95 (includes postage) to CCInc., P.O. Box 227, Allendale, NJ 07401. Phone (201) 236-1666.

DUTCH WONDERLAND FAMILY FUN PARK, 4 mi. e. on US 30, has 48 acres of attractions, including 25 rides, exhibits, shows and gardens. Allow 4 hours minimum. Daily 10-8, May 23-Labor Day; Sat. 10-6, Sun. 11-6, Apr. 18-May 17 and day after Labor Day-Oct. 11. Unlimited-ride pass $19.95; over 59 and ages 3-5, $14.95. Monorail $1.75. AE, DS, MC, VI. Phone (717) 291-1888. *See ad p. 338.*

FARMERS' MARKETS offer such delicacies as souse, schmiercase, cup cheese, schnitz, old-fashioned Bavarian pretzels and shoofly pie.

Bird-in-Hand Farmer's Market, on SR 340, is open Wed.-Sat. 8:30-5:30, July-Oct.; Wed. and Fri.-Sat. 8:30-5:30, Apr.-June and in Nov.; Fri.-Sat. 8:30-5:30, rest of year.

Central Market, Penn Sq., is one of the oldest enclosed markets in the country. Visitors can shop for fresh fruits, vegetables, flowers, meats and baked goods. Tues. and Fri. 6-4, Sat. 6-2.

Meadowbrook Market, 4 mi. e. on SR 23, offers fruits, vegetables, flowers, baked goods, handcrafted items and antiques. Fri. 8-7, Sat. 8-5.

HANDS-ON HOUSE, CHILDREN'S MUSEUM OF LANCASTER is at 2380 Kissel Hill Rd. in a restored Victorian farmhouse. The museum specializes in letting children learn through play. Interactive exhibit areas feature a child-size grocery store, an assembly line in the Whatcha-Ma-Giggle Co., planning and constructing a town and using light to create art.

Allow 1 hour, 30 minutes minimum. Mon.-Sat. 10-5 (also Fri. 5-8), Sun. noon-5, Memorial Day-Labor Day; Tues.-Fri. 11-4 (also Fri. 4-8), Sat. 10-5, Sun. noon-5, rest of year. Admission $4. Under 16 must be with an adult. Phone (717) 569-5437.

HANS HERR HOUSE is 4 mi. s. on US 222, then .7 mi. s. to 1849 Hans Herr Dr. Built in 1719, this is the oldest building in Lancaster County and the oldest documented Mennonite meeting-house in America. The medieval-style Germanic stone house has been depicted in several paintings by Andrew Wyeth, a descendant of Hans Herr. The site includes the restored and furnished house, an exhibit about Mennonite farm life, a blacksmith shop, picnic tables, an orchard and a visitor center.

Allow 1 hour minimum. Mon.-Sat. 9-4, Apr. 1-first weekend in Dec.; closed Thanksgiving. Admission $3.50; ages 7-12, $1. Phone (717) 464-4438.

HERITAGE CENTER MUSEUM OF LANCASTER COUNTY, Penn Sq., occupies the historic 1798 City Hall and the Masonic Lodge Hall of the same period. The museum's exhibits of local folk and decorative arts include furniture, quilts, clocks, silver, textiles and fine art. Changing exhibits are displayed throughout the year. Allow 30 minutes minimum. Tues.-Sat. 10-5 (also Sun. noon-5 in Dec.), Apr.-Dec. Donations. Phone (717) 299-6440.

[SAVE] HISTORIC ROCK FORD PLANTATION, in Lancaster County Park at 881 Rock Ford Rd., is the preserved 18th-century plantation of Edward Hand, adjutant general during the Revolutionary War. A museum in the barn has Zoe and Henry Kauffman's folk items. Tues.-Fri. 10-4, Sun. noon-4, Apr.-Oct. Last tour departs 1 hour before closing. Admission $4.50; over 55, $3.50; ages 6-12, $2. Phone (717) 392-7223.

LANCASTER COUNTY HISTORICAL SOCIETY, 230 N. President Ave., houses items of local and national interest, including genealogical materials. Tues.-Sat. 9:30-4:30 (also Thurs. 4:30-9:30); closed holidays. Museum free. Library $5. Phone (717) 392-4633.

LANCASTER NEWSPAPERS NEWSEUM is 1 blk. s. of the center square at 28 S. Queen St. Window displays depict the evolution of newspapers locally, nationally and internationally. Exhibits include major national headlines and address forms of printing and distribution. Daily 24 hours. Free. Phone (717) 291-8600.

LANCASTER WALKING TOUR, departing from the Lancaster Chamber of Commerce at Queen and Vine sts., is a 90-minute tour of the city with a costumed guide who explains the cultural, economic and religious development of Lancaster. An audiovisual presentation is included. Sun.-Mon. and Wed.-Thurs. at 1, Tues. and Fri.-Sat. at 10 and 1, Apr.-Oct. Fee $5. Phone (717) 392-1776.

[SAVE] ★ LANDIS VALLEY MUSEUM is 2.5 mi. n. on Oregon Pike (SR 272). The 16-acre living-history complex interprets Pennsylvania German rural life before 1900. The many historic buildings include farmsteads, a tavern and a country store. Traditional crafts demonstrations are given April through October. Guided tours are available.

Allow 2 hours minimum. Mon.-Sat. 9-5, Sun. noon-5, Mar.-Dec.; closed holidays except Memorial Day, July 4 and Labor Day. Admission Apr.-Oct. $7; over 60, $6.50; ages 6-12, $5; family rate $19. Admission Nov.-Dec. and in Mar. $5; over 60, $4.50; ages 6-12, $3; family rate $13. Phone (717) 569-0401.

MENNONITE INFORMATION CENTER AND HEBREW TABERNACLE REPRODUCTION are 4.5 mi. e. at 2209 Millstream Rd., just off US 30. The information center has a videotape presentation and exhibits that explain the faith and culture of the Amish and Mennonites. Mennonite "step-on" tour guides are available for 2-hour tours of the Amish farmlands. Adjacent is a reproduction of the Hebrew Tabernacle. Lecture tours about the tabernacle's history, construction, function and significance are available.

Allow 30 minutes minimum. Center open Mon.-Sat. 8-5. Tabernacle tours depart on the hour Mon.-Sat. 8-4, Apr.-Oct.; Mon.-Sat. at 11, 1 and 3, rest of year. Videotape presentations shown every half-hour 8-4:30. Closed Jan. 1, Thanksgiving and Dec. 25. Center free. Tabernacle tours $4; over 64, $3.50; ages 7-12, $2.25. Step-on tour $9 per hour per car (plus a $6 service charge per car). Phone (717) 299-0954.

MILL BRIDGE VILLAGE, 4 mi. e. of jct. US 30 and SR 462, is a restored Colonial mill village with an operating 1738 water-driven gristmill that grinds corn. At the village are working craftsmen, including a blacksmith, hearth broom maker and candle dipper; displays of Amish and Mennonite quilts and handcrafts; and a petting barnyard. Guided tours of an Amish house, school and 1830s print shop also are available.

Entertainment is provided some weekends in the fall. Also included are horse-drawn carriage rides and picnic areas along the mill stream. Village open daily 9:30-5:30, Memorial Day-Labor Day; daily 10-5, Apr. 1-day before Memorial Day and day after Labor Day-Oct. 31. Admission $10; over 55, $8; ages 6-12, $5. AE, DS, MC, VI. Phone (717) 687-6521.

NORTH MUSEUM OF NATURAL HISTORY AND SCIENCE, on the Franklin & Marshall College campus at College and Buchanan aves., contains natural history displays, a planetarium and a children's discovery room. Museum open Tues.-Sat. 9-5, Sun. 1:30-5. Discovery room open Wed.-Sun. 1:30-4:30, late June-Aug. 31; Sat.-Sun. 1:30-4:30, rest of year. Planetarium shows Sat. at 12:30, 2 and 3; Sun. at 2 and 3. Museum admission $2. Planetarium $2.50. Phone (717) 291-3941.

THE PEOPLE'S PLACE—see Intercourse p. 101.

TRINITY LUTHERAN CHURCH, 31 S. Duke St., was originally constructed in 1730 and rebuilt

1761-66. The spire, with statues of apostles Matthew, Mark, Luke and John, dates from 1794. Tours are available by prior arrangement Mon.-Fri. 8:30-4:30. Guide service is available Sun. at 9:45 and noon (after services). Free. Phone (717) 397-2734.

WAX MUSEUM OF LANCASTER COUNTY HISTORY, 4 mi. e. on US 30, presents audiovisual scenes of historical events in Pennsylvania from the 1700s to the present. Visitors can watch a reenactment of an Amish barn raising. Allow 1 hour minimum. Daily 9-8, May 25-Sept. 2; Sun.-Thurs. 9-6, Fri.-Sat. 9-8, Apr. 1-May 24 and Sept. 3-Oct. 31; daily 9-5, rest of year. Admission $5.75; senior citizens $5.25; ages 5-11, $3.25. MC, VI. Phone (717) 393-3679. See ad p. 338.

★**WHEATLAND**, 1120 Marietta Ave., is the 1828 Federal mansion of James Buchanan, the only Pennsylvanian to become president of the United States. He conducted his 1856 presidential campaign from the library. Restored period rooms contain original Buchanan furnishings and decorative objects. Costumed guides conduct tours. Candlelight tours are available the first 2 weeks in December.

One-hour tours begin every half-hour. daily 10-4, Apr.-Nov.; closed Easter and Thanksgiving. Admission $5.50; senior citizens $4.50; students with ID $3.50; ages 6-11, $1.75. MC, VI. Phone (717) 392-8721.

WINERIES

- **Lancaster County Winery**, 8 mi. s. off SR 272, then 1 mi. w. on Baumgardner Rd. and 2 mi. on Rawlinsville Rd. Mon.-Sat. 10-4, Sun. 1-4, Feb.-Dec. Phone (717) 464-3555.

LITITZ (H-9) pop. 8,200, elev. 360'

Dedicated in 1756 as a Moravian community, Lititz was named for the place in Bohemia where the Moravian Church was founded in 1456. Until 1855 the entire community was owned by the church. Linden Hall, one of the oldest girls' residence schools in the United States, was founded by Moravians in 1746. Originally a day school, it began boarding students in 1794. The Lititz Moravian Archives and Museum, at Church Square and Main Street, provides guided tours of the church buildings Memorial Day through Labor Day. Tours are available by appointment only; phone (717) 626-8515.

Self-guiding tours: A brochure outlining a walking tour of historic buildings and houses on E. Main Street is available from the Lititz Historical Foundation at the Johannes Mueller House (see attraction listing).

CANDY AMERICANA MUSEUM AND CANDY OUTLET is in the Wilbur Chocolate Co. building at 48 N. Broad St. The museum displays antique confectionery equipment, including molds, tins, trays, wooden boxes and a collection of more than 200 antique chocolate pots. Visitors can watch hand-dipped candies being made. The museum has a strong aroma of chocolate from the adjoining factory. The candy outlet resembles an old country store.

Mon.-Sat. 10-5; closed Jan. 1-2, Labor Day, Thanksgiving and Dec. 25-26. Free. Phone (717) 626-3249.

GRAVE OF GEN. JOHN A. SUTTER is in the Moravian Cemetery behind the church on E. Main St. It was the discovery of gold on Gen. Sutter's property near Sacramento, Calif., that started the rush of 1849. Sutter lived in Lititz while battling Congress to receive compensation for the California land.

HERITAGE MAP MUSEUM, 55 N. Water St., features more than 100 original 15th- to 19th-century maps from around the world. Allow 1 hour minimum. Daily 10-5. Admission $4; ages 6-12, $3. AE, DS, MC, VI. Phone (717) 626-5002.

JOHANNES MUELLER HOUSE, 137-139 E. Main St., was built in 1792 and consists of a stone house and an adjoining log structure. The log portion contains Mueller's workshop. The stone house is furnished in period. A museum next to the house features a collection of early Lititz artifacts and paintings. Allow 30 minutes minimum. Guided tours are available Mon.-Sat. 10-4, May 1-Memorial Day; Sat.-Mon. 10-4, day after Memorial Day-Dec. 31. Fee $3; ages 6-18, $1.50. Phone (717) 626-7958.

LITITZ SPRINGS PARK, in town on SR 501, is illuminated by thousands of candles on July 4. The celebration dates from the early days of the settlement. Open daily 24 hours.

STURGIS PRETZEL HOUSE is at 219 E. Main St. In 1861 Julius Sturgis established what is said to be the first pretzel bakery in the United States. The bakery dates from 1784, while this first commercial pretzel factory dates from 1861. Handmade soft pretzels are baked in the 200-year-old ovens, and visitors are taught how to twist pretzel dough. Allow 30 minutes minimum. Guided tours Mon.-Sat. 9:30-4:30; closed Jan. 1, Thanksgiving and Dec. 25. Admission $2. Phone (717) 626-4354.

MANHEIM (H-9) pop. 5,000, elev. 400'

Baron William Stiegel, originator of Stiegel glass, founded Manheim. The remains of his house are on Main Street.

Manheim Area Chamber of Commerce: 210 S. Charlotte St., Manheim, PA 17545; phone (717) 665-6330.

PENNSYLVANIA RENAISSANCE FAIRE is on the grounds of the Mount Hope Estate and Winery,

.5 mi. s. of the Pennsylvania Tpke. exit 20 on SR 72. The fair features jousting, 16th-century-style food, drink, theater, artisans, merchants and hundreds of costumed Elizabethan characters.

The 1800 mansion was built by wealthy ironmaster Henry Grubb. Ten acres of vineyards and 20 acres of formal gardens surround the mansion. Tours of the mansion are available only to groups of 15 or more, and reservations are required.

Faire held Sat.-Mon. 10-6, Aug. 2-Labor Day; Sat.-Sun., day after Labor Day-Oct. 5. Admission $16.95; ages 5-11, $7. Phone (717) 665-7021.

MARIETTA (H-8) pop. 2,800, elev. 259'

LE PETIT MUSEUM OF MUSICAL BOXES, 2.2 mi. n. on SR 441 from jct. US 30, then 1.2 mi. w. to 255 West Market St., is in a Federal-style house and features a collection of some 75 music boxes 1820-1900. A guided tour departs hourly. Allow 1 hour minimum. Mon. and Sat. 10-4, Sun. noon-4, Mar.-Dec.; closed Mar. 30, some Sat. in Oct., Thanksgiving and Dec. 25. Admission $3; under 12, $2.50. Phone (717) 426-1154.

 WINERIES

• **Nissley Winery and Vineyards,** 5.5 mi. n. on SR 441, then .5 mi. n.e. on Wickersham Rd. Mon.-Sat. 10-5, Sun. 1-4; closed Jan. 1, Easter, Thanksgiving and Dec. 25. Last tour begins 45 minutes before closing. Phone (717) 426-3514.

MOUNT JOY (H-8) pop. 6,200, elev. 360'

BUBE'S BREWERY, 102 N. Market St., is a 19th-century brewery that operated until Prohibition. Built by Alois Bube, a German immigrant, the brewery is 43 feet below street level in a Victorian hotel, which also houses three restaurants, a brewery museum and an art gallery. Tours last 30 to 40 minutes and are given daily 10-5, June 15-day before Labor Day. Free. Phone (717) 653-2056.

DONEGAL MILLS PLANTATION, 2.5 mi. s.w. on SR 772, then .5 mi. w. via Musser Rd., following signs, includes a tour of a 250-year-old mansion, mill, miller's house, bake house, garden and wildlife areas. Guided tours of the historic village are available Sat.-Sun. noon-6, mid-Mar. through Dec. 31; other times by appointment. Admission $4; ages 6-12, $2. Phone (717) 653-2168.

QUARRYVILLE (I-9) pop. 1,600, elev. 488'

South of Quarryville on US 222 is the restored stone house where artist, inventor and engineer Robert Fulton was born in 1765. His drawings, miniature portraits and invention models, including the steamship *Clermont,* are exhibited on weekends during the summer.

STRASBURG (I-9) pop. 2,600

Though first settled by French Huguenots, Strasburg evolved into a community of German immigrants in the Pennsylvania Dutch Country. The town is noted for its quaint atmosphere; the availability of Amish food, arts and crafts; and its many railroad exhibits, both model and real.

Strasburg Visitors Information Center: One Historic Dr., Strasburg, PA 17579; phone (717) 687-7922.

THE AMISH VILLAGE, 2 mi. n. on SR 896, then 1 mi. s. of US 30, contains an 1840 house furnished in the Old-Order Amish style. In 20- to 25-minute educational tours, guides explain the history, clothing, furniture and Amish way of life. Other buildings include a barn, schoolhouse, blacksmith shop, store and springhouse. Picnicking is permitted.

Daily 9-6, March 14-Labor Day; daily 9-4, day after Labor Day-Oct. 27; daily 10-4, Nov.-Dec.; Sat.-Sun. 10-4, rest of year (weather permitting). Closed Mon.-Thurs. Thanksgiving week and Dec. 24-25. Admission $5.50; ages 6-12, $1.50. MC, VI. Phone (717) 687-8511. *See ad p. 339.*

SAVE CHOO CHOO BARN, TRAINTOWN, U.S.A., e. on SR 741, is a 1,700-square-foot miniature display of Lancaster County and the Pennsylvania Dutch Country. The exhibit has 14 operating toy trains and more than 135 animated and automated figures and vehicles, as well as miniatures of many area landmarks.

Allow 1 hour minimum. Daily 10-5:30, June 1-day before Labor Day; 10-4:30, Apr.-May and Labor Day-Dec. 31. Closed Thanksgiving and Dec. 25. Admission $4; ages 5-12, $2. Phone (717) 687-7911.

GAST CLASSIC MOTORCARS EXHIBIT, 2.5 mi. s. of US 30 or .5 mi. n. of SR 741 on SR 896, displays some 50 vintage vehicles ranging from a 1932 Duesenburg Model J convertible to rock star Dee Snider's 1969 boss 302 Mustang. Other rare and classic cars exhibited are a 1981 Lamborghini Countach; a 1966 German Amphicar, an amphibious car that came with an anchor and rope as standard equipment; a 1948 Tucker Torpedo, one of only 51 produced; and a 1982 DeLorean.

Allow 30 minutes minimum. Daily 9-5; closed Jan. 1, Easter, Thanksgiving and Dec. 24-25. Admission $8; ages 7-12, $4. DS, MC, VI. Phone (717) 687-9500.

HISTORIC CONESTOGA CARRIAGE RIDES leave from the Historic Strasburg Inn on SR 896 at Historic Dr. Passengers tour the Amish farm-

land for 30 minutes aboard a restored Conestoga wagon. Rides aboard other 18th- and 19th-century horse-drawn vehicles also are available. Mon.-Sat. 9-5 (weather permitting); closed major holidays. Conestoga fare $5; other vehicles somewhat higher. Phone (717) 687-7691.

SAVE THE NATIONAL TOY TRAIN MUSEUM, 1.5 mi. e. on SR 741 and .2 mi. n. on Paradise Ln., displays antique and 20th-century toy trains. Five operating layouts can be viewed. A videotape about toy trains also is presented. Allow 1 hour minimum. Daily 10-5, May-Oct. and Dec. 26-31; Sat.-Sun. 10-5 in Apr. and Nov. 1-Dec. 24. Admission $3; over 65, $2.75; ages 5-12, $1.50. Phone (717) 687-8976.

SAVE RAILROAD MUSEUM OF PENNSYLVANIA, 1 mi. e. on SR 741E, traces the history of railroads in Pennsylvania through restored locomotives, railcars and memorabilia. The museum takes visitors from the colorful era of 19th-century woodburning engines to modern streamliners. Exhibits include steam, diesel and electric locomotives, and passenger and freight cars. There are more than 35 cars and about 34 engines as well as a re-created railroad station.

Allow 1 hour, 30 minutes minimum. Mon.-Sat. 9-5, Sun. noon-5, Apr.-Oct.; Tues.-Sat. 9-5, Sun. noon-5, rest of year. Closed Jan. 1, Veterans Day, Thanksgiving and Dec. 25. Admission $6; over 60 $5.50; ages 6-12, $4. Phone (717) 687-8628.

STRASBURG COUNTRY STORE AND CREAMERY, Center Sq., is an early general store in a restored 18th-century building. Features include hand-carved counters and cabinets, old tins, a pot-bellied stove and an 1890 marble and silver soda fountain. Mon.-Sat. 8 a.m.-10 p.m., Sun. 11-10, June-Aug.; Mon.-Thurs. 8-8, Fri.-Sat. 8 a.m.-9 p.m., Sun. 11-5, Sept.-Dec. and Apr.-May; Mon.-Sat. 8-5, Sun. 11-5, rest of year. Free. Phone (717) 687-0766. *See ad p. 340.*

STRASBURG RAIL ROAD CO., 1 mi. e. on SR 741E, provides a scenic 45-minute round trip through Amish country on America's oldest short line, which was chartered in 1832. Steam locomotives and wooden passenger cars are displayed at the depot. Santa Claus rides the train with passengers in December. Picnicking is permitted.

Allow 1 hour minimum. Trips on the hour daily 10-7, July-Aug.; 11-3, Apr.-June and in Sept.; Sat. 11-3, Sun. noon-3, rest of year. Fare $7.75; ages 3-11, $4. Phone (717) 687-7522.

Philadelphia
and Vicinity

The United States was born at the Pennsylvania State House, better known today as Independence Hall, in Philadelphia on July 4, 1776, with the adoption of the Declaration of Independence. The Constitution, drafted there in September 1787, laid the framework for the nation's future. But the seeds of independence were planted a century earlier by William Penn.

Penn, a socially prominent convert to the persecuted Society of Friends (Quakers), resolved to provide a place in which all beliefs could flourish. His opportunity arrived when he asked the king to repay a crown debt to his father with a land grant in the Colonies. Charles II, who was delighted with the prospect of easy payment while ridding the land of an embarrassing rebel, complied.

Penn's vision was simple but revolutionary—persons of all faiths living in harmony and freedom. Even in the Colonies, many of which were founded to foster religious tolerance, freedom of worship was limited to the majority sect. Penn guaranteed personal freedoms by allowing every taxpayer a vote, a prisoner the right to be heard, the accused a trial by jury and taxation only by law. Most of these "guarantees" were part of the existing system in England. The city Penn founded became known as Philadelphia, Greek for "city of brotherly love."

Rising resentment against England in the mid-1700s reached its high point in Philadelphia in 1774, where Colonial representatives met to discuss their grievances and debate their options. The fruit of their wrath was the Declaration of Independence, an open break with England and an explanation for a war that was already in progress. After the war Philadelphia became a rallying site for the successful attempt to unify the independent states. In 1787 representatives meeting in the Pennsylvania State House produced the Constitution of the United States.

In 1790 Philadelphia became the temporary capital of the new United States. The next decade saw the fledgling government enduring numerous tests, among them the issues of the French Revolution, persistent yellow fever epidemics and rising political rivalries. In 1800 the seat of government was moved to the newly constructed city of Washington, along the Potomac between Maryland and Virginia.

Venerable Philadelphia landmarks rub shoulders with modern glass and steel office towers; narrow cobblestone streets intersect broad, busy boulevards; charming Colonial houses hide a few blocks from the business district. Fairmount Park presents a lush green oasis in the midst of urban bustle. Representative of past and present, the gracious elegance of Independence Hall contrasts with the strikingly modern facades of Liberty Place.

Franklin Bridge

Society Hill, extending from Front to 7th streets and Walnut to Lombard streets, is the city's original residential area. Named for the Free Society of Traders, a land promotion company chartered by William Penn to develop the area, the Hill blends past and present as modern buildings mingle with hundreds of restored 18th-century houses. Germantown, in northwest Philadelphia, is another old residential section. Settled mainly by Germans and Dutch, many of its old houses are distinguished by Dutch doors and arched cellar windows.

Philadelphia's society, as legendary as its history, shows an endearingly human side. Anthony J. Drexel Biddle Sr., a colonel in World War I who taught hand-to-hand combat to Marines in World War II and raised alligators in his bathtub, inspired a best-selling novel and Broadway play. Also heralded are residents of the Main Line (once the Main Line of the Pennsylvania Railroad), a century-old swath of beautiful homes and estates rich with prestige.

The University of Pennsylvania, with its ivy-clad walls and shaded paths, dates from 1740 and numbers Benjamin Franklin among its founders. In 1765 it opened the country's first medical school and now ranks among the leading national educational centers. Contributing to the city's reputation as a force in higher education are the area's 88 colleges and universities.

Among these are Drexel University; LaSalle University; St. Joseph's University; Swarthmore College, 11 miles southwest of Philadelphia; Temple University; and Villanova University.

Philadelphia has one of the most beautiful exurban regions of any American city. Beyond the urban tangle sprawl rolling green hills studded with gems, both historical and colorful. In Montgomery County are the old company streets of Valley Forge (*see Valley Forge National Historical Park in the Vicinity section p. 128*), where Washington's men struggled to survive the difficult winter of 1777-78.

Approaches

By Car

The major route from the south is I-95 to Philadelphia International Airport. Follow I-95 to I-676 to the city center; enter the business district at 15th Street. From the north, I-95 leads into the northeastern section of the city. From the west, I-676/US 30 traverses the downtown area as the Vine Street Expressway (I-676), and I-76 leaves the Pennsylvania Turnpike at Valley Forge and enters Philadelphia at the Schuylkill Expressway.

US 1 (Roosevelt Boulevard) traverses northeast Philadelphia, but both the north and south entrances into town are heavily commercialized and rather slow. From the east, both the New Jersey Turnpike and I-295, which run north-south in New Jersey, provide ready access to either US 30, which enters the city center via the Benjamin Franklin Bridge and I-676, or to New Jersey SR 42 (North-South Freeway or Atlantic City Expressway), which approaches the Walt Whitman Bridge and south Philadelphia.

Getting Around

It would be wise to leave your automobile behind when going downtown because the old streets, though arrow straight, also are very narrow. Unless you *must* have your car, allow a bus or cab driver to negotiate the congested, often two-lane, streets.

Street System

Most north-south streets, beginning with Front Street west of the Delaware River, are numbered; east-west streets are named. Broad Street, the major north-south artery, is the equivalent of 14th Street. All downtown north-south streets are alternate one-way with the exception of Broad,

The Informed Traveler

CITY POPULATION: 1,524,200   **ELEVATION:** 9 ft.

Whom To Call

Emergency: 911
Police (non-emergency): 911 (Calls will be transferred to the appropriate department.)
Time and Temperature: time (215) 846-1212; temperature (215) 936-1212

Hospitals: Chestnut Hill Hospital, (215) 248-8200; Germantown Hospital and Medical Center, (215) 951-8000; Hospital of the University of PA, (215) 662-4000; Presbyterian Medical Center of Philadelphia, (215) 662-8000.

Where to Look

Newspapers
Philadelphia has two daily papers—the morning and Sunday Philadelphia *Inquirer* and the afternoon *Daily News.*

Radio and TV
Philadelphia radio station KYW (1060 AM) is an all-news/weather station; WHYY (90.1 FM) is programmed by National Public Radio.
The major TV channels are 3 (CBS), 6 (ABC), 10 (NBC), 12 (PBS) and 29 (FOX). For a complete list of radio and television programs, consult the daily newspapers.

Visitor Information
Information about walking tours and attractions in Philadelphia and its environs can be obtained by writing the Philadelphia Visitors Center at 16th St. and John F. Kennedy Blvd., Philadelphia, PA 19102; phone (215) 636-1666, TDD (215) 636-3403 or (800) 537-7676. The center is open daily 9-5.
Independence National Historical Park also operates a visitor center; it is at 3rd and Chestnut streets in the heart of the historical district; phone (215) 597-8974, or TDD (215) 597-1785

What to Wear

Capricious aptly describes Philadelphia's weather. A warm January day may be followed by gray rain or winter's snowy bluster, while a sweltering summer day may turn suddenly chilly

as a squall sweeps in from the sea. Temperatures range from an average low of 24 and a high of 40 in December, to an average low of 65 and high of 86 in July.

which has two lanes in each direction. Market Street is one-way eastbound between 20th and 15th streets. Westbound motorists should use JFK Boulevard at this point. Chestnut Street is closed to all traffic except buses between 8th and 18th streets from 6 a.m. to 7 p.m.

Since Market Street is the principal east-west artery, north and south numbering begins at this street. Westward numbering begins at Front Street.

Right turns on red are permitted after a full stop, unless otherwise posted. Rush hours in general are 7-9:30 a.m. and 4-6:30 p.m. The speed limit on most streets is 25 mph, or as posted.

Parking

Though chances of getting on-street parking on the clogged downtown streets are virtually zero, some metered parking is permitted on side streets and less traveled avenues: Parking meter rates are 25c for 15 minutes. Rates in the numerous lots and garages range from $2.50 for 30 minutes to a maximum of $11.75 for 24 hours.

What To See

ACADEMY OF NATURAL SCIENCES is at 19th St. and Benjamin Franklin Pkwy. Founded in 1812, it is the oldest continually operating institution of its kind in America. Outstanding among the natural sciences exhibits are the "Discovering Dinosaurs" exhibit, which includes dinosaur bones and eggs. Live animal shows, films and special programs also are offered.

Allow 1 hour, 30 minutes minimum. Mon.-Fri. 10-4:30, Sat.-Sun. 10-5; closed Jan. 1, Thanksgiving and Dec. 25. Admission $7.75; over 65, $7; ages 3-12, $6.75. AE, MC, VI ($25). Phone (215) 299-1000.

AFRO-AMERICAN HISTORICAL AND CULTURAL MUSEUM, n.w. corner of 7th and Arch sts., traces the history of African-American culture in the Americas. The special achievements of African-Americans are documented through artifacts, photographs, multimedia presentations and the works of African-American artists. Allow 2 hours minimum. Tues.-Sat. 10-5, Sun. noon-5; closed major holidays. Admission $4; over 65 and ages 6-17, $2. AE, MC, VI. Phone (215) 574-0380.

SAVE AMERICAN SWEDISH HISTORICAL MUSEUM, 1900 Pattison Ave. in Franklin Delano Roosevelt Park, features 13 permanent galleries as well as changing exhibits. A research library focuses on the history of Swedes in America from the establishment of the New Sweden Colony in 1638 to modern Swedish technology, architecture and fine and decorative arts. Traditional Swedish holidays are celebrated year-round.

Tues.-Fri. 10-4, Sat.-Sun. noon-4; closed legal holidays. Admission $5, over 60 and students with ID $4, under 12 free with adult. MC, VI. Phone (215) 389-1776.

THE ATHENAEUM OF PHILADELPHIA, 219 S. 6th St., is named for Athena, the Greek goddess of wisdom. Founded in 1814, this three-story Italianate Revival building is furnished with American fine and decorative arts from the first half of the 19th century. Changing exhibits, drawn from the reference collections in architectural history and historic design, can be seen in the first floor gallery. Guided tours are offered by appointment.

Allow 30 minutes minimum. Mon.-Tues. and Thurs.-Fri. 9-5, Wed. noon-8; closed holidays.

Transportation

Air travel: Philadelphia International Airport is 6.5 miles south of the business district via I-76 (Schuylkill Expressway) and SR 291 (Penrose Avenue). SEPTA's airport rail line runs daily on the half-hour 6 a.m.-midnight between the airport and Market Street East Station, Suburban Station and 30th Street Station; the fare is $5.

Rail service: Amtrak trains pull into both the main terminal, 30th Street Station, at 30th and Market streets, and the North Philadelphia Station at Broad Street and Glenwood Avenue. Should your destination be mid-city, disembark at 30th Street Station. For Amtrak information phone (215) 824-1600.

Buses: The major bus terminal is Greyhound Lines Inc., (800) 231-2222, at 10th and Filbert streets. New Jersey Transit buses, (215) 569-3752, also depart for southern New Jersey and shore points.

Rental cars: Hertz, 31 S. 19th St., (800) 654-3131 or (800) 654-3080, offers discounts to AAA members. Other companies are listed in the local telephone directory.

Public transport: A system of buses, streetcars, subways and elevateds (Els) serves Philadelphia. Operated by the Southeastern Pennsylvania Transportation Authority (SEPTA), all vehicles charge $1.60, plus 40c for a transfer; exact change is required. Senior citizens ride free in off-peak hours.

A SEPTA Daypass provides unlimited rides on all SEPTA buses, streetcars, subways and Els within the city and a one-way ride on the airport line; the pass is $5. For information about schedules, routes and locations where the Daypass and tokens may be purchased phone (215) 580-7800.

Taxis: Fares for United Cab Association, (215) 238-9500, are $1.80 per mile. Fares for Yellow Cab Co., (215) 922-8400, are $2.80 for the first mile and $1.80 for each additional mile.

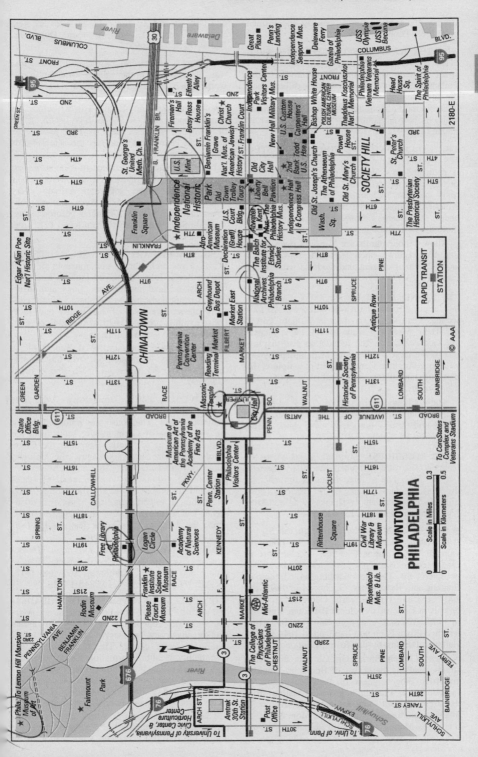

DOWNTOWN
PHILADELPHIA

Library and reading room open by appointment only. Free. Phone (215) 925-2688.

ATWATER KENT MUSEUM—THE PHILADELPHIA HISTORY MUSEUM, 15 S. 7th St., is a small museum with hundreds of artifacts from Philadelphia's past. Featured are exhibits about the city's history and archeology. Allow 30 minutes minimum. Mon. and Wed.-Sun. 10-4; closed major holidays. Admission $3; children $1.50. Phone (215) 922-3031.

THE BALCH INSTITUTE FOR ETHNIC STUDIES, 1 blk. w. of the Liberty Bell at 18 S. 7th St., is dedicated to collecting, preserving and interpreting materials reflecting the nation's multicultural heritage. Changing exhibits focus on America's ethnic, racial and immigrant experiences. A research library has materials about more than 70 ethnic groups.

Allow 1 hour minimum. Museum open Mon.-Sat. 10-4. Library open Tues.-Sat. 10-4. Admission $2, senior citizens and students with ID $1. Phone (215) 925-8090.

THE BARNES FOUNDATION, 300 N. Latch's Ln. in Merion, displays the Albert C. Barnes Art Collection. Featured artists include William Glackens, Henri Matisse, Claude Monet, Pablo Picasso and George Roualt. The foundation also displays one of the largest collections of paintings by artist Pierre Auguste Renoir. African sculpture, Indian rugs and blankets and cubist sculpture also are exhibited.

Allow 2 hours minimum. Fri.-Sat. 9:30-5, Sun. 12:30-5, Sept.-June; closed legal holidays, Good Friday and Easter. Hours may vary; phone ahead. Admission $5. Phone (610) 667-0290.

BETSY ROSS HOUSE, 239 Arch St., is where the Colonial seamstress stitched the first American flag in 1777. The restored home is furnished in the working-class manner of the period. Tues.-Sun. 10-5; closed Jan. 1, Thanksgiving and Dec. 25. Donations. Phone (215) 627-5343.

★ CHRIST CHURCH (Episcopal), on 2nd St. between Market and Arch sts., was the house of worship of 15 signers of the Declaration of Independence. Brass plaques mark the pews once occupied by George Washington, Benjamin Franklin and Betsy Ross. Organized in 1695, the 1727 structure typifies early Georgian architecture. It has one of the oldest Palladian windows in North America. It also contains the font from which William Penn was baptized in 1644 in All-Hallows, Barking-by-the-Tower, London.

Christ Church Burial Ground, 5th and Arch streets, contains the graves of Benjamin Franklin and four other signers of the Declaration of Independence; Franklin's grave is visible from the street. Guided tours are available. Allow 30 minutes minimum. Church open Mon.-Sat. 9-5, Sun. 1-5, Mar. 1-Dec. 23; Wed.-Sat. 9-5, Sun. 1-5, rest of year. Closed Jan. 1, Thanksgiving

and Dec. 25 and 31. Episcopal services are held Sun. at 9 and 11, Wed. at noon. Donations. Phone (215) 922-1695.

CITY HALL, at Penn Sq., Broad and Market sts., was planned to be the tallest structure in the world when construction began in 1871. However, it was surpassed in height by the Washington Monument and Eiffel Tower before its completion in 1901. A 37-foot-high bronze statue of William Penn tops the City Hall tower. The charter in Penn's left hand has the actual words of the charter inscribed upon it.

Ninety-minute guided tours of the interior of City Hall, including the tower, are offered Mon.-Fri. at 12:30; tower tours are offered every quarter-hour Mon.-Fri. 9:30-4:15. Closed holidays. Last tour begins 15 minutes before closing. The 90-minute tours depart from room 121. Free. Phone (215) 686-2840.

CIVIL WAR LIBRARY AND MUSEUM, 1805 Pine St., is a research library and museum of Civil War artifacts. Items displayed include uniforms, weapons, medical instruments, flags and insignias. A room dedicated to Abraham Lincoln contains plaster life-casts of his hands and face. Other exhibits are dedicated to Gens. George G. Meade and Ulysses S. Grant.

Allow 1 hour minimum. Wed.-Sun. 11-4:30; closed holidays. Admission $5; over 65, $4; students with ID $3; ages 3-12, $2. Phone (215) 735-8196.

SAVE CLIVEDEN, 6401 Germantown Ave., was built 1763-67 for Pennsylvania Chief Justice Benjamin Chew. The house was damaged during the 1777 Battle of Germantown; scars from the battle remain in the walls. Home to the Chew family for more than 200 years, the Colonial home is furnished with 18th- and 19th-century pieces, and visitors can view original Chippendale and Federal style family furnishings along with Chinese export porcelain, paintings, documents and other decorative arts. Nestled on 6 acres, the mid-Georgian home features English-style roof urns and garden statuary.

Allow 1 hour, 30 minutes minimum. Thurs.-Sun. noon-4, Apr.-Dec.; closed Easter, Thanksgiving and Dec. 25. Admission $6; ages 6-18, $4. AE, MC, VI. Phone (215) 848-1777.

THE COLLEGE OF PHYSICIANS OF PHILADELPHIA, 19 S. 22nd St. between Chestnut and Market sts., was founded in 1787 by the area's leading physicians and serves as a health information resource center. The C. Everett Koop Community Health Information Center provides up-to-date health information through such mediums as on-line computers, videotapes, journals, pamphlets and a library containing some 500 books written for patients and consumers.

The Mütter Museum contains medical instruments, exhibits detailing the history of medicine within the last 100 years and a re-creation of an early 20th-century doctor's office. Serving the Cause of Science and Humanity is a permanent exhibit that provides an introduction to the museum, information about Dr. Mütter and a depiction of the practice of medicine during his lifetime in the 1830s. Other features include a medicinal plant garden and changing exhibit gallery. Tues.-Sat. 10-4; closed major holidays. Admission $8; over 62, students with ID and ages 6-18, $4. AE, MC, VI. Phone (215) 563-3737.

CORESTATES COMPLEX, S. Broad St. and Pattison Ave., Philadelphia's sports and entertainment complex, consists of two arenas—the CoreStates Center and the CoreStates Spectrum. CoreStates Center is the home of the Philadelphia 76ers, Flyers and Wings; shows, concerts and athletic events also are held here. CoreStates Spectrum houses sporting events, concerts and family shows. Guided tours of the complex are available.

Tours are given Mon.-Fri. at 10, 11, noon and 1, provided no events are scheduled. Fee $6; under 12, $5. Phone (215) 336-3600 for information about scheduled events or 389-9543 for tour information.

DREXEL COLLECTION, 32nd and Chestnut sts., includes antique European and American furniture, a Rittenhouse clock, Boehm porcelain and 19th-century artworks. Mon. 11-5, Tues.-Wed. 9-10:30 and 1:30-5, Thurs.-Fri. 1:30-5; closed school holidays. Free. Phone (215) 895-2424.

EDGAR ALLAN POE NATIONAL HISTORIC SITE, 532 N. 7th St., contains a visitor center, which has exhibits, an audiovisual program and library, and the house where Poe lived 1843-44. Guided tours daily 9-5, June-Oct.; Wed.-Sun. 9-5, rest of year. Closed Jan. 1, Thanksgiving and Dec. 25. Free. Phone (215) 597-8780 (voice or TDD).

ELFRETH'S ALLEY, n. of Arch St. between Front and 2nd sts., is one of many narrow streets lined with quaint restored houses that have stood since the days of Penn's "Greene Countrie Towne." Information about other buildings in the alley is available at the Elfreth's Alley Museum, 126 Elfreth's Alley. Elfreth's Alley Museum open Tues.-Sat. 10-4, Sun. noon-4, Mar.-Dec.; closed holidays. Museum admission $2; under 12, $1; family rate $5 (two adults and up to three children under 12). Phone (215) 574-0560.

★**FAIRMOUNT PARK** is reached by Benjamin Franklin Pkwy. This beautiful park covers 8,579 acres along both sides of the Schuylkill River. The park is threaded by miles of scenic drives, walks, a bicycle route and bridle trails. Visitors can see sculls racing on the Schuylkill, hear band concerts in Pastorious Park or symphony orchestras at Mann Center for the Performing Arts, or visit the numerous museums and historic houses.

The park, founded in 1812, was the site of the Centennial Exposition in 1876. Of almost 200 buildings erected for the fair, only Memorial Hall

and the Ohio House remain. Glendenning Rock Garden and Horticultural Hall Gardens are noteworthy. Within the park boundaries are several Colonial estates (*see Fairmount Park Historic Houses*).

The boathouses along the Schuylkill River are lit at night with strings of white lights that reflect in the water; they are best seen from the Schuylkill Expressway across the river.

Historic RittenhouseTown, on Wissahickon Ave. between Lincoln Dr. and Walnut Ln., was the site of the first hand paper mill in America. The Colonial industrial village was home to more than 40 structures including a paper mill, church, school and fire company. Today seven buildings remain and can be viewed from the outside via a guided walking tour. A museum features exhibits, including an operating diorama of the first paper mill, and an orientation film.

Mon.-Fri. 10-4, Sat.-Sun. noon-4. Admission $4; over 65 and ages 5-12, $2. Reservations are required. Phone (215) 438-5711.

Horticulture Center, off Montgomery Dr. on Belmont Horticulture Dr., includes a landscaped arboretum with a large reflecting pool, Japanese house and garden, seasonal greenhouse displays and outdoor gardens. Allow 30 minutes minimum. Daily 9-3; closed holidays. Donations. Phone (215) 685-0096.

Japanese House and Garden, off Montgomery Dr. at Belmont Mansion Dr., are part of the Horticulture Center. A tea ceremony is held on occasional Sunday afternoons. Allow 1 hour minimum. Tues.-Sun. 11-4, May-Aug.; Sat.-Sun. 11-4, Sept.-Oct. Closed holidays. Admission $2.50; senior citizens and students with ID $2; under 12, $1. Phone (215) 878-5097.

Laurel Hill Cemetery, 3822 Ridge Ave., incorporates striking architecture and landscape design elements into its 95 acres. The grounds are shaded by large trees and contain interesting statuary. Tues.-Sat. 9:30-1:30. Free. Phone (215) 228-8200.

Mann Center for the Performing Arts, 52nd St. and Parkside Ave., is an outdoor amphitheater presenting summer concerts by the Philadelphia Orchestra. Concerts Mon. and Wed.-Thurs. evenings, late June-late July; Pop concerts May-Sept. Single tickets are sold at the box office. Phone (215) 878-7707.

★**Philadelphia Museum of Art,** end of Benjamin Franklin Pkwy. at 26th St., ranks among the world's major art museums. Founded in 1876, the museum's collections offer a full range of both fine and decorative arts from Asia, Europe and the United States. Spanning over 2,000 years, the collections include masterpieces of painting, sculpture, prints and drawings, as well as a wide variety of furniture, silver, glasswork, architectural elements and rooms furnished from historic houses.

Included are works by Paul Cézanne, Claude Monet, Nicolas Poussin, Pierre Auguste Renoir, Peter Paul Rubens and Vincent Van Gogh as well as those by modern artists. The museum displays one of the largest collections of work by Thomas Eakins. Allow 1 hour, 30 minutes minimum. Tues.-Sun. 10-5 (also Wed. 5-8:45); closed holidays. Guided tours are available hourly 10-3. Special programs are presented Wednesday evenings. Admission $8; over 62 and ages 5-18, $5; free to all Sun. 10-1. Limited free parking. AE, MC, VI. Phone (215) 763-8100.

Rodin Museum, Benjamin Franklin Pkwy. and 22nd St., displays a priceless 124-piece collection of Rodin originals and casts, the largest outside Paris. On the grounds is a formal garden with boxwood hedges, trees and a rectangular pool. Audiotape tours are available. Allow 30 minutes minimum. Tues.-Sun. 10-5. Guided tours are available at 1 on the first and third Sat., the second and fourth Sun., and the fourth Wed. of the month. Closed legal holidays. Donations. Tour tape $3. Phone (215) 763-8100.

Zoological Gardens, 3400 W. Girard Ave., contains more than 1,700 mammals, birds and reptiles. A children's zoo provides both contact areas and presentations. Allow 2 hours minimum. Zoo open Mon.-Fri. 9:30-4:45, Sat.-Sun. and holidays 9:30-5:45, Mar.-Nov.; daily 10-4, rest of year. Children's zoo open daily 10-4:30. Closed Jan. 1, Thanksgiving and Dec. 24-25 and 31. Zoo admission $8.50; over 65 and ages 2-11, $6. Tree house admission $1. MC, VI. Phone (215) 243-1100.

FAIRMOUNT PARK HISTORIC HOUSES, along the banks of the Schuylkill River, were the homes of wealthy Philadelphians. Phone (215) 684-7922.

Cedar Grove, Lansdowne Dr., is an 18th-century Quaker farmhouse with a large covered porch. Tues.-Sun. 10-4. Admission $2.50; under 12, $1.25.

Laurel Hill, Kelly Dr. to Fountain Green, following signs, features paneling, delft tiles and an octagonal drawing room with Federal architectural details. Costumed guides conduct tours of the home. Wed.-Fri. 9-4. Admission $2.50; under 12, $1.25.

Lemon Hill, Kelly Dr., is a masterpiece of 19th-century architecture. Wed.-Sun. 10-4. Admission $2.50; under 12, $1.50.

Mount Pleasant, on Fountain Green at 35th St. and Columbia Ave., was the summer home of a Scottish sea captain and privateer. Tues.-Sun. 10-4. Admission $2.50; under 12, $1.

Strawberry Mansion, near Dauphin St. entrance, is the largest of the mansions and is furnished in Empire style. Tues.-Sun. 10-4. Admission $2.50; under 12, $1.

Sweetbriar Mansion, Lansdowne Ave. n. of Girard Ave., captures magnificent views of the Schuylkill from its terrace. Mon., Wed. and Sun. 10-4. Admission $2.50; under 12, $1.

Woodford Mansion, 33rd and Dauphin sts., is a fine example of Colonial architecture and is decorated with a collection of American-crafted furniture. Tues.-Sun. 10-4. Admission $2.50; ages 6-12, $1.

FIREMAN'S HALL—NATIONAL FIRE HOUSE AND MUSEUM OF PHILADELPHIA, 147 N. 2nd St. above Arch St., is housed in a fire house built in 1876. The history of firefighting is depicted using memorabilia, graphics, films and early firefighting equipment. Allow 1 hour minimum. Tues.-Sat. 9-4:30; closed holidays. Free. Phone (215) 923-1438.

FORT MIFFLIN, I-95 s. to Island Ave. exit, then .5 mi. s. to Fort Mifflin Rd., following signs, was built in 1772 by the British to protect the Colonies. Ironically, during the Revolutionary War it was the Americans who used the fort to protect Philadelphia and the Delaware River. The fort was used during the Civil War and for ammunition storage until 1962. Allow 1 hour minimum. Wed.-Sun. 10-4, Apr.-Nov. Admission $4, over 64 and students with ID $2, under 2 free. Phone (215) 685-4192.

SAVE ★FRANKLIN INSTITUTE SCIENCE MUSEUM is at 20th St. and Benjamin Franklin Pkwy. Hands-on exhibits and demonstrations relate to science and industry, computers, physics, astronomy, geography, oceanography, meteorology, mathematics, communications and history. The museum is the national memorial to Benjamin Franklin and contains many of Franklin's personal effects as well as a statue by James Earle Fraser.

Allow 4 hours minimum. Daily 9:30-5; closed major holidays and Dec. 24-25. Admission (including Mandell Center) $9.50; over 62 and ages 4-11, $8.50. Combination ticket including Fels Planetarium *or* Tuttleman Omniverse Theater $12.50; over 62 and ages 4-11, $10.50. Combination ticket including Fels Planetarium and Tuttleman Omniverse Theater $14.50; over 62 and ages 4-11, $12.50. AE, DS, MC, VI. Phone (215) 448-1200.

Fels Planetarium, opened in 1933, is among the country's oldest. Computer-generated images are projected onto the 65-foot-wide planetarium dome. Laser shows are offered Saturday and Sunday. For shows and times phone (215) 448-1200.

Mandell Center displays special exhibits that manifest how science and technology are shaping the 21st century. Cyberzone contains high-speed computers that will open up the world of technology to visitors. Daily 9:30-5 (also Fri.-Sat. 5-9). Admission included with the Franklin Institute Science Museum. Phone (215) 448-1200.

Tuttleman Omniverse Theater projects films of science and adventure onto a four-story, 79-foot-wide domed screen. Diverse topics include space exploration, nature and the human body. The main feature is preceded by "Symphony Philadelphia," a short film about Philadelphia. Mon.-Fri. 10-4, Sat.-Sun. 10-5 (hours may be extended Fri.-Sat.). For shows and times phone (215) 448-1111.

FREE LIBRARY OF PHILADELPHIA, Logan Sq. at 19th and Vine sts., has a variety of exhibits about art, architecture, photography, books and local history. Tours of the rare book room are conducted Mon.-Fri. at 11. Free concerts, films and lecture programs are presented on Sun.; phone for times. Mon.-Wed. 9-9, Thurs.-Fri. 9-6, Sat. 9-5, Sun. 1-5, Sept.-May; Mon.-Wed. 9-9, Thurs.-Fri. 9-6, Sat. 9-5, rest of year. Free. Phone (215) 686-5322.

GERMANTOWN HISTORICAL SOCIETY, 5501 Germantown Ave. on Market Sq., provides an overview of the history of the community from the time of settlement in 1683 to the present. Germantown was America's first German settlement, the scene of the Revolutionary Battle of Germantown, the birthplace of writer Louisa May Alcott, the site of the Underground Railroad and is home to more than 12 historic houses.

Museum and library collections include toys and dolls, quilts, costumes, furniture, genealogy records, photographs and paintings. Guided tours are offered. Allow 2 hours minimum. Information available Sun.-Fri. Library open Tues. and Thurs. 10-4, Sun. 1-5. Admission $4; under 13, $2. Phone (215) 844-1683.

GLORIA DEI (OLD SWEDES') CHURCH, Christian St. at Christopher Columbus Blvd., is believed to be Pennsylvania's oldest church. The church was built in 1700, but its congregation was founded in 1677. Sat.-Sun. 9-5 and by appointment. Phone (215) 389-1513.

HEAD HOUSE SQUARE, bounded by 2nd, Pine, Front and Lombard sts., was Society Hill's New Market when it opened in 1745. The square's picturesque shops include the Dickens Inn, a gourmet shop, restaurant and printshops. Mon.-Sat. 11-9, Sun. 11-6.

HISTORIC BARTRAM'S GARDEN is entered from Lindberg Blvd. w. of 54th St. The 18th century farm of Colonial botanist John Bartram, the estate is now a 44-acre public park on the banks of the Schuylkill. The grounds feature the furnished house, a botanical garden and a wildflower meadow. A guided tour of the house is available. Allow 1 hour minimum. The garden is open daily dawn-dusk. The house is open Wed.-Sun. noon-4, May-Oct.; Wed.-Fri. noon-4, rest of year. Grounds admission free. Guided tour $3. Phone (215) 729-5281.

HISTORICAL SOCIETY OF PENNSYLVANIA, 1300 Locust St., is a museum and research center for American and Pennsylvania history. It contains 15 million rare documents, books, maps, artifacts, prints and genealogical records. A permanent multimedia exhibit, "Finding Philadelphia's Past: Visions and Revisions," explores 300 years of the city's history. Among the displays are the first draft of the Constitution.

Allow 1 hour minimum. Tues. and Thurs.-Sat. 10-5, Wed. 1-9; closed major holidays. Museum $2.50; senior citizens and ages 6-18, $1.50. Library admission charged. Phone (215) 732-6201.

★INDEPENDENCE NATIONAL HISTORICAL PARK, whose main area extends from 2nd to 6th sts. between Walnut and Market sts., includes buildings in Independence Square and others throughout the city that are closely associated with the Colonial period, the founding of the nation and Philadelphia's early role as national capital.

The visitor center for Independence National Historical Park, 3rd and Chestnut streets, presents the 30-minute John Huston film "Independence" throughout the day. Inquire at the center for a walking-tour map and the latest information about all the park's attractions and activities. Building hours vary; phone ahead. Admission is free. To confirm schedules phone (215) 597-8974, or TDD (215) 597-1785.

B. Free Franklin Post Office and Museum, 316 Market St., commemorates Franklin's 1775 appointment as first postmaster general. The only post office operated by the U.S. Postal Service that does not fly the American flag, it is named after Franklin's unique signature-cancellation. It is assumed that his use of "Free" as part of his signature referred to America's struggle for freedom. Philatelists prize the hand-canceled letters from this post office. Daily 9-5; closed Jan. 1 and Dec. 25. Free. Phone (215) 592-1289.

Bishop White House, 309 Walnut St., was built by Pennsylvania's first Protestant Episcopal bishop. The restored house contains many original articles. Building hours vary; phone ahead. Closed Jan. 1 and Dec. 25. Admission $2, under 17 free. Admission is by tour only; obtain tickets at the visitor center on 3rd and Chestnut streets. Phone (215) 597-8974, or TDD (215) 597-1785.

Carpenters' Hall, 320 Chestnut St., was lent by the Carpenters' Co. of Philadelphia for the First Continental Congress in 1774. Inside are a collection of early carpentry tools and chairs used by the Congress. An 11-minute videotape presentation chronicles the history of the Carpenters' Co., which still owns and operates the hall. Tues.-Sun. 10-4, Mar.-Dec.; Wed.-Sun. 10-4, rest of year. Closed Jan. 1, Easter, Thanksgiving and Dec. 24-25. Free. Phone (215) 925-0167.

★ **Congress Hall,** 6th and Chestnut sts., was occupied by the U.S. Congress 1790-1800. On the first floor is the chamber of the House of Representatives; the second floor contains the more elaborate chamber of the Senate and various committee rooms. The hall was the setting for the inaugurations of George Washington (his second) and John Adams. Building hours vary; phone ahead. Closed Jan. 1 and Dec. 25. Free. Phone (215) 597-8974, or TDD (215) 597-1785.

Declaration (Graff) House, s.w. corner of 7th and Market sts., is a reconstruction of the dwelling in which Thomas Jefferson drafted the Declaration of Independence in June 1776. An audiovisual program is shown. Building hours vary; phone ahead. Closed Jan. 1 and Dec. 25. Free. Phone (215) 597-8974, or TDD (215) 597-1785.

Deshler-Morris House, 5442 Germantown Ave., was where George Washington spent the fall of 1793 and the summer of 1794. The restored 1772 house is furnished in period. Tues.-Sat. 1-4, Apr. 1 to mid-Dec.; closed legal holidays. Admission $1, students with ID 50c. Phone (215) 596-1748.

Franklin Court, between 3rd, 4th, Chestnut and Market sts., was once owned by Benjamin Franklin, who lived in Philadelphia from 1722 until his death in 1790. The complex encompasses an underground theater and museum as well as the five Market Street houses, the exteriors of which have been restored to their Franklin era appearances.

In the buildings are the refinished "Aurora" newspaper office, a working reproduction of a 1785 printing press and bindery operation, an ar-

cheological exhibit and a post office. Building hours vary; phone ahead. Closed Jan. 1 and Dec. 25. Free. Phone (215) 597-8974, or TDD (215) 597-1785.

★ **Independence Hall** is between 5th and 6th sts. on Chestnut St. in Independence Square. In this graceful 1732 brick building, the Declaration of Independence and Constitution were signed, the Second Continental Congress decided in 1775 to resist England, and George Washington accepted the role of commander in chief of the Colonial armies. Within the Assembly Room are the inkstand used in signing the Declaration and the "rising sun" chair occupied by Washington during the drafting of the Constitution.

The Assembly Room has been restored to look as it did when used by the Founding Fathers 1775-87. Across the hallway is the restored Pennsylvania Supreme Court Chamber. Upstairs, the Governor's Council Chamber, Long Room and Committee Room have been restored and furnished in period. Admission is by guided tour only; tours are offered regularly throughout the day. Daily 9-5, with extended hours in summer. Free. Phone (215) 597-8974, or TDD (215) 597-1785.

★ **Liberty Bell Pavilion,** 5th, 6th, Market and Chestnut sts., is a glass structure that forms a permanent home for the Liberty Bell, which was moved from Independence Hall on Jan. 1, 1976. Park rangers relate the bell's history. Daily 9-5, with extended hours in summer. The bell can be viewed from the exterior 24 hours a day. Free. Phone (215) 597-8974, or TDD (215) 597-1785.

New Hall Military Museum, on Chestnut between 3rd and 4th sts., is a reconstruction of a 1791 building. The museum commemorates the history of the U.S. Army, Navy and Marine Corps 1775-1805. Hours vary; phone ahead. Closed Jan. 1 and Dec. 25. Free. Phone (215) 597-8974, or TDD (215) 597-1785.

Old City Hall, s.w. corner of 5th and Chestnut sts., was the home of the U.S. Supreme Court 1791-1800. The exterior and the room used by the Supreme Court have been restored. Building hours vary; phone ahead. Closed Jan. 1 and Dec. 25. Free. Phone (215) 597-8974, or TDD (215) 597-1785.

Old St. Joseph's Church, 321 Willings Alley, at 4th St. below Walnut St., was the first Roman Catholic church in Philadelphia. The Marquis de Lafayette and Comte de Rochambeau worshiped in its dim interior. Mon.-Fri. 9-5, Sat. 10-6, Sun. 9-3:30. Phone (215) 923-1733.

St. George's United Methodist Church, 235 N. 4th St. at the Benjamin Franklin Bridge, was dedicated in 1769 and is the oldest Methodist church used continuously for worship. In 1784 St. George's licensed the first African-American Methodist preacher in the United States. The adjoining Methodist Historical Center contains church relics. For guide service ring the bell on

New Street. Allow 30 minutes minimum. Daily 10-3; closed Jan. 1, Thanksgiving and Dec. 25. Free. Phone (215) 925-7788.

★ **Second Bank Of United States,** 420 Chestnut St., is an 1824 structure which now houses Independence National Historical Park's National Portrait Gallery. These 185 late 18th- and early 19th-century portraits, many by Charles Willson Peale, illustrate Philadelphia's role as the capital city 1790-1800. Building hours vary; phone ahead. Closed Jan. 1 and Dec. 25. Admission $2, under 17 free. Phone (215) 597-8974, or TDD (215) 597-1785.

Thaddeus Kosciuszko National Memorial, 3rd and Pine sts., presents exhibits and audiovisual displays, in English and Polish, describing Thaddeus Kosciuszko's contributions to the American Revolution. The home's exterior has been restored. Allow 30 minutes minimum. Daily 9-5, June-Oct.; Tues.-Sat. 9-5, rest of year. Closed Jan. 1, Thanksgiving and Dec. 25. Free. Phone (215) 597-9618.

Todd House, 4th and Walnut sts., was the home of Dolley Payne Todd before her marriage to James Madison, fourth president of the United States. Tour tickets can be obtained at the park visitor center, 3rd and Chestnut streets. Building hours vary; phone ahead. Closed Jan. 1 and Dec. 25. Admission $2, under 17 free. Phone (215) 597-8974, or TDD (215) 597-1785.

INDEPENDENCE SEAPORT MUSEUM, in Penns Landing at 211 S. Columbus Blvd. at Walnut St., relates the maritime heritage of the Delaware River, the bay and its tributaries through interactive exhibits. Permanent exhibits include Homeport Philadelphia, Divers of the Deep, Workshop on the Water, an extensive maritime library, the USS *Becuna* and the USS *Olympia.* Allow 1 hour minimum. Daily 10-5; closed Jan. 1, Thanksgiving and Dec. 25. Admission (including the USS *Becuna,* the USS *Olympia* and the workshop) $7.50; over 65, $6; ages 4-12, $3.50. AE, MC, VI. Phone (215) 925-5439.

USS *Becuna* is a guppy-class submarine commissioned in 1943 to serve in Adm. William Halsey's Seventh Fleet in the South Pacific. Allow 30 minutes minimum. Daily 10-4:30; closed Jan. 1, Thanksgiving and Dec. 25. Admission (including the museum, the USS *Olympia* and the workshop) $7.50; over 65, $6; ages 4-12, $3.50. AE, MC, VI. Phone (215) 922-1898.

USS *Olympia*, Adm. George Dewey's flagship during the Spanish-American War, brought back the body of the Unknown Soldier in 1921. Allow 30 minutes minimum. Daily 10-4:30; closed Jan. 1, Thanksgiving and Dec. 25. Admission (including the museum, the USS *Becuna* and the workshop) $7.50; over 65, $6; ages 4-12, $3.50. AE, MC, VI.

The Workshop on the Water is where boatbuilders can be seen practicing their craft. Models, blueprints and replicas of a variety of small watercraft pay tribute to generations of boatbuilders and enthusiasts. Allow 30 minutes minimum. Daily 10-5; closed Jan. 1, Thanksgiving and Dec. 25. Admission (including the museum, the USS *Becuna* and the USS *Olympia*) $7.50; over 65, $6; ages 4-12, $3.50. AE, MC, VI. Phone (215) 413-8638.

MARIO LANZA INSTITUTE AND MUSEUM, 416 Queen St., is in the Settlement Music School where opera and film star Mario Lanza received his early musical education. The museum displays treasures from Lanza's life, including many portraits and photographs. Among the highlights is a bust of Lanza made behind the Iron Curtain by a Hungarian sculptor. Allow 30 minutes minimum. Mon.-Sat. 10-3:30, Jan.-June and Sept.-Dec.; Mon.-Fri. 10-3:30, rest of year. Closed major and school holidays. Free. Phone (215) 468-3623.

★ **MASONIC TEMPLE,** 1 N. Broad St., was built 1868-73 and is one of the city's striking architectural landmarks. Each of the temple's seven lodge halls exemplifies a different architectural style—Corinthian, Ionic, Italian Renaissance, Norman, Gothic, Oriental and Egyptian. The hallways and stairways are enhanced by chandeliers and paintings, statuary and other artworks. A large stained-glass window overlooks the marble grand staircase.

Tours of the building include the Grand Lodge Museum, a Byzantine-style room housing Masonic treasures. Included in the collection are jewels, George Washington's Masonic apron, furniture, Liverpool and Lowestoft ware, cut glass and statues by William Rush. Visitors must be accompanied by guides. Tours Mon.-Fri. at 10, 11, 1, 2 and 3; Sat. at 10 and 11; closed major holidays and Sat. in July and Aug. Donations. Phone (215) 988-1917.

MORRIS ARBORETUM OF THE UNIVERSITY OF PENNSYLVANIA is at 100 Northwestern Ave., between Germantown and Stenton aves. in Chestnut Hill. Within its 92 acres are 3,500 kinds of trees and shrubs, including North American, European and Asian species. Highlights include the Rose Garden, Swan Pond, Magnolia Slopes and a Victorian house fernery.

Allow 1 hour, 30 minutes minimum. Mon.-Fri. 10-4, Sat.-Sun. 10-5 (10-4, Nov.-Mar.). Guided tours are available Sat.-Sun. at 2. Closed Jan. 1, Thanksgiving and Dec. 24-31. Admission $4; over 65, $3; students with ID $2; under 6 free. Phone (215) 247-5777.

SAVE MUMMERS MUSEUM, 1100 S. 2nd St. at Washington Ave., contains audiovisual and participatory displays, costumes and musical instruments that trace the history of the Mummers and their New Year's Day parade. Guided tours are available by reservation. Allow 1 hour minimum. Tues.-Sat. 9:30-5, Sun. noon-5, Sept.-June;

Tues.-Sat. 9:30-5, rest of year. Closed holidays. String band concerts are given Tues. at 8 p.m., May-Sept. (weather permitting). Admission $2.50; over 55 and ages 6-13, $2. Phone (215) 336-3050.

MUSEUM OF AMERICAN ART OF THE PENN-SYLVANIA ACADEMY OF THE FINE ARTS is at 118 N. Broad St. at Cherry St. Founded in 1805, the museum houses a collection of American art that spans 3 centuries. Featured are works by Mary Cassatt, Richard Diebenkorn, Thomas Eakins, Georgia O'Keeffe, Horace Pippin, Katherine Porter and Benjamin West. The museum building, built in 1876, is an outstanding example of high-Victorian Gothic architecture.

Allow 1 hour minimum. Mon.-Sat. 10-5, Sun. 11-5; closed holidays. Admission $5.95; over 65 and students with ID $4.95; ages 5-11, $3.95; free to all Sun. 3-5. MC, VI. Phone (215) 972-7600.

NATIONAL ARCHIVES PHILADELPHIA BRANCH, 900 Market St., entrance on Chestnut St., contains records that document American history from the First Continental Congress to the present. This branch has Civil and Revolutionary War records and changing exhibitions. Allow 30 minutes minimum. Mon.-Fri. 8-5, second Sat. of each month 8-4. Free. Phone (215) 597-3000.

NATIONAL MUSEUM OF AMERICAN JEWISH HISTORY, 55 N. 5th St. (Independence Mall East) next to the Mikveh Israel Synagogue, offers changing exhibits depicting the contributions Jewish people have made to America. Documents and artifacts preserve the history of Jewish life. Allow 1 hour minimum. Guided tours Mon.-Thurs. 10-5, Fri. 10-3, Sun. noon-5. Admission $2.50; over 65, students with ID and ages 6-18, $1.75. Phone (215) 923-3811.

NATIONAL SHRINE OF ST. JOHN NEUMANN, 5th St. and Girard Ave., contains relics of the life and canonization of the saint. Featured are stained-glass windows depicting his life. His remains are in a glass casket entombed under the main altar. A museum also is available. Allow 1 hour, 30 minutes minimum. The church is open daily 7:30-5. Guided tours are given Mon.-Sat. 9-3. Museum open Mon.-Fri. 7:30-4, Sat.-Sun. 10-4; closed major holidays. Free. Phone (215) 627-3080.

OLD ST. MARY'S CHURCH, 4th St. between Locust and Spruce sts., was founded in 1763 and enlarged in 1810. The second Roman Catholic church in Philadelphia, it became the city's first cathedral in 1810. Daily 9-5. Free. Phone (215) 923-7930.

PENN'S LANDING, between Market and Lombard sts. along the Delaware River, marks the site where William Penn landed in 1682. The 37-acre area, which has several historic ships maintained by the Philadelphia Ship Preservation Guild and a sculpture garden, features concerts, festivals and special exhibitions throughout the year. **Note:** The area will be under construction 1998-99. Phone (215) 629-3200, or 629-6237 for program information.

Gazela of Philadelphia, built in 1883, is the last ship of the Portuguese white fleet. The *Gazela* is the oldest and largest wooden square-rigged vessel still putting out to sea. The ship once departed Lisbon in the spring and returned about 6 months later, laden with salted cod taken from the coastal waters off Eastern Canada. Serving as the maritime ambassador for both the city and the commonwealth, the ship sails to ports along the east coast and Canada. For hours and admission prices phone (215) 923-9030.

Jupiter **Tugboat** was built in 1902 in Camden, N.J. For hours and admission prices phone (215) 923-9030.

PENNSYLVANIA HORTICULTURAL SOCIETY, 100 N. 20th St. on the 5th floor, houses gardening literature; a library is on the 1st floor. Allow 30 minutes minimum. Mon.-Fri. 9-5; closed legal holidays. Free. Phone (215) 988-8800.

★ **PHILADELPHIA MUSEUM OF ART**—
see Fairmount Park p. 111.

[SAVE] **PLEASE TOUCH MUSEUM,** 210 N. 21st St., encourages visitors to use their senses. Children, especially those under 8, will enjoy holding, smelling, listening to and watching a variety of art, science and cultural objects. Special events and weekend theater performances also are available. Allow 1 hour, 30 minutes minimum. Daily 9-6, July 1-Labor Day; 9-4:30, rest of year. Closed Jan. 1, Thanksgiving and Dec. 25. Admission $6.95, under 1 free. Every four children must be accompanied by one adult. AE, MC, VI. Phone (215) 963-0667.

POLISH AMERICAN CULTURAL CENTER MUSEUM, opposite Independence National Historic Park at 308 Walnut St., maintains a portrait collection celebrating well-known Polish figures. Among the scientists, artists and leaders portrayed are freedom fighter Lech Walesa and Revolutionary War hero Gen. Casimir Pulaski. Allow 30 minutes minimum. Mon.-Sat. 10-4, May-Dec.; Mon.-Fri. 10-4, rest of year. Closed holidays. Free. Phone (215) 922-1700.

POWEL HOUSE, 244 S. 3rd St., is a Revolutionary War-era mansion with elegant furnishings and lovely gardens. Allow 30 minutes minimum. Wed.-Sat. 10-4, Aug.-Apr.; noon-5 in May and July; 1-5, rest of year. Closed for special functions and holidays. Last tour begins 30 minutes before closing. Admission $3; over 62 and students with ID $2; under 6 free. Phone (215) 627-0364.

THE PRESBYTERIAN HISTORICAL SOCIETY, at 425 Lombard St., was founded in 1852 to preserve the history of the Presbyterian Church. The museum room houses silver and pewter ware, communion tokens and artifacts from the Colonial period to the present. Other highlights include a portrait gallery featuring church leaders and paintings by such noted artists as Bass Otis, John Neagle and Rembrandt and James Peale. A research library is available. Allow 30 minutes minimum. Mon.-Fri. 8:30-4:30; closed holidays. Free. Library $5. Phone (215) 627-1852.

RODIN MUSEUM—see Fairmount Park p. 112.

SAVE ROSENBACH MUSEUM AND LIBRARY, 2010 Delancey, exhibits paintings, books and manuscripts collected by the Rosenbach brothers. Highlights include manuscripts by Geoffrey Chaucer, Charles Dickens and James Joyce as well as books once owned by Abraham Lincoln and Herman Melville.

Allow 1 hour minimum. Tues.-Sun. 11-4, Sept.-July; closed Dec. 24-25 and major holidays. Last tour begins 1 hour, 15 minutes before closing. Admission $5; senior citizens, students with ID and under 18, $3. Phone (215) 732-1600.

ST. PETER'S CHURCH (Episcopal), 3rd and Pine sts., was erected in 1761. Four signers of the Declaration of Independence worshiped at St. Peter's. If the church is locked, the key can be obtained at 313 Pine St. Mon.-Fri. 9-5, Sat.-Sun. 9-3. Free. Phone (215) 925-5968.

SCHOOL GALLERY OF THE PENNSYLVANIA ACADEMY OF THE FINE ARTS, 1301 Cherry St., has changing exhibits of multimedia works by students, faculty and alumni. Allow 30 minutes minimum. Daily 9-7; closed holidays. Free. Phone (215) 972-7600.

STENTON MANSION, 18th and Windrim sts., was built in 1730 by James Logan, secretary to William Penn. The house, on a 3-acre site, reflects the lives of three generations of the Logan family. Allow 30 minutes minimum. Tues.-Sat. 1-4, Mar. 1-Dec. 15. Admission $5, students with ID $4. Phone (215) 329-7312.

UNITED STATES CUSTOM HOUSE, 2nd and Chestnut sts., houses customs offices, appraisers' stores and other federal offices. Mon.-Fri. 8:30-5; closed holidays. Free.

UNITED STATES MINT, 5th and Arch sts., offers self-guiding audiotape tours that take about 45 minutes. Cameras are prohibited. Daily 9-4:30, July-Aug.; Mon.-Sat. 9-4:30, May-June; Mon.-Fri. 9-4:30, rest of year. Closed holidays. Coining machinery might not be operating Sat.-Sun. and Dec. 23-Jan. 3. Free. Phone (215) 408-0114.

UNIVERSITY OF PENNSYLVANIA, bounded by Chestnut, Pine, 32nd and 40th sts., was founded in 1740; it is currently considered one of the leading educational centers in the nation. In 1765 the country's first medical school was opened at the university. Tours of the campus are available through the Office of Undergraduate Admissions, 1 College Hall. The office is open Mon.-Fri. 8:30-4:30. Free. Phone (215) 898-1000.

Institute of Contemporary Art, 36th and Sansom sts., presents changing exhibitions of contemporary art. Allow 1 hour minimum. Wed.-Sun. 10-5 (also Thurs. 5-7); closed holidays and when exhibitions are being changed. Admission $3; over 65 and students 12-18, $2; free to all Sun. 10-noon. Phone (215) 898-7108.

★The University of Pennsylvania Museum of Archaeology and Anthropology, 33rd and Spruce sts., displays outstanding archeological and anthropological collections from around the world. Exhibits include findings from Ancient Egypt, Asia, Central America, North America, Mesopotamia, Greece and Africa. Food is available.

Allow 1 hour minimum. Tues.-Sat. 10-4:30, Sun. 1-5, day after Labor Day-day before Memorial Day; Tues.-Sat. 10-4:30, rest of year. Closed holidays. Guided tours are given most Sat. and Sun. at 1:30, mid-Sept. to mid-May. Admission $5, senior citizens and students with ID $2.50, under 6 free. Guided tours free. Phone (215) 898-4000.

WOODMERE ART MUSEUM, 4 mi. s. of Pennsylvania Tpke. exit 25 at 9201 Germantown Ave., has paintings and decorative art spanning the 18th, 19th and 20th centuries. The Victorian home and art collection of Charles Knox Smith form the nucleus of the museum. Of particular interest is the collection of 19th-century American paintings, which includes works by Thomas Anshutz, Frederic Church, Jasper Cropsey, Edward Moran and Benjamin West. Changing exhibits often focus on local artists.

Allow 30 minutes minimum. Tues.-Sat. 10-5, Sun. 1-5; closed major holidays. Donations. Phone (215) 247-0476.

ZOOLOGICAL GARDENS—
see Fairmount Park p. 112.

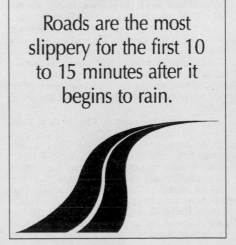

What To Do
Sightseeing

 Bus, Carriage or Trolley Tours

Several companies offer tours of historic Philadelphia via trolley busses, (215) 333-2119; a 20-minute trolley ride along Christopher Columbus Boulevard from Penn's Landing, Christopher Columbus Boulevard and Dock Street, (215) 627-0807; and horse-drawn carriage tours of Independence Park and Society Hill, (215) 923-8516.

 Boat Tours

Riverbus Inc. offers ferry service from Penn's Landing to the Thomas H. Kean New Jersey State Aquarium at Camden in Camden, N.J. *(see attraction listing in the Vicinity section p. 131).* The ferry departs every 30 minutes Mon.-Fri. 8 a.m.-9:45 p.m., Sat. 9 a.m.-11:45 p.m., Sun. 9-7:45, May 15-Sept. 15 (weather permitting); Mon.-Fri. 8-5:45, Sat. 9-7:45, Sun. 9-5:45, rest of year (weather permitting). Fare $2, senior citizens and children $1.50. Phone (609) 365-1400 or (800) 634-4027.

THE *SPIRIT OF PHILADELPHIA*, departing from Columbus Blvd. and Lombard Cir. at Penn's Landing, offers narrated, 2-hour lunch and Sunday brunch cruises on the Delaware River. Dinner and moonlight party cruises also are available. Lunch cruise Mon.-Sat. noon-2, mid-Mar. to mid-Jan. Sunday brunch cruise Sun. 1-3, mid-Mar. to mid-Jan. Closed Dec. 25. Fare $28.90; over 55, $27.80; under 13, $20.10. Parking $6. AE, MC, VI. Phone (215) 923-1419.

 Walking Tours

The heart of historic Philadelphia lends itself to a walking tour. A stroll through the narrow cobblestone streets among restored Georgian and Colonial buildings is the best way to discover the essence of the city and to assimilate its 18th-century atmosphere. A good way to see historic Philadelphia is to combine the walking tour with stops at the attractions along the way. The names of sites listed in detail in the What to See section are printed in bold type. Even if you do not tour a listed site, reading the attraction listing when you reach that point will make the tour more interesting.

A good starting point is **City Hall** at Penn Square. Walking east on Market St., you pass Hechts department store on the right. A few blocks farther on Market at 9th St. is a major shopping mall, the Gallery at Market East, which includes JCPenney and Strawbridge's. Continue east on Market to 7th St., where you will find the shops and restaurants of Market Place East and the **Declaration (Graff) House.** Directly behind the house on 7th St. is **The Balch Institute for Ethnic Studies,** which portrays the ethnic experience in the United States by means of multimedia shows.

Cross 7th St. to the **Atwater Kent Museum—The Philadelphia History Museum.** Upon leaving the museum, take the walkway to the right east to 6th St. Cross 6th and turn left to the **Liberty Bell Pavilion,** which houses the famous symbol of American freedom. From the pavilion, walk south across Chestnut St. to **Independence Hall.**

Within the next three blocks of Chestnut are numerous historical buildings that are part of the **Independence National Historical Park.** They include **Congress Hall** and **Old City Hall,** which flank Independence Hall; **Second Bank of United States;** the **New Hall Military Museum; Carpenters' Hall; Todd House;** and the **Bishop White House.** The visitor center at 3rd and Chestnut sts. has information and exhibits.

Facing Independence Mall is the renovated Philadelphia Bourse. The historic merchants' exchange now houses shops, restaurants and an information center on the first floor.

Just east on Chestnut Street is a path leading to **Franklin Court,** where a steel frame suggests the shape of Franklin's home, destroyed in 1812. Traces of the original foundation are visible.

From Franklin Court, exit onto Market St. and walk east to 2nd St. Take 2nd north to **Christ Church** on the left. Continue north 1.5 blocks, then stroll through **Elfreth's Alley** on the right. The 6-foot-wide alley is lined with a number of quaint, modest houses from the early 1700s. Farther north on 2nd is **Fireman's Hall—National Fire House and Museum of Philadelphia,** a museum depicting the history of firefighting in America with memorabilia, graphics, films and antique equipment.

From this point do an about-face and return to Arch St. Turn right on Arch and walk a half-block to the **Betsy Ross House** on your right. After a visit to this home of the American flag, proceed west on Arch 1.5 blocks to the **United States Mint,** where you can witness the making of pennies, dimes, nickels and quarters.

To end the tour, walk south to Market on 5th St. You will pass the 1783 Free Quaker Meeting House on the right. Once on Market you can choose to walk back to the Gallery East Mall to do some shopping or perhaps rest your feet, relax and refresh at one of the many restaurants in the area. The famous Bookbinders Old Original is tucked away at Second and Walnut sts. This tour takes approximately 5 hours, which allows for a leisurely pace.

Another excellent area for the visitor on foot is **Penn's Landing.** There visitors can view the the USS *Becuna,* the USS *Olympia* and the *Gazela of Philadelphia,* a barkentine that participated in the U.S. Bicentennial celebration in 1976, or catch a glimpse of Philadelphia's nautical past at the **Independence Seaport Museum.**

The Philadelphia Vietnam Veterans Memorial, Christopher Columbus Blvd. and Spruce St., and A World Sculpture Garden, with sculpture given to the city during the Bicentennial, also are at Penn's Landing.

TALK-A-WALK is a self-guiding walking tour of Independence National Historical Park. The tape tour, entitled "Severance Park and Those 'Revolting' Americans," can be obtained through the mail by writing Talk-A-Walk, Sound Publishers, Inc., 30 Waterside Plaza, New York, NY 10010. Fee $12.45 (includes postage and shipping). Phone (212) 686-0356.

Sports and Recreation

Fairmount Park caters to nearly everyone's recreational appetite, with **archery, bicycling, canoeing, fishing, golf, hiking, horseback riding, lawn bowling** and **tennis** available. For information about other municipal facilities, consult the AAA club or the convention and visitors bureau. Running and walking maps are available at downtown hotels.

Philadelphia, with a representative in every major league—**baseball, football, hockey, basketball** and **soccer**—is a paradise for spectator sports fans. The Phillies of baseball's National League and the Eagles of the National Football League play at Philadelphia's Veterans Sport Stadium at South Broad and Pattison streets. The CoreStates Complex, consisting of the CoreStates Spectrum and the CoreStates Center, also is at South Broad and Pattison and plays host to the Philadelphia Flyers of the National Hockey League and the 76ers of the National Basketball Association. To obtain ticket information for the Phillies, phone (215) 463-1000; the Eagles, (215) 463-5500; the 76ers, (215) 339-7676; and the Flyers, (215) 755-9700.

The Philadelphia Phantoms of the American Hockey League and the Philadelphia Kixx, affiliated with the National Soccer League, play at the CoreStates Spectrum. For information about the Phantoms phone (215) 465-4522; for information about the Kixx phone (888) 888-5499.

A familiar sight along the Schuylkill River is the scull, either one-man or crew, skimming the water. Periodic races and spectacular annual rowing regattas can be watched from Fairmount Park.

Polo is played by the suburban Brandywine Polo Club, (610) 268-8692, which has free games on Sunday afternoon from mid-May to September. The Hidden Pond Polo Club, (609) 767-0550, holds matches June through September; fees are $7, senior citizens and children $4. **Cricket** matches are held in Fairmont Park on Saturday and Sunday in the summer.

If you want to play the ponies, Philadelphia Park in Bensalem offers **Thoroughbred racing** all year; phone (215) 639-9000. Garden State Park in Cherry Hill, N.J., offers **Standardbred races** September through December and Thoroughbred races in the winter and spring; phone

(609) 488-8400. Delaware Park near Wilmington, Del., offers Thoroughbred races spring through fall; phone (302) 994-2521.

Note: Policies concerning admittance of children to pari-mutuel betting facilities vary. Phone for information.

Shopping

"Meet me at the eagle" is a time-honored request in Philadelphia, where the baroque bronze bird at Lord & Taylor department store has long marked a gathering spot for friends and been a point of reference for bewildered visitors. The department store also is celebrated for its magnificent pipe organ, which soars several stories above the ground floor and booms forth in daily concerts.

The downtown shopping district extends roughly from 8th to 18th on Market, Chestnut and Walnut streets. Besides Lord & Taylor, Philadelphia has two other department stores of national repute—JCPenney and Strawbridge's, which can be found at The Gallery and Gallery II, the four-level shopping mall at Market East, between 8th, 11th and Market streets. The mall is open Mon.-Sat. 10-7 (10-8 Wed. and Fri.), Sun. noon-5. Along South Street from 2nd to 8th streets are numerous avantgarde shops, galleries and restaurants.

Another renovated historic shopping area is the Philadelphia Bourse, opposite Independence Mall on 5th Street between Chestnut and Market

streets. When it opened in 1895, the Bourse housed a grain and stock exchange, industrial exhibition halls, business offices and banks. Specialty shops and restaurants open onto the Food Court, an oasis for shoppers with its 10-story atrium with live trees and plants. The Bourse is open Mon.-Sat. 10-6.

The China Town Mall, 143 N. 11th St., has Oriental food, products and goods. At the Italian Market, along 9th Street from Christian Street to Dickinson Avenue, vendors sell a variety of wares, including fresh produce, homemade pasta, clothing and spices.

The shops at Liberty Place, between 16th and 17th on Chestnut Street, comprise one of Philadelphia's most elegant malls; the mall is open Mon.-Sat. 10-7 (Wed. 10-8), Sun. noon-6. Market Place East, 701 Market St., occupies an entire city block. Built 1859-1907, this renovated building now houses fine shopping and dining establishments.

For those who get hungry while they shop, there is the Reading Terminal Market, 12th and Filbert streets. In this renovated 19th-century farmers' market, shoppers can find about 80 stalls selling everything from double-yolk eggs to fresh meats to organic vegetables. Ready-to-eat dishes from snapper soup to fried falafel meet the needs of shoppers who have not left time for cooking after they are finished shopping. The market is open Mon.-Sat. 8-6; phone (215) 922-2317.

The upscale shopper will enjoy the Shops at Bellevue, along Broad and Walnut sts. Stores include Alfred Dunhill, Ralph Lauren and Tiffanys. Most of these shops are open Mon.-Sat. 10-6 (Wed. 10-8).

In terms of both quantity and quality, Philadelphia has one of the richest antique markets in the country. You can pick up an unusual $4 china plate or a $40,000 Chippendale highboy, barter for a mustache cup or negotiate for a priceless silver service. Bargains are found mainly in the wholesale/retail district known as Antique Row, the section of Pine east of Broad between 9th and 12th streets.

Prices and quality rise and chances to barter fall in the Upper Pine Street district, along Pine west of Broad between 16th and 18th, on the numbered streets north to Chestnut and along Chestnut between 18th and 20th. In this area are the finest examples of antique art objects and furnishings, displayed in Cadillac-and-kid-glove elegance.

A short drive outside the Philadelphia city limits will take you to one of the area's most extensive malls, The Court and Plaza at King of Prussia, said to be the largest mall on the East Coast. At the intersection of US 202 and North Gulph Road, the mall features several major stores—Bloomingdale's, Hechts, JCPenney, Macy's, Sears and Strawbridge's. Plymouth Meeting Mall, on SR 422 in Plymouth Meeting, is another suburban mall featuring Hess's, IKEA and Strawbridge's.

Franklin Mills, at the Woodhaven Road exit of I-95, is about 16 miles from the center of Philadelphia. The single-level, mile-long concourse boasts nine anchor stores including Brooks Brothers, JCPenney, Marshalls, Nautilus, Neiman-Marcus, Nordstrom, Saks Fifth Avenue, Spiegel and Syms Outlets, and about 225 smaller outlet and discount shops as well as six restaurants, two food courts and a 10-screen movie theater.

Theater and Concerts

The famed Philadelphia Orchestra, one of the country's finer symphonies, presents its winter series in the Academy of Music, which also presents grand opera, the Pennsylvania Ballet, the Philly Pops, musicals and special concerts; phone (215) 893-1999. In summer the orchestra's rich tones ring through Fairmount Park's Mann Center for the Performing Arts. Tickets are sold at the box office; phone (215) 878-7707.

The Police and Firemen's Band thumps out Sousa marches and other rousing favorites in several parks. During the summer, concerts are held on the Great Plaza at Penn's Landing and Kennedy Plaza, 15th Street and JFK Boulevard. Check at the visitor center for times.

Philadelphia theater is very popular. The Forrest Theater presents pre-Broadway and hit shows with name stars, while national touring companies appear at the Annenberg Center and the Merriman Theatre.

There also are numerous regional and community theater companies, including the American Music Festival Theatre, the Arden Theatre, the Bristol Riverside Theater, the Freedom Theater, the Hedgerow Theater, the People's Light and Theatre Company, the Philadelphia Theatre Company, the Philadelphia Festival Theatre of New Plays, the Society Hill Playhouse, the Walnut Street Theatre and the Wilma Theater. College theater can be enjoyed at Temple University or Villanova University's Vasey Theater.

Special Events

Philadelphia's calendar is packed throughout the year with events ranging from the huge Mummers and Thanksgiving Day parades to quaint flower and antique shows and folk festivals.

The world-famous Mummers Parade starts off the new year and attracts some 30,000 costumed Mummers String Bands, fancies and comics. Philadelphia then settles down for the Philadelphia International Auto Show, held in January at the Pennsylvania Convention Center, and the Philadelphia Boat Show, also held in January. The 4-day Chinese New Year occurs sometime between January 21 and February 19 and is celebrated with 10-course banquets at the Chinese Cultural Center in mid-February.

February is Black History Month, a national event that is observed in Philadelphia with exhibitions, lectures and music at the Afro-American Historical and Cultural Museum. PECO Energy Jazz Weekend and the Philadelphia Home Show are held in early February. Also in February, top male players compete in the U.S. Indoor Tennis Championships.

The Philadelphia Flower Show, held in early March at the Convention Center, is one of the nation's largest indoor flower shows. A culinary event not to be missed is The Book and the Cook in mid-April, when world-famous cookbook authors team up with some of Philadelphia's finest chefs to create spectacular dishes. The wearing of the green is toasted during the city's St. Patrick's Day Parade, while the Easter Promenade offers music, entertainment and celebrity guests on South Seaport on Easter Sunday.

The Philadelphia Antiques Show in mid-March is conducted at the 33rd Street Armory. The Penn Relays at Franklin Field in April is one of the world's oldest and largest track meets. Also in the spring, the Mummers String Band Show of Shows is held at the Spectrum. April through June, the Gardens Collaborative, a group of 34 gardens, historic houses and arboretums, stages the World's Largest Garden Party with tours, lectures, workshops, concerts, and family-oriented events and activities. In late April, Valborgsmassoafton, the traditional Swedish welcoming of spring, is observed at the American Swedish Historical Museum.

Guided walking and bus tours of selected homes, gardens and historic buildings in 10 different neighborhoods are offered during the Philadelphia Open House, which runs from late April to May. Also in May is the Africamericas Festival, celebrating African-American culture with entertainment and talent contests. The Dad Vail Regatta is one of the largest college regattas in the country.

Additional events in May include the Rittenhouse Square Flower Market, 18th and Walnut streets; the International Theater Festival for Children at the Annenberg Center, 3680 Walnut St.; the Devon Horse Show and Country Fair, at the Devon Fairgrounds; and Jambalaya Jam, a weekend of Creole and Cajun cooking and jazz at Penn's Landing during Memorial Day weekend.

Summer kicks off with the Rittenhouse Square Fine Arts Annual, Elfreth's Alley Fete Days and the Head House Square Crafts Fair, all held in June.

The SUNOCO Welcome America! festival explodes the last week in June through July to celebrate the country's birth in its hometown. Street parades, boat parades, concerts, sports events and fireworks displays are among the more than 30 scheduled events; phone (215) 636-1666 for more information. August ends with the Philadelphia Folk Festival, which features folk music

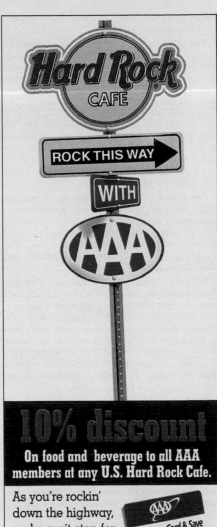

concerts and workshops at suburban Poole Farm in Schwenksville.

September events include the Yo! Philadelphia Festival at Penn's Landing Labor Day Sunday and Monday, the America's Gold Cup equestrian competition at Devon Fairgrounds, the Penn's Landing In-Water Boat Show, the Harvest Show at the Horticulture Center, the Von Steuben Day Parade and The South Street Seven Arts Festival. The Pulaski Day Parade and Columbus Day Parade are in October. The Battle of Germantown is re-enacted in early October, and Super Sunday, a day of hands-on participation at all of the city's cultural and educational institutions, is celebrated in mid-month.

The Convention Center stages the Philadelphia Crafts Show in November, a major exhibition of crafts by the nation's top artisans. Later in November, the holidays begin in grand and traditional fashion with the Philadelphia Thanksgiving Day Parade, complete with celebrities, enormous balloons and national TV coverage.

Following Thanksgiving is the Giant Tinkertoy Extravaganza at the Franklin Institute Science Museum. The Army-Navy Football Classic is held in early December at Veterans Stadium. The Colonial mansions in Fairmount Park come alive in December with all the traditional decorations for the Christmas Tours of Historic Houses. Then Christmas is celebrated in the Swedish tradition with the Lucia Fest and Julmarknad at the American Swedish Historical Museum.

The Philadelphia Vicinity

AUDUBON (H-11)

In the early 1900s some of the country's first feature-length motion pictures were produced a few miles east of Audubon in Betzwood, site of a studio set up by Sigmund Lubin, a noted Philadelphia optician and movie producer. The lot, which accommodated 40 cowboys, 25 Indians and 100 horses, was used to film the "Battle of Shiloh," one of the first epic spectacles filmed.

MILL GROVE, THE AUDUBON WILDLIFE SANCTUARY is off Audubon Rd. to Pawlings Rd., then following signs. On the 175-acre nature preserve is Mill Grove, home in the early 1800s of John James Audubon, noted artist, author and naturalist. Now a museum, the house contains displays of Audubon's paintings, drawings and taxidermy specimens. Numerous trails wind through the grounds, which serve as a bird sanctuary.

Allow 30 minutes minimum. Tues.-Sat. 10-4, Sun. 1-4; closed Jan. 1, Easter, July 4, Thanksgiving and Dec. 25. Grounds open Tues.-Sun. dawn-dusk. Free. Phone (610) 666-5593.

BENSALEM (H-12) pop. 3,000, elev. 70'

BLESSED KATHARINE DREXEL SHRINE, 1663 Bristol Pike, is the gravesite of the founder of the Sisters of the Blessed Sacrament. Born into the wealthy Philadelphia Drexel family in 1858, Katharine Drexel devoted her life to the church and donated her $20 million inheritance to benefit African Americans and American Indians. Daily 1-5. Free. Phone (215) 244-9900.

BRISTOL (H-12) pop. 10,400, elev. 21'

GRUNDY MUSEUM, 610 Radcliffe St., was built in the early 19th century. In later years, when it served as the family home of Sen. Joseph R. Grundy, it was remodeled and furnished in the Victorian style. Allow 30 minutes minimum. Mon.-Fri. 1-4, Sat. 1-3, Sept.-June; Mon.-Fri. 1-4, rest of year. Free. Phone (215) 788-9432.

BROOMALL (I-11)

THOMAS MASSEY HOUSE, 1 mi. s. from SR 3 on Lawrence Rd. at Springhouse Rd., was built in 1696 and is one of the oldest English Quaker homes in Pennsylvania. Restored to its original condition, it contains period furnishings and implements. The grounds include small kitchen gardens and a carriage/woodshed with a blacksmith forge.

Candlelight tours and public dinners are held throughout the winter months. Allow 1 hour minimum. Mon.-Fri. by appointment, Sun. 2-4:30. Admission $2; over 65 and ages 6-18, $1. Reservations are required. Phone (610) 353-3644.

BRYN ATHYN (H-11) pop. 1,100, elev. 200'

BRYN ATHYN CATHEDRAL, SR 232 and Cathedral Rd. in Bryn Athyn, exemplifies Gothic architecture in North America. The church features fine stained-glass windows. Guided tours daily 1-4. Cathedral open daily 11-5; grounds open daily 8-5. Free. Phone (215) 947-0266.

BRYN MAWR (H-11) elev. 412'

HARRITON HOUSE is 1.2 mi. n. of US 30 on Morris Ave., .5 mi. w. on Old Gulph Rd., then n. on Harriton Rd. to entrance. Built in 1704, the two-story stone house was the home of Charles Thomson, secretary of the Continental Congress. The house has some original furnishings and has been restored to its original appearance. The grounds cover 16.5 acres. Guided tours are available by prior arrangement. Picnicking is permitted.

Wed.-Sat. 10-4; other times by appointment. Closed holidays. Admission $2.50, students with ID free. Phone (610) 525-0201.

BUCKINGHAM (H-12) pop. 9,400, elev. 234'

WINERIES

• Buckingham Valley Vineyards and Winery, 1521 SR 413. Tues.-Sat. 11-6, Sun. noon-4. Phone (215) 794-7188.

BUCKS COUNTY

One of the commonwealth's largest and most historic counties, Bucks County stretches into the countryside surrounding northern Philadelphia. This quiet, wooded region bordering the Delaware River is replete with rolling hills, old stone houses and covered bridges. William Penn named the county for its resemblance to Buckinghamshire in England. An interesting driving tour covering much of Bucks County follows the Delaware River along SR 32.

The narrow, winding streets of Doylestown, once an overnight stagecoach stop between Philadelphia and Easton, capture Bucks County's historic charm, as do Fallsington and Washington Crossing Historic Park.

The Delaware Canal, on which construction was begun in 1817, flows through New Hope, an artists' and writers' colony settled along the river. New Hope is known for its natural settings, book and antique shops, art galleries and cafes on the banks of both the river and the canal. The town also is home to one of the nation's oldest and most famous summer theaters, the Bucks County Playhouse.

Places and towns in Bucks County listed individually are Bristol, Doylestown, Dublin, Fallsington, Ivyland, Lahaska, Langhorne, Morrisville, New Hope, Point Pleasant and Washington Crossing Historic Park.

Bucks County Conference & Visitors Bureau: 152 Swamp Rd., Doylestown, PA 18901; phone (215) 345-4552 or (800) 836-2825. *See ad.*

CENTER POINT (H-11)

About 3 miles west on SR 73 in Skippack, Skippack Village contains more than 50 specialty shops and restaurants housed in restored turn-of-the-20th-century homes and buildings.

PETER WENTZ FARMSTEAD, .3 mi. s.e. of jct. SRs 73 and 363, is an 18th-century Pennsylvania German working farm of more than 90 acres with a Georgian-style mansion furnished in period. The house was twice used by George Washington as headquarters during the Revolutionary War. Period craft and farming demonstrations are given on some Saturday afternoons; costumed guides conduct tours.

Allow 1 hour minimum. Tues.-Sat. 10-4, Sun. 1-4; closed major holidays. Last tour begins 30 minutes before closing. Free. Phone (610) 584-5104.

CHADDS FORD (I-10) elev. 129′

Chadds Ford is in the Brandywine Valley, where the Revolutionary War engagement, the Battle of Brandywine, occurred. Chadds Ford also is home to the Wyeth family of artists. A mile-long river walk connects the Brandywine River Museum *(see attraction listing)* with the 18th-century John Chads House, built by a local

innkeeper and ferry operator. The house is open for tours, which include a beehive-oven baking demonstration.

Chadds Ford Historical Society: Box 27, Chadds Ford, PA 19317; phone (610) 388-7376.

SAVE AMERICAN CHRISTMAS MUSEUM, US 1 and Hickory Hill Rd., is housed in an 18th-century stone house. The museum displays collections of Santas in holiday vignettes representing different time periods and traditions. Included are Christmas celebrations of the 1800s, the 1850s, the Victorian era, the 1950s and a contemporary Christmas.

Allow 30 minutes minimum. Mon.-Sat. 9:30-5:30, Sun. noon-5:30, Nov. 1-early Jan.; Tues.-Sat. 9:30-5:30, Sun. noon-5:30, Apr.-Oct.; Sat. 9:30-5:30, Sun. noon-5:30, in Mar. Closed Jan. 1, Easter, Thanksgiving and Dec. 25. Admission Oct.-Dec. $5; over 65, $4; ages 6-13, $2.50. Admission rest of year $3.50; over 65, $3; ages 6-13, $2. DS, MC, VI. Phone (610) 388-0600.

SAVE BRANDYWINE BATTLEFIELD PARK embraces 50 acres along the n. side of US 1, 1 mi. e. of SR 100. The Battle of Brandywine was fought nearby on Sept. 11, 1777. This defeat of the American forces under George Washington left Philadelphia open to advancing British troops. The visitor center contains exhibits about the battle. A reproduction of the farmhouse used

by Washington and the Marquis de Lafayette also are on the grounds.

Allow 1 hour minimum. Tues.-Sat. 9-5, Sun. noon-5; closed non-summer holidays. Admission to historic buildings $3.50; over 60, $2.50; ages 6-12, $1.50; battlefield free. Phone (610) 459-3342.

★BRANDYWINE RIVER MUSEUM, on US 1 just s. of SR 100, is a 19th-century gristmill converted into a museum of American art. Works by three generations of the Wyeth family are featured, with one gallery devoted to the paintings of Andrew Wyeth. The galleries in the restored mill have original beams, pine floors and white plaster walls. One gallery is illuminated by natural light. The museum grounds are landscaped with native plants and wildflowers.

Allow 1 hour, 30 minutes minimum. Daily 9:30-4:30; closed Dec. 25. Admission $5; over 65, students with ID and ages 6-12, $2.50. MC, VI. Phone (610) 388-2700.

CHESTER (I-11) pop. 41,900, elev. 23'

Settled by Swedes and Finns in 1644, Chester is one of the oldest settlements in Pennsylvania. Until its power waned in 1683, it was the most important town in the colony and the seat of its courts. The first meeting of the Pennsylvania Assembly was held in Chester in 1682, the year William Penn arrived.

The Caleb Pusey House, 2 miles west at 15 Race St. on Landingford Plantation in Upland, is a restored cottage built in 1683 of handmade bricks.

COLLEGEVILLE (H-11) pop. 4,200, elev. 155'

BERMAN MUSEUM OF ART, .5 mi. w. on Main St. to the Ursinus College campus, features paintings, sculpture, prints, drawings and historical artifacts. Works of regional artists and turn-of-the-20th-century Pennsylvania artists are highlighted. Allow 1 hour minimum. Tues.-Fri. 10-4, Sat.-Sun. noon-4:30; closed major holidays and Dec. 24-31. Free. Phone (610) 409-3500.

CONCORDVILLE (I-11)

NEWLIN MILL PARK consists of 150 acres on US 1. The restored gristmill, with a 16-foot wheel, dates from 1704. The miller's house, built in 1739, is furnished in period. A blacksmith shop, springhouse and log cabin also are in the park. There are 3 miles of nature trails along the millrace and the stream. Guided tours are available. Picnicking is permitted.

Allow 1 hour minimum. Daily 9-dusk, Mar.-Sept.; 8-5, rest of year. Combined admission to all three buildings $1.50; ages 2-12, 75c. Phone (610) 459-2359.

DOWNINGTOWN (H-10) pop. 7,700, elev. 264'

SPRINGTON MANOR FARM, 5 mi. w. off US 322 on Springton Rd., is a 300-acre demonstration farm. Features include the giant Great Barn, a sheep barn, poultry house and petting area. A nature trail and wildlife pond are on the grounds. Picnicking is permitted. Allow 1 hour minimum. Daily 10-4. Free. Phone (610) 942-2450.

DOYLESTOWN (H-11) pop. 8,600, elev. 351'

Settled in 1735, Doylestown is in Bucks County (see place listing p. 123), one of Pennsylvania's finest farming areas.

Bucks County Conference & Visitors Bureau: 152 Swamp Rd., Doylestown, PA 18901; phone (215) 345-4552 or (800) 836-2825.

FONTHILL MUSEUM, E. Court St. at SR 313, is the castlelike dream house of Dr. Henry Chapman Mercer. Built 1908-10, this concrete mansion was designed by the owner from the inside out; he designed the the interiors of the rooms and then designed the exteriors to accommodate them. The multilevel dwelling has 44 rooms, 32 stairways and more than 200 windows. Works in tile, prints, engravings and memorabilia of Mercer's life are featured.

Allow 1 hour minimum. Mon.-Sat. 10-5, Sun. noon-5; closed Jan. 1, Thanksgiving and Dec. 25. Last tour begins 1 hour before closing. Admission $5; over 65, $4.50; students with ID $1.50; under 6 free. Reservations are required. MC, VI ($20). Phone (215) 348-9461.

SAVE JAMES A. MICHENER ART MUSEUM, 138 S. Pine St., is in the renovated 1884 Bucks County prison. The permanent collection features 19th- and 20th-century regional American art, including many Pennsylvania Impressionists and Daniel Garber's 22-ft. mural, "A Wooded Watershed."

Other highlights include the Mari Sabusawa Michener wing featuring a multimedia exhibition with individual displays about such notable figures as Oscar Hammerstein, Pearl S. Buck, Dorothy Parker and others, as well as changing exhibits from national institutions. A permanent exhibit on author James A. Michener re-creates his Bucks County office where he wrote "Tales of the South Pacific." The Nakashima Reading Room overlooks the courtyard. Food is available.

Allow 1 hour, 30 minutes minimum. Tues.-Fri. 10-4:30, Sat.-Sun. 10-5; closed holidays. Admission $5; over 60, $4.50; students with ID and ages 12-18, $1.50. MC, VI. Phone (215) 340-9800.

SAVE MERCER MUSEUM, Pine and Ashland sts., traces the pre-industrial history of the nation from colonization to the Civil War. Artifacts and implements from the 18th and 19th centuries represent more than 60 crafts and trades. There also are folk art displays and changing exhibits. The Spruance Library has a research collection about Bucks County history, genealogy and the history of trade, crafts and early industry.

Allow 2 hours minimum. Museum open Mon.-Sat. 10-5 (also Tues. 5-9), Sun. noon-5. Library open Wed.-Sat. 10-5, Tues. 1-9. Museum and library closed Jan. 1, Thanksgiving and Dec. 25. Admission $5; over 65, $4.50; students with ID $1.50; under 6 free. Audiotour rental $1. MC, VI. Phone (215) 345-0210.

SAVE MORAVIAN POTTERY AND TILE WORKS, E. Court St. and 130 W. Swamp Rd., is the restored building used by Dr. Henry Chapman Mercer in 1898 for the production of decorative tile and mosaics for public and private buildings through the country. A videotape presentation features Mercer and his production techniques, and a self-guiding tour illustrates the tile-making process. Daily 10-4:45; closed holidays. Last tour departs 45 minutes before closing. Admission $3; over 60, $2.50; ages 7-17, $1.50. Phone (215) 345-6722.

NATIONAL SHRINE OF OUR LADY OF CZESTO-CHOWA (chen-sto-HO-va) is 1.5 mi. n. on SR 611, then 1.5 mi. n.w. on SR 313 and 2 mi. w. on Ferry Rd. On a picturesque tract of 250 acres, the shrine includes a monastery. The upper church's striking stained-glass windows depict 1,000 years of Polish Christianity. "The Holy Trinity," a sculpture above the altar area, is a copy of the painting "Our Lady of Czesto-chowa." Daily 9-5. Free. Phone (215) 345-0600.

EXTON (H-10) elev. 321′

Exton is the site of the Thomas Newcomen Library and Museum, reached via Ship and Newcomen roads. The library features some 3,000 volumes about the history of steam power and its pioneers. The museum traces the development of steam power in the 18th and 19th centuries through actual and working model steam engines and model railroad engines and steamboats. Phone (610) 363-6600.

FALLSINGTON (H-12)

HISTORIC FALLSINGTON is just off Tyburn Rd. between US 1 and US 13. This well-preserved village has pre-Revolutionary, Federal and Victorian buildings, including three Friends meeting-houses around a picturesque square. Also included are restored buildings with period furnishings and a 15-minute audiovisual presentation. Walking tour maps are available.

Allow 1 hour minimum. Guided tours are available on the hour Mon.-Sat. 10-4, Sun. 1-4, May-Oct.; closed major holidays. Admission $3.50; over 65, $2.50; ages 6-18, $1. Reservations are recommended. Phone (215) 295-6567.

FORT WASHINGTON (H-11) elev. 174′

SAVE HOPE LODGE is reached via Pennsylvania Tpke. exit 26S to Pennsylvania Ave., then 3 blks.

to Bethlehem Pike, following signs. Built in 1743 by prosperous Quaker gristmill operator Samuel Morris, the lodge is now filled with antique art and furnishings from the 18th, 19th and 20th centuries. Allow 1 hour minimum. Tues.-Sat. 9-4, Sun. noon-4; closed holidays. Hours may vary; phone ahead. Admission $3.50; over 60, $3; ages 6-12, $1.50. Phone (215) 646-1595.

HORSHAM (H-11) pop. 21,900

SAVE GRAEME PARK, .5 mi. w. off US 611 at 859 County Line Rd., was the home of Sir William Keith, the provincial governor of Pennsylvania 1717-26. Built during his years as governor, the well-preserved stone house is a fine example of 18th-century architecture. Allow 1 hour minimum. Wed.-Sat. 10-4, Sun. noon-4; closed Jan. 1, Thanksgiving, Dec. 25 and state holidays. Admission $3.50; over 60, $3; ages 6-12, $1.50. Phone (215) 343-0965.

IVYLAND (H-11) pop. 500, elev. 257′

THE WAGNER MUSEUM, 900 Jacksonville Rd., chronicles the history of John Wagner & Sons, a manufacturer of gourmet foods, cigars and teas since the mid-1800s. Displays include photographs, business ledgers, labels and packaging, bottles, machinery, signs and a safe. Allow 30 minutes minimum. Mon.-Sat. 10-3:30, Sept.-May; Mon.-Fri. 10-3:30, rest of year. Closed major holidays. Free. Phone (215) 674-5000.

KENNETT SQUARE (I-10) pop. 5,200, elev. 260′

★**LONGWOOD GARDENS** is 3 mi. n.e. of Kennett Square, or about 12 mi. n. of Wilmington, Del., at jct. US 1 and SR 52. Once the country estate of industrialist Pierre S. du Pont, Longwood is famous for its superb outdoor gardens, which include elaborate fountains, two lakes, woodlands, wildflowers, a formal rose garden and greenhouses containing exotic tropical displays.

The 3.5 acres of heated greenhouses and the Conservatory are particularly colorful November through April; masses of flowering plants, some rare, adorn the Conservatory year-round. The chrysanthemums are usually at their best during the first three weeks of November. A Christmas and poinsettia display is featured in December. More than 11,000 types of plants, including water lilies and other blooms, are the main summer outdoor attractions.

Three sets of fountains grace the gardens: one in the Italian Water Garden, one on the stage of the Open-Air Theatre and one in front of the Conservatory. Half-hour illuminated displays take place at the Conservatory Fountain Garden Tuesday, Thursday and Saturday evenings after dark, June through August.

The Peirce-du-Pont House, Pierre du Pont's country home until his death in 1954, contains an exhibit tracing the 300-year historical and horticultural evolution of Longwood Gardens through photographs, artifacts, videotapes and du Pont home movies.

The Fireworks and Fountains program is offered some Friday evenings in summer; advance tickets are required. Performances in the Open-Air Theatre take place every summer; a schedule is available at the visitor center or by sending a self-addressed stamped business envelope to Schedule, Longwood Gardens, P.O. Box 501, Kennett Square, PA 19348-0501.

Allow 2 hours minimum. Visitor center and outdoor gardens daily 9-6, Apr.-Oct. (also Tues., Thurs. and Sat. 6 p.m.-1 hour after dusk, June-Aug.); 9-9, Thanksgiving-Jan. 1; 9-5, rest of year. Conservatory daily 10-6, Apr.-Oct. (also Tues., Thurs. and Sat. 6 p.m.-1 hour after dusk, June-Aug.); 10-9, Thanksgiving-Jan. 1; 10-5, rest of year. Open-Air Theatre performances are given June-Sept. Gardens hours and prices may vary; phone ahead. Gardens admission $12 ($8 on Tues.); ages 16-20, $6; ages 6-15, $2. AE, DS, MC, VI. Phone (610) 388-1000 or (800) 737-5500 in the mid-Atlantic area.

PHILLIPS MUSHROOM MUSEUM, 909 E. Baltimore Pike (US 1), .5 mi. s. jct. SR 52, explains the cultivation and use of mushrooms through photographs, models and a film presentation. Displays show live mushrooms in various stages of growth. Allow 30 minutes minimum. Daily 10-6; closed Jan. 1, Easter, Thanksgiving and Dec. 25. Admission $1.25; over 60, 75c; ages 7-12, 50c. Phone (610) 388-6082.

LAHASKA (H-11)

CAROUSEL WORLD, within Peddler's Village, offers a nostalgic look at the history of the carrousel amusement ride industry. The painstakingly detailed artistry of noted carrousel carvers is displayed, along with miniature representations of a circus and a turn-of-the-20th-century amusement park. Rides are available on a working carrousel that features carved lions and giraffes in addition to horses.

Allow 1 hour minimum. Mon.-Thurs. 10-5:30, Fri.-Sat. 10-9, Sun. 11-5:30, Apr.-Dec.; Mon.-Fri. 10-5:30, Sat. 10-6, rest of year. Closed holidays. Hours may vary; phone ahead. Museum admission $3; over 65, $2.75; children $2. Museum and carrousel ride $3.50, children $2.50. Carrousel ride only $1.50, infants free. Phone (215) 794-8960.

PEDDLER'S VILLAGE is at US 202 and SR 263. Coops from the old Lahaska Chicken Farm have been rebuilt as a charming 42-acre shopping, dining and entertainment complex. Herringbone-patterned brick paths and landscaped gardens enhance this village of more than 80 specialty shops, an inn and restaurants. Special events take place regularly. Allow 2 hours minimum. Mon.-Thurs. 10-5:30, Fri.-Sat. 10-9, Sun. 11-5:30,

Apr.-Dec.; Mon.-Fri. 10-5:30, Sat. 10-6, rest of year. Hours may vary; phone ahead. Closed Jan. 1, Thanksgiving and Dec. 25. Phone (215) 794-4000.

LANGHORNE (H-12) pop. 1,400, elev. 103′

Oxford Valley Mall, US 1 and Oxford Valley Road, is a popular place for shopping in the Langhorne area. The mall's 135 stores include JCPenney, Macy's, Sears and Strawbridges.

SAVE SESAME PLACE is next to Oxford Valley Mall at US 1 and I-95. Water activities include inner tube rides, body flumes and splash pools; a bathing suit is required. Non-water activities feature physical play elements on which children can jump, bounce, slide and climb. Indoor activities include science exhibits and electronic games. Live entertainment includes the Sesame Street characters in walk-around appearances. Food is available.

Allow 5 hours minimum. Daily 9-8 May 16-Labor Day; Sat.-Sun. 9-8, day after Labor Day-Oct. 25. Schedule may vary; phone ahead. Admission $27.95; over 55, $25.15; under 2 free. Second day $9.95. DS, MC, VI. Phone (215) 752-7070. *See color ad p. 119.*

LIMERICK (H-10) pop. 6,700

Little more than a wilderness in 1716, Limerick was first settled by the Brooke family, who named the town after their home in Ireland. Today the area is a residential area. The Farmer's Market of Limerick features some 25 vendors offering various wares Thursday through Sunday.

LIMERICK ENERGY INFORMATION CENTER is 3 mi. w. of the US 422 Limerick/Linfield exit, following signs to 298 Longview Rd. Using water from the Schuylkill and Delaware rivers, the generating station provides electricity to the Delaware Valley. The information center offers displays, films and lectures about energy, nuclear power, plant construction and environmental studies. Allow 30 minutes minimum. Tues.-Fri. 10-4; closed holidays. Free. Phone (610) 495-6767.

LONGWOOD (I-10)

In the midst of the historic Brandywine Valley, Longwood, along with Kennett Square, also is in Chester County—considered the "Mushroom Capital of the World."

Brochures and information are available at the Brandywine Valley Tourist Information Center, located at the entrance to Longwood Gardens. Housed in a 19th-century Quaker meetinghouse, this historic center offers exhibits, videotape presentations and a wide range of visitor information. Across the street is a Quaker cemetery begun in the mid-1800s. The center is open daily 10-5. Phone (610) 388-2900 or (800) 228-9933.

★ **LONGWOOD GARDENS—**
see Kennett Square p. 125.

MEDIA (I-11) pop. 6,000, elev. 210'

Media, named for its central location in Delaware County, was laid out in 1848 after being designated county seat. Midway between Philadelphia and Wilmington, it has remained a thriving business and government center.

Just south of Media on Rose Valley Road in an 1840 gristmill is the 1923 Hedgerow Theatre, one of the oldest repertory theaters in the country. Another sign of the past still rumbles along State Street—an early 20th-century trolley that takes passengers to shops, restaurants and the Delaware County Courthouse.

Delaware County Convention and Visitors Bureau: 200 E. State St., Media, PA 19063; phone (610) 565-3679.

FRANKLIN MINT MUSEUM, 1 mi. s. of SR 452 on US 1, illustrates the history of The Franklin Mint, one of the world's foremost creators of fine collectibles. Fabergé jeweled pieces and works by Norman Rockwell and Andrew Wyeth are displayed. Other highlights include a collection of porcelain dolls, classic cars and Star Trek collectibles. Items include art in bronze, porcelain, precious metals and crystal. Special events are held throughout the year. Mon.-Sat. 9:30-4:30, Sun. 1-4:30; closed holidays. Free. Phone (610) 459-6168.

THE TYLER ARBORETUM, 515 Painter Rd., covers 650 acres of woods and open fields as well as special plant collections. An extensive system of trails leads among the large variety of trees, shrubs and other plants, many of which are labeled. There also is a collection of rhododendrons, a fragrance garden, butterfly garden and bird habitat garden. Lachford Hall is decorated in the period of the 1860s.

Grounds open daily 8 a.m.-dusk. Lachford Hall and Painter Library museums open Sun. 2-5, Apr.-June and Sept.-Oct. Admission $3; ages 3-15, $1. Phone (610) 566-5431.

MORRISVILLE (H-12) pop. 9,800, elev. 21'

[SAVE] **PENNSBURY MANOR,** 5 mi. s. on the Delaware River at 400 Pennsbury Memorial Rd., was the country estate of William Penn. The 43-acre historic site contains the reconstructed 1683 manor house, worker's cottage, a smokehouse, bake-and-brew house, an icehouse, blacksmith shop, stable and horse shelter, as well as farm animals and formal and kitchen gardens. The buildings display 17th- and 18th-century artifacts. Costumed guides conduct tours of the manor. Special events are held throughout the year. Picnicking is permitted in the pavilion.

Allow 1 hour, 30 minutes minimum. Tues.-Sat. 9-5, Sun. noon-5. Phone for tour times and holiday schedule. Last tour begins 1 hour, 30 minutes before closing. Admission $5; over 60, $4.50; ages 6-12, $3; family rate $13. Phone (215) 946-0400.

NEW HOPE (G-12) pop. 1,400, elev. 86'

The picturesque town of New Hope, an artists' and writers' colony, is a favorite spot for antique hunting. There are lovely guest homes and charming restaurants; make reservations early.

Bucks County Playhouse is in a mill dating from the 1780s. Broadway productions are given May through December; phone (215) 862-2041. Mule-drawn barges offer hour-long canal excursions narrated by a folk singer and historian; the barges depart from the south end of New Hope on New Street above SR 32 April through November. Phone (215) 862-2842.

NEW HOPE & IVYLAND RAIL ROAD, jct. Bridge and Stockton sts., offers a 9-mile round-trip ride through the Pennsylvania countryside. The 1925 vintage steam train crosses over Pauline's Trestle, upon which actress Pearl White was bound in the 1914 silent film serial "The Perils of Pauline."

Allow 1 hour minimum. Train departs daily. Departure times vary; phone ahead for schedule. Closed Jan. 1, Thanksgiving and Dec. 24-25. Fare $8.50; over 62, $7.50; ages 2-11, $4.50; under 2, $1.50. MC, VI. Phone (215) 862-2332.

[SAVE] **PARRY MANSION MUSEUM,** S. Main and Ferry sts., was built in 1784 by Benjamin Parry, a wealthy lumbermill owner. The house, owned by Parry's descendants until 1966, has been furnished to reflect 125 years of decorative changes in the home. Allow 1 hour minimum. Fri.-Sun. 1-5, May 1 to mid-Dec. Admission $4; ages 1-12, 50c. Phone (215) 862-5652.

NORRISTOWN (H-11) pop. 30,700, elev. 83'

ELMWOOD PARK ZOO, on Harding Blvd., following signs, exhibits white-tailed deer, waterfowls, cougars and other animals from North America. There also are picnic areas, a children's zoo and petting barn. Animal shows are presented summer weekends. Allow 1 hour minimum. Daily 10-4; closed Jan. 1, Thanksgiving and Dec. 25 and 31. Admission $3; senior citizens and ages 3-12, $1.50. Phone (610) 277-3825.

NOTTINGHAM (I-10)

HERR'S SNACK FOODS, US 1 and SR 272, offers tours that explain snack food production from vegetable washing to packaging. An audiovisual presentation and food samples are available. Allow 1 hour minimum. Mon.-Thurs. 9-3, Fri. 9-noon; closed holidays. Free. Reservations are recommended. Phone (610) 932-6401 or (800) 284-7488.

PAOLI (H-11) elev. 541'

WAYNESBOROUGH, 1 mi. s. of US 30 via SR 252 at 2049 Waynesborough Rd., is the birthplace and former home of Revolutionary War hero Gen. Anthony Wayne. The restored twostory Georgian-style house was built in three sections of native stone quarried on the property. The house is furnished in period and includes a collection of objects that belonged to Wayne and his family. A slide presentation tells the history of the family and the house.

Allow 30 minutes minimum. Tues. and Thurs. 10-4, Sun. 1-4, mid-Mar. to late Dec.; closed holidays. Admission $4; over 62 and ages 7-18, $3. Phone (610) 647-1779.

SAVE **THE WHARTON ESHERICK STUDIO** is between Paoli and Valley Forge. From US 202 take SR 252 n. 1.5 mi. Turn left through a covered bridge and take Yellow Springs Rd. 2.5 mi. to Diamond Rock Rd. Go .5 mi. up a hill and turn right onto Horse Shoe Tr. for .1 mi. One-hour guided tours of the rustic former studio and home of the artist-craftsman feature more than 200 works, including paintings, woodcuts, ceramics, sculpture, furniture and utensils.

Tours Mon.-Fri. require a minimum of $30 per group; there is no minimum requirement Sat.-Sun. Individuals may join a scheduled group tour. Tours Mon.-Sat. 10-5, Sun. 1-5, Mar.-Dec.; closed major holidays. Admission $6; under 12, $3. Reservations are required. Phone (610) 644-5822.

PERKASIE (G-11) pop. 7,900, elev. 414'

THE PEARL S. BUCK HOUSE, 1 mi. s.w. of SR 313 at 520 Dublin Rd. on Green Hills Farm, was the home of author and humanitarian Pearl S. Buck. The 1835 stone farmhouse displays her Nobel and Pulitzer prizes and many personal mementos collected in China. Picnicking is permitted. Guided tours are offered Tues.-Sat. at 10:30, 1:30 and 2:30, Sun. at 1:30 and 2:30, Mar.-Dec.; closed major holidays. Fee $5, over 62 and students with ID $4, under 6 free. Phone (215) 249-0100.

POINT PLEASANT (G-12)

Before its settlement in the mid-1700s, Point Pleasant was the site of Indian quarries for argillite, which was used in making arrowheads and knifeblades. Now another natural resource, the Delaware River, provides many recreational opportunities for area visitors and residents.

 RECREATIONAL ACTIVITIES

Tubing

• **Bucks County River Country**, 2 Walters Ln., P.O. Box 6, Point Pleasant, PA 18950. Other activities are available. Daily 8-5, May-Sept. Phone (215) 297-5000.

POTTSTOWN (H-10) pop. 21,800, elev. 144'

As early as 1714 an iron forge was established north of the present site of Pottstown, and ironmaking quickly became the area's principal industry. When Colonial ironmaster John Potts founded the city in 1752, he named it Pottsgrove. Later, in 1815, it was incorporated as Pottstown. The city remains a busy industrial and trade center.

TriCounty Area Chamber of Commerce: 135 High St., Pottstown, PA 19464; phone (610) 326-2900.

Shopping areas: Coventry Mall, SR 100 and SR 724, is the major shopping center serving the Pottstown area. It includes Boscov's, JCPenney and Sears.

POTTSGROVE MANOR, at SR 100 and W. King St., .7 mi. n. of jct. SR 100 and SR 422 at 100 W. King St., is the restored home of town founder and ironmaster John Potts. Built in 1752, the house contains 18th-century Pennsylvania furnishings. The home features original molding and a dining room, which is considered to be rare in homes built during that period. Allow 1 hour minimum. Tues.-Sat. 10-4, Sun. 1-4; closed major holidays. Free. Phone (610) 326-4014.

VALLEY FORGE (H-10) elev. 98'

Valley Forge began as an iron forge on Valley Creek in the 1740s. A sawmill and gristmill were added by the time of the Revolutionary War, making Valley Forge an important supply center for the Colonists. However, it did not escape the attention of the British, who destroyed the forge and mills in 1777. Only ruins marked the site when George Washington chose Valley Forge for his winter of 1777-78 encampment *(see Valley Forge National Historical Park).*

Valley Forge Convention & Visitors Bureau: 100 West Germantown Pike, Plymouth Meeting, PA 19462; phone (610) 834-1550 or (800) 441-3549.

FREEDOMS FOUNDATION AT VALLEY FORGE, 1601 Valley Forge Rd. (SR 23), was founded in 1949 to promote responsible citizenship. The 105-acre campus features the Independence Garden, the Medal of Honor Grove, the Faith of Our Fathers Chapel and the Credo Monument. The Medal of Honor Grove and the campus are open to the public. Allow 30 minutes minimum. Mon.-Fri. 9-5. Admission to grove and campus $2; under 12, $1. Tours of the other facilities are available by reservation. Phone (610) 933-8825.

★VALLEY FORGE NATIONAL HISTORICAL PARK (H-10)

The 3,600-acre Valley Forge National Historical Park, extending east from the village of Valley Forge along SR 23, was the site of the 6-month winter/spring encampment by the

Continental Army. From Dec. 19, 1777, to June 19, 1778, Gen. George Washington and 12,000 soldiers kept the British Army bottled up in Philadelphia.

During that terrible winter some 2,000 troops died from disease brought on by supply shortages, exposure and poor sanitation. Still, during those 6 months the army was reorganized, Baron von Steuben developed a uniform system of drill and the Continental Army left Valley Forge a better-trained, efficient force.

A self-guiding tour visits the reconstructed huts of Muhlenberg's Brigade, Washington's Headquarters, the Memorial Arch, soldier huts and the original entrenchment lines and fortifications. May through September bus tours and automobile tape tours are available. The tours begin at the visitor center at the junction of SR 23 and N. Gulph Road, where there are exhibits and a short film. For more information contact the Superintendent, Valley Forge National Historical Park, Valley Forge, PA 19481.

Allow 2 hours minimum. The park is open daily 9-5; closed Dec. 25. Free. Phone (610) 783-1077.

NATIONAL MEMORIAL ARCH off SR 23, commemorates the patriotism and suffering of George Washington and the men who were under his command.

WASHINGTON'S HEADQUARTERS, the Potts House, contains Revolutionary War-era furnishings. Allow 30 minutes minimum. Daily 9-5; closed Dec. 25. Admission $2; free to all Dec.-Mar. Admission should be paid at the visitor center.

WASHINGTON MEMORIAL CHAPEL (Episcopal), on SR 23 within the park, contains relics, woodcarvings and windows depicting the history of the country. A bell tower connected with the chapel houses the 58-bell Washington Memorial National Carillon. Free recitals are given Sun. after the 11:15 service, mid-Sept. to mid-June, and Wed. at 8 p.m., July-Aug. Allow 30 minutes minimum. Chapel open Mon.-Sat. 9:30-5, Sun. 12:30-5; closed Jan. 1 and Dec. 25. Donations. Phone (610) 783-0120.

Valley Forge Historical Society Museum, in the Washington Memorial Chapel, displays more than 4,000 artifacts from the winter encampment of the Continental Army 1777-78. Many other items belonged to George and Martha Washington, including a knife that doctors used to "bleed" Washington who was suffering from pneumonia at the time of his death.

Allow 1 hour minimum. Mon.-Sat. 9:30-4, Sun. 1-4:30; closed Jan. 1, Good Friday, Easter, Thanksgiving and Dec. 25. Admission $1.50; under 16, 50c. Phone (610) 783-0535.

World of Scouting Museum, on SR 23 on the grounds of the Washington Memorial Chapel, is housed in a log cabin. The history and traditions of the Boy Scout and Girl Scout movements are chronicled through displays of scouting memorabilia such as uniforms, handbooks, magazines and badges. A separate exhibit contains collections from the 314th Infantry Regiment, which fought in France during World War I. Food is available.

Allow 30 minutes minimum. Fri.-Sun. 11-4, Memorial Day-Labor Day; Sat.-Sun. 11-4, rest of year. Closed holidays. Admission $2; over 60 and under 18, $1. Phone (610) 783-5311.

★ WASHINGTON CROSSING HISTORIC PARK (H-12)

The 500 acres of Washington Crossing Historic Park are divided into two areas. The Thompson Mill section is 1.5 miles southeast of New Hope via SR 32. The Washington Crossing section, 5 miles farther south on SR 32, is connected by bridge with New Jersey's Washington Crossing State Park (see attraction listing p. 48). The park is dedicated to the memory of George Washington and the 2,400 soldiers who crossed the Delaware on Christmas night in 1776 to attack and capture Trenton, N.J., then garrisoned by Hessian mercenaries. A re-enactment of the crossing of the Delaware is held at 1 p.m. on Dec. 25. Picnic facilities are available.

Allow 2 hours minimum. The park, visitor center and historic buildings are open Tues.-Sat. 9-5, Sun. noon-5; closed Jan. 1, Thanksgiving and Dec. 24 and 31. Last tour begins 1 hour before closing. Park admission $1 per private vehicle. Ticket for guided tour/admission to five buildings (Thompson-Neely House, McConkey Ferry Inn, Hibbs House, Bowmans Hill Tower and Taylor House) $4; ages 6-12, $3.50; over 60, $3. Phone (215) 493-4076.

BOWMAN HILL WILDFLOWER PRESERVE is the more northern of the two areas. It includes a 100-acre wildflower preserve with natural history exhibits, 26 hiking trails and indoor exhibits. Tues.-Sat. 9-5, Sun. noon-5. Free. Phone (215) 862-2924.

Bowman's Hill Tower presents a commanding 14-mile view of the Delaware River Valley. Washington Crossing can be seen to the south. An elevator takes visitors to an observation point within the 110-foot tower; the top is then reached by stairs. Tues.-Sun. 10-5, Apr.-Oct.; Sat.-Sun. 10-5, in Nov. Admission included in the five-building ticket. Phone (215) 862-3166.

Memorial Flagstaff marks the graves of the Continental troops who died during the encampment and who were among America's first "unknown soldiers."

Thompson-Neely House, built in 1702, was the scene of many important conferences before the Battle of Trenton. Nearby are the Thompson-Neely Barn and Thompson's Grist Mill. Admission included in the five-building ticket.

WASHINGTON CROSSING SECTION focuses on the site where Gen. George Washington and his troops embarked on their historic crossing.

McConkey Ferry Inn is a restored stone building, the earliest parts of which date from the 1750s. George Washington is believed to have dined at the inn before crossing the Delaware. Admission included in the five-building ticket.

Memorial Building houses a copy of Emanuel Leutze's painting "Washington Crossing the Delaware" and related exhibits. A film depicting the event is shown Mon.-Sat. at 9, 10:30, noon, 1:30 and 3, Sun. at noon, 1:30 and 3; schedule is subject to change. Free.

Taylor House is the restored 1816 home of Mahlon Taylor, an influential businessman of the period. Guided tours are given of the first floor. Admission included in the five-building ticket.

WAYNE (H-11) pop. 900, elev. 400'

CHANTICLEER, 786 Church Rd., is the 1913 former estate of pharmaceutical magnate Adolph Rosengarten, Sr., and his family. Thirty acres of the estate have been fashioned into a series of gardens, complete with a creek, pond and paths for enjoying the diverse plantings. Included are formal gardens; a meadow; a woodland with shrubs, vines and perennials native to Asia; a summer garden; a native wildflower garden; and produce gardens. Allow 1 hour minimum. Wed.-Sat. 10-5, Apr.-Oct. Admission $5, under 17 free. Phone (610) 687-4163.

WEST CHESTER (I-10) pop. 18,500, elev. 424'

Graced by many handsome Greek Revival and Victorian homes, West Chester is surrounded by the rich farmland of Chester County. During the Revolutionary War, several major skirmishes occurred nearby, including the battles of Brandywine and Paoli. In 1842 West Chester became the home of the *Jeffersonian,* one of the few newspapers in the North to support the South. A rioting mob soon wrecked the paper's offices, and eventually the postmaster general prohibited its distribution by mail.

Of architectural interest is the 1704 Brinton House, 5 miles south of West Chester in Dilworthtown, a restored stone house built by a Quaker farmer. The middle-class house is furnished in period and features a walk-in hearth fireplace, leaded casement windows and a Colonial herb garden. The Chester County Courthouse, downtown, was built in 1724.

Chester County Tourist Bureau: 601 Westtown Rd., West Chester, PA 19382; phone (610) 344-6365.

SAVE CHESTER COUNTY HISTORICAL SOCIETY, 225 N. High St., displays early American furniture and decorative arts, including clocks, ceramics, crystal and silver. Changing exhibits feature clothing, textiles, dolls and ceramics. The research library deals with genealogy and area history. Allow 1 hour minimum. Museum Mon.-Sat. 9:30-4:30. Library Mon.-Tues. and Thurs.-Sat. 9:30-4:30, Wed. 1-8. Closed major holidays. Museum admission $5; senior citizens, $4; under 17, $2.50. MC, VI. Phone (610) 692-4800.

 RECREATIONAL ACTIVITIES

Canoeing

• **Northbrook Canoe Co.,** 1810 Beagle Rd., West Chester, PA 19382. Other activities are offered. Daily on the hour 9-4, Apr.-Oct. Phone (610) 793-2279.

Nearby New Jersey

BATSTO

Established in 1766, Batsto became a prominent iron foundry and was of great military importance to the Patriots' cause during the Revolution. The village's prosperity grew after the war; its ironworks, brickyard, gristmill, sawmill and glassworks provided livelihoods for nearly 1,000 people.

Batsto's fortunes dwindled as competition from cheap Pennsylvania coal forced the town's more expensive charcoal-fired furnaces to close in 1855. The town became a virtual ghost town and almost disappeared when fire consumed half its buildings in 1874. Two years later Joseph Wharton, the wealthy Philadelphia financier, bought Batsto and the surrounding 100,000 acres.

BATSTO HISTORIC VILLAGE, on CR 542, is part of the Wharton State Forest's *(see Recreation Chart in New Jersey)* 109,000 acres in the Pine Barrens. The restored 19th-century village includes the restored ironmaster's mansion, sawmill, gristmill, general store, post office and workers' houses. Guided tours of the mansion are available.

Allow a full day. Grounds open daily dawn-dusk. Visitor center open daily 9-4:30. Interpretive programs are offered daily, Memorial Day-Labor Day; Wed.-Sun., rest of year. Closed Jan. 1, Thanksgiving and Dec. 25. Mansion tours $2; ages 6-11, $1. Parking $3 Sat.-Sun. and holidays, Memorial Day-Labor Day. Phone (609) 561-3262.

BURLINGTON pop. 9,800, elev. 13'

One of the first permanent settlements in the western part of the colony, Burlington was established by members of the Society of Friends in 1677. It became the capital of West Jersey and shared that status with Perth Amboy after East and West Jersey united. Its location on the Delaware River between Trenton and Camden made the flourishing port so prosperous that its inhabitants—mainly Quaker settlers and pacifists—were relatively uninvolved with the Revolution.

Still a busy manufacturing and distribution community, Burlington retains much evidence of its past. Though there has been some modernizing of facades, many buildings stand out as having been built in Colonial times.

Among those that are open by appointment are the 1703 Old St. Mary's Church, Broad and Wood streets; the 1685 Revell House, 200 block of Wood Street; the 1784 Friends Meeting House, High Street near Broad Street; the John Hoskins House, 202 High St.; the 1792 Friend's School, York and Penn streets; and the restored carriage house on Smith's Alley between High and Wood streets.

Greater Burlington Chamber of Commerce: P.O. Box 67, Burlington, NJ 08016; phone (609) 387-0963.

BURLINGTON COUNTY HISTORICAL SOCIETY COMPLEX, 2 blks. n. of US 130 at 457 High St., is made up of Corson Poley Center, which contains a library and museum, and three historic homes. The Museum features a jinrikisha made by a local carriage company, case clocks, quilts, decoys and various artifacts. Genealogical holdings are accessible to the public at Delia Biddle Pugh Library. Guided tours are available. Mon.-Thurs. 1-4, Sun. 2-4; closed holidays. Donations. Phone (609) 386-4773.

Bard-How House, 453 High St., was built about 1740. Period furnishings and other accessories decorate the restored house.

Capt. James Lawrence House, 459 High St., is the birthplace of the American naval hero of the War of 1812. As commander of the USS *Chesapeake* when it suffered a beating from the HMS *Shannon,* the mortally wounded Lawrence issued his famous last command, "Don't give up the ship." The house, refurbished to the period during which Lawrence lived, also contains costumes and toys.

James Fenimore Cooper House, 457 High St., is the birthplace of the author of the "Leatherstocking Tales," novels about American frontiersmen and American Indians. "The Last of the Mohicans" and "The Deerslayer" are among the best known of this series, written 1826-41. The 1780 Cooper House has four museum rooms.

CAMDEN pop. 87,500, elev. 25′

The industrial and transportation center of southern New Jersey, Camden began in the 1680s as the site of William Cooper's ferryboat operation on the Delaware River. Becoming the terminus for the Camden & Amboy Railroad in 1834 marked the beginning of the city's real growth. Part of the industrial growth was based on Camden's farm produce.

The deep, broad Delaware provides an excellent port. Shipbuilding boomed during World War I and World War II. The first nuclear-powered merchant ship, the *Savannah,* was built in Camden. Electronic communications, printing and publishing are other major area industries.

Poet Walt Whitman, whose unfettered, subjective style had revolutionized poetic expression in the mid-19th century, lived his last years in Camden. The tomb of the "good gray poet" is in Harleigh Cemetery on Haddon Avenue.

CAMDEN COUNTY HISTORICAL SOCIETY is on Park Blvd. at Euclid Ave.; from US 130 take Haddon Ave. w. to Euclid Ave. The society's museum contains period furniture, antique glass, toys, fire-fighting equipment, 18th- and 19th-century newspapers and an original Victor Talking Machine.

The brick Georgian home, Pomona Hall, built in 1726 and extensively enlarged in 1788, is on the grounds and is furnished in period. The society's library has maps and other historical and genealogical data. Tues. and Thurs. 12:30-4:30, Sun. 1-5, Sept.-July; closed holidays. Admission $2, under 16 free. Library $1. Phone (609) 964-3333.

THOMAS H. KEAN NEW JERSEY STATE AQUARIUM AT CAMDEN is on the banks of the Delaware River, 1.2 mi. w. of I-676 exit 5A to Riverside Dr. via Mickle Blvd. The aquarium features a 760,000-gallon tank containing a submerged shipwreck. Other highlights include a dome that changes color with the weather, a shark area, coral reefs, an outdoor trout stream, a seal tank, an aquatic nursery and interactive exhibits designed to educate and entertain. Approximately 400 species of fish are represented at the facility. Ferry service to the museum is available from the riverfront in Philadelphia. Food is available.

Allow 2 hours minimum. Daily 9:30-5:30, Mar. 16-Sept. 15; Mon.-Fri. 9:30-4:30, Sat.-Sun. 10-5, rest of year. Closed Jan. 1, Thanksgiving and Dec. 25. Admission $10.95; over 64 and students with ID $9.45; ages 3-11, $7.95. Parking $5-$8. Reservations are recommended. AE, DS, MC, VI ($14). Phone (609) 365-3300, or (800) 616-5297 or (888) 463-4744 for ticket reservations.

CLEMENTON pop. 5,600, elev. 96′

CLEMENTON AMUSEMENT PARK & SPLASH WORLD WATER PARK, .7 mi. w. of US 30 on White Horse Ave., is set on the shore of a small lake. The amusement park has rides, carnival games and a children's section with a petting zoo. Three water slides are the attraction at the water park. Bathing suits must be worn at the water park; lockers and changing facilities are available. Picnicking is permitted. Food is available.

Daily noon-10, June 24-Labor Day; Thurs.-Sun. noon-10, May 6-June 23. Water park closes at 8 p.m. Admission to either park $16.95; over 64, $14.41. After 5 (for amusement park) or after 4 (for water park), $12.95; over 64, $11.01. Under 37 inches tall free. Combination ticket $19.95; over 64, $16.96. After 5 (for amusement park) or after 4 (for water park) $16.95; over 64, $14.41. DS, MC, VI. Phone (609) 783-0263.

HADDONFIELD pop. 11,600, elev. 74'

Elizabeth Haddon was sent from England by her sonless father in 1701 to develop 550 acres southeast of Camden. In less than a year the Quaker girl had built a house, begun the colony and proposed marriage to Quaker missionary John Estaugh—he accepted. The romance is the theme of "The Theologian's Tale" in Henry Wadsworth Longfellow's "Tales of a Wayside Inn."

INDIAN KING TAVERN HOUSE MUSEUM, 1.5 blks. n. of Haddon Ave. at 233 Kings Hwy., was built in 1750 and was for many years an important social, political and military center along the historic Kings Highway. The three-story structure is furnished in period and contains historical displays. Allow 30 minutes minimum. Wed.-Sat. 10-noon and 1-4, Sun. 1-4; closed Jan. 1, Thanksgiving and Dec. 25. Free. Phone (609) 429-6792.

MOUNT HOLLY pop. 10,600, elev. 45'

Named after a nearby 183-foot "mountain," Mount Holly is a Quaker town dating from 1676. It served as the capital of the state for 2 months in 1779. John Woolman, the Quaker abolitionist known for his 1774 "Journal," taught at the Old School House. Other historic buildings include the 18th- and 19th-century county buildings on High Street between Garden and Union streets.

Smithville Mansion, 2 miles east in nearby Eastampton, is the Victorian home of Hezekiah B. Smith, former owner of a local foundry. The estate also includes a building devoted to Smith's bicycles and an art gallery. Christmas and Candlelight tours are offered in December; phone (609) 265-5068.

SALEM pop. 6,900, elev. 14'

Settled in 1675 by Quakers, Salem is one of the oldest English settlements on the Delaware River. Its early importance as a port—the Salem River provides good harborage—made it a prize during the Revolutionary War; the city was occupied by the British. After the war Camden surpassed Salem as a shipping center, and attention was turned to commerce based on the surrounding agricultural area.

In addition to supporting some light industry, Salem serves visitors who come to view its 18th-century architecture as well as sportsmen who hunt and fish in the nearby wetlands.

The restored 1721 Alexander Grant House at 79-83 Market St. displays articles from the Colonial and Federal periods. The 1734 Hancock House was the scene of a massacre during the Revolution. In retaliation against the Quaker community for supplying cattle to Gen. George Washington's starving troops at Valley Forge, 300 men under Maj. John Simcoe surprised and killed 30 local men asleep in the house, used as a barracks at the time.

One original resident still lives: the carefully nurtured oak, estimated to be more than 5 centuries old, that guards the entrance to the Friends Burying Ground on West Broadway. Beneath its branches John Fenwick bargained with the Lenni Lenape Indians for the land on which he would establish Salem.

Salem County Chamber of Commerce: 104 Market St., Salem, NJ 08079; phone (609) 935-1415.

FORT MOTT STATE PARK, 104 acres 6 mi. n.w., fronts on the Delaware River. Next to the park is the Finns Point National Cemetery, the burial ground of 2,436 Confederate prisoners of war and 300 Union soldiers. Coastal defense fortifications and structures are in the park. A welcome center is available to those traveling the New Jersey Coastal Heritage Trail. Daily 8-7:30, Memorial Day-Labor Day; 8-4, rest of year. Free. Phone (609) 935-3218.

WOODBURY pop. 10,900, elev. 34'

Of considerable importance during the Revolution, Woodbury was occupied by British troops in November 1777. Gen. Charles Cornwallis chose as his headquarters the home of John Cooper, a Continental Congress member denounced for his patriotism by his pacifist Quaker friends. A number of other 18th-century buildings distinguish Woodbury as a Revolutionary-period community.

"Light Horse" Harry Lee, father of Robert E. Lee, used Woodbury as his headquarters during his campaigns in South Jersey in 1779. Other personages associated with Woodbury are Commodore Stephen Decatur and Capt. James Lawrence, both educated at Woodbury Academy. The Hunter-Lawrence House, 58 N. Broad St., was the boyhood home of Lawrence, known for his dying command, "Don't give up the ship," given during the War of 1812. His home is open to visitors.

Greater Woodbury Chamber of Commerce: Kings Hwy., P.O. Box 363, Woodbury, NJ 08096; phone (609) 845-4056.

RED BANK BATTLEFIELD PARK (Fort Mercer) is 2 mi. w. of US 130 at Riverfront. During the Revolutionary War an earthen redoubt—Fort Mercer—was hastily built at this site to help protect the channels of the Delaware River and the port of Philadelphia from the British forces. In 1777, 400 Patriots under Gen. Nathanael Greene vanquished 1,200 Britons and Hessians led by Count Van Donop.

The house of Ann Whitall, who supposedly continued to spin her wool while the battle raged around her home, has been restored. Park open daily dawn-dusk. House open Wed.-Fri. 9-4, Sat.-Sun. 1-4, Apr.-Sept. Free. Phone (609)853-5120.

Pittsburgh
and Vicinity

Pittsburgh, the nation's largest inland port, is a city of pleasant surprises. Mostly hidden by the hills that surround it, the city literally bursts upon visitors who arrive through tunnels, across bridges, or along scenic hillside roadways. Famous for its Three Rivers—the Allegheny and the Monongahela meet at the "Point" to form the Ohio—Pittsburgh is a blend of modern and historic architecture. "Renaissance" is the word, and Pittsburgh's spectacular rebirth is apparent not only in new buildings, parks and transportation systems, but in philosophy as well. Believing renaissance to be a continuous process that answers to changing times and needs, Pittsburgh refuses to box itself in with an ironclad definition of goals. It continues to unfold itself: A friendly giant whose educational, cultural and recreational aspects are as important as its commercial and industrial facets. Above all, it is a livable place and proud of it.

Pittsburgh's history dates from the 18th-century dispute between the French and English over claims to the Ohio Valley. When the Canadian French established an outpost on the Allegheny River, the English quickly realized their need for a fort to defend their position in the West. Young George Washington, then a major in the Colonial army, selected the area now known as the "Golden Triangle"—the junction of the Monongahela, Allegheny and Ohio rivers. In 1758 Pittsborough was named in honor of the British statesman William Pitt.

After the Revolution the city's position on the three rivers enhanced its commercial value, and Pittsborough—by then called Pittsburgh—grew rapidly. Coal was dug from the hills, the first glassworks was opened and Anschulz's blast furnace, built in 1792, became the precursor of the iron and steel industry. Before the 19th century Pittsburgh boasted a post office, a network of roads and the *Pittsburgh Gazette*, the first newspaper published west of the Allegheny Mountains.

During the 19th century, Pittsburgh plunged headlong into the American industrial age; its iron and steel plants soon won it the nickname "Iron City." This industry and others continued to expand after the Civil War and throughout the early decades of the 20th century. Billows of smoke issuing from a multitude of industrial stacks earned Pittsburgh the unloved nickname "Smoky City." Following World War II awareness of the problems found outlet in concerted, constructive action and regulation. Step by step, a lucrative but grimy past became prologue to a versatile, healthy present.

Pittsburgh's terrain is a picturesque mix of plateaus and hillsides, narrow valleys and rivers spanned by many bridges. Its urban geography is equally arresting: No fewer than 90 neighborhoods are recognized by the city's Planning Department. These areas were established as immigrants arrived to work in the factories or to open businesses; and although most of the groups have long since scattered, the comfortable feeling of neighborhood has remained a dominant, thoroughly Pittsburghian trait.

Approaches
By Car

The primary highway from the north or the south is I-79, which passes through the western edge of the metropolitan area. Intersecting with east-west routes I-76 (Pennsylvania Turnpike) on the north and with I-70 on the south, I-79 funnels traffic into downtown Pittsburgh via controlled-access I-279 (Parkway West) and the Fort Pitt Tunnel from Carnegie.

A second approach is I-279 (Parkway North) from Franklin Plaza, and from the south via Banksville Road and I-279. US 19 Truck Route, using East Street from the north and West Liberty Avenue from the south, carries heavy commercial and industrial traffic into the city.

I-76 carries the bulk of east-west traffic through the Pittsburgh area, interchanging en route with all major arteries; controlled-access I-376 through the eastern suburbs provides the principal link to the heart of the city, arriving downtown via Grant Street exit 3. Two other important east-west highways are US 22 and US 30, which combine upon nearing the city, then join expressways—I-279 on the west and I-376 on the east—before entering the downtown area.

SR 28, first as the Allegheny Valley Expressway, then as E. Ohio Street, follows the north bank of the Allegheny River into the city's North Side, providing a fast route from northeast suburbs. Similarly, SR 60 makes an easy connection from the northwestern suburbs along the south side of the Ohio River, picking up airport traffic before joining with US 22/30.

Getting Around

Street System

Pittsburgh's topography—a maze of hills and ravines sliced at an acute angle by two rivers converging to form a third—permits no consistent geometrical street layout. Instead, there is a patchwork of patterns dictated mainly by the lay of the land. A good street map is necessary for travel in this city.

From the Golden Triangle, major thoroughfares fan out more or less parallel to the Allegheny and Monongahela rivers, with intervening streets perpendicular to the rivers near the Point but following the contours of the hills farther out. Fifth Avenue and Liberty Avenue are the primary arteries.

On the North Side, at least the sections nearest the river, the picture is more regular, with avenues running parallel to the Allegheny and streets perpendicular to it. All the major thoroughfares seem to converge on Allegheny Center, framed by N., E., S. and W. Commons. E. Ohio Street and Western Avenue feed in from the east and west, respectively; East Street, Federal Street, Brighton Avenue and Allegheny Avenue reach the center from the north.

The near edge of the hilly South Side is the only part of the city that employs the designations "East" and "West," using the Smithfield Street Bridge as the dividing line. Carson Street (SR 837), parallel to the river, is the main artery through this area.

For the most part, Pittsburgh's streets are named; there are relatively few areas of consecutively numbered thoroughfares. Two such locations are on the Point, where 1st through 7th avenues are numbered northward from the Monongahela, and inland from the Allegheny River, where numbered streets increase as they proceed upstream.

The Informed Traveler

CITY POPULATION: 358,900   **ELEVATION:** 715 ft.

Whom To Call

Emergency: 911
Police (non-emergency): (412) 255-2916
Time and Temperature: (412) 391-9500

Hospitals: Mercy Providence Hospital, (412) 323-5600; Western Pennsylvania Hospital, (412) 578-5000.

Where to Look

Newspapers

The major daily newspaper is the morning *Post-Gazette.* Smaller daily, weekly and special-interest papers also are published.

Radio and TV

Pittsburgh radio station KDKA (1020 AM) is a news/talk/weather station; WDUQ (90.5 FM) is serviced by National Public Radio.

The major TV channels are 2 (CBS), 4 (ABC), 11 (NBC), 13 (PBS) and 53 (FOX). For a complete list of radio and television programs, consult the daily newspapers.

Visitor Information

Various maps, brochures, calendars of events and lists of sightseeing companies are available at the The Greater Pittsburgh Convention and Visitors Bureau, 4 Gateway Center, 18th floor, Pittsburgh, PA 15222; phone (412) 281-7711 or (800) 359-0758. The bureau is open all year Mon.-Fri. 9-5; closed major holidays.

What to Wear

Pittsburghers frankly admit that their city tends to be a cloudy place. Some form of precipitation falls on about 150 days out of 365, distributing the annual 36 inches fairly evenly through the year. (If that seems like a lot, remember that the remaining 215 days can be enjoyed *sans* umbrella.) In January and February the average high temperature is only 37 and the average low temperature is 21. July and August are the warmest months, and although few days see temperatures reaching into the 90s, the average high of 83 can make quite an impression when combined with the frequently high humidity. Because the July-August average low is 61, a light sweater or other garment sometimes might be handy outdoors.

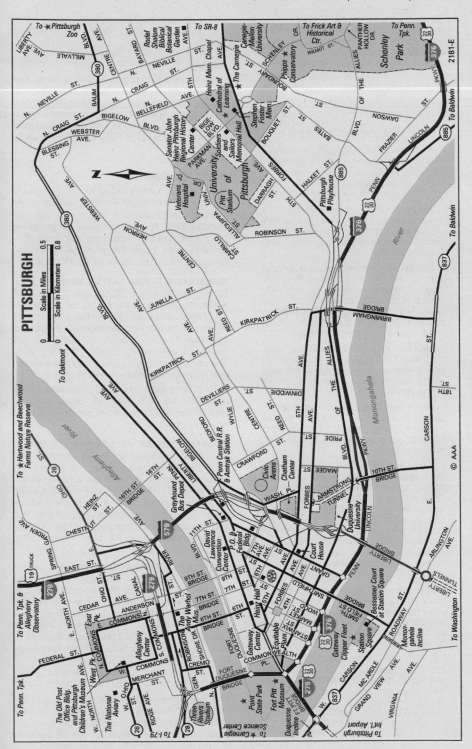

PITTSBURGH

The downtown speed limit, unless otherwise posted, is 25 mph, and on major thoroughfares, 35 mph. Unless a sign prohibits it, turning right at a red light after coming to a complete stop is legal. Similarly, so is turning left from one one-way street onto another. Pedestrians always have the right-of-way, particularly at marked cross-

Transportation

Air travel: The Pittsburgh International Airport, 19 miles west via I-279 and SR 60 (Airport Parkway) is served by numerous major domestic and international carriers, as well as commuter and cargo lines.

Allegheny County Airport, south of the city on Lebanon Church Road in West Mifflin, handles primarily corporate or private aircraft, although air taxis and charter services also are available.

Rail service: Amtrak passenger service's station, (412) 471-6170, is on the lower level of "The Pennsylvanian," formerly Penn Central Station, at Liberty Avenue and Grant Street. The Allegheny Port Authority operates the "T," a three-station subway that loops the city's downtown area.

Buses: The Greyhound Lines Inc. terminal, (800) 231-2222, is at 11th Street and Liberty Avenue. Other bus companies serving the outlying areas are listed in the telephone directory.

Rental cars: Hertz, at the Pittsburgh International Airport, offers discounts to AAA members; phone (412) 472-5955 or (800) 654-3131. Other companies are listed in the telephone directory.

Public transport: Port Authority Transit (PAT) operates a fleet of buses throughout the city, suburbs and surrounding counties. The base fare is $1.25; exact change is required. Various reduced-rate passes and tickets, including weekend passes, are available at PAT's downtown service center, 534 Smithfield St. For route information phone (412) 231-5707. Bus service for the eastern suburbs is provided by the Martin Luther King Jr. East Busway.

Pittsburgh also has a downtown subway and a light rail system for the southern suburbs. The first stage of the light rail system extends 10.5 miles to the South Hills Village shopping mall. Passengers ride free on the subway in the downtown zone.

Taxis: Colonial/Mayflower Cab, (412) 833-3300, People's Cab, (412) 681-3131, and Yellow Cab, (412) 665-8100, are the leading taxi companies. Cabs are metered; the standard fares range from a minimum of $1.50 to $2.50, plus $1 to $1.40 per mile.

walks. Driving during rush hours, about 6:30-9 a.m. and 4-6:30 p.m., should be avoided if possible.

Parking

As in any big city, parking downtown or near the major attractions is at a premium. On-street parking, when a space can be found, is governed by the meter system. However, commercial parking lots and garages are plentiful throughout downtown. Rates range from $2 an hour to $15 a day.

What To See

ALLEGHENY OBSERVATORY, off Perrysville Ave. (US 19) in Riverview Park, is one of the foremost observatories in the world. The surrounding park offers opportunities for swimming (with a city permit), picnicking and tennis. Observatory tours Thurs.-Fri. evenings by appointment, Apr.-Oct. Free. Phone (412) 321-2400.

BEECHWOOD FARMS NATURE RESERVE, is on SR 8, .5 mi. n. of jct. SR 28, then 2 mi. n.e. on Kittanning Pike and 2.5 mi. n. on Dorseyville Rd. Headquarters for the Audubon Society of Western Pennsylvania, Beechwood Farms has more than 90 acres of fields, thickets, ponds and woodlands threaded by 5 miles of hiking trails. The environmental education center has a natural history library and bird observation room.

Trails open daily dawn-dusk. Education center open Tues.-Sat. 9-5, Sun. 1-5; closed holidays. Free. Phone (412) 963-6100, or 963-0201 for events information.

BESSEMER COURT AT STATION SQUARE, s. end of the Smithfield St. Bridge, consists of a riverwalk along which are relics of the region's industrial heritage. Included are a 10-ton Bessemer converter built in 1930; a 25-ton ingot mold; the stern-wheel of the *Jason,* a 1940 steam-powered towboat; and antique railroad cars that have been converted into shops. Allow 30 minutes minimum. Daily 24 hours. Free. Phone (412) 261-2811.

★THE CARNEGIE, 4400 Forbes Ave. across from the Cathedral of Learning, is a cultural complex in the heart of the university area. The Carnegie Performing Arts program sponsors the Music with the Masters series, Jazz Happy Hour and summer concerts in the Sculpture Court. The Carnegie Music Hall, a 2,000-seat auditorium, is home to the Y Music Society, River City Brass Band, Mendelssohn Choir, Opera Theater of Pittsburgh and the Pittsburgh Chamber Music Society. Phone (412) 622-3131.

The Andy Warhol Museum, 117 Sandusky St. on the North Side, is purportedly the most comprehensive single-artist museum in the world devoted to the life and work of one of the most influential artists of the second half of the 20th century. Installations of extensive archival material and more than 500 works of art present the entire range of the Pittsburgh native's creative endeavors as a graphic artist, fine artist, filmmaker, music producer, stage designer, author and publisher. Food is available.

Allow 1 hour minimum .Thurs.-Sat. 11-8, Sun. and Wed. 11-6; closed major holidays. Admission $6; senior citizens $5; students with ID and ages 3-18, $4. AE, MC, VI. Phone (412) 237-8300. *See color ad.*

The Carnegie Library of Pittsburgh, 4400 Forbes Ave. in Oakland, was built in 1895 and is one of the nation's foremost public libraries. It contains more than 4 million items, including books, magazines, newspapers, records, cassettes, photographs and electronic resources. The library is the state's resource library for science and technology. Cultural, educational and recreational programs also are offered. Guided tours are available.

Allow 1 hour minimum. Mon.-Thurs. 9-9, Fri.-Sat. 9-5:30, Sun. 1-5, Sept.-May; Mon.-Thurs. 9-9, Fri.-Sat. 9-5:30, rest of year. Free. Phone (412) 622-3114 or 622-3102 for tour times.

The Carnegie Museum of Art, 4400 Forbes Ave. in Oakland, displays Impressionist and post-Impressionist paintings; 19th- and 20th-century American and European paintings, sculpture and decorative arts; and contemporary art. The museum's film and videotape programs are nationally recognized, and its collection of monumental architectural casts is thought to be unique in the United States. The Heinz Architectural Center surveys past and current architectural expression through the exhibition of architectural drawings, models, photographs, and related materials. Free gallery lectures are given regularly.

Allow 3 hours minimum. Tues.-Sat. 10-5 (also Mon., July-Aug.), Sun. 1-5; closed major holidays. Guided tours are given Sat.-Sun. at 2. Admission (including The Carnegie Museum of Natural Science) $6; senior citizens $5; students with ID and ages 3-18, $4. Phone (412) 622-3131. *See color ad.*

★ **The Carnegie Museum of Natural History,** 4400 Forbes Ave. in Oakland, is known as the "home of the dinosaurs." Dinosaur Hall features 10 full skeletons, including a *Tyrannosaurus rex.* The Walton Hall of Ancient Egypt illustrates daily life through artifacts and interactive computer and videotape programs. Artifacts and displays in Polar World trace the cultural history of Inuit peoples and their adaptation to the Arctic.

In Benedum Hall of Geology, interactive exhibits emphasize Pennsylvania's geology as they show how natural forces shaped the Earth. Masterpiece specimens sparkle in Hillman Hall of Minerals and Gems where visitors can explore crystallography and mineral formations. The Halls of African and North American Wildlife showcase animals in realistic natural habitats. The Discovery Room offers hands-on activities.

Allow 3 hours minimum. Tues.-Sat. 10-5 (also Mon., July-Aug.), Sun. 1-5; closed major holidays. Guided tours are given Sat. at noon and 1, Sun. at 2 and 3. Admission (including The Carnegie Museum of Art) $6; senior citizens $5; students with ID and ages 3-18, $4. Phone (412) 622-3131. *See color ad p. 137.*

SAVE ★**Carnegie Science Center,** One Allegheny Ave. next to Three Rivers Stadium on the North Side, is an "amusement park for the mind" offering more than 250 hands-on exhibits dealing with the advances in science and technology.

The Rangos Omnimax® Theater, which includes a domed, four-story-high screen and a 56-speaker sound system, presents shows about a variety of nature and science topics. Laser light shows are features on Friday and Saturday nights. The Henry Buhl Jr. Planetarium and Observatory probes the inner cosmos and outer space in one of the most technologically sophisticated planetariums in the world.

The Miniature Railroad and Village displays the historical architectural and cultural heritage of western Pennsylvania. Trains speed through a 2,300-square foot detailed miniature landscape which includes 100 animations.

Other highlights include the SciQuest exhibit where visitors can step inside a wind tunnel, feel an earthquake in full motion and check out a tornado. Early Learner's Landing and Science Pier allow youngsters to explore the physical world with their hands and senses; eight interactive modules help visitors understand the work scientists perform and the ways in which science affects our daily lives. The SeaLife Aquarium also is featured.

Allow 4 hours minimum. Daily 10-5 (also Sat. 5-9); closed Jan. 1, Thanksgiving and Dec. 25. Science center or Omnimax theater $6; over 65 and ages 3-18, $4. Science center and Omnimax theater $10; over 65 and ages 3-18, $6. Planetarium, theater and Science Center $12; over 65 and ages 3-18, $8. Parking $3. AE, MC, VI. Phone (412) 237-3400. *See color ad p. 137.*

USS *Requin,* in front of the Carnegie Science Center, is a 300-foot, World War II submarine. Built in May 1945, the sub reached Guam just as the war ended and therefore never saw battle action. Many guides of the 1-hour tour are former submariners, and on weekends the communications room is manned by members of an amateur radio club. There may be a waiting line, and full mobility is necessary for the tour.

Allow 1 hour minimum. Daily 10-5:30, Mar.-Nov. and Dec. 26-31; Sat.-Sun. 10-5:30, rest of year. Closed Jan. 1, Thanksgiving and Dec. 25. Admission $4; senior citizens and ages 3-18, $2. Parking $3. AE, MC, VI. Phone (412) 237-1550.

★**CATHEDRAL OF LEARNING,** the University of Pittsburgh, is on a 14-acre quadrangle at Bigelow Blvd., 5th Ave., Bellefield Ave. and Forbes Ave. The 42-story truncated Gothic stone tower is said to be the tallest skyscraper college building in the Western Hemisphere. Encircling the Commons Room on the first and third floors are 23 nationality classrooms, reflecting styles ranging from classical, Byzantine and Romanesque to Renaissance, Tudor, Empire and folk. Each room was designed and decorated by artists and architects from nations representing Pittsburgh's ethnic heritages.

During the last 3 weeks in December the rooms are decorated in the traditional holiday manner of each nation represented. Allow 1 hour, 30 minutes minimum. Tours Mon.-Fri. 9-3, Sat. 9:30-3, Sun. 11-3. Sat.-Sun. are the best viewing times. Guided tours Apr.-Aug., in Dec. and Sat.-Sun. all year $2; senior citizens $1; ages 8-18, 50c. Fee 50c, rest of year. Reservations are recommended 2 weeks in advance for guided tours; inquire at the information center on the first floor. Phone (412) 624-6000.

CIVIC ARENA, Washington Pl. at Center and Bedford aves. in the Golden Triangle, is a $22 million structure with a stainless steel retractable dome roof three times the size of the dome of St. Peter's in Rome. The multipurpose auditorium is used as a sports arena, theater, convention and concert hall. It is the home of professional hockey's Penguins. Phone (412) 642-1800 or 642-2062 for event information.

DUQUESNE INCLINE affords an excellent opportunity for viewing the city. The lower station is at 1197 W. Carson St., .25 mi. w. of the s. end of the Fort Pitt Bridge. The trip ends at 1220 Grandview Ave., Mount Washington, where restaurants boast panoramas of the Golden Triangle. The incline is not accessible to the physically impaired. Trips depart Mon.-Sat. 5:30 a.m.-12:45 a.m., Sun. and holidays 7 a.m.-12:45 a.m. One-way fare $1; ages 6-11, 50c. Phone (412) 381-1665.

THE FRICK ART & HISTORICAL CENTER, 7227 Reynolds St. in Point Breeze, is a 6-acre complex that includes Pittsburgh industrialist Henry Clay Frick's restored turn-of-the-20th-century home, the reconstructed Alden and Harlow 1897 Greenhouse, and the children's playhouse and bowling alley which is now the visitor center. The Car and Carriage Museum, which exhibits 35 carriages and vintage automobiles, and the Frick Art Museum, which contains Helen Clay Frick's collection of art, also are featured. Food is available.

Grounds open Tues.-Sat. 10-5:30, Sun. noon-6; closed major holidays. Admission to the complex is free. Phone (412) 371-0606.

★**Clayton,** 7227 Reynolds St. in Point Breeze, is the estate of Henry Clay Frick. The only surviving mansion along Pittsburgh's once-famous "Millionaire's Row," the restored Victorian home features original furnishings and personal mementos of the Frick family. Allow 1 hour, 30 minutes minimum. Guided tours are given every 30 minutes Tues.-Sat. 10-4, Sun. noon-5. Admission $6, senior citizens $5, students with ID $4. Tours are not recommended for under age 10. Reservations are required.

Frick Art Museum is at 7227 Reynolds St. at The Frick Art & Historical Center. In a charming landscaped setting across from Frick Park, the Italian Renaissance-style building displays Italian, Flemish and French paintings from the early Renaissance through the 18th century. Also of interest are Italian Renaissance bronzes, 16th-century tapestries and Chinese porcelains. Temporary exhibits, concerts and lectures also are presented.

Allow 1 hour minimum. Tues.-Sat. 10-5:30, Sun. noon-6; closed holidays, except Easter. Free. Phone (412) 371-0600.

★**HARTWOOD,** 215 Saxonburg Blvd., is a 629-acre re-creation of a 16th-century English country estate. A 75-minute tour includes the Gothic Tudor mansion, its collection of English and American antiques, and the estate's formal gardens. Also available are wooded trails, the farm and stable complex, and hayrides.

Allow 1 hour minimum. Guided tours are given on the hour Wed.-Sat. 10-3, Sun. noon-4, Apr.-Dec.; closed major holidays. Hour-long Old English Christmas tours are given mid-Nov. through Dec. 31. Admission $3; over 60 and ages 13-17, $2; ages 6-12, $1.50; under 6, 75c. Reservations are required for all tours. Phone (412) 767-9200.

HEINZ HALL, 6th and Penn aves., is a restored 1926 movie theater. Its excellent acoustics, dramatic decor and architecture now form the backdrop for much of Pittsburgh's cultural activity. Heinz Hall is the home of the Pittsburgh Symphony Orchestra, which presents a variety of popular series during the regular season, including Broadway, Classical, Great Performers, Pops and Summer Casual concerts. Guided tours are given by appointment. Admission $2; under 14, $1. Phone (412) 392-4800.

HEINZ MEMORIAL CHAPEL of the University of Pittsburgh, 5th and S. Bellefield aves. behind the Cathedral of Learning, is a modern French Gothic interdenominational chapel with 73-foot stained-glass windows. Other highlights include the organ, marble altar, carved woodwork and interior and exterior stone carvings. Special programs, concerts, recitals and half-hour guided tours are offered by appointment. Allow 1 hour minimum. Mon.-Fri. 9-4, Sun. 1-5; no guided tours Sun. Free. Phone (412) 624-4157 Mon.-Fri. 8:30-5.

KENNYWOOD PARK is reached by taking exit 9 (Swissvale exit) off I-376, following signs. A traditional family amusement park, Kennywood has four roller coasters, two water coasters, 30 other major rides and 14 children's rides. A wooded grove with picnic shelters is available, and stage shows take place daily at Lake Kennywood. One of only two amusement parks to be named a national historic landmark, Kennywood has buildings dating from 1898. Food is available.

Allow 3 hours minimum. Daily noon-10, mid-May through Labor Day (daily 5-10, Aug. 31-Sept. 4); Sat.-Sun. noon-10, late Apr. to mid-May. Admission $4.95, senior citizens $3.95. All-day ride pass $16.95, Sat.-Sun. $19.95. MC, VI. Phone (412) 461-0500.

MONONGAHELA INCLINE offers a view of the city. The lower station is on W. Carson St. across from Station Square. The terminus is on Grandview Avenue, Mount Washington. An observation deck running approximately .12-mile along Grandview Avenue has circular overhangs providing views of the Golden Triangle. Allow 30 minutes minimum. Mon.-Sat. 5:30 a.m.-12:45 a.m., Sun. and holidays 8:45 a.m.-midnight. One-way fare $1; ages 6-11, 50c. Phone (412) 231-5707.

THE NATIONAL AVIARY, Allegheny Commons West, allows visitors to walk through 23 re-created natural habitats to view more than 250 exotic birds. Allow 1 hour minimum. Daily 9-4:30; closed Dec. 25. Admission $4; over 60, $3; ages 2-12, $2.50. Phone (412) 323-7235.

PITTSBURGH CENTER FOR THE ARTS, 6300 5th Ave. in Mellon Park, has a school and galleries for emerging artists and special projects. Features include regional, national and international exhibitions; classes and workshops for children, adults and the physically and emotionally impaired; concert and dance performances; lectures; an Artcamp for children; and an art shop and gallery where regional and national artists display their works. Mon.-Sat. 10-5:30, Sun. noon-5. Donations. Phone (412) 361-0873.

PITTSBURGH CHILDREN'S MUSEUM is .5 mi. n. via the 6th St. Bridge in the Old Post Office Building at 10 Childrens Way (Allegheny Center). Interactive exhibits relating to human physical and social development are designed for children up to 12 years old. Highlights include puppet shows, storytelling, a hands-on silkscreen printing studio and Stuffee—a 7-foot mascot that turns inside-out to teach anatomy. Safety Street features a real-life street environment with full-scale crosswalks, driveways, intersections, traffic signs and signals, cars and a school bus.

Allow 2 hours minimum. Mon.-Sat. 10-5 (also Fri. 5-8), Sun. noon-5, mid-June through Labor Day; Tues.-Sat. 10-5 (also Fri. 5-8), Sun. noon-5, rest of year. Closed major holidays. Tours of Safety Street are given Mon.-Fri. at 12:30 and 2, Sat. at 12:30 and 2:30, Sun. at 2. Admission $4.50, senior citizens $3.50, under 2 free. Admission $2.50 Thurs. Parking $2. Phone (412) 322-5058.

★ **PITTSBURGH ZOO** is off Butler St. w. of the Highland Park Bridge. The Pittsburgh Zoo is home to more than 4,000 animals, including numerous threatened and endangered species, in 77 acres of natural habitats.

Exhibits include Kids' Kingdom, a children's zoo with a sea lion pool, walk-through kangaroo, deer and goat yards, and a playground; Asian Forest's Siberian tigers; African Savanna's free-roaming elephants, giraffes, zebras and other denizens of the Dark Continent; AquaZoo's living coral reef, penguins and 92,000-gallon shark tank; and Niches of the World's reptiles and small mammals. Food is available.

Allow 2 hours minimum. Daily 10-6, Memorial Day weekend-Labor Day; 9-5, rest of year. Closed Dec. 25. Last admission 1 hour before closing. Admission $6; over 58 and ages 2-13, $4.25. Train ride $1, carrousel ride 75c. Parking $2.50. MC, VI. Phone (412) 665-3640.

★ **POINT STATE PARK,** 36 acres at the confluence of the Allegheny, Monongahela and Ohio rivers, commemorates the British settlement of this frontier outpost in 1754. In the same year, the French seized the area and built Fort Duquesne. The British regained supremacy in 1758 and erected a new fort, which they named Fort Pitt for William Pitt, prime minister of England and friend of the Colonies.

One of the largest fountains in the United States is a focal point of the Golden Triangle. The water is accented by 24 white and gold lights. The fountain, which reaches heights of 150 feet, operates daily from about Easter to mid-November (weather permitting). Park open daily dawn-dusk. Free. Phone (412) 471-0235.

Fort Pitt Blockhouse, built in 1764, is all that remains of the original Fort Pitt, the last reminder of the days when Indian, French, British and Colonial troops fought for possession of the point. Wed.-Sat. 9:30-4, Sun. noon-4. Free. Phone (412) 471-1764.

SAVE ★ **Fort Pitt Museum,** within Point State Park, focuses on the early history of western Pennsylvania and the French and Indian War through models, dioramas, a full-scale reconstructed trader's cabin and artifacts. The museum is in a reproduction of one of the original bastions. An orientation film is shown. The Royal American Regiment performs Sunday at 2:30, mid-June through Labor Day.

Allow 1 hour minimum. Wed.-Sat. 10-4:30, Sun. noon-4:30; closed major holidays, except Memorial Day, July 4 and Labor Day. Admission $4; over 60, $3; ages 6-12, $2. Phone (412) 281-9284.

RODEF SHALOM BIBLICAL BOTANICAL GARDEN, near Carnegie Mellon University at 4905 5th Ave., displays more than 150 varieties of flora—each with a biblical name or reference. The one-third-acre setting is reminiscent of ancient Israel; a stream flowing through the garden represents the River Jordan. Parking is available behind the synagogue. Allow 30 minutes minimum. Sun.-Thurs. 10-2 (also Wed. 7-9 p.m.), Sat. noon-1, June 1-Sept. 15. Free. Phone (412) 621-6566.

SANDCASTLE, I-376 exit 8, following signs along SR 837, is a water park on the Monongahela River with 15 water slides, a lazy river, a giant hot tub, adult and children's pools, boardwalk, go-karts and a miniature golf course. Food is available.

Daily 11-7, weekend after Memorial Day-late Aug. and Labor Day weekend. Club Wet (pool, hot tub and dancing) are available to adults Wed.-Sun. 6 p.m.-1 a.m. and to minors Mon. 8 p.m.-midnight, late May-Labor Day. Admission with slide pass $13.95. Admission with pool pass $7.95, senior citizens $4.95, under 3 free. Go-kart track $3.50. Miniature golf $3.50. Adults Fri.-Sat. evenings $3, Wed.-Thurs. and Sun. evenings $1. Minors Mon. evening $7. MC, VI. Phone (412) 462-6666.

SCHENLEY PARK, 456 acres on Schenley Dr., is one of the city's most popular green spaces. Its lake, playground, picnic areas, tennis courts, baseball fields, trails and golf course offer summer recreation; during the winter there are opportunities for ice skating and cross-country skiing. For further information phone (412) 622-6919, 7-3:30.

★ **Phipps Conservatory,** in Schenley Park, covers 2.5 acres under glass. Highlights include a Japanese Courtyard Garden, Perennial Garden, Victorian Rose Garden, Aquatic Garden and Children's Garden. During spring and fall, flower shows are open daily 9-5. A special flower show also is presented during Christmas. Guided tours are available.

Allow 1 hour minimum. Tues.-Sun. 9-5; closed Thanksgiving, Dec. 25 and the 2 days prior to spring, fall and winter flower shows. Guided tours are given Tues.-Sat. at 11 and 1, Sept.-June; Tues.-Sat. at 1, rest of year. Flower show admission $5; over 59 and students with ID $3.50; ages 2-12, $2. Rest-of-year admission $4; over 59, $3; ages 2-12, $2. Phone (412) 622-6914.

SENATOR JOHN HEINZ PITTSBURGH REGIONAL HISTORY CENTER, 1212 Smallman St., is a museum and research facility devoted to the history and heritage of western Pennsylvania. The museum contains a large collection of premier glass, including blown and etched pieces; antique furnishings; portraits and documents; a library; a children's Discovery Place; an archives; and special exhibits.

Center open daily 10-5. Library and archives open Tues.-Sat. 10-5. Admission $6, senior citizens and students with ID $4.50. MC, VI. Phone (412) 454-6000.

SOLDIERS AND SAILORS MEMORIAL HALL, Fifth Ave. and Bigelow Blvd., honors the memory of veterans of all wars and conflicts. Exhibits feature black military history, Civil War memorabilia, Persian Gulf items, uniforms, photographs and weapons. Film presentations offer insights into American military conflicts and cover topics from the Revolutionary War through the Vietnam War. Guided tours are available by appointment.

Allow 1 hour minimum. Mon.-Fri. 9-4, Sat.-Sun. 1-4; closed major holidays. Free. Reservations are required for films or special tours. Phone (412) 621-4253.

STEPHEN FOSTER MEMORIAL, on the University of Pittsburgh campus, is dedicated to American music and to Foster, a native of Pittsburgh and composer of some of America's best-loved songs. The west wing houses a library and museum. The auditorium presents concerts, the Three Rivers Shakespeare Festival, University Theatre Department productions and Dear Friends, a program of 19th-century American music.

Library and museum open Mon.-Fri. 9-4; closed university holidays. Guided tours $1.50, senior citizens and students $1. Reservations required 2 weeks in advance for guided tours. Phone (412) 624-4100 for more information.

What To Do

Sightseeing

Visitors who prefer to sightsee on their own should stop at the Greater Pittsburgh Convention & Visitors Bureau's Visitor Information Center at 4 Gateway Center, (800) 366-0093, or the Mount Washington Center in the Grandview Avenue Branch of the Carnegie Library, (412) 381-5134. Both centers provide brochures and maps of the Golden Triangle and Mount Washington. The Pittsburgh History and Landmarks Foundation, One Station Sq., Suite 450, offers walking tours and bus tours of a range of historical sites in western Pennsylvania; phone (412) 471-5808.

🚌 Bus Tours

GRAY LINE tours depart from Station Square; pickups are made at major downtown hotels. The company offers three narrated sightseeing tours: Cultural Pittsburgh, Historic Pittsburgh and Pittsburgh and its Rivers. A tour combining Cultural Pittsburgh and Historic Pittsburgh also is available. Reservations are required at least 1 hour prior to departure. Fares include all applicable admission charges. AE, DS, MC, VI. Phone (412) 741-2720 or 761-7000.

The Cultural Pittsburgh Tour is a 2-hour tour that includes stops at the West End Overlook, affording a view of the Golden Triangle; the Cathedral of Learning at the University of Pittsburgh; and PPG Place downtown. Oakland and other downtown sites are seen en route. Tour departs daily at 1 (combination tour at 9:45), Apr.-Oct. Fare $16; ages 6-11, $8. Combination tour $28; ages 6-11, $14.

The Historic Pittsburgh Tour is a 2-hour tour that begins with a ride on the Duquesne Incline to the top of Mount Washington. Calvary Church, Point State Park, historic districts, Millionaires' Row and Three Rivers Stadium are seen en route. Tour departs daily at 9:45, Apr. 1 to mid-Nov. Fare $16; ages 6-11, $8. Combination tour $28; ages 6-11, $14.

Pittsburgh and its Rivers Tour is a 5-hour tour consisting of the Historic Pittsburgh tour and a cruise on Pittsburgh's rivers. Tour departs Mon.-Sat. at 9:45, June 15-Aug. 31. Fare $24; ages 6-11, $12; ages 3-5, $6.

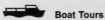 Boat Tours

★**GATEWAY CLIPPER FLEET,** departing from the dock at Station Sq. at W. Carson St. and the Smithfield St. Bridge, provides scenic cruises on the city's three rivers. The 1,000-passenger *Majestic,* the 600-passenger *Gateway Party Liner,* the two 400-passenger *Belles* and the 150-passenger *Good Ship Lollipop* provide not only various narrated sightseeing cruises but Lock and Dam Cruises and Twilight Fountain Cruises as well. Buffet luncheon revue, dinner and moonlight dance cruises also are available.

Cruises depart daily, Memorial Day weekend-Labor Day; otherwise varies. Narrated sightseeing cruises lasting 2-2.5 hours cost $8.50; over 60, $7.50; ages 3-12, $5.50. AE, DI, MC, VI. Phone (412) 355-7980.

Sports and Recreation

That Pittsburghers are avid sports lovers is well known from the city-wide celebrations that followed all the Steelers' Super Bowl victories and the Penguin's Stanley Cup victories. However, the city offers abundant and convenient opportunities for recreational pursuits as well; nearly every imaginable sport or recreational pastime is available. **Boating** is very popular on Pittsburgh's three rivers.

The focus for much recreation is the city and county parks. Frick, Highland and Schenley parks offer ballfields, tennis courts, golf courses and trails for bicycling and hiking. In winter, golf courses and hilly areas are popular for **cross-country skiing.** Information about facilities and current activities in the city parks can be obtained from the City Parks and Recreation Department; phone (412) 255-2676.

Allegheny County's North and South parks have plenty of the above activities as well as swimming pools, nearby bicycle rentals and **ice skating** in winter, the county fairgrounds (South Park) and game preserves. In addition, North Park's lake offers **fishing,** boating and boat rentals. For more information about county park programs and activities contact Allegheny County Parks; phone (412) 392-8455.

Bicycling devotees have the advantage of a city bicycle route that links Highland, Mellon, Frick and Schenley parks. The City Parks and Recreation Department can provide route information; phone (412) 255-2676.

In addition to the courses in the parks, **golf** is available at a number of excellent public courses; consult the telephone directory for listings. Also inquire at your hotel, for some might have a reciprocal golf club agreement for their guests with one of the local private or semiprivate courses.

Hiking is popular, as the number of hiking groups and programs attest. The Sierra Club can furnish information about hiking, canoeing and camping in the area. In winter many of the city's hiking paths become **ski** trails. Besides the cross-country skiing provided by the city and county park areas, Allegheny County's Boyce Park, on Old Frankstown Road in Plum Borough, offers a downhill ski area with four tows, a snow-making machine, instruction and equipment rental. Equipment also can be rented at several ski shops, some of which also arrange ski trips and tours; check the telephone directory.

Horseback riding is available at various locations; stables and riding academies are listed in the local telephone directory. Those who would rather watch equines than ride one can go to the **harness races** at Ladbroke at The Meadows 25 miles south of Pittsburgh, where live harness racing is held year-round; for more information phone (724) 225-9300 or (412) 563-1224 in Pittsburgh. There is **Thoroughbred racing** throughout the year at Mountaineer Park near Chester, W. Va., about an hour from Pittsburgh; phone (304) 387-2400.

Note: Policies concerning admittance of children to pari-mutuel betting facilities vary. Phone for information.

Among the **swimming** pools in Allegheny County, those in Boyce, Settler's Cabin and South Park provide waves for those who yearn for the surf. Fee is $3 for the wave pool, $2 for the waveless.

The county has 78 **tennis** courts; the city operates large complexes in Frick, Highland, McKinley, Mellon and Schenley parks. Courts operate on a first-come-first-served basis. Because some require permits, it is a good idea to check with the city or county parks departments first; phone (412) 255-2676 or (412) 392-8455, respectively.

The National Football League's Steelers are a household word among **football** fans; their home games are played at Three Rivers Stadium. The Pirates are the stars during the **baseball** season. Pro **hockey** is played by the Penguins at the Civic Arena. College sports also are big attractions, particularly the games played by the University of Pittsburgh's Panthers.

Shopping

The Golden Triangle is the core of shopping downtown. Most heavily concentrated in the district around Market Square, 5th, 6th, Wood and Smithfield streets, stores range from specialty shops to such major department stores as Kaufmann's and Saks Fifth Avenue. Most of these have branches in the larger suburban shopping malls. PPG Place, at Market Square, offers shopping as well as noontime concerts in summer. High fashion is the emphasis in Oxford Centre, 301 Grant St., and the Arcade Shops at Fifth Avenue Place.

If you are looking for a novel place to shop or browse, try The Strip which offers open-air and storefront shopping along several block of Penn Avenue east of the Convention Center. Purveyors offer fresh produce, meats and fish, specialty imports, bargain basement housewares, cafes and bars.

Farther out are McIntyre Square, North Hills Village, Northway Mall and Ross Park Mall—all on McKnight Road. The four malls include branches of most of the large department stores. On the Ohio River about 20 minutes from downtown, many Victorian homes in the old community of Sewickley now house antique and specialty shops.

Among Pittsburgh's more popular shopping places are the Shops at Station Square, across the Monongahela River at the south end of the Smithfield Street Bridge at W. Carson Street. A kaleidoscope of 68 specialty shops, eateries and night spots occupies the refurbished 1900s terminal complex of the Pittsburgh & Lake Erie Railroad.

The southern suburbs are served by the area's largest mall, the 190-store Century III Mall in West Mifflin. The 122 stores of South Hills Village are off US 19 between Upper St. Clair and

Bethel Park. In Bethel Park at the intersection of US 19 and Fort Couch Road, Village Square offers 55 stores, including Loehmann's and Silo. Also in the South Hills off US 19 is The Galleria, which features such specialty stores as Ralph Lauren and Tiffanys.

East of downtown, some of the better known shopping areas are on Walnut Street in lively, very trendy Shadyside, where people watching is as rewarding as the fashion and fancy housewares stores; at Forbes and Murray avenues in Squirrel Hill, where delicatessens and other specialty food shops predominate; and on Ellsworth Avenue, with an assortment of boutiques.

Of interest in Oakland is S. Craig Street, where remodeled rowhouses contain specialty shops, art galleries and restaurants. Away from the neighborhood scene on US 22 near the Pennsylvania Turnpike is Monroeville Mall; its 180 stores and other establishments are the commercial heart of this suburban region.

Theater and Concerts

Reflecting the city's metamorphosis from an industrial behemoth to a corporate giant, the city's cultural scene is growing, becoming more varied, more vital and more progressive. This is perhaps most apparent in Pittsburgh's theater offerings.

While as active and excellent as ever, The Carnegie and the universities are no longer alone on the stage. The Pittsburgh Playhouse in Oakland is the site of a wide range of classical and contemporary productions. Contemporary American plays are presented by the City Theatre Company during its October through April season at the New City Theatre in Oakland. The Pittsburgh Public Theatre is a professional Equity company offering classical and modern dramas, including a new play each year.

Among the popular summer series are the productions of the South Park Conservatory Theater. The Three Rivers Shakespeare Festival, held June through August, is a joyous joint effort offering three of the master's works by the City Theatre Company and the University of Pittsburgh Theater.

There are several dinner theaters in the vicinity as well. The Green Tree Marriott and the White Barn Theatre are known for their summer productions. The Fort Pitt Inn leans toward comedy productions.

Dance of many kinds, from folk to the most modern, also is available. As they have for nearly 50 years, the Duquesne University Tamburitzans bring to vivid life the folk dances of Old Europe. The acclaimed Pittsburgh Ballet Theatre performs at the Benedum Center for the Performing Arts October through April. The American Dance Ensemble, the Pittsburgh Black Theatre Dance Ensemble and several other groups stage their productions at the Pittsburgh Playhouse and similar locations.

For orchestral music at its best, the Pittsburgh Symphony has few rivals. This top-flight orchestra packs opulent Heinz Hall September through May for its regular 24-program series as well as for its Pops, Young Peoples' and Tiny Tots' series. An outdoor courtyard with wrought-iron benches, water sculptures and lunchtime performances by local musicians has been added to Heinz Hall. The Pittsburgh Opera performs at the Benedum Center for the Performing Arts, an opulent restored theater.

Contemporary American music is the specialty of the Pittsburgh New Music Ensemble, which performs at Chatham College Chapel. Free chamber music concerts are held at the Frick Art Museum on Sundays, October through April. The Summer Concert in the Parks series provides a variety of free concerts, including bluegrass, folk and jazz in several of the city parks. At Point Park State Park the American Waterways Wind Orchestra presents concerts, folklorists, plays and puppet shows from a floating barge on the river.

The lavish Benedum Center for the Performing Arts, formerly the Stanley Theatre, is home to the Pittsburgh Opera, Civic Light Opera and Pittsburgh Ballet Theatre and also presents first-run Broadway shows.

These are only a few of the possibilities; *Pittsburgh* magazine and the newspaper carry complete listings.

Special Events

Runners take to the streets of the city in early May for the Pittsburgh Marathon. In late May the David Lawrence Convention Centre is the scene of the Folk Festival, an extravaganza of international customs, costumes and cuisines. Also in May, the Shadyside Summer Arts Festival attracts artists, craftsmen, browsers and music aficionados from throughout the area.

During most of June, Pittsburgh celebrates the Three Rivers Arts Festival at Gateway Center, Station Square, Market Square and Point State Park: There are programs and productions of just about everything cultural the city has to offer, including art, dance, music, theater and mime. Also held in June is the Mellon Jazz Festival, featuring 10 days of entertainment from top jazz performers.

The Pittsburgh Three Rivers Regatta occurs the first full weekend in August. Oktoberfest, held in late September, is celebrated at Station Square. Nature's seasonal beauty is feted at Phipps Conservatory with three floral celebrations, the spring, fall and holiday flower shows.

The Pittsburgh Vicinity

AMBRIDGE (G-1) pop. 8,100, elev. 700'

SAVE **OLD ECONOMY VILLAGE,** Great House Square at 14th and Church sts., derives its title from the original town of Economy, built 1824-30 by the Harmony Society *(see Harmony in the Vicinity section)*. Embracing 6.5 acres, the village contains 16 original structures which visitors may tour. The restored buildings include the Museum Building, the Mechanics Building, a store, a wine cellar and the Leader's Home. Guided tours are available.

Allow 1 hour, 30 minutes minimum. Tues.-Sat. 9-5, Sun. noon-5; closed Jan. 1, Veterans Day, Thanksgiving and Dec. 25. Last admission 1 hour before closing. Admission $5; over 60, $4.50; ages 6-12, $3; family rate $13. Phone (724) 266-4500.

BEAVER FALLS (G-1) pop. 10,700, elev. 787′

Beaver Falls, home to Geneva College, is located along the banks of the Beaver River. When the Harmony Society purchased the site in 1859, an industrial boom began which resulted in the area being referred to as a miniature Pittsburgh.

AIR HERITAGE MUSEUM, at the Beaver County Airport, 2 mi. n. on SR 51, houses memorabilia from World War I and World War II, including uniforms, flight suits and airplane models. In an adjacent hangar visitors can observe vintage aircraft being restored. Allow 30 minutes minimum. Mon.-Sat. 10-5, Sun. noon-5. Donations. Phone (724) 843-2820.

BEAVER FALLS HISTORICAL SOCIETY AND MUSEUM is at 1301 Seventh Ave. (SR 18), in the basement of the Carnegie Free Library. Historical items displayed include vintage fire department equipment, china, photo albums, clothing and 1800s Chinese cutlery. A county research center is on the second floor. Allow 1 hour minimum. Historical society and museum open Tues.-Thurs. 10-4, Fri.-Sat. 10-3, Mon. 3-8. Closed holidays. Donations. Phone (724) 846-4340.

CANONSBURG (H-1) pop. 9,200, elev. 936′

THE CHALLENGE CENTER is at 2403 Washington Rd.; from I-79 exit 10 go e. .5 mi. on US 19. This attraction offers participatory sports amusements and adventure games such as laser tag and gladiators. Food is available. Mon. and Thurs.-Fri. 4-11, Sat. noon-11, Sun. noon-9; closed Thanksgiving and Dec. 25. Admission free; activities prices vary. Minimum age for gladiator games is 11. DS, MC, VI. Phone (724) 746-0606.

ELIZABETH (H-2) pop. 1,600. elev. 752′

ROUND HILL EXHIBIT FARM, .5 mi. e. of SR 51 on SR 48, then s. on Round Hill Rd., is a complete small-scale working farm, started in 1790. Highlights include a brick farmhouse built in 1838 and livestock, including dairy and beef

cattle, sheep, pigs, chickens and horses. There also are an adjoining park, a picnic area and duck pond. Dairy cows are milked at 4. Allow 30 minutes minimum. Farm daily 8-dusk. Office Mon.-Fri. 8-4. Free. Phone (412) 384-8555 or 384-4701.

HARMONY (F-2) pop. 2,000, elev. 913′

George Rapp and his Harmony (or Rappite) Society set up their first communal settlement on Connoquenessing Creek in 1804. During the next 10 years about 100 members died and were buried in a little graveyard. The graves, according to custom, were numbered but not marked. This cemetery and a number of substantial brick buildings remain from the original settlement.

In 1814 the society migrated to Indiana and founded New Harmony; 10 years later they returned to Pennsylvania and established the community of Ambridge *(see place listing in the Vicinity section)*.

[SAVE] **HARMONY MUSEUM,** on the Diamond in the town center, preserves relics of the Harmony Society and Mennonites, who acquired the town from the Harmonists. Items are displayed in 19th-century buildings; guided tours are offered. The original Harmonist church tower clock has a single hand that points to the hour. A working replica is displayed in the Grace Church.

Allow 1 hour minimum. Tues.-Sun. 1-4; closed holidays. Admission $3.50; ages 6-13, $1.50. Phone (724) 452-7341.

JEANNETTE (H-3) pop. 11,200

[SAVE] **BUSHY RUN BATTLEFIELD STATE HISTORICAL SITE,** SR 66 n. to SR 993W (Bushy Run Rd.), is the site of a military encounter in 1763 between the British and the American Indians. The British victory at Bushy Run marked the turning point in Pontiac's War. A visitor center displays artifacts and reproductions from the period, and an exhibit describes the battle. Guided and self-guiding tours are offered. Rolling hills and woodlands are available for picnicking.

Allow 30 minutes minimum. Wed.-Sat. 9-5, Sun. noon-5; closed major holidays. Admission $2; senior citizens $1.50; ages 6-12, $1; family rate $5. Phone (724) 527-5584.

MONROEVILLE (G-3) pop. 29,200

SRI VENKATESWARA TEMPLE, on S. McCully Dr., is one of 10 Hindu temples in the United States. It is modeled after a major temple in southern India. The ornate white towers contain representations of Hindu deities. Daily 9-8:30 (also Fri. 8:30-9:30 p.m.), late Apr.-early Oct.; 9-7:30 (also Fri. 7:30-8:30 p.m.), rest of year. Guided tours are available by appointment. Free. Phone (412) 373-3380.

TARENTUM (G-2) pop. 5,700, elev. 777′

TOUR-ED MINE & MUSEUM, SR 28 exit 14, then .1 mi. n. on Bull Creek Rd., offers guided tours of a deep coal mine. The mine car "Old Man Trip" carries visitors one-half-mile down into the mine where the tour begins. Displays feature actual equipment in working condition and illustrate the coal-mining process. A museum exhibits a company store, a miner's log cabin and coal souvenirs and jewelry.

Allow 1 hour minimum. Wed.-Mon. 1-4, Memorial Day weekend-Labor Day. Last tour departs 1 hour before closing. Admission $6; ages 3-12, $3. Phone (724) 224-4720.

WASHINGTON (H-1) pop. 15,900, elev. 1,039'

The Washington and Jefferson College Memorial Library was founded by a gift from Benjamin Franklin. The school is said to be the oldest college west of the Allegheny Mountains. The Duncan Miller Glass Museum, 525 Jefferson Ave., exhibits fine pressed and hand-blown glass.

Washington County is home to 23 of the state's 221 historic covered bridges. A brochure highlighting the bridges is available at the county tourism office at Franklin Mall.

Washington County Tourism Promotion Agency: Franklin Mall, 1500 W. Chestnut St., Washington, PA 15301; phone (724) 228-5520 or (800) 531-4114. *See ad p. 415.*

SAVE **DAVID BRADFORD HOUSE** is at 175 S. Main St. David Bradford was a leader in the 1794 Whiskey Rebellion, a protest against high excise taxes that hurt the grain producers of western Pennsylvania. The house is furnished in 18th-century style. Candlelight tours are featured the first weekend in December. Wed.-Sat. 11-4, Sun. 1-4, May 1 to mid-Dec. Admission $4; over 65, $3.50; ages 6-16, $2. Phone (724) 222-3604.

LeMOYNE HOUSE, 49 E. Maiden St., was the home of antislavery politician and doctor, Francis LeMoyne. Built in 1812, the early Greek Revival-style stone mansion served as LeMoyne's office and apothecary shop and was a station for the underground railroad. The site now houses the Washington County Historical Society headquarters and the LeMoyne Historic Garden. Tues.-Fri. 11-4, Sat.-Sun. noon-4, Feb.-Dec.; closed holidays. Admission $4; under 18, $2. Phone (724) 225-6740.

PENNSYLVANIA TROLLEY MUSEUM is at 1 Museum Rd.; from I-79 exit 8 follow blue Trolley Museum signs. This museum offers trolley rides and has displays of standard-gauge railroad equipment and trolley cars dating from 1894. Special seasonal events are presented. Picnicking is permitted. Allow 1 hour minimum. Daily 11-5, Memorial Day-Labor Day and Dec. 26-31; Sat.-Sun. 11-5, Apr. 1-day before Memorial Day and day after Labor Day-Dec. 24. Admission $5; over 65, $4; ages 2-15, $3. DI, MC, VI. Phone (724) 228-9256.

PLUMER (E-3)

PITHOLE CITY, 1.5 mi. n. on SR 227, then 2.2 mi. e. on a paved road, was a flourishing settlement during the oil boom of the late 1860s. No buildings remain, but cellar holes, streets, a reservoir and abandoned wells still mark the site of the vanished town. The visitor center has exhibits and a brochure outlining a walking tour; other exhibits and markers are along the tour route.

Allow 1 hour minimum. Thurs.-Sun. 10-5, Wed. noon-5, Memorial Day weekend-Labor Day. Guided tours are available on Sun. Admission $2.50; over 60, $2; ages 6-12, 50c; family rate $5.50. Phone (814) 827-2797.

Pocono Mountains Area

In northeastern Pennsylvania, only a 2-hour drive from New York City or Philadelphia, lie the Pocono Mountains. The 2,400 square miles of woodlands with numerous lakes, ponds and clear, rushing rivers are spread across four counties; Carbon, Monroe, Pike and Wayne. Some of the loveliest waterfalls in the East are flanked by blossoming mountain laurel in the spring and brilliant foliage in the fall.

The Poconos are widely known as a recreational resort area. More than 30 golf courses provide challenging sport as well as breathtaking mountain views. Swimming, canoeing, boating and water-skiing can be enjoyed at many of the larger lakes. Lake Wallenpaupack is the third largest lake in Pennsylvania. The preseason stocking of lakes and streams ensures the region's reputation for good fishing, particularly for trout. Deer, bears, rabbits, squirrels, pheasants and grouse attract hunters during designated hunting seasons.

Pocono Mountains Vacation Bureau, Inc.

More than one million skiers and snowboarders annually pray for snow—the earlier the better—and flock to the Poconos' 13 developed ski areas. Many bargain packages and price specials are offered, particularly during midweek when the slopes are less crowded. Snowtubing is a popular pastime and is available at all major ski areas. Frozen lakes and ponds provide natural ice-skating rinks; cross-county skiing, snowmobiling and camping also are possible; phone (717) 421-5565 for fall foliage information and 24-hour updated Pocono ski conditions information.

Pocono Mountains Vacation Bureau: 1004 Main St., Stroudsburg, PA 18360; phone (717) 424-6050 or (800) 762-6667.

Shopping areas: Numerous factory outlet stores make the Pocono Mountains a delight for shoppers. The Pocono Outlet Complex, 9th and Ann streets in Stroudsburg, has more than 30 stores. The Crossings in Tannersville, I-80 exit 45, following signs, features more than 65 stores, including American Tourister, Dansk, Etienne Aigner, London Fog, Oneida, Ralph Lauren, Reebok and Toy Liquidators.

BUSHKILL (F-12)

BUSHKILL FALLS is 2 mi. n.w. off US 209. Rustic bridges and a 2-mile nature trail lead through virgin forests and a scenic gorge to the 300-foot series of eight waterfalls. Bushkill Falls, the largest, drops 100 feet and can be reached by an easy 15-minute walk without climbing. A wildlife exhibit features mounted native birds and animals, while an American Indian exhibit includes a longhouse and examples of arrowheads, spearheads, jewelry, tools and bowls. Comfortable walking shoes are advised. Picnicking, paddleboating and fishing are permitted. Food is available.

Allow 3 hours minimum. Daily 9-dusk, Apr.-Nov. Last admission approximately 1 hour, 30 minutes before closing. All-inclusive admission $7; over 62, $6.25; ages 4-10, $1. DS, MC, VI. For further schedule information phone (717) 588-6682. *See ad.*

POCONO INDIAN MUSEUM, 8 mi. n. on US 209 from I-80, depicts the lifestyle of the Delaware Indians and displays examples of their bark houses, pottery, food and weapons. Many of the items displayed were unearthed in the Delaware Water Gap area. Allow 30 minutes minimum. Daily 9:30-5:30. Admission $3.50; over 62, $2.50; ages 6-16, $2. AE, MC, VI. Phone (717) 588-9338.

DELAWARE WATER GAP NATIONAL RECREATION AREA

Popular with artists and wealthy vacationers during the late 1800s, the Delaware Water Gap is a picturesque break in the Kittatinny Ridge of the Appalachian Mountains. The gap is threaded by the Delaware River, which runs the entire length of the recreation area. Wooded Mt. Tammany and Mt. Minsi rise abruptly about 1,200 feet above the river, which is about 50 feet deep at the gap.

The park encompasses 70,000 acres, in both New Jersey and Pennsylvania, along a 40-mile stretch of the Delaware River. Over 200 miles of scenic roads meander through the valleys and ridges of the park. Trails, wildlife, historic structures and waterfalls can be viewed along the way. A 25-mile portion of the Appalachian Trail winds its way along the Kittatinny Ridge in New Jersey.

A variety of trails are available for such recreational activities as hiking, horseback riding, snowmobiling and cross-country skiing. Camping is permitted in the many area campgrounds. Backcountry camping is permitted only along the Appalachian Trail where special regulations are in effect. Open fires are prohibited. In the summer lifeguards are on duty at Smithfield Beach

and Milford Beach, Pa.; these facilities charge for admission.

Millbrook Village, 12 miles north of the Kittatinny Point Visitor Center along Old Mine Road, is a re-created rural community featuring shops, residences and other buildings of the late 19th century. Interpreters in period dress demonstrate rural lifestyles. The village is open Wed.-Sun. 9-5, early May to mid-Oct. Phone (908) 841-9520 or 841-9531.

Peters Valley, 8 miles northwest of Branchville via US 521, then south on CR 615, has several historic buildings that have been converted into studios for artisans. A gallery also is available; phone (201) 948-5200.

Slateford Farmhouse, in Pennsylvania 3 miles south of I-80 via US 611, following signs, was owned, occupied, farmed and quarried for than 200 years by provincial proprietors, absentee landlords and yeoman farmers. The farmhouse is closed for restoration.

The Kittatinny Point Visitor Center, on I-80 near the toll bridge that crosses the Delaware River into Pennsylvania, has exhibits, audiovisual programs and literature. It is open daily 9-5, early May to mid-Nov.; Sat.-Sun. 9-4:30, rest of year. Hours may vary; phone ahead. Phone (908) 496-4458.

Dingmans Falls Visitor Center, 1 mile west of US 209 near Dingmans Ferry, Pa., offers an audiovisual program, nature exhibits, literature and nature walks and is open daily 9-5, May 1-Nov. 1. Hours may vary; phone ahead. Phone (717) 828-7802. **Note:** The visitor center is closed for renovation.

Bushkill Visitor Center, on US 209, also is closed for renovation; the center is scheduled to reopen spring 1998. The park headquarters,

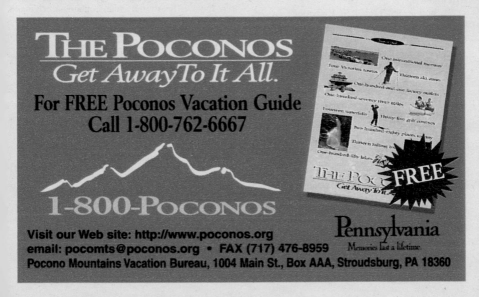

1 mile east of US 209 on River Road in Bush-kill, Pa., is open Mon.-Fri. 8-4:30; closed holidays. Phone (717) 588-2451. *See Recreation Chart.*

HAMLIN (E-10) elev. 555'

One of two Pennsylvania towns called Hamlin, this Hamlin is east of Scranton at SRs 590 and 196. The other Hamlin is north of Lebanon off I-78.

CLAWS 'N' PAWS WILD ANIMAL PARK, 3.5 mi. e. on SR 590, then .7 mi. s. at sign, encompasses some 100 species of exotic animals in a wooded setting. Included are bears, leopards, a snow leopard, monkeys, tigers, giraffes, a rare white tiger and wolves. Also on the grounds is a petting zoo; a farmyard animals exhibit; a birds of prey exhibit; and a walk-in Lory parrot aviary where colorful birds approach visitors. Three different live animal shows take place daily May 1-Labor Day.

Allow 2 hours minimum. Daily 10-6, May-Oct. Last admission is 1 hour, 15 minutes before closing. Admission $8.95; over 65, $7.95; ages 2-11, $5.95. MC, VI. Phone (717) 698-6154. *See ad p. 146.*

HONESDALE (E-11) pop. 5,000, elev. 982'

Established in 1826 as a terminal for canal barges carrying coal to New York markets, Honesdale was the site of the first use of a steam locomotive in the United States. Imported from England to pull coal cars from the mines to the canal, the locomotive "Stourbridge Lion" made its trial run on Aug. 8, 1829. Too heavy for the rails, it was withdrawn from service. A replica can be seen in the county historical museum at 810 Main St.

[SAVE] Stourbridge Line Rail Excursions are offered by the chamber of commerce in April and June through December.

Wayne County Chamber of Commerce: 303 Commercial St., Honesdale, PA 18431; phone (717) 253-1960.

WAYNE COUNTY HISTORICAL SOCIETY MUSEUM, 810 Main St., is housed in the 1860 former office of the D&H Canal Co. Exhibits include "Movin' Energy—The History of the Delaware & Hudson Canal Co. 1828-1898" which features a life-size replica of the first commercial steam engine and the Stourbridge Lion. Other exhibitions include "Faces in Clay—Native Americans of the Upper Delaware" which includes a 3,400-piece archeology collection and changing displays about the history of Wayne County. Also on site is a research library.

Mon. and Wed.-Sat. 10-4, Sun. noon-5, June-Sept.; Mon., Wed. and Fri. 1-4, Sat. 10-4, Oct.-Dec. and Mar.-May; Sat. 10-4, rest of year. Admission $2; ages 12-18, $1. Phone (717) 253-3240.

JIM THORPE (F-10) pop. 5,000, elev. 531'

In the foothills of the Poconos, the town of Jim Thorpe was named after the famous Olympic athlete who won each pentathlon event but the javelin throw in the 1912 Olympic Games in Stockholm. He was later stripped of his honors because of previous "professional" sports activities.

In response to Thorpe's widow's search for a memorial for him, two Pennsylvania communities—Mauch Chunk and East Mauch Chunk—joined forces by incorporating as Jim Thorpe in the mid-1950s. The new community gave the man a final and fitting memorial, while also gaining economic stability for itself. Jim Thorpe was reinstated in the Olympic records in 1982, and the medals he won in the 1912 games were presented to his family. The Jim Thorpe Memorial is a half-mile east on SR 903.

The Harry Packer Mansion, off SR 209, features 400-pound doors made of solid walnut with bronze hardware and etched-glass panels. Self-guiding tours are available; phone (717) 325-8566 to verify schedule. Mauch Chunk Lake Park *(see Recreation Chart),* 4 miles west of town, offers recreational opportunities.

During the first two weekends in December, the town celebrates Old Time Christmas, complete with a Victorian Ball, entertainment and decorations.

Carbon County Tourist Promotion Agency: P.O. Box 90, Jim Thorpe, PA 18229; phone (717) 325-3673 or (888) 546-8467.

ASA PACKER MANSION, off SR 209 on Packer Hill, was the 1860 Victorian home of the well-known 19th-century industrialist and philanthropist Asa Packer. While the exterior has changed somewhat from its original appearance, the interior remains nearly the same, containing original furnishings, woodcarvings and paintings.

Allow 1 hour minimum. Tours are given every 45 minutes daily 11-4:15, day after Memorial Day-Oct. 31; Sat.-Sun. 11-5, in Nov., the first two weekends in Dec. and Apr. 1-late May. Last tour departs at 4:15. Admission $5; ages 7-12, $3. Phone (717) 325-3229.

[SAVE] **H.O. SCALE MODEL TRAIN DISPLAY** is on the second floor of the old Hooven Mercantile Co. building at 41 Susquehanna St. (SR 209) This three-level train display features 13 separate model trains, some pulling as many as 50 railroad cars over nearly 1,100 feet of winding track. The meticulously designed display includes more than 200 miniature buildings, 100 bridges, 1,000 street lights and moving automobiles.

Mon.-Fri. noon-5, Sat.-Sun. 10-5, July-Oct.; Sat.-Sun. noon-5, rest of year. Closed major holidays. Admission $3; over 64, $2; ages 6-14, $1. Phone (717) 386-2297.

JIM THORPE RIVER ADVENTURES departs 1 mi. n. of the Lehigh River Bridge on SR 903, following signs. Write 1 Adventure Ln., Jim Thorpe, PA 18229. Summer rafting float trips are offered July 1 to mid-Sept. White-water rafting trips also are available. Summer rafting float trips $28, children $20; one child free with 2 adults. Minimum age or weight requirements may apply. Reservations are required. Phone (717) 325-2570.

POCONO WHITEWATER RAFTING trips depart 8 mi. n.e. of the Lehigh River Bridge on SR 903. Mountain bike rentals are available. Write Route 903, Jim Thorpe, PA 18229. Summer floats that require paddling are available June 1 to mid-Sept. White-water rafting trips also are available. Summer float trips $33, children $19.95. Under 5 are not permitted. Reservations are recommended. Phone (717) 325-3656 or (800) 944-8392.

ST. MARK'S EPISCOPAL CHURCH, on Race St., contains altars of white Italian marble, large brass gas standards flanking the baptismal font, Tiffany stained-glass windows and one of the oldest operating elevators in the nation. The stone carving behind the altar is a replica of one in St. George Chapel in Windsor Castle. Allow 30 minutes minimum. Daily 1-3:30, Memorial Day-Oct. 31. Donations. Phone (717) 325-2241.

LACKAWAXEN (E-12) pop. 2,800, elev. 687′

ZANE GREY MUSEUM, Scenic Dr., is situated along the Delaware River in the house where Zane Grey began his writing career. Exhibits include photographs, books and personal belongings of the Western author and his wife, Dolly. Guided tours arc available. Allow 30 minutes minimum. Fri.-Sun. noon-5, Memorial Day weekend-Labor Day; Sat.-Sun. noon-4, May 1-day before Memorial Day weekend and day after Labor Day to mid-Oct. Free. Guided tours $2; ages 10-16, $1. Phone (717) 685-4871.

LEHIGHTON (F-10) pop. 5,900, elev. 4,945′

[SAVE] **LEHIGHTON MODEL TRAIN DISPLAY**, 4 mi. w. on SR 443 at 517 Ashtown Dr. within Pocono Museums Unlimited, houses an extensive O-scale model railroad display with 16 operating trains traveling over 2,006 feet of track, a highway with moving automobiles, more than 100 buildings and 10,800 trees, lights, an amusement park, three waterfalls, a lake with live fish and waterfalls as well as a rain storm complete with thunder and lightening. A collection of more than 150 engines and hundreds of cars of rolling stock are displayed.

Allow 1 hour minimum. Wed.-Mon. 10-5, June 1-Labor Day; Wed.-Mon. noon-5, day after Labor Day-Dec. 31; Fri.-Sun. 10-5, rest of year. Closed Jan. 1, Easter, Thanksgiving and Dec. 25. Admission $4; over 60, $3; ages 5-12, $2. Phone (717) 386-3117.

MILFORD (E-12) pop. 1,400

GREY TOWERS, off US 6, following signs, was the home of Gifford Pinchot, two-term governor of Pennsylvania and founder of the USDA Forest Service. The 45-minute tour includes three furnished rooms of memorabilia as well as the gardens, outbuildings and terrace. Allow 1 hour minimum. **Note:** The premises are undergoing renovation and may occasionally be closed to the public; phone to confirm schedule.

Tours on the hour daily 10-4, Memorial Day weekend-Labor Day; Fri.-Mon. 10-4, by appointment Tues.-Thurs., day after Labor Day-Veterans Day; by appointment rest of year. Donations. Phone (717) 296-9630.

THE UPPER MILL, on Sawkill Creek at 150 Water St., is a restored gristmill built in the early 1800s. A three-story water wheel powers the mill. Shops located on the grounds are open year-round. Food is available. Allow 30 minutes minimum. The mill operates daily 10-5, May-Oct.; open by self-guiding tour rest of year. Free. Phone (717) 296-5141.

MOUNT POCONO (F-11) pop. 1,800, elev. 1,658′

From a hundred viewpoints at and near Mount Pocono, the colossal notch of the Delaware Water Gap is plainly visible, even though it is 25 miles away. Southwest of town is Pocono Raceway, where two NASCAR 500 automobile races and other motorsport races are held.

APPLETREE FARM, 1 mi. s. on SR 611 and 1.7 mi. e. on Grange Rd., features buggies, wagons, sleighs, farm machinery and blacksmith and harness shops. Animals can be fed and petted. Pony and horsedrawn wagon rides are available. A pumpkin festival takes place in October. Allow 30 minutes minimum. Daily 10-5, May-Nov.; Sat.-Sun. 10-5, rest of year. Admission $4, under 2 free. Phone (717) 839-7680.

POCONO KNOB, .2 mi. s. on US 611, then e. on Knob Hill Rd. to scenic overlook, is one of the more well-known viewpoints of the region. The panorama extends across the Pocono Mountains into New Jersey and New York.

☀❄❄ RECREATIONAL ACTIVITIES

Horseback Riding

- **Pocono Adventures Stables**, 1 mi. s. on Meadowside Rd. Write HC2, Box 2010, Jim Thorpe, PA 18229. Open daily. Phone (717) 839-6333.

SHAWNEE ON DELAWARE (F-12)

SHAWNEE PLACE PLAY AND WATER PARK, 5 mi. n. of I-80 exit 52 (Marshalls Creek) on US 209, following signs, is an elaborate outdoor play area geared toward ages 3 to 13. Daily magic shows are featured. Attractions include two waterslides, a wading pool and video games, as well as a punch-bag forest, cable glide, net climb, cloud bounce, ball crawl and an adventure river ride. Picnicking is permitted.

Daily 10-5, June 13-Labor Day. Admission $10, adult spectators $5, under 40 inches tall free. AE, DS, MC, VI. Phone (717) 421-7231.

STROUDSBURG (F-11) pop. 5,300, elev. 420'

Col. Jacob Stroud, who served in the French and Indian War, settled in what is now Stroudsburg in 1769. Because of the strategic location 3 miles west of the Delaware Water Gap, Fort Penn was built around his home in 1776. Two years later the post sheltered refugees from the Wyoming Massacre *(see Wyoming p. 161)*. The town was formally established in 1799 when Stroud and his son sold lots in their spaciously platted townsite.

The 1795 Stroud Mansion, built by the colonel for his son, still stands at 9th and Main streets; it serves as headquarters for the Historical Society of Monroe County.

Pocono Mountains Vacation Bureau: 1004 Main St., Stroudsburg, PA 18360; phone (717) 424-6050. *See color ad p. 147.*

SAVE ★ QUIET VALLEY LIVING HISTORICAL FARM, 3.5 mi. s.w. on US 209 Bus. Rte., then 1.5 mi., following signs, is a re-created late-18th-century Pennsylvania-German farm. Costumed guides conduct 90-minute tours. Crafts are demonstrated daily. The farm is open for the Farm Animal Frolic the last two weekends in May, and for the Harvest Festival Columbus Day weekend.

Open Tues.-Sat. 10-5:30, Sun. 1-5:30, June 20-Labor Day. Last tour departs 1 hour, 30 minutes before closing. Admission $6; over 61, $5; ages 3-12, $3.50. Phone (717) 992-6161.

TANNERSVILLE (F-11) elev. 1,276'

CAMELBACK ALPINE SLIDE AND WATERSLIDE is 3.5 mi. n.w. of I-80 Penn. exit 45, following signs. Summer attractions include a 3,200-foot alpine slide, two waterslides, bumper boats, go-karts, a carrousel, kiddie cars, miniature golf, a scenic chairlift, play park and a swimming pool. Free live entertainment is provided Saturday and Sunday afternoons. Food is available; picnicking is permitted.

Allow 3 hours minimum. Daily 10-6, mid-June through Labor Day; Sat.-Sun. 10-5:30, mid-May to mid-June; Sat.-Sun. 11-5, day after Labor Day-Columbus Day; Sat.-Sun. 11-4, day after Columbus Day-early Nov. Alpine slide $5. Five-ride waterslide ticket $5. Combination ticket available. Phone (717) 629-1661.

WHITE MILLS (F-11) elev. 922'

DORFLINGER GLASS MUSEUM, .5 mi. e. of US 6 on Long Ridge Rd., features more than 600 pieces of cut, engraved, etched, gilded and enameled crystal. The crystal is displayed among period antiques and items from the Dorflinger Glassworks. Allow 30 minutes minimum. Wed.-Sat. 10-4, Sun. 1-4, May 16-Nov. 1. Admission $3; over 55, $2.50; ages 6-18, $1.50. Phone (717) 253-1185.

The Dorflinger-Suydam Wildlife Sanctuary offers nature trails for observing indigenous wildlife and waterfowls within its 600 acres. Allow 30 minutes minimum. Daily dawn-dusk. Free. Phone (717) 253-1185.

POINT MARION (I-2) pop. 1,300, elev. 817'

FRIENDSHIP HILL NATIONAL HISTORIC SITE is 3 mi. n. on SR 166. The scenic 661-acre site features the home that Albert Gallatin, treasury secretary for Presidents Jefferson and Madison, built for his first wife, Sophia Allegre, in 1789. A gazebo, built in the late 1800s, typifies the lifestyle of the country gentleman. Mrs. Gallatin's gravesite is nearby.

Ten miles of nature and hiking trails wind through the site. Picnic facilities and self-guiding audio tours are available; guided tours are offered in summer. Allow 1 hour minimum. Daily 8:30-5; closed Dec. 25. Free. Phone (724) 725-9190.

POINT PLEASANT—
see Philadelphia and Vicinity p. 128.

POTTSTOWN—
see Philadelphia and Vicinity p. 128.

POTTSVILLE (G-9) pop. 16,600, elev. 636'

Pottsville was named for John Pott, a pioneer ironworker who built a small iron furnace in 1806. The birth of the city coincided with the beginning of the vital iron and steel industry, which prospered for more than a century.

Pottsville also was the gateway to northeastern Pennsylvania's anthracite coal-mining region. Downtown Pottsville sports the 90-foot-high Henry Clay Monument, a memorial to the presidential candidate who supported legislation favorable to the area's coal industry. The monument, built in 1855, is said to be the nation's oldest cast-iron statue.

Schuylkill Chamber of Commerce: 91 S. Progress Ave., Pottsville, PA 17901; phone (717) 622-1942.

Shopping areas: Schuylkill Mall, 6 miles north on SR 61 or at I-81 exit 36 in Frackville, has about 100 stores, including The Bon Ton and Sears.

YUENGLING BREWERY, 5th and Mahantongo sts., offers tours of America's oldest brewery; it was established in 1829. Visitors observe all facets of the production process and sample the finished product at the tour's end. The many stairways and a few dimly lit areas might present problems for some; sandals and flip-flops are not permitted. Allow 1 hour minimum. Tours depart daily at 10 and 1:30; closed major holidays. Free. Phone (717) 628-4890.

PUNXSUTAWNEY (F-3) pop. 6,800, elev. 1,236'

Each Feb. 2, the nation awaits the prognostication of one of Punxsutawney's most respected citizens: Punxsutawney Phil—the official groundhog of Groundhog Day. As they have each year since 1887, believers trek at dawn to Gobbler's Knob in Sportsman's Park and rout the rodent from his den to determine whether there will be an early spring. The legend that the groundhog's seeing his shadow on Candlemas Day (Feb. 2) predicts 6 more weeks of winter was brought to this country by the German immigrants who settled the area.

Phil is honored not only on Groundhog Day but also by a life-size statue and a groundhog zoo at the Mahoning East Civic Center and the Punxsutawney Groundhog Club, whose membership numbers in the thousands.

Punxsutawney Chamber of Commerce: 124 W. Mahoning St., Punxsutawney, PA 15767; phone (814) 938-7700 or (800) 752-7445.

QUARRYVILLE—
see Pennsylvania Dutch Country p. 104.

READING (H-10) pop. 78,400, elev. 237'

Thomas and Richard Penn, sons of William Penn, founded Reading in 1748 and named it for their ancestral home in England. The settlement was a supply base for forts along the Blue Mountains during the French and Indian War. In Reading originated the first Civil War regiment,

volunteer band, flag and women's aid society. Modern Reading has become a major industrial center, with many clothing manufacturers maintaining retail outlet stores in or near the city.

Reading contains a wealth of 18th- and 19th-century buildings, many noted for their elaborate use of decorative glass and wrought iron. Penn Square, the centerpiece of the city as laid out by the brothers Penn, remains the heart of downtown Reading; historic buildings now house stores and other businesses, and special activities take place on the landscaped pedestrian mall.

Reading has three historic districts: the Callowhill district, which centers on the city's commercial area; the nearby Prince district, which contains well-preserved 19th-century workers' homes, factories and commercial structures; and Centre Park, which displays some of the city's finest Victorian structures.

On the east side of Reading on the summit of Mount Penn is the Pagoda, a seven-story 1908 Japanese-style building that affords panoramas of the city and the Schuylkill Valley; it is home to the Berks Arts Council. About 8 miles northwest via SR 183 is the Blue Marsh Lake Recreation Area *(see Recreation Chart).*

Reading and Berks County Visitors Bureau: P.O. Box 6677, Reading, PA 19610; phone (800) 443-6610.

Shopping areas: The Reading area is known for outlet shopping and features six factory outlet complexes that carry name-brand items ranging from designer clothing and lingerie to baked goods and potato chips. The six complexes are Designers Place, 801 Hill Ave.; Manufacturers Outlet Mall (MOM), SR 10 at I-76 exit 22; The Outlets on Hiesters Lane, 700-800 Hiesters Ln.; Reading Outlet Center, which occupies an entire block between Windsor and Douglass streets; Reading Station, 951 N. 6th St.; and VF Factory Outlet, US 422 and Park Road.

Although better known for its outlet stores, Reading also offers two other major shopping centers. Berkshire Mall, Bern Road off US 422W Bypass, features Hecht's and Sears. Fairground Square, 2 miles north of Reading on US 222, has Boscov's and JCPenney.

BERKS COUNTY HERITAGE CENTER (Gruber Wagon Works), 5 mi. n.w. via SR 183 and Red Bridge Rd., is a restored late 19th-century wagon works. Original tools and equipment are displayed. The 5-mile-long Union Canal Bicycling and Walking Trail is on the grounds; nearby is Wertz's Bridge (also known as Red Bridge), the longest single-span covered bridge in the state. The center also traces the history of transportation on the Union and Schuylkill canals at the C. Howard Heister Canal Center.

Allow 2 hours minimum. Tues.-Sat. and Mon. holidays 10-4, Sun. noon-5, May 1-last Sun. in Oct. Admission to wagon works or canal center $3; over 60, $2.50; ages 7-18, $2. Combination admission for both museums $5; over 60, $4; ages 7-18, $3. Phone (610) 374-8839.

[SAVE] **HISTORICAL SOCIETY OF BERKS COUNTY**, 940 Centre Ave., contains displays that depict local history, including fine arts, industry, transportation and Pennsylvania German arts and crafts. Highlights include the county liberty bell that was rung July 8, 1776, the Dieffenbach organ, a Conestoga wagon and a 1902 Duryea automobile. A hands-on children's museum also is featured. A library contains information about Berks County history and genealogy.

Allow 1 hour minimum. Tues.-Sat. 9-4; closed holidays and holiday weekends. Admission $2.50; senior citizens $2; ages 5-12, $1. Library $4. Phone (610) 375-4375.

MARY MERRITT DOLL MUSEUM, 10 mi. e. on US 422, has rare and quaint dolls dating from about 1725 to the present. Allow 1 hour minimum. Mon.-Sat. 10-4:30, Sun. 1-5; closed major holidays. Admission, including Merritt's Museum of Childhood, $3; over 60, $2.50; ages 5-12, $1.50. Phone (610) 385-3809.

Merritt's Museum of Childhood exhibits papers belonging to William Penn, antique toys, children's carriages, china, glassware and Pennsylvania Dutch pottery and quilts. American Indian baskets, artifacts and pottery also are displayed. Two rooms furnished in period reflect the 1780s. Allow 1 hour minimum. Mon.-Sat. 10-4:30, Sun. 1-5; closed major holidays. Phone (610) 385-3408.

MID-ATLANTIC AIR MUSEUM, SR 183 to the Reading Regional Airport, following signs, displays both military and civilian aircraft. Among the more than 25 airplanes displayed are two classic commercial airliners, a Martin 4-0-4 and a Capitol Airlines Viscount; the first night fighter ever built; a 1944 Douglas DC-3; and a North American B-25 Mitchell. Allow 1 hour minimum. Daily 9:30-4; closed major holidays. Admission $5; ages 6-12, $1. DS, MC, VI. Phone (610) 372-7333.

READING PUBLIC MUSEUM, 500 Museum Rd., presents art, science and history displays ranging from pre-historic times to the present. Changing exhibits, sculptural gardens and a planetarium also are featured. Open Tues.-Sat. 11-5 (also Wed. 5-8), Sun. noon-5; closed Dec. 25. Planetarium shows Sun. at 2 and 3, Wed. at 7. Admission $3; ages 4-17, $2. Phone (610) 371-5850.

RED ROCK (E-9)

RICKETTS GLEN STATE PARK is 4 mi. n. on SR 487. In the Glens Natural Area, 22 waterfalls are formed as Kitchen Creek winds through two deep gorges. There are 21 miles of hiking trails in the park; 5 miles follow the course of Kitchen Creek. Other activities include snowmobiling, boating, fishing, camping, picnicking and swimming. Daily 8-dusk. Free. Fee for camping, cabins or boat rental. Phone (717) 477-5675. *See Recreation Chart and the AAA Mideastern CampBook.*

ROARING SPRING (H-5) pop. 2,600, elev. 1,200'

BARE MEMORIAL FOUNTAIN is in the basin of the spring for which the town of Roaring Spring was named. Varicolored sprays of water rise to a height of 25 feet. It operates daily noon-11, mid-Apr. until freezing weather. Phone (814) 224-5141.

ROCKHILL FURNACE (H-6) pop. 400

EAST BROAD TOP RAILROAD, in Orbisonia, .2 mi. w. of jct. SR 994 and US 522, offers rail excursions on a vintage 1873 narrow-gauge steam train. The 10-mile, 50-minute round trip winds through the Pennsylvania countryside. Picnic facilities are near the station and at Colgate Grove, the turn-around point; passengers may disembark and board a later run.

Allow 1 hour minimum. Trains run Sat. at 11, Sun. at 1 and 3, first weekend in June-Oct. 20; phone for schedule updates. Fare $9; ages 2-12, $6. Phone (814) 447-3011.

Rockhill Trolley Museum, across from the East Broad Top Railroad, chronicles the history of the trolley through photographs and various displays. Excursions on trolleys dating from the 1890s are offered. Open Sat. 10:30-5, Sun. 10:30-4, Memorial Day weekend-Oct. 31. Admission $3; ages 2-11, $1. MC, VI. Phone (610) 437-0448 or (717) 263-3943.

ST. BONIFACE (G-5)

SELDOM SEEN INC., off SR 36, offers electric train rides that carry visitors into an underground coal mine to learn about the past, present and future of coal mining. Tours include a walk through a museum and the mine trip. Allow 2 hours minimum. Tour and mine trip Thurs.-Sun. 11-6, July 1-Labor Day; Sat.-Sun. 11-6, Memorial Day weekend-June 30. Tour only day after Labor Day-Sept. 30. Admission $6; ages 3-12, $3.50. Phone (814) 247-6305.

ST. MARYS (E-5) pop. 5,500, elev. 1,702'

St. Marys was founded in 1842 by a group of persecuted German Catholics from Philadelphia and Baltimore. The city is the center of the powder metal industry.

St. Marys Chamber of Commerce: 126 Center St., St. Marys, PA 15857; phone (814) 781-3804.

STRAUB BREWERY, 303 Sorg St., was founded in 1872. One of the smaller breweries in the country, Straub distributes only in Pennsylvania and eastern Ohio. Allow 30 minutes minimum. Tours Mon.-Fri. 9-noon. Tastings Mon.-Fri. 9-5. Phone ahead for tour information. Closed holidays. Free. Under age 12 are not permitted on tours. Phone (814) 834-2875.

SCHNECKSVILLE (G-10) elev. 669'

TREXLER-LEHIGH COUNTY GAME PRESERVE is 2 mi. w. on Game Preserve Rd. The preserve's 1,200 acres contain about 350 animals representing 50 species. A 25-acre zoo, hiking trails and picnic groves are on the grounds. Special events, activities and educational programs are regularly scheduled. Food is available. Pets are not permitted.

Allow 1 hour minimum. Daily 10-5, Memorial Day weekend-Labor Day; Sat.-Sun. 10-5, last weekend in Apr.-day before Memorial Day weekend and day after Labor Day-Oct. 31. Admission $5; over 60 and ages 2-12, $3. MC, VI. Phone (610) 799-4171.

SCOTTDALE (H-2) pop. 5,200, elev. 1,050'

WEST OVERTON MUSEUMS are 1 mi. n. on SR 819. The complex includes the 1859 "Old Farm" distillery and gristmill, the 1838 Abraham Overholt Homestead, and Springhouse—the birthplace of industrialist Henry Clay Frick. The museums' displays reflect life in a 19th-century rural-industrial village. The 30-minute film "Pillars of Fire," about coke-making operations, is presented regularly.

Guided tours and archives are available. Allow 1 hour, 30 minutes minimum. Tues.-Sat. 10-4, Sun. 1-5, mid-May to mid-Oct. Admission $3; ages 7-12, $1. Phone (724) 887-7910.

SCRANTON (E-10) pop. 81,800, elev. 753'

Four anthracite blast furnaces built in the 1840s and 1850s by the Scranton brothers initiated the growth of Scranton and the area's iron and coal industries. By the end of World War II, the decline of the anthracite industry, due to competition from other fuels, resulted in the development of the Scranton Plan. This plan for revitalizing the economy served as a model for other communities with similar problems.

Scranton has restored parts of its historic downtown as well. At 700 Lackawanna Ave. (I-81 exit 53) is the 1906 Lackawanna Station, a former railroad depot that has been restored and converted into a hotel. Many of the original features of the imposing French Renaissance building have been preserved, including the exterior Indiana limestone facade and the interior Siena marble walls and brass fixtures.

The Suraci and Contemporary galleries at Marywood College, feature paintings, sculpture, prints and photographs. Theater, concerts and musical presentations also are offered throughout the year; phone (717) 348-6207.

Recreational opportunities can be found at nearby Lackawanna State Park *(see Recreation Chart)*. The Lackawanna County Stadium *(see color ad p. 432)*, off I-81 exit 51, is below Montage Mountain. The 10,000-seat facility presents sports events, concerts, festivals and outdoor theater; for baseball fans, it hosts the AAA league Scranton/Wilkes-Barre Red Barons from April through August.

Pennsylvania Northeast Territory Visitors Bureau: 100 Terminal Rd., Wilkes-Barre/Scranton International Airport, Suite 216, Avoca, PA 18641; phone (717) 457-1320 or (800) 229-3526. *See color ad p. 432.*

Shopping areas: One of Scranton's major shopping centers is Viewmont Mall, on US 6 off I-81 exit 57A; Boscov's and Montgomery Ward serve as anchor stores. Boscov's and Montgomery Ward also anchor more than 70 specialty stores in downtown Scranton in The Mall at Steamtown *(see color ad p. 432)*, at Lackawanna and Penn avenues.

ANTHRACITE MUSEUM COMPLEX consists of four sites: the Pennsylvania Anthracite Heritage Museum in McDade Park, the Scranton Iron Furnaces in downtown Scranton, the Museum of Anthracite Mining *(see Ashland p. 65)* and Eckley Miners' Village *(see Hazleton p. 85)*.

Pennsylvania Anthracite Heritage Museum is in McDade Park, off Keyser Ave., following signs. The museum is dedicated to collecting, interpreting and preserving the history and culture of Pennsylvania's hard-coal region. Exhibits feature the immigrants' cultures, ethnic diversity and religion as well as their impact on the region.

Allow 1 hour minimum. Mon.-Sat. 9-5, Sun. noon-5; closed non-summer holidays. Admission $3.50; over 60, $3; ages 6-17, $2. Phone (717) 963-4804.

Scranton Iron Furnaces, Cedar Ave. between Lackawanna Ave. and Moosic St., are four stone smokestacks of blast furnaces built in the 1840s and 1850s. These furnaces were the catalyst for development of the city; in the 1860s they were the second largest producers of iron in the nation. Daily 8 a.m.-dusk. Free. Phone (717) 963-3208.

EVERHART MUSEUM, in Nay Aug Park at the e. end of Mulberry St., houses permanent exhibitions of American Folk, Native American, Oriental and primitive art as well as fine art. Other displays include Dorflinger glass, a dinosaur hall and a bird collection. The museum also presents changing exhibits, lectures and educational programs. Daily noon-5 (also Thurs. 5-8), Apr. 1-Columbus Day; Wed.-Sun. noon-5 (also Thurs. 5-8), rest of year. Closed Jan. 1, Thanksgiving and Dec. 25. Donations. Phone (717) 346-7186.

HOUDINI TOUR AND SHOW, .7 mi. n. of Scranton Expwy. to 1433 N. Main Ave., is dedicated to the memory of famed escape artist and magician Harry Houdini. Visitors can view Houdini memorabilia, including photographs, props and posters, followed by a videotape presentation and a live magic show. Daily 10-5, June 27-Labor Day; 11-3, May 23-June 26 and day after Labor Day-Sept. 13. Schedule varies rest of year; phone ahead. Admission $10; under 10, $8. Phone (717) 342-5555 or 342-8527.

LACKAWANNA COAL MINE TOUR is next to the Pennsylvania Anthracite Heritage Museum in McDade Park. Visitors are taken via railcar 300 feet underground to the floor of the coal mine, then on a guided walking tour through the mine's three veins.Underground temperatures remain at a constant 55 degrees Fahrenheit; jackets are available on loan. Above ground, the Shifting Shanty exhibit room has photomural displays, mining relics and a videotape presentation.

Allow 1 hour minimum. Daily 10-4:30, Apr.-Nov. Fee $6; ages 3-12, $4. DS, MC, VI. Phone (717) 963-6463 or (800) 238-7245. *See color ad p. 432.*

STEAMTOWN NATIONAL HISTORIC SITE is off I-81 exit 53 at jct. Lackawanna Ave. and Cliff St. The 40-acre site is in the former Delaware, Lackawanna and Western railyards, one of the earliest rail lines in northeastern Pennsylvania. The site commemorates the history of steam railroads through one of the country's largest collections of period locomotives and rolling stock.

Visitors can view steam locomotives as well as a working roundhouse, locomotive shop, restoration shop, caboose and other historic rolling stock being restored. A visitor center, a history museum and a technology museum tell the story of American steam railroading. Steam train excursions to Moscow are offered during the summer. In addition, a yard shuttle operates several times daily. Phone (717) 340-5206. Guided tours are available.

The site is open daily 9-5 (weather permitting); closed Jan. 1, Thanksgiving and Dec. 25. Phone for dates and times of excursions and for times of guided tours. Museum admission $7; senior citizens $6; ages 6-12, $2. Excursion fare $10; over 61, $8; under 16, $5. Reservations are recommended for the excursion. MC, VI. Phone (717) 340-5200 or TDD (717) 340-5207. *See color ad p. 432.*

 **RECREATIONAL ACTIVITIES**

Skiing

• **Montage Ski and Summer Recreation Area,** I-81 exit 51. Write P.O. Box 3539, Scranton, PA 18505. Other activities are offered. Daily, Oct.-Apr. Phone (717) 969-7669, or (800) 468-7669 Dec.-Apr.

SHARON (E-1) pop. 17,500, elev. 854′

Evolving from a mill built on the Shenango River in 1802, Sharon is an industrial city that produces steel and steel products.

Shenango Valley Chamber of Commerce: 41 Chestnut St. Sharon, PA 16146; phone (724) 981-5880.

Shopping areas: Reyers, US 62, stocks more than 200,000 pairs of shoes and carries 300 name brands. The Winner, also on US 62, is a four-story women's clothing store.

DAFFIN'S CANDIES CHOCOLATE KINGDOM, .5 mi. e. at 496 E. State St., features large animals sculptured from chocolate, including a 700-pound rabbit and a 400-pound turtle. Numerous other chocolate creations are displayed, and candy-making demonstrations are available by reservation. Allow 30 minutes minimum. Factory tours Mon.-Sat. 9-11:30 and 12:30-3. Free. Reservations are required for tours. Phone (724) 342-2892.

SHARTLESVILLE (G-9)

ROADSIDE AMERICA, on US 22 via the Shartlesville exit from I-78 exit 8, is an extensive exhibit of miniature villages and towns depicting the growth and development of rural America. The 8,000-square-foot exhibit includes model trains that represent more than a half-century's work on the part of the builder.

Allow 1 hour minimum. Daily 9-6:30, July 1-Labor Day; Mon.-Fri. 10-5, Sat.-Sun. 10-6, rest of year. Closed Dec. 25. Admission $4; ages 6-11, $1.50. Phone (610) 488-6241.

SHAWNEE ON DELAWARE—
see Pocono Mountains Area p. 149.

SLIPPERY ROCK (F-2) pop. 3,200

The Old Stone House, built about 1822, is 4 miles south of Slippery Rock near the junction of SRs 173 and 528. The restored tavern and stage-coach stop is furnished in period. The Slippery Rock University History Department offers tours of the house Fri.-Sun., mid-Apr. to mid-Oct.; phone (724) 738-2053.

JENNINGS ENVIRONMENTAL EDUCATION CENTER, 4 mi. s. at SRs 8, 173 and 528, protects remnants of a prairie ecological system that dates back 6,000 years, when a major prairie extended out of the Midwest into Pennsylvania. The system contains a stand of blazing star, a rare, wild prairie flower that blooms in late July. Maple sugaring demonstrations begin in mid-March. Allow 30 minutes minimum. Educational center open Mon.-Fri. 8-4, Sat.-Sun. hours vary. Grounds open daily dawn-dusk. Free. Phone (724) 794-6011.

SMETHPORT (D-5) pop. 1,800, elev. 1,560'

America's First Christmas Store is housed in a turn-of-the-20th-century building about 12 miles northeast on US 6 in Smethport. A variety of unusual Christmas and other gift items is offered; phone (814) 887-5792 or (800) 841-2721.

SOMERSET (H-3) pop. 6,500, elev. 2,250'

[SAVE] SOMERSET HISTORICAL CENTER is 4 mi. n. at SRs 601 and 985. The center examines southwestern Pennsylvania's rural life 1750-1950. A re-created farm includes a maple sugar camp, covered bridge and exhibit halls that contain relics and machinery from western Pennsylvania. Tours begin in the exhibit hall with a 12-minute film about the history of the mountain

barrier area. Guides demonstrate period tools and other items.

Allow 1 hour minimum. Exhibit hall and library open Wed.-Sat. 9-5, Sun. noon-5. Other buildings Wed.-Sun. 9-5, May-Oct. Tours are available Apr.-Nov. Admission $3.50; over 64, $3; ages 6-12, $1.50. Phone (814) 445-6077.

SOUTH TAMAQUA (F-10) pop. 200

STONEHEDGE GARDENS is at 190 Dairy Rd., just e. of jct. SRs 309 and 443. Herb, hosta, water, perennial, nature and chili pepper gardens comprise Stonehedge Gardens' 6 acres. Ponds and a creek also are part of the complex. Guided tours are available. Allow 30 minutes minimum. Daily noon-9; closed Jan. 1 and Dec. 25. Admission $6 Thanksgiving-Jan. 31 during Christmas tree displays; admission by donations rest of year. Guided tours $2.50. DS, MC, VI. Phone (717) 386-4276.

SPRINGS (I-3)

SPRINGS MUSEUM, on SR 669, depicts the lives of Casselman Valley settlers in the mid-18th century. Three buildings house domestic, farm and shop relics. Displays include an early schoolroom, post office, country store and barn. Allow 1 hour minimum. Wed.-Sat. 1-5, Memorial Day weekend-early Oct.; by appointment rest of year. Free. Phone (814) 662-2625.

SPRUCE CREEK (G-6) elev. 777'

[SAVE] INDIAN CAVERNS, 4 mi. n.e. on SR 45, contains limestone formations and American Indian artifacts. The caverns are electrically lighted. Allow 1 hour minimum. Guided tours daily 9-6, June-Aug.; 9-4, Apr.-May and Sept.-Oct. Admission $8; ages 6-12, $4. Phone (814) 632-7578.

STATE COLLEGE (G-6) pop. 38,900, elev. 1,174'

The Pennsylvania State University, founded as an agricultural college in 1855, is located in the fertile Nittany Valley of central Pennsylvania. The school, established to teach methods of soil conservation, became Pennsylvania State College in 1874. A community slowly grew up around the school, and was incorporated as the Borough of State College in 1896. Today Penn State University offers undergraduate degrees in 190 programs and some 150 graduate degree programs. The commonwealth's largest university, Penn State has more than 75,000 students at 23 locations statewide, including nearly 40,000 in State College.

Centre County Convention & Visitors Bureau: 1402 S. Atherton St., State College, PA 16801; phone (814) 231-1400 or (800) 358-5466.

PENNSYLVANIA STATE UNIVERSITY, in University Park, is noted for its attractive campus. For tour information contact the office of University Relations; phone (814) 865-2501.

Note: Visitors' parking is provided for a fee daily until 9 p.m. (central campus) and until 5 p.m. (other areas).

College of Agricultural Sciences welcomes visitors to the dairy, beef and sheep research center, deer pens, creamery and flower gardens. Allow 30 minutes minimum. Mon.-Fri. 8-5. Free.

Earth and Mineral Sciences Museum, in the Edward Steidle Building, contains gemstones, minerals, fossils and mineral industries-related art. Allow 30 minutes minimum. Mon.-Fri. 9-4:30; closed university holidays, Jan. 1. and Dec. 25-31. Free. Phone (814) 865-6427.

Frost Entomological Museum, Curtin Rd., houses more than 500,000 insects, including mounted, live, land and aquatic specimens. There are numerous exhibits, photographs and models. Guided tours are available on request. Allow 30 minutes minimum. Mon.-Fri. 9:30-4:30; closed major holidays. Free. Phone (814) 863-2865.

Old Main, the Central Administration building, was built 1856-62 and rebuilt 1929-30. It contains the Land Grant Frescoes, by American scene painter Henry Varnum Poor. Mon.-Fri. 8-5; closed holidays. Free. Phone (814) 865-7517.

Palmer Museum of Art, Curtin Rd., offers exhibits of American and international paintings, sculpture, prints, drawings and decorative arts. Guided tours are available by appointment. Allow 30 minutes minimum. Tues.-Sat. 10-4:30, Sun. noon-4; closed holidays. Free. Phone (814) 865-7672.

Penn State Football Hall of Fame, McKean Rd. in the Greenberg Sports Complex, exhibits memorabilia of the Penn State Nittany Lions football teams, the Heisman trophy and photographs of former players. Allow 30 minutes minimum. Mon.-Fri. 8:30-4:30, Sat.-Sun. 11-3 (Sat. hours might vary during home football games); closed during semester breaks. Free. Phone (814) 865-0412.

Penn State Room University Archives, in the Pattee Library, offers a nostalgic look at campus history. Exhibits dating from 1855 include publications, photographs, artworks and furniture. Allow 30 minutes minimum. Mon.-Fri. 9:30-5, Sat. 9-1; closed major holidays. Free. Phone (814) 865-7931.

STRASBURG—
see Pennsylvania Dutch Country p. 104.

STROUDSBURG—
see Pocono Mountains Area p. 150.

SUNBURY (F-8) pop. 11,600, elev. 446′
Sunbury, on Shamokin Creek and the Susquehanna River, was the site of Pennsylvania's largest frontier fort, Fort Augusta. The powder magazine from the 1756 fort still stands. The Hunter House, 1150 N. Front St., contains a research library and exhibits pertaining to the fort.

Sunbury boasted one of the world's first three-wire, central-station, incandescent electric lighting plants. It was built by Thomas Edison in 1883. The plant was treated with much suspicion by the townspeople, most of whom were afraid to cross the threshold to look inside.

At S. Second Street are the Blue Bird Gardens, featuring a variety of trees, azaleas and rhododendrons. The gardens reach peak bloom March through May. On SR 147 is the Shikellamy Marina & Fabridam, where a 3,000-acre lake is formed by what is said to be the world's largest inflatable dam.

Central Susquehanna Valley Chamber of Commerce: US 11/15, Shamokin Dam, PA 17876; phone (717) 743-4100.

Shopping areas: Susquehanna Valley Mall, on US 11/15, is the main local shopping center. Its major stores are The Bon Ton, Boscov's, JCPenney and Sears.

TANNERSVILLE—
see Pocono Mountains Area p. 150.

TARENTUM—
see Pittsburgh and Vicinity p. 144.

TITUSVILLE (D-3) pop. 6,400, elev. 1,174′
American Indians used the slick film on Oil Creek to mix their war paints, and enterprising settlers bottled and sold it as a medicinal concoction called "Seneca Oil." Not until 1859, when Col. Edwin Drake drilled a well, did oil begin to revolutionize industry and spur progress around the world. Titusville's status as birthplace of the oil industry earned Oil Creek Valley its title of "the valley that changed the world," and the city became a wealthy boom town overnight. Pennsylvania was the nation's number one oil producer until 1891, when production peaked and the oil industry began striking richer fields in the West.

Titusville Chamber of Commerce: 116 W. Central Ave., Titusville, PA 16354; phone (814) 827-2941.

SAVE ★ **DRAKE WELL MUSEUM** is .5 mi. s. on SR 8, then 1.2 mi. e. on E. Bloss St. The museum marks the spot where Edwin Drake drilled the world's first commercially successful oil well in 1859. Exhibits deal with the origin of the oil industry. Photographs and outdoor working oil field equipment trace the history of the modern petroleum industry. Included are a replica of Drake's well, an operating oil lease, a steel drilling rig, pumping jacks and oil transportation cars. A 25-minute videotape presentation details Col. Edwin Drake's efforts.

A 10-mile paved bicycle trail and 30 miles of hiking trails connect Drake Well and Oil Creek

State Park (see Recreation Chart). Special events are held in the spring and fall. Allow 1 hour, 30 minutes minimum. Mon.-Sat. 9-5, Sun. noon-5, May-Oct.; Tues.-Sat. 9-5, Sun. noon-5, rest of year. Closed winter holidays. Admission $4; over 60, $3.50; ages 6-12, $2; family rate $10. Phone (814) 827-2797.

[SAVE] OIL CREEK AND TITUSVILLE RAILROAD, 409 S. Perry St., offers 2.5-hour train trips in restored 1930s passenger cars. A tour guide and an audio recording describe the history and scenery of the area, which is known for its 19th-century oil boom. The only operating railway post office car in the United States resumed service in 1990 after an almost 40-year absence. A renovated freight station built in 1896 also is displayed. Trains also depart from the Drake Well Museum (see attraction listing), south of Titusville, and Rynd Farm, north of Oil City.

Train departs from the Perry Street station Wed.-Sun. at 2, July-Aug.; Sat.-Sun. at 2, June 13-30 and Sept. 1-27; Wed.-Fri. at 2, Sat.-Sun. at 11:45 and 3:15, Sept. 30-Oct. 31. Departure times are later from the other two stations. Fare $10; over 60, $9; ages 3-17, $6. Reservations are suggested. DS, MC, VI. Phone (814) 676-1733.

TOWANDA (D-9) pop. 3,200, elev. 771'

Towanda was the boyhood home of composer Stephen Collins Foster and the home of staunch Abraham Lincoln supporter David Wilmot, who founded the Republican Party.

Towanda Chamber of Commerce: P.O. Box 146, Towanda, PA 18848; phone (717) 268-2732.

FRENCH AZILUM, 8 mi. s.e. on SR 187, then 3 mi. e., following signs, was founded in 1793 as a refuge for French nobility fleeing the Revolution. About 50 log buildings were erected. After Napoleon's pardon, many immigrants left the area. Highlights include five log cabins, the 1836 Laporte House containing period furnishings, a 14-minute videotape about the site's history, a museum and a library. Guided tours, nature trails and a picnic pavilion are available.

Wed.-Sun. 11-4, June-Aug.; Sat.-Sun. 11-4:30 in May and Sept.-Oct. Last tour begins 30 minutes before closing. Admission $4.50; senior citizens $4; ages 6-18, $3. Phone (717) 265-3376.

TROY (D-8) pop. 1,800, elev. 1,136'

[SAVE] FARM MUSEUM (BRADFORD COUNTY HERITAGE ASSOCIATION) is on SR 14 in Alparon Park, .5 mi. n. of jct. US 6. Exhibits, which include re-creations of a general store, ice house, blacksmith shop and woodworking shop, allow visitors to imagine what rural life was like in America's past. Examples of agricultural equipment and farming implements also are displayed.

Allow 1 hour minimum. Mon. and Fri.-Sat. 10-4, Sun. noon-4, late Apr.-late Oct. Admission $2.50, senior citizens $2, under 6 free. Phone (717) 297-3410.

TYRONE (G-5) pop. 1,800, elev. 909'

BLAND'S PARK, 12 mi. n. on Old US 220, is an 8-acre amusement park. Highlights include more than 30 rides, an interactive water park, an 18-hole miniature golf course, go-karts and miniature train rides. Food is available. Park open Tues.-Sun. at noon (miniature golf and go-kart areas open daily), June-Aug.; Sat.-Sun. at noon, in May and Sept. Closing times vary. All-day ride or water park pass $5.95. Combination pass $7.95. Miniature golf Mon.-Thurs. $2.95, Fri.-Sun. $3.50. Go-karts $3. MC, VI. Phone (814) 684-3538.

GARDNER'S CANDY MUSEUM, 30 W. 10th St., is in an 1890s-era candy store. A re-created candy kitchen, candy-making utensils, Easter bunny molds, candy boxes and other memorabilia are displayed. A 15-minute videotape depicts the history of the business. Food is available. Allow 1 hour minimum. Mon.-Sat. 9:30-9, Sun. 1-9; closed major holidays. Free. Phone (814) 684-0857.

UNIONTOWN (I-3) pop. 12,000, elev. 1,022'

Uniontown, in the bituminous coking coal district of western Pennsylvania, is a major producer of coke, steel, glass and iron. The birthplace of Gen. George C. Marshall, Uniontown is near the grave of another general, Edward Braddock, who is buried southeast of town near Farmington (see Fort Necessity National Battlefield p. 76). About 5 miles west on US 40 is Searights Tollhouse, which was built in 1835. Tours of the tollhouse are given mid-May to mid-October.

Central Fayette Chamber of Business and Industry: 11 Pittsburgh St., P.O. Box 2124, Uniontown, PA 15401; phone (724) 437-4571 or (800) 916-9365.

[SAVE] LAUREL CAVERNS is 5 mi. e. on US 40, then 5 mi. s. on Caverns Park Rd. A maze cave with more than 2 miles of passages, the caverns have been explored since the late 1700s. Guided tours include the "Grand Canyon" and other limestone formations. A view from Chestnut Ridge covers two states and 4,000 square miles. An indoor miniature golf course also is available.

Cavern temperatures remain at a constant 52 degrees Fahrenheit; visitors should dress accordingly. Allow 1 hour minimum. Daily 9-5, May-Oct.; Sat.-Sun. 9-5, Mar.-Apr. and in Nov. Admission $8; over 65, $7; ages 12-17, $6; ages 6-11, $5. DS, MC, VI. Phone (724) 438-3003.

UPPER DELAWARE SCENIC AND RECREATIONAL RIVER

The Upper Delaware Scenic and Recreational River comprises 73 miles of the Upper Delaware River from just north of Matamoras to Hancock, N.Y. Along this stretch the river changes from long, placid eddies to swift water and Class I and II rapids. It is paralleled on the New York side by SR 97, which has a number of scenic overlooks. The best road from which to see the river on the Pennsylvania side is the northern section of SR 191, which at times is only a few feet above the water.

Almost all land along the river is privately owned; public river access areas are located on both the Pennsylvania and New York shores. Private campgrounds and canoe liveries are available near the river.

The Upper Delaware was an important transportation route for American Indians and early settlers. In 1828 the Delaware and Hudson Canal opened, bringing boatloads of coal from the Pennsylvania interior to the port of New York. However, problems soon developed at the point where the canal crossed the river: Slow-moving boats being towed across the river and along the canal were constantly colliding with the huge log and timber rafts that were coursing down the river to sawmills and shipyards in Trenton, N.J., and Philadelphia.

To solve the problem, the canal company approved a plan to "build the canal above the water." John Roebling, who later designed the Brooklyn Bridge, built the Delaware Aqueduct to cross the river and carry canal traffic from Lackawaxen, Pa., to Minisink Ford, N.Y. The aqueduct is considered to be the oldest existing wire suspension bridge in America. The adjacent tollhouse contains exhibits interpreting the history of the Delaware and Hudson Canal, John Roebling and the Delaware Aqueduct. It is open weekends Memorial Day weekend through mid-October.

Wildlife in the area includes bears, beavers, white-tailed deer, minks, muskrats, otters, rabbits and squirrels. Birds include bald eagles, ospreys, great egrets, great blue herons, turkey vultures, Canada geese and several varieties of hawks and ducks.

On the banks of the Upper Delaware Scenic and Recreational River lies the Zane Grey Museum *(see Lackawaxen p. 149)*. The renowned Western author began his writing career and lived at the site with his wife Dolly 1905-18.

Recreational opportunities include boating, canoeing, fishing and rafting. In summer the National Park Service offers a variety of cultural, natural history and recreational activities.

Information stations, located at some public boating access sites, may be staffed on weekends Memorial Day weekend through Labor Day. An information center on Main Street in Narrowsburg is open weekends 9:30-4:30, May-Oct. Phone (717) 685-4871.

VALLEY FORGE—
see Philadelphia and Vicinity p. 128.

★ VALLEY FORGE NATIONAL HISTORICAL PARK—
see Philadelphia and Vicinity p. 128.

VOLANT (F-1) pop. 200, elev. 944′

Volant grew up around a gristmill built on Neshannock Creek in 1812. The restored mill is now the centerpiece of Main Street, which is lined with quaint shops and restaurants. Amish buggies are a common sight on the roadways.

Shopping areas: The Volant Mill features handmade Amish furniture, pottery, dried flowers, pictures and crafts. A nearby caboose and three train cars have been restored and also house specialty shops, as does The Barns at Potters Run Landing.

WARREN (D-3) pop. 11,100, elev. 1,174′

KINZUA DAM is 6 mi. e. via US 6 and SR 59. Several overlooks provide scenic views of the dam and reservoir. Boating, fishing and swimming are permitted. Allow 1 hour minimum. The bridge roadway spanning the dam is open to pedestrians daily (weather permitting) 9-3:30. A visitor center in the Big Bend Access Area is open daily 10-4, June-Aug.; Sat.-Sun. 10-4, Sept.-Oct. Free. Phone (814) 726-0661, or 726-0164 for lake conditions.

WARREN COUNTY HISTORICAL SOCIETY, 210 4th Ave., is housed in an Italian Renaissance house built in 1873. Period rooms include a formal parlor, a Victorian room and a general store. A research library contains archives, genealogy records and a photograph collection. Allow 30 minutes minimum. Mon.-Fri. 8:30-4:30, Sat. 9-noon; closed holidays. Admission $1, under 18 free. Phone (814) 723-1795.

WASHINGTON—
see Pittsburgh and Vicinity p. 145.

★ WASHINGTON CROSSING HISTORIC PARK—
see Philadelphia and Vicinity p. 129.

WATERFORD (D-2) pop. 1,600, elev. 1,192′

Waterford, which grew up around an American post established in the area in the late 1700s, dates back to the French Fort LeBoeuf, built in 1753. A 21-year-old George Washington, then a major in the British Virginia Militia, delivered a message from Gov. Robert Dinwiddie asking the French to withdraw from the area. The French refused, and eventually tensions erupted into the French and Indian War. A model of the fort is at the Fort LeBoeuf Museum at 123 S. High St.

Also of interest on S. High Street is the Amos Judson House, a restored two-story Federal Greek Revival home built in 1820. Across the

TOURBOOK*MARK*

AAA DIAMOND RATING SYSTEM

◆◆◆◆◆ Luxurious, World-Class

◆◆◆◆ Top Class, Excellent Service

◆◆◆ Very Comfortable, Well-Appointed

◆◆ Comfortable, Pleasant and Casual

◆ Basic Comfort, Unpretentious but Good

LODGING LISTING SYMBOLS

🐕 Pets Allowed

🏊 Outdoor Swimming Pool

🏊 Indoor Swimming Pool

💼 Dataports and/or Business Services

✈ Airport Transportation

🏋 Exercise/Whirlpool/Sauna Facilities

ECTV Extended Cable TV

CTV Cable TV

♿ Fully Accessible

🚶 Semi-Accessible

✕ Non-Smoking Available

👂 Hearing Impaired

S Fire Protection Sprinklers

D Smoke Detectors

SAVE Official appointment lodging offering special savings

AAA OFFICIAL APPOINTMENT

LODGING CLASSIFICATIONS

B&B – Bed & Breakfast, smaller establishment, personal attention, rooms individually decorated, at home feeling, breakfast included, limited parking.

COMPLEX– Combination of two or more classifications.

COTTAGE – Individual cabin or villa usually containing one housekeeping unit. May have separate living room/bedroom. Not required to offer daily housekeeping service.

COUNTRY INN– Larger operation than a B&B, decor may include antiques, dining room where breakfast and dinner are served.

HOTEL – Multistory building provides full service. Usually includes food service, conference space, pool and exercise equipment, room service and convenience shops. Limited or offsite parking.

LODGE – Two or more stories with all facilities in one building, usually has food and beverage service.

MOTEL – Usually one to two stories offering limited service. Food service limited to a snack bar.

MOTOR INN – Offers moderate service, building two or more stories. Usually has recreational facilities and food service. May have limited meeting space. Ample parking.

RANCH – Any classification featuring outdoor, Western-style recreation. Facilities may vary in size.

SUBCLASSIFICATIONS

APARTMENT – Four or more stories with over half of rental units equipped for housekeeping; includes kitchen, living and sleeping areas. Apartment may not offer full daily maid service.

CONDOMINIUM – Destination property located in a resort area. Units include bedroom, kitchen and living room. Not required to offer full daily maid service.

HISTORIC – Restored structures more than 50 years old. Reflects the ambiance of yesteryear. Rooms may lack some modern amenities, often shared baths. Owner operated and food service usually available.

RESORT – Applies to any other type of lodging, vacation atmosphere with extensive recreational facilities. Rates may include meals.

SUITE – Bedroom(s) and living room, which may or may not be closed off from bedroom.

REMEMBER

AAA inspectors assign ratings by evaluating lodging establishments based on their classification.

Thus, "Hotels" are rated in comparison to other "Hotels," etc.

Refer to all the details in the introductory material preceding the lodging section of the TourBook®.

street is the restored Eagle Hotel, a Federal- and Georgian-style structure built in 1826. An old covered bridge is 1 mile off the end of E. First Street on a dirt road. Events include Community Heritage Days in July. Swimming, boating, fishing and camping are available at nearby Lake LeBoeuf (*see Recreation Chart*).

WAYNE—
see Philadelphia and Vicinity p. 130.

WAYNESBORO (I-7) pop. 9,600, elev. 713′

Tucked into rolling hills and surrounded by peach and apple orchards, Waynesboro dates back to 1749. Like many other towns in the vicinity, it lays claim to a historical footnote; abolitionist John Brown taught Sunday school nearby while preparing for his ill-fated Harper's Ferry raid. Later, Waynesboro became an early 20th-century retreat for Washington, D.C., residents seeking escape from summer heat and humidity.

Waynesboro Chamber of Commerce: 323 E. Main St., Waynesboro, PA 17268; phone (717) 762-7123.

RENFREW MUSEUM AND PARK, 1010 E. Main St., houses a 300-piece pottery collection and the Nicodemus Collection of Decorative Arts, featuring ceramics, quilts, painted furniture and metalware. Items dating 1790-1830 are displayed in a home-like setting. Special holiday programs are offered in December; phone for schedule. The park has nature and hiking trails, a picnic area and a 150-seat pavilion. Guided tours are available by appointment.

Allow 1 hour minimum. Park open daily dawn-dusk. Museum open Thurs. and Sat.-Sun. 1-4, late Apr.-Oct. 31; closed July 4. Admission $3; over 55, $2.50; ages 7-12, $1.50. Phone (717) 762-4723.

WAYNESBURG (I-1) pop. 4,300, elev. 938′

Waynesburg was named for Revolutionary War hero Gen. "Mad" Anthony Wayne. The town is the seat of Greene County, which was named for another Revolutionary War hero, Gen. Nathanael Greene. A statue of Greene is atop the 1850 county courthouse, a fine example of Greek Revival architecture. Also in town is Waynesburg College, one of the first colleges in the United States to grant degrees to women.

Greene County Tourist Promotion Agency: 17 S. Washington St., Waynesburg, PA 15370; phone (724) 627-8687.

GREENE COUNTY HISTORICAL MUSEUM is 3 mi. e. via I-79 exit 3 on old SR 21. The museum is housed in a 52-room mid-Victorian structure that formerly housed the county's "Poor Farm." Fourteen rooms are furnished in period—from Colonial times through the Victorian era. The exhibits include American Indian artifacts, salt-glaze pottery, quilts, glassware and a country store. Picnicking is permitted.

Allow 1 hour minimum. Wed-Fri. 10-4, Sat.-Sun. noon-4, May-Aug.; Thurs.-Sun. noon-4, Sept.-Oct. Admission $2.50; ages 6-14, $1.50. Phone (724) 627-3204.

WELLSBORO (D-7) pop. 3,400, elev. 1,315′

If Wellsboro's gas-lit streets, town green and Victorian mansions seem vaguely reminiscent of Massachusetts or Vermont, it is because the town was founded by New England colonists in 1806. In the mountainous region of north-central Pennsylvania, Wellsboro is an all-year recreation center and the gateway to the "Grand Canyon" of Pennsylvania.

Wellsboro Chamber of Commerce: 114 Main St., P.O. Box 733, Wellsboro, PA 16901; phone (717) 724-1926.

GRAND CANYON OF PENNSYLVANIA, 10 mi. w. on SR 660, was formed by the Pine Creek River. Fifty miles long and up to 1,000 feet deep, it is the highlight of the Endless Mountain area, which includes several state parks and state-owned game lands. The area offers spectacular panoramas; Leonard Harrison and Colton Point state parks (*see Recreation Chart and the AAA Mideastern CampBook*) encompass the east and west rims, respectively. Many primitive areas are accessible only by narrow gravel roads. Daily dawn-dusk. Free.

WEST CHESTER—
see Philadelphia and Vicinity p. 130.

WHITE HAVEN (F-10) pop. 1,100, elev. 1,120′

White Haven is a year-round outdoor recreation destination. White-water rafting is popular on the Lehigh River spring through fall, and nearby Hickory Run State Park (*see Recreation Chart*) offers snowmobiling and cross-country skiing in winter.

 RECREATIONAL ACTIVITIES
White-water Rafting

• **Lehigh Rafting Rentals**, off I-80 exit 40, .5 mi. e. on SR 940, then n. on Main St. Write P.O. Box 296, White Haven, PA 18661. Daily Mar. 1-Thanksgiving. Phone (717) 443-4441, or (800) 291-7238 within a 300-mi. radius.

• [SAVE] **Whitewater Challengers Raft Tours**, 6 mi. s. of I-80 exit 40 just off Weatherly-White Haven Rd. Write P.O. Box 8, White Haven, PA 18661. White-water rafting daily 8-6, Mar.-June and Sept.-Oct. Summer rafting in calmer waters daily 8-6, July-Aug. Phone (717) 443-9532, (800) 443-8554 or (800) 443-7238.

WHITE MILLS—
see Pocono Mountains Area p. 150.

WILKES-BARRE (E-10) pop. 47,500, elev. 593′

In the Wyoming Valley on the Susquehanna River, Wilkes-Barre was named for John Wilkes and Isaac Barre, members of the British Parliament and Colonial sympathizers. They also are honored by a monument in Public Square.

The Wyoming Valley was the scene of the Yankee-Pennamite Wars, a land struggle between Pennsylvania and Connecticut that lasted 1769-85. Many skirmishes were fought on Wilkes-Barre's River Common, a 35-acre park on River Street between North and South streets. Within the park, which dates from 1770, are the Luzerne County Court House and numerous historic markers. Eventually Congress ruled in favor of Pennsylvania, though Connecticut did not relinquish its claims to the disputed area until 1800.

Wilkes-Barre's "face" has changed several times since its early days. Once a center of the anthracite coal-mining region, industry is now diversified. After the city and surrounding valley were damaged by Hurricane Agnes in 1972, Wilkes-Barre underwent significant renovation.

The F.M. Kirby Center for the Performing Arts is housed in a restored 1930s Art Deco movie palace. The center is home to the Northeastern Philharmonic Orchestra and Ballet Theatre Pennsylvania. It offers a full program of drama, comedy, opera and musicals.

The Wyoming Historical and Geological Society operates a museum at 69 S. Franklin St. with exhibits about the coal-mining industry as well as American Indian artifacts, rocks, minerals and fossils of local origin; phone (717) 822-1727.

Harness racing takes place at Pocono Downs, on SR 315. Frances Slocum State Park *(see Recreation Chart)* offers a variety of recreational facilities. Scenic Ricketts Glen State Park is 30 miles west via SR 118 in Red Rock *(see place listing p. 152 and Recreation Chart).*

Note: Policies concerning admittance of children to pari-mutuel betting facilities vary. Phone for information.

Luzerne County Tourist Promotion Agency: 56 Public Square, Wilkes-Barre, PA 18701; phone (717) 819-1877 or (888) 905-2872.

Shopping areas: The Wyoming Valley Mall on Bus. Rte. 309 offers more than 100 stores, including The Bon Ton, JCPenney, Kaufmann's and Sears. Downtown shopping, featuring numerous specialty shops, centers around an outdoor mall covered by a canopy to protect shoppers from the weather.

NATHAN DENISON HOUSE—
see Forty Fort p. 76.

SORDONI ART GALLERY, 150 S. River St., is on the campus of Wilkes University. The gallery displays paintings, sculpture, watercolors, photographs and other media of late 19th- and 20th-century American artists. Exhibits are changed monthly; the gallery usually closes for the changeover. Daily noon-5; closed major holidays. Free. Phone (717) 831-4325.

WILLIAMSPORT (E-8) pop. 32,300, elev. 528′

Now a manufacturing city, Williamsport was known as a great lumber center until the forests were depleted in the 1890s. Millionaires' Row, along W. Fourth Street, is lined with Victorian mansions once owned by the lumber barons.

Little League baseball originated in Williamsport in 1939, and each August the city is host to the Little League World Series. On West Fourth Street south of Max M. Brown Memorial Park is Carl. E. Stotz Field, the original Little League field which has been named after the league's founder.

Williamsport Chamber of Commerce: 454 Pine St., Williamsport, PA 17701; phone (717) 326-1971.

Shopping areas: Lycoming Mall, I-80 Lycoming Mall exit, features The Bon Ton, JCPenney, Kaufmann's and Sears. The Old Jail Center, 154 W. Third St., features shops and art galleries in a renovated 1868 jailhouse.

SAVE CHILDREN'S DISCOVERY WORKSHOP, 343 W. Fourth St., is a hands-on museum for ages 3-11. Exhibits include Kid Science, Playhouse Theatre, Exploration of the Mind, the Kid Clinic, Human Habitrail, Ice Cream Parlor, Shadow Wall, a 129-ft. suspension maze and Construct-a-Space. Various programs and activities take place regularly. Allow 1 hour minimum. Tues.-Sat. 10-4, Sun. 1-4, June-Aug.; Tues.-Fri. and Sun. 1-5, Sat. 11-5, rest of year. Admission $3.50, under 2 free. Phone (717) 322-5437.

HERDIC TROLLEY TOUR departs from the Trolley Gazebo in front of the Sheraton Inn Downtown. The tour acquaints visitors with Williamsport's areas of interest, including Millionaires' Row. Complete with a taped narration, passengers can view the impressive mansions built by the town's lumber barons. Tours Tues., Thurs. and Sat., June-Aug. Times vary; phone ahead. Fare $2. Phone (717) 326-2500 or (800) 248-9287.

HIAWATHA RIVERBOAT TOURS, 4 mi. w. in Susquehanna State Park at the base of Arch St. offers 1-hour paddle-wheeler cruises along the Susquehanna River. A narrator describes the history of the river. Sightseeing cruises depart Tues.-Sat. at 1, 2:30 and 4, Sun. at 1, 2:30 and 4

June-Aug.; Sat. at 11:30, 1, 2:30 and 4, Sun. at 1, 2:30 and 4, in May and Sept.-Oct. Schedule may vary; phone ahead. Tickets are sold one hour before departure. Fare $7; over 60, $6.50; under 12, $3. MC, VI. Phone (717) 326-1221 or (800) 358-9900.

SAVE **LITTLE LEAGUE BASEBALL MUSEUM**, 1.2 mi. s. on US 15, is next to the field where the annual Little League World Series is held. Displays interpret the history and growth of Little League Baseball since its founding in 1939. Exhibits include Little League memorabilia, original uniforms and major league players' Little League items.

Allow 1 hour minimum. Mon.-Sat. 9-7, Sun. noon-7, Memorial Day-Labor Day; Mon.-Sat. 9-5, Sun. noon-5, rest of year. Closed Jan. 1, Thanksgiving and Dec. 25. Admission $5; over 62, $3; ages 5-13, $1.50. Phone (717) 326-3607.

SAVE **LYCOMING COUNTY HISTORICAL MUSEUM**, SR 180 Maynard St. exit to 858 W. Fourth St., exhibits artifacts from 10,000 B.C. to the present. Exhibits include a blacksmith shop, carpenter shop, Victorian parlor and gristmill. Displays about the lumber industry, American Indians and The Shempp Toy Train Collection also are featured.

Allow 1 hour minimum. Tues.-Fri. 9:30-4, Sat. 11-4, Sun. 1-4, May-Oct.; Tues.-Fri. 9:30-4, Sat. 11-4, rest of year. Closed major holidays. Admission $3.50; over 65, $3; under 12, $1.50; free to all third Sun. of the month. MC, VI. Phone (717) 326-3326.

WOMELSDORF (G-9) pop. 2,300, elev. 434'

SAVE **CONRAD WEISER HOMESTEAD**, 26 acres .5 mi. e. on US 422, was the home of Conrad Weiser, Colonial interpreter and peacemaker during the French and Indian War. Tours, a park and picnic facilities are available. Allow 1 hour minimum. Wed.-Sat. 9-5, Sun. noon-5; closed holidays, except Memorial Day, July 4 and Labor Day. Admission $2.50; over 60, $2; ages 6-12, $1; family rate $6. Phone (610) 589-2934.

WOODWARD (F-7)

WOODWARD CAVE, 2 mi. w. off SR 45, following signs, is one of the state's largest caverns. A 1-hour, half-mile guided tour visits five rooms. The cave maintains a constant temperature of 48 degrees Fahrenheit. Daily 9-7, May 15-Labor Day; 10-5, Mar. 15-May 14 and day after Labor Day-Nov. 15. Last tour departs 1 hour before closing. Admission $10; ages 5-15, $5. Phone (814) 349-9800 or 349-8252.

WYOMING (E-10) pop. 3,300, elev. 557'

With the outbreak of the Revolution, the Wyoming Valley's importance as a granary led to a number of attacks by Tory and American Indian forces. On July 3, 1778, 1,200 Indians and renegade whites defeated 300 frontiersmen 4 miles north of Kingston near Forty Fort, leaving the settlements of the Wyoming Valley unprotected. The next day the Indians passed up and down the valley in a series of raids that became known as the Wyoming Massacre. In reprisal, Gen. John Sullivan led an expedition up the Susquehanna River, devastating the area and breaking the Indians' grip on the region.

A monument at 4th Street and Wyoming Avenue marks the site of a grave for victims of the Wyoming Massacre.

YORK (I-8) pop. 42,200, elev. 375'

York served as the national capital Sept. 30, 1777, to June 27, 1778, while the British occupied Philadelphia. It was in York that Congress received the news of Gen. John Burgoyne's surrender, adopted the Articles of Confederation, issued the first National Thanksgiving Proclamation and learned that France was to send aid to the Colonies.

Many farmers' markets specialize in Pennsylvania Dutch and German cuisine, including the Central Market House, 34 W. Philadelphia St.; Farmers' Market, 380 W. Market St.; and the New Eastern Market, 201 Memory Ln.

Visitors Information Center: 1618 Toronita St., York, PA 17402; phone (717) 843-6660.

Self-guiding tours: A brochure that describes a historical walking tour of 34 landmark buildings in downtown York can be obtained for $1 at various locations in town or at the York County Convention and Visitors Bureau, 1 Market Way E., P.O. Box 1229, York, PA 17405; phone (717) 848-4000 or (888) 858-9675.

Shopping areas: The Galleria, 2 miles east of I-83 on US 30, is the area's largest mall; anchor stores are The Bon Ton, Boscov's, JCPenney and Sears. West Manchester Mall, 1 mile west of I-83 on US 30, and York Mall Merchants, off I-83 exit 8E, are other major shopping centers. West Manchester features The Bon Ton and Hecht Co.; the major store at York Mall Merchants is Montgomery Ward.

A number of factory outlet complexes also provide shopping opportunities. Meadowbrook Village, 2 miles east of I-83 on US 30 across from the Galleria, features Christmas Tree Hill, Danskin, Pfaltzgraff and Talbots. East Prospect Factory Outlet, 16 W. Maple St. in East Prospect, offers Gantner Swimwear.

Old Tollgate Village, east of I-83 exit 4 on US 74, has more than two dozen shops offering specialty items, gifts and handmade crafts.

AGRICULTURE AND INDUSTRIAL MUSEUM OF YORK COUNTY, with locations at 480 E. Market St. and 217 W. Princess St., focuses on the history of the Golden Age of industrial development that occurred from the Civil War to World War I.

Exhibits and displays highlight industrial equipment and agricultural products manufactured or used in York County. A children's play area is available.

Allow 1 hour minimum. Tues., Thurs. and Sat. 10-4; otherwise by appointment. Closed major holidays. Admission (each museum) $2; ages 4-12, $1. Phone (717) 852-7007.

Agriculture Museum is at 480 E. Market St. Visitors can view York County's farm heritage from the practices of American Indians through modern day techniques. A 19th-century furnished worker's house is on-site.

Industrial Museum is at 217 W. Princess St. Various displays include pottery, a howitzer, a gristmill and a full-size Phineas Davis locomotive model.

BOB HOFFMAN WEIGHTLIFTING HALL OF FAME is off I-83N exit 11, at 3300 Board Rd. Exhibits detail the history of Olympic lifting, powerlifting, bodybuilding and strongman competitions. Mon.-Fri. 10-6 (also Wed. and Fri. 6-8 p.m.), Sat. 10-5. Free. Phone (717) 767-6481.

★**HISTORICAL SOCIETY OF YORK COUNTY**, 250 E. Market St., has a gallery with changing exhibits, a museum depicting life in York County up to the 20th century and a genealogical library. The museum also has a reproduction of the original York village square, and a gallery devoted to transportation features a Conestoga freight wagon and York County's early automobile industry.

Museum and gallery Mon.-Sat. 9-5, Sun. 1-4. Library Mon.-Sat. 9-5. Closed major holidays. Museum $2.50; senior citizens $2.25; ages 6-13, $1.25. Library $4. Combination admission ticket to museum and gallery, Bonham House, Golden Plough Tavern, General Horatio Gates House and Bobb Log House $7.50; senior citizens $6.50; ages 6-13, $3.50. MC, VI. Phone (717) 848-1587.

Bonham House, 152 E. Market St., depicts various periods in American life through a Victorian parlor, an early 20th-century library and a Federal dining room. The museum displays Oriental porcelains, ivories and bronzes as well as silver, china and glass. Guided tours are offered Tues.-

Sat. at 10:30 and 3:30 by reservation. Fee $2; senior citizens $1.50; ages 6-13, $1. Phone (717) 848-1587.

★**Golden Plough Tavern, General Horatio Gates House** and **Bobb Log House**, 157 W. Market St., are restored 18th-century buildings. The half-timbered brick frontier tavern was built in the 1740s and housed travellers as well as Congressional delegates. The stone General Horatio Gates House was the scene of the Conway Cabal meeting, at which Marquis de Lafayette prevented the overthrow of Gen. George Washington as head of the Continental Army; Gen. Gates was the hero of the Battle of Saratoga. The log house is an example of homes built along Pennsylvania's frontier around the turn of the 19th century; furnishings are typical of that period and region. Mon.-Sat. 10-4, Sun. 1-4; closed major holidays. Admission $4; senior citizens $3.50; ages 6-13, $2.

RODNEY C. GOTT MUSEUM and the Harley-Davidson assembly plant are .7 mi. e. of jct. I-83 and US 30, at US 30 and Eden Rd. Exhibits range from the original 1906 Harley-Davidson motorcycle to current models. In the plant, which can be visited by guided tour only, visitors can see a motorcycle roll off the assembly line about every 2.5 minutes. It takes approximately two-and-one-half hours to assemble a Harley. Closed-toe shoes are required; cameras are prohibited on plant tour.

Combined plant and museum tours are offered Mon.-Fri. at 10 and 1:30; plant closed holidays and during shutdown for new model changeover. Museum tours are offered Mon.-Fri. at 12:30, Sat. at 10, 11, 1 and 2; closed major holidays and Sat. before Mon. holidays. Free. Under 12 are not admitted to the plant Phone (717) 848-1177, ext. 2900.

YORK COUNTY COLONIAL COURT HOUSE, W. Market St. and Pershing Ave., is a reconstruction of the courthouse in which the Continental Congress voted to adopt the Articles of Confederation. A sound-and-light show is presented. Guided tours are available. Mon.-Sat. 10-4, Sun. 1-4 and by appointment, Mar.-Dec. Last tour begins 1 hour before closing. Admission $1; ages 6-16, 50c. Phone (717) 846-1977 or 755-4392.

About Lodgings & Restaurants

Lodging and restaurant listings appear after this section. Both types of properties are listed alphabetically (with lodgings listed first) under the city or town in which they physically are located or in some circumstances under the nearest recognized city or town. Major restaurant chains are not listed due to their widespread notoriety. To help you plan your trip, towns and cities that contain AAA RATED® lodgings or restaurants are printed in red on AAA/CAA regional, state, provincial and Triptik maps. The TourBook includes special accommodation "spotting" maps to help you find lodgings and restaurants. (See Maps, page 164.)

Using lodging listings

To use this book most effectively, read the sample lodging listing along with the explanation of the terms. The location given to pinpoint a facility is based on major reference points, most often highway junctions. Air conditioning, phones, color TV and private baths are not mentioned if available in all rooms. All showers are tub showers unless otherwise noted. If the term "movie" is denoted in the listing, guests can view the movie through a TV channel; there may be an additional charge. Deposits and fees for pets are stated in the listing. Please verify the property's pet policy when making reservations and inquire about any restrictions.

If parking is provided on the premises at no charge, it is not mentioned in the listing. Other parking conditions such as no parking available, off-site parking, street parking only or off-site valet parking, and any charges, are specifically noted in the listing. **Check-in** times are shown only if they are after 3 p.m.; **check-out** times are shown only if they are before 10 a.m. Service charges are not shown unless they are $1 or more, or at least 5 percent of the room rate.

What the SAVE means

Show Your Card & Save® (SYCS) participants are denoted by the SAVE icon found just below a lodging's name to the right of the AAA/CAA emblem. This icon represents a 10% discount off the published rates printed in the lodging listing for AAA/CAA members.

Only properties that are Official Appointments (see What the 🆎 or 🅐 means) may have a SAVE icon displayed in their listing.

Many properties are part of AAA's chain lodging program. To ensure receiving the best available rate these properties have to offer AAA/CAA members, visit your local AAA/CAA office to make reservations or call the following 800 numbers. Phone (800) 228-1222 for these chain participants: Clarion, Comfort Inn, Econo Lodge, Quality Inn, Rodeway and Sleep Inns; (800) 432-

9755 for Days Inn; (800) 916-2221 for Hilton; (800) 532-1496 for Hyatt; and (800) 221-4731 for La Quinta.

To receive the Show Your Card & Save discount, be sure to identify yourself as a AAA/CAA member when making reservations and show your AAA/CAA card at registration to verify the discount. The Show Your Card & Save discount may not be used in conjunction with other discounts.

Dining establishments that contain a SAVE icon in their listing have agreed to offer AAA/CAA members either discounts or a free item with their purchase. Restrictions may apply; refer to individual restaurant listings for details. Participating locations will also display a Show Your Card & Save decal on their window or door.

What the 🆎 or 🅐 means

Lodgings and restaurants approved by AAA/CAA are eligible for our Official Appointment Program, which permits the display and advertising of the 🆎 or 🅐 emblem. The 🆎 or 🅐 under a property name identifies that property as an Official Appointment establishment with a special interest in serving AAA/CAA members.

Some Official Appointment listings include the following special amenities: free breakfast; early check-in/late check-out; free room upgrade (subject to availability); free local phone calls; free daily newspaper; and preferred room, such as ocean view, poolside, etc. (subject to availability).

This does not imply that these amenities are exclusively offered by these properties. Please remember to identify yourself as a AAA/CAA member when making reservations and present your card at registration.

The ⊕ or ⊛ sign helps traveling members—like you—find accommodations on which they can depend. These properties want AAA/CAA business.

Rate options and discounts

Annually, lodging operators are requested to update rates, rate options and discounts for TourBook publication. Properties are not required to offer a discount to AAA/CAA members. However, if they choose to offer a minimum 10% discount, the [SAVE] icon appears in the listing. If the property chooses not to offer a discount, then one of the following rate options must be selected:

(1) Guaranteed Rates—The establishment guarantees AAA/CAA members will not be charged more than the maximum rates printed in the TourBook.

(2) Rates Subject To Change—Rates may vary for the life of the TourBook, however are guaranteed not to exceed a 15% increase on rates printed in the TourBook.

To receive the rates noted in the TourBook, you *must* identify yourself as a AAA/CAA member and request them when making reservations. Show your AAA/CAA card at registration and verify the rate.

Rates for Special Events: Lodgings may temporarily increase their room rates or modify their policies during a special event. Examples of such

events range from Mardi Gras and the Kentucky Derby to college football homecoming games, holidays and state fairs.

Senior Discount: Some establishments offer the senior discount with either the **Guaranteed Rates** option or the **Rates Subject to Change** option. Where the words "senior discount" are included in a listing, a minimum discount of 10 percent off the prevailing or guaranteed rates is available to AAA/CAA members who are 60 years of age or older. You *must* identify yourself as a AAA/CAA member *and* request the senior discount when making reservations. Show your AAA/CAA card at registration and verify the rate and discount. **Note:** Members may take the senior discount or the Show Your Card & Save® discount (denoted by the [SAVE] icon), but not both. The senior discount may not be used in conjunction with other discounts and might not apply during special events.

Rate lines: Rates printed are based on rack rates and last room availability, and are rounded to the nearest dollar. Rates do not include taxes and discounts. Alaska rates are in U.S. dollars; rates for Canadian lodgings are in Canadian dollars.

Maps

Area maps are used for large geographical areas in which there are many towns containing lodgings and restaurants. Because the maps are on such a small scale, lodgings and restaurants are not shown, but the towns that have these types of facilities are printed in magenta type.

Spotting maps are used for large metropolitan areas to assist you in locating the facilities listed in the Lodgings & Restaurants section of your book. These maps locate, or "spot," lodgings with a black-background numeral (⓴, for example); restaurants are spotted with a white-background numeral (⑳, for example). Indexes found near the map match the number symbol to the property. **Downtown/city spotting maps** are provided when spotted facilities are very concentrated.

Starred points of interest also appear on these maps. **Vicinity spotting maps** (Greater, North, South, for example) spot those accommodations that are outside the downtown or city area but are within the metropolitan area. Roads required to find a lodging or dining facility, airports, major landmarks and starred points of interest are shown on vicinity spotting maps. The names of suburban communities that have AAA RATED® accommodations are shown in magenta type.

Driving distance maps located in the For Your Information section of the book are intended to be used only for trip-distance and driving-time planning. Refer to more detailed AAA/CAA maps available from your club for actual route numbers.

Making reservations

When making reservations, you must identify yourself as a AAA/CAA member. Give all pertinent information about your planned stay. Request written confirmation to guarantee: type of room, rate, dates of stay, and cancellation and refund policies. **Note:** Age restrictions may apply.

Most establishments give full deposit refunds if they have been notified at least 48 hours before the normal check-in time. However, when making reservations, confirm the property's deposit, cancellation and refund policies. Some properties may charge a cancellation or handling fee. When this applies, "handling fee imposed" will appear in the listing. If you cancel too late, you have little recourse if a refund is denied. When an establishment requires a full or partial payment in advance, and your trip is cut short, a refund may not be given.

When canceling reservations, call the lodging immediately. Make a note of the date and time you called, the cancellation number if there is one, and the name of the person who handled the cancellation. If your AAA/CAA club made your reservation, allow them to make the cancellation for you as well so you will have proof of cancellation.

When you are charged more than the rate listed in the TourBook, under the option **Guaranteed Rates,** or you qualify for the **Senior Discount** and did not receive it, question the additional charge. If management refuses to adhere to the published rate, pay for the room and submit your receipt and membership number to AAA/CAA *within 30 days (see Tell us what you think, page 5).* Include all pertinent information: dates of stay, rate paid, itemized paid receipts, number of persons in your party, the room number you occupied, and list any extra room equipment used. A refund of the amount paid in excess of the stated maximum will be made when our investigation indicates that unjustified charging has occurred.

Lodging Reservation and Deposit Definitions

RESERVATION: A temporary hold on lodgings, usually until 4 or 6 p.m. on the arrival date.

RESERVATION CONFIRMATION: Once the reservation process is complete, a "confirmation number" is assigned to the guest for future reference. When ample notice is given, a copy of the reservation details and confirmation number is mailed to the guest.

CREDIT CARD GUARANTEED RESERVATION: When reserved lodgings have been secured with a credit card number, the room will be held for the first night regardless of arrival time, but will be billed to the credit card if the guest fails to arrive at all (is a "no show"). Credit card guarantees usually pertain to the first night only.

RESERVATION DEPOSIT: These funds are collected from the guest in advance of arrival to secure reserved lodgings. A reservation deposit can be in the form of cash, check, money order, credit card transaction or other means to transfer funds. One or more days' payment may be required depending on the length of the stay.

PREPAID RESERVATION: Reserved lodgings that are fully paid in advance of arrival.

CANCELLATION POLICY: Published terms/conditions set by lodging by which the guest can cancel a reservation and recover all, or a portion of, the deposit/full payment. Sometimes a "service charge" or "handling fee" is levied regardless of how far in advance the reservation was cancelled.

CANCELLATION NUMBER: Upon receipt of a cancellation, it is customary for lodgings to assign a "cancellation number" that is given to the caller for future reference.

When you find your room is not as specified, and you have written confirmation of reservations for a certain type of accommodation, you should be given the option of choosing a different room or finding one elsewhere. Should you choose to go elsewhere and a refund is refused or resisted, sub-mit the matter to AAA/CAA *within* 30 days along with complete documentation, including your rea-sons for refusing the room and copies of your written confirmation and any receipts or canceled checks associated with this problem.

Guest safety

In order to be approved for listing in AAA/CAA TourBooks for the United States and Canada, all lodgings must comply with AAA's guest room se-curity requirements. In response to AAA/CAA members' concern about their safety at properties, AAA RATED® accommodations must have dead-bolt locks on all guest room entry doors and con-necting room doors. If the area outside the guest room door is not visible from inside the room through a window or door panel, viewports must be installed on all guest room entry doors. Bed and breakfast properties and country inns are not required to have viewports. Ground floor and eas-ily accessible sliding doors must be equipped with some other type of secondary security locks.

Field inspectors view a percentage of rooms at each property. Because it is not feasible for the in-spectors to evaluate every room in every lodging establishment, AAA cannot guarantee that there are working locks on all doors and windows in all guest rooms.

Travelers are faced with the task of protecting themselves while in a strange environment. Al-though there is no way to guarantee absolute pro-tection from crime, the experts—law enforcement officials—advise travelers to take a pro-active ap-proach to securing their property and ensuring their safety. A few simple precautions can save a vacation:

- Make sure the hotel desk clerk does not an-nounce your room number; if so, quietly re-quest a new room assignment.

- Ask front desk personnel which areas of town to avoid and what, if any, special precautions should be taken when driving a rental car (some criminals target tourists driving rental cars).

- Never open the door to a stranger; use the peephole and request identification. If you are still unsure, call the front desk to verify the identity of the person and the purpose of his/her visit.

- Carry money separately from credit cards or use a "fanny pack." Carry your purse close to your body and your wallet in an inside coat or front trouser pocket. Never leave luggage unat-tended, and use your business address, if possi-ble, on luggage tags.

- Beware of distractions staged by would-be scam artists, especially groups of children that surround you or a stranger who accidently spills something on you. They may be lifting your wallet.

- If using an automatic teller machine (ATM), choose one in a well-lit area with plenty of foot traffic, such as one at a grocery store. Machines inside establishments are the safest to use.

- Use room safes or safety deposit boxes pro-vided by the hotel. Store all valuables out of sight, even when you are in the room.

- Law enforcement agencies consider card-key (electronic) door locks the most secure.

Hotel/Motel fire safety

The AAA/CAA inspection program is designed to provide you with the most useful information for se-lecting the lodgings best suited to your needs. Be-cause of the highly specialized skills needed to conduct professional fire safety inspections, how-ever, AAA/CAA inspectors cannot assess fire safety.

All guest rooms must be equipped with an opera-tional, single-station smoke detector, and all pub-lic areas must have operational smoke detectors or an automatic sprinkler system. (**Note:** Some Canadian lodgings are an exception to this re-quirement. There may be some Canadian proper-ties that were approved prior to 1988 that use heat sensors in place of smoke detectors and/or auto-matic sprinkler systems.) The type of fire protec-tion a lodging provides is identified with symbols (see the Sample Listing). At each establishment whose listing shows these symbols, a AAA/CAA inspector has evaluated a sampling of the rooms and verified that this equipment is in place.

For additional fire safety information read the page posted on the back of your guest room door, or write the National Fire Protection Association, 1 Batterymarch Park, P.O. Box 9101, Quincy, MA 02269-9101.

Access for disabled

Certain properties listed in this book have symbols indicating they are either *Fully Accessible or Semi-Accessible*. This two-tiered standard was developed to meet members' varying degrees of accessibility needs.

🔥 *Fully Accessible* properties meet the needs of those who are significantly disabled and primarily confined to a wheelchair. A fully accessible lodging will provide at least one guest room meeting the designated criteria. A traveler with these disabilities will be able to park and access public areas, including restrooms, check-in facilities and at least one food and beverage outlet. A *Fully Accessible* restaurant indicates that parking, dining rooms and restrooms are accessible.

🔥 *Semi-Accessible* properties meet the needs of those who are disabled but have some mobility and are not confined to a wheelchair. Such travelers would include the elderly, people using a cane or walker, or a disabled individual with good mobility but a limited arm or hand range of motion. A semi-accessible lodging will provide at least one guest room meeting the designated criteria. A traveler with these disabilities will be able to park and access public areas, including restrooms, check-in facilities and at least one food and beverage outlet. A *Semi-Accessible* restaurant indicates that parking, dining rooms and restrooms are accessible.

A property with a 🔥 symbol has the following equipment available for *Hearing Impaired* travelers: TDD at front desk or switchboard; visual notification of fire alarm, incoming telephone calls, door knock or bell; closed caption decoder available; text telephone or TDD available for guest room use; telephone amplification device available, with shelf and electric outlet next to guest room telephone.

AAA/CAA urges members with disabilities to always phone ahead to fully understand the accommodation's offerings. Some properties do not fully comply with AAA/CAA's exacting accessibility standards but may offer some property design standards that meet the needs of some guests with disabilities.

AAA/CAA does not evaluate recreational facilities, banquet rooms or convention and meeting facilities for accessibility. Call a property directly to inquire about your needs for these areas.

The criteria used by AAA/CAA do not represent the full scope of the Americans With Disabilities Act of 1990 Accessibility Guidelines (ADAAG); they are, however, consistent with the ADAAG. Members can obtain the brochure AAA Accessibility Criteria for Travelers With Disabilities, which describes the specific criteria pertaining to the *Fully Accessible* and *Semi-Accessible* standards, from their local AAA/CAA club.

The 𝐀𝐀𝐀 Diamonds

Lodgings and restaurants are assigned ratings from one to five diamonds, which reflect the overall quality of the establishment or dining experience.

Lodgings

Properties must satisfy a set of minimum requirements that reflect the basic lodging needs members have identified. Ratings are assigned according to the property's classification, which appears beneath the diamond rating in the lodging listing. A one-diamond property still is better than one-third of the lodgings in operation. Lodgings listed without ratings were undergoing construction or renovation at the time of inspection and are noted as such in the listing. "Best available" indicates the property does not meet AAA requirements, but is listed as a service.

◆ Good but modest accommodations. Establishments are functional, emphasizing clean and comfortable rooms. They must meet the basic needs of comfort and cleanliness.

◆◆ Maintain the attributes offered at the one diamond level, while showing noticeable enhancements in room decor and quality of furnishings. They may be recently constructed or older properties, both targeting the needs of a budget-oriented traveler.

◆◆◆ Offer a degree of sophistication. Additional amenities, services and facilities may be offered. There is a marked upgrade in physical attributes, services and comfort.

◆◆◆◆ Excellent properties displaying a high level of service and hospitality. These properties offer a wide variety of amenities and upscale facilities in the guest rooms, on the grounds and in the public areas.

◆◆◆◆◆ World-class properties exhibiting an exceptionally high degree of service; striking, luxurious facilities; and many extra amenities. Guest services are executed and presented in a flawless manner. The guest is pampered by a professional, attentive staff. The properties' facilities and operation help set industry standards in hospitality and service.

Restaurants

Ratings are assigned based on conditions noted at the time of the evaluation. The condition of one or more aspects may limit the overall rating, which is not an average of the rating criteria. Food quality is the most critical to the overall rating. Restaurants are classified by cuisine type. Some listings include additional information, such as the availability of a senior citizen menu, children's menu or "early bird specials," if offered at least 5 days a week. The dinner price range is approximate and includes a salad or appetizer, an entree, a vegetable and a non-alcoholic beverage for one person. Taxes and tip are not included.

◆ Provides a simple, family or specialty meal in clean, pleasant surroundings. Food is basic and wholesome. Service is casual, limited or self-serve. Decor is informal.

◆◆ More extensive menus for family or adult dining. Food is prepared with standard ingredients. Service is attentive but may be informal, casual, limited or self-serve. The decor presents a unified theme that is comfortable but also may be trendy, casual or upbeat.

◆◆◆ An upscale or special family dining experience. Food is cooked to order and creatively prepared with quality ingredients. A wine list is available. A skilled, often uniformed staff provides service. The usually professional and inviting decor projects a trendy, upbeat, casual or formal atmosphere.

◆◆◆◆ A high degree of sophistication, thus creating an adult dining experience. Complex food is creatively presented. An extensive wine list is offered. The service staff, often formally attired, is professionally trained. The decor is distinctive, stylish and elegant; some establishments are casual while still offering refinement or formality.

◆◆◆◆◆ A memorable occasion—the ultimate in adult dining. Food shows the highest culinary skills, evident in all areas of preparation and presentation. An extensive wine list is available. A professional staff—often in formal attire—provides flawless and pampering service. The decor has classic details, often formal and reflects comfort and luxury.

Lodging Classifications

BED AND BREAKFAST (limited service)—Usually a smaller establishment emphasizing personal attention. Guest rooms may lack some modern amenities such as TVs, phones, etc., and may have shared bathrooms. A Continental or full hot breakfast is served and is included in the room rate.

COMPLEX (service varies depending on type of lodgings)—A combination of two or more kinds of lodging classifications.

COTTAGE (limited service)—Individual bungalow, cabin or villa that may have a separate living room and bedroom(s). Although basic cleaning supplies must be provided, cottages are not required to offer daily housekeeping service.

COUNTRY INN (moderate service)—Although similar in definition to a bed and breakfast, country inns are usually larger in size. Offers a dining room reflecting the ambiance of the inn. At a minimum, breakfast and dinner are served.

HOTEL (full service)—A multistory building usually including a coffee shop, dining room, lounge, a pool and exercise equipment, room service, convenience shops, valet laundry and full banquet and meeting facilities.

LODGE (moderate service)—Typically several stories with all facilities in one building. Located in vacation, ski, fishing areas, etc. Usually has food and beverage service.

MOTEL (limited service)—Usually one or two stories. Food service, if any, consists of a limited facility or snack bar. Often has a pool or playground.

MOTOR INN (moderate service)—Usually a two or three story facility offering recreational facilities and food service.

RANCH (moderate service)—May be any classification featuring outdoor, Western-style recreation. Accommodations and facilities may vary in size.

Subclassifications

APARTMENT—Usually four or more stories. Each unit typically provides a full kitchen, living room and one or more bedrooms; studios may be available. Although basic cleaning supplies must be available, apartments are not required to offer daily housekeeping service.

CONDOMINIUM—Each unit consists of a bedroom, living room and kitchen. Kitchens are separate from bedrooms and are fully equipped with appliances, cooking utensils and table settings. Although basic cleaning supplies must be available, condominiums are not required to offer daily housekeeping service.

HISTORIC—Accommodations in restored structures more than 50 years old, reflecting the ambiance of yesteryear and the surrounding area. Rooms may lack some modern amenities and have shared baths. Usually owner-operated and food service is often available.

RESORT—Vacation atmosphere offering extensive recreational facilities for such specific interests as golf, tennis, fishing, etc. Rates may include meals under American or Modified American plans.

SUITE—One or more bedrooms and a living room/sitting area which is closed off by a full wall.

Remember

AAA/CAA inspectors assign diamond ratings by evaluating lodging establishments based on their classification. Thus, "Hotels" are rated in comparison with other "Hotels," and so on with all classifications.

Sample Lodging Listing

THE HODGES INN Guaranteed Rates **Phone: 555/555-5555** ②⓪
ⒶⒶⒶ ⓈⒶⓋⒺ 2/1-3/8 [CP] 1P: $59- 79 2P/1B: $59- 79 2P/2B: $59- 79 XP: $6 F1⑧
◆◆◆ 3/9-1/31 [CP] 1P: $49- 69 2P/1B: $49- 69 2P/2B: $49- 69 XP: $6 F1⑧
Motor Inn **Location:** From I-20 exit 185; just n; intersection US 78 & SR 21S. US 78 & SR 21 36203 (PO Box 5555, OX
FORD). Fax: 555/555-5556. **Terms:** Weekly rates; pets. **Facility:** 194 rooms. 2 stories; interior/exterior corr
dors; whirlpool; playground, shaded picnic area. **Dining & Entertainment:** Restaurant; 6 am-midnight; cockta
lounge; entertainment. **Services:** Fee: coin laundry. **All Rooms:** coffeemakers, free & pay movies
Some Rooms: microwaves, refrigerators, safes, whirlpools. **Cards:** AE, CB, DI, DS, JCB, MC, V
Special Amenities: Early check-in/late check-out and free newspaper. 🛏 ⚊ 🏊 ✈ ⒸⓉⓋ ⊠ Ⓓ

① ⒶⒶⒶ or ⒸⒶⒶ — AAA/CAA Official Appointment (see pg. 163)

ⓈⒶⓋⒺ — Show Your Card and Save (see pg. 163)

NOTE: the Guaranteed Rates or Rates Subject to Change will not appear wher
the SAVE icon is present

◆◆◆ — Diamond Rating (see pg. 168)

Motor Inn — Lodging Classification (see pg. 169)

② Rate lines show from left to right: dates the rates in that line are effective, any
meal plan included in the rate (CP=Continental Plan of pastry, juice and anothe
beverage or may offer expanded breakfast items; BP=Breakfast Plan of full ho
breakfast; AP=American Plan of three meals daily; MAP=Modified America
Plan of two meals daily; EP=European Plan, where rate includes room only)
number of Persons/Beds allowed/provided for the rates shown, the rate
charged, the extra person (XP) charge and, if applicable, the family pla
indicator (F17=children 17 and under stay free; D17=discount for children 1
and under; F=children stay free; D=discounts for children). The establishmen
may limit the number of children to whom the family plan applies.

③ Rate Options (see pg. 164)

④ ②⓪ — Spotting map indicator (see pg. 164)

⑤ 🛏 — Pets allowed   ⒺⒸⓉⓋ — Extended Cable TV

⚊ — Outdoor swimming pool   🖢 — Fully accessible

⚊ — Swimming pool   🏠 — Semi-accessible

🏊 — Dataports and/or business services   ⊠ — Non-smoking available

✈ — Airport transportation   🎧 — Hearing impaired

🏋 — Exercise/whirlpool/sauna facilities Ⓓ — Smoke detectors

ⒸⓉⓋ — Cable TV   Ⓢ — Fire protection sprinklers

Lodging Evaluation Criteria

Regardless of the diamond rating, properties listed by AAA/CAA are required to provide:

- Clean and well-maintained facilities   • A well-kept appearance
- Hospitable staff   • Comfortable furnishings and pleasant decor

Each guest room is required to have:

- Comfortable beds and good quality   • At least one chair
  bedding   • Adequate illumination at each task
- Adequate towels and supplies   area

NEW JERSEY

ABSECON—*see Atlantic City & Vicinity p. 180.*

ALLAMUCHY—300

LODGING

THE INN AT PANTHER VALLEY	Guaranteed Rates			Phone: 908/852-6000

All Year   1P: $75   2P/1B: $75   2P/2B: $75   XP: $10   F16
Location: I-80 exit 19, 0.8 mi s. CR 517 07820 (PO Box 183). Fax: 908/850-1503. **Terms:** No pets.
Facility: 100 rooms. 8 extended stay & 4 fireplace rooms, extra charge; 2-bedroom/2-bath suite; 2 stories;
interior/exterior corridors. **Dining:** Restaurant; 6:30 am-10 pm; $10-$20. **All Rooms:** free movies.
Cards: AE, CB, DI, MC, VI.

◆◆◆
Motor Inn

RESTAURANT

MATTAR'S	**Lunch:** $9-$15	**Dinner:** $15-$24	Phone: 908/852-2300

◆◆◆
Ethnic

Location: I-80, exit 19; 1 mi s on CR 517. 07820. **Hours:** 11:30 am-2 & 5-10 pm, Fri-11 pm, Sat 5 pm-11
pm, Sun 2 pm-9 pm. Closed major holidays. **Reservations:** suggested; weekends. **Features:** health
conscious menu items; cocktails & lounge; a la carte. A sophisticated dining experience awaits; attractive
dining rooms, good service & wonderfully prepared culinary treats to delight everyone's taste. Upscale casual. **Cards:** AE,
CB, DI, DS, MC, VI.

ANDOVER—800

LODGINGS

CROSSED KEYS B&B	Rates Subject to Change			Phone: 973/786-6661

All Year [BP]   1P: $100- 150   2P/1B: $100- 150 2P/2B: $100- 150 XP: $25
Location: I-80, exit 25, US 206 N 8 mi, 1.5 mi w on CR 603, just n of jct CR 606 & 603. 289 Peguest Rd
07821. Fax: 973/786-6320. **Terms:** Age restrictions may apply; reserv deposit, 15 day notice; no pets.
Facility: 5 rooms. Whirlpool rm, extra charge. Handling fee imposed; 2 stories; interior corridors. **Cards:** AE,
MC, VI.

◆◆◆
Historic Bed
& Breakfast

HOLIDAY MOTEL	Rates Subject to Change			Phone: 973/786-5260

All Year   1P: $70   2P/1B: $70   2P/2B: $76   XP: $6
Location: Westbound I-80, exit 25; 8 mi n US 206, eastbound I-80, exit 19; 7 mi n on CR 17 to jct 206, 1 mi
n. 708 US Hwy 206 07821. Fax: 973/786-7627. **Terms:** No pets. **Facility:** 19 rooms. 1 story; exterior corridors.
Cards: AE, DS, MC, VI.

◆◆
Motel

Atlantic City & Vicinity

ATLANTIC CITY—38,000   (See map p. 172; index below)

**To help you more easily locate accommodations in the Atlantic City area, the following
index and map show lodgings and restaurants within Atlantic City area.**

Index of Establishments on the ATLANTIC CITY ACCOMMODATIONS Spotting Map

Sun N' Surf .... ❶	Holiday Inn Boardwalk Hotel .... ㉓
Lido Motel .... ❷	Days Inn/Atlantic City-Boardwalk .... ㉕
Trump Marina Casino Resort .... ❸	Atlantic City Travelodge .... ㉘
Best Western Envoy Inn .... ❹	Howard Johnson Hotel....................... ㉚
Sands Hotel & Casino........................... ❻	
Resorts Casino Hotel .... ❽	RESTAURANTS
The Flagship Resort .... ❾	Harbor View .... ①
Howard Johnson .... ⑩	Caruso's.. ③
Knights Inn .... ⑪	Ivanka's .... ④
The Madison House Hotel.................... ⑰	China Moon.................................... ⑤
Trump Plaza Hotel & Casino................. ⑳	Cafe 21 .... ⑥
Atlantic City Hilton Casino Resort .... ㉒	

LODGINGS

ATLANTIC CITY HILTON CASINO RESORT			Phone: 609/347-7111	㉒

6/19-9/17   1P: $205- 290   2P/2B: $205- 290 XP: $20   F12
5/1-6/18, 9/18-12/4 &
4/10-4/30   1P: $175- 255   2P/2B: $175- 255 XP: $20   F12
12/5-4/9   1P: $125- 220   2P/2B: $125- 220 XP: $20   F12
Location: On the boardwalk. Boston & The Boardwalk 08401 (PO Box 1737). Fax: 609/236-7804.
Terms: Check-in 4 pm; reserv deposit, 3 day notice; package plans; 2 night min stay, weekends; no pets. **Facility:** 814 rooms.
Luxurious accommodations, many rooms with good ocean view & some with oceanfront public areas with an accent on el-
egance. Handling fee imposed; 23 stories; interior corridors; beach, saunas, steamrooms, whirlpools. Fee: parking. **Dining &
Entertainment:** 3 dining rooms, 2 restaurants; 24 hours; $9-$35; cocktails/lounge; casino; 24-hour room service; also,
Caruso's, see separate listing; nightclub. **Services:** valet laundry. Fee: massage; valet parking. **Recreation:** swimming.
All Rooms: free & pay movies. **Some Rooms:** refrigerators, safes, whirlpools. Fee: VCR's. **Cards:** AE, CB, DI, DS, MC.
Special Amenities: Free room upgrade and preferred room (each subject to availability with advanced reservations).
See color ad p 18)

◆◆◆◆
Hotel

DIAMONDS tell the story—read The   Diamonds.

(See map below)

ATLANTIC CITY TRAVELODGE — Guaranteed Rates — Phone: 609/348-3137 — **28**
◆
| | | 5/24-9/15 | 1P: $89- 159 | 2P/1B: $89- 159 | 2P/2B: $89- 159 | XP: $15 | F14 |
Motel   5/1-5/23 & 9/16-4/30   1P: $59- 99   2P/1B: $59- 99   2P/2B: $59- 99   XP: $15   F14
Location: Just w of the boardwalk. 154 S North Carolina Ave 08401. Fax: 609/822-0060. **Terms:** Sr discount; reserv deposit, 3 day notice; no pets. **Facility:** 56 rooms. 5 stories; exterior corridors. **All Rooms:** free movies. **Cards:** AE, DS, MC, VI.   [CTV] [X] [D]

BEST WESTERN ENVOY INN — Rates Subject to Change — Phone: 609/344-7117 — **4**
◆◆
7/1-9/6 [CP]   2P/1B: $98- 165   2P/2B: $98- 165   XP: $10   F12
Motel   12/1-4/30 [CP]   2P/1B: $58- 125   2P/2B: $58- 125   XP: $10   F12
5/1-6/30 & 9/7-11/30 [CP]   2P/1B: $78- 125   2P/2B: $78- 125   XP: $10   F12
Location: Pacific & New York aves. 1416 Pacific Ave 08401. Fax: 609/344-5659. **Terms:** No pets. **Facility:** 75 rooms. 5 whirlpool suites with refrigerator & microwave, $150-$250, rates for up to 2 persons; 4 stories; interior corridors. **All Rooms:** free movies. **Cards:** AE, CB, DI, DS, MC, VI.   [CTV] [X] [D] [S]

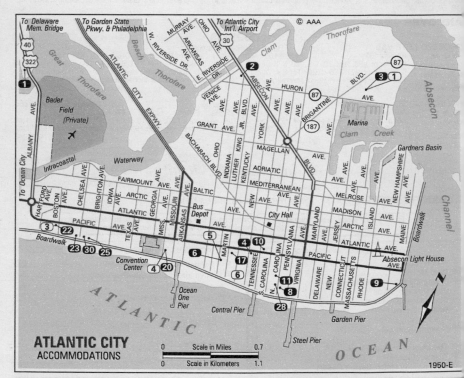

ATLANTIC CITY
ACCOMMODATIONS

1950-E

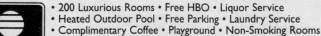

(See map p. 172)

DAYS INN/ATLANTIC CITY-BOARDWALK   Phone: 609/344-6101   🅾
🆂🆂🆂 SAVE   Fri & Sat 5/15-9/30   2P/1B: $70- 345 2P/2B: $70- 345 XP: $10   F16
            Fri & Sat 5/1-5/14, Sun-Thurs
◆◆   5/15-9/30 & Fri & Sat
Motor Inn   10/1-4/30   2P/1B: $60- 345 2P/2B: $60- 345 XP: $10   F16
            Sun-Thurs 5/1-5/14 &
            10/1-4/30   2P/1B: $50- 345 2P/2B: $50- 345 XP: $10   F16
Location: On the boardwalk. Boardwalk & Morris Ave 08401. Fax: 609/348-5335. **Terms:** No pets. **Facility:** 106 rooms. Modest rooms, most with balcony; some with ocean view. 5 stories; interior corridors; amusement arcade. **Dining & Entertainment:** Restaurant; 7 am-8 pm, 5/1-9/30 to 10 pm; $6-$13; cocktails/lounge. **Services:** Fee: valet parking. **All Rooms:** free movies. **Some Rooms:** Fee: refrigerators. **Cards:** AE, DS, MC, VI.   🛌 CTV ⊠ D S

THE FLAGSHIP RESORT   Rates Subject to Change   Phone: 609/343-7447   🅾
◆◆◆   1/3-3/31   1P: $69- 199 2P/1B: $69- 199 2P/2B: $69- 199 XP: $15
Suite Hotel 5/1-1/2 & 4/1-4/30   1P: $99- 199 2P/1B: $99- 199 2P/2B: $99- 199 XP: $15
Location: At the boardwalk; 2 mi n on Atlantic Ave. 60 N Maine Ave 08401. Fax: 609/344-3545. **Terms:** Check-in 4 pm; reserv deposit; no pets. **Facility:** 205 rooms. 32 stories; interior corridors. **Dining:** Restaurant, deli; 7 am-11 pm, hours vary off season; deli 7 am-10 pm; $10-$22. **All Rooms:** efficiencies. Fee: movies. **Cards:** AE, CB, DI, DS, JCB, MC, VI.   🛌 ECTV ⊠ D S

HOLIDAY INN BOARDWALK HOTEL   Phone: 609/348-2200   🅾
🆂🆂🆂 SAVE   7/2-9/6   1P: $125- 179 2P/1B: $125- 179 2P/2B: $125- 179 XP: $15   F19
            5/1-7/1 & 9/7-10/31   1P: $98- 140 2P/1B: $98- 140 2P/2B: $98- 140 XP: $15   F19
◆◆◆   11/1-11/26 & 3/1-4/30   1P: $88- 130 2P/1B: $88- 130 2P/2B: $88- 130 XP: $15   F19
Hotel   11/27-2/28   1P: $78- 108 2P/1B: $78- 108 2P/2B: $78- 108 XP: $15   F19
            Location: On the boardwalk. Chelsea Ave & Boardwalk 08401. Fax: 609/345-5110. **Terms:** Reserv deposit, 3 day notice; weekly/monthly rates; BP avail; package plans; 2 night min stay, weekends; no pets. **Facility:** 220 rooms. Contemporary high-rise; most rooms with ocean view. Voice mail, pool cabana. 20 stories; interior corridors. **Dining & Entertainment:** Restaurant; 7 am-10 pm; $10-$25; cocktails/lounge. **Services:** valet laundry; valet parking. **All Rooms:** coffeemakers. Fee: movies. **Some Rooms:** Fee: refrigerators. **Cards:** AE, CB, DI, DS, JCB, MC, VI.
(See color ad p 175)   🛌 🍴 ✈ CTV ⊠ D S

Checkout time is noted in the listing if the required time is before 10 a.m.

INSIDE YOU'LL FIND A WELCOME THAT'S MADE US THE WORLD'S FAVORITE CASINO.

Foxwoods Resort Casino is now even more breathtaking than ever. The new 800-room Grand Pequot Tower, the AAA four-diamond rated Great Cedar Tower and the AAA three-diamond rated Two Trees Inn offer a total of over 1400 luxurious rooms and suites. With gourmet restaurants and more table games, slot machines and chances to win. Plus, all hotels honor AAA discounts.

Foxwoods is entertainment with stars like Celine Dion, Reba McEntire and David Copperfield. There's also a health spa, fabulous shops and plenty of free parking.

With its Hotels, Restaurants, Gaming and Entertainment, it's no wonder that Foxwoods has become the hottest entertainment destination in the country.

THE WONDER OF THE CONNECTICUT WOODS.

Call 1-800-PLAY-BIG or your Travel Professional.
Exit 92 off I-95 in Southeast Connecticut.
Mashantucket Pequot Tribal Nation.

(See map p. 172)

OWARD JOHNSON   Rates Subject to Change   Phone: 609/344-4193   [10]
        Fri & Sat 6/22-9/15   2P/2B: $98- 195 XP: $15   F18
        Fri & Sat 5/1-6/21 &
◆◆   9/16-4/30   2P/2B: $88- 195 XP: $15   F18
Motor Inn   Sun-Thurs 6/22-9/15   2P/2B: $78- 98 XP: $15   F18
        Sun-Thurs 5/1-6/21 &
        9/16-4/30   2P/2B: $45- 75 XP: $15   F18

Location: At Pacific & Tennessee aves, just w of boardwalk, between casinos. 1339 Pacific Ave 08401. Fax: 609/348-1263.
Terms: Sr. discount; no pets. Facility: 71 rooms. 3 stories; interior corridors. Dining: Coffee shop; 7 am-4 pm, 6/22-9/15 to
pm; $8-$10. All Rooms: free movies. Some Rooms: 4 efficiencies. Cards: AE, CB, DI, DS, JCB, MC, VI.
(See color ad below)

GOING UP? Expect elevators in establishments of three or
more stories. We tell you in the listings if there are none.

(See map p. 172)

HOWARD JOHNSON HOTEL   Phone: 609/344-7071 3
⊕ SAVE   6/30-8/27   1P: $99- 179   2P/2B: $99- 179 XP: $15   F1
◆   5/1-6/29 & 8/28-10/29 1P: $89- 139   2P/2B: $89- 139 XP: $15   F1
          10/30-11/26   1P: $69- 109   2P/2B: $69- 109 XP: $15   F1
Hotel   11/27-4/30   1P: $59- 99   2P/2B: $59- 99 XP: $15   F1
Location: Just w of the boardwalk. Chelsea Ave & Boardwalk 08401. Fax: 609/344-0878. **Terms:** Rese
deposit, 3 day notice; BP, MAP avail; package plans; 2 night min stay, weekends; no pets. **Facility:** 121 rooms. Catering
bus groups; most rooms with 2 double beds. 5 stories; interior corridors; sauna, steamroom, whirlpool; game roor
Dining & Entertainment: Restaurant; 7 am-2:30 & 4:30-10 pm; $10-$16; cocktails/lounge. **Services:** valet laundr
Some Rooms: Fee: refrigerators. **Cards:** AE, DI, DS, MC, VI. **Special Amenities:** Free newspaper and free roo
upgrade (subject to availability with advanced reservations). *(See color ad p 175)*

⊠ ⊕ ⊕ CTV ⊠ ⊘ D S

KNIGHTS INN   Rates Subject to Change   Phone: 609/345-0155   1
◆   7/1-8/31   2P/1B: $75- 150 2P/2B: $75- 150 XP: $10   F1
Motel   5/1-6/30   2P/1B: $50- 125 2P/2B: $50- 125 XP: $10   F1
          9/1-10/31 & 3/1-4/30   2P/1B: $45- 110 2P/2B: $45- 110 XP: $10   F1
          11/1-2/28   2P/1B: $40- 75 2P/2B: $40- 75 XP: $10   F1
Location: Downtown, just w of boardwalk. 124 S North Carolina Ave 08401. Fax: 609/345-4556. **Terms:** Sr. discount; r
pets. **Facility:** 25 rooms. 2 stories; exterior corridors. **All Rooms:** free movies. **Cards:** AE, DS, MC, VI.

ECTV ⊠ C

LIDO MOTEL   Phone: 609/344-1975   ⊘
⊕ SAVE   Fri & Sat 6/19-9/12 1P: $50- 110 2P/1B: $50- 110 2P/2B: $50- 110 XP: $5   D
◆   Fri & Sat 5/1-6/18 &
         9/13-4/30   1P: $50- 85 2P/1B: $50- 85 2P/2B: $50- 85 XP: $5   D
Motel   Sun-Thurs   1P: $40- 75 2P/1B: $40- 75 2P/2B: $40- 75 XP: $5   D
Location: 1.5 mi w of boardwalk on US 30. 1600 Absecon Blvd 08401. **Terms:** Reserv deposit; week
rates; **Facility:** 27 rooms. 1 story; exterior corridors. **All Rooms:** free movies, combo or shower baths. **Cards:** AE, CB, D
DS, MC. **Special Amenities:** Early check-in/late check-out and free local telephone calls. *(See color ad below)*

⊠ CTV C

 SAVE   Look for this icon in the restaurant listings. These restaurants
offer special values or discounts to AAA members.

See map p. 172)

THE MADISON HOUSE HOTEL   Phone: 609/345-1400   [17]
[AAA] [SAVE]   Fri & Sat 5/1-9/30 & 4/1-4/30   1P: $85- 150   2P/1B: $89- 159   2P/2B: $89- 159   XP: $10   F12
        Fri & Sat 10/1-3/31   1P: $55- 130   2P/1B: $59- 129   2P/2B: $59- 129   XP: $10   F12
◆◆   Sun-Thurs 5/1-9/30 &
Historic Hotel 4/1-4/30   1P: $65- 95   2P/1B: $69- 99   2P/2B: $69- 99   XP: $10   F12
        Sun-Thurs 10/1-3/31   1P: $45- 65   2P/1B: $39- 69   2P/2B: $39- 69   XP: $10   F12
Location: Just e of jct Pacific Ave & Dr Martin Luther King Blvd (Illinois Ave). 123 S Dr Martin Luther King Blvd 08401.
Fax: 609/347-7265. **Terms:** Package plans; 2 night min stay, weekends in season; no pets. **Facility:** 210 rooms. Limited
service hotel. Some compact guest rooms. On National Register of Historic Places. $1 charge for outgoing phone call; 14 sto-
ries; interior corridors. **Fee:** parking; recreation facilities at the Sands Hotel & Casino. **Dining & Entertainment:** Coffee
shop; 7-11 am; 24-hour cocktail lounge. **Services:** valet laundry. **All Rooms:** free movies. **Some Rooms:** honor bars,
coffeemakers. **Fee:** refrigerators. **Cards:** AE, DI, DS, MC. *(See color ad p 176)*   [icons]

TAXES—state, city and local—are extra.
Allow for them; our listed rates do not.

(See map p. 172)

RESORTS CASINO HOTEL Rates Subject to Change Phone: 609/344-6000
◆◆◆ 6/19-9/17 1P: $150- 250 2P/1B: $150- 250 2P/2B: $150- 250 XP: $10 F1
Hotel 5/1-6/18 & 9/18-4/30 1P: $100- 200 2P/1B: $100- 200 2P/2B: $100- 200 XP: $10 F1
Location: Oceanfront, at east end of North Carolina Ave. 1133 Boardwalk 08401. Fax: 609/340-7684
Terms: Check-in 4 pm; reserv deposit; 2 night min stay, weekends; no pets. **Facility:** 662 rooms. 9-15 stories; interior corridors. Fee: parking. **Dining:** 3 dining rooms, 5 restaurants; 24 hours; $12-$30. **All Rooms:** free & pay movies. **Cards:** AE, MC, VI.
Roll in showers. 🛍 🛍 CTV ⊠ D S

SANDS HOTEL & CASINO Rates Subject to Change Phone: 609/441-4000
◆◆◆ Fri & Sat 2P/1B: $199- 259 2P/2B: $199- 259 XP: $15 F1
Hotel Sun-Thurs 2P/1B: $109- 199 2P/2B: $109- 199 XP: $15 F1
Location: E end of Indiana Ave, just w of the boardwalk. Indiana Ave & Brighton Park 08401
Fax: 609/441-4630. **Terms:** Sr. discount; reserv deposit; no pets. **Facility:** 532 rooms. Handling fee imposed; 21 stories; interior corridors. Fee: parking. **Dining:** 4 dining rooms, restaurant, coffee shop; 24 hours; $10-$35; also, China Moon, see separate listing. **All Rooms:** free & pay movies. **Cards:** AE, CB, DI, DS, MC, VI.
Roll in showers. CTV ⊠ D S

SUN N' SURF Phone: 609/344-2515
AAA SAVE Fri & Sat 6/19-9/12 1P: $50- 110 2P/1B: $50- 110 2P/2B: $50- 110 XP: $5-10 D1
  Fri & Sat 5/1-6/18 &
◆ 9/13-4/30 1P: $50- 85 2P/1B: $50- 85 2P/2B: $50- 85 XP: $5 D1
Motel Sun-Thurs 6/14-9/6 1P: $40- 75 2P/1B: $45- 75 2P/2B: $45- 75 XP: $5 D1
  Sun-Thurs 5/1-6/13 &
  9/7-4/30 1P: $40- 75 2P/1B: $40- 75 2P/2B: $40- 75 XP: $5 D1
Location: 1.5 mi w on US 40. 1600 Albany Ave 08401. Fax: 609/383-1937. **Terms:** Reserv deposit; weekly/monthly rates; small pets only, $25 dep req. **Facility:** 25 rooms. 1 story; exterior corridors. **Services:** Fee: area transportation, to casinos. **All Rooms:** free movies, shower baths. **Cards:** AE, DI, DS, MC, VI. **Special Amenities:** Early check-in/late check-out and free local telephone calls. *(See color ad p 176)* 🐾 🛍 CTV D

TRUMP MARINA CASINO RESORT Phone: 609/441-2000
AAA SAVE 6/30-9/3 1P: $110- 325 2P/1B: $110- 325 2P/2B: $110- 325 XP: $15 F1
◆◆◆◆ 5/1-6/29 & 9/4-4/30 1P: $80- 305 2P/1B: $80- 305 2P/2B: $80- 305 XP: $15 F1
Hotel **Location:** On SR 87, 0.8 mi n of US 30; at Frank S Farley Marina. Huron Ave & Brigantine Blvd 08401
Fax: 609/345-7604. **Terms:** Check-in 4 pm; reserv deposit; package plans; no pets. **Facility:** 728 rooms. Large bayside casino with spacious guest rooms featuring fine view of the city or marina. 23 two-bedroom units; 14-27 stories; interior corridors; luxury level rooms; wading pool, saunas, steamroom, whirlpools; 4 lighted tennis courts; health club, shuffleboard. **Dining & Entertainment:** 3 dining rooms, 3 restaurants, coffee shop; 24 hours; $6-$37; cocktails/lounge; 24-hour room service; also, Harbor View, see separate listing; name entertainment, nightclub. **Services:** valet laundry. Fee: massage, area transportation, limo service; valet parking. **Recreation:** jogging. **All Rooms:** Fee: movies. **Some Rooms:** microwaves, radios, refrigerators, whirlpools. Fee: VCR's. **Cards:** AE, CB, DI, DS, JCB, MC, VI. *(See ad below)* 🛍 🍴 📶 CTV ⊠ 🐾 D S

(See map p. 172)

TRUMP PLAZA HOTEL & CASINO

(AAA) ◆◆◆◆ Hotel

	Rates Subject to Change			
6/12-9/12	1P: $185- 240	2P/1B: $185- 240	2P/2B: $185- 240	XP: $10	F18
5/1-6/11, 9/13-11/30 &					
3/13-4/30	1P: $160- 185	2P/1B: $160- 185	2P/2B: $160- 185	XP: $10	F18
12/1-3/12	1P: $120- 145	2P/1B: $120- 145	2P/2B: $120- 145	XP: $10	F18

Phone: 609/441-6000   20

Location: The Boardwalk at Mississippi Ave 08401 (PO Box 1980). Fax: 609/441-7881. **Terms:** Check-in 4 pm; 2 night min stay, weekends in season; no pets. **Facility:** 904 rooms. 47 whirlpool rms, extra charge; 35 stories; interior corridors. Fee: parking. **Dining:** 4 dining rooms, 2 restaurants, 2 cafeterias, coffee shop, deli; 24 hours; $7-$37; also, Ivanka's, see separate listing. **All Rooms:** free & pay movies. **Cards:** AE, CB, DI, DS, MC, VI. ⊇ ⒺⒸⓉⓋ ✕ 🌀 Ⓓ Ⓢ

RESTAURANTS

CAFE 21

(AAA) (SAVE) ◆◆ Ethnic

Lunch: $5-$14   **Dinner:** $7-$40   Phone: 609/347-3300   6

Location: On the boardwalk, between Kentucky & New York aves. 1523 Boardwalk 08401. **Hours:** 8 am-10 pm, Fri & Sat-midnight. **Reservations:** suggested; weekends. **Features:** casual dress; children's menu; cocktails; street parking; a la carte. Eclectic cafe with a wide ranging menu spotlighting authentic Brazilian, Portuguese, Mexican, Southern American & Italian cuisine. Also, standard fare & vegetarian offerings. Chef/owner. **Cards:** AE, DI, DS, MC, VI. **Special Value: 20% discount on the price of any entree, excluding beverages, tax and gratuity.**

CARUSO'S

◆◆◆ Italian

Dinner: $20-$37   Phone: 609/347-7111   3

Location: On the boardwalk; in Atlantic City Hilton Casino Resort. Boston Ave & Boardwalk 08401. **Hours:** 6 pm-11 pm, Sun 10:30 am-2:30 pm. Closed: Mon & Tues. **Reservations:** suggested. **Features:** Sunday brunch; cocktails; fee for parking & valet parking; a la carte. Traditional & contemporary Italian specialties presented in a magnificent countryside setting. **Cards:** AE, CB, DI, DS, JCB, MC, VI. ✕

CHINA MOON

◆◆◆ Chinese

Dinner: $15-$30   Phone: 609/441-4100   5

Location: E end of Indiana Ave, just w of the boardwalk; in Sands Hotel & Casino. Indiana Ave & Brighton Pk 08401. **Hours:** 6 pm-11 pm. Closed: Wed & Thurs. **Reservations:** suggested. **Features:** dressy casual; cocktails; valet parking; a la carte. Traditional Cantonese & American-style Chinese cuisine. In an atmosphere of opulent refinement. **Cards:** AE, CB, DS, MC, VI. ✕

HARBOR VIEW

◆◆◆ Seafood

Dinner: $18-$37   Phone: 609/441-2000   1

Location: On SR 87, 0.8 mi n of US 30; at Frank S Farley Marina; in Trump Marina Casino Resort. Huron Ave & Brigantine Blvd 08401. **Hours:** 6 pm-10 pm, Sat-11 pm, Sun 10 am-3:30 pm. Closed: Mon. **Reservations:** suggested. **Features:** dressy casual; Sunday brunch; cocktails; fee for parking & valet parking; a la carte. Excellent view of the marina & city skyline compliments skilled preparation of quality seafood. Superior dessert. **Cards:** AE, CB, DI, DS, JCB, MC, VI. ✕

IVANKA'S

◆◆◆ Continental MC, VI.

Dinner: $23-$37   Phone: 609/441-6000   4

Location: The Boardwalk at Mississippi Ave; in Trump Plaza Hotel & Casino. **Hours:** 6 pm-11 pm. Closed: Thurs & Fri. **Reservations:** required. **Features:** semi-formal attire; cocktails; fee for parking & valet parking; a la carte. Elegant dining room. Attentive, professional service. Very good wine list. **Cards:** AE, CB, DI, DS,

The Atlantic City Vicinity

ABSECON—7,300

LODGINGS

COMFORT INN-NORTH

(AAA) (SAVE) ◆◆◆ Motel DS, MC, VI.

All Year [CP]	1P: $49- 109	2P/1B: $49- 109	2P/2B: $49- 109	XP: $10	F17

Phone: 609/641-7272

Location: Garden St Pkwy exit 40, 2.5 mi e on US 30 southbound; northbound U-turn through Atlantic City Service Plaza & return to exit 40. 539 Absecon Blvd 08201. Fax: 609/646-3286. **Terms:** Reserv deposit; package plans; no pets. **Facility:** 205 rooms. Some rooms with Atlantic City skyline view. 7 stories; interior corridors. **Services:** valet laundry. **All Rooms:** free movies. **Some Rooms:** refrigerators. **Cards:** AE, CB, DI 🌀 🌀 ⒸⓉⓋ ✕ 🌀 Ⓓ Ⓢ

DAYS INN-ABSECON/ATLANTIC CITY

(AAA) (SAVE) ◆◆ Motel

5/1-9/30 [CP]	1P: $50- 150	2P/1B: $50- 150	2P/2B: $50- 160	XP: $5	F18
10/1-11/30 & 4/1-4/30 [CP]	1P: $45- 95	2P/1B: $45- 95	2P/2B: $45- 95	XP: $5	F18
12/1-3/31 [CP]	1P: $40- 95	2P/1B: $40- 95	2P/2B: $40- 95	XP: $5	F18

Phone: 609/652-2200

Location: On US 30, 0.5 mi e of Garden State Pkwy, exit 40 southbound; northbound U-turn through Atlantic City Service Plaza, s to exit 40. 224 E White Horse Pike (US 30) 08201. Fax: 609/748-8005. **Terms:** Weekly/monthly rates; pets, $10.60 extra charge. **Facility:** 102 rooms. 3 stories; exterior corridors; small pool. **Services:** Fee: coin laundry. **All Rooms:** free movies. **Some Rooms:** whirlpools. **Cards:** AE, DI, DS, MC, VI. 🌀 🌀 ⒸⓉⓋ ✕ Ⓓ

ECONO LODGE

(AAA) (SAVE) ◆◆ Motel

Fri & Sat 5/1-9/30 & 4/1-4/30 [CP]	1P: $61	2P/1B: $75	2P/2B: $75	XP: $5	F18
10/1-3/31 [CP]	1P: $30- 40	2P/1B: $40- 54	2P/2B: $40- 60	XP: $5	F18
Sun-Thurs 5/1-9/30 & 4/1-4/30 [CP]	1P: $50	2P/1B: $55	2P/2B: $55	XP: $5	F18

Phone: 609/652-3300

Location: From Garden State Pkwy, 0.5 mi e of exit 40 (southbound); from Atlantic City Expwy exit 12, 2 mi n on CR 575 then 4 mi e on US 30. 328 White Horse Pike 08201. Fax: 609/652-8885. **Terms:** Reserv deposit; weekly rates; no pets. **Facility:** 62 rooms. Most rooms ground floor. Handling fee imposed; 1-2 stories; exterior corridors. **All Rooms:** free movies. **Some Rooms:** coffeemakers, microwaves, refrigerators. **Cards:** AE, CB, DI, DS, MC. **Special Amenities: Free breakfast and free local telephone calls.** ⒸⓉⓋ ✕ Ⓓ

EXECUTIVE LODGE

◆◆ Motel

	Rates Subject to Change		
6/6-9/5	2P/1B: $45- 95	2P/2B: $45- 95	
5/2-6/5	2P/1B: $40- 75	2P/2B: $40- 75	
5/1-5/1 & 9/6-4/30	2P/1B: $35- 55	2P/2B: $35- 55	

Phone: 609/484-9555

Location: On US 30, 1.5 mi e of Garden State Pkwy, exit 40. 300 Absecon Blvd 08201. **Terms:** Sr. discount; no pets. **Facility:** 23 rooms. Rates for up to 4 persons; 2 stories; exterior corridors. **All Rooms:** free movies. **Cards:** AE, DS, MC, VI. ⒸⓉⓋ ✕ Ⓓ

FAIRFIELD INN BY MARRIOTT-ATLANTIC CITY NORTH   Phone: 609/646-5000

ⓐⓐⓐ SAVE	7/1-8/31 [CP]	1P:	$65- 119	2P/1B:	$75- 129	2P/2B:	$65- 119	XP: $10		F18
	6/1-6/30 & 9/1-9/30 [CP]	1P:	$55- 110	2P/1B:	$65- 120	2P/2B:	$55- 110	XP: $10		F18
◆◆◆	5/1-5/31, 10/1-11/30 &									
	4/1-4/30 [CP]	1P:	$45- 99	2P/1B:	$55- 109	2P/2B:	$45- 99	XP: $10		F18
Motel	12/1-3/31 [CP]	1P:	$40- 70	2P/1B:	$50- 80	2P/2B:	$40- 70	XP: $10		F18

Location: 1.5 mi e on US 30, northbound U-turn through Atlantic City Service Plaza & s to exit 40. 405 E Absecon Blvd 08201. Fax: 609/383-8744. **Terms:** Check-in 4 pm; reserv deposit; package plans; no pets. **Facility:** 200 rooms. Contemporary rooms. 6 stories; interior corridors. **Services:** valet laundry. **All Rooms:** free & pay movies. **Some Rooms:** refrigerators, whirlpools. **Cards:** AE, CB, DI, DS, MC, VI. **Special Amenities:** Early check-in/late check-out and preferred room (subject to availability with advanced reservations). (See color ad p 173)

HAMPTON INN   Rates Subject to Change   Phone: 609/652-2500

◆◆◆	Fri & Sat [CP]	1P: $109- 136	2P/1B: $109- 136	2P/2B: $109- 136		
Motel	Sun-Thurs 5/1-5/31 &					
	9/8-4/30 [CP]	1P: $59- 96	2P/1B: $59- 96	2P/2B: $59- 96		
	Sun-Thurs 6/1-9/7 [CP]	1P: $59- 82	2P/1B: $59- 82	2P/2B: $55- 82		

Location: From Garden State Pkwy, 0.8 mi e, exit 40 (southbound); from AC Expwy exit 12, left 3 mi, then e on US 30, follow signs for Pomona. 240 E White Horse Pike (US 30) 08201. Fax: 609/652-2212. **Terms:** No pets. **Facility:** 129 rooms. Rates for up to 4 persons; 4 stories; interior corridors. **All Rooms:** free movies. **Cards:** AE, CB, DI, DS, MC, VI.

MARRIOTT'S SEAVIEW RESORT   Rates Subject to Change   Phone: 609/748-1990

◆◆◆	7/3-9/7 [BP]	1P: $224	2P/1B: $224	2P/2B: $224	
Resort Hotel	5/1-7/2, 9/8-11/22 &				
	4/13-4/30 [BP]	1P: $204	2P/1B: $204	2P/2B: $204	
	11/23-4/12 [BP]	1P: $125	2P/1B: $125	2P/2B: $125	

Location: On US 9, 2.5 mi ne of US 30 (White Horse Pike). 401 S New York Rd 08201-9727. Fax: 609/652-2307. **Terms:** Sr. discount; check-in 4 pm; reserv deposit, 10 day notice; no pets. **Facility:** 300 rooms. 3-4 stories; interior corridors. **Dining:** Dining room, restaurant; 6:30 am-11 pm; $10-$30. **All Rooms:** free & pay movies. **Cards:** AE, DI, DS, MC, VI. Roll in showers.

STARLITE MOTOR INN   Phone: 609/645-7499

ⓐⓐⓐ SAVE	5/22-9/5 & 12/26-12/31	2P/1B: $40- 89	2P/2B: $45- 95	XP: $5		F15
	9/6-12/25	2P/1B: $35- 69	2P/2B: $35- 69	XP: $5		F15
◆◆	5/1-5/21 & 1/1-4/30	2P/1B: $45- 59	2P/2B: $45- 59	XP: $5		F15

Motel   **Location:** On US 30, just w of jct US 9; 1.5 mi e of Garden State Pkwy, exit 40. 461 White Horse Pike 08201. **Terms:** Weekly/monthly rates; no pets. **Facility:** 29 rooms. Many rooms with king bed. Handling fee imposed; 2 stories; exterior corridors. **Dining:** Restaurant nearby. **All Rooms:** free movies. **Some Rooms:** radios, refrigerators. **Cards:** AE, DI, DS, MC, VI. **Special Amenities:** Early check-in/late check-out and free local telephone calls.

SUPER 8 MOTEL-ABSECON/ATLANTIC CITY   Phone: 609/652-2477

ⓐⓐⓐ SAVE	Fri & Sat 5/1-10/31	1P: $45- 120	2P/1B: $45- 120	2P/2B: $50- 125	XP: $5		F12
	Fri & Sat 11/1-4/30	1P: $45- 85	2P/1B: $45- 85	2P/2B: $50- 90	XP: $5		F12
◆◆	Sun-Thurs 5/1-10/31	1P: $35- 50	2P/1B: $35- 50	2P/2B: $40- 55	XP: $5		F12
Motel	Sun-Thurs 11/1-4/30	1P: $35- 45	2P/1B: $35- 45	2P/2B: $40- 50	XP: $5		F12

Location: Southbound 1.5 mi w on US 30 or 0.5 mi e of Garden State Pkwy, exit 40; northbound return to exit 40 by reversing direction through Absecon Rest Area. 229 E White Horse Pike (US 30) 08201. Fax: 609/748-0666. **Terms:** No pets. **Facility:** 57 rooms. 2 whirlpool rms, extra charge; max 4 persons per room; 2 stories; exterior corridors. **All Rooms:** free movies. **Cards:** AE, CB, DI, DS, MC, VI.

RESTAURANT

RAM'S HEAD INN RESTAURANT   **Lunch:** $10-$14   **Dinner:** $18-$36   Phone: 609/652-1700

ⓐⓐⓐ   **Location:** On US 30, 2.8 mi w of US 9, exit 40 off Garden State Pkwy (southbound). 9 W White Horse Pike 08201. **Hours:** noon-3 & 5-9:30 pm, Sat 5 pm-10 pm, Sun 1:30 pm-7:30 pm. Closed: 7/4, 9/1, 12/24 & Mon.

◆◆◆◆   **Reservations:** suggested. **Features:** semi-formal attire; children's menu; cocktails & lounge; valet parking; a la carte. Nicely landscaped grounds. Elegant dining rooms in converted mansion. **Cards:** AE, CB, DI, DS, MC, VI.

American

BARGAINTOWN—1,600

RESTAURANTS

COUSIN'S COUNTRY HOUSE   **Lunch:** $7-$11   **Dinner:** $13-$30   Phone: 609/927-5777

◆◆◆   **Location:** Jct Fire (CR 651) & Zion (CR 615) rds; GSP, exit 36, 1 mi s on CR 651. 3373 Bargaintown Rd 08234-5916. **Hours:** 11 am-2:30 & 3-10 pm, Fri & Sat-10:30 pm, Sun brunch 10:30 am-1:30 pm. Closed: 1/1, 12/24 & 12/25. **Reservations:** accepted. **Features:** dressy casual; children's menu; early bird specials; carryout; cocktails & lounge; entertainment. Upscale casual dining in 150 year old house surrounded by lovely gardens, ponds & fountains. Eclectic European influenced cuisine. **Cards:** AE, DI, MC, VI.

JULIANO'S RESTAURANT   **Lunch:** $4-$11   **Dinner:** $14-$20   Phone: 609/927-6363

◆◆   **Location:** Jct Zion Rd (CR 615) & Ocean Heights Ave (Alt CR 559). 2264 Ocean Heights Ave 08232.

Italian   **Hours:** 11:30 am-3 & 4-10 pm, Fri & Sat-11 pm. Closed: 11/26 & 12/25. **Reservations:** suggested. **Features:** casual dress; children's menu; early bird specials; carryout; cocktails & lounge. Family style dining, featuring seafood, veal, steak & pasta. Entrees can be served over any pasta dish. **Cards:** AE, MC, VI.

BUENA—4,400

LODGING

ECONO LODGE   Phone: 609/697-9000

ⓐⓐⓐ SAVE	Fri & Sat 5/1-11/1 [CP]	1P: $60	2P/1B: $60	2P/2B: $70	XP: $10		F17
	Fri & Sat 11/2-4/30 [CP]	1P: $50	2P/1B: $50	2P/2B: $60	XP: $10		F17
◆◆	Sun-Thurs [CP]	1P: $45	2P/1B: $45	2P/2B: $55	XP: $10		F17

Motel   **Location:** Jct SR 40 & SR 54. 146 Old Tuckahoe Rd 08310. Fax: 609/697-9000. **Terms:** Weekly rates; no pets. **Facility:** 45 rooms. Handling fee imposed; 2 stories; interior corridors. **Dining:** Restaurant nearby. **All Rooms:** free movies. **Some Rooms:** coffeemakers, radios, whirlpools. Fee: microwaves, refrigerators. **Cards:** AE, CB, DI, DS, JCB, MC, VI.

CARDIFF—500

LODGING

HOWARD JOHNSON
◆ ◆
Motel

Rates Subject to Change

Phone: 609/641-3131

5/1-9/9 [CP]	1P: $135	2P/1B: $135	2P/2B: $99	XP: $25	F17
9/10-1/1 [CP]	1P: $99	2P/1B: $99	2P/2B: $69	XP: $25	F17
1/2-4/30 [CP]	1P: $65	2P/1B: $65			

Location: Atlantic City Expwy exit 9, 1 mi e. 2580 Tilton Rd 08234. **Fax:** 609/641-0555. **Terms:** Sr. discount; check-in 4 pm; reserv deposit; no pets. **Facility:** 94 rooms. 2 stories; interior/exterior corridors. **All Rooms:** free movies. **Cards:** AE, DI, DS, MC, VI. *(See ad p 179)*

◄ ⊞ CTV ⊠ ◨ Ⓓ

HAMMONTON—12,200

LODGING

RAMADA INN OF HAMMONTON
◆ ◆ ◆
Motor Inn

Rates Subject to Change

Phone: 609/561-5700

2P/2B: $45- 95 XP: $10 F18

Location: Atlantic City Expwy exit 28, 3 mi n on SR 54, 1 mi e on SR 30. 308 White Horse Pike 08037. **Fax:** 609/561-2392. **Terms:** Sr. discount; reserv deposit; no pets. **Facility:** 103 rooms. 2 stories; exterior corridors. **Dining:** Restaurant; 7 am-11 pm; $6-$16. **Cards:** AE, DI, DS, MC, VI.

◄ CTV ⊠ Ⓓ

MAYS LANDING—2,100

LODGING

ABBOTT HOUSE BED & BREAKFAST
◆ ◆
Historic Bed
& Breakfast

Rates Subject to Change

Phone: 609/625-4400

2P/1B: $89 2P/2B: $99 XP: $15

Location: Just w of jct US 40 & SR 50. 6056 Main St 08330. **Terms:** Age restrictions may apply; reserv deposit, 7 day notice; no pets. **Facility:** 4 rooms. Handling fee imposed; 3 stories, no elevator; interior corridors; smoke free premises. **Cards:** AE, DS.

⊠ Ⓓ Ⓢ

NORTHFIELD—7,300

RESTAURANT

GIOVANNI'S, THE BEST OF ITALY
◆
Italian

Lunch: $4-$6   Dinner: $6-$13   Phone: 609/383-1155

Location: Garden State Pkwy exit 36, 0.3 mi n on Fire Rd, 1 mi e. 801 Tilton Ave 08225. **Hours:** 11 am-10:30 pm. Closed major holidays. **Features:** casual dress; children's menu; carryout.

PLEASANTVILLE—16,000

LODGINGS

COMFORT INN VICTORIAN
ⒶⒶⒶ ⓈⒶⓋⒺ
◆ ◆ ◆
Motel

Phone: 609/646-8880

All Year [CP]   1P: $60- 180 2P/1B: $60- 180 2P/2B: $60- 180 XP: $15   F12
Location: On US 40/322, 1 mi w of US 9; 1.7 mi e of Garden State Pkwy exit 36. 6817 Black Horse Pike 08234 (PO Box 739, EGG HARBOR TOWNSHIP, 08234-9176). **Fax:** 609/272-9176. **Terms:** No pets. **Facility:** 117 rooms. Comfortable, well-maintained rooms; voice mail. 2 stories; interior corridors; putting green; small pool. **Services:** Fee: coin laundry, area transportation, to casino. **Recreation:** jogging. **All Rooms:** coffeemakers, free & pay movies. **Some Rooms:** refrigerators. **Cards:** AE, CB, DI, DS, MC, VI. **Special Amenities:** Free breakfast and free room upgrade (subject to availability with advanced reservations). *(See color ad p 177)*

⊞ ⊕ CTV ⊠ Ⓓ

DAYS INN ATLANTIC CITY-PLEASANTVILLE
ⒶⒶⒶ ⓈⒶⓋⒺ
◆ ◆ ◆
Motel

Phone: 609/641-4500

5/1-12/31 [CP]   2P/2B: $49- 199 XP: $5   F12
1/1-4/30 [CP]   2P/2B: $49- 129 XP: $5   F12
Location: Exit 36 of Garden State Pkwy at Tilton Rd; on CR 563, just s of US 40. (6708 Tilton Rd, EGG HARBOR TOWNSHIP, 08234). **Fax:** 609/645-8295. **Terms:** Weekly/monthly rates; no pets. **Facility:** 117 rooms. 5 stories; interior corridors; designated smoking area. **Dining:** Restaurant nearby. **Services:** area transportation, to casino. Fee: coin laundry. **All Rooms:** free & pay movies. **Some Rooms:** coffeemakers, efficiency, microwaves, refrigerators. **Cards:** AE, CB, DI, DS, JCB, MC, VI. **Special Amenities:** Free breakfast. *(See ad p 173)*

◄ ⊞ ⊕ CTV ⊠ Ⓓ Ⓢ

HOLIDAY INN EXPRESS-ATLANTIC CITY WEST
◆ ◆ ◆
Motel

Rates Subject to Change

Phone: 609/484-1500

5/31-8/31 [CP]	1P: $118	2P/1B: $118	2P/2B: $118	XP: $25	F12
5/1-5/30 & 9/1-9/30 [CP]	1P: $99	2P/1B: $99	2P/2B: $99	XP: $25	F12
10/1-4/30 [CP]	1P: $79	2P/1B: $79	2P/2B: $79	XP: $25	F12

Location: On US Rt 40/322, 0.5 mi w of US Rt 9; 0.3 mi e of Garden State Pkwy, exit 36 northbound, exit 37 southbound. 6811 Black Horse Pike 08234. **Fax:** 609/645-9657. **Terms:** Sr. discount; check-in 4 pm; no pets. **Facility:** 196 rooms. 4 stories; interior corridors. **All Rooms:** free & pay movies. **Cards:** AE, CB, DI, DS, MC, VI. *(See ad p 179)*

◄ ⊞ CTV ⊠ ◨ Ⓓ Ⓢ

SHERATON HOTEL-ATLANTIC CITY WEST
◆ ◆ ◆
Hotel

Rates Subject to Change

Phone: 609/272-0200

5/1-10/29   1P: $129- 169 2P/1B: $129- 169 2P/2B: $129- 169 XP: $25   D12
10/30-4/30   1P: $99- 129 2P/1B: $99- 129 2P/2B: $99- 129 XP: $25   D12
Location: On US 40/322, 0.3 mi w of jct US 9; or 0.5 mi e of Garden State Pkwy, exit 36 northbound, exit 37 southbound. 6821 Black Horse Pike 08234. **Fax:** 609/646-3703. **Terms:** Sr. discount; check-in 4 pm; no pets. **Facility:** 213 rooms. 6 stories; interior corridors. **Dining:** Restaurant; 6:30 am-11 pm; $18-$25. **All Rooms:** free & pay movies. **Cards:** AE, CB, DI, DS, JCB, MC, VI. *(See ad p 179)*

◄ ⊞ CTV ⊠ ◨ Ⓓ Ⓢ

RESTAURANTS

EAST BAY CRAB & GRILLE
◆ ◆
Seafood

Lunch: $5-$7   Dinner: $11-$19   Phone: 609/272-7721

Location: On US 40 & 322, at Cardiff Circle; in Fashion Shopping Plaza. 6701 Black Horse Pk 08234. **Hours:** 11:30 am-10 pm, Fri & Sat-10:30 pm. Closed: 12/25. **Reservations:** accepted. **Features:** casual dress; children's menu; early bird specials; carryout; cocktails & lounge; a la carte. Bright, contemporary decor. Lively atmosphere. Specialties include seafood, steak, chicken & ribs; all-you-can-eat nights. **Cards:** AE, CB, DI, DS, MC, VI.

⊠

SHORE DINER
◆
Continental

Lunch: $5-$9   Dinner: $7-$18   Phone: 609/641-3669

Location: From Garden State Pkwy, exit 36. 6710 Tilton Rd 08234. **Hours:** 7 am-midnight. Closed: 12/25. **Features:** casual dress; children's menu; carryout; cocktails; a la carte. Casual, family dining, offering large portions. **Cards:** AE, DS, MC, VI.

SOMERS POINT—11,200

LODGING

RESIDENCE INN BY MARRIOTT AT GREATE BAY RESORT & COUNTRY CLUB   Phone: 609/927-6400

6/20-9/14 [CP]	2P/1B: $130	2P/2B: $176	XP: $10
5/1-6/19 & 9/15-11/14 [CP]	2P/1B: $117	2P/2B: $144	XP: $10
11/15-4/30 [CP]	2P/1B: $80	2P/2B: $107	XP: $10

Apartment Motel **Location:** 1 mi e of Garden State Pkwy, exit 30 (southbound only); 1 mi e of Garden State Pkwy, exit 29 (northbound only). 900 Mays Landing Rd 08244. Fax: 609/926-0145. **Terms:** Package plans; 2 night min stay, weekends in season; small pets only, $50 dep req. **Facility:** 119 rooms. Residential, townhouse atmosphere. Spacious units, some bi-level. Some units with fireplace. Complimentary evening hospitality hour with hors d'oeuvres Mon-Thurs 5-7 pm; 2 stories; exterior corridors. Fee: golf privileges. **Dining:** Restaurant nearby. **Services:** Fee: coin laundry. **All Rooms:** coffeemakers, kitchens, microwaves, free movies, refrigerators. **Some Rooms:** Fee: VCR's. **Cards:** AE, CB, DI, DS, MC, VI. **Special Amenities: Free breakfast and free newspaper.**

RESTAURANT

CRAB TRAP RESTAURANT   **Lunch:** $6-$11   **Dinner:** $11-$26   Phone: 609/927-7377

Steak and Seafood **Location:** Exit 30; 1.5 mi e of Garden State Pkwy (southbound) at Egg Harbor Toll Plaza North; jct SR 52 & CR 559; on the circle. 2 Broadway 08244. **Hours:** 11 am-10 pm, Fri & Sat-11 pm. Closed: 12/25. **Features:** casual dress; children's menu; early bird specials; cocktails & lounge; entertainment. Featuring a variety of seafood dishes & steak; homemade baked goods. Overlooking Great Egg Harbor Bay. Outdoor cocktail deck avail in season. **Cards:** AE, CB, DI, DS, MC, VI.

WEST ATLANTIC CITY—1,300

LODGINGS

BEST WESTERN BAYSIDE RESORT   Rates Subject to Change   Phone: 609/641-3546

6/1-8/31	1P: $75- 125	2P/1B: $75- 125	2P/2B: $75- 125	XP: $10 F16
9/1-10/31	1P: $65- 115	2P/1B: $65- 115	2P/2B: $65- 115	XP: $10 F16
5/1-5/31 & 4/1-4/30	1P: $55- 95	2P/1B: $55- 95	2P/2B: $55- 95	XP: $10 F16
11/1-3/31	1P: $45- 85	2P/1B: $45- 85	2P/2B: $45- 85	XP: $10 F16

Motor Inn **Location:** On US 40/322; 4 mi e of jct US 9; from Atlantic City Expwy exit 2, 1 mi w. 8029 Black Horse Pike 08232. Fax: 609/641-4329. **Terms:** Sr. discount; reserv deposit; no pets. **Facility:** 110 rooms. 2 stories; interior corridors; designated smoking area. **Dining:** Restaurant; 7 am-7 pm; $8-$10. **All Rooms:** free movies. **Cards:** AE, CB, DI, DS, MC, VI.

COMFORT INN-ATLANTIC CITY/WEST   Rates Subject to Change   Phone: 609/645-1818

7/2-8/31 [CP]	1P: $59- 149	2P/1B: $59- 149	2P/2B: $59- 149	XP: $10 F18
9/1-10/31 [CP]	1P: $55- 139	2P/1B: $55- 139	2P/2B: $55- 139	XP: $10 F18
5/1-7/1 [CP]	1P: $49- 129	2P/1B: $49- 129	2P/2B: $49- 129	XP: $10 F18
11/1-4/30 [CP]	1P: $35- 119	2P/1B: $35- 119	2P/2B: $35- 119	XP: $10 F18

Motel **Location:** On US 40/322, 3 mi e of jct US 9; e of Garden State Pkwy exit 36. 7095 Black Horse Pike 08232. Fax: 609/383-0228. **Terms:** Sr. discount; check-in 4 pm; no pets. **Facility:** 194 rooms. 2-3 stories; interior corridors. **Dining:** Coffee shop; 7 am-11 am, Sat & Sun-11:30 am. **All Rooms:** free & pay movies. **Cards:** AE, CB, DI, DS, MC, VI. *See ad p 172)*

RAMADA LIMITED-WEST ATLANTIC CITY   Phone: 609/646-5220

Fri & Sat [CP]	1P: $55- 195	2P/1B: $55- 195	2P/2B: $55- 195	XP: $15 F12
Sun-Thurs [CP]	1P: $35- 75	2P/1B: $35- 75	2P/2B: $35- 75	XP: $15 F12

Motel **Location:** On US 40/322; from Atlantic City Expy, exit 2, 1.3 mi w. 8037 Black Horse Pike 08232. Fax: 609/646-2802. **Terms:** Check-in 4 pm; weekly/monthly rates; package plans; no pets. **Facility:** 141 rooms. 5 stories; interior/exterior corridors. **Services:** Fee: coin laundry. **All Rooms:** free & pay movies. **Some Rooms:** Fee: refrigerators. **Cards:** AE, CB, DI, DS, MC, VI. **Special Amenities: Early check-in/late check-out and free breakfast.** *(See color ad p 177)*

ATLANTIC HIGHLANDS—4,600

RESTAURANT

HOFBRAUHAUS   **Dinner:** $19-$24   Phone: 732/291-0224

German **Location:** 301 Ocean Blvd 07716. **Hours:** 4 pm-10 pm, Sat & Sun noon-11 pm. Closed: 12/24 & 12/25. **Reservations:** suggested; weekends. **Features:** casual dress; children's menu; carryout; cocktails & lounge; a la carte. German motif inn perched high above the ocean serving Bavarian home-style cuisine, plus steak & seafood entrees. Also American entrees. Entertainment on weekends. **Cards:** AE, DI, MC, VI.

AVALON—1,800

RESTAURANT

TORTILLA FLATS   **Lunch:** $4-$9   **Dinner:** $6-$13   Phone: 609/967-5658

Mexican **Location:** Exit 13 off Garden State Pkwy, 3.5 mi se on CR 601, then 0.3 mi n. 2540 Dune Dr 08202. **Hours:** Open 5/1-11/30 & 4/1-4/30; noon-10 pm, Sat & Sun-11 pm. Closed: 4/12, 11/26 & 12/1-3/15. **Features:** casual dress; children's menu; carryout; street parking; a la carte. Great Mexican & Southwestern cuisine. Daily specials. Smoke free premises. **Cards:** AE, MC, VI.

AVON BY THE SEA—2,200

LODGINGS

ATLANTIC VIEW INN   Rates Subject to Change   Phone: 732/774-8505

5/15-9/15 [BP]	1P: $75- 150	2P/1B: $75- 160	2P/2B: $75- 160	XP: $35
5/1-5/14 & 9/16-4/30 [BP]	1P: $70- 110	2P/1B: $80- 120	2P/2B: $80- 120	XP: $30

Bed & Breakfast **Location:** From jct Ocean Ave, just w. 20 Woodland Ave 07717. Fax: 732/869-0187. **Terms:** Age restrictions may apply; reserv deposit; no pets, dog on premises. **Facility:** 12 rooms. 2 & 3 night min stay, weekends in season; 3 stories, no elevator; interior corridors; smoke free premises. **Dining:** Breakfast served 8-10:30 am. **Cards:** AE, MC, VI.

CASHELMARA BED & BREAKFAST INN   Rates Subject to Change   **Phone:** 732/776-8727
◆◆◆   All Year [BP]   1P: $75- 150   2P/1B: $75- 150   2P/2B: $75- 150   XP: $18
Bed &   **Location:** From Ocean Blvd, just w. 22 Lakeside Ave 07717. Fax: 732/988-5819. **Terms:** No pets, dog on
Breakfast   premises. **Facility:** 14 rooms. 2 whirlpool rms, extra charge; 3 stories; interior corridors; smoke free premises.
   Cards: AE, DS, MC, VI.   (CTV) (X) (D)

BARGAINTOWN—see Atlantic City & Vicinity p. 181.

BASKING RIDGE—3,100   (See map p. 206; index p. 205)

LODGING

OLDE MILL INN   Rates Subject to Change   **Phone:** 908/221-1100   [1]
◆◆◆   All Year [CP]   1P: $155   2P/1B: $165   2P/2B: $165   XP: $10   F5
Motor Inn   **Location:** Jct I-287, exit 30B (2nd ramp). 225 US 202 & N Maple Ave 07920. Fax: 908/221-1560. **Terms:** Sr.
   discount; no pets. **Facility:** 102 rooms. Whirlpool rm, extra charge; 2 stories; interior/exterior corridors.
Dining: The Grain House at the Olde Mill Inn, see separate listing. **All Rooms:** Fee: movies. **Some Rooms:** 4 efficiencies.
2 kitchens. **Cards:** AE, DI, DS, MC, VI.   (CTV) (X) (D)

RESTAURANT

THE GRAIN HOUSE AT THE
OLDE MILL INN   Historical   **Lunch:** $7-$11   **Dinner:** $11-$20   **Phone:** 908/221-1150   [1]
◆◆   **Location:** Jct I-287, exit 30B (2nd ramp); in Olde Mill Inn. US 202 & Maple Ave 07920. **Hours:** Mon-Sat
American   11:30 am-3 & 5-10 pm; Sun 10 am-2 & 5-9 pm. Closed: 12/25. **Reservations:** accepted; for 5 or more
   Features: casual dress; Sunday brunch; children's menu; health conscious menu items; carryout; cocktails &
lounge; a la carte. Historic, converted 1768 barn. Early American theme decor with fireplace. **Cards:** AE, DI, DS, MC, VI.
   (X)

BAY HEAD—1,200

LODGINGS

BAY HEAD GABLES   Rates Subject to Change   **Phone:** 732/892-9844
◆◆◆   6/11-9/15 [BP]   2P/1B: $100- 195
Bed &   5/1-6/10 & 9/16-12/31 [BP]   2P/1B: $95- 175
Breakfast   **Location:** N end on SR 35S. 200 Main Ave 08742. Fax: 732/295-2196. **Terms:** Open 5/1-12/31; age
   restrictions may apply; reserv deposit, 10 day notice; 2 night min stay; no pets. **Facility:** 11 rooms. Handling
fee imposed; 3 stories; interior corridors; smoke free premises. **Cards:** AE, DS, MC, VI.   (X) (D)

CONOVERS BAY HEAD INN   Rates Subject to Change   **Phone:** 732/892-4664
◆◆◆   All Year [BP]   2P/1B: $140- 225
Historic Bed   **Location:** Between Forsythe & Johnson sts on SR 35S. 646 Main Ave 08742. Fax: 732/892-8748
& Breakfast   **Terms:** Age restrictions may apply; reserv deposit, 14 day notice; 2 night min stay, weekends; no pets.
   Facility: 12 rooms. Handling fee imposed; 3 stories, no elevator; interior corridors; smoke free premises.
Cards: AE, MC, VI.   (X) (D)

GRENVILLE HOTEL   Rates Subject to Change   **Phone:** 732/892-3100
◆◆◆   5/29-9/30 [CP]   2P/1B: $90- 275   XP: $25
Historic   5/1-5/28, 10/1-11/1 &
Country Inn   4/1-4/30 [CP]   2P/1B: $65- 229   XP: $25
   11/2-3/31 [CP]   2P/1B: $60- 179   XP: $25
Location: SR 35S at Bridge Ave, just w of ocean. 345 Main Ave (SR 35) 08742. Fax: 732/892-0599. **Terms:** Reserv
deposit, 7 day notice; 2 night min stay, 6/1-9/30; no pets. **Facility:** 31 rooms. Handling fee imposed; 4 stories; interior corridors. **Dining:** Grenville by the Sea, see separate listing. **Cards:** AE, DI, DS, MC, VI.   (CTV) (D) (S)

RESTAURANT

GRENVILLE BY THE SEA   Historical   **Lunch:** $6-$10   **Dinner:** $16-$24   **Phone:** 732/892-3100
◆◆◆   **Location:** SR 35S at Bridge Ave, just w of ocean; in Grenville Hotel. 345 Main Ave 08742. **Hours:** 11:30
American   am-2:30 & 5-9 pm, Fri & Sat-9:30 pm, Sun brunch 10:30 am-2 pm. Closed: 12/25 & Mon except 7/1-8/31
   Reservations: suggested. **Features:** dressy casual; health conscious menu items; wine only; street parking;
a la carte. Quietly elegant yet relaxed dining room. Creative entrees including stellar in-house dessert. Renault Winery (New
Jersey) wines. **Cards:** AE, DI, DS, MC, VI.

BEACH HAVEN—1,500

LODGINGS

AMBER STREET INN   Rates Subject to Change   **Phone:** 609/492-161
◆◆◆   5/1-9/15 [CP]   2P/1B: $95- 165   XP: $10
Historic Bed   **Location:** 7 mi s on Long Beach Blvd (which becomes Bay Ave) from SR 72 causeway, then just e. 11
& Breakfast   Amber St 08008. Fax: 609/492-9165. **Terms:** Open 5/1-9/15; age restrictions may apply; reserv deposit, 1
   day notice; 2 night min stay, 7/1-8/30; no pets. **Facility:** 6 rooms. Open weekends only 2/1-4/30 & 9/15-11/30
3 stories, no elevator; interior corridors; smoke free premises. **Some Rooms:** A/C.   (X) (D)

ENGLESIDE INN   Rates Subject to Change   **Phone:** 609/492-125
(AAA)   5/24-5/26 & 6/12-9/8   2P/2B: $150- 299   XP: $12   F
   9/9-9/14   2P/2B: $92- 148   XP: $10   F
◆◆   5/27-6/11 & 9/15-12/31   2P/2B: $82- 142   XP: $10   F
Motor Inn   5/1-5/23 & 1/1-4/30   2P/2B: $75- 122   XP: $10   F
   Location: 7.3 mi s of SR 72 causeway to Engleside Ave, just e. 30 Engleside Ave 08008
Fax: 609/492-9175. **Terms:** Reserv deposit, 30 day notice, 30 days in season; 4 night min stay, weekends in season; pets
9/16-5/3 only; $10 extra charge. **Facility:** 72 rooms. 3 stories, no elevator; exterior corridors. **Dining:** Restaurant; 8 am-noo
& 5-9 pm; closed Mon & Tues for dinner off season; $8-$22. **Some Rooms:** 38 efficiencies. **Cards:** AE, DI, DS, MC, VI.
   Roll in showers.   (⌂) (🛏) (CTV) (X) (D)

JOLLY ROGER   Rates Subject to Change   **Phone:** 609/492-693
◆◆   5/20-9/7   2P/1B: $110- 130   2P/2B: $110- 130
Motel   9/8-9/30   2P/1B: $90- 110   2P/2B: $90- 110
   5/1-5/19, 10/1-12/31 &
   4/1-4/30   2P/1B: $65- 75   2P/2B: $65- 75
Location: SR 72 causeway, 9 mi s on Long Beach Blvd (which becomes Bay Ave). 5416 S Bay Ave 0800
Fax: 609/492-6676. **Terms:** Open 5/1-12/31 & 4/1-4/30; reserv deposit, 5 day notice; 3 night min stay, weekends in season
no pets. **Facility:** 12 rooms. 3 stories, no elevator; interior/exterior corridors. **Cards:** AE, MC, VI.   (CTV) (D)

SEA SPRAY MOTEL   Rates Subject to Change   **Phone:** 609/492-4944
ⒶⒶ   6/26-9/7   1P: $108- 132   2P/1B: $108- 132   2P/2B: $108- 132
            5/1-6/25 & 9/8-10/15   1P: $50- 60   2P/1B: $50- 60   2P/2B: $50- 60
◆◆   **Location:** From jct Rt 72 & Long Beach Blvd, 8.5 mi s. 2600 S Bay Ave 08008. **Fax:** 609/492-5824.
Motel   **Terms:** Open 5/1-10/15; reserv deposit, 14 day notice; no pets. **Facility:** 52 rooms. 2-3 night min stay in
          summer. Efficiencies & suites for up to 8 persons. 5 units with washer/dryer; 2 stories; exterior corridors.
All Rooms: free movies. **Some Rooms:** 11 efficiencies, 5 kitchens. **Cards:** AE, MC, VI.   🏊 ⓒⓣⓥ ✕ Ⓓ

RESTAURANT

THE GREEN GABLES INN & RESTAURANT   **Phone:** 609/492-3553
◆◆◆   **Location:** Just e of Long Beach Blvd. 212 Centre St 08008. **Hours:** seatings at 6 pm & 8:30 pm.
Nouvelle **Reservations:** required. **Features:** casual dress; street parking; prix fixe. Leisurely romantic dining in
American charming Victorian home. The menu changes frequently. Dietary restrictions catered to. Afternoon tea avail.
          Outdoor dining weather permitting. Smoke free premises. **Cards:** AE, MC, VI.   ✕

BEESLEYS POINT—900

RESTAURANT

TUCKAHOE INN RESTAURANT & TAVERN   **Lunch:** $4-$8   **Dinner:** $11-$21   **Phone:** 609/390-3322
◆◆   **Location:** On US 9, at the southern terminus of the Great Egg Harbor Beesley's Point Bridge. 1 Harbor Rd
American   & Rt 9 08223. **Hours:** 11 am-11 pm. Closed: 12/25. **Features:** casual dress; children's menu; early bird
          specials; carryout; cocktails & lounge. Overlooks scenic Great Egg Harbor; lively atmosphere & hearty
portioning; seasonal outdoor deck; weekend entertainment. **Cards:** AE, DS, MC, VI.   ✕

BELLMAWR—See Philadelphia & Vicinity p. 388.

BELMAR—5,900

LODGINGS

BELMAR MOTOR LODGE   Rates Subject to Change   **Phone:** 732/681-6600
◆   Fri & Sat 5/22-9/7   1P: $115   2P/1B: $115   2P/2B: $115   XP: $10   F12
Motel   Sun-Thurs 5/22-9/7   1P: $88   2P/1B: $88   2P/2B: $88   XP: $10   F12
          Fri & Sat 5/1-5/21   1P: $60- 70 2P/1B: $60- 70 2P/2B: $60- 70 XP: $10   F12
          Sun-Thurs 5/1-5/21 &
          9/8-4/30   1P: $50- 67 2P/1B: $50- 67 2P/2B: $50- 67 XP: $10   F12
Location: On SR 35; at 10th Ave, opposite Shark River Marina. 910 River Rd 07719. **Fax:** 732/681-6604. **Terms:** Sr.
discount; reserv deposit, 3 day notice; no pets. **Facility:** 55 rooms. 2 stories; interior corridors. **All Rooms:** free movies.
Cards: AE, DI, MC, VI.   🏊 ⓒⓣⓥ ✕ Ⓓ

DOWN THE SHORE BED & BREAKFAST   Rates Subject to Change   **Phone:** 732/681-9023
◆◆   5/15-9/12 [BP]   1P: $80- 90 2P/1B: $80- 90 2P/2B: $80- 90 XP: $20
Bed &   5/1-5/14 & 9/13-4/30 [BP] 1P: $55- 65 2P/1B: $55- 65 2P/2B: $55- 65 XP: $20
Breakfast **Location:** From jct Ocean Ave, just w. 201 Seventh Ave 07719-2204. **Fax:** 732/681-7795. **Terms:** Age
          restrictions may apply; reserv deposit, 14 day notice; small pets only. **Facility:** 3 rooms. Handling fee imposed;
2 stories; interior corridors; smoke free premises.   🐾 ✕ Ⓓ

THE INN AT THE SHORE   Guaranteed Rates   **Phone:** 732/681-3762
◆◆   5/1-9/30 [CP]   1P: $60- 120 2P/1B: $60- 120 2P/2B: $60- 120 XP: $20   F10
Historic Bed 10/1-4/30 [CP]   1P: $55- 90 2P/1B: $55- 90 2P/2B: $55- 90 XP: $20   F10
& Breakfast **Location:** Jct Ocean Ave, just w. 301 Fourth Ave 07719. **Fax:** 732/280-1914. **Terms:** Sr. discount; reserv
          deposit, 14 day notice; 2 night min stay, weekends 7/1-8/31; no pets. **Facility:** 12 rooms. 2 stories; interior cor-
ridors; designated smoking area. **All Rooms:** free movies. **Cards:** AE, MC, VI.   ⓒⓣⓥ ✕ Ⓓ

BERNARDSVILLE—6,600   (See map p. 206; index p. 205)

LODGING

THE BERNARDS INN   **Phone:** 908/766-0002   🔢
ⒶⒶ Ⓢ▲ⓥⒺ   All Year [CP]   2P/1B: $110- 210
          Location: Downtown; jct Mine Brook Rd (US 202) & Mt Airy Rd (CR 525), just s. 27 Mine Brook Rd 07924.
◆◆◆◆   **Fax:** 908/766-4604. **Terms:** Check-in 4 pm; no pets. **Facility:** 20 rooms. 3 stories, no elevator; interior corri-
Historic dors. **Dining:** Dining room, see separate listing. **All Rooms:** free movies. **Cards:** AE, CB, DI, MC, VI.
Country Inn   ⓒⓣⓥ Ⓓ Ⓢ

RESTAURANTS

THE BERNARDS INN   Historical   **Lunch:** $8-$14   **Dinner:** $25-$32   **Phone:** 908/766-0002   🔢
ⒶⒶ   **Location:** Downtown; jct Mine Brook Rd (US 202) & Mt Airy Rd (CR 525) just s; in The Bernards Inn. 27 Mine
          Brook Rd 07924. **Hours:** 11:30 am-3 & 5:30-10 pm, Fri & Sat-11 pm. Closed major holidays & Sun.
◆◆◆◆   **Features:** health conscious menu items; cocktails & lounge; entertainment; a la carte. Contemporary award
American winning progressive American cuisine with a French flair using top ingredients & emphasizing light, natural
          sauces. Excellent wine list. Jackets suggested. **Cards:** AE, DI, MC, VI.   ✕

ECCOQUI   **Lunch:** $10-$23   **Dinner:** $10-$23   **Phone:** 908/221-0040   🔢
◆◆◆   **Location:** Near center of town, just n. 107 Route 202 07920. **Hours:** 11:30 am-10 pm, Fri & Sat-11 pm, Sun
Italian   2 pm-9 pm, Sat noon-11 pm. Closed: 11/26 & 12/25. **Features:** health conscious menu items; carryout;
          cocktails & lounge. Casual but neat. High energy bistro. Colorful contemporary pizza & pasta from open
kitchen. Daily specials. **Cards:** AE, DI, MC, VI.   ✕

GIRAFE   **Lunch:** $9-$15   **Dinner:** $15-$28   **Phone:** 908/221-0017   🔢
◆◆◆   **Location:** I-287, exit 30B, 0.5 mi s on US 202. 95 Morristown Rd (US 202) 07920. **Hours:** 11:30 am-2 & 5-9
American pm, Fri & Sat-10 pm, Sun 4:30 pm-7:30 pm. Closed major holidays. **Reservations:** suggested. **Features:**
          health conscious menu; cocktails & lounge; a la carte. Jackets preferred. $15.95 3-course prixe
fixe lunch. **Cards:** AE, DI, MC, VI.   ✕

BLACKWOOD—See Philadelphia & Vicinity p. 388.

BORDENTOWN—See Philadelphia & Vicinity p. 388.

BRADLEY BEACH—4,500

RESTAURANT

LA NONNA PIANCONES   **Lunch:** $6-$11   **Dinner:** $9-$18   **Phone:** 732/775-0906
◆◆   **Location:** From jct SR 71 & SR 33, 0.5 mi s. 800-802 Main St 07720. **Hours:** 11:30 am-10 pm, Fri & Sat-11
Italian   pm, Sun 2 pm-9 pm. Closed: 1/1, 11/26 & 12/25. **Features:** casual dress; health conscious menu items;
carryout; cocktails & lounge; street parking; a la carte. New generation Italian cuisine. Specialty food shop &
bakery adjacent. Sun-Thurs early bird specials. Generous portions. Parking lot behind restaurant. **Cards:** AE, DI, DS, MC,
VI.

BRIDGEPORT—See Philadelphia & Vicinity p. 389.

BRIDGETON—18,900

LODGING

DAYS INN   Rates Subject to Change   **Phone:** 609/455-1500
◆◆   All Year [CP]   1P: $55   2P/1B: $55   2P/2B: $60   XP: $5   F12
Motel   **Location:** 1 mi e on SR 49. 500 E Broad St 08302. Fax: 609/451-1556. **Terms:** No pets. **Facility:** 31 rooms.
2 stories; exterior corridors. **All Rooms:** free movies. **Cards:** AE, DI, DS, MC, VI.   (CTV) (X) (D)

BROOKLAWN—See Philadelphia & Vicinity p. 389.

BUDD LAKE—7,300

RESTAURANT

BUDD LAKE DINER-RESTAURANT   **Lunch:** $7-$19   **Dinner:** $7-$19   **Phone:** 204/691-9100
◆   **Location:** I-80, exit 26 westbound, 0.5 mi w; eastbound exit 27, make U-turn, just w. 120 US 46W 07828.
American   **Hours:** 24 hours. Closed: 12/25. **Features:** children's menu; carryout; minimum charge-$13. Daily specials.
Extensive menu. **Cards:** AE, MC, VI.   (X)

BUENA—See Atlantic City & Vicinity p. 181.

BURLINGTON—See Philadelphia & Vicinity p. 389.

CALDWELL—7,500   (See map p. 206; index p. 205)

RESTAURANT

MEZZANOTTE   **Lunch:** $9-$22   **Dinner:** $12-$24   **Phone:** 973/403-8500   (155)
◆◆◆   **Location:** I-280, exit 7, 1.5 mi n to Bloomfield Ave; 1.5 m w. 115 Bloomfield Ave 07006. **Hours:** 11:30
Italian   am-2:30 & 5-10 pm, Mon from 5 pm, Wed & Thurs-10:30 pm, Fri & Sat 5 pm-11 pm & Sun 4 pm-10 pm.
Closed: 11/26, 12/24 & 12/25. **Features:** casual dress; carryout; valet parking; a la carte. Upscale open
kitchen style. Chic, modern decor. Contemporary Italian dishes featuring fresh fish, veal, pork & pasta. Chicken Mezzanotte
is a signature dish. Own desserts. **Cards:** AE, DI, MC, VI.

CAPE MAY—4,700

LODGINGS

THE ABBEY BED & BREAKFAST   Guaranteed Rates   **Phone:** 609/884-4506
◆◆◆   6/15-9/30 [BP]   1P: $100- 280   2P/1B: $100- 280 2P/2B: $100- 280
Historic Bed   5/1-6/14, 10/1-1/1 & 4/1-4/30
& Breakfast   [BP]   1P: $80- 175   2P/1B: $80- 175 2P/2B: $80- 175
Location: Center, just w of Beach Ave. 34 Gurney St at Columbia Ave 08204. Fax: 609/884-2379.
Terms: Open 5/1-1/1 & 4/1-4/30; age restrictions may apply; reserv deposit, 30 day notice; no pets. **Facility:** 14 rooms. 3- tc
4-night min stay weekends 6/15-9/30. Open weekends only 11/1-12/31. Handling fee imposed; 3 stories, no elevator; interior
corridors; smoke free premises. **Some Rooms:** A/C. **Cards:** DS, MC, VI.   (X) (D)

THE BRASS BED INN
◆◆   Historic Bed & Breakfast   Rates Subject to Change   Phone: 609/884-2302

6/16-9/15 [BP]	2P/1B:	$95- 165	2P/2B:	$95- 165
5/1-6/15 & 4/1-4/30 [BP]	2P/1B:	$95- 130	2P/2B:	$95- 130
9/16-12/31 [BP]	2P/1B:	$85- 130	2P/2B:	$85- 130
2/1-3/31 [BP]	2P/1B:	$75- 120	2P/2B:	$75- 120

Location: Center. 719 Columbia Ave 08204. Fax: 609/884-2296. **Terms:** Open 5/1-12/31 & 2/1-4/30; age restrictions may apply; reserv deposit, 7 day notice; no pets. **Facility:** 9 rooms. 3 night min stay weekends, 2 night min stay weekends off season. Handling fee imposed; 3 stories, no elevator; interior corridors; smoke free premises. **Some Rooms:** A/C. **Cards:** MC, VI. ⊗ D

CARROLL VILLA BED & BREAKFAST
AAA   ◆◆   Historic Country Inn   Rates Subject to Change   Phone: 609/884-9619

	1P	2P/1B	2P/2B	XP
9/19-1/5 [BP]	1P: $68- 135	2P/1B: $78- 145	2P/2B: $145	XP: $20
5/22-9/18 [BP]	1P: $88- 150	2P/1B: $98- 160	2P/2B: $140	XP: $20
5/1-5/21 [BP]	1P: $68- 130	2P/1B: $78- 160	2P/2B: $140	XP: $20
1/6-4/30 [BP]	1P: $58- 120	2P/1B: $68- 130	2P/2B: $130	XP: $20

Location: Just w of Beach Ave. 19 Jackson St 08204. Fax: 609/884-0264. **Terms:** Reserv deposit, 10 day notice; 2 night min stay, weekends & 7/1-8/31; no pets. **Facility:** 22 rooms. Handling fee imposed; 3 stories, no elevator; interior corridors; smoke free premises. **Dining:** Dining room; 8 am-2:30 & 5:30-10 pm; hours may vary off season; also, The Mad Batter Restaurant, see separate listing. **Cards:** AE, DI, DS, MC, VI. *(See color ad p 186)* CTV ⊗ D S

COLVMNS BY THE SEA
◆◆◆   Historic Bed & Breakfast   Rates Subject to Change   Phone: 609/884-2228

	1P	2P/1B	2P/2B	XP	
All Year [BP]	1P: $130- 215	2P/1B: $140- 225	2P/2B: $175- 225	XP: $40	F18

Location: Between Baltimore & Brooklyn aves. 1513 Beach Dr 08204. Fax: 609/884-4789. **Terms:** Sr. discount; age restrictions may apply; reserv deposit, 30 day notice; 3 night min stay, 7/1-8/31; no pets. **Facility:** 11 rooms. Handling fee imposed; 3 stories, no elevator; interior corridors; smoke free premises. **All Rooms:** no A/C. **Cards:** MC, VI. ECTV ⊗ D S

GINGERBREAD HOUSE
◆◆◆   Historic Bed & Breakfast   Rates Subject to Change   Phone: 609/884-0211

	1P	2P/1B	2P/2B	XP
6/16-9/15 [CP]	1P: $108- 150	2P/1B: $118- 190	2P/2B: $118- 190	XP: $25
Thurs-Sun 5/1-6/15, 9/16-12/31 & 4/1-4/30 [CP]	1P: $105- 150	2P/1B: $115- 170	2P/2B: $115- 170	XP: $25
Mon-Wed 5/1-6/15, 9/16-12/31 & 4/1-4/30 [CP]	1P: $65- 125	2P/1B: $70- 145	2P/2B: $70- 145	XP: $25

Location: Center, just w of Beach Ave. 28 Gurney St 08204. Fax: 609/884-1825. **Terms:** Open 5/1-12/31 & 4/1-4/30; age restrictions may apply; reserv deposit; no pets. **Facility:** 6 rooms. 2-4 night min stay when weekend included. Handling fee imposed; 3 stories, no elevator; interior corridors; smoke free premises. **Some Rooms:** A/C. **Cards:** MC, VI. ⊗ D

HERITAGE MOTOR INN
AAA   ◆◆   Motel   Rates Subject to Change   Phone: 609/884-7300

	2P/1B	2P/2B	XP
6/26-9/7	2P/1B: $125- 140	2P/2B: $125- 175	XP: $15
6/12-6/25 & 9/8-9/26	2P/1B: $90- 115	2P/2B: $90- 115	XP: $15
5/29-6/11 & 9/27-10/11	2P/1B: $74- 90	2P/2B: $74- 90	XP: $15
5/1-5/28 & 10/12-1/4	2P/1B: $56- 80	2P/2B: $56- 80	XP: $15

Location: At Stockton Pl, opposite Convention Hall facing ocean. 721 Beach Dr 08204. Fax: 609/884-7566. **Terms:** Open 5/1-1/4; reserv deposit, 21 day notice; 3 night min stay, 7/1-9/30; no pets. **Facility:** 21 rooms. 7 efficiencies 6/27-9/7 $155-$165 for up to 4 persons; weekend nights, $10 extra charge. Handling fee imposed; 2 stories; exterior corridors. **Cards:** AE, DS, MC, VI. ECTV D

HERITAGE SOUTHWINDS
AAA   ◆◆   Motel   Rates Subject to Change   Phone: 609/884-7300

	2P/1B	2P/2B	XP
6/26-9/7	2P/1B: $115- 130	2P/2B: $115- 175	XP: $15
6/12-6/25 & 9/8-9/26	2P/1B: $85- 110	2P/2B: $85- 110	XP: $15
5/29-6/11 & 9/27-10/11	2P/1B: $69- 85	2P/2B: $69- 85	XP: $15
5/1-5/28, 10/12-1/4 & 4/3-4/30	2P/1B: $51- 75	2P/2B: $51- 75	XP: $15

Location: Just off Beach Dr. 14 Patterson Ave 08204. Fax: 609/884-7566. **Terms:** Open 5/1-1/4 & 4/3-4/30; reserv deposit, 21 day notice; 3 night min stay, in season; no pets. **Facility:** 17 rooms. 10 efficiencies 6/27-9/7, $155-$165 for up to 4 persons; 2 bedroom units, $550-$925 weekly; weekend nights, $10 extra charge. Handling fee imposed; 2 stories; exterior corridors. **Some Rooms:** A/C. **Cards:** AE, DS, MC, VI. D

THE INN ON OCEAN
AAA   ◆◆◆   Historic Bed & Breakfast   Rates Subject to Change   Phone: 609/884-7070

	1P	2P/1B	2P/2B
5/1-12/31 & 2/14-4/30 [BP]	1P: $99- 295	2P/1B: $99- 295	2P/2B: $99- 295

Location: Just w of Beach Ave. 25 Ocean St 08204. Fax: 609/884-1384. **Terms:** Open 5/1-12/31 & 2/14-4/30; age restrictions may apply; reserv deposit; no pets. **Facility:** 5 rooms. Handling fee imposed; 3 stories, no elevator; interior corridors; smoke free premises. **Cards:** AE, CB, DI, DS, MC, VI. ECTV ⊗ D

LA MER MOTOR INN
AAA   ◆◆◆   Motor Inn   Rates Subject to Change   Phone: 609/884-9000

	2P/1B	2P/2B	XP
6/26-9/7	2P/1B: $120- 136	2P/2B: $136- 161	XP: $15
6/12-6/25 & 9/8-9/20	2P/1B: $100- 118	2P/2B: $118- 138	XP: $15
5/22-6/11 & 9/21-10/20	2P/1B: $68- 89	2P/2B: $89- 114	XP: $15
5/1-5/21	2P/1B: $60- 70	2P/2B: $70- 85	XP: $15

Location: At Pittsburgh Ave. 1317 Beach Ave 08204. Fax: 609/884-5004. **Terms:** Open 5/1-10/20; reserv deposit, 14 day notice; 3 night min stay, 6/15-9/30; no pets. **Facility:** 67 rooms. 18 efficiencies, $153-$159 in season, weekends $15 extra per night. Handling fee imposed; 1-2 stories; exterior corridors. **Dining:** Dining room; also, Waters Edge Restaurant, see separate listing. **Cards:** AE, CB, DI, DS, MC, VI. ⊋ ECTV D

THE MAINSTAY
◆◆◆   Bed & Breakfast   Rates Subject to Change   Phone: 609/884-8690

	2P/1B	2P/2B	XP
All Year [BP]	2P/1B: $145- 250	2P/2B: $160- 320	XP: $35

Location: At Stockton Pl; just n of Ocean St. 635 Columbia Ave 08204. **Terms:** Age restrictions may apply; reserv deposit, 60 day notice; 3 night min stay, weekends 6/1-9/30; no pets. **Facility:** 16 rooms. Handling fee imposed; 2-3 stories, no elevator; interior corridors; smoke free premises. **Some Rooms:** A/C. ECTV ⊗ D

MANOR HOUSE
◆◆◆   Historic Bed & Breakfast   Rates Subject to Change   Phone: 609/884-4710

	2P/1B
5/1-12/31 & 2/1-4/30 [BP]	2P/1B: $82- 225

Location: Between Ocean & Franklin sts. 612 Hughes St 08204. Fax: 609/898-0471. **Terms:** Open 5/1-12/31 & 2/1-4/30; age restrictions may apply; 3 night min stay, 7/1-8/31; no pets. **Facility:** 10 rooms. 3 stories, no elevator; interior corridors; designated smoking area. **Cards:** DS, MC, VI. CTV ⊗ D

MARQUIS DE LAFAYETTE HOTEL

Phone: 609/884-3500

(AAA) [SAVE]

◆ ◆

Motor Inn

5/28-10/23 [BP]	1P: $300	2P/1B: $308	2P/2B: $308	XP: $18
5/1-5/27 [BP]	1P: $158	2P/1B: $161	2P/2B: $166	XP: $18
10/24-1/1 [BP]	1P: $124	2P/1B: $132	2P/2B: $132	XP: $18
1/2-4/30 [BP]	1P: $114	2P/1B: $124	2P/2B: $124	XP: $18

Location: Between Decatur & Ocean sts. 501 Beach Dr 08204 (PO Box 31). Fax: 609/884-0669. **Terms:** Check-in 4 pm; reserv deposit, 10 day notice; package plans; pets, $20 extra charge, $50 dep req. **Facility:** 73 rooms. Unique Victorian-style decor in traditional hotel rooms, efficiencies & suites. All units overlooking the ocean, with patio or balcony; rocking chairs provided. Handling fee imposed; 3-6 stories; interior/exterior corridors; sauna. **Dining & Entertainment:** Restaurant; 8 am-9 pm, to 10 pm in season; $9-$30; cocktails/lounge; also, Top of The Marq, see separate listing. **Services:** Fee: coin laundry. **All Rooms:** coffeemakers, free movies. **Some Rooms:** 43 efficiencies, refrigerators. **Cards:** AE, DS, MC, VI. **Special Amenities: Free breakfast and free room upgrade (subject to availability with advanced reservations).**

MONTREAL INN

Rates Subject to Change

Phone: 609/884-7011

(AAA)

◆ ◆ ◆

Apartment
Motor Inn

6/12-9/6	2P/1B: $80- 159	2P/2B: $80- 159	XP: $9
5/22-6/11 & 9/7-9/26	2P/1B: $55- 120	2P/2B: $55- 120	XP: $6
5/8-5/21 & 9/27-10/12	2P/1B: $45- 89	2P/2B: $45- 89	XP: $6
5/1-5/7, 10/13-11/24 & 3/8-4/30	2P/1B: $37- 80	2P/2B: $37- 80	XP: $6

Location: At Madison Ave. 1028 Beach Ave 08204. Fax: 609/884-4559. **Terms:** Open 5/1-11/24 & 3/8-4/30; reserv deposit, 14 day notice; no pets. **Facility:** 70 rooms. Handling fee imposed; 4 stories; exterior corridors. **Dining:** Restaurant; 8 am-10 pm 5/15-10/15;; $9-$23. **All Rooms:** free movies. **Cards:** AE, DI, DS, MC, VI.

PERIWINKLE INN

Rates Subject to Change

Phone: 609/884-9200

(AAA)

◆ ◆ ◆

Motel

6/26-9/7	2P/1B: $128- 159	2P/2B: $156- 178	XP: $15
6/9-6/25	2P/1B: $105- 123	2P/2B: $98- 129	XP: $15
5/26-6/8	2P/1B: $68- 90	2P/2B: $85- 95	XP: $15
5/1-5/25, 9/8-10/18 & 4/4-4/30	2P/1B: $54- 75	2P/2B: $69- 79	XP: $15

Location: Between Madison & Philadelphia aves. 1039 Beach Ave 08204 (PO Box 220). **Terms:** Open 5/1-10/18 & 4/4-4/30; reserv deposit, 14 day notice; 3 night min stay, in season; no pets. **Facility:** 50 rooms. Handling fee imposed; 3 stories; exterior corridors. **Some Rooms:** 14 efficiencies.

QUEENS HOTEL

Guaranteed Rates

Phone: 609/884-1613

(AAA)

◆ ◆ ◆

Historic Hotel

6/19-9/13	1P: $150- 230	2P/1B: $160- 240	2P/2B: $250	XP: $25
5/1-6/18 & 9/14-12/31	1P: $80- 205	2P/1B: $90- 215	2P/2B: $160- 210	XP: $25
1/1-4/30	1P: $65- 175	2P/1B: $75- 185	2P/2B: $135- 180	XP: $25

Location: Center, at Ocean St, just w of Beach Ave. 601 Columbia Ave 08204. **Terms:** Reserv deposit, 21 day notice; no pets. **Facility:** 9 rooms. 2 night min stay weekends 11/1-3/31; 3 night min stay 4/1-10/31. Handling fee imposed; 3 stories, no elevator; interior corridors; smoke free premises. **Cards:** MC, VI. *(See color ad below)*

THE QUEEN VICTORIA

Guaranteed Rates

Phone: 609/884-8702

(AAA)

◆ ◆ ◆

Historic Bed
& Breakfast

6/19-9/13 [BP]	1P: $170- 270	2P/1B: $180- 270	2P/2B: $195- 270	XP: $25
5/1-6/18 & 9/14-12/31 [BP]	1P: $100- 225	2P/1B: $110- 235	2P/2B: $125- 235	XP: $25
1/1-4/30 [BP]	1P: $80- 200	2P/1B: $100- 210	2P/2B: $100- 210	XP: $25

Location: Center, between Hughes & Columbia sts; just w of Beach Dr. 102 Ocean St 08204. **Terms:** Reserv deposit, 21 day notice; no pets. **Facility:** 23 rooms. 2-3 night min stay weekends. Handling fee imposed; 3 stories, no elevator; interior/exterior corridors; smoke free premises. **Cards:** MC, VI.

(See color ad below)

WE GO TOGETHER!

See the sights near your overnight lodging.
The front of this TourBook shows the way.

SEA CREST INN
Rates Subject to Change
Phone: 609/884-4561

(AAA)
6/18-9/6
2P/1B: $109- 224 2P/2B: $129- 249 XP: $21

6/4-6/17 & 9/7-9/19
2P/1B: $85- 199 2P/2B: $88- 199 XP: $24

◆◆◆
5/1-6/3, 9/20-10/30 &

Motel
4/15-4/30
2P/1B: $75- 150 2P/2B: $78- 160 XP: $24

10/31-11/15
2P/1B: $57- 90 2P/2B: $66- 99 XP: $24

Location: Between Patterson & Broadway aves. 101 Beach Ave 08204. Fax: 609/898-9675. **Terms:** Open 5/1-11/15 & 4/15-4/30; reserv deposit, 14 day notice; no pets. **Facility:** 55 rooms. 2-3 night min stay some weekends. Handling fee imposed; 4 stories; exterior corridors. **All Rooms:** efficiencies. **Cards:** CB, DI, DS, MC, VI. *(See color ad below)*

(⇔) (ECTV) (D)

THE SOUTHERN MANSION
Phone: 609/884-7171

(AAA) (SAVE)
Sun-Thurs 5/1-10/31 & Fri &

Sat [CP]
1P: $175- 350 2P/1B: $175- 350 2P/2B: $175- 350 XP: $35

◆◆◆
Sun-Thurs 11/1-4/30 [CP]
1P: $75- 195 2P/1B: $75- 195 2P/2B: $75- 195 XP: $35

Historic Bed & Breakfast
Location: Jct Jefferson & Washington sts. 720 Washington St 08204. Fax: 609/898-0492. **Terms:** Reserv deposit, 21 day notice; 2 night min stay, weekends; no pets. **Facility:** 24 rooms. 1863 American bracketed Villa style home designed by Samuel Sloan, furnished with Roccoco antiques & reproductions; private guest dining room serves breakfast, lunch & dinner. Handling fee imposed; 4 stories, no elevator; interior/exterior corridors; smoke free premises; lawn games. **Dining:** Dining room nearby. **Services:** valet laundry. **All Rooms:** refrigerators, combo or shower baths. **Some Rooms:** VCR's. **Cards:** AE, MC, VI. *(See color ad below)*

(📶) (ECTV) (✕) (D) (S)

VICTORIAN LACE INN
Rates Subject to Change
Phone: 609/884-1772

◆◆
7/1-8/31 Weekly [EP]
2P/1B: $875-1200 2P/2B: $875-1200

Historic Bed & Breakfast
5/1-6/30, 9/1-10/18 &

4/1-4/30 Daily [BP]
2P/1B: $95- 200 2P/2B: $95- 200 XP: $20 F10

Location: At Jefferson St, just w of Beach Ave. 901 Stockton Ave 08204. **Terms:** Open 5/1-10/18 & 4/1-4/30; reserv deposit; 2 night min stay, weekends; no pets. **Facility:** 4 rooms. Also open 12/1-12/15, $95-$180 for up to 2 persons; 2-3 stories, no elevator; interior/exterior corridors; smoke free premises. **All Rooms:** A/C.
Some Rooms: A/C.

(ECTV) (✕) (D)

WHITE DOVE COTTAGE
Phone: 609/884-0613

(AAA) (SAVE)
6/11-9/9 [BP]
1P: $110- 200 2P/1B: $125- 215 XP: $25

◆◆◆
5/1-6/10, 9/10-12/31 &

3/27-4/30 [BP]
1P: $90- 170 2P/1B: $105- 195 XP: $25

Historic Bed & Breakfast
1/1-3/26 [BP]
1P: $85- 165 2P/1B: $100- 180 XP: $25

Location: Between Ocean & Franklin sts. 619 Hughes St 08204. **Terms:** Age restrictions may apply; reserv deposit, 21 day notice; weekly rates; package plans; 2 night min stay, in season & weekends; no pets. **Facility:** 6 rooms. 1866 'second empire'-style residence. Owner displays a unique, extensive teddy bear collection in main parlor. Handling fee imposed; 3 stories, no elevator; interior/exterior corridors; smoke free premises; beach passes & beach chairs. **All Rooms:** free movies, safes, shower baths, no phones. **Some Rooms:** refrigerators, whirlpools. **Special Amenities: Free newspaper and free room upgrade (subject to availability with advanced reservations).**

(CTV) (✕) (D)

RESTAURANTS

AXELSSONS'S BLUE CLAW RESTAURANT   **Dinner:** $20-$25   **Phone:** 609/884-5878
⬥⬥⬥ (AAA)   **Location:** From southern terminus of Garden State Pkwy 1.3 mi e on CR 621 (Ocean Dr). 991 Ocean Dr
08204. **Hours:** 5 pm-10 pm. Closed: Mon-Thurs 10/1-4/20, Mon-Wed 4/21-6/14, also Sun 11/1-4/10 except
Steak and   holidays. **Reservations:** suggested. **Features:** dressy casual; children's menu; cocktails & lounge. Fine
Seafood   dining with a view of the working fishing fleet; specializing in seafood, chicken, veal, pasta & Black Angus
beef; game specialties occasionally avail; the Clippership Pub exemplifies northern European pub tradition.
Cards: DI, MC, VI.   ✕

410 BANK STREET Historical   **Dinner:** $25-$35   **Phone:** 609/884-2127
⬥⬥⬥   **Location:** Just w of the mall, between Broad & Lafayette Sts. 410 Bank St 08204. **Hours:** Open 5/15-10/14;
Seafood   5 pm-10:30 pm. **Reservations:** suggested. **Features:** dressy casual; a la carte. Bustling, informal ambience
in a restored 1840 carriage house. Upscale menu with some New Orleans-style influences; market-fresh
seafood & prime steak. No alcohol served; BYOB. **Cards:** AE, DI, DS, MC, VI.   ✕

FRESCOS Historical   **Dinner:** $20-$30   **Phone:** 609/884-0366
⬥⬥⬥   **Location:** Just w of the mall, between Broad & Lafayette sts. 412 Bank St 08204. **Hours:** Open 5/1-10/15 &
Italian   4/1-4/15; 5 pm-10 pm. **Reservations:** suggested. **Features:** dressy casual; children's menu; a la carte.
Excellent northern & regional Italian cuisine; homemade pasta, fresh seafood & dessert made on premises.
Cozy candle lit setting in a restored 1880 Victorian cottage. No alcohol served; BYOB. Smoke free premises. **Cards:** AE, DI,
DS, MC, VI.   ✕

LOBSTER HOUSE   **Lunch:** $5-$12   **Dinner:** $16-$38   **Phone:** 609/884-8296
(AAA)   **Location:** At the wharf; e of s end of Cold Spring Bridge. Fisherman's Wharf 08204. **Hours:** 11:30 am-3 &
5-10 pm, 6/19-9/30 11:30 am-3 & 4:30-10 pm, Sun 2 pm-9 pm, 4/6-9/30, 4 pm-10 pm. Closed: 11/26, 12/24
⬥⬥   & 12/25. **Features:** casual dress; children's menu; carryout; cocktails & lounge. Overlooking harbor. Fresh
Seafood   fish market on property. **Cards:** AE, DS, MC, VI.

THE MAD BATTER RESTAURANT Historical   **Lunch:** $8-$10   **Dinner:** $15-$23   **Phone:** 609/884-5970
(AAA) SAVE   **Location:** Just w of Beach Ave; at Carroll Villa Bed & Breakfast. 19 Jackson St 08204. **Hours:** 8 am-2:30 &
5:30-10 pm. Closed: 11/26, 12/25 & 1/3-1/15. **Reservations:** suggested; for dinner. **Features:** casual dress;
⬥⬥⬥   children's menu; carryout; street parking; a la carte. Eclectic menu featuring homemade bread & dessert;
American informal service, casual ambience. 1882 Victorian hotel, now a bed-and-breakfast. **Cards:** AE, DS, MC, VI.
Special Value: $1 off the price of a dinner entree. *(See color ad p 186)*   ✕

MERION INN Historical   **Lunch:** $6-$13   **Dinner:** $14-$32   **Phone:** 609/884-8363
(AAA)   **Location:** Center; at jct Decatur St & Columbia Ave. 106 Decatur St 08204. **Hours:** Open 5/1-12/31 &
4/5-4/30; noon-2:30 & 5-10 pm. Closed: Mon-Thurs off season. **Reservations:** suggested. **Features:** dressy
⬥⬥⬥   casual; children's menu; early bird specials; cocktails & lounge. Specializing in fresh traditional seafood
Steak and entrees, char-grilled steak & classic cocktails. Desserts prepared from own recipes. Victorian atmosphere.
Seafood   Wed-Sat in season, late night menu & live entertainment. **Cards:** AE, CB, DI, DS, MC, VI.   ✕

THE PETER SHIELDS RESTAURANT   **Lunch:** $8-$13   **Dinner:** $17-$24   **Phone:** 609/884-6491
⬥⬥⬥   **Location:** At Beach Dr & Trenton Ave. 1301 Beach Dr 08204. **Hours:** 5 pm-10 pm, Sun 10 am-2 pm.
American Closed: 12/25. **Reservations:** suggested. **Features:** dressy casual; Sunday brunch; health conscious menu
items; wine only. Classically elegant dining amidst the romantic ambience provided by this large
turn-of-century colonial Georgian style mansion. **Cards:** AE, CB, DI, DS, MC, VI.   ✕

PILOT HOUSE   **Lunch:** $5-$15   **Dinner:** $5-$23   **Phone:** 609/884-3449
⬥⬥   **Location:** At jct of Carpenters Ln & Decatur St; on Washington St Mall. 142 Decatur St 08204. **Hours:** 11:30
Steak and am-11 pm. Closed: 11/26, 12/25 & 12/26. **Reservations:** suggested. **Features:** casual dress; children's
Seafood   menu; early bird specials; carryout; cocktails & lounge; street parking. In the center of Victorian Historic
District. Fireside or patio dining. **Cards:** AE, DS, MC, VI.   ✕

SPIAGGI RESTAURANT   **Dinner:** $14-$24   **Phone:** 609/884-3504
⬥⬥⬥   **Location:** At jct Beach Dr & Decatur St. 429 Beach Dr 08204. **Hours:** Open 5/1-10/30; 5 pm-10 pm. Closed:
Regional Mon. **Reservations:** suggested. **Features:** casual dress; cocktails & lounge; minimum charge-$14; street
Italian   parking. Regional Italian cuisine prepared with a creative flair. Porch dining area offers a terrific view of the
ocean & beach, lending itself to a decidedly grown-up audience. Age restrictions apply. Smoke free
premises. **Cards:** AE, DI, DS, MC, VI.   ✕

TOP OF THE MARQ   **Dinner:** $14-$30   **Phone:** 609/884-3500
(AAA)   **Location:** Between Decatur & Ocean sts; in Marquis de Lafayette Hotel. 501 Beach Dr 08204. **Hours:** 5:30
pm-9 pm, to 10 pm in season. Closed: Mon-Thurs 10/15-5/7. **Reservations:** accepted. **Features:** casual
⬥⬥⬥   dress; children's menu; early bird specials; cocktails & lounge. Excellent view of the ocean. **Cards:** AE, CB,
American DI, DS, MC, VI.   ✕

THE WASHINGTON INN Historical   **Dinner:** $18-$27   **Phone:** 609/884-5697
(AAA)   **Location:** Center. 801 Washington St 08204. **Hours:** 5 pm-10 pm; Wed-Sun 11/1-4/30 5 pm-9 pm. Closed:
11/26, 12/24, 12/25 & 1/4-2/16. **Reservations:** suggested. **Features:** cocktails & lounge; street parking; a la
⬥⬥⬥   carte. An 1848 colonial plantation home. Wine cellar with extensive collection of wines. Upscale casual
American atmosphere. **Cards:** AE, CB, DI, DS, MC, VI.   ✕

WATERS EDGE RESTAURANT   **Dinner:** $17-$26   **Phone:** 609/884-1717
⬥⬥⬥   **Location:** At Pittsburgh Ave; in La Mer Motor Inn. 1317 Beach Ave 08204. **Hours:** 5 pm-10 pm, Fri & Sat-11
American pm 7/1-8/31. Closed: 11/26, Mon-Thurs 10/15-4/1, Tues 4/1-6/30 & 9/15-10/14. **Reservations:** suggested.
Features: dressy casual; Sunday brunch; children's menu; carryout; cocktails & lounge; street parking. a la
carte. Outstanding view of the ocean from both the casually elegant dining room & outdoor terrace. Extensive list of wines
by the glass. **Cards:** AE, CB, DI, DS, MC, VI.   ✕

CAPE MAY COURT HOUSE—4,500

LODGINGS

THE DOCTORS INN AT KINGS GRANT   Rates Subject to Change   **Phone:** 609/463-9330
◆◆◆   5/15-9/9 [BP]   1P: $135- 170   2P/1B: $135- 175   XP: $20   D14
Historic   5/1-5/14 & 9/10-4/30 [BP]   1P: $115- 150   2P/1B: $120- 155   XP: $20   D14
Country Inn   **Location:** At Main (US 9) & Mechanic sts. 2 N Main St 08210. **Fax:** 609/463-9650. **Terms:** Sr. discount; reserv deposit, 14 day notice; no pets. **Facility:** 6 rooms. Handling fee imposed; 3 stories, no elevator; interior corridors; smoke free premises. **Dining:** Bradbury's Fine Dining, see separate listing. **Cards:** AE, MC, VI.
(CTV) (X) (D) (S)

HY-LAND MOTOR INN   Rates Subject to Change   **Phone:** 609/465-7305
◆   6/15-9/7   1P: $75- 85   2P/1B: $75- 85   2P/2B: $75- 85   XP: $5
Motel   5/1-6/14 & 9/8-10/1   1P: $60- 65   2P/1B: $60- 65   2P/2B: $60- 65   XP: $5
   10/2-4/30   1P: $50- 55   2P/1B: $50- 55   2P/2B: $50- 55   XP: $5
Location: On Garden State Pkwy; just s of Stone Harbor exit, at MM 9.6. 38 E Mechanic St 08210 (PO Box 97). **Fax:** 609/465-8776. **Terms:** Reserv deposit; 2 night min stay, weekends in season; no pets. **Facility:** 34 rooms. 10 efficiencies, $80-$90; $60-$70 off season, 3-night min stay. Rates for up to 4 persons in season. Handling fee imposed; 1-2 stories; exterior corridors. **Cards:** AE, DI, MC, VI.
(symbols) (CTV) (D)

RESTAURANT

BRADBURY'S FINE DINING   Historical   **Lunch:** $7-$10   **Dinner:** $23-$34   **Phone:** 609/463-9331
◆◆◆   **Location:** At Main (US 9) & Mechanic sts; in The Doctors Inn at Kings Grant. 2 N Main St 08210. **Hours:** 11 am-2 & 5-8 pm, Fri & Sat 5 pm-10 pm, Sun 11 am-2 pm. Closed: 12/25, Mon & Tues for lunch & Sun for dinner. **Reservations:** suggested. **Features:** Sunday brunch; health conscious menu. Intimately elegant dining in mid-19th century Italianate mansion; upscale casual atmosphere; menu features European & American dishes. Smoke free premises. **Cards:** AE, MC, VI.
(X)

CARDIFF—*See Atlantic City & Vicinity p. 182.*

CARLSTADT—5,500   (See map p. 210; index p. 209)

LODGING

HAMPTON INN - MEADOWLANDS   Rates Subject to Change   **Phone:** 201/935-9000   (70)
◆◆◆   All Year [CP]   1P: $68- 73   2P/1B: $78- 83   2P/2B: $78- 83   XP: $10   F18
Motel   **Location:** NJ Tpk, exit 16W, Rt 3 w to SR 17N; 1 mi e. 304 Paterson Plank Rd 07072. **Fax:** 201/935-9410. **Terms:** Sr. discount; no pets. **Facility:** 121 rooms. Whirlpool suites, $85-$130 microwaves & refrigerators; 5 stories; interior corridors. **All Rooms:** free & pay movies. **Cards:** AE, CB, DI, DS, MC, VI.
Roll in showers. (symbols) (CTV) (X) (symbol) (D) (S)

RESTAURANT

NICK'S OAK ROOM   **Lunch:** $8-$15   **Dinner:** $18-$26   **Phone:** 201/460-1777   (36)
◆◆◆   **Location:** NJ Tpk exit 16W; SR 3W to SR 17N, 1.5 mi n to Paterson Plank Rd, then 0.3 mi e. 335 Paterson Plank Rd 07072. **Hours:** noon-9:30 pm, Sat 5 pm-11 pm. Closed major holidays. **Reservations:** suggested.
Continental   **Features:** casual dress; health conscious menu items; cocktails & lounge; entertainment; a la carte. Sophisticated, multi-level dining rooms. **Cards:** AE, CB, MC, VI.
(X)

CARTERET—19,000   (See map p. 206; index p. 205)

LODGING

HOLIDAY INN   Rates Subject to Change   **Phone:** 732/541-9500   (6)
◆◆◆   All Year   1P: $102- 142   2P/1B: $110- 142   2P/2B: $110- 142   XP: $8   F19
Motor Inn   **Location:** At tpk exit 12. 1000 Roosevelt Ave 07008. **Fax:** 732/541-9640. **Terms:** Sr. discount; small pets only. **Facility:** 118 rooms. 2 stories; interior corridors. **Dining:** Restaurant; 6:30 am-10 pm, seafood buffet Fri & Sat, Sunday brunch 9:30 am-2 pm; $8-$24. **All Rooms:** free & pay movies. **Cards:** AE, CB, DI, DS, JCB, MC, VI.
(symbols) (symbols) (CTV) (X) (symbol) (D)

CEDAR GROVE—12,100   (See map p. 206; index p. 205)

RESTAURANT

IL TULIPANO   **Lunch:** $10-$25   **Dinner:** $14-$27   **Phone:** 973/256-9300   (152)
AAA   **Location:** 1.5 mi s on SR 23 from jct US 46. 1131 Pompton Ave 07009. **Hours:** noon-2:30 & 6-10 pm, Sat & Sun from 6 pm. Closed major holidays, Sat, Sun & Mon for lunch. **Reservations:** suggested.
◆◆◆◆   **Features:** health conscious menu items; cocktails & lounge; a la carte. A well-lit dining room highlighted by crystal tulip chandeliers & original artwork, creates a warm & intimate spring time atmosphere to enjoy
Italian   wonderful house specialties. Banquet facilities. Dinner valet. Jackets & ties preferred. **Cards:** AE, CB, DI, MC, VI. *(See ad p 212)*
(symbol)

CHATHAM—8,000   (See map p. 206; index p. 205)

RESTAURANT

FRESH FIELDS CAFE   **Lunch:** $9-$11   **Dinner:** $17-$23   **Phone:** 973/377-4072   (163)
◆◆◆   **Location:** In Hickory Square Mall; jct Shunpike Rd & Green Village Rd. 641 Shunpike Rd 07928.
American   **Hours:** noon-2 & 5:30-10 pm, Sun 4 pm-8 pm. Closed: Mon. **Features:** a la carte. Fresh made, seasonal cuisine in relaxed upscale casual, cozy restaurant. Smoke free premises. **Cards:** MC, VI.
(X)

CHERRY HILL—*See Philadelphia & Vicinity p. 390.*

CHESTER—1,200

RESTAURANT

LARISON'S TURKEY FARM INN   **Lunch:** $6-$10   **Dinner:** $12-$15   **Phone:** 908/879-5521
◆   **Location:** Jct US 206 & SR 24, nw corner. 2 W Main St 07930. **Hours:** 11 am-9 pm. Closed: 12/24.
American   **Features:** casual dress; children's menu; health conscious menu items; carryout; cocktails & lounge. Country style family dining; casual atmosphere; petting farm & Turkey Roost Country Store. **Cards:** AE, DI, DS, MC, VI.
(X)

CLARK—14,600   (See map p. 206; index p. 205)

LODGING

HOLIDAY INN SELECT   Phone: 752/574-0100   [120]
(AAA) [SAVE]   Mon-Thurs   1P: $130- 140   2P/1B: $140- 150 2P/2B: $140- 150   XP: $10   F12
               Fri-Sun   1P: $106   2P/1B: $116   2P/2B: $116   XP: $10   F12
◆◆◆   **Location:** Just e of Garden State Pkwy, exit 135. 36 Valley Rd 07066. Fax: 752/815-0661. **Terms:** No pets.
Motor Inn   **Facility:** 191 rooms. 6 stories; interior corridors. **Dining:** Restaurant; 6 am-11 pm; $10-$19. **All Rooms:** free
movies. **Cards:** AE, DI, DS, JCB, MC, VI.   [≥] [CTV] [X] [⌀] [D] [S]

CLIFTON—71,700   (See map p. 210; index p. 209)

LODGING

RAMADA INN   Phone: 973/778-6500   [1]
(AAA) [SAVE]   Mon-Thurs   1P: $89- 125   2P/1B: $89- 125   2P/2B: $89- 125   XP: $15   F18
               Fri-Sun   1P: $75- 125   2P/1B: $75- 125   2P/2B: $75- 125   XP: $15   F18
◆◆◆   **Location:** On SR 3 eastbound, 2.5 mi e of Garden State Pkwy, exit 153, NJ Tpk exit 16W, 4.5 mi w on SR
Motor Inn   3, U-turn on Main Ave. 265 Rt 3E 07014. Fax: 973/778-8724. **Terms:** AP, BP, CP avail; package plans; small
pets only. **Facility:** 183 rooms. 4 stories; interior corridors; sauna. **Dining & Entertainment:** Restaurant;
6:30 am-10 pm; $9-$14; cocktails/lounge. **Services:** Fee: coin laundry. **All Rooms:** free & pay movies. **Some Rooms:** 4
kitchens, refrigerators. Fee: microwaves. **Cards:** AE, CB, DI, DS, JCB, MC, VI.   [🛏] [≥] [🖼] [🖼] [CTV] [X] [⌀] [D] [S]

RESTAURANTS

CAVALIER CAFE   **Lunch:** $8-$15   **Dinner:** $15-$20   Phone: 973/778-5008   [3]
◆◆   **Location:** SR 3 w to Broad St exit, w then n; SR 3 e to Broad St exit, n. 1168 Broad St 07013.
American   **Hours:** 11:30 am-10 pm, Sat 4:30 pm-midnight. Closed: 1/1, 11/26, 12/25 & Sun. **Reservations:** suggested;
weekends. **Features:** casual dress; health conscious menu items; carryout; cocktails & lounge;
entertainment; a la carte. Eclectic menu featuring Italian, French, Cajun & Continental cuisine. **Cards:** AE, DI, MC, VI.

CHENGDU 46   **Lunch:** $10-$11   **Dinner:** $10-$22   Phone: 973/777-8855   [1]
◆◆◆   **Location:** Garden State Pkwy (SB) exit 154, 1 mi w (NB) 153B, 1 mi w. 1105 Rt 46E 07013. **Hours:** noon-3
Chinese   & 5-10:30 pm, Fri-11:30 pm, Sat 5 pm-11:30 pm, Sun 1 pm-10:30 pm. Closed: 11/26 & Mon.
Reservations: suggested. **Features:** cocktails & lounge; minimum charge-$10 for dinner; a la carte.
Soothing, sophisticated, softly lighted dining room. Authentic Sichuan cuisine. Showy flambe dessert presentations. Jackets
recommended. **Cards:** AE, DI, MC, VI.

CLINTON—2,100

LODGING

HOLIDAY INN SELECT-CLINTON   Rates Subject to Change   Phone: 908/735-5111
◆◆◆   All Year   1P: $93   2P/1B: $93   2P/2B: $93   XP: $8   F18
Motor Inn   **Location:** I-78, exit 15 just nw on SR 173W. 111 Rt 173 08809. Fax: 908/730-9768. **Terms:** No pets.
Facility: 142 rooms. 5 stories; interior corridors. **Dining:** Restaurant; 6:30 am-2 & 5-10 pm, Sat & Sun from
7 am; $12-$20. **All Rooms:** free & pay movies. **Cards:** AE, DI, DS, MC, VI.   [≥] [CTV] [X] [D] [S]

COLESVILLE—100

LODGING

HIGH POINT COUNTRY INN   Rates Subject to Change   Phone: 973/702-1860
◆   All Year   1P: $50- 60   2P/1B: $55- 75   2P/2B: $55- 75   XP: $5   F8
Motel   **Location:** 1 mi n of town center. 1328 SR 23 N 07461. Fax: 973/702-1860. **Terms:** Pets, $5 extra charge.
Facility: 15 rooms. 1 story; exterior corridors. **Cards:** DS, MC, VI.   [🛏] [≥] [X] [D]

DAYTON—4,300

LODGING

DAYS INN OF SOUTH BRUNSWICK   Rates Subject to Change   Phone: 732/329-3000
◆   5/15-9/10 [CP]   1P: $54- 85   2P/1B: $59- 85   2P/2B: $59- 85   XP: $5   F12
Motel   5/1-5/14 & 9/11-4/30 [CP] 1P: $54   2P/1B: $59   2P/2B: $59   XP: $5   F12
Terms: Sr. discount; no pets. **Facility:** 51 rooms. 2 stories; exterior corridors. **All Rooms:** free movies. **Cards:** AE, CB, DI,
DS, MC, VI.   [CTV] [X] [D]

EAST BRUNSWICK—43,500

LODGINGS

BRUNSWICK HILTON AND TOWERS   Rates Subject to Change   Phone: 732/828-2000
◆◆◆   9/15-12/31   1P: $180- 205   2P/1B: $200- 225 2P/2B: $200- 225   XP: $20   F18
Hotel   1/1-2/28   1P: $150- 175   2P/1B: $170- 195 2P/2B: $170- 195   XP: $20   F18
5/1-9/14 & 3/1-4/30 1P: $99- 175   2P/1B: $99- 195   2P/2B: $99- 195   XP: $20   F18
Location: NJ Tpk exit 9, 18 N, first right on service road. 3 Tower Center Blvd 08816. Fax: 732/828-6958. **Terms:** Check-in
4 pm; small pets only. **Facility:** 405 rooms. 15 stories; interior corridors. **Dining:** Restaurant; 7 am-10:30 pm; $12-$27.
All Rooms: free & pay movies. **Cards:** AE, CB, DI, DS, JCB, MC, VI. *(See color ad p 18)*
                                                                    [🛏] [≥] [CTV] [X] [⌀] [D] [S]

MCINTOSH INN OF EAST BRUNSWICK   Rates Subject to Change   Phone: 732/238-4900
◆◆◆   All Year [CP]   1P: $52- 63   2P/1B: $61- 67   2P/2B: $58- 63   XP: $7   F18
Motel   **Location:** On SR 18 N between Rue Ln & Racetrack Rd; 4 mi s from exit 9, NJ Tpk. 764 Rt 18 N 08816.
Fax: 732/257-2023. **Terms:** Sr. discount; no pets. **Facility:** 107 rooms. 2 stories; interior/exterior corridors.
All Rooms: free movies. **Cards:** AE, CB, DI, MC, VI. *(See color ad p 220, p 234 & p 353)*
                                                    Roll in showers. [CTV] [X] [⌀] [D]

EAST HANOVER—9,900   (See map p. 206; index p. 205)

LODGING

RAMADA INN & CONFERENCE CENTER   **Phone: 973/386-5622**   🔢 17

Mon-Thurs	1P:	$89- 117	2P/1B:	$89- 117	2P/2B:	$99- 127	XP: $10	F18
Fri-Sun	1P:	$59- 89	2P/1B:	$59- 89	2P/2B:	$69- 99	XP: $10	F18

♦♦♦ **Location:** I-287 exit 39, 4 mi e on SR 10 westbound. 130 Rt 10W 07936. Fax: 973/386-5724.
Motor Inn   **Terms:** Weekly/monthly rates; small pets only. **Facility:** 254 rooms. 5 stories; interior corridors. Fee: miniature golf, driving range. **Dining & Entertainment:** Restaurant; 6:30 am-midnight; $8-$18; health conscious menu items; cocktails/lounge. **Services:** complimentary evening beverages, Mon-Fri; area transportation, within 8 mi. Fee: coin laundry. **All Rooms:** free & pay movies. **Some Rooms:** microwaves, refrigerators. Fee: VCR's. **Cards:** AE, CB, DI, DS, JCB, MC, VI.

RESTAURANTS

ARCATA RISTORANTE   **Lunch: $11-$17**   **Dinner: $13-$24**   **Phone: 973/887-4949**   🔢 16
♦♦♦♦ **Location:** On SR 10E, 3.8 mi e of I-287, northbound exit 39, southbound exit 39B, 1.5 mi w of Livingston
Northern   Circle. 341 SR 10 E 07936. **Hours:** 11:30 am-2:30 & 5-10 pm, Fri & Sat-11 pm, Sun 3 pm-9 pm.
Italian   **Reservations:** suggested; weekends. **Features:** health conscious menu items; cocktails & lounge; a la
carte. Warmly elegant yet informal decor. Business casual dress. Fish & veal specialties. **Cards:** AE, DI, MC,
VI.

RILLO'S   **Lunch: $7-$13**   **Dinner: $10-$18**   **Phone: 973/887-0580**   🔢 15
♦♦ **Location:** On SR 10W, 2 mi w of Livingston Cir, I-287 exit 35; 3.8 mi e on SR 10. 190 Rt 10 W 07936.
Northern   **Hours:** 11:30 am-10 pm, Wed-Sat to 11 pm, Sun 4 pm-10 pm. Closed: 1/1, 12/25 & Mon.
Italian   **Reservations:** suggested; weekends. **Features:** health conscious menu; carryout; cocktails & lounge; a la
carte. Many pasta & veal specialties. **Cards:** AE, DI, MC, VI.

EAST RUTHERFORD—7,900   (See map p. 210; index p. 209)

LODGINGS

FAIRFIELD INN BY MARRIOTT   Guaranteed Rates   **Phone: 201/507-5222**   🔢 6

All Year [CP]	1P:	$89- 99	2P/1B:	$89- 99	2P/2B:	$89- 99

♦♦♦ **Location:** NJ Tpk eastern spur exit 16W, SR 3W to SR 17N, 1.5 mi n to Paterson Plank Rd (SR 120), just
Motel   e; I-80 exit 64B, 3 mi s on SR 17 to Paterson Plank Rd, just e. 850 SR 120 07073. Fax: 201/507-0744.
Terms: No pets. **Facility:** 140 rooms. 4 whirlpool rms, $99; 5 stories; interior corridors. **All Rooms:** free & pay movies.
Cards: AE, DI, DS, MC, VI.

SHERATON MEADOWLANDS   Rates Subject to Change   **Phone: 201/896-0500**   🔢 5

Sun-Thurs	1P: $160	2P/1B: $160	2P/2B: $160	XP: $20	F17
Fri & Sat 9/1-4/30	1P: $119	2P/1B: $119	2P/2B: $119	XP: $20	F17
Fri & Sat 5/1-8/31	1P: $109	2P/1B: $109	2P/2B: $109	XP: $20	F17

♦♦♦ **Location:** NJ Tpk exit 16W (from western spur), sports complex 1st right after toll (3E) to Sheraton Plaza Dr. 2
Hotel   Meadowlands Plaza 07073. Fax: 201/896-9696. **Terms:** Sr. discount; pets. **Facility:** 425 rooms. Whirlpool rm, extra charge;
21 stories; interior corridors. **Dining:** Restaurant; 6 am-11 pm; $8-$20. **All Rooms:** free & pay movies. **Cards:** AE, CB, DI,
DS, JCB, MC, VI.

RESTAURANTS

PARK & ORCHARD   **Lunch: $8-$17**   **Dinner: $13-$24**   **Phone: 201/939-9292**   🔢 8
♦♦♦ **Location:** NJ Tpk exit 16W; SR 3W, 1 mi n on SR 17; after 2nd light Union Ave w to Hackensack St, just n,
southbound SR 17 Union Ave exit Rutherford. 240 Hackensack St 07073. **Hours:** noon-4 & 5-10 pm, Sat
♦♦   from 5 pm, Sun 2 pm-9 pm. Closed major holidays & Mon for lunch. **Features:** casual dress; children's
American   menu; health conscious menu; cocktails & lounge. Natural foods restaurant. Crayfish pasta a popular
signature dish. A Grand Award Winner offering one of the top wine lists in the world. Seafood, pasta &
chicken entrees. **Cards:** AE, DI, DS, MC, VI.

SONOMA GRILL   **Lunch: $10-$14**   **Dinner: $17-$25**   **Phone: 201/507-8989**   🔢 7
♦♦♦ **Location:** NJ Tpk, exit 16W, 0.5 mi on SR 3W to SR 17N, 1.5 mi to Paterson Plank Rd exit, just w to
American   Enoch, just n. 64 Hoboken Rd 07073. **Hours:** 11:30 am-2:30 & 5-10 pm, Fri & Sat-11 pm, Sun 4 pm-8:30
pm. Closed major holidays, Sun 6/1-8/31 & Mon 9/1-5/31. **Reservations:** suggested. **Features:** cocktails &
lounge; a la carte. Innovative, creative contemporary American cuisine with California, Asian & Southwest influences.
Hand-selected exceptionally good wine list. Upscale casual dress; relaxed friendly atmosphere. **Cards:** AE, DI, MC, VI.

EAST WINDSOR—15,100

LODGINGS

DAYS INN   Rates Subject to Change   **Phone: 609/448-3200**

5/1-9/6 [CP]	1P: $59- 104	2P/1B: $59- 104	2P/2B: $65- 109	XP: $10	F12
9/7-4/30 [CP]	1P: $52- 82	2P/1B: $52- 82	2P/2B: $59- 89	XP: $10	F12

♦♦♦ **Location:** NJ Tpk, exit 8, just e. 460 Rt 33 E 08520. Fax: 609/448-8447. **Terms:** Sr. discount; pets.
Motor Inn   **Facility:** 100 rooms. 3 stories; interior corridors. **Dining:** Restaurant; 4 pm-10 pm, Fri & Sat-midnight; $6-$16.
All Rooms: free & pay movies. **Cards:** AE, DI, DS, MC, VI.

RAMADA INN & CONFERENCE CENTER   **Phone: 609/448-7000**

5/1-8/31	1P: $62- 125	2P/1B: $62- 125	2P/2B: $69- 125	XP: $10	F12
9/1-4/30	1P: $62- 102	2P/1B: $62- 102	2P/2B: $69- 109	XP: $10	F12

♦♦♦ **Location:** NJ Tpk, exit 8, just e then just n via Woodside Ave. 399 Monmouth St 08520. Fax: 609/443-6227.
Motor Inn   **Terms:** Monthly rates; package plans; no pets. **Facility:** 200 rooms. Within minutes of historic Princeton. 4
whirlpool rms, extra charge; 4 stories; interior corridors; sauna; game room, basketball & volleyball courts, par
course fitness trail. **Dining & Entertainment:** Restaurant; 7 am-10 pm, Sun & Mon-9 pm; $9-$19; health conscious menu
items; cocktails/lounge. **Services:** valet laundry. **All Rooms:** free & pay movies. **Some Rooms:** Fee: refrigerators.
Cards: AE, CB, DI, DS, MC, VI. **Special Amenities:** Early check-in/late check-out and free newspaper.

EATONTOWN—13,800

LODGING

SHERATON HOTEL & CONFERENCE CENTER　　　　　　　　　　　　**Phone:** 732/542-6500
AAA SAVE　All Year　　　1P: $109- 145　2P/1B: $124- 159　2P/2B: $124- 159　XP: $15　　F17
◆◆◆　**Location:** On SR 35 northbound, 0.5 mi s of jct SR 36. 6 Industrial Way East 07724. Fax: 732/542-6607.
Hotel　**Terms:** BP, CP avail; package plans; no pets. **Facility:** 208 rooms. 11 whirlpool rms, extra charge. Handling
　　fee imposed; 6 stories; interior corridors; whirlpool. **Dining & Entertainment:** 2 restaurants; 7 am-10:30 pm,
　　$9-$23; health conscious menu items; cocktails/lounge. **Services:** valet laundry. **All Rooms:** coffeemakers,
free & pay movies. **Some Rooms:** Fee: microwaves, refrigerators, VCR's. **Cards:** AE, DI, DS, MC, VI. **Special Amenities:**
Free newspaper. *(See color ad below)*　　　　　　🛏 🛏 🛁 🛗 CTV ⊠ 🛏 D S

EDISON—88,700　　(See map p. 206; index p. 205)

LODGINGS

CROWNE PLAZA AT RARITAN CENTER　Rates Subject to Change　　**Phone:** 732/225-8300　🔟
◆◆◆　All Year　　1P: $135　　2P/1B: $135　　　2P/2B: $135
Hotel　**Location:** 0.5 mi se of tpk, exit 10; on CR 514 keep right after tolls. 125 Raritan Center Pkwy 08837.
ridors. Fax: 732/225-0037. **Terms:** Sr. discount; pets, $25 extra charge. **Facility:** 274 rooms. 12 stories; interior cor-
Dining: Restaurant; 6:30 am-11 pm, Sun-10 pm; $7-$23. **All Rooms:** free & pay movies. **Cards:** AE, DI, DS, MC, VI.
　　　　　　　　　　　　　　　　　　🛏 🛏 CTV ⊠ 🛏 D S

RED ROOF INN　　　　　　Rates Subject to Change　　　　**Phone:** 732/248-9300　㉒
◆◆　6/1-8/31　　1P: $52- 66　2P/1B: $61- 75　2P/2B: $73　　XP: $9　F18
Motel　5/1-5/31 & 3/1-4/30　1P: $48- 63　2P/1B: $57- 71　2P/2B: $68　XP: $8　F18
　　9/1-10/31　　1P: $46- 58　2P/1B: $54- 66　2P/2B: $58　XP: $8　F18
　　11/1-2/28　　1P: $43- 53　2P/1B: $50- 60　2P/2B: $53　XP: $7　F18
Location: Northbound on I-287, exit Durham Ave & return to I-287 southbound, exit Metuchen & New Durham Rd. 860 New
Durham Rd 08817. Fax: 732/248-9326. **Terms:** Pets. **Facility:** 132 rooms. 2 stories; exterior corridors. **All Rooms:** free &
pay movies. **Cards:** AE, CB, DI, DS, MC, VI.　　　🛏 CTV ⊠ 🛏 D

WELLESLEY INN　　　　　　　　　　　　　　　**Phone:** 732/287-0171　㉟
AAA SAVE　All Year [CP]　　1P: $77- 105　2P/1B: $86- 110　2P/2B: $129　　XP: $5　F18
　　Location: On US 1 southbound; 1 mi s of I-287. 831 US 1S 08817. Fax: 732/287-8364.
◆◆　**Terms:** Weekly/monthly rates; small pets only. **Facility:** 100 rooms. 3 stories; interior corridors.
Motel　**Services:** valet laundry. **All Rooms:** free & pay movies. **Some Rooms:** coffeemakers, microwaves,
refrigerators. **Cards:** AE, DI, DS, MC, VI. **Special Amenities: Free breakfast and free local telephone
calls.** *(See color ad opposite inside back cover)*　　　🛏 🛁 CTV ⊠ 🛏 D S

RESTAURANTS

EDISON DINER　　　**Lunch:** $5-$7　　　**Dinner:** $8-$12　　**Phone:** 732/985-3335　㉟
◆　**Location:** From jct I-287, 3 mi s; from jct SR 18, 1 mi n. 101 US 1S 08817. **Hours:** 24 hours
American　**Features:** children's menu; early bird specials; senior's menu; carryout. Shiny, well-lighted family eatery.
　　Cards: AE, DI, DS, MC, VI.　　　　　　　　　　　　　　⊠

JACK COOPER'S CELEBRITY DELI & RESTAURANT　**Lunch:** $6-$9　**Dinner:** $8-$15　**Phone:** 732/549-4580　㉟
◆　**Location:** 0.3 mi w of US 1; located in Tano Mall. 1199 Amboy Ave 08837. **Hours:** 9 am-9 pm. Closed major
American　holidays & Mon. **Features:** children's menu; health conscious menu items; carryout. A Jewish deli restaurant
　　also serving updated cuisine. **Cards:** AE, DS, MC, VI.　　　　　　　　　　⊠

ELIZABETH—109,700　　(See map p. 210; index p. 209)

LODGINGS

HAMPTON INN-NEWARK AIRPORT　　　Rates Subject to Change　　**Phone:** 908/355-0500　㉖
◆◆◆　All Year [CP]　　1P: $95- 105　2P/1B: $105- 115　2P/2B: $98- 108　XP: $10　F12
Motel　**Location:** NJ Tpk, exit 13A; on US 1 & 9N, U-turn on McClellan St. 1128-38 Spring St 07207.
Fax: 908/355-4343. **Terms:** No pets. **Facility:** 152 rooms. Up to 4 persons in room; 5 stories; interior corridors.
All Rooms: free & pay movies. **Cards:** AE, CB, DI, DS, JCB, MC, VI.　🛗 CTV 🛏 ⊠ 🛏 D S

NEWARK AIRPORT HILTON HOTEL　　　Rates Subject to Change　　**Phone:** 908/351-3900　㉖
AAA　All Year　　　1P: $155　　2P/1B: $165　　2P/2B: $165　　XP: $10　F1
◆◆◆　**Location:** NJ Tpk exit 13A, on US 1 & 9N, U-turn on McClellan St. 1170 Spring St 07201.
Hotel　Fax: 908/351-9556. **Terms:** Reserv deposit; small pets only. **Facility:** 376 rooms. 12 stories; interior corridors.
Dining: Restaurant; 6:30 am-11 pm, Sat & Sun from 7 am; $10-$24. **All Rooms:** free & pay movies.
Cards: AE, CB, DI, DS, JCB, MC, VI. *(See color ad p 18)*　🛏 🛏 🛗 CTV 🛏 ⊠ 🛏 D S

(See map p. 210)

WYNDHAM GARDEN HOTEL-NEWARK AIRPORT   Rates Subject to Change   **Phone:** 908/527-1600   **27**
◆◆◆   Sun-Thurs   1P: $109   2P/1B: $119   2P/2B: $119
Hotel   Fri & Sat   1P: $79   2P/1B: $79   2P/2B: $79
       Location: New Jersey Tpk exit 13A; Rtes 1 & 9S, to North Ave W, right turn at 2nd light 0.3 mi. 901 Spring St 07201. Fax: 908/527-1327. **Terms:** Reserv deposit; no pets. **Facility:** 260 rooms. 11 stories; interior corridors. **Dining:** Restaurant; 6:30 am-2 & 5-10 pm; $9-$30. **All Rooms:** Fee: movies. **Cards:** AE, DI, DS, JCB, MC, VI.
(See color ad below)   Roll in showers.

ENGLEWOOD—24,900   (See map p. 210; index p. 209)

LODGING

RADISSON HOTEL ENGLEWOOD   Rates Subject to Change   **Phone:** 201/871-2020   **8**
◆◆◆   Sun-Thurs 9/14-12/18   1P: $129   2P/1B: $129   2P/2B: $129
Hotel   Sun-Thurs 5/1-6/28   1P: $119   2P/1B: $119   2P/2B: $119
       Fri & Sat 5/1-6/28, 6/29-9/13,
       Fri & Sat 9/14-12/18 &
       12/19-4/30   1P: $99   2P/1B: $99   2P/2B: $99
Location: Van Brunt exit, off SR 4W. 401 S Van Brunt St 07631. Fax: 201/871-7116. **Terms:** Sr. discount; reserv deposit; pets, $25 fee. **Facility:** 192 rooms. 9 stories; interior corridors. **Dining:** Restaurant; 6:30 am-10 pm; $10-$18. **All Rooms:** free & pay movies. **Cards:** AE, CB, DI, DS, JCB, MC, VI.

FAIRFIELD—7,600   (See map p. 206; index p. 205)

LODGINGS

BEST WESTERN FAIRFIELD EXECUTIVE INN   **Phone:** 973/575-7700   **11**
   Sun-Thurs [BP]   1P: $84- 157   2P/1B: $97- 170   2P/2B: $97- 170   XP: $13   F18
      Fri & Sat [BP]   1P: $56- 164   2P/1B: $56- 164   2P/2B: $56- 164   XP: $13   F18
◆◆◆   **Location:** I-80 westbound exit 52 & 1.5 mi w on US 46 eastbound, I-80 eastbound exit 47B & 5.5 mi e.
Motor Inn   216-234 Rt 46E 07004. Fax: 973/575-4653. **Terms:** Weekly/monthly rates; weekend rates avail; no pets. **Facility:** 170 rooms. 14 whirlpool rms, $92-$150; 4 stories; interior corridors; sauna, steamroom, whirlpool; 3 guest rooms with exercise equipment & rooms with video game, pool table, air hockey & electronic dart board in game room. **Dining & Entertainment:** Restaurant; 6 am-11 pm, Sat & Sun from 7 am; $10-$20; health conscious menu items; cocktails/lounge; entertainment. **Services:** area transportation. Fee: coin laundry. **All Rooms:** coffeemakers, free & pay movies, refrigerators. **Some Rooms:** microwaves. **Cards:** AE, CB, DI, DS, MC, VI. **Special Amenities: Free breakfast and free newspaper.** *(See color ad below)*

(See map p. 206)

MEADOWLANDS PLAZA HOTEL — Rates Subject to Change — Phone: 973/227-4333 **14**
◆◆
Motor Inn — Sun-Thurs [CP] — 1P: $65 — 2P/1B: $65 — 2P/2B: $70 — XP: $5 — F10
Fri & Sat [CP] — 1P: $45 — 2P/1B: $50 — 2P/2B: $50 — XP: $5 — F10
Location: I-80 westbound exit 52, 1 mi w on US 46 eastbound; I-80 eastbound exit 47B, 6 mi e. 286 Route 46E 07004. Fax: 973/227-5399. **Terms:** Sr. discount; no pets. **Facility:** 70 rooms. 3 stories; interior corridors. **Dining:** Restaurant; 7 am-10 pm, Sat & Sun from 5 pm; $9-$20. **Cards:** AE, CB, DI, DS, JCB, MC, VI. (CTV)(X)(D)(S)

RADISSON HOTEL & SUITES — Rates Subject to Change — Phone: 973/227-9200 **12**
◆◆
Hotel — All Year — 1P: $179- 189 — 2P/1B: $189- 199 — 2P/2B: $189- 199 — XP: $10 — F17
Location: Westbound I-80 exit 52, eastbound exit Caldwells 47B, 7 mi e. 690 US 46E 07004. Fax: 973/227-4308. **Terms:** Sr. discount; small pets only, $50 dep req. **Facility:** 204 rooms. Handling fee imposed; 5 stories; interior corridors. **Dining:** Restaurant; 6:30 am-10:30 pm, Fri-Sun from 7 am; $14-$25. **All Rooms:** free & pay movies. **Some Rooms:** 12 efficiencies. **Cards:** AE, CB, DI, DS, JCB, MC, VI. (icons) (CTV)(X)(?)(D)(S)

RAMADA INN — Rates Subject to Change — Phone: 973/575-1742 **13**
◆◆◆
Motor Inn — Mon-Thurs — 1P: $99- 150 — 2P/1B: $99- 150 — 2P/2B: $99- 150 — XP: $10 — F18
Fri-Sun — 1P: $79- 140 — 2P/1B: $79- 140 — 2P/2B: $79- 140 — XP: $10 — F18
Location: I-80 westbound exit 52; I-80 eastbound, exit Caldwells 47B, 7 mi e on US 46, exit Passaic Ave. 38 Two Bridges Rd 07004. Fax: 973/575-9567. **Terms:** Small pets only. **Facility:** 176 rooms. 2 stories; interior corridors. **Dining:** Restaurant; 6:30 am-10 pm; $9-$15. **All Rooms:** free & pay movies. **Cards:** AE, CB, DI, DS, JCB, MC, VI.
Roll in showers. (icons) (CTV)(&)(X)(?)(D)

FLEMINGTON—4,000

LODGINGS

CABBAGE ROSE INN — Rates Subject to Change — Phone: 908/788-0247
◆◆◆
Historic Bed — Fri-Sun [BP] — 1P: $80- 125 — 2P/1B: $80- 125 — XP: $15
& Breakfast — Mon-Thurs [BP] — 1P: $75- 115 — 2P/1B: $75- 115 — XP: $15
Location: Center. 162 Main St 08822. Fax: 908/788-0247. **Terms:** Age restrictions may apply; reserv deposit, 7 day notice; no pets. **Facility:** 5 rooms. Handling fee imposed; 2 stories; interior corridors; smoke free premises. **Cards:** AE, DS, MC, VI. (X)(D)

JERICA HILL-A BED & BREAKFAST INN — Rates Subject to Change — Phone: 908/782-8234
◆◆◆
Historic Bed — Fri-Sun [BP] — 1P: $100- 115 — 2P/1B: $100- 115 — XP: $20
& Breakfast — Mon-Thurs [BP] — 1P: $85 — 2P/1B: $90 — XP: $20
Location: Just e of Main St between Church & Williams sts. 96 Broad St 08822. Fax: 908/782-8234. **Terms:** Age restrictions may apply; reserv deposit, 7 day notice; 2 night min stay, most weekends; no pets. **Facility:** 5 rooms. 2 stories; interior corridors; smoke free premises. **Cards:** AE, MC, VI. (X)(D)

THE RAMADA INN — Rates Subject to Change — Phone: 908/782-7472
◆◆
Motor Inn — 5/1-10/31 — 1P: $74 — 2P/1B: $84 — 2P/2B: $84 — XP: $10 — F18
11/1-4/30 — 1P: $68 — 2P/1B: $78 — 2P/2B: $78 — XP: $10 — F18
Location: 0.5 mi s of the circle. 250 Hwy US 202 & SR 31 08822. Fax: 908/782-1975. **Terms:** Reserv deposit; pets, $10 extra charge. **Facility:** 103 rooms. 2 stories; exterior corridors. **Dining:** Restaurant; 6:30 am-11 pm; $11-$20. **All Rooms:** Fee: movies. **Some Rooms:** 25 efficiencies, kitchen. **Cards:** AE, CB, DI, DS, MC, VI. (icons) (CTV)(X)(?)(D)

RESTAURANTS

RATTLESNAKE GRILL — Lunch: $8-$14 — Dinner: $8-$14 — Phone: 908/788-7772
◆◆
American — **Location:** From Flemington Circle, 1.5 mi s (northbound side). 208 Rts 202/31 08822. **Hours:** 11:30 am-10 pm, Fri-11 pm, Sat noon-11 pm, Sun noon-9:30 pm. Closed: 11/26 & 12/25. **Features:** casual dress; children's menu; carryout; cocktails & lounge; a la carte. American cuisine with southwestern regional flair. Upbeat decor. **Cards:** AE, DI, MC, VI. (X)

THE UPPER CRUST-A CRAFTY TEA ROOM — Lunch: $7-$9 — Dinner: $13-$17 — Phone: 908/788-9750
◆◆
American — **Location:** Downtown. 146 Main St 08822. **Hours:** 11:30 am-5 pm, Thurs-Sat to 9 pm. Closed major holidays & Sun. **Reservations:** suggested; weekends. **Features:** casual dress; health conscious menu items; carryout; a la carte. Inviting dining rooms in Victorian house. Selections of contemporary entrees include beef, vegetarian, seafood & fish. Assorted tea, soda & coffee. Own desserts. Smoke free premises. **Cards:** MC, VI. (X)

FLORHAM PARK—8,500   (See map p. 206; index p. 205)

LODGING

HAMILTON PARK EXECUTIVE CONFERENCE CENTER — Rates Subject to Change — Phone: 973/377-2424 **27**
◆◆◆
Hotel — Sun-Thurs [EP] — 1P: $170 — 2P/1B: $170 — 2P/2B: $170 — XP: $20 — F18
Fri & Sat [CP] — 1P: $119 — 2P/1B: $119 — 2P/2B: $119 — XP: $20 — F18
Location: 2 mi w on CR 510, 1 mi s on (Park Ave) CR 623. 175 Park Ave 07932. Fax: 973/377-6108. **Terms:** No pets. **Facility:** 219 rooms. 5 stories; interior corridors. **Dining:** Restaurant; 6:45-9:30 am, 11-2 & 6-10 pm, Sun brunch 11 am-2 pm; $20-$35. **All Rooms:** free & pay movies. **Cards:** AE, CB, DI, DS, MC, VI. (icons) (CTV)(X)(?)(D)(S)

RESTAURANT

THE AFTON — Lunch: $7-$12 — Dinner: $14-$19 — Phone: 973/377-1871 **28**
(AAA)
◆◆
American — **Location:** Opposite Auto Club at S Orange Ave (CR 510) & Hanover Rd. 2 Hanover Rd 07932. **Hours:** 11:30 am-2:30 & 5-9 pm, Sat 11:30 am-3 & 5-9 pm, Sun noon-8 pm, Sun brunch 11 am-2 pm. Closed: 12/25 & Mon. **Reservations:** suggested. **Features:** casual dress; children's menu; early bird specials; carryout; cocktails & lounge. Family owned colonial inn. **Cards:** AE, CB, DI, MC, VI. (X)

FORKED RIVER—200

RESTAURANT

CAPTAIN'S INN — Lunch: $6-$12 — Dinner: $12-$25 — Phone: 609/693-3351
◆
Seafood — **Location:** Garden State Pkwy exit 74 (southbound), 3 mi e on Lacey Rd; exit 69 (northbound) 2 mi on 532E n 4 mi on US 9, & 0.8 mi on Lacey Rd to dock. 08731. **Hours:** 11:45 am-10 pm. Closed: 12/25 **Features:** children's menu; early bird specials; carryout; cocktails & lounge. Extensive seafood menu; view of Forked River, docking facilities avail. **Cards:** AE, DI, MC, VI. (X)

FORT LEE—32,000 (See map p. 210; index p. 209)

LODGINGS

EXECUTIVE INN AT FORT LEE **Phone:** 201/461-7000 ⑩
AAA SAVE All Year [CP] 1P: $84- 94 2P/1B: $94- 109 XP: $10 F17
◆◆ Motel
Location: 0.5 mi w of George Washington Bridge. 2300 Rt 4 W 07024. Fax: 201/461-3338. **Terms:** No pets. **Facility:** 60 rooms. 2 stories; exterior corridors. **Services:** valet laundry. **All Rooms:** refrigerators, VCR's. **Some Rooms:** whirlpools. **Cards:** AE, CB, DI, DS, MC, VI. **Special Amenities: Early check-in/late check-out and free breakfast.**

FORT LEE HILTON **Phone:** 201/461-9000 ⑪
AAA SAVE All Year 1P: $135 2P/1B: $147 2P/2B: $147 XP: $12 F18
◆◆◆ Hotel
Location: 1 mi w of GW Bridge; U-turn on Jones Rd; I-95 & I-80 eastbound, local lanes exit 71 Broad Ave-Leonia to Broad Ave, 0.5 mi e. 2117 Rt 4 E 07024. Fax: 201/585-9807. **Terms:** AP, BP, CP avail; package plans; no pets. **Facility:** 235 rooms. Convenient access to George Washington Bridge. Whirlpool & regrigerator suites, extra charge; 15 stories; interior corridors; luxury level rooms; sauna, whirlpool. **Dining & Entertainment:** 2 restaurants; 6:30 am-11 pm; $12-$28; health conscious menu items; cocktails/lounge; nightclub. **Services:** valet laundry; area transportation, within 5 mi. **All Rooms:** coffeemakers, free movies. **Some Rooms:** refrigerators. **Cards:** AE, CB, DI, DS, JCB, MC, VI. **Special Amenities: Early check-in/late check-out and free newspaper.** *(See color ad p 18)*

FRENCHTOWN—1,500

LODGING

HUNTERDON HOUSE Rates Subject to Change **Phone:** 908/996-3632
◆◆◆ Fri-Sun [BP] 2P/1B: $110- 145 XP: $15
Historic Bed & Breakfast Mon-Thurs [BP] 2P/1B: $85- 100 XP: $15
Location: Center of town, just w of jct SR 12. 12 Bridge St 08825. Fax: 908/996-0942. **Terms:** Sr. discount; age restrictions may apply; reserv deposit, 10 day notice; no pets. **Facility:** 7 rooms. Handling fee imposed; 3 stories, no elevator; interior corridors; smoke free premises. **Cards:** AE, MC, VI.

RESTAURANT

THE FRENCHTOWN INN Historical **Lunch:** $9-$15 **Dinner:** $22-$27 **Phone:** 908/996-3300
◆◆◆ French
Location: Center of town; just w of jct SR 12. 7 Bridge St 08825. **Hours:** noon-2 & 6-9 pm, Sat-9:30 pm, Sun noon-2:45 & 5:30-8:30 pm. Closed: 1/1, 12/25 & Mon. **Reservations:** suggested. **Features:** Sunday brunch; cocktails & lounge; a la carte. Upscale casual. Cozy, romantic dining room or casual grill/bar room. Top wine list. Creative award winning cuisine. Prixe fixe avail on Sat. **Cards:** AE, DI, MC, VI.

GARFIELD—26,700 (See map p. 210; index p. 209)

RESTAURANT

GOODFELLAS RISTORANTE & BAR **Lunch:** $7-$15 **Dinner:** $11-$23 **Phone:** 973/478-4000 (55)
◆◆ South Italian
Location: US 46, 1 mi sw via Outwater Ln to Midland Ave, just n. 661 Midland Ave 07026. **Hours:** noon-3:30 & 5-10:30 pm, Sat 5 pm-11 pm. Closed: Sun. **Reservations:** suggested. **Features:** cocktails & lounge; valet parking; a la carte. Business casual dress. Olde country ambience restaurant serving comfort food. **Cards:** AE, DI, MC, VI.

GLEN ROCK—10,900 (See map p. 210; index p. 209)

RESTAURANT

GLEN ROCK INN **Lunch:** $7-$12 **Dinner:** $10-$20 **Phone:** 201/445-2362 (52)
AAA ◆ American
Location: SR 208 to CR 507 (Maple Ave), 1 mi n to Rock Rd, 0.3 mi w. 222 Rock Rd 07452. **Hours:** 11:30 am-midnight, Sun from 11 am. Closed: 12/25. **Reservations:** suggested; weekends. **Features:** casual dress; Sunday brunch; children's menu; early bird specials; health conscious menu items; carryout; cocktails & lounge; street parking; a la carte. Hometown comfortable restaurant. **Cards:** AE, DI, DS, MC, VI.

HACKENSACK—37,000 (See map p. 210; index p. 209)

LODGING

BEST WESTERN ORITANI HOTEL Rates Subject to Change **Phone:** 201/488-8900 (74)
◆◆ All Year [CP] 1P: $90- 115 2P/1B: $90- 115 2P/2B: $90- 115 XP: $8 F
Motel
Location: Jct Rt 4 & Hackensack Ave, just n; adjacent to Riverside Square Mall. 414 Hackensack Ave 07601. Fax: 201/488-5456. **Terms:** Sr. discount; no pets. **Facility:** 99 rooms. 4 stories; interior corridors. **All Rooms:** free & pay movies. **Cards:** AE, CB, DI, DS, MC, VI.

RESTAURANT

STONY HILL INN Historical **Lunch:** $13-$22 **Dinner:** $15-$29 **Phone:** 201/342-4085 ㊶
AAA ◆◆◆ Continental
Location: I-80 westbound local lanes from GW Bridge exit 64B & right; I-80 eastbound local lane exit 64 (SR 17S), exit Terrace Ave, 0.3 mi n. 231 Polifly Rd 07601. **Hours:** 11:30 am-3 & 5:30-10:30 pm, Sat seatings 5:30 pm-7 pm & after 9:15 pm, Sun 3 pm-10 pm. Closed: 12/25. **Reservations:** suggested. **Features:** semi-formal attire; health conscious menu items; cocktails & lounge; valet parking; a la carte. Elegant classic Georgian; on National Register of Historic Places. **Cards:** AE, CB, DI, MC, VI.

HAMBURG—2,600

RESTAURANT

ROADHOUSE RESTAURANT **Lunch:** $4-$7 **Dinner:** $7-$12 **Phone:** 973/702-8801
◆◆ Italian
Location: Jct SR 94; just n. 87 SR 23 07419. **Hours:** 11:30 am-9 pm, Fri & Sat-10 pm. Closed major holidays. **Features:** early bird specials; senior's menu; carryout; cocktails & lounge. Casual family dining. Pasta, burgers, steak, seafood & pizza specials. Homemade dessert. **Cards:** AE, DS, MC, VI.

HAMMONTON—*See Atlantic City & Vicinity p. 182.*

Service Charges - See Using lodging listings.

HARDYSTON—5,300

RESTAURANT

HENRI'S COUNTRY MANOR   **Dinner:** $12-$20   **Phone:** 973/209-1816
◆◆   **Location:** On SR 94, 0.8 mi n jct SR 23. 137 Rt 94 07460. **Hours:** 5 pm-10 pm, Sun 10 am-9 pm. Closed:
American   12/25. **Features:** casual dress; children's menu; health conscious menu items; carryout; cocktails & lounge;
a la carte. Early bird specials Mon, Wed & Thurs. Tues pasta nite. Rural locale. **Cards:** AE, DI, DS, MC, VI.
🅇

HASBROUCK HEIGHTS—11,500   (See map p. 210; index p. 209)

LODGINGS

CROWNE PLAZA   **Phone:** 201/288-6100   🏷️15
🆎 SAVE   Sun-Thurs   1P: $140- 160   2P/1B: $140- 160 2P/2B: $140- 160 XP: $20   F18
           Fri & Sat   1P: $122- 142   2P/1B: $122- 142 2P/2B: $122- 142 XP: $20   F18
◆◆◆   **Location:** E I-80 local lanes exit 64B (westbound), 64 (eastbound), just s on SR 17S. 650 Terrace Ave
Hotel   07604. Fax: 201/288-4717. **Terms:** Weekly/monthly rates; package plans; small pets only. **Facility:** 355 rooms.
Upscale luxury hotel with easy access for major highways. Handling fee imposed; 14 stories; interior corridors;
luxury level rooms; saunas. **Dining & Entertainment:** Restaurant; 6:30 am-11 pm; $11-$35; cocktails/lounge; entertainment.
Services: valet laundry. **All Rooms:** coffeemakers, free & pay movies. **Some Rooms:** microwaves, refrigerators.
Cards: AE, DI, DS, MC, VI.   Roll in showers. 🍴 ⛵ 📶 💺 CTV 🅇 💈 D S

HOLIDAY INN   **Phone:** 201/288-9600   🏷️14
🆎 SAVE   Mon-Thurs   1P: $99- 119   2P/1B: $99- 119 2P/2B: $109- 129 XP: $10   F12
           Fri-Sun   1P: $79- 99   2P/1B: $79- 99   2P/2B: $89- 109 XP: $10   F12
◆◆   **Location:** On SR 17 southbound; 1 mi s of jct I-80, exit 64B westbound, exit 64 eastbound. 283 Rt 17S
Motor Inn   07604. Fax: 201/288-4527. **Terms:** No pets. **Facility:** 246 rooms. 2-5 stories; interior corridors. **Dining &
Entertainment:** Restaurant; 6:30 am-2:30 & 4-10 pm, Sat & Sun from 7 am; $10-$20; health conscious
menu items; cocktails/lounge; nightclub. **Services:** valet laundry; area transportation, to local businesses. **All Rooms:** free &
pay movies, combo or shower baths. **Some Rooms:** coffeemakers, microwaves, refrigerators. **Cards:** AE, CB, DI, DS, MC,
VI. **Special Amenities:** Early check-in/late check-out and free room upgrade (subject to availability with advanced
reservations).   Roll in showers. ⛵ 📶 💺 CTV 💈 🅇 💈 D

HAZLET—22,000

LODGING

WELLESLEY INN   Rates Subject to Change   **Phone:** 732/888-2800
◆◆   5/1-9/30 & 4/1-4/30 [CP]   1P: $119   2P/1B: $119   2P/2B: $119   XP: $5   F18
Motel   10/1-3/31 [CP]   1P: $79- 84   2P/1B: $84- 89 2P/2B: $89- 94   XP: $5   F18
Location: Garden State Parkway, exit 117, 1.5 mi s on SR 35, U-turn Hazlet Ave. 3215 SR 35N 07730.
Fax: 732/888-2902. **Terms:** Sr. discount; small pets only. **Facility:** 89 rooms. 3 stories; interior corridors. **All Rooms:** free
movies. **Cards:** AE, CB, DI, DS. *(See color ad opposite inside back cover)*   🍴 CTV 🅇 💈 D S

HIGHTSTOWN—5,100

RESTAURANT

JACK BAKER'S LOBSTER SHANTY   **Lunch:** $5-$13   **Dinner:** $8-$26   **Phone:** 609/443-6600
◆   **Location:** On SR 33, 4.3 mi e of tpk exit 8. Rt 33 & Perrineville Rd 08520. **Hours:** 11:30 am-2 & 4:30-9 pm,
Seafood   Sat-10 pm, Sun noon-8:30 pm, in summer Fri 11:30 am-2 & 4:30-10 pm, Sat-10:30 pm. Closed: 12/25.
Reservations: suggested; for 8 or more. **Features:** children's menu; early bird specials; health conscious
menu; carryout; cocktails & lounge; a la carte. Casual family dining. **Cards:** AE, DI, MC, VI.   🅇

HOBOKEN—33,400   (See map p. 210; index p. 209)

RESTAURANTS

ARTHUR'S TAVERN   **Lunch:** $6-$15   **Dinner:** $6-$15   **Phone:** 201/656-5009   🏷️48
◆◆   **Location:** Downtown; corner Washington & 3rd St. 237 Washington 07030. **Hours:** 11:30 am-11 pm, Fri &
Steakhouse   Sat-midnight, Sun 2 pm-10 pm. Closed: 11/26 & 12/25. **Features:** casual dress; cocktails & lounge; fee for
parking. A bustling tavern. Steak, burgers & sandwiches in a relaxing casual atmosphere. **Cards:** AE, DI, DS,
MC, VI.

THE BRASS RAIL   **Lunch:** $6-$18   **Dinner:** $6-$18   **Phone:** 201/659-7074   🏷️49
◆   **Location:** Corner Washington & 2nd St. 135 Washington 07030. **Hours:** noon-10 pm, Sat-11 pm, Sun 11
Continental   am-midnight. Closed: 12/25. **Reservations:** suggested; weekends. **Features:** casual dress; health conscious
menu items; carryout; cocktails & lounge; a la carte. Brasserie on 1st floor open for lunch & dinner; Sun
brunch 11 am-4 pm. **Cards:** AE, DI, MC, VI.   🅇

RISTORANTE GERRINO   **Lunch:** $9-$14   **Dinner:** $11-$20   **Phone:** 201/656-7731   🏷️46
◆◆   **Location:** On corner of 1st & River sts. 96 River St 07030. **Hours:** noon-10 pm, Fri & Sat-11 pm. Closed
Italian   major holidays & Sun. **Reservations:** suggested; for 4 or more. **Features:** casual dress; health conscious
menu items; carryout; cocktails & lounge; street parking; a la carte. A popular, relaxing bistro. Rooftop dining
in summer. 2nd & River St parking lot validation. **Cards:** AE, DI, DS, MC, VI.   🅇

HO-HO-KUS—3,900

RESTAURANT

CLAUDE'S HO-HO-KUS INN   Historical   **Lunch:** $7-$16   **Dinner:** $18-$27   **Phone:** 201/445-4115
◆◆◆   **Location:** Southbound SR 17 1 mi w via Sheridan Ave; northbound W Linwood Ave-Ridgewood exit, 1.5 mi
French   w, 1 mi n on Maple. Franklin Tpk & Sheridan Ave 07423. **Hours:** noon-2 & 5-9 pm, Fri-9:30 pm, Sat 5 pm-10
pm, Sun noon-2 & 3-8 pm. Closed: 1/1 & 12/25. **Reservations:** suggested. **Features:** semi-formal attire;
Sunday brunch; health conscious menu; cocktails & lounge; a la carte, also prix fixe. Charming historical landmark. Formal
service, valet parking for dinner. **Cards:** AE, CB, DI, MC, VI.

HOPE—1,700

RESTAURANT

INN AT MILLRACE POND   Country Inn   **Dinner:** $19-$25   **Phone:** 908/459-4884
◆◆◆   **Location:** I-80 exit 12; 1 mi s on CR 521, left at blinker on CR 519; at Inn at Millrace Pond. Rt 519 07844.
American   **Hours:** 5 pm-9 pm, Sat-10 pm, Sun noon-7 pm. Closed: 12/25. **Reservations:** suggested; weekends.
Features: health conscious menu items; cocktails & lounge. Seasonal menu featuring original cuisine,
fresh-baked bread & dessert. Upscale casual. **Cards:** AE, CB, DI, MC, VI.   🔥 ☒

ISELIN—16,100   (See map p. 206; index p. 205)

LODGING

SHERATON AT WOODBRIDGE PLACE   Rates Subject to Change   **Phone:** 732/634-3600   123
◆◆◆   Sun-Thurs [EP]   1P: $140- 160   2P/1B: $150- 170 2P/2B: $150- 170 XP: $10   F17
Hotel   Fri & Sat [CP]   1P: $79   2P/1B: $79   2P/2B: $79   XP: $10   F17
Location: 2 mi s of jct SR 9; diagonal to Woodbridge Center. 515 Rt 1S 08830. **Fax:** 732/634-0258.
Terms: No pets. **Facility:** 253 rooms. Handling fee imposed; 7 stories; interior corridors. **Dining:** Dining room, restaurant; 6
am-11 pm; $9-$30. **All Rooms:** free & pay movies. **Cards:** AE, CB, DI, DS, MC, VI.   ➳ ➳ CTV ☒ D S

JAMESBURG—5,300

LODGING

HOLIDAY INN CENTER POINT   Rates Subject to Change   **Phone:** 609/655-4775
◆◆   All Year   1P: $105- 174 2P/1B: $110- 174 2P/2B: $120- 174 XP: $10   F18
Motor Inn   **Location:** NJ Tpk exit 8A, follow sign for Monroe/Jamesburg. 390 Forsgate Dr 08831. **Fax:** 609/655-5254.
Terms: Sr. discount; reserv deposit; no pets. **Facility:** 150 rooms. 6 stories; interior corridors.
Dining: Restaurant; 6:30 am-10 pm; $11-$25. **All Rooms:** free & pay movies. **Some Rooms:** 10 efficiencies. **Cards:** AE,
CB, DI, DS, JCB, MC, VI.   ➳ ♿ CTV ☒ 🏊 D S

RESTAURANT

FIDDLEHEAD'S RESTAURANT   **Lunch:** $6-$9   **Dinner:** $11-$22   **Phone:** 732/521-0878
◆◆◆   **Location:** NJ Tpk exit 8A, 3 mi e to Railroad Ave, just n. 27 E Railroad Ave 08831. **Hours:** 11:30 am-2:30 &
American   5-9 pm, Fri & Sat-10 pm, Sun 4 pm-8 pm. Closed: Mon. **Reservations:** suggested. **Features:** casual dress;
children's menu; health conscious menu; carryout; a la carte. Eclectic menu includes some Thai influence,
assorted pasta, seafood, beef, lamb & chicken, prepared by certified executive chef. Own desserts. Smoke free premises.
Cards: AE, MC, VI.   ☒

JERSEY CITY—228,500   (See map p. 210; index p. 209)

LODGING

HOLLAND MOTOR LODGE   Guaranteed Rates   **Phone:** 201/963-6200   18
🅰🅰🅰   All Year [CP]   1P: $52- 65 2P/1B: $57- 65 2P/2B: $62- 70 XP: $5   F18
◆   **Location:** NJ Tpk, exit 14C, 3 mi e following signs to Holland Tunnel, at entrance to tunnel. Holland Tunnel
Motel   Plaza E 07302. **Fax:** 201/420-5091. **Terms:** Small pets only. **Facility:** 71 rooms. 3 stories; interior corridors.
All Rooms: free & pay movies. **Cards:** AE, CB, DI, DS, MC, VI.   🛏 CTV D

RESTAURANTS

CASA DANTE   **Lunch:** $11-$14   **Dinner:** $14-$26   **Phone:** 201/795-2750   12
◆◆◆   **Location:** Downtown; just e jct Kennedy Blvd. 737 Newark Ave 07306. **Hours:** 11:30 am-10:30 pm, Sat 4
Continental   pm-11 pm. Closed major holidays & Sun. **Reservations:** suggested. **Features:** cocktails & lounge; valet
parking; a la carte. Congenial family ambience in European decor. Upscale casual attire. Classically
prepared cuisine. **Cards:** AE, DI, DS, MC, VI.   ☒

PRONTO CENA RISTORANTE   **Lunch:** $8-$22   **Dinner:** $8-$22   **Phone:** 201/435-0004   13
◆◆◆   **Location:** From jct Grand & Washington sts just s. 87 Sussex St 07302. **Hours:** 11:30 am-10 pm, Thur &
Italian   Fri-11 pm, Sat 4 pm-11 pm, Sun 11:30 am-9 pm. Closed major holidays. **Reservations:** suggested.
Features: casual dress; carryout; cocktails; street parking; a la carte. Upscale casual trattoria. Creative
Tuscan specialties including game entrees. Reasonably priced Italian wines. Own desserts. **Cards:** AE, DI, MC, VI.   ☒

KENDALL PARK—7,100

RESTAURANT

SHOGUN 27 JAPANESE CUISINE   **Lunch:** $6-$10   **Dinner:** $10-$24   **Phone:** 732/422-1117
◆◆   **Location:** SR 27 at corner Sand Hill Rd. 3376 Hwy 27 08824. **Hours:** 11:30 am-2:30 & 4:30-10 pm, Fri-11
Chinese   pm, Sat 4:30 pm-11 pm, Sun 4 pm-9:30 pm. Closed: 11/26. **Reservations:** suggested; weekends.
Features: casual dress; children's menu; health conscious menu items; carryout; cocktails & lounge.
Individual dining in tatami rooms, hibachi dining & sushi bar. **Cards:** AE, DI, MC, VI.   ☒

KENILWORTH—7,600   (See map p. 206; index p. 205)

RESTAURANT

GOLDEN PALACE   **Lunch:** $7-$14   **Dinner:** $10-$21   **Phone:** 908/276-8884   123
◆◆   **Location:** Center; Garden State Pkwy exit 138, 0.8 mi w on Boulevard; between N 20th & N 21st. 504
Chinese   Boulevard 07033. **Hours:** 11:30 am-9:30 pm, Fri & Sat-10:30 pm, Sun noon-9:30 pm.
Reservations: suggested; weekends. **Features:** casual dress; health conscious menu items; carryout; street
parking; a la carte. Conservative soft decor. Well prepared cuisine. **Cards:** AE, MC, VI.

KEYPORT—7,600

RESTAURANT

YE COTTAGE INN   **Lunch:** $7-$13   **Dinner:** $9-$25   **Phone:** 732/264-1263
◆   **Location:** W Front St, 0.3 mi s CR 6. 149 W Front St 07735. **Hours:** noon-10 pm, Fri & Sat-11 pm. Closed:
Seafood   Mon. **Reservations:** suggested; for 6 or more. **Features:** casual dress; children's menu; early bird specials;
health conscious menu items; carryout; cocktails & lounge. View of pier & harbor. Also serving steak, veal,
chicken & pasta. **Cards:** AE, DI, DS, MC, VI.   ☒

LAKEWOOD—45,000

LODGING

BEST WESTERN LEISURE INN   Phone: 732/367-0900
AAA **SAVE**   5/1-9/30   1P: $85- 95   2P/1B: $95   2P/2B: $95   XP: $10   F16
          10/1-4/30   1P: $53- 66   2P/1B: $57- 76 2P/2B: $53- 66 XP: $10   F16
◆◆   **Location:** On SR 70, just w of Garden State Pkwy exit 88 southbound; 2.5 mi e of US 9. 1600 Rt 70 08701.
Motor Inn   Fax: 732/370-4928. **Terms:** Weekly/monthly rates; no pets. **Facility:** 105 rooms. Handling fee imposed; 2 sto-
ries; interior/exterior corridors. **Dining & Entertainment:** Restaurant; 7 am-10:30 pm, Sat & Sun from 7:30
am; $10-$17; health conscious menu items; cocktails/lounge. **Services:** Fee: coin laundry. **All Rooms:** free movies, VCR's.
Some Rooms: Fee: microwaves, refrigerators, whirlpools. **Cards:** AE, CB, DI, DS, MC, VI. **Special Amenities: Free room
upgrade and preferred room (each subject to availability with advanced reservations).**   [ad] [CTV] [X] [D]

RESTAURANT

IL CAMINO   **Lunch:** $7-$11   **Dinner:** $9-$18   Phone: 732/364-4461
◆◆   **Location:** On US 9, 1.5 mi n of jct SR 70. 515 River Ave 08701. **Hours:** 11:30 am-10 pm, Fri & Sat noon-11
Italian   pm. **Closed:** 11/26 & 12/25. **Reservations:** suggested. **Features:** children's menu; carryout; cocktails; a la
carte. Warm, inviting family restaurant. Native Italian chef serves authentic cuisine, including own desserts.
Espresso/cappuccino. **Cards:** AE, MC, VI.

LAMBERTVILLE—3,900

LODGINGS

CHIMNEY HILL BED & BREAKFAST   Rates Subject to Change   Phone: 609/397-1516
◆◆◆   Fri & Sat [BP]   1P: $120- 170   2P/1B: $135- 175   XP: $30
Historic Bed Sun-Thurs [BP]   1P: $75- 95   2P/1B: $85- 105   XP: $30
& Breakfast **Location:** From jct SR 29 & Swan St, just n to Studdiford St, 1.5 mi e (Studdiford St changes to Goat Hill
Rd). 207 Goat Hill Rd 08530. Fax: 609/397-9353. **Terms:** Sr. discount; age restrictions may apply; reserv
deposit, 14 day notice; no pets. **Facility:** 8 rooms. Phones on request. Accessible area with coffee maker, refrigerator & re-
freshments (butler pantry). Handling fee imposed; 3 stories; interior corridors; smoke free premises. **Cards:** AE, MC, VI.
                                                                                          [X] [D]

THE INN AT LAMBERTVILLE STATION   Rates Subject to Change   Phone: 609/397-4400
AAA   All Year [CP]   1P: $85- 160   2P/1B: $85- 160 2P/2B: $95- 180 XP: $15   F12
          Location: Center, s of the Free Bridge. 11 Bridge St 08530. Fax: 609/397-9744. **Terms:** No pets. **Facility:** 45
◆◆◆   rooms. Whirlpool suites, $125-$225; 3 stories; interior corridors. **Dining:** The Lambertville Station, see
Motor Inn   separate listing. **Cards:** AE, CB, DI, MC, VI.   [CTV] [D]

LAMBERTVILLE HOUSE-A NATIONAL HISTORIC INN   Phone: 609/397-0200
AAA **SAVE**   All Year [CP]   1P: $159- 299   2P/1B: $159- 299
          Location: Downtown. 32 Bridge St 08530. Fax: 609/397-0511. **Terms:** Reserv deposit, 5 day notice; no
◆◆◆   pets. **Facility:** 26 rooms. Historic refurbished inn. Some rooms with balcony, 23 with gas fireplace. 4 stories;
Historic Hotel interior corridors; smoke free premises; 8 two-person whirlpools. **Services:** valet laundry.
          All Rooms: whirlpools. **Some Rooms:** refrigerators. **Cards:** AE, DS, MC, VI. [ad] [CTV] [X] [D] [S]

RESTAURANT

THE LAMBERTVILLE STATION Historical   **Lunch:** $6-$9   **Dinner:** $11-$18   Phone: 609/397-8300
AAA   **Location:** Center; s of the Free Bridge, near the Inn at Lambertville Station. 11 Bridge St 08530.
          Hours: 11:30 am-3 & 4-10 pm, Fri & Sat-11 pm, Sun 10:30 am-3 & 4-10 pm. **Reservations:** suggested; 6 or
◆◆   more. **Features:** casual dress; Sunday brunch; early bird specials; health conscious menu items; cocktails
American   lounge; a la carte. Restored train station alongside scenic Delaware River. **Cards:** AE, CB, MC, VI.   [X]

LAWRENCEVILLE—6,400

LODGINGS

MCINTOSH INN OF PRINCETON   Rates Subject to Change   Phone: 609/896-3700
◆◆   All Year [CP]   1P: $52- 62   2P/1B: $57- 67 2P/2B: $57- 67 XP: $7   F18
Motel   **Location:** 0.3 mi n of exit 67A off I-295, on US 1 adjacent to Quaker Bridge Mall. 3270 Brunswick Pike
08648. Fax: 609/896-2544. **Terms:** Sr. discount; no pets. **Facility:** 115 rooms. 4 stories; interior corridors.
All Rooms: free movies. **Cards:** AE, CB, DI, MC, VI. *(See color ad p 220, p 234 & p 353)*
                                                      Roll in showers. [CTV] [X] [🛇] [D]

RED ROOF INN-PRINCETON   Rates Subject to Change   Phone: 609/896-3388
◆◆   All Year   1P: $48   2P/1B: $55   2P/2B: $56   XP: $7   F18
Motel   **Location:** On US 1, just n of exit 67A of I-295. 3203 Brunswick Pike 08648. Fax: 609/896-4919.
          Terms: Pets. **Facility:** 149 rooms. 2 stories; exterior corridors. **All Rooms:** free & pay movies. **Cards:** AE,
CB, DI, DS, MC, VI.   [🛏] [CTV] [X] [🛇] [D]

RESTAURANTS

ACACIA   **Lunch:** $9-$11   **Dinner:** $18-$20   Phone: 609/895-9885
◆◆◆   **Location:** I-295, exit 7B, on US 206. 2637 Main St 08648. **Hours:** noon-2:30 & 6-9:30 pm, Fri-10 pm, Sat
American   5:30 pm-10 pm, Sun 5 pm-9 pm. **Closed:** major holidays. **Reservations:** suggested. **Features:** health
conscious menu items; a la carte. Progressive American cuisine. Creative, beautifully presented fish, seafood
& meat. Own stunning desserts. Smoke free premises. **Cards:** AE, DS, MC, VI.   [X]

THE NEW NEW YORK DELICATESSEN RESTAURANT   **Lunch:** $7-$13   **Dinner:** $7-$13   Phone: 609/520-0087
◆   **Location:** In Mercer Mall; sw corner jct I-295. 3357 Route 1 S 08648. **Hours:** 7 am-10 pm, Sat-12:30 am,
American   Sun-10 pm. **Closed:** 4/12 & 12/25. **Features:** children's menu; carryout. Friendly family style eatery offering
New York deli quality ingredients plus made-on-premises desserts. **Cards:** AE, DI, DS, MC, VI.   [X]

PALACE OF ASIA   **Lunch:** $6-$8   **Dinner:** $7-$15   Phone: 609/987-0606
◆◆◆   **Location:** In Mercer Mall; US 1N, at jct I-95/295 & US 1. 400 Mercer Mall 08648. **Hours:** 11:30 am-11 pm.
Ethnic   **Closed:** major holidays. **Reservations:** suggested; weekends. **Features:** casual dress; Sunday brunch;
health conscious menu items; carryout; cocktails. Soft, pleasing decor. Exotic Indian food. Extensive menu.
Smoke free premises. **Cards:** AE, DI, DS, MC, VI.   [X]

LEDGEWOOD—1,000   (See map p. 206; index p. 205)

LODGING

DAYS INN   Rates Subject to Change   **Phone: 973/347-5100** 🆔
◆◆   All Year   1P: $85   2P/1B: $85- 95 2P/2B: $85- 95 XP: $8   F18
Motor Inn   **Location:** Westbound I-80, exit 27, 2 mi e on 46E; eastbound I-80, exit 27 (thru 206N & 183N), 2 mi e on 46E. 1691 US 46 W 07852. Fax: 973/347-6356. **Terms:** Sr. discount; no pets. **Facility:** 98 rooms. 2 stories; interior corridors. **Dining:** Restaurant; 7 am-9 pm, Sat & Sun from 8 am; $7-$18. **All Rooms:** free movies. **Cards:** AE, DS, MC, VI. Roll in showers. 🖥️🆗♿🚫🐾📶Ⓓ

LONG BRANCH—28,700

LODGING

OCEAN PLACE HILTON RESORT & SPA   Rates Subject to Change   **Phone: 732/571-4000**
◆◆◆   6/1-9/30   1P: $160- 195 2P/1B: $180- 215 2P/2B: $180- 215 XP: $20   F18
Hotel   5/1-5/31, 10/1-10/31 &
        4/1-4/30   1P: $130- 160 2P/1B: $150- 180 2P/2B: $150- 180 XP: $20   F18
        11/1-3/31   1P: $140   2P/1B: $130- 160 2P/2B: $130- 160 XP: $20   F18
Location: Garden State Pkwy, exit 105, 7 mi w on SR 36 to Ocean Blvd, just s. 1 Ocean Blvd 07740. Fax: 732/571-3314. **Terms:** Check-in 4 pm; reserv deposit; no pets. **Facility:** 254 rooms. Handling fee imposed; 12 stories; interior corridors. **Dining:** Restaurant; 6 am-10 pm; $8-$28. **All Rooms:** free & pay movies. **Some Rooms:** 2 efficiencies. **Cards:** AE, CB, DI, DS, MC, VI. *(See color ad p 18)* 📶📶🖥️🚫ⒹⓈ

RESTAURANT

CASA COMIDA   **Lunch:** $5-$16   **Dinner:** $8-$16   **Phone: 732/229-7774**
◆◆   **Location:** Jct SR 36 & Branchport Ave, just n & e. 336 Branchport Ave 07740. **Hours:** 4 pm-10 pm, Fri &
Mexican   Sat-11 pm; also Wed-Fri 11:30 am-2 pm. Closed: Mon. **Features:** children's menu; health conscious menu items; carryout; cocktails & lounge; a la carte. Inviting, comfortable family atmosphere. Authentic freshly prepared cuisine. Friendly, relaxed service. **Cards:** AE, MC, VI. 🚫

LYNDHURST—18,300   (See map p. 210; index p. 209)

LODGINGS

NOVOTEL MEADOWLANDS   **Phone: 201/896-6666** 🆔
🅰🅰🅰 [SAVE]   Sun-Thurs   1P: $99   2P/1B: $99   2P/2B: $99   XP: $10   F16
        Fri & Sat   1P: $79   2P/1B: $79   2P/2B: $79   XP: $10   F16
◆◆◆   **Location:** NJ Tpk western spur exit 16W, w on SR 3 & s on SR 17. 1 Polito Ave 07071. Fax: 201/896-1309.
Hotel   **Terms:** Package plans; pets. **Facility:** 219 rooms. 6 stories; interior corridors; sauna, whirlpool. **Dining & Entertainment:** Restaurant; 6 am-11 pm; $10-$20; health conscious menu items; cocktails/lounge; entertainment. **Services:** Fee: coin laundry. **All Rooms:** free & pay movies. **Some Rooms:** microwaves, refrigerators, safes. **Cards:** AE, CB, DI, DS, JCB, MC, VI. *(See ad below)* 🐾📶🐕♿🖥️🔒🚫📶ⒹⓈ

QUALITY INN-SPORTS COMPLEX   Rates Subject to Change   **Phone: 201/933-9800** 🆔
◆◆   All Year   1P: $63- 75 2P/1B: $66- 85 2P/2B: $66- 85 XP: $10   F18
Motor Inn   **Location:** NJ Tpk, exit 16W, SR 3W, s on SR 17. 10 Polito Ave 07071. Fax: 201/933-0658. **Terms:** Sr. discount; no pets. **Facility:** 145 rooms. 2 stories; interior corridors. **Dining:** Restaurant; 6:30 am-midnight; $8-$17. **All Rooms:** free & pay movies. **Cards:** AE, CB, DI, DS, JCB, MC, VI. 📶♿🖥️🚫📶Ⓓ

RESTAURANT

LA DOLCE VITA   **Lunch:** $10-$16   **Dinner:** $11-$22   **Phone: 201/935-4260** ⑱
◆◆   **Location:** From SR 3W exit Ridge Rd, 0.8 mi s, 0.5 mi w. 316 Valley Brook Ave 07071. **Hours:** noon-10:30
Italian   pm, Fri-11 pm, Sat 4 pm-11:30 pm, Sun 1 pm-10 pm. **Reservations:** suggested. **Features:** casual dress; health conscious menu items; carryout; cocktails & lounge; a la carte. Traditional cuisine. **Cards:** AE, DI, DS, MC, VI. 🚫

MADISON—15,900   (See map p. 206; index p. 205)

RESTAURANTS

L' ALLEGRIA   **Lunch:** $12-$20   **Dinner:** $12-$20   **Phone: 973/377-6808** ⑮⑨
🅰🅰🅰   **Location:** Center, at jct Prospect & Main sts. 9-11 Prospect St 07940. **Hours:** 11:30 am-3 & 5-11 pm, Sat from 5 pm, Sun 3 pm-9 pm. Closed: 11/26, 12/25 & 1/1. **Reservations:** suggested. **Features:** casual dress;
◆◆◆   health conscious menu items; cocktails & lounge; a la carte. Ambience of a casually sophisticated
Italian   Mediterranean courtyard. **Cards:** AE, CB, DI, DS, MC, VI. 🚫

THE MEETING PLACE   **Lunch:** $12-$15   **Dinner:** $10-$20   **Phone: 973/966-0252** ⑮⑧
◆◆◆   **Location:** Center on Main St (SR 124). 54 Main St 07940. **Hours:** 11:30 am-10 pm, Sat from 5 pm, Sun 5
American pm-9 pm. **Features:** casual dress; health conscious menu items; cocktails & lounge; street parking; a la carte. **Cards:** AE, DI, MC, VI. 🚫

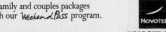

(See map p. 206)

3 CENTRAL **Lunch:** $7-$13 **Dinner:** $11-$20 **Phone:** 973/514-1333 [161]
◆◆ **Location:** Center, jct of Central & Main. 3 Central Ave 07940. **Hours:** 11:30 am-2:30 & 5-9:30 pm, Fri-10
Italian pm, Sat 5 pm-10 pm; Sun 5 pm-9 pm. Closed major holidays. **Reservations:** suggested; weekends.
  Features: casual dress; health conscious menu items; carryout. Fresh seafood, pasta. BYOB. **Cards:** AE,
CB, DI, MC, VI. ⊠

MAHWAH—17,900

LODGINGS

COURTYARD BY MARRIOTT Rates Subject to Change **Phone:** 201/529-5200
◆◆◆ Mon-Thurs 1P: $114- 129 2P/1B: $114- 129 2P/2B: $124- 139
Motel Fri-Sun 1P: $69- 89 2P/1B: $69- 89 2P/2B: $74- 94
  Location: SR 17S, just s of jct I-287 exit 66. 140 SR 17S 07430. **Fax:** 201/529-1991. **Terms:** Sr. discount;
no pets. **Facility:** 146 rooms. 3 stories; interior corridors. **Dining:** Mon-Thurs 6 pm-10 pm, breakfast or a la carte.
All Rooms: free & pay movies. **Cards:** AE, DI, DS, MC, VI. *(See color ad below)* (♿) [CTV] ⊠ 🐾 [D] [S]

RAMADA INN Rates Subject to Change **Phone:** 201/529-5880
◆◆◆ All Year 1P: $96- 106 2P/1B: $111- 116 2P/2B: $106- 116 XP: $10 F16
Motor Inn **Location:** On SR 17S, 0.8 mi s of I-287, exit 66. 180 Rt 17S 07430. **Fax:** 201/529-4767. **Terms:** No pets.
  Facility: 128 rooms. 5 refrigerators avail; 4 stories; interior corridors. **Dining:** Restaurant; 6:30 am-11 pm,
Sat & Sun from 7 am; $7-$16. **All Rooms:** free & pay movies. **Some Rooms:** 12 efficiencies. **Cards:** AE, CB, DI, DS, JCB,
MC, VI. (♿) [CTV] ⊠ 🐾 [D]

SHERATON CROSSROADS HOTEL Guaranteed Rates **Phone:** 201/529-1660
◆◆◆ Sun-Thurs 1P: $99- 135 2P/1B: $119- 155 2P/2B: $119- 155 XP: $20 F18
Hotel Fri & Sat 1P: $99- 109 2P/1B: $99- 109 2P/2B: $99- 109 XP: $20 F18
  Location: At jct SR 17N & exit 66 of I-287. 1 International Blvd, Rt 17 07495. **Fax:** 201/529-4709. **Terms:** Sr.
discount; pets. **Facility:** 225 rooms. 22 stories; interior corridors. **Dining:** Dining room, coffee shop; 6 am-10 pm, Fri &
Sat-11 pm; $15-$21. **All Rooms:** free & pay movies. **Cards:** AE, CB, DI, DS, JCB, MC, VI.
  [🛏] (♿) [CTV] ⊠ 🐾 [D] [S]

RESTAURANT

MASON JAR **Lunch:** $5-$10 **Dinner:** $9-$18 **Phone:** 201/529-2302
ⒶⒶⒶ **Location:** Jct SR 17S & US 202 (Ramapo Valley Rd), just w. 221 Ramapo Valley Rd 07430. **Hours:** 11:15
  am-11 pm, Fri & Sat-midnight. Closed: 11/26, 12/25 & Easter. **Features:** Sunday brunch; carryout; cocktails
◆ & lounge. Southern style hickory barbecue. Wood fired stone hearth pizza ovens for individually
American made-to-order pizza. Steak, seafood, chicken, hamburgers & pasta. Daily specials. **Cards:** AE, DI, MC, VI.
  ⊠

MANALAPAN—100

RESTAURANT

PEKING PAVILION **Lunch:** $6-$11 **Dinner:** $7-$15 **Phone:** 732/308-9700
◆◆ **Location:** From Freehold Race Mall, 1 mi w. 110 Hwy 33 W 07726. **Hours:** 11:30 am-10 pm, Fri-11 pm, Sat
Chinese 5 pm-11 pm. Closed: 7/4, 11/26 & 12/25. **Features:** casual dress; carryout; cocktails & lounge; a la carte.
  Award winning restaurateur. Well prepared traditional cuisine as well as steak, veal & lamb. **Cards:** AE. ⊠

MAPLE SHADE—*See Philadelphia & Vicinity p. 390.*

MARMORA—700

LODGING

ECONO LODGE Rates Subject to Change **Phone:** 609/390-3366
ⒶⒶⒶ Fri & Sat 6/1-9/30 1P: $110- 179 2P/1B: $110- 199 2P/2B: $110- 199 XP: $8 F14
  Sun-Thurs 6/1-9/30 1P: $75- 85 2P/1B: $75- 85 2P/2B: $75- 85 XP: $8 F14
◆◆ Fri & Sat 5/1-5/31 &
Motel 10/1-4/30 1P: $75 2P/1B: $75 2P/2B: $75 XP: $8 F14
  Sun-Thurs 5/1-5/31 &
  10/1-4/30 1P: $35 2P/1B: $35 2P/2B: $35 XP: $8 F14
Location: On US 9, just s of Garden State Pkwy, exit 25. 119 Rt 9 S 08223. **Fax:** 609/390-0193. **Terms:** Sr. discount; reserv
deposit; no pets. **Facility:** 54 rooms. 1 story; exterior corridors. **Cards:** AE, DI, DS, MC, VI. (♿) [CTV] ⊠ [D]

MATAWAN—9,300

RESTAURANT

BART'S MODERN CONTINENTAL CUISINE **Lunch:** $6-$10 **Dinner:** $12-$22 **Phone:** 732/566-0267
◆◆ **Location:** From jct SR 34 & Main St (SR 79), 1 mi n; GSP, exit 117 sw to Matawan. 74 Main St 07747.
Continental **Hours:** 11:30 am-10 pm, Fri-11 pm, Sat 5 pm-11 pm, Sun 2 pm-9 pm. Closed major holidays.
  Reservations: suggested; weekends. **Features:** children's menu; carryout; cocktails. A welcoming friendly
ambience. Dine in cozy old church. Creative cuisine at reasonable prices. **Cards:** AE, DI, DS, MC, VI. ⊠

MAYS LANDING—*See Atlantic City & Vicinity p. 182.*

MCAFEE—1,400

LODGING

DAYS INN — Rates Subject to Change — **Phone:** 973/827-4666
◆◆
Motel

		2P/1B:	$59-	69	2P/2B:	$69-	84	XP:	$7	F18
5/16-10/15 & 12/15-3/15										
5/1-5/15, 10/16-12/14 & 3/16-4/30		2P/1B:	$49-	59	2P/2B:	$59-	69	XP:	$7	F18

Location: 0.3 mi s. 15 Rt 94 07428. **Fax:** 973/827-1466. **Terms:** Reserv deposit; pets. **Facility:** 37 rooms. Handling fee imposed; 2 stories; exterior corridors. **Cards:** AE, DI, DS, MC, VI. Roll in showers. 🛒 CTV ✕ D

MEDFORD—*See Philadelphia & Vicinity p. 391.*

MENDHAM—4,900   (See map p. 206; index p. 205)

RESTAURANT

THE BLACK HORSE INN & PUB Historical   **Lunch:** $8-$15   **Dinner:** $8-$26   **Phone:** 973/543-7300   127
◆◆   **Location:** Center; on SR 24. 1 W Main St 07945. **Hours:** 11:30 am-11 pm, Sun 11:30 am-8 pm. Closed:
American   12/25. **Reservations:** suggested. **Features:** children's menu; carryout; cocktails & lounge; entertainment; a
            la carte. Quaint historic coach inn. Vallet parking dinner only. **Cards:** AE, CB, DI, MC, VI.   ✕

METUCHEN—12,800   (See map p. 206; index p. 205)

RESTAURANT

CAFE ABBRACI   **Lunch:** $9-$13   **Dinner:** $13-$21   **Phone:** 732/548-6077   118
◆◆◆   **Location:** From I-287 s, Metuchen exit, 1 mi n; from I-287 n, make U-turn on New Durham Rd exit, 1 mi n.
Northern   140 Durham Ave 08840. **Hours:** 11:45 am-2 & 5-10 pm, Fri & Sat-11 pm, Sun 4 pm-9 pm. Closed major
Italian   holidays. **Features:** casual dress; carryout; a la carte. Upscale cuisine in contemporary ambience. Osso
            Buco, Arugula crusted salmon are favorites. Own desserts. Smoke free premises. **Cards:** AE, MC, VI.   ✕

MIDDLESEX—13,100   (See map p. 206; index p. 205)

RESTAURANT

ADAM'S CAFE   **Lunch:** $10-$13   **Dinner:** $11-$20   **Phone:** 732/424-2121   180
◆◆◆   **Location:** From jct SR 529, 2.5 mi e. 619 Bound Brook Rd 08846. **Hours:** 11 am-10 pm, Sat & Sun noon-10
Italian   pm. **Reservations:** suggested. **Features:** health conscious menu items; carryout; a la carte. Handsome
            contemporary decor. Refined, creative continental Italian cuisine. BYOB. **Cards:** AE, DI, MC, VI.   ✕

MILFORD—1,300

RESTAURANT

THE SHIP INN RESTAURANT & BREWERY   **Lunch:** $5-$8   **Dinner:** $6-$17   **Phone:** 908/995-0188
◆   **Location:** Downtown. 61 Bridge St 08848. **Hours:** 11:30 am-10 pm. Closed: 11/25 & 11/26.
American   **Reservations:** required; for dinner. **Features:** health conscious menu items; cocktails & lounge; street
            parking. Contemporary European cuisine. House made sausage. Fish & chips made from own beer batter &
fresh potatoes. Smoked pork loin. Non-filtered ales & hard ciders on draft. **Cards:** AE, DI, MC, VI.   ✕

MILLBURN—18,600   (See map p. 206; index p. 205)

RESTAURANT

40 MAIN STREET RESTAURANT & CAFE MAIN   **Lunch:** $4-$12   **Dinner:** $15-$25   **Phone:** 973/376-4444   131
◆◆◆   **Location:** Downtown. 40 Main St 07041. **Hours:** 11:30 am-10 pm, Fri-11 pm, Sat 5:30 pm-11 pm. Closed
American   major holidays, Sun & Mon (restaurant only). **Reservations:** suggested. **Features:** casual dress; children's
            menu; health conscious menu items; cocktails; street parking; a la carte. Charming dining room serves
creative gourmet cuisine. Livelier cafe features pasta, burgers & pizza. **Cards:** AE, DI, MC, VI.   ✕

MILLVILLE—26,000

LODGING

COUNTRY INN BY CARLSON   Guaranteed Rates   **Phone:** 609/825-3100
◆◆◆   All Year [CP]   1P: $70- 85 2P/1B: $75- 85 2P/2B: $75- 85 XP: $5   F18
Motor Inn **Location:** SR 55, exit 26, 0.5 mi w following signs to Wheaton Village. 1125 Village Dr & Wade Blvd 08332.
Fax: 609/825-1317. **Terms:** Sr. discount; no pets. **Facility:** 100 rooms. 4 suites, $125-$135; 2 stories; interior
corridors. **Dining:** Restaurant; 7 am-9 pm, Fri & Sat-10 pm; $5-$13. **All Rooms:** free movies. **Cards:** AE, CB, DI, DS, MC,
VI. *(See color ad below)*   🛏 CTV ✕ D S

MONMOUTH JUNCTION—1,600

LODGINGS

DAYS INN   Phone: 732/329-4555
🔺🔺🔺 SAVE

| | 5/25-6/13 [CP] | 1P: | $80 | 2P/1B: | $90- | 95 | 2P/2B: | $99- | 105 | XP: | $10 | | F12 |

5/1-5/24 & 6/14-4/30 [CP]   1P: $45- 50   2P/1B: $55- 65 2P/2B: $65- 90 XP: $7   F12
◆◆   **Location:** On US 1 southbound, 0.5 mi n of Raymond Rd. 4191, Rt 1 08852. Fax: 732/329-1041.
Motel   **Terms:** Reserv deposit, 3 day notice; no pets. **Facility:** 73 rooms. 3 whirlpool rms, extra charge; 2 stories; exterior corridors. **Some Rooms:** Fee: microwaves, refrigerators, VCR's. **Cards:** AE, DI, DS, MC, VI.
Special Amenities: Free breakfast and free room upgrade (subject to availability with advanced reservations).

🔲 CTV ✖ 🌀 D

RED ROOF INN/NORTH PRINCETON   Rates Subject to Change   Phone: 732/821-8800
◆◆   5/1-10/31   1P: $46- 56   2P/1B: $53- 64 2P/2B: $64   XP: $8   F18
Motel 11/1-4/30   1P: $36- 46   2P/1B: $44- 53 2P/2B: $53   XP: $7   F18
       Location: On US 1 southbound at New Rd. 208 New Rd 08852. Fax: 732/821-5171. **Terms:** Small pets
only. **Facility:** 119 rooms. 3 stories; exterior corridors. **All Rooms:** free & pay movies. **Cards:** AE, CB, DI, DS, MC, VI.

🔲 CTV ✖ 🌀 D S

RESIDENCE INNS BY MARRIOTT   Rates Subject to Change   Phone: 732/329-9600
◆◆◆   Mon-Thurs [CP]   1P: $139   2P/1B: $139   2P/2B: $159
Apartment Fri-Sun [CP]   1P: $89   2P/1B: $89   2P/2B: $109
Motel   **Location:** On US 1 southbound, 0.5 mi s of Raymond Rd. 4225 Rt 1 08540 (PO Box 8388, PRINCETON,
08543). Fax: 732/329-8422. **Terms:** Pets, $10 extra charge. **Facility:** 208 rooms. 2 stories; interior/exterior corridors. **All Rooms:** kitchens, free & pay movies. **Cards:** AE, CB, DI, DS, MC, VI.

🔲 CTV ✖ 🌀 D

MONTCLAIR—37,300   (See map p. 206; index p. 205)

RESTAURANT

THAI CHEF RESTAURANT   **Dinner:** $9-$17   Phone: 973/783-4994   (177)
◆◆◆   **Location:** From jct CR 506 & SR 23, just se. 664 Bloomfield Ave 07042. **Hours:** 5 pm-10 pm, Fri & Sat-11
Ethnic   pm. Closed major holidays. **Features:** minimum charge-$10; street parking; a la carte. Exquisite Thai cuisine
VI.   in sleekly sophisticated yet comfortable cozy restaurant. Outdoor seating weather permitting. **Cards:** AE, MC,

✖

MORRISTOWN—16,200   (See map p. 206; index p. 205)

LODGINGS

BEST WESTERN MORRISTOWN INN   Phone: 973/540-1700   (40)
🔺🔺🔺 SAVE   All Year   1P: $96- 115   2P/1B: $106- 125 2P/2B: $106- 125 XP: $10   F17
       Location: I-287 exit 35, just w on US 24, just s. 270 South St 07960. Fax: 973/267-0241. **Terms:** No pets.
◆◆   **Facility:** 60 rooms. 3 stories; interior corridors. **All Rooms:** free movies. **Some Rooms:** 15 efficiencies.
Motor Inn   **Cards:** AE, CB, DI, DS, JCB, MC, VI.

CTV ✖ 🌀 D

PLAN AHEAD FOR ECONOMY

- Select the optimum route in terms of distance and type of highway. A AAA Travel Counselor can assist you.
- Travel light and avoid using a car-top rack. The less weight and wind resistance, the better the gas mileage.
- Combine short trips, such as visits, errands and shopping.

(See map p. 206)

THE MADISON HOTEL
Phone: 973/285-1800 42

					XP: $10	F18
♦♦♦	Mon-Thurs [CP]	1P: $119- 139	2P/1B: $119- 139		XP: $10	F18
	Fri-Sun [CP]	1P: $109- 129	2P/1B: $109- 129		XP: $10	F18

Motor Inn Location: I-287 exit 35, 1.5 mi e on US 124 (Madison Ave). 1 Convent Rd & Rt 124 07960. Fax: 973/540-8566. Terms: Reserv deposit; no pets. Facility: 190 rooms. 3 whirlpool rms, extra charge; 4 stories; interior corridors. Dining: Rod's 1890's Restaurant, see separate listing. All Rooms: free & pay movies.
Cards: AE, CB, DI, DS, MC, VI. *(See color ad p 204)* 🕾 📺 ⊠ 🐾 D

RESTAURANTS

CALALOO CAFE Lunch: $8-$11 Dinner: $9-$16 Phone: 973/993-1100 44
♦ Location: Center on SR 24; from I-287 exit 35, 0.8 mi s. 190 South St 07960. Hours: 11:30 am-11 pm,
American Fri-midnight, Sat noon-midnight, Sun 11 am-3 & 4-10 pm. Closed major holidays. Reservations: suggested; Sun for brunch. Features: casual dress; children's menu; health conscious menu; cocktails & lounge; a la carte. Featuring fresh fish & pasta. Popular, bustling atmosphere. Comedy cafe Fri & Sat. Reservations required for all shows. Cards: AE, DI, MC, VI. ⊠

ROD'S 1890'S RESTAURANT Lunch: $7-$17 Dinner: $21-$30 Phone: 973/539-6666 43
♦♦ Location: I-287 exit 35, 1.5 mi e on US 124 (Madison Ave); in The Madison Hotel. Madison Ave 07961.
American Hours: 11:30 am-11 pm, Sun 11 am-3 & 4-10 pm. Closed: 12/25. Reservations: suggested. Features: Sunday brunch; children's menu; early bird specials; health conscious menu items; carryout; salad bar; cocktails & lounge; entertainment; valet parking; a la carte. Presidential & Wanamaker railcars add to the Victorian charm & ambience of the many dining rooms. Jackets preferred at dinner. Cards: AE, CB, DI, DS, MC, VI.

MOUNT ARLINGTON—3,600

LODGING

FOUR POINTS HOTEL BY SHERATON Guaranteed Rates Phone: 973/770-2000

♦♦♦	5/1-10/31 & 3/1-4/30	1P: $105- 115	2P/1B: $105- 119 2P/2B: $105- 119	XP: $10	F18
Hotel	11/1-2/28	1P: $89- 99	2P/1B: $99- 109 2P/2B: $99- 109	XP: $10	F18

Location: I-80, exit 30, just n. 15 Howard Blvd 07856. Fax: 973/770-1287. Terms: Sr. discount; small pets only, $50 dep req. Facility: 124 rooms. 5 stories; interior corridors. Dining: Restaurant; 6:30 am 10:30 pm, Sat & Sun from 7 am; $8-$16. All Rooms: free & pay movies. Cards: AE, DI, DS, MC, VI. 🕾 🕾 📺 ⊠ 🐾 D S

MOUNT HOLLY—See Philadelphia & Vicinity p. 391.

MOUNT LAUREL—See Philadelphia & Vicinity p. 391.

MOUNT OLIVE

LODGING

WYNDHAM GARDEN HOTEL Rates Subject to Change Phone: 973/448-1100
♦♦♦ All Year [BP] 1P: $115 2P/1B: $125 2P/2B: $125 XP: $10
Hotel Location: I-80, exit 25, just n. 1000 International Dr 07828. Fax: 973/448-1200. Terms: Reserv deposit; no pets. Facility: 141 rooms. 5 stories; interior corridors. Dining: Restaurant; 6:30 am-10 pm; $15-$22.
All Rooms: Fee: movies. Cards: AE, DI, DS, MC, VI. *(See color ad p 212)* Roll in showers. 🕾 📺 ⊠ 🐾 D S

NEW JERSEY METRO

> **AREA CODE CHANGE** - Effective December 6, 1997 with permissive dialing beginning June 1, 1997, certain cities in the New Jersey Metro area changed their area code from 908 to 732. These changes are reflected in the individual property listings.

To help you more easily locate accommodations in the New Jersey Metro area, the following index and map show lodgings and restaurants in multiple cities. Listings for these establishments are found under the heading for the city in which they are located. THe New Jersey Metro area map comprises: Basking Ridge, Bernardsville, Caldwell, Carteret, Cedar Grove, Chatham, Clark, East Hanover, Edison, Fairfield, Florham Park, Iselin, Kenilworth, Ledgewood, Madison, Mendham, Metuchen, Middlesex, Millburn, Montclair, Morristown, New Providence, Parsippany, Piscataway, Randolph, Rockaway, Scotch Plains, South Plainfield, Short Hills, Summit, Totowa, Union, Warren, Wayne, Westfield, West Orange, Whippany and Woodbridge.

Index of Establishments on the NEW JERSEY METRO AREA ACCOMMODATIONS Spotting Map

BASKING RIDGE
Olde Mill Inn 1

RESTAURANT
The Grain House at the Olde Mill Inn .... (1)

CARTERET
Holiday Inn 6

FAIRFIELD
🏨 Best Western Fairfield Executive Inn.......... 11
Radisson Hotel & Suites...................... 12
Ramada Inn 13
Meadowlands Plaza Hotel 14

EAST HANOVER
🏨 Ramada Inn & Conference Center 17

RESTAURANTS
Rillo's 15
Arcata Ristorante 16

EDISON
Crowne Plaza at Raritan Center............... 19
🏨 Wellesley Inn................................... 20
Red Roof Inn.................................... 22

RESTAURANTS
Jack Cooper's Celebrity Deli & Restaurant....... (19)
Edison Diner .... (20)

FLORHAM PARK
Hamilton Park Executive Conference Center 27

RESTAURANT
🏨 The Afton .... (28)

LEDGEWOOD
Days Inn 34

MORRISTOWN
🏨 Best Western Morristown Inn................. 40
🏨 The Madison Hotel............................ 42

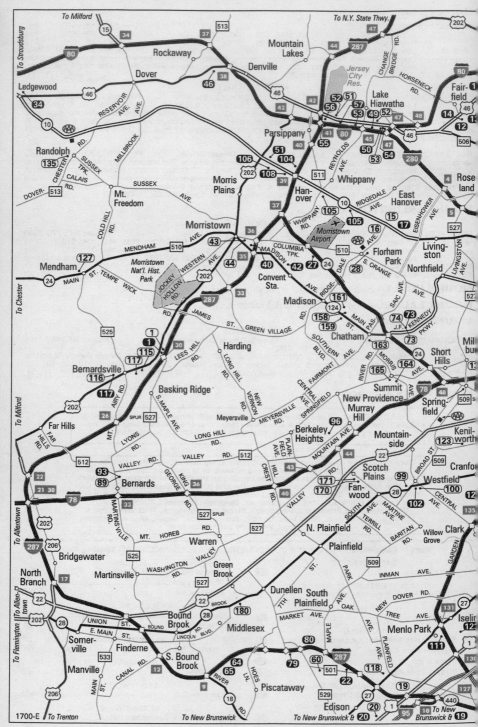

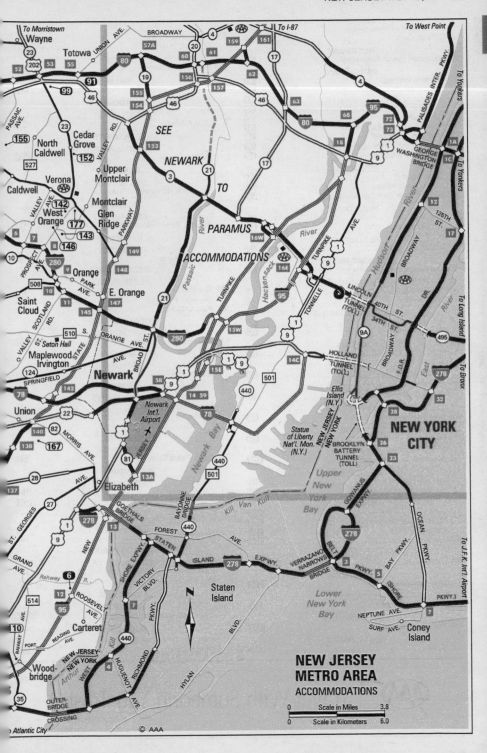

NEW JERSEY METRO AREA
ACCOMMODATIONS

Scale in Miles 0 — 3.8
Scale in Kilometers 0 — 6.0

© AAA

RESTAURANTS

Rod's 1890's Restaurant 43
Calaloo Cafe 44

ROCKAWAY

Mountain Inn of Rockaway 46

PARSIPPANY

Ramada Limited 49
Holiday Inn-Parsippany 50
Parsippany Hilton 51
Embassy Suites 52
Red Roof Inn 53
Howard Johnson Express Inn 54
Sheraton Tara Hotel 55
Hampton Inn - Parsippany 56
Days Inn-Parsippany 57

RESTAURANT

Caffe' Sport 51
Eccola, Italian Bistro 52
Harold's New York Deli Restaurant 53

PISCATAWAY

Wyndham Garden Hotel 64
Embassy Suites Hotel 65

RESTAURANT

Al Dente 60

SHORT HILLS

The Hilton at Short Hills 73

RESTAURANT

The Dining Room 73
The Terrace 74

SOUTH PLAINFIELD

Holiday Inn 79
Ramada Limited 80

TOTOWA

Holiday Inn-Totowa 91

WARREN

Somerset Hills Hotel 93

RESTAURANT

Christine's 89

NEW PROVIDENCE

Best Western Murray Hill Inn 96

WAYNE

Holiday Inn 99

WESTFIELD

Westfield Inn-Best Western 102

RESTAURANTS

Ken Marcotte 99
Northside Trattoria 100

WHIPPANY

Summerfield Suites-Hanover 104
Courtyard by Marriott 105
Hanover Marriott 106
Howard Johnson Inn 108

RESTAURANT

Il Capriccio 105

WOODBRIDGE

Woodbridge Hilton 111

RESTAURANT

The Reo Restaurant & Diner 110

BERNARDSVILLE

The Bernards Inn 117

RESTAURANTS

Girafe 115
The Bernards Inn 116
Eccoqui 117

CLARK

Holiday Inn Select 120

ISELIN

Sheraton at Woodbridge Place 123

METUCHEN

RESTAURANT

Cafe Abbraci 118

KENILWORTH

RESTAURANT

Golden Palace 123

MENDHAM

RESTAURANT

The Black Horse Inn & Pub 127

MILLBURN

RESTAURANT

40 Main Street Restaurant & Cafe Main 131

RANDOLPH

RESTAURANT

Casa de Pasta 135

WEST ORANGE

RESTAURANTS

The Manor 142
Highlawn Pavilion 143
Pals Cabin 146

CEDAR GROVE

RESTAURANT

Il Tulipano 152

CALDWELL

RESTAURANT

Mezzanotte 155

MADISON

RESTAURANTS

The Meeting Place 158
L' Allegria 159
3 Central 161

CHATHAM

RESTAURANT

Fresh Fields Cafe 163

SUMMIT

RESTAURANTS

J B Winberie 164
Souffle' 165

UNION

RESTAURANT

Mario's Trattoria 167

SCOTCH PLAINS

RESTAURANTS

Ginamarie's Ristorante 170
Stage House Inn 171

MONTCLAIR

RESTAURANT

Thai Chef Restaurant 177

MIDDLESEX

RESTAURANT

Adam's Cafe 180

NEWARK—275,200   (See map p. 210; index below)

> **AREA CODE CHANGE - Effective December 6, 1997 with permissive dialing beginning June 1, 1997, certain cities in the Northern New Jersey area changed their area code from 201 to 973. These changes are reflected in the individual property listings.**

To help you more easily locate accommodations in the Newark area, the following index and map show lodgings and restaurants in multiple cities. Listings for these establishments are found under the heading for the city in which they are located. The Newark area map comprises: Carlstadt, Clifton, East Rutherford, Elizabeth, Englewood, Fort Lee, Garfield, Glen Rock, Hackensack, Hasbrouck Heights, Hoboken, Jersey City, Lyndhurst, Newark, North Bergen, Paramus, Saddle Brook, Secaucus, Teaneck and Weehawken.

Airport Accommodations

Listings for these establishments are found under the heading for the city in which they are located.

NEWARK

Airport Marriott, at airport/NEWARK
Courtyard by Marriott, 1.5 mi from main terminal/NEWARK
Ⓦ **Days Inn-Newark Airport, 0.5 mi from main terminal/NEWARK**
Hampton Inn-Newark Airport, 0.75 mi n of main terminal/ELIZABETH
Ⓦ **Howard Johnson Hotel, 2 mi from main terminal/NEWARK**
Ⓦ **Newark Airport Hilton Hotel, 1 mi n from main terminal/ELIZABETH**
Ramada Inn-Newark International Airport, 0.3 mi from main terminal/NEWARK
Sheraton Hotel Newark Airport, 2 mi ne from main terminal/NEWARK
Wyndham Garden Hotel-Newark Airport, 0.5 mi from main terminal/ELIZABETH

Index of Establishments on the NEWARK to PARAMUS ACCOMMODATIONS Spotting Map

CLIFTON
Ⓦ Ramada Inn .... ❶

RESTAURANTS
Chengdu 46 .... ①
Cavalier Cafe .... ③

EAST RUTHERFORD
Sheraton Meadowlands .... ❺
Fairfield Inn by Marriott.................... ❻

RESTAURANTS
Sonoma Grill................................ ⑦
Ⓦ Park & Orchard........................... ⑧

ENGLEWOOD
Radisson Hotel Englewood .... ❽

FORT LEE
Ⓦ Executive Inn at Fort Lee .... ❿
Ⓦ Fort Lee Hilton .... ⓫

HASBROUCK HEIGHTS
Ⓦ Holiday Inn .... ⓮
Ⓦ Crowne Plaza .... ⓯

TEANECK
Marriott at Glenpointe .... ⓰

JERSEY CITY
Ⓦ Holland Motor Lodge .... ⓲

RESTAURANTS
Casa Dante................................. ⑫
Pronto Cena Ristorante .... ⑬

LYNDHURST
Ⓦ Novotel Meadowlands .... ㉓
Quality Inn-Sports Complex................. ㉔

RESTAURANT
La Dolce Vita .... ⑱

ELIZABETH
Hampton Inn-Newark Airport .... ㉖
Wyndham Garden Hotel-Newark Airport .... ㉗
Ⓦ Newark Airport Hilton Hotel .... ㉘

NEWARK
Ramada Inn-Newark International Airport .... ㉝
Sheraton Hotel Newark Airport .... ㉞
Ⓦ Days Inn-Newark Airport .... ㉟
Courtyard by Marriott...................... ㊲
Hilton Gateway............................. ㊳
Ⓦ Howard Johnson Hotel................... ㊴
Airport Marriott .... ㊵

RESTAURANTS
Priscilla's .... ㉓

Tony Da Caneca............................ ㉕
Ⓦ Don Pepe .... ㉖

NORTH BERGEN
Days Inn................................... ㊸

PARAMUS
Howard Johnson Lodge .... ㊹
Holiday Inn .... ㊺
Radisson Inn Paramus .... ㊻

SADDLE BROOK
Ⓦ Holiday Inn and Conference Center....... ㊾
Marriott Hotel .... ㊿
Howard Johnson Plaza Hotel 51

SECAUCUS
Ⓦ Radisson Suite Hotel Meadowlands........... 54
Ⓦ Courtyard by Marriott.................... 55
Red Roof Inn-Meadowlands................. 56
The Holiday Inn Harmon Meadow........... 57
Meadowlands Hilton 58
Hampton Inn 59
Howard Johnson Inn 61
Embassy Suites-Meadowlands 65

RESTAURANT
Ⓦ Lantana Restaurant...................... 31

WEEHAWKEN
Ⓦ Ramada Suite Hotel...................... 68

CARLSTADT
Hampton Inn - Meadowlands................ 70

RESTAURANT
Nick's Oak Room........................... 36

HACKENSACK
Best Western Oritani Hotel.................. 74

RESTAURANT
Ⓦ Stony Hill Inn........................... 41

HOBOKEN
RESTAURANTS
Ristorante Gerrino 46
Arthur's Tavern 48
The Brass Rail 49

GLEN ROCK
RESTAURANT
Ⓦ Glen Rock Inn.......................... 52

GARFIELD
RESTAURANT
Goodfellas Ristorante & Bar 55

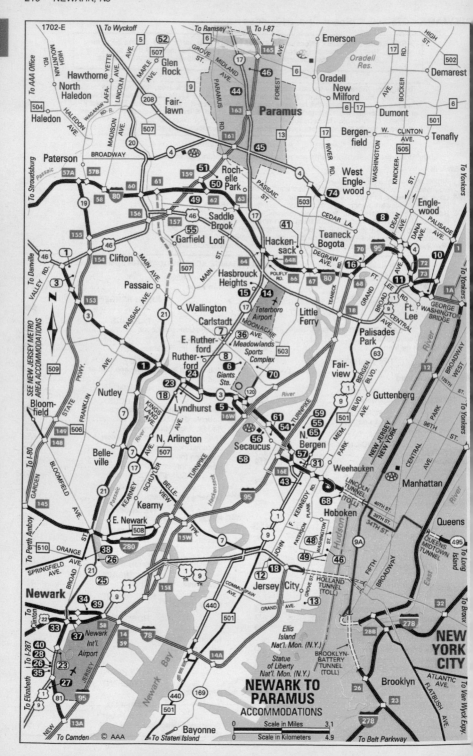

1702-E

To Wyckoff · To Ramsey · To I-87

Emerson

Oradell Res.

Demarest

Oradell New Milford

Paramus

Bergenfield

Tenafly

Hawthorne
North Haledon
Haledon

Glen Rock

Fair-lawn

Dumont

Paterson

Rochelle Park

West Englewood

Englewood

Saddle Brook

Garfield Lodi

Hacken-sack

Teaneck
Bogota

Ft. Lee

Clifton

Passaic

Hasbrouck Heights

GEORGE WASHINGTON BRIDGE

Wallington

Carlstadt

Tetarboro Airport

Little Ferry

Palisades Park

E. Rutherford
Rutherford

Meadowlands Sports Complex

Giants Sta.

Fair-view

Guttenberg

Nutley

Lyndhurst

Bloomfield

N. Arlington

Secaucus

N. Bergen

Weehauken

Manhattan

Belleville

Kearny

E. Newark

Hoboken

Queens

Newark

Newark Int'l. Airport

Jersey City

Ellis Island Nat'l. Mon. (N.Y.)

Statue of Liberty Nat'l. Mon. (N.Y.)

Brooklyn

NEW YORK CITY

Bayonne

NEWARK TO PARAMUS
ACCOMMODATIONS

Scale in Miles   3.1
Scale in Kilometers   4.9

© AAA   To Staten Island

To Camden

To Belt Parkway

(See map p. 210)

LODGINGS

AIRPORT MARRIOTT
◆◆◆ Hotel
	Mon-Thurs	1P: $195	2P/1B: $195	2P/2B: $195	XP: $20
	Fri-Sun	1P: $89	2P/1B: $89	2P/2B: $89	

Rates Subject to Change Phone: 973/623-0006 ⑩ F18
Location: Northbound NJ Tpk exit 13A, southbound exit 14 to airport. Newark International Airport 07114. Fax: 973/623-7618. **Terms:** Check-in 4 pm; reserv deposit; small pets only. **Facility:** 590 rooms. Up to 4 persons in room weekends; 10 stories; interior corridors. **Dining:** Dining room, restaurant; 6 am-11 pm; Sat & Sun from 7 am; $14-$25; also, Priscilla's, see separate listing. **All Rooms:** free & pay movies. **Cards:** AE, CB, DI, DS, JCB, MC, VI.

COURTYARD BY MARRIOTT
◆◆◆ Motor Inn
Rates Subject to Change Phone: 973/643-8500 ㊲ F17
Sun-Thurs 1P: $119 2P/1B: $129 2P/2B: $129 XP: $10 F17
Fri & Sat 1P: $79 2P/1B: $89 2P/2B: $89 XP: $10 F17
Location: NJ Tpk exit 14, 1 mi SW via US 1 & 9S; I-78W exit 58B to US 1 & 9S, local lanes; I-78E exit 58A to US 1 & 9S, local lanes. 600 US 1 & 9S 07114. Fax: 973/648-0662. **Terms:** No pets. **Facility:** 146 rooms. Rates for up to 4 persons on weekends; 3 stories; interior corridors. **Dining:** Restaurant; 6:30 am-1 & 5-10 pm; $8-$15. **All Rooms:** free & pay movies. **Cards:** AE, DI, DS, MC, VI. *(See color ad below)*

DAYS INN-NEWARK AIRPORT
ⒶⒶⒶ Ⓢ̲ⓐ̲ⓥ̲ⓔ̲
◆◆ Motor Inn
All Year 1P: $65- 100 2P/1B: $70- 110 2P/2B: $70- 110 XP: $5 ㉟ F12
Phone: 973/242-0900
Location: Exit 14 of NJ Tpk & 1.5 mi on US 1 & 9S. 450 US 1S 07114. Fax: 973/242-8480. **Terms:** Weekly/monthly rates; package plans; no pets. **Facility:** 191 rooms. 8 stories; interior corridors. **Dining & Entertainment:** Restaurant; 6:30 am-midnight, Fri & Sat from 7 am; $9-$21; cocktails/lounge. **Services:** Fee: coin laundry. **All Rooms:** free & pay movies. **Some Rooms:** Fee: microwaves, refrigerators. **Cards:** AE, CB, DI, DS, MC, VI. *(See ad below)*

HILTON GATEWAY
◆◆◆ Hotel
Rates Subject to Change Phone: 973/622-5000 ㊳
All Year 1P: $135 2P/1B: $135
Location: 3 mi w of exit 15E of NJ Tpk via Raymond Blvd, connecting to Penn Station, NJ Transit, Path & Amtrak. Gateway Center-Raymond Blvd 07102. Fax: 973/622-2644. **Terms:** Reserv deposit; no pets. **Facility:** 253 rooms. Up to 4 persons in room; 10 stories; interior corridors. Fee: parking. **Dining:** Dining room, restaurant; 6 am-11 pm; $10-$20. **All Rooms:** free & pay movies. **Cards:** AE, CB, DI, DS, MC, VI. *(See color ad p 18)*

(See map p. 210)

HOWARD JOHNSON HOTEL   Phone: 973/344-1500   39

(AAA) [SAVE]   All Year   1P: $70- 100   2P/2B: $70- 100
◆◆   **Location:** Tpk exit 14, 2nd right after toll booth via service road & right 0.3 mi. 50 Port St 07114.
Motor Inn   Fax: 973/344-3311. **Terms:** No pets. **Facility:** 171 rooms. Long-term secure valet parking. 3 stories; interior
             corridors. **Dining & Entertainment:** Coffee shop; 6 am-midnight; $7-$15; cocktails/lounge. **Services:**
             Fee: coin laundry. **All Rooms:** free movies. **Cards:** AE, CB, DI, DS, MC, VI. **Special Amenities:** Free room
upgrade and preferred room (each subject to availability with advanced reservations). *(See ad below)*

[icons]

RAMADA INN-NEWARK
INTERNATIONAL AIRPORT   Rates Subject to Change   Phone: 973/824-4000   33
◆◆   All Year   1P: $90- 120   2P/1B: $100- 130 2P/2B: $100- 130 XP: $10   F18
Motor Inn   **Location:** On US 1 & 9 southbound, exit 14 off NJ Tpk. 550 Rt 1 & 9S 07114. Fax: 973/824-4100.
             Terms: No pets. **Facility:** 342 rooms. 5 stories; interior corridors. **Dining:** Restaurant, coffee shop; 6 am-1
am; $10-$16. **All Rooms:** free & pay movies. **Cards:** AE, CB, DI, DS, JCB, MC, VI.   [icons]

(See map p. 210)

SHERATON HOTEL NEWARK AIRPORT

◆◆
Hotel

	Rates Subject to Change			
Sun-Thurs 1/1-4/30	1P: $189	2P/1B: $189	2P/2B: $189	XP: $10 F16
Sun-Thurs 5/1-12/31	1P: $184	2P/1B: $184	2P/2B: $184	XP: $10 F16
Fri & Sat 1/1-4/30	1P: $95	2P/1B: $95	2P/2B: $95	XP: $10 F16
Fri & Sat 5/1-12/31	1P: $89	2P/1B: $89	2P/2B: $89	XP: $10 F16

Phone: 973/690-5500 🟦34

Location: NJ Tpk exit 14; via service road, 2nd right after toll booth. 128 Frontage Rd 07114. Fax: 973/465-7195. **Terms:** Sr. discount; small pets only. **Facility:** 502 rooms. 12 stories; interior corridors. Fee: parking. **Dining:** Dining room, restaurant; 6:30 am-11 pm; $15-$25. **All Rooms:** free & pay movies. **Cards:** AE, CB, DI, DS, MC, VI.

🛏 🚲 🛧 CTV ✕ 🛁 D S

RESTAURANTS

DON PEPE
🔺🔺🔺
◆◆
Ethnic

Lunch: $7-$11   Dinner: $12-$23   Phone: 973/623-4662 🟦26
Location: Just n of Raymond Blvd. 844 McCarter (US 22) Hwy 07102. **Hours:** 11:30 am-10 pm, Fri & Sat-11 pm, Sun 1 pm-10 pm. Closed: 11/26 & 12/25. **Features:** casual dress; cocktails & lounge; a la carte. Warm wall murals lend a feeling of the Spanish countryside. Fresh seafood specialties. **Cards:** AE, DI, DS, MC, VI.
✕

PRISCILLA'S
◆◆◆
Continental

Lunch: $11-$17   Dinner: $18-$31   Phone: 973/623-0006 🟦23
Location: Northbound NJ Tpk exit 13A, southbound exit 14 to airport; in Airport Marriott. Newark Int'l Airport 07114. **Hours:** 11:30 am-2 & 5:30-10 pm, Sat from 5:30 pm. Closed major holidays & Sun. **Reservations:** suggested. **Features:** health conscious menu items; cocktails & lounge; valet parking; a la carte. Business casual dress. Upscale dining at the airport. **Cards:** AE, DI, DS, JCB, MC, VI.
✕

TONY DA CANECA
◆◆
Ethnic

Lunch: $7-$15   Dinner: $12-$20   Phone: 973/589-6882 🟦25
Location: On corner of Elm Rd & Houston St; in Ironbound section. 72 Elm Rd 07105. **Hours:** 11:30 am-10 pm, Fri & Sat-11 pm, Sun noon-10 pm. **Reservations:** suggested; weekends. **Features:** casual dress; health conscious menu items; carryout; cocktails & lounge; a la carte. Authentic Portuguese & Spanish cuisine. Featuring pork with clams Alentejana, rabbit stew & suckling pig with pepper sauce. **Cards:** AE, DI, DS, MC, VI.

NEW BRUNSWICK—41,700

RESTAURANTS

THE FROG AND THE PEACH   Historical   Lunch: $9-$16   Dinner: $18-$30   Phone: 732/846-3216
◆◆◆
Nouvelle
American

Location: Just w of jct SR 27 & 18 via Albany St to Neilson St, just e. 29 Dennis St 08901. **Hours:** 11:30 am-2:30 & 5:30-10:30 pm, Sat from 5:30 pm, Sun 4:30 pm-9:30 pm. Closed major holidays. **Reservations:** suggested. **Features:** dressy casual; health conscious menu items; cocktails & lounge; a la carte. Contemporary dining in sophisticated renovated brownstone. Bar menu avail on patio from 2:30 pm. Smoke free premises. **Cards:** AE, CB, DI, DS, MC, VI.
✕

LA FONTANA RISTORANTE
🔺🔺🔺
◆◆◆◆
Italian

Lunch: $15-$20   Dinner: $23-$31   Phone: 732/249-7500
Location: Downtown, corner Spring Alley & Albany sts. 120 Albany St 08901. **Hours:** 11:30 am-2:30 & 5-10 pm, Sat 5 pm-11 pm. Closed: Sun. **Reservations:** suggested. **Features:** semi-formal attire; cocktails; valet parking; a la carte. Old world romantic ambience. Professionally attentive, yet friendly wait staff. Classic preparation of entrees from all regions of Italy. Excellent wine list, including many half-bottles. **Cards:** AE, DI, MC, VI.
✕

PANICO'S
◆◆◆◆
Italian

Lunch: $13-$18   Dinner: $18-$30   Phone: 732/545-6100
Location: Downtown, just e of jct George & Church sts. 103 Church St 08901. **Hours:** 11:30 am-2:30 & 5:30-10 pm, Fri-11 pm, Sat 5:30 pm-11 pm. Closed major holidays & Sun. **Reservations:** suggested. **Features:** semi-formal attire; cocktails & lounge; fee for parking; a la carte. Creative cuisine; all made on premises. Award winning wine list. Excellent professional wait staff. Simple elegance with a touch of sophistication. Jackets required for gentleman for dinner. Validated parking in garage opposite. **Cards:** AE, DI, DS, MC, VI.
✕

ZIA GRILL
◆◆
Southwest
American

Lunch: $6-$12   Dinner: $16-$28   Phone: 732/249-1551
Location: Just e of jct SR 27 & 18 via Albany St to Neilson St, just n to Dennis St. 19 Dennis St 08901. **Hours:** 11:30 am-2:30 & 5:30-10:30 pm, Sat from 5:30 pm, Sun 4 pm-9 pm. Closed major holidays. **Reservations:** suggested; weekends. **Features:** casual dress; carryout; cocktails & lounge; a la carte. High energy, upscale casual ambience. Innovative cuisine. Outstanding selection of flavored tequilas. Own desserts. Espresso/cappuccino. **Cards:** AE, MC, VI.
✕

NEW PROVIDENCE—11,400   (See map p. 206; index p. 205)

LODGING

BEST WESTERN MURRAY HILL INN
🔺🔺🔺 SAVE
◆◆
Motor Inn

Phone: 908/665-9200 🟦96
All Year   1P: $105- 130   2P/1B: $115- 140   2P/2B: $115- 140   XP: $10 F17
Location: I-78 eastbound exit 44, westbound exit 43, 1.5 mi in New Providence; jct South St & Central Ave. 535 Central Ave 07974. Fax: 908/665-9562. **Terms:** No pets. **Facility:** 76 rooms. 3 stories; interior corridors. **Dining:** Restaurant; 6:30 am-9:30 pm, Sat & Sun 7 am-10 pm; $13-$16. **All Rooms:** free & pay movies. **Some Rooms:** 23 efficiencies. **Cards:** AE, CB, DI, DS, JCB, MC, VI.
CTV ✕ 🛁 D

NEWTON—7,800

LODGING

THE WOODEN DUCK BED & BREAKFAST
◆◆◆
Bed &
Breakfast

Rates Subject to Change   Phone: 973/300-0395
All Year [BP]   1P: $100- 120   2P/1B: $100- 120   2P/2B: $100- 120   XP: $30
Location: I-80, exit 25; 7.8 mi n on US 206 to Goodale Rd, 1.5 mi e. 140 Goodale Rd 07860. Fax: 973/300-0395. **Terms:** Age restrictions may apply; reserv deposit, 7 day notice; no pets. **Facility:** 5 rooms. 2 stories; interior/exterior corridors; smoke free premises. **Cards:** AE, DS, MC, VI. 🚲 CTV ✕ D

NORTH BERGEN—48,400   (See map p. 210; index p. 209)

LODGING

DAYS INN
◆◆
Motor Inn

Rates Subject to Change   Phone: 201/348-3600 🟦43
All Year   1P: $69- 79   2P/1B: $69- 79   2P/2B: $84- 99   XP: $15 F12
Location: From jct SR 3, just s. 2750 Tonnelle Ave (US 1 & 9) 07047. Fax: 201/330-8932. **Terms:** Reserv deposit; no pets. **Facility:** 250 rooms. Whirlpool suite, extra charge; 12 stories; interior corridors. **Dining:** Restaurant; 6:30 am-midnight; $10-$17. **All Rooms:** free movies. **Cards:** AE, CB, DI, DS, MC, VI.
🚲 CTV ✕ D

NORTH BRUNSWICK—31,300

RESTAURANT

ARTHUR'S TAVERN **Lunch:** $4-$12 **Dinner:** $5-$12 **Phone:** 732/828-1117
◆◆ **Location:** Exit 9 of NJ Tpk, Rt 18 n 0.5 mi, 2 mi s on US 1, n 0.5 mi. 644 Georges Rd 08902. **Hours:** 11:30
Steakhouse am-11 pm, Fri & Sat-midnight, Sun 2 pm-10 pm. Closed: 11/26 & 12/25. **Features:** casual dress; carryout;
cocktails & lounge; a la carte. Inviting pub atmosphere. Local favorite for steak. **Cards:** AE, DI, MC, VI. ⊠

NORTHFIELD—*See Atlantic City & Vicinity p. 182.*

NORTH WILDWOOD—5,000

LODGINGS

CANDLELIGHT INN **Phone:** 609/522-6200
ⒶⒶⒶ ⟨SAVE⟩ 5/15-10/19 [BP] 1P: $110- 140 2P/1B: $120- 150 2P/2B: $115- 260 XP: $20
  5/1-5/14 & 10/20-4/30 [BP] 1P: $75- 115 2P/1B: $95- 125 2P/2B: $85- 225 XP: $20
◆◆◆ **Location:** At 24th & Central aves; from Garden St Pkwy, exit 6, 3 mi se on SR 147 (which becomes NJ
Historic Bed Ave), 1.2 mi s on NJ Ave, just e to Central Ave. 2310 Central Ave 08260. Fax: 609/522-6125. **Terms:** Age
& Breakfast restrictions may apply; reserv deposit, 15 day notice; weekly rates; package plans; 3 night min stay,
  weekends 7/1-8/31; no pets. **Facility:** 10 rooms. Turn-of-the-century Queen Anne Victorian structure with wrap-
around veranda. Authentic antique furnishings. Carriage house suites, whirlpool tub & fireplace $140-$225. Handling fee imposed; 4 stories, no elevator; interior/exterior corridors; smoke free premises; whirlpool; lawn games. **Services:** area
transportation, to bus terminal. **All Rooms:** free movies, combo or shower baths, no phones. **Some Rooms:** coffeemakers,
microwaves, refrigerators, VCR's, whirlpools. **Cards:** AE, DS, MC, VI. **Special Amenities: Free breakfast and free local
telephone calls.** 📵 CTV ⊠ D

EUROPEAN Rates Subject to Change **Phone:** 609/729-4622
ⒶⒶⒶ 6/28-8/24 & 8/30-9/2 1P: $84 2P/1B: $84 2P/2B: $96 XP: $10 F6
  6/21-6/27 & 8/25-8/29 1P: $70 2P/1B: $70 2P/2B: $85 XP: $8 F6
◆◆ 6/7-6/20 & 9/3-10/18 1P: $42 2P/1B: $42 2P/2B: $50 XP: $8 F6
Motel 5/10-6/6 1P: $38 2P/1B: $38 2P/2B: $42 XP: $8 F6
  Location: 3rd & Ocean aves; exit 6 off Garden State Pkwy, 3 mi se on SR 147 (which becomes New Jersey
Ave) to 3rd Ave, 0.5 mi e. 300 Ocean Ave 08260. **Terms:** Open 5/10-10/18; reserv deposit, 14 day notice; no pets.
Facility: 20 rooms. Handling fee imposed; 2 stories; exterior corridors. **All Rooms:** efficiencies. **Cards:** AE, DS, MC, VI.
(See color ad p 240) 🛥 CTV D

HARBOR LIGHT MOTOR INN Guaranteed Rates **Phone:** 609/729-5567
ⒶⒶⒶ 7/4-9/2 2P/2B: $80- 140 XP: $10
  6/23-7/3 2P/2B: $70- 125 XP: $10
◆◆ 6/14-6/22 2P/2B: $50- 102 XP: $10
Motel 5/1-6/13 & 9/3-10/15 2P/2B: $40- 85 XP: $10
  Location: Exit 6 off Garden State Pkwy, 3 mi se on SR 147 (which becomes New Jersey Ave) to 3rd Ave,
then 0.5 mi e. 301 Ocean Ave 08260. Fax: 609/522-5935. **Terms:** Open 5/1-10/15; reserv deposit, 14 day notice; 3 night
min stay, in season; no pets. **Facility:** 45 rooms. Rates are for up to 4 persons. Handling fee imposed; 3 stories, no elevator;
exterior corridors. **Some Rooms:** 43 efficiencies. **Cards:** AE, DS, MC, VI. *(See color ad opposite title page & p 241)*
  🛥 CTV D

ISLE OF CAPRI MOTEL Guaranteed Rates **Phone:** 609/522-1991
◆◆ 6/28-9/5 1P: $64- 70 2P/1B: $72- 78 2P/2B: $78- 90 XP: $8 F8
Motel 6/12-6/27 & 9/6-9/20 1P: $40 2P/1B: $44- 46 2P/2B: $48- 56 XP: $6 F8
  5/1-6/11 & 9/21-10/1 1P: $38 2P/1B: $40- 42 2P/2B: $40- 46 XP: $6 F8
Location: From Garden State Pkwy exit 6, 3 mi se on SR 147 (which becomes New Jersey Ave), to 5th Ave, 0.5 mi e. 500
Ocean Ave At 5th Ave 08260. **Terms:** Open 5/1-10/1; 3 night min stay, 6/25-9/7; no pets. **Facility:** 20 rooms. 2 stories; exterior
corridors. **Some Rooms:** 5 efficiencies. **Cards:** MC, VI. *(See ad p 238)* 🛥 CTV D

IVANHOE MOTEL Rates Subject to Change **Phone:** 609/522-5874
◆◆ 7/1-8/31 2P/2B: $80- 150 XP: $12
Motel 6/1-6/30 & 9/1-9/30 2P/2B: $50- 110 XP: $12
  5/1-5/31 & 10/1-10/31 2P/2B: $50- 80 XP: $5
  4/1-4/30 2P/2B: $45- 60 XP: $5
Location: Garden State Pkwy, exit 6, 3 mi se on SR 147 (which becomes New Jersey Ave) to 21st Ave, 0.5 mi e. 430 E
21st Ave 08260. Fax: 609/523-2323. **Terms:** Open 5/1-10/31 & 4/1-4/30; reserv deposit; no pets. **Facility:** 40 rooms. Rates for
2 adults & 2 children; 2 stories; exterior corridors. **Some Rooms:** 29 efficiencies, 9 kitchens. **Cards:** AE, CB, DI, DS, MC,
VI. 🛥 CTV D

LONG BEACH LODGE Rates Subject to Change **Phone:** 609/522-1520
ⒶⒶⒶ 7/24-8/31 2P/1B: $81 2P/2B: $103- 155 XP: $10 F6
  7/16-7/23 2P/1B: $72 2P/2B: $95- 136 XP: $10 F6
◆◆ 6/2-7/15 & 9/1-9/19 2P/1B: $49- 56 2P/2B: $59- 106 XP: $8 F6
Motel 5/1-6/1 & 9/20-10/13 2P/1B: $49 2P/2B: $53- 79 XP: $8 F6
  Location: Garden State Pkwy, exit 6, 3 mi s on SR 147 to New Jersey Ave, 0.5 mi s to 9th Ave, then 0.5 mi
e. 539 E 9th Ave 08260. Fax: 609/522-0538. **Terms:** Open 5/1-10/13; reserv deposit, 14 day notice; no pets. **Facility:** 24
rooms. Rates for up to 4 persons in season. Handling fee imposed; 3 stories, no elevator; exterior corridors.
All Rooms: efficiencies. **Cards:** AE, DS, MC, VI. *(See color ad p 238)* 🛥 CTV D

THE MALI KAI Rates Subject to Change **Phone:** 609/522-2866
ⒶⒶⒶ 7/2-9/6 2P/1B: $119- 152 2P/2B: $119- 152 XP: $10 F6
  6/12-7/1 & 9/7-9/11 2P/1B: $75- 103 2P/2B: $75- 103 XP: $10 F6
◆◆ 5/25-6/11 2P/1B: $59- 69 2P/2B: $59- 69 XP: $8-10 F6
Condo Motel 5/1-5/24, 9/12-10/25 &
  4/1-4/30 2P/1B: $35- 59 2P/2B: $35- 59 XP: $8-10 F6
Location: Garden State Pkwy, exit 6, 3 mi se on SR 147 (which becomes New Jersey Ave) to 19th Ave, 0.5 mi e. 417 E
19th St 08260. Fax: 609/523-1583. **Terms:** Open 5/1-10/25 & 4/1-4/30; reserv deposit, 14 day notice; 3 night min stay,
7/12-8/17; no pets. **Facility:** 41 rooms. Rates for up to 4 persons. Handling fee imposed; 5 stories; exterior corridors.
All Rooms: efficiencies, free movies. **Cards:** DS, MC, VI. 🛥 CTV D

MATADOR OCEANFRONT RESORT MOTEL
ⒶⒶⒶ
◆◆
Motel

	7/14-8/26	Guaranteed Rates			**Phone:** 609/522-9451	
	7/14-8/26	2P/1B: $90	2P/2B: $105- 175	XP: $10		
	7/1-7/13 & 8/27-9/4	2P/1B: $80	2P/2B: $95- 150	XP: $10		
	6/16-6/30	2P/1B: $70	2P/2B: $78- 125	XP: $10		
	5/1-6/15 & 9/5-10/15	2P/1B: $55	2P/2B: $65- 110	XP: $10		

Location: Garden State Pkwy, exit 6, 3.8 mi se on SR 147(which becomes New Jersey Ave) to 16th Ave, 0.5 mi e. 511 E 16th Ave & Beach 08260. Fax: 609/522-4452. **Terms:** Open 5/1-10/15; reserv deposit, 14 day notice; 3 night min stay; no pets. **Facility:** 62 rooms. Handling fee imposed; 4 stories; exterior corridors. **Some Rooms:** 41 efficiencies, 2 kitchens. **Cards:** AE, DS, MC, VI. *(See color ad p 241)* 🅿️ ⓒⓣⓥ Ⓓ

MEDITERRANEAN MOTEL
ⒶⒶⒶ
◆◆
Motel

	6/28-8/24 & 8/30-9/2	Rates Subject to Change			**Phone:** 609/522-0112		
	6/28-8/24 & 8/30-9/2	1P: $68	2P/1B: $72	2P/2B: $72- 96	XP: $10	F6
	6/21-6/27 & 8/25-8/29	1P: $50	2P/1B: $55	2P/2B: $70- 85	XP: $8	F6
	6/7-6/20 & 9/3-9/29	1P: $38	2P/1B: $40	2P/2B: $42- 50	XP: $8	F6
	5/10-6/6	1P: $32	2P/1B: $36	2P/2B: $38- 42	XP: $8	F6

Location: At Ocean & 5th aves; exit 6 off Garden State Pkwy, 3 mi se on SR 147 (which becomes New Jersey Ave) to 5th Ave, 0.5 mi e. 405 Ocean Ave 08260. **Terms:** Open 5/10-9/29; reserv deposit, 14 day notice; 3 night min stay, weekends in season; no pets. **Facility:** 33 rooms. Open Fri-Sun only 5/7-5/15. Winter phone number (215) 271-6882. Handling fee imposed; 3 stories, no elevator; exterior corridors. **All Rooms:** free movies. **Some Rooms:** 22 efficiencies. **Cards:** AE, DS, MC, VI. *(See color ad p 240)* 🅿️ ⓒⓣⓥ ✕ Ⓓ

PANORAMIC MOTEL AND APARTMENTS
◆◆
Motel

	7/1-8/31	Rates Subject to Change		**Phone:** 609/522-1181	
	7/1-8/31	2P/2B: $80- 150	XP: $12		
	6/1-6/30 & 9/1-9/30	2P/2B: $50- 110	XP: $12		
	5/1-5/31 & 10/1-10/31	2P/2B: $50- 80	XP: $5		
	4/1-4/30	2P/2B: $45- 60	XP: $5		

Location: Garden State Pkwy, exit 6, 3 mi se on SR 147 (which becomes New Jersey Ave) to 21st Ave; 0.5 mi e. 2101 Surf Ave 08260. Fax: 609/523-2323. **Terms:** Open 5/1-10/31 & 4/1-4/30; reserv deposit; no pets. **Facility:** 25 rooms. Rates for 2 adults & 2 children; 2 stories; exterior corridors. **Some Rooms:** 23 efficiencies, 2 kitchens. **Cards:** AE, CB, DI, DS, MC, VI. 🅿️ ⓒⓣⓥ Ⓓ

SURF SONG MOTEL
◆◆◆
Motel

	7/9-8/28	Rates Subject to Change		**Phone:** 609/523-0003	
	7/9-8/28	1P: $103- 125	2P/1B: $103- 125	XP: $10	
	6/11-7/8 & 8/29-9/2	1P: $61- 103	2P/1B: $61- 103	XP: $10	
	5/1-5/23, 9/19-10/31 &				
	3/15-4/30	1P: $31- 43	2P/1B: $31- 43	XP: $6	
	5/24-6/10 & 9/3-9/18	1P: $50- 89	2P/1B: $50- 89	XP: $6	

Location: Garden State Pkwy exit 6, 3.5 mi se on SR 147 (which becomes New Jersey Ave) to 18th Ave, then 0.4 mi e. 1800 Ocean Ave 08260. Fax: 609/523-8984. **Terms:** Open 5/1-10/31 & 3/15-4/30; reserv deposit, 14 day notice; no pets. **Facility:** 60 rooms. Handling fee imposed; 5 stories; exterior corridors. **All Rooms:** free movies. **Cards:** AE, CB, DI, DS, MC, VI. 🅿️ ⓒⓣⓥ Ⓓ

RESTAURANTS

PIRO'S VILLAGE RESTAURANT
◆◆
Italian

Dinner: $9-$25   **Phone:** 609/729-0401
Location: Garden State Pkwy exit 6, 3 mi se on SR 147 (which becomes New Jersey Ave) to 19th Ave, then just w. 1901 New York Ave 08260. **Hours:** Open 5/1-10/15; 5 pm-10 pm. **Reservations:** suggested. **Features:** casual dress; children's menu; carryout; cocktails & lounge. **Cards:** MC, VI.

SPAGHETTI REEF
◆◆
Seafood

Dinner: $15-$20   **Phone:** 609/729-3344
Location: Garden State Pkwy, exit 6, 3 mi se on SR 147 (New Jersey Ave) to New York Ave, just n to Anglesea Dr. 119 W Anglesea Dr 08260. **Hours:** 5 pm-10 pm. Closed: 9/30-3/31. **Reservations:** suggested. **Features:** casual dress; children's menu; early bird specials; carryout; cocktails & lounge. Seafood, steak, veal & chicken prepared with an Italian flair; seasonal outdoor dining deck; very good view of ocean inlet. **Cards:** AE, DS, MC, VI.

OCEAN CITY—15,500

LODGINGS

BEACH CLUB HOTEL
ⒶⒶⒶ
◆◆◆
Motor Inn

	6/12-9/7	Rates Subject to Change		**Phone:** 609/399-8555	
	6/12-9/7	2P/2B: $185- 265	XP: $10	F6	
	9/8-9/19	2P/2B: $124- 170	XP: $10	F6	
	5/8-6/11 & 9/20-10/18	2P/2B: $76- 140	XP: $10	F6	
	5/1-5/7	2P/2B: $70- 112	XP: $10	F6	

Location: 13th St & Ocean Ave; at the ocean boardwalk. 1280 Boardwalk Ave 08226. Fax: 609/398-4739. **Terms:** Open 5/1-10/18; reserv deposit, 7 day notice; 3 night min stay, 7/1-9/3; no pets. **Facility:** 82 rooms. Handling fee imposed; 4 stories; interior corridors. **Dining:** Restaurant; 7 am-9 pm; $7-$16. **All Rooms:** Fee: movies. **Some Rooms:** 2 kitchens. **Cards:** AE, MC, VI. 🅿️ ⓔⓒⓣⓥ ✕ 🅿️ Ⓓ

CASTLE BY THE SEA
ⒶⒶⒶ
◆◆◆
Historic Bed
& Breakfast

	6/1-8/31 [BP]	Guaranteed Rates			**Phone:** 609/398-3555	
	6/1-8/31 [BP]	1P: $109- 219	2P/1B: $109- 219	2P/2B: $109- 219	XP: $15	F
	5/1-5/31, 9/1-10/31 &					
	4/1-4/30 [BP]	1P: $109- 209	2P/1B: $109- 209	2P/2B: $109- 209	XP: $15	F
	11/1-3/31 [BP]	1P: $99- 199	2P/1B: $99- 199	2P/2B: $99- 199	XP: $15	F

Location: At 7th St & Ocean Ave. 701 Ocean Ave 08226. Fax: 609/398-8742. **Terms:** Age restrictions may apply; reserv deposit, 6 day notice; 2 night min stay, Saturday check-in; no pets. **Facility:** 9 rooms. 3 stories, no elevator; interior corridors; smoke free premises. **All Rooms:** free movies. **Cards:** AE, DS, MC, VI. ⓒⓣⓥ ✕ Ⓓ

CROSSINGS MOTOR INN
ⒶⒶⒶ
◆◆
Motel

	7/2-9/7 [CP]	Rates Subject to Change			**Phone:** 609/398-4433	
	7/2-9/7 [CP]	1P: $119- 144	2P/1B: $119- 144	2P/2B: $119- 144	XP: $10	F12
	6/19-7/1 [CP]	1P: $89- 114	2P/1B: $89- 114	2P/2B: $89- 114	XP: $10	F12
	5/22-6/18 & 9/8-9/17 [CP]	1P: $69- 94	2P/1B: $69- 94	2P/2B: $69- 94	XP: $10	F12
	5/1-5/21 & 9/18-9/30 [CP]	1P: $49- 74	2P/1B: $49- 74	2P/2B: $49- 74	XP: $10	F12

Location: Garden State Pkwy exit 25, 3 mi e; 0.3 mi w of ocean beaches on the south end of town. 3420 Haven Ave 08226. Fax: 609/525-0490. **Terms:** Open 5/1-9/30; reserv deposit, 7 day notice; 2 night min stay, weekends, 7/1-8/31; pets, $15 extra charge, off season. **Facility:** 70 rooms. Weekend rates higher. Handling fee imposed; 3 stories; exterior corridors. **All Rooms:** free movies. **Some Rooms:** 10 efficiencies. **Cards:** AE, DS, MC, VI. 🅿️ 🅿️ ⓔⓒⓣⓥ ✕ Ⓓ

THE FLANDERS HOTEL
◆◆◆
Suite Hotel

Rates Subject to Change

Phone: 609/399-1000

7/2-9/2	1P: $269- 299	2P/1B: $269- 299	2P/2B: $269- 299	XP: $15	F3
5/23-7/1 & 9/3-10/13	1P: $169	2P/1B: $169	2P/2B: $169	XP: $15	F3
5/1-5/22, 10/14-12/31 & 3/28-4/30	1P: $139	2P/1B: $139	2P/2B: $139	XP: $10	F3
1/1-3/27	1P: $119	2P/1B: $119	2P/2B: $119	XP: $10	F3

Location: Garden St Pkwy, exit 30, 3 mi e to Ocean Ave, 0.3 mi s. 719 E 11th St 08226 (PO Box 29). Fax: 609/399-0194. **Terms:** Check-in 4 pm; reserv deposit, 3 day notice; no pets. **Facility:** 95 rooms. Handling fee imposed; 9 stories; interior corridors. Fee: parking. **All Rooms:** efficiencies. **Cards:** AE, DS, MC, VI.   Roll in showers. ⚐ ECTV D S

THE FORUM MOTOR INN
(AAA)
◆◆
Motel

Rates Subject to Change

Phone: 609/399-8700

6/16-9/11		2P/2B: $86- 160	XP: $10
5/24-6/15 & 9/12-9/18			
5/1-5/23 & 9/19-10/14		2P/2B: $66- 120	XP: $10
		2P/2B: $66- 96	XP: $10

Location: 8th St between Ocean & Atlantic aves, just w of the ocean boardwalk. 800 Atlantic Ave & 8th St 08226 (Box 448). Fax: 609/399-8704. **Terms:** Open 5/1-10/14; 3 night min stay, 7/1-8/31; no pets. **Facility:** 57 rooms. 2-3 stories; interior/exterior corridors. **Dining:** Coffee shop; 7 am-3 pm 5/15-9/15. **Some Rooms:** 2 efficiencies. **Cards:** MC, VI.   ⚐ CTV

IMPALA ISLAND INN
(AAA)
◆◆
Motor Inn

Rates Subject to Change

Phone: 609/399-7500

6/12-9/7		2P/2B: $127- 175	XP: $10	F16
9/8-9/19		2P/2B: $77- 125	XP: $10	F16
5/1-6/11 & 9/20-4/30		2P/2B: $61- 92	XP: $10	F16

Location: Ocean Ave at 10th St, just w of boardwalk. 1001 Ocean Ave 08226. Fax: 609/398-4379. **Terms:** Reserv deposit, 7 day notice; 3 night min stay, 6/16-9/3; no pets. **Facility:** 109 rooms. Handling fee imposed; 2 stories; exterior corridors. **Dining:** Restaurant; 8 am-8 pm, closed 10/31-3/1; $6-$15. **All Rooms:** Fee: movies. **Some Rooms:** 9 kitchens. **Cards:** AE, MC, VI.   ⚐ ECTV X D

NORTHWOOD INN
(AAA) SAVE
◆◆
Historic Bed
& Breakfast

Phone: 609/399-6071

7/1-10/1 [CP]		2P/1B: $110- 160	2P/2B: $140- 150	XP: $15
5/15-6/30 [CP]		2P/1B: $100- 150	2P/2B: $130- 140	XP: $15
5/1-5/14, 10/2-1/2 & 2/1-4/30 [CP]	1P: $90- 140	2P/1B: $130		XP: $15

Location: Garden State Pkwy, exit 30, e on 9th St to Wesley Ave, 0.5 mi n; at 4th St. 401 Wesley Ave 08226. Fax: 609/399-4472. **Terms:** Open 5/1-1/2 & 2/1-4/30; age restrictions may apply; reserv deposit, 7 day notice; weekly rates; BP avail, weekends; package plans; 2 night min stay, weekends; no pets. **Facility:** 8 rooms. 1894 Queen Anne Victorian converted to Colonial Victorian style in 1910. Light, airy rooms with tasteful contemporary furnishings. Small art gallery on property. Closed 11/26 & 12/25. 3 stories, no elevator; interior corridors; smoke free premises; whirlpool; pool table, videos avail. **Dining:** Full breakfast served weekends. **Services:** area transportation, to train & bus terminals. **Recreation:** bicycles. **All Rooms:** combo or shower baths, no phones. **Some Rooms:** VCR's, whirlpools. **Cards:** AE, MC, VI. **Special Amenities:** Early check-in/late check-out and free breakfast.   ⚐ ⊞ CTV X D S

PORT-O-CALL HOTEL
(AAA) SAVE
◆◆◆
Hotel

Phone: 609/399-8812

6/20-9/6		2P/2B: $175- 275	XP: $15	F12
5/23-6/19 & 9/7-11/2		2P/2B: $95- 195	XP: $15	F12
5/1-5/22 & 11/3-4/30		2P/2B: $75- 145	XP: $15	F12

Location: Between 15th & 16th sts, at the ocean boardwalk. 1510 Boardwalk 08226. Fax: 609/399-0387. **Terms:** Reserv deposit, 3 day notice, 7 day 6/21-9/2. Handling fee imposed; package plans; 3 night min stay, weekends, 7/1-8/31; no pets. **Facility:** 99 rooms. Up-to-date high-rise at the shore; some rooms with excellent ocean view, all with private balcony. 1 two-bedroom unit with private swimming pool access, $2600-$4400 wkly in season; 1 three-bedroom whirlpool unit, $2800-$4600 wkly in season; 10 stories; interior corridors; beachfront; beach, saunas; beauty salon. **Dining:** Dining room; 8 am-2 & 5:30-9 pm; 9/16-5/26 8 am-11 & noon-2; dinner Fri & Sat 5-8 pm; $10-$20. **Services:** area transportation. Fee: coin laundry. **Recreation:** swimming. **All Rooms:** coffeemakers, refrigerators. Fee: movies. **Some Rooms:** microwaves. **Cards:** AE, CB, DI, DS, MC.   ⚐ ⊞ ⊕ ⊞ ECTV X ⚐ D S

SCARBOROUGH INN
(AAA) SAVE
◆◆◆
Historic Bed
& Breakfast

Phone: 609/399-1558

7/11-9/2 [CP]	2P/1B: $100- 175	2P/2B: $100- 175	XP: $20
6/13-7/10 [CP]	2P/1B: $95- 145	2P/2B: $95- 145	XP: $20
5/2-6/12 & 9/3-10/13 [CP]	2P/1B: $75- 135	2P/2B: $75- 135	XP: $20

Location: Garden State Pkwy exit 30, e on CR 52 to Ocean Ave, just n of 7th St. 720 Ocean Ave 08226. Fax: 609/399-4173. **Terms:** Open 5/2-10/13; reserv deposit, 7 day notice; weekly rates; package plans; 2 night min stay; no pets. **Facility:** 24 rooms. Turn-of-the-century Victorian inn features rooms nicely finished with a variety of antiques & an attractive guest library. Convenient to boardwalk & beach. Children welcome. 4 two-bedroom units. Handling fee imposed; 4 stories, no elevator; interior corridors; smoke free premises; bike racks avail. **Dining:** Restaurant nearby. **Services:** Fee: coin laundry. **All Rooms:** combo or shower baths. **Some Rooms:** efficiency, microwaves, whirlpools. Fee: refrigerators. **Cards:** AE, DS, MC, VI. **Special Amenities:** Free breakfast and free local telephone calls.   ⊞ CTV X D

SERENDIPITY BED & BREAKFAST
(AAA)
◆◆
Historic Bed
& Breakfast

Guaranteed Rates

Phone: 609/399-1554

5/24-9/30 [BP]	1P: $85- 135	2P/1B: $85- 135	2P/2B: $85- 135
5/1-5/23 & 10/1-4/30 [BP]	1P: $75- 125	2P/1B: $75- 125	2P/2B: $75- 125

Location: Garden State Pkwy, exit 30; 3 mi e on 9th St; just e of Ocean Ave. 712 9th St 08226. Fax: 609/399-1527. **Terms:** Age restrictions may apply; reserv deposit, 7 day notice; 2 night min stay, weekends; no pets. **Facility:** 6 rooms. Handling fee imposed; 3 stories, no elevator; interior corridors; smoke free premises. **Cards:** AE, DS, MC, VI.   CTV X D

WATSON'S REGENCY SUITES
◆◆◆
Suite Motel

Rates Subject to Change

Phone: 609/398-4300

6/25-9/6		2P/2B: $229- 259	XP: $15
5/1-6/24 & 9/7-10/9		2P/2B: $149	XP: $10
10/10-12/31		2P/2B: $119	XP: $10
1/1-4/30		2P/2B: $99	XP: $10

Location: Garden State Pkwy exit 30, e to Ocean Ave, at 9th St. 901 Ocean Ave 08226. Fax: 609/398-0197. **Terms:** Check-in 4 pm; reserv deposit, 3 day notice; no pets. **Facility:** 80 rooms. Rates for up to 4 persons. Handling fee imposed; 5 stories; interior corridors. **Cards:** AE, DS, MC, VI.   ⚐ ⚐ ECTV X D S

RESTAURANTS

COUSIN'S RESTAURANT & CATERING   **Dinner:** $19-$28   **Phone:** 609/399-9462
◆◆   **Location:** Just s of 1st St. 104 Asbury Ave 08226. **Hours:** Open 5/1-11/1; 4 pm-9 pm, Fri & Sat-10 pm
Continental   6/1-8/31. **Reservations:** suggested. **Features:** casual dress; children's menu; early bird specials; street
            parking. Extensive offering of homemade favorites, including lasagna, veal parmigiana & pasta alfredo. Also
chicken, seafood & steak. Dessert made on premises. Bustling atmosphere, popular with locals. "Family style" take out
menu. Smoke free premises. **Cards:** DS, MC, VI.   ⊠

THE CULINARY GARDEN   **Lunch:** $5-$13   **Dinner:** $12-$20   **Phone:** 609/399-3713
ⒶⒶⒶ   **Location:** 9th St & Central Ave. 841 Central Ave 08226. **Hours:** 8 am-2 & 5-9 pm 6/1-9/4, 11 am-2 & 5-8 pm
            3/5-5/31 Sun 8 am-2 & 5-9 pm. **Reservations:** suggested; in summer. **Features:** casual dress; children's
◆◆   menu; early bird specials; carryout; a la carte. Selection of gourmet to downhome cooking unique
Continental preparation, homemade dessert. **Cards:** AE, DS, MC, VI.   ⊠

PARAMUS—25,100   (See map p. 210; index p. 209)

LODGINGS

HOLIDAY INN   Rates Subject to Change   **Phone:** 201/843-5400   ㊺
◆◆◆   All Year   1P: $76- 100 2P/1B: $76- 100 2P/2B: $76- 100
Motor Inn   **Location:** On SR 17 northbound, n of jct SR 4; Garden State Pkwy northbound exit 161, southbound exit
163. 50 Rt 17 N 07652. Fax: 201/712-0434. **Terms:** Sr. discount; no pets. **Facility:** 80 rooms. Rates for up to
4 persons; 2 stories; interior corridors. **Dining:** Restaurant; 6:30 am-10 pm; $8-$20. **All Rooms:** free movies. **Cards:** AE,
CB, DI, DS, JCB, MC, VI.   ⊠ 🖅 ⊠ ⒹⓈ

HOWARD JOHNSON LODGE   Guaranteed Rates   **Phone:** 201/265-4200   ㊹
◆◆   All Year   1P: $70- 85 2P/1B: $70- 85 2P/2B: $80- 90 XP: $7   F18
Motor Inn   **Location:** 0.5 mi n of Garden St Pkwy northbound exit 163, U-turn on Midland Ave-Glen Rock to 17S;
Garden State Pkwy southbound, exit 165 4 mi s on SR 17. 393 Rt 17S 07652. Fax: 201/265-0247. **Terms:** Sr.
discount; small pets only. **Facility:** 81 rooms. 3 stories; interior corridors. **All Rooms:** free movies. **Cards:** AE, CB, DI, DS,
MC.   🛏 🖅 ⊠ 🎬 ⒹⓈ

RADISSON INN PARAMUS   Guaranteed Rates   **Phone:** 201/262-6900   ㊻
◆◆   All Year   1P: $140   2P/1B: $140   2P/2B: $140   XP: $10   F17
Motor Inn   **Location:** On service road (From Rd) w of Garden State Pkwy exit 165; northbound Ridgewood exit
            (shopping center), southbound Oradell (shopping center). 601 From Rd 07652. Fax: 201/262-4955.
Terms: Sr. discount; small pets only. **Facility:** 119 rooms. 2 stories; interior corridors. **Dining:** Restaurant; 6:30 am-10 pm,
Sat & Sun from 7 am; $12-$21. **All Rooms:** free & pay movies. **Cards:** AE, CB, DI, DS, JCB, MC, VI.
                                                           🛏 🖅 ⊠ 🎬 ⒹⓈ

PARK RIDGE—8,100

LODGING

PARK RIDGE MARRIOTT HOTEL   Rates Subject to Change   **Phone:** 201/307-0800
◆◆◆   Sun-Thurs   1P: $169   2P/1B: $169   2P/2B: $169
Hotel   Fri & Sat   1P: $79- 95   2P/1B: $79- 95 2P/2B: $79- 95
            Location: Southbound Garden State Pkwy, U-turn thru Food Fuel Service Plaza to Garden State Pkwy
northbound, exit 172, right 300 yds on Grand Ave & 0.5 mi s on Mercedes. 300 Brae Blvd 07656. Fax: 201/307-0859.
Terms: Check-in 4 pm; reserv deposit; no pets. **Facility:** 289 rooms. 4 stories; interior corridors. **Dining:** Dining room,
restaurant; 6:30am-2:30 & 5-10 pm; $9-$30. **All Rooms:** free & pay movies. **Cards:** AE, CB, DI, DS, MC, VI.
                             Roll in showers. 🖅 🖅 ⊠ 🎬 ⒹⓈ

RESTAURANT

VALENTINO'S   **Lunch:** $12-$15   **Dinner:** $13-$20   **Phone:** 201/391-2230
◆◆◆   **Location:** From jct Grand Ave, 1 mi s. 103 Spring Valley Rd 07656. **Hours:** 11:30 am-2:30 & 5-10 pm, Fri &
Italian   Sat-11 pm. Closed major holidays & Sun. **Features:** semi-formal attire; health conscious menu items;
            carryout; cocktails & lounge; a la carte. Intimate rooms for comfortable, leisurely dining. Continental Italian
cuisine prepared to order. Own desserts. **Cards:** AE, DI, DS, MC, VI.   ⊠

PARSIPPANY—48,500   (See map p. 206; index p. 205)

LODGINGS

DAYS INN-PARSIPPANY   **Phone:** 973/335-0200   ㊼
ⒶⒶⒶ SAVE   All Year [CP]   1P: $78   2P/1B: $84   2P/2B: $84   XP: $5   F16
            Location: 0.3 mi w of jct I-287 & US 202; I-80 exit 42, 0.5 mi e. 3159 Rt 46 07054. Fax: 973/263-3094.
◆◆   **Terms:** Weekly/monthly rates; pets. **Facility:** 120 rooms. 2 whirlpool rms, extra charge; 2 stories;
Motor Inn   interior/exterior corridors; wading pool. **Dining:** Restaurant nearby. **Services:** valet laundry. **All Rooms:** free
            movies. **Some Rooms:** 4 kitchens. Fee: microwaves, refrigerators. **Cards:** AE, CB, DI, DS, JCB, MC, VI.
Special Amenities: Free breakfast and free local telephone calls.   🛏 🖅 🆓 ⊠ ⒹⓈ

EMBASSY SUITES   Rates Subject to Change   **Phone:** 973/334-1440   ㊾
◆◆◆   Sun-Thurs [BP]   1P: $179   2P/1B: $209   2P/2B: $209   XP: $30   F18
Suite Hotel Fri & Sat [BP]   1P: $114   2P/1B: $114   2P/2B: $139   XP: $25   F18
            Location: I-80, exit 42 to US 202N; just ne of jct US 202 & Rt 46W. 909 Parsippany Blvd 07054.
Fax: 973/402-1188. **Terms:** Sr. discount; no pets. **Facility:** 274 rooms. 5 stories; interior corridors. **Dining:** Caffe' Sport, see
separate listing. **All Rooms:** efficiencies, free & pay movies. **Cards:** AE, CB, DI, DS, JCB, MC, VI.
                                                           🖅 ⊠ 🎬 ⒹⓈ

HAMPTON INN - PARSIPPANY   Rates Subject to Change   **Phone:** 973/263-0095   ㊽
◆◆◆   Fri & Sat [CP]   1P: $69- 135 2P/1B: $69- 135 2P/2B: $69- 135
Motor Inn   Sun-Thurs [CP]   1P: $104- 115 2P/1B: $104- 115 2P/2B: $104- 115
            Location: I-80, exit 42; 0.5 mi e to jct SR 46 & Cherry Hill Rd, sw corner. 3535 Rt 46 07054.
Fax: 973/263-6133. **Terms:** No pets. **Facility:** 100 rooms. Rates for up to 4 persons; 4 stories; interior corridors.
Dining: Restaurant; 11:30 am-2 & 5-10 pm; Sat from 5 pm; Closed Sun. **All Rooms:** free & pay movies. **Cards:** AE, CB, DI,
DS, JCB, MC, VI.   Roll in showers. ⊠ ⊠ 🎬 ⒹⓈ

(See map p. 206)

HOLIDAY INN-PARSIPPANY — Rates Subject to Change — Phone: 973/263-2000   50
♦♦♦   Sun-Thurs   1P: $75- 100   2P/1B: $75- 100   2P/2B: $75- 100
Motel   Fri & Sat   1P: $65- 80   2P/1B: $65- 80   2P/2B: $65- 80
Location: ON US 46, just w of jct I-80; westbound exit 47, eastbound exit 45, 0.8 mi e. 707 Rt 46E 07054.
Fax: 973/299-9029. **Terms:** Sr. discount; no pets. **Facility:** 153 rooms. Up to 4 persons in room; 4 stories; interior corridors. **Dining:** Harold's New York Deli Restaurant, see separate listing. **All Rooms:** free & pay movies. JCB, MC, VI.

HOWARD JOHNSON EXPRESS INN — Rates Subject to Change — Phone: 973/882-8600   54
♦♦   All Year [CP]   1P: $45- 49   2P/1B: $49- 55   2P/2B: $55- 58   XP: $6   F13
Motel   **Location:** I-80 westbound exit 47, eastbound exit 45, 1 mi e. 625 Rt 46 E 07054. Fax: 973/882-3493.
Terms: Sr. discount; small pets only. **Facility:** 118 rooms. Handling fee imposed; 3 stories; exterior corridors.
All Rooms: free & pay movies. **Cards:** AE, CB, DI, DS, MC, VI.

PARSIPPANY HILTON — Rates Subject to Change — Phone: 973/267-7373   51
♦♦♦   Mon-Thurs   1P: $150- 160   2P/1B: $150- 160   2P/2B: $150- 160   XP: $10   F17
Hotel   Fri-Sun   1P: $79   2P/1B: $79   2P/2B: $75
Location: In Hilton Court; I-287 northbound exit 39, southbound exit 39B, 1.3 mi w on SR 10. 1 Hilton Court 07054. Fax: 973/984-2896. **Terms:** Pets. **Facility:** 508 rooms. 6 stories; interior corridors. **Dining:** Dining room, restaurant; 6:30 am-11:45 pm, Sat & Sun from 7 am; $10-$35. **All Rooms:** free & pay movies. **Cards:** AE, CB, DI, DS, JCB, MC, VI.
(See color ad p 18)

RAMADA LIMITED — Rates Subject to Change — Phone: 973/263-0404   49
♦♦♦   All Year [CP]   1P: $80- 105   2P/1B: $80- 105   2P/2B: $80- 105   XP: $5   F18
Motel   **Location:** I-80 westbound exit 47; eastbound exit 45, 0.5 mi e. 949 Rt 46 E 07054. Fax: 973/263-4057.
Terms: Reserv deposit; small pets only. **Facility:** 72 rooms. 2 stories; interior corridors. **All Rooms:** free movies. **Cards:** AE, CB, DI, DS, JCB, MC, VI.

RED ROOF INN — Rates Subject to Change — Phone: 732/334-3737   53
♦♦   All Year   1P: $75- 89   2P/1B: $84- 98   2P/2B: $90- 110   XP: $9   F18
Motel   **Location:** On US 46, w of I-80, westbound exit 47, eastbound exit 45 then 0.5 mi e. 855 US 46E 07054.
Fax: 732/334-1984. **Terms:** Pets. **Facility:** 108 rooms. 2 stories; exterior corridors. **All Rooms:** free & pay movies. **Cards:** AE, CB, DI, DS, MC, VI.

SHERATON TARA HOTEL — Rates Subject to Change — Phone: 973/515-2000   55
♦♦♦   Mon-Thurs   1P: $199- 210   2P/1B: $199- 210   2P/2B: $199- 210   XP: $20   F17
Hotel   Fri-Sun   1P: $89- 109   2P/1B: $89- 109   2P/2B: $89- 109   XP: $20   F17
Location: At jct I-80 & I-287; access from US 46, opposite reservoir. 199 Smith Rd 07054.
Fax: 973/515-9798. **Terms:** No pets. **Facility:** 390 rooms. 6 stories; interior corridors. **Dining:** Dining room, restaurant; 6:30 am-11 pm; $15-$28. **All Rooms:** free & pay movies. **Cards:** AE, CB, DI, DS, MC, VI.

RESTAURANTS

CAFFE' SPORT — Lunch: $7-$12 — Dinner: $9-$15 — Phone: 973/402-8080   51
♦♦   **Location:** I-80, exit 42 to US 202N; just ne of jct US 202 & Rt 46W; in Embassy Suites. 909 Parsippany
Italian   Blvd 07054. **Hours:** 11 am-11 pm. Closed: 12/25. **Features:** casual dress; children's menu; health conscious menu items; carryout; cocktails & lounge; a la carte. **Cards:** AE, CB, DI, JCB, MC, VI.

ECCOLA, ITALIAN BISTRO — Lunch: $9-$16 — Dinner: $9-$16 — Phone: 973/334-8211   52
♦♦   **Location:** On US 46W, w of I-80, westbound exit 47; eastbound exit 45, 0.3 mi e. 1082 Rt 46W 07054.
Northern   **Hours:** 11:30 am-10 pm, Sat noon-11 pm, Sun 2 pm-9 pm. Closed: 11/26 & 12/25. **Features:** casual dress;
Italian   carryout; cocktails; a la carte. Bustling, high energy bistro, serving homemade pasta, wood-oven pizza, osso bucco, chicken entrees & homemade dessert. Casually chic ambience. **Cards:** AE, DI, MC, VI.

HAROLD'S NEW YORK DELI RESTAURANT — Lunch: $5-$15 — Dinner: $5-$15 — Phone: 973/335-3339   53
♦♦   **Location:** ON US 46, just w of I-80; westbound exit 47, eastbound exit 45, 0.8 mi e; in Holiday
American   Inn-Parsippany. 707 US 46 E 07054. **Hours:** 7 am-11 pm, Fri & Sat-midnight, Sun-9 pm.
Features: children's menu; health conscious menu items; carryout; cocktails & lounge; a la carte. A bright inviting full service restaurant serving top quality home-cured meat, pickles, dessert including New York style cheesecake, plus a wide variety of complete dinner. **Cards:** AE, MC, VI.

PEMBERTON—See Philadelphia & Vicinity p. 393.

PENNS GROVE—See Philadelphia & Vicinity p. 393.

PHILLIPSBURG—15,800

LODGINGS

HOLIDAY INN CONFERENCE CENTER — Rates Subject to Change — Phone: 908/454-9771
♦♦♦   All Year   2P/1B: $99   2P/2B: $99   XP: $10   F12
Motor Inn   **Location:** I-78, exit 3, just n. 1314 US Hwy 22 08865. Fax: 908/859-2502. **Terms:** Sr. discount; no pets.
Facility: 134 rooms. 2 stories; interior/exterior corridors. **Dining:** Restaurant; 6 am-10 pm, Sat & Sun from 7 am; $10-$18. **All Rooms:** Fee: movies. **Some Rooms:** 3 efficiencies. **Cards:** AE, DI, DS, MC, VI.

PHILLIPSBURG INN — Guaranteed Rates — Phone: 908/454-6461
♦♦   All Year   1P: $68   2P/1B: $68   2P/2B: $78   XP: $10   F12
Motel   **Location:** I-78 exit 3, just n. 1315 US 22 W 08865. Fax: 908/454-3034. **Terms:** Sr. discount; no pets.
Facility: 73 rooms. 2 stories; interior corridors. **All Rooms:** free movies. **Cards:** AE, CB, DI, DS, MC.
Roll in showers.

PISCATAWAY—47,100   (See map p. 206; index p. 205)

LODGINGS

EMBASSY SUITES HOTEL	Rates Subject to Change			Phone: 732/980-0500	65
◆◆◆	Sun-Thurs [BP]	1P: $175	2P/1B: $195	2P/2B: $185	XP: $20	F18
Hotel	Fri & Sat [BP]	1P: $99	2P/1B: $99	2P/2B: $119	XP: $20	F18

Location: I-287, exit 5 (SR 18), just s on Highland Park to Centennial Ave, in Office Park. 121 Centennial Ave 08854. Fax: 732/980-9473. **Terms:** Sr. discount; no pets. **Facility:** 220 rooms. 5 stories; interior corridors. **Dining:** Restaurant; 11:30-2 & 5-10 pm; $9-$20. **All Rooms:** free & pay movies. **Cards:** AE, CB, DI, DS, JCB, MC, VI.

⊇ CTV ⊠ ⌕ D S

WYNDHAM GARDEN HOTEL	Rates Subject to Change			Phone: 732/980-0400	64
◆◆◆	Sun-Thurs	1P: $89	2P/1B: $99	2P/2B: $99	XP: $10	F12
Hotel	Fri & Sat	1P: $59	2P/1B: $59	2P/2B: $59	XP: $10	F12

Location: I-287, exit 5 (Highland Park) to Centennial Ave; 0.5 mi left. 21 Kingsbridge Rd 08854. Fax: 732/980-0973. **Terms:** No pets. **Facility:** 165 rooms. 5 stories; interior corridors. **Dining:** Restaurant; $9-$15. **All Rooms:** Fee: movies. **Cards:** AE, CB, DI, DS, JCB, MC, VI. *(See color ad below)*

Roll in showers. ⊇ CTV ⊠ ⌕ D S

RESTAURANT

AL DENTE	Lunch: $12-$16	Dinner: $12-$25	Phone: 732/985-8220	60

◆◆◆ **Location:** From jct US 1 & Plainfield Ave, 3 mi nw. 1665 Stelton Rd 08854. **Hours:** 11:30 am-2:30 & 5:30-10
Italian pm, Fri-11 pm, Sat 5 pm-11 pm. Closed: Sun & 12/25. **Reservations:** suggested. **Features:** health conscious menu items; carryout; cocktails & lounge; a la carte. Upscale casual and/or business attire. Unusual, creative & stylistic cuisine in casually elegant decor with Old World detail. Excellent wine list. **Cards:** AE, DI, MC, VI. ⊠

PLEASANTVILLE—*See Atlantic City & Vicinity p. 182.*

POINT PLEASANT BEACH—5,100

LODGINGS

MARINER'S COVE MOTOR INN	Rates Subject to Change			Phone: 732/899-0060	
ⒶⒶⒶ	Fri & Sat 6/16-9/5	1P: $140	2P/1B: $140	2P/2B: $145	XP: $15	F16
	Fri & Sat 5/1-6/15 & 9/6-9/16	1P: $102	2P/1B: $102	2P/2B: $115	XP: $15	F16
◆◆	Sun-Thurs 6/16-9/5	1P: $105	2P/1B: $105	2P/2B: $112	XP: $15	F16
Motel	Sun-Thurs 5/1-6/15, 9/6-9/16, 9/17-12/31 & 2/1-4/30	1P: $45- 89	2P/1B: $45- 89	2P/2B: $45- 89	XP: $7	F16

Location: 0.8 mi e of SR 35 following signs to beach. 50 Broadway 08742. Fax: 732/701-0260. **Terms:** Open 5/1-12/31 & 2/1-4/30; reserv deposit, 7 day notice, in season; no pets. **Facility:** 24 rooms. Closed 1/1-2/15; 2 stories; exterior corridors. **Cards:** AE, MC, VI.

⊇ CTV D

SURFSIDE MOTEL	Rates Subject to Change			Phone: 732/899-1109	
ⒶⒶⒶ	Fri & Sat 5/1-6/30 & 9/1-4/30		2P/2B: $42- 152	XP: $20	F15
	Fri & Sat 7/1-8/31	2P/1B: $142	2P/2B: $151	XP: $20	F15
◆◆	Sun-Thurs 5/1-6/30 & 9/1-4/30		2P/2B: $42- 121	XP: $20	F15
Motel	Sun-Thurs 7/1-8/31	2P/1B: $112	2P/2B: $121	XP: $20	F15

Location: 2 blks from ocean; 0.5 mi e jct SR 35, follow signs to beach area. 101 Broadway 08742. **Terms:** Reserv deposit, 7 day notice; no pets. **Facility:** 27 rooms. Handling fee imposed; 2 stories; exterior corridors. **Cards:** AE, DS, MC, VI.

⊇ CTV D

RESTAURANTS

BARMORES SHRIMP BOX	Dinner: $11-$25	Phone: 732/899-1637

◆◆ **Location:** 0.5 mi e of US 35 via Broadway & left at Inlet Dr. 75 Inlet Dr 08742. **Hours:** 4 pm-9 pm, Sun from
Seafood 1 pm. Closed: 11/1-3/15. **Features:** casual dress; children's menu; early bird specials; health conscious menu items; carryout; salad bar; cocktails & lounge; a la carte. Overlooking Manasquan Inlet. **Cards:** AE, DI,
MC, VI. ⊠

JACK BAKER'S WHARFSIDE	Lunch: $8-$13	Dinner: $13-$20	Phone: 732/892-9100

◆ **Location:** 0.5 mi e of SR 35, follow signs to beach area, left on Boston. 101 Channel Dr 08742.
Seafood **Hours:** 11:30 am-9:30 pm, Fri-10 pm, Sat-10:30 pm, Sun-9 pm; in winter 11:30 am-9 pm, Fri-9:30 pm, Sat-10 pm, Sun-8:30 pm. Closed: 12/25. **Features:** children's menu; early bird specials; carryout; cocktails & lounge. Overlooking Manasquan Inlet. **Cards:** AE, CB, DI, MC, VI. ⊠

SOUTHERN HOUSE   **Lunch:** $7-$13   **Dinner:** $7-$13   **Phone:** 732/899-7427
◆   **Location:** On SR 35 N. 501 Washington Ave 08742. **Hours:** noon -10 pm, Fri & Sat-11 pm. Closed: 11/26 &
American   12/25. **Features:** casual dress; children's menu; carryout; cocktails & lounge; a la carte. Southern style ribs, chicken, & meat w/beans, slaw & sweet potato pie & more. Served in a casual, kickback atmosphere.
Cards: AE, DI, MC, VI.

PRINCETON—12,000

LODGINGS

THE FORRESTAL AT PRINCETON HOTEL & CONFERENCE CENTER   **Phone:** 609/452-7800
🔺🔺🔺 SAVE   Fri & Sat   1P: $160- 185   2P/1B: $185- 205   2P/2B: $185- 205   XP: $10   F12
◆◆◆   Sun-Thurs   1P: $94- 119   2P/1B: $94- 119   2P/2B: $94- 119
Hotel   **Location:** Off US 1, northbound 2.5 mi n of CR 571; in the Princeton Forrestal Center. 100 College Rd E
08540. Fax: 609/452-7883. **Terms:** Package plans; no pets. **Facility:** 290 rooms. On 25 acres of peaceful
wooded grounds. 3 stories; interior corridors; saunas, whirlpool; 4 lighted tennis courts; par fitness course, ping
pong, pool room, video games. **Dining & Entertainment:** 2 restaurants; 6:45-9 am, 11:30-2:30 & 5:30-10:30 pm; $14-$20;
health conscious menu items; cocktails/lounge; buffet breakfast & lunch avail. **Services:** valet laundry; area transportation;
within 8 mi; valet parking. Fee: massage. **Recreation:** jogging. Rental: bicycles. **All Rooms:** honor bars, coffeemakers.
Fee: movies. **Some Rooms:** refrigerators. Fee: VCR's. **Cards:** AE, CB, DI, DS, MC, VI. **Special Amenities:** Early
check-in/late check-out and preferred room (subject to availability with advanced reservations).
Roll in showers.

HOLIDAY INN-PRINCETON   **Phone:** 609/452-2400
🔺🔺 SAVE   All Year   1P: $98   2P/1B: $108   2P/2B: $108   XP: $10   F17
◆◆◆   **Location:** On US 1 southbound, jct Ridge Rd; 3 mi n of CR 571. 4355 US 1 at Ridge Rd 08540.
Motor Inn   Fax: 609/452-2494. **Terms:** Package plans; no pets. **Facility:** 240 rooms. 6 stories; interior corridors.
Dining & Entertainment: Restaurant; 6:30 am-10 pm, Sat & Sun from 7 am; $8-$17; health conscious
menu items; cocktails/lounge. **Services:** valet laundry. **All Rooms:** coffeemakers, free & pay movies.
Some Rooms: Fee: microwaves, refrigerators. **Cards:** AE, DI, DS, JCB, MC, VI. **Special Amenities: Free local telephone
calls and free newspaper.**   Roll in showers.

HYATT REGENCY-PRINCETON   **Phone:** 609/987-1234
🔺🔺🔺🔺 SAVE   Sun-Thurs   1P: $159   2P/1B: $159   2P/2B: $159   XP: $25   F17
◆◆◆◆   Fri & Sat   1P: $109   2P/1B: $109   2P/2B: $109   XP: $25   F17
Hotel   **Location:** On US 1 northbound; 0.5 mi s of CR 571; in Carnegie Office Complex. 102 Carnegie Center
08540. Fax: 609/987-2584. **Terms:** Package plans; no pets. **Facility:** 348 rooms. Atrium hotel in semi-rural
area. Comedy club on premises. 4 stories; interior corridors; saunas, whirlpool; 2 tennis courts. **Dining &
Entertainment:** Cocktails/lounge; entertainment; nightclub. **Services:** valet laundry. Fee: valet parking.
All Rooms: coffeemakers, free & pay movies. **Some Rooms:** whirlpools. Fee: microwaves, refrigerators, VCR's. **Cards:** AE,
CB, DI, DS, JCB, MC, VI.   Roll in showers.

NASSAU INN
◆◆◆ Motor Inn
Phone: 609/921-7500
All Year — Rates Subject to Change — 1P: $179 2P/1B: $199 2P/2B: $199
Location: Palmer Sq town center. 10 Palmer Sq 08542. Fax: 609/921-9385. **Terms:** No pets. **Facility:** 215 rooms. 5 stories; interior corridors. Fee: parking. **Dining:** 2 restaurants; 7 am-10:30 pm; $13-$20. **All Rooms:** free & pay movies. **Cards:** AE, DI, MC, VI. Roll in showers. CTV ⊠ 🌀 D S

NOVOTEL PRINCETON HOTEL
ⒶⒶⒶ SAVE ◆◆ Motor Inn
Phone: 609/520-1200
Mon-Thurs — 1P: $99-169 2P/1B: $99-169 2P/2B: $99-169 XP: $15 F16
Fri-Sun — 1P: $89 2P/1B: $89 2P/2B: $89 XP: $15 F16
Location: On US 1; exit 67 off I-295, 3 mi n of jct CR 526 & 571; in Princeton Corporate Center. 100 Independence Way 08540. Fax: 609/520-0594. **Terms:** BP avail; small pets only. **Facility:** 180 rooms. Close proximity to corporate parks, attractions & shopping centers. 1 parlor suite avail. Handling fee imposed; 4 stories; interior corridors; whirlpool. **Dining & Entertainment:** Restaurant; 6 am-10:30 pm; $9-$17; health conscious menu items; cocktails/lounge. **Services:** complimentary evening beverages; valet laundry. Fee: massage. **All Rooms:** free & pay movies. **Some Rooms:** Fee: microwaves, refrigerators. **Cards:** AE, DI, DS, MC, VI. *(See ad p 220)*
🍴 🏊 🐕 ♿ CTV 🔥 ⊠ 🌀 D S

PALMER INN-BEST WESTERN
ⒶⒶⒶ SAVE ◆◆ Motor Inn
Phone: 609/452-2500
All Year [CP] — 1P: $89-114 2P/1B: $99-124 2P/2B: $99-124 XP: $10 F17
Location: On US 1 southbound, 2 mi s of jct CR 526 & 571. 3499 US 1S 08540. Fax: 609/452-1371. **Terms:** No pets. **Facility:** 105 rooms. 2 stories; interior/exterior corridors. **Dining:** Restaurant; 6:30 am-9:30 & 11:30-10 pm, Sat & Sun 7 am-10 & noon-9 pm; $8-$15. **All Rooms:** free movies. **Some Rooms:** 6 efficiencies. **Cards:** AE, CB, DI, DS, JCB, MC, VI.
🏊 CTV ⊠ 🌀 D S

PRINCETON MARRIOTT FORRESTAL VILLAGE
◆◆◆ Hotel
Phone: 609/452-7900
Sun-Thurs — Rates Subject to Change — 1P: $149 2P/1B: $149 2P/2B: $149
Fri & Sat — 1P: $99 2P/1B: $99 2P/2B: $99
Location: On US 1 southbound, 1.5 mi n of CR 571. 201 Village Blvd; Forrestal V 08540. Fax: 609/452-1223. **Terms:** No pets. **Facility:** 294 rooms. Up to 4 persons in room; 6 stories; interior corridors. **Dining:** Dining room, restaurant; 6 am-11 pm; $7-$25. **All Rooms:** free & pay movies. **Cards:** AE, CB, DI, DS, MC, VI.
🏊 🏊 CTV 🔥 ⊠ 🌀 D S

SUMMERFIELD SUITES HOTEL
◆◆◆ Suite Motel
Phone: 609/951-0009
Sun-Thurs [CP] — Rates Subject to Change — 1P: $179 2P/1B: $189 2P/2B: $199
Fri & Sat [CP] — 1P: $139 2P/1B: $149 2P/2B: $169
Location: US 1S just past Ridge Rd. 4375 US 1 S 08543. Fax: 609/951-0696. **Terms:** Sr. discount; small pets only, $200-$300 fee. **Facility:** 124 rooms. Handling fee imposed; 3 stories; interior/exterior corridors. **All Rooms:** kitchens, free movies. **Cards:** AE, DI, DS, MC, VI.
🍴 🏊 CTV ⊠ 🌀 D S

RESTAURANTS

LAHIERE'S
◆◆◆ American
Lunch: $7-$13 **Dinner: $16-$26** **Phone: 609/921-2798**
Location: On Witherspoon at Nassau St (SR 27). 11 Witherspoon 08542. **Hours:** 11:30 am-2:30 & 5:30-10 pm, Sat 11:30 am-2 & 5:30-10 pm. Closed major holidays & Sun. **Reservations:** suggested. **Features:** casual dress; health conscious menu items; cocktails & lounge; a la carte. In the center of historic Princeton. Smoking in bar eating area only. Validated parking avail at Park & Shop Lot on Spring St. Landmark owned by same family for over 70 years. **Cards:** AE, CB, DI, MC, VI. ⊠

LE PLUMET ROYAL
◆◆◆ French
Lunch: $13-$16 **Dinner: $21-$35** **Phone: 609/924-1707**
Location: Jct SR 206 & Nassau St, just w on SR 206 (Bayard Ln). 20 Bayard Ln 08540. **Hours:** 11:30 am-2:30 & 5:30-9:30 pm, Sat 11:30 am-2:30 & 5:30-9 pm, Sun 11:30 am-2:30 & 5:30-9 pm. **Reservations:** suggested. **Features:** semi-formal attire; Sunday brunch; health conscious menu items; cocktails & lounge; valet parking; a la carte. Gracious dining in romantic Queen Anne Colonial house. Cuisine has light, contemporary touches. California & French extensive wine list. Own desserts. Expresso/cappuccino. Smoking in lounge. **Cards:** AE, MC, VI. ⊠

MEDITERRA
◆◆◆ Ethnic
Lunch: $7-$13 **Dinner: $12-$18** **Phone: 609/252-9680**
Location: Downtown, from jct Nassau & Witherspoon sts, just w. 49 Nulfish St 08540. **Hours:** 11:30 am-2:30 & 5-10 pm, Fri & Sat noon-2:30 & 5-11 pm. Closed major holidays. **Features:** casual dress; health conscious menu; cocktails; fee for parking; a la carte. Blend of cuisine from Mediterranean countries. Upscale casual bistro. Tapas bar. Smoke free premises. **Cards:** AE, MC, VI. ⊠

MEXICAN VILLAGE RESTAURANT
◆◆ Mexican
Lunch: $6-$9 **Dinner: $7-$13** **Phone: 609/924-5143**
Location: 0.5 mi e; just s of jct Witherspoon St. 42 Leigh Ave 08540. **Hours:** 11:30 am-2 & 5-9:30 pm, Fri & Sat-10 pm, Sun 4 pm-9:30 pm. Closed major holidays. **Reservations:** required; for 6 or more. **Features:** children's menu; carryout. Authentic Mexican favorite for over 15 years. Chile Rellenos, Chimichangas plus a variety of grill entrees including Chipotle Carne Asada. **Cards:** AE, DS, MC, VI. ⊠

TERESA'S PIZZETTA CAFFE
◆ Italian
Lunch: $7-$10 **Dinner: $7-$14** **Phone: 609/921-1974**
Location: Downtown, just w jct Nassau St on Palmer Sq (opposite entrance to Nassau Inn). 19-23 Palmer Sq E 08542. **Hours:** 11 am-11 pm, Fri & Sat-midnight, Sun noon-10 pm. Closed: 11/26 & 12/25. **Features:** health conscious menu items; carryout; cocktails; fee for parking; a la carte. Upscale casual trattoria serving rustic cuisine updated & lightened for the modern palate. Moderate priced wine list. Wood oven pizzas. Expresso/cappuccino. Smoke free premises. **Cards:** AE, MC, VI. ⊠

RAMSEY—13,200

LODGINGS

HOWARD JOHNSON MOTOR LODGE
ⒶⒶⒶ SAVE ◆ Motor Inn
Phone: 201/327-4500
All Year [CP] — 1P: $45-80 2P/1B: $55-90 2P/2B: $55-90 XP: $10 F18
Location: From I-287, 1.5 mi s on SR 17 southbound. 1255 Rt 17S 07446. Fax: 201/327-5911. **Terms:** Reserv deposit, 7 day notice; weekly/monthly rates; no pets. **Facility:** 50 rooms. Some rooms with balcony or patio facing interior courtyard. 2 stories; exterior corridors. **Dining:** Restaurant; Japanese-American; 11:30 am-2:30 & 4:30-10 pm, Fri-Sun 4 pm-11 pm; $8-$20; cocktails. **Services:** valet laundry. **All Rooms:** free movies. **Some Rooms:** refrigerators. **Cards:** AE, DI, DS, MC, VI. **Special Amenities:** Free breakfast and free local telephone calls.
🏊 🐕 CTV ⊠ D

THE INN AT RAMSEY
Phone: 201/327-6700

AAA SAVE ♦♦ Motor Inn
All Year [CP] 1P: $69- 120 2P/1B: $69- 120 2P/2B: $69- 120 XP: $5 F12
Location: 1315 SR 17S 07446. Fax: 201/327-6709. **Terms:** Weekly/monthly rates; pets. **Facility:** 81 rooms. Theme rooms avail. Lively bar/restaurant. 35 whirlpool rms, extra charge; 2 stories; interior corridors. **Dining & Entertainment:** Restaurant; 7 am-midnight; $10-$20; cocktails/lounge. **Services:** valet laundry. **All Rooms:** free movies, VCR's. **Some Rooms:** Fee: microwaves, refrigerators. **Cards:** AE, CB, DI, DS, MC, VI. **Special Amenities:** Free breakfast and free newspaper.

🛏 🍽 CTV ⊠ D

WELLESLEY INN
Phone: 201/934-9250
♦♦ Motel
All Year [CP] Rates Subject to Change
1P: $68- 90 2P/1B: $75- 97 2P/2B: $75- 97 XP: $5 F18
Location: Rt 17 at Airmont Rd. 946 Rt 17N 07446. Fax: 201/934-9719. **Terms:** Sr. discount; pets, $5 extra charge. **Facility:** 89 rooms. 3 stories; interior corridors. **All Rooms:** free & pay movies. **Cards:** AE, CB, DI, DS, JCB, MC, VI. *(See color ad opposite inside back cover)*

🛏 CTV ⊠ 🍴 D S

RESTAURANT

CAFE PANACHE **Lunch:** $9-$14 **Dinner:** $18-$24 Phone: 201/934-0030
♦♦♦ French
Location: Downtown. 130 E Main 07446. **Hours:** noon-2 & 5:30-9 pm, Fri-10 pm, Sat seatings at 6 pm, 6:30 pm, 8:30 pm & 9 pm. Closed major holidays & Sun. **Reservations:** suggested. **Features:** semi-formal attire; health conscious menu items; a la carte. Creative gourmet food in a casual but quietly elegant dining room. Daily fresh fish entrees. Homemade pasta, bread & dessert. Smoke free premises. **Cards:** AE, CB, DI, MC, VI. ⊠

RANDOLPH—20,000 (See map p. 206; index p. 205)

RESTAURANT

CASA DE PASTA **Lunch:** $5-$10 **Dinner:** $10-$20 Phone: 973/584-3700 (135)
♦♦♦ Italian
Location: 0.3 mi n jct Dover-Chester Rd & Sussex Tpk. 1438 Sussex Tpk 07969. **Hours:** 11:30 am-11 pm, Sat from 5 pm, Sun 4 pm-10 pm. Closed: 11/26, 12/25, 12/24 for dinner & Mon. **Features:** casual dress; health conscious menu items; carryout; cocktails & lounge. Bustling rustic inn. **Cards:** AE, DS, MC, VI.

RARITAN—5,800

RESTAURANT

MAX'S CUCINA ITALIANO **Lunch:** $9-$13 **Dinner:** $10-$20 Phone: 908/725-4553
♦♦♦ Italian
Location: Downtown; sw corner of Wall & Somerset sts. 63 W Somerset St 08869. **Hours:** 11:30 am-10 pm, Fri-11 pm, Sat 5 pm-11 pm, Sun 5 pm-10 pm. Closed: 7/4, 11/26 & 12/25. **Reservations:** suggested. **Features:** health conscious menu items; carryout; cocktails & lounge; a la carte. Sophisticated understated bistro serving regional cuisine. Mostly Italian wines including quality wines by the glass. Professional wait staff. Free parking behind restaurant. **Cards:** AE, DI, MC, VI.

RED BANK—10,600

LODGINGS

COURTYARD BY MARRIOTT
Phone: 732/530-5552
♦♦♦ Motor Inn
All Year Rates Subject to Change
1P: $114 2P/1B: $124 2P/2B: $124 XP: $10 F12
Location: Garden State Parkway, exit 109, just e. 245 Half Mile Rd 07701. Fax: 732/530-5756. **Terms:** Sr. discount; check-in 4 pm; reserv deposit; no pets. **Facility:** 146 rooms. 3 stories; interior corridors. **Dining:** Restaurant; breakfast buffet Mon-Thurs; dinner 6 pm-10 pm; $8-$12. **All Rooms:** free & pay movies. **Cards:** AE, DS, MC, VI. *(See color ad below)*

🏊 CTV ⊠ 🍴 D S

MOLLY PITCHER INN
Phone: 732/747-2500
♦♦♦ Historic Motor Inn
All Year Rates Subject to Change
1P: $89- 179 2P/1B: $89- 179 2P/2B: $89- 179 XP: $10 F16
Location: 0.3 mi s of Navesink River bridge on SR 35. 88 Riverside Ave 07701. Fax: 732/747-2713. **Terms:** Sr. discount; no pets. **Facility:** 106 rooms. 4 stories; interior corridors. **Dining:** Restaurant; 6:30 am-10 pm; $18-$26. **All Rooms:** free movies. **Cards:** AE, DI, MC, VI.

CTV ⊠ D S

THE OYSTER POINT HOTEL
Phone: 732/530-8200
♦♦♦ Motor Inn
All Year Rates Subject to Change
1P: $100- 120 2P/1B: $100- 120 2P/2B: $100- 120 XP: $10 F12
Location: Just e of SR 35 on the Navasink River. 146 Bodman Place 07701. Fax: 732/747-1875. **Terms:** Sr. discount; no pets. **Facility:** 58 rooms. 11 whirlpool rms, extra charge. Rates for up to 4 persons; 5 stories; interior corridors. **Dining:** Restaurant; $10-$25. **All Rooms:** free movies. **Cards:** AE, DI, MC, VI.

CTV ⊠ 🍴 D S

IT COULD HAPPEN. Some lodgings require advance payment when you check in, and if your trip is cut short a refund may be impossible.

RESTAURANT

PEKING PAVILION   **Lunch:** $6-$9   **Dinner:** $7-$15   **Phone:** 732/219-0888
◆◆◆   **Location:** From jct Maple Ave (US35), just w. 58 Oakland St 07701. **Hours:** 11 am-2:30 & 5-10 pm; Fri &
Northern   Sat to 11 pm. **Reservations:** accepted; for parties of 6 or more. **Features:** dressy casual; carryout; cocktails
Chinese   & lounge; a la carte. Upscale casual dress. Hunan & Szechuan cuisines. **Cards:** AE, MC, VI.   ⊠

RIDGEWOOD—24,800

RESTAURANT

CAFE WINBERIE   **Lunch:** $7-$13   **Dinner:** $7-$13   **Phone:** 201/444-3700
◆   **Location:** Downtown; just n of jct Ridgewood Ave. 30 Oak St 07450. **Hours:** 11:30 am-11 pm. Closed:
American   12/25. **Features:** casual dress; Sunday brunch; children's menu; carryout; cocktails & lounge; street parking;
a la carte. Casual eatery serving contemporary cuisine. **Cards:** AE, DI, DS, MC, VI.   ⊠

ROCKAWAY—6,200   (See map p. 206; index p. 205)

LODGING

MOUNTAIN INN OF ROCKAWAY   **Phone:** 973/627-8310 **46**
ⒶⒶⒶ ⑤ⓐⓥⓔ   All Year [CP]   1P: $50- 70 2P/1B: $50- 70 2P/2B: $55- 70 XP: $5   F15
◆   **Location:** From I-80, Denville exit to Rt 46, 1 mi w. 156 Rt 46E 07866. **Fax:** 973/627-0556.
Motel   **Terms:** Weekly/monthly rates; no pets. **Facility:** 88 rooms. 2 stories; interior corridors. **Dining:** Restaurant;
$10-$20; health conscious menu items; cocktails. **Services:** valet laundry. **All Rooms:** free movies.
Some Rooms: 16 efficiencies, microwaves, refrigerators. **Cards:** AE, CB, DI, DS, MC, VI.
Special Amenities: Free breakfast and preferred room (subject to availability with advanced reservations).

      🛴 🛇 CTV ⊠ D

ROSELLE PARK—12,800

RESTAURANT

COSTAS RESTAURANT   **Lunch:** $10-$15   **Dinner:** $15-$25   **Phone:** 908/241-1131
◆◆   **Location:** Garden State Pkwy exit 137, 1 mi e on SR 28, just n. 120 Chestnut St 07204. **Hours:** noon-3 &
Italian   5-10 pm, Sat 4 pm-11 pm, Sun 2 pm-10 pm. **Reservations:** suggested; weekends. **Features:** casual dress;
health conscious menu items; carryout; cocktails & lounge; fee for parking; a la carte. Casual elegance
serving freshly prepared cuisine. **Cards:** AE, DI, MC, VI.

RUMSON—6,700

RESTAURANT

FROMAGERIE   **Lunch:** $10-$15   **Dinner:** $20-$30   **Phone:** 732/842-8088
ⒶⒶⒶ   **Location:** Jct SR 34 (Ridge Rd) & Two Rivers Ave. 26 Ridge Rd 07760. **Hours:** 11:30 am-2:30 & 5-10 pm,
    Fri & Sat-11 pm, Sun 4 pm-10 pm. Closed: 12/25. **Reservations:** suggested. **Features:** semi-formal attire;
◆◆◆◆   cocktails & lounge; a la carte. Warm country elegance for fine dining. Comfortable yet professional wait staff.
French   Excellent wine list. Own desserts. Jackets required at dinner. Valet parking for dinner. **Cards:** AE, CB, DI,
MC, VI.

RUNNEMEDE—*See Philadelphia & Vicinity p. 393.*

SADDLE BROOK—13,300   (See map p. 210; index p. 209)

LODGINGS

HOLIDAY INN AND CONFERENCE CENTER   Rates Subject to Change   **Phone:** 201/843-0600 **49**
ⒶⒶⒶ   Mon-Thurs   1P: $109   2P/1B: $109   2P/2B: $109
◆◆   Fri-Sun   1P: $89   2P/1B: $89   2P/2B: $89
    Location: I-80 exit 62 to Midland Ave, Garden State Pkwy exit 159 direction Saddle Brook, just e to Kenny
Hotel   Pl. 50 Kenney Pl 07663. **Fax:** 201/843-2822. **Terms:** Small pets only. **Facility:** 144 rooms. Rates for up to 4
persons; 12 stories; interior corridors. **Dining:** Restaurant; 6:30 am-10 pm; $9-$17. **All Rooms:** free & pay
movies. **Cards:** AE, CB, DI, DS, JCB, MC, VI.   🛏 🛴 CTV ⊠ 🛇 D Ⓢ

HOWARD JOHNSON PLAZA HOTEL   Rates Subject to Change   **Phone:** 201/845-7800 **51**
◆◆   Mon-Thurs   1P: $79- 139 2P/1B: $79- 139 2P/2B: $79- 139 XP: $10   F18
Motor Inn   Fri-Sun   1P: $69- 99 2P/1B: $69- 99 2P/2B: $69- 99
    Location: Jct I-80 exit 62 (Saddle Brook); Garden State Pkwy exit 159 (Saddle Brook). 129 Pehle Ave
07663. **Fax:** 201/845-7061. **Terms:** Sr. discount; no pets. **Facility:** 141 rooms. Handling fee imposed; 8 stories; interior corridors. **Dining:** Restaurant; 6:30 am-10:30 pm; $8-$20. **All Rooms:** free movies. **Cards:** AE, CB, DI, DS, MC, VI.

      🛴 CTV ⊠ 🛇 D Ⓢ

MARRIOTT HOTEL   Rates Subject to Change   **Phone:** 201/843-9500 **50**
◆◆◆   Sun-Thurs 5/1-12/31 &
Hotel   2/22-4/30   1P: $149   2P/1B: $149   2P/2B: $149
    Sun-Thurs 1/1-2/21   1P: $139   2P/1B: $139   2P/2B: $139
    Fri & Sat 5/1-12/31 &
    2/22-4/30   1P: $89   2P/1B: $89   2P/2B: $89
    Fri & Sat 1/1-2/21   1P: $79   2P/1B: $79   2P/2B: $79
Location: I-80 exit 62 (Midland Ave) & Garden State Pkwy exit 159. Jct I-80 & Garden State Pkwy 07663.
Fax: 201/843-7760. **Terms:** No pets. **Facility:** 221 rooms. 12 stories; interior corridors. **Dining:** Restaurant; 6:30 am-11 pm,
Fri & Sat-midnight; $7-$22. **All Rooms:** free & pay movies. **Cards:** AE, CB, DI, DS, JCB, MC, VI.
    Roll in showers.   🛴 🛴 CTV ⊠ 🛇 D Ⓢ

SADDLE RIVER—3,000

RESTAURANT

SADDLE RIVER INN   **Lunch:** $10-$19   **Dinner:** $24-$30   **Phone:** 201/825-4016
◆◆◆◆   **Location:** SR 17, Saddle River/Woodcliff Lake exit, just w to light, behind ne corner. 2 Barnstable Ct 07458.
Continental   **Hours:** noon-2 & 6-10 pm, Sat 6, 7 & 8:30 & 9:30 pm seatings. Closed: Sun & Mon. **Features:** semi-formal
attire; a la carte. Sumptuous, contemporary American-French cuisine served to top waiter staff in converted
old barn. Long-lived award winning restaurant. Jackets required in the evening. Diners may bring their own alcoholic
beverage. No service fee. Smoke free premises. **Cards:** AE, MC, VI.   ⊠

SCOTCH PLAINS—21,200   (See map p. 206; index p. 205)

RESTAURANTS

GINAMARIE'S RISTORANTE   **Lunch:** $12-$19   **Dinner:** $14-$24   **Phone:** 908/322-3133   ⟨170⟩
◆◆◆   **Location:** From US 22, 0.5 mi e via Park Ave; in CVC Pharmacy Bldg. 514 Park Ave 07076. **Hours:** 11:30
Italian   am-2:30 & 5:30-10 pm, Fri & Sat-11 pm. Closed: 12/25 & Sun. **Reservations:** suggested. **Features:** casual dress; cocktails & lounge; a la carte. Chic, modern decor. Well chosen wine list compliments such entrees as Osso Buco, Moroccan-spiced tuna, Bistecca alla Senese. Variety of pasta. Own dessert. Smoke free premises. **Cards:** AE, DI, MC, VI.   ⊠

STAGE HOUSE INN   Historical   **Lunch:** $10-$17   **Dinner:** $21-$31   **Phone:** 908/322-4224   ⟨171⟩
◆◆◆   **Location:** Corner Park Ave & Front St, 0.3 mi e jct US 22. 366 Park Ave 07076. **Hours:** 11:30 am-2:30 &
French   5:30-9:30 pm, Fri-10 pm. Sat 5:30 pm-10 pm, Sun 4 pm-8 pm. Closed major holidays & Mon. **Reservations:** suggested. **Features:** semi-formal attire; health conscious menu items; cocktails & lounge; a la carte. A 1746 stagecoach retreat converted into a charming inn. **Cards:** AE, DI, DS, MC, VI.   ⊠

SECAUCUS—14,100   (See map p. 210; index p. 209)

LODGINGS

COURTYARD BY MARRIOTT   **Phone:** 201/617-8888   ⟨55⟩
⟨AAA⟩ ⟨SAVE⟩   All Year   1P: $150   2P/1B: $160   2P/2B: $160   XP: $10   F18
◆◆◆   **Location:** Eastern NJ Tpk spur, northbound exit 16E, southbound exit 17, just e on SR 3. 455 Harmon
Motel   Meadow Blvd 07094. Fax: 201/319-0035. **Terms:** Package plans, weekends; no pets. **Facility:** 165 rooms. Vicinity of Meadowlands Sports Complex. Meadowlands Convention Center, nearby & 2 mi from Secaucus Outlet Center. Close New York City access via Lincoln Tunnel. 7 stories; interior corridors. Fee: passes for nearby health club. **Dining:** Breakfast only; 6:30-10:30 am, Sat & Sun 7-11:30 am; restaurant nearby. **Services:** valet laundry. **All Rooms:** coffeemakers, free & pay movies. **Some Rooms:** refrigerators. Fee: microwaves. **Cards:** AE, CB, DI, DS, MC, VI. **Special Amenities:** Early check-in/late check-out and preferred room (subject to availability with advanced reservations). *(See color ad below)*   ⟨icons⟩ (CTV) ⟨icons⟩ ⊠ ⟨icons⟩ (S)

EMBASSY SUITES-MEADOWLANDS   Rates Subject to Change   **Phone:** 201/864-7300   ⟨65⟩
◆◆◆   Sun-Thurs [BP]   1P: $160- 190   2P/1B: $180- 210   2P/2B: $190- 220   XP: $25   F12
Suite Hotel   Fri & Sat [BP]   1P: $150- 180   2P/1B: $160- 190   2P/2B: $160- 200   XP: $25   F12
Location: Eastern NJ Tpk spur, northbound exit 16E, southbound exit 17, just e on SR 3 to Harmon Meadow Blvd. 455 Plaza Dr 07094. Fax: 201/864-5391. **Terms:** Reserv deposit; small pets only, $150 dep req. **Facility:** 261 rooms. 9 stories; interior corridors. **Dining:** Restaurant; 11:30 am-11 pm; $8-$18. **All Rooms:** efficiencies, free & pay movies. **Cards:** AE, CB, DI, DS, JCB, MC, VI.   ⟨icons⟩ (CTV) ⟨icons⟩ ⊠ ⟨icons⟩ (S)

HAMPTON INN   Rates Subject to Change   **Phone:** 201/867-4400   ⟨59⟩
◆◆◆   All Year [CP]   1P: $82- 97   2P/1B: $93- 97   2P/2B: $97   XP: $10   F18
Motel   **Location:** Eastern Tpk spur, northbound exit 16E, southbound exit 17, just e on SR 3. 250 Harmon Meadow Blvd 07094. Fax: 201/865-7932. **Terms:** No pets. **Facility:** 151 rooms. 7 stories; interior corridors.
All Rooms: free & pay movies. **Cards:** AE, CB, DI, DS, MC, VI.   (CTV) ⟨icons⟩ ⊠ ⟨icons⟩ (D) (S)

THE HOLIDAY INN HARMON MEADOW   Rates Subject to Change   **Phone:** 201/348-2000   ⟨57⟩
◆◆◆   5/1-6/30, 9/7-12/31 &
Hotel   3/16-4/30   1P: $129   2P/1B: $129   2P/2B: $139   XP: $10   F18
   7/1-9/6 & 1/1-3/15   1P: $109- 119   2P/1B: $109- 119   2P/2B: $109- 119   XP: $10   F18
Location: NJ Tpk, exits 16E, 17, or 16W via SR 3 to Harmon Meadow Blvd. 300 Plaza Dr 07094. Fax: 201/348-6035. **Terms:** Sr. discount; no pets. **Facility:** 160 rooms. 8 stories; interior corridors. **Dining:** Restaurant; 6:30 am-10 pm; $9-$18. **All Rooms:** free & pay movies. **Cards:** AE, CB, DI, DS, JCB, MC, VI.   (CTV) ⊠ ⟨icons⟩ (D) (S)

(See map p. 210)

HOWARD JOHNSON INN
◆
Motel
Guaranteed Rates
All Year   1P: $75- 90 2P/1B: $75- 90 2P/2B: $90- 95 XP: $10
Phone: 201/864-1400 **61** F18
Location: Service road off Rt 3 to NJ Tpk. 875 Paterson Plank Rd 07094. Fax: 201/864-9845. **Terms:** Sr. discount; reserv deposit; no pets. **Facility:** 74 rooms. 2 stories; interior corridors. **All Rooms:** free movies.
Cards: AE, CB, DI, DS, MC, VI.
🛏 Ⓧ Ⓓ

MEADOWLANDS HILTON
◆◆◆
Hotel
Guaranteed Rates
All Year   1P: $119   2P/1B: $119   2P/2B: $119   XP: $10
Phone: 201/348-6900 **58** F16
Location: Between eastern & western spurs of NJ Tpk exits 16E, 17 or 16W via SR 3 at Meadowlands Pkwy. 2 Harmon Plaza 07094. Fax: 201/348-4436. **Terms:** No pets. **Facility:** 296 rooms. 14 stories; interior corridors. **Dining:** Restaurant; 6:30 am-11 pm; $12-$21. **All Rooms:** free & pay movies. **Cards:** AE, CB, DI, DS, MC, VI.
(See color ad p 18)
🛏 CTV Ⓧ 🍸 Ⓓ Ⓢ

RADISSON SUITE HOTEL MEADOWLANDS
🅰🅰🅰 SAVE
◆◆◆
Hotel
Sun-Thurs   1P: $179   2P/1B: $189   2P/2B: $199   XP: $10
Fri & Sat   1P: $119- 129 2P/1B: $129- 139 2P/2B: $149- 159 XP: $10
Phone: 201/863-8700 **54** F18 F18
Location: In Mill Creek Mall, between eastern & western spurs of NJ Tpk exits 16E, 17 or 16W via SR 3 & Harmon Meadow Blvd. 350 Rt 3W, Mill Creek Dr 07094. Fax: 201/863-6209. **Terms:** Reserv deposit; monthly rates; package plans; small pets only. **Facility:** 151 rooms. 9 stories; interior corridors. **Dining &**
Entertainment: Restaurant; 6:30 am-3 & 4-10 pm; $9-$20; health conscious menu items; cocktails/lounge.
Services: complimentary evening beverages, Sun-Thurs; area transportation, to local businesses. Fee: coin laundry.
All Rooms: coffeemakers, efficiencies, no utensils, microwaves, free & pay movies, refrigerators. **Some Rooms:** whirlpools.
Fee: VCR's. **Cards:** AE, CB, DI, DS, JCB, MC, VI.
🐾 🛏 🍴 ✈ 🏋 CTV Ⓧ 🍸 Ⓓ Ⓢ

RED ROOF INN-MEADOWLANDS
◆◆
Motel
Rates Subject to Change
All Year   1P: $80- 94 2P/1B: $92- 106 2P/2B: $100   XP: $12
Phone: 201/319-1000 **56** F18
Location: Between eastern & western spurs of NJ Tpk, exits 16E, 17 or 16W via SR3 exit Meadowlands Pkwy. 15 Meadowlands Pkwy 07094. Fax: 201/319-1097. **Terms:** Small pets only. **Facility:** 172 rooms. 3 stories; exterior corridors. **All Rooms:** free movies. **Cards:** AE, CB, DI, DS, MC, VI.
🐾 CTV Ⓧ 🍸 Ⓓ

RESTAURANT

LANTANA RESTAURANT
🅰🅰🅰
◆◆◆
Northern
Italian
Lunch: $8-$19   Dinner: $11-$26   Phone: 201/867-1065 **31**
Location: New Jersey Turnpike, exit 16E or 17, just e. 1148 Paterson Plank Rd 07094. **Hours:** 11:30 am-3 & 5-10 pm, Sat 5 pm-midnight, Sun 4 pm-10 pm. Closed: 1/1 & 12/25. **Reservations:** required; weekends.
Features: casual dress; children's menu; early bird specials; health conscious menu items; cocktails; valet parking; a la carte. Long established local favorite. Dover sole, creative veal entrees plus pasta & chicken.
Cards: AE, DI, DS, MC, VI.
Ⓧ

SHORT HILLS (See map p. 206; index p. 205)

LODGING

THE HILTON AT SHORT HILLS
🅰🅰🅰 SAVE
◆◆◆◆
Hotel
All Year   1P: $215- 316 2P/1B: $235- 316 2P/2B: $235- 316 XP: $20
Phone: 973/379-0100 **73** F17
Location: Exit 142 off Garden State Pkwy to I-78W, 4 mi exit SR 24, 2.5 mi to Kennedy Pkwy exit. 41 John F Kennedy Pkwy 07078. Fax: 973/379-6870. **Terms:** Package plans; weekends; no pets. **Facility:** 300 rooms. Opposite Short Hills Mall & adjacent to a forested wetlands refuge. Warmly elegant public areas with stunning floral displays. Gracious white glove service. 10 stories; interior corridors; luxury level rooms; saunas, whirlpool; aerobic instruction, extensive spa & fitness facility. Fee: 3 tennis courts; personal trainer. **Dining & Entertainment:** Cocktail lounge; afternoon tea; also, The Dining Room, The Terrace, see separate listing. **Services:** valet laundry; area transportation, to mall. Fee: massage; valet parking. **All Rooms:** free & pay movies. **Some Rooms:** coffeemakers, 8 efficiencies, microwaves, refrigerators. Fee: VCR's. **Cards:** AE, CB, DI, DS, JCB, MC, VI. **Special Amenities:** Free newspaper and preferred room (subject to availability with advanced reservations). *(See color ad below & p 18)*
🛏 🛏 🍴 ✈ 🏋 CTV Ⓧ 🍸 Ⓓ Ⓢ

RESTAURANTS

THE DINING ROOM
🅰🅰🅰
◆◆◆◆
Continental
Dinner: $58   Phone: 973/379-0100 **73**
Location: Exit 142 off Garden State Pkwy to I-78W, 4 mi exit SR 24, 2.5 mi to Kennedy Pkwy exit; in The Hilton at Short Hills. 41 John F Kennedy Pkwy 07078. **Hours:** 6 pm-10:30 pm. Closed: Sun.
Reservations: required. **Features:** semi-formal attire; health conscious menu items; cocktails & lounge; valet parking; prix fixe, a la carte. Intimate, formal dining room. Harpist provides peaceful background music nightly. Imaginative menu reflects seasonal influences with stunning food presentations. **Cards:** AE, CB, DI, DS, JCB, MC, VI.
♿ Ⓧ

(See map p. 206)

THE TERRACE
Lunch: $10-$15   Dinner: $18-$24   Phone: 973/379-0100   (74)
Location: Exit 142 off Garden State Pkwy to I-78W, 4 mi exit SR 24, 2.5 mi to Kennedy Pkwy exit; in The
Hilton at Short Hills. 41 John F Kennedy Pkwy 07078. **Hours:** 6:30 am-11 pm. **Reservations:** required; for
◆◆◆◆   brunch. **Features:** casual dress; Sunday brunch; children's menu; health conscious menu items; cocktails &
American   lounge; valet parking; a la carte. Multi-purpose casual restaurant with a formal edge. Extensive menu
selections. Stunning food presentations. Lavish Sun brunch buffet. **Cards:** AE, CB, DI, DS, JCB, MC, VI.

⊠

SHREWSBURY—3,100

RESTAURANT

SHADOWBROOK
Dinner: $20-$25   Phone: 732/747-0200
◆◆◆   **Location:** Just n of jct White St & SR 35. SR 35 07702. **Hours:** 5:30 pm-9 pm, Sat-10 pm, Sun 3 pm-9 pm.
Continental   Closed: 12/24 & Mon. **Reservations:** suggested. **Features:** semi-formal attire; children's menu; health
conscious menu items; cocktails & lounge; valet parking. Victorian & Empire rooms in converted Georgian
mansion overlooking gardens. **Cards:** AE, MC, VI.

SOMERSET—22,100

LODGINGS

DOUBLETREE HOTEL   Rates Subject to Change   Phone: 732/469-2600
◆◆◆   Sun-Thurs   1P: $134   2P/1B: $134   2P/2B: $134   XP: $15   F18
Hotel   Fri & Sat   1P: $84   2P/1B: $84   2P/2B: $84   XP: $15   F18
Location: I-287 exit 6, (direction Bound Brook) n on CR 527 to Davidson Ave, 0.5 mi sw in Atrium Corp
Park. 200 Atrium Dr 08873. Fax: 732/469-4617. **Terms:** Sr. discount; no pets. **Facility:** 361 rooms. 6 stories; interior corridors.
Dining: 2 restaurants; 6:30 am-midnight; $12-$25. **All Rooms:** free & pay movies. **Cards:** AE, DI, DS, MC, VI.

🛏 🛏 CTV ⊠ 🖊 D S

HAMPTON INN   Rates Subject to Change   Phone: 732/563-1600
◆◆◆   Sun-Thurs [CP]   1P: $68- 95   2P/1B: $78- 95   2P/2B: $78- 95
Motel   Fri & Sat [CP]   1P: $60- 80   2P/1B: $60- 80   2P/2B: $60- 80
Location: I-287, exit 6, just n on CR 527 (direction Bound Brook), 0.8 mi sw. 255 Davidson Ave 08873.
Fax: 732/563-9775. **Terms:** Sr. discount; no pets. **Facility:** 109 rooms. Rates for up to 4 persons; 5 stories; interior corridors.
All Rooms: free movies. **Some Rooms:** 29 efficiencies. **Cards:** AE, CB, DI, MC, VI. *(See color ad below)*
Roll in showers. CTV ⊠ 🖊 D S

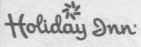

HOLIDAY INN-SOMERSET
◆◆◆   Mon-Thurs   1P: $119- 129   2P/1B: $119- 129   2P/2B: $119- 129
      Fri-Sun   1P: $89- 129   2P/1B: $89- 129   2P/2B: $89- 129
Hotel   **Location:** I-287 exit 6, (direction Bound Brook) just n on CR 527, 0.5 mi sw. 195 Davidson Ave 08873.
Phone: 732/356-1700
Fax: 732/356-0939. **Terms:** Sr. discount; pets, $50 dep req. **Facility:** 284 rooms. Rates for up to 4 persons; 6 stories; interior
corridors. **Dining:** Restaurant; 6:30 am-10:30 pm; $10-$20. **All Rooms:** Fee: movies. **Cards:** AE, CB, DI, DS, MC, VI.
(See color ad p 226)

QUALITY INN-SOMERSET
     All Year   1P: $55- 68   2P/1B: $55- 68   2P/2B: $62   XP: $5   F18
Phone: 732/469-5050
    Location: Just s of I-287, exit 6; (direction New Brunswick) on CR 527. 1850 Easton Ave 08873.
◆◆   Fax: 732/469-6870. **Terms:** Monthly rates; no pets. **Facility:** 112 rooms. 2 stories; interior/exterior corridors;
Motor Inn   saunas, whirlpool. **Dining & Entertainment:** Restaurant; 6:30 am-10 pm; $10-$15; health conscious menu
    items; cocktails/lounge. **Services:** Fee: coin laundry. **All Rooms:** coffeemakers, free movies, refrigerators.
Some Rooms: 6 efficiencies, microwaves. **Cards:** AE, CB, DI, DS, MC, VI. **Special Amenities: Early check-in/late
check-out and free newspaper.**

RAMADA INN SOMERSET
    Sun-Thurs   1P: $103   2P/1B: $113   2P/2B: $113   XP: $10   F18
    Fri & Sat   1P: $75   2P/1B: $85   2P/2B: $85   XP: $10   F18
Phone: 732/560-9880
◆◆   **Location:** I-287 exit 7 just sw via Weston Canal Rd (Cottontail Ln signage). 60 Cottontail Ln 08873.
Motor Inn   Fax: 732/356-7455. **Terms:** Reserv deposit; monthly rates; package plans, weekends; pets. **Facility:** 125
    rooms. 5 stories; interior corridors; sauna. **Dining:** Restaurant; 6:30 am-10 pm, Sat & Sun from 7 am;
$7-$15; health conscious menu items; cocktails. **Services:** area transportation, to local businesses. Fee: coin laundry.
All Rooms: coffeemakers, free & pay movies, refrigerators. **Some Rooms:** 8 efficiencies, microwaves. **Cards:** AE, CB, DI,
DS, MC, VI.

SOMERSET MARRIOTT HOTEL
◆◆◆   Sun-Thurs   1P: $124- 139   2P/1B: $124- 139   2P/2B: $124- 139   XP: $15   F16
      Fri & Sat   1P: $69   2P/1B: $69   2P/2B: $69   XP: $15   F16
Phone: 732/560-0500
Hotel   **Location:** I-287 exit 6, (direction Bound Brook) just n on CR 527 to Davidson Ave, just sw. 110 Davidson
Ave 08873. Fax: 732/560-3669. **Terms:** No pets. **Facility:** 440 rooms. 3-11 stories; interior corridors. **Dining:** Restaurant;
6:30 am-11 pm; $10-$19. **All Rooms:** free & pay movies. **Cards:** AE, CB, DI, DS, JCB, MC, VI.
    Roll in showers.

SUMMERFIELD SUITES HOTEL
◆◆◆   Sun-Thurs [CP]   1P: $145   2P/1B: $145   2P/2B: $159   XP: $10   F16
      Fri & Sat [CP]   1P: $129   2P/1B: $129   2P/2B: $159   XP: $10   F16
Phone: 732/356-8000
Suite Motel   **Location:** I-287 exit 6, (direction Bound Brook) just n on CR 527 to Davidson Ave, 0.8 mi sw. 260 Davidson
Ave 08873. Fax: 732/356-0782. **Terms:** Check-in 4 pm; small pets only, $5 extra charge, $150 dep req. **Facility:** 140 rooms.
2 stories; interior/exterior corridors. **All Rooms:** kitchens, free movies. **Cards:** AE, DI, DS, MC, VI.

RESTAURANTS

THE MCATEERS   **Lunch:** $6-$8   **Dinner:** $13-$20   **Phone: 732/469-2522**
◆   **Location:** I-287 exit 6 (direction New Brunswick), 0.8 mi s. 1714 Easton Ave 08873. **Hours:** 11 am-10:30
Continental   pm, Fri-11 pm, Sat 5 pm-11 pm, Sun 1 pm-9 pm. **Closed:** 12/25 & Mon. **Reservations:** suggested.
    Features: casual dress; early bird specials; health conscious menu items; cocktails. Valet parking dinner
only. Pianist Thur, Fri & Sat dinner. **Cards:** AE, DI, DS, MC, VI.

TRATTORIA NICOLA   **Lunch:** $8-$13   **Dinner:** $14-$21   **Phone: 732/745-4846**
◆◆◆   **Location:** I-287 exit 6, 1.8 mi se on Easton Ave (SR 527). 900 Easton Ave 08873. **Hours:** 11:30 am-2 &
Northern   5-10 pm, Fri-11 pm, Sat 5 pm-11 pm, Sun 4 pm-9 pm. Closed major holidays. **Reservations:** suggested.
Italian   **Features:** health conscious menu items; carryout; minimum charge-$15; a la carte. Casual, cozy restaurant
    serving hearty gourmet cuisine. Own desserts. Espresso, cappuccino. BYOB. Smoke free premises.
Cards: AE, CB, DI, MC, VI.

SOMERS POINT—*See Atlantic City & Vicinity p. 183.*

SOUTH PLAINFIELD—20,500   (See map p. 206; index p. 205)

LODGINGS

HOLIDAY INN   Rates Subject to Change   **Phone: 908/753-5500**   ⑲
◆◆   Sun-Thurs   1P: $94- 114   2P/1B: $94- 114   2P/2B: $94- 114
Motor Inn   Fri & Sat   1P: $59- 69   2P/1B: $59- 69   2P/2B: $59- 69
    Location: I-287 northbound, left off Durham Ave exit ramp, first right, 1 mi w on Hadley Rd, southbound exit
Edison; adjacent Middlesex Mall. 4701 Stelton Rd 07080. Fax: 908/753-5500. **Terms:** Sr. discount; small pets only.
Facility: 173 rooms. Weekend rates for up to 4 persons; 4 stories; interior corridors. **Dining:** Restaurant; 6:30 am-10 pm,
Sat & Sun from 7 am; $9-$20. **All Rooms:** free & pay movies. **Cards:** AE, CB, DI, DS, MC, VI.

RAMADA LIMITED   Rates Subject to Change   **Phone: 908/753-8900**   ⑳
◆◆   All Year [CP]   1P: $48- 63   2P/1B: $48- 63   2P/2B: $48- 63   XP: $10   F18
Motel   **Location:** From I-287, exit CR 529N to light, then 0.8 mi ne. 2989 Hamilton Blvd 07080. Fax: 908/769-4359.
    Terms: No pets. **Facility:** 143 rooms. 4 stories; interior corridors. **All Rooms:** free & pay movies.
Some Rooms: A/C. **Cards:** AE, DI, DS, MC, VI.

SPARTA—8,900

RESTAURANT

KROGH'S RESTAURANT Historical   **Lunch:** $6-$8   **Dinner:** $10-$18   **Phone: 973/729-8428**
◆   **Location:** Center town, jct Winona Pkwy. 23 White Deer Plaza 07871. **Hours:** 11:30 am-10 pm, Sun noon-9
American   pm. Closed major holidays. **Reservations:** suggested. **Features:** children's menu; carryout; cocktails &
    lounge. Pub-style atmosphere; view of Lake Mohawk. **Cards:** AE, CB, DI, DS, MC, VI.

SPRINGFIELD (UNION COUNTY)

LODGING

HOLIDAY INN
◆◆   All Year [BP]
Motor Inn
Rates Subject to Change
1P: $90   2P/1B: $90   2P/2B: $90   XP: $10   F18
Phone: 973/376-9400
Location: On SR 22 westbound, 4 mi w of Garden State Pkwy; northbound exit 140, southbound exit 140A. 304 Rt 22W 07081. Fax: 973/376-9534. **Terms:** Sr. discount; pets. **Facility:** 194 rooms. Rates for up to 4 persons; 4 stories; interior corridors. **Dining:** Restaurant; 7 am-10 pm; $8-$14. **All Rooms:** free & pay movies. **Cards:** AE, CB, DI, DS, JCB, MC, VI.

SPRING LAKE—3,500

LODGINGS

THE BREAKERS HOTEL
◆◆◆   6/20-9/14
Hotel   5/1-6/19 & 9/15-4/30
Rates Subject to Change
2P/1B: $150- 300   2P/2B: $150- 200   XP: $30   F18
2P/1B: $84- 190   2P/2B: $84- 120   XP: $30   F18
Phone: 732/449-7700
Location: Across from beach. 1507 Ocean Ave 07762. Fax: 732/449-0161. **Terms:** Reserv deposit, 10 day notice; no pets. **Facility:** 64 rooms. 4 stories; interior corridors. **Dining:** Dining room; 8 am-4 & 5-10 pm, Mon-8 pm, Fri & Sat-11 pm, Sun 8 am-9 pm, closed 12/20-1/31; $12-$22. **Cards:** AE, CB, DI, MC, VI. *(See ad below)*

THE CHATEAU
(AAA) (SAVE)   6/12-9/12
               5/1-6/11, 9/13-10/31 &
◆◆◆   4/23-4/30
Historic   11/1-4/22
Country Inn
1P: $125- 140   2P/1B: $135- 175   2P/2B: $160- 175   XP: $15   F11

1P: $69- 99   2P/1B: $79- 129   2P/2B: $94- 129   XP: $15   F11
1P: $55- 75   2P/1B: $65- 85   2P/2B: $75- 85   XP: $15   F11
Phone: 732/974-2000
Location: Jct SR 71 & Warren Ave, 0.5 mi e just w of Lake Divine Park. 500 Warren Ave 07762. Fax: 732/974-0007. **Terms:** Reserv deposit, 10 day notice; monthly rates; package plans; no pets. **Facility:** 38 rooms. Victorian inn, circa 1888. Some fireplaces avail. Many marble baths, some with soaking tub. 3 night min stay weekends when including Sat 7/1-8/31, 2 night min stay weekends 4/29-6/26 & 9/9-10/30; 3 stories; interior corridors; lake view; beach & tennis passes. **Dining:** Continental breakfast 4/25-10/29, weekends 10/30-4/24, complimentary continental breakfast Mon-Fri during winter. **Services:** valet laundry. **Rental:** bicycles. **All Rooms:** refrigerators, safes, combo or shower baths, VCR's. **Some Rooms:** coffeemakers, 2 kitchens, microwaves, whirlpools. **Cards:** AE, DI, DS, MC, VI. **Special Amenities: Free local telephone calls and preferred room (subject to availability with advanced reservations).** *(See color ad p 229)*

HAMILTON HOUSE INN
◆◆◆   5/15-9/15 [BP]
Bed &   5/1-5/14 & 9/16-4/30 [BP]
Breakfast
Rates Subject to Change
1P: $145- 225   2P/1B: $145- 225
1P: $115- 175   2P/1B: $115- 175
Phone: 732/449-8282
Location: From jct Ocean Ave, just w. 15 Mercer Ave 07762. Fax: 732/449-0206. **Terms:** Age restrictions may apply; reserv deposit, 14 day notice; 2 night min stay, weekends in season; no pets. **Facility:** 8 rooms. 3 stories; interior corridors; smoke free premises. **Cards:** AE, DI, DS, MC, VI.

THE HEWITT WELLINGTON HOTEL
◆◆◆   All Year [CP]
Historic
Country Inn
Rates Subject to Change
2P/1B: $140- 280
Phone: 732/974-1212
XP: $40
Location: On s side of lake at 2nd Ave. 200 Monmouth Ave 07762. Fax: 732/974-2338. **Terms:** Sr. discount; age restrictions may apply; reserv deposit, 10 day notice; 2 night min stay, weekends in season; no pets. **Facility:** 29 rooms. 3 stories, no elevator; interior corridors. **Dining:** Dining room; also, Whispers, see separate listing. **All Rooms:** free movies. **Cards:** AE, DS, MC, VI.

LA MAISON
◆◆◆
Historic Bed
& Breakfast

Rates Subject to Change

5/15-9/19 [BP]   2P/1B: $155- 285
5/1-5/14, 9/20-11/7 &
2/1-4/30 [BP]   2P/1B: $125- 220
11/8-12/31 [BP]   2P/1B: $115- 200

Phone: 732/449-0969
XP: $40

XP: $40

Location: 4 blks from ocean. 404 Jersey Ave 07762. Fax: 732/449-4860. **Terms:** Open 5/1-12/31 & 2/1-4/30; age restrictions may apply; reserv deposit, 10 day notice; 3 night min stay, weekends; no pets. **Facility:** 9 rooms. Cottage unit, seasonal only. 1 room w/double whirlpool tub. Handling fee imposed; 3 stories, no elevator; interior corridors; smoke free premises. **Cards:** AE, DI, DS, MC, VI.   CTV ✕ D

NORMANDY INN
◆◆◆
Historic Bed
& Breakfast

Rates Subject to Change

5/21-9/30 [BP]   1P: $90- 276   2P/1B: $121- 286 2P/2B: $146- 158 XP: $10-20
5/1-5/20 & 10/1-4/30 [BP]   1P: $72   2P/1B: $96- 215 2P/2B: $117- 126 XP: $10-20

Phone: 732/449-7172

Location: 1/2 blk from ocean. 21 Tuttle Ave 07762. Fax: 732/449-1070. **Terms:** Reserv deposit, 10 day notice; no pets. **Facility:** 19 rooms. 2 night min stay weekends 3/11-11/30, 3 night min stay weekends 7/1-8/31, 2 night min stay mid-week 7/1-8/31. Handling fee imposed; 3 stories, no elevator; interior corridors; smoke free premises.
Some Rooms: kitchen. **Cards:** AE, CB, DI, DS, MC, VI.   CTV ✕ D

THE OCEAN HOUSE
◆
Historic Bed
& Breakfast

Rates Subject to Change

5/1-10/1 [CP]   1P: $70- 110   2P/1B: $80- 140 2P/2B: $110- 150 XP: $20

Phone: 732/449-9090

Location: Just w of jct Ocean Ave. 102 Sussex Ave 07762. **Terms:** Open 5/1-10/1; reserv deposit, 5 day notice; no pets, dog on premises. **Facility:** 34 rooms. 3 stories; interior corridors; designated smoking area.
Cards: MC, VI.   ✕ D

SEACREST BY THE SEA
◆◆◆
Historic Bed
& Breakfast

Rates Subject to Change

5/16-9/30 [BP]   2P/1B: $159- 189
5/1-5/15 & 10/1-4/30 [BP]   2P/1B: $145- 159

Phone: 732/449-9031

Location: Just w from ocean. 19 Tuttle Ave 07762. Fax: 732/974-0403. **Terms:** Age restrictions may apply; reserv deposit; no pets. **Facility:** 12 rooms. 2-room suite $195-$239 with fireplace & soaking tub; whirlpool & fireplace suite $225-$249. Handling fee imposed; 3 stories, no elevator; interior corridors; smoke free premises. **Cards:** AE, MC, VI.   CTV ✕ D

RESTAURANT

WHISPERS
◆◆◆
Continental

Dinner: $18-$25

Phone: 732/449-3330

Location: On s side of lake at 2nd Ave; in The Hewitt Wellington Hotel. 200 Monmouth Ave 07762.
Hours: 5:30 pm-9 pm, Fri & Sat-10 pm. Closed: Mon, Tues & 1/1-1/31. **Reservations:** suggested.
Features: street parking; a la carte. Upscale casual dress. Creative, colorful entrees. BYOB. Smoke free premises. **Cards:** DI, MC, VI.   ✕

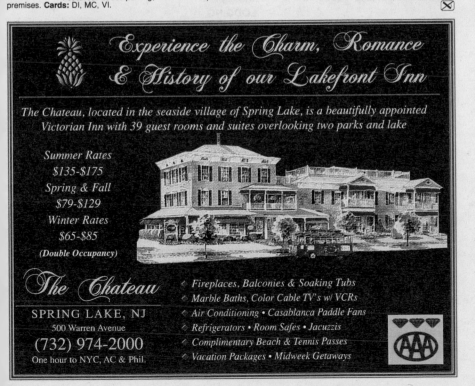

SPRING LAKE HEIGHTS—5,300

RESTAURANT

OLD MILL INN
◆◆
American

Lunch: $9-$13 **Dinner:** $18-$30 **Phone:** 732/449-1800
Location: At Ocean Rd between SR 35 & 71. Old Mill Rd 07762. **Hours:** 11:30 am-10 pm, Fri & Sat-11 pm, Sun 11 am-9:30 pm. Closed: Mon 10/1-5/15. **Reservations:** suggested. **Features:** casual dress; children's menu; early bird specials; health conscious menu items; cocktails & lounge; a la carte. Pleasant dining rooms overlooking Old Mill Pond. Large selection. Reservations advised for Sun brunch, 11 am-3 pm. **Cards:** AE, DI, MC, VI.

STANHOPE—3,400

LODGING

THE WHISTLING SWAN INN
◆◆◆.
Bed &
Breakfast

Rates Subject to Change **Phone:** 973/347-6369
All Year [BP] 1P: $85- 135 2P/1B: $90- 140 XP: $20
Location: Center; I-80 exit 27B, SR 183/206N 1 mi to Main St, 0.5 mi w. 110 Main St 07874. **Fax:** 973/347-3391. **Terms:** Age restrictions may apply; reserv deposit; no pets. **Facility:** 10 rooms. Suite with VCR & refrigerator. Handling fee imposed; 3 stories, no elevator; interior corridors; smoke free premises.
All Rooms: Fee: movies. **Cards:** AE, DS, MC, VI. CTV X D

RESTAURANT

BLACK FOREST INN
◆◆◆
Continental

Lunch: $9-$13 **Dinner:** $16-$22 **Phone:** 973/347-3344
Location: I-80, exit 25 to US 206N; 1 mi n on right. 249 US 206 N 07874. **Hours:** 11:30 am-2 & 5-10 pm, Sat from 5 pm, Sun 1 pm-9 pm. Closed: 1/1, 12/24 & 12/25 & Tues. **Reservations:** suggested.
Features: casual dress; health conscious menu items; cocktails & lounge; a la carte. Delightful Old World charm; authentic German house specialties. Freshly made desserts. **Cards:** AE, DI, MC, VI. 🦽 X

SUMMIT—19,800 (See map p. 206; index p. 205)

RESTAURANTS

J B WINBERIE
◆
American

Lunch: $8-$11 **Dinner:** $8-$11 **Phone:** 908/277-4224 (164)
Location: Downtown, jct Springfield Ave. 2 Kent Place Blvd 07901. **Hours:** 11:30 am-11 pm, Fri & Sat-midnight, Sun 10 am-10 pm. Closed: 11/26 & 12/25. **Features:** casual dress; Sunday brunch; children's menu; carryout; cocktails & lounge; fee for parking; a la carte. Comfortable family neighborhood eatery.
Cards: AE, DI, DS, MC, VI.
X

SOUFFLE'
◆◆◆
French

Lunch: $7-$12 **Dinner:** $16-$24 **Phone:** 908/598-0717 (165)
Location: Downtown; corner Summit Ave. 7 Union Pl 07901. **Hours:** 11:30 am-2:30 & 5-11 pm, Fri & Sat-11 pm, Sun 4 pm-9 pm. Closed: Mon. **Reservations:** suggested. **Features:** carryout; street parking; a la carte, also prix fixe. Warm yet sophisticated cozy restaurant serving classic souffle as well as contemporary delicacies such as pastrami salmon, oie gras, rack of lamb, bouillabaisse. **Cards:** AE, MC, VI. 🦽 X

TEANECK—37,800 (See map p. 210; index p. 209)

LODGING

MARRIOTT AT GLENPOINTE
◆◆◆
Hotel

Rates Subject to Change **Phone:** 201/836-0600 ⓰
Sun-Thurs 1P: $185- 195 2P/1B: $200- 210 2P/2B: $200- 210
Fri & Sat 1P: $97- 115 2P/1B: $97- 115 2P/2B: $97- 115
Location: From I-80 (I-95); westbound local lanes exit 70, (Teaneck), eastbound local lanes exit 70 to 70B. 100 Frank W Burr Blvd 07666. **Fax:** 201/836-0638. **Terms:** Sr. discount; check-in 4 pm; no pets. **Facility:** 341 rooms. 15 stories; interior corridors. **Dining:** Restaurant; 6:30 am-10 pm; $10-$15. **All Rooms:** free & pay movies. **Cards:** AE, CB, DI, DS, JCB, MC, VI. 🛏 🕂 CTV 👤 X 🐕 D S

THOROFARE—*See Philadelphia & Vicinity p. 393.*

TINTON FALLS—12,400

LODGINGS

COURTYARD BY MARRIOTT
◆◆◆
Motel

Rates Subject to Change **Phone:** 732/389-2100
Fri & Sat 5/1-9/30 1P: $105 2P/1B: $115 2P/2B: $125 XP: $10 F16
Sun-Thurs 5/1-9/30 &
10/1-4/30 1P: $99 2P/1B: $99- 109 2P/2B: $99- 109 XP: $10 F16
Fri & Sat 10/1-4/30 1P: $69- 89 2P/1B: $69- 89 2P/2B: $69- 89 XP: $10 F16
Location: Garden State Pkwy, exit 105, 1st jughandle after toll, n. 600 Hope Rd 07724. **Fax:** 732/389-1727. **Terms:** Check-in 4 pm; no pets. **Facility:** 120 rooms. 3 stories; interior corridors. **All Rooms:** free & pay movies. **Cards:** AE, DI, DS, MC, VI. 🛏 CTV X 🐕 D S

HOLIDAY INN AT TINTON FALLS — Rates Subject to Change — Phone: 732/544-9300
◆◆ All Year 1P: $99- 109 2P/1B: $109- 119 2P/2B: $109- 119 XP: $10 F18
Hotel **Location:** Garden State Pkwy, exit 105. 700 Hope Rd 07724. Fax: 732/544-8049. **Terms:** Sr. discount; no pets. **Facility:** 171 rooms. 5 stories; interior corridors. **Dining:** Restaurant; 6:30 am-11 pm; $9-$15.
All Rooms: free & pay movies. **Cards:** AE, DI, DS, MC, VI. *(See ad p 230)* (CTV) (X) (🔊) (D) (S)

RED ROOF INN — Rates Subject to Change — Phone: 732/389-4646
◆◆ 5/1-9/30 1P: $60- 80 2P/1B: $65- 80 2P/2B: $66- 86 XP: $10 F18
Motel 3/1-4/30 1P: $50- 58 2P/1B: $56- 64 2P/2B: $56- 64 XP: $10 F18
10/1-2/28 1P: $40- 50 2P/1B: $50- 61 2P/2B: $50- 61 XP: $10 F18
Location: Garden State Pkwy exit 105, right at 1st light after toll. 11 Centre Plaza 07724. Fax: 732/389-4509. **Terms:** Small pets only. **Facility:** 119 rooms. 3 stories; exterior corridors. **All Rooms:** free & pay movies. **Cards:** AE, CB, DI, DS, MC, VI.
(🐾) (CTV) (X) (🔊) (D)

RESIDENCE INN BY MARRIOTT — Rates Subject to Change — Phone: 732/389-8100
◆◆◆ 5/1-11/22 [CP] 1P: $135 2P/1B: $135 2P/2B: $145
Apartment 3/1-4/30 [CP] 1P: $130 2P/1B: $130 2P/2B: $140
Motel 11/23-2/28 [CP] 1P: $120 2P/1B: $120 2P/2B: $130
Location: Garden State Pkwy, exit 105, 1st jughandle after toll, immediate left before Courtyard by Marriott, just n then e. 90 Park Rd 07724. Fax: 732/389-1573. **Terms:** Pets, $150 extra charge, 7 night min stay. **Facility:** 96 rooms. Rates for up to 4 persons; 2 stories; exterior corridors. **All Rooms:** kitchens, free movies. **Cards:** AE, DI, DS, JCB, MC, VI.
(🐾) (🍳) (CTV) (X) (🔊) (D)

SUNRISE SUITES HOTEL — Rates Subject to Change — Phone: 732/389-4800
◆◆ 6/15-9/15 [CP] 1P: $129 2P/1B: $139 2P/2B: $159 XP: $10 F
Suite Motel 5/1-6/14 [CP] 1P: $99 2P/1B: $109 2P/2B: $129 XP: $10 F
9/16-4/30 [CP] 1P: $79 2P/1B: $99 2P/2B: $109 XP: $10 F
Location: Garden State Pkwy, exit 105, 1st right at Hope Rd after toll. 3 Centre Plaza 07724. Fax: 732/389-0137. **Terms:** Sr. discount; reserv deposit; pets, $50 dep req. **Facility:** 96 rooms. 3 stories; interior/exterior corridors.
All Rooms: free movies. **Some Rooms:** 20 efficiencies. **Cards:** AE, CB, DI, DS, JCB, MC, VI. (🐾) (🍳) (CTV) (X) (🔊) (D)

TOMS RIVER—7,500

LODGINGS

HOLIDAY INN — Rates Subject to Change — Phone: 732/244-4000
◆◆ 5/25-9/6 1P: $99- 114 2P/1B: $99- 114 2P/2B: $99- 114 XP: $10 F19
Motor Inn 5/1-5/24 & 9/7-4/30 1P: $84 2P/1B: $84 2P/2B: $84 XP: $10 F19
Location: Garden State Pkwy exit 82, 1 mi e on SR 37. 290 Hwy 37E 08753. Fax: 732/244-4000.
Terms: Small pets only. **Facility:** 123 rooms. 4 stories; interior corridors. **Dining:** Restaurant; 6:30 am-10 pm, Sat & Sun from 7 am; $9-$17. **All Rooms:** free & pay movies. **Cards:** AE, CB, DI, DS, JCB, MC, VI. (🐾) (🍳) (CTV) (X) (🔊) (D) (S)

HOWARD JOHNSON MOTOR LODGE-TOMS RIVER — Phone: 732/244-1000
(AAA) (SAVE) 7/1-9/15 [CP] 1P: $75- 85 2P/1B: $90- 98 2P/2B: $120- 139 XP: $10 F18
5/25-6/30 [CP] 1P: $70- 90 2P/1B: $80- 90 2P/2B: $85- 100 XP: $6 F18
◆◆ 9/16-3/30 [CP] 1P: $65- 70 2P/1B: $70- 75 2P/2B: $75- 85 XP: $6 F18
Motor Inn 5/1-5/24 & 3/31-4/30 [CP] 1P: $60- 70 2P/1B: $65- 75 2P/2B: $70- 85 XP: $6 F18
Location: Garden State Pkwy exit 82, 1 mi e on SR 37. 955 Hooper Ave 08753. Fax: 732/505-3194.
Terms: Pets, $10 extra charge. **Facility:** 96 rooms. 2 stories; interior corridors. **Dining:** Restaurant; 11:30 am-9 pm; $7-$19.
All Rooms: free movies. **Cards:** AE, CB, DI, DS, MC, VI. (🐾) (🍳) (CTV) (X) (🔊) (D)

QUALITY INN — Rates Subject to Change — Phone: 732/341-2400
◆◆◆ 6/27-9/1 [CP] 1P: $109 2P/1B: $119 2P/2B: $119 XP: $10 D
Motor Inn 5/1-6/26 & 9/2-4/30 [CP] 1P: $79 2P/1B: $89 2P/2B: $89 XP: $10 D
Location: 1.5 mi w of Garden State Pkwy, exit 82A. 815 SR 37 W 08755. Fax: 732/341-6469. **Terms:** Sr. discount; check-in 4 pm; no pets. **Facility:** 100 rooms. 6 whirlpool rms, extra charge; 2 stories; interior corridors.
Dining: Restaurant; noon-9 pm; $6-$15. **All Rooms:** free movies. **Cards:** AE, CB, DI, DS, JCB, MC, VI. (🍳) (CTV) (X) (🔊) (D) (S)

RAMADA INN & SUITES-TOMS RIVER/LAKEWOOD — Phone: 732/905-2626
(AAA) (SAVE) 5/26-9/7 1P: $85- 115 2P/1B: $90- 120 2P/2B: $85- 115 XP: $10 F12
5/1-5/25 & 9/8-4/30 1P: $62- 90 2P/1B: $69- 95 2P/2B: $62- 69 XP: $10 F12
◆◆◆ **Location:** At jct US 9 & SR 70, 2.5 mi w of exit 88 of Garden State Pkwy southbound, 3.5 mi n of exit 83
Motor Inn northbound. 2373 Rt 9 08755. Fax: 732/905-8735. **Terms:** Pets. **Facility:** 126 rooms. Continental breakfast Mon-Fri only. 2-room executive suites; 2 with fireplace, 2 whirlpool rms, extra charge; 3 stories; interior corridors; whirlpool; 1 tennis court; outdoor basketball court. **Dining & Entertainment:** Restaurant; 7 am-10 pm, Sat from 7:30 am, Sun 7:30 am-9 pm, non-smoking restaurant; $8-$21; health conscious menu items; cocktails/lounge. **Services:** Fee: coin laundry. **All Rooms:** free & pay movies. **Some Rooms:** coffeemakers, 24 efficiencies, microwaves, safes. Fee: refrigerators. **Cards:** AE, CB, DI, DS, MC, VI. **Special Amenities:** Free breakfast and free newspaper.
(🐾) (🍳) (🍽) (♿) (CTV) (X) (🔊) (D) (S)

RESTAURANTS

JACK BAKER'S LOBSTER SHANTY — Lunch: $8-$13 — Dinner: $13-$20 — Phone: 732/240-4800
◆ **Location:** 0.5 mi e of Garden State Pkwy exit 81; just e of jct SR 166, overlooking Toms River across from
Seafood Huddy Park. 4 Robbins Pkwy 08753. **Hours:** 11:30 am-9:30 pm, Fri-10 pm, Sat-10:30 pm, Sun-9 pm; in winter 11:30 am-9 pm, Fri-9:30 pm, Sat-10 pm, Sun-9 pm. Closed: 12/25. **Features:** children's menu; early bird specials; carryout; salad bar; cocktails & lounge; fee for parking. Variety of daily specials, raw bar. Municipal parking lot opposite with meters. **Cards:** AE, DI, CB, MC, VI. (♿) (X)

KING'S WOK — Lunch: $5-$6 — Dinner: $7-$11 — Phone: 732/286-1505
◆ **Location:** Garden State Pkwy exit 82, just s; in Stello Towne Center. 1226 SR 166 08753. **Hours:** 11 am-10
Chinese pm, Fri & Sat-11 pm, Sun noon-10 pm. Closed: 11/26. **Features:** casual dress; early bird specials; carryout; a la carte. Szechuan, Hunan & Cantonese cuisines. Soft, soothing decor. Gracious service. **Cards:** AE, CB,
MC, VI. (X)

THE OLD TIME TAVERN — Lunch: $6-$10 — Dinner: $10-$18 — Phone: 732/505-5307
◆ **Location:** Jct SR 37 & 166, just n. Rt 166 Dove Mall 08753. **Hours:** 11:30 am-11 pm, Sun-10 pm. Closed:
American 12/25. **Features:** casual dress; children's menu; early bird specials; health conscious menu; carryout; cocktails & lounge; a la carte. Casual family restaurant with an extensive, varied menu including pizza, pasta, steak & prime rib. Good selection of beer. **Cards:** AE, CB, DI, MC, VI. (X)

TOTOWA—10,200   (See map p. 206; index p. 205)

LODGING

HOLIDAY INN-TOTOWA
◆◆◆
Motor Inn

		Guaranteed Rates				Phone: 973/785-9000	91
Mon-Thurs	1P: $99	2P/1B: $99	2P/2B: $99	XP: $10	F18
Fri-Sun	1P: $84	2P/1B: $84	2P/2B: $84	XP: $10	F18

Location: On US 46W, 2.5 mi w of jct SR 3; I-80 westbound exit 55A at 1st left, I-80 eastbound to US 46E, to Totowa Union Blvd exit, then 1st right. 1 US 46 W 07512. Fax: 973/785-3031. **Terms:** Sr. discount; no pets. **Facility:** 155 rooms. 5 stories; interior corridors. **Dining:** Restaurant; 7 am-10 pm; $8-$18. **All Rooms:** free & pay movies. **Cards:** AE, DI, DS, MC, VI.

🛏 CTV ⊠ 🔌 D

TRENTON—88,700

RESTAURANTS

DIAMOND'S
◆◆◆
Italian

Lunch: $6-$16	Dinner: $13-$27	Phone: 609/393-1000

Location: From jct US 1 & SR 33, 2 mi e. 132 Kent St 08611. **Hours:** 11:30 am-2:30 & 4:30-midnight. Closed major holidays. **Reservations:** suggested; for dinner. **Features:** cocktails; valet parking. Upscale casual dress. Award winning wine list. **Cards:** AE, DI, DS, MC, VI.

LARRY PERONI'S WATERFRONT
◆
Continental

Lunch: $7-$12	Dinner: $10-$19	Phone: 609/882-0303

Location: I-95 exit 1, 1 mi n. SR 29, River Rd 08628. **Hours:** 11:30 am-10 pm, Fri & Sat-11 pm, Sun-9 pm. Closed: 12/25. **Reservations:** suggested; weekends. **Features:** casual dress; Sunday brunch; children's menu; carryout; cocktails & lounge; a la carte. Quaint dining rooms with rustic ambience. Large selection of continental cuisine. **Cards:** AE, CB, DI, MC, VI.

TUCKERTON—3,000

RESTAURANT

THE GRAPEVINE
◆◆
Seafood

Dinner: $10-$24	Phone: 609/296-7799

Location: On US 9, 1 mi n. 364 E Main St 08087. **Hours:** 4 pm-9 pm, Fri & Sat-10 pm, Sun 2 pm-9 pm. Closed major holidays, Mon, Tues & 1/1-2/10. **Reservations:** suggested. **Features:** casual dress; children's menu; early bird specials; health conscious menu items; carryout; cocktails & lounge; a la carte. Comfortable family atmosphere. **Cards:** AE, MC, VI.

⊠

UNION—492,400   (See map p. 206; index p. 205)

RESTAURANT

MARIO'S TRATTORIA
◆
Italian

Lunch: $5-$13	Dinner: $11-$17	Phone: 908/687-3250	167

Location: Garden State Pkwy exit 139, 0.5 mi e. 495 Chestnut St 07083. **Hours:** 11 am-11 pm, Fri-midnight, Sat 4 pm-midnight, Sun 1 pm-10 pm. Closed: 12/25. **Reservations:** suggested; weekends. **Features:** casual dress; early bird specials; health conscious menu items; carryout; cocktails & lounge; a la carte. Neighborhood favorite. **Cards:** AE, DI, DS, MC, VI.

⊠

VERNON—1,300

LODGING

THE GREAT GORGE RESORT
◆◆◆
Resort
Cottage

	Rates Subject to Change			Phone: 973/827-2222	
6/17-9/5 & 12/15-3/15	2P/1B: $175- 219	2P/2B: $219- 299	XP: $80	F15
5/1-6/16, 9/6-12/14 & 3/16-4/30	2P/1B: $125- 169	2P/2B: $169- 224	XP: $55	F15

Location: From jct SR 23, 5 mi n. Rt 94N 07462 (PO Box 848, MCAFEE, 07428). Fax: 973/827-8115. **Terms:** Check-in 4 pm; reserv deposit, 3 day notice; 2 night min stay, weekends; no pets. **Facility:** 105 rooms. 3-4 stories; exterior corridors. **Dining:** Restaurant, deli; 7 am-9 pm, Fri & Sat-10 pm; $14-$22. **All Rooms:** kitchens. **Cards:** AE, DI, MC, VI.

🛏 🛏 CTV D

VOORHEES—See Philadelphia & Vicinity p. 393.

WALL

LODGING

COMFORT INN   **Phone:** 732/449-6146
AAA **SAVE**   6/21-9/7 [CP]   1P: $90- 175   2P/1B: $90- 175   2P/2B: $90- 175   XP: $10   F18
◆   5/1-6/20 & 9/8-4/30 [CP]   1P: $50- 100   2P/1B: $50- 100   2P/2B: $50- 100   XP: $10   F18
                 Location: Exit 98 off Garden State Pkwy to I-195 & to Wall Township, 1.5 mi s. 1909 SR 35 07719 (PO Box
Motel   14, SPRING LAKE, 07762). Fax: 732/449-6556. **Terms:** Reserv deposit; no pets. **Facility:** 70 rooms. Handling
nearby. **All Rooms:** free movies. **Some Rooms:** 8 efficiencies, no utensils, microwaves. Fee: refrigerators. **Cards:** AE, CB,
DI, DS, JCB, MC, VI. **Special Amenities: Free breakfast and free local telephone calls.**

WARREN—10,800   (See map p. 206; index p. 205)

LODGING

SOMERSET HILLS HOTEL   Rates Subject to Change   **Phone:** 908/647-6700   **93**
◆◆◆   Sun-Thurs   1P: $165   2P/1B: $175   2P/2B: $175   XP: $10   F16
Hotel   Fri & Sat 5/1-12/14   1P: $125   2P/1B: $125   2P/2B: $125   XP: $10   F16
                 Fri & Sat 12/15-4/30   1P: $99   2P/1B: $99   2P/2B: $99   XP: $10   F16
Location: I-78 exit 33; just n CR 525. 200 Liberty Corner Rd 07059. Fax: 908/647-8053. **Terms:** Sr. discount; small pets
only. **Facility:** 111 rooms. 3 whirlpool suites; 5 stories; interior corridors. **Dining:** Christine's, see separate listing.
All Rooms: free & pay movies. **Some Rooms:** 9 efficiencies. **Cards:** AE, DI, MC, VI.

RESTAURANT

CHRISTINE'S   **Lunch:** $11-$19   **Dinner:** $20-$25   **Phone:** 908/647-6700   **89**
◆◆◆   **Location:** I-78 exit 33, 0.3 mi n CR 525; in Somerset Hills Hotel. 200 Liberty Corner Rd 07059. **Hours:** 11
Italian   am-3 & 5-10 pm, Fri-11 pm, Sat 5 pm-11 pm, Sun 10:30 am-2:30 pm. Closed major holidays & Sun for
                 dinner. **Reservations:** suggested; weekends. **Features:** casual dress; Sunday brunch; cocktails & lounge;
entertainment; a la carte. Upscale Old World dining room featuring upscale cuisine with made on premises desserts.
Cards: AE, CB, DI, DS, MC, VI.

WAYNE—47,000   (See map p. 206; index p. 205)

LODGING

HOLIDAY INN   Rates Subject to Change   **Phone:** 973/256-7000   **99**
◆◆◆   All Year   1P: $75- 91   2P/1B: $75- 91   2P/2B: $75- 91   XP: $6   F18
Motor Inn   **Location:** I-80 westbound Butler-Verona exit 53 thru 23S, service road off US 46 eastbound Caldwells exit
                 47, 7 mi e on US 46 to service road. 334 US 46E/Service Rd 07470. Fax: 973/890-5406. **Terms:** Sr.
discount; no pets. **Facility:** 139 rooms. 2 stories; exterior corridors. **Dining:** Restaurant; 6:30 am-11 pm; $10-$19.
All Rooms: free & pay movies. **Cards:** AE, CB, DI, DS, JCB, MC, VI.

WEEHAWKEN—12,400   (See map p. 210; index p. 209)

LODGING

RAMADA SUITE HOTEL   **Phone:** 201/617-5600   **68**
AAA **SAVE**   All Year [CP]   1P: $119- 219   2P/1B: $139- 239   2P/2B: $139- 239   XP: $20   F18
                 Location: In Lincoln Harbor Complex. 500 Harbor Blvd 07087. Fax: 201/617-5627. **Terms:** Reserv deposit;
◆◆◆   monthly rates; package plans; small pets only, $75 dep req. **Facility:** 244 rooms. Overlooking New York Harbor
Suite Hotel with magnificent view of Midtown Manhattan skyline; conveniently located to Lincoln Tunnel & Lincoln Harbor
                 Ferry which departs to Midtown & Lower Manhattan daily from hotel dock. 10 stories; interior corridors.
Dining: Restaurant; 11:30 am-3 & 5-11 pm; $18-$25; cocktails. **Services:** complimentary evening beverages; valet laundry;
area transportation, within 5 mi. **All Rooms:** coffeemakers, microwaves, free & pay movies, refrigerators.
Some Rooms: VCR's. **Cards:** AE, CB, DI, DS, MC, VI.

WEST ATLANTIC CITY—*See Atlantic City & Vicinity p. 183.*

WESTFIELD—28,900   (See map p. 206; index p. 205)

LODGING

WESTFIELD INN-BEST WESTERN   **Phone:** 908/654-5600   **102**
AAA **SAVE**   All Year [CP]   1P: $97- 125   2P/1B: $107- 135   2P/2B: $107- 135   XP: $10   F17
                 Location: On SR 28; 4 mi w of Garden State Pkwy, exit 137. 435 North Ave W 07090. Fax: 908/654-6483.
◆◆   **Terms:** No pets. **Facility:** 40 rooms. 2 stories; interior corridors. **All Rooms:** free movies. **Some Rooms:** 15
Motel   efficiencies. **Cards:** AE, CB, DI, DS, JCB, MC, VI.

RESTAURANTS

KEN MARCOTTE   **Lunch:** $9-$11   **Dinner:** $19-$24   **Phone:** 908/233-2309   **99**
◆◆◆   **Location:** Downtown; just w of jct Broad St. 115 Elm St 07090. **Hours:** 11:30 am-2:30 & 5:30-9 pm, Fri-10
American   pm, Sat 5:30 pm-10 pm, Sun 4:30 pm-8 pm. Closed major holidays. **Reservations:** suggested.
                 Features: health conscious menu; cocktails; street parking; a la carte. Contemporary, creative entrees
emphasizing fresh ingredients. Good wine list. Expresso/cappuccino. Understated elegance of old bank building with art
deco touches. Upscale casual. **Cards:** AE, DI, MC, VI.

NORTHSIDE TRATTORIA   **Lunch:** $6-$10   **Dinner:** $10-$15   **Phone:** 908/232-7320   **100**
◆   **Location:** Between North Ave & Broad St. 16 Prospect St 07090. **Hours:** 11:30 am-9:30 pm, Fri & Sat-10
Regional   pm, Sun 5 pm-9 pm. Closed major holidays. **Features:** casual dress; health conscious menu items; carryout;
Italian   a la carte. Imported pasta house specials, homemade stuffed pizza & foccaccio. Smoke free premises.
                 Cards: AE, MC, VI.

KNOW THE ZERO HOUR. Confirm the checkout time with the
front desk employee before planning your departure time.

WEST LONG BRANCH—7,700

LODGING

MCINTOSH INN OF WEST LONG BRANCH   Rates Subject to Change   Phone: 732/542-7900
◆◆   5/1-9/28 [CP]   1P: $59- 70 2P/1B: $66- 77 2P/2B: $66- 77 XP: $7   F18
Motel   9/29-4/30 [CP]   1P: $42- 52 2P/1B: $49- 59 2P/2B: $49- 59 XP: $7   F18
            Location: Garden State Pkwy exit 105, 4 mi e on SR 36; 1 mi e of jct SR 35. 294 Rt 36E 07764.
Fax: 732/542-7356. **Terms:** Sr. discount; no pets. **Facility:** 117 rooms. 4 stories; interior corridors. **All Rooms:** free movies.
Cards: AE, CB, DI, MC, VI. *(See color ad p 220, p 353 & below)*   Roll in showers. (CTV) (X) (∅) (D)

WEST ORANGE—39,100   (See map p. 206; index p. 205)

RESTAURANTS

HIGHLAWN PAVILION Historical   **Lunch:** $7-$15   **Dinner:** $15-$25   Phone: 973/731-3463   (143)
◆◆◆◆   **Location:** 0.3 mi n of I-280 exit 8B, 0.3 mi e on Eagle Rock Ave. Eagle Rock Reservation 07052.
American   **Hours:** noon-3 & 5:30-9:30 pm, Fri-10:30 pm, Sat 5 pm-11 pm, Sun 5 pm-9:30 pm. Closed: 12/24.
            Reservations: suggested. **Features:** semi-formal attire; health conscious menu items; cocktails & lounge;
valet parking; a la carte. 1900's casino on 412 acre park site. Magnificent view of northern New Jersey & Manhattan skyline.
Outdoor patio. Thurs-Sat pianist. **Cards:** AE, DI, DS, MC, VI.
                                                                                                            (X)

THE MANOR   **Lunch:** $9-$14   **Dinner:** $17-$30   Phone: 973/731-2360   (142)
(AAA)   **Location:** I-280, exit 8B, 1 mi n on CR 577 (Prospect Ave). 111 Prospect Ave 07052. **Hours:** noon-2:30 &
            6-9:30 pm, Sat from 6 pm, Sun noon-8 pm, Lobster buffet Tue-Sat, Sun candlelight buffet noon-7 pm, Wed
◆◆◆◆   Lunch buffet 11:30-3 pm. Closed: 12/24 & Mon. **Reservations:** required. **Features:** semi-formal attire;
Continental   cocktails & lounge; valet parking; a la carte. Long-standing award winning, local favorite with formal gardens.
            Everything prepared in-house. Smoke free premises. **Cards:** AE, DI, DS, MC, VI.
                                                                                                            (X)

PALS CABIN   **Lunch:** $6-$12   **Dinner:** $12-$19   Phone: 973/731-4000   (146)
(AAA)   **Location:** Just n of I-280, exit 8B. 265 Prospect Ave 07052. **Hours:** 8 am-11 pm, Sat-midnight.
◆   **Reservations:** suggested; weekends. **Features:** children's menu; carryout; cocktails & lounge. Landmark
American   restaurant, rustic decor. Family-owned since 1932. Valet parking, dinner only. **Cards:** AE, CB, DI, DS, MC,
            VI.
                                                                                                            (X)

WEST WINDSOR—16,000

RESTAURANT

SUNNY GARDEN   **Lunch:** $5-$7   **Dinner:** $7-$17   Phone: 609/520-1881
◆◆   **Location:** US 1S, just n of I-295/95. 15 Farber Rd 08540. **Hours:** 11:30 am-10 pm, Fri & Sat-11 pm. Closed:
Chinese   11/26. **Reservations:** accepted. **Features:** carryout. Sushi bar. Spacious, bright & airy garden room decor.
            Lunch buffet avail. Bring your own bottle. Smoke free premises. **Cards:** AE, MC, VI.
                                                                                                            (X)

Never leave valuables in your car!

Garages and parking lots may
not be legally responsible for
the loss or theft of articles
from your car.

WHIPPANY   (See map p. 206; index p. 205)

LODGINGS

COURTYARD BY MARRIOTT
◆◆◆
Motel

	Rates Subject to Change			
Sun-Thurs	1P: $119	2P/1B: $129	2P/2B: $129	XP: $10
Fri & Sat	1P: $69	2P/1B: $79	2P/2B: $79	XP: $10

Phone: 973/887-8700 **105** F F

Location: I-287 exit 39, 1.5 mi e. 157 SR 10E 07981. Fax: 973/887-8068. **Terms:** No pets. **Facility:** 149 rooms. 3 stories; interior corridors. **Dining:** Breakfast buffet avail. **All Rooms:** free & pay movies. **Cards:** AE, CB, DI, DS, MC, VI. *(See color ad below)*

HANOVER MARRIOTT
◆◆◆
Hotel

	Rates Subject to Change		
Sun-Thurs	1P: $195	2P/1B: $205	2P/2B: $205
Fri & Sat	1P: $99	2P/1B: $99	2P/2B: $99

Phone: 973/538-8811 **106**

Location: I-287, southbound exit 39B, northbound exit 39, 0.5 mi w. 1401 Rt 10E 07981. Fax: 973/538-0291. **Terms:** Sr. discount; check-in 4 pm; small pets only. **Facility:** 353 rooms. 8 stories; interior corridors. **Dining:** Dining room, restaurant; 6:30 am-11 pm, Sat & Sun from 7 am; $7-$28. **All Rooms:** free & pay movies. **Cards:** AE, CB, DI, DS, JCB, MC, VI.

HOWARD JOHNSON INN
AAA SAVE
◆◆
Motor Inn

	1P: $85	2P/1B: $95	2P/2B: $90	XP: $10
All Year [CP]				

Phone: 973/539-8350 **103** F

Location: I-287, exit 39B southbound, 39 northbound, just w. 1255 Rt 10E 07981. Fax: 973/539-9338. **Terms:** Weekly/monthly rates; package plans; small pets only. **Facility:** 108 rooms. 2 stories; interior corridors. **Dining:** Restaurant; 6 am-11 pm; $8-$15; health conscious menu items. **Services:** area transportation, within 10 mi. Fee: coin laundry. **All Rooms:** free & pay movies. **Some Rooms:** efficiency, no utensils, microwaves, refrigerators. **Cards:** AE, DI, DS, MC, VI.   Roll in showers.

SUMMERFIELD SUITES-HANOVER
◆◆◆
Motel

	Rates Subject to Change			
All Year [BP]	1P: $120- 180	2P/1B: $120- 180	2P/2B: $169- 280	XP: $10

Phone: 973/605-1001 **104** F18

Location: I-287, exit 39, Rt 10W, just nw. 1 Ridgedale Ave 07981. Fax: 973/605-8338. **Terms:** Sr. discount; pets, $300 fee, $15 extra charge. **Facility:** 136 rooms. 3 stories; interior corridors. **All Rooms:** free movies. **Cards:** AE, CB, DI, DS, JCB, MC, VI.   Roll in showers.

RESTAURANT

IL CAPRICCIO
AAA
◆◆◆◆
Italian

Lunch: $10-$16   **Dinner:** $15-$26   **Phone:** 973/884-9175 **105**

Location: 1 mi e of I-287. 633 SR 10 07981. **Hours:** 11:30 am-2:30 & 5-10 pm, Fri-11 pm, Sat 5 pm-11 pm. Closed major holidays & Sun. **Reservations:** suggested. **Features:** semi-formal attire; cocktails & lounge; entertainment; a la carte. Elegant decor. Progressive Italian cuisine. Award winning wine list. Valet dinner only. **Cards:** AE, DI, MC, VI.

WHITEHOUSE—900

RESTAURANT

THE RYLAND INN
AAA
◆◆◆◆
French

Lunch: $10-$16   **Dinner:** $26-$33   **Phone:** 908/534-4011

Location: On SR 22 W, 1 mi e. 08888. **Hours:** 11:30 am-2 & 5:30-10 pm, Sat from 5:30 pm, Sun 4 pm-9 pm. Closed major holidays. **Reservations:** suggested. **Features:** semi-formal attire; health conscious menu items; cocktails & lounge; a la carte, also prix fixe. Grand country manor with intimate dining rooms. Modern regional French cuisine using own garden herbs & vegetables. Jacket required at dinner. Valet parking Fri-Sun evenings. Cigar room. Smoke free premises. **Cards:** AE, DI, DS, MC, VI.

WHITE HOUSE STATION—1,300

LODGING

HOLLY THORN HOUSE
AAA
◆◆◆◆
Historic Bed
& Breakfast

	Rates Subject to Change		
All Year [BP]	1P: $115- 150	2P/1B: $115- 150	XP: $25

Phone: 908/534-1616

Location: 3 mi s of US 22; on CR 620 4 mi e of jct CR 523. 143 Readington Road 08889. Fax: 908/534-9017. **Terms:** Age restrictions may apply; no pets. **Facility:** 5 rooms. 2 stories; interior corridors; smoke free premises. **Dining:** Breakfast 7-9 am, buffet after 9 am on weekends. **Cards:** AE, DS, MC, VI.

WILDWOOD—4,500

LODGINGS

AA HEART OF WILDWOOD MOTELS
Phone: 609/522-4090

		Rates Subject to Change					
	7/12-8/29 & 9/4-9/6	2P/1B:	$75- 100	2P/2B:	$92- 150	XP: $10	F16
	6/21-7/11 & 8/30-9/3	2P/1B:	$70- 92	2P/2B:	$82- 135	XP: $10	F16
Motel	5/22-6/20	2P/1B:	$52- 85	2P/2B:	$60- 110	XP: $10	F16
	5/1-5/21, 9/7-10/11 & 4/1-4/30	2P/1B:	$40- 60	2P/2B:	$48- 90	XP: $10	F16

Location: Garden State Pkwy exit 4B, 3 mi se on SR 47, 0.5 mi n. 3915 & 4002 Ocean Ave 08260. Fax: 609/522-4224.
Terms: Open 5/1-10/11 & 4/1-4/30; reserv deposit, 14 day notice; 3 night min stay, weekends in season; no pets. **Facility:** 77 rooms. 3 two-bedroom efficiencies, $115-$180. Rates are for 2 adults & 2 children. Handling fee imposed; 2 stories; exterior corridors. **All Rooms:** free movies. **Cards:** AE, DS, MC, VI. *(See color ad below)*

ALA MOANA MOTEL
Phone: 609/729-7666

		Rates Subject to Change				
	7/11-8/16	2P/1B:	$96- 110	2P/2B:	$96- 110	XP: $6-10
	7/3-7/10 & 8/17-8/28	2P/1B:	$85- 95	2P/2B:	$85- 95	XP: $6-10
	5/27-7/2	2P/1B:	$63- 79	2P/2B:	$63- 79	XP: $6-10
Motel	5/15-5/26 & 8/29-9/30	2P/1B:	$45- 60	2P/2B:	$45- 60	XP: $6-10

Location: Garden State Pkwy, exit 4B, 3 mi se on SR 47, 0.4 mi s. 5300 Atlantic Ave 08260. Fax: 609/523-1753. **Terms:** Open 5/15-9/30; reserv deposit, 7 day notice; no pets. **Facility:** 43 rooms. 2-3 night min stay 7/1-8/31. Handling fee imposed; 3 stories, no elevator; exterior corridors. **All Rooms:** efficiencies, free movies. **Cards:** AE, DS, MC, VI.

With your AAA membership card and exclusive Hertz discount card, you are recognized all over the world as a special customer.

CYPRESS INN — Phone: 609/729-1110

7/12-8/22	2P/1B: $79	2P/2B: $105- 143	XP: $8	F12
Motel 6/21-7/11 & 8/23-9/6	2P/1B: $66	2P/2B: $85- 114	XP: $8	F12
6/2-6/20	2P/1B: $53	2P/2B: $70- 95	XP: $8	F12
5/1-6/1, 9/7-10/15 & 4/1-4/30	2P/1B: $40	2P/2B: $55- 79	XP: $8	F12

Rates Subject to Change
Location: Garden State Pkwy, exit 4B, 3 mi se on SR 47 to Atlantic Ave, just n. 303 E Andrews Ave 08260. **Fax:** 609/523-0468. **Terms:** Open 5/1-10/15 & 4/1-4/30; reserv deposit; no pets. **Facility:** 24 rooms. 3 stories, no elevator; exterior corridors. **Some Rooms:** 20 efficiencies. **Cards:** AE, MC, VI. *(See color ad p 236)*

DAYS INN SUITES — Phone: 609/522-0331

5/22-5/25, 7/2-7/5 & 7/10-9/6 [CP]	2P/1B: $118	2P/2B: $150- 175	XP: $10	F12
7/6-7/9 [CP]	2P/1B: $95	2P/2B: $138- 147	XP: $10	F12
Suite Motel 6/5-7/1 & 9/7-9/20 [CP]	2P/1B: $60- 80	2P/2B: $70- 108	XP: $10	F12
5/1-5/21, 5/26-6/4, 9/21-10/18 & 4/5-4/30 [CP]	2P/1B: $50- 60	2P/2B: $62- 92	XP: $10	F12

Location: 4B exit off Garden State Pkwy, 3 mi se on SR 47, just n on Ocean Ave. 4610 Ocean & Andrews aves 08260. **Fax:** 609/522-2018. **Terms:** Open 5/1-10/18 & 4/5-4/30; reserv deposit, 14 day notice; package plans; 3 night min stay, 7/15-8/27; no pets. **Facility:** 36 rooms. Comfortable contemporary furnishings. Handling fee imposed; 5 stories; exterior corridors; oceanview; wading pool; game room. **Dining:** Restaurant nearby. **Services:** Fee: coin laundry. **All Rooms:** refrigerators. **Some Rooms:** coffeemakers, 35 efficiencies. Fee: microwaves. **Cards:** AE, DI, DS, MC, VI. *(See ad below)*

THE DIPLOMAT MOTEL — Phone: 609/729-5200

5/22-5/26 & 7/3-7/6	2P/1B: $90- 110	2P/2B: $105- 125	XP: $5-10	F12
7/7-9/3	2P/1B: $72- 90	2P/2B: $92- 125	XP: $5-10	F12
5/27-7/2 & 9/4-9/7	2P/1B: $45- 90	2P/2B: $45- 95	XP: $5-10	F12
Condo Motel 5/1-5/21, 9/8-10/25 & 4/15-4/30	2P/1B: $35- 50	2P/2B: $45- 75	XP: $5-10	F12

Guaranteed Rates
Location: Garden State Pkwy, exit 4B, 3 mi se on SR 47 to Atlantic Ave, then 0.8 mi n. 225 E Wildwood Ave 08260. **Fax:** 609/729-2949. **Terms:** Open 5/1-10/25 & 4/15-4/30; reserv deposit, 14 day notice; 3 night min stay, in season; no pets. **Facility:** 88 rooms. Handling fee imposed; 5 stories; exterior corridors. **All Rooms:** efficiencies, free movies. **Cards:** MC, VI. *(See color ad opposite title page)*

ROOM RESERVATIONS: Mail in your advance deposit early to make certain that space is held for you.

KNOLL'S RESORT MOTEL

(AAA) (SAVE)
♦ ♦
Motel

		Phone: 609/522-8211		
7/1-9/6	2P/2B:	$94- 109	XP: $10	D13
5/21-6/30	2P/2B:	$69- 79	XP: $10	D13
9/7-10/11	2P/2B:	$52- 62	XP: $10	D13
5/1-5/20 & 10/12-4/30	2P/2B:	$39- 49	XP: $10	D13

Location: Garden State Pkwy, exit 48, 3 mi se on SR 47, 0.4 mi n. 4111 Atlantic Ave 08260. **Fax:** 609/522-0687. **Terms:** Reserv deposit, 14 day notice; weekly rates; package plans; 3 night min stay; no pets. **Facility:** 40 rooms. 1 blk to beach & boardwalk. Handling fee imposed; 3 stories, no elevator; exterior corridors; barbecue grills. **Dining:** Restaurant nearby. **Services:** area transportation, to bus terminal. **All Rooms:** coffeemakers, free movies, refrigerators. **Some Rooms:** microwaves, VCR's. **Cards:** AE, DS, MC, VI. **Special Amenities:** Free local telephone calls and preferred room (subject to availability with advanced reservations). *(See color ad p 237 & opposite title page)*

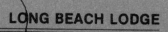

GEM FINDER: The Table of Contents is a diamond mine of where-to-find-it information.

Graceful down home attitudes, seaside ambience and warm caring service along with an unequalled array of superb family activities, great restaurants and the cleanest, biggest beaches at the Jersey Shore are what you can expect from every **M**orey Hospitality Property.

We not only offer three of the finest vacation accommodations on the entire seaboard, but also great rates on Morey's Piers Vacation Magic Passes where your family can enjoy more than 100 rides and attractions on our piers and waterparks. Of course, there's also pre and post season packages, discounts on championship golf and special rates for any size group.

Coast awhile with us... and discover an ocean of extraordinary vacation possibilities.

Pan American
H O T E L
Crocus Road & Ocean Road
Wildwood Crest, NJ 08260
609-522-6936

PORT ROYAL
H O T E L
Palm Road & Beach
Wildwood Crest, NJ 08260
609-729-2000

SEAPOINTE
VILLAGE RESORT
9900 Seapointe Blvd.
Wildwood Crest, NJ 08260
Rentals 609-729-0600
Sales 609-729-7100
By Seapointe Village Realty

* ©Aladdin Color Inc., Florence, NJ 08518

LE VOYAGEUR MOTEL
Rates Subject to Change
Phone: 609/522-6407

		2P/1B:	$66-	74	2P/2B:	$83-	105	XP:	$10	F5
	6/25-9/3									
	6/18-6/24	2P/1B:	$59		2P/2B:	$66-	85	XP:	$8	F5
	5/19-6/17 & 9/4-9/29	2P/1B:	$40-	45	2P/2B:	$47-	59	XP:	$6-8	F5
Motel	5/1-5/18, 9/30-10/30 &									
	4/15-4/30	2P/1B:	$37		2P/2B:	$40-	51	XP:	$6	F5

Location: Garden St Pkwy, exit 4B; 3 mi se on SR 47 to Pacific Ave, just n to Andrews Ave, then just e. 232 E Andrews Ave 08260. Fax: 609/523-1834. **Terms:** Open 5/1-10/30 & 4/15-4/30; reserv deposit, 21 day notice; no pets. **Facility:** 33 rooms. Rates for up to 4 persons in season. Handling fee imposed; 2-3 stories, no elevator; exterior corridors. **All Rooms:** free movies. **Some Rooms:** 14 efficiencies. **Cards:** AE, MC, VI. *(See color ad below)* 🅰 CTV D

MARLANE MOTEL
Rates Subject to Change
Phone: 609/522-7463

		1P:	$67-	73		2P/2B:	$79-	83	XP:	$10	D10
	7/13-8/16										
Motel	6/29-7/12 & 8/17-8/23	1P:	$59-	65		2P/2B:	$69-	75	XP:	$10	D10
	8/24-9/2	1P:	$50-	55		2P/2B:	$60-	65	XP:	$10	D10
	5/1-6/28 & 9/3-10/10	1P:	$39-	47		2P/2B:	$39-	57	XP:	$10	D10

Location: Garden State Pkwy, exit 4B, 3 mi se on SR 47, 0.5 mi n on Atlantic Ave to Montgomery Ave. 4310 Atlantic Ave 08260. Fax: 609/522-7463. **Terms:** Open 5/1-10/10; reserv deposit, 14 day notice; no pets. **Facility:** 27 rooms. Fri & Sat, $30 extra charge. Handling fee imposed; 2 stories; exterior corridors. **All Rooms:** free movies. **Cards:** AE, MC, VI.

🅰 CTV D

INK CHAMPAGNE MOTEL   Guaranteed Rates   Phone: 609/522-4857

Motel

7/12-9/6	2P/1B:	$80-	89	2P/2B:	$80-	89	XP: $10	F6
6/14-7/11	2P/1B:	$70-	72	2P/2B:	$70-	72	XP: $10	F6
5/1-6/13 & 9/7-9/30	2P/1B:	$50		2P/2B:	$50		XP: $10	F6

ocation: From exit 4B off Garden State Pkwy, 3 mi se on SR 47, just s. 4910 Atlantic Ave 08260. Fax: 609/522-9374. **erms:** Open 5/1-9/30; reserv deposit, 7 day notice; 3 night min stay, weekends; no pets. **Facility:** 24 rooms. 2-room efficiency nits for up to 4 persons, $125. Handling fee imposed; 3 stories, no elevator; exterior corridors. **Cards:** DS, MC, VI.

ECTV D

UARTER DECK I   Phone: 609/522-5415

Motel

7/1-9/6		2P/2B:	$79-	99	XP: $10
6/19-6/30		2P/2B:	$60-	75	XP: $8
5/1-6/18 & 9/3-10/15		2P/2B:	$39-	59	XP: $8

Location: From Garden State Pkwy, exit 4B, 3 mi se on SR 47, 0.8 mi n on Atlantic Ave to Pine Ave. 320 E Pine Ave 08260. **Terms:** Open 5/1-10/15; reserv deposit, 30 day notice; 3 night min stay, 7/1-8/31; no pets. **acility:** 30 rooms. Handling fee imposed; 3 stories, no elevator; exterior corridors. **Cards:** DS, MC, VI. *See color ad opposite title page)*

CTV D

UARTER DECK II   Phone: 609/522-4512

otel

7/1-9/6		2P/2B:	$99-	119	XP: $10	F14
6/19-6/30		2P/2B:	$69-	95	XP: $8	F14
5/1-6/18 & 9/7-9/30		2P/2B:	$59-	75	XP: $8	F14

Location: Garden St Pkwy, exit 4B, 3 mi se on SR 47, 0.8 mi n on Atlantic Ave to Pine Ave. 3200 Atlantic Ave 08260. **Terms:** Open 5/1-9/30; reserv deposit, 30 day notice; 3 night min stay, 7/1-8/31; no pets. **acility:** 52 rooms. Handling fee imposed; 5 stories; exterior corridors. **Some Rooms:** 6 efficiencies. **Cards:** DS, MC, VI. *See color ad opposite title page)*

CTV D

IVIERA RESORT MOTEL   Rates Subject to Change   Phone: 609/522-5353

otel

6/25-8/31		2P/2B:	$102-	210	XP: $6-12	D12
5/26-6/24		2P/2B:	$80-	190	XP: $6-12	D12
9/1-9/9		2P/2B:	$68-	180	XP: $6-12	D12
5/1-5/25 & 9/11-10/15		2P/2B:	$62-	180	XP: $6-12	D12

Location: From exit 4B, off Garden St Pkwy, 3 mi se on SR 47, 0.5 mi n on Ocean Ave. 325 E Spencer Ave 8260 (PO Box 127). Fax: 609/522-3992. **Terms:** Open 5/1-10/15; reserv deposit, 14 day notice; 3 night min stay, in eason; no pets. **Facility:** 31 rooms. Handling fee imposed; 3 stories, no elevator; exterior corridors. **Some Rooms:** 9 ficiencies, 3 kitchens. **Cards:** AE, DS, MC, VI.

CTV D

ROYAL CANADIAN MOTEL

🛆🛆🛆

7/2-8/29 [CP]	2P/1B:	$85- 135	2P/2B:	$85- 135	XP:	$10
6/26-7/1 [CP]	2P/1B:	$75- 100	2P/2B:	$75- 100	XP:	$8
5/29-6/25 & 8/30-9/19 [EP]	2P/1B:	$60- 85	2P/2B:	$60- 85	XP:	$5
5/1-5/28, 9/20-10/30 &						
4/1-4/30 [EP]	2P/1B:	$45- 65	2P/2B:	$45- 65	XP:	$5

◆◆

Motel

Guaranteed Rates   Phone: 609/522-095

Location: Garden State Pkwy, exit 4B, 3 mi se on SR 47, 0.8 mi n. 3300 Atlantic Ave 08260 (PO Box 856
Fax: 609/522-3290. **Terms:** Open 5/1-10/30 & 4/1-4/30; reserv deposit, 14 day notice; 3 night min stay, weekends 7/1-8/3
no pets. **Facility:** 86 rooms. Handling fee imposed; 4 stories; exterior corridors. **Some Rooms:** 32 efficiencies. **Cards:** A
DS, MC, VI. *(See color ad opposite title page)*   📶 CTV ⬜

SEA GULL MOTEL

◆◆

Motel

7/4-9/2	2P/1B:	$78- 97	2P/2B:	$68- 136	XP:	$4-8	F
5/23-7/3	2P/1B:	$55- 70	2P/2B:	$44- 78	XP:	$4-8	F
9/3-10/12	2P/1B:	$55	2P/2B:	$32- 72	XP:	$4-8	F
5/1-5/22	2P/1B:	$53	2P/2B:	$38- 62	XP:	$4-5	F

Rates Subject to Change   Phone: 609/522-333

Location: Garden State Pkwy, exit 4B; 3 mi se on SR 47, 0.5 mi s. 5305 Atlantic Ave 08260. Fax: 609/729-892
Terms: Open 5/1-10/12; reserv deposit, 14 day notice; 2 night min stay, weekends in season; no pets. **Facility:** 66 room
Rates for 2 adults with 2 children. 2- & 3-room efficiency apts $550-$770 weekly, 7/9-8/28. Handling fee imposed; 2-3 storie
no elevator; exterior corridors. **Some Rooms:** 30 efficiencies. **Cards:** AE, DS, MC, VI.   📶 CTV ⬜

SEA-N-SUN RESORT MOTEL

🛆🛆🛆

◆◆

Motel

6/26-8/31	2P/2B:	$108- 150	XP: $6-12	D
6/5-6/25 & 9/1-9/12	2P/2B:	$80- 130	XP: $6-12	D
5/1-6/4 & 9/13-10/15	2P/2B:	$65- 98	XP: $6-12	D

Rates Subject to Change   Phone: 609/522-282

Location: Garden State Pkwy, exit 4B, 3 mi se on SR 47, 0.5 mi n. 3909 Ocean Ave 08260 (PO Box 12
Fax: 609/522-3992. **Terms:** Open 5/1-10/15; reserv deposit, 14 day notice; 3 night min stay, in season;
pets. **Facility:** 21 rooms. Handling fee imposed; 2 stories; exterior corridors. **Some Rooms:** 4 efficiencies. **Cards:** AE, D
MC, VI.   CTV ⬜

TOWER MOTEL

◆

Motel

6/29-8/24	2P/1B:	$55- 65	2P/2B:	$65- 75	XP:	$6	F
8/25-10/5	2P/1B:	$28- 45	2P/2B:	$33- 55	XP:	$6	F
5/11-6/28	2P/1B:	$28- 45	2P/2B:	$38- 52	XP:	$6	F

Rates Subject to Change   Phone: 609/522-58

Location: Garden State Pkwy exit 4B, SR 47 (Rio Grande Ave) 2.5 mi se. 430 W Rio Grande Ave 08260. **Terms:** Op
5/11-10/5; reserv deposit, 14 day notice; 2 night min stay, weekends 7/1-8/31; no pets. **Facility:** 30 rooms. 2 stories; exter
corridors. **All Rooms:** free movies. **Some Rooms:** 6 efficiencies. **Cards:** AE, DS, MC, VI.   📶 CTV ✖ ⬜

RESTAURANTS

ALFE'S RESTAURANT   **Lunch:** $5-$11   **Dinner:** $15-$33   **Phone:** 609/729-57

◆◆

Italian

Location: Garden State Pkwy, exit 6, 3 mi se on SR 147 (which becomes New Jersey Ave), 0.7 mi s. 34
New Jersey Ave 08260. **Hours:** 11 am-2 am, Sun from 4 pm to 3 am in summer. Closed: 12/24 & 12/
Reservations: suggested. **Features:** casual dress; children's menu; early bird specials; carryout; cocktails
lounge. Bustling atmosphere. Featuring seafood, veal & a variety of pasta. **Cards:** AE, DI, MC, VI.

BOATHOUSE RESTAURANT   **Lunch:** $5-S15   **Dinner:** $10-$20   **Phone:** 609/729-53

◆◆

American

Location: Garden State Pkwy exit 4B, SR 47 s to se side of bridge. 506 W Rio Grande Ave 082
Hours: Open 5/1-10/15 & 4/15-4/30; 11:30 am-10 pm; Crabdeck open Fri & Sat-midnight. **Features:** cas
dress; children's menu; early bird specials; cocktails & lounge; entertainment. Waterfront dining room, a
deck dining overlooking bay. Seafood also featured on menu. Lunch is served on the crab deck only. **Cards:** AE, CB,
DS, MC, VI.

CHIARELLA'S RISTORANTE & SIDEWALK CAFE   **Lunch:** $4-S9   **Dinner:** $11-$20   **Phone:** 609/522-41

🛆🛆🛆

◆◆

Italian

Location: Garden State Pkwy exit 4B, SR 47 s to NJ Ave; n to Taylor Ave. 100 E Taylor Ave 082
Hours: 11:30 am-11 pm; late night menu 11 pm-2 am. Closed: Mon & Tues 2/15-6/1; 12/15-2/
Reservations: suggested. **Features:** casual dress; children's menu; carryout; cocktails & lounge; a la ca
Family oriented. Family owned & operated for 26 years. Pizza menu avail. **Cards:** AE, CB, DI, DS, MC, VI

THE CRAB HOUSE AT TWO MILE LANDING   **Lunch:** $5-$7   **Dinner:** $5-$15   **Phone:** 609/522-13

◆◆

Seafood

MC, VI.

Location: 1 mi s of Wildwood Crest. Ocean Dr 08260. **Hours:** Open 5/2-10/13; noon-10 p
Features: casual dress; children's menu; carryout; cocktails & lounge. Traditional Maryland crab house w
a diversified menu. Waterfront; additional deck dining area overlooks the marina. **Cards:** AE, CB, DI, I

DUFFER'S RESTAURANT & ICE CREAM PARLOR   **Lunch:** $7-$10   **Dinner:** $14-$21   **Phone:** 609/729-18

🛆🛆🛆

◆

American

Location: From exit 4B off Garden State Pkwy, 3 mi se on SR 47, 0.4 mi s. 5210 Pacific Ave 082
Hours: Open 5/1-9/30; 8 am-1 am. **Features:** casual dress; children's menu; carryout; a la carte. Liv
family oriented atmosphere. Restaurant also has old fashioned ice cream parlor, gift shop, arcade
miniature golf course. Smoke free premises. **Cards:** DS, MC, VI.

THE TWO MILE INN RESTAURANT   **Dinner:** $13-$21   **Phone:** 609/522-13

🛆🛆🛆

◆◆◆

Seafood

Location: 1 mi s of Wildwood Crest, n of Cape May. Ocean Dr 08260. **Hours:** Open 5/3-10/13; 4:30 pm
pm. **Features:** casual dress; children's menu; cocktails & lounge. Waterfront location with great view & w
good seafood in comfortable setting. **Cards:** AE, CB, DI, DS, MC, VI.

WILDWOOD CREST—3,600

LODGINGS

ACACIA BEACHFRONT MOTEL & CONDOMINIUM   Rates Subject to Change   **Phone: 609/729-2233**

7/6-8/25		2P/2B:	$99- 163	XP: $9	F10
6/16-7/5 & 8/26-9/7		2P/2B:	$88- 146	XP: $9	F10
9/8-9/30		2P/2B:	$50- 87	XP: $7	F10
5/3-6/15		2P/2B:	$36- 86	XP: $7	F10

Location: Garden State Pkwy exit 4B; SR 47 se 3 mi to Atlantic Ave, 2.1 mi s. 9101 Atlantic Ave 08260. Fax: 609/522-2294. **Terms:** Open 5/3-9/30; reserv deposit, 14 day notice; 3 night min stay, in season; no pets. **Facility:** 52 rooms. Rates for up to 4 persons, in season. Handling fee imposed; 4 stories; exterior corridors. **Cards:** AE, DS, MC, VI.

ADMIRAL MOTEL   Rates Subject to Change   **Phone: 609/522-7704**

6/28-9/8		2P/2B:	$90- 175	XP: $10	
6/14-6/27		2P/2B:	$55- 105	XP: $10	
5/1-6/13 & 9/9-10/13		2P/2B:	$45- 85	XP: $10	

Motor Inn   **Location:** Garden State Pkwy, exit 4B, 3 mi se on SR 47 to Ocean Ave, 1.2 mi s. 7200 Ocean Ave 08260. **Terms:** Open 5/1-10/13; reserv deposit, 14 day notice; no pets. **Facility:** 60 rooms. Rates for up to 4 persons in units & 6 in efficiencies. Handling fee imposed; 4 stories; interior/exterior corridors. **Dining:** Restaurant; 7 am-10 pm; $7-$14. **Some Rooms:** 39 efficiencies. **Cards:** AE, DI, DS, MC, VI.

ADVENTURER MOTOR INN   Rates Subject to Change   **Phone: 609/729-1200**

6/30-9/2		2P/2B:	$135- 215	XP: $12	F3
6/13-6/29		2P/2B:	$98- 165	XP: $10	F3
5/1-6/12, 9/3-10/30 &					
4/10-4/30		2P/2B:	$55- 110	XP: $10	F3

Motor Inn   **Location:** Ocean Ave & Morning Glory; exit 4B off Garden State Pkwy, se on SR 47, 0.3 mi s. 5401 Ocean Ave 08260 (PO Box 1506). Fax: 609/523-0505. **Terms:** Open 5/1-10/30 & 4/10-4/30; reserv deposit, 14 day notice; 3 night min stay, 7/1-8/31; no pets. **Facility:** 104 rooms. Rates for up to 4 persons; 6 stories; interior corridors. **Dining:** Restaurant; 7 am-8 pm; $5-$14. **Some Rooms:** 75 efficiencies. **Cards:** DS, MC, VI. *(See color ad p 244 & opposite title page)*

AMERICAN SAFARI MOTEL   Rates Subject to Change   **Phone: 609/522-0157**

7/11-8/15		2P/2B:	$93- 150	XP: $5-8	
7/1-7/10 & 8/16-8/22		2P/2B:	$84- 130	XP: $5	
6/20-6/30 & 8/23-9/6		2P/2B:	$50- 104	XP: $5	
5/1-6/19 & 9/7-10/13		2P/2B:	$40- 80	XP: $5	

Motel   **Location:** From Garden State Pkwy exit 4B, 3 mi se on SR 47, 0.4 mi s. 5610 Ocean Ave 08260. **Terms:** Open 5/1-10/13; reserv deposit, 21 day notice; 3 night min stay, 7/1-8/31; no pets. **Facility:** 25 rooms. Rates for up to 4 persons. Handling fee imposed; 3 stories, no elevator; exterior corridors. **All Rooms:** free movies. **Some Rooms:** 12 efficiencies. **Cards:** AE, DS, MC, VI.

AQUA BEACH RESORT   Rates Subject to Change   **Phone: 609/522-6507**

7/9-8/21	2P/1B:	$112- 118	2P/2B:	$124- 130	XP: $10	F17
6/14-7/8	2P/1B:	$100- 118	2P/2B:	$117- 130	XP: $10	F17
8/22-9/15 & 10/16-11/1	2P/1B:	$44- 112	2P/2B:	$51- 124	XP: $10	F17
5/1-6/13, 9/16-10/15 &						
4/1-4/30	2P/1B:	$40- 71	2P/2B:	$45- 82	XP: $10	F17

Complex   **Location:** Exit 4B Garden State Pkwy, 3 mi se on SR 47, 0.3 mi s. 5501 Ocean Ave 08260. Fax: 609/522-8535. **Terms:** Open 5/1-11/1 & 4/1-4/30; reserv deposit, 14 day notice; 3 night min stay, 7/1-8/31; no pets. **Facility:** 123 rooms. 3 two-bedroom suites. In-season rates for 4-6 persons. Handling fee imposed; 5 stories; exterior corridors. **Dining:** Coffee Shop; 6 am-4 pm. **All Rooms:** free movies. **Cards:** DS, MC, VI. *(See color ad below)*

ARMADA BY-THE-SEA   Rates Subject to Change   **Phone: 609/729-3000**

7/13-8/24	2P/1B:	$130- 142	2P/2B:	$122- 159	XP: $10	F7
6/21-7/12 & 8/25-9/2	2P/1B:	$105- 119	2P/2B:	$96- 137	XP: $10	F7
5/24-6/20	2P/1B:	$75- 82	2P/2B:	$67- 87	XP: $8-10	F7
5/3-5/23 & 9/3-10/14	2P/1B:	$56- 67	2P/2B:	$55- 72	XP: $6	F7

Motel   **Location:** Garden State Pkwy exit 4B, 3 mi se on SR 47 to Ocean Ave, 0.8 mi s. 6503 Ocean Ave 08260. Fax: 609/729-7472. **Terms:** Open 5/3-10/14; reserv deposit, 14 day notice; no pets. **Facility:** 58 rooms. Rates for up to 4 persons in season. Handling fee imposed; 5 stories; exterior corridors. **Some Rooms:** 45 efficiencies. **Cards:** AE, DS, MC, VI.

TTACHE RESORT MOTEL   Rates Subject to Change   **Phone:** 609/522-0241
◆◆◆

7/13-8/29	2P/2B: $115- 180	XP: $10
6/20-7/12 & 8/30-9/6	2P/2B: $85- 160	XP: $10
5/30-6/19 & 9/7-9/19	2P/2B: $60- 90	XP: $5
5/1-5/29, 9/20-10/15 &		
4/29-4/30	2P/2B: $50- 70	XP: $5

Motel

ocation: From Garden State Pkwy, exit 4B, 3 mi se on SR 47, 0.3 mi s on Ocean Ave to Heather Rd. 5711 Ocean Ave 8260. **Terms:** Open 5/1-10/15 & 4/29-4/30; reserv deposit, 21 day notice; no pets. **Facility:** 42 rooms. Rates 6/25-9/5 for up to 4 persons. Handling fee imposed; 3 stories; exterior corridors. **Cards:** AE, MC, VI.

EACH COLONY MOTEL   Rates Subject to Change   **Phone:** 609/522-4037
ⒶⒶ

7/11-8/29	2P/2B: $92- 112	XP: $10
6/26-7/10 & 8/30-9/6	2P/2B: $75- 98	XP: $10
6/4-6/25 & 9/7-9/19	2P/2B: $52- 65	XP: $7
5/8-6/3 & 9/20-10/18	2P/2B: $35- 45	XP: $5

◆◆
Motel

Location: Exit 4B off Garden State Pkwy, 3 mi se on SR 47, 1.2 mi s on Ocean Ave to Stockton Ave. 500 E tockton Ave 08260. **Terms:** Open 5/8-10/18; reserv deposit, 21 day notice; no pets. **Facility:** 26 rooms. Weekend rate in eason $8 extra charge. Handling fee imposed; 2 stories; exterior corridors. **All Rooms:** free movies. **Some Rooms:** 14 fficiencies. **Cards:** MC, VI. *(See ad below)*

EAU RIVAGE MOTOR INN   Rates Subject to Change   **Phone:** 609/729-2121
ⒶⒶ

7/12-8/17	2P/2B: $110- 190	XP: $10
6/28-7/11 & 8/18-9/2	2P/2B: $95- 175	XP: $10
6/1-6/27 & 9/3-9/8	2P/2B: $55- 150	XP: $8
5/1-5/31 & 9/9-10/13	2P/2B: $52- 90	XP: $8

◆◆◆
uite Motel

Location: Exit 4B off Garden State Pkwy, 3 mi se on SR 47, 2.2 mi s. 9103 Atlantic Ave 08260. ax: 609/729-2752. **Terms:** Open 5/1-10/13; reserv deposit, 21 day notice; 3 night min stay, in season; no pets. **Facility:** 49 ooms. Rates for up to 4 people in season. Handling fee imposed; 4 stories; exterior corridors. **Dining:** Coffee shop; 7 am-4 m. **Cards:** MC, VI. *(See color ad below)*

EL-AIR MOTEL   Rates Subject to Change   **Phone:** 609/522-4235
ⒶⒶ

7/10-9/6	2P/2B: $109- 150	XP: $7	F18
6/19-7/9	2P/2B: $75- 130	XP: $7	F18
5/1-6/18 & 9/7-10/12	2P/2B: $40- 90	XP: $5	F18

◆◆
otel

Location: From exit 4B of Garden State Pkwy, 3 mi se on SR 47, 0.3 mi s. 5510 Ocean Ave 08260. **Terms:** Open 5/1-10/12; reserv deposit, 14 day notice; 3 night min stay, 7/1-8/31; no pets. **Facility:** 27 rooms. ates for up to 4 persons. Handling fee imposed; 2 stories; exterior corridors. **All Rooms:** free movies. **Some Rooms:** 12 ficiencies. **Cards:** MC, VI.

BISCAYNE MOTEL   Rates Subject to Change   Phone: 609/522-444

ⒶⒶⒶ	7/6-9/1		2P/2B: $90- 160	XP: $8-10
	6/21-7/5		2P/2B: $75- 145	XP: $8-10
◆◆◆	6/13-6/20		2P/2B: $60- 105	XP: $8
Motel	5/1-6/12 & 9/2-10/15		2P/2B: $60- 95	XP: $8

Location: Garden State Pkwy, exit 4B; 3 mi se on SR 47, 1.5 mi s. 7807 Atlantic Ave 08260. **Terms:** Ope 5/1-10/15; reserv deposit, 14 day notice; no pets. **Facility:** 33 rooms. 7 night min stay in apts & 3 night in motel units, season. Handling fee imposed; 3 stories, no elevator; exterior corridors. **Some Rooms:** 20 efficiencies. **Cards:** MC, VI.

⌦ CTV ⌂

BRISTOL PLAZA RESORT   Rates Subject to Change   Phone: 609/729-123

ⒶⒶⒶ	7/12-8/24	2P/1B: $133- 186	2P/2B: $133- 186	XP: $10	F
	6/29-7/11 & 8/25-9/3	2P/1B: $111- 155	2P/2B: $111- 155	XP: $10	F
◆◆◆	6/19-6/28	2P/1B: $98- 127	2P/2B: $98- 127	XP: $6-10	F
Motel	5/1-6/18, 9/4-11/15 &				
	4/1-4/30	2P/1B: $42- 90	2P/2B: $42- 90	XP: $6	F

Location: Exit 4B off Garden State Pkwy, 3 mi se on SR 47, 0.8 mi s. 6407 Ocean Ave 08260. Fax: 609/729-936 **Terms:** Open 5/1-11/15 & 4/1-4/30; reserv deposit, 14 day notice; no pets. **Facility:** 55 rooms. Handling fee imposed; 5 sto ries; exterior corridors. **All Rooms:** free movies. **Some Rooms:** 40 efficiencies. **Cards:** AE, DS, MC, VI. *(See ad below)*

⌦ CTV ✕ ⌂

CARA MARA MOTEL   Guaranteed Rates   Phone: 609/522-695

ⒶⒶⒶ	7/3-9/4		2P/2B: $104- 195	XP: $10	F
	6/15-7/2		2P/2B: $70- 129	XP: $8-10	F
◆◆	5/1-6/14 & 9/5-10/20		2P/2B: $40- 129	XP: $8-10	F
Motel					

Location: Exit 4B off Garden State Pkwy, 3.5 mi se on SR 47, 1 mi s. 6701 Atlantic Ave 0826 Fax: 609/523-1583. **Terms:** Open 5/1-10/20; reserv deposit, 14 day notice; 3 night min stay, in season; r pets. **Facility:** 45 rooms. Handling fee imposed; 3 stories, no elevator; exterior corridors. **Some Rooms:** 34 efficiencie **Cards:** AE, MC, VI.

⌦ CTV ⌂

CARIBBEAN MOTEL   Phone: 609/522-829

ⒶⒶⒶ Ⓢⓐⓥⓔ	6/9-9/2	1P: $63- 115	2P/1B: $63- 115	2P/2B: $63- 115	XP: $10	F
	5/1-6/8 & 4/16-4/30	1P: $45- 66	2P/1B: $45- 66	2P/2B: $45- 66	XP: $6	F
◆◆	9/3-10/15	1P: $54- 64	2P/1B: $54- 64	2P/2B: $54- 64	XP: $6	F
Motel						

Location: From exit 4B off Garden State Pkwy, 3 mi se on SR 47, 0.3 mi s. 5600 Ocean Ave 0826 **Terms:** Open 5/1-10/15 & 4/16-4/30; reserv deposit, 21 day notice; package plans; no pets. **Facility:** 30 room Traditional motel rooms & 1 room efficiencies. Sun deck & picnic barbecue facilities. Located 200 feet from the beach. Rate for up to 4 persons 6/8-9/1; 2 stories; exterior corridors; wading pool, small heated pool; game room & shuffleboar **Dining:** Restaurant nearby. **Services:** Fee: coin laundry. **All Rooms:** coffeemakers, refrigerators. **Some Rooms:** efficiencies, microwaves. **Cards:** MC, VI.

🍴 CTV ⌂

CARRIAGE STOP MOTEL

Phone: 609/522-640

Rates Subject to Change

	2P/1B:	2P/2B:	XP:
7/1-9/6	$121- 139	$131- 149	$10
5/1-6/30	$80- 112	$84- 113	$10
9/7-10/19	$60- 72	$63- 75	$10

Motel

Location: Garden State Pkwy, exit 4B, 3 mi se on SR 47, 1.6 mi s on Atlantic Ave. 400 E St Paul A 08260. Fax: 609/522-0066. **Terms:** Open 5/1-10/19; reserv deposit, 14 day notice, 3 night min stay, 7/1-8/3 no pets. **Facility:** 31 rooms. Rates for up to 4 persons. Handling fee imposed; 3 stories, no elevator; exterior corrido **All Rooms:** efficiencies, free movies. **Cards:** AE, DS, MC, VI.

COMMANDER BY THE SEA

Phone: 609/522-280

	2P/1B:	2P/2B:	XP:
7/1-8/24	$80	$130- 150	$10
6/16-6/30 & 8/25-9/2	$65	$98- 130	$10
5/23-6/15 & 9/3-9/20	$42- 52	$65- 94	$8
5/1-5/22 & 9/21-10/15	$45	$50- 80	$8

Motel

Location: SR 47 exit 4B off Garden State Pkwy, 2 mi se, 2 mi s. 8803 Atlantic Ave 08260. **Terms:** Op 5/1-10/15; reserv deposit, 14 day notice; package plans; 3 night min stay, in season; no pets. **Facility:** 40 rooms. Most un with sitting rooms. A family oriented motel. Complimentary morning coffee. Rates for up to 4 persons in season. Handling f imposed; 3 stories, no elevator; exterior corridors; beachfront; beach, wading pool; video games & pool tab **Dining:** Restaurant nearby. **Services:** Fee: coin laundry. **Recreation:** swimming; bicycles. **All Rooms:** refrigerato **Some Rooms:** 31 efficiencies, microwaves. **Cards:** MC, VI. **Special Amenities:** Free local telephone calls and preferre room (subject to availability with advanced reservations).

COMPASS FAMILY RESORT

Phone: 609/522-69

Rates Subject to Change

	2P/1B:	2P/2B:	XP:
7/14-8/20	$97- 119	$97- 119	$8
6/26-7/13 & 8/21-9/3	$77- 97	$77- 97	$4
5/1-6/25, 9/4-10/31 & 4/1-4/30	$45- 69	$45- 69	$4

Motel

Location: Exit 4B off Garden State Pkwy, 3 mi se on SR 47, 0.8 mi s. 6501 Atlantic Ave 082 Fax: 609/729-9363. **Terms:** Open 5/1-10/31 & 4/1-4/30; reserv deposit, 14 day notice; no pets. **Facility:** 50 rooms. Rates are up to 4 persons, 7/13-8/21. Handling fee imposed; 3 stories; exterior corridors. **Some Rooms:** 25 efficiencies. **Cards:** AE, D MC, VI.

CRUSADER RESORT MOTOR INN

Phone: 609/522-69

	2P/1B:	2P/2B:	XP:
7/13-9/1	$137- 143	$160- 198	$12
6/22-7/12	$113- 138	$127- 178	$12
5/24-6/21 & 9/2-9/14	$77- 95	$93- 128	$6
5/1-5/23, 9/15-10/13 & 4/10-4/30	$55- 75	$67- 95	$6

Motor Inn

Location: At Ocean Ave & Cardinal Rd, exit 4B off Garden State Pkwy 3 mi se on SR 47, 0.5 mi s. 6101 Ocean Ave 082 (PO Box 1308). Fax: 609/522-2280. **Terms:** Open 5/1-10/13 & 4/10-4/30; reserv deposit, 14 day notice; package plans, night min stay, in season; no pets. **Facility:** 60 rooms. 1- & 2-room motel rooms & efficiencies, some with private balcony sundeck. Handling fee imposed; 3 stories; exterior corridors; beachfront; beach, wading pool, sauna; beach volleyball, ga room, ping pong & shuffleboard. **Dining:** Restaurant; 7 am-9 pm; $5-$10. **Services:** Fee: coin launc **Recreation:** children's program in season; swimming. **All Rooms:** coffeemakers, microwaves, free movies, refrigerato combo or shower baths. **Some Rooms:** 39 efficiencies. Fee: VCR's. **Cards:** MC, VI. *(See color ad p 247)*

EL CORONADO MOTOR INN

Phone: 609/729-10

Rates Subject to Change

	2P/1B:	2P/2B:	XP:	
9/1-10/19	$48- 138	$50- 242	$5	F
7/2-8/31	$127- 137	$129- 237	$10	F
5/22-7/1	$73- 111	$75- 209	$10	F
5/1-5/21	$43- 50	$45- 91	$5	F

Motor Inn

Location: Garden State Pkwy exit 4B to SR 47, 3 mi se, 1.8 mi s on Atlantic Ave. 8501 Atlantic Ave 082 Fax: 609/729-6557. **Terms:** Open 5/1-10/19; 3 night min stay, in season; no pets. **Facility:** 113 rooms. Handling fee impos 6 stories; interior corridors. **Dining:** Coffee shop; 7:30 am-4 pm. **All Rooms:** free movies. **Some Rooms:** 63 efficienci **Cards:** AE, DS, MC, VI. *(See color ad p 247)*

FLEUR DE LIS

Phone: 609/522-01

Rates Subject to Change

	1P:	2P/1B:	2P/2B:	XP:
7/2-8/28	$100- 170	$100- 170	$100- 160	$10
6/20-7/1 & 8/29-9/3	$85- 120	$85- 120	$85- 120	$10
5/22-6/19 & 9/4-9/20	$57- 85	$57- 85	$57- 80	$10
5/1-5/21, 9/21-10/13 & 4/11-4/30	$49- 67	$49- 67	$49- 62	$10

Motel

Location: 3 mi se on SR 47, exit 4B off Garden State Pkwy, 0.6 mi s on Ocean Ave. 6105 Ocean Ave 082 Fax: 609/523-0893. **Terms:** Open 5/1-10/13 & 4/11-4/30; reserv deposit, 14 day notice; no pets. **Facility:** 44 rooms. 3 ni min stay in season, 4 night min stay in efficiencies. Rates for up to 4 persons in season. Weekends $10 extra. Handling imposed; 3 stories, no elevator; exterior corridors. **Cards:** MC, VI. *(See color ad opposite title page)*

GONDOLIER MOTEL

Phone: 609/522-69

Rates Subject to Change

	2P/2B:	XP:
7/17-8/22	$125- 189	$7-10
5/22-6/18 & 9/7-9/13	$69- 160	$7
6/19-7/16 & 8/23-9/6	$110- 155	$10
5/1-5/21 & 9/14-10/15	$49- 67	$7

Motel

Location: On the beach at Lavender Rd; from Garden State Pkwy, exit 4B, 3 mi se on SR 47 to Ocean A 0.4 mi s. 5701 Ocean Ave 08260. Fax: 609/522-8379. **Terms:** Open 5/1-10/15; reserv deposit, 14 day notice; no pe **Facility:** 43 rooms. Rates are for up to 4 persons. Handling fee imposed; 3 stories; interior/exterior corrido **Some Rooms:** 25 efficiencies. **Cards:** DI, DS, MC, VI. *(See color ad opposite title page & p 247)*

GRANADA MOTEL

Phone: 609/522-90

Rates Subject to Change

	2P/1B:	2P/2B:	XP:
6/26-8/29	$82- 85	$135- 179	$10
6/12-6/25 & 8/30-9/3	$59- 69	$98- 139	$10
5/22-6/11 & 9/4-9/19	$42- 51	$78- 104	$8
5/1-5/21 & 9/20-10/18	$42	$55- 86	$8

Motel

Location: SR 47 exit 4B off Garden State Pkwy; 3 mi se, 2 mi s. 8801 Atlantic Ave at Topeka Ave 082 Fax: 609/523-1583. **Terms:** Open 5/1-10/18; reserv deposit, 14 day notice; 3 night min stay, in season; no pets. **Facility:** rooms. Rates for up to 4 persons in season. Handling fee imposed; 3 stories, no elevator; exterior corridors. **Cards:** AE, MC, VI. *(See ad p 238)*

HAWAII KAI MOTOR INN
(AAA)
◆◆
Motel

Rates Subject to Change
7/4-8/17 & 8/29-9/2	2P/1B:	$94-	122	2P/2B:	$94-	122	XP: $10	F5
6/23-7/3 & 8/18-8/28	2P/1B:	$80-	100	2P/2B:	$80-	100	XP: $10	F5
5/1-6/22 & 9/3-9/30	2P/1B:	$59-	79	2P/2B:	$59-	79	XP: $10	F5

Phone: 609/522-8181

Location: Garden State Pkwy, exit 4B, 3 mi se on SR 47, 1.5 mi s. 7504 Ocean Ave 08260. **Terms:** Open 5/1-9/30; reserv deposit, 21 day notice; 3 night min stay, weekends 7/1-8/31; no pets. **Facility:** 30 rooms. Rates for up to 4 persons in season. Handling fee imposed; 3 stories, no elevator; exterior corridors. **Cards:** AE, MC, VI. ☎ (CTV) (D)

HIALEAH RESORT MOTEL
◆◆
Apartment
Motel

Rates Subject to Change
7/10-8/19				
6/30-7/9 & 8/20-8/31	2P/2B:	$80- 100	XP: $5	F3
5/25-6/29 & 9/1-9/17	2P/2B:	$70- 91	XP: $5	F3
5/1-5/24, 9/18-10/30 &	2P/2B:	$45- 66	XP: $5	F3
4/15-4/30	2P/2B:	$40- 55	XP: $5	F3

Phone: 609/522-6655

Location: Exit 4B off Garden State Pkwy 3 mi se on SR 47, 0.7 mi s. 6211 Atlantic Ave at Wisteria Rd 08260. Fax: 609/522-1529. **Terms:** Open 5/1-10/30 & 4/15-4/30; reserv deposit, 14 day notice; 3 night min stay, in season; no pets. **Facility:** 52 rooms. Handling fee imposed; 3 stories, no elevator; exterior corridors. **Some Rooms:** 42 efficiencies. **Cards:** AE, DS, MC, VI. ☎ (CTV) (D)

IMPERIAL 500 MOTEL
◆◆
Motel

Rates Subject to Change
7/3-9/7	2P/2B:	$90- 110	XP: $10
6/19-7/2	2P/2B:	$75- 85	XP: $5
5/1-6/18 & 9/8-10/18	2P/2B:	$40- 60	XP: $5

Phone: 609/522-6063

Location: Garden State Pkwy exit 4B, SR 47 se to Atlantic Ave, 1 mi s. 6601 Atlantic Ave 08260. Fax: 609/522-7643. **Terms:** Open 5/1-10/18; reserv deposit, 45 day notice; no pets. **Facility:** 45 rooms. Rates for up to 4 persons 7/2-9/2; 3 stories, no elevator; exterior corridors. **Some Rooms:** 26 efficiencies. **Cards:** DS, MC, VI. ☎ (CTV) (D)

JOLLY ROGER MOTEL
◆◆
Motel

Rates Subject to Change
7/18-8/29	2P/2B:	$103- 160	XP: $7	F5
7/3-7/17 & 8/30-9/6	2P/2B:	$98- 135	XP: $5	F5
6/5-7/2 & 9/7-9/19	2P/2B:	$87- 119	XP: $5	F5
5/15-6/4 & 9/20-9/27	2P/2B:	$54- 75	XP: $3	F5

Phone: 609/522-6915

Location: Exit 4B off Garden State Pkwy 3 mi se on SR 47, 1 mi s. 6805 Atlantic Ave 08260. Fax: 609/729-2051. **Terms:** Open 5/15-9/27; reserv deposit, 14 day notice; 3 night min stay, in season; no pets. **Facility:** 74 rooms. Handling fee imposed; 3 stories, no elevator; exterior corridors. **Dining:** Coffee shop; 7:30 am-4 pm in season. **Some Rooms:** 30 efficiencies. **Cards:** MC, VI. *(See color ad opposite title page)* ☎ (CTV) (D)

LOTUS MOTOR INN
(AAA)
◆◆◆
Motel

Rates Subject to Change
7/19-8/29 [CP]	2P/2B:	$114- 156	XP: $10
5/22-5/24, 6/26-7/18 &			
8/30-9/6 [CP]	2P/2B:	$89- 142	XP: $10
6/5-6/25 & 9/7-9/19 [CP]	2P/2B:	$65- 108	XP: $5-10
5/1-5/21, 5/25-6/4 &			
9/20-10/20 [EP]	2P/2B:	$40- 79	XP: $5-10

Phone: 609/522-6300

Location: Exit 4B off Garden State Pkwy, 3 mi se on SR 47, 1 mi s. 6900 Ocean Ave 08260. Fax: 609/729-0203. **Terms:** Open 5/1-10/20; reserv deposit, 14 day notice; 2 night min stay, weekends, 7/1-8/31; no pets. **Facility:** 62 rooms. Handling fee imposed; 5 stories; exterior corridors. **All Rooms:** free movies. **Some Rooms:** 52 efficiencies. **Cards:** DS, MC, VI. *(See color ad below)* ☎ (CTV) (X) (D)

MADRID OCEAN RESORT
(AAA)
◆◆
Motor Inn

Rates Subject to Change
7/1-9/6	2P/1B:	$109-	135	2P/2B:	$139- 149	XP: $10
6/19-6/30 & 9/7-9/19	2P/1B:	$80-	90	2P/2B:	$95- 105	XP: $10
6/1-6/18	2P/1B:	$65-	70	2P/2B:	$80- 90	XP: $10
5/8-5/31 & 9/20-10/4	2P/1B:	$45-	55	2P/2B:	$55- 70	XP: $10

Phone: 609/729-1600

Location: Off 8000 blk of Atlantic Ave; exit 4B off Garden State Pkwy, 3 mi se on SR 47, 1.5 mi s on Atlantic Ave to Miami Ave. 427 E Miami Ave 08260. Fax: 609/729-8483. **Terms:** Open 5/8-10/4; reserv deposit, 14 day notice; no pets. **Facility:** 54 rooms. Rates based on 2 adults & 2 children aged 12 & under. Rates Fri-Sun $10 higher. Handling fee imposed; 5 stories; exterior corridors. **Dining:** Restaurant; 7 am-9 pm; off season 8 am-4 pm; $3-$13. **Some Rooms:** 24 efficiencies. **Cards:** AE, MC, VI. *(See color ad p 250)* ☎ (CTV) (D)

THE MARINER RESORT MOTEL

Rates Subject to Change   Phone: 609/522-1849

7/3-8/24 & 9/4-9/7	2P/1B:	$90-	95	2P/2B:	$105-	130	XP:	$10	
8/25-9/3	2P/1B:	$82-	87	2P/2B:	$95-	110	XP:	$10	
6/20-7/2	2P/1B:	$65-	80	2P/2B:	$72-	90	XP:	$10	
5/1-6/19 & 9/8-4/30	2P/1B:	$45-	66	2P/2B:	$50-	72	XP:	$8-10	

Motel   **Location:** From exit 4B off Garden State Pkwy, 3 mi se on SR 47, 1.6 mi s on Atlantic Ave. 407 E Monterey Ave 08260. Fax: 609/522-0429. **Terms:** Reserv deposit, 14 day notice; no pets. **Facility:** 14 rooms. Max rates for up to 4 persons 7/1-9/1. Handling fee imposed; 2 stories; exterior corridors. **All Rooms:** efficiencies. **Cards:** AE, DS, MC, VI.   (CTV) (D)

MARKAY MOTEL

Rates Subject to Change   Phone: 609/522-5326

6/28-8/29	2P/1B:	$58-	70	2P/2B:	$75-	120	XP: $10	F12
6/19-6/27 & 8/30-9/3	2P/1B:	$49-	62	2P/2B:	$58-	68	XP: $5-10	F12
5/22-6/18 & 9/4-9/16	2P/1B:	$45		2P/2B:	$50-	60	XP: $5	F12
5/1-5/21 & 9/17-10/1	2P/1B:	$32-	38	2P/2B:	$36-	58	XP: $5	F12

Motel   **Location:** Garden State Pkwy, exit 4B, 3 mi se on SR 47, 0.4 mi s. 5701 Atlantic Ave 08260. **Terms:** Open 5/1-10/1; reserv deposit, 15 day notice; 3 night min stay, 7/1-8/31; no pets. **Facility:** 20 rooms. Handling fee imposed; 2 stories; exterior corridors. **Some Rooms:** 7 efficiencies. **Cards:** AE, MC, VI.   (CTV) (D)

MONTA CELLO MOTEL

Phone: 609/522-4758

7/4-9/1	2P/2B:	$57-	95	XP: $4-7	F5
9/2-10/4	2P/2B:	$56-	78	XP: $4-6	F5
5/15-7/3	2P/2B:	$34-	74	XP: $4	F5

Motel   **Location:** Garden State Pkwy exit 4B, 3 mi se on SR 47, 2 mi s on New Jersey Ave to jct Denver Ave, then just e. 8400 Seaview Ave 08260. **Terms:** Open 5/15-10/4; reserv deposit, 14 day notice; package plans; no pets. **Facility:** 21 rooms. 1 two-bedroom unit. 3 night min stay in efficiency units with rates for up to 6 persons during 5/15-10/4 at $58-$134. Handling fee imposed; 2 stories; exterior corridors; wading pool; barbecue grills. **All Rooms:** refrigerators, combo or shower baths. **Some Rooms:** microwaves. **Cards:** MC, VI. **Special Amenities:** Free local telephone calls and preferred room (subject to availability with advanced reservations).   (ECTV) (D)

NASSAU INN

Guaranteed Rates   Phone: 609/729-9077

7/3-9/1	2P/1B:	$95-	120	2P/2B:	$135-	180	XP:	$10
6/20-7/2	2P/1B:	$85		2P/2B:	$95-	105	XP:	$8
5/30-6/19 & 9/2-9/14	2P/1B:	$70		2P/2B:	$75-	90	XP:	$8
5/1-5/29, 9/15-10/14 &								
4/25-4/30	2P/1B:	$55		2P/2B:	$68-	80	XP:	$8

Motel   **Location:** From exit 4B off Garden State Pkwy, 3 mi se on SR 47, 0.7 mi s. 6201 Ocean Ave at Sweetbriar Rd 08260. Fax: 609/729-2208. **Terms:** Open 5/1-10/14 & 4/25-4/30; reserv deposit, 14 day notice; no pets. **Facility:** 56 rooms. 7/2-9/6 max rates for up to 4 persons. Handling fee imposed; 5 stories; exterior corridors. **Some Rooms:** 40 efficiencies. **Cards:** DS, MC, VI. *(See color ad below & opposite title page)*   (CTV) (D)

THE OCEAN HOLIDAY MOTOR INN

Rates Subject to Change   Phone: 609/729-2900

7/11-8/23	2P/2B: $125- 174	XP: $10	F6
6/27-7/10 & 8/24-9/1	2P/2B: $110- 135	XP: $10	F6
5/23-6/26 & 9/2-9/13	2P/2B: $75- 115	XP: $10	F6
5/1-5/22 & 9/14-10/19	2P/2B: $45- 65	XP: $10	F6

Motel
Location: Garden State Pkwy, exit 4B, 3 mi se on SR 47, 0.8 mi s. 6501 Ocean Ave 08260. Fax: 609/523-1024. **Terms:** Open 5/1-10/19; reserv deposit, 14 day notice; 3 night min stay, 7/1-8/31; no pets. **Facility:** 58 rooms. Handling fee imposed; 5 stories; exterior corridors. **Some Rooms:** 53 efficiencies. **Cards:** AE, MC, VI. *(See color ad below)*
Roll in showers.

OCEANVIEW MOTEL

Rates Subject to Change   Phone: 609/522-6656

7/10-8/29	2P/2B: $105- 160	XP: $10
6/19-7/9	2P/2B: $95- 145	XP: $10
6/12-6/18	2P/2B: $65- 99	XP: $6
5/1-6/11 & 8/30-10/13	2P/2B: $55- 80	XP: $6

Motel
Location: Garden State Pkwy exit 4B, 3 mi se on SR 47 to Ocean Ave, 1.5 mi s. 7201 Ocean Ave 08260. Fax: 609/522-6793. **Terms:** Open 5/1-10/13; reserv deposit, 14 day notice; no pets. **Facility:** 110 rooms. Handling fee imposed; 4 stories; exterior corridors. **Some Rooms:** 64 efficiencies. **Cards:** DS, MC, VI. *(See color ad below)*

PAN AMERICAN HOTEL
[AAA] 7/3-9/7
6/12-7/2
◆◆◆ 5/29-6/11 & 9/8-9/19
Motor Inn 5/1-5/28 & 9/20-10/11

Rates Subject to Change
2P/1B: $133
2P/1B: $80- 112
2P/1B: $78
2P/1B: $62

2P/2B: $160- 197 XP: $6-12   F:
2P/2B: $92- 162 XP: $6-12   F:
2P/2B: $85- 106 XP: $6   F:
2P/2B: $72- 91 XP: $6   F:

Phone: 609/522-693(

Location: At Crocus Rd; exit 4B off Garden State Pkwy, 3 mi se on SR 47, then 0.5 mi s. 5901 Ocean Av(08260. Fax: 609/522-6937. **Terms:** Open 5/1-10/11; reserv deposit, 14 day notice; no pets. **Facility:** 78 rooms. Max rates 6/27 9/1 for up to 4 persons. Handling fee imposed; 4 stories; interior corridors. **Dining:** Dining room; 7:30 am-9 pm in season off season 7:30 am-3 pm; $3-$17. **Some Rooms:** 49 efficiencies. **Cards:** MC, VI.
(See color ad p 239 & opposite title page)   [≋] [CTV] [D

PARADISE INN MOTEL
◆◆ 7/4-7/7, 7/15-8/24 & 8/30-9/2
Motel 6/15-7/3, 7/8-7/14 &
8/25-8/29
5/15-6/14 & 9/3-9/30

Rates Subject to Change
2P/2B: $112- 145 XP: $10

2P/2B: $75- 89 XP: $7
2P/2B: $55- 66 XP: $6

Phone: 609/729-500(

Location: Garden St Pkwy, exit 4B, 3.5 mi se on SR 47, 1.8 mi s on Atlantic Ave to Denver Ave. 405 E Denver Ave 0826(Fax: 609/522-7077. **Terms:** Open 5/15-9/30; reserv deposit, 10 day notice; 3 night min stay, 7/1-8/31; no pets. **Facility:** 4(rooms. Handling fee imposed; 3 stories; exterior corridors. **Some Rooms:** 37 efficiencies. **Cards:** MC, VI.   [≋] [CTV] [D

PORT ROYAL HOTEL
[AAA] 7/3-9/7
6/26-7/2
◆◆◆ 6/19-6/25
Motor Inn 5/8-6/18 & 9/8-10/12

Guaranteed Rates
2P/1B: $134- 143
2P/1B: $112- 118
2P/1B: $100- 104
2P/1B: $84- 88

2P/2B: $160- 196 XP: $12   F
2P/2B: $133- 163 XP: $12   F
2P/2B: $112- 132 XP: $6   F
2P/2B: $92- 113 XP: $6   F

Phone: 609/729-200(

Location: Exit 4B off Garden State Pkwy, 3 mi se on SR 47, 1 mi s. 6801 Ocean Ave 0826(Fax: 609/729-2051. **Terms:** Open 5/8-10/12; reserv deposit, 14 day notice; 4 night min stay, in season; no pets. **Facility:** 10(rooms. 50 efficiencies, $185-$191 in season. Handling fee imposed; 6 stories; interior corridors. Fee: parkin(**Dining:** Restaurant; 8 am-3 pm; 6/15-9/6 to 8 pm; $9-$16. **Cards:** MC, VI. *(See color ad p 239 & opposite title page)*   [≋] [CTV] [D

REGES OCEANFRONT RESORT
[AAA] 7/17-8/22
6/26-7/16 & 8/23-9/7
◆◆◆ 6/12-6/25 & 9/8-9/19
Motel 5/8-6/11 & 9/20-10/12

Rates Subject to Change
2P/1B: $150- 199 2P/2B: $150- 199 XP: $15   F1
2P/1B: $140- 190 2P/2B: $140- 190 XP: $15   F1
2P/1B: $103- 159 2P/2B: $103- 159 XP: $15   F1
2P/1B: $65- 88 2P/2B: $65- 88 XP: $15   F1

Phone: 609/729-930(

Location: Garden State Pkwy, exit 4B, 3 mi se on SR 47 to Atlantic Ave, 2.5 mi s to Trenton Ave. 920(Atlantic Ave 08260. Fax: 609/729-1829. **Terms:** Open 5/8-10/12; reserv deposit, 14 day notice; no pets. **Facility:** 75 rooms Handling fee imposed; 8 stories; interior/exterior corridors. **Dining:** Coffee shop; 7 am-6 pm. **Some Rooms:** 45 efficiencies **Cards:** AE, DI, DS, MC, VI. *(See color ad opposite title page & below)*   [≋] [CTV] [∅] [D

SEAPOINTE VILLAGE
[AAA] 7/5-8/29 Weekly
6/21-7/4 Weekly
◆◆◆ 5/1-6/20 & 8/30-4/30 Weekly
Condo
Complex

Rates Subject to Change
2P/2B: $1155-2975
2P/2B: $945-2520
2P/2B: $665-1995

Phone: 609/729-060(

Location: Garden State Pkwy, exit 4B 3 mi se to Atlantic Ave, 3 mi s. 9900 Seapointe Blvd 0826(Fax: 609/729-1829. **Terms:** Check-in 4 pm; 2 night min stay, off season; no pets. **Facility:** 248 rooms. Ha(dling fee imposed; 2-7 stories; interior/exterior corridors. **Dining:** Deli; 8:30 am-5:30 pn **All Rooms:** kitchens, free movies. *(See color ad p 239 & opposite title page)*   [≋] [CTV] [X] [D] [S

TANGIERS MOTEL
[AAA] 7/2-7/5, 7/10-8/22 & 9/4-9/6
5/22-5/24, 6/12-7/1, 7/6-7/9 &
◆◆ 8/23-9/3
Motel 5/25-6/11 & 9/7-9/11
5/1-5/21, 9/12-10/13 &
4/11-4/30

Rates Subject to Change
2P/1B: $118

2P/1B: $86- 95
2P/1B: $54- 64

2P/1B: $45

2P/2B: $110- 130 XP: $10   F

2P/2B: $67- 101 XP: $10   F
2P/2B: $46- 72 XP: $7-10   F

2P/2B: $41- 53 XP: $5   F

Phone: 609/522-141(

Location: At Sweet Briar Rd & Atlantic Ave; Garden State Pkwy, exit 4B, 3 mi se on SR 47, 0.7 mi s. 6201 Atlantic Av 08260. Fax: 609/522-8524. **Terms:** Open 5/1-10/13 & 4/11-4/30; reserv deposit, 14 day notice; 3 night min stay, 6/28-9/2; n(pets. **Facility:** 50 rooms. Handling fee imposed; 3 stories, no elevator; exterior corridors. **Dining:** Coffee shop; 5/16-9/17, am-2 pm; 4/15-5/15 & 9/18-10/16 to 11 am. **Cards:** AE, MC, VI.   [≋] [CTV] [X] [C

TEMPO RESORT MOTEL Rates Subject to Change Phone: 609/523-0700

ⒶⒶⒶ
5/23-5/26 & 7/3-9/1		2P/2B:	$89- 110	XP: $10	F12
6/22-7/2		2P/2B:	$69- 85	XP: $10	F12
◆◆ | 5/27-6/21 | | 2P/2B: | $39- 55 | XP: $5 | F12 |
Motel | 5/1-5/22 & 9/2-10/31 | | 2P/2B: | $35- 49 | XP: $5 | F12 |

Location: Garden State Pkwy, exit 4B, 3 mi se on SR 47, 1.5 mi s. 7801 Atlantic Ave 08260. Fax: 609/523-0700. **Terms:** Open 5/1-10/31; reserv deposit, 14 day notice; 3 night min stay, 7/1-8/31; no pets. **Facility:** 19 rooms. Handling fee imposed; 2 stories; exterior corridors. **Some Rooms:** 14 efficiencies. **Cards:** AE, DS, MC, VI.

📶 [CTV] [D]

TOPAZ MOTEL Rates Subject to Change Phone: 609/522-2723

ⒶⒶⒶ
7/12-8/29	2P/1B:	$87		2P/2B:	$77- 92	XP: $6	F5
7/3-7/11	2P/1B:	$77		2P/2B:	$72- 82	XP: $6	F5
◆◆ | 6/6-6/28 & 8/30-9/3 | 2P/1B: | $65 | | 2P/2B: | $60- 70 | XP: $6 | F5 |
Motel | 5/1-6/5, 6/29-7/2 & 9/4-10/1 | 2P/1B: | $50 | | 2P/2B: | $45- 55 | XP: $6 | F5 |

Location: From Garden State Pkwy; exit 4B, 2.5 mi se on SR 47, to Park Blvd, 1.1 mi s to Primrose Rd, 0.3 mi e. 7010 Seaview Ave & Primrose Rd 08260. **Terms:** Open 5/1-10/1; reserv deposit, 14 day notice; no pets. **Facility:** 21 rooms. 1 three-room efficiency for 4-8 persons avail, $70-$120; 2 night min stay weekends in season. Handing fee imposed; 2 stories; exterior corridors. **Some Rooms:** 17 efficiencies. **Cards:** MC, VI.

📶 [CTV] [D]

WATERWAYS MOTEL Guaranteed Rates Phone: 609/522-2255

◆◆
7/3-9/7	1P:	$59- 130	2P/1B:	$59- 140	2P/2B:	$59- 140	XP:	$9
5/23-7/2 & 9/8-9/27	1P:	$40- 70	2P/1B:	$40- 80	2P/2B:	$40- 80	XP:	$4
Motel | 5/1-5/22 & 9/28-10/12 | 1P: | $32- 50 | 2P/1B: | $32- 50 | 2P/2B: | $32- 50 | XP: | $4 |

Location: Garden State Pkwy exit 4B, 3 mi se on SR 47 to Ocean Ave, 1.2 mi s. 7204 Ocean Ave 08260. **Terms:** Open 5/1-10/12; reserv deposit, 21 day notice; no pets. **Facility:** 25 rooms. Rates for up to 4 persons in efficiencies & 2-room suites, 3 persons in motel rooms, 5/01-6/30 & 9/4-10/14 for 2 persons. Handling fee imposed; 3 stories, no elevator; exterior corridors. **All Rooms:** free movies. **Some Rooms:** 20 efficiencies. **Cards:** AE, DS, MC, VI. *(See color ad p 251)*

📶 [CTV] [D]

RESTAURANTS

THE CAPTAIN'S TABLE RESTAURANT Dinner: $10-$27 Phone: 609/522-2939

ⒶⒶⒶ
◆◆
American

Location: From SR 47 exit 4B, 3 mi se, 0.5 mi s. 8701 Atlantic Ave 08260. **Hours:** Open 5/8-9/20; 8 am-noon & 4:30-10 pm, Sun 8 am-1 & 4:30-10 pm. **Reservations:** suggested. **Features:** casual dress; children's menu; early bird specials; carryout; minimum charge-$10. Family oriented. Dining room offers a nice view of the beach. **Cards:** AE, CB, DI, DS, MC, VI.

❌

DUFFY'S ON THE LAKE Dinner: $10-$24 Phone: 609/522-1815

◆◆
American

Location: From Garden State Pkwy exit 4B, 2.8 mi se on SR 47, 1.5 mi s. 7601 New Jersey Ave 08260. **Hours:** Open 5/3-10/18; 4:30 pm-9:30 pm. **Reservations:** suggested. **Features:** casual dress; children's menu; early bird specials; street parking. Family oriented. Dining room offers an excellent view of the bay. **Cards:** AE, DS, MC, VI.

❌

WINSLOW—*See Philadelphia & Vicinity p. 395.*

WOODBRIDGE—93,100 (See map p. 206; index p. 205)

LODGING

WOODBRIDGE HILTON Rates Subject to Change Phone: 732/494-6200 [111]

◆◆◆
Mon-Thurs	1P:	$115- 154	2P/1B:	$115- 154	2P/2B:	$115- 154	XP: $15	F18
Fri-Sun	1P:	$86	2P/1B:	$86	2P/2B:	$86	XP: $15	F18

Hotel **Location:** Exit 131A of Garden State Pkwy; NJ Tpk exit 11 to Garden State Pkwy N. 120 Wood Ave S 08830. Fax: 732/603-7777. **Terms:** No pets. **Facility:** 200 rooms. 11 stories; interior corridors. **Dining:** Dining room, restaurant, coffee shop; 6 am-11 pm; $10-$25. **All Rooms:** free movies. **Cards:** AE, DI, DS, MC, VI. *(See color ad p 18)*

🛏 🏋 [CTV] ❌ 🏊 [D] [S]

RESTAURANT

THE REO RESTAURANT & DINER Lunch: $5-$8 Dinner: $7-$13 Phone: 732/634-9200 [110]

◆
American

Location: Jct SR 35 (Amboy Ave) & Main St, just n. 392 Amboy Ave 07095. **Hours:** 24 hours. **Closed:** 12/25. **Features:** children's menu; carryout. Friendly, family atmosphere. Brightly lighted. **Cards:** AE, MC, VI.

❌

WOODCLIFF LAKE—5,300

LODGING

WOODCLIFF LAKE HILTON Rates Subject to Change Phone: 201/391-3600

ⒶⒶⒶ
◆◆◆
Hotel

All Year	1P: $126	2P/1B: $126	2P/2B: $126

Location: Northbound Garden State Pkwy exit 171, left on Glen Rd from exit ramp, right on Chestnut Ridge Road 0.5 mi to Tice Blvd, just left. 200 Tice Blvd 07675. Fax: 201/391-4572. **Terms:** Reserv deposit; pets. **Facility:** 334 rooms. 4 stories; interior corridors. **Dining:** Restaurant; 6:30 am-11 pm, Sat & Sun from 7 am; Sun Brunch seatings at 11 am & 1 pm; $8-$26. **All Rooms:** free & pay movies. **Cards:** AE, CB, DI, DS, JCB, MC, VI. *(See color ad p 18)* Roll in showers. 🛁 🛏 🛏 🏋 [CTV] ❌ 🏊 [D]

WOOD-RIDGE—7,500

RESTAURANT

ASSAGGIA RISTORANTE Lunch: $6-$14 Dinner: $8-$20 Phone: 201/933-0330

◆◆◆
Italian

Location: From jct SR 17 & Moonachie Ave, just w to Hackensack St. 187 Hackensack St 07075. **Hours:** noon-3 & 5-10 pm, Fri & Sat-11 pm. **Closed:** 1/1, 12/25 & Sun. **Reservations:** suggested; weekends. **Features:** cocktails; a la carte. Casual, comfortable quietly sophisticated restaurant serving regional Italian food. Italian wine list from small top Italian wineries. Homemade pasta & dessert. **Cards:** AE, DI, MC, VI.

❌

PENNSYLVANIA

> **AREA CODE CHANGE** - Effective April 29, 1998 with permissive dialing beginning February 1, 1998, certain cities in the Western Pennsylvania area changed their area code from 412 to 724. These changes are reflected in the individual property listings.

ABBOTTSTOWN—500

LODGING

THE INN AT THE ALTLAND HOUSE
Phone: 717/2⬛

⬛ ⬛ All Year [CP] 1P: $72 2P/1B: $82 XP: $10
Location: Just s on SR 194 from jct US 30. Center Sq Rt 30 17301 (PO Box 448). Fax: 717/2
◆◆◆ **Terms:** Reserv deposit; weekly/monthly rates; package plans; small pets only, in designated
Historic **Facility:** 9 rooms. 18th-century structure, rooms feature contemporary furnishings with historical ac
Country Inn whirlpool rms, $82-$92. 2 efficiencies, $125. Rates for up to 2 persons; 3 stories, no elevator; interior c
Dining & Entertainment: Restaurant; 5 pm-10 pm, Fri & Sat-11 pm, Sun-9 pm; $7-$14; cocktai
dining room, see separate listing. **All Rooms:** combo or shower baths. **Some Rooms:** refrigerators. **Cards:** AE, DS
Special Amenities: Free breakfast and free room upgrade (subject to availability with advanced reservations

⬛ ⬛ CTV ⬛

RESTAURANT

THE ALTLAND HOUSE Historical **Lunch:** $9-$27 **Dinner:** $9-$27 Phone: 717/2⬛
◆◆◆ **Location:** Just s on SR 194 from jct US 30; in The Inn at the Atland House. Center Sq Rt 3⬛
American **Hours:** 11 am-9 pm, Sun-7 pm. Closed: 12/25. **Reservations:** suggested; weekends. **Features**
casual; Sunday brunch; children's menu; carryout; cocktails & lounge. Inviting decor in 1790 la
Homemade soup, bread & dessert. Smoke free premises. **Cards:** AE, DS, MC, VI.

> **Towns under which AAA-approved lodging and dining facilities are listed are shown in red on AAA maps.**

ADAMSTOWN—*See Pennsylvania Dutch Country p. 330.*

AKRON—*See Pennsylvania Dutch Country p. 330.*

ALLENTOWN—105,100

LODGINGS

ALLENTOWN COMFORT SUITES   Phone: 610/437-9100
All Year [CP]   1P: $89- 120   2P/1B: $99- 120   2P/2B: $99- 120   XP: $10   F18
Location: Hamilton Blvd, exit off I-78, 0.5 mi n opposite Dorney Park. 3712 Hamilton Blvd 18103.
Fax: 610/437-0221. **Terms:** Monthly rates; package plans; no pets. **Facility:** 122 rooms. Large, attractive
rooms. 4 stories; interior corridors. **Dining & Entertainment:** Dining room; 11 am-1 am; $10-$20;
cocktails/lounge. **Services:** valet laundry; area transportation, within 10 mi. **All Rooms:** microwaves, free
movies, refrigerators, VCR's. **Some Rooms:** whirlpools. **Cards:** AE, CB, DI, DS, JCB, MC, VI. **Special Amenities: Free
breakfast and preferred room (subject to availability with advanced reservations).**

ALLENTOWN HILTON   Phone: 610/433-2221
All Year   1P: $85   2P/1B: $85   2P/2B: $85   XP: $10   F18
Location: 9th & Hamilton sts. 904 Hamilton Mall 18101. Fax: 610/433-6455. **Terms:** Package plans; no pets.
Facility: 224 rooms. Attractively furnished guest rooms & public areas. 9 stories; interior corridors; sauna;
game room. Fee: parking. **Dining & Entertainment:** Dining room; 6:30 am-2:30 & 5:30-10 pm; $5-$20;
cocktails/lounge. **Services:** valet laundry. **All Rooms:** coffeemakers, free movies. **Some Rooms:**
Fee: refrigerators. **Cards:** AE, CB, DI, DS, MC, VI. *(See color ad p 18)*

ALLENWOOD MOTEL   Rates Subject to Change   Phone: 610/395-3707
All Year   2P/2B: $40- 45   XP: $5   F3
Location: 0.5 mi e on US 22 from tpk exit 33, 0.8 mi s on SR 309, w on Tilghman St to light, 0.8 mi n on
Hausman Rd to dead end. 1058 Hausman Rd 18104. **Terms:** Reserv deposit; pets, $5 dep req. **Facility:** 22
rooms. Handling fee imposed; 1 story; exterior corridors. **Cards:** AE, DS, MC, VI.

DAYS INN   Rates Subject to Change   Phone: 610/797-1234
5/1-9/30   1P: $65- 99   2P/1B: $79- 125   2P/2B: $79- 125   XP: $5
10/1-4/30   1P: $55- 79   2P/1B: $60- 79   2P/2B: $60- 79   XP: $5
Location: Just n of jct I-78/SR 309; exit 18 (Lehigh St) eastbound, exit 18A westbound. 2622 Lehigh St
18103. Fax: 610/797-3452. **Terms:** No pets. **Facility:** 36 rooms. Whirlpool rm, $95-$125; 2 stories; interior corridors.
All Rooms: free movies. **Cards:** AE, CB, DI, DS, JCB, MC, VI.

DAYS INN CONFERENCE CENTER   Rates Subject to Change   Phone: 610/395-3731
6/16-9/8 [CP]   1P: $65- 125   2P/1B: $75- 125   2P/2B: $75- 125   XP: $6   F12
5/1-6/15 & 9/9-12/31 [CP]   1P: $59- 85   2P/1B: $65- 89   2P/2B: $65- 89   XP: $6   F12
1/1-4/30 [CP]   1P: $45- 70   2P/1B: $49- 75   2P/2B: $49- 75   XP: $6   F12
Location: 4.5 mi w on SR 309, n of jct US 22; 0.5 mi e of tpk exit 33; off SR 309 via Bulldog Dr access road. 1151 Bulldog
Dr 18104. Fax: 610/395-9899. **Terms:** Sr. discount; check-in 4 pm; pets, $15 extra charge. **Facility:** 282 rooms. Extended stay
rooms avail with refrigerator & microwave, $275-$300 weekly; 1-2 stories; interior/exterior corridors. **Dining:** Restaurant;
6:30 am-10 pm, Sat & Sun from 7 am; $6-$15. **All Rooms:** free movies. **Cards:** AE, DI, DS, MC, VI. *(See ad below)*

ECONO LODGE   Phone: 610/797-2200
All Year   1P: $55- 85   2P/1B: $75- 110   2P/2B: $75- 110   XP: $5   F16
Location: SR 309/I-78, exit 18, 0.8 mi n on Lehigh St. 2115 Downyflake Ln 18103. Fax: 610/797-2818.
Terms: No pets. **Facility:** 49 rooms. Comfortably decorated rooms. 4 suites with whirlpool, $95-150; 2 stories;
interior/exterior corridors. **Dining:** Restaurant nearby. **All Rooms:** free movies. **Some Rooms:**
Fee: microwaves, refrigerators. **Cards:** AE, DI, DS, MC, VI. **Special Amenities: Early check-in/late
check-out and free breakfast.**

HOLIDAY INN EXPRESS   Phone: 610/435-7880
6/1-9/30 [CP]   1P: $65- 95   2P/1B: $65- 95   2P/2B: $65- 95   XP: $7   F18
5/1-5/31 & 10/1-4/30 [CP]   1P: $54- 95   2P/1B: $54- 95   2P/2B: $54- 95   XP: $7   F18
Location: US 22, 15th St exit, just n. 1715 Plaza Ln 18104. Fax: 610/432-2555. **Terms:** Package plans;
small pets only, $10 extra charge. **Facility:** 83 rooms. 4 stories; interior corridors; whirlpool. **Services:** valet
laundry. **All Rooms:** free movies. **Some Rooms:** Fee: refrigerators. **Cards:** AE, CB, DI, DS, MC, VI.
Special Amenities: Free breakfast and free local telephone calls.

HOLIDAY INN EXPRESS HOTEL & SUITES   Rates Subject to Change   **Phone:** 610/437-925?
◆◆◆   5/1-10/31 & 4/1-4/30 [CP]   1P: $99- 159   2P/1B: $99- 159   2P/2B: $99- 159   XP: $10   F1?
Motel   11/1-3/31 [CP]   1P: $79- 130   2P/1B: $79- 130   2P/2B: $79- 130   XP: $10   F1?
Location: Just n of I-78, exit 16. 3620 Hamilton Blvd 18104. **Fax:** 610/437-9541. **Terms:** Sr. discount; reser
deposit; no pets. **Facility:** 70 rooms. 3 stories; interior corridors. **All Rooms:** free movies. **Some Rooms:** 2 efficiencies
Cards: AE, DI, DS, JCB, MC, VI.   Roll in showers.

HOWARD JOHNSON LODGE   **Phone:** 610/439-400?
⚠⚠⚠ [SAVE]   6/15-9/6 [CP]   1P: $59- 90   2P/1B: $59- 125   2P/2B: $59- 125   XP: $5   F1
5/1-6/14, 9/7-12/31 &
◆◆   1/1-4/30 [CP]   1P: $39- 85   2P/1B: $42- 99   2P/2B: $42- 99   XP: $5   F1
Motel   **Location:** Hamilton Blvd exit 16 off I-78, 1.5 mi n on US 222. 3220 Hamilton Blvd 18103
Fax: 610/439-8947. **Terms:** Weekly/monthly rates; small pets only, $30 dep req. **Facility:** 43 rooms. Interio
corridors. **Dining:** Restaurant nearby. **All Rooms:** microwaves, free movies, refrigerators. **Some Rooms:** whirlpools
Cards: AE, CB, DI, DS, MC, VI. **Special Amenities:** Free breakfast and free local telephone calls.

MCINTOSH INN OF ALLENTOWN   Rates Subject to Change   **Phone:** 610/264-753?
◆◆   All Year [CP]   1P: $48- 55   2P/1B: $57- 64   2P/2B: $57- 64   XP: $7   F1
Motel   **Location:** US 22, exit Airport Rd S. 1701 Catasauqua Rd 18103. **Fax:** 610/264-5474. **Terms:** Sr. discoun
no pets. **Facility:** 107 rooms. 2 stories; interior/exterior corridors. **All Rooms:** free movies. **Cards:** AE, CB
DI, MC, VI. *(See color ad p 297)*   Roll in showers.

MICROTEL INN   **Phone:** 610/266-907?
⚠⚠⚠ [SAVE]   7/15-8/31   1P: $50   2P/1B: $54
5/1-7/14 & 9/1-10/31   1P: $44   2P/1B: $48
◆◆   11/1-4/30   1P: $42   2P/1B: $46
Motel   **Location:** At Airport Rd S exit of US 22. 1880 Steelstone Rd 18103. **Fax:** 610/266-0377. **Terms:** Pets
Facility: 105 rooms. 3 stories; interior corridors. **All Rooms:** free & pay movies, combo or shower bath?
Some Rooms: Fee: microwaves, refrigerators. **Cards:** AE, CB, DI, DS, MC, VI. **Special Amenities:** Early check-in/late
check-out and preferred room (subject to availability with advanced reservations).
Roll in showers.

RAMADA INN-ALLENTOWN/WHITEHALL   **Phone:** 610/439-103?
⚠⚠⚠ [SAVE]   7/1-10/31 [CP]   1P: $75- 90   2P/1B: $75- 95   2P/2B: $75- 95   XP: $5   F1
5/1-6/30 & 11/1-12/31 [CP]   1P: $80   2P/1B: $85   2P/2B: $85   XP: $5   F1
◆◆◆   1/1-4/30 [CP]   1P: $55- 70   2P/1B: $55- 75   2P/2B: $55- 75   XP: $5   F1
Motor Inn   **Location:** US 22, MacArthur Rd N exit to Grape St exit, turn around, hotel 0.3 mi on right. 1500 McArthu
Rd 18052. **Fax:** 610/770-1425. **Terms:** Weekly/monthly rates; package plans; no pets. **Facility:** 122 rooms.
whirlpool rms, extra charge; 2 stories; interior corridors; wading pool. **Dining & Entertainment:** Restaurant; 6:30 am-10 pn
$6-$19; cocktails/lounge; entertainment. **Services:** complimentary evening beverages, with dinner; valet laundry; are
transportation, within 5 mi. **All Rooms:** free movies. **Some Rooms:** coffeemakers. Fee: refrigerators, VCR's. **Cards:** AE, D
DS, MC, VI.

RED ROOF INN   Rates Subject to Change   **Phone:** 610/264-540?
◆◆   All Year   1P: $46- 90   2P/1B: $56- 100   2P/2B: $56- 110   XP: $8   F1
Motel   **Location:** Just s of US 22, exit Airport Rd S. 1846 Catasauqua Rd 18103. **Fax:** 610/264-7618. **Terms:** Sma
pets only. **Facility:** 115 rooms. 3 stories; exterior corridors. **All Rooms:** free & pay movies. **Cards:** AE, CB
DI, DS, MC, VI.

SHERATON INN-JETPORT   **Phone:** 610/266-100?
⚠⚠⚠ [SAVE]   All Year   1P: $99   2P/1B: $109   2P/2B: $109   XP: $10   F1
Location: On SR 987N (Airport Rd), 0.5 mi n of jct SR 22. 3400 Airport Rd 18103. **Fax:** 610/266-188?
◆◆◆   **Terms:** Package plans; pets; in carriers. **Facility:** 147 rooms. Property has a mix of traditional motel rooms
Motor Inn   suites with a few suites designed to accommodate businessman work stations. 2-3 stories, no elevator; inte
rior corridors; sauna, whirlpool. **Dining & Entertainment:** Restaurant; 6:30 am-10 pm; $9-$2?
cocktails/lounge; entertainment; nightclub. **Services:** valet laundry; area transportation, within 10 m
All Rooms: coffeemakers, free & pay movies. **Some Rooms:** microwaves, refrigerators, VCR's. **Cards:** AE, CB, DI, D?
MC, VI. **Special Amenities:** Early check-in/late check-out.

RESTAURANTS

ABE'S PLACE   **Lunch:** $5-$17   **Dinner:** $8-$17   **Phone:** 610/435-173?
◆   **Location:** Just w of jct 17th & Allen sts. 1741 Allen St 18104. **Hours:** 11 am-3 pm; Wed & Thurs-9 pm; Su
American   3 pm-9 pm. **Closed:** Sat, Fri for dinner & Jewish holidays. **Reservations:** accepted. **Features:** casual dres
children's menu; carryout; a la carte. Authentic New York Glatt kosher deli. Smoke free premises. **Cards:** A?
DS, MC, VI.

AMBASSADOR RESTAURANT   **Lunch:** $5-$8   **Dinner:** $15-$22   **Phone:** 610/432-202?
⚠⚠⚠   **Location:** 0.3 mi e of I-78 exit 16. 3750 Hamilton Blvd 18103. **Hours:** 11:30 am-2:30 & 5-10 pm. Close
11/26, 12/25 & Sun. **Reservations:** suggested; weekends. **Features:** casual dress; children's menu; heal
◆◆◆   conscious menu items; cocktails & lounge; a la carte. Very well prepared steak & seafood in a pleasa
Continental   Spanish atmosphere. Some Spanish selections. **Cards:** AE, CB, DI, DS, MC, VI.

THE BRASS RAIL RESTAURANT   **Lunch:** $3-$8   **Dinner:** $5-$14   **Phone:** 610/797-192?
⚠⚠⚠   **Location:** S on Lehigh St at jct I-78, exit 18. 3015 Lehigh St 18103. **Hours:** 7 am-midnight, Fri & Sat-1 a?
◆   Sun 8 am-10 pm. **Closed:** 4/12, 11/26 & 12/25. **Features:** casual dress; children's menu; carryout; cockta
American   & lounge. Complete breakfast menu. **Cards:** AE, DS, MC, VI.

BRASS RAIL RESTAURANT   **Lunch:** $4-$8   **Dinner:** $6-$14   **Phone:** 610/434-938?
⚠⚠⚠   **Location:** Downtown, at jct 12th & Hamilton sts. 1137 Hamilton St 18101. **Hours:** 7 am-10 pm, Fri & Sat-
pm, Sun 8 am-10 pm. **Closed:** 4/12, 11/26 & 12/25. **Features:** casual dress; children's menu; carryou
◆   cocktails & lounge. Family dining in historic area. Ample portions. Complete breakfast menu. **Cards:** AE, D
American   MC, VI.

THE SHANTY RESTAURANT   **Lunch:** $7-$16   **Dinner:** $15-$27   **Phone:** 610/437-53?
◆◆   **Location:** At 19th & Tilghman sts. 617 N 19th St 18104-4333. **Hours:** 11:30 am-10 pm, Fri & Sat-11 p
Seafood   Sun 11 am-9 pm. **Closed:** major holidays. **Reservations:** suggested. **Features:** casual dress; Sunday brunc
children's menu; carryout; salad bar; cocktails & lounge. Lively atmosphere, open kitchen, family owned
operated for more than 20 years. **Cards:** AE, CB, DI, DS, MC, VI.

WALP'S PA DUTCH FAMILY RESTAURANT   Lunch: $3-$7   Dinner: $5-$14   Phone: 610/437-4841
Location: 1.5 mi s of US 22 jct Union Blvd & Airport Rd (SR 987). 911 Union Blvd 18103. Hours: 6:30 am-10 pm, Mon-9 pm. Closed: 7/4 & 12/25. Reservations: suggested. Features: casual dress; children's menu; early bird specials; carryout; cocktails & lounge. Famous Pennsylvania Dutch style cooking. Family owned & operated since 1936. Cards: AE, DS, MC, VI.
Regional
American

ALLISON PARK—See Pittsburgh & Vicinity p. 406.

ALTOONA—51,900

LODGINGS

DAYS INN   Phone: 814/944-9661
All Year   1P: $60- 65   2P/1B: $70- 75   2P/2B: $70- 75   XP: $7   F12
Location: I-99/ US 220, exit Frankstown Rd; 0.4 mi w on Frankstown Rd, just n. 3306 Pleasant Valley Blvd 16602. Fax: 814/944-9557. Terms: Reserv deposit; no pets. Facility: 111 rooms. Large rooms with 25" TV, hair dryer, iron & ironing board. 2 stories; interior corridors; designated smoking area; whirlpool.
Motel
Dining: Restaurant nearby. Services: Fee: coin laundry. All Rooms: coffeemakers, microwaves, free & pay movies, refrigerators. Cards: AE, CB, DI, DS, JCB, MC, VI. Special Amenities: Free local telephone calls and free room upgrade (subject to availability with advanced reservations).

HOLIDAY INN   Phone: 814/944-4581
5/1-10/31   1P: $64   2P/1B: $69   2P/2B: $69   XP: $5   F18
11/1-4/30   1P: $59   2P/1B: $64   2P/2B: $64   XP: $5   F18
Location: I-99/US 220, exit Frankstown Rd; 0.4 mi w on Frankstown Rd, 0.5 mi n. 2915 Pleasant Valley
Motor Inn
Blvd 16602. Fax: 814/943-4996. Terms: Reserv deposit; no pets. Facility: 139 rooms. Some rooms face courtyard/pool area & others able to park at room. 2 whirlpool rms, extra charge; 2 stories; exterior corridors; designated smoking area. Dining & Entertainment: Restaurant; 7 am-2 & 5-10 pm, Sun-8 pm; $9-$15; cocktails/lounge. Services: Fee: coin laundry. All Rooms: coffeemakers. Fee: movies, safes. Some Rooms: microwaves, refrigerators. Cards: AE, CB, DI, DS, JCB, MC, VI. Special Amenities: Early check-in/late check-out and free room upgrade (subject to availability with advanced reservations).

HOWARD JOHNSON EXPRESS INN   Rates Subject to Change   Phone: 814/946-7601
All Year [CP]   1P: $45- 50   2P/1B: $50- 55   2P/2B: $45- 50   XP: $5   F12
Location: Just n of I-99/US 220, exit Plank Rd. 1500 Sterling St 16602. Fax: 814/946-5162. Terms: Sr.
Motel
discount; pets. Facility: 112 rooms. 1 story; exterior corridors. All Rooms: free & pay movies.
Some Rooms: 11 efficiencies. Cards: AE, CB, DI, DS, JCB, MC, VI.

RESTAURANTS

ALLEGRO   Lunch: $4-$8   Dinner: $11-$30   Phone: 814/946-5216
Location: Broad Ave & 40th St. 3926 Broad Ave 16601. Hours: 4 pm-9:30 pm, Sat-10 pm, Fri 11:30 am-1 & 4-9:30 pm. Closed major holidays & Sun. Reservations: suggested. Features: casual dress; children's menu; health conscious menu items; cocktails & lounge. 4 course dinner with extensive selection of seafood, veal, steak & chicken entrees. Cards: AE, DI, DS, MC, VI.
Italian

INELLI'S ITALIAN VILLA   Dinner: $8-$19   Phone: 814/943-8510
Location: I-99/US 220, exit 17th St, 0.9 mi w on 17th, just w. 1808 4th Ave 16602. Hours: 5 pm-9 pm, Fri & Sat-10 pm. Closed major holidays, Sun & Mon. Reservations: suggested. Features: casual dress; health conscious menu items; cocktails & lounge; street parking; area transportation; a la carte. Relaxed neighborhood dining featuring veal, seafood, steak, traditional pasta dishes & tableside flambe. Small parking lot. Cards: AE, DS, MC, VI.
Italian

ALUM BANK

LODGING

WEST VU INN   Phone: 814/839-2632
All Year   1P: $28   2P/1B: $32   2P/2B: $36   XP: $4   F14
Location: On SR 56, just e of jct SR 96. (RR 1, Box 366, 15521). Fax: 814/839-9371.
Terms: Weekly/monthly rates; pets, $4 extra charge. Facility: 16 rooms. A few microwaves avail for weekly rentals. 8 kitchen units, $34-$42, rate for up to 2 persons; 1 story; exterior corridors. All Rooms: free movies. Some Rooms: refrigerators. Cards: DS, MC, VI.
Motel

ANNVILLE—4,300

LODGING

WATARA CREEK INN   Phone: 717/865-3259
5/1-11/30 & 3/1-4/30 [BP]   1P: $50- 70   2P/1B: $60- 80   XP: $15
12/1-2/28 [BP]   1P: $43- 58   2P/1B: $51- 68   XP: $13
Location: On Jonestown Rd; from I-81, 0.5 mi s on SR 934, just w at Harper's Tavern. 17003 (RD 2, Box 692). Terms: Weekly/monthly rates; no pets. Facility: 10 rooms. Country setting. Inviting rooms, with sun dried
Historic Bed
Breakfast
sheets. 1 two-bedroom unit. 3 stories, no elevator; interior corridors; smoke free premises. Dining: Restaurant nearby. All Rooms: combo or shower baths, no phones. Cards: AE, DI, DS, MC, VI. Special Amenities: Free breakfast and free room upgrade (subject to availability with advanced reservations).

ARCHBALD—6,300   (See map p. 418; index p. 417)

RESTAURANT

GARRETT'S FAMILY RESTAURANT   Lunch: $2-$5   Dinner: $5-$14   Phone: 717/876-2503   85
Location: 1 mi n. 474 Main St 18403. Hours: 11 am-11 pm. Closed: 4/7, 7/4, 11/26 & 12/25.
American
Reservations: suggested; weekends. Features: casual dress; children's menu; carryout; cocktails & lounge; street parking; a la carte. Family style dining room with adjacent Irish pub. Cards: DS, MC, VI.

ARDMORE—See Philadelphia & Vicinity p. 375.

AVONDALE—See Philadelphia & Vicinity p. 375.

BAINBRIDGE—See Pennsylvania Dutch Country p. 331.

BARKEYVILLE—300

LODGING

DAYS INN
◆ ◆
Motel

Rates Subject to Change
1P: $49- 59   2P/1B: $49- 59 2P/2B: $54   XP: $6   F1
Location: From I-80 exit 3, just n on SR 8. (RD 1, HARRISVILLE, 16038). Fax: 814/786-9693
Terms: Reserv deposit; pets. **Facility:** 83 rooms. 2 stories; exterior corridors. **All Rooms:** free movies
Cards: AE, DI, DS, JCB, MC, VI.

Phone: 814/786-790

 ⒣ ⒸⓉⓋ ⊠ Ⓓ

BARTONSVILLE—See Pocono Mountains Area p. 420.

BATH—2,400

RESTAURANT

BARN HOUSE VILLAGE RESTAURANT   **Lunch:** $5-$10   **Dinner:** $10-$18   **Phone:** 610/837-123
◆
American
Location: At jct SR 987 & 329. 7401 Airport Rd 18014. **Hours:** 7 am-9 pm, Fri & Sat-11 pm. Closed: 1/1 &
12/25. **Reservations:** accepted. **Features:** casual dress; children's menu; carryout; cocktails & lounge
Bustling family dining atmosphere with country motif; menu features steak, seafood, port, chicken & vea
Cards: AE, DS, MC, VI.
⊠

BEAVER—See Pittsburgh & Vicinity p. 406.

BEAVER FALLS—See Pittsburgh & Vicinity p. 406.

BEDFORD—3,100

LODGINGS

BEST WESTERN BEDFORD INN
ⒶⒶⒶ ⓈⰛⓋⒺ
◆ ◆ ◆
Motor Inn

5/1-10/31   1P: $46- 56   2P/1B: $54- 64 2P/2B: $54- 64 XP: $8   F1
11/1-4/30   1P: $38- 48   2P/1B: $46- 56 2P/2B: $46- 56 XP: $8   F1
Location: I-70/76, exit 11, 0.3 mi n. Business Route 220 N 15522 (RD 2, Box 33B). Fax: 814/623-7120
Terms: Monthly rates; package plans; pets, $50 dep req. **Facility:** 105 rooms. 1-2 stories; exterior corridors
sauna, whirlpool; video rental library, small game room. **Dining:** Restaurant; 6:30 am-11 & 5-10 pm, Sat
Sun 6:30 am-10 pm; $7-$13; cocktails. **Services:** Fee: coin laundry. **All Rooms:** coffeemakers, free movies. **Some Rooms**
Fee: VCR's. **Cards:** AE, CB, DI, DS, MC, VI. **Special Amenities: Free local telephone calls and free newspaper.**
(See color ad below)

Phone: 814/623-900

⒣ ⒟ ⒴ ⒨ ⒺⒸⓉⓋ ⊠ Ⓓ

ECONO LODGE
◆
Motor Inn

Rates Subject to Change
5/1-10/31   1P: $39- 58   2P/1B: $45- 65 2P/2B: $45- 65 XP: $6   F1
11/1-4/30   1P: $32- 45   2P/1B: $36- 50 2P/2B: $36- 50 XP: $6   F1
Location: I-70/76, exit 11, 0.3 mi n on US 220 business route. RD 2, US 220N 15522. Fax: 814/623-5455
Terms: Sr. discount; reserv deposit; pets, $4 extra charge. **Facility:** 32 rooms. 2 stories; interior corridors
Dining: Restaurant; 6 am-10 pm; $6-$12. **All Rooms:** free movies. **Cards:** AE, DS, MC, VI.

Phone: 814/623-517

⒣ ⒺⒸⓉⓋ ⊠ Ⓓ

HAMPTON INN OF BEDFORD
ⒶⒶⒶ ⓈⰛⓋⒺ
Motel

All Year [CP]   1P: $74- 76   2P/1B: $80- 82 2P/2B: $80- 82 XP: $6   F1
Too new to rate; **Location:** I-70/76 (PA Tpk) exit 1, just s on US 220 business route. (RD 2, Box 6, 15522
Fax: 814/624-0106. **Terms:** Reserv deposit, 15 day notice; small pets only, $5 extra charge. **Facility:** 7
rooms. Scheduled to open November 1997; 4 stories; interior corridors; whirlpool. **Dining:** Restaura
nearby. **All Rooms:** free movies. **Some Rooms:** whirlpools. Fee: microwaves, refrigerators. **Cards:** AE, CB, DI, DS, MC, V
Special Amenities: Free breakfast and free local telephone calls. (See color ad p 259)

Phone: 814/624-010

⒣ ⒟ ⒴ ⒨ ⒺⒸⓉⓋ ⊠ Ⓓ Ⓢ

HOST INN
ⒶⒶⒶ ⓈⰛⓋⒺ
◆
Motel

All Year   1P: $26- 28   2P/1B: $32- 34 2P/2B: $35- 37 XP: $5   F1
Location: I-70/76 (PA Tpk) exit 11, just n on US 220 business route. (RD 2 Box 18, 15522). **Terms:** Rese
deposit; weekly/monthly rates; pets. **Facility:** 18 rooms. Basic budget lodging. 1 story; exterior corridor
smoke free premises. **Dining:** Restaurant nearby. **All Rooms:** free movies, combo or shower bath
Some Rooms: microwaves, refrigerators. **Cards:** AE, CB, DI, DS, MC, VI. **Special Amenities: Free loc
telephone calls and preferred room (subject to availability with advanced reservations).**

Phone: 814/623-951

⒣ ⒺⒸⓉⓋ ⊠ Ⓓ

JANEY LYNN MOTEL   Phone: 814/623-9515

Motel

5/1-10/31   1P: $27- 32   2P/1B: $31- 36   2P/2B: $35- 40   XP: $4   D6
11/1-4/30   1P: $22- 27   2P/1B: $26- 31   2P/2B: $30- 35   XP: $4   D6
Location: I-70/76, exit 11, 1.4 mi s on US 220 business route. 15522 (RD 5, Box 367). **Terms:** Reserv deposit; weekly rates; small pets only, $4 extra charge. **Facility:** 21 rooms. Appealing view at rear. 1 two-bedroom unit. 1-2 stories; exterior corridors. **All Rooms:** free movies. **Some Rooms:** microwaves, radios, refrigerators. **Cards:** AE, CB, DI, DS, MC, VI. **Special Amenities: Free local telephone calls and preferred room (subject to availability with advanced reservations).**

JUDY'S MOTEL-PA DUTCH HERITAGE   Guaranteed Rates   Phone: 814/623-9118

Motel

All Year   1P: $24   2P/1B: $28   2P/2B: $33   XP: $3   D8
Location: I-70/76 (PA Tpk), exit 11, 1.5 mi s on US 220 business route. (RD 5 Box 370, 15522). **Terms:** Reserv deposit, 3 day notice; no pets. **Facility:** 12 rooms. 1 story; exterior corridors. **Cards:** DS, MC, VI.

MIDWAY MOTEL   Rates Subject to Change   Phone: 814/623-8107

Motel

5/1-11/25   1P: $29- 32   2P/1B: $34- 38   2P/2B: $42- 47   XP: $3   D10
11/26-4/30   1P: $22- 27   2P/1B: $27- 30   2P/2B: $34- 40   XP: $3   D10
Location: I-70/76, exit 11, just n on US 220 business route. 15522 (RD 2, Box 13A). Fax: 814/623-5618. **Terms:** Sr. discount; reserv deposit, 3 day notice; small pets only, $5 extra charge. **Facility:** 33 rooms. 1-2 stories; exterior corridors. **All Rooms:** free movies. **Cards:** AE, DI, DS, MC, VI.

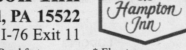

MOTEL TOWN HOUSE   Phone: 814/623-5138

AAA SAVE
◆◆◆

Fri & Sat 5/1-10/31	1P:	$32-	42	2P/1B:	$40-	60	2P/2B:	$45-	65	XP:	$5	F18
Sun-Thurs 5/1-10/31	1P:	$32-	40	2P/1B:	$37-	45	2P/2B:	$45-	50	XP:	$5	F18
11/1-4/30	1P:	$30-	40	2P/1B:	$35-	45	2P/2B:	$45-	50	XP:	$5	F18

Motel   **Location:** I-70/76 (PA Tpk), exit 11, 2.5 mi s on US 220 business route. 200 S Richard St 15522.
Fax: 814/623-9123. **Terms:** Reserv deposit, 15 day notice; weekly rates; small pets only, $5 extra charge.
Facility: 19 rooms. Basic economy lodgings. 2 stories; exterior corridors. **Dining:** Restaurant nearby. **All Rooms:** free
movies. **Some Rooms:** microwaves, refrigerators. **Cards:** AE, CB, DI, DS, MC, VI. **Special Amenities:** Early check-in/late
check-out and free local telephone calls. *(See color ad p 259)*   (icons)

QUALITY INN BEDFORD   Phone: 814/623-5188

AAA SAVE
◆◆◆

6/1-10/31	1P:	$63	2P/1B:	$69	2P/2B:	$69	XP:	$6	F18
5/1-5/31 & 11/1-4/30	1P:	$54	2P/1B:	$60	2P/2B:	$60	XP:	$6	F18

Motor Inn   **Location:** I-70/76, exit 11, just n on US 220 business route. (RD 2, Box 171, 15522). Fax: 814/623-0814.
Terms: Package plans; pets. **Facility:** 66 rooms. Executive rooms with dataport telephones. 1-2 stories;
interior/exterior corridors. **Dining:** The Arena Restaurant, see separate listing. **Services:** valet laundry.
All Rooms: coffeemakers. **Some Rooms:** Fee: microwaves, refrigerators. **Cards:** AE, CB, DI, DS, JCB, MC, VI.
Special Amenities: Free local telephone calls and free newspaper.   (icons)

SUPER 8 MOTEL   Phone: 814/623-5880

◆◆   All Year [CP]   Rates Subject to Change
                                   1P: $44- 49 2P/1B: $49- 54 2P/2B: $51- 56 XP: $6   F12
Motel   **Location:** I-70/76 (PA Tpk) exit 11, 0.3 mi n on US 220 business route. (RD 2, Box 32A, 15522).
Fax: 814/623-5880. **Terms:** Small pets only, in designated rooms. **Facility:** 57 rooms. 3 stories, no elevator;
interior corridors. **All Rooms:** free movies. **Cards:** AE, CB, DI, DS, JCB, MC, VI. *(See color ad p 259)*   (icons)

RESTAURANTS

THE ARENA RESTAURANT   Lunch: $3-$6   Dinner: $9-$20   Phone: 814/623-8074

AAA   **Location:** I-70/76, exit 11, just n on US 220 business route; in Quality Inn Bedford. 15522. **Hours:** 7 am-10
            pm, Sun-9 pm. Closed: 1/1, 12/25 & 12/26. **Reservations:** suggested; weekends. **Features:** casual dress;
◆◆◆   children's menu; carryout; salad bar; cocktails & lounge. Featuring prime rib, steak, seafood & pasta. Lunch
American   buffet Mon-Sat. **Cards:** AE, CB, DI, DS, MC, VI.   (icon)

ED'S STEAK HOUSE   Lunch: $4-$14   Dinner: $7-$19   Phone: 814/623-8894

AAA   **Location:** I-70/76 (PA Tpk), exit 11, 0.3 mi n on US 220 business route. 15522. **Hours:** 7 am-9 pm, Fri &
            Sat-10 pm; winter hours may vary. Closed: 11/26 & 12/25. **Reservations:** suggested. **Features:** casual
◆◆   dress; children's menu; carryout; cocktails & lounge. Coffee shop & four dining rooms, very popular locally.
Steak and   **Cards:** AE, MC, VI.   (icon)
Seafood

BENSALEM—*See Philadelphia & Vicinity p. 375.*

BENTON—1,000

LODGING

THE RED POPPY BED & BREAKFAST   Guaranteed Rates   Phone: 717/925-5823

◆◆◆   All Year [BP]   1P: $55- 75 2P/1B: $65- 85 2P/2B: $75
Historic Bed   **Location:** 0.5 mi n on SR 487 from n jct with SR 239. RR 2, Box 82 17814. **Terms:** Reserv deposit, 7 day
& Breakfast   notice; pets. **Facility:** 4 rooms. 2 stories; interior corridors; smoke free premises. **All Rooms:** no A/C.
                 Cards: MC, VI.   (icons)

BERWICK—11,000

LODGING

RED MAPLE INN   Rates Subject to Change   Phone: 717/752-6220

◆   All Year   1P: $40- 60 2P/1B: $50- 70 2P/2B: $50- 70 XP: $5-10   D12
Motel   **Location:** 2.2 mi n on US 11 from I-80, exit 36. (RR 3-US Rt 11, 18603). Fax: 717/759-0533. **Terms:** Reserv
                 deposit, 3 day notice; small pets only, $5 extra charge; $50 dep req. **Facility:** 18 rooms. 1 story; exterior cor-
ridors. **All Rooms:** free movies. **Cards:** DS, MC, VI.   (icons)

BERWYN—*See Philadelphia & Vicinity p. 375.*

BETHEL (BERKS COUNTY)

LODGING

COMFORT INN-MIDWAY   Phone: 717/933-8888

AAA SAVE
◆◆◆

6/1-9/30 [CP]	1P:	$52-	67	2P/1B:	$58-	75	2P/2B:	$62-	78
5/1-5/31 & 10/1-4/30 [CP]	1P:	$48-	57	2P/1B:	$52-	67	2P/2B:	$58-	75

Motel   **Location:** Just w of I-78, exit 5. 41 Diner Dr 19507. Fax: 717/933-9845. **Terms:** Check-in 4 pm; pets, $10
            extra charge. **Facility:** 72 rooms. Contemporary guest rooms with modern cherry finish furnishings. 3 stories;
            interior corridors; game room. **Dining:** Restaurant nearby. **All Rooms:** free movies, combo or shower baths.
Some Rooms: whirlpools. Fee: microwaves, refrigerators. **Cards:** AE, CB, DI, DS, JCB, MC, VI. **Special Amenities:** Free
breakfast and free newspaper.   Roll in showers.   (icons)

BETHEL PARK—*See Pittsburgh & Vicinity p. 406.*

BETHLEHEM—71,400

LODGINGS

COMFORT INN   Guaranteed Rates   Phone: 610/865-6300

◆◆   All Year [CP]   1P: $58- 74 2P/1B: $70- 90 2P/2B: $70- 90 XP: $6   F18
Motel   **Location:** Just s of US 22, exit SR 191. 3191 Highfield Dr 18017. Fax: 610/865-5074. **Terms:** Sr. discount;
            pets, $6 extra charge. **Facility:** 116 rooms. 2 stories; interior/exterior corridors. **All Rooms:** free movies.
Cards: AE, CB, DI, DS, JCB, MC, VI.   (icons)

COMFORT SUITES
◆◆◆ All Year [CP]
Suite Motel
Rates Subject to Change   Phone: 610/882-9700
1P: $80- 150   2P/1B: $85- 150   XP: $10   F18
Location: Center, W 3rd & Brodhead sts (3rd St exit from SR 378). 120 W 3rd St 18015. Fax: 610/882-4389. **Terms:** Sr. discount; small pets only, $8 extra charge. **Facility:** 124 rooms. 4 stories; interior corridors. **Dining:** Restaurant; 4:30 pm-midnight; $6-$15. **All Rooms:** free movies. **Cards:** AE, CB, DI, DS, MC, VI.

COURTYARD BY MARRIOTT
◆◆◆ Fri & Sat
Motel Sun-Thurs
Rates Subject to Change   Phone: 610/317-6200
1P: $84- 120   2P/1B: $84- 120   2P/2B: $84- 120
1P: $84- 95   2P/1B: $84- 95   2P/2B: $84- 95
Location: 0.8 mi se off US 22 (Airport Rd S exit) on Catasauqua Rd. 2160 Motel Dr 18018. Fax: 610/317-2606. **Terms:** Reserv deposit; no pets. **Facility:** 114 rooms. 3 stories; interior corridors. **Dining:** Coffee shop; 6:30 am-10 am, Sat & Sun 7 am-11 am. **All Rooms:** free & pay movies. **Cards:** AE, DI, DS, MC, VI.
Roll in showers.

FAIRFIELD INN BY MARRIOTT
◆◆◆ All Year [CP]
Motel
Rates Subject to Change   Phone: 610/867-8681
1P: $62- 69   2P/1B: $62- 69   2P/2B: $62- 69
Location: 0.8 mi se off US 22 (Airport Rd S exit) on Catasauqua Rd. 2140 Motel Dr 18018. Fax: 610/758-9000. **Terms:** Sr. discount; no pets. **Facility:** 103 rooms. 3 whirlpool rms, extra charge; 3 stories; interior corridors. **All Rooms:** free & pay movies. **Cards:** AE, CB, DI, DS, MC, VI.
Roll in showers.

HAMPTON INN & SUITES
◆◆◆ All Year [CP]
Suite Motel
Rates Subject to Change   Phone: 610/868-2442
1P: $89- 150   2P/1B: $99- 160   2P/2B: $99- 160
Location: Off US 22, Center St & SR 512 exit. US Rt 22 & 512 18017. Fax: 610/867-0136. **Terms:** No pets. **Facility:** 110 rooms. 3 stories; interior corridors. **All Rooms:** free movies. **Some Rooms:** 28 efficiencies. **Cards:** AE, CB, DI, DS, JCB, MC, VI.
Roll in showers.

HOLIDAY INN HOTEL & CONFERENCE CENTER
◆◆◆ All Year [CP]
Motor Inn
Rates Subject to Change   Phone: 610/866-5800
1P: $85- 125   2P/1B: $95- 135   2P/2B: $95- 135   XP: $10   F18
Location: Off US 22, Center St & SR 512 exit. US 22 & 512 18017. Fax: 610/867-9120. **Terms:** Sr. discount; reserv deposit; small pets only. **Facility:** 192 rooms. 2 stories; interior/exterior corridors. **Dining:** Restaurant; 6:30 am-10 pm; $10-$19. **All Rooms:** free & pay movies. **Cards:** AE, CB, DI, DS, JCB, MC, VI.
Roll in showers.

RESIDENCE INN BY MARRIOTT
◆◆◆ All Year [CP]
Apartment
Motel
Rates Subject to Change   Phone: 610/317-2662
2P/1B: $94   2P/2B: $129
Location: 0.8 mi se off US 22 (Airport Rd S exit) on Catasauqua Rd. 2180 Motel Dr 18018. Fax: 610/317-2663. **Terms:** Sr. discount; check-in 4 pm; reserv deposit; pets, $100 extra charge. **Facility:** 120 rooms. 3 stories; interior corridors. **All Rooms:** free & pay movies. **Some Rooms:** 84 efficiencies, 36 kitchens. **Cards:** AE, CB, DI, DS, JCB, MC, VI.

WYDNOR HALL INN
ⒶⒶⒶ Fri & Sat
Sun-Thurs
◆◆◆
Historic Bed
& Breakfast
Rates Subject to Change   Phone: 610/867-6851
1P: $100- 130   2P/1B: $110- 140   XP: $20   F10
1P: $75- 90   2P/1B: $85- 100   XP: $20   F10
Location: I-78 exit 20, 0.3 mi s to Saucon Valley Rd, 2.3 mi e to SR 378, 1.5 mi n to Black River Rd, 0.3 mi w to Old Philadelphia Pk, 0.3 mi s. 3612 Old Philadelphia Pk 18015-5320. Fax: 610/866-2062. **Terms:** Reserv deposit, 10 day notice; no pets. **Facility:** 5 rooms. 2 night min stay weekends 5/1-6/30 & 9/1-10/31. Handling fee imposed; 3 stories, no elevator; interior corridors; smoke free premises. **Cards:** AE, CB, DI, DS, MC, VI.

RESTAURANTS

PANE 'E VINO   Lunch: $6-$10   Dinner: $11-$23   Phone: 610/691-7125
◆◆
Italian
Location: 0.5 mi s of jct US 22. 1267 Schoenersville Rd 18017. **Hours:** 11 am-11 pm. Closed: 1/1 & 12/25. **Features:** casual dress; carryout. Family operated. Lively, romantic atmosphere with tasteful wall mural scenes of Old Italy. Features authentic cuisine of both North & South Italy, including brick oven pizza. Complimentary glass of wine & homemade garlic bread. Smoke free premises. **Cards:** AE, MC, VI.

THE SUN INN   Historical   Lunch: $5-$8   Dinner: $11-$22   Phone: 610/974-9451
◆◆◆
American
Location: Downtown, in historic district. 564 Main St 18018. **Hours:** 11 am-9 pm; Fri & Sat-10 pm. Closed: 1/1, 11/26, 12/24 & 12/25. **Reservations:** suggested. **Features:** casual dress; children's menu; cocktails. Traditional dining in an authentic Colonial setting; serving guests since 1758. **Cards:** AE, DS, MC, VI.

BIRD-IN-HAND—See Pennsylvania Dutch Country p. 331.

BLAIRSVILLE—3,600

LODGING

COMFORT INN
◆◆◆ All Year [CP]
Motel
Rates Subject to Change   Phone: 724/459-7100
1P: $61- 99   2P/1B: $61- 99   2P/2B: $67- 99   XP: $6   F18
Location: On US 22, 1 mi w of jct of US 119. (RR 1 Box 22, 15717). Fax: 724/459-7192. **Terms:** Sr. discount; no pets. **Facility:** 72 rooms. 2 stories; interior corridors. **Cards:** AE, CB, DI, DS, MC, VI.
Roll in showers.

RESTAURANT

CHESTNUT RIDGE INN ON THE GREEN   Dinner: $13-$26   Phone: 724/459-7191
ⒶⒶⒶ
◆◆◆
Continental
Location: 2 mi e on US 22/119, exit US 119N, just s. 15717. **Hours:** 5 pm-9 pm, Fri & Sat-10 pm. Closed major holidays & Sun. **Reservations:** suggested. **Features:** semi-formal attire; health conscious menu items; cocktails; a la carte. Fine dining at scenic golf course complex. **Cards:** AE, DI, DS, MC, VI.

BLAKESLEE—200

LODGING

BLUE BERRY MOUNTAIN INN   **Phone: 717/646-7144**
(AAA) (SAVE)   All Year [BP]   1P: $110- 125   2P/1B: $110- 125   2P/2B: $110- 125   XP: $10-20
◆◆◆   **Location:** I-80, exit 43, 3.5 mi n on SR 115, just ne on Thomas Rd, then to the end of Edmund Dr. Edmund
Bed &   Dr 18610 (HC 1, Box 1102). Fax: 717/646-6269. **Terms:** Reserv deposit, 28 day notice; 2 night min stay,
Breakfast   weekends; small pets only, $40 dep req. **Facility:** 6 rooms. Modern well-appointed guest rooms in charming
inn nestleed on 440 acres amid Pocono mountain streams, lakes & ponds. One suite with kitchen. Handling
fee imposed; 2 stories; interior corridors; smoke free premises; whirlpool; billiard room; barbecue & picnic facilities. **Recreation:** swimming, boating, canoeing, fishing; hiking trails. **All Rooms:** combo or shower baths, no phones.
Some Rooms: coffeemakers, microwaves, radios, refrigerators, VCR's. **Cards:** AE, DS, MC, VI. **Special Amenities:** Early
check-in/late check-out and free local telephone calls.   🛏 🛍 ⊕ CTV ⊠ D S

BLAWNOX—*See Pittsburgh & Vicinity p. 406.*

BLOOMFIELD—*See Pittsburgh & Vicinity p. 406.*

BLOOMSBURG—12,400

LODGINGS

BUDGET HOST PATRIOT INN   Rates Subject to Change   **Phone: 717/387-1776**
(AAA)   All Year   1P: $42- 50   2P/1B: $48- 60   2P/2B: $48- 60   XP: $5-10   F16
◆◆   **Location:** On US 11, 0.5 mi s of jct I-80, eastbound exit 36A, westbound exit 36S. 6305 New Berwick Hwy
Motor Inn   17815. Fax: 717/387-9611. **Terms:** No pets. **Facility:** 48 rooms. 1 story; interior corridors.
Dining: Restaurant; 11 am-2 & 4-10 pm, Fri-10 pm, Sat 8 am-11 & 4-10 pm, Sun 8 am-noon, closed Mon;
$6-$14. **All Rooms:** free & pay movies. **Cards:** AE, CB, DI, DS, MC, VI. *(See color ad p 254)*
                                                                          CTV ⊠ D

ECONO LODGE AT BLOOMSBURG   **Phone: 717/387-0490**
(AAA) (SAVE)   All Year   1P: $45- 95   2P/1B: $45- 95   2P/2B: $48- 95   XP: $6-8   F18
◆◆   **Location:** I-80 exit 34; on SR 42. 189 Columbia Mall Dr 17815 (RD#5 Box 290). Fax: 717/387-0893.
Motel   **Terms:** Pets, $10 extra charge. **Facility:** 80 rooms. Nice rooms next to mall & convenient to interstate. 1 two-
bedroom unit. 2 stories; interior corridors. **Dining:** Restaurant nearby. **All Rooms:** free movies.
Some Rooms: coffeemakers. **Cards:** AE, CB, DI, DS, JCB, MC, VI. **Special Amenities:** Free local
telephone calls and free room upgrade (subject to availability with advanced reservations).
                                                                    🛏 ⊕ CTV ⊠ 🏊 D

THE INN AT TURKEY HILL   Rates Subject to Change   **Phone: 717/387-1500**
◆◆◆   All Year [CP]   1P: $87- 145   2P/2B: $94- 185   XP: $15   F12
Country Inn   **Location:** I-80 westbound, exit 35A; eastbound, exit 35, just e. 991 Central Rd 17815. Fax: 717/784-3718.
Terms: Check-in 4 pm; pets, $15 extra charge. **Facility:** 23 rooms. 7 whirlpool rms with fireplace $95-$185;
1-2 stories; interior/exterior corridors. **Dining:** Dining room, see separate listing. **Cards:** AE, CB, DI, DS, MC.
                                                                          🛏 CTV ⊠ D

QUALITY INN AT BUCKHORN   **Phone: 717/784-5300**
(AAA) (SAVE)   All Year [CP]   1P: $45- 100   2P/1B: $50- 100   2P/2B: $55- 105   XP: $5-8   F18
◆◆   **Location:** On SR 42 at I-80 exit 34, just n. 1 Buckhorn Rd 17815. Fax: 717/387-0367. **Terms:** Pets, $10
Motel   extra charge, in smoking rooms. **Facility:** 120 rooms. Convenient access to interstate & shopping mall across
the street. 2 stories; interior corridors. **Dining & Entertainment:** Cocktail lounge; restaurant nearby.
All Rooms: coffeemakers, free movies. **Some Rooms:** refrigerators. **Cards:** AE, CB, DI, DS, JCB, MC, VI.
Special Amenities: Free breakfast and free local telephone calls.   🛏 CTV ⊠ 🏊 D

RESTAURANT

THE INN AT TURKEY HILL   **Dinner:** $16-$23   **Phone: 717/387-1500**
◆◆◆   **Location:** I-80 westbound, exit 35A; eastbound, exit 35, just e; in The Inn At Turkey Hill. 991 Central Rd
Regional   17815. **Hours:** 6 pm-8 pm, Fri & Sat 5-9 pm. Closed: 1/1. **Reservations:** suggested. **Features:** cocktails &
American   lounge; a la carte. Intimate country dining with gourmet touch. 3 distinct dining rooms overlooking beautiful
landscaped courtyard. **Cards:** AE, CB, DI, DS, MC, VI.   ⊠

BLUE BELL—*See Philadelphia & Vicinity p. 375.*

BLUE MOUNTAIN

LODGING

KENMAR MOTEL   **Phone: 717/423-5915**
(AAA) (SAVE)   5/1-11/30 & 4/1-4/30 [CP]   1P: $36- 45   2P/1B: $45- 55   2P/2B: $50- 70   XP: $5
        12/1-3/31 [CP]   1P: $30- 35   2P/1B: $40- 45   2P/2B: $45- 55   XP: $5
◆◆   **Location:** I-76 (PA Tpk) exit 15, just e on SR 997N. 17788 Cumberland Hwy 17240. **Terms:** Reserv deposit;
Motel   weekly/monthly rates; pets, $3 extra charge, in designated rooms. **Facility:** 15 rooms. Well-maintained prop-
erty. Quiet location. Family owned & operated for over 25 years. 1 unit with 3 double beds, $65-$85; 1 story;
exterior corridors. **All Rooms:** free movies. **Some Rooms:** efficiency, no utensils, radios, refrigerators. **Cards:** AE, DS, MC,
VI.   🛏 🛍 ⊠ D

BOALSBURG—2,200

RESTAURANT

DUFFY'S BOALSBURG TAVERN   Historical   **Lunch:** $4-$7   **Dinner:** $14-$19   **Phone: 814/466-6241**
◆◆   **Location:** Center; just s on Church St from jct US 322 business route & SR 45. 113 E Main St 16827.
American   **Hours:** 11:30 am-2 & 5-10 pm, Sat from 9 am, Sun 4 pm-9 pm. Closed: 1/1, 11/26 & 12/25.
Reservations: accepted; main dining rm. **Features:** casual dress; children's menu; health conscious menu;
carryout; cocktails & lounge; a la carte. In 1819 stone building. Several dining rooms reflecting the period with authentic
fireplaces. The tavern serves a varied menu from sandwiches to dinner. 19th-century ambience. Smoke free premises.
Cards: AE, DI, DS, MC, VI.   ⊠

BOILING SPRINGS—2,000

RESTAURANT

BOILING SPRINGS TAVERN   Historical   **Lunch:** $9-$11   **Dinner:** $11-$19   **Phone:** 717/258-3614
◆◆◆   **Location:** Downtown on the Square. 1 E First St 17007. **Hours:** 11:30 am-2:30 & 5-9:30 pm, Sat 11:30
American   am-2 & 5-9:30 pm. Closed major holidays, Sun & Mon. **Reservations:** suggested. **Features:** casual dress;
health conscious menu items; cocktails & lounge; a la carte. 1932 Federal style inn of native limestone
featuring fresh fish & aged western beef entrees. **Cards:** AE, MC, VI.   ⓧ

BOYERTOWN—3,800

LODGINGS

MEL-DOR MOTEL   Rates Subject to Change   **Phone:** 610/367-2626
◆   5/1-9/6 & 4/1-4/30 [CP]   1P: $43- 52   2P/1B: $44- 50   2P/2B: $53   XP: $5   F14
Motel   9/7-3/31 [CP]   1P: $39- 46   2P/1B: $41- 48   2P/2B: $48   XP: $5   F14
Location: 1 mi n of Boyertown at New Berlinville exit off SR 100. 494 Swamp Creek Rd 19545 (PO Box
349, NEW BERLINVILLE). Fax: 610/367-2626. **Terms:** Reserv deposit; small pets only, no cats. **Facility:** 18 rooms. 1 story;
exterior corridors. **All Rooms:** free movies. **Cards:** AE, DS, MC, VI.   🛏 ⓒⓉⓥ Ⓓ

TWIN TURRETS INN   Guaranteed Rates   **Phone:** 610/367-4513
◆◆◆   All Year [BP]   1P: $75   2P/1B: $95- 120   2P/2B: $95   XP: $15
Historic Bed   **Location:** Off SR 100 Boyertown exit, 1 mi w on SR 73. 11 E Philadelphia Ave 19512. Fax: 610/369-7898.
& Breakfast   **Terms:** Sr. discount; age restrictions may apply; reserv deposit; no pets. **Facility:** 10 rooms. 3 stories; interior
corridors; smoke free premises. **All Rooms:** free movies. **Cards:** AE, DS, MC, VI.   ⓒⓉⓥ ⓧ Ⓓ

BRADDOCK HILLS—See Pittsburgh & Vicinity p. 407.

BRADFORD—9,600

LODGINGS

GLENDORN-A LODGE IN THE COUNTRY   Rates Subject to Change   **Phone:** 814/362-6511
◆◆◆◆   All Year [AP]   1P: $285   2P/1B: $345- 545
Historic   **Location:** Main & Corydon, follow Corydon 4.3 mi w to signs. 1032 W Corydon 16701. Fax: 814/368-9923.
Country Inn   **Terms:** Age restrictions may apply; reserv deposit, 30 day notice; 2 night min stay, weekends; no pets.
Facility: 9 rooms. Closed 1/1-1/31; 1-2 stories; interior/exterior corridors. **Dining:** Dining room; 8-10 am,
lunch seating at 1 pm, dinner seating at 7:30 pm. Public by reservation only. **Some Rooms:** A/C. **Cards:** AE, MC, VI.
🛥 Ⓓ

HOWARD JOHNSON HOTEL AT BRADFORD   **Phone:** 814/362-4501
ⒶⒶⒶ SAVE   All Year   1P: $64- 76   2P/1B: $68- 86   2P/2B: $68- 86   XP: $10   F18
Location: Just s, southbound off US 219, Forman St exit, northbound off US 219, Elm St exit. 100 Davis St
◆◆   16701 (PO Box 523). Fax: 814/362-2709. **Terms:** Monthly rates; AP avail; no pets. **Facility:** 120 rooms. 3 sto-
Motor Inn   ries; interior/exterior corridors. **Dining & Entertainment:** Dining room; 6:30 am-2 & 5-9:30 pm; $5-$12;
cocktails/lounge. **Services:** valet laundry. **All Rooms:** free movies. **Cards:** AE, CB, DI, DS, JCB, MC, VI.
Special Amenities: Free newspaper.   🛥 🍴 ⓒⓉⓥ ⓧ Ⓓ

RESTAURANT

CARNEGIES   **Lunch:** $4-$6   **Dinner:** $5-$21   **Phone:** 814/362-9717
◆◆   **Location:** Just s of center. 27 Congress St 16701. **Hours:** 10:30 am-10 pm. Closed major holidays & Sun.
American   **Reservations:** suggested. **Features:** casual dress; children's menu; early bird specials; health conscious
menu items; carryout; cocktails & lounge; fee for parking. In restored library building, located in Bradford's
historic district. Building is registered in the National Register of Historic Places. **Cards:** AE, DS, MC, VI.   ⓧ

BREEZEWOOD—200

LODGINGS

BEST WESTERN PLAZA MOTOR LODGE   **Phone:** 814/735-4352
ⒶⒶⒶ SAVE   All Year   1P: $37- 42   2P/1B: $41- 46   2P/2B: $43- 52   XP: $4   F12
Location: Jct I-70 & Rt 30. 15533 (HCR 2, Box 7). Fax: 814/735-3036. **Terms:** No pets. **Facility:** 89 rooms.
◆◆   2 stories; exterior corridors. **Dining:** Restaurant nearby. **Cards:** AE, CB, DI, DS, MC. **Special Amenities:**
Motel   Early check-in/late check-out and free local telephone calls.   🛥 ⒺⒸⓉⓥ ⓧ Ⓓ

BREEZEWOOD RAMADA INN   **Phone:** 814/735-4005
ⒶⒶⒶ SAVE   5/1-10/31   1P: $49- 59   2P/1B: $59- 79   2P/2B: $59- 79   XP: $8   F18
◆◆◆   11/1-4/30   1P: $41- 49   2P/1B: $49- 59   2P/2B: $49- 59   XP: $8   F18
Motor Inn   **Location:** I-70/76, exit 12, just e on US 30. Jct I-70 & Rt 30 (PO Box 307, 15533). Fax: 814/735-3228.
Terms: BP avail; package plans; pets, $50 dep req. **Facility:** 125 rooms. Good size rooms. 2 stories; interior
corridors; sauna, whirlpool; playground. **Dining:** Prime Rib Restaurant, see separate listing.
All Rooms: coffeemakers, free & pay movies. **Cards:** AE, CB, DI, DS, JCB, MC. **Special Amenities:** Free local telephone
calls and free newspaper. *(See color ad p 264)*   🐾 🛥 🍴 🏋 ⓒⓉⓥ ⓧ Ⓓ

COMFORT INN OF BREEZEWOOD   **Phone:** 814/735-2200
ⒶⒶⒶ SAVE   All Year [CP]   1P: $40- 60   2P/1B: $50- 70   2P/2B: $50- 75   XP: $6   F18
Location: I-70/76, exit 12, just e on US 30. I-70 & US 30 (PO Box 309, 15533). Fax: 814/735-4910.
◆◆◆   **Terms:** Reserv deposit, 15 day notice; package plans; small pets only, $5 extra charge. **Facility:** 118 rooms.
Motor Inn   Contemporary rooms. 2-3 stories, no elevator; interior corridors. **Dining:** Restaurant; 5 pm-9 pm, closed
11/1-4/1; $6-$16; cocktails. **All Rooms:** free movies. **Cards:** AE, CB, DI, DS, JCB, MC, VI.
Special Amenities: Free breakfast and free newspaper. *(See color ad p 264)*   🛏 🍴 ⒺⒸⓉⓥ ⓧ Ⓓ

ECONO LODGE   **Phone:** 814/735-4341
ⒶⒶⒶ SAVE   5/1-10/31   1P: $45- 69   2P/1B: $49- 73   2P/2B: $49- 73   XP: $6   F18
◆◆   11/1-4/30   1P: $39- 63   2P/1B: $45- 69   2P/2B: $45- 69   XP: $6   F18
Motor Inn   **Location:** I-70/76 (PA Tpk) exit 12, just w on US 30. I-70 & Rt 30 15533 (RD 1, Box 101A).
Fax: 814/735-4899. **Terms:** Weekly rates; no pets. **Facility:** 81 rooms. Very basic. 1-2 stories; exterior corridors. **Dining:** Restaurant; Food court; 24 hours; $6-$10. **Services:** Fee: coin laundry. **All Rooms:** free
movies. **Some Rooms:** coffeemakers. **Cards:** AE, CB, DI, DS, MC, VI. **Special Amenities:** Early check-in/late check-out
and free local telephone calls. *(See color ad p 265)*   🛥 🍴 ⒺⒸⓉⓥ ⓧ Ⓓ

Do you need a room AND an 18-hole golf course?
Let the **ResortsIndex lead you** to accommodations
with on-site recreational facilities.

QUALITY INN-BREEZE MANOR

Phone: 814/735-4311

		1P:		2P/1B:		2P/2B:		XP:		
AAA SAVE	6/11-10/31	1P:	$46- 78	2P/1B:	$50- 78	2P/2B:	$65- 78	XP:	$5	F18
	5/1-6/10	1P:	$43- 70	2P/1B:	$48- 70	2P/2B:	$62- 70	XP:	$5	F18
◆◆	3/1-4/30	1P:	$41- 66	2P/1B:	$46- 66	2P/2B:	$56- 66	XP:	$5	F18
Motel	11/1-2/28	1P:	$39- 62	2P/1B:	$42- 62	2P/2B:	$55- 62	XP:	$5	F18

Location: I-70/76 (PA Tpk), exit 12, 0.3 mi e on US 30. I-70 & US 30 (RD 1, Box 36, 15533). Fax: 814/735-3433. **Terms:** No pets. **Facility:** 50 rooms. 21 large, modern "executive" rooms, attractively appointed. Family owned & operated since 1953. 1-2 stories; exterior corridors; wading pool; playground. **Dining:** Restaurant nearby. **Services:** Fee: coin laundry. **Recreation:** jogging. **All Rooms:** coffeemakers, free movies. **Some Rooms:** radios. **Cards:** AE, CB, DI, DS, JCB, MC, VI. **Special Amenities:** Free local telephone calls and preferred room (subject to availability with advanced reservations). *(See color ad below)*   ⊠ ECTV ⊠ D

WILTSHIRE MOTEL

Phone: 814/735-4361

AAA SAVE	5/1-10/31 & 4/1-4/30	1P:	$33	2P/2B:	$42	XP:	$4
	11/1-3/31	1P:	$30	2P/2B:	$40	XP:	$4

◆
Motel
Location: I-70/76 (PA Tpk) exit 12, just w on US 30 at jct SR 126. (HC 2, Box 1, 15533). **Terms:** Reserv deposit; small pets only. **Facility:** 12 rooms. 1 story; exterior corridors. **All Rooms:** free movies. **Cards:** AE, DS, MC, VI.   🛏 ECTV ⊠ D

RESTAURANT

PRIME RIB RESTAURANT

Lunch: $4-$7   **Dinner:** $9-$16   **Phone:** 814/735-4005

AAA SAVE
◆◆
American
Location: I-70/76, exit 12, just e on US 30; in Breezewood Ramada Inn. US Rt 30E 15533. **Hours:** 6:30 am-10 pm. Closed: 12/25. **Reservations:** suggested. **Features:** casual dress; salad bar; cocktails & lounge. Casual dining experience. **Cards:** AE, CB, DI, DS, JCB, MC, VI. **Special Value:** 10% discount on the price of any entree, excluding beverages, tax and gratuity. *(See color ad p 264)*   ⊠

BRIDGEVILLE—See Pittsburgh & Vicinity p. 407.

BROOKVILLE—4,200

LODGINGS

BUDGET HOST GOLD EAGLE INN

Guaranteed Rates   Phone: 814/849-7344

AAA
All Year [CP]   1P: $30- 40   2P/1B: $35- 48   2P/2B: $38- 50   XP: $5

◆
Motor Inn
Location: I-80, exit 13; 0.5 mi s on SR 36. 250 W Main St 15825. Fax: 814/849-7345. **Terms:** Small pets only. **Facility:** 29 rooms. 1 story; exterior corridors; designated smoking area. **Dining:** Gold Eagle Restaurant, see separate listing. **Some Rooms:** 3 efficiencies. **Cards:** AE, DS, MC, VI. *(See color ad p 254)*   🛏 ECTV ⊠ D

HOLIDAY INN EXPRESS

◆◆ Motor Inn

Phone: 814/849-8381

Fri & Sat [CP]	1P: $50- 60	2P/1B: $57- 67	2P/2B: $57- 67	XP: $7	F18
Sun-Thurs [CP]	1P: $50	2P/1B: $57	2P/2B: $57	XP: $7	F18

Location: I-80, exit 13; just s on SR 36. 235 Allegheny Blvd 15825. Fax: 814/849-8386. **Terms:** Pets, $5 extra charge. **Facility:** 68 rooms. 2 stories; interior corridors; designated smoking area. **Services:** Fee: coin laundry. **All Rooms:** free movies. **Cards:** AE, CB, DI, DS, MC, VI. **Special Amenities:** Early check-in/late check-out and free room upgrade (subject to availability with advanced reservations).

HOWARD JOHNSON

◆ Motor Inn

Rates Subject to Change

Phone: 814/849-3335

All Year	1P: $38- 44	2P/1B: $43- 49	2P/2B: $43- 49	XP: $6	F18

Location: I-80 exit 13, just n on SR 36. 245 Allegheny Blvd 15825. Fax: 814/849-8302. **Terms:** Sr. discount; pets. **Facility:** 40 rooms. 2 stories; interior corridors. **Dining:** Coffee shop; 24 hours. **All Rooms:** free movies. **Cards:** AE, DI, DS, MC, VI.

SUPER 8 MOTEL

◆◆ Motel

Rates Subject to Change

Phone: 814/849-8840

Fri & Sat 5/1-3/31	1P: $47	2P/1B: $54	2P/2B: $54	XP: $12	F12
Sun-Thurs 5/1-3/31	1P: $42	2P/1B: $49	2P/2B: $49	XP: $12	F12
4/1-4/30	1P: $39	2P/1B: $46	2P/2B: $46	XP: $13	F12

Location: On SR 36; just n of I-80, exit 13. 251 Allegheny Blvd 15825. Fax: 814/849-8840. **Terms:** Sr. discount; reserv deposit; small pets only, $5 fee with permission. **Facility:** 57 rooms. 3 stories, no elevator; interior corridors; designated smoking area. **All Rooms:** free & pay movies. **Cards:** AE, CB, DI, DS, JCB, MC, VI.

RESTAURANTS

GOLD EAGLE RESTAURANT

◆◆ Steak and Seafood

Dinner: $9-$30

Phone: 814/849-8251

Location: I-80, exit 13; 0.5 mi s on SR 36; in Budget Host Gold Eagle Inn. 250 W Main St 15825. **Hours:** 4 pm-9:30 pm, Fri & Sat-10 pm, Sun-9 pm. Closed major holidays. **Reservations:** suggested; weekends. **Features:** casual dress; children's menu; health conscious menu items; cocktails & lounge. Country inn atmosphere with cozy rustic barn interior decor & featuring fresh seafood, steak & chicken entrees. **Cards:** AE, DS, MC, VI.

THE MEETING PLACE

◆◆ American

Lunch: $4-$6   **Dinner:** $5-$12   **Phone: 814/849-2557**

Location: Center, opposite courthouse. 209 Main St 15825. **Hours:** 8 am-9 pm, Sun 10 am-7 pm. Closed major holidays. **Features:** casual dress; children's menu; cocktails & lounge; street parking. Located in the heart of town, built in 1871. **Cards:** AE, DS, MC, VI.

BURNHAM—2,200

LODGINGS

THE CLARION INN OF LEWISTOWN

◆◆ Motor Inn

Rates Subject to Change

Phone: 717/248-4961

All Year	1P: $59- 75	2P/1B: $59- 75	2P/2B: $59- 75	XP: $5	F19

Location: Just e of jct US 322 Burnham exit; 3.1 mi n of jct US 22 & 522. 13015 Ferguson Valley Rd 17009. Fax: 717/242-3013. **Terms:** Pets. **Facility:** 118 rooms. 2 stories; exterior corridors. **Dining:** Restaurant; 6 am-2 & 5-10 pm; $10-$17. **All Rooms:** free movies. **Cards:** AE, DI, DS, JCB, MC, VI.

SUPER 8 MOTEL-LEWISTOWN

◆◆ Motel

Rates Subject to Change

Phone: 717/242-8888

All Year [CP]	1P: $45	2P/1B: $50	2P/2B: $50	XP: $5	F16

Location: Just w of jct US 322, Burnham exit, 3.1 mi n of jct US 22 & 522. 12688 Ferguson Valley Rd 17009. Fax: 717/242-9401. **Terms:** Sr. discount; no pets. **Facility:** 57 rooms. 2 stories; interior corridors. **All Rooms:** free & pay movies. **Cards:** AE, CB, DI, DS, MC, VI.   Roll in showers.

RESTAURANT

LUBA'S RESTAURANT

◆◆ American

Dinner: $10-$20

Phone: 717/248-4566

Location: From US 322 Burnham exit, 0.8 mi e on E Ferguson Rd/W Freedom Ave. 205 W Freedom Ave 17009. **Hours:** 4 pm-9 pm, Fri & Sat-10 pm. Closed: Sun & Mon. **Features:** casual dress; children's menu; health conscious menu; carryout; cocktails. Ample portions. Also petit menu avail. **Cards:** AE, CB, DI, DS, MC, VI.

BUSHKILL—See Pocono Mountains Area p. 421.

BUTLER—See Pittsburgh & Vicinity p. 407.

CAMPBELLTOWN—1,600—See also HERSHEY.

LODGING

VILLAGE MOTEL

◆ Motel

Rates Subject to Change

Phone: 717/838-4761

6/19-8/30		2P/1B: $52	2P/2B: $60	XP: $4	
5/22-6/18		2P/1B: $48	2P/2B: $56	XP: $4	
5/1-5/21, 8/31-12/13 & 2/12-4/30		2P/1B: $36	2P/2B: $42	XP: $4	

Location: 0.5 mi w on US 322. (PO Box 76, 17010). Fax: 717/838-5574. **Terms:** Open 5/1-12/13 & 2/12-4/30; reserv deposit; no pets. **Facility:** 32 rooms. Handling fee imposed; 1-2 stories; exterior corridors. **Some Rooms:** efficiency. **Cards:** AE, DS, MC, VI. *(See color ad p 303)*

CAMP HILL—7,800   (See map p. 292; index p. 291)

LODGINGS

HAMPTON INN CAMP HILL/MECHANICSBURG

◆◆ Motor Inn

Phone: 717/737-6711   **48**

All Year	1P: $40	2P/1B: $43- 48	2P/2B: $48	XP: $5	F12

Location: 0.8 mi w of US 15 on Carlisle Pike (Market St extended). 3721 Market St 17011. Fax: 717/737-6514. **Terms:** Weekly rates; no pets. **Facility:** 58 rooms. Independently owned & operated, not associated with national chain. 3 two-bedroom units. 1-2 stories; interior/exterior corridors; whirlpool. **Dining & Entertainment:** Restaurant; 11 am-11 pm; $4-$14; cocktails/lounge. **Services:** Fee: coin laundry. **All Rooms:** combo or shower baths. **Cards:** AE, CB, DI, MC, VI. *(See ad p 296)*

(See map p. 292)

RADISSON PENN HARRIS HOTEL & CONVENTION CENTER   Phone: 717/763-7117   [49]
🆔 [SAVE]   All Year   1P: $69   2P/1B: $72   2P/2B: $72   XP: $10   F16
♦♦♦   **Location:** Jct US 11, 15 & Erford Rd. 1150 Camp Hill By-Pass 17011. Fax: 717/763-4518. **Terms:** Monthly
Motor Inn   rates; package plans; small pets only, $75 dep req. **Facility:** 257 rooms. Colonial styling with spacious grounds
in a quiet suburban area. 2 stories; interior/exterior corridors. **Dining & Entertainment:** Dining room,
restaurant; 6:30 am-10 pm, Fri & Sat-11 pm; $9-$15; cocktails/lounge; nightclub. **Services:** valet laundry;
area transportation; to malls. **All Rooms:** free & pay movies, combo or shower baths. **Some Rooms:** coffeemakers.
Fee: refrigerators. **Cards:** AE, CB, DI, DS, MC, VI. **Special Amenities: Early check-in/late check-out and free room
upgrade (subject to availability with advanced reservations).** *(See color ad p 394)*

Roll in showers. [icons] [D] [S]

RESTAURANTS

HARDING'S RESTAURANT   **Lunch:** $5-$10   **Dinner:** $10-$17   Phone: 717/761-7539   [14]
🆔   **Location:** US 15, exit Wesley Dr; 1.2 mi n. 3817 Gettysburg Rd 17011. **Hours:** 11:30 am-2:30 & 4:30-9 pm,
♦♦   Thurs & Fri-10 pm, Sat 5 pm-10 pm. Closed major holidays & Sun. **Reservations:** suggested. **Features:**
American   casual dress; children's menu; early bird specials; carryout; cocktails. Club type atmosphere
featuring prime rib, crab cakes, pasta & weekly specials. **Cards:** AE, DI, DS, MC, VI.   [icon]

KOSTA'S FINE CUISINE   **Lunch:** $6-$13   **Dinner:** $10-$19   Phone: 717/761-8617   [13]
🆔 [SAVE]   **Location:** US 11 & 15N to N 21st St, just w. 451 N 21st St 17011. **Hours:** 11:30 am-10:30 pm. Closed:
♦♦♦   11/26, 12/24 & 12/25. **Reservations:** suggested. **Features:** casual dress; Sunday brunch; children's menu;
Italian   health conscious menu items; carryout; cocktails & lounge; a la carte. Mediterranean menu influence with
pasta, steak & seafood entrees; homemade dessert. **Cards:** AE, CB, DI, DS, MC, VI. **Special Value: 10%
discount on the price of any entree, excluding beverages, tax and gratuity.**   [icon]

CANADENSIS—*See Pocono Mountains Area p. 421.*

CARBONDALE—10,700

RESTAURANTS

BEN-MAR RESTAURANT   **Lunch:** $3-$7   **Dinner:** $8-$18   Phone: 717/282-5970
♦♦   **Location:** Center, on US 6. 89 N Main St 18407. **Hours:** 8 am-10 pm, Fri & Sat-11 pm, Sun-9 pm. Closed:
Italian   12/25. **Reservations:** suggested; Sat. **Features:** casual dress; children's menu; early bird specials; carryout;
cocktails & lounge. Warm inviting atmosphere. Selection of Italian, seafood, beef, veal & poultry. American
cuisine also avail. **Cards:** AE, CB, DI, DS, MC, VI.   [icon]

GRIFF'S CORNER RESTAURANT   **Lunch:** $3-$5   **Dinner:** $6-$8   Phone: 717/282-2052
♦   **Location:** In town, corner of Lincoln & N Church, just e of US 6. 49 N Church St 18407. **Hours:** 6:30 am-4
American   pm, Wed-Sat to 8 pm, Sun-2 pm. Closed major holidays. **Reservations:** accepted. **Features:** casual dress;
children's menu; senior's menu; carryout; street parking. Home cooking in family style restaurant. Friendly
atmosphere.   [icon]

CARLISLE—18,400

LODGINGS

APPALACHIAN MOTOR INN   Phone: 717/245-2242
🆔 [SAVE]   All Year   1P: $40- 65   2P/1B: $40- 65   2P/2B: $45- 75 XP: $5   F12
♦♦   **Location:** On US 11, 1.2 mi n of PA Tpk, I-76 exit 16; 0.5 mi n of I-81, exit 17 (southbound) or exit 17A
Motor Inn   (northbound). 1825 Harrisburg Pike 17013. Fax: 717/258-4881. **Terms:** No pets. **Facility:** 200 rooms. Along
busy commercial hwy; popular trucker lodging. 2 stories; interior corridors. **Dining & Entertainment:**
Restaurant; 24 hours; $5-$7; cocktails/lounge. **Services:** Fee: coin laundry. **All Rooms:** free & pay movies.
Some Rooms: coffeemakers, whirlpools. **Cards:** AE, CB, DI, DS, MC, VI. **Special Amenities: Early check-in/late
check-out and free local telephone calls.**   [icons] [D] [S]

DAYS INN CARLISLE   Guaranteed Rates   Phone: 717/258-4147
♦♦♦   All Year [CP]   1P: $55- 99   2P/1B: $55- 99   2P/2B: $55- 99 XP: $5   F18
Motel   **Location:** Just se of I-81, exit 13. 101 Alexander Spring Rd 17013. Fax: 717/258-1207. **Terms:** Small pets
only, $6 extra charge, in smoking rooms. **Facility:** 136 rooms. Whirlpool rm, $75-$120; 2-3 stories; interior cor-
ridors; designated smoking area. **Cards:** AE, CB, DI, DS, MC, VI.   Roll in showers. [icons] [D]

ECONO LODGE — Guaranteed Rates — **Phone:** 717/249-7775
◆◆ Motel
All Year 1P: $40- 75 2P/1B: $44- 75 2P/2B: $48- 85 XP: $5 F18
Location: On US 11 at jct I-81, exit 17; Tpk I-76, 0.8 mi n from exit 16. 1460 Harrisburg Pike 17013. Fax: 717/249-4457. **Terms:** Sr. discount; small pets only, $5 extra charge, in smoking rooms. **Facility:** 72 rooms. 2 stories; exterior corridors; designated smoking area. **Cards:** AE, CB, DI, DS, MC, VI.

EMBERS INN AND CONVENTION CENTER — Rates Subject to Change — **Phone:** 717/243-1717
AAA ◆◆ **Motor Inn**
5/1-10/31 1P: $63- 68 2P/1B: $73 2P/2B: $68 XP: $5 F12
11/1-4/30 1P: $44 2P/1B: $54 2P/2B: $49 XP: $5 F12
Location: 0.4 mi n of jct I-81 exit 17 southbound or exit 17A northbound; 1.2 mi n of PA Tpk exit 16. 1700 Harrisburg Pike 17013. Fax: 717/243-6648. **Terms:** Sr. discount; pets. **Facility:** 272 rooms. 3 efficiency suites, $110-$170; 1 story; interior corridors. **Dining:** Restaurant; 7 am-9 pm; $13-$20. **All Rooms:** free movies. **Cards:** AE, CB, DI, DS, MC, VI. *(See color ad p 267)*

HAMPTON INN CARLISLE — **Phone:** 717/240-0200
AAA SAVE ◆◆◆ **Motel**
All Year [CP] 1P: $69- 119 2P/1B: $79- 129
Location: Just n of PA Tpk, exit 16. 1164 Harrisburg Pike 17013. Fax: 717/249-5145. **Terms:** No pets. **Facility:** 94 rooms. 3 stories; interior corridors; designated smoking area; whirlpool, small heated indoor pool. **Services:** Fee: coin laundry. **All Rooms:** free movies, combo or shower baths. **Some Rooms:** coffeemakers, microwaves, refrigerators, whirlpools. **Cards:** AE, CB, DI, DS, MC, VI. **Special Amenities: Free breakfast and free local telephone calls.** *(See color ad below)*
Roll in showers.

HOLIDAY INN CARLISLE — Rates Subject to Change — **Phone:** 717/245-2400
◆◆◆ Motor Inn
All Year 1P: $55- 95 2P/1B: $62- 100 2P/2B: $66- 104 XP: $10 F19
Location: Just se of I-81 exit 17; 0.8 mi n of Tpk I-76, exit 16. 1450 Harrisburg Pike 17013. Fax: 717/245-9070. **Terms:** Reserv deposit; pets, $10 extra charge. **Facility:** 100 rooms. 2 stories; interior corridors. **Dining:** Restaurant; 6:30 am-2 & 5-10 pm; $9-$16. **All Rooms:** free movies. **Cards:** AE, DI, DS, JCB, MC, VI.

MOTEL 6 — Rates Subject to Change — **Phone:** 717/249-7622
◆◆ Motel
All Year 1P: $33- 50 2P/1B: $39- 56 2P/2B: $39- 56 XP: $3-6 F17
Location: Just s of PA Tpk, exit 16. 1153 Harrisburg Pike 17013. Fax: 717/249-0597. **Terms:** Pets. **Facility:** 118 rooms. 1 story; exterior corridors; designated smoking area. **All Rooms:** free movies. **Some Rooms:** efficiency. **Cards:** AE, CB, DI, DS, MC, VI.
Roll in showers.

PHEASANT FIELD BED & BREAKFAST — **Phone:** 717/258-0717
AAA SAVE ◆◆◆ **Historic Bed & Breakfast**
All Year [BP] 1P: $60- 90 2P/1B: $65- 95 XP: $10
Location: I-76, exit 16; 0.4 mi n on US 11, 2.3 mi se on S Middlesex Rd, 0.4 mi e on Ridge Dr, just s. 150 Hickorytown Rd 17013. Fax: 717/258-0717. **Terms:** Age restrictions may apply; check-in 4 pm; reserv deposit, 3 day notice; no pets. **Facility:** 4 rooms. 200 year-old federal style brick farmhouse that was former stop on underground railroad with quiet & serene rural location close to Appalachian Trail. Horse boarding avail, $20. Handling fee imposed; 2 stories; interior corridors; designated smoking area; 1 tennis court. **Some Rooms:** phones. **Cards:** AE, MC, VI. **Special Amenities: Free breakfast and free local telephone calls.**

QUALITY INN CARLISLE — Rates Subject to Change — **Phone:** 717/243-6000
◆◆◆ Motel
5/1-10/15 1P: $54- 89 2P/1B: $54- 89 2P/2B: $54- 89 XP: $5 F18
10/16-12/31 1P: $50- 60 2P/1B: $50- 60 2P/2B: $50- 60 XP: $5 F18
1/1-4/30 1P: $50- 54 2P/1B: $50- 54 2P/2B: $50- 54 XP: $5 F18
Location: US 11 at jct I-81, exit 17; 0.8 mi n of Tpk I-76, exit 16. 1255 Harrisburg Pike 17013. Fax: 717/258-4123. **Terms:** Sr. discount; pets. **Facility:** 96 rooms. 2 stories; interior corridors; designated smoking area. **All Rooms:** free movies. **Cards:** AE, CB, DI, DS, MC, VI.

RODEWAY INN — **Phone:** 717/249-2800
AAA SAVE ◆◆ **Motel**
6/11-9/5 [CP] 1P: $59 2P/1B: $59 2P/2B: $59 XP: $5 F18
5/1-6/10 & 9/6-4/30 [CP] 1P: $49 2P/1B: $49 2P/2B: $49 XP: $5 F18
Location: 0.8 mi n of PA Tpk I-76, exit 16; 0.3 mi s of jct I-81, exit 17. 1239 Harrisburg Pike 17013. Fax: 717/249-9444. **Terms:** Weekly/monthly rates; small pets only. **Facility:** 101 rooms. Along a busy commercial hwy; park at rooms. 10 efficiencies, $49-$54 for up to 2 persons; 1 story; exterior corridors; designated smoking area; video movie rentals. **Dining:** Restaurant nearby. **All Rooms:** free movies. **Some Rooms:** coffeemakers, microwaves, radios, refrigerators. Fee: VCR's. **Cards:** AE, CB, DI, DS, MC, VI. **Special Amenities: Free breakfast and free local telephone calls.**

SUPER 8 MOTEL
Rates Subject to Change   **Phone:** 717/249-7000
(AAA)   All Year   1P: $40- 95   2P/1B: $45- 100 2P/2B: $45- 100 XP: $3   F12
◆◆   **Location:** 0.5 mi n of jct I-81, exit 17; 1.3 mi n of Tpk, exit 16. 1800 Harrisburg Pike 17013.
Motel   Fax: 717/249-9070. **Terms:** Sr. discount; reserv deposit; no pets. **Facility:** 111 rooms. 2 stories; interior/exterior
corridors; designated smoking area. **All Rooms:** free movies. **Some Rooms:** 16 efficiencies. **Cards:** AE,
CB, DI, DS, MC, VI.   (ECTV) (⌂) (✕) (D)

RESTAURANTS

CALIFORNIA CAFE Historical   **Lunch:** $6-$10   **Dinner:** $10-$18   **Phone:** 717/249-2028
◆◆   **Location:** Just s on SR 34 (S. Hanover) from jct of US 11/SR 74/SR 34. 38 W Pomfret St 17013. **Hours:** 11
French   am-2 & 5-9 pm. Closed major holidays. **Reservations:** suggested. **Features:** casual dress; health conscious
menu items; carryout; cocktails; street parking. In Historical Carlisle District with casual sophistication;
specializing in French cuisine with California accents; offering espresso & cappuccino; 4 course dinner avail. Smoke free
premises. **Cards:** AE, DI, DS, MC, VI.   (✕)

EMPIRE   **Lunch:** $6-$10   **Dinner:** $16-$30   **Phone:** 717/258-4888
◆◆◆   **Location:** Downtown; just n of square. 109 N Hanover St 17013. **Hours:** 11 am-2 & 5-10 pm, Sat from 5
Continental   pm, Sun 11 am-3 pm. Closed major holidays, Mon & Tues. **Reservations:** suggested. **Features:** casual
dress; Sunday brunch; health conscious menu items; street parking; a la carte. Innovative international
cuisine. Smoke free premises. **Cards:** AE, DI, DS, MC, VI.   (✕)

RILLO'S   **Dinner:** $6-$21   **Phone:** 717/243-6141
◆◆   **Location:** 0.4 mi w of I-81, exit 15 & just s on Spruce. 50 Pine St 17013. **Hours:** 5 pm-9:30 pm, Fri &
Italian   Sat-10:30 pm, Sun-9 pm. Closed major holidays & Mon. **Reservations:** suggested; weekends.
Features: casual dress; children's menu; senior's menu; carryout; cocktails & lounge; a la carte. Full range
of Italian favorites & specialties. **Cards:** AE, DI, MC, VI.   (✕)

SUNNYSIDE RESTAURANT   **Lunch:** $5-$9   **Dinner:** $11-$21   **Phone:** 717/243-5712
◆◆   **Location:** I-81, exit 17; 4 mi s on US 11. 850 N Hanover St 17013. **Hours:** 11 am-10 pm. Closed major
American   holidays & Sun. **Reservations:** accepted. **Features:** casual dress; children's menu; senior's menu; carryout;
cocktails & lounge. Across from Army War College entry; specializing in steak, broiled crab cakes &
Mediterrean style dishes. **Cards:** AE, DS, MC, VI.   (✕)

CASHTOWN—300—*See also GETTYSBURG.*

LODGING

CASHTOWN INN   Guaranteed Rates   **Phone:** 717/334-9722
◆◆◆   5/1-12/31 & 4/1-4/30 [BP]   1P: $95- 145 2P/1B: $95- 145   XP: $15   F18
    1/1-3/31 [BP]   1P: $81- 124 2P/1B: $81- 124   XP: $15   F18
Historic   **Location:** On US 30, 0.7 mi s on High St, just w. 1325 Old US 30 17310 (PO Box 103). Fax: 717/334-1442.
Country Inn   **Terms:** Age restrictions may apply; reserv deposit, 10 day notice; 2 night min stay, weekends 5/1-11/30; no
pets. **Facility:** 7 rooms. Handling fee imposed; 3 stories, no elevator; interior/exterior corridors; designated smoking area.
Dining: Dining room; 11:30 am-3 & 5-8 pm, Fri & Sat-9 pm, Sun 11:30 am-3 pm. Closed Mon, 12/21-12/28, Tues & Wed for
lunch; $16-$23. **Cards:** DS, MC, VI.   (ECTV) (✕) (D)

CENTER SQUARE—*See Philadelphia & Vicinity p. 376.*

CHADDS FORD—*See Philadelphia & Vicinity p. 376.*

CHALK HILL—*See Laurel Highlands p. 311.*

CHAMBERSBURG—16,600

LODGINGS

CHAMBERSBURG TRAVELODGE   **Phone:** 717/264-4187
(AAA) (SAVE)   All Year [BP]   1P: $51   2P/1B: $59   2P/2B: $68   XP: $7   F18
◆◆   **Location:** I-81, exit 6, 0.8 mi w on US 30. 565 Lincoln Way E 17201. Fax: 717/264-2446.
Motor Inn   **Terms:** Weekly/monthly rates; package plans; pets. **Facility:** 52 rooms. On busy commercial hwy. 3 stories;
exterior corridors. **Dining:** Restaurant; 6 am-2 & 5-9 pm, Sat from 7 am, Sun 7 am-2 pm; $8-$15; cocktails.
Services: valet laundry. **All Rooms:** coffeemakers, free movies, combo or shower baths.
Some Rooms: refrigerators. **Cards:** AE, CB, DI, DS, JCB, MC, VI. **Special Amenities: Free breakfast and free local
telephone calls.**   (🛏) (🍴) (ECTV) (✕) (D)

COMFORT INN-CHAMBERSBURG   **Phone:** 717/263-6655
(AAA) (SAVE)   5/1-10/31 [CP]   1P: $68- 88   2P/1B: $74- 94   2P/2B: $74- 94 XP: $5   F17
    11/1-4/30 [CP]   1P: $66- 76   2P/1B: $72- 82   2P/2B: $72- 82 XP: $5   F17
◆◆◆   **Location:** I-81, exit 8, just e then just s on SR 997. 3301 Blackgap Rd 17201. Fax: 717/263-6655.
Motel   **Terms:** No pets. **Facility:** 65 rooms. Attractive & modern. Shopping mall adjacent. 5 whirlpool rms, extra
charge; 2 stories; interior corridors; whirlpool. **Dining:** Restaurant nearby. **All Rooms:** free movies.
Some Rooms: Fee: VCR's. **Cards:** AE, CB, DI, DS, JCB, MC, VI. **Special Amenities: Free breakfast and free
newspaper.**   (🌐) (🍴) (🛁) (CTV) (✕) (D) (S)

DAYS INN   **Phone:** 717/263-1288
(AAA) (SAVE)   5/1-10/31 & 4/1-4/30 [CP] 1P: $55- 60 2P/1B: $63- 68 2P/2B: $63- 68 XP: $8   F17
    11/1-3/31 [CP]   1P: $50- 55   2P/1B: $58- 63 2P/2B: $58- 63 XP: $8   F17
◆◆◆   **Location:** I-81, exit 6, just e on US 30. 30 Falling Spring Rd 17201. Fax: 717/263-1313. **Terms:** Weekly
Motel   rates; small pets only. **Facility:** 107 rooms. Busy commercial location. Data port telephones avail. 3 stories; in-
terior corridors. **Dining:** Restaurant nearby. **Services:** Fee: coin laundry. **All Rooms:** free movies.
Fee: safes. **Some Rooms:** microwaves, refrigerators. **Cards:** AE, CB, DI, DS, JCB, MC, VI. **Special Amenities: Free
breakfast.** *(See color ad p 270)*   (🛏) (🍴) (ECTV) (✕) (D)

ECONO LODGE   **Phone:** 717/264-8005
(AAA) (SAVE)   9/23-10/31 [CP]   1P: $44   2P/1B: $48   2P/2B: $52   XP: $5   F18
    5/1-9/22 & 4/1-4/30 [CP] 1P: $42   2P/1B: $46   2P/2B: $50   XP: $5   F18
    11/1-3/31 [CP]   1P: $40   2P/1B: $44   2P/2B: $48   XP: $5   F18
◆◆   **Location:** I-81, exit 5, just w on SR 316. 1110 Sheller Ave 17201. Fax: 717/263-7720. **Terms:** No pets.
Motel   **Facility:** 61 rooms. Up-to-date budget lodgings; busy commercial district. 2 stories; interior corridors; video
rental library. **Dining & Entertainment:** Cocktail lounge; restaurant nearby. **Services:** Fee: coin laundry.
Some Rooms: coffeemakers, microwaves, radios, refrigerators. Fee: VCR's. **Cards:** AE, CB, DI, DS, JCB, MC, VI.
Special Amenities: Free breakfast and free local telephone calls.   (🍴) (ECTV) (✕) (D)

FAIRFIELD INN BY MARRIOTT
◆◆◆
Motel

Rates Subject to Change

		1P:	2P/1B:		2P/2B:		XP:	
6/1-10/31 [CP]		$62- 75	$69- 85		$69- 85		$7	F17
5/1-5/31 & 4/1-4/30 [CP]		$60- 70	$67- 80		$67- 80		$7	F17
11/1-3/31 [CP]		$58- 67	$65- 75		$65- 75		$7	F17

Phone: 717/264-1200

Location: I-81, exit 5, just e on SR 316. 1122 Wayne Ave 17201. Fax: 717/264-0095. **Terms:** Sr. discount; no pets. **Facility:** 74 rooms. 3 stories; interior corridors. **All Rooms:** free movies. **Cards:** AE, CB, DI, DS, MC, VI.
(See color ad below)
Roll in showers.

HAMPTON INN
(AAA) (SAVE)
◆◆◆
Motel

All Year [CP] 1P: $62 2P/1B: $69 2P/2B: $69

Phone: 717/261-9185

Location: I-81 exit 5, just e on SR 316. 955 Lesher Rd 17201. Fax: 717/261-1984. **Terms:** Monthly rates; no pets. **Facility:** 124 rooms. Stylish & modern with good size rooms & attractive marble lobby. 2 person rates for up to 5 persons; 3 stories; interior corridors. **Dining:** Restaurant nearby. **Services:** valet laundry. **All Rooms:** free movies, refrigerators, combo or shower baths. **Cards:** AE, CB, DI, DS, MC.
Special Amenities: Free breakfast and free local telephone calls.   Roll in showers.

HOLIDAY INN
(AAA) (SAVE)
◆◆
Motor Inn

All Year [CP] 1P: $55- 65 2P/1B: $62- 72 2P/2B: $62- 72 XP: $7 F19

Phone: 717/263-3400

Location: I-81 exit 5, just w on SR 316. 1095 Wayne Ave 17201. Fax: 717/263-3400. **Terms:** BP avail; package plans; pets. **Facility:** 139 rooms. Large rooms in busy commercial area. 2 stories; interior/exterior corridors; wading pool. **Dining & Entertainment:** Restaurant; 6 am-2 & 5-10 pm; $9-$16; cocktails/lounge. **Services:** valet laundry. **All Rooms:** free movies. **Some Rooms:** Fee: refrigerators. **Cards:** AE, CB, DI.
Special Amenities: Free breakfast and preferred room (subject to availability with advanced reservations).

HOWARD JOHNSON INN
(AAA) (SAVE)
◆◆◆
Motor Inn

All Year 1P: $47- 58 2P/1B: $55- 68 2P/2B: $56- 70 XP: $7 F17

Phone: 717/263-9191

Location: I-81, exit 6, just w on US 30. 1123 Lincoln Way E 17201. Fax: 717/263-4752. **Terms:** Reserv deposit; monthly rates; no pets. **Facility:** 132 rooms. In busy commercial district. 3 stories; interior corridors; sauna; video rental library. **Dining & Entertainment:** Restaurant; 6 am-11 pm; 12/1-3/31, 6 am-10 pm, Fri & Sat-11 pm; $6-$10; cocktails/lounge. **Services:** valet laundry. **All Rooms:** coffeemakers, refrigerators.
Some Rooms: Fee: VCR's. **Cards:** AE, CB, DI, DS, JCB, MC, VI. **Special Amenities: Free local telephone calls and free newspaper.**

RODEWAY INN
(AAA) (SAVE)
◆
Motel

		1P:	2P/1B:		2P/2B:		XP:	
5/1-10/31 & 4/1-4/30		$36- 41	$36- 43		$43		$5	F18
11/1-3/31		$25- 28	$33		$38		$5	F18

Phone: 717/264-4108

Location: I-81, exit 6, 1.3 mi e on US 30. 1620 Lincoln Way E 17201. **Terms:** Reserv deposit; weekly rates, off season; small pets only, in designated rooms. **Facility:** 40 rooms. Basic budget lodgings. 1-2 stories; exterior corridors; picnic pavillion. **Dining:** Restaurant nearby. **All Rooms:** combo or shower baths.
Some Rooms: coffeemakers, refrigerators. **Cards:** AE, DI, DS, MC, VI. **Special Amenities: Free local telephone calls and free newspaper.**

SHULTZ VICTORIAN MANSION B & B
♦♦♦
Historic Bed
& Breakfast

Rates Subject to Change

5/1-12/31 [BP]	1P:	$58-	83	2P/1B:	$63-	85	2P/2B:	$68	XP: $15
1/1-4/30 [BP]	1P:	$53-	73	2P/2B:	$63-	78	2P/2B:	$68	XP: $15

Phone: 717/263-3371

Location: On US 11, 0.8 mi n of jct US 30. 756 Philadelphia Ave 17201. **Terms:** Age restrictions may apply; check-in 4 pm; reserv deposit, 3 day notice; no pets. **Facility:** 7 rooms. 1 suite with kitchen & whirlpool, $98-$115, for up to 2 persons. Handling fee imposed; 3 stories, no elevator; interior corridors; smoke free premises. **Some Rooms:** kitchen. **Cards:** MC, VI.

ECTV ✖ D

RESTAURANTS

COPPER KETTLE RESTAURANT
♦♦♦
American

DS, MC, VI.

Dinner: $8-$20

Phone: 717/264-3109

Location: On US 30, 0.3 mi w of I-81, exit 6. 1049 Lincoln Way E 17201. **Hours:** 5 pm-9:30 pm. Closed major holidays & Sun. **Reservations:** suggested. **Features:** casual dress; children's menu; cocktails & lounge. Small, attractively decorated dining rooms in converted home. Prime rib specialty. **Cards:** AE, DI,

✖

SCHOENBERGER'S
♦♦
American

Dinner: $10-$23

Phone: 717/263-1137

Location: On US 30, 1.3 mi w of I-81, exit 6. 346 Lincoln Way E 17201. **Hours:** 4 pm-10 pm. Closed major holidays. **Reservations:** suggested. **Features:** casual dress; children's menu; carryout; cocktails & lounge. Since 1936. Specialties are steak & seafood. **Cards:** AE, CB, DI, DS, MC, VI.

✖

CLARION—6,500

LODGINGS

COMFORT INN-CLARION
♦♦♦
Motel

Rates Subject to Change

5/1-10/31 [CP]	1P:	$64-	84	2P/1B:	$64-	84	2P/2B:	$64-	84	XP: $10	F17
11/1-4/30 [CP]	1P:	$59-	79	2P/1B:	$59-	79	2P/2B:	$59-	79	XP: $10	F17

Phone: 814/226-5230

Location: I-80 exit 9, just n on SR 68. Dolby St 16214 (PO Box 385). Fax: 814/226-5231. **Terms:** No pets. **Facility:** 81 rooms. 2 stories; interior corridors. **All Rooms:** Fee: movies. **Cards:** AE, CB, DI, DS, MC, VI.

CTV f̂ ✖ D

HOLIDAY INN
♦♦♦
Motor Inn

Rates Subject to Change

All Year	1P:	$69-	89	2P/1B:	$69-	89	2P/2B:	$69-	89

Phone: 814/226-8850

Location: I-80, exit 9; 0.5 mi n on SR 68. Rt 68 & I-80 16214. Fax: 814/226-9055. **Terms:** Reserv deposit; pets. **Facility:** 121 rooms. Free breakfast with room Mon-Fri; 2 stories; interior corridors. **Dining:** Restaurant; 6:30 am-10 pm; $8-$18. **All Rooms:** free & pay movies. **Cards:** AE, CB, DI, DS, JCB, MC, VI.

Roll in showers. 🛏 ⤳ ECTV f̂ ✖ D

SUPER 8
🆎 SAVE
♦♦
Motel

All Year [CP]

1P:	$50-	70	2P/1B:	$55-	75	2P/2B:	$60-	75	XP: $5	F12

Phone: 814/226-4550

Location: I-80 exit 9, just n. Hwy 68 16214 (Rt 3, Box 253). Fax: 814/227-2337. **Terms:** Pets. **Facility:** 99 rooms. Quiet landscaped setting with parking at rooms. 9 efficiencies, $43.95-$48.95; 1 story; exterior corridors; designated smoking area; small pool; video rentals. **All Rooms:** free movies. **Some Rooms:** coffeemakers, radios, refrigerators. Fee: VCR's. **Cards:** AE, CB, DI, DS, MC, VI. **Special Amenities: Free breakfast and free local telephone calls.**

🛏 ECTV ✖ D

RESTAURANT

CLARION CLIPPER RESTAURANT
🆎
♦
American

Lunch: $3-$5   **Dinner:** $6-$12

Phone: 814/226-7950

Location: From I-80 exit 9, north on SR 68. 16214. **Hours:** 6:30 am-10 pm. Closed: 11/26 & 12/25. **Features:** casual dress; Sunday brunch; children's menu; health conscious menu items; carryout; salad bar; cocktails & lounge. Family dining. Generous portions. Convenient parking. Homemade soup, broasted chicken local favorite. **Cards:** AE, DS, MC, VI.

✖

CLARK—600

LODGING

TARA-A COUNTRY INN
🆎
♦♦♦♦
Historic
Country Inn

DS, MC, VI.

Rates Subject to Change

Sat [BP]	1P:	$175- 355	2P/1B:	$175- 355	XP: $58	F12
Sun-Fri [BP]	1P:	$150- 325	2P/1B:	$150- 325	XP: $13	F12

Phone: 724/962-3535

Location: Exit 1N from I-80, 8 mi n on Rt 18. 3665 Valley View Rd 16113. Fax: 724/962-3250. **Terms:** Reserv deposit, 7 day notice; no pets. **Facility:** 27 rooms. 3 stories, no elevator; interior corridors; smoke free premises. **Dining:** Dining room; 7-10 am, 11-3 & 5-8 pm, Fri & Sat-9 pm, Sun noon-7 pm. Reservations suggested; $14-$22; also, Ashley's, see separate listing. **All Rooms:** free movies. **Cards:** AE,

⤳ CTV ✖ D S

RESTAURANT

ASHLEY'S
♦♦♦♦
American

Phone: 724/962-3535

Location: Exit 1N from I-80, 8 mi n on Rt 18; in Tara-A Country Inn. 3665 Valley View Rd 16113. **Hours:** 6 pm-8 pm, Fri & Sat-8:30 pm. Closed: 12/25. **Reservations:** required. **Features:** formal attire; health conscious menu items; cocktails & lounge; entertainment; prix fixe. An elegant & sophisticated setting with skilled, attentive service. Smoke free premises. **Cards:** AE, DS, MC, VI.

✖

CLARKS SUMMIT—5,400   (See map p. 418; index p. 417)

LODGINGS

DAYS INN SCRANTON-NORTH
🆎 SAVE
♦♦
Motel

All Year [CP]

1P:	$49-	52	2P/1B:	$59-	63	2P/2B:	$63	XP: $4	F18

Phone: 717/586-9100   92

Location: On US Rt 6 & 11 at I-81, exit 58 & PA Tpk (I-476), exit 39. 811 Northern Blvd 18411. Fax: 717/586-9111. **Terms:** Package plans; no pets. **Facility:** 66 rooms. 4 stories; interior corridors. **Dining:** Restaurant nearby. **All Rooms:** combo or shower baths. **Some Rooms:** Fee: VCR's. **Cards:** AE, DI, DS, MC. **Special Amenities: Free breakfast and free local telephone calls.**

CTV ✖ 🅰 D

THE INN AT NICHOLS VILLAGE
🆎 SAVE
♦♦♦♦
Motor Inn

All Year

1P:	$109- 179	2P/1B:	$119- 179	2P/2B:	$139- 169	XP: $10	F18

Phone: 717/587-1135   94

Location: On US 6 & 11, 0.5 mi w of tpk exit 39 & I-81 exit 58. 1101 Northern Blvd 18411. Fax: 717/586-7140. **Terms:** Weekly/monthly rates; package plans; no pets. **Facility:** 135 rooms. Patios, courtyards & gardens. Beautifully furnished rooms, immaculately kept. Whirlpool suites avail; 2-4 stories; interior corridors; saunas. **Dining:** Restaurant, coffee shop; also, So-Journer, Ryah House, see separate listing. **Services:** valet laundry. Fee: massage. **All Rooms:** free & pay movies, refrigerators. **Some Rooms:** coffeemakers, microwaves. Fee: VCR's. **Cards:** AE, CB, DI, DS, MC, VI. **Special Amenities: Free local telephone calls and free room upgrade (subject to availability with advanced reservations).** (See color ad p 430)

⤳ 🍴 ♨ 🍴 CTV ✖ D

(See map p. 418)

RAMADA PLAZA HOTEL　　　　　　　　　　　　　　　　　　　Phone: 717/586-2730　🆕
🔷🔷🔷 5/1-10/31　　　　1P: $79- 95　　　　2P/2B:　$89- 95　XP: $10　　F17
Motor Inn 11/1-4/30　　　　1P: $69- 95　　　　2P/2B:　$79- 95　XP: $10　　F17
　　　　Location: On US 6 & 11, 0.3 mi w of tpk exit 39 & I-81 exit 58. 820 Northern Blvd 18411.
　　　　Fax: 717/587-0740. **Terms:** Package plans; no pets. **Facility:** 104 rooms. Comfortable rooms 6 mi from downtown Scranton. 5 stories; interior corridors. **Dining & Entertainment:** Restaurant; 6:30 am-10 pm; $11-$19;
cocktails/lounge. **Services:** valet laundry; area transportation. **All Rooms:** coffeemakers. Fee: movies. **Some Rooms:**
Fee: refrigerators. **Cards:** AE, CB, DI, DS, JCB, MC, VI. **Special Amenities: Free local telephone calls and free
newspaper.**

TRAVELODGE　　　　　　Rates Subject to Change　　　　　　Phone: 717/586-1211　🆕
🔷🔷 All Year [CP]　　　　1P: $40- 50　2P/1B:　$55- 69　2P/2B:　$55- 69　XP:　$5　　F17
Motel　**Location:** On US 6 & 11 southbound, 0.5 mi e of tpk exit 39 & I-81 exit 58. 649 Northern Blvd 18411.
　　　　Fax: 717/586-7928. **Terms:** Sr. discount; pets, $5 extra charge. **Facility:** 32 rooms. 2 stories; exterior corridors.
Cards: AE, CB, DI, DS, MC.

RESTAURANTS

RYAH HOUSE　　　　　　**Dinner:** $19-$33　　　　　　　　　Phone: 717/587-4124　54
🔷🔷🔷 **Location:** On US 6 & 11, 0.5 mi w of tpk exit 39 & I-81 exit 58; in The Inn at Nichols Village. 1101 Northern
Regional Blvd 18411. **Hours:** 4:30 pm-10 pm, Sat-11 pm. Closed major holidays & Sun. **Reservations:** suggested.
American **Features:** casual dress; health conscious menu; cocktails & lounge. Fine dining in a casual, but upscale
　　　　atmosphere. Fireside lounge. Fine wine list. **Cards:** AE, CB, DI, DS, MC, VI.

SO-JOURNER　　　　**Lunch:** $6-$8　　　　**Dinner:** $10-$14　　　Phone: 717/586-5517　55
🔷🔷 **Location:** On US 6 & 11, 0.5 mi w of tpk exit 39 & I-81 exit 58; in The Inn at Nichols Village. 1101 Northern
American Blvd 18411. **Hours:** 6 am-10 pm. Closed: 12/25. **Features:** casual dress; children's menu; early bird
　　　　specials; health conscious menu; carryout; cocktails. Informal family dining in contemporary atmosphere.
Specializing in freshly made entrees, homemade bread & dessert. **Cards:** AE, CB, DI, DS, MC, VI.

CLAY—See Pennsylvania Dutch Country p. 332.

CLEARFIELD—6,600

LODGINGS

BEST WESTERN MOTOR INN　　　　　　　　　　　　　　　　Phone: 814/765-2441
　　　　All Year　　　　1P: $51- 58　2P/1B:　$55- 64　2P/2B:　$60- 68　XP:　$4　　F18
🔷🔷 **Location:** 0.4 mi ne of I-80, exit 19. Rt 879 16830 (PO Box 286). Fax: 814/765-5221. **Terms:** Small pets
Motor Inn only. **Facility:** 122 rooms. 2 stories; interior corridors; small heated indoor pool closed 12/1-4/15. **Dining &
　　　　Entertainment:** Restaurant; 6 am-10 pm; $9-$15; cocktails/lounge; entertainment. **Services:** Fee: coin
laundry. **All Rooms:** free movies. **Cards:** AE, CB, DI, DS, MC, VI. **Special Amenities: Free local
telephone calls and free newspaper.**

BUDGET INN　　　　　　　　　　　　　　　　　　　　　　　Phone: 814/765-2639
　　　　All Year　　　　1P: $25- 28　2P/1B:　$28- 31　2P/2B:　$32- 40　XP:　$4　　F10
🔷 **Location:** I-80 exit 19, 1.5 mi sw on SR 879, 1.2 mi e. Rt 322 E 16830 (RD 2, Box 297). Fax: 814/765-2639.
Motel　**Terms:** Weekly rates; pets, $3 extra charge. **Facility:** 29 rooms. 1 story; interior/exterior corridors; designated
　　　　smoking area. **Dining:** Restaurant nearby. **Some Rooms:** Fee: microwaves, refrigerators. **Cards:** AE, DS,
MC, VI. **Special Amenities: Early check-in/late check-out and free local telephone calls.**

DAYS INN　　　　　　　　　　　　　　　　　　　　　　　　Phone: 814/765-5381
　　　　All Year [CP]　　　　1P: $39- 65　2P/1B:　$45- 65　2P/2B:　$44- 75　XP:　$6　　F18
🔷🔷 **Location:** I-80 exit 19, just sw on SR 879. Rt 879 16830 (RR 2, Box 245B). Fax: 814/765-7885.
Motor Inn **Terms:** Small pets only. **Facility:** 119 rooms. 2 stories; exterior corridors; video movie rentals. **Dining &
　　　　Entertainment:** Restaurant; 6:30 am-noon & 4-9 pm; cocktails/lounge. **Some Rooms:** microwaves,
refrigerators. Fee: VCR's. **Cards:** AE, CB, DI, DS, MC, VI. **Special Amenities: Free breakfast and free
newspaper.**

RODEWAY INN　　　　　　　　　　　　　　　　　　　　　Phone: 814/765-7587
🔷🔷 5/1-10/31 [CP]　　1P: $35- 45　2P/1B:　$38- 55　2P/2B:　$40- 65　XP:　$4　　F18
　　　　11/1-4/30 [CP]　　1P: $30- 40　2P/1B:　$34- 49　2P/2B:　$36- 59　XP:　$4　　F18
Motel　**Location:** Off I-80, exit 19; 1.5 mi sw on SR 879, 1.3 mi e on US 322. US 322E 16830 (RR 2, Box 297B).
　　　　Fax: 814/765-7587. **Terms:** Weekly rates; small pets only. **Facility:** 34 rooms. 2 stories; exterior corridors; designated smoking area. **Dining:** Restaurant nearby. **Some Rooms:** coffeemakers. Fee: refrigerators.
Cards: AE, CB, DI, DS, MC, VI. **Special Amenities: Free breakfast and free local telephone calls.**

SUPER 8 MOTEL-CLEARFIELD　　　　Rates Subject to Change　　　Phone: 814/768-7580
🔷🔷 Fri & Sat　　　　1P: $50- 70　2P/1B:　$55- 75　2P/2B:　$58- 75　XP:　$5　　F12
Motel　Sun-Thurs　　　　1P: $45- 65　2P/1B:　$49- 70　2P/2B:　$53- 70　XP:　$5　　F12
　　　　Location: Just s of I-80, exit 19. Rt 879 16830 (RR 2, Box 242C). Fax: 814/768-7580. **Terms:** Pets, with
permission. **Facility:** 50 rooms. 2 stories; interior corridors; designated smoking area. **All Rooms:** free movies. **Cards:** AE,
CB, DI, DS, JCB, MC, VI.　　　　　　　　　　　　Roll in showers.

RESTAURANT

DUTCH PANTRY　　　　**Lunch:** $6-$9　　　　　**Dinner:** $6-$9　　　Phone: 814/765-2137
🔷 **Location:** Just s of I-80, exit 19. RD 2 Box 244 16830. **Hours:** 6 am-10 pm. Closed: 12/25.
American **Features:** casual dress; children's menu; carryout; a la carte. Casual family dining; homemade soup; some
　　　　homemade dessert. **Cards:** AE, DS, MC, VI.

CLYMER—1,500

RESTAURANT

LUIGI'S RISTORANTE   **Lunch:** $4-$11   **Dinner:** $5-$12   **Phone:** 724/254-4777
◆◆   **Location:** Downtown on SR 286. 625 Franklin St 15728. **Hours:** 11am-10 pm, Fri & Sat-11 pm, Sun noon-8
Italian   pm. Closed major holidays. **Features:** casual dress; children's menu; carryout; cocktails & lounge; street
parking; a la carte. Specializing in Southern Italian homemade pasta dishes with friendly service & hearty
portions. **Cards:** DS, MC, VI.   ⊠

CONCORDVILLE—See Philadelphia & Vicinity p. 376.

CONNEAUT LAKE—700

RESTAURANT

MAMA BEAR'S COUNTRY INN RESTAURANT   **Lunch:** $5-$8   **Dinner:** $6-$12   **Phone:** 814/382-3115
AAA   **Location:** 1 mi w on US 6, 1.5 mi n. 11531 SR 618 16316. **Hours:** Open 5/22-9/13; 8 am-9 pm.
Features: No A/C; casual dress; children's menu; carryout; salad bar; a la carte. Homestyle cooking with a
◆   family atmosphere. Daily specials. **Cards:** MC, VI.
American

CONSHOHOCKEN—See Philadelphia & Vicinity p. 376.

CONYNGHAM—2,100

LODGINGS

DAYS INN-HAZLETON/CONYNGHAM   **Phone:** 717/788-5887
AAA [SAVE]   All Year [CP]   1P: $57- 60   2P/1B: $62- 65   2P/2B: $62- 65   XP: $6   F18
Location: On SR 93, just s of jct I-80 exit 38; or I-81 exit 41, 4 mi n. SR 93 18222 (RR 2, Box 304,
◆◆   DRUMS). Fax: 717/788-3929. **Terms:** Reserv deposit; weekly/monthly rates; small pets only, $5 extra
Motel   charge, no pets in summer. **Facility:** 62 rooms. 5 suites, $65-$85; 3 stories, no elevator; interior corridors.
All Rooms: free movies. **Cards:** AE, CB, DI, DS, MC, VI. **Special Amenities:** Free breakfast and free
local telephone calls. (See color ad p 299)   🛏 CTV ⊠ 🕭 D

LOOKOUT MOTOR LODGE   **Phone:** 717/788-4131
AAA [SAVE]   5/1-10/31 [CP]   1P: $42   2P/2B: $48   XP: $5
11/1-4/30 [CP]   1P: $36   2P/2B: $40   XP: $5
◆◆   **Location:** On SR 93 (Hazleton-Berwick Hwy), 1.3 mi n of jct I-80 exit 38, 6.3 mi n of jct I-81, exit 41. SR 93
Motel   18222 (RD 2, Box 130, DRUMS). **Terms:** Reserv deposit; no pets. **Facility:** 19 rooms. 1 story; exterior corri-
dors. **Cards:** AE, DS, MC, VI.   CTV ⊠ D

RESTAURANT

TOM'S KITCHEN FAMILY RESTAURANT   **Lunch:** $4-$12   **Dinner:** $4-$12   **Phone:** 717/788-3808
AAA   **Location:** On SR 93, 2 mi s of I-80, exit 38, 2 mi n of I-81, exit 41. Rt 93 18219-0894. **Hours:** 7 am-8 pm,
Sun from 8 am. Closed: 1/1, 4/7, 11/26 & 12/25. **Features:** casual dress; children's menu; carryout. Family
◆   dining; daily specials. Smoke free premises.   ⊠
American

COOKSBURG—100

LODGING

CLARION RIVER LODGE   **Phone:** 814/744-8171
AAA [SAVE]   All Year   1P: $67- 114   2P/1B: $72- 124   XP: $15
Location: 5.8 mi n on River Rd, along the Clarion River; from jct SR 36 & 899, 2 mi ne on Greenwood River
◆◆◆   Rd, 3 mi sw following signs. River Rd 16217 (HC 1 Box 22D). Fax: 814/744-8553. **Terms:** Reserv deposit,
Lodge   10 day notice; weekly rates; AP, BP avail; no pets. **Facility:** 20 rooms. Remote inn, nestled on a hill at edge
of Cook Forest State Park. Handling fee imposed; 2 stories; interior corridors. **Dining:** The Blue Heron
Restaurant, see separate listing. **Services:** valet laundry. **Recreation:** fishing; cross country skiing, snowmobiling; hiking
trails. **All Rooms:** coffeemakers, free movies, refrigerators. **Some Rooms:** Fee: VCR's. **Cards:** AE, DS, MC, VI.
🍴 CTV ⊠ D

RESTAURANT

THE BLUE HERON RESTAURANT   **Lunch:** $9-$21   **Dinner:** $15-$30   **Phone:** 814/744-8171
◆◆◆   **Location:** 5.8 mi n on River Rd, along the Clarion River; from jct SR 36 & 899, 2 mi ne on Greenwood River
Continental   Rd, 3 mi sw following signs; in Clarion River Lodge. River Road 16217. **Hours:** 11:30 am-8 pm.
Reservations: suggested. **Features:** casual dress; children's menu; health conscious menu items; cocktails
& lounge. Good selection of well prepared food in remote, peaceful & scenic setting. **Cards:** AE, DS, MC, VI.   ⊠

COOPERSBURG—2,600

LODGING

TRAVELODGE   **Phone:** 610/282-1212
AAA [SAVE]   6/16-9/29   1P: $49- 95   2P/1B: $49- 95   2P/2B: $49- 95   XP: $10   D12
5/1-6/15, 9/30-12/31 &
◆◆   4/15-4/30   1P: $45- 85   2P/1B: $45- 85   2P/2B: $45- 85   XP: $5   D12
Motel   1/1-4/14   1P: $40- 75   2P/1B: $40- 75   2P/2B: $40- 75   XP: $5   D12
Location: Center, on SR 309. 321 S 3rd St 18036. Fax: 610/282-1052. **Terms:** Reserv deposit, 3 day notice;
weekly rates; no pets. **Facility:** 34 rooms. 2 stories; exterior corridors. **Dining:** Restaurant nearby.
All Rooms: coffeemakers, microwaves, free movies, refrigerators. **Some Rooms:** whirlpools. Fee: VCR's. **Cards:** AE, DS,
MC, VI. **Special Amenities: Free breakfast and preferred room (subject to availability with advanced reservations).**
CTV ⊠ D

CORAOPOLIS—See Pittsburgh & Vicinity p. 408.

CORRY—7,200

LODGING

DAY LILY INN BED & BREAKFAST
◆◆◆   All Year [BP]
Bed &
Breakfast
Rates Subject to Change   **Phone:** 814/664-9047
1P: $60   2P/1B: $60   2P/2B: $60- 70 XP: $10
Location: Just n, then just w on W Smith St. 49 W Smith St 16407. **Terms:** Reserv deposit; no pets.
Facility: 7 rooms. 3 stories, no elevator; interior corridors; smoke free premises. **All Rooms:** free movies.
Cards: AE, DS, MC, VI.
(CTV) (X) (D)

COUDERSPORT—2,900

LODGING

WESTGATE INN
(AAA)
◆◆
Motel
Rates Subject to Change   **Phone:** 814/274-0400
1P: $49   2P/1B: $59   2P/2B: $64   XP: $4   F12
Location: 1 mi w. US 6W 16915. Fax: 814/274-8607. **Terms:** Check-in 3:30 pm; reserv deposit; no pets.
Facility: 34 rooms. 1 story; interior corridors. **All Rooms:** free movies. **Cards:** AE, DI, DS, MC, VI.
(CTV) (X) (D)

RESTAURANT

ERWAYS FAMILY RESTAURANT
(AAA)
◆
American
Lunch: $4-$12   **Dinner:** $6-$14   **Phone:** 814/274-8862
Location: 1 mi w on US 6, next to Westgate Inn. Route 6 West 16915. **Hours:** 6 am-9 pm. Closed: 12/25.
Features: casual dress; children's menu; health conscious menu items; carryout; a la carte. Country charm
& decor, also features bakery, deli & dairy products from the Erway Family Farm. Menu ranges from soup &
sandwiches to sit-down dinner, as well as a variety of fresh baked pie. **Cards:** AE, DS, JCB, MC, VI.
(X)

COVENTRYVILLE—See Philadelphia & Vicinity p. 376.

CRABTREE—See Laurel Highlands p. 311.

CRAFTON—See Pittsburgh & Vicinity p. 409.

CRESCO—See Pocono Mountains Area p. 421.

CRYSTAL LAKE—300

RESTAURANT

OLIVERI'S RESTAURANT & LAKESIDE CAFE
(AAA) (SAVE)
◆◆◆
American
Lunch: $4-$8   **Dinner:** $13-$25   **Phone:** 717/222-3181
Location: From I-81, exit 62; 3.5 mi e on SR 107E, 8 mi n on SR 247N, at Oliveri's Crystal Lake Hotel. RD
1 18407. **Hours:** noon-midnight. Closed: 12/24 & 12/25. **Reservations:** suggested; weekends.
Features: casual dress; children's menu; carryout; cocktails & lounge. Italian influence. All dishes made to
order, including pasta, salad, veal, pastry & unique ice cream. Outdoor dining lakeside in season.
Family-owned & operated for more than 50 years. **Cards:** AE, DS, MC, VI. **Special Value: $1 off the price
of a dinner entree.**
(X)

DALLAS—7,600

LODGING

PONDA-ROWLAND BED & BREAKFAST
◆◆
Bed &
Breakfast
Guaranteed Rates   **Phone:** 717/639-3245
1P: $75- 105 2P/1B: $75- 105 2P/2B: $75- 105 XP: $10-30
Location: 6 mi n on SR 309 from jct SR 415, 1 mi e following signs. RR 1 Box 349 18612.
Fax: 717/639-5531. **Terms:** Check-in 4 pm; reserv deposit, 8 day notice; no pets, kennel on premises for
guests. **Facility:** 5 rooms. 2 stories; interior corridors; designated smoking area. **Dining:** Breakfast served
8:30-9 am. **Cards:** AE, DS, MC, VI.
(X) (D)

RESTAURANT

OVERBROOK
◆◆◆
Italian
Dinner: $9-$25   **Phone:** 717/675-2223
Location: SR 309, just w on Center St, 0.3 mi n on Pioneer Ave, 0.5 mi w. 259 Overbrook Rd 18612.
Hours: 5 pm-10 pm. Closed: 1/1, 11/26, 12/25 & Sun. **Reservations:** suggested; weekends.
Features: casual dress; children's menu; carryout; cocktails & lounge. Specializing in seafood, veal & pasta.
Cozy, intimate atmosphere. **Cards:** MC, VI.
(X)

DANVILLE—5,200

LODGINGS

DAYS INN CONFERENCE CENTER
◆◆
Motor Inn
Rates Subject to Change   **Phone:** 717/275-5510
1P: $52- 69 2P/1B: $58- 75 2P/2B: $58- 75 XP: $6   F18
Location: I-80, exit 33. 50 Sheraton Rd 17821. Fax: 717/275-7918. **Terms:** Sr. discount; no pets.
Facility: 146 rooms. 2 stories; interior/exterior corridors. **Dining:** Restaurant; 6:30 am-10:30 & 5-9 pm;
$8-$20. **Cards:** AE, CB, DI, DS, JCB, MC, VI.
(≈) (CTV) (X) (D)

HOWARD JOHNSON LODGE
◆
Motel
Rates Subject to Change   **Phone:** 717/275-5100
5/1-10/31   1P: $48- 65 2P/1B: $53- 75 2P/2B: $53- 75 XP: $5   F17
11/1-4/30   1P: $40- 45 2P/1B: $45- 55 2P/2B: $45- 55 XP: $5   F17
Location: I-80, exit 33, just n on SR 54. 15 Valley West Rd 17821. Fax: 717/275-1886. **Terms:** Sr. discount;
no pets. **Facility:** 77 rooms. 2 stories; interior corridors. **All Rooms:** free movies. **Cards:** AE, CB, DI, DS, JCB, MC, VI.
(≈) (CTV) (X) (D)

TRAVELODGE
(AAA) (SAVE)
◆
Motel
          Phone: 717/275-4640
6/15-9/30   1P: $49- 89 2P/1B: $59- 89 2P/2B: $69- 79
5/1-6/14 & 10/1-4/30   1P: $45- 79 2P/1B: $62- 79 2P/2B: $62- 75
Location: On SR 54, just sw of jct I-80, exit 33. 35 Sheraton Rd 17821. Fax: 717/275-2064. **Terms:** Reserv
deposit; no pets. **Facility:** 118 rooms. Rates for up to 4 persons; 2 stories; exterior corridors.
Dining: Restaurant nearby. **All Rooms:** coffeemakers, free movies. **Some Rooms:** radios. **Cards:** AE, DI,
DS, MC, VI. **Special Amenities: Free local telephone calls and free newspaper.**
(≈) (🍴) (ECTV) (X) (D)

RESTAURANTS

THE OLD HARDWARE RESTAURANT　　　　**Lunch:** $3-$7　　　**Dinner:** $7-$16　　　**Phone:** 717/275-6615
Location: Downtown, just s of US 11. 336 Mill St 17821. **Hours:** 11 am-8 pm, Fri & Sat-9 pm, Sun 11:30
am-2 pm. Closed major holidays. **Reservations:** suggested. **Features:** casual dress; children's menu; health
conscious menu items; carryout; a la carte. Well-prepared entrees served in attractive, country atmosphere
American　　for a taste of the past. Banquet facilities avail. **Cards:** AE, DS, MC, VI.

PINE BARN INN RESTAURANT　　　　**Lunch:** $5-$10　　　**Dinner:** $13-$22　　　**Phone:** 717/275-2071
Location: 0.5 mi n of US 11, follow signs to Geisinger Medical Center; in The Pine Barn Inn. 1 Pine Barn Pl
American　17821. **Hours:** 7 am-10 pm, Sat from 8 am, Sun 8 am-8 pm. Closed major holidays.
Reservations: suggested; Sat. **Features:** casual dress; children's menu; carryout; cocktails & lounge; a la
carte. Rustic country atmosphere in a converted barn; specializing in New England seafood with live Maine lobster. Dessert
baked on premises. **Cards:** AE, CB, DI, DS, MC, VI.

DELMONT—See Pittsburgh & Vicinity p. 409.

DENVER—See Pennsylvania Dutch Country p. 332.

DICKSON CITY—6,300　　(See map p. 418; index p. 417)

LODGING

QUALITY HOTEL　　　　　　　Rates Subject to Change　　　　　　**Phone:** 717/383-9979　　　85
◆◆　　5/1-9/5 [CP]　　　　　1P: $65　　2P/1B:　$75　　　2P/2B:　$75
Hotel　　9/6-4/30 [CP]　　　　1P: $65　　2P/1B:　$65　　　2P/2B:　$65
Location: I-81 exit 57A, 2 mi e on US 6; from PA Tpk Northeast Extension, Clarks Summit exit, 4.5 mi e on
US 6. 1946 Scranton-Carbondale Hwy 18508-1144. Fax: 717/383-1756. **Terms:** Pets. **Facility:** 85 rooms. 4 stories; interior
corridors. **Dining:** Dining room; 5 pm-10 pm; $5-$27. **All Rooms:** free & pay movies. **Cards:** AE, CB, DS, JCB, MC, VI.
(See color ad p 431 & p 431)

DONEGAL—See Laurel Highlands p. 311.

DOUGLASSVILLE—1,200

LODGING

ECONO LODGE　　　　　　　Rates Subject to Change　　　　　　　**Phone:** 610/385-3016
◆◆　　5/1-11/30 [CP]　　1P: $43- 63　2P/1B:　$47- 77　2P/2B:　$60- 99　XP: $10　　F18
Motel　　12/1-4/30 [CP]　　1P: $38- 56　2P/1B:　$45- 61　2P/2B:　$49- 68　XP: $10　　F18
Location: On Rt 422, from Pottstown 422 W 10 mi, from Reading 422 E 10 mi. 387 Ben Franklin Hwy
19518. Fax: 610/385-3016. **Terms:** Sr. discount; reserv deposit; small pets only, $10 extra charge, $20 dep req. **Facility:** 24
rooms. Handling fee imposed; 2 stories; exterior corridors. **All Rooms:** free movies. **Cards:** AE, CB, DI, DS, JCB, MC, VI.

DRINKER　(See map p. 418; index p. 417)

RESTAURANT

MY BROTHERS PLACE　　　　　　**Dinner:** $15-$23　　　　　**Phone:** 717/689-4410　　77
Location: 0.8 mi w on SR 590; 5 mi e of jct SR 590 & 435 at Elmhurst. SR 590 18444. **Hours:** 4 pm-10 pm,
Sun from 1 pm. Closed: Tues & 1/6-2/14. **Reservations:** accepted. **Features:** casual dress; children's menu;
health conscious menu items; carryout; salad bar; cocktails & lounge. Cozy atmosphere; good selection of
American　seafood & beef. Prime rib specials on weekends. **Cards:** AE, CB, DI, DS, MC, VI. **Special Value: $3 off the
price of a dinner entree.**

DRUMS—600　　(See map p. 418; index p. 417)

LODGING

ECONO LODGE　　　　　　　　　　　　　　　　　　**Phone:** 717/788-4121　　113
Fri & Sat 5/17-10/31 [CP]　　1P: $55- 60　2P/1B:　$85- 90　2P/2B:　$70- 85　XP: $7　　F18
Sun-Thurs 5/17-10/31 [CP]　1P: $50- 55　2P/1B:　$60- 65　2P/2B:　$55- 60　XP: $7　　F18
◆◆　　5/1-5/16 & 11/1-4/30 [CP]　1P: $45- 48　2P/1B:　$54- 59　2P/2B:　$50- 54　XP: $7　　F18
Motel　　**Location:** I-80 exit 39, 0.3 mi n on SR 309, I-81 exit 42, e to 309S, following signs. SR 309 & I-80 18222
(RR 1, Box 1470). Fax: 717/788-3317. **Terms:** Reserv deposit, 3 day notice; weekly/monthly rates; no pets.
Facility: 42 rooms. 2 stories; exterior corridors. **Dining:** Restaurant nearby. **All Rooms:** free movies.
Some Rooms: refrigerators. **Cards:** AE, DS, MC, VI. **Special Amenities: Free local telephone calls and free room
upgrade (subject to availability with advanced reservations).**

RESTAURANTS

COUNTRYSIDE FAMILY RESTAURANT　　　　**Dinner:** $6-$11　　　　　**Phone:** 717/788-6213　　59
Location: On SR 309, 0.9 mi s of I-80, exit 39. SR 309 & Edgewood Rd 18222. **Hours:** 7 am-9 pm. Closed:
12/25. **Reservations:** accepted. **Features:** casual dress; children's menu; carryout. Family style dining
amidst country decor. Smoke free premises. **Cards:** AE, DS, MC, VI.
American

EDGEWOOD IN THE PINES RESTAURANT　　　**Dinner:** $8-$20　　　　　**Phone:** 717/788-1101　　60
Location: From jct I-80, exit 39; 1 mi s on SR 309, 0.8 mi w. Edgewood Rd 18222. **Hours:** 5 pm-10 pm,
Sun noon-8 pm, open weekends only 1/2-3/31. Closed: 1/1, 12/24, 12/25, Mon & Tues. **Features:** casual
dress; children's menu; carryout; cocktails & lounge. Very attractive setting. **Cards:** MC, VI.
American

DU BOIS—8,300

LODGINGS

BEST WESTERN INN & CONFERENCE CENTER　　　　　　　　**Phone:** 814/371-6200
5/1-10/31 [CP]　　1P: $48- 54　2P/1B:　$60- 66　2P/2B:　$54- 60　XP: $6　　F18
11/1-4/30 [CP]　　1P: $44- 50　2P/1B:　$56- 62　2P/2B:　$50- 56　XP: $6　　F18
◆◆◆　　**Location:** I-80, exit 16 or 17, at jct US 219 & SR 255. 82 N Park Pl 15801. Fax: 814/371-4608. **Terms:** No
Motel　　pets. **Facility:** 60 rooms. Opposite DuBois campus, Penn State. 2 stories; interior corridors; designated
smoking area; playground. **Dining:** Restaurant nearby. **Services:** Fee: coin laundry. **All Rooms:** free
movies, combo or shower baths. **Some Rooms:** refrigerators. **Cards:** AE, CB, DI, DS, MC, VI. **Special Amenities: Free
breakfast and free newspaper.**

HAMPTON INN
◆◆◆
Motel
All Year [CP]
1P: $59- 64 2P/1B: $59- 64 2P/2B: $59- 64
Phone: 814/375-1000
Location: 0.5 mi s of I-80, exit 17. RD 8, Box 3A-Route 255 15801. Fax: 814/375-4668. **Terms:** Sr. discount; reserv deposit; no pets. **Facility:** 96 rooms. 3 stories; interior corridors; designated smoking area.
All Rooms: free & pay movies. **Cards:** AE, DI, DS, MC, VI.
Roll in showers. [ECTV] [ℹ] [✕] [D] [S]

HOLIDAY INN
[AAA] [SAVE]
◆◆◆
Motor Inn
Phone: 814/371-5100
All Year [BP]
1P: $59- 82 2P/1B: $59- 88 2P/2B: $59- 88 XP: $6   F19
Location: I-80, exit 16; just s on US 219. US 219 & I-80 15801. Fax: 814/375-0230. **Terms:** Package plans; pets. **Facility:** 159 rooms. 2 stories; interior corridors; wading pool, heated pool open summer. **Dining & Entertainment:** Restaurant; 6:30 am-2 & 5-10 pm, Sat & Sun from 7 am; free breakfast Mon-Fri; cocktails/lounge. **Services:** area transportation, within 6 mi. Fee: coin laundry. **All Rooms:** free & pay movies. **Some Rooms:** Fee: refrigerators. **Cards:** AE, CB, DI, DS, MC, VI. **Special Amenities:** Free newspaper.
(See color ad below)
[🛏] [🍴] [➕] [ECTV] [✕] [D]

RAMADA INN
[AAA] [SAVE]
◆
Motor Inn
Phone: 814/371-7070
All Year
1P: $50- 65 2P/1B: $60- 75 2P/2B: $60- 75 XP: $10   F18
Location: I-80, exit 17; just s. Rt 255 & I-80 15801. Fax: 814/371-1055. **Terms:** AP, EP avail; package plans; small pets only. **Facility:** 96 rooms. 2 stories; small indoor pool. **Dining & Entertainment:** Restaurant; 6:30 am-11 & 5:30-10 pm; $10-$16; cocktails/lounge. **Services:** Fee: coin laundry. **All Rooms:** free & pay movies. **Some Rooms:** coffeemakers, refrigerators, whirlpools. **Cards:** AE, CB, DI, DS, JCB, MC, VI.
Special Amenities: Early check-in/late check-out and free local telephone calls.
[🛏] [🍴] [ECTV] [✕] [D]

RESTAURANT

THUNDERBIRD RESTAURANT & LOUNGE
◆◆
American
VI.
Dinner: $13-$21
Phone: 814/371-0799
Location: 2.6 mi s on US 219 from SR 255, 1 mi s on US 119, 1 mi w. Rt 322 15851. **Hours:** 5 pm-9 pm. Closed: 12/25, Sun & Mon. **Reservations:** suggested; weekends. **Features:** casual dress; children's menu; cocktails & lounge. Rustic atmosphere with fireplace serving steak, seafood & chops. **Cards:** AE, DS, MC,

DUNCANSVILLE—1,300

LODGING

WYE MOTOR LODGE
[AAA]
◆◆
Motel
Rates Subject to Change
5/1-10/31   1P: $30- 34 2P/1B: $36- 38 2P/2B: $38- 40 XP: $3   F12
11/1-4/30   1P: $29- 32 2P/1B: $32- 34 2P/2B: $34- 36 XP: $3   F12
Phone: 814/695-4407
Location: I-99/US 220, exit Plank Rd, 2.5 mi s on Plank Rd; at jct US 22 & Plank Rd. 200 N 220 Bus 16635. Fax: 814/695-7283. **Terms:** Reserv deposit; no pets. **Facility:** 38 rooms. 1 story; exterior corridors; designated smoking area. **Cards:** AE, DS, MC, VI.
[ECTV] [✕] [D]

DUNMORE—15,400   (See map p. 418; index p. 417)

LODGINGS

DAYS INN
[AAA] [SAVE]
◆◆
Motel
Phone: 717/348-6101 [1]
All Year [CP]
1P: $60- 66 2P/1B: $65- 76 2P/2B: $65- 76 XP: $5   F18
Location: Jct SR 347 & I-81, exit 55A. 1226 O'Neil Hwy 18512. Fax: 717/348-5064. **Terms:** Package plans; pets, $3 extra charge. **Facility:** 90 rooms. Very decorative rooms. 4 stories; interior corridors. **Dining:** Restaurant nearby. **All Rooms:** free movies, refrigerators, combo or shower baths. **Some Rooms:** microwaves. Fee: VCR's. **Cards:** AE, DI, DS, MC, VI. **Special Amenities: Early check-in/late check-out and free breakfast.**
[🛏] [CTV] [✕] [D]

ECONO LODGE SCRANTON NORTHEAST
[AAA] [SAVE]
◆◆
Motel
Phone: 717/346-8782 [4]
5/1-10/31 & 4/1-4/30 [CP] 1P: $40- 85 2P/1B: $50- 85 2P/2B: $50- 95 XP: $5   F16
11/1-3/31 [CP]   1P: $40- 60 2P/1B: $50- 75 2P/2B: $50- 75 XP: $5   F16
Location: On SR 347; 0.3 mi e of I-81, exit 55 (Throop exit). 1027 O'Neill Hwy 18512. Fax: 717/346-7825. **Terms:** Reserv deposit, 7 day notice; package plans; no pets. **Facility:** 32 rooms. Handling fee imposed; 2 stories; exterior corridors. **Dining:** Restaurant nearby. **All Rooms:** free movies. **Cards:** AE, DI, DS, MC, VI.
Special Amenities: Free breakfast.
[CTV] [✕] [D]

HOLIDAY INN-SCRANTON EAST
◆◆◆
Motor Inn
Rates Subject to Change
7/1-4/30   1P: $86 2P/1B: $96 2P/2B: $96 XP: $10   F19
5/1-6/30   1P: $79 2P/1B: $89 2P/2B: $89 XP: $10   F19
Phone: 717/343-4771 [3]
Location: I-380/84, exit 1 (Tigue St), 0.3 mi e of jct I-81. 200 Tigue St 18512. Fax: 717/343-5171. **Terms:** Sr. discount; pets. **Facility:** 139 rooms. Suites, $125-$165; 3 stories; interior/exterior corridors. **Dining:** Restaurant; 6:30 am-10 pm; $9-$18. **All Rooms:** free movies. **Cards:** AE, CB, DI, DS, JCB, MC, VI. *(See color ad p 431)*
[🛏] [🚐] [➕] [CTV] [✕] [D]

DUPONT—3,000   (See map p. 418; index p. 417)

LODGING

HOLIDAY INN EXPRESS Rates Subject to Change Phone: 717/654-3300 **123**
◆◆◆   Fri & Sat [CP]   1P: $79   2P/1B: $79   2P/2B: $79
Motor Inn   Sun-Thurs [CP]   1P: $69   2P/1B: $69   2P/2B: $69
Location: Just e of I-81, exit 49A. 18641 (30 Concorde Dr, PITTSTON). Fax: 717/883-7301. **Terms:** No pets. **Facility:** 100 rooms. 5 stories; interior corridors. **Dining:** Restaurant; 11 am-11 pm; $7-$16. **All Rooms:** free & pay movies. **Cards:** AE, MC, VI.
Roll in showers. 🛬 CTV 🛏 ✕ 🎦 D S

EAGLES MERE—100

LODGINGS

CRESTMONT INN Phone: 717/525-3519
AAA SAVE   All Year [BP]   1P: $89- 148   2P/1B: $89- 148 2P/2B: $89- 148 XP: $25
◆◆◆   **Location:** Just n on SR 42 (Eagle Mere Ave), just w on Lakewood Ave. Crestmont Dr 17731.
Historic   Fax: 717/525-3534. **Terms:** Age restrictions may apply; reserv deposit, 5 day notice; weekly/monthly rates;
Country Inn package plans; no pets. **Facility:** 13 rooms. Tastefully decorated rooms on 8 acres of lawn, gardens & nature trails in quaint town amidst abundant, unspoiled forests with numerous outdoor activities. Handling fee imposed; 2 stories; interior corridors; designated smoking area; nearby golf; guest access to private Eagles Mere Lake; 6 tennis courts; croquet, shuffleboard, adjoins Wyoming State Forest. **Dining & Entertainment:** Restaurant; 8-9:30 am & 6-8 pm; with reservations; $10-$20; cocktails/lounge. **Recreation:** canoeing; cross country skiing; bicycles, hiking trails. Fee: tobogganing. **All Rooms:** free movies, no phones. **Some Rooms:** A/C, refrigerators, VCR's, whirlpools. **Cards:** MC, VI. **Special Amenities: Free breakfast and preferred room (subject to availability with advanced reservations).** 🛬 🕥 CTV ✕ D

SHADY LANE BED & BREAKFAST Guaranteed Rates Phone: 717/525-3394
◆◆   All Year [BP]   1P: $65   2P/1B: $85   2P/2B: $85   XP: $15
Bed &   **Location:** Just s on Allegheny Ave from PA Rt 42. Allegheny Ave 17731 (PO Box 314). **Terms:** Age
Breakfast restrictions may apply; reserv deposit, 10 day notice; no pets. **Facility:** 8 rooms. 1 carriage house, $100-$125; 1 story; interior corridors; smoke free premises. **All Rooms:** no A/C. **Some Rooms:** efficiency. CTV ✕ D

EASTON—26,300

LODGINGS

BEST WESTERN EASTON INN Phone: 610/253-9131
AAA SAVE   6/21-11/25 [CP]   1P: $70- 85   2P/1B: $80- 95 2P/2B: $80- 95 XP: $10 F12
        5/1-6/20 & 4/1-4/30 [CP] 1P: $65- 75   2P/1B: $75- 80 2P/2B: $75- 80 XP: $10 F12
◆◆◆   1/1-3/31 [CP]   1P: $55- 60   2P/1B: $65- 70 2P/2B: $65- 70 XP: $10 F12
Motel   11/26-12/31 [CP]   1P: $49- 59   2P/1B: $59- 65 2P/2B: $59- 65 XP: $10 F12
Location: US 22, 4th St (SR 611) exit, just e to 3rd St, 0.5 mi s; or I-78 exit 22, 1 mi n following signs. 185 S Third St 18042. Fax: 610/252-5145. **Terms:** Weekly rates; small pets only. **Facility:** 85 rooms. Comfortably furnished guest rooms. 4 stories; interior corridors; pool closed 1/1-3/31. **Dining & Entertainment:** Restaurant. 4 pm-10 pm; $8-$22; cocktails/lounge. **All Rooms:** microwaves, refrigerators. Fee: movies. **Some Rooms:** Fee: whirlpools. **Cards:** AE, CB, DI, DS, MC, VI. **Special Amenities: Early check-in/late check-out.** 🛒 🕥 🕥 CTV ✕ 🎦 D

DAYS INN Rates Subject to Change Phone: 610/253-0546
◆◆   5/1-10/31 & 4/1-4/30 [CP] 1P: $45- 100   2P/1B: $56- 100 2P/2B: $56- 100 XP: $4 F18
Motel   11/1-12/31 & 1/1-3/31 [CP] 1P: $45- 56   2P/1B: $56- 75 2P/2B: $56- 75 XP: $4 F18
Location: US 22, exit 25th St, just e on N Service Rd. 2555 Nazareth Rd 18042. Fax: 610/252-8952. **Terms:** Pets, $5 extra charge. **Facility:** 84 rooms. 4 stories; interior corridors. **All Rooms:** free movies. **Cards:** AE, DS, JCB, MC, VI. 🛒 CTV ✕ 🎦 D S

EAST PETERSBURG—See Pennsylvania Dutch Country p. 333.

EAST STROUDSBURG—See Pocono Mountains Area p. 423.

EBENSBURG—3,900

LODGINGS

COMFORT INN Rates Subject to Change Phone: 814/472-6100
◆◆◆   5/1-10/28 [CP]   1P: $54- 59   2P/1B: $65   2P/2B: $65   XP: $6 F17
Motel   10/29-4/30 [CP]   1P: $49- 55   2P/1B: $60   2P/2B: $60   XP: $6 F17
Location: Just e on US 22 from jct of US 219. 111 Cook Rd 15931. Fax: 814/472-4960. **Terms:** Sr. discount; pets, $6 extra charge, $25 dep req. **Facility:** 78 rooms. 8 whirlpool rms, extra charge; 3 stories; interior corridors; designated smoking area. **All Rooms:** free movies. **Cards:** AE, CB, DI, DS, JCB, MC, VI.
Roll in showers. 🛒 🕥 ECTV 🛏 D S

THE NOON-COLLINS INN Phone: 814/472-4311
AAA SAVE   5/1-10/31 [BP]   1P: $55   2P/1B: $60   2P/2B: $60   XP: $15   D
        11/1-4/30 [BP]   1P: $50   2P/1B: $55   2P/2B: $55   XP: $15   D
◆◆   **Location:** Downtown, just e of jct High & Center sts. 114 E High St 15931. Fax: 814/472-6946.
Historic   **Terms:** Reserv deposit, 7 day notice; no pets. **Facility:** 7 rooms. 1834 restored historic federal style country
Country Inn inn. Phones avail; 2 stories; interior corridors; designated smoking area. **Dining:** Dining room; 11 am-2 & 5-8 pm, Fri & Sat-9 pm, closed Sun & Mon; $10-$16; cocktails. **Services:** guest laundry. **All Rooms:** shower baths, no phones. **Cards:** AE, CB, DI, DS, MC, VI. **Special Amenities: Free breakfast and free local telephone calls.** ✕ D

EDINBORO—7,700

LODGING

RAMADA INN Phone: 814/734-5650
AAA SAVE   5/1-10/9   1P: $85   2P/1B: $85   2P/2B: $85   XP: $5-15 F18
◆   10/10-4/30   1P: $55   2P/1B: $60   2P/2B: $60   XP: $5-10 F18
Motor Inn   **Location:** 2 mi e of I-79, exit 38. Rt 6N 16412. Fax: 814/734-7532. **Terms:** Weekly rates; package plans; no pets. **Facility:** 105 rooms. 2 stories; interior corridors; saunas. Fee: 18 holes golf. **Dining & Entertainment:** Dining room; 7 am-2 & 4-10pm; $6-$18; cocktails/lounge. **Services:** Fee: coin laundry. **All Rooms:** free & pay movies. **Some Rooms:** microwaves, refrigerators. **Cards:** AE, CB, DI, DS, MC, VI. **Special Amenities: Free local telephone calls and free newspaper.** 🕥 🕥 ✕ D

ELIZABETHTOWN—*See Pennsylvania Dutch Country p. 333.*

EMLENTON—800

LODGING

WHIPPLE TREE INN & FARM
◆◆
Bed &
Breakfast

Rates Subject to Change
5/1-10/31 & 4/1-4/30 [BP]   1P: $50- 60   2P/1B: $50- 60   2P/2B: $50- 60   XP: $10   **Phone:** 724/867-9543   F5
Location: I-80 exit 5, 1 mi e on SR 208, 1 mi n. Big Bend Rd 16373 (Rd #3, Box 285). **Terms:** Open 5/1-10/31 & 4/1-4/30; reserv deposit, 3 day notice; pets, $10 stall fee for horses. **Facility:** 4 rooms. Handling fee imposed; 2 stories; interior corridors. **Cards:** MC, VI.

EMMAUS—11,200

LODGING

LEIBERT GAP MANOR BED & BREAKFAST
◆◆◆
Bed &
Breakfast

Rates Subject to Change
All Year [BP]   1P: $75- 140   2P/1B: $90- 150   XP: $20   **Phone:** 610/967-1242
Location: I-476 PA Tpk exit 32, e on SR 663 to SR 309N (I-78) exit 17, SR 29S (Cedar Crest Blvd), just e on Chestnut to 10th S, 1 mi s. 4502 S Mountain Dr 18049 (PO Box 623). **Terms:** Age restrictions may apply; no pets. **Facility:** 4 rooms. 3 stories; interior corridors; smoke free premises. **Cards:** AE, CB, DI, MC, VI.

RESTAURANT

THE FARMHOUSE RESTAURANT
◆◆◆
French

Dinner: $18-$24   **Phone:** 610/967-6225
Location: I-78, exit 17; 3 mi s on SR 29 (Cedar Crest Blvd), 0.3 mi w. 1449 Chestnut St 18049. **Hours:** 5 pm-9 pm, Fri & Sat-10 pm. Closed: 1/1 & 12/25. **Reservations:** suggested. **Features:** casual dress; cocktails & lounge; a la carte. Intimate dining in a early 1800's farmhouse. Smoke free premises. **Cards:** AE, DI, DS, MC, VI.

EMPORIUM—2,500

RESTAURANT

CABIN KITCHEN RESTAURANT
(AAA)
◆
American

Lunch: $3-$10   Dinner: $3-$10   **Phone:** 814/486-0528
Location: Directly w of Broad St. 24 W Fourth St 15834. **Hours:** 6 am-8 pm, Sun from 7 am. **Reservations:** accepted. **Features:** casual dress; children's menu; health conscious menu items; carryout; street parking. Hearty home cooked meals served in a casual diner atmosphere.

ENOLA—6,000   (See map p. 292; index p. 291)

LODGING

QUALITY INN HARRISBURG-ENOLA
(AAA) (SAVE)
◆◆
Motel

Phone: 717/732-0785   **11**
5/1-10/31 [CP]   1P: $59   2P/1B: $76   2P/2B: $66   XP: $7   F18
11/1-4/30 [CP]   1P: $49   2P/1B: $66   2P/2B: $56   XP: $7   F18
Location: 1 mi s of I-81, exit 215. 501 N Enola Rd 17025. Fax: 717/732-7860. **Terms:** Pets. **Facility:** 72 rooms. Spacious rooms. Handling fee imposed; 2 stories; interior corridors; video movie rentals. **Dining:** Restaurant nearby. **Services:** Fee: coin laundry. **All Rooms:** coffeemakers, free movies. **Some Rooms:** Fee: VCR's. **Cards:** AE, CB, DI, DS, JCB, MC, VI. **Special Amenities: Free local telephone calls and free newspaper.**

RESTAURANT

VISAGGIO'S RISTORANTE
◆◆◆
Italian

Lunch: $7-$12   Dinner: $11-$24   **Phone:** 717/697-8082   (2)
Location: 1.1 mi w of I-81, exit 18, just n. 6990 Wertzville Rd 17025. **Hours:** 11 am-2 pm, Sat 5 pm-9 pm. Closed major holidays & Sun 6/1-8/31. **Reservations:** suggested. **Features:** casual dress; carryout; cocktails & lounge. Relaxing atmosphere. **Cards:** AE, MC, VI.

EPHRATA—*See Pennsylvania Dutch Country p. 333.*

ERIE—108,700

LODGINGS

COMFORT INN
◆◆◆
Motel

Rates Subject to Change
5/1-10/31 [CP]   1P: $80- 109   2P/1B: $90- 149   2P/2B: $90- 149   XP: $10   F17
11/1-4/30 [CP]   1P: $60- 80   2P/1B: $75- 139   2P/2B: $75- 139   XP: $10   F17
Location: I-90 exit 6, just s. 8051 Peach St 16509. Fax: 814/864-1367. **Terms:** Sr. discount; no pets. **Facility:** 110 rooms. 2 stories; interior corridors. **All Rooms:** free movies. **Cards:** AE, CB, DI, DS, MC, VI.   **Phone:** 814/866-6666

DAYS INN
◆◆◆
Motel

Rates Subject to Change
5/1-10/1 [CP]   1P: $80   2P/1B: $100   2P/2B: $100   XP: $5   F17
10/2-10/31 [CP]   1P: $53   2P/1B: $63   2P/2B: $63   XP: $5   F17
11/1-4/30 [CP]   1P: $50   2P/1B: $57   2P/2B: $57   XP: $5   F17
Location: On SR 97, at jct I-90, exit 7. 7415 Schultz Rd 16509. Fax: 814/866-0463. **Terms:** Sr. discount; reserv deposit; pets, $5 extra charge, in limited rooms. **Facility:** 113 rooms. 4 stories; interior corridors. **All Rooms:** free movies. **Cards:** AE, CB, DI, DS, JCB, MC, VI.   **Phone:** 814/868-8521

ECONO LODGE
◆◆◆
Motel

Rates Subject to Change
5/1-10/31 [CP]   1P: $79- 149   2P/1B: $89- 149   2P/2B: $89- 149   XP: $10   F
11/1-4/30 [CP]   1P: $59- 139   2P/1B: $79- 139   2P/2B: $79- 139   XP: $10   F
Location: I-90 exit 6, just s. 8050 Peach St 16509. Fax: 814/864-6218. **Terms:** Sr. discount; no pets. **Facility:** 97 rooms. 3 stories; interior corridors. **All Rooms:** free movies. **Cards:** AE, CB, DI, DS, MC, VI.   **Phone:** 814/866-5544
Roll in showers.

GLASS HOUSE INN
(AAA)
◆◆◆
Motel

Guaranteed Rates
5/22-9/7 [CP]   1P: $65- 75   2P/1B: $65- 75   2P/2B: $82- 92   XP: $5-7   **Phone:** 814/833-7751
5/1-5/21 & 9/8-4/30 [CP]   1P: $48- 58   2P/1B: $48- 58   2P/2B: $58- 68   XP: $5
Location: On US 20, 0.3 mi w of jct SR 832, 1 mi w of I-79 exit 43. 3202 W 26th St 16506. Fax: 814/833-4222. **Terms:** Reserv deposit; no pets. **Facility:** 30 rooms. 1 story; exterior corridors. **Cards:** AE, CB, DI, DS, MC, VI. *(See color ad p 279)*

HAMPTON INN ERIE   Rates Subject to Change   **Phone:** 814/835-4200
◆◆◆   5/14-9/10 [CP]   1P: $102   2P/1B: $102   2P/2B: $102
Motel   5/1-5/13 & 9/11-4/30 [CP]   1P: $70   2P/1B: $77   2P/2B: $77
     Location: I-79 exit 44 B, 1.7 mi w on Rt 5. 3041 W 12th St 16505. Fax: 814/835-5212. **Terms:** No pets.
Facility: 100 rooms. 3 stories; interior corridors. **All Rooms:** free movies. **Cards:** AE, CB, DI, DS, MC, VI.

HOLIDAY INN-DOWNTOWN   **Phone:** 814/456-2961
Ⓐ Ⓢ   All Year [BP]   1P: $79   2P/1B: $89   2P/2B: $89
     Location: 1 mi s at 18th & Peach sts. 18 W 18th St 16501. Fax: 814/456-7067. **Terms:** MAP avail; no pets.
◆◆   **Facility:** 134 rooms. 4 stories; exterior corridors. **Dining & Entertainment:** Dining room; 6:30 am-2 & 5-10
Motor Inn   pm; $6-$14; cocktails/lounge. **Services:** guest laundry. **All Rooms:** coffeemakers. Fee: movies.
     Some Rooms: refrigerators. **Cards:** AE, DI, DS, JCB, MC, VI. **Special Amenities:** Free breakfast and free
newspaper. *(See color ad below)*

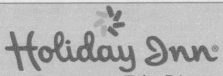

The best reservation is a *confirmed* reservation.

LAKE ERIE LODGE
◆◆ Motel
| | | Guaranteed Rates | | | | | | Phone: 814/833-9855 |

5/21-9/7 [CP] 1P: $63- 73 2P/1B: $63- 73 2P/2B: $82- 92 XP: $5-7
5/1-5/20 & 9/8-4/30 [CP] 1P: $46- 56 2P/1B: $46- 56 2P/2B: $56- 66 XP: $5-7
Location: I-79 exit 44B, 1.5 mi w on Rt 5, just n. 1015 Peninsula Dr 16505. Fax: 814/835-3493.
Terms: Reserv deposit; no pets. Facility: 19 rooms. 1 story; exterior corridors. Cards: MC, VI. *(See color ad p 279)*
🛇 CTV ⊠ D

MICROTEL ERIE
◆◆ Motel
Rates Subject to Change Phone: 814/864-1010
5/22-9/6 1P: $54 2P/1B: $54 XP: $4 F18
5/1-5/21, 9/7-11/1 &
3/30-4/30 1P: $40 2P/1B: $45 XP: $4 F18
11/2-3/29 1P: $35 2P/1B: $40 XP: $4 F18
Location: 0.3 mi s on SR 19 from I-90 exit 6. 8100 Peach St 16509. Fax: 814/866-6661. Terms: Pets, $4 extra charge.
Facility: 101 rooms. 3 stories; interior corridors. All Rooms: free & pay movies. Cards: AE, CB, DI, DS, MC, VI.
Roll in showers. 🛇 ECTV ⊠ 🎱 D S

RAMADA INN
AAA SAVE
◆◆ Motor Inn
Phone: 814/825-3100
5/23-9/8 & 12/30-12/31 1P: $80- 90 2P/1B: $80- 90 2P/2B: $80- 90 XP: $10 F18
9/9-10/31 1P: $65- 75 2P/1B: $65- 75 2P/2B: $65- 70 XP: $10 F18
5/1-5/22 & 3/1-4/30 1P: $55- 60 2P/1B: $55- 60 2P/2B: $55- 60 XP: $10 F18
11/1-12/29 & 1/1-2/28 1P: $49- 55 2P/1B: $49- 55 2P/2B: $49- 55 XP: $10 F18
Location: On SR 8, at I-90 exit 8. 6101 Wattsburg Rd 16509. Fax: 814/825-0857. Terms: Small pets only,
$10 extra charge. Facility: 122 rooms. 2 stories; interior corridors; wading pool, whirlpool; basketball & volleyball court.
Dining: Dining room; 6:30 am-1 & 5-9:30 pm; $6-$13; cocktails. Services: Fee: coin laundry. All Rooms: coffeemakers,
free movies. Some Rooms: Fee: VCR's. Cards: AE, CB, DI, DS, JCB, MC, VI. Special Amenities: Free newspaper and
free room upgrade (subject to availability with advanced reservations). 🛇 🛇 🛇 🛇 ⊠ D

RED ROOF INN
◆◆ Motel
Rates Subject to Change Phone: 814/868-5246
5/22-9/7 1P: $45- 79 2P/1B: $55- 79 2P/2B: $61- 79 XP: $10 F18
5/1-5/21 1P: $42- 54 2P/1B: $52- 61 2P/2B: $58- 79 XP: $10 F18
10/25-4/30 1P: $36- 48 2P/1B: $47- 55 2P/2B: $52- 79 XP: $10 F18
9/8-10/24 1P: $40- 51 2P/1B: $49- 58 2P/2B: $55- 79 XP: $10 F18
Location: On SR 97, at I-90 exit 7. 7865 Perry Hwy 16509. Fax: 814/868-5450. Terms: Small pets only. Facility: 110 rooms.
2 stories; interior/exterior corridors. All Rooms: free & pay movies. Cards: AE, CB, DI, DS, MC, VI. 🛇 ⊠ D

RESIDENCE INN BY MARRIOTT
◆◆◆ Suite Motel
Rates Subject to Change Phone: 814/864-2500
5/1-9/3 [CP] 1P: $99- 199 2P/1B: $99- 199 2P/2B: $169- 279
9/4-4/30 [CP] 1P: $89- 149 2P/1B: $89- 149 2P/2B: $139- 229
Location: I-90 exit 6, just s. 8061 Peach St 16509. Fax: 814/864-0688. Terms: Sr. discount; no pets.
Facility: 78 rooms. 3 stories; interior corridors. All Rooms: efficiencies, free movies. Cards: AE, CB, DI, DS, MC, VI.
Roll in showers. 🛇 🛇 🛇 ⊠ 🎱 D S

RODEWAY INN
AAA SAVE
◆◆ Motel
Phone: 814/899-1919
5/22-9/14 1P: $50- 80 2P/1B: $60- 90 2P/2B: $60- 90 XP: $5 F18
5/1-5/21 & 9/15-4/30 1P: $30- 40 2P/1B: $40- 50 2P/2B: $40- 50 XP: $5 F18
Location: Just n on SR 531 fromI-90, exit 10 at the Travel Port Truck Stop. 4050 Depot Rd 16510.
Fax: 814/899-7918. Terms: Pets, $8 extra charge. Facility: 36 rooms. 2 stories; exterior corridors.
Dining: Restaurant; 24 hours; $8-$10. All Rooms: coffeemakers. Some Rooms: radios. Cards: AE, DI, DS,
MC, VI. Special Amenities: Free local telephone calls and free newspaper. 🛇 ⊠ D

SPENCER HOUSE BED & BREAKFAST
AAA
◆
Bed & Breakfast
Rates Subject to Change Phone: 814/454-5984
All Year [BP] 1P: $70- 90 2P/1B: $75- 95 2P/2B: $75 XP: $15 F6
Location: W of downtown. 519 W 6th St 16507. Fax: 814/456-5091. Terms: Reserv deposit, 7 day notice;
no pets. Facility: 5 rooms. Handling fee imposed; 3 stories; interior corridors; smoke free premises.
Cards: AE, DS, MC, VI. CTV ⊠ D

SUPER 8 MOTEL
AAA SAVE
◆◆
Motor Inn
Phone: 814/864-9200
All Year 1P: $69- 99 2P/1B: $69- 99 2P/2B: $69- 99 XP: $6 F18
Location: On SR 97, at I-90 exit 7. 8040 Perry Hwy 16509. Fax: 814/864-3743. Terms: Weekly/monthly
rates; package plans; pets. Facility: 216 rooms. 2-4 stories; interior/exterior corridors. Dining: Dining room,
restaurant; 6:30 am-2 & 5-10 pm; $10-$22; cocktails. Services: valet laundry. Fee: childcare.
All Rooms: coffeemakers. Fee: movies. Some Rooms: 2 kitchens, no utensils. Fee: refrigerators.
Cards: AE, CB, DI, DS, JCB, MC, VI. Special Amenities: Free newspaper and free room upgrade (subject to
availability with advanced reservations). *(See color ad below)* 🛇 🛇 🛇 🛇 CTV ⊠ D

RESTAURANTS

THE MARKETPLACE GRILL   **Lunch:** $5-$7   **Dinner:** $7-$11   **Phone:** 814/455-7272
◆◆ **Location:** Just s of public docks. 319 State St 16507. **Hours:** 11:30 am-10 pm. Fri & Sat-11 pm. Closed
American major holidays & Sun. **Features:** children's menu; senior's menu; health conscious menu items; carryout;
cocktails & lounge; street parking; a la carte. Casual dining in renovated factory. Validated parking in Hamot
Parking on 3rd St. Daily lunch buffet, $3.95. **Cards:** AE, DI, DS, MC, VI. [⊠]

PUFFERBELLY ON FRENCH STREET   **Lunch:** $5-$8   **Dinner:** $9-$15   **Phone:** 814/454-1557
Ⓐ **Location:** Just se of public dock. 414 French St 16507. **Hours:** 11:30 am-9:30 pm, Fri & Sat-11 pm, Sun 11
am-8 pm. **Reservations:** suggested; for dinner. **Features:** casual dress; Sunday brunch; children's menu;
◆◆ health conscious menu items; carryout; cocktails & lounge; street parking. Historic 1907 fire station.
American **Cards:** AE, DS, MC, VI. [⊠]

ERWINNA—100

LODGING

GOLDEN PHEASANT INN   Guaranteed Rates   **Phone:** 610/294-9595
◆◆ All Year [CP]   1P: $75- 135   2P/1B: $85- 155   XP: $10
Historic **Location:** On SR 32, 0.5 mi n of jct of Dark Hollow Rd. 763 River Rd 18920. Fax: 610/294-9882.
Country Inn **Terms:** Age restrictions may apply; reserv deposit, 14 day notice; 2 night min stay, weekends; small pets
only. **Facility:** 6 rooms. 1-2 stories; interior/exterior corridors; smoke free premises. **Dining:** Dining room,
see separate listing. **Cards:** AE, CB, DI, DS, MC, VI. [🛏][⊠][D]

RESTAURANT

GOLDEN PHEASANT INN   Country Inn   **Dinner:** $21-$27   **Phone:** 610/294-9595
◆◆ **Location:** On SR 32, 0.5 mi n of jct of Dark Hollow Rd; in Golden Pheasant Inn. 763 River Rd 18920.
French **Hours:** 5:30 pm-10:30 pm, Sun 11 am-8 pm. Closed: Mon. **Reservations:** suggested. **Features:** dressy
casual; Sunday brunch; carryout; cocktails & lounge; a la carte. Classic French cuisine served in Historic
1857 mule-barge rest stop. Located between the Delaware River & canal. Features breast of pheasant normandy, rack of
lamb & crab cake brittany. Smoking permitted in lounge only. **Cards:** AE, CB, DI, DS, MC, VI. [⊠]

ESSINGTON—*See Philadelphia & Vicinity p. 376.*

EXTON—*See Philadelphia & Vicinity p. 377.*

FAIRFIELD—500—*See also GETTYSBURG.*

RESTAURANT

THE HISTORIC FAIRFIELD INN   Historical   **Lunch:** $5-$9   **Dinner:** $10-$16   **Phone:** 717/642-5410
◆◆ **Location:** Center, on SR 116. 15 W Main St 17320. **Hours:** 11 am-2 & 5-8:30 pm. Closed major holidays,
American Sun & Mon. **Reservations:** suggested; evenings. **Features:** casual dress; carryout; cocktails & lounge.
Historic inn circa 1757. 19th-century stagecoach stop. In operation since 1823. **Cards:** AE, MC, VI. [⊠]

FAIRVILLE—*See Philadelphia & Vicinity p. 377.*

FAYETTEVILLE—3,000

LODGING

WHITE SPOT MOTEL   Guaranteed Rates   **Phone:** 717/352-2144
Ⓐ 5/1-10/31 & 4/1-4/30   1P: $39   2P/1B: $42   2P/2B: $45   XP: $3
◆ 11/1-3/31   1P: $36   2P/1B: $38   2P/2B: $41   XP: $3
Motel **Location:** On US 30, 1 mi w of jct SR 997. 5651 Lincoln Way E 17222. **Terms:** Small pets only, $1 extra
charge. **Facility:** 20 rooms. 1 story; exterior corridors. **Dining:** Restaurant; 6 am-8 pm, Fri & Sat-9 pm, Sun
7 am-8 pm, Mon-2 pm; $6-$11. **Cards:** AE, DS, MC, VI. [🛏][ECTV][⊠][D]

FLEETWOOD—3,400

RESTAURANT

MOSELEM SPRINGS INN   **Lunch:** $4-$10   **Dinner:** $10-$19   **Phone:** 610/944-8213
◆◆ **Location:** On US 222 at jct SR 662. 19522. **Hours:** 11:30 am-9 pm, Fri & Sat-10 pm. Closed: 12/24 &
American 12/25. **Reservations:** accepted. **Features:** casual dress; cocktails & lounge. Colonial atmosphere of a
country inn. Featuring a variety of country smoked meat, smoked on premises since 1852. **Cards:** AE, CB,
DI, MC, VI. [⊠]

FOGELSVILLE—900

LODGINGS

CLOVERLEAF MOTEL   Rates Subject to Change   **Phone:** 610/395-3367
◆ All Year   2P/1B: $40- 47   2P/2B: $40- 47   XP: $4   F12
Motel **Location:** On SR 100, s of US 22, left first traffic light & immediate left on service road, at end of service
road. 327 Star Rd 18051 (PO Box 213). **Terms:** Reserv deposit; pets. **Facility:** 12 rooms. Weekend rates
higher 7/1-9/30; 1 story; exterior corridors. **Cards:** AE, DS, MC, VI. [🛏][ECTV][⊠][D]

GLASBERN   Rates Subject to Change   **Phone:** 610/285-4723
◆◆ Fri & Sat 9/16-11/16 [BP]   1P: $115- 375   2P/1B: $165- 375   2P/2B: $185- 375   XP: $20
Country Inn 5/1-9/15, Sun-Thurs
9/16-11/16 & 11/17-4/30 [BP]   1P: $100- 300   2P/1B: $115- 300   2P/2B: $140- 300   XP: $20
Location: From US 22/I-78, exit 14B (SR 100); 0.3 mi n to first light w on Main St, 0.6 mi w on Church St, 0.8 mi nw. 2141
Packhouse Rd 18051. Fax: 610/285-2862. **Terms:** Age restrictions may apply; check-in 4 pm; reserv deposit, 7 day notice; 2
night min stay, weekends; no pets. **Facility:** 22 rooms. Handling fee imposed; 2-3 stories; no elevator; interior/exterior corridors. **Dining:** Dining room, see separate listing. **All Rooms:** free movies. **Cards:** MC, VI. [🍴][CTV][⊠][D]

HAMPTON INN-ALLENTOWN   Rates Subject to Change   **Phone:** 610/391-1500
◆◆ All Year [CP]   1P: $68- 75   2P/1B: $73- 81   2P/2B: $73- 81
Motel **Location:** Jct SR 100 & US 22/I-78; exit 14A, 0.3 mi; Wm Penn Business Center. 7471 Keebler Way 18106.
Fax: 610/391-0386. **Terms:** Sr. discount; no pets. **Facility:** 124 rooms. 5 stories; interior corridors.
All Rooms: free & pay movies. **Cards:** AE, DI, DS, MC, VI. [CTV][🏋][⊠][🏊][D][S]

HOLIDAY INN CONFERENCE CENTER   Rates Subject to Change   Phone: 610/391-100
◆◆◆   All Year   1P: $103   2P/1B: $113   XP: $10   F1
Motor Inn   **Location:** 0.3 mi s of jct I-78 exit 14A & SR 100S. 7736 Adrian Dr 18031 (PO Box 22226, LEHIGH VALLE
18002). Fax: 610/391-1664. **Terms:** No pets. **Facility:** 182 rooms. 3 stories; interior corridors. **Dining:** Dinir
room; 6:30 am-10 pm; $10-$15. **All Rooms:** free & pay movies. **Cards:** AE, CB, DI, DS, MC, VI.

SLEEP INN   Phone: 610/395-660
Motel   Under construction; **Location:** On SR 100, s of I-78 (US 22), left 1st traffic light & immediate left on servic
road at end. 327 Star Rd 18051. **Terms:** Sr. discount; **Facility:** 62 rooms. 2 whirlpool rms, extra charge. Scheduled to open June 1998; 3 stories; interior corridors. **Cards:** AE, DS, MC, VI.   Roll in showers. CTV ⊗ D S

RESTAURANT

GLASBERN   Dinner: $24-$38   Phone: 610/285-472
◆◆◆   **Location:** From US 22/I-78 exit 14B (SR 100), 0.3 mi n to 1st light, w on Main St, 0.5 mi w on Church S
American   0.5 mi nw to Packhouse Rd, 1 mi nw; in Glasbern. 2141 Packhouse Rd 18051. **Hours:** 6 pm-8 pr
Reservations: required. **Features:** dressy casual; cocktails. American cuisine served in idyllic great hall of
country inn converted from a 19th-century, post-and- beam German bank barn. Smoke free premises. **Cards:** MC, VI.

FOX CHAPEL—See Pittsburgh & Vicinity p. 409.

FRACKVILLE—4,700

LODGINGS

ECONO LODGE   Phone: 717/874-383
AAA SAVE   All Year [CP]   1P: $36- 76   2P/1B: $40- 76 2P/2B: $40- 76 XP: $5   F1
Location: On SR 61N, exit 36W off I-81. 501 S Middle St 17931. Fax: 717/874-4660. **Terms:** No pet
◆◆   **Facility:** 39 rooms. 2 stories; exterior corridors. **Dining:** Restaurant nearby. **All Rooms:** free movie
Motel   **Cards:** AE, CB, DI, DS, JCB, MC, VI. **Special Amenities:** Free breakfast and free local telephone calls.

CTV ⊗

GRANNY'S BUDGET HOST INN   Rates Subject to Change   Phone: 717/874-040
AAA   All Year   1P: $37- 41   2P/1B: $41- 45 2P/2B: $41- 45 XP: $3   F
Location: I-81, exit 36W, 03. mi nw on SR 61, 0.3 mi n on Altamont Blvd. 115 W Coal St 1793
◆◆   Fax: 717/874-1872. **Terms:** Pets, $25 dep req. **Facility:** 34 rooms. 2 stories; interior/exterior corridor
Motor Inn   **Dining:** Restaurant; 6 am-9:30 pm; $7-$10. **All Rooms:** free movies. **Cards:** AE, DI, DS, MC, VI.
(See color ad p 254)

MOTEL 6   Rates Subject to Change   Phone: 717/874-122
AAA   All Year   1P: $40   2P/1B: $45   2P/2B: $45   XP: $6
Location: Off I-81 via exit 36W, 0.3 mi nw on SR 61, 0.3 mi n. 701 Altamont Blvd 17931 (PO Box D
◆◆   Fax: 717/874-0297. **Terms:** No pets. **Facility:** 55 rooms. 1-2 stories; interior/exterior corridors. **Cards:** A
Motel   DS, MC, VI.   CTV ⊗

FRANKLIN (VENANGO COUNTY)

LODGINGS

IDLEWOOD MOTEL   Phone: 814/437-300
AAA SAVE   All Year   1P: $28   2P/1B: $31   2P/2B: $34   XP: $3   F
Location: 1.5 mi s on US 62 & SR 8. (RD 5, Box 640, FRANKLIN, 16323). **Terms:** Reserv deposit; week
◆   rates; no pets. **Facility:** 17 rooms. Efficiency unit, $37 for up to 2 persons; exterior corridors; luxury lev
Motel   rooms. **Dining:** Restaurant nearby. **All Rooms:** combo or shower baths. **Cards:** AE, DI, DS, MC, V
Special Amenities: Free local telephone calls and preferred room (subject to availability wi
advanced reservations).   CTV

THE INN AT FRANKLIN   Phone: 814/437-303
AAA SAVE   All Year [CP]   1P: $60   2P/1B: $65   2P/2B: $70   XP: $5   F
Location: Center; on US 62 & SR 8. 1411 Liberty St 16323. Fax: 814/432-7481. **Terms:** Small pets on
◆◆ $10 extra charge. **Facility:** 82 rooms. 6 stories; interior corridors. **Dining & Entertainment:** Dining room;
Motor Inn   am-2 & 5-10 pm; $8-$16; cocktails/lounge. **Services:** valet laundry. **Fee:** movie
Some Rooms: refrigerators. **Cards:** AE, CB, DI, DS, JCB, MC, VI. **Special Amenities:** Free breakfast ar
free room upgrade (subject to availability with advanced reservations).

QUO VADIS BED & BREAKFAST   Rates Subject to Change   Phone: 814/432-420
AAA   All Year [BP]   1P: $60- 80   2P/1B: $60- 80 2P/2B: $80   XP: $10
Location: Corner of 15th & Liberty sts. In historic district. 1501 Liberty St 16323. **Terms:** Reserv deposit,
◆◆   day notice; no pets. **Facility:** 6 rooms. 2 stories; interior corridors. **Cards:** AE, MC, VI.   ⊗
Bed &
Breakfast

FRAZER (CHESTER COUNTY)—See Philadelphia & Vicinity p. 377.

FRYSTOWN—200

LODGING

MOTEL OF FRYSTOWN   Guaranteed Rates   Phone: 717/933-46
◆   All Year   1P: $32   2P/1B: $37   2P/2B: $42   XP: $5   F
Motel   **Location:** Jct I-78 & SR 645 exit 2, just e on service road. 90 Fort Motel Dr 17067. **Terms:** Pets. **Facility:**
rooms. 1 story; exterior corridors. **Cards:** AE, DS, MC, VI.

GALETON—1,400

LODGING

PINE LOG MOTEL   Rates Subject to Change   Phone: 814/435-64
AAA   All Year   1P: $37   2P/1B: $40- 45 2P/2B: $45- 50 XP: $6
Location: 9 mi w. 5156 US Rt 6 W 16948 (PO Box 151, 16922). Fax: 814/435-8539. **Terms:** Sr. discou
◆   pets. **Facility:** 10 rooms. 1 story; exterior corridors. **All Rooms:** free movies, no A/C. **Cards:** AE, DS, M
Motel   VI.

GETTYSBURG—7,000—*See also CASHTOWN, FAIRFIELD & ORRTANNA.*

LODGINGS

APPLEFORD INN Rates Subject to Change **Phone:** 717/337-1711
5/1-12/31 & Fri & Sat
1/1-4/30 [BP] 1P: $80- 95 2P/1B: $95- 140 2P/2B: $105- 150 XP: $15
Sun-Thurs 1/1-4/30 [BP] 1P: $70- 85 2P/1B: $85- 110 2P/2B: $95- 120 XP: $10
Location: Just n on US 15 business route. 218 Carlisle St 17325. Fax: 717/334-6228. **Terms:** Sr. discount; age restrictions may apply; reserv deposit, 10 day notice; 2 night min stay, weekends 4/1-10/31; no pets. **Facility:** 10 rooms. 3 stories, no elevator; interior corridors; smoke free premises. **Cards:** AE, DS, MC, VI.

(Historic Bed & Breakfast)

BALADERRY INN AT GETTYSBURG **Phone:** 717/337-1342
All Year [BP] 1P: $84- 102 2P/1B: $94- 112 2P/2B: $97 XP: $15
Location: US 15, 1.1 mi se on SR 97, just sw on McAllister Mill Rd, 0.5 mi s on Blacksmith Shop Rd, then just s. 40 Hospital Rd 17325. Fax: 717/337-1342. **Terms:** Age restrictions may apply; reserv deposit, 5 day notice; package plans; 2 night min stay, weekends 4/1-11/30; no pets. **Facility:** 8 rooms. Charming rooms on 4 quiet country acres adjacent to the battlefields. 2 stories; interior corridors; smoke free premises; 1 tennis court. **All Rooms:** combo or shower baths. **Cards:** AE, CB, DI, DS, MC, VI. **Special Amenities:** Free local telephone calls and free room upgrade (subject to availability with advanced reservations).

(Historic Bed & Breakfast)

BEST WESTERN GETTYSBURG HOTEL EST. 1797 **Phone:** 717/337-2000
10/1-10/31 1P: $90- 150 2P/1B: $90- 150 2P/2B: $90- 150
7/1-8/31 1P: $92- 150 2P/1B: $99- 150 2P/2B: $99- 150 XP: $5 F16
5/1-6/30, 9/1-9/30 &
11/1-4/30 1P: $79- 135 2P/1B: $79- 135 2P/2B: $79- 135 XP: $5 F16
Location: Center. 1 Lincoln Sq 17325. Fax: 717/337-2075. **Terms:** Package plans; no pets. **Facility:** 83 rooms. Completely restored historic hotel; stylish traditional lobby & comfortable rooms. Some units with gas fireplace. 6 stories; interior corridors; video rental library, outdoor facilities at Gettysburg College. **Dining:** Dining room; 7 am-10:30 & 5-9 pm; $14-$18; cocktails. **Services:** valet laundry. **Recreation:** jogging. **Some Rooms:** whirlpools. Fee: refrigerators, VCR's. **Cards:** AE, CB, DI, DS, JCB, MC, VI. **Special Amenities:** Free local telephone calls and free room upgrade (subject to availability with advanced reservations). *(See color ad p 284)*

(Historic Hotel)

BLUE SKY MOTEL Guaranteed Rates **Phone:** 717/677-7736
6/12-8/29 2P/1B: $49 2P/2B: $54 XP: $4
5/1-6/11, 8/30-10/31 &
4/1-4/30 2P/1B: $38 2P/2B: $39 XP: $4
11/1-3/31 2P/1B: $29 2P/2B: $34 XP: $4
Location: 4.5 mi n on SR 34. 2585 Biglerville Rd 17325. Fax: 717/677-6794. **Terms:** No pets. **Facility:** 16 rooms. 1 story; exterior corridors. **Some Rooms:** efficiency. **Cards:** AE, CB, DI, DS, MC, VI. *(See color ad below)*

(Motel)

THE BRAFFERTON INN Rates Subject to Change **Phone:** 717/337-3423
All Year [BP] 2P/1B: $90- 125 2P/2B: $90- 125 XP: $10 D
Location: Just e on US 30. 44 York St 17325. **Terms:** Age restrictions may apply; 2 night min stay, weekends 4/1-11/30; no pets. **Facility:** 10 rooms. 1-3 stories, no elevator; interior corridors; smoke free premises. Fee: parking. **Cards:** AE, DS, MC, VI.

(Historic Bed & Breakfast)

BUDGET HOST THREE CROWNS MOTOR LODGE Rates Subject to Change **Phone:** 717/334-3168
6/19-8/22 1P: $62 2P/1B: $62 2P/2B: $62 XP: $5 F12
5/22-6/18 & 8/23-10/17 1P: $45 2P/1B: $50 2P/2B: $50 XP: $5 F12
5/1-5/21 & 4/2-4/30 1P: $40 2P/1B: $45 2P/2B: $45 XP: $5 F12
10/18-4/1 1P: $30 2P/1B: $35 2P/2B: $35 XP: $5 F12
Location: 0.5 mi s on US 15 business route, at jct SR 134. 205 Steinwehr Ave 17325. **Terms:** Sr. discount; no pets. **Facility:** 29 rooms. 1 story; exterior corridors. **Cards:** AE, DS, MC, VI. *(See color ad p 284 & p 254)*

(Motel)

DON'T WAIT FOR THE BIG CHILL.
Check the blanket supply in your room when you arrive;
you might not be able to get extras during the night.

COLLEGE MOTEL   **Phone:** 717/334-673
AAA SAVE   6/13-9/6   2P/1B: $68- 88 2P/2B: $68- 88 XP: $5   F1
           9/7-11/1   2P/1B: $58- 88 2P/2B: $58- 88 XP: $5   F1
◆◆   5/1-6/12   2P/1B: $49- 76 2P/2B: $49- 76 XP: $5   F1
Motel   11/2-4/30   2P/1B: $39- 68 2P/2B: $39- 68 XP: $5   F1
           Location: 0.4 mi n on US 15 business route. 345 Carlisle St 17325. **Terms:** Reserv deposit; no pets
Facility: 21 rooms. Handling fee imposed; 1 story; exterior corridors. **Cards:** AE, MC, VI.   ⟨ECTV⟩ ⟨✕⟩ ⟨C

COLONIAL MOTEL   **Phone:** 717/334-312
AAA SAVE   6/13-9/6   2P/1B: $64- 88 2P/2B: $64- 88 XP: $5   F1
           9/7-11/1   2P/1B: $58- 88 2P/2B: $58- 88 XP: $5   F1
◆◆   5/1-6/12   2P/1B: $49- 76 2P/2B: $49- 76 XP: $5   F1
Motel   11/2-4/30   2P/1B: $39- 68 2P/2B: $39- 68 XP: $5   F1
           Location: Just n on US 15 business route. 157 Carlisle St 17325. **Terms:** Reserv deposit; no pets
Facility: 30 rooms. Handling fee imposed; 2 stories; exterior corridors. **Cards:** AE, MC, VI.   ⟨ECTV⟩ ⟨✕⟩ ⟨C

THE COLTON MOTEL   Rates Subject to Change   **Phone:** 717/334-551
AAA   6/19-8/22   1P: $52- 65 2P/1B: $52- 65 2P/2B: $52- 65 XP: $5   F1
           5/22-6/18 & 8/23-10/17   1P: $40- 48 2P/1B: $40- 48 2P/2B: $40- 48 XP: $5   F1
◆   5/1-5/21 & 4/2-4/30   1P: $35- 48 2P/1B: $35- 48 2P/2B: $35- 48 XP: $5   F1
Motel   10/18-4/1   1P: $29- 34 2P/1B: $29- 34 2P/2B: $29- 34 XP: $5   F1
           Location: On US 15 business route, just s of jct SR 134. 232 Steinwehr Ave 17325. **Terms:** Reserv depos
3 day notice; small pets only, $5 extra charge. **Facility:** 25 rooms. 4 oversized rms, $42-$135 sleeps 6-8 persons; 1-2 storie
exterior corridors. **Cards:** AE, DS, MC, VI. *(See ad p 285)*   ⟨🛏⟩ ⟨➔⟩ ⟨ECTV⟩ ⟨✕⟩ ⟨C

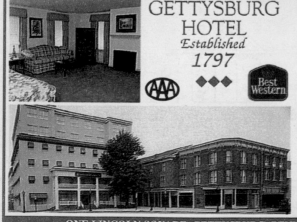

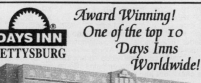

COMFORT INN Phone: 717/337-24•

🆎 SAVE   6/12-9/6 [CP]   1P: $90- 95   2P/1B: $89- 95 2P/2B: $89- 95 XP: $7   F
          5/1-6/11 & 9/7-10/31 [CP] 1P: $75- 79   2P/1B: $75- 79 2P/2B: $75- 79 XP: $7   F
◆◆◆   4/1-4/30 [CP]   1P: $69- 79   2P/1B: $69- 79 2P/2B: $69- 79 XP: $7   F
Motel   11/1-3/31 [CP]   1P: $47- 55   2P/1B: $47- 55 2P/2B: $47- 55 XP: $7   F
          Location: 1 mi e on US 30. 871 York Rd 17325. Fax: 717/337-0831. **Terms:** Reserv deposit; package plan;
no pets. **Facility:** 81 rooms. Contemporary rooms. 3 whirlpool rms, $69-$140 for up to 2 persons; 2 stories; interior corridor,
whirlpool. **Dining:** Restaurant nearby. **All Rooms:** free movies. **Some Rooms:** Fee: microwaves, refrigerators. **Cards:** A
CB, DI, DS, JCB, MC, VI. **Special Amenities:** Free breakfast and free newspaper. (➔) (🏍) ECTV (X) (D) (

DAYS INN GETTYSBURG   Rates Subject to Change   Phone: 717/334-00
◆◆◆   6/6-9/1 & 10/1-11/2   1P: $80- 95   2P/1B: $90- 105 2P/2B: $90- 100 XP: $5   F
Motel   5/1-6/5 & 9/2-9/30   1P: $67- 85   2P/1B: $78- 95 2P/2B: $78- 95 XP: $5   F
          4/1-4/30   1P: $61- 76   2P/1B: $71- 90 2P/2B: $72- 82 XP: $5   F
          11/3-3/31   1P: $54- 68   2P/1B: $60- 75 2P/2B: $60- 75 XP: $5   F
Location: 1 mi e on US 30. 865 York Rd 17325. Fax: 717/337-1002. **Terms:** No pets. **Facility:** 112 rooms. 3 whirlpool rm
$110-$150 for up to 2 persons; 5 stories; interior corridors. **All Rooms:** free movies. **Cards:** AE, CB, DI, DS, JCB, MC, VI.
(See ad p 285) (➔) ECTV (X) (D) (

ECONO LODGE   Phone: 717/334-67
🆎 SAVE   6/5-10/31 [CP]   1P: $55- 75   2P/1B: $55- 89 2P/2B: $59- 89 XP: $5   F
          5/1-6/4 [CP]   1P: $45- 66   2P/1B: $45- 66 2P/2B: $49- 66 XP: $5   F
◆   11/1-4/30 [CP]   1P: $36- 39   2P/1B: $36- 45 2P/2B: $39- 49 XP: $5   F
Motel   **Location:** 0.5 mi s on SR 97. 945 Baltimore Pike 17325. Fax: 717/334-6580. **Terms:** No pets. **Facility:**
          rooms. 1-2 stories; interior/exterior corridors. **Dining:** Restaurant nearby. **Some Rooms:** radios. **Cards:** A
DI, DS, MC, VI. **Special Amenities:** Free breakfast and free local telephone calls. *(See ad p 285)* (➔) ECTV (X) (

EISENHOWER INN AND CONFERENCE CENTER   Rates Subject to Change   Phone: 717/334-81
◆◆   5/1-10/31 & 4/1-4/30   1P: $87- 130   2P/2B: $87- 130 XP: $7   F
Motor Inn 11/1-3/31   1P: $73- 120   2P/2B: $73- 120 XP: $7   F
          Location: 5 mi s on US 15 business route. 2634 Emmitsburg Rd 17325. Fax: 717/334-6066. **Terms:**
discount; no pets. **Facility:** 203 rooms. 2 stories; interior corridors. **Dining:** Restaurant, deli; 7 am-2 & 5-9:30 pm; $9-$
All Rooms: free movies. **Cards:** AE, DI, DS, MC, VI. (➔) (CTV) (X) (

THE GASLIGHT INN   Phone: 717/337-91
🆎 SAVE   Fri & Sat 5/1-11/14 &
          4/1-4/30 [BP]   1P: $110- 140   2P/1B: $110- 140 2P/2B: $140   XP: $20
◆◆◆   Sun-Thurs 5/1-11/14, Fri &
Historic Bed Sat 11/15-3/31 & Sun-Thurs
& Breakfast   4/1-4/30 [BP]   1P: $100- 130   2P/1B: $100- 130 2P/2B: $130   XP: $20
          Sun-Thurs 11/15-3/31 [BP] 1P: $85- 115   2P/1B: $85- 115 2P/2B: $115   XP: $20
Location: Just s on US 15 business route from jct US 30, then just e. 33 E Middle St 17325. Fax: 717/337-96
Terms: Age restrictions may apply; reserv deposit, 8 day notice; weekly/monthly rates; package plans; 2 night min st
weekends 10/1-10/31; no pets. **Facility:** 8 rooms. Charming, cheerful 1872 Victorian with contemporary furnishings & mode
conveniences; including color cable TV/VCR's on request, some gas fireplaces & some rooms with steam showers. Handl
fee imposed; 3 stories, no elevator; interior corridors; smoke free premises; small video library. **Dining:** Dinner avail
guests Mon-Sat with 24 hr notice; restaurant nearby. **All Rooms:** combo or shower baths. **Some Rooms:** whirlpoo
Cards: AE, DS, MC, VI. **Special Amenities:** Early check-in/late check-out and free local telephone calls. (🏍) (X) (

GETTYSTOWN INN BED & BREAKFAST   Rates Subject to Change   Phone: 717/334-21
◆◆   5/1-11/30 & 3/13-4/30 [BP]   2P/1B: $85- 105   XP: $6
Historic 12/1-3/12 [BP]   2P/1B: $55- 75   XP: $6
Country Inn **Location:** Just n of jct SR 134 & US 15 business route. 89 Steinwehr Ave 17325. Fax: 717/334-69
          Terms: Sr. discount; age restrictions may apply; reserv deposit; no pets. **Facility:** 5 rooms. 2 stori
interior/exterior corridors; smoke free premises. **Dining:** Springhouse Tavern at the Dobbin House, see separate listi
Cards: AE, MC, VI. *(See ad p 285)* ECTV (X) (

AMPTON INN
Phone: 717/338-9121

5/1-10/31 [CP]	1P:	$69- 169	2P/1B:	$69- 169	2P/2B:	$69- 169	XP: $8	F18
11/1-4/30 [CP]	1P:	$49- 109	2P/1B:	$49- 109	2P/2B:	$49- 109	XP: $8	F18

Location: Just w on US 30 from jct US 15. 1280 York Rd 17325. Fax: 171/338-9180. **Terms:** No pets. **Facility:** 77 rooms. Thoroughly modern. 8 king 'studies' with separate work area & sleeper sofa. 4 two-bedroom units. 8 whirlpool rms, extra charge; 4 stories; interior corridors; whirlpool. **Dining:** Restaurant arby. **Services:** Fee: coin laundry. **All Rooms:** free movies. **Some Rooms:** microwaves, refrigerators. **Cards:** AE, DI, DS, C, VI. **Special Amenities:** Free breakfast and free local telephone calls. *(See color ad below)*
Roll in showers.

ERITAGE MOTOR LODGE
Phone: 717/334-9281

Rates Subject to Change

6/1-12/1	1P:	$56- 85	2P/1B:	$56- 60	2P/2B:	$65- 85	XP: $10
5/1-5/31 & 4/1-4/30	1P:	$47- 64	2P/1B:	$50- 55	2P/2B:	$58- 64	XP: $10
12/2-3/31	1P:	$47- 54	2P/1B:	$47- 54	2P/2B:	$47- 54	XP: $10

Location: Just sw on SR 97 from jct US 15 business route. 64 Steinwehr Ave 17325. **Terms:** Reserv deposit; small pets only, $5 extra charge. **Facility:** 35 rooms. Handling fee imposed; 1-2 stories; terior/exterior corridors. **All Rooms:** free movies. **Cards:** AE, DS, MC, VI.
Roll in showers.

ERR TAVERN & PUBLICK HOUSE
Phone: 717/334-4332

All Year [BP]	1P:	$65- 170	2P/1B:	$65- 170	XP: $10

Location: 1.5 mi w on US 30. 900 Chambersburg Rd 17325. Fax: 717/334-3332. **Terms:** Age restrictions may apply; check-in 4 pm; reserv deposit; weekly rates; no pets. **Facility:** 12 rooms. Restored 19th century public house with extensive modern addition. Some rooms very spacious. Handling fee imposed; 3 stories, no elevator; interior corridors; designated smoking area. **Dining & Entertainment:** Cocktail lounge; afternoon tea; dining room, see separate listing. **All Rooms:** combo or shower baths. **Some Rooms:** microwaves, frigerators, VCR's, whirlpools. **Cards:** AE, DS, MC, VI. **Special Amenities:** Free breakfast and free newspaper. ee color ad below)

OLIDAY INN-BATTLEFIELD
Phone: 717/334-6211

Rates Subject to Change

5/1-9/6 & 4/1-4/30	1P:	$89- 110	2P/1B:	$89- 110	2P/2B:	$89- 110	XP: $7	F19
9/7-10/31	1P:	$79- 110	2P/1B:	$79- 110	2P/2B:	$79- 110	XP: $7	F19
11/1-3/31	1P:	$59- 89	2P/1B:	$59- 89	2P/2B:	$59- 89	XP: $7	F19

cation: At jct US 15 business route & SR 97. 516 Baltimore St 17325. Fax: 717/334-7183. **Terms:** Pets. **Facility:** 102 oms. 5 stories; exterior corridors. **Dining:** Restaurant; 7 am-10 pm, Sun 7 am-2 & 5-10 pm; $12-$20. **All Rooms:** free ovies. **Cards:** AE, CB, DI, DS, JCB, MC, VI.
Roll in showers.

– OPENED IN JULY 1996 –

- 75 Rooms – Suites – Family Rooms
- Free Continental Breakfast
- Indoor Pool – Jacuzzi
- Exercise Room – Spa
- King & Queen Beds
- Beautifully Landscaped
- Smoking & Non-Smoking Rooms
- Kids Stay Free

100% SATISFACTION GUARANTEED
1280 YORK RD. RT 30 EAST
717-338-9121
GETTYSBURG

the Herr Tavern & Publick House

717-334-4332
herrtav@cvn.net
Route 30 West (1 mile) Gettysburg
Call **1-800-362-9494** for Reservations

Circa 1815
- Relaxed dining with American Cuisine
- Lodging in the first Confederate hospital
- Jacuzzi tubs, fireplaces, and queen size beds
- Adjacent lounge with beach volleyball
- room discounts

HOLIDAY INN EXPRESS OF GETTYSBURG
Phone: 717/337-14(

(AAA) (SAVE)
5/1-10/31 & 4/1-4/30 [CP]   1P: $70- 109   2P/1B: $70- 109   2P/2B: $70- 109   XP: $10   F
11/1-3/31 [CP]   1P: $45- 69   2P/1B: $45- 69   2P/2B: $45- 69   XP: $10   F
◆◆◆   **Location:** 1 mi e on US 30. 869 York Rd 17325. Fax: 717/337-0159. **Terms:** No pets. **Facility:** 51 room
Motel   Contemporary rooms. 2 stories; interior corridors; whirlpool. **Dining:** Restaurant nearby. **Services:** va
laundry. **All Rooms:** free movies. **Some Rooms:** efficiency, no utensils. Fee: microwaves, refrigerato
Cards: AE, CB, DI, DS, JCB, MC, VI. **Special Amenities: Free breakfast and free local telephone calls.**

HOMESTEAD MOTOR LODGE   Rates Subject to Change   Phone: 717/334-38(
(AAA)   6/9-9/5   2P/1B: $49- 65   2P/2B: $58- 69   XP: $6
◆   5/1-6/8, 9/6-11/30 & 4/1-4/30   2P/1B: $39- 49   2P/2B: $46- 59   XP: $6
Motel   **Location:** On US 30, 0.5 mi e of jct US 15 bypass. 1650 York Rd 17325. **Terms:** Sr. discount; Op
5/1-11/30 & 4/1-4/30; no pets. **Facility:** 10 rooms. 1 story; exterior corridors; smoke free premise
Cards: AE, DS, MC, VI.

HOWARD JOHNSON INN   Rates Subject to Change   Phone: 717/334-118
(AAA)   5/1-11/21 & 3/26-4/30   1P: $60- 100   2P/1B: $60- 100   2P/2B: $60- 100
11/22-3/25   1P: $38- 40   2P/1B: $48- 50   2P/2B: $48- 50
◆◆   **Location:** 1 mi s on US 15 business route; just s of jct SR 134. 301 Steinwehr Ave 1732
Motel   Fax: 717/334-1188. **Terms:** Sr. discount; small pets only. **Facility:** 77 rooms. 2 stories; interior/exterior co
dors. **All Rooms:** free movies. **Some Rooms:** efficiency. **Cards:** AE, CB, DI, DS, MC, VI. *(See ad p 80)*

JAMES GETTYS HOTEL   Phone: 717/337-133
(AAA) (SAVE)
5/1-11/30 & 3/15-4/30 [CP]   1P: $115- 135   2P/1B: $115- 135   2P/2B: $115- 135   XP: $15   F
12/1-3/14 [CP]   1P: $85- 105   2P/1B: $85- 105   2P/2B: $85- 105   XP: $15   F
◆◆◆   **Location:** Just w on US 30. 27 Chambersburg St 17325. Fax: 717/334-2103. **Terms:** Reserv deposit; week
Historic Bed   rates; no pets. **Facility:** 11 rooms. Small hotel with almost 200 years of rich Gettysburg history. On Natior
& Breakfast   Register of Historic Places. 4 stories; interior corridors; smoke free premises. **Dining:** Restaurant near
Services: valet laundry. **All Rooms:** coffeemakers, efficiencies, microwaves, refrigerators, combo or show
baths. **Some Rooms:** VCR's. **Cards:** AE, DS, MC, VI. **Special Amenities: Free breakfast and free room upgra
(subject to availability with advanced reservations).**

QUALITY INN GETTYSBURG MOTOR LODGE   Rates Subject to Change   Phone: 717/334-11(
◆◆◆   5/1-11/21 & 3/26-4/30   1P: $63- 126   2P/1B: $63- 126   2P/2B: $63- 126
Motel   11/22-3/25   1P: $40- 50   2P/1B: $50- 70   2P/2B: $50- 70
Location: 1 mi s on US 15 business route, just s of jct SR 134. 380 Steinwehr Ave 1732
Fax: 717/334-1103. **Terms:** Sr. discount; small pets only. **Facility:** 109 rooms. 2 stories; interior/exterior corrido
All Rooms: free movies. **Cards:** AE, CB, DI, DS, JCB, MC, VI. *(See ad p 80)*

QUALITY INN LARSON'S   Phone: 717/334-31
(AAA) (SAVE)
5/1-11/1 & 3/27-4/30 [CP]   1P: $60- 86   2P/1B: $60- 86   2P/2B: $66- 86   XP: $5   F
11/2-3/26 [CP]   1P: $42- 78   2P/1B: $46- 78   2P/2B: $49- 78   XP: $5   F
◆◆◆   **Location:** 0.8 mi w on US 30. 401 Buford Ave 17325. Fax: 717/334-1813. **Terms:** Package plans; no pe
Motor Inn   **Facility:** 41 rooms. Free admission to General Lee's Headquarters Museum on premises. Quiet setting ad
cent to battlefield. 1 whirlpool rm, extra charge; 1 story; exterior corridors. **Dining:** Muldoon's Grill, s
separate listing. **Services:** valet laundry. **Some Rooms:** refrigerators. **Cards:** AE, CB, DI, DS, JCB, MC,
Special Amenities: Free breakfast and free newspaper.

RED CARPET INN-PERFECT REST MOTEL   Phone: 717/334-13(
(AAA) (SAVE)
6/1-9/3   1P: $50   2P/1B: $55   2P/2B: $60- 69   XP: $5
5/10-5/31 & 9/4-10/31   1P: $46   2P/1B: $50   2P/2B: $58   XP: $5
◆   5/1-5/9 & 3/29-4/30   1P: $38- 40   2P/1B: $42- 44   2P/2B: $46- 48   XP: $5
Motel   11/1-3/28   1P: $34   2P/1B: $38   2P/2B: $42   XP: $5
Location: 4.5 mi s on US 15 business route. 2450 Emmitsburg Rd 17325. Fax: 717/334-50:
Terms: Reserv deposit; weekly rates; no pets. **Facility:** 25 rooms. Quiet setting bordered by farmland. 1 two-bedroom un
Handling fee imposed; 1 story; exterior corridors. **All Rooms:** free movies. **Some Rooms:** refrigerators. **Cards:** AE, CB,
DS, MC, VI. **Special Amenities: Free local telephone calls and preferred room (subject to availability with advanc
reservations).** *(See ad p 285)*

RESTAURANTS

ALEXANDER DOBBIN DINING ROOMS
IN THE DOBBIN HOUSE TAVERN   Historical   **Dinner:** $17-$22   Phone: 717/334-21
◆◆◆   **Location:** Just n of jct SR 134 & US 15 business route; adjacent to Gettysburg Inn Bed & Breakfast.
American   Steinwehr Ave 17325. **Hours:** 5 pm-9 pm. Closed major holidays. **Reservations:** required. **Features:** cas
dress; children's menu; cocktails; minimum charge-$7.50; also prix fixe. Relaxed fine dining in cozy histo
rooms, areas dating as far back as 1776. Excellent roast duck. Smoke free premises. **Cards:** AE, MC, VI.

FARNSWORTH HOUSE   Historical   **Dinner:** $13-$18   Phone: 717/334-88
(AAA)   **Location:** Just s on US 15 business route; in Farnsworth House Inn. 401 Baltimore St 17325. **Hours:**
pm-9:30 pm; noon-3 pm 7/1-9/1. Closed: 1/1, 11/26 & 12/25. **Reservations:** suggested. **Features:** cas
◆◆   dress; children's menu; cocktails & lounge. Civil War period house with bullet holes. Lunch served in summ
American   garden. **Cards:** AE, DS, MC, VI.

THE HERR TAVERN & PUBLICK HOUSE   Historical   **Lunch:** $5-$8   **Dinner:** $14-$20   Phone: 717/334-43
(AAA)   **Location:** 1.5 mi w on US 30; in Herr Tavern & Publick House. 900 Chambersburg Rd 17325. **Hours:**
am-9 pm, Fri 11 am-3 & 5-9 pm, Sat 11:30 am-3 & 5-9 Pm, Sun from 5 pm. Closed major holida
◆◆◆   **Reservations:** suggested; weekends. **Features:** casual dress; children's menu; carryout; cocktails & loun
American   Relaxed dining in comfortable atmosphere of 1816 public house with some modern additions. **Cards:** /
DS, MC, VI. *(See color ad p 287)*

MULDOON'S GRILL   **Lunch:** $3-$6   **Dinner:** $5-$12   Phone: 717/334-22
(AAA)   **Location:** 0.8 mi w on US 30; in Quality Inn Larson's. 401 Buford Ave 17325. **Hours:** 11 am-9 pm. Clos
12/25. **Reservations:** accepted. **Features:** casual dress; children's menu; carryout; cocktails & lounge. Ir
◆◆   pub setting. **Cards:** AE, DS, MC, VI.
American

SPRINGHOUSE TAVERN AT THE DOBBIN HOUSE   Historical **Lunch:** $5-$16   **Dinner:** $7-$16   **Phone:** 717/334-2100
(AAA)   **Location:** Just n of jct SR 134 & US 15 business route; in Gettystown Inn Bed & Breakfast. 89 Steinwehr
◆◆   Ave 17325. **Hours:** 11:30 am-10 pm. Closed major holidays. **Features:** casual dress; children's menu;
American   cocktails & lounge. Unique ambience in cozy tavern circa 1776. Once a slave hideout & Civil War hospital.
Sandwiches, salads, ribs, steak & "pecan pye". Smoke free premises. **Cards:** AE, MC, VI. *(See ad p 285)*
[X]

WHIT'S LANDING   **Lunch:** $4-$9   **Dinner:** $10-$22   **Phone:** 717/337-9611
◆◆   **Location:** 0.8 mi s on US 15 business route. 226 Steinwehr Ave 17325. **Hours:** 11 am-8 pm. Closed: Mon,
American   Tues & 12/22-1/3. **Features:** casual dress; carryout; cocktails. Relaxed dining with nautical theme. Features
seafood selections. **Cards:** AE, CB, DI, DS, MC, VI.   [X]

GIBSONIA—*See Pittsburgh & Vicinity p. 409.*

GINTHER—200

LODGING

PINES MOTEL   Rates Subject to Change   **Phone:** 717/668-0100
◆   Fri & Sat 5/1-10/31   1P: $35- 45   2P/1B: $38-   45   2P/2B: $45-   65   XP: $5   F12
Motel   Sun-Thurs 5/1-10/31   1P: $35   2P/1B: $38   2P/2B: $42   XP: $5   F12
11/1-4/30   1P: $28   2P/1B: $32   2P/2B: $38   XP: $5   F12
Location: 2 mi s on SR 309 from I-81 exit 39 (McAdoo/Tamaqua). SR 309 18252 (RD 4 Box 349A, TAMAQUA). **Terms:** No
pets. **Facility:** 20 rooms. 1 story; exterior corridors. **All Rooms:** free movies. **Cards:** AE, DS, MC, VI.   [icons]

GLENSIDE—*See Philadelphia & Vicinity p. 378.*

GRANTVILLE—800

LODGINGS

ECONO LODGE   **Phone:** 717/469-0631
(AAA) (SAVE)   5/1-9/30 & 4/1-4/30 [CP]   1P: $45-   65   2P/1B: $45-   65   2P/2B: $45-   65   XP: $5   F18
10/1-3/31 [CP]   1P: $40-   50   2P/1B: $40-   50   2P/2B: $40-   50   XP: $5   F18
◆◆   **Location:** I-81, exit 28. 252 Bow Creek Rd 17028. Fax: 717/469-0843. **Terms:** No pets. **Facility:** 101 rooms.
Motel   Convenient interstate access. 4 whirlpool rms, $70-$110 for up to 2 persons. Handling fee imposed; 2-3 sto-
DS, MC, VI. **Special Amenities: Free breakfast.**   ries; exterior corridors. **All Rooms:** free movies. **Some Rooms:** refrigerators. Fee: VCR's. **Cards:** AE, DI,
[icons]

HAMPTON INN-GRANTVILLE/HARRISBURG/HERSHEY   Rates Subject to Change   **Phone:** 717/469-7689
◆◆◆   5/1-10/31 & 4/1-4/30   1P: $78- 160   2P/1B: $78- 160   2P/2B: $78- 160
Motel   11/1-3/31   1P: $60- 100   2P/1B: $60- 100   2P/2B: $60- 100
Location: I-81, exit 28. 255 Bow Creek Rd 17028. Fax: 717/469-2337. **Terms:** Sr. discount; no pets.
Facility: 79 rooms. 4 stories; interior corridors. **All Rooms:** free movies. **Cards:** AE, DI, DS, MC, VI.
Roll in showers.   [icons]

HOLIDAY INN HARRISBURG-HERSHEY AREA, I-81   Rates Subject to Change   **Phone:** 717/469-0661
◆◆◆   Fri & Sat 6/23-9/2   1P: $149- 199   2P/2B: $149- 199   XP: $10   F18
Motor Inn   Sun-Thurs 6/23-9/2   1P: $129- 179   2P/2B: $129- 179   XP: $10   F18
5/1-6/22 & 9/3-4/30   1P: $99- 159   2P/2B: $99- 159   XP: $10   F18
Location: At I-81, exit 28. 604 Station Rd 17028. Fax: 717/469-7755. **Terms:** Sr. discount; reserv deposit, 6/1-8/31; pets.
Facility: 195 rooms. 4 stories; interior corridors. **Dining:** Dining room, restaurant; 6:30 am-10 pm; $4-$15. **All Rooms:**
Fee: movies. **Cards:** AE, CB, DI, DS, JCB, MC, VI. *(See ad p 305 & p 294)*
Roll in showers.   [icons]

GREENCASTLE—3,600

LODGINGS

COMFORT INN   **Phone:** 717/597-8164
(AAA) (SAVE)   All Year [CP]   1P: $48-   53   2P/1B: $56-   61   2P/2B: $56-   61   XP: $6   F18
Location: I-81, exit 2, just s on US 11. 50 Pine Dr 17225. Fax: 717/597-5050. **Terms:** Monthly rates;
◆◆◆   package plans; no pets. **Facility:** 71 rooms. Contemporary rooms, some with recliner. 3 stories; interior corri-
Motor Inn   dors; saunas, whirlpools; aerobics instruction, small video game room, video rental library. Fee: racquetball
courts. **Dining:** Restaurant; 7 am-9 pm, Fri & Sat-10 pm; $6-$13. **Services:** valet laundry.
Recreation: jogging. **All Rooms:** free movies. **Some Rooms:** Fee: VCR's. **Cards:** AE, DI, DS, JCB, MC, VI.
Special Amenities: Free local telephone calls and free newspaper.   [icons]

RODEWAY INN   **Phone:** 717/597-7762
(AAA) (SAVE)   5/1-10/31   1P: $40-   45   2P/1B: $40   2P/2B: $45
11/1-4/30   1P: $35-   40   2P/1B: $35   2P/2B: $40
◆◆   **Location:** I-81 exit 3, just e on SR 16. 10835 John Wayne Dr 17225. Fax: 717/597-7156. **Terms:** Weekly
Motel   rates; no pets. **Facility:** 36 rooms. Economy lodgings at busy truck stop operation. Rates for up to 5 persons;
2 stories; exterior corridors. **Dining:** Restaurant; 24 hours; $7-$12. **Services:** Fee: coin laundry.
All Rooms: coffeemakers, free movies. **Cards:** AE, DS, MC, VI. **Special Amenities: Free local telephone calls and free
newspaper.**   [icons]

RESTAURANT

ANTRIM HOUSE   **Lunch:** $6-$16   **Dinner:** $6-$16   **Phone:** 717/597-8111
(AAA) (SAVE)   **Location:** I-81, exit 3; 0.6 mi w on SR 16. 104 E Baltimore St 17225. **Hours:** 6 am-9 pm, Sun 7 am-7 pm.
Closed: 1/1, 12/24, 12/25 & 12/31. **Reservations:** accepted. **Features:** casual dress; children's menu;
◆◆   carryout; salad bar; buffet. Homestyle cooking for both buffet & plate items. Homemade dessert & pie. Sat
American   breakfast buffet. Originally built in 1859. **Cards:** AE, DS, MC, VI. **Special Value: 20% discount on the price
of any entree, excluding beverages, tax and gratuity.**   [X]

GREENSBURG—*See Laurel Highlands p. 311.*

GREEN TREE—*See Pittsburgh & Vicinity p. 410.*

GROVE CITY—8,200

LODGINGS

AMERIHOST INN-GROVE CITY　　　　　　　　　　　　Phone: 724/748-5836

🆎 SAVE　All Year [CP]　　　　　1P: $64- 89　2P/1B: $74- 99　2P/2B: $69- 94　XP: $5　　F16

◆◆◆　Location: Exit 31 off I-79, just w. 1924 Leesburg Rd 16127. Fax: 724/748-5486. Terms: No pets. Facility: 61

Motel　rooms. 2 stories; interior corridors; sauna, whirlpool. All Rooms: coffeemakers, free movies. Some Rooms: microwaves, refrigerators. Cards: AE, CB, DI, DS, MC, VI. Special Amenities: Free breakfast and free newspaper. (See ad p 254)

LYNNROSE BED & BREAKFAST　　　　Guaranteed Rates　　　　　Phone: 724/458-6425

◆◆　All Year [BP]　　　　1P: $50- 65　2P/1B: $60- 70　2P/2B: $60- 65　XP: $10　F12

Bed &　Location: Just s of downtown. 114 W Main St 16127. Terms: Reserv deposit; pets. Facility: 5 rooms. 2 sto-

Breakfast　ries; interior corridors; designated smoking area. All Rooms: free movies. Cards: DS, MC, VI.

SNOW GOOSE INN　　　　　　　　　　　　　　　Phone: 724/458-4644

🆎 SAVE　All Year [BP]　　　　2P/1B: $65　　　2P/2B: $65

◆　Location: Across from entrance to Grove City College. 112 E Main St 16127. Terms: Reserv deposit; no

Bed &　pets. Facility: 4 rooms. 2 stories; interior corridors; designated smoking area. Cards: MC, VI.

Breakfast

GWYNEDD—*See Philadelphia & Vicinity p. 378.*

HALLSTEAD—1,300

LODGING

COLONIAL BRICK MOTEL　　　　　　　　　　　　　Phone: 717/879-2162

🆎 SAVE　All Year　　　　1P: $63- 83　2P/1B: $63- 83　2P/2B: $63- 83　XP: $7　D12

◆◆　Location: I-81, Great Bend-Hallstead exit 68. US 11 18822 (PO Box AD). Fax: 717/879-5213.

Motel　Terms: Weekly rates; package plans; no pets. Facility: 53 rooms. Tastefully decorated rooms in light commer-

cial area with convenient interstate access. 2 stories; interior corridors. Dining: Restaurant nearby. Some Rooms: 7 efficiencies, kitchen, microwaves, radios, refrigerators. Cards: AE, DS, MC, VI.

Special Amenities: Early check-in/late check-out and free local telephone calls. (See color ad below)

HAMLIN—*See Pocono Mountains Area p. 423.*

HANOVER (YORK COUNTY)

LODGINGS

BEECHMONT INN　　　　　　　　　　　　　　　Phone: 717/632-3013

🆎 SAVE　All Year [BP]　　　1P: $80- 135　2P/1B: $80- 135　2P/2B: $95　XP: $10

◆◆◆　Location: 0.3 mi n on SR 194 from SR 94. 315 Broadway 17331. Terms: Age restrictions may apply; reserv

Historic Bed　deposit; package plans; 2 night min stay, weekends in suites; no pets. Facility: 7 rooms. 1830

& Breakfast　home with Federal period ambience. TV, VCR & dataport avail on request. Handling fee imposed; 2 stories; interior corridors; smoke free premises. Dining: Afternoon refreshments. All Rooms: combo or shower baths. Some Rooms: coffeemakers, kitchen, microwaves, refrigerators, whirlpools. Cards: AE, DS, MC, VI.

Special Amenities: Free breakfast and free local telephone calls.

HAMPTON INN　　　　　　　Rates Subject to Change　　　　　　Phone: 717/633-1117

◆◆◆　4/1-4/30 [CP]　　　1P: $66- 80　2P/1B: $71- 85　2P/2B: $71- 85

Motel　5/24-9/12 [CP]　　1P: $68- 73　2P/1B: $83- 88　2P/2B: $73

9/13-3/31 [CP]　　1P: $63- 78　2P/1B: $68- 83　2P/2B: $68

5/1-5/23 [CP]　　1P: $62- 77　2P/1B: $67- 82　2P/2B: $67

Location: 1.4 mi n on SR 94, then just e. 309 Wilson Ave 17331. Fax: 717/633-7599. Terms: No pets. Facility: 83 rooms. Rates for up to 4 persons; 3 stories; interior corridors. All Rooms: free & pay movies. Cards: AE, CB, DI, DS, JCB, MC, VI. Roll in showers.

HANOVER SUPER 8 MOTEL　　　　Rates Subject to Change　　　　Phone: 717/630-8888

◆◆　All Year [CP]　　　1P: $50　　　　　　　2P/2B: $55　XP: $5　D12

Motel　Location: 1.5 mi n on SR 94. 40 Wetzel Dr 17331. Fax: 717/630-9124. Terms: Sr. discount; reserv deposit; 7 day notice; no pets. Facility: 46 rooms. 2 whirlpool rms, $78.88 for up to 2 persons; 2 stories; interior corridors. Cards: AE, CB, DI, DS, MC, VI.

▌ARFORD—1,100

LODGING

PARTNERS INN BED & BREAKFAST   Rates Subject to Change   **Phone:** 717/434-2233
♦   Fri-Sun [BP]   1P: $95   2P/1B: $95   2P/2B: $95
▪storic Bed   Mon-Thurs [CP]   1P: $65   2P/1B: $65   2P/2B: $65
Breakfast   **Location:** I-81 exit 65, 3 mi s on SR 547. 1 N Harmony Rd 18823 (PO Box 300). **Terms:** Age restrictions
                 may apply; reserv deposit, 14 day notice; 2 night min stay, weekends; no pets. **Facility:** 3 rooms. Handling fee
▪posed; 3 stories, no elevator; interior corridors; smoke free premises. **All Rooms:** no A/C. **Cards:** AE, DS, MC, VI.

[X] [D]

▌ARMARVILLE—See Pittsburgh & Vicinity p. 411.

▌ARRISBURG—52,400   (See map p. 292; index below)

> To help you more easily locate accommodations in the Harrisburg area, the following
> index and map show lodgings and restaurants. Listings for these estab-
> lishments are found under the heading for the city in which they are located. The Harris-
> burg area map comprises: **Camp Hill, Enola, Harrisburg, Mechanicsburg, New
> Cumberland and Wormleysburg.**

Index of Establishments on the HARRISBURG ACCOMMODATIONS Spotting Map

NEW CUMBERLAND
Farm Fortune Bed & Breakfast **1**
Fairfield Inn Harrisburg West **3**
Days Inn - Harrisburg South **5**
McIntosh Inn **7**
Harrisburg Holiday Inn Hotel & Conference
    Center **9**

RESTAURANT
Coakley's Restaurant & Irish Pub . . . . ①

ENOLA
Quality Inn Harrisburg-Enola **11**

RESTAURANT
Visaggio's Ristorante . . . . ②

HARRISBURG
Inn at Felicita **13**
Harrisburg Hilton & Towers **14**
Budgetel Inn **15**
Doubletree Club Hotel **18**
Comfort Inn East **20**
Budgetel Inn - Harrisburg Airport **21**
Holiday Inn Harrisburg East-Airport **22**
Days Inn North **24**
Super 8 Motel-North **28**
Sheraton Inn Harrisburg **29**
Residence Inn by Marriott Harrisburg-Hershey . . . **30**
Red Roof Inn-South **31**
Red Roof Inn-North **32**
Harrisburg Marriott **33**
Econo Lodge **35**
Holiday Inn Express-Riverfront **36**
Best Western Capital Plaza **37**
Daystop Harrisburg **38**
Ramada Inn on Market Square **39**
Wyndham Garden Hotel **40**
Best Western Country Oven **41**

Sleep Inn **42**
Super 8 Motel Harrisburg/Hershey **43**
Travelodge **44**
Hampton Inn Harrisburg East **45**
Howard Johnson Harrisburg/Hershey **46**
Days Inn-Harrisburg Airport **47**

RESTAURANTS
Malley's Restaurant . . . . ③
Ashley's . . . . ④
Progress Grill . . . . ⑤
Maverick Restaurant . . . . ⑥
Country Oven Restaurant . . . . ⑦
Finley's American Restaurant . . . . ⑧
The Golden Sheaf . . . . ⑨

CAMP HILL
Hampton Inn Camp Hill/Mechanicsburg **48**
Radisson Penn Harris Hotel & Convention
    Center **49**

RESTAURANTS
Kosta's Fine Cuisine . . . . ⑬
Harding's Restaurant . . . . ⑭

MECHANICSBURG
Comfort Inn West **51**
Best Western Plantation Inn **52**
Amber Inn **53**
Homewood Suites - Harrisburg West **54**
Holiday Inn Harrisburg-West **55**
Hampton Inn-Harrisburg West **56**
Econo Lodge **57**

RESTAURANT
Isaac's Restaurant & Deli . . . . ⑳

WORMLEYSBURG
RESTAURANT
Catalano's . . . . ㉕

LODGINGS

▌EST WESTERN CAPITAL PLAZA   **Phone:** 717/545-9089   **37**
[SAVE]   All Year   1P: $55- 61   2P/1B: $59- 65   2P/2B: $63   XP: $4   F18
                Location: Just n of I-81, exit 24. 150 Nationwide Dr 17110. Fax: 717/545-7926. **Terms:** Small pets only.
• ♦   **Facility:** 121 rooms. Along busy hwy. 3 stories; interior/exterior corridors; game room. **Dining:** Restaurant
▪tel   nearby. **Services:** Fee: coin laundry. **All Rooms:** free movies. **Some Rooms:** Fee: microwaves,
               refrigerators, VCR's. **Cards:** AE, CB, DI, DS, JCB, MC, VI. **Special Amenities:** Early check-in/late
▪eck-out and free local telephone calls.

[🛏] [🛁] [ECTV] [X] [🔲] [D]

▌EST WESTERN COUNTRY OVEN   **Phone:** 717/652-7180   **41**
[SAVE]   6/1-11/2   1P: $83- 89   2P/1B: $83- 89   2P/2B: $83- 89   XP: $3   F13
                5/1-5/31   1P: $76- 82   2P/1B: $76- 82   2P/2B: $76- 82   XP: $3   F13
• ♦ ♦   11/3-4/30   1P: $55- 62   2P/1B: $60- 71   2P/2B: $65- 76   XP: $3   F13
▪tor Inn   **Location:** I-81, exit 26B northbound or exit 26 southbound. 300 N Mountain Rd 17112. Fax: 717/541-8991.
               Terms: Weekly/monthly rates, in winter; pets. **Facility:** 49 rooms. Attractive country styling in rooms & public
▪as; on attractive grounds. 2 stories; interior corridors. **Dining:** Country Oven Restaurant, see separate listing.
▪ Rooms: free movies. **Cards:** AE, CB, DI, DS, MC, VI. **Special Amenities:** Early check-in/late check-out and free
▪om upgrade (subject to availability with advanced reservations). (See color ad p 293)

[🛏] [🛁] [ECTV] [X] [D]

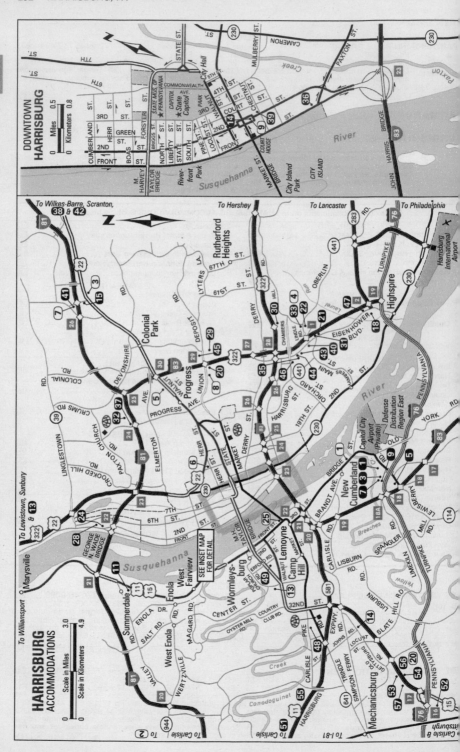

DOWNTOWN HARRISBURG

HARRISBURG ACCOMMODATIONS

(See map p. 292)

UDGETEL INN
All Year [CP]　　　　Rates Subject to Change
1P: $58- 69　2P/1B: $65- 75　2P/2B: $65- 75
Phone: 717/540-9339　**15**
Location: I-81 exit 26A northbound, exit 26 southbound. 200 N Mountain Rd 17112. Fax: 717/540-9486.
Terms: Sr. discount; pets. **Facility:** 67 rooms. 3 stories; interior corridors. **All Rooms:** free movies.
Cards: AE, CB, DI, DS, MC, VI. *(See color ad below)*

UDGETEL INN - HARRISBURG AIRPORT
All Year [CP]　　　　Rates Subject to Change
1P: $43- 58　2P/1B: $50- 65　2P/2B: $55　　XP: $7　F18
Phone: 717/939-8000　**21**
Location: Just se of I-283, exit 1. 990 Eisenhower Blvd 17111. Fax: 717/939-0500. **Terms:** Sr. discount;
small pets only. **Facility:** 114 rooms. Rates for up to 4 persons; 3 stories; interior corridors. **All Rooms:** free
pay movies. **Cards:** AE, CB, DI, DS, MC, VI. *(See color ad below)*

OMFORT INN EAST
6/1-10/31 [CP]　　　　Rates Subject to Change
1P: $79- 99　2P/1B: $79- 99　2P/2B: $79- 99
5/1-5/31 & 11/1-4/30 [CP]　1P: $69- 89　2P/1B: $69- 89　2P/2B: $69- 89
Phone: 717/561-8100　**20**
Location: I-83 exit 29; just w. 4021 Union Deposit Rd 17109. Fax: 717/561-1357. **Terms:** Sr. discount;
serv deposit; pets. **Facility:** 115 rooms. Rates for up to 4 persons; 5 stories; interior corridors. **All Rooms:** free & pay
ovies. **Cards:** AE, CB, DI, DS, JCB, MC, VI.

AYS INN-HARRISBURG AIRPORT
6/11-9/5 [CP]　　　　Rates Subject to Change
1P: $69- 89　2P/1B: $69- 89　2P/2B: $69- 89　XP: $5　F18
5/1-6/10 & 9/6-4/30 [CP]　1P: $59- 89　2P/1B: $59- 89　2P/2B: $59- 89　XP: $5　F18
Phone: 717/939-4147　**47**
Location: I-76, exit 19; I-283, exit 2W (Highspire). 17057 (800 Eisenhower Blvd, MIDDLETOWN).
ax: 717/939-5291. **Terms:** Sr. discount; pets. **Facility:** 82 rooms. Weekend rate, $5 extra per night, 6/11-9/5; 2 stories; ex-
rior corridors. **All Rooms:** free & pay movies. **Cards:** AE, CB, DI, DS, JCB, MC, VI.

AYS INN NORTH
5/1-10/31 [CP]　　　　
1P: $49- 84　2P/1B: $54- 89　2P/2B: $54- 84　XP: $5　F11
11/1-4/30 [CP]　　　　1P: $42- 69　2P/1B: $48- 79　2P/2B: $48- 79　XP: $5　F11
Phone: 717/233-3100　**24**
Location: I-81 exit 22, just n on N Front St. 3919 N Front St 17110. Fax: 717/233-6415. **Terms:** Weekly
rates; no pets. **Facility:** 116 rooms. Some rooms with view of river; pleasant breakfast room. 3 stories; exterior
corridors; playground. **Dining:** Restaurant nearby. **Services:** Fee: coin laundry. **All Rooms:** free & pay
ovies. **Some Rooms:** Fee: microwaves, refrigerators. **Cards:** AE, CB, DI, DS, JCB, MC, VI. **Special Amenities: Free
eakfast.** *(See ad p 294)*

(See map p. 292)

DAYSTOP HARRISBURG   Phone: 717/652-9578
AAA SAVE   5/1-9/4, 10/31-11/30 &
◆   3/1-4/30   1P: $50   2P/1B: $55   2P/2B: $55   XP: $6   F
                9/5-10/30   1P: $45   2P/1B: $50   2P/2B: $50   XP: $6   F
Motor Inn   12/1-2/28   1P: $40   2P/1B: $45   2P/2B: $45   XP: $6   F
                Location: I-81 & SR 39 exit 27, adjacent to truck stop. 7848 Linglestown Rd 17112 (PO Box 6535
Fax: 717/657-5012. **Terms:** Check-in 4 pm; no pets. **Facility:** 31 rooms. Pleasant rooms. 2 stories; exterior corridors; gam
room. **Dining:** Restaurant; 24 hours; $7-$10. **Services:** Fee: coin laundry. **All Rooms:** free movie
Some Rooms: microwaves, refrigerators. **Cards:** AE, DS, MC, VI. **Special Amenities:** Early check-in/late check-out an
free local telephone calls.

DOUBLETREE CLUB HOTEL   Rates Subject to Change   Phone: 717/939-1600
◆◆◆   6/1-9/6 [CP]   1P: $90- 105   2P/1B: $100- 115 2P/2B: $100- 115 XP: $10   F
Motor Inn   5/1-5/31 & 9/7-4/30 [CP]   1P: $80- 95   2P/1B: $90- 105 2P/2B: $90- 105 XP: $10   F
                Location: Just n of I-76, exit 19; just w of I-283, exit 2W (Highspire). (815 S. Eisenhower Blvd
MIDDLETOWN, 17057). Fax: 717/939-8763. **Terms:** Sr. discount; check-in 4 pm; no pets. **Facility:** 176 rooms. Suites ava
$85-$120; 6 stories; interior corridors. **Dining:** Dining room; 5 pm-10 pm; $9-$15. **All Rooms:** free & pay movie
Cards: AE, CB, DI, DS, MC, VI. *(See color ad p 295)*

ECONO LODGE   Phone: 717/561-1885
AAA SAVE   9/25-10/15   1P: $40- 80   2P/1B: $45- 85   2P/2B: $45- 85   XP: $5   F
◆◆   5/1-9/24   1P: $45- 55   2P/1B: $45- 65   2P/2B: $45- 70   XP: $5   F
Motel   10/16-4/30   1P: $40- 50   2P/1B: $45- 60   2P/2B: $45- 65   XP: $5   F
                Location: 0.5 mi n on Eisenhower Blvd from jct I-283, exit 1 & SR 441, exit 19 PA Tpk. 495 Eisenhow
                Blvd 17111. Fax: 717/561-1888. **Terms:** Reserv deposit; weekly rates; no pets. **Facility:** 30 rooms. Lar
rooms. Handling fee imposed; 2 stories; interior corridors. **Dining:** Restaurant nearby. **All Rooms:** free movie
Some Rooms: Fee: refrigerators. **Cards:** AE, CB, DI, DS, JCB, MC, VI. **Special Amenities:** Early check-in/late check-o
and free room upgrade **(subject to availability with advanced reservations).**

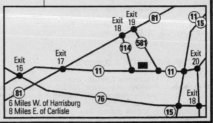

(See map p. 292)

HAMPTON INN HARRISBURG EAST   Phone: 717/545-9595
AAA SAVE   3/8-4/30 [CP]   1P: $78- 94   2P/1B: $91- 99   2P/2B: $89
            7/25-10/31 [CP]   1P: $79- 92   2P/1B: $89- 99   2P/2B: $89
♦♦♦   5/1-7/24 [CP]   1P: $76- 92   2P/1B: $89- 99   2P/2B: $86
Motel   11/1-3/7 [CP]   1P: $70- 83   2P/1B: $83- 88   2P/2B: $78
            Location: I-83 exit 29, just e. 4230 Union Deposit Rd 17111. Fax: 717/545-6907. **Terms:** No pe
Facility: 145 rooms. Handsomely decorated public areas. Rates for up to 4 persons; 5 stories; interior corridors; whirlpo
Dining: Restaurant nearby. **Services:** Fee: coin laundry. **All Rooms:** free movies. **Some Rooms:** microwaves, refrigerato
Cards: AE, CB, DI, DS, MC, VI.

HARRISBURG HILTON & TOWERS   Phone: 717/233-6000
AAA SAVE   All Year   1P: $134   2P/1B: $144   2P/2B: $144   XP: $10
            Location: Center. One North 2nd St 17101. Fax: 717/233-6271. **Terms:** Package plans; no pe
♦♦♦♦   **Facility:** 341 rooms. Attractive public areas. 15 stories; interior corridors; luxury level rooms; in-room vid
Hotel   games. Fee: parking. **Dining & Entertainment:** Restaurant; 6:30 am-11 pm, Sat & Sun from 7 am; S8-S2
            cocktail lounge; also, The Golden Sheaf, see separate listing; entertainment. **Services:** valet laundry; ar
transportation, to Amtrak station. Fee: valet parking. **All Rooms:** free & pay movies, refrigerators, combo or shower bath
Some Rooms: Fee: microwaves. **Cards:** AE, CB, DI, DS, MC, VI. **Special Amenities: Free newspaper.**
(See color ad p 18)   Roll in showers.

HARRISBURG MARRIOTT   Rates Subject to Change   Phone: 717/564-5511
♦♦♦   All Year   1P: $92- 159   2P/1B: $92- 159 2P/2B: $92- 159 XP: $10
Hotel   **Location:** Just e of I-283, exit 1. 4650 Lindle Rd 17111. Fax: 717/564-6173. **Terms:** Check-in 4 pm; rese
            deposit; no pets. **Facility:** 348 rooms. 10 stories; interior corridors. **Dining:** Ashley's, see separate listin
All Rooms: free & pay movies. **Cards:** AE, CB, DI, DS, JCB, MC, VI.
                                                         Roll in showers.

HOLIDAY INN EXPRESS-RIVERFRONT   Phone: 717/233-1611
AAA SAVE   5/1-10/31 & 4/15-4/30 [CP] 1P: $79- 99   2P/1B: $79- 99 2P/2B: $79- 99
            11/1-4/14 [CP]   1P: $59- 89   2P/1B: $59- 89 2P/2B: $59- 89
♦♦♦   **Location:** Center, 0.5 mi n of I-83 exit 23. 525 S Front St 17104. Fax: 717/233-1611. **Terms:** Small p
Motor Inn   only, $10 extra charge. **Facility:** 117 rooms. Overlooking Susquehanna River. 2 stories; interior/exterior co
            dors; gameroom. **Dining:** Restaurant; 11:30 am-2:30 & 5-10 pm; $9-$17; cocktails. **Services:** a
transportation, within 10 mi. Fee: coin laundry. **All Rooms:** free movies, combo or shower baths. **Some Room**
Fee: refrigerators. **Cards:** AE, CB, DI, DS, MC, VI. **Special Amenities: Free breakfast and free local telephone calls.**
                                                         Roll in showers.

ee map p. 292)

◗LIDAY INN HARRISBURG EAST-AIRPORT Rates Subject to Change **Phone: 717/939-7841** 🅲🅲
◆◆ All Year 2P/1B: $131 2P/2B: $131 XP: $12 F18
★tor Inn **Location:** Just e of I-283, exit 1. 4751 Lindle Rd 17111. Fax: 717/939-9317. **Terms:** Sr. discount; check-in 4 pm; reserv deposit; no pets. **Facility:** 299 rooms. 2-3 stories; interior corridors. **Dining:** Dining room; 6:30
⊩-2 & 5-10 pm; $10-$19. **All Rooms:** free & pay movies. **Cards:** AE, CB, DI, DS, MC, VI. *(See color ad p 296)*

🛏️ 🚗 ⊬ ECTV ✕ 🔗 Ⓓ

◗WARD JOHNSON HARRISBURG/HERSHEY **Phone: 717/564-6300** 🆖
Ⓢ SAVE 9/6-10/31 [CP] 1P: $59 2P/2B: $99
◆ 5/1-9/5 [CP] 1P: $59 2P/2B: $89
◆ 11/1-4/30 [CP] 1P: $39 2P/2B: $59
★tel **Location:** 0.7 mi n on Eisenhower Blvd from jct I-283, exit 1. 473 Eisenhower Blvd 17111. Fax: 717/564-4840. **Terms:** Weekly/monthly rates; small pets only. **Facility:** 174 rooms. 2 stories; interior cor-
⊩rs; wading pool. **Dining:** Restaurant nearby. **Services:** valet laundry; area transportation, within 5 mi. **All Rooms:** free
⊮vies. **Some Rooms:** microwaves. Fee: refrigerators. **Cards:** AE, CB, DI, DS, MC, VI. **Special Amenities: Free breakfast
d free newspaper.**

🛏️ 🚗 ⊬ ⊬ ⊬ ECTV ✕ Ⓓ

◗ AT FELICITA **Phone: 717/599-5301** 🅱
Ⓢ SAVE All Year [CP] 1P: $85 2P/1B: $85
◆◆ **Location:** I-81 exit 23W, 5 mi nw on US 22, 3.8 mi e on SR 443. 2201 Fishing Creek Valley Rd 17112. Fax: 717/599-5623. **Terms:** Reserv deposit; weekly rates; package plans; no pets. **Facility:** 13 rooms. Small
⊩untry Inn country inn with big resort facilities. Guest rooms furnished in a country look, some small rooms. 3 stories; no elevator; interior corridors; smoke free premises; sauna, whirlpool; 1 lighted tennis court; bocci ball, horse-
⊩es, sand volleyball. **Dining & Entertainment:** Dining room; 4 pm-10 pm, Sun brunch 11 am-1 pm. Closed Mon; $15-$20;
⊩ktails/lounge. **Services:** Fee: massage. **Recreation:** hiking trails. **All Rooms:** combo or shower baths. **Cards:** AE, CB,
⊦DS, JCB, MC, VI. **Special Amenities: Free breakfast and free newspaper.** *(See ad below)*

🚗 ⊬ ⊬ ECTV ✕ Ⓓ

◗MADA INN ON MARKET SQUARE Rates Subject to Change **Phone: 717/234-5021** 🆖
◆ 5/1-11/25 & 4/1-4/30 1P: $115 2P/1B: $125 2P/2B: $125 XP: $10 F18
  11/26-3/31 1P: $109 2P/1B: $119 2P/2B: $119 XP: $10 F18
★tel **Location:** 2nd & Chestnut sts. 23 S 2nd St 17101. Fax: 717/234-2347. **Terms:** Sr. discount; no pets.
⊩cility: 190 rooms. 10 stories; interior corridors. Fee: parking. **Dining:** Dining room; 6:30 am-2 & 5-10 pm, Sat & Sun from
⊩m; $10-$18. **All Rooms:** free & pay movies. **Cards:** AE, CB, DI, DS, MC, VI.
Roll in showers. 🚗 ⊬ CTV ⌂ ✕ Ⓓ Ⓢ

◗D ROOF INN-NORTH Rates Subject to Change **Phone: 717/657-1445** 🅱
◆ All Year 1P: $40- 47 2P/1B: $49- 61 2P/2B: $54 XP: $9 F18
★tel **Location:** At I-81 exit 24, just n on Progress Ave. 400 Corporate Cir 17110. Fax: 717/657-2775.
  Terms: Pets. **Facility:** 110 rooms. 2 stories; interior/exterior corridors. **All Rooms:** free movies. **Cards:** AE,
⊦, DI, DS, MC, VI. Roll in showers. 🛏️ CTV ✕ 🔗 Ⓓ

(See map p. 292)

RED ROOF INN-SOUTH
◆◆ Motel

| | Rates Subject to Change | | | | Phone: 717/939-1331 |
7/1-8/31 1P: $51- 61 2P/1B: $60- 73 2P/2B: $76 XP: $10
6/1-6/30 & 10/1-10/31 1P: $40- 51 2P/1B: $54- 66 2P/2B: $51 XP: $9
5/1-5/31, 9/1-9/30 &
11/1-4/30 1P: $33- 47 2P/1B: $41- 51 2P/2B: $48 XP: $7
Location: Just e of I-283, exit 1. 950 Eisenhower Blvd 17111. Fax: 717/939-8266. **Terms:** Pets. **Facility:** 110 rooms. 2 stori interior/exterior corridors. **All Rooms:** free & pay movies. **Cards:** AE, CB, DI, DS, MC, VI.
Roll in showers.

RESIDENCE INN BY MARRIOTT HARRISBURG-HERSHEY Rates Subject to Change Phone: 717/561-1900
◆◆◆ Apartment Motel
All Year [CP] 1P: $116 2P/1B: $125 2P/2B: $143
Location: Just e on US 322 from jct I-83; exit Penhar Dr. 4480 Lewis Rd 17111. Fax: 717/561-86 **Terms:** Sr. discount; pets, $5 extra charge, $50 dep req. **Facility:** 80 rooms. 2 stories; exterior corrido **All Rooms:** kitchens, free movies. **Cards:** AE, CB, DI, MC, VI.

SHERATON INN HARRISBURG
◆◆ Motor Inn
Rates Subject to Change Phone: 717/561-2800
11/1-4/30 1P: $75- 110 2P/1B: $85- 125 2P/2B: $85- 135 XP: $10
5/1-10/31 1P: $100- 105 2P/1B: $105- 110 2P/2B: $105- 125 XP: $10
Location: I-83, exit 29; Just e on Union Deposit Rd, 0.5 mi s. 800 East Park Dr 17111. Fax: 717/561-83 **Terms:** Small pets only, $20 dep req. **Facility:** 174 rooms. 3 stories; interior corridors. **Dining:** Dining room; 6:30-10:30 a 11:30-2 & 5-10 pm; $10-$17. **All Rooms:** free & pay movies. **Cards:** AE, CB, DI, DS, MC, VI.

SLEEP INN
(AAA) SAVE
◆◆ Motel
Phone: 717/540-9100
6/2-9/4 [CP] 1P: $52 2P/1B: $59- 79 2P/2B: $69- 89 XP: $10
5/1-6/1 & 3/31-4/30 [CP] 1P: $49 2P/1B: $52- 62 2P/2B: $59- 89 XP: $10
9/5-3/30 [CP] 1P: $42 2P/1B: $45- 69 2P/2B: $45- 79 XP: $10
Location: I-81, exit 27. 7930 Linglestown Rd 17112. Fax: 717/671-8514. **Terms:** Weekly/monthly rates; pe $5 extra charge. **Facility:** 42 rooms. 2 stories; interior corridors. **All Rooms:** free movies, combo or sho baths. **Cards:** AE, DI, DS, MC, VI.

SUPER 8 MOTEL HARRISBURG/HERSHEY
(AAA) SAVE
◆◆ Motel
Phone: 717/564-7790
6/6-10/15 [CP] 1P: $45- 63 2P/1B: $55- 63 2P/2B: $55- 63 XP: $5
5/1-6/5 [CP] 1P: $38- 46 2P/1B: $46- 55 2P/2B: $46- 55 XP: $5
10/16-4/30 [CP] 1P: $35- 42 2P/1B: $45- 50 2P/2B: $45- 50 XP: $5
Location: I-283 exit 1 (Swatara), just w, 0.5 mi n. 4131 Executive Park Dr 17111. Fax: 717/564-07 **Terms:** No pets. **Facility:** 48 rooms. Large appealing rooms. 2 stories; interior corridors; video libra Fee: private club pool adjacent to property. **Dining:** Restaurant nearby. **Cards:** AE, CB, DI, DS, MC, VI. **Special Ameniti Free breakfast and free local telephone calls.**

SUPER 8 MOTEL-NORTH
(AAA)
◆◆ Motor Inn
Rates Subject to Change Phone: 717/233-5891
All Year 1P: $42- 55 2P/1B: $50- 60 2P/2B: $55- 70 XP: $5
Location: I-81 exit 22, 0.8 mi n. 4125 N Front St 17110. Fax: 717/233-5891. **Terms:** Sr. discount; pe **Facility:** 57 rooms. 2 stories; exterior corridors. **Dining:** Restaurant; 7-11 am, 11:30-2 & 5-9 pm; Sat 6 am-11& 5-9 pm; Sun 8-11:30 am; $12-$20. **All Rooms:** free & pay movies. **Cards:** AE, CB, DI, DS, MC,

TRAVELODGE
(AAA) SAVE
◆◆ Motel
Phone: 717/564-3876
All Year 1P: $35- 55 2P/1B: $35- 55 2P/2B: $45- 65 XP: $5
Location: I-283 exit 1 & SR 441, 0.5 mi n. 631 S Eisenhower Blvd 17111. Fax: 717/561-08 **Terms:** Reserv deposit; small pets only, $5 in cage. **Facility:** 52 rooms. Handling fee imposed; 1 story; exte corridors. **All Rooms:** coffeemakers, free movies, combo or shower baths. **Some Rooms:** VCF whirlpools. **Cards:** AE, CB, DI, DS, JCB, MC, VI. **Special Amenities:** Early check-in/late check-out a free local telephone calls.

WYNDHAM GARDEN HOTEL
◆◆◆ Motor Inn
Rates Subject to Change Phone: 717/558-9500
All Year 1P: $89- 109 2P/1B: $99- 119 2P/2B: $99- 119 XP: $10
Location: Just w of I-283, exit 1. 765 Eisenhower Blvd 17111. Fax: 717/558-8956. **Terms:** Pets. **Facility:** rooms. 6 stories; interior corridors. **Dining:** Dining room; 6 am-2:30 & 5-10 pm; $6-$19. **All Rooms:** fre pay movies. **Cards:** AE, CB, DI, DS, JCB, MC, VI.

RESTAURANTS

ASHLEY'S
◆◆◆ American
JCB, MC, VI.
Lunch: $7-$12 Dinner: $15-$20 Phone: 717/564-5511
Location: Just e of I-283, exit 1; in Harrisburg Marriott. 4560 Lindle Rd 17111. **Hours:** 6 am-11 pm, F Sat-midnight, Sun 7 am-11 pm. **Reservations:** suggested. **Features:** casual dress; Sunday brun children's menu; cocktails & lounge. Daily lunch buffet $7.95 & Sun buffet $13.95. **Cards:** AE, CB, DI,

COUNTRY OVEN RESTAURANT
(AAA) SAVE
◆◆◆ American
Lunch: $5-$7 Dinner: $10-$20 Phone: 717/652-7180
Location: I-81, exit 26B northbound or exit 26 southbound; in Best Western Country Oven. 300 N Moun Rd 17112. **Hours:** 6:30 am-9 pm, Fri & Sat-9:30 pm, Sun-8 pm. Closed: 12/25. **Reservations:** sugges **Features:** casual dress; children's menu; carryout; cocktails & lounge. Popular dining specializing in seafo prime rib, roast turkey & Betty's homemade desserts including peanut butter pie & apple dumplings. Ei coffee shop or formal dining room atmosphere avail. **Cards:** AE, CB, DI, DS, MC, VI. **Special Value:** $1 the price of a dinner entree. (See color ad p 293)

FINLEY'S AMERICAN RESTAURANT
◆ American
Lunch: $5-$11 Dinner: $6-$15 Phone: 717/564-4270
Location: 0.3 mi w of I-83, exit 29 (Union Deposit Rd). 3951 Union Deposit Rd 17109. **Hours:** 11 am pm, Fri & Sat-11 pm. Closed: 11/26 & 12/25. **Features:** casual dress; children's menu; carryout. Ca family dining. Seasonally updated specialties. **Cards:** AE, DI, DS, MC, VI.

THE GOLDEN SHEAF
◆◆◆◆ Regional American
Lunch: $9-$15 Dinner: $18-$28 Phone: 717/237-6400
Location: Center; in Harrisburg Hilton & Towers. One N 2nd St 17101. **Hours:** 11:30 am-2 & 5:30-10 Closed major holidays & Sun. **Reservations:** suggested. **Features:** semi-formal attire; cocktails; fee for v parking; a la carte. Seasonal specialty menu, intimate fine dining. Winemaker specialty dinners hos monthly. Member Chaine des Rotisseurs. Smoke free premises. **Cards:** AE, CB, DI, DS, JCB, MC, VI.

(See map p. 292)

MALLEY'S RESTAURANT   **Lunch:** $5-$9   **Dinner:** $12-$19   **Phone:** 717/652-9947 ③
◆◆   **Location:** I-81, exit 26 (southbound) or 26A (northbound), 0.3 mi s on N Mountain Rd, just e on US 22. 6085
American   Allentown Blvd 17112. **Hours:** 11 am-3 & 5-10 pm, Fri-11 pm, Sat 5 pm-11 pm, Sun 4 pm-10 pm. Closed:
1/1, 5/25, 9/7, 12/25 & 12/26. **Reservations:** suggested. **Features:** casual dress; carryout; cocktails &
lounge. Relaxed dining in pleasant atmosphere. **Cards:** AE, CB, DI, MC, VI. ✗

MAVERICK RESTAURANT   **Lunch:** $5-$11   **Dinner:** $9-$22   **Phone:** 717/233-7688 ⑥
◆◆   **Location:** I-83, exit 30W, 2.8 mi w on US 22 by-pass. 1851 Arsenal Blvd 17103. **Hours:** 11 am-10 pm, Sat
Continental   4:30 pm-10:30 pm. Closed major holidays & Sun. **Reservations:** suggested. **Features:** casual dress;
children's menu; carryout; cocktails & lounge. Family owned since 1961. Fresh seafood, aged beef, lamb &
veal capably served in warm, comfortable supper club ambience. **Cards:** AE, CB, DI, MC, VI. ✗

PROGRESS GRILL   **Dinner:** $14-$25   **Phone:** 717/652-7348 ⑤
◆◆◆   **Location:** I-83, exit 30W (Progress); 0.9 mi w. 3526 Walnut St 17109. **Hours:** 4 pm-11 pm. Closed major
Steak and   holidays, Sun & 6/28-7/4. **Reservations:** required. **Features:** casual dress; children's menu; health
Seafood   conscious menu items; carryout; cocktails & lounge. Upscale casual dining. Noted for their seafood
preparation. **Cards:** AE, DI, MC, VI. ✗

HAVERTOWN—*See Philadelphia & Vicinity p. 378.*

HAWLEY—*See Pocono Mountains Area p. 423.*

HAZLETON—24,700

LODGINGS

BEST WESTERN GENETTI MOTOR LODGE   **Phone:** 717/454-2494

		1P:		2P/1B:		2P/2B:		XP:		
5/1-10/31 [CP]		$55-	75	$60-	80	$69-	89	$7		F12
11/1-4/30 [CP]		$39-	55	$49-	59	$55-	75	$7		F12

◆◆   **Location:** 2 mi n on SR 309, 6 mi s on SR 309 from I-80 exit 39. 32nd & N Church St 18201 (RR 2, Box
Motel   37). **Fax:** 717/455-7793. **Terms:** Weekly/monthly rates; small pets only. **Facility:** 89 rooms. Well-appointed
guest rooms. 7 whirlpool suites, $120-$150; 3 stories; interior/exterior corridors; playground.
Dining: Restaurant nearby. **Services:** Fee: coin laundry. **All Rooms:** combo or shower baths. **Some Rooms:** microwaves,
refrigerators. Fee: VCR's. **Cards:** AE, CB, DI, MC, VI. **Special Amenities:** Early check-in/late check-out and free room
upgrade (subject to availability with advanced reservations). *(See color ad below)* 🛏 🛄 🛁 CTV ✗ 🐾 D

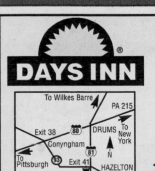

HAZLETON MOTOR INN
Phone: 717/459-1451

AAA SAVE

♦ Motel

DS, MC, VI.

5/1-9/30 1P: $32- 42 2P/1B: $35- 45 2P/2B: $35- 47 XP: $5 F12
10/1-4/30 1P: $30- 35 2P/1B: $35- 38 2P/2B: $35- 38 XP: $5 F12
Location: 0.5 mi e. 615 E Broad St 18201. Fax: 717/459-6264. **Terms:** Reserv deposit; weekly/monthly rates; pets. **Facility:** 25 rooms. Handling fee imposed; 2 stories; interior corridors. **Dining:** Restaurant nearby. **Some Rooms:** coffeemakers, 3 efficiencies, microwaves, radios, refrigerators. **Cards:** AE, CB, DI, [icons]

HOLIDAY INN
Phone: 717/455-2061

♦♦♦

Motor Inn

Rates Subject to Change
5/1-10/31 & 4/1-4/30 1P: $65- 89 2P/1B: $65- 89 2P/2B: $65- 89
11/1-3/31 1P: $55 2P/1B: $55 2P/2B: $55
Location: 2 mi n on SR 309; 6 mi s on SR 309 from I-80 exit 39; from I-81, exit 41, 0.5 mi s on SR 93, 1 mi e on Airport Rd, 0.7 mi s on SR 309. (Rt 309, Box 28, 18201). Fax: 717/455-9387. **Terms:** Sr. discount; pets. **Facility:** 107 rooms. 2 stories; exterior corridors. **Dining:** Restaurant; 6 am-2 & 5-10 pm; $7-$16. **All Rooms:** free & pay movies. **Cards:** AE, CB, DI, DS, MC, VI. *(See color ad below)* [icons]

RESTAURANTS

CARMEN'S
Lunch: $3-$6 Dinner: $5-$17 Phone: 717/455-5521

♦♦

Italian

Location: Center. 44 E Broad St 18201. **Hours:** 11 am-9 pm, Sun 8 am-8 pm. Closed: 12/25. **Reservations:** suggested; weekends. **Features:** casual dress; children's menu; early bird specials; senior's menu; health conscious menu; carryout; salad bar; cocktails & lounge; buffet. Homemade dessert. Seafood, fowl & steak specialties. **Cards:** AE, DI, MC, VI. [icon]

MIKE DUBATTO'S LIBRARY LOUNGE RESTAURANT
Dinner: $8-$17 Phone: 717/455-3920

AAA

♦♦

Italian

Location: E on SR 93, behind Dubatto's Family Restaurant. 615 E Broad St 18201. **Hours:** 4:30 pm-11 pm. Closed major holidays & Sun. **Reservations:** suggested. **Features:** casual dress; carryout; cocktails & lounge. Attractive atmosphere. Traditional Northern cuisine. Fresh fish nightly. **Cards:** AE, MC, VI.

SCATTON'S RESTAURANT
Dinner: $11-$20 Phone: 717/455-6630

AAA

♦♦♦

Steak and Seafood

Location: From I-81 exit 40, 3 mi n on SR 924, 1 mi n on SR 309, just w on 22nd St; from I-80 exit 39, 6 mi s on SR 309 to 22nd St. 1008 N Vine St 18201. **Hours:** 5 pm-10 pm. Closed major holidays & Sun. **Reservations:** accepted. **Features:** casual dress; children's menu; senior's menu; carryout; cocktails & lounge. Featuring homemade pasta, fresh seafood, chicken, veal, steak & chops. Very good cuisine. Chef/owner for 14 years. Walk-ins welcome. Ample parking. **Cards:** AE, CB, DI, DS, MC, VI. [icon]

HEIDELBERG—See Pittsburgh & Vicinity p. 411.

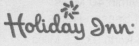

HERMITAGE—15,300

LODGINGS

COLLINS MOTEL Rates Subject to Change **Phone:** 724/981-6150
AAA All Year 1P: $39- 49 2P/1B: $42- 55 2P/2B: $49- 62
◆ **Location:** I-80, exit 1N, 3 mi n on SR 18N to US 62N, then 0.8 mi n. 4036 E State St 16148. **Terms:** Reserv
Motel deposit, 7 day notice; no pets. **Facility:** 13 rooms. 1 story; exterior corridors. **All Rooms:** free movies.
Cards: MC, VI. (CTV) (X) (D)

HOLIDAY INN-SHARON/HERMITAGE Rates Subject to Change **Phone:** 724/981-1530
◆◆ 6/30-4/30 1P: $90 2P/1B: $90 2P/2B: $90
Motor Inn 5/1-6/29 1P: $80 2P/1B: $80 2P/2B: $80
Location: On SR 18, at jct I-80 exit 1N. 3200 S Hermitage Rd 16159. Fax: 724/981-1518. **Terms:** Sr.
discount; small pets only. **Facility:** 180 rooms. 3 stories; interior corridors. **Dining:** Dining room; 6:30 am-10 pm; $10-$20.
All Rooms: free movies. **Cards:** AE, CB, DI, DS, JCB, MC, VI. (🐾) (🏊) (CTV) (X) (D)

RESTAURANT

COMBINE BROS BAR & GRILLE **Lunch:** $6-$8 **Dinner:** $9-$16 **Phone:** 724/983-1057
◆◆ **Location:** 1 mi n on SR 18 from I-80, exit 1N. 2376 S Hermitage Rd 16159. **Hours:** 11 am-10 pm, Fri &
Italian Sat-11 pm. Closed: 1/1, 11/26, 12/25, Sun & Mon. **Features:** carryout; cocktails & lounge. Hearty portions;
owner/chef. Homemade bread, pastry, sauces, sausage & meatballs. Very popular, expect 20-45 min wait
after 6 pm. Seafood & steak also. **Cards:** AE, DS, MC, VI. (X)

HERSHEY—11,900—See also CAMPBELLTOWN & PALMYRA (LEBANON COUNTY).

LODGINGS

BEST WESTERN INN-HERSHEY **Phone:** 717/533-5665
AAA SAVE 6/19-9/7 [CP] 1P: $149- 169 2P/1B: $154- 174 2P/2B: $149- 169 XP: $10 F17
5/1-6/18 [CP] 1P: $119- 139 2P/1B: $124- 144 2P/2B: $119- 139 XP: $10 F17
◆◆◆ 9/8-4/30 [CP] 1P: $79- 129 2P/1B: $84- 134 2P/2B: $79- 129 XP: $10 F17
Motel **Location:** Just e on US 422 from jct US 322. US 422 & Sipe Ave 17033 (PO Box 364). Fax: 717/533-5675.
Terms: Package plans; no pets. **Facility:** 122 rooms. 3 stories; interior/exterior corridors; wading pool, whirl-
pool. **Dining:** Restaurant nearby. **Services:** Fee: coin laundry. **All Rooms:** free movies, refrigerators. **Some Rooms:**
Fee: microwaves, VCR's. **Cards:** AE, CB, DI, DS, MC, VI. **Special Amenities:** Free breakfast and free newspaper.
(See color ad p 304) (🏊) (🎯) (CTV) (X) (D)

CHOCOLATETOWN MOTEL

| | | Rates Subject to Change | | | | | **Phone:** 717/533-2330 |

Location info:

CHOCOLATETOWN MOTEL
(AAA)
♦♦
Motel

7/3-9/6
6/12-7/2
5/1-6/11, 9/7-10/17 &
4/1-4/30
10/18-12/15 & 3/1-3/31

Rates Subject to Change

	2P/1B:	$79-	84	2P/2B:	$89	XP:	$5
	2P/1B:	$56-	65	2P/2B:	$69	XP:	$5
	2P/1B:	$45-	49	2P/2B:	$53-	59	XP: $5
	2P/1B:	$40-	44	2P/2B:	$48-	54	XP: $5

Location: 2 mi e on US 422 from jct of SR 743. 1806 E Chocolate Ave 17033. **Terms:** Open 5/1-12/15 & 3/1-4/30; reserv deposit, 3 day notice; no pets. **Facility:** 26 rooms. Handling fee imposed; 2 stories; interior/exterior corridors. **Cards:** AE, DS, MC, VI. *(See color ad below)*

COCOA MOTEL   Phone: 717/534-1243
AAA SAVE 6/27-9/7   1P: $70- 95 2P/1B: $75- 95 2P/2B: $80- 135 XP: $5   F18
          5/1-6/26 & 3/15-4/30   1P: $50- 75 2P/1B: $55- 75 2P/2B: $60- 115 XP: $5   F18
◆   9/8-10/6   1P: $40- 65 2P/1B: $45- 65 2P/2B: $50- 95 XP: $5   F18
Motel   10/7-12/22 & 2/13-3/14   1P: $40- 60 2P/1B: $45- 60 2P/2B: $50- 85 XP: $5   F18
          Location: Just s on SR 743 from jct of US 322. 914 Cocoa Ave 17033. Fax: 717/533-4822. **Terms:** Open
5/1-12/22 & 2/13-4/30; reserv deposit; weekly rates; no pets. **Facility:** 14 rooms. Park at rooms. Comfortable rooms. 1 story;
exterior corridors. **All Rooms:** coffeemakers, refrigerators. **Cards:** AE, DS, MC, VI. **Special Amenities: Free local
telephone calls.**   [CCTV] [X] [D]

COCOA NIGHTS MOTEL   Rates Subject to Change   Phone: 717/533-2384
AAA   6/24-8/31   2P/1B: $80- 88 2P/2B: $78- 88 XP: $5
          6/1-6/23   2P/1B: $44- 68 2P/2B: $44- 68 XP: $5
◆ ◆   5/1-5/31, 9/1-10/25 &
Motel   3/1-4/30   2P/1B: $38- 64 2P/2B: $38- 64 XP: $5
          10/26-12/13 & 2/14-2/28   2P/1B: $38- 40 2P/2B: $38- 40 XP: $5
Location: 1.5 mi e on US 422 from jct of SR 743. 1518 E Chocolate Ave 17033. Fax: 717/533-3078. **Terms:** Open
5/1-12/13 & 2/14-4/30; reserv deposit, 3 day notice; no pets. **Facility:** 27 rooms. Handling fee imposed; 1-2 stories;
interior/exterior corridors. **Cards:** MC, VI. *(See color ad below)*   [⚲] [CCTV] [X] [D]

COMFORT INN   Phone: 717/566-2050

7/6-9/6 [CP]	1P: $139- 195	2P/1B: $149- 205	2P/2B: $149- 205	XP: $10	F18
5/8-7/5 [CP]	1P: $79- 185	2P/1B: $89- 195	2P/2B: $89- 195	XP: $10	F18
5/1-5/7 & 9/7-4/30 [CP]	1P: $69- 179	2P/1B: $79- 189	2P/2B: $79- 189	XP: $10	F18

Motel   **Location:** At jct US 322, 422 & SR 39; just off Hershey Park Dr. 1200 Mae St 17036. Fax: 717/566-8656.
Terms: Package plans; no pets. **Facility:** 125 rooms. 7 stories; interior corridors. **Services:** area transportation, within 5 mi. Fee: coin laundry. **Some Rooms:** coffeemakers, microwaves, refrigerators. Fee: VCR's. **Cards:** AE, DI, DS, MC, VI. **Special Amenities: Free breakfast and free local telephone calls.** (See color ad below)

DAYS INN HERSHEY   Rates Subject to Change   Phone: 717/534-2162

6/13-10/13 [CP]	1P: $80- 129	2P/1B: $90- 139	2P/2B: $90- 139	XP: $6	F12
5/1-6/12 & 10/14-4/30 [CP]	1P: $59- 109	2P/1B: $69- 119	2P/2B: $69- 119	XP: $6	F12

Motel   **Location:** Center, on US 422. 350 W Chocolate Ave 17033. Fax: 717/533-6409. **Terms:** Sr. discount; no pets. **Facility:** 75 rooms. 4 stories; interior corridors. **Cards:** AE, CB, DI, DS, JCB, MC, VI.

HERSHEY ECONO LODGE   Phone: 717/533-2515

5/28-8/31	1P: $118			XP: $10	F18
5/1-5/27, 9/1-10/15 & 3/1-4/30	1P: $75		2P/2B: $128		
			2P/2B: $80	XP: $5	F18
10/16-2/28	1P: $55		2P/2B: $60	XP: $5	F18

Motel   **Location:** Just e on US 422 from jct of US 322. 115 Lucy Ave 17033 (PO Box 737). Fax: 717/533-2543.
Terms: Reserv deposit; no pets. **Facility:** 48 rooms. Near Hershey Medical Center. 3 stories; exterior corridors. **Dining:** Restaurant nearby. **Some Rooms:** coffeemakers. **Cards:** AE, DS, MC, VI. **Special Amenities: Free breakfast.**

THE HERSHEY LODGE & CONVENTION CENTER   Phone: 717/533-3311

5/22-9/6	1P: $148- 168	2P/1B: $158- 178	2P/2B: $158- 178	XP: $15	F17
9/7-11/12	1P: $128- 148	2P/1B: $138- 158	2P/2B: $138- 158	XP: $15	F17
5/1-5/21 & 11/13-12/31	1P: $108- 128	2P/1B: $118- 138	2P/2B: $118- 138	XP: $15	F17
1/1-4/30	1P: $98- 118	2P/1B: $108- 128	2P/2B: $108- 128	XP: $15	F17

Resort Motor Inn   **Location:** 2.5 mi w on US 422 from jct of US 322. W Chocolate Ave & Univ Dr 17033-0446 (PO Box 446). Fax: 717/533-9642. **Terms:** Check-in 4 pm; reserv deposit; MAP avail; package plans; no pets. **Facility:** 667 rooms. Very attractive, spacious public areas & grounds. Parking at some rooms. 6 two-bedroom units. Handling fee imposed; 2 stories; interior/exterior corridors; miniature golf; wading pool, saunas, whirlpool; 4 lighted tennis courts; game room. **Dining & Entertainment:** 2 restaurants; 7 am-9 pm; $8-$18; cocktails/lounge. **Services:** valet laundry. **Recreation:** recreation program; jogging. Fee: bicycles. **All Rooms:** coffeemakers, free & pay movies, combo or shower baths. **Some Rooms:** A/C. Fee: refrigerators. **Cards:** AE, CB, DI, DS, MC, VI. **Special Amenities: Free newspaper and free room upgrade (subject to availability with advanced reservations).** (See ad p 302)
Roll in showers.

HOLIDAY INN EXPRESS OF HERSHEY   **Phone:** 717/583-0500

(AAA) (SAVE) 5/1-10/31 & 4/1-4/30 [CP]   1P: $89- 139 2P/1B: $89- 139 2P/2B: $89- 139 XP: $10   F19

◆◆◆   11/1-3/31 [CP]   1P: $69- 99 2P/1B: $69- 99 2P/2B: $69- 99 XP: $10   F19

Location: Just nw of Jct US 322, 422 & SR 39. 610 Walton Ave 17036 (610 Walton Ave, HUMMELSTOWN).

Motel   Fax: 717/583-0564. **Terms:** Reserv deposit; small pets only, $10 extra charge, $35 dep req. **Facility:** 78 rooms. Attractive, comfortably appointed guest rooms & public area. 3 stories; interior corridors; whirlpool, small indoor heated pool; game room. **Dining:** Restaurant nearby. **Services:** Fee: coin laundry. **All Rooms:** free movies, combo or shower baths. **Some Rooms:** coffeemakers, microwaves, refrigerators. **Cards:** AE, CB, DI, DS, MC, VI. **Special Amenities:** Free breakfast and free newspaper. *(See color ad below)*

Roll in showers. 🐕 📶 ♿ ECTV 🚭 ✕ D S

THE HOTEL HERSHEY   **Phone:** 717/533-2171

(AAA) (SAVE) 5/22-9/6   1P: $228- 248 2P/1B: $238- 258 2P/2B: $238- 258 XP: $25   F18

        9/7-11/12   1P: $208- 228 2P/1B: $218- 238 2P/2B: $218- 238 XP: $25   F18

◆◆◆◆ 5/1-5/21 & 11/13-12/31 1P: $188- 208 2P/1B: $198- 218 2P/2B: $198- 218 XP: $25   F18

Resort Hotel 1/1-4/30   1P: $178- 198 2P/1B: $188- 208 2P/2B: $188- 208 XP: $25   F18

Location: 2.3 mi n on SR 39W from jct US 322. Hotel Rd 17033 (PO Box 400). Fax: 717/534-8887.
Terms: Check-in 4 pm; reserv deposit, 3 day notice; BP, MAP avail; package plans; no pets. **Facility:** 236 rooms. A historical hotel on a hilltop with view of surrounding area. 5 stories; interior corridors; 2 wading pools, saunas, whirlpool; 3 tennis courts. Fee: 9 holes golf; balloon rides, bocci ball, carriage rides. **Dining & Entertainment:** Restaurant; $8-$35; cocktails/lounge; live entertainment Thurs-Sun; 24-hour room service; also, The Circular Dining Room, see separate listing. **Services:** valet laundry; area transportation, to Amtrak station; valet parking. Fee: childcare; massage. **Recreation:** nature trails; jogging. Fee: cross country skiing, tobogganing. Rental: bicycles. **All Rooms:** free & pay movies. **Some Rooms:** coffeemakers, whirlpools. Fee: refrigerators, VCR's. **Cards:** AE, CB, DI, DS, MC, VI. **Special Amenities:** Free newspaper and free room upgrade (subject to availability with advanced reservations). *(See ad p 302)*

🛏 🛏 📶 ♿ ECTV ✕ 📞 D

MILTON MOTEL   Rates Subject to Change   **Phone:** 717/533-4533

(AAA) 7/3-8/29   2P/1B: $66- 76 2P/2B: $79- 109 XP: $5

      6/5-7/2 & 8/30-9/6   2P/1B: $59- 69 2P/2B: $69- 99 XP: $5

◆◆◆ 5/1-6/4 & 9/7-4/30   2P/1B: $39- 49 2P/2B: $49- 59 XP: $5

Motel   **Location:** 2 mi e on US 422 from jct SR 743. 1733 E Chocolate Ave 17033. Fax: 717/533-0369.
Terms: Reserv deposit, in season; no pets. **Facility:** 31 rooms. 2 stories; interior/exterior corridors.
All Rooms: free movies. **Cards:** AE, DI, DS, MC, VI. *(See color ad p 305)*

🛏 ECTV ✕ D

Check out our **bold** listings!

RODEWAY INN HERSHEY　　　　　　　　　　　　　　　　　　　　**Phone:** 717/533-7054

		1P:		2P/1B:		2P/2B:		XP:	
6/19-9/5 [CP]		1P:	$109- 185	2P/1B:	$119- 195	2P/2B:	$119- 195	XP:	$10	F18
5/1-6/18 & 1/4-4/30 [CP]		1P:	$75- 175	2P/1B:	$85- 185	2P/2B:	$85- 185	XP:	$10	F18
9/6-10/5 [CP]		1P:	$75- 170	2P/1B:	$82- 180	2P/2B:	$82- 180	XP:	$10	F18
10/6-12/23 [CP]		1P:	$72- 160	2P/1B:	$80- 165	2P/2B:	$82- 165	XP:	$10	F18

Motel　　**Location:** Just s of US 422 (Chocolate Ave) on SR 743, just w. 43 W Areba Ave 17033. Fax: 717/533-3405.
Terms: Open 5/1-12/23 & 1/4-4/30; reserv deposit; no pets. **Facility:** 22 rooms. Pleasant rooms in quiet residential area. 4 two-bedroom units. 2 stories; exterior corridors. **All Rooms:** coffeemakers, refrigerators. **Some Rooms:** 10 efficiencies, kitchen, microwaves. **Cards:** AE, CB, DI, DS, MC, VI. **Special Amenities:** Free local telephone calls and free newspaper. *(See color ad p 306)*

SPINNER'S INN　　　　　　　　Rates Subject to Change　　　　　　　**Phone:** 717/533-9157

	2P/1B:		2P/2B:		XP:	
7/3-8/31 [CP]	2P/1B:	$79	2P/2B:	$99- 119	XP:	$5
6/4-7/2 & 9/1-9/6 [CP]	2P/1B:	$69	2P/2B:	$89- 109	XP:	$5
5/1-6/3 & 9/7-4/30 [CP]	2P/1B:	$49	2P/2B:	$59- 69	XP:	$5

Motor Inn　　**Location:** 1 mi e on US 422. 845 E Chocolate Ave 17033. Fax: 717/534-1189. **Terms:** Sr. discount; reserv deposit; no pets. **Facility:** 52 rooms. 1-2 stories; interior/exterior corridors. **Dining:** Catherine's at Spinner's, see separate listing. **All Rooms:** free movies. **Cards:** AE, CB, DI, DS, MC, VI. *(See color ad below)*

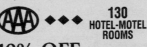

WHITE ROSE MOTEL   Phone: 717/533-9876

(AAA) (SAVE)   7/3-9/5   2P/1B: $108   2P/2B: $108   XP: $5   F17
◆◆◆   6/5-7/2   2P/1B: $85   2P/2B: $85   XP: $5   F17
            5/1-6/4 & 4/1-4/30   2P/1B: $53   2P/2B: $64   XP: $5   F17
Motel   9/6-3/31   2P/1B: $44   2P/2B: $55   XP: $5   F17
            Location: 1.3 mi e on US 422 from jct SR 743. 1060 E Chocolate Ave 17033-1293. Fax: 717/533-6923.
Terms: Reserv deposit; weekly rates, off season; no pets. **Facility:** 24 rooms. Attractive guest rooms. Handling fee imposed;
2 stories; exterior corridors; designated smoking area. **Dining:** Restaurant nearby. **All Rooms:** free movies, refrigerators,
combo or shower baths. **Fee:** VCR. **Some Rooms:** efficiency. **Cards:** AE, DS, MC, VI. **Special Amenities: Free local
telephone calls.** (See color ad p 301)   Roll in showers.   ☕ 🖥 ⓔⓒⓣⓥ ⊠ Ⓓ

RESTAURANTS

CATHERINE'S AT SPINNER'S   **Dinner:** $9-$20   Phone: 717/533-9050
(AAA) (SAVE)   **Location:** 1 mi e on US 422; in Spinner's Inn. 845 E Chocolate Ave 17033. **Hours:** 4 pm-10 pm. Closed
            major holidays, Sun & Mon. **Reservations:** suggested. **Features:** casual dress; children's menu; carryout;
◆◆◆   cocktails & lounge. Casually elegant decor. Innovative American cuisine featuring beef, veal & seafood
American   favorites. Also, continental cuisine. **Cards:** AE, CB, DI, DS, MC, VI. **Special Value: $1 off the price of a
            dinner entree.** (See color ad p 307)   ⊠

THE CIRCULAR DINING ROOM   **Lunch:** $10-$20   **Dinner:** $20-$35   Phone: 717/533-2171
◆◆◆◆   **Location:** 2.3 mi n on SR 39W from jct US 322; in The Hotel Hershey. Hotel Rd 17033. **Hours:** 7-10 am,
Continental 11:30-2 & 5:30-10 pm. **Reservations:** required; for dinner. **Features:** semi-formal attire; Sunday brunch;
            children's menu; health conscious menu items; cocktails & lounge; valet parking; a la carte. Mediterranean
atmosphere with grand hotel style dining. Live entertainment Thurs-Sun. Nightly prix fixe menu avail. Breakfast & lunch
buffets. Smoke free premises. **Cards:** AE, CB, DI, DS, MC, VI.

HEARTH RESTAURANT   **Lunch:** $4-$8   **Dinner:** $7-$18   Phone: 717/533-3311
◆◆   **Location:** 1.5 mi w on US 322 & 422; in Hershey Lodge & Convention Center. W Chocolate Ave & Univ Dr
American   17033-0446. **Hours:** 7-11 am, 11:30-2 & 5-9 pm, Sun noon-9 pm. **Reservations:** accepted.
            Features: casual dress; children's menu; salad bar; cocktails. Early American decor. Smoke free premises.
Cards: AE, DI, DS, MC, VI.   ⊠

HOLLIDAYSBURG—5,600

RESTAURANT

THE DREAM FAMILY RESTAURANT   **Lunch:** $7-$13   **Dinner:** $7-$13   Phone: 814/696-3384
◆◆   **Location:** 0.6 mi e on US 22 from SR 36. 1500 Allegheny St 16648. **Hours:** 8 am-9 pm, Fri & Sat-10 pm.
American   Closed major holidays. **Features:** casual dress; children's menu; carryout. Variety of entrees, salad &
            sandwiches with large selection of bakery items. **Cards:** AE, DS, MC, VI.   ⊠

HONESDALE—See Pocono Mountains Area p. 424.

HONEY BROOK (CHESTER COUNTY)—See Philadelphia & Vicinity p. 378.

HOPWOOD—See Laurel Highlands p. 312.

HORSHAM—See Philadelphia & Vicinity p. 378.

HUNTINGDON—6,800

LODGING

HUNTINGDON MOTOR INN   Rates Subject to Change   Phone: 814/643-1133
◆◆   All Year   1P: $37- 44   2P/1B: $46- 65 2P/2B: $54- 65 XP: $4   F12
Motor Inn   **Location:** On US 22 at jct SR 26. (PO Box 353, 16652). Fax: 814/643-1331. **Terms:** Small pets only, $10
            extra charge. **Facility:** 48 rooms. 1-2 stories; exterior corridors. **Dining:** Restaurant; 7 am-2 & 5-10 pm,
closed Sun; $5-$18. **Cards:** AE, CB, DI, DS, MC.   🐾 ⓔⓒⓣⓥ ⊠ Ⓓ

INDIANA (INDIANA COUNTY)

LODGINGS

BEST WESTERN UNIVERSITY INN   Rates Subject to Change   Phone: 724/349-9620
◆◆   8/1-10/31 [BP]   1P: $55   2P/1B: $59   2P/2B: $65
Motor Inn   5/1-7/31 & 11/1-4/30 [BP] 1P: $51   2P/1B: $51   2P/2B: $55
            Location: 0.6 mi n of US 422, exit Wayne Ave. 1545 Wayne Ave 15701. Fax: 724/349-2620. **Terms:** Sr
discount; no pets. **Facility:** 107 rooms. 2 stories; interior corridors. **Dining:** Restaurant; 6:30 am-1 & 5-9 pm, Sat 8 am-1 &
5-9 pm, Sun 8 am-1 pm; $6-$13. **All Rooms:** free & pay movies. **Cards:** AE, CB, DI, DS, MC, VI.   ☕ ⓔⓒⓣⓥ ⊠ Ⓓ

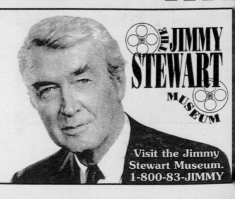

CHARBERT FARM BED AND BREAKFAST Phone: 724/726-8264
(AAA) (SAVE) All Year [BP] 1P: $55- 95 2P/1B: $55- 95 2P/2B: $95 XP: $20
◆◆ **Location:** sw of Indiana; 1.3 mi w on SR 56 from jct SR 286, 1.1 mi w on J. George's Rd, just n. 2439
Bed & Laurel Rd 15701 (PO Box 1415, INDIANA). Fax: 724/726-1132. **Terms:** Reserv deposit, 7 day notice;
Breakfast weekly/monthly rates; small pets only, stay outside home. **Facility:** 4 rooms. Renovated 1850's farmhouse on
108 acres in quiet picturesque country setting. 2 stories; interior corridors; designated smoking area.
Services: guest laundry. **Recreation:** canoeing, fishing; hiking trails. **All Rooms:** no A/C.
Some Rooms: radios, phones. **Cards:** MC, VI. **Special Amenities:** Early check-in/late check-out and free room
upgrade (subject to availability with advanced reservations). (🛏) (X) (D)

COMFORT INN INDIANA Rates Subject to Change Phone: 724/465-7000
◆◆◆ All Year [CP] 1P: $58- 80 2P/2B: $64- 86 XP: $6 F18
Motel **Location:** 0.7 mi e of US 422, exit Oakland Ave. 1350 Indian Springs Rd 15701. Fax: 724/465-7892.
Terms: Sr. discount; reserv deposit; no pets. **Facility:** 71 rooms. 3 stories; interior corridors; designated
smoking area. **All Rooms:** free movies. **Cards:** AE, DI, DS, MC, VI. Roll in showers. (ECTV) (f̂) (X) (D) (S)

HOLIDAY INN HOLIDOME Rates Subject to Change Phone: 724/463-3561
◆◆◆ All Year 1P: $69- 89 2P/1B: $69- 89 2P/2B: $69- 89
Motor Inn **Location:** 1 mi n of US 422, exit Wayne Ave. 1395 Wayne Ave 15701. Fax: 724/463-8006. **Terms:** Reserv
deposit; pets. **Facility:** 159 rooms. 2 stories; interior/exterior corridors. **Dining:** Restaurant; 6 am-2 & 4-10
pm, Sat & Sun from 7 am. Sun brunch avail; $6-$18. **All Rooms:** free movies. **Some Rooms:** kitchen. **Cards:** AE, CB, DI,
DS, JCB, MC, VI. *(See ad p 308)* Roll in showers. (🛏) (≈) (⊀) (ECTV) (X) (D)

RESTAURANTS

DEAN'S RESTAURANT **Dinner:** $8-$12 Phone: 724/349-3326
◆◆ **Location:** Downtown. 533 Philadelphia St 15701. **Hours:** 6:30 am-9 pm. Closed: 12/25.
American **Reservations:** accepted. **Features:** casual dress; children's menu; salad bar; a la carte. Breakfast, lunch &
dinner avail. Back parking lot. **Cards:** DS, MC, VI. (X)

ROUKI'S RESTAURANT & DELI **Lunch:** $3-$6 **Dinner:** $3-$6 Phone: 724/465-7200
◆ **Location:** Downtown. 665 Philadelphia St 15701. **Hours:** 7:30 am-6 pm. Closed major holidays & Sun.
American **Features:** casual dress; children's menu; health conscious menu items; carryout; street parking; a la carte.
Specialty sandwiches, salad, soup & dessert. **Cards:** MC, VI. (X)

INDUSTRY—*See Pittsburgh & Vicinity p. 411.*

INTERCOURSE—*See Pennsylvania Dutch Country p. 333.*

JENNERSTOWN—*See Laurel Highlands p. 313.*

JERMYN—2,300 (See map p. 418; index p. 417)

RESTAURANTS

EARL'S TOWNHOUSE FAMILY RESTAURANT **Lunch:** $2-$7 **Dinner:** $8-$20 Phone: 717/876-1210 (69)
(AAA) **Location:** Center. 539-541 Washington Ave 18433. **Hours:** 11 am-midnight, Sun 8 am-10 pm. Closed: 4/4 &
◆ 12/25. **Features:** casual dress; Sunday brunch; children's menu; carryout; cocktails & lounge. Family dining
with expansive selection. **Cards:** AE, DS, MC, VI.
American

WINDSOR INN **Lunch:** $4-$6 **Dinner:** $5-$7 Phone: 717/876-4600 (70)
(AAA) **Location:** On SR 107, 0.3 mi s of jct US 6. 669-671 Washington Ave 18433. **Hours:** 4 pm-10 pm, Tues &
◆ Wed-11:30 pm, Thurs-Sat 9 am-11:30 pm. Closed major holidays. **Features:** casual dress; children's menu;
carryout; cocktails & lounge. Famous for hot wings. Rustic decor. **Cards:** AE, DS, MC, VI.
American

WOODLAND INN **Dinner:** $11-$18 Phone: 717/876-1672 (73)
◆◆◆ **Location:** From US 6, 0.5 mi se on SR 107, 1.3 mi s. 1 S Washington Ave 18433. **Hours:** 4 pm-10 pm, Sun
Continental 3 pm-9 pm. Closed: 1/1, 7/4, 12/24-12/26 & Mon. **Reservations:** suggested; Fri & Sat. **Features:** casual
dress; health conscious menu; carryout; cocktails & lounge. Leisurely dining featuring excellent variety of
entrees. **Cards:** AE, DS, MC, VI.

JIM THORPE—*See Pocono Mountains Area p. 424.*

JOHNSTOWN—*See Laurel Highlands p. 313.*

KANE—4,600

LODGING

KANE VIEW MOTEL Phone: 814/837-8600
(AAA) (SAVE) All Year 1P: $36 2P/1B: $39 2P/2B: $46 XP: $2 F12
◆ **Location:** 1 mi e on US 6. US Rt 6 16735 (RD 1, Box 91A). **Terms:** Monthly rates; pets. **Facility:** 20 rooms.
Motel Spacious grounds with wooded area. 1 story; exterior corridors. **Recreation:** nature trails; cross country
skiing, snowmobiling. **All Rooms:** combo or shower baths, no A/C. **Cards:** AE, DS, MC, VI.
Special Amenities: Early check-in/late check-out and preferred room (subject to availability with
advanced reservations). (🛏) (CTV) (X) (D)

KENNETT SQUARE—*See Philadelphia & Vicinity p. 378.*

EXTRA PERSON (XP) rates include only the standard room equipment.
There may be an additional charge for cots, rollaways and baby beds.

KING OF PRUSSIA—*See Philadelphia & Vicinity p. 378.*

KINTNERSVILLE—*See Philadelphia & Vicinity p. 380.*

KITTANNING—5,100

LODGINGS

COMFORT INN
◆◆◆   All Year [CP]   1P: $55- 75   2P/1B: $55- 75 2P/2B: $59- 75 XP: $10   F18
Motel   **Location:** 0.8 mi w via US 422, at jct SR 268; SR 28,exit 19A. 16201 (Hilltop Plaza, Rd 8, P O Box 14).
Rates Subject to Change   **Phone:** 724/543-5200
Fax: 724/543-5455. **Terms:** Sr. discount; small pets only. **Facility:** 70 rooms. 3 stories; interior corridors.
All Rooms: free movies. **Cards:** AE, CB, DI, DS, JCB, MC, VI.   Roll in showers. (symbols)

QUALITY INN ROYLE   **Phone:** 724/543-1159
(AAA) (SAVE)   All Year [CP]   1P: $50   2P/1B: $54   2P/2B: $54   XP: $4   F18
            Location: 1.8 mi w via US 422, at jct SR 268; SR 28, exit 19A. 405 Butler Rd 16201. Fax: 724/543-1159.
◆◆◆   **Terms:** Reserv deposit; no pets. **Facility:** 58 rooms. Exceptionally well maintained property. 2 stories;
Motel   interior/exterior corridors. **Dining:** Restaurant nearby. **Services:** valet laundry. **All Rooms:** coffeemakers,
free movies. **Some Rooms:** refrigerators. Fee: VCR's. **Cards:** AE, CB, DI, DS, JCB, MC, VI.
Special Amenities: Free local telephone calls and free newspaper.   (symbols)

RODEWAY INN KITTANNING   **Phone:** 724/543-1100
(AAA) (SAVE)   All Year   1P: $44- 46   2P/1B: $50- 52 2P/2B: $52- 56 XP: $5   F18
            Location: 1 mi e of Kittanning on US 422; e of jct US 422 & SR 66 & 28; SR 28, exit 19A. US 422 E 16201
◆   (RD 6, Box 279G). Fax: 724/543-1526. **Terms:** Weekly/monthly rates; no pets. **Facility:** 20 rooms. 2 stories;
Motel   exterior corridors. **Services:** valet laundry. **All Rooms:** coffeemakers, combo or shower baths.
Some Rooms: Fee: microwaves, refrigerators. **Cards:** AE, CB, DI, DS, MC, VI. **Special Amenities:** Early
check-in/late check-out and free local telephone calls.   (symbols)

KNOX—700

RESTAURANT

WOLF'S DEN RESTAURANT   **Lunch:** $6-$9   **Dinner:** $10-$18   **Phone:** 814/797-1105
◆◆   **Location:** At I-80 exit 7. 16232. **Hours:** 11:30 am-9 pm, Fri & Sat-10 pm. Closed: 12/25.
American   **Reservations:** suggested; on weekends. **Features:** casual dress; Sunday brunch; children's menu; early
bird specials; carryout; cocktails & lounge; a la carte. Served in attractively remodeled 1831 barn.
Cards: AE, DS, MC, VI.   (symbol)

KULPSVILLE—*See Philadelphia & Vicinity p. 380.*

KUTZTOWN—4,700

LODGINGS

CAMPUS INN   **Phone:** 610/683-8721
(AAA) (SAVE)   All Year   1P: $40- 70   2P/1B: $50- 75 2P/2B: $50- 75 XP: $5   F10
            Location: US 222 Kutztown/Virginsville exit, 1 mi e. 15080 Kutztown Rd 19530. Fax: 610/683-8721.
◆◆   **Terms:** Reserv deposit, 3 day notice; weekly rates; small pets only. **Facility:** 29 rooms. 2 whirlpool rms, extra
Motel   charge; 2 stories; exterior corridors. **Some Rooms:** microwaves, refrigerators. **Cards:** AE, CB, DI, DS, MC,
VI. **Special Amenities:** Free breakfast and free local telephone calls.   (symbols)

LINCOLN MOTEL   **Phone:** 610/683-3456
(AAA) (SAVE)   All Year   1P: $35- 65   2P/1B: $45- 70 2P/2B: $45- 70 XP: $5   F10
            Location: US 222, Kutztown/Virginsville exit. Main St 19530 (RD 4 Box 171). **Terms:** Reserv deposit, 3 day
◆◆   notice; weekly rates; small pets only. **Facility:** 14 rooms. Cozy rooms with contemporary appointments. 1 story;
Motel   exterior corridors. **Dining:** Restaurant nearby. **All Rooms:** combo or shower baths. **Cards:** AE, DI, DS, MC,
VI. **Special Amenities:** Free local telephone calls.   (symbols)

LACKAWAXEN—*See Pocono Mountains Area p. 424.*

LAHASKA—*See Philadelphia & Vicinity p. 380.*

LAKEVILLE—*See Pocono Mountains Area p. 424.*

LAMPETER—*See Pennsylvania Dutch Country p. 334.*

LANCASTER—*See Pennsylvania Dutch Country p. 334.*

LANDENBERG—*See Philadelphia & Vicinity p. 381.*

LANGHORNE—*See Philadelphia & Vicinity p. 381.*

LATROBE—*See Laurel Highlands p. 313.*

IF THE ROOM YOU GET ISN'T THE ROOM YOU RESERVED . . .

Do you have written confirmation?

Has the management offered you a choice of
another room there or elsewhere?

Know what to do. **Read the Making Reservations
section in About Lodgings & Restaurants.**

Laurel Highlands

CHALK HILL—400

LODGING

THE LODGE AT CHALK HILL
Rates Subject to Change
Phone: 724/438-8880
Fri & Sat [CP]   1P: $73   2P/2B: $78   XP: $10   F15
Sun-Thurs [CP]   1P: $60   2P/2B: $72   XP: $10   F15
Location: Just w on US 40. (Rt 40E, Box 240, 15421). Fax: 724/438-1685. **Terms:** Check-in 4 pm; reserv
Motel
deposit; pets, $5 extra charge. **Facility:** 61 rooms. 6 kitchens, $74.95; Fri & Sat, $90.95; 1 story; exterior cor-
ridors. **All Rooms:** free movies. **Cards:** AE, DS, MC, VI. *(See color ad p 318)* 🖭 ✗ Ⓓ

RESTAURANT

THE STONE HOUSE RESTAURANT Historical   **Lunch:** $8-$19   **Dinner:** $8-$19   Phone: 724/329-8876
Location: 0.5 mi e on US 40. US 40W 15421. **Hours:** 11:30 am-9 pm, Fri & Sat-10 pm. Closed: 12/25.
Reservations: suggested. **Features:** casual dress; children's menu; carryout; cocktails & lounge. In restored
American
historic hotel, circa 1822. Also featuring Italian fare. **Cards:** AE, DS, MC, VI. ✗

CRABTREE—1,000

RESTAURANT

CARBONE'S
Dinner: $9-$18
Phone: 724/834-3430
Location: Center, 3 mi s of US 22. Rt 119 15624. **Hours:** 4:30 pm-9 pm, Fri & Sat-10 pm. Closed major
Italian
holidays & Sun. **Features:** casual dress; children's menu; cocktails & lounge; a la carte. Traditional favorites
& specialty pizzas. **Cards:** AE, CB, DI, DS, MC, VI. ✗

DONEGAL—2,400

LODGING

MOUNTAIN VIEW BED & BREAKFAST
Phone: 724/593-6349
All Year [BP]   1P: $85- 95   2P/1B: $125- 140 2P/2B: $155   XP: $15
Location: Off SR 31; 1 mi e of exit 9 (PA Tpk), 0.5 mi s. 10 Mountain View Rd 15628. Fax: 724/593-6345.
Terms: Age restrictions may apply; no pets. **Facility:** 6 rooms. Restored 1850's Georgian farmhouse & barn
Historic Bed
with period furnishings in quiet pastoral setting with magnificent view of surrounding Laurel Mountain. Formal
& Breakfast
breakfast served in dining room. 1 two-bedroom unit. 2 stories; interior/exterior corridors; designated smoking
area. **Dining:** Afternoon tea. **All Rooms:** combo or shower baths. **Some Rooms:** phones. **Cards:** AE, CB,
DI, DS, MC, VI. **Special Amenities:** Free local telephone calls and free room upgrade **(subject to availability with
advanced reservations).** ✗ Ⓓ

RESTAURANT

CANDLELIGHT RESTAURANT   **Lunch:** $4-$10   **Dinner:** $4-$10   Phone: 724/593-6301
Location: Just w of PA Tpk, exit 9. Rt 31 15628. **Hours:** 7 am-9 pm, Fri & Sat-10 pm. Closed: 11/26 &
American
12/25. **Features:** casual dress; Sunday brunch; children's menu; carryout; salad bar; cocktails; a la carte.
MC, VI.
Dinner buffet Fri. Breakfast & dinner buffet Sat. Lunch & dinner buffet Sun. Homemade dessert. **Cards:** DS,
✗

GREENSBURG—16,300

LODGINGS

COMFORT INN GREENSBURG
Phone: 724/832-2600
5/26-9/9 [CP]   1P: $71- 99   2P/1B: $76- 109 2P/2B: $76- 109 XP: $5   F18
5/1-5/25 & 9/10-4/30 [CP] 1P: $69- 99   2P/1B: $71- 109 2P/2B: $71- 109 XP: $5   F18
Location: On US 30, 3.5 mi e of jct US 119. 1129 E Pittsburgh St 15601. Fax: 724/834-3442. **Terms:** No
Motel
pets. **Facility:** 77 rooms. Large baths & rooms; hilltop location. 3 stories; interior corridors; designated smoking
area; video movie rentals. **Dining:** Restaurant nearby. **Services:** valet laundry. **All Rooms:** free movies.
Some Rooms: whirlpools. Fee: microwaves, refrigerators, VCR's. **Cards:** AE, CB, DI, DS, JCB, MC, VI. **Special Amenities:**
Free breakfast and free local telephone calls. 🖭 ♨ ᴇᴄᴛᴠ ✗ Ⓓ Ⓢ

KNIGHTS INN-GREENSBURG   Rates Subject to Change   **Phone:** 724/836-7100
◆◆   All Year   1P: $47- 56   2P/1B: $53- 71 2P/2B: $57   XP: $7   F18
Motel   **Location:** On US 119, just s of jct US 30. 1215 S Main St 15601. Fax: 724/837-5390. **Terms:** Sr. discount;
            no pets. **Facility:** 110 rooms. 11 efficiencies, $6 extra charge for up to 2 persons; 1 story; exterior corridors.
All Rooms: free movies. **Some Rooms:** 11 efficiencies. **Cards:** AE, CB, DI, DS, MC, VI.   (ECTV) (X) (D)

MOUNTAIN VIEW INN   **Phone:** 724/834-5300
(AAA) (SAVE)   All Year [CP]   1P: $62- 175   2P/1B: $62- 175 2P/2B: $88- 175 XP: $8   F16
            Location: On US 30, 5.3 mi e of US 119. 1001 Village Dr 15601. Fax: 724/834-5304. **Terms:** Reserv
◆◆◆   deposit; package plans; no pets. **Facility:** 93 rooms. Restored 1924 historic inn accented with antiques with
Hotel   varied room sizes & styles & some suites with fireplace. 4 stories; interior corridors; designated smoking area.
            Dining: 1776 Tavern-light menu & beverage; cocktails; dining room, see separate listing. **Services:** valet
laundry. **All Rooms:** coffeemakers, free movies, combo or shower baths. **Some Rooms:** 7 efficiencies, microwaves, radios,
refrigerators, whirlpools. Fee: VCR's. **Cards:** AE, CB, DI, DS, MC, VI. **Special Amenities: Free breakfast and free local
telephone calls.** (See color ad below)   Roll in showers.   (icons) (ECTV) (∱) (X) (D) (S)

RESTAURANTS

MOUNTAIN VIEW INN Historical   **Lunch:** $4-$11   **Dinner:** $12-$22   **Phone:** 724/834-5300
(AAA)   **Location:** On US 30, 5.3 mi e of jct of US 119; in Mountain View Inn. 1001 Village Dr 15601. **Hours:** 6:30
            am-10 pm. Closed: 12/23-12/27. **Reservations:** suggested. **Features:** dressy casual; children's menu; early
◆◆◆   bird specials; health conscious menu; cocktails & lounge; a la carte. Elegant country inn atmosphere; lighter
American   fare at lunch; family style meals on Sun. **Cards:** AE, CB, DI, DS, MC, VI.   (X)

VALLOZZI'S   **Lunch:** $5-$10   **Dinner:** $10-$22   **Phone:** 724/836-7663
◆◆◆   **Location:** 3.6 mi e of jct of US 119. Rt 30E 15601. **Hours:** 11 am-10 pm, Fri-11 pm, Sat 4 pm-11 pm.
Italian   Closed major holidays & Sun. **Reservations:** required. **Features:** dressy casual; children's menu; health
            conscious menu items; cocktails & lounge; valet parking; a la carte. Northern Italian specialties featured in
seafood, beef & chicken entrees in relaxed dining atmosphere. **Cards:** AE, DI, MC, VI.

HOPWOOD—2,000

LODGING

HOPWOOD MOTEL   **Phone:** 724/437-7591
(AAA) (SAVE)   Fri & Sat 5/1-10/31   1P: $38- 40 2P/1B: $48- 50 2P/2B: $51- 55 XP: $3   F11
            Sun-Thurs & Fri & Sat
◆   11/1-4/30   1P: $36- 38 2P/1B: $46- 48 2P/2B: $48- 50 XP: $3   F11
Motel   **Location:** 0.5 mi e on US 40 Business-Hopwood exit off George C. Marshall Pkwy. 15401 (RD 2, Box 661,
            UNIONTOWN). **Terms:** Reserv deposit, 3 day notice; no pets. **Facility:** 15 rooms. 1 story; exterior corridors.
Cards: DS, MC, VI.   (ECTV) (D)

A CLASSIC AMERICAN INN

*A Laurel Highlands Tradition of
Fine Dining and Premiere Lodging
for over 70 years*

♦ **Award-Winning Guest Rooms & American Cuisine**
♦ **Lovely Gardens, Sweeping Views, Swimming Pool**
♦ **Superb Wedding and Meeting Facility**
♦ **Free Continental Breakfast**

*Unique Getaway Packages and
Year-Round Special Events*

1-800-537-8709
RESERVATIONS
Route 30 East Greensburg

LAUREL HIGHLANDS

RESTAURANTS

CHEZ GERARD   Historical   **Phone: 724/437-9001**
◆◆◆   **Location:** Center. Rt 40E 15445. **Hours:** 11:30 am-2 & 5:30-10 pm. Closed major holidays & Tues.
Traditional   **Reservations:** suggested. **Features:** dressy casual; Sunday brunch; cocktails & lounge; prix fixe. Renovated
French   historic place dating back to 1790. French chefs come here to learn English & earn certificates as culinary
ambassadors. Very traditional French menu with adaptations for local products. **Cards:** AE, DI, DS, MC, VI.

THE SUN PORCH   **Lunch:** $4-$7   **Dinner:** $9-$13   **Phone:** 724/439-5734
◆◆   **Location:** 0.5 mi e on US 40 business route, Hopwood exit off George C Marshall Pkwy. 15445. **Hours:** 11
American   am-8 pm, Fri-9 pm, Sat 4 pm-9 pm. Closed: 1/1, 12/25 & Mon. **Features:** casual dress; children's menu;
carryout; salad bar. Casual dining in light, cheerful surroundings. Offers extensive buffet at dinner.
Cards: CB, DI, DS, MC, VI.

JENNERSTOWN—600

RESTAURANT

GREEN GABLES   **Lunch:** $5-$8   **Dinner:** $10-$24   **Phone:** 814/629-9220
◆◆   **Location:** 0.5 mi n on SR 985. 7712 Somerset Pike 15547. **Hours:** Open 5/1-12/31 & 4/1-4/30; noon-8 pm,
American   Fri & Sat-9 pm. Closed: 12/25, Tues 9/2-12/31 & Mon. **Reservations:** suggested. **Features:** casual dress;
children's menu; cocktails. Picturesque setting with stream in rear. Companion facility to popular dinner
theater, can be crowded on matinee days. Open some weekends in winter, call for days & times. **Cards:** AE, DI, DS, MC, VI.

JOHNSTOWN—28,100

LODGINGS

COMFORT INN   **Phone:** 814/266-3678
(AAA) [SAVE]   All Year [CP]   1P: $55- 60 2P/1B: $61- 66 2P/2B: $61- 66 XP: $6   F18
Location: Just e of US 219, exit Elton (SR 756). 455 Theatre Dr 15904. **Terms:** Small
◆◆◆   pets only, $6 extra charge. **Facility:** 117 rooms. Across from Richland Mall. 27 whirlpool rms, $85-$95; 5 sto-
Motel   ries; interior corridors; whirlpool, small heated indoor pool; video movie rentals. **Dining:** Restaurant nearby.
Services: Fee: coin laundry. **All Rooms:** VCR's. **Some Rooms:** microwaves, radios, refrigerators.
Cards: AE, CB, DI, DS, JCB, MC, VI. **Special Amenities: Free breakfast and free newspaper.**

HAMPTON INN   **Phone:** 814/262-7700
(AAA) [SAVE]   All Year [CP]   1P: $62   2P/1B: $67   2P/2B: $67
Motel   Too new to rate; **Location:** US 219, exit Elton (SR 756); just e on SR 756, just n on Donald Ln, then just w.
129 Commerce Ct 15904. Fax: 814/262-7800. **Terms:** Reserv deposit; no pets. **Facility:** 70 rooms. Scheduled
to open November 1997; 3 stories; interior corridors; video rentals. **All Rooms:** free movies.
Some Rooms: microwaves, refrigerators, whirlpools. Fee: VCR's. **Cards:** AE, CB, DI, DS, MC, VI. **Special Amenities: Free
breakfast and free local telephone calls.**   Roll in showers.

HOLIDAY INN DOWNTOWN   Guaranteed Rates   **Phone:** 814/535-7777
◆◆◆   All Year   1P: $79- 84 2P/1B: $79- 84 2P/2B: $79- 84
Hotel   **Location:** Downtown; corner Market & Vine sts. 250 Market St 15901. Fax: 814/539-1393. **Terms:** Sr.
discount; pets. **Facility:** 164 rooms. 6 stories; interior corridors; designated smoking area.
Dining: Restaurant; 7 am-10 pm; seasonal sidewalk cafe; $10-$16. **All Rooms:** Fee: movies. **Cards:** AE, CB, DI, DS, JCB,
MC, VI. *(See ad p 90)*   Roll in showers.

HOLIDAY INN EXPRESS JOHNSTOWN   Rates Subject to Change   **Phone:** 814/266-8789
◆◆◆   All Year [CP]   1P: $59- 64 2P/1B: $59- 64 2P/2B: $59- 64
Motel   **Location:** Just e of US 219, exit Windber (SR 56E). 1440 Scalp Ave 15904. Fax: 814/266-5285. **Terms:** Sr.
discount; pets. **Facility:** 108 rooms. 3 stories; interior corridors. **All Rooms:** free movies. **Cards:** AE, CB, DI,
DS, JCB, MC, VI.   Roll in showers.

MOTEL 6   Rates Subject to Change   **Phone:** 814/536-1114
◆◆   All Year   1P: $55   2P/1B: $58   2P/2B: $58   XP: $3   F17
Motel   **Location:** Downtown at jct of SR 271 & 403. 430 Napoleon Pl 15901. Fax: 814/536-0022. **Terms:** Sr.
discount; reserv deposit; small pets only, 1 per room. **Facility:** 47 rooms. 3 stories; interior corridors; desig-
nated smoking area. **All Rooms:** free movies. **Cards:** AE, CB, DI, DS, MC, VI.
Roll in showers.

SLEEP INN   Rates Subject to Change   **Phone:** 814/262-9292
◆◆   All Year [CP]   1P: $49- 53 2P/1B: $59   2P/2B: $55   XP: $6   F18
Motel   **Location:** Just e of US 219, exit Elton (SR 756). 453 Theatre Dr 15904. Fax: 814/262-0486. **Terms:** Sr.
discount; reserv deposit; pets, $6 extra charge. **Facility:** 62 rooms. 3 stories; interior corridors.
All Rooms: free movies. **Cards:** AE, CB, DI, DS, MC, VI.   Roll in showers.

RESTAURANT

LOMBARDO'S   **Lunch:** $5-$8   **Dinner:** $8-$19   **Phone:** 814/266-4247
◆◆   **Location:** 0.8 mi w of US 219, exit Scalp Ave. 935 Scalp Ave 15904. **Hours:** 11 am-10 pm, Sat 4 pm-11 pm,
Italian   Sun 11 am-8 pm. Closed major holidays. **Reservations:** suggested; weekends. **Features:** casual dress;
children's menu; carryout; cocktails; a la carte. Variety of traditional & specialty Italian entrees. **Cards:** AE,
DI, DS, MC, VI.

LATROBE—9,300

RESTAURANTS

DISALVO'S STATION RESTAURANT   Historical   **Lunch:** $5-$8   **Dinner:** $8-$18   **Phone:** 724/539-0500
◆◆◆   **Location:** Downtown. 325 McKinley Ave 15650. **Hours:** 11 am-10 pm, Sat from 4 pm, Sun 10 am-9 pm.
Italian   Closed: 1/1, 12/25 & Mon. **Reservations:** suggested. **Features:** casual dress; Sunday brunch; children's
menu; early bird specials; health conscious menu items; cocktails & lounge; fee for parking; a la carte.
Renovated Pennsylvania railroad station built in 1903. Large dining & socializing complex with 5 distinct dining areas &
downstairs nightclub. Free parking in evening. **Cards:** AE, CB, DI, DS, MC, VI.

SLEEPY HOLLOW INN   **Lunch:** $5-$10   **Dinner:** $11-$25   **Phone:** 724/537-5454
◆◆◆   **Location:** On US 30; 5.6 mi e of jct of SR 981. Rt 30E 15650. **Hours:** 11 am-2:30 & 4-9 pm, Fri & Sat-10
Nouvelle   pm, Sun-9 pm. Closed: 1/1 & 12/25. **Reservations:** suggested. **Features:** dressy casual; Sunday brunch;
American   children's menu; health conscious menu; cocktails & lounge; a la carte. Casual fine dining in rustic inn with
    woodland mountain stream view from atrium dining section; featuring creative entrees, soup & dessert. Verify
winter hours. **Cards:** AE, MC, VI.   ⊠

TORY'S BAR-B-QUE & ALE   **Lunch:** $5-$10   **Dinner:** $5-$10   **Phone:** 724/539-7427
◆   **Location:** On US 30, 0.5 mi e of jct SR 981. Rt 30E 15650. **Hours:** 11 am-9 pm, Fri & Sat-10 pm. Closed
American   major holidays. **Features:** casual dress; children's menu; senior's menu; carryout; salad bar; cocktails; a la
    carte. Barbecue dinners, various sandwich selections. **Cards:** DS, MC, VI.   ⊠

LIGONIER—1,600

RESTAURANT

COLONIAL INN   **Lunch:** $5-$10   **Dinner:** $9-$29   **Phone:** 724/238-6604
◆◆◆   **Location:** 1.5 mi w on US 30 from jct SR 711. Rt 30W 15658. **Hours:** 11:30 am-2:30 & 5-10 pm, Fri &
American   Sat-11 pm, Sun noon-9 pm. Closed: 1/1, 11/26, 12/25 & Mon. **Reservations:** suggested; weekends.
    Features: casual dress; Sunday brunch; health conscious menu items; cocktails & lounge; a la carte. Quiet
country dining. Nouvelle dishes & seafood specialties. Homemade soup & dessert. Lunch buffet daily. **Cards:** AE, DS, MC,
VI.   ⟨ẑ⟩ ⊠

NEW STANTON—2,100

LODGINGS

HOWARD JOHNSON INN   **Phone:** 724/925-3511
(AAA) [SAVE]   5/1-9/14 [CP]   2P/1B: $61-   77   2P/2B: $66-   78   XP: $5   F18
    9/15-10/31 & 4/1-4/30 [CP]   2P/1B: $49-   66   2P/2B: $59-   72   XP: $5   F18
◆◆◆   11/1-3/31 [CP]   2P/1B: $49-   61   2P/2B: $55-   65   XP: $5   F18
Motel   **Location:** 0.5 mi sw of I-76 & tpk exit 8 or I-70, exit 26. 112 W Byers Ave 15672 (PO Box 214).
    Fax: 724/925-3511. **Terms:** Weekly/monthly rates, winter & fall; no pets. **Facility:** 87 rooms. Many rooms with
private balcony facing pool; some with parking at room & all with voice mail & hair dryer. 1-2 stories; interior/exterior corridors;
designated smoking area; playground; video movie rentals. **Dining:** Restaurant nearby. **Services:** valet laundry.
Some Rooms: microwaves. Fee: refrigerators, VCR's. **Cards:** AE, CB, DI, DS, MC, VI. **Special Amenities:** Free breakfast
and free local telephone calls.   ⟨≈⟩ ⟨▥⟩ [ECTV] ⊠ [D]

RAMADA INN   **Phone:** 724/925-6755
(AAA) [SAVE]   All Year   1P: $58-   95   2P/2B: $74-   92   XP: $6   F18
    Too new to rate; **Location:** 110 N Main St/Byers Ave 15672 (PO Box 747). Fax:724/925-3097.
Motel   **Terms:** Reserv deposit, 10 day notice; **Facility:** 155 rooms. Scheduled to open November 1997. **Cards:** AE,
    CB, DI, DS, MC, VI. **Special Amenities:** Early check-in/late check-out and free local telephone calls.
(See color ad below)   [D]

RESTAURANT

LATAVOLA RISTORANTE   **Lunch:** $7-$10   **Dinner:** $9-$23   **Phone:** 724/925-9440
◆◆◆   **Location:** 0.5 mi s of I-76/PA Tpk, exit 8; just s of I-70, exit 26. 400 S Center Ave 15672. **Hours:** 11:30
Italian   am-10 pm, Sat 5 pm-11 pm. Closed major holidays & Sun. **Reservations:** suggested. **Features:** dressy
casual; health conscious menu items; cocktails & lounge; a la carte. Northern Italian with continental cuisine
flair featuring fresh seafood, beef, chicken & specialty pasta entrees. **Cards:** AE, DI, MC, VI.   🐁 ⊠

SOMERSET—6,500

LODGINGS

BEST WESTERN EXECUTIVE INN   **Phone:** 814/445-3996
🅰️🅰️🅰️ 〔SAVE〕   Fri & Sat [CP]   1P: $45- 65   2P/1B: $55- 75   2P/2B: $55- 75   XP: $5   F12
   Sun-Thurs [CP]   1P: $39- 59   2P/1B: $45- 65   2P/2B: $45- 65   XP: $5   F12
◆◆◆   **Location:** I-70/76 (Pa Tpk) exit 10, just e. 165 Water Works Rd 15501. Fax: 814/445-3808. **Terms:** Reserv
Motel   deposit; small pets only. **Facility:** 58 rooms. Modern rooms. Commerical location, adjacent to bus station. 3
   stories; interior corridors; video rental library. **Dining:** Restaurant nearby. **All Rooms:** combo or shower
baths. **Some Rooms:** Fee: VCR's. **Cards:** AE, CB, DI, DS, MC, VI. **Special Amenities: Free breakfast and free local
telephone calls.** (See color ad below)   Roll in showers.   🛏️ 🖐️ 📺 ⊠ D

BUDGET HOST INN   Rates Subject to Change   **Phone:** 814/445-7988
◆◆   Fri & Sat   1P: $40- 50   2P/1B: $40- 60   2P/2B: $45- 70   XP: $5   F12
Motel   Sun-Thurs   1P: $33- 38   2P/1B: $33- 40   2P/2B: $33- 40   XP: $5   F12
   Location: I-70/76 (PA Tpk) exit 10, 0.3 mi s. 799 N Center Ave 15501. **Terms:** Sr. discount; pets, $5 extra
charge. **Facility:** 27 rooms. 2 stories; exterior corridors. **All Rooms:** free movies. **Cards:** AE, CB, DI, DS, MC, VI.
(See color ad p 254)   🛏️ 📺 ⊠ D

THE BUDGET INN   **Phone:** 814/443-6441
🅰️🅰️🅰️ 〔SAVE〕   Fri & Sat   1P: $23- 50   2P/1B: $28- 55   2P/2B: $35- 50   XP: $3   F12
   Sun-Thurs   1P: $20- 30   2P/1B: $25- 35   2P/2B: $28- 38   XP: $3   F12
◆◆   **Location:** I-70/76 (PA Tpk) exit 10, 0.4 mi s. 736 N Center Ave 15501. Fax: 814/445-3763. **Terms:** Reserv
Motel   deposit, 5 day notice; weekly rates; small pets only. **Facility:** 16 rooms. Up-to-date budget accommodations;
   busy commercial location. 1-2 stories; interior corridors. **Dining:** Restaurant nearby. **All Rooms:** free movies,
combo or shower baths. **Some Rooms:** microwaves, refrigerators. **Cards:** AE, DS, MC, VI. **Special Amenities: Free local
telephone calls and free room upgrade (subject to availability with advanced reservations).** (See color ad below)
   🛏️ 📺 ⊠ D

DAYS INN-SOMERSET   Rates Subject to Change   **Phone:** 814/445-9200
◆◆   Fri & Sat 12/24-3/31 [CP]   1P: $54   2P/1B: $54   2P/2B: $58
Motel   5/1-12/23, Sun-Thurs
   12/24-3/31 & 4/1-4/30 [CP]   1P: $44- 54   2P/1B: $44- 54   2P/2B: $48- 58
Location: I-70/76 (PA Tpk) exit 10, just e. 220 Water Works Rd 15501. Fax: 814/445-9222. **Terms:** Sr. discount; small pets
only. **Facility:** 105 rooms. Rates for up to 4 persons; 2 stories; exterior corridors. **Cards:** AE, DI, DS, JCB, MC, VI.
   🛏️ 📺 ⊠ D

DOLLAR INN
(AAA)
◆◆
Motel

		1P:		2P/1B:		2P/2B:		XP:		
Fri & Sat		$25-	35	$30-	40		$35-	50	$5	D10
Sun-Thurs		$25-	32	$28-	35		$30-	40	$5	D10

Rates Subject to Change   **Phone:** 814/445-2977

Location: I-70/76 (PA Tpk) exit 10, just e via Water Works Rd then 0.5 mi n on SR 601. 1146 N Center Ave 15501. Fax: 814/443-6205. **Terms:** Sr. discount; reserv deposit, 4 day notice; pets, $5 extra charge, in designated rooms. **Facility:** 15 rooms. 1 story; exterior corridors. **All Rooms:** free movies. **Cards:** AE, CB, DI, DS, MC, VI. *(See color ad below)*

(🛏️) (ECTV) (✕) (D)

ECONOMY INN
(AAA) (SAVE)
◆◆
Motel

		1P:		2P/1B:		2P/2B:		XP:		
Fri & Sat [CP]		$50-	65	$50-	70		$65-	79	$5	D
Sun-Thurs [CP]		$35-	49	$45-	55		$55-	65	$5	D

Phone: 814/445-4144

Location: I-70/76 (PA Tpk) exit 10, just e via Water Works Rd then 0.5 mi n on SR 601. (RD 2, Box 5, SR 601, 15501). Fax: 814/445-3763. **Terms:** Reserv deposit; weekly rates; no pets. **Facility:** 19 rooms. Attractive economy lodgings; good-sized rooms with many extra amenities, including cordless telephone, hair dryer, iron & ironing board. 2 whirlpool rms, extra charge. Handling fee imposed; 1 story; interior corridors; whirlpool; playground, picnic area, game room. **Dining:** Restaurant nearby. **Services:** area transportation, within 15 mi; winter plug-ins. Fee: coin laundry. **All Rooms:** microwaves, free movies, refrigerators, VCR's. **Cards:** AE, DS, MC, VI. **Special Amenities: Free breakfast and free local telephone calls.** *(See color ad below)*

(📶) (🍴) (🛏️) (♿) (ECTV) (✕) (D)

HAMPTON INN
◆◆◆
Motel

		1P:		2P/1B:		2P/2B:	
Fri & Sat 1/1-3/15 [CP]		$80		$80		$80	
5/1-12/31, Sun-Thurs							
1/1-3/15 & 3/16-4/30 [CP]		$59-	68	$70-	73	$64	

Rates Subject to Change   **Phone:** 814/445-9161

Location: I 70/76 (PA Tpk) exit 10, just sw. 324 Laurel Crest Rd 15501. Fax: 814/445-9162. **Terms:** No pets. **Facility:** 112 rooms. Rates for up to 4 persons; 5 stories; interior corridors. **All Rooms:** free movies. **Cards:** AE, CB, DI, DS, MC, VI.

Roll in showers. (🏊) (ECTV) (✕) (D) (S)

HOLIDAY INN
(AAA) (SAVE)
◆◆
Motor Inn

		1P:		2P/1B:		2P/2B:		XP:		
All Year		$69-	89	$75-	95		$75-	95	$10	F18

Phone: 814/445-9611

Location: I-70/76, exit 10, just s. 202 Shaffer St 15501 (PO Box 191). Fax: 814/445-5815. **Terms:** Weekly/monthly rates; BP avail; small pets only, in designated rooms. **Facility:** 102 rooms. Contemporary rooms; kings with recliner chairs. 2-3 stories, no elevator; interior corridors; wading pool; game room, video rental library. **Dining & Entertainment:** Restaurant; 6:30 am-1 & 6-9 pm; $9-$16; cocktails/lounge. **Services:** valet laundry. **All Rooms:** free movies. **Some Rooms:** coffeemakers. Fee: VCR's. **Cards:** AE, CB, DI, DS, JCB, MC, VI. **Special Amenities: Free local telephone calls and free room upgrade (subject to availability with advanced reservations).**

(🛏️) (🏊) (🍴) (ECTV) (✕) (D)

THE INN AT GEORGIAN PLACE
◆◆◆
Historic Bed
& Breakfast

		1P:		2P/1B:			XP:	
All Year [BP]		$95-	185	$95-	185		$10	

Rates Subject to Change   **Phone:** 814/443-1043

Location: I-70/76 (PA Tpk) exit 10, just e via Water Works Rd, then 0.5 mi n on SR 601; at Horizon Outlet Center. 800 Georgian Place Dr 15501. Fax: 814/445-3047. **Terms:** Sr. discount; age restrictions may apply; pets. **Facility:** 11 rooms. Public tours avail Mon-Fri, 1:30 pm, $3 per person; 3 stories, no elevator; interior corridors. **Dining:** Dining room; noon-4 pm. **All Rooms:** free movies. **Cards:** AE, CB, DI, DS, MC, VI.

(🛏️) (ECTV) (✕) (D)

KNIGHTS INN   Rates Subject to Change   **Phone:** 814/445-8933
◆◆   Fri & Sat 12/17-3/12   1P: $48   2P/1B: $58   2P/2B: $60   XP: $10   F18
Motel   5/1-12/16, Sun-Thurs
            12/17-3/12 & 3/13-4/30   1P: $46   2P/1B: $46   2P/2B: $53   XP: $7   F18
Location: I-70/76 (PA Tpk) exit 10, just s. 585 Ramada Rd 15501. Fax: 814/445-9745. **Terms:** Sr. discount; pets.
Facility: 112 rooms. 10 efficiencies, $58.95-$68.95, rates for up to 2 persons; 1 story; exterior corridors. **All Rooms:** free
movies. **Cards:** AE, CB, DI, DS, MC, VI.   🐾 ⛵ ECTV ✕ D

QUILL HAVEN COUNTRY INN   Rates Subject to Change   **Phone:** 814/443-4514
◆◆◆   All Year [BP]   1P: $75- 95   2P/1B: $75- 95   XP: $10   F5
Historic Bed **Location:** I-70/76 (PA Tpk) exit 10, just e via Water Works Rd, then 1.1 mi n on SR 601. 1519 N Center Ave
& Breakfast   15501. Fax: 814/445-1376. **Terms:** Check-in 4 pm; reserv deposit, 14 day notice; no pets. **Facility:** 4 rooms.
2 stories; interior corridors; smoke free premises. **All Rooms:** free movies. **Cards:** MC, VI.   ECTV ✕ D

RAMADA INN   **Phone:** 814/443-4646
🅰🅰🅰 SAVE   All Year   1P: $62- 88   2P/1B: $72- 98 2P/2B: $72- 98 XP: $10   F17
             Location: I-70/76 (PA Tpk) exit 10, just s. Exit 10 PA Turnpike 15501 (PO Box 511). Fax: 814/445-7539.
◆◆◆   **Terms:** Weekly rates; BP avail; package plans; small pets only. **Facility:** 152 rooms. Attractive enclosed court-
Motor Inn   yard. 2 stories; interior corridors; saunas, whirlpool. **Dining & Entertainment:** Cocktail lounge; also, Myron's,
             see separate listing; entertainment. **Services:** valet laundry. **All Rooms:** free movies.
Some Rooms: coffeemakers. Fee: refrigerators. **Cards:** AE, DI, DS, MC, VI. **Special Amenities: Free local telephone
calls and free room upgrade (subject to availability with advanced reservations).** *(See color ad below)*
                                                                                🐾 ⛵ 🛎 ECTV ✕ D

RESTAURANTS

GRAPEVINE CAFE   **Lunch:** $5-$9   **Dinner:** $6-$15   **Phone:** 814/445-6622
◆◆   **Location:** I-70/76 (PA Tpk) exit 10, jsut e via Water Works Rd, then 1.7 mi n on SR 601. 1640 N Center Ave
American   15501. **Hours:** 11 am-9 pm, Fri & Sat-10 pm, Sun-8 pm. Closed major holidays. **Reservations:** suggested; 6
or more. **Features:** casual dress; Sunday brunch; children's menu; carryout; cocktails & lounge. Casual
family dining with some excellent Italian specialties, including "wedding soup", a rich broth swimming with meatballs, chicken
& fresh spinach. **Cards:** AE, DS, MC, VI.   ✕

JIMMY'S AMERICAN BISTRO   **Lunch:** $5-$12   **Dinner:** $7-$12   **Phone:** 814/444-1111
🅰🅰🅰 SAVE   **Location:** 1 mi e on Pleasant Ave, then just ne on SR 31. 373 E Main St 15501. **Hours:** 11 am-9 pm, Fri &
             Sat-10 pm, Sun-8 pm. Closed major holidays. **Reservations:** suggested; 6 or more. **Features:** casual dress;
◆◆   children's menu; carryout; cocktails. Excellent homemade Italian-American specialties, cheerful ambience.
American   **Cards:** AE, DS, MC, VI. **Special Value: 20% discount on the price of any entree, excluding beverages,
tax and gratuity.** *(See color ad p 316)*   ✕

MYRON'S   **Lunch:** $5-$8   **Dinner:** $8-$15   **Phone:** 814/443-4646
◆◆   **Location:** I-70/76 (PA Tpk), exit 10, just s; in Ramada Inn. **Hours:** 6:30-11 am, 11:30-2 & 5-10 pm, Sun from
American   7 am. **Reservations:** accepted. **Features:** casual dress; Sunday brunch; children's menu; salad bar;
cocktails & lounge; entertainment. Informal family dining. Lunch buffet weekdays; nightly specials.
Cards: AE, CB, DI, DS, JCB, MC, VI.   ✕

PINE GRILL RESTAURANT   **Lunch:** $3-$5   **Dinner:** $5-$14   **Phone:** 814/445-2102
◆◆   **Location:** 0.3 mi s of I-76 & I-70, PA Tpk exit 10. 800 N Center Ave 15501. **Hours:** 7 am-10 pm. Closed:
American   12/25. **Reservations:** accepted. **Features:** casual dress; children's menu; carryout; cocktails & lounge.
Relaxed dining. Homemade desserts. **Cards:** AE, MC, VI.   ✕

Relax over good food: Follow the recommendations
in the Lodgings & Restaurants listings.

STAHLSTOWN—600

RESTAURANT

THE BRASS DUCK   **Lunch:** $5-$9   **Dinner:** $13-$30   **Phone:** 724/593-7440
◆◆   **Location:** Just e of jct SR 130 & 711. Main & Diamond 15687. **Hours:** noon-8:30 pm, Sat 9:40 pm, Sun 11
American   am-8:40 pm. Closed major holidays & Tues. **Reservations:** suggested. **Features:** casual dress; Sunday
brunch; children's menu; health conscious menu items; cocktails & lounge. Offering a variety of creative
entrees & featuring duck creations. **Cards:** AE, CB, DI, DS, MC, VI.   ⊠

UNIONTOWN—12,000

LODGINGS

HERITAGE INN   **Phone:** 724/437-7829
🆎 [SAVE]   Fri & Sat 5/1-10/31   2P/1B: $59-   79   2P/2B: $59-   79   XP: $5
     Sun-Thurs 5/1-10/31   2P/1B: $45-   69   2P/2B: $45-   69   XP: $5
◆◆   11/1-4/30   2P/1B: $38-   59   2P/2B: $38-   59   XP: $5
Motel   **Location:** 0.6 mi w on US 40. 222 West Main St 15401. Fax: 724/437-8717. **Terms:** Reserv deposit; weekly
rates, off season; no pets. **Facility:** 19 rooms. 1 story; exterior corridors. **Dining:** Restaurant nearby.
Services: valet laundry. **All Rooms:** free movies. **Some Rooms:** microwaves, refrigerators. **Cards:** AE, DS, MC, VI.
Special Amenities: Free local telephone calls. *(See color ad below)*   🅂 ♿ 🄴🄲🅃🅅 ⊠ (D)

HOLIDAY INN   Rates Subject to Change   **Phone:** 724/437-2816
◆◆◆   All Year   1P: $79-   95   2P/1B: $79-   95   2P/2B: $79-   95
Motor Inn   **Location:** 1.8 mi w on US 40. 700 W Main St 15401. Fax: 724/437-3505. **Terms:** Sr. discount; pets.
Facility: 179 rooms. 2 stories; interior corridors. **Dining:** Dining room; 6:30 am-2 & 4:30-10 pm; $10-$19.
All Rooms: free movies. **Cards:** AE, CB, DI, DS, JCB, MC, VI.   🍴 ♿ 🄴🄲🅃🅅 ⊠ (D)

INNE AT WATSON'S CHOICE   Rates Subject to Change   **Phone:** 724/437-4999
◆◆◆   All Year [BP]   1P: $89- 125   2P/1B: $89- 125
Historic Bed   **Location:** 3 mi w on SR 21 from jct US 40/119, 0.3 mi nw, following signs. (RD 3, Box 363, 15401).
& Breakfast   **Terms:** Age restrictions may apply; reserv deposit, 7 day notice; 2 night min stay, weekends; no pets.
Facility: 7 rooms. 2 stories; interior corridors; smoke free premises. **Cards:** AE, DS, MC, VI.   ⊠ (D)

M G MOTEL   Phone: 724/437-0506

		1P:	$43	2P/1B:	$43	2P/2B:	$49
	5/1-10/15						
	10/16-4/30	1P:	$39	2P/1B:	$39	2P/2B:	$45

Location: 2.2 mi w on Rt 40W. (RD 6, Box 130, 15401). **Terms:** Reserv deposit; weekly rates; no pets.
Motel   **Facility:** 10 rooms. Compact rooms. 1 story; exterior corridors; basketball hoop. **Cards:** AE, DS, MC, VI.
Special Amenities: Early check-in/late check-out and free local telephone calls. [ECTV] [D]

MOUNT VERNON INN   Phone: 724/437-2704

		1P:	$38- 73	2P/1B:	$42- 78	2P/2B:	$42- 78	XP:	$5	F18
	5/1-10/31 [BP]									
	11/1-4/30 [BP]	1P:	$33- 68	2P/1B:	$37- 73	2P/2B:	$37- 73	XP:	$5	F18

Location: 0.5 mi w on US 40. 180 W Main St 15401. Fax: 724/437-2737. **Terms:** Weekly/monthly rates;
Motor Inn   small pets only, $10 extra charge, $25 dep req. **Facility:** 46 rooms. Convenient downtown location. Live band,
loud music some nights. 1-3 stories; interior/exterior corridors. **Dining & Entertainment:** Restaurant; 11
am-11 pm; $7-$14; cocktails/lounge; entertainment. **All Rooms:** combo or shower baths. **Some Rooms:** refrigerators.
Cards: AE, CB, DI, DS, MC, VI. **Special Amenities: Early check-in/late check-out and free breakfast.**
[icons]

RESTAURANTS

COAL BARON RESTAURANT   **Dinner:** $8-$20   Phone: 724/439-0111
Location: 4 mi w on US 40. Rt 40 W 15401. **Hours:** 4 pm-11 pm, Sun noon-8 pm. Closed major holidays &
Continental   Mon. **Reservations:** suggested. **Features:** casual dress; children's menu; early bird specials; carryout;
cocktails & lounge; valet parking. Flambe desserts, popular for beef & veal dishes. Extensive wine list.
Cards: AE, CB, DI, DS, MC, VI.

MELONI'S   **Lunch:** $5-$7   **Dinner:** $6-$14   Phone: 724/437-2061
Location: Center. 105 W Main St 15401. **Hours:** 11 am-10 pm, Fri & Sat-11 pm, Sun noon-9 pm. Closed
major holidays. **Features:** casual dress; children's menu; carryout; cocktails & lounge. Some American fare.
Cards: MC, VI.
Italian

WINDBER—4,800

RESTAURANT

RIZZO'S RESTAURANT   **Dinner:** $7-$17   Phone: 814/467-7908
Location: Just n from jct SR 56 & 160, just e. 2200 Graham Ave 15963. **Hours:** 3 pm-midnight, Sun 11
Italian   am-7 pm (last seating). Closed major holidays & Mon. **Reservations:** suggested; weekends.
Features: casual dress; children's menu; cocktails & lounge; a la carte. Homemade soup, dessert & pasta
with traditional favorites & specialty entrees. **Cards:** MC, VI. [X]

LAVANSVILLE—100

RESTAURANT

OAKHURST TEA ROOM   **Lunch:** $3-$10   **Dinner:** $7-$16   Phone: 814/443-2897
Location: 1.4 mi w on SR 31. SR 31 15501. **Hours:** 11 am-9 pm, Sun-8 pm; smorgasbord Tues-Sat 4 pm-9
pm, Tues-Sat lunch buffet 11 am-3 pm & Sunday Brunch 11 am-2 pm. Closed: 12/25 & Mon.
American   **Features:** casual dress; children's menu; early bird specials; carryout; salad bar; cocktails & lounge. Country
dining serving smorgasbord & family-style meals. Homemade soup, bread & dessert; popular bread stuffing
ball. **Cards:** AE, DS, MC, VI. [X]

LEBANON (LEBANON COUNTY)

LODGING

QUALITY INN LEBANON VALLEY   Phone: 717/273-6771

		1P:	$80- 109	2P/1B:	$90- 109	2P/2B:	$90- 109	XP:	$7	F18
	7/1-9/1									
	9/2-10/31	1P:	$78- 99	2P/1B:	$82- 99	2P/2B:	$82- 99	XP:	$7	F18
	5/1-6/30	1P:	$76- 99	2P/1B:	$81- 99	2P/2B:	$81- 99	XP:	$7	F18
	11/1-4/30	1P:	$72- 83	2P/1B:	$77- 93	2P/2B:	$77- 93	XP:	$7	F18

Location: 0.5 mi s on SR 72. 625 Quentin Rd 17042. Fax: 717/273-4882. **Terms:** Weekly/monthly rates;
Motor Inn   package plans; no pets. **Facility:** 130 rooms. Convenient midtown location. 1-5 stories; interior/exterior corridors; wading pool.
Dining & Entertainment: Dining room; 6 am-1:30 & 5-9 pm, Sun 7 am-11, noon-2 & 5-8 pm; $10-$23; cocktails/lounge.
Services: valet laundry. **All Rooms:** coffeemakers, combo or shower baths. **Some Rooms:** Fee: refrigerators. **Cards:** AE,
CB, DI, DS, JCB, MC, VI. **Special Amenities: Free newspaper and free room upgrade (subject to availability with
advanced reservations).** *(See color ad p 307)*   Roll in showers. [icons]

LEMONT—2,600

RESTAURANT

THE VICTORIAN MANOR RESTAURANT   **Dinner:** $15-$28   Phone: 814/238-5534
Location: Center. 901 Pike St 16851. **Hours:** 5 pm-9 pm. Closed major holidays & Mon.
Continental   **Reservations:** suggested. **Features:** semi-formal attire; cocktails & lounge. Fine dining in 1890's converted
residence. Smoke free premises. **Cards:** AE, DI, DS, MC, VI. [X]

LEOLA—*see Pennsylvania Dutch Country p. 348.*

LEVITTOWN—*See Philadelphia & Vicinity p. 381.*

PARKING FACILITIES
Hotels—Outlined in listings.
Other lodging classifications—Described in listings only if not free.

LEWISBURG—5,800

LODGINGS

BEST WESTERN COUNTRY CUPBOARD INN   Rates Subject to Change   **Phone:** 717/524-5500
(AAA)   All Year [CP]   1P: $70- 150   2P/1B: $80- 160   2P/2B: $80- 160   XP: $6   F
◆◆◆   **Location:** I-80 exit 30A (Lewisburg), 4.8 mi s. Rt 15N 17837 (PO Box 46). **Fax:** 717/524-4291. **Terms:** Sr.
Motor Inn   discount; no pets. **Facility:** 106 rooms. 2-3 stories; interior corridors. **Dining:** Restaurant, see separate
listing. **All Rooms:** free movies. **Cards:** AE, CB, DI, DS, MC, VI. *(See ad below)*   ☒ ⊙ ⊠ Ⓓ

BRYNWOOD INN   **Phone:** 717/524-2121
(AAA) [SAVE]   All Year [CP]   1P: $50- 73   2P/1B: $61- 73   2P/2B: $56- 73   XP: $6   F16
◆◆◆   **Location:** S of I-80 exit 30A, close to Bucknell University. Rt 15 & 45 17837. **Fax:** 717/524-4932
Motel   **Terms:** Monthly rates; small pets only. **Facility:** 17 rooms. Spacious units with very nice furniture. 2 stories;
interior corridors. **Dining:** Restaurant nearby. **All Rooms:** free movies. **Some Rooms:** microwaves
Fee: refrigerators. **Cards:** AE, DI, MC, VI. **Special Amenities: Free breakfast and free local telephone**
calls.   ⊞ ⊛ ⊙ ⊠ Ⓓ

LEWISBURG-DAYS INN   **Phone:** 717/523-1171
(AAA) [SAVE]   All Year   1P: $59- 133   2P/1B: $65- 133   2P/2B: $71- 133   XP: $6   F17
◆◆   **Location:** On US 15, 0.5 mi n of jct SR 45. US Rt 15 17837 (PO Box 253). **Fax:** 717/524-4667
Motel   **Terms:** Small pets only. **Facility:** 108 rooms. Suites, $104-$131; 2 stories; exterior corridors.
Dining: Restaurant nearby. **Some Rooms:** whirlpools. Fee: microwaves, refrigerators, VCR's. **Cards:** AE
DI, DS, JCB, MC, VI. **Special Amenities: Free room upgrade (subject to availability with advanced**
reservations). *(See ad below)*   ⊞ ⊠ ⊛ ⊛ ⊙ ⊠ Ⓓ

RESTAURANTS

COUNTRY CUPBOARD RESTAURANT   **Lunch:** $5-$11   **Dinner:** $6-$11   **Phone:** 717/523-3211
(AAA)   **Location:** I-80, exit 30A (Lewisburg) 4.8 mi s; adjacent to Best Western Country Cupboard Inn. 17837
◆◆   **Hours:** 7 am-9 pm. Closed: 12/25. **Features:** casual dress; children's menu; carryout; salad bar; buffet
American   Popular, colonial style family restaurant, also regional specialties. Smoke free premises. **Cards:** DS, MC, VI.
(See ad below)   ⊠

TEMPERANCE HOUSE   **Lunch:** $6-$11   **Dinner:** $9-$16   **Phone:** 717/524-2558
◆◆   **Location:** 0.5 mi e on SR 45 from jct US 15, just n. 50 N 2nd St 17837. **Hours:** 11:30 am-10:45 pm
American   Fri-11:45 pm, Sat 4 pm-11:45 pm. Closed major holidays & Sun. **Reservations:** suggested
Features: casual dress; carryout; cocktails. Relaxed dining, daily specials featured. **Cards:** AE, DS, MC, VI.
⊠

LIGONIER—*See Laurel Highlands p. 314.*

LINE LEXINGTON—*See Philadelphia & Vicinity p. 381.*

LINFIELD—*See Philadelphia & Vicinity p. 381.*

LIONVILLE—*See Philadelphia & Vicinity p. 381.*

LITITZ—*See Pennsylvania Dutch Country p. 348.*

LOCK HAVEN—9,200

LODGING

BEST WESTERN-LOCK HAVEN	Rates Subject to Change			**Phone:** 717/748-3297	

◆◆   All Year [CP]   1P: $60- 90   2P/1B: $60- 90   2P/2B: $60- 90   XP: $5   F16
Motel   **Location:** Just s on E Walnut St from jct US 220, SR 120W exit. 101 E Walnut St 17745. Fax: 717/748-5390. **Terms:** Sr. discount; pets, $4 extra charge. **Facility:** 67 rooms. 4 stories; interior corridors. **All Rooms:** free & pay movies. **Cards:** AE, CB, DI, DS, MC.   🛏 ➕ ᴇᴄᴛᴠ 🈳 ✖ 🅓

LUMBERVILLE—*See Philadelphia & Vicinity p. 382.*

LUZERNE—3,200

RESTAURANT

ANDY PERUGINO'S RESTAURANT   **Lunch:** $3-$6   **Dinner:** $6-$26   **Phone:** 717/287-9315
◆   **Location:** From Cross Valley Expwy southbound exit 5, right on Bennett, 0.3 mi to Carpenter, right on
Italian   Carpenter, right on Charles St; northbound exit 6, back to exit 5. 258 Charles St 18709. **Hours:** 11 am-2 & 4-11 pm, Sat from 4 pm. Closed: 1/1, 3/30, 11/26, 12/25, Sun & 8/1-8/8. **Reservations:** suggested; weekends. **Features:** casual dress; children's menu; early bird specials; carryout; cocktails & lounge. Also, American dishes; hearty portions. **Cards:** AE, DS, MC, VI.   ✖

MALVERN—*See Philadelphia & Vicinity p. 382.*

MANSFIELD—3,500

LODGINGS

COMFORT INN   Rates Subject to Change   **Phone:** 717/662-3000
◆◆◆   10/1-10/31 [CP]   1P: $65- 81   2P/1B: $75- 91   2P/2B: $75- 91   XP: $6   F18
Motel   5/1-9/30 & 4/1-4/30 [CP]   1P: $61- 79   2P/1B: $71- 89   2P/2B: $71- 89   XP: $6   F18
   11/1-3/31 [CP]   1P: $59- 77   2P/1B: $69- 87   2P/2B: $69- 87   XP: $6   F18
Location: Jct US 15 & US 6. 300 Gateway Dr 16933. Fax: 717/662-2551. **Terms:** Sr. discount; pets. **Facility:** 100 rooms. 2 stories; interior corridors. **All Rooms:** free movies. **Cards:** AE, CB, DI, DS, JCB, MC, VI.   🛏 ᴄᴛᴠ ✖ 🅓 🆂

MANSFIELD INN   **Phone:** 717/662-2136
🆓 ꜱᴀᴠᴇ   5/1-12/1 [CP]   1P: $49   2P/1B: $59   2P/2B: $65   XP: $5   F18
   12/2-4/30 [CP]   1P: $45   2P/1B: $55   2P/2B: $60   XP: $5   F18
◆◆◆   **Location:** Just s on Bus US 15 from jct Rt 6. 26 S Main St 16933. Fax: 717/662-2067. **Terms:** Pets, $5
Motel   extra charge. **Facility:** 25 rooms. Attractively appointed rooms in small downtown area. 1 story; exterior corridors. **Dining:** Restaurant nearby. **Services:** winter plug-ins. **All Rooms:** coffeemakers, free movies.
Cards: AE, CB, DI, DS, MC, VI. **Special Amenities:** Free breakfast and free local telephone calls.
(See color ad below)   🛏 ᴄᴛᴠ ✖ 🅓

WEST'S DELUXE MOTEL   **Phone:** 717/659-5141
🆓 ꜱᴀᴠᴇ   All Year   1P: $32   2P/1B: $40- 45   2P/2B: $45   XP: $5   F10
◆   **Location:** 3.5 mi s on US 15. 16933 (RD 1, Box 97). Fax: 717/659-5851. **Terms:** Reserv deposit; package
Motel   plans; pets. **Facility:** 20 rooms. Nice rooms in country setting. 1 story; exterior corridors; picnic area.
Dining & Entertainment: Restaurant; 4 pm-9 pm, Fri & Sat-9:30 pm, Sun 11 am-8 pm; $7-$15; cocktails/lounge. **Services:** winter plug-ins. **All Rooms:** coffeemakers, combo or shower baths.
Some Rooms: refrigerators. Fee: VCR's. **Cards:** AE, DS, MC, VI. **Special Amenities:** Free local telephone calls.   🛏 🛋 ᴄᴛᴠ ✖ 🅓

MARIETTA—*See Pennsylvania Dutch Country p. 348.*

MARSHALLS CREEK—*See Pocono Mountains Area p. 425.*

MATAMORAS—*See Pocono Mountains Area p. 425.*

MAYFIELD—1,900

RESTAURANT

ALEXANDER'S FAMILY RESTAURANT   **Lunch:** $5-$9   **Dinner:** $8-$16   **Phone:** 717/876-9993
(AAA)   **Location:** On US 6. **Hours:** 8 am-2 am. Closed: 12/24 & 12/25. **Reservations:** accepted. **Features:** casual
◆◆   dress; children's menu; carryout; cocktails & lounge. Family restaurant featuring fresh seafood, beef & pork.
American   On-premise baking. **Cards:** AE, DS, MC, VI.   ⊠

MCMURRAY—*See Pittsburgh & Vicinity p. 411.*

MEADVILLE—14,300

LODGINGS

DAYS INN   **Phone:** 814/337-4264
(AAA) (SAVE)   5/1-10/31   1P: $65- 80   2P/1B: $65- 86 2P/2B: $70- 91 XP: $6   F18
        11/1-4/30   1P: $60- 71   2P/1B: $60- 76 2P/2B: $59- 79 XP: $6   F18
◆◆   **Location:** On US 6 & 322; from I-79 exit 36, 0.5 mi e. 18360 Conneaut Lake Rd 16335. Fax: 814/337-7304.
Motor Inn   **Terms:** Package plans; pets, $5 extra charge, $25 dep req. **Facility:** 163 rooms. 2 stories; interior corridors;
    whirlpool. **Dining & Entertainment:** Dining room; 7 am-2 & 5-10 pm; $8-$15; cocktails/lounge.
Services: valet laundry. **All Rooms:** free movies. Fee: safes. **Some Rooms:** radios. Fee: microwaves, refrigerators, VCR's.
Cards: AE, CB, DI, DS, MC, VI. **Special Amenities:** Free newspaper and free room upgrade **(subject to availability
with advanced reservations).** *(See color ad below)*   🍴 ⚖ 📶 📺 ⊠ D

HOLIDAY INN EXPRESS   **Phone:** 814/724-6012
(AAA) (SAVE)   All Year [CP]   1P: $65- 75   2P/1B: $65- 75 2P/2B: $65- 75
◆◆◆   **Location:** Exit 36A off I-79, 0.3 mi w on US 322. 18240 Conneaut Lake Rd 16335. Fax: 814/337-2617.
Motel   **Terms:** No pets. **Facility:** 68 rooms. 3 stories; interior/exterior corridors. **All Rooms:** free movies.
    Cards: AE, DS, JCB, MC, VI. *(See color ad below)*   📺 ⊠ 🚭 D S

SUPER 8 MOTEL   Rates Subject to Change   **Phone:** 814/333-8883
◆◆   All Year   1P: $42   2P/1B: $48   2P/2B: $48   XP: $6   F14
Motel   **Location:** I-79 exit 36B, 0.5 mi w on US 322. 845 Conneaut Lake Rd 16335. Fax: 814/333-8883.
    Terms: Small pets only, $20 dep req. **Facility:** 62 rooms. Weekends 5/1-11/1, $5 extra charge; 3 stories;
interior/exterior corridors. **All Rooms:** free & pay movies. **Cards:** AE, DI, DS, MC, VI.   🍴 📺 ⊠ D S

RESTAURANT

SANDALINI'S
◆◆
American

Lunch: $5-$9   Dinner: $10-$18   Phone: 814/724-1286
Location: Exit 36A off I-79, 0.3 mi e on US 322. 18228 Conneaut Lake Rd 16335. **Hours:** 11 am-1 am.
Closed: 12/25. **Features:** casual dress; children's menu; early bird specials; health conscious menu;
carryout; cocktails. Bistro cafe atmosphere. **Cards:** AE, DS, MC, VI.   [X]

MECHANICSBURG—9,500   (See map p. 292; index p. 291)

LODGINGS

AMBER INN   Phone: 717/766-9006   53
[AAA] [SAVE]   All Year   1P: $34- 53 2P/1B: $39- 53 2P/2B: $44- 59 XP: $5   F12
◆◆   **Location:** PA Tpk exit 17, 1 mi on on US 15, Wesley Dr exit, just w & just on Gettysburg Rd. 1032 Audubon
Motel   Rd 17055. **Terms:** Reserv deposit; no pets. **Facility:** 15 rooms. Handling fee imposed; 1 story; exterior corri-
           dors; designated smoking area. **All Rooms:** combo or shower baths. **Some Rooms:** efficiency, microwaves,
           refrigerators. **Cards:** AE, DS, MC, VI.   [ECTV] [X] [D]

BEST WESTERN PLANTATION INN   Phone: 717/766-0238   52
[AAA] [SAVE]   5/1-11/1 & 4/15-4/30 [CP] 1P: $66- 75   2P/2B: $72- 85 XP: $5   F12
           11/2-4/14 [CP]   1P: $56- 75   2P/2B: $62- 78 XP: $5   F12
◆◆◆   **Location:** On US 15 at PA Tpk I-76, exit 17. 381 Cumberland Pkwy 17055. Fax: 717/697-9329. **Terms:** No
Motel   pets. **Facility:** 35 rooms. Pleasant setting adjacent to Chip & Putt Par 3 golf course. 2 stories; exterior corri-
           dors; designated smoking area. Fee: 9 holes golf. **Services:** Fee: coin laundry. **All Rooms:** combo or
shower baths. **Some Rooms:** microwaves, refrigerators. **Cards:** AE, DI, DS, MC, VI. **Special Amenities: Free local
telephone calls.**   [jacuzzi] [ECTV] [D]

COMFORT INN WEST   Rates Subject to Change   Phone: 717/790-0924   51
◆◆◆   All Year [CP]   1P: $59- 68 2P/1B: $65- 73 2P/2B: $65- 73 XP: $6   F18
Motel   **Location:** 1 mi w on US 11 from jct of Carlisle Pike & US 11. 6325 Carlisle Pike 17055. Fax: 717/691-9385.
           Terms: Sr. discount; no pets. **Facility:** 125 rooms. 4 stories; interior corridors. **All Rooms:** free movies.
Cards: AE, CB, DI, DS, JCB, MC, VI. *(See ad p 295)*   [ECTV] [X] [D]

DAYS INN HARRISBURG WEST   Phone: 717/766-3700
[AAA] [SAVE]   All Year   1P: $59- 135 2P/1B: $69- 135 2P/2B: $79- 135 XP: $10   F16
           Too new to rate; **Location:** 1012 Wesley Dr 17055. Fax: 717/766-8380. **Facility:** 64 rooms. Handling fee im-
Motel   posed. Scheduled to open May 1997. **Cards:** AE, CB, DI, DS, MC, VI. **Special Amenities: Free breakfast
and free local telephone calls.**   [D] [S]

ECONO LODGE   Phone: 717/766-4728   57
[AAA] [SAVE]   5/1-10/31   1P: $32- 47 2P/1B: $40- 55 2P/2B: $40- 55 XP: $6   F18
           11/1-4/30   1P: $30- 45 2P/1B: $35- 50 2P/2B: $35- 50 XP: $6   F18
◆◆   **Location:** PA Tpk, exit 17; 1 mi n on US 15 to Wesley Dr exit, just w, 0.8 mi s. 650 Gettysburg Rd 17055.
Motel   Fax: 717/766-4728. **Terms:** Reserv deposit; no pets. **Facility:** 41 rooms. Park at rooms. 1 story; exterior cor-
           ridors. **All Rooms:** free movies, shower baths. **Cards:** AE, DI, DS, MC, VI. **Special Amenities: Free room
upgrade and preferred room (each subject to availability with advanced reservations).** *(See color ad p 295)*
                                                                          [jacuzzi] [X] [D]

HAMPTON INN-HARRISBURG WEST   Rates Subject to Change   Phone: 717/691-1300   56
◆◆◆   All Year [CP]   1P: $85   2P/1B: $89   2P/2B: $86- 89 XP: $6   F18
Motel   **Location:** PA Tpk exit 17, 1 mi n on US 15 exit Rossmoyne Rd. 4950 Ritter Rd 17055. Fax: 717/691-9692.
           Terms: Reserv deposit; no pets. **Facility:** 129 rooms. Rates for up to 4 persons; 4 stories; interior corridors.
All Rooms: free movies. **Cards:** AE, CB, DI, DS, MC, VI.   [jacuzzi] [ECTV] [symbol] [X] [D] [S]

HOLIDAY INN HARRISBURG-WEST   Rates Subject to Change   Phone: 717/697-0321   55
◆◆◆   9/25-10/8   1P: $106   2P/1B: $106   2P/2B: $106   XP: $10   F18
Motor Inn   5/1-9/24 & 10/9-4/30   1P: $94   2P/1B: $94   2P/2B: $94   XP: $10   F18
           Location: Just w on Carlisle Pike from jct of Carlisle Pike & US 11. 5401 Carlisle Pike 17055.
Fax: 717/697-7594. **Terms:** Sr. discount; pets, $50 dep req. **Facility:** 218 rooms. 5 whirlpool rms, extra charge; 2 stories; ex-
terior corridors. **Dining:** Restaurant; 6:30 am-9 pm; $4-$13. **All Rooms:** free & pay movies. **Cards:** AE, CB, DI, DS, MC, VI.
                                                                    [symbol] [jacuzzi] [symbol] [ECTV] [D]

HOMEWOOD SUITES - HARRISBURG WEST Rates Subject to Change   Phone: 717/697-4900   54
◆◆◆   All Year [CP]   1P: $112- 125 2P/1B: $122- 135 2P/2B: $122- 135 XP: $10   F18
Suite Motel **Location:** PA Tpk exit 17, 1 mi n on US 15, exit Rossmoyne Rd. 5001 Ritter Rd 17055. Fax: 717/697-9101.
           Terms: Sr. discount; reserv deposit; no pets. **Facility:** 84 rooms. 2 stories; interior corridors; designated
smoking area. **All Rooms:** kitchens, free movies. **Cards:** AE, DI, DS, MC, VI. Roll in showers. [ECTV] [symbol] [X] [symbol] [D] [S]

RESTAURANT

ISAAC'S RESTAURANT & DELI   Lunch: $3-$7   Dinner: $3-$7   Phone: 717/766-1111   20
◆   **Location:** PA Tpk exit 17, 1 mi n on US 15, exit Rossmoyne Rd. 4940 Ritter Rd 17055. **Hours:** 10 am-9 pm,
American   Fri & Sat-10 pm, Sun 11 am-9 pm. Closed major holidays. **Features:** casual dress; children's menu; health
           conscious menu items; carryout; a la carte. Specializing in a variety of unique sandwiches & desserts.
Cards: AE, DS, MC, VI.   [symbol] [X]

MEDIA—*See Philadelphia & Vicinity p. 382.*

MENDENHALL—*See Philadelphia & Vicinity p. 382.*

MERCER—2,400

LODGINGS

COLONIAL INN MOTEL   Phone: 724/662-5600
[AAA] [SAVE]   5/1-9/30 & 4/1-4/30   1P: $29   2P/1B: $32   2P/2B: $36   XP: $5   F14
           10/1-3/31   1P: $24- 27 2P/1B: $26- 29 2P/2B: $32- 36 XP: $5   F14
◆   **Location:** I-80 exit 2; 3.5 mi n on Rte 19. 383 N Perry Hwy 16137 (Rt 19N). **Terms:** Reserv deposit; weekly
Motel   rates; small pets only. **Facility:** 21 rooms. Quiet location. Handling fee imposed; 1 story; interior/exterior corri-
           dors. **Cards:** AE, DS, MC, VI. **Special Amenities: Free local telephone calls and preferred room
(subject to availability with advanced reservations).**   [symbol] [CTV] [X] [D]

HOWARD JOHNSON LODGE   Phone: 724/748-3030
🔺🔺 🅢🅐🅥🅔 All Year   1P: $72   2P/1B: $76   2P/2B: $79   XP: $6   F18
🔹🔹🔹   **Location:** On US 19, at I-80 exit 2. 835 Perry Hwy 16137. **Fax:** 724/748-3484. **Terms:** Package plans; pets.
Motor Inn   **Facility:** 102 rooms. 2 stories; interior corridors; saunas; playground. **Dining:** Restaurant; 6 am-midnight;
$5-$10; cocktails. **Services:** Fee: coin laundry. **All Rooms:** coffeemakers, free movies.
Some Rooms: VCR's. **Cards:** AE, CB, DI, DS, MC, VI. **Special Amenities:** Free local telephone calls and
free newspaper. *(See color ad below)*   🐕 🛏 📶 🍴 📺 ☒ 🎣 🄳

MEHARD MANOR BED & BREAKFAST   Guaranteed Rates   Phone: 724/662-2489
🔹🔹🔹   All Year [BP]   1P: $60- 70   2P/1B: $70- 85   XP: $10   F12
Historic Bed **Location:** Just n of town square. 146 N Pitt St 16137. **Terms:** Reserv deposit; no pets. **Facility:** 4 rooms. 3
& Breakfast   stories; interior corridors; smoke free premises. **Cards:** DS, MC, VI.   ☒ 🄳

RESTAURANTS

BENJAMIN'S   **Lunch:** $5-$8   **Dinner:** $7-$12   Phone: 724/662-4301
🔹   **Location:** 1 mi e from sq on SR 58. 787 Mercer-Grove City Rd 16137. **Hours:** 11 am-11 pm. Closed major
American holidays. **Features:** casual dress; children's menu; carryout; cocktails & lounge. **Cards:** AE, DS, MC, VI.

TIMBERS Historical   **Dinner:** $10-$20   Phone: 724/662-4533
🔺🔺🔺   **Location:** 2 mi n on Rt 19 off I-80, exit 2, 1 mi sw on SR 62. **Hours:** 3 pm-10 pm, Fri & Sat 11:30 am-11
pm; Sun-8 pm. Closed: 1/1, 11/26, 12/25 & Mon. **Reservations:** suggested; weekends. **Features:** children's
🔹🔹   menu; carryout; cocktails & lounge. 1872 restored farm & country store, featuring steak & seafood.
American   **Cards:** AE, DS, MC, VI.

MERCERSBURG—1,600

LODGING

THE MERCERSBURG INN   Rates Subject to Change   Phone: 717/328-5231
🔹🔹🔹   All Year [BP]   2P/1B: $115- 225 2P/2B: $115- 225 XP: $25
Historic   **Location:** Just e on SR 16. 405 S Main 17236. **Fax:** 717/328-3403. **Terms:** Age restrictions may apply;
Country Inn reserv deposit, 7 day notice; 2 night min stay, weekends 10/1-10/31; no pets. **Facility:** 15 rooms. 1 whirlpool
rm, extra charge. Handling fee imposed; 3 stories, no elevator; interior corridors; smoke free premises.
Dining: Dining room; Fri & Sat seatings at 6 pm & 8 pm; $45. **Cards:** DS, MC, VI.   ☒ 🄳

RESTAURANT

JAMES BUCHANAN PUB & RESTAURANT Historical **Lunch:** $4-$6 **Dinner:** $10-$20 **Phone:** 717/328-3008
🔹🔹   **Location:** Center, on SR 16, 75 & 416. 15 N Main St 17236. **Hours:** 11 am-9 pm, Fri & Sat-10 pm. Closed:
Continental 11/26, 12/25, 3/30, Sun & Mon. **Reservations:** suggested. **Features:** casual dress; carryout; cocktails.
Relaxed dining in boyhood home of 15th President of the United States, James Buchanan. **Cards:** AE, DS,
MC, VI.   ☒

MIDDLETOWN (DAUPHIN COUNTY)

RESTAURANT

ALFRED'S VICTORIAN RESTAURANT Historical **Lunch:** $5-$12 **Dinner:** $15-$25 **Phone:** 717/944-5373
🔹🔹🔹   **Location:** On SR 441, 3.3 mi s of SR 230. 38 N Union St 17057. **Hours:** 11:30 am-2 & 5-10 pm, Sat from 5
Continental pm, Sun 3 pm-9 pm. Closed major holidays. **Reservations:** suggested. **Features:** health conscious menu
items; cocktails; street parking; a la carte. Tuscan Regional Northern Italian specialties served in elegant
Victorian setting; casual sophistication with no tie required. Casual lunch menu. **Cards:** AE, DI, DS, MC, VI.   ☒

MIFFLINVILLE—1,300

LODGING

SUPER 8 MOTEL   Rates Subject to Change   Phone: 717/759-6778
🔹🔹   All Year   1P: $40   2P/2B: $50   XP: $5   F12
Motor Inn   **Location:** Just n of I-80, exit 37. (Box E, 18631). **Fax:** 717/759-6738. **Terms:** Pets, $20 dep req. **Facility:** 30
rooms. 1 story; exterior corridors. **Dining:** Restaurant; 6 am-10 pm; $7-$24. **Cards:** AE, DI, DS, MC, VI.
🛏 📺 ☒ 🄳

MILESBURG—1,100

LODGING

HOLIDAY INN
◆◆◆
Motor Inn

Rates Subject to Change
All Year   1P: $70- 115   2P/1B: $70- 115 2P/2B: $70- 115 XP: $10   F13
Location: 0.4 mi n of jct I-80, exit 23. Rt 150 16853 (PO Box 538). Fax: 814/355-2651. **Terms:** Sr. discount; small pets only. **Facility:** 115 rooms. Handling fee imposed; 2 stories; interior corridors. **Dining:** Restaurant; 6 am-11 & 5-11 pm; $6-$12. **All Rooms:** free & pay movies. **Cards:** AE, CB, DI, DS, JCB, MC, VI.
Phone: 814/355-7521
Roll in showers. [icons] ECTV [icons]

MILFORD (PIKE COUNTY)—See Pocono Mountains Area p. 425.

MILLERSVILLE—See Pennsylvania Dutch Country p. 348.

MONESSEN—See Pittsburgh & Vicinity p. 411.

MONROEVILLE—See Pittsburgh & Vicinity p. 411.

MONTGOMERY (LYCOMING COUNTY)

LODGING

NORTHWOOD MOTEL
[AAA] [SAVE]
◆
Motel

5/1-9/30 & 4/2-4/30   1P: $34   2P/1B: $37   2P/2B: $39   XP: $2   D
10/1-4/1   1P: $29   2P/1B: $31   2P/2B: $33   XP: $2   D
Location: 8 mi s of Williamsport. (RD 2, Box 583 US Rt 15, MONTGOMERY, 17752). **Terms:** Reserv deposit; weekly rates; no pets. **Facility:** 10 rooms. Quiet rural location along hwy. 1 story; exterior corridors; 2 18-hole public golf courses & a 9-hole executive course across the street. **All Rooms:** microwaves, refrigerators. **Cards:** AE, DS, MC, VI. **Special Amenities:** Free local telephone calls and preferred room (subject to availability with advanced reservations).
Phone: 717/547-6624
[icons] CTV [X] [D]

MONTGOMERYVILLE—See Philadelphia & Vicinity p. 383.

MONTOURSVILLE—5,000

LODGING

WILLIAMSPORT SUPER 8 MOTEL
◆◆
Motel

Rates Subject to Change
All Year   1P: $44   2P/2B: $49   XP: $5   F16
Location: Just s of I-180, Warrensville Rd exit. 2815 Old Montoursville Rd 17754. Fax: 717/368-8555. **Terms:** Sr. discount; no pets. **Facility:** 43 rooms. 3 stories, no elevator; interior corridors. **All Rooms:** free movies. **Cards:** AE, CB, DI, DS, JCB, MC, VI.
Phone: 717/368-8111
CTV [X] [D] [S]

RESTAURANT

HILLSIDE RESTAURANT
◆◆
American

Dinner: $6-$19
Location: From I-180 (US 220), Faxon exit, 1 mi n on North Way Rd, 1 mi 2725 Four Mile Dr 17754. **Hours:** 4:30-10 pm. Closed: 11/26, 12/24-12/26, Sun & Easter. **Reservations:** suggested; weekends. **Features:** casual dress; children's menu; health conscious menu items; carryout; cocktails & lounge. Attractive, 2 level dining room with lovely view. Also, some Continental fare. Banquet facilities & off premise catering avail. Can accommodate bus tours at anytime with advance notice. **Cards:** AE, DI, DS, MC, VI.
Phone: 717/326-6779
[X]

MONTROSE—2,000

LODGING

RIDGE HOUSE
[AAA]
◆◆
Historic Bed
& Breakfast

Guaranteed Rates
All Year [CP]   1P: $40   2P/2B: $55   XP: $10   D
Location: I-81 exit 67, 0.5 mi w on SR 492, 1 mi s on US 11, 8 mi w on SR 706. 6 Ridge St 18801. **Terms:** Reserv deposit; small pets only, in pet carrier. **Facility:** 5 rooms. Handling fee imposed; 2 stories; interior corridors. **All Rooms:** no A/C.
Phone: 717/278-4933
[icons] [X] [D]

RESTAURANT

THE MONTROSE HOUSE RESTAURANT & INN
◆◆
American

Lunch: $3-$6   Dinner: $11-$18   **Phone: 717/278-1124**
Location: On SR 29, just s of jct SR 706. 26 S Main St 18801. **Hours:** 11 am-2 & 5-8:30 pm, Fri-9:30 pm, Sat 5 pm-9:30 pm, Sun 5 pm-8:30 pm. Closed: 1/1, 7/4 & 12/25. **Reservations:** suggested. **Features:** casual dress; carryout; cocktails & lounge. Fine dining in a rustic atmosphere in the heart of the Endless Mountains. **Cards:** CB, DI, DS, MC, VI.
[X]

MOOSIC—5,300   (See map p. 418; index p. 417)

LODGINGS

COURTYARD BY MARRIOTT
◆◆◆
Motel

Rates Subject to Change
All Year   1P: $69- 89   2P/1B: $69- 89 2P/2B: $69- 89 XP: $10   F18
Location: I-81, exit 51, 0.5 mi se on Montage Mountain Rd. 16 Glenmaura National Blvd 18507. Fax: 717/969-2110. **Terms:** No pets. **Facility:** 120 rooms. 3 stories; interior corridors. **Dining:** Coffee shop; 6:30 am-1 & 5-10 pm; Sat & Sun from 7 am; $4-$10. **All Rooms:** free & pay movies. **Cards:** AE, DI, DS, MC, VI.
Phone: 717/969-2100 **71**
Roll in showers. [icons] CTV [icons] [X] [icons] [D] [S]

DAYS INN-MONTAGE
[AAA] [SAVE]
◆
Motel

5/1-8/31 [CP]   1P: $50- 55   2P/1B: $50- 55 2P/2B: $60   XP: $5   F16
9/1-4/30 [CP]   1P: $40- 50   2P/1B: $40- 50 2P/2B: $55   XP: $5   F16
Location: I-81, exit 51, US 11 2 mi s; I-81 exit 50, US 11 0.3 mi n. 4130 Birney Ave 18507. Fax: 717/457-4479. **Terms:** Reserv deposit, 30 day notice; pets, $5 dep req. **Facility:** 46 rooms. Some large rooms. 1 two-bedroom unit. Handling fee imposed; 2 stories; interior/exterior corridors. **Dining:** Restaurant nearby. **Services:** Fee: coin laundry. **All Rooms:** free movies, combo or shower baths. **Some Rooms:** coffeemakers, microwaves, refrigerators, whirlpools. **Cards:** AE, DI, DS, MC, VI. **Special Amenities:** Early check-in/late check-out and free breakfast. (See color ad p 431)
Phone: 717/457-6713 **70**
[icons] CTV [X] [D]

(See map p. 418)

RESTAURANT

MARVELOUS MUGGS RESTAURANT & PUB   **Lunch:** $5-$8   **Dinner:** $7-$17   **Phone:** 717/961-1551   53
◆◆   **Location:** I-81, exit 51, by Comfort Suites. 20 Montage Mountain Rd 18507. **Hours:** 11 am-11 pm, Fri &
American   Sat-midnight, Sun-10 pm. **Closed:** 11/26, early 12/24 & 12/25. **Reservations:** call ahead seat.
Features: casual dress; children's menu; health conscious menu items; carryout; cocktails & lounge.
Comfortable family dining with customer photos adorning walls; upscale casual & a separate lounge area. **Cards:** AE, MC,
VI.
f X

MORGANTOWN—900

LODGING

HOLIDAY INN-HOLIDOME   Rates Subject to Change   **Phone:** 610/286-3000
◆◆◆   All Year   1P: $79- 99 2P/1B: $89- 109 2P/2B: $89- 109 XP: $5   F
Motor Inn   **Location:** Just s of exit 22 off PA Tpk & SR 10. 230 Cherry St (Rt 10) 19543. **Fax:** 610/286-0520. **Terms:** Sr.
discount; no pets. **Facility:** 195 rooms. 4 stories; interior corridors. **Dining:** Restaurant; 6 am-2 & 5-10 pm;
$6-$17. **All Rooms:** free & pay movies. **Cards:** AE, CB, DI, DS, MC, VI.
⊇ CTV X ⌨ D S

RESTAURANT

THE WINDMILL RESTAURANT   **Lunch:** $6-$15   **Dinner:** $6-$15   **Phone:** 610/286-5980
AAA SAVE   **Location:** On SR 10 & 23, 0.5 mi w of jct Hwy 76. Rts 10 & 23 19543. **Hours:** 7 am-10 pm, Fri & Sat-11
pm. **Closed:** 11/26 & 12/25. **Features:** casual dress; children's menu; early bird specials; senior's menu;
◆   carryout. Casual dining. Features homemade pie & bread. **Cards:** AE, DS, MC, VI. **Special Value:** 10%
American   **discount on the price of any entree, excluding beverages, tax and gratuity.**   X

MOUNTAIN TOP—800

RESTAURANT

DAMENTI'S RESTAURANT   **Dinner:** $19-$32   **Phone:** 717/788-2004
◆◆◆   **Location:** On SR 309, 1.3 mi n of I-80, exit 39. 1307 S Mountain Blvd 18707. **Hours:** 5 pm-10 pm, Sun 4
Continental   pm-9 pm. **Closed** major holidays & Mon. **Reservations:** required. **Features:** casual dress; cocktails &
lounge. Intimate fine dining in rural setting. Features steak, seafood, veal & pasta dishes. **Cards:** AE, MC,
VI.   X

MOUNT JOY—See Pennsylvania Dutch Country p. 348.

MOUNT PLEASANT—4,100

RESTAURANT

THE BARN RESTAURANT   Historical   **Lunch:** $9-$15   **Dinner:** $9-$23   **Phone:** 724/547-4500
◆◆◆   **Location:** Jct SR 31 & 982. RD 2, Box 523A 15666. **Hours:** 11:30 am-9:30 pm. **Closed** major holidays &
American   Mon. **Reservations:** suggested. **Features:** dressy casual; children's menu; health conscious menu items;
cocktails & lounge; a la carte. Rustic historic barn with fashionable, intimate interior featuring contemporary
retro cuisine. **Cards:** AE, DS, MC, VI.   f X

MOUNT POCONO—See Pocono Mountains Area p. 426.

MURRYSVILLE—See Pittsburgh & Vicinity p. 412.

MYERSTOWN—3,200

LODGINGS

LANTERN LODGE MOTOR INN   **Phone:** 717/866-6536
AAA SAVE   5/1-10/31 & 4/15-4/30   1P: $59- 90 2P/1B: $70   2P/2B: $95   XP: $10   F12
11/1-4/14   1P: $50- 80 2P/1B: $60   2P/2B: $70- 80 XP: $10   F12
◆◆◆   **Location:** Just n of US 422, on SR 501. 411 N College St 17067. **Fax:** 717/866-6536. **Terms:** Reserv
Motor Inn   deposit; no pets. **Facility:** 80 rooms. 3-bedroom homes, $150-$175 for up to 2 persons, $20 extra person. 1
whirlpool suite, $225 for up to 4 persons; 2 stories; interior corridors. **Dining:** Dining room, see separate
listing. **All Rooms:** free movies. **Some Rooms:** 3 kitchens. **Cards:** AE, CB, DI, DS, MC, VI.   CTV X D

MOTEL SKANDIA   Rates Subject to Change   **Phone:** 717/866-6447
◆◆   Fri & Sat 5/1-1/1 & 3/1-4/30 1P: $50- 65 2P/1B: $50- 65 2P/2B: $60- 75 XP: $7   F12
Motel   Sun-Thurs 5/1-1/1 & 3/1-4/30 1P: $39- 54 2P/1B: $44- 59 2P/2B: $49- 64 XP: $7   F12
Location: 2 mi e on SR 422. 922 E Lincoln Ave 17067. **Terms:** Open 5/1-1/1 & 3/1-4/30; reserv deposit, 3
day notice; no pets. **Facility:** 15 rooms. 1-2 stories; exterior corridors. **Cards:** AE, DS, MC, VI.   ECTV X D

RESTAURANT

LANTERN LODGE DINING ROOM   **Lunch:** $4-$8   **Dinner:** $12-$21   **Phone:** 717/866-6536
◆◆◆   **Location:** Just n of US 422 on SR 501; in Lantern Lodge Motor Inn. 411 N College St 17067. **Hours:** 7-11
Continental   am, 11:30-2 & 5-10 pm, Sun-9 pm. **Reservations:** suggested. **Features:** casual dress; Sunday brunch;
children's menu; health conscious menu items; carryout; cocktails & lounge. Weekend entertainment.
Cards: AE, CB, DI, DS, MC, VI.   X

NAZARETH—5,700

LODGING

CLASSIC VICTORIAN BED & BREAKFAST   Guaranteed Rates   **Phone:** 610/759-8276
◆◆◆   All Year [BP]   1P: $80- 105 2P/1B: $80- 105 2P/2B: $80- 105 XP: $15
Historic Bed   **Location:** 5 mi n on SR 191 from US 22; 0.5 mi from town center in historic district; on SR 191, 2 mi w of
& Breakfast   US 33. 35 N New St 18064. **Fax:** 610/434-1889. **Terms:** Check-in 4 pm; reserv deposit, 10 day notice; no
pets. **Facility:** 3 rooms. Handling fee imposed; 2 stories; interior corridors; smoke free premises. **Cards:** AE,
MC, VI.   CTV X D

RESTAURANT

NEWBURG INN   **Lunch:** $4-$10   **Dinner:** $11-$27   **Phone:** 610/759-8528
◆◆   **Location:** On SR 191, 2 mi n of US 22. 4357 Newburg Rd 18064. **Hours:** 11:30 am-2:30 pm & 5-9:30 pm,
American   Sat from 5 pm, Sun noon-7:30 pm. **Closed** major holidays. **Reservations:** suggested. **Features:** casual
dress; children's menu; carryout; salad bar; cocktails & lounge. Specializing in prime rib & fresh seafood. Hot
bar served at lunch Mon-Fri. **Cards:** AE, CB, DI, DS, MC, VI.   X

NEW BERLIN—900

LODGING

THE INN AT NEW BERLIN Guaranteed Rates **Phone:** 717/966-0321
All Year [BP]   1P: $85- 175   2P/1B: $85- 175   XP: $20   D
Location: Center, at intersection of SR 304 & 204, 8 mi w of US 15. 321 Market St 17855-0390 (PO Box
390). Fax: 717/966-9557. **Terms:** Reserv deposit, 7 day notice; no pets. **Facility:** 7 rooms. 2 two-bedroom
Historic units, $135-$165; 3 stories; interior corridors; smoke free premises. **Dining:** Gabriel's Restaurant, see
Country Inn separate listing. **Cards:** DS, MC, VI.   Ⓓ

RESTAURANT

GABRIEL'S RESTAURANT Country Inn   **Lunch:** $6-$8   **Dinner:** $13-$20   **Phone:** 717/966-0321
Location: Center, at intersection of SR 304 & 204, 8 mi w of US 15; in The Inn at New Berlin. 321 Market St
Continental 17855-0390. **Hours:** 10 am-2 & 4:30-8:30 pm. Closed: 12/25, Mon, Tues & 1/1-1/14.
Reservations: suggested. **Features:** cocktails; a la carte. Good menu variety offering creative selections.
Smoke free premises. **Cards:** DS, MC, VI.   ⊠

NEW CASTLE—28,300

LODGING

COMFORT INN   **Phone:** 724/658-7700
All Year [CP]   1P: $62- 68 2P/1B: $66- 72 2P/2B: $67- 73 XP: $6   F18
Location: Exit 29 off I-79, 11 mi w on US 422; exit Rt 60S off I-80 to US 422E, 7 mi to New Castle exit.
Motel 1740 New Butler Rd 16101. Fax: 724/658-7727. **Terms:** Reserv deposit; weekly/monthly rates; pets, $6 extra
charge. **Facility:** 79 rooms. 8 whirlpool rms, extra charge; 2 stories; interior corridors; sauna. **Services:** valet
laundry. **All Rooms:** free & pay movies. **Some Rooms:** microwaves, radios, refrigerators. **Cards:** AE, CB,
DI, DS, MC, VI.   🛏 🕸 🛅 ⊠ Ⓓ Ⓢ

NEW COLUMBIA—500

LODGING

NEW COLUMBIA COMFORT INN   **Phone:** 717/568-8000
All Year   1P: $54- 67 2P/1B: $59- 75 2P/2B: $59   XP: $5   F18
Location: I-80 exit 30A, US 15/New Columbia exit. (PO Box 62, 17856). Fax: 717/568-0660. **Terms:** Pets.
Motor Inn **Facility:** 120 rooms. Facility carved out in rural area set back from, but with convenient access to interstate.
8 whirlpool rms, extra charge; 2 stories; interior corridors; game room. **Dining & Entertainment:** Restaurant;
7 am-9 pm; cocktail lounge. **Services:** Fee: coin laundry. **All Rooms:** free & pay movies.
Some Rooms: microwaves, refrigerators. **Cards:** AE, CB, DI, DS, JCB, MC, VI. **Special Amenities:** Free room upgrade
and preferred room (each subject to availability with advanced reservations). 🛏 ➡ 🕸 ⒸⓉⓋ 🔥 ⊠ Ⓓ Ⓢ

NEW CUMBERLAND—7,700 (See map p. 292; index p. 291)

LODGINGS

DAYS INN - HARRISBURG SOUTH   **Phone:** 717/774-4156   ❺
6/1-10/31   1P: $55   2P/2B: $65 XP: $5 F12
5/1-5/31 & 11/1-4/30   1P: $39   2P/2B: $49 XP: $5 F12
Motor Inn **Location:** Just ne of I-83, exit 18; 0.5 mi s of PA Tpk exit 18. 353 Lewisberry Rd 17070. Fax: 717/774-2040.
Terms: Pets, $5 extra charge. **Facility:** 62 rooms. 2 stories; interior corridors; small pool; video movie rentals.
Dining & Entertainment: Restaurant; 7 am-11 & 5-9 pm; $5-$9; cocktails/lounge. **Services:** Fee: coin
laundry. **All Rooms:** free movies. **Some Rooms:** radios. Fee: VCR's. **Cards:** AE, CB, DI, DS, MC, VI. **Special Amenities:**
Early check-in/late check-out and preferred room (subject to availability with advanced reservations).
🛏 ⒸⓉⓋ ⊠ Ⓓ

FAIRFIELD INN HARRISBURG WEST Rates Subject to Change **Phone:** 717/774-6200   ❸
6/2-11/2 [CP]   1P: $45- 65 2P/1B: $45- 65 2P/2B: $65
Motel 5/1-6/1 [CP]   1P: $50- 60 2P/1B: $50- 60 2P/2B: $50- 60
11/3-12/31 & 1/1-4/30 [CP] 1P: $39- 49 2P/1B: $39- 49 2P/2B: $39- 49
Location: Just ne of PA Tpk I-76, exit 18; just ne of I-83 exit 18A (Limekiln Rd). 175 Beacon Hill Blvd 17070.
Fax: 717/774-6200. **Terms:** Sr. discount; no pets. **Facility:** 105 rooms. 3 stories; interior/exterior corridors. **All Rooms:** free
movies. **Cards:** AE, DI, DS, MC, VI. *(See color ad p 295)*   ⒸⓉⓋ 🔥 ⊠ Ⓓ Ⓢ

FARM FORTUNE BED & BREAKFAST Rates Subject to Change **Phone:** 717/774-2683   ❶
All Year [BP]   1P: $57- 75 2P/1B: $65- 85 2P/2B: $65- 85 XP: $15
Historic Bed **Location:** I-83, exit 18A; 0.5 mi e. 204 Limekiln Rd 17070. **Terms:** Age restrictions may apply; reserv
& Breakfast deposit, 7 day notice; no pets. **Facility:** 4 rooms. 3 stories, no elevator; interior corridors; smoke free prem-
ises. **Cards:** AE, DI, DS, MC, VI.   ⒸⓉⓋ ⊠ Ⓓ

HARRISBURG HOLIDAY INN HOTEL &
CONFERENCE CENTER   Rates Subject to Change **Phone:** 717/774-2721   ❾
5/1-10/31 & 4/1-4/30 1P: $69- 119 2P/1B: $69- 119 2P/2B: $69- 119 XP: $10 F18
Motor Inn 11/1-3/31   1P: $49- 94 2P/1B: $49- 94 2P/2B: $49- 94 XP: $10 F18
Location: Just e of I-83, exit 18A; just n of I-76 PA Tpk, exit 18. PA Turnpike, exit 18 & I-83 17070 (PO Box
A). Fax: 717/774-2485. **Terms:** Sr. discount; small pets only, $10 fee. **Facility:** 196 rooms. Handling fee imposed; 2 stories;
interior corridors; designated smoking area. **Dining:** Dining room; 6:30 am-2 & 5-9 pm, Fri & Sat-10 pm; $11-$17.
All Rooms: free & pay movies. **Cards:** AE, CB, DI, DS, JCB, MC, VI. Roll in showers. 🛏 ➡ 🛅 ⒸⓉⓋ ⊠ Ⓓ

MCINTOSH INN Rates Subject to Change **Phone:** 717/774-8888   ❼
6/28-9/1 [CP]   1P: $51- 60 2P/1B: $58   2P/2B: $64 XP: $7 F18
Motel 5/1-6/27 & 9/2-10/26 [CP] 1P: $46- 55 2P/1B: $53   2P/2B: $59 XP: $7 F18
10/27-4/30 [CP]   1P: $42- 51 2P/1B: $49   2P/2B: $55 XP: $7 F18
Location: Just n of PA Tpk, exit 18; just e of I-83, exit 18A. 130 Limekiln Rd 17070. Fax: 717/774-7717. **Terms:** Sr.
discount; no pets. **Facility:** 88 rooms. 3 stories; interior/exterior corridors. **All Rooms:** free movies. **Cards:** AE, CB, DI, MC,
VI. *(See color ad p 297)* Roll in showers. 🔥 ⊠ 🎦 Ⓓ Ⓢ

(See map p. 292)

RESTAURANT

COAKLEY'S RESTAURANT & IRISH PUB   Lunch: $4-$8   Dinner: $6-$16   Phone: 717/774-5556   ①
🔺🔺 SAVE   **Location:** I-83 exit 18A, 0.8 mi e on Limekiln Rd, 0.5 mi n on Poplar Ave; 0.5 mi e on 3rd St. 305 Bridge St
◆◆   17070. **Hours:** 11 am-11 pm, Fri & Sat-midnight, Sun noon-10 pm. Closed major holidays.
American   **Reservations:** suggested. **Features:** casual dress; children's menu; health conscious menu; carryout;
gratuity.   cocktails & lounge; a la carte. Slow roasted prime rib a specialty. Outdoor dining in season. **Cards:** AE, DI,
DS, MC, VI. **Special Value: 10% discount on the price of any entree, excluding beverages, tax and
⊠

NEW HOLLAND—See Pennsylvania Dutch Country p. 349.

NEW HOPE—See Philadelphia & Vicinity p. 383.

NEW KENSINGTON—See Pittsburgh & Vicinity p. 412.

NEW OXFORD—1,600

RESTAURANT

INN 94   **Lunch:** $8-$11   **Dinner:** $10-$20   **Phone:** 717/624-4665
◆◆   **Location:** 3 mi n on SR 94 from jct US 30. 4805 Carlisle Pike 17350. **Hours:** 10:30 am-9 pm, Fri & Sat-10
American   pm, Sun 11 am-7 pm. Closed: 12/24-12/26. **Reservations:** suggested; weekends. **Features:** casual dress;
children's menu; carryout; cocktails & lounge. Relaxed dining. Varied menu, including quality steak
well-prepared. **Cards:** AE, DS, MC, VI.   ⊠

NEW SMITHVILLE

LODGING

SUPER 8 MOTEL   **Phone:** 610/285-4880
🔺🔺 SAVE   5/1-9/30 & 4/1-4/30   1P: $45   2P/1B: $49   2P/2B: $53   XP: $4   F12
10/1-3/31   1P: $41   2P/1B: $45   2P/2B: $49   XP: $4   F12
◆◆   **Location:** I-78, exit 13. 2160 Golden Key Rd 19530. Fax: 610/285-4452. **Terms:** No pets. **Facility:** 38 rooms.
Motel   Queen suite, $57; 2 stories; interior corridors. **Dining:** Restaurant nearby. **All Rooms:** free movies.
Cards: AE, DI, DS, MC, VI.   ⒸⓉⓋ ⊠ Ⓓ

NEW STANTON—See Laurel Highlands p. 314.

NEWTOWN (BUCKS COUNTY)—See Philadelphia & Vicinity p. 384.

NEWTOWN SQUARE—See Philadelphia & Vicinity p. 384.

NEW WILMINGTON—2,700

RESTAURANT

THE TAVERN Historical   **Lunch:** $9-$11   **Dinner:** $13-$20   **Phone:** 724/946-2020
◆◆   **Location:** On SR 208, at jct SR 158 & 956. 108 N Market St 16142. **Hours:** 11:30 am-2 & 5-8 pm, Sun
American   noon-6:30 pm. Closed: 7/4, 11/26, 12/25 & Tues. **Reservations:** suggested. **Features:** casual dress; a la
carte. Good down home country fare, sticky rolls & calling the menu, long standing traditions. Afternoon tea
& weekend breakfast buffet avail. **Cards:** AE, DS, MC, VI.   ⊠

NORTHAMPTON (NORTHAMPTON COUNTY)

RESTAURANT

THE ATLAS HOTEL   **Dinner:** $6-$20   **Phone:** 610/261-1766
◆◆   **Location:** At E 10th St & Siegfried Ave. 366-368 E 10th St 18067. **Hours:** 4 pm-9 pm, Fri & Sat-10 pm, lite
American   menu avail-11 pm. Closed: 1/1, 12/24, 12/25, Sun & Mon. **Reservations:** suggested. **Features:** casual
dress; children's menu; carryout; cocktails & lounge; street parking. Cozy family-style dining room featuring
steak, veal & chicken. Sandwiches, pizza & other convenience foods also avail. **Cards:** MC, VI.   ⊠

NORTH EAST—4,600

LODGINGS

GRAPE ARBOR INN BED & BREAKFAST   Rates Subject to Change   **Phone:** 814/725-5522
🔺   All Year   1P: $85- 165   2P/1B: $85- 165   XP: $15
◆◆◆   **Location:** Exit 11 off I-90, 2 mi n on Rt 89, just e. 51/55 E Main St 16428. Fax: 814/725-8471.
Bed &   **Terms:** Reserv deposit, 7 day notice; no pets. **Facility:** 6 rooms. Handling fee imposed; 2 stories; interior cor-
Breakfast   ridors; smoke free premises. **Cards:** AE, DS, MC, VI.   ⒺⒸⓉⓋ ⊠ Ⓓ

SUPER 8 MOTEL   Rates Subject to Change   **Phone:** 814/725-4567
◆   All Year   1P: $34- 47   2P/1B: $38- 49 2P/2B: $47- 70 XP: $5   F12
Motel   **Location:** Exit 11 off I-90, just n on Rt 89. 11021 Side Hill Rd 16428. Fax: 814/725-4887. **Terms:** Sr.
MC, VI.   discount; no pets. **Facility:** 45 rooms. 1 story; exterior corridors. **All Rooms:** free movies. **Cards:** AE, DS,
ⒺⒸⓉⓋ ⊠ Ⓓ

NOTTINGHAM (CHESTER COUNTY)—See Philadelphia & Vicinity p. 384.

Look for the 🔺🔺🔺 in our listings!

OAKDALE—*See Pittsburgh & Vicinity p. 412.*

OAKLAND—*See Pittsburgh & Vicinity p. 413.*

OAKMONT—*See Pittsburgh & Vicinity p. 413.*

OIL CITY—11,900

LODGING

HOLIDAY INN Phone: 814/677-1221
[AAA] [SAVE]   All Year   1P: $61- 69   2P/1B: $71- 76   2P/2B: $73- 78   XP: $10   F18
◆◆   **Location:** Downtown. 1 Seneca St 16301. Fax: 814/677-0492. **Terms:** Package plans; pets. **Facility:** 105
Motor Inn   rooms. 2 whirlpool rms, extra charge; 5 stories; interior/exterior corridors. **Dining & Entertainment:** Dining
room; 7 am-2 & 5-9 pm; $8-$16; cocktails/lounge. **Services:** valet laundry. **All Rooms:** coffeemakers, free
movies. Fee: safes. **Some Rooms:** microwaves, refrigerators. **Cards:** AE, CB, DI, DS, MC, VI.
**Special Amenities: Early check-in/late check-out and free room upgrade (subject to availability with advanced
reservations).** [🛏] [🏊] [🛍] [ECTV] [✕] [D]

ORRTANNA—200—*See also GETTYSBURG.*

LODGING

HICKORY BRIDGE FARM BED & BREAKFAST   Rates Subject to Change   Phone: 717/642-5261
◆◆◆   Fri-Sun [BP]   1P: $60   2P/1B: $89- 125   2P/2B: $89- 125
Country Inn   Mon-Thurs [BP]   1P: $50   2P/1B: $79- 110   2P/2B: $79- 110
Location: SW end of town, following signs. 96 Hickory Bridge Rd 17353. Fax: 717/642-6419. **Terms:** Reserv
deposit, 7 day notice; 2 night min stay, weekends; no pets. **Facility:** 7 rooms. 3-bedroom unit in farmhouse $79-$225. 2 whirlpool rms, $110-$125 rates for up to 2 persons; 1-2 stories; exterior corridors; smoke free premises. **Dining:** Restaurant, see
separate listing. **Cards:** DS, MC, VI. *(See ad p 285)* [✕] [D]

RESTAURANT

HICKORY BRIDGE FARM RESTAURANT   Historical   **Dinner:** $17   Phone: 717/642-5261
◆◆   **Location:** SW end of town, following signs; in Hickory Bridge Farm Bed & Breakfast. 96 Hickory Bridge Rd
American   17353. **Hours:** 5 pm-8 pm, Sun noon-3 pm. Closed: Mon-Thurs. **Reservations:** suggested.
Features: casual dress; children's menu; prix fixe. Farm-style service; 140 year-old barn. Smoke free
premises. **Cards:** MC, VI. *(See ad p 285)* [✕]

ORWIGSBURG—2,800

LODGING

FORT MOTEL   Rates Subject to Change   Phone: 717/366-2091
◆   All Year   1P: $35   2P/1B: $40   2P/2B: $45   XP: $5   F10
Motel   **Location:** On SR 61, 2 mi s of jct SR 443. RD 1, Box 1223 17961. **Terms:** No pets. **Facility:** 12 rooms. 1 story;
exterior corridors. **Cards:** DS, MC, VI. [CTV] [D]

RESTAURANT

LEIBENSPERGER'S DEER LAKE INN   **Lunch:** $6-$18   **Dinner:** $10-$26   Phone: 717/366-1135
[AAA]   **Location:** On SR 61, 4.5 mi s of jct SR 443. 17961. **Hours:** 11 am-2 & 5-9 pm, Fri & Sat-10 pm, Sun
noon-9 pm. Closed: 12/25 & Mon. **Reservations:** suggested; Fri & Sat. **Features:** casual dress; children's
◆◆   menu; early bird specials; carryout; cocktails; a la carte. Specializing in roast duckling with orange sauce,
American   crabmeat imperial & roast prime rib of beef; served in a warm, congenial & cozy atmosphere. **Cards:** AE,
CB, DI, DS, MC, VI.

OSTERBURG—400

RESTAURANT

SLICK'S IVY STONE RESTAURANT   **Lunch:** $3-$7   **Dinner:** $7-$13   Phone: 814/276-3131
[AAA]   **Location:** 2 mi n on unmarked Old US 220 from jct I-99/US 220, Osterburg/St Clairsville exit. Old Route 220
16667. **Hours:** Open 5/1-12/23 & 4/1-4/30; 11 am-8:30 pm, Sat from 4 pm, Sun 11 am-8 pm. Closed: Mon.
◆◆   **Reservations:** accepted. **Features:** casual dress; children's menu; carryout; salad bar. Colonial atmosphere.
American   Featuring family-style meals. Homemade soup, bread & dessert, famous for fried chicken, roast turkey &
waffles. Ample portions. **Cards:** MC, VI. [✕]

OTTSVILLE—*See Philadelphia & Vicinity p. 384.*

PALM—*See Philadelphia & Vicinity p. 385.*

PALMYRA (LEBANON COUNTY)—*See also HERSHEY.*

LODGING

PALMYRA MOTEL   Rates Subject to Change   Phone: 717/838-1324
[AAA]   7/10-8/27   2P/1B: $58- 68   2P/2B: $68- 78   XP: $5
6/7-7/9   2P/1B: $46- 58   2P/2B: $59- 68   XP: $5
◆◆   5/1-6/6, 8/28-9/22 & 4/2-4/29   2P/1B: $38- 46   2P/2B: $44- 54   XP: $5
Motor Inn   9/23-12/13 & 2/12-4/1   2P/1B: $28- 35   2P/2B: $36- 44   XP: $5
Location: 1 mi e on US 422. 1071 E Main St 17078. Fax: 717/838-1399. **Terms:** Open 5/1-12/13 &
2/12-4/29; reserv deposit, 3 day notice; no pets. **Facility:** 30 rooms. 1-2 stories; interior/exterior corridors.
Dining: Restaurant; 5:30 am-9 pm; $6-$15. **Cards:** AE, DS, MC, VI. *(See color ad p 303)* [🏊] [ECTV] [✕] [D]

PARADISE (LANCASTER COUNTY)—*See Pennsylvania Dutch Country p. 349.*

Pennsylvania Dutch Country

ADAMSTOWN—1,100

LODGINGS

ADAMSTOWN INN
Rates Subject to Change
Phone: 717/484-0800
◆◆◆ All Year [CP] 1P: $63- 100 2P/1B: $70- 125
Historic Bed **Location:** Center. 62 W Main St 19501. **Terms:** Age restrictions may apply; reserv deposit, 14 day notice; 2
& Breakfast night min stay, weekends; no pets, pets on premises. **Facility:** 4 rooms. Handling fee imposed; 2 stories; interior corridors; smoke free premises. **Cards:** MC, VI.
⊠ Ⓓ

THE BARNYARD INN
Phone: 717/484-1111
ⒶⒶⒶ (SAVE) All Year [BP] 1P: $75- 120 2P/1B: $75- 120 2P/2B: $75- 120 XP: $25
Location: 1 mi nw via Main St/Old Lancaster Pike. 2145 Old Lancaster Pike 19501 (PO Box 273).
◆◆◆ Fax: 717/484-0722. **Terms:** Age restrictions may apply; reserv deposit, 10 day notice; weekly/monthly rates;
Historic Bed no pets, pets on premises. **Facility:** 4 rooms. Animal-loving owners with a menagerie of cozy rooms decorated
& Breakfast with a whimsical touch & a real-life zoo out back. 2 stories; interior corridors; smoke free premises; badminton, croquet. **Recreation:** bicycles. **All Rooms:** combo or shower baths, no phones. **Cards:** MC, VI.
Special Amenities: Free local telephone calls.
🐾 ECTV ⊠ Ⓓ

BLACK FOREST INN
Rates Subject to Change
Phone: 717/484-4801
ⒶⒶⒶ 5/1-11/30 & 4/1-4/30 [CP] 1P: $43- 89 2P/1B: $43- 99 2P/2B: $43- 99 XP: $10   F12
12/1-3/31 [CP] 1P: $38- 54 2P/1B: $38- 54 2P/2B: $43- 58 XP: $10   F12
◆◆ **Location:** On SR 272; 2.8 mi n of Tpk, exit 21. 500 Lancaster Ave 19501 (PO Box 457). **Terms:** Pets, $8
Motel extra charge. **Facility:** 19 rooms. Handling fee imposed; 1 story; exterior corridors. **Cards:** DS, MC, VI.
🛏 🖃 CTV ⊠ Ⓓ

RESTAURANT

STOUDT'S BLACK ANGUS STEAK HOUSE **Lunch:** $5-$30 **Dinner:** $18-$30 **Phone:** 717/484-4385
ⒶⒶⒶ **Location:** 2.8 mi n of tpk exit 21 on SR 272. **Hours:** 5 pm-11 pm, Sat from noon, Sun noon-9 pm. Closed:
1/1, 11/26 & 12/25. **Reservations:** suggested. **Features:** casual dress; children's menu; carryout; cocktails &
◆◆◆ lounge. Victorian decor. German beer garden weekends in summer. Authentic selection of German cuisine.
Steakhouse Micro-brewery on premises. Homemade beer bread & soup. **Cards:** AE, CB, DI, MC, VI.
⊠

AKRON—3,900

LODGINGS

BOXWOOD INN
Guaranteed Rates
Phone: 717/859-3466
ⒶⒶⒶ 5/1-12/31 & 2/1-4/30 [BP] 1P: $95- 160 2P/1B: $95- 160 2P/2B: $95 XP: $10
Location: SR 272, 0.5 mi e on Main St, 0.3 mi s on Diamond St. 12 Tobacco Rd 17501 (Box 203).
◆◆◆ Fax: 717/859-4507. **Terms:** Open 5/1-12/31 & 2/1-4/30; reserv deposit; 2 night min stay, weekends
Historic Bed 10/1-10/31; no pets. **Facility:** 5 rooms. 2 stories; interior/exterior corridors; smoke free premises. **Cards:** AE,
& Breakfast MC, VI.
ECTV ⊠ Ⓓ

MOTEL AKRON
Rates Subject to Change
Phone: 717/859-1654
ⒶⒶⒶ 6/20-11/1 1P: $44- 49 2P/1B: $44- 49 2P/2B: $49- 56 XP: $5   F6
5/1-6/19 & 4/1-4/30 1P: $40- 45 2P/1B: $40- 45 2P/2B: $45- 50 XP: $5   F6
◆◆ 11/2-3/31 1P: $35- 40 2P/1B: $35- 40 2P/2B: $39- 45 XP: $5   F6
Motel **Location:** Just s on SR 272. 116 S 7th St 17501. **Terms:** Reserv deposit, 3 day notice; no pets. **Facility:** 23
rooms. Weekends $5 extra charge, 4/1-11/1. Handling fee imposed; 1 story; exterior corridors; smoke free
premises. **Cards:** MC, VI. *(See color ad p 331)*
ECTV ⊠ Ⓓ

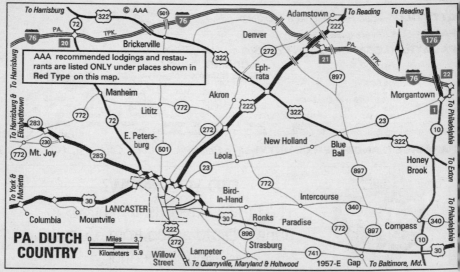

RESTAURANT

AKRON RESTAURANT ◆ American
Lunch: $7-$14   **Dinner:** $7-$14   **Phone:** 717/859-1181
Location: 0.5 mi s on SR 272. 333 S 7th St 17501. **Hours:** 6 am-8 pm, Sun 11 am-7 pm. Closed major holidays. **Features:** casual dress; children's menu; early bird specials; carryout. Home-style cooking & atmosphere; also counter service. **Cards:** DS, MC, VI.   ☒

BAINBRIDGE—900

RESTAURANT

VILLAGE HOMESTEAD RESTAURANT ◆ American
Lunch: $5-$12   **Dinner:** $5-$12   **Phone:** 717/426-2740
Location: Just se on SR 441. 2141 River Rd 17502. **Hours:** 5:30 am-8 pm; Sun 11 am-2 pm. Closed: 12/25. **Reservations:** accepted. **Features:** casual dress; children's menu; carryout. Pennsylvania Dutch home-cooked meals. Counter seating avail. Smoke free premises. **Cards:** DS, MC, VI.   ☒

BIRD-IN-HAND—500

LODGINGS

AMISH COUNTRY MOTEL ◆◆ Motel
Rates Subject to Change   **Phone:** 717/768-8396
6/26-9/6   2P/2B: $79   XP: $8   F17
5/15-6/25 & 9/7-10/24   2P/2B: $65- 75   XP: $8   F17
5/1-5/14, 10/25-11/28 & 4/1-4/30   2P/2B: $49- 59   XP: $8   F17
Location: 1 mi e on SR 340. 3013 Old Philadelphia Pike 17505 (PO Box 73). **Terms:** Open 5/1-11/28 & 4/1-4/30; reserv deposit; no pets. **Facility:** 25 rooms. Weekends 9/1-11/30, $5 extra charge; 1-2 stories; exterior corridors. **Cards:** AE, DS, MC, VI.   ⊠ ECTV ☒ D

BIRD-IN-HAND FAMILY INN ◆◆◆ Motor Inn
Rates Subject to Change   **Phone:** 717/768-8271
6/19-9/6   2P/2B: $86- 99   XP: $8   F16
9/7-10/31   2P/2B: $75- 99   XP: $8   F16
5/1-6/18   2P/2B: $70- 85   XP: $8   F16
11/1-4/30   2P/2B: $49- 69   XP: $8   F16
Location: 0.3 mi e on SR 340. 2740 Old Philadelphia Pike 17505 (PO Box 402). Fax: 717/768-1117. **Terms:** Reserv deposit; no pets. **Facility:** 100 rooms. 2 whirlpool rms, $30 extra charge. 1 efficiency unit, $10 extra charge. Weekends 8/30-11/30, $5 extra charge; 1-2 stories; interior/exterior corridors. **Dining:** Restaurant; 6 am-9 pm, in winter-8 pm, closed Sun; $6-$10. **Cards:** AE, CB, DI, DS, MC, VI. (See ad starting on p 338)   ⊠ ⊠ ECTV ☒ D

VILLAGE INN OF BIRD-IN-HAND ◆◆ Historic Bed & Breakfast
Rates Subject to Change   **Phone:** 717/293-8369
6/26-10/24 [CP]   2P/2B: $89- 145   XP: $10   F12
5/1-6/25 & 10/25-4/30 [CP]   2P/2B: $69- 120   XP: $10   F12
Location: Center; on SR 340. 2695 Old Philadelphia Pike 17505 (PO Box 253). Fax: 717/768-1117. **Terms:** Reserv deposit; no pets. **Facility:** 11 rooms. 3 stories, no elevator; interior corridors. **Cards:** AE, CB, DI, DS, MC, VI.   ECTV ☒ D

RESTAURANTS

AMISH BARN RESTAURANT ⒶⒶⒶ SAVE ◆ American
Lunch: $6-$8   **Dinner:** $10-$13   **Phone:** 717/768-8886
Location: 1.1 mi e on SR 340. 3029 Old Philadelphia Pike 17505. **Hours:** Open 5/1-12/31 & 4/1-4/30; 8 am-8 pm. Closed: 12/25. **Reservations:** accepted. **Features:** casual dress; children's menu; carryout; salad bar. Family style dining featuring traditional Pennsylvania Dutch favorites. **Cards:** AE, DS, MC, VI. **Special Value:** $1 off the price of a dinner entree.   ☒

PLAIN & FANCY FARM DINING ROOM ◆ Regional American
Lunch: $14   **Dinner:** $14   **Phone:** 717/768-4400
Location: 2 mi e on SR 340. 3121 Old Philadelphia Pike 17505. **Hours:** 11:30 am-8 pm; noon-7 pm 1/1-3/31. Closed: 12/24 & 12/25. **Reservations:** suggested; weekends. **Features:** casual dress. Family-style seating. Small parties share tables & heaping plates of Pennsylvania Dutch favorites. Children 4-11 years, $5.95. Smoke free premises. **Cards:** AE, DS, MC, VI. (See ad starting on p 338)   ☒

LEARN THE ESCAPE CLAUSES.
Read Hotel/Motel fire safety in
About Lodgings & Restaurants
for advice on how to deal with a lodging fire.

CLAY—300

LODGING

CLEARVIEW FARM BED & BREAKFAST
Guaranteed Rates   **Phone:** 717/733-6333
All Year [BP]   2P/1B: $95- 145
Location: 4 mi w on US 322 from jct SR 272, 1 mi n. 355 Clearview Rd 17522. **Fax:** 717/733-6333.
Terms: Age restrictions may apply; check-in 4 pm; 2 night min stay, weekends; no pets. **Facility:** 5 rooms. 3 stories, no elevator; interior corridors; smoke free premises. **Cards:** DS, MC, VI.
Historic Bed & Breakfast
(See ad starting on p 338)   🗙 Ⓓ

DENVER—2,900

LODGINGS

BLACK HORSE LODGE AND SUITES
Phone: 717/336-7563
Fri & Sat 5/1-10/24 [CP]   2P/1B: $69- 109   2P/2B: $79- 119   XP: $10   F12
Sun-Thurs 5/1-10/24 &
4/16-4/30 [CP]   2P/1B: $69- 89   2P/2B: $79- 99   XP: $10   F12
10/25-4/15 [CP]   2P/1B: $65- 79   2P/2B: $69- 89   XP: $10   F12
Motor Inn
Location: I-76 (PA Tpk) exit 21, 1 mi w to SR 272, then 0.3 mi n. 2180 N Reading Rd 17517 (PO Box 343).
Fax: 717/336-1110. **Terms:** Weekly/monthly rates; package plans; pets, in designated rooms. **Facility:** 74 rooms. Variety of room types; balcony or patio. 4 luxury suites with kitchen, $169-$229, rate for up to 2 persons; 1-2 stories; interior/exterior corridors; playground, outdoor health stations, picnic pavilion. **Dining:** Dining room, see separate listing. **Services:** Fee: coin laundry. **All Rooms:** coffeemakers. **Some Rooms:** 2 efficiencies, microwaves, refrigerators, whirlpools. **Cards:** AE, CB, DI, DS, MC, VI. **Special Amenities:** Free breakfast and free local telephone calls. *(See color ad below)*
🛏 ⊇ ⅏ 🗙 Ⓓ

COCALICO CREEK BED & BREAKFAST
Rates Subject to Change   **Phone:** 717/336-0271
All Year [BP]   1P: $58- 73   2P/1B: $72- 87   XP: $12   D10
Location: I-76 (PA Tpk) exit 21, 1 mi w to SR 272, 1.5 mi s on SR 272, 1.5 mi w on Church & Main sts, just
Historic Bed & Breakfast   s. 224 S 4th St 17517. **Terms:** Reserv deposit, 10 day notice; no pets, pets on premises. **Facility:** 4 rooms.
Handling fee imposed; 2 stories; interior corridors; smoke free premises. **Cards:** MC, VI.   🗙 Ⓓ

COMFORT INN
Phone: 717/336-4649
7/1-10/31 [CP]   1P: $60- 130   2P/1B: $60- 130   2P/2B: $60- 130   XP: $8   F18
5/1-6/30 & 11/1-4/30 [CP]   1P: $60- 90   2P/1B: $60- 90   2P/2B: $60- 90   XP: $8   F18
Location: I-76 (PA Tpk) exit 21, 1 mi w to SR 272, then just s. 2015 N Reading Rd 17517.
Motel
Fax: 717/336-5501. **Terms:** Weekly/monthly rates; small pets only, $10 extra charge, in designated rooms.
Facility: 45 rooms. Comfortable contemporary rooms. 2 night min stay last weekend in April, June & Sept; 2
stories; interior corridors. **Dining:** Restaurant nearby. **Services:** valet laundry. **All Rooms:** free movies. **Cards:** AE, DS, MC, VI. **Special Amenities:** Free local telephone calls and free newspaper.
🛏 🏊 🏋 ⅏ 🗙 Ⓓ

HOLIDAY INN-LANCASTER COUNTY
Phone: 717/336-7541
Fri & Sat   1P: $59- 99   2P/1B: $59- 99   2P/2B: $59- 99   XP: $8   F12
Sun-Thurs   1P: $49- 89   2P/1B: $49- 89   2P/2B: $49- 89   XP: $8   F12
Location: I-76 (PA Tpk) exit 21, 1 mi w to SR 272, then just s exit 21 & Rt 272. (PO Box 129, 17517).
Motor Inn
Fax: 717/336-0515. **Terms:** Weekly/monthly rates; package plans; no pets. **Facility:** 110 rooms. 2-person rate for up to 4 persons; 2 stories; interior corridors; video rental library. **Dining:** Restaurant; 6:30 am-2 & 5-10 pm; $10-$15; cocktails. **Services:** Fee: coin laundry. **All Rooms:** free movies. **Some Rooms:** coffeemakers. Fee: VCR's. **Cards:** AE, CB, DI, DS, JCB, MC, VI. **Special Amenities:** Free local telephone calls and free room upgrade (subject to availability with advanced reservations).
⊇ 🏋 ⅏ 🗙 Ⓓ

PENNSYLVANIA DUTCH MOTEL
Rates Subject to Change   **Phone:** 717/336-5559
5/1-10/31 & 4/1-4/30   2P/1B: $46   2P/2B: $50   XP: $3   F10
11/1-3/31   2P/1B: $36   2P/2B: $40   XP: $3   F10
Motel
Location: I-76 (PA Tpk) exit 21, 1 mi w to SR 272, then 0.5 mi n. 2275 N Reading Rd 17517.
Terms: Reserv deposit; pets. **Facility:** 20 rooms. 1 story; exterior corridors. **Cards:** VI.
🛏 ⅏ Ⓓ

RESTAURANTS

THE BLACK HORSE RESTAURANT & TAVERN
Lunch: $5-$15   **Dinner:** $14-$28   **Phone:** 717/336-6555
Location: I-76 (PA Tpk) exit 21, 1 mi w to SR 272, then 0.3 mi n; in Black Horse Lodge and Suites. 2170 N
Reading Rd 17517. **Hours:** 11:30 am-10 pm, Sun-9 pm; Tavern 11 am-11 pm. Closed: 1/1, 11/26 & 12/25.
Reservations: suggested. **Features:** casual dress; children's menu; cocktails & lounge. Homemade soup &
American   dessert; specialties are Maryland crab cakes, barbecued ribs & pork tenderloins. All beef is certified Angus.
Cards: AE, CB, DI, DS, MC, VI.   🗙

ZINN'S DINER   **Lunch:** $3-$10   **Dinner:** $3-$10   **Phone:** 717/336-2210
AAA   **Location:** I-76 (PA Tpk) exit 21, 1 mi w to SR 272, then 0.4 mi n. 2270 N Reading Rd 17517. **Hours:** 6
◆◆   am-11 pm. **Closed:** 12/25. **Features:** casual dress; children's menu; health conscious menu; carryout.
Regional   Excellent Pennsylvania Dutch cooking, from pot pies to shoo-fly pies with a variety of standard favorites.
American   Informal family atmosphere. Popular with locals & tourists alike. Family owned & operated since 1950.
    Cards: DS, MC, VI.   ⊠

EAST PETERSBURG—4,200

RESTAURANT

HAYDN ZUG'S   Historical   **Lunch:** $4-$10   **Dinner:** $15-$30   **Phone:** 717/569-5746
◆◆   **Location:** On the square; jct of SR 72 & 722. 1987 State St 17520. **Hours:** 11:30 am-2 & 5-9 pm, Sat from
American   5 pm. Closed major holidays, Sun & Mon. **Reservations:** suggested. **Features:** casual dress; children's
    menu; carryout; cocktails & lounge. Well-prepared meals served in colonial atmosphere. Built in 1852.
Half-dinners avail. **Cards:** AE, DI, DS, MC, VI.   ⊠

ELIZABETHTOWN—10,000

LODGINGS

HOLIDAY INN EXPRESS ELIZABETHTOWN (HERSHEY AREA)   Rates Subject to Change   **Phone:** 717/367-4000
◆◆◆   5/1-10/31 [CP]   1P: $89   2P/1B: $89   2P/2B: $89   XP: $10   F18
Motel   11/1-4/30 [CP]   1P: $79   2P/1B: $79   2P/2B: $79   XP: $10   F18
    Location: SR 283, Elizabethtown/Rheems exit. 147 Merts Dr 17022. **Fax:** 717/367-0292. **Terms:** Sr.
discount; reserv deposit, 7 day notice; no pets. **Facility:** 82 rooms. 4 whirlpool rms, extra charge; 2 stories; interior corridors.
Some Rooms: efficiency. **Cards:** AE, DI, DS, MC, VI.   Roll in showers.   CTV ⑤ ⊠ 🕾 D Ⓢ

WEST RIDGE GUEST HOUSE   Rates Subject to Change   **Phone:** 717/367-7783
AAA   All Year [BP]   1P: $60- 120   2P/1B: $60- 120   2P/2B: $80   XP: $15   D12
    Location: 5.5 mi se from SR 283 via SR 743S, SR 230E, SR 743S, then w. 1285 W Ridge Rd 17022.
◆◆◆   **Fax:** 717/367-8468. **Terms:** Reserv deposit, 5 day notice; no pets. **Facility:** 9 rooms. 2 stories; interior corri-
Bed &   dors; smoke free premises. **Cards:** AE, DI, DS, MC, VI.   ECTV ⊠ D
Breakfast

EPHRATA—12,100

LODGING

HISTORIC SMITHTON COUNTRY INN   Rates Subject to Change   **Phone:** 717/733-6094
AAA   Fri-Sun [BP]   1P: $95- 140   2P/1B: $105- 150   XP: $20-35
    Mon-Thurs [BP]   1P: $65- 110   2P/1B: $75- 120   XP: $20-35
◆◆◆   **Location:** On US 322, just w of jct SR 272. 900 W Main St 17522. **Terms:** Check-in 3:30 pm; reserv
Historic Bed   deposit, 14 day notice; 2 night min stay, Sat; pets, 1 dog only. **Facility:** 8 rooms. 3 stories, no elevator; inte-
& Breakfast   rior corridors; smoke free premises. **Cards:** AE, MC, VI.   🛏 ⊠ D

RESTAURANTS

FAMILY TIME RESTAURANT   **Lunch:** $5-$10   **Dinner:** $6-$11   **Phone:** 717/738-4231
AAA   **Location:** On US 322, 1.8 mi w of jct SR 272. 1737 W Main St 17522. **Hours:** 11 am-8 pm, Fri & Sat-9 pm.
    Closed 12/25. **Reservations:** accepted. **Features:** casual dress; children's menu; salad bar. Pennsylvania
◆   Dutch smorgasbord. Seafood buffet Sat 3 pm-9 pm, $19. Smoke free premises. **Cards:** DS, MC, VI.   ⊠
American

ISAAC'S RESTAURANT & DELI   **Lunch:** $4-$8   **Dinner:** $4-$8   **Phone:** 717/733-7777
◆   **Location:** On SR 272, just n of jct US 322, in Cloister Shopping Center. 120 N Reading Rd 17522.
American   **Hours:** 10 am-9 pm, Fri & Sat-10 pm, Sun 11 am-9 pm. Closed: 1/1, 11/26 & 12/25. **Features:** casual dress;
    children's menu; carryout. Pterodactyls, penguins & prairie chickens on the menu at lively deli with a flair for
inventive sandwiches whimsically named. **Cards:** AE, DS, MC, VI.   ⊠

THE RESTAURANT AT DONECKERS   **Lunch:** $9-$14   **Dinner:** $16-$28   **Phone:** 717/738-9501
◆◆◆   **Location:** 2 mi w on US 322 from jct US 222, 0.5 mi n. 333 N State St 17522. **Hours:** 11 am-10 pm. Closed
French   major holidays, Sun & Wed. **Reservations:** suggested; weekends. **Features:** dressy casual; children's
    menu; health conscious menu items; cocktails. Relaxed dining. Expertly prepared entrees with an American
flair. Varied menu. Braille & large print menus avail. Smoke-free lunch hour. **Cards:** AE, DI, DS, MC, VI.   ⊠

WAHTNEY'S INN   Historical   **Dinner:** $8-$17   **Phone:** 717/733-2014
◆◆   **Location:** 4 mi w on US 322 from jct SR 272. 2415 W Main St 17522. **Hours:** 4 pm-10 pm, Fri & Sat-11 pm,
American   Sun-9 pm. Closed major holidays. **Reservations:** suggested. **Features:** casual dress; children's menu;
    carryout; cocktails & lounge. Relaxed dining in former hotel. International cuisine. **Cards:** AE, DS, MC, VI.
    ⊠

INTERCOURSE—1,200

LODGINGS

BEST WESTERN INTERCOURSE VILLAGE INN   Rates Subject to Change   **Phone:** 717/768-3636
AAA   Fri & Sat   2P/2B: $69- 109   XP: $6   F12
    Sun-Thurs   2P/2B: $59- 99   XP: $6   F12
◆◆◆   **Location:** On SR 772, just se of SR 340. Rt 340 & 772 17534 (PO Box 40). **Fax:** 717/768-7622. **Terms:** No
Motor Inn   pets. **Facility:** 40 rooms. 5 suites with refrigerator, microwave & wet bar, $30 extra charge; 2 stories;
    interior/exterior corridors; smoke free premises. **Dining:** Restaurant; 6 am-8 pm; closed Sun; $6-$12.
Cards: AE, CB, DI, DS, MC, VI. *(See color ad p 334)*   ECTV ⊠ D

HARVEST DRIVE FAMILY MOTEL   Rates Subject to Change   **Phone:** 717/768-7186
◆◆   6/19-10/31   2P/1B: $64- 75   2P/2B: $64- 75   XP: $5   F14
Motor Inn   5/1-6/18   2P/1B: $64- 69   2P/2B: $64- 69   XP: $5   F14
    4/2-4/30   2P/1B: $54- 59   2P/2B: $54- 59   XP: $5   F14
    11/1-4/1   2P/1B: $49- 59   2P/2B: $49- 59   XP: $5   F14
Location: 0.5 mi w on SR 340, 0.7 mi s on Clearview Rd, then just w. 3370 Harvest Dr 17534 (PO Box 498).
Fax: 717/768-4513. **Terms:** Reserv deposit; no pets. **Facility:** 51 rooms. 1-2 stories; exterior corridors. **Dining:** Restaurant;
7 am-7 pm; 11/1-4/1 8 am-7 pm; $5-$12. **Cards:** AE, DS, MC, VI.   ECTV ⊠ D

INTERCOURSE VILLAGE BED & BREAKFAST SUITES   Rates Subject to Change   Phone: 717/768-2626
Bed &   All Year [BP]   2P/1B: $89- 169   XP: $29
Breakfast   Too new to rate; **Location:** Center. Main St, Rt 340 17534 (PO Box 340). **Facility:** 12 rooms. Scheduled to open March 1998. **Cards:** AE, MC, VI.   (D)

TRAVELERS REST MOTEL   Guaranteed Rates   Phone: 717/768-8731
◆◆◆   6/26-9/6 [CP]   2P/2B: $75- 89   XP: $8   F17
Motel   5/15-6/25 & 9/7-10/24 [CP]   2P/2B: $65- 85   XP: $8   F17
   5/1-5/14, 10/25-12/6 &
   2/5-4/30 [CP]   2P/2B: $45- 59   XP: $8   F17
Location: 0.5 mi e on SR 340. 3701 Old Philadelphia Pike 17534 (PO Box 128). **Terms:** Open 5/1-12/6 & 2/5-4/30; reserv deposit; no pets. **Facility:** 40 rooms. 1 story; exterior corridors. **Cards:** AE, DS, MC, VI. *(See ad starting on p 338)*

(CTV) (X) (D)

LAMPETER—800

LODGINGS

AUSTRALIAN WALKABOUT INN B&B   Phone: 717/464-0707
(AAA) (SAVE)   5/1-10/31 & 4/1-4/30 [BP]   1P: $99- 159   2P/1B: $99- 189   2P/2B: $99- 225   XP: $25
   11/1-3/31 [BP]   1P: $99- 139   2P/1B: $99- 169   2P/2B: $99- 169   XP: $25
◆◆◆   **Location:** Just w on SR 741. 837 Village Rd 17537 (PO Box 294). Fax: 717/464-2501. **Terms:** Age
Historic Bed   restrictions may apply; reserv deposit, 14 day notice; package plans, Sun-Thurs; no pets. **Facility:** 5 rooms.
& Breakfast   Attractive rooms with many antiques. Authentic Australian-style bed & breakfast inn. Rural village setting. Handling fee imposed; 3 stories; interior/exterior corridors; smoke free premises; croquet. **All Rooms:** combo or
shower baths, no phones. **Some Rooms:** whirlpools. **Cards:** AE, MC, VI. **Special Amenities: Free breakfast and free
local telephone calls.**

(CTV) (X) (D)

BED & BREAKFAST-THE MANOR   Rates Subject to Change   Phone: 717/464-9564
◆◆   5/15-10/31 [BP]   2P/1B: $79- 99   2P/2B: $79- 99   XP: $35   D12
Bed &   5/1-5/14 & 11/1-4/30 [BP]   2P/1B: $79- 89   2P/2B: $79- 89   XP: $35   D12
Breakfast   **Location:** Just w on SR 741. 830 Village Rd 17537 (PO Box 416). **Terms:** Reserv deposit, 7 day notice; no
pets. **Facility:** 6 rooms. Handling fee imposed; 2 stories; interior/exterior corridors; smoke free premises.
Cards: MC, VI.

(≋) (+) (X) (D)

LANCASTER—55,600

LODGINGS

BEST WESTERN EDEN RESORT INN & CONFERENCE CENTER   Phone: 717/569-6444
(AAA) (SAVE)   7/1-10/29   1P: $99- 159   2P/2B: $99- 159   XP: $10   F18
   5/1-6/30   1P: $89- 139   2P/2B: $89- 139   XP: $10   F18
◆◆◆   10/30-4/30   1P: $84- 119   2P/2B: $84- 119   XP: $10   F18
Motor Inn   **Location:** At jct US 30 & SR 272. 0.3 mi n on SR 272. 222 Eden Rd 17601. Fax: 717/569-4208.
Terms: Reserv deposit; weekly/monthly rates; AP, BP avail; package plans; pets. **Facility:** 274 rooms. 16 two-
bedroom units. 40 family units with full kitchen $175-$249. Handling fee imposed; 3 stories; interior/exterior corridors; wading
pool, saunas, whirlpool; 1 lighted tennis court; playground, basketball, shuffleboard. **Dining & Entertainment:** Dining room,
restaurant; 6:30 am-11 pm, Sun brunch 10:30 am-2 pm; $10-$20; cocktails/lounge; entertainment. **Services:** Fee: coin
laundry. **All Rooms:** coffeemakers. Fee: movies. **Some Rooms:** microwaves, refrigerators, whirlpools. **Cards:** AE, CB, DI,
DS, MC, VI. **Special Amenities: Early check-in/late check-out and preferred room (subject to availability with
advanced reservations).** *(See color ad p 335)*   (≋)(≋)(≋)(⌘)(⌘)(ECTV)(X)(D)

CLASSIC INN   Rates Subject to Change   Phone: 717/291-4576
◆◆   6/24-11/13   1P: $49- 79   2P/1B: $49- 89   2P/2B: $59- 99   XP: $10
Motel   5/1-6/23 & 11/14-4/30   1P: $39- 49   2P/1B: $49- 59   2P/2B: $49- 69   XP: $5
   Location: 5 mi e on SR 30. 2302 Lincoln Hwy E 17602. Fax: 717/291-1762. **Terms:** Reserv deposit; no
pets. **Facility:** 18 rooms. 1 room with efficiency & whirlpool, $99-$135. Handling fee imposed; 2 stories; interior/exterior corridors; smoke free premises. **Cards:** AE, DS, MC, VI.   (ECTV)(X)(D)

COMFORT INN-SHERWOOD KNOLL   Guaranteed Rates   Phone: 717/898-2431
◆◆◆   All Year [CP]   1P: $68- 88   2P/1B: $80- 105   2P/2B: $99- 105   XP: $8   F18
Motor Inn   **Location:** 5 mi w on US 30, at Centerville exit. 500 Centerville Rd 17601. Fax: 717/898-2344. **Terms:** Sr.
discount; small pets only, $5 extra charge. **Facility:** 166 rooms. 6 whirlpool rms, $105-$150 for up to 2 per-
sons; 3 stories; interior corridors. **Dining:** Dining room; 6:45 am-2 & 5-9:30 pm, Sun 7:45 am-1 & 4:30-8:30 pm; $8-$15.
All Rooms: free movies. **Cards:** AE, CB, DI, DS, JCB, MC, VI.   (⌘)(≋)(ECTV)(X)(D)

CONTINENTAL INN   Guaranteed Rates   **Phone:** 717/299-0421
△△△   6/19-9/7   2P/1B: $73- 82 2P/2B: $85- 96 XP: $10   F15
        9/8-11/29   2P/1B: $54- 74 2P/2B: $64- 84 XP: $7   F15
◆ ◆   5/1-6/18 & 3/27-4/30   2P/1B: $57- 61 2P/2B: $67- 71 XP: $7   F15
Motor Inn   11/30-3/26   2P/1B: $48- 50 2P/2B: $52- 54 XP: $7   F15
        Location: 5 mi e on US 30. 2285 Lincoln Hwy E 17602. Fax: 717/293-8512. **Terms:** Reserv deposit; no
pets. **Facility:** 165 rooms. 4 whirlpool rms, extra charge; 2 stories; exterior corridors. **Dining:** Dining room; 7:30 am-10:30 &
6-9 pm, Fri-9:30 pm, Sat 8 am-11 & 6-9:30 pm, Sun 8 am-11 & 6-9 pm; $8-$17. **Cards:** AE, DI, DS, MC.
(See color ad below)

Come see a place where the scenery stares back.

Unforgettable surroundings, plus the charm of another country, another century.
Discover it all in one place. The one with two names.

Lancaster County, Pennsylvania Dutch Country.

Everywhere you look, it looks like Just Plain Fun.

PREMIUM PA DUTCH PACKAGES

Theatre Package	Amish Experience Package	Golf Package
$109-$139	$73-$103	$111-$141

Rates are per person for two nights. Summer rates higher.

For preferred lodging reservations and a free Map & Visitors Guide,
call toll-free 24 hours a day: **1-800-PA DUTCH (800-735-2629).**

Just *plain* fun.

Pennsylvania
Memories last a lifetime.

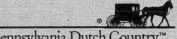

Pennsylvania Dutch Country™
Lancaster County

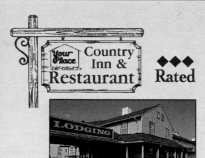

COUNTRY LIVING INN   Rates Subject to Change   Phone: 717/295-7295

◆◆◆

6/27-10/30			2P/2B:	$77- 97	XP: $8	F5
Motel 5/1-6/26 & 2/16-4/30			2P/2B:	$56- 86	XP: $8	F5
10/31-2/15			2P/2B:	$46- 75	XP: $8	F5

Location: On SR 340, 2 mi e of jct US 30. 2406 Old Philadelphia Pike 17602. Fax: 717/295-0994. **Terms:** Reserv deposit; no pets. **Facility:** 34 rooms. 1 whirlpool rm, $130; 2 stories; interior corridors. **Cards:** MC, VI.

ECTV ⊠ D

ECONO LODGE NORTH   Phone: 717/299-6900

🔺🔺 SAVE

6/16-8/31	1P: $59- 79	2P/1B: $59- 79	2P/2B: $59- 79	XP: $5	F18
9/1-10/31	1P: $44- 75	2P/1B: $47- 75	2P/2B: $53- 75	XP: $5	F18
5/1-6/15	1P: $39- 65	2P/1B: $41- 65	2P/2B: $41- 65	XP: $5	F18
Motel 11/1-4/30	1P: $32- 65	2P/1B: $33- 65	2P/2B: $36- 65	XP: $5	F18

◆◆

Location: 4.5 mi e on US 30. 2165 US Hwy 30 E 17602. Fax: 717/299-6900. **Terms:** No pets. **Facility:** 49 rooms. 2 stories; interior corridors. **Cards:** AE, DS, MC, VI.

ECTV ⊠ D

ECONO LODGE SOUTH

Phone: 717/397-1900

(AAA) [SAVE]
◆◆
Motel

		1P:	2P/1B:		2P/2B:		XP:	
6/16-8/31		$59- 79	$59- 79		$59- 79		$5	F18
9/1-10/31		$44- 75	$47- 75		$53- 75		$5	F18
5/1-6/15		$39- 65	$41- 65		$41- 65		$5	F18
11/1-4/30		$32- 65	$33- 65		$36- 65		$5	F18

Location: 4.5 mi e on US 30. 2140 US Hwy 30E 17602. Fax: 717/299-6900. **Terms:** No pets. **Facility:** 44 rooms. 2 stories; interior corridors. **Cards:** AE, DS, MC, VI.

[ECTV] [X] [D]

FAIRFIELD INN BY MARRIOTT

Rates Subject to Change

Phone: 717/581-1800

(AAA)
◆◆◆
Motel

		1P:		2P/1B:		2P/2B:		XP:	
5/16-10/20 [CP]		$79		$79		$79		$5	F18
5/1-5/15 & 10/21-4/30 [CP]		$69		$69		$69		$5	F18

Location: On SR 72; jct SR 283. 150 Granite Run Dr 17601. Fax: 717/581-1810. **Terms:** No pets. **Facility:** 133 rooms. 3 stories; interior corridors. **All Rooms:** free & pay movies. **Cards:** AE, DI, DS, MC, VI. Roll in showers. [≥] [CTV] [&] [X] [⌂] [D] [S]

FULTON STEAMBOAT INN

Rates Subject to Change

Phone: 717/299-9999

(AAA)
◆◆◆
Motor Inn

		2P/2B:		XP:	
Fri & Sat		$58- 130		$10	
Sun-Thurs		$47- 130		$10	

Location: Jct US 30 & SR 896. (PO Box 333, STRASBURG, 17579). Fax: 717/299-9992. **Terms:** Check-in 3:30 pm; reserv deposit; 2 night min stay, weekends; no pets. **Facility:** 96 rooms. 3 stories; interior corridors. **Dining:** Restaurant; 7 am-9 pm, Fri & Sat-10 pm; $9-$20. **All Rooms:** Fee: movies. **Cards:** AE, DS, MC, VI.

(See color ad below)

[≥] [ECTV] [D]

GARDENS OF EDEN BED & BREAKFAST

◆◆◆
Historic Bed
& Breakfast

Rates Subject to Change

Phone: 717/393-5179

		1P:		2P/1B:	2P/2B:	XP:	
All Year [BP]		$85		$85- 130	$130	$20	

Location: 0.8 mi ne on SR 23E from jct US 30, 0.4 mi e. 1894 Eden Rd 17601. Fax: 717/393-7722. **Terms:** Age restrictions may apply; reserv deposit, 7 day notice; 2 night min stay, weekends; no pets. **Facility:** 4 rooms. Handling fee imposed; 2 stories; interior/exterior corridors; designated smoking area. **Some Rooms:** efficiency. **Cards:** MC, VI.

[ECTV] [X] [D]

GARDEN SPOT MOTEL

Rates Subject to Change

Phone: 717/394-4736

(AAA)
◆◆
Motel

		2P/1B:		2P/2B:		XP:	
6/25-9/6		$54		$63		$5	
5/1-6/24 & 9/7-10/31		$50		$54		$5	
11/1-11/30 & 3/27-4/30		$44		$48		$5	

Location: 5 mi e on US 30. 2291 US 30E 17602. **Terms:** Open 5/1-11/30 & 3/27-4/30; no pets. **Facility:** 19 rooms. 1 story; exterior corridors. **Dining:** Coffee shop; 7:30-11 am. **Cards:** AE, DS, MC, VI.

[ECTV] [X] [D]

HAMPTON INN-LANCASTER

Rates Subject to Change

Phone: 717/299-1200

◆◆◆
Motel

		1P:	2P/1B:		2P/2B:	
6/17-10/27 [CP]		$92- 112	$111		$103	
4/15-4/30 [CP]		$87- 104	$104		$97	
5/1-6/16 [CP]		$83- 100	$100		$93	
10/28-4/14 [CP]		$73- 89	$89		$83	

Location: 3.3 mi e on US 30 at Greenfield Rd exit, 0.4 mi n. 545 Greenfield Rd 17601. Fax: 717/299-1155. **Terms:** Sr. discount; reserv deposit; no pets. **Facility:** 129 rooms. Rates for up to 4 persons; 4 stories; interior corridors. **All Rooms:** free movies. **Cards:** AE, CB, DI, DS, MC, VI. Roll in showers. [≥] [ECTV] [X] [D] [S]

HILTON GARDEN INN-LANCASTER

Rates Subject to Change

Phone: 717/560-0880

◆◆◆
Motor Inn

		1P:		2P/1B:		2P/2B:		XP:	
All Year		$129- 169		$129- 169		$129- 169		$10	F18

Location: On SR 72; jct SR 72 & 283. 101 Granite Run Dr 17601. Fax: 717/560-5400. **Terms:** No pets. **Facility:** 156 rooms. 2 stories; interior corridors. **Dining:** Restaurant; 6:30 am-2 & 5-10 pm, Sat & Sun 7 am-noon & 5-10 pm; $12-$22. **All Rooms:** free & pay movies. **Cards:** AE, CB, DI, DS, MC, VI. *(See color ad p 18)*

[≥] [CTV] [X] [D] [S]

HOLIDAY INN-HISTORIC DISTRICT

Rates Subject to Change

Phone: 717/393-0771

◆◆◆
Motor Inn

		1P:		2P/1B:		2P/2B:	
7/1-10/31		$99		$99		$99	
5/1-6/30 & 11/1-4/30		$79		$79		$79	

Location: 0.5 mi s on SR 501 from jct US 30. 1492 Lititz Pike 17601. Fax: 717/299-6238. **Terms:** Sr. discount; no pets. **Facility:** 160 rooms. 2 stories; exterior corridors. **Dining:** Dining room; 6 am-1 & 5-10 pm; $9-$16. **All Rooms:** free & pay movies. **Cards:** AE, CB, DI, DS, JCB, MC, VI. *(See color ad p 343)*

[≥] [CTV] [X] [D]

HOLIDAY INN LANCASTER HOST HOTEL & CONFERENCE CENTER   Guaranteed Rates   **Phone:** 717/299-5500
◆◆◆
Resort Motor
Inn

		1P	2P/1B	2P/2B	XP	
	7/1-10/31	1P: $139- 159	2P/1B: $139- 159	2P/2B: $139- 159	XP: $15	F18
	5/1-6/30 & 4/1-4/30	1P: $109- 129	2P/1B: $109- 129	2P/2B: $109- 129	XP: $15	F18
	11/1-3/31	1P: $99- 109	2P/1B: $99- 109	2P/2B: $99- 109	XP: $15	F18

Location: 5 mi e on US 30. 2300 Lincoln Hwy E 17602. Fax: 717/295-5139. **Terms:** Sr. discount; check-in 4 pm; no pets. **Facility:** 330 rooms. 2-4 stories; interior corridors. **Dining:** Dining room, restaurant; 6:30 am-10 pm; $11-$20. **All Rooms:** free & pay movies. **Cards:** AE, CB, DI, DS, MC, VI. *(See color ad p 344)* 🛏 🛏 📶 ECTV ✕ D S

HOLIDAY INN-VISITORS CENTER   Rates Subject to Change   **Phone:** 717/299-2551
◆◆◆
Motor Inn

		1P	2P/1B	2P/2B
	5/1-10/31	1P: $89- 99	2P/1B: $89- 99	2P/2B: $89- 99
	11/1-4/30	1P: $79- 89	2P/1B: $79- 89	2P/2B: $79- 89

Location: 3.3 mi e on US 30 at Greenfield Rd exit, just n. 521 Greenfield Rd 17602. Fax: 717/397-0220. **Terms:** Sr. discount; no pets. **Facility:** 189 rooms. Double occupancy rates for up to 4 persons; 2-4 stories; interior/exterior corridors. **Dining:** Restaurant; 6 am-2 & 5-10 pm, Sat & Sun from 7 am; $8-$17. **All Rooms:** free & pay movies. **Cards:** AE, CB, DI, DS, MC, VI. *(See color ad below)* 🛏 🛏 CTV ✕ D

HOTEL BRUNSWICK   Guaranteed Rates   **Phone:** 717/397-4801
◆◆◆
Hotel

		1P	2P/1B	2P/2B	XP	
	5/1-10/31	1P: $60- 78	2P/1B: $70- 88	2P/2B: $75- 83	XP: $6	F17
	11/1-4/30	1P: $52- 70	2P/1B: $62- 80	2P/2B: $65- 75	XP: $6	F17

Location: Corner of Chestnut & Queen sts. 17608 (PO Box 749). Fax: 717/397-4991. **Terms:** Sr. discount; small pets only, $100 dep req. **Facility:** 225 rooms. 9 stories; interior corridors. **Dining:** Restaurant; 7 am-1:30 & 5:30-9 pm; breakfast & lunch buffet Mon-Fri; $7-$19. **All Rooms:** Fee: movies. **Cards:** AE, CB, DI, DS, MC, VI.
Roll in showers. 🐾 🛏 ECTV ✕ D S

HOWARD JOHNSON INN   **Phone:** 717/397-7781
AAA SAVE
◆◆
Motor Inn

		1P	2P/1B	2P/2B	XP	
	6/17-10/31	1P: $46- 89	2P/1B: $48- 89	2P/2B: $48- 89	XP: $7	F18
	5/1-6/16 & 11/1-4/30	1P: $35- 59	2P/1B: $39- 65	2P/2B: $42- 65	XP: $7	F18

Location: 4 mi e on US 30. 2100 US Hwy 30 E 17602. Fax: 717/397-6340. **Terms:** Package plans; no pets. **Facility:** 112 rooms. All rooms with patio or balcony. Handling fee imposed; 2 stories; interior corridors; playground. **Dining & Entertainment:** Restaurant; 6 am-midnight, Fri & Sat-1 am; $8-$16; cocktails/lounge. **All Rooms:** free movies. **Some Rooms:** refrigerators. **Cards:** AE, CB, DI, DS, MC, VI. **Special Amenities:** Free local telephone calls. 🛏 🍴 ECTV ✕ D

THE KING'S COTTAGE   Rates Subject to Change   **Phone:** 717/397-1017
AAA
◆◆◆
Historic Bed
& Breakfast

		2P/1B	XP
	All Year [BP]	2P/1B: $100- 175	XP: $25

Location: 1.5 mi e on US 462. 1049 E King St 17602. Fax: 717/397-3447. **Terms:** Age restrictions may apply; check-in 2 pm; reserv deposit, 7 day notice; 2 night min stay, weekends; no pets. **Facility:** 9 rooms. Carriage house with whirlpool bath & fireplace, $175-$195. Handling fee imposed; 3 stories; interior/exterior corridors; smoke free premises. **Cards:** DI, DS, MC, VI. ✕ D

KNIGHTS INN   **Phone:** 717/299-8971
AAA SAVE
◆◆
Motel

		1P	2P/1B	2P/2B	XP	
	6/15-10/31	1P: $65	2P/1B: $65	2P/2B: $77	XP: $5	F8
	5/1-6/14, 11/1-11/30 & 3/1-4/30	1P: $55	2P/1B: $55	2P/2B: $67	XP: $5	F8
	12/1-2/28	1P: $39	2P/1B: $39	2P/2B: $49	XP: $5	F8

Location: 4.5 mi e on US 30. 2151 Lincoln Hwy E 17602. Fax: 717/392-2403. **Terms:** Reserv deposit; weekly rates; no pets. **Facility:** 66 rooms. 1-3 stories; interior/exterior corridors. **Dining:** Restaurant nearby. **All Rooms:** free movies, combo or shower baths. **Cards:** AE, DS, MC, VI. 🛏 ECTV ✕ D

MCINTOSH INN OF LANCASTER
◆◆ Motel

6/28-11/9 [CP]	1P:	$57-	67	2P/1B:	$64-	74	2P/2B:	$64-	74	XP: $7 F18
5/1-6/27 & 4/4-4/30 [CP]	1P:	$50-	58	2P/1B:	$57-	65	2P/2B:	$57-	65	XP: $7 F18
11/10-4/3 [CP]	1P:	$40-	48	2P/1B:	$43-	55	2P/2B:	$43-	55	XP: $7 F18

Rates Subject to Change Phone: 717/299-9700
Location: 5 mi e on US 30. 2307 Lincoln Hwy E 17602. Fax: 717/392-3576. **Terms:** Sr. discount; no pets. **Facility:** 98 rooms. 3 stories; interior/exterior corridors. **All Rooms:** free movies. **Cards:** AE, CB, DI, MC, VI. *(See color ad p 297)*
Roll in showers. 📠 ECTV ✕ D S

O'FLAHERTY'S DINGELDEIN HOUSE BED & BREAKFAST Rates Subject to Change Phone: 717/293-1723
Ⓐ◆◆◆
Historic Bed & Breakfast

All Year [BP]	1P:	$80- 100	2P/1B:	$80- 100	2P/2B:	$70-	95	XP: $15

Location: 1.5 mi e on SR 462. 1105 E King St 17602. Fax: 717/293-1947. **Terms:** Reserv deposit, 7 day notice; 2 night min stay, weekends in season; no pets. **Facility:** 5 rooms. Handling fee imposed; 3 stories, no elevator; interior corridors; smoke free premises. **Cards:** DS, MC, VI.
✕ D

OREGON BED & BREAKFAST Rates Subject to Change Phone: 717/656-2644
◆
Historic Bed & Breakfast

5/1-10/31 [BP]	2P/1B:	$55-	77	2P/2B:	$55-	77	XP: $12 F7
11/1-4/30 [BP]	2P/1B:	$44-	66	2P/2B:	$44-	66	XP: $12 F7

Location: At jct SR 272 & 722; 1 mi n from US 222, Oregon Pike exit. 1500 Oregon Rd 17540 (LEOLA). **Terms:** Reserv deposit; 2 night min stay, weekends; no pets. **Facility:** 4 rooms. Handling fee imposed; 2 stories; interior corridors; smoke free premises. **Cards:** AE, DS, MC, VI.
✕ D

QUALITY INN & SUITES Phone: 717/569-0477
Ⓐ SAVE
Motor Inn

7/1-10/31	1P:	$79-	99	2P/1B:	$79- 110	2P/2B:	$79- 110	XP: $6 F18
5/1-6/30	1P:	$69-	99	2P/1B:	$76- 105	2P/2B:	$76- 105	XP: $6 F18
11/1-4/30	1P:	$59-	89	2P/1B:	$59-	94	2P/2B:	$59-	94	XP: $6 F18

Location: On SR 272; 2 mi n of jct US 30. 2363 Oregon Pike 17601. Fax: 717/569-6479. **Terms:** Reserv deposit; pets, $25 dep req. **Facility:** 82 rooms. Quiet rural setting. 2 whirlpool rms, $140. Handling fee imposed; 1 story; interior/exterior corridors. **Dining & Entertainment:** Cocktail lounge. **All Rooms:** coffeemakers. **Some Rooms:** refrigerators. Fee: VCR's. **Cards:** AE, CB, DI, DS, JCB, MC, VI. **Special Amenities:** Free breakfast and free local telephone calls.
🐾 📠 🛎 ECTV ✕ D

ROCKVALE VILLAGE INN Rates Subject to Change Phone: 717/293-9500
◆◆◆
Motel

6/30-11/4	1P:	$89-	99	2P/1B:	$89-	99	2P/2B:	$89- 99	XP: $8 F12
5/1-6/29, 11/5-12/31 & 4/2-4/30	1P:	$59-	69	2P/1B:	$59-	89	2P/2B:	$59- 89	XP: $8 F12
1/1-4/1	1P:	$45-	69	2P/1B:	$45-	79	2P/2B:	$45- 79	XP: $8 F12

Location: 6.5 mi e on US 30, in Rockvale Square Outlets. 24 S Willowdale Dr 17602. Fax: 717/293-8558. **Terms:** Reserv deposit; no pets. **Facility:** 113 rooms. 2 stories; interior corridors. **Dining:** Coffee shop; 7 am-2 pm. **All Rooms:** free movies. **Cards:** AE, DI, DS, MC, VI.
📠 ECTV ✕ D

RODEWAY INN ITALIAN VILLA EAST Phone: 717/397-4973
Ⓐ SAVE
Motor Inn

5/1-9/10	1P:	$58-	82	2P/1B:	$58-	82	2P/2B:	$58-	82	XP: $8 F16
9/11-10/31	1P:	$48-	75	2P/1B:	$48-	75	2P/2B:	$48-	75	XP: $8 F16
11/1-4/30	1P:	$32-	58	2P/1B:	$32-	58	2P/2B:	$32-	58	XP: $8 F16

Location: 5 mi e on US 30. 2331 Lincoln Hwy E 17602. Fax: 717/393-7819. **Terms:** No pets. **Facility:** 60 rooms. 2 stories; interior/exterior corridors. **Dining & Entertainment:** Restaurant; 4 pm-10 pm; $10-$15; cocktails/lounge. **All Rooms:** coffeemakers, free movies. **Cards:** AE, DI, DS, MC, VI.
📠 ECTV ✕ D

THE 1722 MOTOR LODGE Rates Subject to Change Phone: 717/397-4791
◆◆
Motel

6/12-8/31 [CP]	2P/2B:	$49-	69	XP: $5 F14
9/1-11/8 [CP]	2P/2B:	$43-	59	XP: $5 F14
5/1-6/11 & 4/3-4/30 [CP]	2P/2B:	$39-	53	XP: $5 F14
11/9-4/2 [CP]	2P/2B:	$29-	39	XP: $5 F14

Location: 0.8 mi w on SR 340 from US 30. 1722 Old Philadelphia Pike 17602. **Terms:** Sr. discount; no pets. **Facility:** 21 rooms. 1 story; exterior corridors. **Cards:** MC, VI.
ECTV ✕ D

SUNSET VALLEY MOTEL Rates Subject to Change Phone: 717/656-2091
◆
Motel

5/24-10/31	1P:	$59	2P/1B:	$59	2P/2B:	$59	XP: $5
5/1-5/23, 11/1-11/15 & 3/15-4/30	1P:	$55	2P/1B:	$55	2P/2B:	$55	XP: $5
11/16-3/14	1P:	$45	2P/1B:	$45	2P/2B:	$45	XP: $5

Location: 5 mi e on SR 23; 3 mi e of US 30. 2288 New Holland Pike 17601. **Terms:** Reserv deposit; no pets. **Facility:** 20 rooms. 1 story; exterior corridors. **Cards:** MC, VI.
ECTV ✕ D

SUPER 8 MOTEL Rates Subject to Change Phone: 717/393-8888
◆◆
Motel

6/15-10/31	1P:	$56	2P/1B:	$69	2P/2B:	$74	XP: $5 F16
5/1-6/14	1P:	$46	2P/1B:	$51	2P/2B:	$56	XP: $5 F16
11/1-4/30	1P:	$39	2P/1B:	$44	2P/2B:	$50	XP: $5 F16

Location: 4.5 mi e on SR 30. 2129 Lincoln Hwy E 17602. Fax: 717/393-8888. **Terms:** Sr. discount; small pets only, $25 dep req. **Facility:** 101 rooms. 3 stories; interior corridors. **All Rooms:** free movies. **Cards:** AE, CB, DI, DS, MC, VI.
🐾 ECTV ✕ D S

WILLOW VALLEY FAMILY RESORT & CONFERENCE CENTER Rates Subject to Change Phone: 717/464-2711
Ⓐ◆◆◆
Resort Motor Inn

6/19-9/6	1P:	$114- 154	2P/1B:	$114- 154	2P/2B:	$114- 154	XP: $10 F5
9/7-11/24	1P:	$104- 144	2P/1B:	$104- 144	2P/2B:	$104- 144	XP: $10 F5
5/1-6/18 & 3/26-4/30	1P:	$94- 134	2P/1B:	$94- 134	2P/2B:	$94- 134	XP: $10 F5
11/25-3/25	1P:	$84- 124	2P/1B:	$84- 124	2P/2B:	$84- 124	XP: $10 F5

Location: 3.8 mi s on US 222. 2416 Willow St Pike 17602. Fax: 717/464-4784. **Terms:** Reserv deposit; 2 night min stay, weekends; no pets. **Facility:** 352 rooms. 10 whirlpool rms, extra charge. Handling fee imposed; 1-5 stories; interior/exterior corridors. **Dining:** 2 restaurants; 6 am-9 pm; $6-$16. **All Rooms:** free movies. **Cards:** AE, CB, DI, DS, MC, VI. *(See color ad p 346)*
📠 📠 ✈ ECTV ✕ D

OUR PLACE COUNTRY INN Rates Subject to Change Phone: 717/393-3413
Ⓐ◆◆◆
Motor Inn

6/15-10/31 [CP]	1P:	$69- 79	2P/1B:	$79- 109	2P/2B:	$79- 109	XP: $7 F17
5/1-6/14 & 11/1-4/30 [CP]	1P:	$49- 59	2P/1B:	$49- 79	2P/2B:	$49- 79	XP: $7 F17

Location: 4.5 mi e on US 30. 2133 Lincoln Hwy E 17602. Fax: 717/393-2889. **Terms:** No pets. **Facility:** 125 rooms. 2 stories; interior corridors. **Dining:** Restaurant; 11 am-2 am, 4/1-10/31 6 am-10 & 11-2 am; $8-$15. **All Rooms:** free & pay movies. **Cards:** AE, DS, MC, VI. *(See color ad p 340)*
Roll in showers. 📠 ECTV ✕ D S

RESTAURANTS

D & S BRASSERIE Historical   **Lunch:** $4-$7   **Dinner:** $9-$17   **Phone:** 717/299-1694
Location: 2 mi e on SR 462. 1679 Lincoln Hwy E 17602. **Hours:** 11:30 am-2 & 5-10 pm, Fri & Sat-11 pm.
Closed: 11/26 & 12/25. **Reservations:** suggested. **Features:** casual dress; children's menu; carryout;
cocktails & lounge. Relaxed dining in a converted 1925 home. Outdoor deck in season. **Cards:** AE, DI, DS,
American   MC, VI.

FINLEY'S AMERICAN RESTAURANT   **Lunch:** $6-$9   **Dinner:** $7-$14   **Phone:** 717/392-7801
Location: 5 mi e on US 30. 2175 Lincoln Hwy E 17602. **Hours:** 11 am-10 pm, Fri & Sat-11 pm. Closed:
American   11/26 & 12/25. **Features:** casual dress; children's menu; carryout. Seasonally updated specialties.
Cards: AE, DI, DS, MC, VI.

FINLEY'S AMERICAN RESTAURANT   **Lunch:** $5-$9   **Dinner:** $6-$14   **Phone:** 717/393-0611
Location: 3 mi w on SR 462. 2020 Columbia Ave 17603. **Hours:** 11 am-10 pm, Fri & Sat-11 pm. Closed:
American   11/26 & 12/25. **Features:** casual dress; children's menu; carryout; a la carte. Casual family dining.
Seasonally updated specialties. **Cards:** AE, DI, DS, MC, VI.

HORSE INN RESTAURANT   **Dinner:** $9-$24   **Phone:** 717/392-5528
Location: Access via 200 blk of N Marshall St in alley. 225 N Marshall St 17602. **Hours:** 5 pm-10 pm, Fri &
Sat-10:30 pm, Sun-9 pm. Closed major holidays & Mon. **Reservations:** suggested. **Features:** casual dress;
children's menu; carryout; cocktails; street parking; a la carte. Very rustic & casual atmosphere in a 2-story
American   building; specializing in steak & seafood, with some vegetarian entrees. Also parking lot at corner of Marshall
& Fulton sts. **Cards:** AE, DS, MC, VI.

ISAAC'S RESTAURANT & DELI   **Lunch:** $5-$7   **Dinner:** $5-$7   **Phone:** 717/560-7774
Location: On SR 72, just n of jct SR 72 & 283; in Granite Run Square. 1559 Manheim Pike 17601.
American   **Hours:** 10 am-9 pm, Fri & Sat-10 pm, Sun from 11 am. Closed major holidays. **Features:** casual dress;
children's menu; carryout. Grilled sandwiches, named after birds, plants & flowers. **Cards:** AE, DS, MC, VI.

ISAAC'S RESTAURANT & DELI   **Lunch:** $5-$7   **Dinner:** $5-$7   **Phone:** 717/393-6067
Location: 3.3 mi e on US 30 at Greenfield Rd exit, 0.3 mi n. 555 Greenfield Rd 17601. **Hours:** 10 am-9 pm,
American   Fri & Sat-10 pm, Sun 11 am-9 pm. Closed: 1/1, 11/26 & 12/25. **Features:** casual dress; children's menu;
carryout. Grilled sandwiches, named after birds, plants & flowers. **Cards:** AE, DS, MC, VI.

ISAAC'S RESTAURANT & DELI   **Lunch:** $4-$6   **Dinner:** $4-$6   **Phone:** 717/394-5544
Location: Just n of Town Square, in Central Market Mall. 44 N Queen St 17603. **Hours:** 10 am-9 pm.
American   Closed major holidays & Sun. **Features:** casual dress; children's menu; carryout; street parking. Grilled
sandwiches, named after birds, plants & flowers. **Cards:** AE, DS, MC, VI.

ISAAC'S RESTAURANT & DELI   **Lunch:** $5-$7   **Dinner:** $5-$7   **Phone:** 717/393-1199
Location: US 30 at Centerville Rd exit, just s on Centerville Rd; in Sycamore Court Plaza. 245 Centerville
American   Rd 17603. **Hours:** 10 am-9 pm, Fri & Sat-10 pm, Sun from 11 am. Closed major holidays. **Features:** casual
MC, VI.   dress; children's menu; carryout. Grilled sandwiches, named after birds, plants & flowers. **Cards:** AE, DS,

KOUNTRY KITCHEN   **Lunch:** $6-$12   **Dinner:** $6-$12   **Phone:** 717/394-2291
Location: On SR 501; 0.5 mi s of US 30. 1500 Oregon Pike 17601. **Hours:** 7 am-8:30 pm. Closed: 12/25.
Features: casual dress; children's menu; carryout; a la carte. Country-style cooking served in country
American   atmosphere. Ample portions; homemade soup & some dessert. Smoke free premises.

MARKET FARE RESTAURANT   **Lunch:** $5-$10   **Dinner:** $11-$22   **Phone:** 717/299-7090
SAVE   **Location:** At corner of Grant & Market sts. 50 W Grant St 17603. **Hours:** 11 am-2:30 & 5-10 pm, Mon-9 pm,
Sun 11 am-2 & 5-9 pm. Closed major holidays. **Reservations:** suggested. **Features:** dressy casual; Sunday
Regional   brunch; children's menu; carryout; cocktails & lounge; fee for parking. Contemporary decor. Seafood & pasta
American   entrees are specialties. Also Continental & Cajun cuisines. **Cards:** AE, DI, DS, MC, VI. **Special Value:** 10%
discount on the price of any entree, excluding beverages, tax and gratuity.

THE OLDE GREENFIELD INN   **Lunch:** $5-$8   **Dinner:** $10-$20   **Phone:** 717/393-0668
Location: 3.3 mi e on US 30 at Greenfield Rd exit, 0.5 mi n. 595 Greenfield Rd 17601. **Hours:** 11 am-2 &
5-10 pm, Mon from 5 pm, Sat from 8 am, Sun 8 am-2 pm. Closed major holidays. **Reservations:** suggested.
Features: casual dress; Sunday brunch; children's menu; carryout; cocktails & lounge. Kid-friendly fine
American   dining with good array of fresh seafood & steak. Patio dining in season. **Cards:** AE, DI, DS, MC, VI.

THE PRESSROOM   **Lunch:** $6-$9   **Dinner:** $6-$20   **Phone:** 717/399-5400
Location: Jct Market & King sts. 26-28 W King St 17603. **Hours:** 11:30 am-3 & 5-9:30 pm, Fri & Sat-10:30
pm. Closed major holidays, Sun & Mon. **Reservations:** suggested. **Features:** dressy casual; children's
menu; carryout; cocktails & lounge. Lively, industrial style bistro in renovated historic Steinman Hardware
American   Building. **Cards:** AE, MC, VI.

THE RESTAURANT AT AVENUES   **Lunch:** $4-$7   **Dinner:** $8-$20   **Phone:** 717/299-3456
Location: Corner of King & Prince sts. 10 S Prince St 17603. **Hours:** 11:30 am-midnight, Sat from 5 pm,
Sun 5 pm-9 pm. Closed major holidays. **Reservations:** suggested. **Features:** casual dress; carryout;
American   cocktails & lounge; street parking; a la carte. Large selection of imported & micro-brew beers. Creative pasta
dishes & homemade pizza. **Cards:** AE, DI, DS, MC, VI.

STOCKYARD INN   **Lunch:** $6-$10   **Dinner:** $13-$25   **Phone:** 717/394-7975
Location: 0.5 mi s off US 30; on US 222S. 1147 Lititz Pike 17601. **Hours:** 11:30 am-9 pm, Fri-9:30 pm, Sat
& Mon 4 pm-9 pm. Closed: 1/1, 12/25 & Sun. **Reservations:** suggested. **Features:** dressy casual; children's
menu; cocktails. Former home of President James Buchanan. Some continental entrees. **Cards:** AE, MC, VI.
American

TOBIAS S FROGG   **Lunch:** $6-$8   **Dinner:** $10-$16   **Phone:** 717/394-8366
Location: 2.5 mi w on SR 462. 1766 Columbia Ave 17603. **Hours:** 11 am-midnight, Wed-Sat to 1 am.
American   Closed major holidays. **Reservations:** suggested. **Features:** casual dress; children's menu; health conscious
menu items; carryout; cocktails & lounge. Relaxed atmosphere. Several house specialties. **Cards:** AE, DI,
DS, MC, VI.

LEOLA—1,000

RESTAURANT

LOG CABIN RESTAURANT   **Dinner: $16-$30**   **Phone: 717/626-1181**
(AAA)   **Location:** US 30, 5.5 mi n on SR 272, 0.5 mi w on Rosehill Rd; 0.3 mi s on Log Cabin Rd & just e. 11 Leroy
             Forest Dr 17540. **Hours:** 5 pm-10 pm, Sun 4 pm-9 pm. Closed major holidays. **Reservations:** suggested.
◆◆◆   **Features:** semi-formal attire; children's menu; cocktails & lounge. Attractive decor featuring genuine 18th &
American   19th century paintings. Rural location. **Cards:** AE, MC, VI.   ⊠

LITITZ—8,300

LODGINGS

GENERAL SUTTER INN   Rates Subject to Change   **Phone: 717/626-2115**
◆◆◆   All Year   1P: $60- 90 2P/1B: $75- 105 2P/2B: $75- 105 XP: $5
Historic   **Location:** On the square, SR 501. 14 E Main St 17543. Fax: 717/626-0992. **Terms:** Reserv deposit; small
Country Inn pets only. **Facility:** 13 rooms. Handling fee imposed; 3 stories, no elevator; interior corridors. **Dining:** Dining
             room, coffee shop; 7 am-3 & 5-9 pm, Fri & Sat-9:30 pm, Sun-8 pm; $14-$19. **Cards:** AE, DS, MC, VI.
                                                                                        🛏 CTV D

SWISS WOODS BED & BREAKFAST   Rates Subject to Change   **Phone: 717/627-3358**
(AAA)   All Year [BP]   1P: $80- 105 2P/1B: $95- 150 2P/2B: $123- 130 XP: $15
             Location: 4 mi n on SR 501, 1 mi w on Brubaker Valley Rd, just n. 500 Blantz Rd 17543.
◆◆◆   Fax: 717/627-3483. **Terms:** Age restrictions may apply; 2 night min stay, weekends 4/1-1/2; no pets.
Bed &   **Facility:** 7 rooms. 2 stories; interior corridors; smoke free premises. **All Rooms:** Fee: movies. **Cards:** AE,
Breakfast   DS, MC, VI.   ⊠ D

MARIETTA—2,800

RESTAURANTS

JOSEPHINE'S CAFE & RESTAURANT Historical   **Dinner: $13-$20**   **Phone: 717/426-2003**
(AAA) [SAVE] **Location:** 2.2 mi n on SR 441 from jct US 30, 1.5 mi w. 324 W Market St 17547. **Hours:** 5 pm-9 pm, also
             open for lunch Tues-Fri 11:30 am-2 pm. Closed major holidays & Sun. **Reservations:** suggested.
◆◆◆   **Features:** dressy casual; cocktails. Restored late 18th century inn. Beef, seafood & chicken featured.
French   **Cards:** MC, VI. **Special Value:** $1 off the price of all entrees.   ⊠

RAILROAD HOUSE RESTAURANT Country Inn   **Lunch: $9-$15**   **Dinner: $12-$20**   **Phone: 717/426-4141**
◆◆   **Location:** 2.2 mi n on SR 441 from jct US 30, 1.3 mi w on Market St, just s on Perry St; in Railroad House
American   Restaurant Bed & Breakfast. 280 W Front St 17547. **Hours:** 11 am-2 & 5-9 pm, Fri & Sat-10 pm, Sun 11
             am-9 pm. Closed: 1/1, 12/24, 12/25 & Mon. **Reservations:** suggested. **Features:** dressy casual; Sunday
brunch; carryout; cocktails & lounge. Also Continental cuisine. Beef, poultry, seafood & pasta featured. Patio dining in
season. **Cards:** MC, VI.   ⊠

MILLERSVILLE—8,100

LODGING

BEST WESTERN THE INN AT MILLERSVILLE   Rates Subject to Change   **Phone: 717/872-4600**
◆◆◆   5/1-11/15 & 4/1-4/30 [CP]   1P: $89- 109 2P/1B: $89- 109 2P/2B: $89- 109 XP: $10   F18
Motel   11/16-12/31 [CP]   1P: $79- 99 2P/1B: $79- 99 2P/2B: $79- 99 XP: $10   F18
             1/1-3/31 [CP]   1P: $69- 89 2P/1B: $69- 89 2P/2B: $69- 89 XP: $10   F18
Location: 1.3 mi e on SR 999 from jct SR 741, 0.8 mi s on N Duke St, 0.5 mi e on Frederick St, just s. 101 Shenks Ln
17551. Fax: 717/872-8050. **Terms:** Sr. discount; reserv deposit; small pets only. **Facility:** 59 rooms. 1 kitchen suite, $109-
$149. Handling fee imposed; 2 stories; interior corridors. **Cards:** AE, DI, DS, MC, VI.
                                                  Roll in showers. 🛒 ECTV ⊠ D S

MOUNT JOY—2,800

LODGINGS

CAMERON ESTATE INN   Rates Subject to Change   **Phone: 717/653-1773**
◆◆◆   All Year [BP]   2P/1B: $125- 300   XP: $10
Historic   **Location:** Rheems exit SR 283, 3.5 mi s on Cloverleaf & Colebrook rds, 0.3 mi w on Donegal Springs Rd;
Country Inn adjacent to Donegal Presbyterian Church. 1855 Mansion Ln 17552. Fax: 717/653-8334. **Terms:** Age
             restrictions may apply; reserv deposit, 7 day notice; 2 night min stay, weekends; no pets. **Facility:** 17 rooms.
Handling fee imposed; 3 stories, no elevator; interior corridors; smoke free premises. **Dining:** Dining room, see separate
listing. **Cards:** AE, CB, DI, DS, MC, VI.   ⊠ D

HILLSIDE FARM B & B   Rates Subject to Change   **Phone: 717/653-6697**
◆◆   All Year [BP]   1P: $55- 70 2P/1B: $55- 70 2P/2B: $55- 72 XP: $10
Bed &   **Location:** SR 283 Salunga exit, 1.2 mi sw then 0.3 nw. 607 Eby Chiques Rd 17552. Fax: 717/653-5233.
Breakfast   **Terms:** Check-in 4 pm; reserv deposit, 7 day notice; no pets. **Facility:** 5 rooms. Interior corridors; smoke free
             premises. **Cards:** DS, MC, VI.   ⊠ D

RESTAURANTS

ALOIS RESTAURANT Historical   **Dinner: $26**   **Phone: 717/653-2057**
(AAA)   **Location:** Just n of SR 230 on N Market St; in Bube's Brewery. 102 N Market St 17552. **Hours:** 5:30 pm-9
             pm, Fri & Sat 5 pm-10 pm, Sun 5 pm-8 pm. Closed major holidays & Mon. **Reservations:** suggested.
◆◆◆   **Features:** semi-formal attire; cocktails & lounge; prix fixe. Fine gourmet dining in restored 1800's Victorian
American   hotel/brewery. Varied, multi-course meal featuring several cuisine types. **Cards:** AE, DS, MC, VI.   ⊠

CAMERON ESTATE INN RESTAURANT Historical   **Dinner: $20-$32**   **Phone: 717/653-1773**
◆◆◆   **Location:** Rheems exit SR 283, 3.5 mi s on Cloverleaf & Colebrook rds, 0.3 mi w on Donegal Springs Rd;
Continental adjacent to Donegal Presbyterian Church, in Cameron Estate Inn. 1895 Donegal Springs Rd 17552.
             Hours: 6 pm-8 pm, Fri & Sat 5:30 pm-9 pm. Closed: 11/26, 12/24, 12/25, Sun & Mon.
Reservations: required; weekends. **Features:** semi-formal attire; Sunday brunch; cocktails. Candlelight dining in early
19th-century manor house. Some classic American fare. Smoke free premises. **Cards:** AE, DI, DS, MC, VI.   ⊠

THE CATACOMBS Historical **Dinner:** $17-$30 **Phone:** 717/653-2056
△△△
Location: Just n of SR 230 on N Market St; in Bube's Brewery. 102 N Market St 17552. **Hours:** 5:30 pm-9
◆◆ pm, Fri & Sat 5 pm-10 pm, Sun 5 pm-9:45 pm. Closed major holidays. **Reservations:** suggested.
American **Features:** casual dress; children's menu; cocktails & lounge. Underground lagering cellars of 19th-century
brewery; outdoor bier garten in summer. Hearty portions. Medieval feast on selected Sun, 5 pm-9 pm, $30.
On National Register of Historic Places. **Cards:** AE, DS, MC, VI. ⊠

COUNTRY TABLE RESTAURANT **Lunch:** $6-$11 **Dinner:** $6-$11 **Phone:** 717/653-4745
△△△
Location: 1 mi e on SR 230. 740 E Main St 17552. **Hours:** 6 am-8 pm, Fri & Sat-9 pm. Closed major
◆ holidays & Sun. **Features:** casual dress; children's menu; carryout. Freshly prepared Pennsylvania Dutch
American home cooked meals. Homemade dessert. Smoke free premises. ⊠

GROFF'S FARM **Lunch:** $5-$8 **Dinner:** $15-$24 **Phone:** 717/653-2048
△△△
Location: 0.5 mi w on Marietta Ave (SR 772), 1 mi s. 650 Pinkerton Rd 17552. **Hours:** 11:30 am-1:30 &
◆◆◆ 5-7:30 pm, Sat seatings at 5 pm or 8 pm; Sun 10 am-2 pm. Closed: 12/24 & 12/25. **Reservations:** required;
American for dinner. **Features:** casual dress; Sunday brunch; children's menu; cocktails; a la carte. Authentic
Pennsylvania fare served in original 1756 farm house. Individual family-style seatings. Homemade bread,
soup & dessert. **Cards:** AE, DI, DS, MC, VI. ⊠

THE WATERING TROUGH **Lunch:** $3-$7 **Dinner:** $8-$17 **Phone:** 717/653-6181
◆◆ **Location:** 1.2 mi w on SR 230. 905 W Main St 17552. **Hours:** 11 am-2 & 5-10 pm, Sun 11 am-10 pm.
American Closed: 1/1, 11/26 & 12/25. **Reservations:** suggested; weekends. **Features:** casual dress; children's menu;
carryout; cocktails & lounge. Casual, dining from "wings to filet". Outdoor dining in season. **Cards:** MC, VI.
⊠

NEW HOLLAND—4,500

LODGINGS

COMFORT INN	Rates Subject to Change				Phone: 717/355-9900	
◆◆◆	5/1-10/31 & 4/15-4/30 [CP]	1P: $63	2P/1B: $76	2P/2B: $83	XP: $7	F16
Motel	11/1-4/14 [CP]	1P: $57	2P/1B: $67	2P/2B: $73	XP: $7	F16

Location: Just e on SR 23. 624 W Main St 17557. Fax: 717/354-4193. **Terms:** Sr. discount; no pets.
Facility: 70 rooms. 4 whirlpool rms, $89 for up to 2 persons; 8 executive rms with refrigerator & microwave, $79 for up to 2
persons; 2 stories; interior corridors. **Cards:** AE, CB, DI, DS, JCB, MC, VI. ⓔⒸⓉⓥ ⊠ Ⓓ Ⓢ

COUNTRY SQUIRE MOTOR INN	Rates Subject to Change			Phone: 717/354-4166	
◆◆	6/10-11/10	1P: $55	2P/2B: $60	XP: $5	F12
Motel	5/1-6/9, 11/11-12/6 &				
	3/1-4/30	1P: $45	2P/2B: $50	XP: $5	F12
	12/7-2/28	1P: $40	2P/2B: $45	XP: $5	F12

Location: 0.8 mi e on SR 23. 504 E Main St 17557. Fax: 717/354-8697. **Terms:** No pets. **Facility:** 24 rooms. 1 story; exterior
corridors. **Dining:** Coffee shop; 6-11 am, Sun 7 am-1 pm; Ice cream shoppe. **Cards:** AE, DI, DS, MC, VI. ⓔⒸⓉⓥ ⊠ Ⓓ

THE HOLLANDER MOTEL	Guaranteed Rates					Phone: 717/354-4377	
△△△	6/13-11/2	1P: $52- 55	2P/1B: $52- 55	2P/2B: $59- 65	XP: $5	F6
◆	5/1-6/12 & 3/31-4/30	1P: $45- 48	2P/1B: $45- 48	2P/2B: $48- 50	XP: $5	F6
Motel	11/3-3/30	1P: $36- 39	2P/1B: $36- 39	2P/2B: $38- 45	XP: $5	F6

Location: Just e on SR 23. 320 E Main St 17557. Fax: 717/355-9714. **Terms:** Sr. discount; reserv deposit, 3
day notice; pets, $5 extra charge, in designated rooms. **Facility:** 17 rooms. Handling fee imposed; 1 story; ex-
terior corridors. **Cards:** AE, CB, DI, DS, MC, VI. 🐾 ⓔⒸⓉⓥ ⊠ Ⓓ

RESTAURANT

PEOPLE'S RESTAURANT **Lunch:** $5-$12 **Dinner:** $5-$12 **Phone:** 717/354-2276
△△△
Location: Town center; on SR 23. 140 W Main St 17557. **Hours:** 7 am-8 pm, Sun 11 am-7 pm. Closed
major holidays & Sat. **Features:** casual dress; children's menu; carryout. Established 1907. Home cooked
◆◆ meals, soup & dessert. Smoke free premises. **Cards:** MC, VI. ⊠
American

PARADISE (LANCASTER COUNTY)—4,400

LODGING

BEST WESTERN REVERE MOTOR INN						Phone: 717/687-7683	
△△△ Ⓢ Ⓐ Ⓥ Ⓔ	5/22-5/24 & 6/19-10/31 [CP]	1P: $76	2P/1B: $79- 89	2P/2B: $79- 89	XP: $5	F12
	5/1-5/21, 5/25-6/18,					
◆◆◆	11/1-11/28 & 4/2-4/30 [CP]	1P: $59	2P/1B: $59- 69	2P/2B: $59- 69	XP: $5	F12
Motor Inn	11/29-4/1 [CP]	1P: $54	2P/1B: $49- 69	2P/2B: $49- 69	XP: $5	F12

Location: 0.3 mi w on US 30. 3063 Lincoln Hwy E 17562 (PO Box 336, PARADISE). Fax: 717/687-6141.
Terms: Reserv deposit; no pets. **Facility:** 29 rooms. Suites, $89-$129; 4 whirlpool rms, extra charge; 2 stories; exterior corri-
dors. **Dining & Entertainment:** Dining room, coffee shop; 11 am-3 & 5-10 pm, Sun 4 pm-9 pm; $10-$18; cocktails/lounge.
All Rooms: coffeemakers, free movies, refrigerators. **Some Rooms:** microwaves, radios. **Cards:** AE, CB, DI, DS, MC, VI.
Special Amenities: Free breakfast and free local telephone calls. 🏊 🅵 ⓔⒸⓉⓥ ⊠ Ⓓ

RONKS—400

LODGINGS

BLACK FOREST COUNTRY LODGE	Rates Subject to Change				Phone: 717/393-2550	
△△△	6/30-11/4	1P: $79- 89	2P/1B: $79- 89	2P/2B: $79- 89	XP: $8	F12
	5/1-6/29, 11/5-12/31 &					
◆◆	4/2-4/30	1P: $49- 69	2P/1B: $49- 79	2P/2B: $49- 79	XP: $8	F12
Motel	1/1-4/1	1P: $49- 59	2P/1B: $49- 59	2P/2B: $49- 59	XP: $8	F12

Location: Just n on SR 896 from jct US 30. 21 Eastbrook Rd 17572. **Terms:** No pets. **Facility:** 55 rooms. 2
stories; interior corridors. **Cards:** AE, DS, MC, VI. ⓔⒸⓉⓥ ⊠ Ⓓ Ⓢ

CHERRY LANE MOTOR INN　　　　　　　　　　　　　　　　　　　Phone: 717/687-7646

(AAA) (SAVE)	5/23-9/8		2P/1B:	$69- 89	2P/2B:	$69- 89	XP:	$6	F12
	9/9-11/15		2P/1B:	$59- 89	2P/2B:	$59- 89	XP:	$6	F12
◆◆	5/1-5/22 & 3/27-4/30		2P/1B:	$53- 59	2P/2B:	$59- 75	XP:	$6	F12
Motel	11/16-3/26		2P/1B:	$45- 59	2P/2B:	$45- 64	XP:	$6	F12

Location: 1.5 mi e on US 30 from jct SR 896, 0.3 mi n. 84 N Ronks Rd 17572. **Terms:** Reserv deposit, 3 day notice; no pets. **Facility:** 41 rooms. 2 stories; interior/exterior corridors. **Cards:** AE, DS, MC, VI. *(See color ad p 341)*

🛜 ⓔⓒⓣⓥ ⓧ Ⓓ

DAYS INN　　　　　　　　　　　　　　　　　　　　　　　　　Phone: 717/390-1800

(AAA) (SAVE)	5/1-10/31 & 4/1-4/30 [CP]	1P: $48- 85	2P/1B:	$52- 85	2P/2B:	$52- 85	XP:	$5	F18
◆◆◆	11/1-3/31 [CP]	1P: $45- 57	2P/1B:	$49- 69	2P/2B:	$49- 69	XP:	$5	F18

Location: Just n on SR 896 from jct US 30. 34 E Brooks Rd 17572. Fax: 717/390-1800. **Terms:** Reserv
Motel　　deposit, 7 day notice; no pets. **Facility:** 52 rooms. Contemporary economy lodgings; close to popular outlet center. 1 whirlpool rm, $10 extra charge. Handling fee imposed; 2 stories; interior corridors; indoor pool privileges at Howard Johnson-Lancaster. **Dining:** Restaurant nearby. **All Rooms:** free & pay movies, refrigerators. **Some Rooms:** microwaves. **Cards:** AE, DS, MC, VI. **Special Amenities:** Free breakfast and free local telephone calls. *(See color ad p 336)*

🛜 ⓔⓒⓣⓥ ⓧ Ⓓ Ⓢ

OLDE AMISH INN　　　　　　　　Rates Subject to Change　　　　　　　Phone: 717/393-3100

(AAA)	6/21-9/6		2P/2B:	$67- 77	XP:	$6	F12
	9/7-11/1		2P/2B:	$65- 73	XP:	$6	F12
◆◆◆	5/1-6/20 & 3/31-4/30		2P/2B:	$58- 68	XP:	$6	F12
Motel	11/2-12/22 & 2/1-3/30		2P/2B:	$45- 55	XP:	$6	F12

Location: Just n on SR 896 from jct US 30. 33 Eastbrook Rd 17572. **Terms:** Open 5/1-12/22 & 2/1-4/30; reserv deposit; no pets. **Facility:** 25 rooms. 2 stories; interior/exterior corridors. **Cards:** AE, DS, MC, VI. *(See ad starting on p 338)*

ⓔⓒⓣⓥ ⓧ Ⓓ

QUIET HAVEN MOTEL　　　　　　Rates Subject to Change　　　　　　　Phone: 717/397-6231

◆	6/15-10/31		2P/2B:	$58	XP:	$3
Motel	5/1-6/14 & 4/1-4/30		2P/2B:	$48	XP:	$3
	11/1-3/31		2P/2B:	$36	XP:	$3

Location: 0.5 mi s on SR 896 from jct SR 340, 0.3 mi e. 2556 Siegrist Rd 17572. **Terms:** Reserv deposit, 3 day notice; no pets. **Facility:** 15 rooms. 1 story; exterior corridors.

ⓔⓒⓣⓥ Ⓓ

WEATHERVANE MOTOR COURT　　Rates Subject to Change　　　　　　　Phone: 717/397-3398

◆◆	5/1-10/31 [CP]		2P/2B:	$45- 65	XP:	$5	F12
Motel	11/1-4/30 [CP]		2P/2B:	$32- 55	XP:	$5	F12

Location: Just n on SR 896 from jct US 30. 15 Eastbrook Rd 17572 (PO Box 281). **Terms:** Reserv deposit, 3 day notice; no pets. **Facility:** 34 rooms. $5 surcharge holiday weekends & 2 night min stay; 1 story; exterior corridors. **Cards:** MC, VI.

ⓔⓒⓣⓥ Ⓓ

RESTAURANT

MILLER'S SMORGASBORD　　**Lunch:** $18　　　　　**Dinner:** $18　　　　Phone: 717/687-6621
◆◆　　**Location:** On US 30, 1.8 mi e of jct SR 896. 2811 Lincoln Hwy E 17572. **Hours:** noon-8 pm, from 8 am
American　　6/1-10/31, Sat & Sun 8 am-8:30 pm 11/1-5/31. Closed: 12/24 & 12/25. **Features:** casual dress; buffet. Informal dining, children prices avail. Smoke free premises. **Cards:** AE, DS, MC, VI.
(See ad starting on p 338)

ⓧ

SMOKETOWN—300

LODGINGS

MILL STREAM COUNTRY INN　　Rates Subject to Change　　　　　　Phone: 717/299-0931

(AAA)	6/19-9/6	1P: $81		2P/2B:	$89	XP:	$10	F5
	9/7-10/30	1P: $79		2P/2B:	$86	XP:	$10	F5
◆◆◆	5/1-6/18	1P: $65		2P/2B:	$67	XP:	$10	F5
Motel	10/31-4/30	1P: $61		2P/2B:	$65	XP:	$10	F5

Location: 0.3 mi s on SR 896 from jct SR 340. 170 Eastbrook Rd 17576. Fax: 717/295-9326 **Terms:** Reserv deposit; no pets. **Facility:** 52 rooms. 2-3 stories, no elevator; exterior corridors. **Dining:** Coffee shop 7-11:30 am, closed Sun & 12/25; continental breakfast for guests only on Sun. **All Rooms:** free movies. **Cards:** AE, DS, MC, VI.

🛜 ➕ ⓔⓒⓣⓥ ⓧ Ⓓ

SMOKETOWN MOTOR LODGE　　Rates Subject to Change　　　　　　Phone: 717/397-6944

(AAA)	6/12-10/31	2P/1B: $56- 76	2P/2B:	$56- 76	XP:	$5	
	5/1-6/11 & 4/1-4/30 [CP]	2P/1B: $46- 66	2P/2B:	$46- 66	XP:	$5	
◆◆	11/1-3/31 [CP]	2P/1B: $40- 60	2P/2B:	$40- 60	XP:	$5	

Location: Just s on SR 896 from jct SR 340. 190 Eastbrook Rd 17576. **Terms:** Reserv deposit, 14 day notice; no pets. **Facility:** 17 rooms. 2 stories; interior corridors. **Some Rooms:** 2 efficiencies. **Cards:** AE, DS, MC, VI.

ⓔⓒⓣⓥ ⓧ Ⓓ

RESTAURANT

GOOD 'N PLENTY RESTAURANT　　**Lunch:** $14　　　**Dinner:** $14　　　Phone: 717/394-7111
(AAA)　　**Location:** 1 mi n on SR 896 from US 30; 0.5 mi s of SR 340. Eastbrook Rd 17576. **Hours:** 11:30 am-8 pm.
◆　　Closed: 12/25, 12/28, 2/7 & Sun. **Features:** casual dress; carryout. Pennsylvania Dutch fare. Original farmhouse dates from 1871. Small parties share tables; family style service. Children ages 4-10, $6.13.
Regional American　　Smoke free premises. **Cards:** MC, VI. *(See ad starting on p 338)*

ⓧ

STRASBURG—2,600

LODGINGS

AMISH LANTERNS MOTEL　　　Rates Subject to Change　　　　　　Phone: 717/687-7839

(AAA)	6/12-9/6	2P/1B: $58- 68	2P/2B:	$68- 78	XP:	$6	F12
	5/1-6/11, 9/7-11/5 & 4/2-4/30	2P/1B: $48- 58	2P/2B:	$58- 68	XP:	$6	F12
◆◆	11/6-4/1	2P/1B: $36- 42	2P/2B:	$44- 48	XP:	$6	F12

Location: 0.3 mi n on SR 896; 2.5 mi s of US 30. 17579 (PO Box 16). Fax: 717/687-3908. **Terms:** Reserv deposit, 3 day notice; no pets. **Facility:** 33 rooms. 1-2 stories; exterior corridors. **Dining:** Coffee shop; 7-11 am 3/15-11/30. **Cards:** AE, DS, MC, VI. *(See ad starting on p 338)*

🛜 ⓔⓒⓣⓥ ⓧ Ⓓ

CARRIAGE HOUSE MOTOR INN
Rates Subject to Change **Phone:** 717/687-7651

⏺	Fri & Sat [CP]		2P/2B:	$59- 89	XP: $6	F12
	Sun-Thurs [CP]		2P/2B:	$39- 69	XP: $6	F12

◆ ◆ **Location:** 0.3 mi e on SR 896 & 741. 144 E Main St 17579. **Terms:** No pets. **Facility:** 14 rooms. 1 story; exterior corridors. **Cards:** AE, DS, MC, VI.
Motel

(ECTV) (X) (D)

DUTCH TREAT MOTEL
Rates Subject to Change **Phone:** 717/687-7998

⏺	6/26-9/6	2P/1B: $52- 62	2P/2B:	$64- 68	XP: $5	D5
	5/1-6/25, 9/7-10/31 &					
◆ ◆	3/26-4/30	2P/1B: $42- 48	2P/2B:	$50- 60	XP: $5	D5
Motel	11/1-3/25	2P/1B: $36	2P/2B:	$40- 48	XP: $5	D5

Location: 2 mi s on SR 896 from jct US 30. (265 Herr Rd, RONKS, 17572). Fax: 717/687-7291.
Terms: Reserv deposit, 3 day notice; no pets. **Facility:** 25 rooms. 1 story; exterior corridors. **Cards:** AE, DS, MC, VI.

(🏊) (ECTV) (X) (D)

HISTORIC STRASBURG INN
Rates Subject to Change **Phone:** 717/687-7691

⏺	5/1-10/31 [BP]	1P: $119- 129	2P/1B: $119- 129	2P/2B: $119- 129	XP: $15	F12
	11/1-12/31 [BP]	1P: $99- 109	2P/1B: $99- 109	2P/2B: $99- 109	XP: $15	F12
◆ ◆ ◆	1/1-4/30 [BP]	1P: $79- 99	2P/1B: $79- 99	2P/2B: $79- 99	XP: $15	F12

Country Inn **Location:** 0.5 mi n on SR 896, 2.5 mi s of US 30. One Historic Dr 17579. Fax: 717/687-6098. **Terms:** Reserv deposit; pets, $12 extra charge, $25 dep req; dogs only. **Facility:** 101 rooms. Suites, $40 extra charge; deluxe rms with refrigerator/coffeemaker, $15 extra charge; 6 king rms, $30 extra charge; 2 whirlpool rms, extra charge; 2 stories; interior/exterior corridors. **Dining:** Dining room, restaurant; 7-10 am, 11:30-2 & 5-9 pm, Fri & Sat-9:30 pm; $10-$40. **Cards:** AE, CB, DI, DS, MC, VI. *(See color ad p 341)*

(🐕) (🏊) (ECTV) (X) (D)

STRASBURG VILLAGE INN
Rates Subject to Change **Phone:** 717/687-0900

⏺ (SAVE)	6/10-10/28 [BP]		2P/1B: $79- 119	2P/2B: $79- 119	XP: $10	F5
	5/1-6/9 [BP]		2P/1B: $64- 109	2P/2B: $64- 109	XP: $10	F5
◆ ◆ ◆	10/29-4/30 [BP]		2P/1B: $54- 99	2P/2B: $54- 99	XP: $10	F5

Historic Bed **Location:** Center; at jct SR 741 & 896. 1 W Main St, Centre Sq 17579. **Terms:** Reserv deposit, 5 day
& Breakfast notice; package plans; 2 night min stay, weekends in season; no pets. **Facility:** 11 rooms. Attractively appointed rooms in 1788 structure, formerly a tavern. 2 stories; interior corridors; smoke free premises. **Dining:** Breakfast served at Creamery next door Mon-Sat; continental breakfast Sun in the Inn; restaurant nearby. **All Rooms:** no phones. **Some Rooms:** whirlpools. **Cards:** AE, DS, MC, VI. **Special Amenities:** Free breakfast and preferred room (subject to availability with advanced reservations). *(See ad starting on p 338)*

(ECTV) (X) (D)

RESTAURANTS

HERSHEY FARM RESTAURANT OF FAMILY TIME **Lunch:** $7-$13 **Dinner:** $8-$15 **Phone:** 717/687-8635

⏺ **Location:** Jct US 30, 1.5 mi s on SR 896; in Family Time at Hershey Farm Motor Inn & Restaurant. 240 Hartman Bridge Rd 17572. **Hours:** 7:30 am-8 pm. Closed: 1/1 & 12/25. **Reservations:** suggested; weekends. **Features:** casual dress; children's menu; carryout; salad bar; buffet. Pennsylvania Dutch home cooked meals from popular smorgasbord, also menu service. Smoke free premises. **Cards:** DS, MC, VI. (X)
Regional
American

ISAAC'S RESTAURANT & DELI **Lunch:** $5-$8 **Dinner:** $5-$8 **Phone:** 717/687-7699

◆ **Location:** 0.5 mi e on SR 741, in the Shops of Traintown. RT 741 E 17579. **Hours:** 7 am-8 pm. Closed major holidays. **Features:** casual dress; children's menu; carryout; a la carte. Lengthy menu of inspired deli fare, featuring inventive sandwich combinations, salad & pizza. Smoke free premises. **Cards:** AE, DS, MC, VI.
American
VI.

(X)

WILLOW STREET

LODGING

THE APPLE BIN INN
Rates Subject to Change **Phone:** 717/464-5881

◆ ◆	All Year [BP]	1P: $95- 135	2P/1B: $95- 135	XP: $10

Bed & **Location:** From jct 222, 272, 741, 0.5 mi s on Sr 272, just e on W Willow Rd, then n on SR 272. 2835
Breakfast Willow St Pike 17584. Fax: 717/464-1818. **Terms:** Age restrictions may apply; reserv deposit, 7 day notice; 2 night min stay, weekends; no pets. **Facility:** 5 rooms. 1 story; interior corridors; smoke free premises. **Cards:** AE, MC, VI.

(ECTV) (X) (D)

Philadelphia & Vicinity

PHILADELPHIA—1,585,600   (See map p. 354; index below)

To help you more easily locate accommodations in the Greater Philadelphia area, the following two indexes and maps show lodgings and restaurants in multiple cities. Listings for these establishments are found under the heading for the city in which they are located. The Philadelphia area map comprises: Ardmore, Bensalem, Conshohocken, Essington, Glenside, Havertown, Horsham, Langhorne, Levittown, Philadelphia, Plymouth Meeting, Springfield (Delaware County), Trevose, and Willow Grove, PA; also including Bellmawr, Brooklawn, Burlington, Cherry Hill, Maple Shade, Medford, Mount Laurel, Mount Holly, Runnemede and Voorhees, NJ.

Airport Accommodations

Listings for these establishments are found under the heading for the city in which they are located.

PHILADELPHIA

Ⓦ Comfort Inn Airport, 2.5 mi sw of airport/ESSINGTON
Courtyard By Marriott Airport, on Bartram Ave 1.5 mi n of terminal/PHILADELPHIA
Ⓦ Days Inn/Philadelphia Int'l Airport, 1.5 mi e of terminal on SR 291/PHILADELPHIA
Embassy Suites-Philadelphia Airport, 1.5 mi nw of airport/PHILADELPHIA
Ⓦ Holiday Inn-Airport, 2.5 mi sw of airport/ESSINGTON
Ⓦ Philadelphia Airport Hilton, 1.5 mi e of Terminal on SR 291/PHILADELPHIA
Philadelphia Airport Marriott, at terminal/PHILADELPHIA
Philadelphia Airport Residence Inn, 1.5 mi e of terminal on SR 291/PHILADELPHIA
Radisson Hotel Philadelphia Airport, 2 mi sw of airport/PHILADELPHIA
Ramada Inn-Philadelphia International Airport, SR 291, 2.3 mi w of terminal/ESSINGTON
Red Roof Inn-Airport, 2.8 mi sw of airport/ESSINGTON
Ⓦ Westin Suites, 1.5 mi e of terminal on SR 291/PHILADELPHIA

Index of Establishments on the DOWNTOWN PHILADELPHIA ACCOMMODATIONS Spotting Map

Ⓦ Penn's View Hotel .... ❶
The Warwick .... ❷
Wyndham Franklin Plaza Hotel.............. ❸
Ⓦ Four Seasons Hotel............................... ❹
Walnut St Inn .... ❺
Ⓦ Holiday Inn-Independence Mall .... ❻
Holiday Inn Select Philadelphia Center City ...... ❼
Sheraton University City...................... ❽
The Latham .... ❾
Comfort Inn Downtown-Historic Area............ ❿
Ⓦ Holiday Inn-Express Midtown .... ⓫
Ⓦ The Rittenhouse Hotel & Condominium
Residences .... ⓬
The Doubletree Hotel Philadelphia.............. ⓭
Shippen Way Inn .... ⓮
Korman Suites Hotel .... ⓯
Ⓦ Penn Tower Hotel.................................. ⓰
Ⓦ Embassy Suites Center City................ ⓱
Best Western Independence Park Inn .... ⓲
Sheraton Society Hill........................... ⓳
Ⓦ The Thomas Bond House .... ⓴
Omni Hotel at Independence Park.............. ㉑
Ⓦ The Ritz-Carlton, Philadelphia .... ㉒
Ⓦ Park Hyatt Philadelphia at the Bellevue ...... ㉔
Ⓦ Best Western Center City Hotel.............. ㉕
Ⓦ Clarion Suites .... ㉖
Philadelphia Marriott .... ㉗
Ⓦ Ten-Eleven Clinton .... ㉘

RESTAURANTS
Ⓦ Founder's... ①
Ⓦ Ristorante Panorama .... ②
Fountain Restaurant .... ③
Ⓦ Bookbinder's Old Original..................... ⑤
Philadelphia Fish & Company .... ⑧
Ⓦ South Street Souvlaki........................... ⑨
Ralphs' Italian Restaurant .... ⑩
Ⓦ London Grill .... ⑪
Ⓦ Le Bec-Fin .... ⑫
McCrossen's Tavern .... ⑬
Jack's Firehouse Restaurant .... ⑭
The Garden... ⑮

Ⓦ Deux Cheminees .... ⑯
Ⓦ Bookbinder's 15th St Seafood House .... ⑰
Di Lullo... ⑱
Susanna Foo .... ⑲
Ⓦ Tree Tops Restaurant .... ⑳
Ⓦ The Monte Carlo Living Room............. ㉑
Nicholas, Nicholas, The Restaurant............ ㉒
Orfeo Cafe by Day-Restaurant by Night .... ㉓
Palm Restaurant................................. ㉔
Zocalo... ㉕
Azalea .... ㉗
Ⓦ Bistro Romano .... ㉛
Brasil's... ㉞
Ⓦ Chanterelles....................................... ㊲
Ⓦ Ciboulette.. ㊳
Circa .... ㊶
Ⓦ City Tavern... ㊷
Cutters .... ㊸
Dickens Inn .... ㊹
Dimitri's.. ㊻
Dock Street Brewing Company Brewery &
Restaurant .... ㊼
Essene Cafe .... ㊾
Fez Moroccan Cuisine .... ㊿
Imperial Inn 51
Ⓦ The Inn Philadelphia.......................... 52
Kabul, Cuisine of Afghanistan 53
Kat Man Du... 54
Mia's.. 60
Zanzibar Blue 62
Ⓦ Overtures 63
Ⓦ Palladium Restaurant 65
Pamplona 68
Passage To India 70
Rangoon Burmese Restaurant 72
Ⓦ Ristorante Primavera 73
The Ritz-Carlton Grill Room................. 74
Singapore Kosher Vegetarian Restaurant...... 75
Striped Bass 79
Swann Lounge & Cafe 80

In the listings, the meal plan included in the rates follows the open dates.

See map p. 354)

LODGINGS

BEST WESTERN CENTER CITY HOTEL **Phone:** 215/568-8300 25
5/1-10/31 1P: $99- 119 2P/1B: $109- 129 2P/2B: $109- 129 XP: $10 F18
11/1-4/30 1P: $89- 109 2P/1B: $99- 119 2P/2B: $99- 119 XP: $10 F18
Location: On 22nd St, just n of Benjamin Franklin Pkwy. 501 N 22nd St 19130. Fax: 215/557-0259.
Terms: Monthly rates; package plans; small pets only, $10 extra charge. **Facility:** 183 rooms. 3 stories; interior corridors. **Dining & Entertainment:** Coffee shop; 7 am-10 am; cocktail lounge. **Services:** valet laundry.
All Rooms: free movies. **Some Rooms:** Fee: refrigerators. **Cards:** AE, CB, DI, DS, JCB, MC, VI. **Special Amenities:** Preferred room (subject to availability with advanced reservations). *(See color ad below)*

BEST WESTERN INDEPENDENCE PARK INN Guaranteed Rates **Phone:** 215/922-4443 18
All Year [CP] 1P: $130- 155 2P/1B: $140- 175 2P/2B: $140- 175 XP: $10 F18
Historic Hotel **Location:** In Independence Park Historic District, between 2nd & 3rd sts. 235 Chestnut St 19106.
Fax: 215/922-4487. **Terms:** Sr. discount; small pets only, $10 extra charge. **Facility:** 36 rooms. 5 stories; interior corridors. Fee: parking. **All Rooms:** free movies. **Cards:** AE, CB, DI, DS, MC, VI. *(See color ad p 356)*

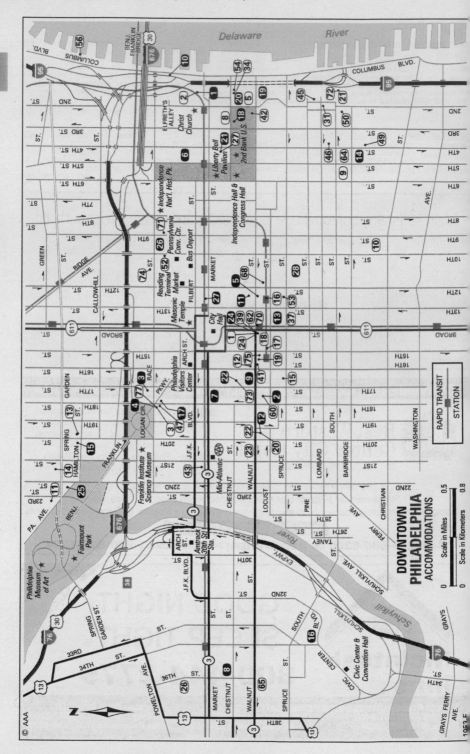

(See map p. 354)

CLARION SUITES
AAA SAVE
◆◆◆
Suite Hotel
Phone: 215/922-1730 26
All Year [CP]   1P: $99   2P/1B: $99   2P/2B: $99   XP: $10   F18
Location: In Chinatown, just e of Convention Center. 1010 Race St 19107. Fax: 215/922-6258. **Terms:** Check-in 4 pm; package plans; small pets only, $10 extra charge. **Facility:** 96 rooms. 1-bedroom suites with living room & kitchen in restored & converted 1890 Bentwood Rocker factory; on National Register of Historic Places. 10 two-bedroom units. 8 stories; interior corridors. Fee: parking. **Dining & Entertainment:** 5 am-midnight; cocktail lounge; restaurants nearby. **Services:** valet laundry. **All Rooms:** kitchens, utensil deposit, free movies, refrigerators. **Some Rooms:** microwaves. **Cards:** AE, CB, DI, DS, JCB, MC, VI. **Special Amenities:** Free breakfast and free room upgrade (subject to availability with advanced reservations). *(See color ad p 356)*

COMFORT INN DOWNTOWN-HISTORIC AREA
◆◆
Motel
Rates Subject to Change   Phone: 215/627-7900 10
All Year [CP]   1P: $95   2P/1B: $95   2P/2B: $95   XP: $10   F18
Location: I-95, Historic Area exit, to Columbus Blvd & Race St. 100 N Columbus Blvd 19106. Fax: 215/238-0809. **Terms:** Sr. discount; no pets. 10 stories; interior corridors. Fee: parking. **All Rooms:** Fee: movies. **Cards:** AE, CB, DI, DS, JCB, MC, VI. *(See color ad p 356)*

THE DOUBLETREE HOTEL PHILADELPHIA
◆◆◆
Hotel
Rates Subject to Change   Phone: 215/893-1600 13
Sun-Thurs   1P: $149   2P/1B: $169   2P/2B: $169   XP: $20   F18
Fri & Sat   1P: $125   2P/1B: $125   2P/2B: $125   XP: $20   F18
Location: Broad & Locust sts 19107. Fax: 215/893-1663. **Terms:** Sr. discount; reserv deposit; no pets. **Facility:** 427 rooms. 26 stories; interior corridors. Fee: parking. **Dining:** Dining room; 6:30 am-10:30 pm; $9-$23. **All Rooms:** free & pay movies. **Cards:** AE, CB, DI, DS, JCB, MC, VI.   Roll in showers.

EMBASSY SUITES CENTER CITY
AAA SAVE
◆◆◆
Suite Hotel
Phone: 215/561-1776 17
Sun-Thurs [BP]   1P: $169- 209   2P/1B: $184- 224   2P/2B: $184- 224   XP: $15   F18
Fri & Sat [BP]   1P: $115- 179   2P/1B: $130- 194   2P/2B: $130- 194   XP: $15   F18
Location: Downtown, at 18th St & Benjamin Franklin Pkwy. 1776 Benjamin Franklin Pkwy 19103. Fax: 215/963-0122. **Terms:** Check-in 4 pm; reserv deposit; package plans; no pets. **Facility:** 288 rooms. 28 stories; interior corridors; sauna; children's playroom. Fee: parking. **Dining & Entertainment:** Restaurant; 7 am-1 am; $10-$17; cocktails/lounge. **Services:** complimentary evening beverages. Fee: coin laundry; valet parking. **All Rooms:** coffeemakers, microwaves, free & pay movies, refrigerators, combo or shower baths. **Some Rooms:** VCR's. **Cards:** AE, CB, DI, DS, JCB, MC. **Special Amenities:** Free breakfast and free newspaper.
Roll in showers.

Bring The Troops.

Take the family to the Valley Forge area this year! Experience Valley Forge National Historical Park's spectacular foliage, historical attractions, and seasonal events. Shop the East Coast's largest mall. Enjoy affordable hotels and restaurants suiting every taste. For a free Visitors Guide or to make a reservation, call toll-free **1.888.VISIT VF**

See the following towns listed in the Philadelphia Vicinity section of the TourBook for Valley Forge area lodging:

Berwyn	Chadds Ford	Horsham	Lahaska	Plymouth Meeting	Wayne
Boyertown	Exton	King of Prussia	Lionville	Pottstown	Willow Grove
	Frazer	Kulpsville	Malvern	St. Davids	

Pennsylvania
Memories last a lifetime.™

Valley Forge
PENNSYLVANIA

1.888.VISIT VF
www.valleyforge.org

(See map p. 354)

FOUR SEASONS HOTEL
AAA
◆◆◆◆◆
Hotel

Rates Subject to Change
Sun-Thurs   1P: $265- 335   2P/1B: $265- 335   2P/2B: $295- 365   XP: $30
Fri & Sat   1P: $205- 295   2P/1B: $205- 295   2P/2B: $225- 325   XP: $30

Phone: 215/963-1500
F16
F16

Location: At corner 18th & Benjamin Franklin Pkwy. 1 Logan Sq 19103. **Fax:** 215/963-9506. **Terms:** Pets
Facility: 371 rooms. 8 stories; interior corridors. **Dining:** Fountain Restaurant, Swann Lounge & Cafe, see
separate listing. **All Rooms:** free & pay movies. **Cards:** AE, CB, DI, DS, JCB, MC, VI.
Roll in showers. 📶 🚗 ♿ CTV ✕ 🕸 D S

(See map p. 354)

HOLIDAY INN-EXPRESS MIDTOWN   Phone: 215/735-9300 **11**
(AAA) (SAVE)   All Year [CP]   1P: $97   2P/1B: $97   2P/2B: $97
◆◆◆   **Location:** Just e of Broad St. 1305 Walnut St 19107. **Fax:** 215/732-2682. **Terms:** No pets. **Facility:** 166 rooms.
Motel   Conveniently located to historic, cultural & shopping districts. Parking garage has a vehicle height restriction of
            6 ft, 5 inches. 20 stories; interior corridors; rooftop pool with southern exposure. Fee: parking.
            Dining: Restaurant nearby. **Services:** valet laundry. **All Rooms:** free & pay movies. **Cards:** AE, CB, DI, DS,
MC, VI. **Special Amenities: Free breakfast and free local telephone calls.** (See color ad p 357)

HOLIDAY INN-INDEPENDENCE MALL   Phone: 215/923-8660 **6**
(AAA) (SAVE)   All Year   1P: $95- 159   2P/1B: $95- 169 2P/2B: $95- 169   XP: $10   F18
◆◆◆   **Location:** In historic district between 4th & 5th sts. 400 Arch St 19106. **Fax:** 215/923-4633. **Terms:** Check-in
Hotel   4 pm; monthly rates; package plans; no pets. **Facility:** 364 rooms. Excellent colonial flair in the decor; public
            areas with fine Indian & Oriental antiques. 8 stories; interior corridors. Fee: parking. **Dining &**
            Entertainment: Dining room, coffee shop; 6:30 am-10:30 pm; $5-$25; cocktails/lounge. **Services:** Fee: coin
laundry. **All Rooms:** free & pay movies. **Some Rooms:** Fee: refrigerators, VCR's. **Cards:** AE, CB, DI, DS, MC, VI.
(See color ad p 359)

HOLIDAY INN SELECT PHILADELPHIA CENTER CITY   Rates Subject to Change   Phone: 215/561-7500 **7**
◆◆◆   All Year   1P: $130- 180   2P/1B: $130- 180 2P/2B: $130- 180   XP: $20   F18
Hotel   **Location:** Downtown, between 18th & 19th sts. 1800 Market St 19103. **Fax:** 215/561-4484. **Terms:** Reserv
            deposit; pets, $25 extra charge, $125 dep req. **Facility:** 445 rooms. 25 stories; interior corridors.
Dining: Restaurant, coffee shop; 6 am-11 pm, pub offerings after 11 pm; $8-$20. **All Rooms:** free & pay movies.
Cards: AE, CB, DI, DS, JCB, MC, VI.   Roll in showers.

KORMAN SUITES HOTEL   Rates Subject to Change   Phone: 215/569-7000 **15**
◆◆◆   Sun-Thurs   1P: $119   2P/1B: $119   2P/2B: $149
Hotel   Fri & Sat   1P: $109   2P/1B: $109   2P/2B: $139
            Location: 20th St at Hamilton St. 2001 Hamilton St 19130. **Fax:** 215/569-1422. **Terms:** No pets.
Facility: 125 rooms. 28 stories; interior corridors. **Dining:** Restaurant; 6:30-10:30 am, 11-2:30 & 5:30-10:30 pm; $11-$19.
All Rooms: free movies. **Some Rooms:** 80 efficiencies, 45 kitchens. **Cards:** AE, DI, MC, VI.

THE LATHAM   Rates Subject to Change   Phone: 215/563-7474 **9**
◆◆◆   All Year   1P: $195   2P/1B: $215   2P/2B: $215   XP: $20   F18
Hotel   **Location:** Center, at 17th & Walnut sts. 135 S 17th St 19103. **Fax:** 215/563-4034. **Terms:** No pets.
            Facility: 139 rooms. 14 stories; interior corridors. Fee: parking. **Dining:** Dining room; 6:30 am-10:30 pm, Sat
& Sun from 7:30 am; $11-$23. **All Rooms:** free movies. **Cards:** AE, CB, DI, DS, JCB, MC, VI. (See ad below)

(See map p. 354)

OMNI HOTEL AT INDEPENDENCE PARK   Rates Subject to Change   **Phone: 215/925-0000**   21
◆◆◆◆   5/1-6/30 & 9/9-12/31   1P: $189   2P/1B: $189   2P/2B: $189   XP: $20
Hotel   7/1-9/8 & 1/1-4/30   1P: $159   2P/1B: $159   2P/2B: $159   XP: $20
Location: Chestnut St at 4th St. 401 Chestnut St 19106. Fax: 215/925-1263. **Terms:** Check-in 4 pm; reserv deposit; no pets. **Facility:** 150 rooms. 14 stories; interior corridors. Fee: parking. **Dining:** Azalea, see separate listing. **All Rooms:** free & pay movies. **Cards:** AE, CB, DI, DS, JCB, MC, VI.

PARK HYATT PHILADELPHIA AT THE BELLEVUE   **Phone: 215/893-1776**   24
(AAA) (SAVE)   All Year   1P: $195   2P/1B: $195   2P/2B: $195
Location: Broad & Walnut St 19102. Fax: 215/893-9698. **Terms:** Package plans; small pets only.
◆◆◆◆   **Facility:** 170 rooms. Outstanding public areas. Including day spa, salon & upscale retail outlets. Restored Historic Hotel   French Renaissance hotel occupying the top 7 floors of Bellevue Building. 19 stories; interior corridors; driving range; saunas, whirlpools; racquetball courts; squash courts; aerobic studios, basketball court. Fee: parking; roller blading. **Dining & Entertainment:** Lounge menu available; cocktails/lounge; 24-hour room service; afternoon tea; also, Founder's, see separate listing. **Services:** valet laundry. Fee: massage; valet parking. **Recreation:** jogging. **All Rooms:** honor bars, free & pay movies, VCR's. **Some Rooms:** refrigerators. **Cards:** AE, CB, DI, DS, JCB, MC, VI.

PENN'S VIEW HOTEL   **Phone: 215/922-7600**   1
(AAA) (SAVE)   All Year [CP]   2P/1B: $130- 185   XP: $15   F12
Location: At Front & Market sts; I-95, southbound exit 17, northbound exit 16. 14 N Front St 19106.
◆◆◆   Fax: 215/922-7642. **Terms:** Reserv deposit; package plans; weekends; no pets. **Facility:** 38 rooms. 1828 Historic Hotel   structure, formerly a warehouse, with elegant rooms & some upscale details; a few rooms with gas fireplace. Closed 12/24 & 12/25. 5 stories; interior corridors. Fee: parking. **Dining & Entertainment:** Restaurant; $10-$22; cocktails/lounge; also, Ristorante Panorama, see separate listing. **Services:** valet laundry. **All Rooms:** free movies, combo or shower baths. **Some Rooms:** whirlpools. **Cards:** AE, CB, DI, JCB, MC, VI. **Special Amenities:** Free breakfast and free newspaper.

(See map p. 354)

PENN TOWER HOTEL   Phone: 215/387-8333   [16]
AAA SAVE   All Year   1P: $149- 174   2P/1B: $169- 204   2P/2B: $169- 204   XP: $20   F12
◆◆◆   **Location:** W of I-76 South St exit, facing University of PA Medical Center. Civic Center Blvd & 34th St
Hotel   19104-4385. Fax: 215/386-8306. **Terms:** Reserv deposit; no pets. **Facility:** 117 rooms. Well appointed rooms.
21 stories; interior corridors. Fee: parking. **Dining & Entertainment:** Dining room; 6:30 am-11 & 11:30-8:30
pm; $7-$17; cocktails/lounge. **Services:** valet laundry. **All Rooms:** free & pay movies.
Some Rooms: coffeemakers, VCR's. Fee: refrigerators. **Cards:** AE, DI, DS, MC, VI. **Special Amenities: Free newspaper
and free room upgrade (subject to availability with advanced reservations).** *(See ad p 360)*

PHILADELPHIA MARRIOTT   Rates Subject to Change   Phone: 215/625-2900   [27]
◆◆◆   All Year   1P: $230   2P/1B: $250   2P/2B: $250   XP: $20
Hotel   **Location:** Downtown; opposite Convention Center. 1201 Market St 19107. Fax: 215/625-6000.
Terms: Check-in 4 pm; reserv deposit, 3 day notice; small pets only, $100 dep req. **Facility:** 1198 rooms. 1
whirlpool rm, extra charge, rates for up to 4 persons; 23 stories; interior corridors. Fee: parking. **Dining:** Dining room, 2
restaurants; 6:30 am-11 pm; $10-$25. **All Rooms:** free & pay movies. **Cards:** AE, DI, DS, JCB, MC, VI.
Roll in showers.

THE RITTENHOUSE HOTEL &   Phone: 215/546-9000   [12]
CONDOMINIUM RESIDENCES   Rates Subject to Change
AAA   Sun-Thurs   1P: $280- 315   2P/1B: $305- 340   2P/2B: $305- 340   XP: $25   F17
Fri & Sat   1P: $170- 190   2P/1B: $170- 190   2P/2B: $170- 190   XP: $25   F17
◆◆◆◆◆ **Location:** 210 W Rittenhouse Sq 19103. Fax: 215/732-3364. **Terms:** Pets. **Facility:** 98 rooms. 33 stories; in-
Hotel   terior corridors. **Dining:** Dining room; 6:30 am-11 pm, Fri & Sat-midnight; $12-$35; also, Tree Tops
Restaurant, see separate listing. **All Rooms:** free movies. **Cards:** AE, CB, DI, DS, MC, VI. A Preferred
Hotel.

THE RITZ-CARLTON, PHILADELPHIA   Rates Subject to Change   Phone: 215/563-1600   [22]
AAA   All Year   1P: $305-1250   2P/1B: $305- 950   2P/2B: $305-1250
◆◆◆◆ **Location:** 17th & Chestnut St at Liberty Pl 19103. Fax: 215/567-2822. **Terms:** No pets. **Facility:** 290 rooms.
15 stories; interior corridors. Fee: parking. **Dining:** The Ritz-Carlton Grill Room, see separate listing.
Hotel   **All Rooms:** free & pay movies. **Cards:** AE, CB, DI, DS, JCB, MC, VI.

SHERATON SOCIETY HILL   Rates Subject to Change   Phone: 215/238-6000   [19]
◆◆◆   6/29-9/8   1P: $135- 230   2P/1B: $155- 230   2P/2B: $155- 230   XP: $20   F17
Hotel   5/1-6/28   1P: $130- 230   2P/1B: $150- 230   2P/2B: $150- 230   XP: $20   F17
9/9-4/30   1P: $99- 230   2P/1B: $99- 230   2P/2B: $99- 230   XP: $20   F17
Location: Off I-95, Historic District Center City exit 16, 0.5 mi n on Delaware Ave to Dock St, at 2nd & Walnut sts. One
Dock St 19106. Fax: 215/922-2709. **Terms:** Reserv deposit; no pets. **Facility:** 365 rooms. 4 stories; interior corridors.
Fee: parking. **Dining:** Restaurant; 6:30 am-10:30 pm; $11-$26. **All Rooms:** free & pay movies. **Cards:** AE, CB, DI, DS, MC,
VI. *(See color ad p 353)*

SHERATON UNIVERSITY CITY   Rates Subject to Change   Phone: 215/387-8000   [8]
◆◆◆   All Year   1P: $145   2P/1B: $155   2P/2B: $155   XP: $10   F17
Hotel   **Location:** 0.5 mi w of I-76 exit 39, at jct Chestnut & 36th sts. 3501 Chestnut St 19104. Fax: 215/387-7920.
Terms: Reserv deposit; no pets. **Facility:** 375 rooms. 8 suites, $210-$320; 20 stories; interior corridors.
Fee: parking. **Dining:** Dining room, deli; 7 am-11 pm; $8-$19. **All Rooms:** free & pay movies. **Cards:** AE, CB, DI, DS, JCB,
MC, VI.

SHIPPEN WAY INN   Guaranteed Rates   Phone: 215/627-7266   [14]
◆◆   All Year [CP]   1P: $75- 95   2P/1B: $80- 110   2P/2B: $90   XP: $10
Historic Bed   **Location:** Between 4th & 5th sts. 418 Bainbridge St 19147. Fax: 215/627-7781. **Terms:** Age restrictions may
& Breakfast   apply; reserv deposit, 3 day notice; no pets, cat on property. **Facility:** 9 rooms. 3 stories, no elevator;
interior/exterior corridors; designated smoking area. **All Rooms:** free movies. **Cards:** AE, MC, VI.

TEN-ELEVEN CLINTON   Phone: 215/923-8144   [28]
AAA SAVE   All Year [CP]   2P/1B: $125- 175   2P/2B: $135- 185   XP: $15   F6
◆◆◆   **Location:** Downtown, between Spruce & Pine sts & 10th & 11th sts. 1011 Clinton St 19107.
Historic Bed   Fax: 215/923-5757. **Terms:** Reserv deposit, 14 day notice; weekly/monthly rates; no pets. **Facility:** 7 rooms.
& Breakfast   Elegantly decorated apartments in 1836 Federal style townhouse with seasonal private courtyard. All units
have a working gas fireplace. 3 stories, no elevator; interior corridors; smoke free premises; off site parking
only. **Dining:** Restaurant nearby. **Services:** Fee: coin laundry. **All Rooms:** coffeemakers, microwaves,
refrigerators, VCR's. **Some Rooms:** efficiency, 6 kitchens. **Cards:** AE, MC, VI. **Special Amenities: Free breakfast and free
local telephone calls.**

THE THOMAS BOND HOUSE   Phone: 215/923-8523   [20]
AAA SAVE   All Year [CP]   2P/1B: $90- 160   2P/2B: $115- 125   XP: $15
◆◆   **Location:** In historic district. 129 S 2nd St 19106. Fax: 215/923-8504. **Terms:** Weekly rates; 2 night min
Historic Bed   stay, weekends 3/1-10/31; no pets. **Facility:** 12 rooms. A restored, early American guest house, listed in Na-
& Breakfast   tional Register of Historic Places. Some small rooms; few rooms with gas fireplace. 4 stories, no elevator; in-
terior corridors. Fee: parking. **Dining:** Full breakfast provided on weekends; restaurant nearby.
Services: valet laundry. **All Rooms:** free movies, combo or shower baths. **Some Rooms:** whirlpools.
Cards: AE, CB, DI, DS, MC, VI.

WALNUT ST INN   Rates Subject to Change   Phone: 215/546-7000   [5]
◆◆   All Year [CP]   1P: $95- 145   2P/1B: $95- 145   2P/2B: $95- 145   XP: $15   F13
Historic Hotel   **Location:** Downtown, between 12th & 13th sts. 1208 Walnut St 19107. Fax: 215/546-7573. **Terms:** No pets.
Facility: 25 rooms. 7 stories; interior corridors. Fee: parking. **Cards:** AE, CB, DI, DS, MC, VI.

(See map p. 354)

THE WARWICK   Rates Subject to Change   Phone: 215/735-6000   ②
◆◆◆   5/1-5/31, 9/14-11/14 &
Hotel   3/2-4/30   1P: $130- 170   2P/1B: $145- 180   2P/2B: $145- 180   XP: $15   F16
             6/1-9/13 & 11/15-3/1 1P: $125- 145   2P/1B: $140- 165   2P/2B: $140- 165   XP: $15   F16
Location: Jct 17th & Locust sts. 1701 Locust St 19103-6179. Fax: 215/790-7766. **Terms:** No pets. **Facility:** 153 rooms. 20 stories; interior corridors. **Fee:** parking. **Dining:** Dining room, restaurant, coffee shop; 6:30 am-11 pm; $8-$26; also, Mia's, see separate listing. **All Rooms:** Fee: movies. **Cards:** AE, CB, DI, DS, MC, VI.   ⊞ⓒ⊠🄳🄳🅂

WYNDHAM FRANKLIN PLAZA HOTEL   Rates Subject to Change   Phone: 215/448-2000   ③
◆◆◆   All Year   1P: $109- 238   2P/1B: $109- 238   2P/2B: $109- 238   XP: $20   F18
Hotel   **Location:** 17th & Race sts 19103. Fax: 215/448-2864. **Terms:** Reserv deposit; no pets. **Facility:** 758 rooms. 26 stories; interior corridors. **Fee:** parking. **Dining:** Dining room, restaurant; 6:30 am-11 pm; $10-$30.
All Rooms: Fee: movies. **Cards:** AE, CB, DI, DS, JCB, MC, VI.   Roll in showers. ➁⊞ⓒ⊠🄳🄳🅂

RESTAURANTS

AZALEA   **Lunch:** $11-$16   **Dinner:** $18-$30   Phone: 215/925-0000   ㉗
◆◆◆◆   **Location:** Chestnut St at 4th St; in Omni Hotel at Independence Park. 401 Chestnut St 19106.
American **Hours:** 6:30-10:30 am, 11:30-2 & 5:30-9 pm, Fri-9:30 pm, Sat 7 am-11 & 5:30-10 pm, Sun 7 am-2 & 5:30-9 pm. **Reservations:** suggested. **Features:** dressy casual; Sunday brunch; children's menu; cocktails & lounge; street parking & fee for valet parking; a la carte, also prix fixe. Contemporary American restaurant serving exceptional regional foods. Country club casual dress code. **Cards:** AE, CB, DI, DS, MC, VI.   ⊠

BISTRO ROMANO   **Dinner:** $10-$18   Phone: 215/925-8880   ㉛
ⒶⒶⒶ 🆂🅰🆅🅴 **Location:** On Lombard St, between Front & 2nd sts. 120 Lombard St 19147. **Hours:** 4:30 pm-11 pm, Fri & Sat-midnight, Sun-10 pm. Closed: 11/26 & 12/25. **Reservations:** suggested; weekends. **Features:** casual
◆◆   dress; children's menu; health conscious menu; carryout; cocktails & lounge; street parking; area
Italian transportation; a la carte. Mystery cafe dinner theater & valet parking Fri & Sat. **Cards:** AE, CB, DI, DS, MC, VI. **Special Value: 20% discount on the price of any entree, excluding beverages, tax and gratuity.** ⊠

BOOKBINDER'S OLD ORIGINAL Historical **Lunch:** $7-$19   **Dinner:** $18-$40   Phone: 215/925-7027   ⑤
ⒶⒶⒶ   **Location:** At 2nd & Walnut sts. 125 Walnut St 19106. **Hours:** 11:45 am-10 pm, Sat from 4:30 pm, Sun 3
◆◆   pm-9 pm. Closed: 1/1, 11/26, 12/24 & 12/25. **Reservations:** suggested. **Features:** casual dress; children's
Seafood menu; health conscious menu items; carryout; cocktails & lounge; fee for valet parking; a la carte. Famous restaurant established in 1865. Large selection of seafood. Free valet parking at lunch. **Cards:** AE, DI, DS, MC, VI.   ⊠

BOOKBINDER'S 15TH ST SEAFOOD HOUSE **Lunch:** $7-$14   **Dinner:** $16-$33   Phone: 215/545-1137 ⑰
ⒶⒶⒶ 🆂🅰🆅🅴 **Location:** Center, between Walnut & Locust sts. 215 S 15th St 19102. **Hours:** 11:30 am-10 pm, Sat 4 pm-11
◆   pm, Sun 3 pm-10 pm. Closed: 11/26 & 12/25. **Reservations:** suggested. **Features:** casual dress; children's
Seafood menu; carryout; cocktails & lounge; fee for parking; a la carte. Well-known family operation. Bustling atmosphere. **Cards:** AE, CB, DI, DS, MC, VI. **Special Value: 10% discount on the price of any entree, excluding beverages, tax and gratuity.**   ⊠

BRASIL'S   **Dinner:** $17-$24   Phone: 215/413-1700   ㉞
◆◆   **Location:** Between Front & 2nd sts. 112 Chestnut St 19106. **Hours:** 5 pm-10 pm, Fri & Sat-11 pm, Sun 4
Ethnic   pm-10 pm. Closed: 4/12, 11/26 & 12/25. **Reservations:** suggested; weekends. **Features:** casual dress; carryout; cocktails; street parking. Simple dining room divided by aquariums & faux waterfalls. Festive, casual atmosphere. Brazilian menu features beef, chicken & seafood, none of which are hot/spicy. **Cards:** AE, CB, DI, MC, VI.   ⊠

CHANTERELLES   **Dinner:** $26-$31   Phone: 215/735-7551   ㊲
ⒶⒶⒶ 🆂🅰🆅🅴 **Location:** Between 13th & Broad sts. 1312 Spruce St 19107. **Hours:** 5:30-10 pm, Fri & Sat-11 pm. Closed major holidays & Sun. **Reservations:** suggested. **Features:** dressy casual; cocktails; street parking; a la
◆◆◆◆   carte, also prix fixe. Fine dining in a tiny facility with minimalist decor & elegant table appointments. Upscale
French   casual atmosphere. Eclectic menu variety reflects a creative fusion of Regional, French & Pacific Rim influences. Smoke free premises. **Cards:** AE, CB, DI, MC, VI. **Special Value: 10% discount on the price of any entree, excluding beverages, tax and gratuity.**   ⊠

CIBOULETTE Historical   **Lunch:** $15-$25   **Dinner:** $40-$60   Phone: 215/790-1210   ㊴
ⒶⒶⒶ   **Location:** Between Walnut & Broad sts; in the Bellevue Building. 200 S Broad St 19102. **Hours:** 5:30-9 pm,
        Fri & Sat-10:30 pm; Lunch Tues-Fri noon-2 pm. Closed major holidays & Sun. **Reservations:** suggested.
◆◆◆◆   **Features:** dressy casual; cocktails & lounge; fee for parking & valet parking; a la carte. Upscale casual
French   dining, French Provencale cuisine served in Regal French Renaissance setting. All menu items are presented in appetizer portion. **Cards:** AE, MC, VI.   ⊠

CIRCA   **Lunch:** $8-$13   **Dinner:** $12-$21   Phone: 215/545-6800   ㊶
◆◆◆   **Location:** Between 15th & 16th sts. 1518 Walnut St 19102. **Hours:** 11:30 am-2:30 & 5-10 pm, Thurs &
Continental Fri-11 pm, Sat 5 pm-11 pm, Sun 4:30 pm-9 pm. Closed: Mon for lunch. Call for hours major holidays.
        Features: dressy casual; health conscious menu; carryout; cocktails & lounge; street parking & fee for valet parking; a la carte. Upscale dining. Imaginative dishes with Mediterranean flair. The grand marble-walled building once housed a bank; a downstairs dining room is inside the old bank vault. Dancing Fri & Sat from 10 pm during spring, fall & winter. **Cards:** AE, DI, MC, VI.   ⊠

CITY TAVERN   **Lunch:** $15-$22   **Dinner:** $18-$34   Phone: 215/413-1443   ㊷
ⒶⒶⒶ   **Location:** Corner of 2nd & Walnut sts. 138 S 2nd St 19106. **Hours:** 11:30 am-10 pm, Fri & Sat-11 pm,
        Sun-8 pm. **Reservations:** suggested. **Features:** casual dress; children's menu; cocktails & lounge; street
◆◆◆   parking; a la carte. Faithful re-creation of a colonial tavern. A culinary experience inspired by the customs &
American foods of the 18th century. Colonial American. Costumed wait staff. Outdoor dining, weather permitting. **Cards:** AE, CB, DI, DS, MC, VI.   ⊠

CUTTERS   **Lunch:** $7-$15   **Dinner:** $11-$24   Phone: 215/851-6262   ㊸
◆◆   **Location:** In the Commerce Square building on Market St. 2005 Market St 19103. **Hours:** 11:30 am-10 pm,
American Fri-11 pm, Sat 4:30 pm-11 pm. Closed: Sun. **Features:** casual dress; children's menu; early bird specials; carryout; cocktails & lounge; a la carte. Casual upscale dining. Specialities include fresh fish & steak.
Cards: AE, DI, DS, MC, VI.   ⊠

(See map p. 354)

DEUX CHEMINEES Historical   **Dinner:** $68   **Phone:** 215/790-0200   ⑯
Location: Downtown, between 12th & 13th sts. 1221 Locust St 19107. **Hours:** 5:30 pm-8:30 pm, Sat-9:30 pm. Closed major holidays Sun & Mon. **Reservations:** suggested. **Features:** dressy casual; health conscious menu; cocktails; fee for parking; prix fixe. Distinctive fine dining, showcases an excellent offering of game & specialty items. Smoke free premises. **Cards:** AE, CB, DI, MC, VI.
Regional
French

DICKENS INN   **Lunch:** $13-$18   **Dinner:** $17-$30   **Phone:** 215/928-9307   ㊺
Location: At Head House Square. 421 S 2nd St 19147. **Hours:** 11:30 am-3 & 5-10 pm, Sun dinner 4 pm-9 pm. Closed: 1/1 & 12/25. **Reservations:** suggested. **Features:** casual dress; Sunday brunch; carryout; cocktails & lounge; fee for parking; a la carte. Traditional English foods as well as dishes with a European flair served in a 1780 building renovated to portray the era of Charles Dickens. Illustrations from his novels decorate the walls. Imported ale & beer. **Cards:** AE, CB, DI, DS, MC, VI.
Continental

DI LULLO   **Lunch:** $8-$12   **Dinner:** $17-$28   **Phone:** 215/546-2000   ⑱
Location: Opposite Academy of Music. 1407 Locust St 19102. **Hours:** 5:30 pm-10 pm. Closed major holidays & Sun. **Reservations:** suggested. **Features:** dressy casual; cocktails & lounge; fee for parking; a la carte. Elegant surroundings. Smoke free premises. **Cards:** AE, CB, DI, MC, VI.
Northern
Italian

DIMITRI'S   **Dinner:** $6-$18   **Phone:** 215/625-0556   ㊻
Location: 3rd & Catherine St, in Queens Village area. 795 S 3rd St 19147. **Hours:** 5:30 pm-11 pm, Sun-10 pm. Closed: 4/12, 11/26, 12/24-1/1. **Features:** casual dress; carryout; street parking; a la carte. Small, popular & very lively dining room with an open kitchen; Greek cuisine with other Mediterranean flairs; BYOB. Smoke free premises.

DOCK STREET BREWING COMPANY
BREWERY & RESTAURANT   **Lunch:** $4-$10   **Dinner:** $10-$16   **Phone:** 215/496-0413   ㊼
Location: In Two Logan Square Bldg, at 18th & Cherry sts. Two Logan Sq 19103. **Hours:** 11:30 am-midnight, Fri & Sat noon-2 am, Sun-11 pm. Closed: 9/7, 11/26 & 12/25. **Reservations:** suggested; for 6 or more. **Features:** dressy casual; carryout; cocktails & lounge; street parking; a la carte. Philadelphia's only full-grain brewery serving classic brewed-on-premises beer. **Cards:** AE, CB, DI, DS, MC, VI.
American

ESSENE CAFE   **Phone:** 215/922-1146   ㊾
Location: At Monroe & 4th sts. 719 S 4th St 19147. **Hours:** 9 am-8 pm. **Features:** casual dress; carryout; street parking. Well stocked juice bar, stylish no-meat, no-dairy menu. "Commissary"-type, with no wait service. Prices are per pound. Smoke free premises. **Cards:** DS, MC, VI.
Vegetarian

FEZ MOROCCAN CUISINE   **Dinner:** $10-$20   **Phone:** 215/925-5367   ㊿
Location: Between South & Bainbridge sts. 620 S 2nd St 19147. **Hours:** 5 pm-10:30 pm, Fri & Sat-11 pm. Closed: 11/26 & 12/25. **Reservations:** suggested; weekends. **Features:** casual dress; carryout; cocktails; street parking; prix fixe, a la carte. Dining room is a re-creation of a Moroccan wedding tent. Choose from a 6- or 8-course feast. Belly dancer performs weekends & special affairs. **Cards:** AE, DS, MC, VI.
Moroccan

FOUNDER'S Historical   **Lunch:** $11-$18   **Dinner:** $21-$35   **Phone:** 215/893-1776   ①
Location: On Broad St, between Walnut & Locust sts; in Park Hyatt Philadelphia at the Bellevue. 1415 Chancellor Ct 19102. **Hours:** 7 am-2 & 5:30-10 pm, Fri & Sat-11 pm, Sun 7 am-11 pm. **Reservations:** suggested. **Features:** semi-formal attire; Sunday brunch; children's menu; early bird specials; carryout; cocktails & lounge; fee for parking & valet parking; a la carte, also prix fixe. Elegant classical decor. Gracious service. **Cards:** AE, CB, DI, DS, MC, VI.
Continental

FOUNTAIN RESTAURANT   **Lunch:** $15-$18   **Dinner:** $27-$36   **Phone:** 215/963-1500   ③
Location: At corner 18th & Benjamin Franklin Pkwy; in Four Seasons Hotel. One Logan Sq 19103. **Hours:** 6:30 am-2:30 & 6-11 pm, Sat & Sun from 7 am. **Reservations:** suggested. **Features:** semi-formal attire; Sunday brunch; children's menu; health conscious menu items; cocktails & lounge; entertainment; fee for valet parking; a la carte, also prix fixe. Rich African mahogany accents & gracious table appointments; refined elegance. Innovative menu changes seasonally; table d'hote menu daily. **Cards:** AE, CB, DI, DS, JCB, MC, VI.
Continental

THE GARDEN   **Lunch:** $10-$24   **Dinner:** $20-$35   **Phone:** 215/546-4455   ⑮
Location: Downtown, on Spruce St, between 16th & 17th sts. 1617 Spruce St 19103. **Hours:** 11:30 am-1:30 & 5:30-9 pm, Sat 5:30 pm-9:30 pm. Closed major holidays, Sun & Mon for lunch. **Reservations:** suggested. **Features:** casual dress; early bird specials; cocktails & lounge; fee for valet parking; a la carte. Converted townhouse with garden dining in summer. Reduced fee parking avail. American cuisine with Continental influences. **Cards:** AE, CB, DI, MC, VI.
American

IMPERIAL INN   **Lunch:** $6-$7   **Dinner:** $9-$20   **Phone:** 215/627-2299   ㊾
Location: In Chinatown. 142-46 N 10th St 19107. **Hours:** 11 am-12:30 am, Fri & Sat-2 am, Sun-midnight. **Reservations:** suggested. **Features:** casual dress; carryout; cocktails; fee for parking; a la carte. Variety of Szechuan, Mandarin & Cantonese dishes. Authentic Dim Sum 11 am-3 pm. **Cards:** AE, CB, DI, MC, VI.
Chinese

THE INN PHILADELPHIA   **Dinner:** $14-$29   **Phone:** 215/732-2339   ㊾
Location: Between Locust & Spruce sts, just e of the Academy of Music. 251-253 S Camac St 19107. **Hours:** 5:30 pm-10:30 pm. Closed: 1/1 & Mon. **Reservations:** suggested. **Features:** casual dress; Sunday brunch; cocktails & lounge; street parking. 3 exceedingly tasteful dining areas. The Green Room is an intimately-scaled formal room. Traditional Great room with 2 fireplaces, contemporary Gallery. Seasonal patio dining. Fee for valet parking Sat evening. **Cards:** AE, CB, DI, DS, MC, VI.
American

JACK'S FIREHOUSE RESTAURANT   **Lunch:** $4-$10   **Dinner:** $15-$22   **Phone:** 215/232-9000   ⑭
Location: Just e of jct 22nd St & Fairmount Ave. 2130 Fairmount Ave 19130. **Hours:** 11:30 am-2:30 & 5-10:30 pm; Sun Brunch 11 am-2:30 pm. Closed major holidays. **Reservations:** suggested. **Features:** dressy casual; children's menu; cocktails & lounge; street parking; a la carte. Upscale casual dining in a converted firehouse. **Cards:** AE, MC, VI.
American

KABUL, CUISINE OF AFGHANISTAN   **Dinner:** $13-$19   **Phone:** 215/922-3676   ㊾
Location: Between 2nd & Front sts. 106 Chestnut St 19106. **Hours:** 4:30 pm-10 pm, Fri & Sat 5 pm-11 pm, Sun 4:30 pm-9 pm. Closed: Mon. **Reservations:** suggested. **Features:** casual dress; carryout; fee for parking. Featuring traditional kabobs of marinated chicken, lamb or beef. Appetizers such as scallion-filled dumplings with yogurt sauce. Many vegetable dishes. **Cards:** AE, DI, DS, MC, VI.
Ethnic

(See map p. 354)

KAT MAN DU   Lunch: $7-$13   Dinner: $10-$20   Phone: 215/629-7400   56
◆◆   **Location:** Between Spring Garden & Callowhill sts, Pier 25 N. 417 N Columbus Blvd 19123. **Hours:** Open
American   5/1-9/30 & 4/15-4/30; 11:30 am-2 am. **Reservations:** suggested. **Features:** No A/C; casual dress; Sunday
brunch; children's menu; early bird specials; carryout; cocktails & lounge; entertainment; fee for valet parking;
a la carte. Lively American bistro with island flair. Live music nightly. 9 live shows per week & 10 DJ shows. **Cards:** AE, CB,
DI, DS, MC, VI.

LE BEC-FIN   Lunch: $36   Dinner: $102   Phone: 215/567-1000   12
AAA   **Location:** Between 15th & 16th sts. 1523 Walnut St 19102. **Hours:** Lunch seatings at 11:30 am & 1:30 pm
Mon-Fri; dinner seatings Mon-Thurs at 6 pm & 9 pm, Fri & Sat 6 pm & 9:30 pm. Closed major holidays &
◆◆◆◆◆   Sun. **Reservations:** required. **Features:** formal attire; cocktails & lounge; prix fixe. Formal dining in a lavish
French   setting; Louis XVI decor. Exquisite table appointments. Menu changes seasonally & offers outstanding
variety. Valet parking, evenings. **Cards:** AE, CB, DI, DS, MC, VI.

LONDON GRILL   Lunch: $5-$12   Dinner: $15-$22   Phone: 215/978-4545   11
AAA   **Location:** Just w of jct 22nd St & Fairmount Ave. 2301 Fairmount Ave 19130. **Hours:** 11:30 am-3 &
5:30-10:30 pm, Sun 11 am-2:30 & 4-9 pm. **Closed:** 1/1, 11/26 & 12/25. **Reservations:** suggested.
◆◆   **Features:** casual dress; Sunday brunch; children's menu; health conscious menu items; carryout; cocktails &
Nouvelle   lounge; minimum charge-$15; a la carte. Friendly neighborhood dining. Lighter fare menu avail. Eclectic
American   menu. **Cards:** AE, CB, DI, DS, MC, VI.

MCCROSSEN'S TAVERN   Lunch: $7-$17   Dinner: $7-$17   Phone: 215/854-0923   13
◆◆   **Location:** 20th St between Hamilton & Spring Gardens sts. 529 N 20th St 19130. **Hours:** 11:30 am-11 pm.
Italian   **Reservations:** accepted. **Features:** casual dress; carryout; cocktails & lounge; street parking; a la carte.
Bustling intimately casual atmosphere. American & Italian cuisine with a Mediterranean flair. **Cards:** AE, DI,
DS, MC, VI.

MIA'S   Lunch: $12-$20   Dinner: $13-$26   Phone: 215/545-4655   60
◆◆◆   **Location:** Jct 17th & Locust sts; in The Warwick. 1701 Locust St 19103-6179. **Hours:** 6:30 am-11 pm.
Continental   **Reservations:** suggested. **Features:** casual dress; Sunday brunch; cocktails & lounge; fee for parking &
valet parking; a la carte. Cozy, sophisticated dining, specializing in Mediterranean cuisine. 45 wines avail by
the glass. **Cards:** AE, CB, DI, MC, VI.

THE MONTE CARLO LIVING ROOM   Dinner: $26-$32   Phone: 215/925-2220   21
AAA   **Location:** South St at 2nd St. 150 South St 19147. **Hours:** 6 pm-10:30 pm, Sat from 5:30 pm, Sun 5
pm-9:30 pm. Closed major holidays. **Reservations:** suggested. **Features:** semi-formal attire; cocktails &
◆◆◆◆   lounge; fee for valet parking; a la carte. Intimate dining room in trendy Queen's Village area. Reserved
Italian   atmosphere. Features fresh domestic & imported seafood. Formal service. **Cards:** AE, DI, MC, VI.

NICHOLAS, NICHOLAS, THE RESTAURANT   Dinner: $24-$36   Phone: 215/546-8440   22
◆◆◆◆   **Location:** In the Rittenhouse Hotel & Condominium Residences. 210 W Rittenhouse Square 19103.
Continental   **Hours:** 5:30 pm-10:30 pm, Fri & Sat-11 pm. Closed: Sun. **Reservations:** suggested. **Features:** dressy
casual; cocktails & lounge; fee for valet parking; a la carte. Mutedly opulent dining room overlooking famous
Rittenhouse Square. Featuring seafood, prime steak & veal dishes. Smoke free premises. **Cards:** AE, CB, DI, DS, MC, VI.

ORFEO CAFE BY DAY-RESTAURANT BY NIGHT   Lunch: $3-$7   Dinner: $13-$23   Phone: 215/567-5000   23
◆◆   **Location:** Downtown, on Walnut St; midway between 20th & 21st sts. 2029 Walnut St 19103. **Hours:** 10
Ethnic   am-10 pm, Fri & Sat-11 pm, Sun-5 pm. Closed: 1/1, 11/26, 12/24 & 12/25. **Reservations:** accepted.
Features: casual dress; Sunday brunch; early bird specials; carryout; cocktails; street parking; a la carte.
Eclectic continental cuisine with Mediterranean & Asian accent. Featured in an intimate bistro atmosphere within a historic
19th-century brownstone. Smoke free premises. **Cards:** AE, DI, MC, VI.

OVERTURES   Dinner: $15-$25   Phone: 215/627-3455   64
AAA   **Location:** Just s of South St, between 4th & 5th sts. 609 E Passyunk Ave 19147. **Hours:** 6 pm-10 pm, Sun
5 pm-9:30 pm. Closed major holidays & Mon. **Reservations:** required; weekends. **Features:** dressy casual;
◆◆◆   street parking; a la carte. Dine elegantly in the main dining room with its Old World atmosphere. Less formal
Provincial   enclosed porch with cafe tables & almost-outdoor feel. **Cards:** AE, CB, DI, MC, VI.
French

PALLADIUM RESTAURANT   Lunch: $6-$12   Dinner: $10-$19   Phone: 215/387-3463   65
AAA   **Location:** I-76 exit 38, 0.5 mi w on Market St, 0.5 mi s on 36th St to campus parking, just s. 3601 Locust
Walk 19104. **Hours:** 11:30 am-2:30 & 5-9 pm, Fri & Sat-10 pm. Closed: Sun, 8/16-8/22 & 12/22-1/2.
◆◆   **Reservations:** suggested. **Features:** casual dress; early bird specials; health conscious menu; carryout;
Continental   cocktails & lounge; a la carte. On the University of PA campus in a restored Collegiate Gothic building.
Cards: AE, CB, DI, DS, MC, VI.

PALM RESTAURANT   Lunch: $8-$14   Dinner: $14-$25   Phone: 215/546-7256   24
◆◆   **Location:** Corner of Walnut & Broad sts. 200 S Broad St 19102. **Hours:** 11:30 am-11 pm, Sat from 5 pm,
American   Sun 4:30 pm-9 pm. Closed major holidays. **Reservations:** suggested. **Features:** casual dress; carryout;
cocktails & lounge; fee for parking & valet parking; a la carte. In shops at the Bellevue. Upbeat, high-energy
atmosphere. **Cards:** AE, CB, DI, MC, VI.

PAMPLONA   Dinner: $8-$17   Phone: 215/627-9059   68
◆◆   **Location:** Corner of 12th & Locust sts. 225 S 12th St 19107. **Hours:** 5:30 pm-10 pm; Fri & Sat-11 pm.
Spanish   Closed: 1/1, 11/26, 12/24 & 12/25. **Features:** casual dress; carryout; beer & wine only; street parking; a la
carte. Gloriously theatrical space dominated by oversized Picasso-inspired murals. Sleek, yet relaxed. Tapas
style menu. Smoke free premises. **Cards:** AE, DI, MC, VI.

PASSAGE TO INDIA   Lunch: $7-$18   Dinner: $7-$18   Phone: 215/732-7300   70
◆◆   **Location:** Corner of Juniper & Walnut sts. 1320 Walnut St 19107. **Hours:** 11:30 am-2:30 & 5-9:30 pm, Fri &
Northern Indian   Sat-10:30 pm. Closed: 11/26 & 12/25. **Reservations:** suggested; weekends. **Features:** casual dress;
Sunday brunch; carryout; cocktails; street parking; a la carte. Fat free, clay oven prepared cuisine. Daily
lunch buffet, $6-$8. **Cards:** AE, CB, DI, DS, MC, VI.

(See map p. 354)

PHILADELPHIA FISH & COMPANY   **Lunch:** $10-$17   **Dinner:** $21-$26   **Phone:** 215/625-8605   ⑧
◆◆   **Location:** Just w of 2nd & Chestnut sts. 207 Chestnut St 19106. **Hours:** 11:30 am-10 pm, Fri 11:30 am-4 &
Seafood   5-midnight, Sat noon-3 & 4:30-midnight, Sun 3 pm-10 pm. Closed: 1/1, 11/26 & 12/24-12/26.
          Reservations: suggested. **Features:** casual dress; children's menu; health conscious menu; cocktails &
lounge; street parking; a la carte. Innovatively prepared seafood, lively atmosphere. Seasonal outdoor dining patio.
Cards: AE, DI, MC, VI.   ☒

RALPHS' ITALIAN RESTAURANT   **Lunch:** $6-$9   **Dinner:** $8-$18   **Phone:** 215/627-6011   ⑩
◆   **Location:** South Philadelphia. 760 S 9th St 19147. **Hours:** noon-9:45 pm, Fri & Sat-10:45 pm. Closed: 11/26
South Italian   & 12/25. **Reservations:** suggested. **Features:** casual dress; carryout; cocktails; street parking; a la carte.
          Family run operation in the Italian market area since the early 1900's, making it the the oldest family owned
Italian restaurant in the country. Offering simple, home cooked cuisine.   ☒

RANGOON BURMESE RESTAURANT   **Lunch:** $5-$10   **Dinner:** $8-$10   **Phone:** 215/829-8939   ㉑
◆   **Location:** In Chinatown. 112-114 N 9th St 19107. **Hours:** 11:30 am-9 pm, Fri 11:30 am-10 pm, Sat 1 pm-10
Ethnic   pm, Sun 1 pm-9 pm. Closed major holidays. **Features:** health conscious menu; carryout; street parking; a la
          carte. Burmese cuisine. The menu combines ingredients from Indian, Thai & Chinese cooking traditions, with
distinctive & delicious results. **Cards:** MC, VI.

RISTORANTE PANORAMA   Historical   **Lunch:** $10-$14   **Dinner:** $13-$19   **Phone:** 215/922-7800   ②
⏺⏺   **Location:** At Front & Market sts; I-95, southbound exit 17, northbound exit 16; in Penn's View Hotel. 14 N
          Front St 19106. **Hours:** noon-2:30 & 5:30-10 pm, Fri & Sat-11 pm. Closed: 1/1, 12/24 & 12/25.
◆◆◆   **Reservations:** suggested. **Features:** cocktails & lounge; fee for parking; a la carte. Contemporary northern
Regional   Italian cuisine. World class wine bar with 120 selections on the cruvinet system. Homemade pasta, sauce &
Italian   dessert. Wine cellar. **Cards:** AE, CB, DI, MC, VI.   ☒

RISTORANTE PRIMAVERA   **Dinner:** $15-$25   **Phone:** 215/925-7832   ㉒
⏺   **Location:** South St District. 146 South St 19147. **Hours:** 5:30 pm-10:30 pm, Sun-9:30 pm, Fri & Sat-11 pm.
◆◆   Closed major holidays. **Features:** casual dress; carryout; cocktails; fee for parking & valet parking; a la carte.
Italian   Homemade pasta & fish specials daily.

THE RITZ-CARLTON GRILL ROOM   **Lunch:** $10-$20   **Dinner:** $18-$35   **Phone:** 215/563-1600   ㉓
◆◆◆◆   **Location:** In The Ritz-Carlton, Philadelphia. 17th & Chestnut St at Liberty Pl 19103. **Hours:** 11:30 am-2:30 &
American   5:30-10:30 pm, Sun 5:30 am-11:30 & 5:30-10:30 pm. **Reservations:** suggested. **Features:** semi-formal
          attire; children's menu; health conscious menu; cocktails & lounge; fee for parking & valet parking; a la carte,
also prix fixe. Regional fare, including hearty steak, chops & seafood served in a club-like setting, enhanced with rich
mahogany & oil paintings. **Cards:** AE, CB, DI, DS, JCB, MC, VI.   ☒

SINGAPORE KOSHER VEGETARIAN
RESTAURANT   **Lunch:** $7-$10   **Dinner:** $7-$10   **Phone:** 215/922-3288   ㉔
◆◆   **Location:** Corner of 11th & Race sts, in Chinatown. 1029 Race St 19107. **Hours:** 11:30 am-10:30 pm, Fri &
Chinese   Sat-midnight. **Features:** casual dress; health conscious menu; carryout; street parking; a la carte. Dishes
          based on fresh & dried vegetables along with mock meat & seafood dishes made from grains, glutens & soy
product. **Cards:** AE, DI, DS, MC, VI.

SOUTH STREET SOUVLAKI   **Lunch:** $5-$11   **Dinner:** $5-$11   **Phone:** 215/925-3026   ⑨
ⓐⓐⓐ   **Location:** At South & 5th sts. 509 South St 19147. **Hours:** 11 am-10 pm, Fri & Sat-11 pm, Sun noon-10 pm.
          Closed: 1/1, 11/26, 12/25 & Mon. **Features:** casual dress; carryout; cocktails; street parking; a la carte.
◆   Traditionally prepared cuisine, made on premises & served in modest dining room.
Greek

STRIPED BASS   **Lunch:** $14-$18   **Dinner:** $29-$46   **Phone:** 215/732-4444   ㉕
◆◆◆◆   **Location:** Sw corner of 15th & Walnut sts. 1500 Walnut St 19102. **Hours:** 11:30 am-2:30 & 5-11 pm, Fri &
Seafood   Sat-11:30 pm, Sun 5 pm-10 pm; Sun brunch 11 am-2:30 pm, 9/8-6/30. Closed major holidays.
          Reservations: suggested. **Features:** dressy casual; cocktails & lounge; fee for valet parking; a la carte.
Stylish, marble pillars. 30-foot marquetry ceiling, colorful Oriental rug, potted palms & spectacular flower arrangements set
the mood. Saturday brunch 11 am-2:30 pm. Smoke free premises. **Cards:** AE, DI, MC, VI.   ☒

SUSANNA FOO   **Lunch:** $9-$17   **Dinner:** $15-$24   **Phone:** 215/545-2666   ⑲
◆◆◆   **Location:** Between 15th & 16th sts. 1512 Walnut St 19102. **Hours:** 11:30 am-2:30 & 5:30-10 pm, Fri &
Chinese   Sat-11 pm. Closed major holidays & Sun. **Reservations:** suggested. **Features:** semi-formal attire; carryout;
          cocktails; fee for parking & valet parking; a la carte. Excellent selection of imaginative & unorthodox
preparations that offer an adventure in gastronomy. Atmosphere has a formal edge. **Cards:** AE, CB, DI, MC, VI.   ☒

SWANN LOUNGE & CAFE   **Lunch:** $6-$20   **Dinner:** $13-$23   **Phone:** 215/963-1500   ㉗
◆◆◆◆   **Location:** At corner 18th & Benjamin Franklin Pkwy; in Four Seasons Hotel. One Logan Sq 19103.
Continental   **Hours:** 11:30 am-1 am, Sun from 10 am. **Reservations:** accepted. **Features:** dressy casual; Sunday
          brunch; children's menu; health conscious menu; cocktails & lounge; entertainment; fee for valet parking; a la
carte. Relaxed elegant environment with view of Logan Circle. Seasonal menu changes. **Cards:** AE, CB, DI, DS, JCB, MC,
VI.   ☒

TREE TOPS RESTAURANT   **Lunch:** $15-$25   **Dinner:** $20-$35   **Phone:** 215/546-9000   ⑳
ⓐⓐⓐ   **Location:** In The Rittenhouse Hotel & Condominium Residences. 210 W Rittenhouse Sq 19103.
          Hours: 6:30 am-11 pm. **Reservations:** suggested. **Features:** dressy casual; Sunday brunch; children's
◆◆◆◆   menu; health conscious menu; cocktails; fee for valet parking; a la carte. Upscale solarium enclosed dining
American   room with gracious ambience, overlooks famous Rittenhouse Square; offering innovative American Regional
          cuisine. **Cards:** AE, CB, DI, DS, MC, VI.   ☒

ZANZIBAR BLUE   **Lunch:** $8-$16   **Dinner:** $16-$22   **Phone:** 215/732-4500   ㉖
◆◆◆   **Location:** Center, corner of Broad & Walnut sts. 200 S Broad St 19102. **Hours:** 11:30 am-2:30 & 5:30-11
Northern   pm, Fri-midnight, Sat 5:30 pm-midnight, Sun jazz brunch 11 am-2:30 & 5:30-11 pm. Closed major holidays.
American   **Reservations:** suggested. **Features:** dressy casual; cocktails & lounge; entertainment; fee for parking; a la
          carte. Eclectic international menu served in upscale club atmosphere. Live jazz entertainment nightly from 7
pm Sun, 8:30 pm Mon-Thurs & from 9 pm Fri & Sat. Cover charge applies some evenings. Smoke free premises.
Cards: AE, CB, DI, MC, VI.   ☒

(See map p. 354)

ZOCALO
◆◆
Regional
Mexican

Lunch: $6-$11   **Dinner:** $18-$25   **Phone:** 215/895-0139 ㉖
Location: Just n of Market St, on 36th St. 3600 Lancaster Ave 19104. **Hours:** noon-2:30 & 5:30-10 pm
Fri-11 pm, Sat 5:30 pm-11 pm, Sun 5 pm-9:30 pm. Closed major holidays. **Reservations:** suggested
weekends. **Features:** casual dress; children's menu; cocktails & lounge; a la carte. Bright bold southwes
decor. Philadelphia's only hand made corn tortillas. Smoke free premises. **Cards:** AE, DI, DS, MC, VI. ☒

GREATER PHILADELPHIA (See map p. 368; index below)

Index of Establishments on the PHILADELPHIA & VICINITY ACCOMMODATIONS Spotting Map

BENSALEM
Comfort Inn .... ㉚
Courtyard by Marriott Bensalem .... ㉛
Hampton Inn Philadelphia North East .... ㉝
⊕ Holiday Inn-Philadelphia Northeast .... ㉞
McIntosh Inn of Bensalem .... ㉟

RESTAURANT
Fisher's Tudor House .... ㉟

LEVITTOWN
⊕ Comfort Inn Levittown/Bristol .... ㊲

GREATER PHILADELPHIA
⊕ Adam's Mark Hotel .... ㊵
Radisson Hotel Philadelphia Airport .... ㊶
⊕ Days Inn .... ㊷
⊕ Westin Suites .... ㊸
⊕ Days Inn/Philadelphia Int'l Airport .... ㊹
⊕ Philadelphia Airport Hilton .... ㊺
Embassy Suites-Philadelphia Airport .... ㊻
Chestnut Hill Hotel .... ㊼
Philadelphia Airport Marriott.................. ㊽
Philadelphia Airport Residence Inn........... ㊾
⊕ Roosevelt Inn .... ㊿
⊕ Club Hotel By Doubletree .... ㊿②
⊕ Best Western Hotel Philadelphia Northeast.... ㊿③
Courtyard By Marriott Airport................. ㊿④
Holiday Inn City Line .... ㊿⑥
⊕ Holiday Inn Philadelphia Stadium........... ㊿⑦
Philadelphia Marriott West .... ㊿⑧

RESTAURANTS
Cafe Flower Shop .... ⑨⓪
Cafe Zesty.................................. ⑨①
Jake's...................................... ⑨④
Joseph's.................................... ⑨⑤
Kansas City Prime........................... ⑨⑦
Le Bus .... ⑨⑧
Pollo Rosso................................. ⑩⓪
Sonoma .... ⑩①
Stephen's................................... ⑩③
Umbria .... ⑩⑤
La Collina Restaurant .... ⑩⑥
The Marker .... ⑩⑦
Fishers Seafood Restaurant .... ⑩⑧
⊕ Country Club Restaurant................... ⑩⑨

HORSHAM
Residence Inn by Marriott-Willow Grove........ ㉖⓪
Horsham Days Inn............................ ㉖②

PLYMOUTH MEETING
⊕ Doubletree Guest Suites .... ㉖⑥

ESSINGTON
Ramada Inn-Philadelphia International Airport.... ⑦⓪
⊕ Holiday Inn-Airport .... ⑦①
Red Roof Inn-Airport .... ⑦③
⊕ Comfort Inn Airport......................... ⑦④

RESTAURANT
The Logoon Restaurant & Nite Club .... ⑪⑦

WILLOW GROVE
Courtyard by Marriott-Willow Grove............. ⑦⑨
Hampton Inn-Willow Grove .... ⑧⓪

TREVOSE
⊕ Howard Johnson Hotel....................... ⑧⑤
Red Roof Inn................................ ⑧⑨
⊕ Holiday Inn Select Bucks County............. ⑨⓪
Radisson Hotel of Philadelphia Northeast........ ⑨①

BELLMAWR, NJ
⊕ Bellmawr Motor Inn......................... ⑨⑨

LANGHORNE
Red Roof Inn-Oxford Valley .... ⑩⑧
⊕ Sheraton Bucks County Hotel .... ⑪⓪
McIntosh Inn of Oxford Valley................. ⑪①

RUNNEMEDE, NJ
⊕ Holiday Inn-Runnemede..................... ⑪⑤
⊕ Comfort Inn .... ⑪⑥

CHERRY HILL, NJ
Residence Inn by Marriott .... ⑫⓪
Four Points-Cherry Hill by ITT Sheraton .... ⑫①
Holiday Inn-Cherry Hill .... ⑫③
⊕ Days Inn .... ⑫④
Hilton at Cherry Hill .... ⑫⑤
⊕ Howard Johnson Express Inn & Conference
    Center .... ⑫⑥

RESTAURANTS
⊕ La Campagne .... ⑬③
Caffe Lamberti .... ⑬④
⊕ Andreotti's Viennese Cafe & Pastry Shop .... ⑬⑤
Siri's Thai French Cuisine .... ⑬⑥

MAPLE SHADE, NJ
⊕ Rodeway Inn .... ⑬⓪

MOUNT LAUREL, NJ
Radisson Hotel.............................. ⑬④
Courtyard by Marriott........................ ⑬⑨
⊕ Track & Turf Motel .... ⑬⑥
Super 8 Motel .... ⑬⑦
Red Roof Inn................................ ⑬⑧
⊕ Travelodge Hotel and Conference Center ..... ⑬⑨
Quality Inn.................................. ⑭⓪
McIntosh Inn of Mount Laurel .... ⑭①
⊕ Red Carpet Inn .... ⑭②
Summerfield Suites Hotel..................... ⑭③
Hampton Inn Mt Laurel....................... ⑭④
Doubletree Guest Suites Hotel .... ⑭⑥

RESTAURANT
Sage Diner .... ⑭⓪

MOUNT HOLLY, NJ
Howard Johnson Motor Lodge .... ⑮⓪
⊕ Best Western Burlington Inn .... ⑮①

RESTAURANT
Robin's Nest .... ⑭⑤

BROOKLAWN, NJ
⊕ Days Inn .... ⑮⑧

VOORHEES, NJ
Hampton Inn .... ⑯⓪

RESTAURANTS
Mama Ventura's............................. ⑭⑧
Somsak-Thai Cuisine .... ⑭⑨

BURLINGTON, NJ
RESTAURANT
⊕ Cafe Gallery.............................. ⑮①

ARDMORE
RESTAURANT
⊕ Thai Pepper Restaurant..................... ⑮④

HAVERTOWN
RESTAURANT
⊕ Nais Cuisine .... ⑮⑦

(See map p. 368)

CONSHOHOCKEN		MEDFORD, NJ	
RESTAURANT		RESTAURANT	
Spring Mill Cafe	161	Beau Rivage Restaurant	170
GLENSIDE		SPRINGFIELD (DELAWARE COUNTY)	
RESTAURANT		RESTAURANT	
Alfio's Restaurant	166	Caffe Bellissimo Seafood Italiano Ristorante	174

LODGINGS

ADAM'S MARK HOTEL Phone: 215/581-5000 40
AAA SAVE Mon-Thurs 1P: $159 2P/1B: $175 2P/2B: $175 XP: $15 F18
Fri-Sun 1P: $99 2P/1B: $99 2P/2B: $99
◆◆◆ **Location:** On US 1 (City Ave), just s of I-76, Schuylkill Expwy, exit 33. City Ave at Monument Rd 19131.
Hotel **Fax:** 215/581-5069. **Terms:** Reserv deposit; package plans; no pets. **Facility:** 515 rooms. Impressive public areas. Comfortably appointed rooms. Hair salon, travel agency & car rentals on premises. 3 two-bedroom units. 23 stories; interior corridors; saunas, whirlpool; racquetball courts. Fee: parking. **Dining & Entertainment:** Dining room, restaurant; 6 am-midnight; $8-$30; cocktails/lounge; also, The Marker, see separate listing; entertainment. **Services:** valet laundry. Fee: childcare; valet parking. **All Rooms:** Fee: movies. **Some Rooms:** whirlpools. Fee: refrigerators, VCR's. **Cards:** AE, CB, DI, DS, JCB, MC, VI. **Special Amenities: Free newspaper and free room upgrade (subject to availability with advanced reservations).** (See color ad below)

BEST WESTERN HOTEL PHILADELPHIA NORTHEAST Phone: 215/464-9500 53
AAA SAVE 5/1-10/31 [CP] 1P: $98 2P/1B: $98 2P/2B: $105 XP: $5 F18
1/1-4/30 [CP] 1P: $70 2P/1B: $70 2P/2B: $75 XP: $5 F18
◆◆◆ 11/1-12/31 [CP] 1P: $65 2P/1B: $65 2P/2B: $70 XP: $5 F18
Motor Inn **Location:** 3 mi s on US 1, from PA Tpk exit 28. 11580 Roosevelt Blvd 19116. Fax: 215/464-8511. **Terms:** Weekly/monthly rates; package plans; no pets. **Facility:** 100 rooms. 2 stories; interior corridors; wading pool; playground, shuffleboard, sand volleyball. **Dining & Entertainment:** Coffee shop; 9 am-9 pm, Sun-noon; $4-$8; cocktail lounge. **Services:** Fee: coin laundry. **All Rooms:** free movies. **Some Rooms:** 6 efficiencies, no utensils, microwaves, refrigerators, whirlpools. **Cards:** AE, CB, DI, DS, JCB, MC, VI. **Special Amenities: Early check-in/late check-out and free breakfast.** (See color ad below)

CHESTNUT HILL HOTEL Rates Subject to Change Phone: 215/242-5905 47
◆◆◆ All Year [CP] 1P: $110- 150 2P/1B: $120- 150 2P/2B: $120- 150 XP: $10 F12
Historic Hotel **Location:** I-276 exit 25; 5.5 mi e on Germantown Pike. 8229 Germantown Ave 19118. Fax: 215/242-8778. **Terms:** No pets. **Facility:** 28 rooms. 2-4 stories; interior corridors. **Dining:** Pollo Rosso, see separate listing. **All Rooms:** free movies. **Cards:** AE, CB, DI, MC, VI.

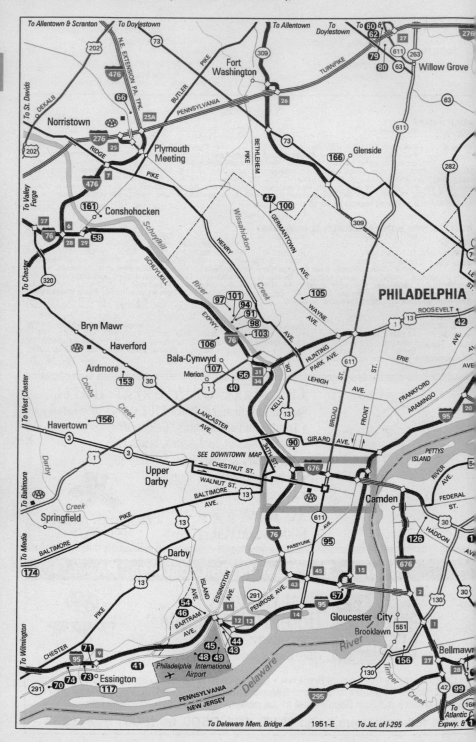

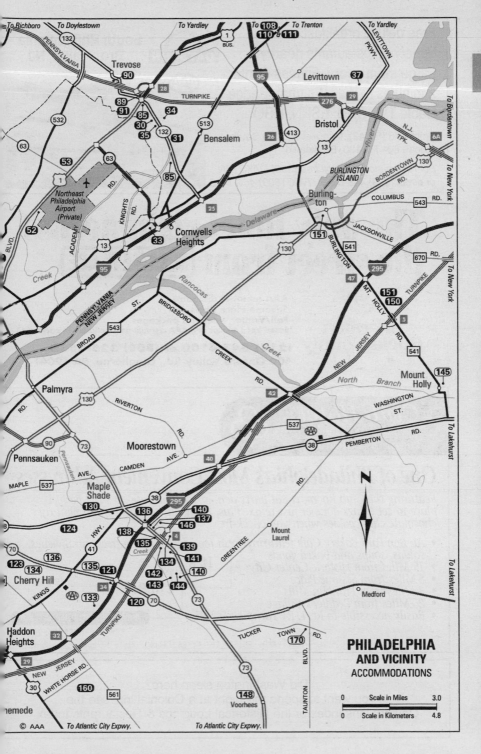

PHILADELPHIA
AND VICINITY
ACCOMMODATIONS

© AAA

Did Washington sleep here?
If you want to spend the night at a Colonial inn, see the
Country Inns Index or the Historical Lodgings & Restaurants Index.

(See map p. 368)

CLUB HOTEL BY DOUBLETREE

Phone: 215/671-9600   52   F17

All Year   1P: $109   2P/1B: $119   XP: $10

Location: 5 mi s on US 1, from PA Tpk exit 28. 9461 Roosevelt Blvd 19114. Fax: 215/464-7759. **Terms:** No pets. **Facility:** 188 rooms. Nicely appointed public areas & rooms with quality cherry finish furnishings. 4 suites avail; 6 stories; interior corridors. **Dining & Entertainment:** Coffee shop; 6 am-11 pm; $4-$9; cocktails/lounge. **Services:** Fee: coin laundry. **All Rooms:** coffeemakers, free & pay movies. **Some Rooms:** Fee: microwaves, refrigerators. **Cards:** AE, DI, DS, MC, VI. **Special Amenities: Early check-in/late check-out and free room upgrade (subject to availability with advanced reservations).** *(See color ad p 370)*

Roll in showers.

Motor Inn

COURTYARD BY MARRIOTT AIRPORT

Rates Subject to Change   **Phone: 215/365-2200**   54

	1P	2P/1B	2P/2B
5/1-12/31 & Sun-Thurs			
1/1-4/30	$124	$124	$124
Fri & Sat 1/1-4/30	$59- 79	$59- 79	$59- 79

Location: I-95 southbound exit 10 (airport), bearing right on exit ramp to light, just n; I-95 northbound exit 10, follow 291E signs until light, 1 mi n. 8900 Bartram Ave 19153. Fax: 215/365-6905. **Terms:** No pets. **Facility:** 152 rooms. 12 suites, $125-$135. Handling fee imposed; 4 stories; interior corridors. **Dining:** Restaurant; 6:30 am-9:30 & Sun & Sun 8 am-noon & 6-10 pm, room service 5 pm-9:30 pm; $9-$17. **All Rooms:** free & pay movies. **Cards:** AE, CB, DI, MC, VI. *(See color ad below)*

Motor Inn

DAYS INN

Phone: 215/289-9200   42   F12

All Year [CP]   1P: $65   2P/1B: $60- 65   2P/2B: $70   XP: $7

Location: I-76 exit 34 US 1N (Roosevelt Blvd), 5.3 mi n; PA Tpk exit 28, 12 mi s on US 1. 4200 Roosevelt Blvd 19124. Fax: 215/289-9200. **Terms:** Reserv deposit; no pets. **Facility:** 116 rooms. 6 whirlpool rms, extra charge; 2 stories; interior corridors. **Dining:** Restaurant nearby. **All Rooms:** free movies. **Cards:** AE, CB, DI, DS, JCB, MC, VI. **Special Amenities: Free breakfast and free local telephone calls.**

Motel

DAYS INN/PHILADELPHIA INT'L AIRPORT

Phone: 215/492-0400   44

	1P	2P/1B	2P/2B	XP
5/1-10/31 & 2/1-4/30	$98- 118	$98- 118	$98- 118	$15 F16
11/1-1/31	$69- 89	$69- 89	$69- 89	$15 F16

Location: Jct I-95 & SR 291 exit 11 northbound; exit 13 southbound. 4101 Island Ave 19153. Fax: 215/365-6035. **Terms:** Monthly rates; BP avail; package plans; no pets. **Facility:** 177 rooms. 5 stories; interior corridors. **Dining & Entertainment:** Dining room; 6 am-2 & 5-10 pm, food service in lounge-midnight; $8-$16; health conscious menu; cocktails/lounge. **Services:** Fee: coin laundry. **Recreation:** jogging. **All Rooms:** coffeemakers, free & pay movies. **Some Rooms:** microwaves, refrigerators. Fee: VCR's. **Cards:** AE, CB, DI, DS, MC, VI.

Motor Inn

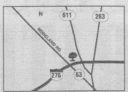

(See map p. 368)

EMBASSY SUITES-PHILADELPHIA AIRPORT Rates Subject to Change **Phone:** 215/365-4500 🔢46
◆◆◆   Mon-Thurs [BP]   1P: $169   2P/1B: $169   2P/2B: $169
Hotel   Fri-Sun [BP]   1P: $109   2P/1B: $119   2P/2B: $119
         Location: From jct I-95 & Essington Ave, just n on Essington Ave, just w. 9000 Bartram Ave 19153.
Fax: 215/365-3195. **Terms:** Sr. discount; no pets. **Facility:** 263 rooms. 5 stories; interior corridors. **Dining:** Dining room; 11 am-11 pm; $8-$15. **All Rooms:** free & pay movies. **Cards:** AE, DI, DS, JCB, MC, VI.
Roll in showers. (icons)

HOLIDAY INN CITY LINE   Rates Subject to Change   **Phone:** 215/477-0200 🔢56
◆◆◆   All Year   1P: $107   2P/1B: $107   2P/2B: $107   XP: $10   F18
Hotel   **Location:** On US 1, just s of I-76 (Schuylkill Expwy), exit 33. 4100 Presidential Blvd 19131.
         Terms: Check-in 4 pm; no pets. **Facility:** 344 rooms. 8 stories; interior corridors.
Dining: Dining room; 6:30 am-10 pm, Sat & Sun from 7 am; $7-$18. **All Rooms:** free & pay movies. **Cards:** AE, CB, DI, DS, JCB, MC, VI. *(See color ad below)*
(icons)

HOLIDAY INN PHILADELPHIA STADIUM   1P: $119   2P/1B: $119   **Phone:** 215/755-9500 🔢57
(AAA)(SAVE)   All Year   2P/2B: $119   XP: $10   F18
         Location: Jct of I-76 & I-95, w end of Walt Whitman Bridge. 10th St & Packer Ave 19148.
◆◆◆   Fax: 215/462-6947. **Terms:** BP avail; no pets. **Facility:** 238 rooms. Good size rooms with varied appointments.
Hotel   11 stories; interior corridors. **Dining & Entertainment:** Restaurant; 6:30 am-midnight; $9-$22; cocktails/lounge; entertainment, nightclub. **Services:** valet laundry. **All Rooms:** free & pay movies.
Some Rooms: Fee: microwaves, refrigerators. **Cards:** AE, CB, DI, DS, JCB, MC, VI. **Special Amenities:** Free room upgrade and preferred room (each subject to availability with advanced reservations).
(icons)

(See map p. 368)

PHILADELPHIA AIRPORT HILTON   Guaranteed Rates   **Phone: 215/365-4150**   45
All Year   1P: $115   2P/1B: $115   2P/2B: $115   XP: $10   F18
Location: Jct I-95 & SR 291 exit 11 northbound; exit 13 southbound. 4509 Island Ave 19153.
Fax: 215/365-3002. **Terms:** Sr. discount; pets, $25 extra charge. **Facility:** 331 rooms. 9 stories; interior corridors. **Dining:** Restaurant; 6 am-11 pm; $7-$28. **All Rooms:** free & pay movies. **Cards:** AE, CB, DI, DS, MC, VI. *(See color ad p 18)*   Roll in showers.
Hotel

PHILADELPHIA AIRPORT MARRIOTT   Rates Subject to Change   **Phone: 215/492-9000**   48
All Year   1P: $179- 199   2P/1B: $179- 199   2P/2B: $179- 199
Hotel   **Location:** Jct I-95 & SR 291, exit 10. Arrivals Rd 19153. Fax: 215/492-6799. **Terms:** No pets. **Facility:** 419
rooms. 14 stories; interior corridors. Fee: parking. **Dining:** Dining room; 6:30 am-11 pm; $10-$20.
All Rooms: free & pay movies. **Cards:** AE, CB, DI, DS, JCB, MC, VI.   Roll in showers.

PHILADELPHIA AIRPORT RESIDENCE INN   Rates Subject to Change   **Phone: 215/492-1611**   49
Mon-Thurs [CP]   1P: $155   2P/1B: $155   2P/2B: $175
Fri-Sun [CP]   1P: $109   2P/1B: $109   2P/2B: $150
Apartment   **Location:** From I-95 (northbound, exit 11 or southbound, exit 13), 0.3 mi e on SR 291. 4630 Island Ave
Motel   19153. Fax: 215/492-1665. **Terms:** Pets, $6 extra charge, $100 dep req. **Facility:** 102 rooms. 2 stories;
interior/exterior corridors. **All Rooms:** kitchens, free movies. **Cards:** AE, DI, DS, MC, VI.
Roll in showers.

PHILADELPHIA MARRIOTT WEST   Rates Subject to Change   **Phone: 610/941-5600**   58
All Year   1P: $179   2P/1B: $199   2P/2B: $199   XP: $20
Hotel   **Location:** I-476 exit 6, 0.5 mi s on SR 23; I-76, exit 28B eastbound or exit 29 westbound, 0.5 mi s on SR
23. 111 Crawford St 19428. Fax: 610/941-4425. **Terms:** No pets. **Facility:** 286 rooms. Handling fee imposed;
17 stories; interior corridors. **Dining:** Restaurant; 6 am-11 pm; $15-$25. **All Rooms:** free & pay movies. **Cards:** AE, CB, DI,
DS, JCB, MC, VI.

RADISSON HOTEL PHILADELPHIA AIRPORT   Rates Subject to Change   **Phone: 610/521-5900**   41
Sun-Thurs   1P: $139- 149   2P/1B: $149- 159   2P/2B: $149- 159   XP: $10   F18
Fri & Sat   1P: $89- 109   2P/1B: $89- 109   2P/2B: $89- 109   XP: $10   F18
Hotel   **Location:** On SR 291, 1 mi e of jct SR 420, I-95 Essington/SR 420 exit 9A. 500 Stevens Dr 19113.
Fax: 610/521-4362. **Terms:** Sr. discount; check-in 4 pm; no pets. **Facility:** 353 rooms. 12 stories; interior corridors.
Dining: Restaurant; 6:30 am-11 pm; $8-$19. **All Rooms:** free & pay movies. **Cards:** AE, CB, DI, DS, JCB, MC, VI.

ROOSEVELT INN   Rates Subject to Change   **Phone: 215/338-7600**   51
All Year   1P: $50- 55   2P/1B: $55- 60   2P/2B: $55- 60   XP: $5   F12
Location: On US 1, 0.5 mi n of jct SR 73; 6 mi s of PA Tpk, exit 28. 7600 Roosevelt Blvd 19152.
Fax: 215/338-7609. **Terms:** Sr. discount; no pets. **Facility:** 106 rooms. 2 stories; interior corridors.
Motor Inn   **All Rooms:** free movies. **Cards:** AE, MC, VI. *(See ad below)*

WESTIN SUITES   **Phone: 215/365-6600**   43
Mon-Thurs   1P: $170   2P/1B: $170   2P/2B: $170   XP: $20   F18
Fri-Sun   1P: $89   2P/1B: $89   2P/2B: $89   XP: $20   F18
Location: Jct I-95 & SR 291 exit 11 (northbound), exit 13 (southbound). 4101 Island Ave 19153.
Fax: 215/492-8471. **Terms:** No pets. **Facility:** 251 rooms. Atrium style hotel at Gateway Center. 1-bedroom
suites with living room. 8 stories; interior corridors; sauna, steamroom, whirlpool; game room, horseshoes,
sand volleyball. **Dining & Entertainment:** Restaurant; 6 am-11 pm; $9-$21; cocktails/lounge. **Services:** valet laundry.
Recreation: jogging. **All Rooms:** coffeemakers, free & pay movies, refrigerators. **Some Rooms:** honor bars, microwaves,
whirlpools. Fee: VCR's. **Cards:** AE, CB, DI, DS, MC, VI.

RESTAURANTS

CAFE FLOWER SHOP   Lunch: $6-$8   Dinner: $13-$19   **Phone: 215/232-1076**   90
Location: 25th St just n of Fairmount Ave. 2501 Meredith St 19130. **Hours:** 6 pm-10 pm, Wed-Fri 11 am-3 &
American   5-10 pm, Sat 9 am-2:30 & 5-9:30 pm, Sun 9 am-2:30 pm. Closed: 11/26 & 12/25. **Features:** street parking; a
la carte. Indoor garden. Noted for their Sat & Sun brunch. Homestyle cooking from scratch. Outdoor dining in
season. Smoke free premises. **Cards:** AE, MC, VI.

CAFE ZESTY   Lunch: $8-$12   Dinner: $14-$30   **Phone: 215/483-6226**   91
Location: In Manayunk; off of Interstate 76, exit 31. 4382 Main St 19127. **Hours:** 11 am-10 pm, Fri & Sat-11
Ethnic   pm. Closed major holidays. **Reservations:** suggested. **Features:** casual dress; Sunday brunch; carryout;
cocktails & lounge; street parking & fee for valet parking; a la carte. Greco-Roman cuisine; the open kitchen
is in full view of the dining room. Smoke free premises. **Cards:** AE, DI, DS, MC, VI.

(See map p. 368)

COUNTRY CLUB RESTAURANT   Lunch: $4-$8   Dinner: $7-$14   Phone: 215/722-0500   (109)
AAA   **Location:** On SR 73, 1 mi nw of jct US 1 (Roosevelt Blvd). 1717 Cottman Ave 19111. **Hours:** 7 am-11 pm,
◆   Wed & Thurs-midnight, Fri & Sat-1 am. Closed: 12/25. **Reservations:** suggested; for 6 or more.
American   **Features:** children's menu; early bird specials; health conscious menu; carryout; cocktails; a la carte.
Bustling family restaurant & diner. Menu features sandwiches, comfort foods & extensive selection of freshly
baked pastry. **Cards:** AE, DI, DS, MC, VI.   ☒

FISHERS SEAFOOD RESTAURANT   Lunch: $4-$6   Dinner: $7-$16   Phone: 215/725-6201   (108)
◆◆   **Location:** Jct US 1 & SR 73 (Cottman Ave), 0.8 mi w on SR 73, just n. 7312 Castor Ave 19152. **Hours:** 11
Seafood   am-9 pm, Fri & Sat-10 pm, Sun noon-9 pm. Closed: 11/26, 12/25 & Mon. **Reservations:** suggested; for 5 or
more. **Features:** casual dress; children's menu; early bird specials; health conscious menu; carryout;
cocktails & lounge; a la carte. Popular. Nicely prepared food served in attractive dining rooms. Bakery. **Cards:** DS, MC, VI.   ☒

JAKE'S   Lunch: $11-$24   Dinner: $23-$34   Phone: 215/483-0444   (94)
◆◆◆   **Location:** In Manayunk, between Levering & Grape sts. 4365 Main St 19127. **Hours:** 11:30 am-2:30 &
Nouvelle   5:30-9:30 pm, Fri & Sat-10:30 pm, Sun 10:30 am-2:30 & 5-9 pm. **Reservations:** suggested.
American   **Features:** Sunday brunch; health conscious menu; carryout; cocktails; street parking & fee for valet parking;
a la carte. Popular crowded bistro in fashionable shopping district. Upscale casual atmosphere. Creative food
presentations reflect very modern & imaginative cuisine influences. Smoke free premises. **Cards:** AE, DI, MC, VI.   ☒

JOSEPH'S   Lunch: $6-$10   Dinner: $15-$27   Phone: 215/755-2770   (95)
◆◆   **Location:** Between 13th & Passyunk Ave. 1915 E Passyunk Ave 19148. **Hours:** noon-10 pm, Fri-midnight,
Italian   Sat 4 pm-midnight, Sun & Mon 4 pm-10 pm. Closed: 1/1, 11/26 & 12/25. **Reservations:** required; weekends.
Features: casual dress; carryout; cocktails & lounge; street parking; a la carte. South Philly friendly, with
bountiful portions. Fee for valet parking Fri & Sat nights. **Cards:** AE, MC, VI.

KANSAS CITY PRIME   Dinner: $17-$29   Phone: 215/482-3700   (97)
◆◆◆   **Location:** In Manayunk district; I-76 exit 31, 0.3 mi n on Green Ln, 0.3 mi e. 4417 Main St 19127.
Steak and   **Hours:** 5:30 pm-11 pm, Sun-10 pm. Closed: 11/26. **Reservations:** suggested. **Features:** casual dress;
Seafood   carryout; cocktails & lounge; fee for valet parking; a la carte. Specializing in char-grilled steak & seafood
presented in a comfortably sophisticated atmosphere. **Cards:** AE, CB, DI, DS, MC, VI.   ☒

LA COLLINA RESTAURANT   Lunch: $9-$16   Dinner: $15-$27   Phone: 610/668-1780   (106)
◆◆◆   **Location:** I-76, exit 31 Belmont Ave just s, Jefferson Ave just s. 37-41 Ashland Ave 19004. **Hours:** 11:30
Northern   am-2:30 & 5:30-10 pm, Fri-11 pm, Sat 5:30 pm-11 pm. Closed major holidays & Sun.
Italian   **Reservations:** suggested. **Features:** semi-formal attire; health conscious menu; cocktails & lounge; valet
parking; a la carte. Elegant dining with Italian ambience. Seafood is a specialty. **Cards:** AE, CB, DI, MC, VI.

LE BUS   Lunch: $6-$9   Dinner: $10-$16   Phone: 215/487-2663   (98)
◆   **Location:** From I-76, exit 31; 0.3 mi n on Green Ln, 0.5 mi e on Main St. 4266 Main St 19127. **Hours:** 11
American   am-10 pm, Wed-Fri to 11 pm, Sat 9:30 am-11:30 pm, Sun 9:30 am-10 pm. Closed: 11/26 & 12/25
Reservations: required; for 6 persons. **Features:** casual dress; children's menu; carryout; cocktails &
lounge; street parking; a la carte. Lively, family oriented atmosphere. Homemade bread, pasta, pastry & dessert. Sat & Sun
brunch. **Cards:** MC, VI.   ☒

THE MARKER   Lunch: $8-$15   Dinner: $12-$30   Phone: 215/581-5010   (107)
◆◆◆◆   **Location:** On US 1 (City Ave), just s of I-76, Schuylkill Expwy, exit 33; in Adam's Mark Hotel. City Ave at
American   Monument Rd 19131. **Hours:** 11:30 am-2:30 & 5:30-10:30 pm, Fri & Sat-11 pm; Sunday brunch seatings at
10:30 am & 2 pm, reservations recommended. **Reservations:** suggested. **Features:** semi-formal attire; early
bird specials; cocktails; valet parking; a la carte. Fine dining in elegant atmosphere. Nicely presented entrees. **Cards:** AE,
CB, DI, DS, JCB, MC, VI. *(See color ad p 367)*   ☒

POLLO ROSSO   Dinner: $14-$21   Phone: 215/248-9338   (100)
◆◆   **Location:** From I-276, exit 25; 5.5 mi e on Germantown Pike; in Chestnut Hill Hotel. 8229 Germantown Ave
Italian   19118. **Hours:** 5 pm-10 pm, Fri & Sat-11 pm, Sun-9:30 pm. Closed: 11/26, 12/24 & 12/25
Reservations: suggested. **Features:** casual dress; children's menu; carryout; cocktails; a la carte. Features
a wood-burning pizza oven & a menu built around pasta & grilled dishes. **Cards:** AE, CB, DI, MC, VI.   ☒

SONOMA   Lunch: $6-$11   Dinner: $9-$14   Phone: 215/483-9400   (101)
◆◆   **Location:** In Manayunk district; I-76 exit 31, 0.3 mi n on Green Ln, 0.3 mi e. 4411 Main St 19127. **Hours:** 11
Italian   am-11 pm, Fri & Sat-midnight. **Reservations:** suggested; for 6 or more. **Features:** casual dress; Sunday
brunch; early bird specials; health conscious menu; carryout; cocktails & lounge; fee for valet parking; a la
carte. "Italifornia" cuisine, which combines the fresh herbs, olive oil & vegetable components of Italian cooking with the fun &
casual elements of California eating. **Cards:** AE, DI, DS, MC, VI.   ☒

STEPHEN'S   Dinner: $18-$40   Phone: 215/487-3136   (103)
◆◆◆   **Location:** Just n of Main St. 105 Shurs Ln 19127. **Hours:** 5:30 pm-10 pm, Fri & Sat-11 pm, Sun 5 pm-9 pm
Ethnic   Closed major holidays & Mon. **Reservations:** suggested. **Features:** carryout; cocktails & lounge; street
parking; a la carte. Located in trendy Manayunk District. Upscale casual dining atmosphere in renovated
Victorian stone house. Mediterranean cuisine with emphasis on Italian. **Cards:** AE, DI, MC, VI.

UMBRIA   Dinner: $20-$30   Phone: 215/242-6470   (105)
◆◆◆   **Location:** Between Germantown, Mount Pleasant & Mount Airy. 7131 Germantown Ave 19119. **Hours:** 6
American   pm-9 pm. Closed major holidays & Mon. **Reservations:** required. **Features:** casual dress; street parking; a
la carte. Intimate, chic bistro featuring an eclectic menu. Smoke free premises.   ☒

The Philadelphia Vicinity

ARDMORE—12,600   (See map p. 368; index p. 366)

RESTAURANT

THAI PEPPER RESTAURANT **Lunch:** $5-$7 **Dinner:** $8-$17 **Phone:** 610/642-5951 [153]
(AAA) [SAVE] **Location:** Center on US 30. 64 E Lancaster Ave 19003. **Hours:** 11:30 am-3 & 5-10 pm, Fri & Sat 5
◆◆ pm-10:30 pm, Sun 4 pm-9:30 pm. **Reservations:** suggested; weekend. **Features:** casual dress; carryout;
Ethnic street parking; a la carte. Extensive menu with variety of Thai specialties including tofu & curry dishes.
Smoke free premises. **Cards:** AE, DI, DS, MC, VI. **Special Value: $3 off the price of a dinner entree.** [X]

AVONDALE—1,000

RESTAURANT

THE FARM HOUSE RESTAURANT **Lunch:** $5-$10 **Dinner:** $15-$27 **Phone:** 610/268-2235
◆◆◆ **Location:** From SR 41, center of town, 2 mi n on Church St, 0.5 mi w. 514 McCue Rd 19311. **Hours:** 11:30
Continental am-3 & 5-9 pm. **Closed:** 1/1, 12/24 & 12/25. **Reservations:** suggested. **Features:** dressy casual; cocktails &
lounge. 18th century farm house charmingly decorated in country antiques & folk art. Seasonal outdoor
dining patio overlooks 18-hole golf course. Specialties include crab cakes, lamb & veal. **Cards:** AE, DS, MC, VI. [X]

BENSALEM—3,000   (See map p. 368; index p. 366)

LODGINGS

COMFORT INN Rates Subject to Change **Phone:** 215/245-0100 [30]
◆◆◆ All Year [CP] 1P: $85- 115 2P/1B: $85- 115 2P/2B: $90- 100 XP: $10 F16
Motel **Location:** Just se on SR 132 from jct US 1. 3660 Street Rd 19020. **Fax:** 215/245-1851. **Terms:** Sr. discount;
pets, $25 dep req. **Facility:** 141 rooms. 2 king suites, $119. Handling fee imposed; 3 stories; interior/exterior
corridors. **All Rooms:** free movies. **Cards:** AE, DI, DS, MC, VI. [🐾] [ECTV] [X] [🖊] [D]

COURTYARD BY MARRIOTT BENSALEM Rates Subject to Change **Phone:** 215/639-9100 [31]
◆◆◆ 5/1-9/30 1P: $109 2P/1B: $109 2P/2B: $119
Motor Inn 10/1-4/30 1P: $89 2P/1B: $89 2P/2B: $89
Location: 1 mi se on SR 132 from jct US 1. 3327 Street Rd 19020. **Fax:** 215/639-4598. **Terms:** Check-in 4
pm; no pets. **Facility:** 167 rooms. 6 stories; interior corridors. **Dining:** Coffee shop; 6:30-10:30 am, Sat & Sun 7-11 am.
All Rooms free & pay movies **Cards:** AE, CB, DI, DS, JCB, MC, VI. *(See color ad p 371)*
Roll in showers. [🛁] [CTV] [X] [🖊] [D] [S]

HAMPTON INN PHILADELPHIA NORTH EAST Rates Subject to Change **Phone:** 215/245-5222 [33]
◆◆◆ All Year [CP] 1P: $79- 109 2P/1B: $91- 115 2P/2B: $85- 109
Motel **Location:** Jct US 13 & I-95, Woodhaven Rd exit, 0.3 mi w on US 13. 1329 Bristol Pike 19020.
Fax: 215/245-1314. **Terms:** Sr. discount; no pets. **Facility:** 141 rooms. 2 whirlpool rms, $115-$135; 3 stories;
interior corridors. **All Rooms:** free movies. **Cards:** AE, CB, DI, DS, MC, VI. [🛁] [CTV] [🔥] [X] [🖊] [D] [S]

HOLIDAY INN-PHILADELPHIA NORTHEAST **Phone:** 215/638-1500 [34]
(AAA) [SAVE] 5/29-9/7 1P: $109 2P/1B: $109 2P/2B: $109
◆◆ 5/1-5/28 & 9/8-4/30 1P: $94 2P/1B: $94 2P/2B: $94
Motor Inn **Location:** On SR 132, just se of jct US 1. 3499 Street Rd 19020. **Fax:** 215/638-8547. **Terms:** Check-in 4
pm; monthly rates; package plans; no pets. **Facility:** 117 rooms. Guest rooms with varied appointments
ranging from vintage to contemporary. 2 stories; interior/exterior corridors; wading pool. **Dining &**
Entertainment: Restaurant; 6:30 am-2 & 5-10 pm, Sun-9 pm; $6-$15; cocktails/lounge. **Services:** Fee: coin laundry.
All Rooms: free & pay movies. **Some Rooms:** coffeemakers. **Cards:** AE, CB, DI, DS, JCB, MC, VI. **Special Amenities:**
Early check-in/late check-out and free newspaper. [🛁] [🍴] [CTV] [X] [🖊] [D]

MCINTOSH INN OF BENSALEM Rates Subject to Change **Phone:** 215/245-0111 [35]
◆◆ 6/29-8/30 [CP] 1P: $55- 69 2P/1B: $75- 83 2P/2B: $72- 79 XP: $7 F18
Motel 5/1-6/28 & 8/31-4/30 [CP] 1P: $50- 56 2P/1B: $57- 63 2P/2B: $57- 63 XP: $7 F18
Location: Just se on SR 132 from jct US 1. 3671 Street Rd 19020. **Fax:** 215/244-4999. **Terms:** Sr. discount;
no pets. **Facility:** 111 rooms. Weekend rates may be higher; 5 stories; interior corridors. **All Rooms:** free movies.
Cards: AE, CB, DI, MC, VI. *(See color ad p 353)* Roll in showers. [CTV] [♿] [X] [🖊] [D] [S]

RESTAURANT

FISHER'S TUDOR HOUSE **Lunch:** $4-$10 **Dinner:** $8-$24 **Phone:** 215/244-9777 [85]
◆◆ **Location:** On SR 132, 2 mi w of jct I-95. 1858 Street Rd 19020. **Hours:** 11 am-10 pm, Sun 1 pm-9 pm.
Seafood **Closed:** 11/26, 12/25 & Mon. **Reservations:** suggested. **Features:** casual dress; children's menu; carryout;
cocktails & lounge. Popular restaurant serving nicely prepared food. Bakery. **Cards:** AE, DS, MC, VI. [X]

BERWYN—3,200

LODGING

RESIDENCE INN BY MARRIOTT Rates Subject to Change **Phone:** 610/640-9494
◆◆◆ 11/23-12/31 [CP] 1P: $165 2P/1B: $165 2P/2B: $199
Apartment 5/1-11/22 & 1/1-4/30 [CP] 1P: $155 2P/1B: $155 2P/2B: $169
Motel **Location:** From US 202, Devon exit, then SR 252 (Swedesford Rd) 1 mi s. 600 W Swedesford Rd 19312.
Fax: 610/993-0330. **Terms:** Sr. discount; reserv deposit, 7 day notice; pets, $6 extra charge, $100 dep req.
Facility: 88 rooms. 2 stories; exterior corridors. **All Rooms:** kitchens, free movies. **Cards:** AE, CB, DI, JCB, MC, VI.
[🐾] [🛁] [CTV] [X] [D]

BLUE BELL—6,100

RESTAURANT

BLUE BELL INN Historical **Lunch:** $6-$12 **Dinner:** $15-$25 **Phone:** 215/646-2010
◆◆◆ **Location:** On SR 73, 1.5 mi e of jct US 202. 601 Skippack Pike 19422. **Hours:** 11:30 am-2:30 & 4:30-10
American pm. Closed major holidays, Sun & Mon. **Reservations:** suggested. **Features:** dressy casual; children's
menu; early bird specials; carryout; cocktails & lounge; entertainment; a la carte. Since 1743, the Blue Bell
Inn has been serving guests food & beverage & was marked on George Washington's military maps of 1777. Today guests
enjoy well-prepared food served in a contemporary & spacious atmosphere. **Cards:** AE, MC, VI. [X]

CENTER SQUARE—700

RESTAURANT

TIFFANY DINING PLACE & GAZEBO   **Dinner:** $10-$19   **Phone:** 610/272-1888
◬
Location: On US 202, 0.3 mi ne of jct SR 73. 799 Dekalb Pike 19422. **Hours:** 5 pm-10 pm, Fri-11 pm, Sat
♦♦   4:15 pm-11 pm, Sun 10:30 am-2 & 3:30-10 pm. Closed: 12/25. **Reservations:** suggested. **Features:** casual
American   dress; Sunday brunch; children's menu; early bird specials; health conscious menu; salad bar; cocktails &
lounge. Popular eatery in Victorian style dining rooms. Featuring some mesquite grill items. Fresh fish.
Extensive salad bar. **Cards:** AE, DI, DS, MC, VI.   ⊠

CHADDS FORD—1,200

LODGING

BRANDYWINE RIVER HOTEL   **Phone:** 610/388-1200
◬ SAVE   All Year [CP]   1P: $125- 169   2P/1B: $125- 169 2P/2B: $125- 169   XP: $10   F12
Location: 2 mi w of US 202, at jct US 1 & SR 100. (PO Box 1058, 19317). Fax: 610/388-1200.
♦♦♦   **Terms:** Reserv deposit, 14 day notice; weekly/monthly rates; package plans; small pets only, $20, must be in
Motel   a cage. **Facility:** 40 rooms. Colonial ambience in historic setting; Queen Anne cherrywood furnishings. 10
whirlpool suites with fireplace, $149-$169. Handling fee imposed; 2 stories; interior corridors.
Dining: Afternoon tea; restaurant nearby. **Services:** valet laundry. **All Rooms:** free movies, combo or shower baths.
Fee: VCR. **Some Rooms:** coffeemakers. Fee: refrigerators. **Cards:** AE, CB, DI, DS, MC, VI. **Special Amenities: Free
breakfast and free newspaper.**   Roll in showers. 🛏 🍴 🈷 📶 CTV ⊠ D

RESTAURANT

CHADDS FORD INN RESTAURANT   Historical   **Lunch:** $6-$13   **Dinner:** $18-$30   **Phone:** 610/388-7361
♦♦   **Location:** On US 1 at jct SR 100. 19317. **Hours:** 11:30 am-2 & 5:30-10 pm, Fri & Sat 5 pm-10:30 pm, Sun
Regional   11 am-2 & 4-9 pm. Closed: 1/1, 7/4, 12/24 & 12/25. **Reservations:** suggested. **Features:** casual dress
American   Sunday brunch; children's menu; carryout; cocktails & lounge; a la carte. Dating from 1736, several dining
rooms with Brandywine decor. Innovative menu. **Cards:** AE, DI, DS, MC, VI.   ⊠

CONCORDVILLE—600

LODGING

BEST WESTERN CONCORDVILLE HOTEL & CONFERENCE CTR   **Phone:** 610/358-9400
◬ SAVE   All Year [CP]   1P: $109- 119   2P/1B: $119   2P/2B: $119   XP: $15   F12
Location: At jct US 322 W & 1. (US 322 & US 1, 19331). Fax: 610/358-9381. **Terms:** Monthly rates
♦♦♦   package plans; no pets. **Facility:** 116 rooms. English country style hotel. Spacious deluxe guest rooms, suites
Hotel   & parlors. 6 whirlpool rms, $175-$200; 5 stories; interior corridors; sauna, whirlpool; aerobic instruction, hair
salon, travel agency, tanning bed. **Dining & Entertainment:** Cocktails/lounge; also, Concordville Inn, see
separate listing. **Services:** valet laundry. Fee: massage. **All Rooms:** honor bars, free movies. **Some Rooms:** refrigerators
Fee: VCR's. **Cards:** AE, CB, DI, DS, JCB, MC, VI. **Special Amenities: Free newspaper and free room upgrade (subject
to availability with advanced reservations).**   ⇔ 🍴 🈯 🈷 CTV ⊠ 🈁 D S

RESTAURANT

CONCORDVILLE INN   **Lunch:** $8-$21   **Dinner:** $22-$30   **Phone:** 610/459-2230
♦♦   **Location:** At jct US 322 W & US 1; in Best Western Concordville Hotel & Conference Ctr. 780 Baltimore
American   Pike 19331. **Hours:** 11 am-3 & 5-10 pm, Sun 1 pm-9 pm. Closed: 12/25. **Reservations:** suggested
VI.   **Features:** casual dress; children's menu; carryout; cocktails & lounge. Rustic decor. **Cards:** AE, DI, DS, MC
⊠

CONSHOHOCKEN—8,100   (See map p. 368; index p. 366)

RESTAURANT

SPRING MILL CAFÉ   **Lunch:** $8-$15   **Dinner:** $17-$22   **Phone:** 610/828-2550   161
♦♦♦   **Location:** Rt 76W, Conshohocken exit, over Fayette Bridge right on Elm St, left on Sandy St, right on Hector
Ethnic   St, then right. 164 Barren Hill Rd 19428. **Hours:** 9 am-10 pm. Closed: 7/4, 11/26 & 12/25
Reservations: suggested. **Features:** casual dress; Sunday brunch; carryout; a la carte. Intimate bistro
Housed in a rustic building that was once a post office. Featuring French, Mediterranean & Vietnamese cuisine. Afternoon
tea served.   ⊠

COVENTRYVILLE—400

RESTAURANT

COVENTRY FORGE INN RESTAURANT   Country Inn   **Dinner:** $16-$26   **Phone:** 610/469-6222
♦♦♦   **Location:** 5 mi s of Pottstown, 1.5 mi w of jct SR 100, off SR 23. 3360 Coventryville Rd 19465. **Hours:** 5:30
French   pm-9 pm, Sat 5 pm-10 pm. Closed major holidays, Sun & Mon. **Reservations:** suggested
Features: semi-formal attire; cocktails; a la carte. Fine cuisine served in 18th-century inn. Extensive wine
cellar. Sat prix fixe, $38.50. **Cards:** AE, CB, DI, MC, VI.   ⊠

ESSINGTON   (See map p. 368; index p. 366)

LODGINGS

COMFORT INN AIRPORT   **Phone:** 610/521-9800   74
◬ SAVE   All Year [CP]   1P: $66- 105   2P/1B: $66- 105   2P/2B: $66- 105   XP: $5   F
Location: On SR 291, just s of jct SR 420, 0.3 mi s of I-95 Essington exit SR 420. 53 Industrial Hwy 19029
♦♦♦   Fax: 610/521-4847. **Terms:** Weekly/monthly rates; small pets only, $10 extra charge. **Facility:** 150 rooms
Motel   Comfortably decorated units & public areas with contemporary decor. 10 whirlpool rms, extra charge; 3 stories
interior corridors. **Dining:** Restaurant nearby. **Services:** valet laundry. **All Rooms:** free & pay movies
Some Rooms: Fee: microwaves, refrigerators. **Cards:** AE, DI, DS, MC, VI. **Special Amenities: Free breakfast and free
newspaper.**   🛏 🍴 🈯 🈷 CTV ⊠ 🈁 D S

HOLIDAY INN-AIRPORT   **Phone:** 610/521-2400   🅦
◬ SAVE   All Year   1P: $119   2P/1B: $129   2P/2B: $129   XP: $10   F1
Location: On SR 291 at jct SR 420; 0.3 mi se of I-95, exit 9A, Essington 420. 45 Industrial Hwy 19029
♦♦♦   Fax: 610/521-1605. **Terms:** Pets. **Facility:** 303 rooms. 6 stories; interior corridors. **Dining & Entertainment:**
Motor Inn   Dining room, coffee shop; 7 am-2 & 5-10 pm; $13-$18; cocktails/lounge. **Services:** valet laundry
All Rooms: free & pay movies. **Some Rooms:** coffeemakers. Fee: refrigerators. **Cards:** AE, CB, DI, DS
MC, VI. **Special Amenities: Free room upgrade and preferred room (each subject to availability with advanced
reservations).** *(See color ad p 357)*   🛏 ⇔ 🈯 🈷 🈷 CTV ⊠ 🈁 D S

(See map p. 368)

RAMADA INN-PHILADELPHIA INTERNATIONAL AIRPORT   Guaranteed Rates   **Phone:** 610/521-9600   70
◆◆◆   All Year   1P: $75   2P/1B: $75   2P/2B: $75
Hotel   **Location:** I-95, exit 9A; 0.5 mi w on SR 291. 76 Industrial Hwy 19029. Fax: 610/521-9388. **Terms:** Small pets only. **Facility:** 292 rooms. 7 stories; interior corridors. **Dining:** Restaurant; 6 am-11 pm; $10-$17.
All Rooms: Fee: movies. **Cards:** AE, CB, DI, DS, MC, VI. *(See ad p 360)*   [icons]

RED ROOF INN-AIRPORT   Rates Subject to Change   **Phone:** 610/521-5090   73
◆◆   5/1-10/31   2P/2B: $71   2P/2B: $71   XP: $7   F18
Motel   11/1-4/30   2P/1B: $67   2P/2B: $67   XP: $7   F18
    Location: On SR 291, just s of jct SR 420; 0.3 mi se of I-95, exit 9A, Essington SR 420. 49 Industrial Hwy 19029. Fax: 610/521-4019. **Terms:** Small pets only. **Facility:** 134 rooms. 2-3 stories; exterior corridors. **All Rooms:** free & pay movies. **Cards:** AE, CB, DI, DS, MC, VI.   [icons]

RESTAURANT

THE LOGOON RESTAURANT & NITE CLUB   **Dinner:** $10-$20   **Phone:** 610/521-1400   117
◆◆   **Location:** Just s of I-95, exit 9A, on SR 420. 101 Taylor Ave 19029. **Hours:** 11 am-10 pm, Fri & Sat-11 pm.
Seafood   Closed: 12/25. **Reservations:** suggested. **Features:** casual dress; carryout; cocktails & lounge; entertainment; fee for valet parking; a la carte. Live bands Wed, Fri & Sat nights. Dynamic atmosphere. Smoke free premises. **Cards:** AE, DI, DS, MC, VI.   [icon]

EXTON—2,600

LODGINGS

DULING-KURTZ HOUSE & COUNTRY INN   Rates Subject to Change   **Phone:** 610/524-1830
◆◆◆   Fri & Sat [CP]   1P: $80- 120   2P/1B: $80- 120   2P/2B: $80- 120   XP: $25
Country Inn   Sun-Thurs [CP]   1P: $55- 79   2P/1B: $55- 79   2P/2B: $55- 79   XP: $25
    Location: 1 mi w on SR 30, from jct SR 100, 0.5 mi s. 146 S Whitford Rd 19341. Fax: 610/524-6258. **Terms:** Age restrictions may apply; no pets. **Facility:** 15 rooms. 3 stories; interior corridors. **Dining:** Dining room, see separate listing. **All Rooms:** free movies. **Cards:** AE, CB, DI, DS, MC, VI.   [icons]

HOLIDAY INN EXPRESS   Rates Subject to Change   **Phone:** 610/524-9000
◆◆◆   All Year [CP]   1P: $72   2P/1B: $72   2P/2B: $72   XP: $5   F18
Motel   **Location:** Jct US 30 & SR 100, 3 mi s of PA Tpk, exit 23. 120 N Pottstown Pike 19341. Fax: 610/524-7259. **Terms:** Small pets only. **Facility:** 124 rooms. 4 stories; interior corridors. **All Rooms:** free & pay movies. **Cards:** AE, CB, DI, DS, JCB, MC, VI.   [icons]

RESTAURANTS

CHINA ROYAL   **Lunch:** $5-$7   **Dinner:** $8-$15   **Phone:** 610/363-1553
◆◆   **Location:** Jct US 30 & SR 100, 4 mi s of PA Tpk, exit 23. 201-30 W Lincoln Hwy 19341. **Hours:** 11:30
Chinese   am-9:30 pm, Sat-10 pm, Sun noon-9 pm. Closed: 11/26 & 12/25. **Reservations:** suggested. **Features:** casual dress; carryout; a la carte. Attractive restaurant, with an extensive menu selection. **Cards:** AE, DS, MC, VI.   [icon]

DULING-KURTZ HOUSE & COUNTRY INN   **Lunch:** $12-$18   **Dinner:** $22-$38   **Phone:** 610/524-1830
◆◆◆   **Location:** 1 mi w on SR 30, from jct SR 100, 0.5 mi s; in Duling-Kurtz House & Country Inn. 146 S Whitford
Continental   Rd 19341. **Hours:** 11:30 am-3 & 5-11 pm, Sat from 5 pm, Sun from 3 pm. **Reservations:** suggested. **Features:** semi-formal attire; cocktails & lounge; a la carte. Seven intimate dining rooms in 1830's country inn, all furnished in antiques. Menu features veal, lamb & farm raised game. **Cards:** AE, CB, DI, DS, MC, VI.   [icon]

FAIRVILLE—200

LODGING

FAIRVILLE INN   Rates Subject to Change   **Phone:** 610/388-5900
◆◆◆   All Year [CP]   1P: $140- 195   2P/1B: $140- 195   2P/2B: $140- 195   XP: $15
Country Inn   **Location:** 2 mi s on SR 52 from US 1. Rt 52 19357 (PO Box 219, MENDENHALL). Fax: 610/388-5902. **Terms:** Age restrictions may apply; reserv deposit, 5 day notice; no pets. **Facility:** 15 rooms. Handling fee imposed; 2 stories; interior/exterior corridors. **Cards:** AE, DS, MC, VI.   [icons]

FRAZER (CHESTER COUNTY)

LODGINGS

MCINTOSH INN OF MALVERN   Rates Subject to Change   **Phone:** 610/651-0400
◆◆   All Year [CP]   1P: $65- 71   2P/1B: $72- 78   2P/2B: $72   XP: $6   F18
Motel   **Location:** On US 30 at jct SR 29. One Moorehall Rd 19355. Fax: 610/647-9434. **Terms:** Sr. discount; no pets. **Facility:** 91 rooms. 12 large rooms with microwave & refrigerator, $67.95-$74.95; 4 stories; interior corridors. **All Rooms:** free movies. **Cards:** AE, CB, DI, MC. *(See color ad p 353)*   [icons]

SHERATON GREAT VALLEY HOTEL   Rates Subject to Change   **Phone:** 610/524-5500
◆◆◆   Sun-Thurs   1P: $115- 150   2P/1B: $125- 160   2P/2B: $125- 160   XP: $10   F17
Motor Inn   Fri & Sat   1P: $99- 115   2P/1B: $99- 115   2P/2B: $99- 115   XP: $10   F17
    Location: On SR 30 & jct SR 202. 707 Lancaster Pike 19355. Fax: 610/524-1808. **Terms:** Sr. discount; check-in 4 pm; no pets. **Facility:** 154 rooms. Presidential suite, $395 for up to 5 persons; drawing room suites, $195; Ambassador suite $295; 5 stories; interior corridors. **Dining:** Restaurant; also, The White Horse Tavern, see separate listing. **All Rooms:** free & pay movies. **Cards:** AE, CB, DI, DS, MC, VI. *(See color ad p 379)*   [icons]

RESTAURANT

THE WHITE HORSE TAVERN   **Lunch:** $7-$20   **Dinner:** $13-$30   **Phone:** 610/594-2650
◆◆◆   **Location:** On SR 30 & jct SR 202; in Sheraton Great Valley Hotel. 707 Lancaster Pike 19355. **Hours:** 6
Continental   am-10 pm, Sat 7:30 am-11:30 & 6-10 pm, Sun 7:30 am-2:30 & 5:30-9:30 pm. **Reservations:** suggested. **Features:** Sunday brunch; children's menu; early bird specials; senior's menu; cocktails & lounge; also prix fixe. Upscale casual dining in 5 intimate dining rooms of restored 18th century Colonial farmhouse. **Cards:** AE, CB, DI, DS, MC, VI.   [icon]

GLENSIDE—8,700 (See map p. 368; index p. 366)

RESTAURANT

ALFIO'S RESTAURANT   **Lunch:** $4-$11   **Dinner:** $7-$19   **Phone:** 215/885-3787   (166)
◆◆   **Location:** PA Turnpike exit 27 (Willow Grove), 5 mi s on Easton Rd, 0.5 mi w on Glenside, just n. 15
Italian   Limekiln Pike 19038. **Hours:** 11:30 am-10 pm, Fri-11 pm, Sat 4 pm-11 pm; Sun 4 pm-9 pm. Closed major
holidays & Mon. **Reservations:** suggested; weekends. **Features:** casual dress; carryout; cocktails. Pasta,
seafood & veal entrees. Caesar salad is a specialty. **Cards:** AE, DI, DS, MC, VI.   (X)

GWYNEDD—600

RESTAURANT

WILLIAM PENN INN   **Lunch:** $7-$16   **Dinner:** $19-$32   **Phone:** 215/699-9272
◆◆◆   **Location:** At jct US 202 & Sumneytown Pike. 1017 Dekalb Pike 19436. **Hours:** 11:30 am-2:30 &
Continental   Sat 11:30 am-2:30 & 4:30-10 pm, Sun 10:30 am-8 pm. Closed: 12/25. **Reservations:** suggested.
Features: formal attire; Sunday brunch; children's menu; early bird specials; health conscious menu;
carryout; cocktails & lounge; a la carte. Long established; serving extensive menu of international dishes. Smoke free
premises. **Cards:** AE, CB, DI, DS, MC, VI.   (X)

HAVERTOWN—30,000 (See map p. 368; index p. 366)

RESTAURANT

NAIS CUISINE   **Dinner:** $13-$23   **Phone:** 610/789-5983   (156)
(AAA)   **Location:** Ne of I-476 & SR 3, on W Benedict Ave, just off Darby Rd. 13-17 W Benedict Ave 19083.
Hours: 5 pm-9 pm, Fri & Sat-10 pm. Closed: 1/1. **Reservations:** suggested. **Features:** dressy casual;
◆◆   carryout; street parking; a la carte. French style cooking with an Oriental flair. Opposite city parking lot.
French   **Cards:** AE, MC, VI.   (X)

HONEY BROOK (CHESTER COUNTY)

LODGING

WAYNEBROOK INN   Rates Subject to Change   **Phone:** 610/273-2444
◆◆◆   Fri & Sat   1P: $78- 205   2P/1B: $78- 205   2P/2B: $128   XP: $8   F18
Historic Bed   Sun-Thurs   1P: $58- 150   2P/1B: $58- 150   2P/2B: $108   XP: $8   F18
& Breakfast   **Location:** Jct of US 322 & SR 10 (Main St). (PO Box 610, HONEY BROOK, 19344). **Fax:** 610/273-2137.
Terms: Small pets only. **Facility:** 20 rooms. 4 stories; interior corridors. **Cards:** AE, MC, VI.
  (🛏) (CTV) (X) (D)

HORSHAM—15,100 (See map p. 368; index p. 366)

LODGINGS

HORSHAM DAYS INN   Rates Subject to Change   **Phone:** 215/674-2500   (62)
◆◆◆   All Year [CP]   1P: $88- 96   2P/1B: $88- 96   2P/2B: $88- 96   XP: $6   F
Motel   **Location:** On SR 611N, exit 27 off PA tpk, 1 mi n on SR 611 (Easton Rd). 245 Easton Rd 19044.
Fax: 215/674-0145. **Terms:** No pets. **Facility:** 171 rooms. 4 stories; interior corridors. **All Rooms:** free & pay
movies. **Cards:** AE, CB, DI, DS, MC, VI.   (🕂) (CTV) (X) (🕭) (D) (S)

RESIDENCE INN BY MARRIOTT-WILLOW GROVE   Rates Subject to Change   **Phone:** 215/443-7330   (60)
◆◆◆   All Year [CP]   1P: $139   2P/1B: $139   2P/2B: $169
Apartment   **Location:** From PA Tpk exit 27, 1 mi n on SR 611, 1.3 mi w on Dresher Rd. 3 Walnut Grove Dr 19044.
Motel   **Fax:** 215/443-7330. **Terms:** Pets, $150 extra charge. **Facility:** 118 rooms. 28 two-bedroom suites, $169; 2 sto-
ries; exterior corridors. **All Rooms:** free movies. **Cards:** AE, DI, DS, MC, VI.
  (🛏) (🏊) (🕂) (CTV) (🕭) (X) (🕭) (D) (S)

KENNETT SQUARE—5,200

LODGINGS

LONGWOOD INN   **Phone:** 610/444-3515
(AAA) (SAVE)   All Year [CP]   1P: $74   2P/1B: $80   2P/2B: $80   XP: $6   F12
Location: On US 1; 0.5 mi s of Longwood Gardens. 815 E Baltimore Pike 19348. Fax: 610/444-4285.
◆◆   **Terms:** Weekly/monthly rates; no pets. **Facility:** 28 rooms. Very attractive landscaping in season. 1 story; ex-
Motor Inn   terior corridors. **Dining & Entertainment:** Lite fare menu in lounge 5 pm-9 pm; cocktail lounge. **All Rooms:**
breakfast.   Fee: VCR. **Cards:** AE, DI, DS, MC, VI. **Special Amenities:** Early check-in/late check-out and free
breakfast.   (🕭) (CTV) (X) (D)

SCARLETT HOUSE   **Phone:** 610/444-9592
(AAA) (SAVE)   All Year [BP]   1P: $85- 135   2P/1B: $85- 135   2P/2B: $135   XP: $30
Location: 5 blks w. 503 W State St 19348. Fax: 610/925-0373. **Terms:** Age restrictions may apply; check-in
◆◆◆   4 pm; reserv deposit, 5 day notice; weekly rates; no pets, pet on premises. **Facility:** 4 rooms. Stone mano
Historic Bed   built in Foursquare architectural style. Attractively furnished with Victorian antiques circa late 1800's. Handling
& Breakfast   fee imposed; 3 stories; interior corridors; smoke free premises. **All Rooms:** no phones. **Cards:** AE, DS, MC
VI. **Special Amenities:** Early check-in/late check-out and free breakfast.   (X) (D)

KING OF PRUSSIA—18,400

LODGINGS

BEST WESTERN-THE INN AT KING OF PRUSSIA   **Phone:** 610/265-4500
(AAA) (SAVE)   1/1-4/30 [CP]   1P: $105- 115   2P/1B: $105- 115   2P/2B: $115- 125   XP: $10   F12
   5/1-12/31 [CP]   1P: $95- 105   2P/1B: $95- 105   2P/2B: $105- 115   XP: $10   F12
◆◆◆   **Location:** On US 202N & S Gulph Rd, 1.3 mi e of tpk exit 24, e of I-76 exit 26A westbound, 26B eastbound.
Motel   127 S Gulph Rd 19406. Fax: 610/337-0672. **Terms:** Weekly/monthly rates; package plans; no pets.
Facility: 168 rooms. Garden type property. 18 executive rooms with upgraded amenities $85-$105; 2 stories;
interior/exterior corridors. **Dining:** Restaurant nearby. **Services:** Fee: coin laundry. **All Rooms:** free & pay movies, combo o
shower baths. **Some Rooms:** Fee: whirlpools. **Cards:** AE, CB, DI, DS, MC, VI. **Special Amenities:** Free breakfast and
free newspaper. (See color ad p 379)   Roll in showers. (🏊) (🕭) (🕂) (CTV) (X) (🕭) (D)

OMFORT INN VALLEY FORGE
Phone: 610/962-0700
All Year [CP] 1P: $77- 129 2P/1B: $87- 139 2P/2B: $77- 139 XP: $10 F17
Location: On US 202N, 0.7 mi ne of I-76, exit 26; from PA Tpk exit 24 (Valley Forge) 1 mi ne. 550 W Dekalb Pike 19406. Fax: 610/962-0218. Terms: Monthly rates; no pets. Facility: 121 rooms. 5 stories; interior corridors. Dining: Restaurant nearby. Services: valet laundry. All Rooms: free & pay movies, combo or shower baths. Some Rooms: honor bars, coffeemakers, refrigerators, VCR's. Cards: AE, CB, DI, DS, JCB, C, VI. Special Amenities: Free breakfast and free newspaper.
Roll in showers.

AIRFIELD BY MARRIOTT-VALLEY FORGE
Rates Subject to Change
Phone: 610/337-0700
All Year [CP] 1P: $95 2P/1B: $95 2P/2B: $95
Location: Just off US 202N, 1 mi e of Tpk exit 24; just n of I-76, exit 25. 258 Mall Blvd 19406. Fax: 610/337-7027. Terms: Sr. discount; no pets. Facility: 80 rooms. 5 stories; interior corridors.
ll Rooms: free & pay movies. Cards: AE, CB, DI, DS, MC, VI.

AMPTON INN
Rates Subject to Change
Phone: 610/962-8111
All Year [CP] 1P: $85- 95 2P/1B: $99- 103 2P/2B: $97 XP: $8 F17
Location: On US 202N, 0.7 mi ne of I-76, exit 26B; from PA Tpk exit 24 (Valley Forge), 1 mi ne. 530 Dekalb Pike 19406. Fax: 610/962-5494. Terms: No pets. Facility: 148 rooms. 7 stories; interior corridors.
ll Rooms: free movies. Cards: AE, CB, DI, DS, JCB, MC, VI.

OLIDAY INN OF KING OF PRUSSIA
Phone: 610/265-7500
All Year 1P: $109- 119 2P/1B: $119 2P/2B: $119 XP: $10 F18
Location: Just w off US 202N, 1 mi e of tpk exit 24; just n of I-76 exit 25. 260 Mall Blvd 19406. Fax: 610/265-4076. Terms: Package plans; no pets. Facility: 225 rooms. Comfortable guest rooms; located adjacent to a large shopping mall. 5 stories; interior corridors; sauna, whirlpool, heated indoor lap pool; racquetball courts; indoor track. Dining & Entertainment: Dining room; 6:30 am-10 pm, Sat & Sun from 7 am; -$16; cocktails/lounge; entertainment. Services: valet laundry. All Rooms: free & pay movies. ome Rooms: refrigerators. Cards: AE, CB, DI, DS, MC, VI.

CINTOSH INN OF KING OF PRUSSIA
Rates Subject to Change
Phone: 610/768-9500
All Year [CP] 1P: $65- 67 2P/1B: $70 2P/2B: $71 XP: $5 F18
Location: 0.5 mi n of jct US 202 on SR 363 (Gulph Rd), exit 24 off PA Tpk. 260 N Gulph Rd 19406. Fax: 610/768-0225. Terms: Sr. discount; no pets. Facility: 212 rooms. 7 stories; interior corridors.
ll Rooms: free movies. Cards: AE, CB, DI, MC, VI. *(See color ad p 353)* Roll in showers.

HE PARK RIDGE AT VALLEY FORGE
Rates Subject to Change
Phone: 610/337-1800
All Year 1P: $179 2P/1B: $189 2P/2B: $189 XP: $10 F12
Location: On SR 363 (N Gulph Rd) 0.3 mi w of I-76, exit 24. 480 N Gulph Rd 19406. Fax: 610/337-4624. Terms: Sr. discount; no pets. Facility: 265 rooms. 6 stories; interior corridors. Dining: The Coppermill arvest, see separate listing. All Rooms: free & pay movies. Cards: AE, CB, DI, DS, JCB, MC, VI.
Roll in showers.

SHERATON VALLEY FORGE AND PLAZA SUITES HOTEL   Rates Subject to Change   Phone: 610/337-20●
♦♦♦   All Year   1P: $98- 130   2P/1B: $98- 142 2P/2B: $98- 142
Hotel   **Location:** On SR 363 (N Gulph Rd), 1.3 mi n of tpk exit 24 & I-76, exit 24; at Valley Forge Conventi●
Plaza. 1160 First Ave 19406. Fax: 610/768-3222. **Terms:** No pets. **Facility:** 480 rooms. Various theme suit●
$125-$175; 6-15 stories; interior corridors. **Dining:** 2 dining rooms, restaurant; 6:30 am-11 pm; $9-$30. **All Rooms:** free●
pay movies. **Cards:** AE, CB, DI, DS, MC, VI.   Roll in showers. 🖼️ 🖶 CTV ✕ 🖉 D ◻

RESTAURANTS

THE BARONS INNE   **Lunch:** $7-$13   **Dinner:** $20-$30   Phone: 610/265-25●
♦♦♦   **Location:** On SR 363 (N Gulph Rd) 0.3 mi w of I-76, exit 24. 499 N Gulph Rd 19406. **Hours:** 11 am-2:30
Continental   5-10 pm, Sat from 5 pm. Closed major holidays & Sun. **Reservations:** suggested. **Features:** dressy casu●
VI.   health conscious menu; carryout; cocktails & lounge. Elegant dining in Old World charm. **Cards:** AE, DI, M

CARLUCCI'S GILL N' GRILLE   **Lunch:** $7-$22   **Dinner:** $7-$22   Phone: 610/265-06●
♦♦   **Location:** Just s of jct US 202N & SR 363 (S Gulph Rd). 795 West DeKalb Pike 19406. **Hours:** 11 am-
Steak and   pm, Sun 10 am-10 pm. Closed: 12/25. **Reservations:** suggested. **Features:** casual dress; family brunc●
Seafood   children's menu; carryout; cocktails & lounge; a la carte. Bustling casual atmosphere. Menu features stea●
seafood, veal & chicken with Mediterranean & California influences. Sandwiches, pizza & other convenien●
foods avail. **Cards:** AE, DS, MC, VI.

CHARLEY'S PLACE   **Lunch:** $4-$8   **Dinner:** $8-$20   Phone: 610/337-86●
♦   **Location:** On SR 363 (N Gulph Rd), 0.5 mi n of jct US 202. N Gulph Rd & Mall Blvd 19406. **Hours:** 11:
American   am-10:30 pm, Fri-11 pm, Sat noon-11 pm, Sun 10:30 am-9:30 pm. Closed: 12/25. **Reservations:** suggeste●
Features: casual dress; Sunday brunch; children's menu; early bird specials; carryout; cocktails & loung●
Brandywine decor. Casual family dining. **Cards:** AE, CB, DI, DS, MC, VI.   ◻

THE COPPERMILL HARVEST   **Lunch:** $10-$15   **Dinner:** $18-$35   Phone: 610/337-18●
♦♦♦   **Location:** On SR 363 (N Gulph Rd), 0.3 mi w of I-76, exit 24; in The Park Ridge at Valley Forge. 480
American   Gulph Rd 19406. **Hours:** 6:30 am-2:30 & 5:30-10 pm. **Reservations:** suggested. **Features:** casual dres●
Sunday brunch; children's menu; early bird specials; carryout; cocktails & lounge; a la carte, buffet. Casu●
yet elegant atmosphere. Bountiful kiosk buffets. Menu features seafood, steak & pasta creatively prepared. **Cards:** AE, C●
DI, DS, JCB, MC, VI.   ◻

KENNEDY SUPPLEE MANSION RESTAURANT Historical **Lunch:** $8-$12 **Dinner:** $16-$26 **Phone:** 610/337-37●
♦♦♦   **Location:** From I-76 exit 24, 0.7 mi w on SR 363 n Gulph Rd to SR 23W, 0.3 mi. 1100 W Valley Forge ●
Continental   19406. **Hours:** 11:30 am-2 & 5:30-10 pm, Sat 5:30-10:30 pm. Closed major holidays & Su●
Reservations: suggested. **Features:** semi-formal attire; cocktails & lounge; valet parking; a la carte. Built ●
1852 with Italianate architectural detail. Elegant setting for very well prepared entrees. Private dining rooms avail. Smo●
free premises. **Cards:** AE, MC, VI.   ◻

KOBE   **Dinner:** $17-$33   Phone: 610/337-12●
♦♦♦   **Location:** On US 202N, 0.3 mi w of I-76, exit 26A; in Valley Forge Hilton. 251 W DeKalb Pike 1940●
Ethnic   **Hours:** 6 pm-10 pm, Sat from 4:30 pm, Sun 6 pm-9 pm. Closed: 1/1, 11/26 & 12/2●
Reservations: suggested. **Features:** casual dress; children's menu; senior's menu; cocktails & lounge.
very entertaining Japanese Hibachi house featuring the chef as the star attraction. Sushi bar. Smoke free premise●
Cards: AE, DI, JCB, MC, VI.   ◻

KINTNERSVILLE—200

LODGINGS

THE BUCKSVILLE HOUSE   Rates Subject to Change   Phone: 610/847-89●
♦♦♦   All Year [BP]   1P: $100- 130   2P/1B: $100- 130   XP: $35
Historic Bed   **Location:** 2 mi n on SR 412 (Durham Rd) from jct SR 611. 4501 Durham Rd, Rt 412 18930-161●
& Breakfast   Fax: 610/847-8948. **Terms:** Age restrictions may apply; reserv deposit, 7 day notice; 2 night min sta●
weekends; no pets. **Facility:** 5 rooms. 3 stories, no elevator; interior/exterior corridors; smoke free premise●
Cards: AE, DS, MC, VI.   ✕ ◻

LIGHTFARM   Phone: 610/847-32●
AAA SAVE   All Year [BP]   1P: $85- 125   2P/1B: $99- 145 2P/2B: $115- 150   XP: $20   D●
♦♦♦   **Location:** 0.5 mi s on Berger Rd from SR 412. 2042 Berger Rd 18930. Fax: 610/847-2926. **Terms:** A●
Historic Bed   restrictions may apply; reserv deposit, 7 day notice; small pets only, $15 fee, $15 dep req. **Facility:** 4 room●
& Breakfast   1815 farm with original floors. Very attractive public areas with period furnishings. Working farm. Archaeologi●
site & artifacts on property. 1 two-bedroom unit. 2 night minimum stay weekends & 10/1-10/31. Handling f●
imposed; 3 stories, no elevator; interior corridors; smoke free premises; whirlpool. **Recreation:** hiking tra●
All Rooms: combo or shower baths, no phones. **Some Rooms:** VCR's. **Cards:** AE, DS, MC, VI. **Special Amenities:** Fr●
breakfast and free local telephone calls.   🖳 🖬 CTV ✕ ◻

KULPSVILLE—5,200

LODGING

HOLIDAY INN-KULPSVILLE   Rates Subject to Change   Phone: 215/368-38●
♦♦♦   Sun-Thurs   1P: $79   2P/1B: $84- 89 2P/2B: $84   XP: $5   F●
Motor Inn   Fri & Sat   1P: $69   2P/1B: $69 2P/2B: $69   XP: $5   F●
Location: PA Tpk Northeast Extension I-476, exit 31. 1750 Sumneytown Pike 19443. Fax: 215/368-782●
Terms: Pets, $20 extra charge, at designated times. **Facility:** 183 rooms. 4 stories; interior corridors. **Dining:** Restaura●
6:45 am-2 & 5:30-10 pm; $5-$15. **All Rooms:** Fee: movies. **Cards:** AE, CB, DI, DS, MC, VI.   🖳 🖼️ CTV ✕ ◻

LAHASKA—200

LODGING

GOLDEN PLOUGH INN   Phone: 215/794-40●
AAA SAVE   All Year [CP]   1P: $105- 325   2P/1B: $105- 325 2P/2B: $105- 325   XP: $15
♦♦♦   **Location:** On SR 202 in Peddlers Village. SR 202 & Street Rd 18931. Fax: 215/794-4008. **Terms:** Rese●
Motor Inn   deposit; package plans; no pets. **Facility:** 60 rooms. Elegant guest rooms decorated in American coun●
charm. Seven different buildings scattered throughout unique shopping village. Winding brick paths throu●
pockets of flower gardens and antique shops. Suites, $200-$325; 3 stories; interior corridors. **Dining**
Entertainment: Dining room; 7 am-11 pm, Sun-9 pm; $12-$18; cocktails/lounge. **Services:** valet laund●
All Rooms: coffeemakers, refrigerators, combo or shower baths. **Some Rooms:** 4 kitchens, whirlpools. **Cards:** AE, CB, ●
DS, MC, VI.   🖬 CTV ✕ ◻

RESTAURANT

OCK 'N BULL RESTAURANT **Lunch:** $6-$10 **Dinner:** $15-$25 **Phone:** 215/794-4010
Location: On SR 263 in Peddler's Village. SR 263 & Street Rd 18931. **Hours:** 11 am-3 & 5-9 pm, Fri-10 pm, Sat 4 pm-10 pm, Sun 10 am-3 & 4-8 pm. Closed: 1/1, 12/25 & 12/24 for dinner. **Reservations:** suggested; for dinner. **Features:** casual dress; Sunday brunch; cocktails & lounge; a la carte. Bustling atmosphere. Good array of traditional favorites. Appealing decor accented by an eclectic collection of folk art. In the heart of a unique shopping area. **Cards:** AE, DI, DS, MC, VI.

ANDENBERG

LODGING

ORNERSTONE INN BED & BREAKFAST Rates Subject to Change **Phone:** 610/274-2143
All Year [BP] 1P: $65- 140 2P/1B: $75- 150 2P/2B: $75- 150 XP: $10-25
istoric Bed Breakfast **Location:** 5.1 mi s on Neward Rd from US 1 (Toughkenamon exit); at jct of Buttonwood Rd. 300 Buttonwood Rd 19350. Fax: 610/274-0734. **Terms:** Reserv deposit, 10 day notice; 2 night min stay, weekends 4/1-10/31; no pets, pets on premises. **Facility:** 11 rooms. Handling fee imposed; 1-3 stories, no elevator; interior/exterior orridors; smoke free premises. **Some Rooms:** 6 efficiencies. **Cards:** AE, DS, MC, VI.

ANGHORNE—1,400 (See map p. 368; index p. 366)

LODGINGS

CINTOSH INN OF OXFORD VALLEY Rates Subject to Change **Phone:** 215/757-4500 [111]
All Year [CP] 1P: $65- 86 2P/1B: $65- 86 2P/2B: $72- 86 XP: $7 F18
otel **Location:** Just e of I-95, Oxford Valley Rd exit, 0.5 mi n of Sesame Place. 3101 W Cabot Blvd 19047. Fax: 215/757-0196. **Terms:** No pets. **Facility:** 89 rooms. 4 stories; interior corridors. **All Rooms:** free ovies. **Cards:** AE, CB, DI, MC, VI. *(See color ad p 353)* Roll in showers.

ED ROOF INN-OXFORD VALLEY Rates Subject to Change **Phone:** 215/750-6200 [108]
5/1-8/31 2P/1B: $54- 75 2P/2B: $76- 80 XP: $7 F18
otel 9/1-9/30 & 4/1-4/30 2P/1B: $62- 71 2P/2B: $66- 77 XP: $7 F18
10/1-3/31 2P/1B: $54- 71 2P/2B: $64- 71 XP: $7 F18
Location: Just e of I-95, Oxford Valley Rd exit, 0.5 mi n of Sesame Place. 3100 Cabot Blvd W 19047. Fax: 215/750-6205. **Terms:** Small pets only. **Facility:** 91 rooms. 3 stories; exterior corridors. **All Rooms:** free & pay movies. **Cards:** AE, CB, DI, S, MC, VI.

HERATON BUCKS COUNTY HOTEL **Phone:** 215/547-4100 [110]
7/31-9/7 1P: $179 2P/1B: $194 2P/2B: $194 XP: $15 F17
6/12-7/30 1P: $169 2P/1B: $184 2P/2B: $184 XP: $15 F17
5/1-6/11 1P: $159 2P/1B: $174 2P/2B: $174 XP: $15 F17
9/8-4/30 1P: $135 2P/1B: $154 2P/2B: $154 XP: $15 F17
otel **Location:** 0.8 mi e of I-95, exit Oxford Valley Rd; opposite Sesame Place. 400 Oxford Valley Rd 19047. ax: 215/269-3400. **Terms:** Reserv deposit; package plans; no pets. **Facility:** 186 rooms. Family oriented property located di-ctly across from Sesame Place & local shopping mall. Large guest rooms, nicely decorated. 15 stories; interior corridors; xury level rooms; wading pool, saunas, steamrooms, whirlpool; hair salon. **Dining & Entertainment:** Restaurant; 6:30 m-10:30 pm, Fri-11 pm, Sat 7 am-11 pm, Sun 7 am-10 pm, Sun brunch 11 am-2:30 pm; $10-$20; cocktails/lounge. ervices: Fee: coin laundry. **Recreation:** children's evening arts & crafts center in summer. **All Rooms:** free & pay movies, ombo or shower baths. **Some Rooms:** Fee: microwaves, refrigerators, VCR's. **Cards:** AE, CB, DI, DS, MC, VI. pecial Amenities: Early check-in/late check-out and preferred room (subject to availability with advanced servations). (See color ad p 370) Roll in showers.

EVITTOWN—55,400 (See map p. 368; index p. 366)

LODGING

OMFORT INN LEVITTOWN/BRISTOL **Phone:** 215/547-5000 [37]
6/1-9/3 [CP] 1P: $65- 75 2P/1B: $75- 85 XP: $10 F15
5/1-5/31 & 9/4-4/30 [CP] 1P: $55- 65 2P/1B: $65- 75 XP: $10 F15
otel **Location:** 0.4 mi n, Pennsylvania Tpk, exit 29. 6401 Bristol Pk 19057. Fax: 215/547-9698. **Terms:** Small pets only. **Facility:** 72 rooms. Traditional motel rooms, offering good, comfortable economy style accommoda-tions. 2 whirlpool king rms, $85-$95; 2 stories; interior corridors. **Dining:** Restaurant nearby. **All Rooms:** free ovies. **Some Rooms:** radios, whirlpools. Fee: microwaves, refrigerators. **Cards:** AE, DI, DS, MC, VI. **Special Amenities:** ree breakfast and preferred room (subject to availability with advanced reservations).

INE LEXINGTON—700

RESTAURANT

OTO'S RESTAURANT **Lunch:** $4-$7 **Dinner:** $6-$14 **Phone:** 215/822-1948
Location: Rt 309 & Hilltown Pike 18932. **Hours:** 7 am-11 pm, Fri & Sat-midnight, Sun-10 pm. Closed: 12/25. merican **Features:** casual dress; children's menu; early bird specials; senior's menu; health conscious menu. Family style restaurant. Banquet facilities. Smoke free premises. **Cards:** MC, VI.

INFIELD—700

LODGING

HEARER ELEGANCE BED & BREAKFAST Rates Subject to Change **Phone:** 610/495-7429
All Year [BP] 1P: $60- 125 2P/1B: $75- 140 XP: $10
istoric Bed Breakfast **Location:** US 422, Limerick/Linfield exit, just s to Linfield-Trappe Rd, 1.4 mi w to jct Main & Church sts. 154 Main St 19468. Fax: 610/495-7814. **Terms:** Age restrictions may apply; reserv deposit, 7 day notice; no pets. **Facility:** 7 rooms. 3 stories, no elevator; interior corridors; smoke free premises. **All Rooms:** free movies. ards: AE, DS, MC, VI.

IONVILLE—400

LODGINGS

XTON COMFORT INN **Phone:** 610/524-8811
All Year [CP] 1P: $60- 65 2P/1B: $70- 75 2P/2B: $70 XP: $5 F18
otel **Location:** Jct SR 113 & 100; 0.5 mi s of tpk, exit 23. 5 N Pottstown Pike 19341. Fax: 610/524-0562. **Terms:** Pets, $5 extra charge. **Facility:** 104 rooms. 8 whirlpool rms, extra charge; 4 stories; interior corridors; small heated indoor pool. **Dining:** Restaurant nearby. **Services:** Fee: coin laundry. **All Rooms:** free & pay movies. **Some Rooms:** Fee: microwaves, refrigerators. **Cards:** AE, DI, DS, MC, VI. **Special Amenities:** ee local telephone calls and free newspaper.

HAMPTON INN
◆◆◆   All Year [CP]   1P: $83- 89 2P/1B: $89- 95 2P/2B: $89- 95   Guaranteed Rates   Phone: 610/363-555
Motel   **Location:** Jct SR 113 & 100; 0.5 mi s of tpk, exit 23. 4 N Pottstown Pike 19341. Fax: 610/363-496
Terms: Pets. **Facility:** 122 rooms. 4 stories; interior corridors. **All Rooms:** free & pay movies. **Cards:** A
CB, DI, DS, MC, VI.

HOLIDAY INN HOTEL & CONFERENCE CENTER   Rates Subject to Change   Phone: 610/363-11
◆◆   All Year [BP]   1P: $82- 109 2P/1B: $82- 109 2P/2B: $82- 109 XP: $8   F
Motor Inn   **Location:** 0.5 mi s of jct SR 113 & 100; 1.1 mi s of Tpk, exit 23. 815 N Pottstown Pike 19341-159
Fax: 610/524-2329. **Terms:** Sr. discount; pets. **Facility:** 213 rooms. 4 stories; interior corridor
Dining: Restaurant; 6:30 am-2 & 5:30-10 pm, Sun 6:30 am-2 pm; $9-$18. **All Rooms:** free & pay movies. **Cards:** AE, C
DI, MC, VI.

RESTAURANT

THE STRANGE BREW BAGEL BISTRO   Lunch: $3-$9   Phone: 610/363-028
◆   **Location:** From jct SR 100, 1 mi n on US 113. 255 Gordon Dr 19341. **Hours:** 7 am-3 pm. Closed: 11/26
American   12/25. **Features:** casual dress; carryout. Specializing in homemade soup & bagels. **Cards:** MC, VI.

LUMBERVILLE—200

LODGING

1740 HOUSE   Rates Subject to Change   Phone: 215/297-56
(AAA)   Fri & Sat [BP]   1P: $113   2P/1B: $113   2P/2B: $113   XP: $20
Sun-Thurs [BP]   1P: $65   2P/1B: $75   2P/2B: $75   XP: $20
◆◆◆   **Location:** On SR 32. River Rd 18933. Fax: 215/297-5956. **Terms:** Age restrictions may apply; rese
Country Inn   deposit, 7 day notice; 2 night min stay, weekends; no pets. **Facility:** 24 rooms. 1 suite; Fri & Sat $125, Su
Thurs $113; 2 stories; interior corridors. *(See ad p 383)*

RESTAURANT

CUTTALOSSA INN   Lunch: $7-$13   Dinner: $18-$28   Phone: 215/297-50
◆◆   **Location:** On Rt 32. River Rd 18933. **Hours:** 11 am-2 & 5-9 pm. Closed: 1/1, 12/24, 12/25 & Su
American   **Reservations:** suggested; in winter. **Features:** dressy casual; health conscious menu; cocktails & lounge;
la carte. A unique old inn turned restaurant. Wonderfully landscaped grounds in season overlooking waterf
Patio dining & outdoor bar in colorful garden. **Cards:** AE, MC, VI.

MALVERN—2,900

LODGING

THE DESMOND, GREAT VALLEY HOTEL   Rates Subject to Change   Phone: 610/296-98
◆◆◆   Mon-Thurs   1P: $119- 129 2P/1B: $134- 140 2P/2B: $134- 140 XP: $15   F
Hotel   Fri-Sun   1P: $95- 129 2P/1B: $95- 125 2P/2B: $110- 140 XP: $15   F
Location: 0.5 mi w of US 202, SR 29 exit; in Great Valley Corporate Center. 1 Liberty Blvd 1935
Fax: 610/889-9869. **Terms:** Sr. discount; no pets. **Facility:** 194 rooms. 4 stories; interior corridors. **Dining:** Restaurant; 6:
am-10:30 pm. Seasonal outdoor dining terrace avail; $9-$33; also, The Hunt Room, see separate listing. **All Rooms:** free
pay movies. **Cards:** AE, DI, DS, MC, VI.

RESTAURANTS

THE HUNT ROOM   Lunch: $10-$18   Dinner: $19-$33   Phone: 610/296-98
◆◆◆   **Location:** 0.5 mi w of US 202, SR 29 exit; in Great Valley Corporate Center; in The Desmond, Great Vall
Regional   Hotel. 1 Liberty Blvd 19355. **Hours:** 6:30 am-2:30 & 5-10 pm, Fri-11 pm, Sat 7 am-3 & 5-11 pm, Sun
American   am-2:30 & 5-10 pm. Closed: 12/25. **Reservations:** suggested. **Features:** dressy casual; Sunday brunc
children's menu; early bird specials; health conscious menu; cocktails & lounge. Subdued elegant ambienc
Menu revised seasonally. **Cards:** AE, CB, DI, DS, MC, VI.

MARGARET KUO'S MANDARIN   Lunch: $6-$10   Dinner: $9-$20   Phone: 610/647-54
◆◆   **Location:** On US 30, 0.5 mi w of jct SR 29. 190 Lancaster Ave 19355. **Hours:** 11:30 am-10 pm, Fri & Sat-
Chinese   pm, Sun-9 pm. Closed: 11/26. **Reservations:** suggested; weekends. **Features:** casual dress; carryout; a
carte. Classic Mandarin & Szechuan cuisine. Lunch buffet Mon-Fri. Dim Sum served Fri-Sun. Smoke fr
premises. **Cards:** AE, MC, VI.

MEDIA—6,000

LODGING

MCINTOSH INN OF MEDIA   Rates Subject to Change   Phone: 610/565-58
◆◆   All Year [CP]   1P: $54- 56 2P/1B: $61   2P/2B: $63   XP: $7   F
Motel   **Location:** Just s on SR 352 from US 1. Rt US 1 & 352 19063. Fax: 610/565-7748. **Terms:** Sr. discount;
pets. **Facility:** 84 rooms. 2-3 stories; exterior corridors. **All Rooms:** free movies. **Cards:** AE, CB, DI, MC, V
(See color ad p 353)

MENDENHALL—600

LODGING

MENDENHALL INN HOTEL & CONFERENCE CENTER   Rates Subject to Change   Phone: 610/388-21
◆◆◆   All Year [CP]   1P: $104   2P/1B: $114   2P/2B: $114   XP: $15
Motor Inn   **Location:** On SR 52, 1 mi s of jct US 1. Rt 52 Kennett Pike 19357 (PO Box 606). Fax: 610/388-118
Terms: No pets. **Facility:** 70 rooms. 4 suites, $145-$195. Handling fee imposed; 3 stories; interior/exterior c
ridors. **Dining:** Dining room, see separate listing. **All Rooms:** free movies. **Cards:** AE, CB, DI, DS, MC, VI.

RESTAURANT

MENDENHALL INN   Lunch: $9-$15   Dinner: $22-$38   Phone: 610/388-11
◆◆◆   **Location:** On SR 52, 1 mi s of jct US 1; in Mendenhall Inn Hotel & Conference Center. Rt 52 Kennett Pi
Continental   19357. **Hours:** 11:30 am-2:30 & 5-10 pm, Sun 10 am-2 & 4-8 pm. Closed: 12/25. **Reservations:** suggeste
Features: dressy casual; Sunday brunch; children's menu; cocktails & lounge; valet parking. Elegant dini
in traditional style; menu features various game birds. **Cards:** AE, CB, DI, DS, MC, VI.

MONTGOMERYVILLE—9,100

LODGINGS

EST WESTERN MONTGOMERYVILLE   Phone: 215/699-8800
AAD SAVE   All Year [CP]   1P: $71- 94 2P/1B: $71- 94 2P/2B: $79- 89 XP: $5   F12
♦♦   **Location:** On US 309, 0.3 mi s of jct W US 202. 969 Bethlehem Pike 18936. Fax: 215/699-7747. **Terms:** No
Motor Inn   pets. **Facility:** 61 rooms. Budget oriented property featuring average size guest rooms & decor. 1-2 stories;
exterior corridors. **Dining & Entertainment:** Restaurant; 5 pm-9 pm; $8-S15; cocktails/lounge.
Services: valet laundry; area transportation, within 8 mi. **All Rooms:** free movies. **Some Rooms:** 6
efficiencies. Fee: microwaves, refrigerators. **Cards:** AE, CB, DI, DS, MC, VI. **Special Amenities: Free breakfast and free
newspaper.**   (symbols) CTV X (symbols)

COMFORT INN   Rates Subject to Change   Phone: 215/361-3600
♦♦♦   All Year [CP]   1P: $83- 129 2P/1B: $97- 110 2P/2B: $88- 132 XP: $5   F18
Motel   **Location:** On SR 309, 0.3 mi n of jct, 463 & US 202. 678 Bethlehem Pike 18936. Fax: 215/361-7949.
Terms: Sr. discount; no pets. **Facility:** 84 rooms. 31 whirlpool rms, extra charge; 3 stories; interior corridors.
Some Rooms: 6 efficiencies. **Cards:** AE, DI, DS, MC, VI.   (symbols) CTV X (D)(S)

NEW HOPE—1,400

LODGINGS

ARON BURR HOUSE INN & CONFERENCE CENTER   Guaranteed Rates   Phone: 215/862-2343
♦♦   All Year [CP]   1P: $90- 170 2P/1B: $90- 199   XP: $20
Historic Bed   **Location:** 0.5 mi w of SR 32, at W Bridge & Chestnut sts. 80 W Bridge St (SR 179) 18938.
Breakfast   Fax: 215/862-2570. **Terms:** Reserv deposit, 10 day notice; 2 night min stay, weekends; pets, $20 extra
charge, in designated rooms. **Facility:** 7 rooms. 3 gas fireplace suites, $180-$200; 3 stories, no elevator; in-
terior corridors; smoke free premises. **Cards:** MC, VI.   (symbols) CTV X (D)

EST WESTERN NEW HOPE INN   Phone: 215/862-5221
AAD SAVE   Fri & Sat   1P: $100- 149 2P/1B: $100- 149 2P/2B: $100- 149
Sun-Thurs   1P: $85- 99   2P/1B: $85- 99   2P/2B: $79- 99
Motor Inn   **Location:** 2 mi s on US 202, 1 mi w of jct SR 179. 6426 Lower York Rd 18938. Fax: 215/862-5847.
Terms: Reserv deposit; package plans; small pets only, $20 extra charge. **Facility:** 152 rooms. Well main-
tained property with very comfortable guest rooms offering a pleasant, modern decor. In a quiet area sur-
rounded by lots of trees & shrubs. Manicured lawn & pool area. 3 stories; exterior corridors; 1 tennis court; shuffleboard.
Dining & Entertainment: Restaurant; 7 am-10 & 5-10 pm, Sat & Sun 7-11 am; $9-$16; cocktails/lounge. **Services:**
fee: coin laundry. **All Rooms:** free movies. **Cards:** AE, CB, DI, DS, MC, VI. **Special Amenities: Free local telephone
calls and free newspaper.**   (symbols) CTV X (symbols)(D)

HE FOX & HOUND BED & BREAKFAST OF NEW HOPE   Guaranteed Rates   Phone: 215/862-5082
AAD   Fri & Sat [BP]   1P: $115- 165 2P/1B: $115- 165 2P/2B: $115- 165 XP: $20
Sun-Thurs [CP]   1P: $65- 115 2P/1B: $65- 115 2P/2B: $65- 115 XP: $10
♦♦♦   **Location:** 1 mi s on SR 179. 246 W Bridge St 18938. Fax: 215/862-5082. **Terms:** Age restrictions may
Historic Bed   apply; reserv deposit, 10 day notice; 2 night min stay, weekends; no pets. **Facility:** 8 rooms. 3 rooms with gas
Breakfast   fireplace and/or whirlpool $90-$115, Fri & Sat $145-$165; 3 stories, no elevator; interior/exterior corridors.
Cards: AE, MC, VI.   X (D)

HE MANSION INN   Rates Subject to Change   Phone: 215/862-1231
AAD   All Year [BP]   1P: $160- 265 2P/1B: $160- 265
Location: Center, on SR 32. 9 S Main St 18938 (PO Box 117). Fax: 215/862-0277. **Terms:** Age restrictions
♦♦♦♦   may apply; reserv deposit, 10 day notice; 2 night min stay, weekends; no pets. **Facility:** 9 rooms. 3 stories, no
Historic Bed   elevator; interior/exterior corridors; smoke free premises. **All Rooms:** free movies. **Cards:** AE, MC, VI.
Breakfast   (symbols) CTV X (D)

EW HOPE MOTEL IN THE WOODS   Phone: 215/862-2800
AAD SAVE   Fri & Sat   2P/1B: $64- 89 2P/2B: $64- 89 XP: $10
Sun-Thurs   2P/1B: $59- 84 2P/2B: $59- 84 XP: $10
♦   **Location:** 1 mi s on SR 179, e of jct US 202. 400 W Bridge St 18938. Fax: 215/862-3962. **Terms:** Reserv
Motel   deposit, 14 day notice; 2 night min stay, weekends; small pets only, $20 fee. **Facility:** 28 rooms. An older but
well maintained property featuring large 2-bed guest rooms & average size 1-bed guest rooms. Tall, mature
shade trees dot the property offering wonderful shady areas throughout property & around the pool. Handling fee imposed; 1
story; exterior corridors. **Dining:** Restaurant nearby. **All Rooms:** refrigerators, combo or shower baths. **Cards:** AE, DI, DS,
MC, VI. **Special Amenities: Free local telephone calls and preferred room (subject to availability with advanced
reservations).**   (symbols) ECTV X (D)

PINEAPPLE HILL BED & BREAKFAST　　　　　　　　　　　　　　　　　　Phone: 215/862-179
(AAA) SAVE　All Year [BP]　　　　　　1P: $83- 171　2P/1B: $94- 182　2P/2B: $182　　　XP: $30
◆◆◆　　Location: 4.6 mi s on SR 32. 1324 River Rd 18938. Fax: 215/862-5273. Terms: Reserv deposit, 5 da
　　　　notice; 2 night min stay, weekends; no pets. Facility: 8 rooms. Handling fee imposed; 3 stories, no elevato
Historic Bed　interior/exterior corridors; smoke free premises. Cards: AE, DS, MC, VI.
& Breakfast

THE WEDGWOOD INN　　　　　　　　　　　　　　　　　　　　　　　Phone: 215/862-252
(AAA) SAVE　All Year [CP]　　　　　　1P: $75- 185　2P/1B: $80- 199　　　　　　XP: $20
◆◆◆　　Location: 0.5 mi w of SR 32. 111 W Bridge St (SR 179) 18938. Fax: 215/862-2570. Terms: Reserv depos
　　　　10 day notice; weekly/monthly rates; package plans; 2 night min stay, weekends; pets, $20 extra charge,
Historic Bed　designated rooms. Facility: 12 rooms. Consists of 2 side-by-side Victorian homes with registration & breakfa
& Breakfast　served in the Wedgwood House. Charming decor in both homes, with some rooms featuring compact siz
　　　　bathrooms. Close to shops & restaurants. 6 gas fireplace suites, $180-$200; 2 stories; interior/exterior cor
dors; smoke free premises. Dining: Restaurant nearby. All Rooms: combo or shower baths. Some Rooms: coffeemaker
kitchen, microwaves, refrigerators, phones, VCR's. Cards: AE, MC, VI. Special Amenities: Free breakfast and free loc
telephone calls.

RESTAURANTS

CENTRE BRIDGE INN　Country Inn　　　　　　Dinner: $22-$29　　　　　Phone: 215/862-204
◆◆◆　　Location: 4 mi n, at jct SR 32 & 263. 18938. Hours: 5:30 pm-9:30 pm, Fri & Sat-10 pm, Sun 11:30 am-2:3
Continental　　& 3:30-9 pm. Closed: 12/25. Reservations: suggested. Features: dressy casual; Sunday brunch; cocktails
　　　　lounge. Informal dining in a quaint, rustic setting. Friendly, attentive service. Features fresh fish & homemac
dessert. Patio dining in season. Cards: AE, MC, VI.

LA BONNE AUBERGE　　　　　　　Dinner: $30-$42　　　　　　　　　　Phone: 215/862-246
(AAA) SAVE　Location: Just s on Main St, 1 mi w on Mechanic St, follow to rear of Village 2 townhouse complex, ne
　　　　tennis courts & pool. Village 2 18938. Hours: 6 pm-9 pm, Sun 5:30 pm-8:30 pm. Closed: 12/25, Mon
◆◆◆◆　Tues. Reservations: required. Features: semi-formal attire; cocktails & lounge; a la carte. Fine dining in
French　　beautifully landscaped 18th-century farmhouse. Gracious dining room appointments. Unpretentious, attentiv
　　　　service, classic food. Smoking not permitted in dining room. 5-course prix fix menu Wed & Thurs, $4
Smoke free premises. Cards: AE, MC, VI. Special Value: 10% discount on the price of any entree, excludin
beverages, tax and gratuity.

THE LANDING RESTAURANT　　　　Lunch: $5-$10　　　Dinner: $18-$24　　　Phone: 215/862-571
◆◆◆　　Location: Just n of jct W SR 179. 22 N Main St 18938. Hours: 11 am-4 & 5-10 pm, Fri & Sat-11 pr
Regional　　Closed: 11/26 & 12/25. Features: casual dress; cocktails & lounge; a la carte. Casual fine dining
American　　charmingly intimate dining room with fireplaces or on seasonal flower bedecked brick patio. Feature
　　　　Regional American cuisine prepared with the freshest ingredients. Raw bar. Smoke free premise
Cards: CB, DI, DS, MC, VI.

NEWTOWN (BUCKS COUNTY)

LODGINGS

THE BRICK HOTEL　　　　　　　　Rates Subject to Change　　　　　　　Phone: 215/860-831
◆◆◆　　　　　　　　　　1P: $80- 135　2P/1B: $80- 135　2P/2B: $110- 120
Historic　　Location: I-95 Newtown exit, 5 mi w to S State St, just n to Center; Corner Washington Ave & State St. 1
Country Inn　Washington Ave 18940. Fax: 215/860-8084. Terms: Check-in 4 pm; no pets. Facility: 13 rooms. 3 stories, n
　　　　elevator; interior corridors. Dining: Dining room; 11 am-10 pm, Fri & Sat-11 pm, Sun 10 am-9:30 pr
$9-$19. Cards: AE, DS, MC, VI.

YE OLDE TEMPERANCE HOUSE　　　Rates Subject to Change　　　　　　Phone: 215/860-047
◆◆◆　　All Year [CP]　　　　　1P: $95- 135　2P/1B: $95- 135　2P/2B: $135
Historic　　Location: I-95 Newtown exit, 3 mi w to S State St, 0.9 mi n to center. 5 S State St 1894
Country Inn　Fax: 215/860-7773. Terms: No pets. Facility: 13 rooms. 3 stories, no elevator; interior corrido
　　　　Dining: Dining room; 4 pm-10 pm, Sat-11 pm, Sun 11 am-3 & 4-9 pm; $12-$22. Cards: AE, DI, MC, VI.

NEWTOWN SQUARE—11,300

RESTAURANT

ALBERTO'S NEWTOWN SQUIRE　Historical　　Lunch: $6-$16　　Dinner: $16-$26　　Phone: 610/356-970
◆◆◆　　Location: On SR 252, 0.5 mi s of jct with SR 3. 191 S Newtown Street Rd 19073. Hours: 11:30 am-2:30
Italian　　4:30-10 pm, Fri & Sat-11 pm, Sunday brunch 11 am-2:30 pm & Sun dinner 4 pm-9 pm. Closed: 5/25, 9/7
　　　　12/25. Features: dressy casual; early bird specials; cocktails & lounge; valet parking; a la carte, also p
fixe. Northern Italian & American cuisine served in elegantly refurbished 1798 colonial stone farmhouse with fireplaces
additions. Menu features prime rib, rack of lamb, grilled fish & large pasta variety. Cards: AE, CB, DI, MC, VI.

NOTTINGHAM (CHESTER COUNTY)

RESTAURANT

NOTTINGHAM INN　　　　　　　Lunch: $6-$9　　　　　Dinner: $6-$14　　　　Phone: 610/932-405
◆◆　　　Location: On US 272, 0.5 mi s of jct US 1. 190 Baltimore Pike 19362. Hours: 6 am-3 pm, Thurs-Sat also
Continental　pm-10 pm, Sun 3 pm-8 pm. Closed: 12/25 & Mon. Reservations: required; weekends. Features: casu
　　　　dress; children's menu; carryout; cocktails & lounge. Casual dining in a country setting. Very good varie
menu, specializing in grilled seafood, pasta & steak. Cards: AE, DS, MC, VI.

OTTSVILLE—300

LODGING

FRANKENFIELD FARM BED & BREAKFAST　Rates Subject to Change　　　　Phone: 610/847-277
◆◆◆　　All Year [BP]　　　　　1P: $95- 150　2P/1B: $95- 150
Historic Bed　Location: 2 mi se on Durham Rd from jct SR 611, following signs. 93 Frankenfield Rd 18942 (PO Box 23
& Breakfast　Fax: 610/847-2771. Terms: Age restrictions may apply; reserv deposit, 14 day notice; 2 night min sta
　　　　weekends; no pets, pet on premises. Facility: 4 rooms. Separate guest house with whirlpool & fireplace, $19
Handling fee imposed; 3 stories, no elevator; interior/exterior corridors; smoke free premises. Cards: AE, DS, MC, VI.

PALM—400

RESTAURANT

CAB FRYE'S TAVERN Historical **Lunch:** $7-$14 **Dinner:** $16-$30 **Phone:** 215/679-9935
AAA [SAVE] **Location:** Just nw on SR 29. 914 Gravel Pike 18070. **Hours:** 11:30 am-2 & 5-10 pm. Closed major holidays,
Sun & Sat-Tues for lunch. **Reservations:** suggested. **Features:** casual dress; carryout; cocktails & lounge. 4
◆◆◆ charming dining rooms in historic 1830 3-story brick country farmhouse. Menu features game & Swiss
Continental entrees, dover sole & Scottish lobster with an emphasis on wild mushrooms in preparation. **Cards:** AE, DS,
MC, VI. **Special Value: $1 off price of a breakfast or lunch entree.** [X]

PIPERSVILLE—600

LODGING

THE VICTORIAN PEACOCK BED & BREAKFAST Rates Subject to Change **Phone:** 215/766-1356
AAA Fri & Sat 5/1-1/1 & 4/1-4/30
[CP] 1P: $90- 140 2P/1B: $95- 145
◆◆◆ Sun-Thurs 5/1-1/1, 1/2-3/31
Bed & & 4/1-4/30 [CP] 1P: $60- 100 2P/1B: $65- 105
Breakfast Fri & Sat 1/2-3/31 [CP] 1P: $80- 120 2P/1B: $85- 125
Location: 2.9 mi w on Dark Hollow Rd from jct W SR 32 in Erwinna. 309 E Dark Hollow Rd 18947.
Fax: 215/766-1356. **Terms:** Age restrictions may apply; reserv deposit, 7 day notice; 2 night min stay, weekends in season;
no pets. **Facility:** 5 rooms. Handling fee imposed; 3 stories; interior corridors; smoke free premises. **Cards:** MC, VI.
[pool] [X] [D]

PLYMOUTH MEETING—6,200 (See map p. 368; index p. 366)

LODGING

DOUBLETREE GUEST SUITES Rates Subject to Change **Phone:** 610/834-8300 [66]
AAA Sun-Thurs 1P: $174 2P/1B: $194 2P/2B: $194 XP: $20 F18
Fri & Sat 1P: $119 2P/1B: $119 2P/2B: $119 XP: $20 F18
◆◆◆ **Location:** I-276, exit 25, just w on Plymouth Rd, just e on Germantown Pike; just e on Hickory Rd. 640 W
Suite Hotel Germantown Pike 19462. Fax: 610/834-7813. **Terms:** Sr. discount; no pets. **Facility:** 252 rooms. 7 stories; in-
terior corridors. **Dining:** Dining room; 6:30-10:30 am, 11-2:30 & 5-10:30 pm, Sat & Sun from 7 am; $10-$24.
All Rooms: free & pay movies. **Cards:** AE, CB, DI, DS, JCB, MC, VI. [pool] [tv] [CTV] [X] [jacuzzi] [D] [S]

POINT PLEASANT—800

LODGING

TATTERSALL INN Rates Subject to Change **Phone:** 215/297-8233
AAA All Year [BP] 1P: $60- 120 2P/1B: $70- 130 XP: $15
Location: 0.5 mi n on SR 32, at jct of Cafferty & River rds. 16 Cafferty Rd 18950 (PO Box 569).
◆◆◆ Fax: 215/297-5093. **Terms:** Reserv deposit, 10 day notice; no pets. **Facility:** 6 rooms. 2 stories; interior corri-
Historic Bed dors; designated smoking area. **Cards:** AE, DS, MC, VI. [X] [D]
Breakfast

POTTSTOWN—21,800

LODGINGS

COMFORT INN Rates Subject to Change **Phone:** 610/326-5000
◆◆◆ All Year [CP] 1P: $64- 89 2P/1B: $64- 89 2P/2B: $64- 89 XP: $7 F18
Motel **Location:** On SR 100, 1 mi n of jct US 422. 99 Robinson St 19464. Fax: 610/970-7230. **Terms:** Sr. discount;
small pets only, $25 dep req. **Facility:** 121 rooms. 4 stories; interior corridors. **All Rooms:** free & pay
movies. **Cards:** AE, CB, DI, DS, JCB, MC. [pets] [pool] [CTV] [X] [jacuzzi] [D] [S]

DAYS INN **Phone:** 610/970-1101
AAA [SAVE] 5/1-10/31 [CP] 1P: $43 2P/1B: $43 2P/2B: $55- 85 XP: $5 F
11/1-4/30 [CP] 1P: $34 2P/1B: $34 2P/2B: $45 XP: $5 F
◆◆ **Location:** Just off SR 663, 0.5 mi e of jct SR 100. 29 High St 19464. Fax: 610/327-8643. **Terms:** Weekly
Motel rates; pets, $10 extra charge. **Facility:** 60 rooms. 2 stories; exterior corridors. **Dining:** Restaurant nearby.
All Rooms: free movies. **Some Rooms:** Fee: refrigerators. **Cards:** AE, CB, DI, DS, MC, VI.
Special Amenities: Free breakfast. [pets] [pool] [CTV] [X] [D]

HOLIDAY INN EXPRESS Guaranteed Rates **Phone:** 610/327-3300
◆◆◆ All Year [CP] 1P: $69 2P/1B: $69 2P/2B: $69 XP: $5 F18
Motel **Location:** Jct US 422 & Armand Hammer Blvd exit. 1600 Industrial Hwy 19464. Fax: 610/327-9447.
Terms: Sr. discount; pets, $25 extra charge. **Facility:** 119 rooms. 4 stories; interior corridors.
All Rooms: free & pay movies. **Cards:** AE, CB, DI, DS, JCB, MC, VI. [pets] [pool] [CTV] [f] [X] [jacuzzi] [D] [S]

RAMADA INN-POTTSTOWN **Phone:** 610/326-6700
AAA [SAVE] All Year 1P: $49- 59 2P/1B: $64 2P/2B: $54 XP: $5 F18
Location: Just e of SR 100 on W King St. Rt 100 & W King St 19464. Fax: 610/970-2665. **Terms:** Weekly
◆◆ rates; no pets. **Facility:** 100 rooms. 2 stories; exterior corridors. **Dining:** Restaurant; 6:30 am-10 & 5-9 pm;
Motel $6-$16; cocktails. **Services:** valet laundry. **Some Rooms:** Fee: microwaves, refrigerators. **Cards:** AE, DI,
DS, MC, VI. **Special Amenities: Free room upgrade and preferred room (each subject to availability**
with advanced reservations). [pool] [pets] [CTV] [X] [D]

QUAKERTOWN—9,000

LODGINGS

BEST WESTERN MOTOR INN **Phone:** 215/536-2500
AAA [SAVE] All Year 1P: $67- 77 2P/1B: $77- 87 2P/2B: $77- 87 XP: $8 F17
Location: E of jct SR 313 & 309. 1446 W Broad St 18951. Fax: 215/536-2508. **Terms:** No pets. **Facility:** 40
◆◆◆ rooms. Comfortably furnished guest rooms. 2 stories; interior corridors. **Dining:** Breakfast room for guests
Motel only, 6-10 am; restaurant nearby. **Services:** Fee: coin laundry. **Cards:** AE, CB, DI, DS, MC, VI.
Special Amenities: Free local telephone calls. [pets] [tv] [CTV] [X] [D]

ECONO LODGE
Phone: 215/538-300
All Year [CP]   1P: $45- 70 2P/1B: $50- 70 2P/2B: $50- 75 XP: $5   F1
Location: Jct SR 663 & exit 32 off ne extension of PA Tpk (I-476). 1905 John Fries Hwy 1895
Fax: 215/538-2311. **Terms:** Reserv deposit; weekly rates; no pets. **Facility:** 43 rooms. 4 whirlpool rms, ext charge; 2 stories; exterior corridors. **Dining:** Restaurant nearby. **All Rooms:** coffeemakers, microwaves, fre
Motel   movies, refrigerators. **Some Rooms:** Fee: VCR's. **Cards:** AE, CB, DI, DS, JCB, MC, VI.   CTV ⊠ C

QUAKERTOWN RODEWAY INN
Phone: 215/536-760
Fri & Sat 5/1-9/2 [CP]   1P: $60- 70 2P/1B: $60- 70 2P/2B: $60- 70 XP: $5   F1
Sun-Thurs 5/1-9/2 [CP]   1P: $50- 55 2P/1B: $50- 60 2P/2B: $50- 60 XP: $5   F1
9/3-4/30 [CP]   1P: $50- 55 2P/1B: $55- 60 2P/2B: $55- 60 XP: $5   F1
Motel   **Location:** Just e of NE Extention PA Tpk (I-476), exit 32. 1920 SR 663 18951. Fax: 215/536-592
Terms: Reserv deposit; weekly rates; package plans; small pets only, $5 extra charge. **Facility:** 40 rooms. story; exterior corridors. **Dining:** Restaurant nearby. **All Rooms:** microwaves, free movies, refrigerators, combo or show baths. **Some Rooms:** radios, whirlpools. **Cards:** AE, DI, DS, MC, VI. **Special Amenities:** Early check-in/late check-o and free local telephone calls.   🛏 📵 CTV ⊠ C

ST. DAVIDS

LODGING

RADNOR HOTEL
Rates Subject to Change
Phone: 610/688-580
◆◆◆   All Year   1P: $145   2P/1B: $155   2P/2B: $155   XP: $10   F1
Motor Inn   **Location:** 0.3 mi w of intersection I-476 exit 5 & US 30. 591 E Lancaster Ave 19087. Fax: 610/341-329
Terms: Sr. discount; no pets. **Facility:** 170 rooms. 4 stories; interior corridors. **Dining:** Dining room; 6:3
am-11 pm, Fri & Sat-midnight; $7-$19. **All Rooms:** Fee: movies. **Some Rooms:** 2 efficiencies. **Cards:** AE, CB, DI, DS, M(
VI.   Roll in showers. 📵 CTV ⊠ 🛁 C

SPRINGFIELD (DELAWARE COUNTY) (See map p. 368; index p. 366)

RESTAURANT

CAFFE BELLISSIMO SEAFOOD
ITALIANO RISTORANTE
Lunch: $5-$11   **Dinner:** $12-$24   Phone: 610/328-2300   17
◆◆   **Location:** 1 mi e of I-476, exit 2; in Springfield Square South Shopping Center. 1001 Baltimore Pike 1906
Italian   **Hours:** noon-10 pm, Fri & Sat-11 pm. Closed: 12/25. **Features:** casual dress; children's menu; carryou cocktails & lounge. Lively atmosphere, innovative Northern & Southern Italian cuisine. Large pasta portion
made on premise. Open brick oven pizza. **Cards:** AE, DS, MC, VI.   ▷

TREVOSE (See map p. 368; index p. 366)

LODGINGS

HOLIDAY INN SELECT BUCKS COUNTY
Phone: 215/364-2000   9
5/1-8/31   1P: $109- 139 2P/1B: $109- 139 2P/2B: $109- 139 XP: $10   F1
9/1-4/30   1P: $79- 99 2P/1B: $79- 99 2P/2B: $79- 99 XP: $10   F1
◆◆◆   **Location:** On SR 132; 1 mi nw of I-276 (PA Tpk), exit 28 via US 1S. 4700 Street Rd 1905
Hotel   Fax: 215/364-7197. **Terms:** Reserv deposit; weekly/monthly rates; package plans; no pets. **Facility:** 21 rooms. A family & business oriented property. For families the guest rooms are large & comfortable; for bus ness travelers, the top floor is locked off with a separate key. Guest rooms are modern with large working space. 2 suite $225; 6 stories; interior corridors; luxury level rooms; sauna, whirlpool. **Dining & Entertainment:** Restaurant; 6:30 am-2 5-10 pm; $12-$24; cocktails/lounge. **Services:** Fee: coin laundry. **Recreation:** activity center in summe **All Rooms:** coffeemakers, free & pay movies. **Some Rooms:** Fee: refrigerators. **Cards:** AE, CB, DI, DS, MC, V **Special Amenities: Early check-in/late check-out and preferred room (subject to availability with advance reservations).** *(See color ad p 372)*   🏊 📵 🛗 CTV 🛐 ⊠ 🛁 D 🔒

HOWARD JOHNSON HOTEL
Phone: 215/638-4554   8
5/1-9/8   1P: $55- 70 2P/1B: $55- 80 2P/2B: $55- 80 XP: $5   F1
9/9-4/30   1P: $45- 60 2P/1B: $45- 60 2P/2B: $45- 60 XP: $5   F1
◆◆   **Location:** US 1, 0.5 mi s of PA Tpke exit 28. 2779 Rt 1N 19053. Fax: 215/638-708
Motor Inn   **Terms:** Weekly/monthly rates; package plans; no pets. **Facility:** 88 rooms. Comfortable budget oriented pro erty. Guest rooms offer a modern decor. 5 whirlpool suites, $95-$149; 3 stories; interior corridors; video game
room. **Dining:** Restaurant; 6:30 am-2 & 5-10 pm; $8-$15; cocktails. **Services:** valet laundry. **All Rooms:** free movie
Some Rooms: refrigerators. **Cards:** AE, DI, DS, MC, VI. **Special Amenities: Free newspaper.** *(See color ad below)*   🏊 📵 CTV ⊠ D 🔒

(See map p. 368)

RADISSON HOTEL OF PHILADELPHIA NORTHEAST   Guaranteed Rates   **Phone:** 215/638-8300   91
◆◆◆   All Year   1P: $120   2P/1B: $130   2P/2B: $130   XP: $10   F18
Hotel   **Location:** On US 1; 1 mi s of tpk exit 28, jct Roosevelt Blvd & Old Lincoln Hwy. (US Route 1 at Old Lincoln Hwy, 19053-6894). Fax: 215/638-4377. **Terms:** Sr. discount; reserv deposit; no pets. **Facility:** 281 rooms. 6 stories; interior corridors. **Dining:** Restaurant; 6:30 am-2 & 5-10 pm; Sat & Sun from 7 am; $10-$20. **All Rooms:** free & pay movies. **Cards:** AE, CB, DI, DS, JCB, MC. *(See color ad p 394)*

Roll in showers. 🛏 🛏 🚫 CTV 🚫 ✂ 🏊 D S

RED ROOF INN   Rates Subject to Change   **Phone:** 215/244-9422   89
◆◆   5/1-10/31   1P: $50- 60   2P/1B: $56- 73   2P/2B: $66- 90   XP: $10   F18
Motel   1/1-4/30   1P: $40- 60   2P/1B: $48- 63   2P/2B: $56- 73   XP: $9   F18
    11/1-12/31   1P: $37- 53   2P/1B: $46- 60   2P/2B: $54- 70   XP: $8   F18
Location: On US 1; 0.5 mi s from exit 28 off PA Tpk. 3100 Lincoln Hwy 19053. Fax: 215/244-9469. **Terms:** Small pets only.
Facility: 162 rooms. 2 stories; exterior corridors. **All Rooms:** free & pay movies. **Cards:** AE, CB, DI, DS, MC, VI.

🛏 CTV 🚫 ✂ 🏊 D

WARMINSTER—32,800

LODGING

REGENCY 265 MOTOR INN   Rates Subject to Change   **Phone:** 215/674-2200
AAA   All Year   1P: $50- 60   2P/1B: $55- 60   2P/2B: $60- 70   XP: $5
◆   **Location:** On SR 132, 1.8 mi se of jct SR 263. 265 E Street Rd 18974. Fax: 215/443-7854. **Terms:** Sr. discount; no pets. **Facility:** 52 rooms. 2 stories; interior/exterior corridors. **All Rooms:** free movies.
Motel   **Cards:** AE, DI, DS, MC, VI.   CTV 🚫 D

WASHINGTON CROSSING—800

LODGING

INN TO THE WOODS BED & BREAKFAST   **Phone:** 215/493-1974
AAA SAVE   Fri & Sat [BP]   2P/1B: $145- 185   XP: $25
    Sun-Thurs [BP]   2P/1B: $95- 135   XP: $25
◆◆◆   **Location:** I-95, New Hope exits 31 & 31B, 1 mi n on Taylorsville Rd, 0.5 mi w on Mount Eyre Rd, 0.5 mi n
Bed &   on Walker Rd, 0.5 mi e. 150 Glenwood Rd 18977. Fax: 215/493-7592. **Terms:** Age restrictions may apply;
Breakfast   weekly/monthly rates; package plans; 2 night min stay, on weekends; no pets. **Facility:** 6 rooms. In a quiet
    residential area, surrounded by lush shrubbery on a large manicured lawn, this modern home features an
eclectic decor & art collection. Guest rooms are cozy & decorated in their own unique charm. 3 stories, no elevator; interior
corridors; smoke free premises. **Recreation:** hiking trails. **All Rooms:** combo or shower baths. **Some Rooms:** phones.
Cards: AE, MC, VI. **Special Amenities:** Free local telephone calls and free room upgrade (subject to availability with
advanced reservations).   CTV 🚫 D

WAYNE—900

LODGINGS

COURTYARD BY MARRIOTT   Rates Subject to Change   **Phone:** 610/687-6633
◆◆◆   All Year   1P: $79- 136
Motor Inn   **Location:** On US 30 in Devon Square Business Center. 762 W Lancaster Ave 19087. Fax: 610/687-1150.
    Terms: Sr. discount; no pets. **Facility:** 149 rooms. 12 suites, $129-$139; 3 stories; interior corridors.
Dining: Coffee shop; 6:30-10 am, Sat & Sun 7 am-noon. **All Rooms:** free & pay movies. **Cards:** AE, CB, DI, DS, JCB, MC,
VI. *(See color ad p 371)*   🛏 CTV 🚫 ✂ 🏊 D S

COURTYARD BY MARRIOTT-VALLEY FORGE   Rates Subject to Change   **Phone:** 610/687-6700
◆◆◆   All Year   1P: $69- 122   2P/1B: $69- 122   2P/2B: $69- 122
Motor Inn   **Location:** From US 202, Warner Rd exit, 0.5 mi s on Swedesford Rd. 1100 Drummers Ln 19087.
    Fax: 610/687-1149. **Terms:** Sr. discount; no pets. **Facility:** 150 rooms. 3 stories; interior corridors.
Dining: Coffee shop; 6:30-10 am, Sat & Sun 7-11 am. **All Rooms:** free & pay movies. **Cards:** AE, DI, DS, MC, VI.
(See color ad p 371)   🛏 CTV 🚫 ✂ 🏊 D S

VALLEY FORGE MARRIOTT SUITES   Rates Subject to Change   **Phone:** 610/647-6700
◆◆◆   Mon-Fri   1P: $159   2P/1B: $189   2P/2B: $189   XP: $10
Suite Hotel   Sat & Sun   1P: $89- 129   2P/1B: $89- 129   2P/2B: $89- 129
    Location: US 202 at Chesterbrook Blvd exit; in Chesterbrook Complex. 888 Chesterbrook Blvd 19087-5684.
Fax: 610/408-8323. **Terms:** No pets. **Facility:** 229 rooms. 5 stories; interior corridors. **Dining:** Restaurant; 6:30-10 am,
11-2:30 & 5-10 pm, Sat-11 pm, Sun brunch 11 am-3 & 5-10 pm; $8-$19. **All Rooms:** free & pay movies. **Cards:** AE, CB, DI,
DS, JCB, MC, VI.   Roll in showers. 🛏 🚫 CTV 🚫 ✂ 🏊 D S

RESTAURANTS

J B WINBERIE RESTAURANT & BAR   **Lunch:** $7-$12   **Dinner:** $7-$14   **Phone:** 610/293-9333
◆◆   **Location:** On SR 252, just n of jct with US 202. 1164 Valley Forge Rd 19087. **Hours:** 11:30 am-11 pm, Fri &
American   Sat-midnight. Closed: 11/26 & 12/25. **Reservations:** accepted; for 6 or more. **Features:** Sunday brunch;
    children's menu; carryout; cocktails & lounge; valet parking. Circa 1740's colonial inn dining, specializing in
fresh seafood, pasta & sandwich menu. Lively atmosphere & seasonal outdoor dining patio. Smoke free premises.
Cards: AE, CB, DI, DS, MC, VI.   ✂

LA FOURCHETTE   **Dinner:** $18-$28   **Phone:** 610/687-8333
◆◆◆   **Location:** Downtown; on US 30, just n. 110 N Wayne Ave 19087. **Hours:** 6 pm-10 pm, Sun 11 am-2 & 6-9
French   pm. Closed major holidays. **Reservations:** suggested. **Features:** Sunday brunch; health conscious menu;
    cocktails & lounge; street parking; a la carte. Upscale casual, warm country French Provincial atmosphere.
Gracious service. Creative freshly prepared cuisine. Extensive wine list. **Cards:** AE, CB, DI, DS, MC, VI.   ✂

SAMUELS   **Lunch:** $7-$15   **Dinner:** $23-$33   **Phone:** 610/687-2840
◆◆◆   **Location:** In Spread Eagle Village at Lancaster Ave, (US 30) & Eagle Rd. 503 W Lancaster Ave 19087.
American   **Hours:** 11:30 am-2:30 & 6-10 pm, Sun, Mon & Tues-9 pm. Closed major holidays. **Reservations:** suggested. **Features:** dressy casual; Sunday brunch; cocktails & lounge; a la carte. A menu
changing with the seasons featuring very well prepared entrees in a Contemporary American cuisine. **Cards:** AE, CB, DI,
DS, MC, VI.   ✂

VILLA STRAFFORD   **Lunch:** $7-$16   **Dinner:** $20-$33   **Phone:** 610/964-1116
◆◆◆   **Location:** Just n of SR 30. 115 Strafford Ave 19087. **Hours:** 11:30 am-2:30 & 5:30-10 pm, Sat from 5:30
Continental   pm. **Closed:** 7/4, 12/25 & Sun. **Reservations:** suggested. **Features:** semi-formal attire; early bird specials;
health conscious menu items; cocktails & lounge; a la carte. Live jazz on Fri & Sat evenings. Formal dining
in elegant setting. **Cards:** AE, CB, DI, MC, VI.   ⊠

WEST CHESTER—18,000

RESTAURANT

DILWORTHTOWN INN Historical   **Dinner:** $17-$25   **Phone:** 610/399-1390
AAA   **Location:** 4 mi s on US 202 & 322, 0.3 mi w; in historic Dilworth Town Village. **Hours:** 5:30 pm-10 pm, Sat
5 pm-10:30 pm, Sun 3 pm-9 pm. **Reservations:** required. **Features:** semi-formal attire; cocktails & lounge; a
◆◆◆   la carte. Candlelight dining in restored historic inn. French influence. Very extensive wine list. **Cards:** AE,
Continental   CB, DI, DS, MC, VI.   ⊠

WILLOW GROVE—16,300   (See map p. 368; index p. 366)

LODGINGS

COURTYARD BY MARRIOTT-WILLOW GROVE   Rates Subject to Change   **Phone:** 215/830-0550   🆗79
◆◆◆   Sun-Thurs   1P: $145- 162   2P/1B: $145- 162   2P/2B: $145- 162
Motor Inn   Fri & Sat   1P: $105- 115   2P/1B: $105- 115   2P/2B: $105- 115
Location: Just n on SR 611 from jct PA Tpk, exit 27. 2350 Easton Rd, Rt 611 19090. **Fax:** 215/830-0572.
Terms: Sr. discount; check-in 4 pm; no pets. **Facility:** 149 rooms. 3 stories; interior corridors. **Dining:** Coffee shop; 6:30-10
am, Sat & Sun 7-11:30 am. **All Rooms:** free & pay movies. **Cards:** AE, DI, DS, MC, VI. *(See color ad p 371)*
🛰 CTV 🛁 ⊠ 🐾 D S

HAMPTON INN-WILLOW GROVE   Rates Subject to Change   **Phone:** 215/659-3535   🆗80
◆◆◆   All Year [CP]   1P: $109   2P/1B: $119   2P/2B: $119
Motel   **Location:** 0.3 mi s on SR 611 from jct PA Tpk, exit 27. 1500 Easton Rd 19090. **Fax:** 215/659-4040.
Terms: Reserv deposit; no pets. **Facility:** 150 rooms. Max rate for up to 4 persons; 5 stories; interior corridors.
All Rooms: free & pay movies. **Cards:** AE, CB, DI, MC, VI.   CTV 🛁 ⊠ 🐾 D S

WRIGHTSTOWN—400

LODGING

HOLLILEIF BED & BREAKFAST   Rates Subject to Change   **Phone:** 215/598-3100
AAA   All Year [BP]   1P: $75- 160   2P/1B: $85- 160   XP: $20
Location: 0.4 mi s of SR 232. 677 Durham Rd (SR 413) 18940. **Terms:** Age restrictions may apply; reserv
◆◆   deposit, 7 day notice; 2 night min stay, some weekends; no pets. **Facility:** 5 rooms. 2 rooms feature gas fire-
Historic Bed   place; 3 stories, no elevator; interior corridors; smoke free premises. **Cards:** AE, DS, MC, VI.   ⊠ D
& Breakfast

Nearby New Jersey

BELLMAWR—12,600   (See map p. 368; index p. 366)

LODGING

BELLMAWR MOTOR INN   **Phone:** 609/931-6300   🆗99
AAA SAVE   Fri & Sat   1P: $48   2P/1B: $48   2P/2B: $52   XP: $4   F12
◆   Sun-Thurs   1P: $38   2P/1B: $44   2P/2B: $48   XP: $4   F12
Motel   **Location:** I-295, exit 28, 0.6 mi s; or New Jersey Tpk, exit 3; just n. 312 S Black Horse Pike (SR 168)
08031. **Fax:** 609/931-8350. **Terms:** Reserv deposit; weekly rates; no pets. **Facility:** 28 rooms. Modest rooms
for travellers on a budget. $2 key deposit; 2 stories; exterior corridors. **Dining:** Restaurant nearby.
Services: winter plug-ins. **All Rooms:** free movies. **Cards:** AE, CB, DI, DS, MC, VI. **Special Amenities:** Early
check-in/late check-out and preferred room (subject to availability with advanced reservations).   CTV ⊠ D

BLACKWOOD—5,100

LODGING

HOWARD JOHNSON EXPRESS INN   **Phone:** 609/228-4040
AAA SAVE   Fri & Sat [CP]   1P: $59- 95   2P/1B: $59- 95   2P/2B: $59- 95   XP: $7   F17
◆◆   Sun-Thurs [CP]   1P: $55- 89   2P/1B: $55- 89   2P/2B: $55- 89   XP: $7   F17
Motel   **Location:** On SR 168 just s of SR 42; from NJ Turnpike exit 3, 3.7 mi s. 832 N Black Horse Pike 08012.
Fax: 609/227-7544. **Terms:** Weekly rates; pets; $10 extra charge. **Facility:** 100 rooms. Traditional motel rooms
& 1 bedroom suites, most quite spacious. 17 whirlpool or Roman bath rms, $69-$95; 3 stories, no elevator; ex-
terior corridors. **Dining:** Restaurant nearby. **Services:** Fee: coin laundry. **All Rooms:** free movies. **Some Rooms:**
Fee: microwaves, refrigerators. **Cards:** AE, CB, DI, DS, JCB, MC, VI. **Special Amenities:** Early check-in/late check-out
and free newspaper.   🐾 🛰 🍴 CTV ⊠ 🐾 D

BORDENTOWN—4,300

LODGINGS

BEST WESTERN INN   **Phone:** 609/298-8000
AAA SAVE   5/1-6/30 & 9/4-9/30 [CP]   1P: $70- 80   2P/1B: $70- 85   2P/2B: $85   XP: $5   F16
◆◆   10/1-4/30 [CP]   1P: $64- 67   2P/1B: $69- 72   2P/2B: $72   XP: $5   F16
Motor Inn   7/1-9/3 [CP]   1P: $95   2P/1B: $115   XP: $5   F16
Location: Tpk exit 7, 0.8 mi n on US 206N. 1068 US 206N 08505. **Fax:** 609/291-9757. **Terms:** Reserv
deposit; package plans; small pets only. **Facility:** 102 rooms. Spacious accommodations; close proximity to
major highway. 3 stories; exterior corridors; saunas, whirlpool, small heated indoor pool; video games in all rooms. **Dining &
Entertainment:** Restaurant; 7 am-10 & 5-9:30 pm; $10-$21; health conscious menu items; cocktails/lounge. **Services:** valet
laundry. **All Rooms:** free & pay movies, refrigerators. **Cards:** AE, DI, DS, MC, VI. **Special Amenities:** Early check-in/late
check-out and free local telephone calls. *(See color ad p 232)*   🐾 🍴 🍴 CTV ⊠ 🐾 D

DAYS INN-BORDENTOWN   Phone: 609/298-6100
[AAA] [SAVE] 5/22-9/7   1P: $85- 95 2P/1B: $85- 95 2P/2B: $95- 105 XP: $10 F12
              5/1-5/21 & 9/8-4/30   1P: $55- 59 2P/1B: $55- 59 2P/2B: $55- 59 XP: $10 F12
◆◆   **Location:** Tpk exit 7, 0.8 mi n on US 206N. 1073 US 206N 08505. Fax: 609/298-7509. **Terms:** Package
Motor Inn   plans, weekends & summer; small pets only. **Facility:** 131 rooms. 2 stories; interior/exterior corridors.
              Dining & Entertainment: Restaurant; 6:30 am-10 & 5-9 pm; $7-$16; health conscious menu items;
cocktails/lounge. **Services:** valet laundry. **All Rooms:** free movies. **Some Rooms:** refrigerators. **Cards:** AE, CB, DI, DS,
CB, MC, VI.
                                                        🛏 🛳 🅼 CTV ✕ D

IMPERIAL INN   Rates Subject to Change   Phone: 609/298-3355
◆   Fri & Sat   1P: $45- 65 2P/1B: $45- 65 2P/2B: $45- 65 XP: $5
Motel   Sun-Thurs   1P: $40- 55 2P/1B: $40- 55 2P/2B: $40- 55 XP: $5
             Location: NJ Tpk, exit 7; 0.8 mi s. 3312 Rt 206 08505. Fax: 609/298-4617. **Terms:** No pets. **Facility:** 29
rooms. 2 whirlpool rms, extra charge; 1 story; exterior corridors. **All Rooms:** free movies. **Cards:** AE, DI, DS, MC, VI.
                                                           CTV ✕ 🌀 D

RAMADA INN BORDENTOWN   Rates Subject to Change   Phone: 609/298-3200
◆◆   5/1-9/1   1P: $75- 95 2P/1B: $75- 95 2P/2B: $75- 95 XP: $10 F18
Motor Inn   9/2-4/30   1P: $60- 80 2P/1B: $60- 80 2P/2B: $60- 80 XP: $10 F18
             Location: Tpk exit 7, 0.8 mi n. 1083 US 206N 08505. Fax: 609/298-8845. **Terms:** Sr. discount; reserv
deposit; small pets only. **Facility:** 95 rooms. 2 stories; interior corridors. **Dining:** Restaurant; $8-$11. **All Rooms:** free
movies. **Cards:** AE, DS, MC.
                                                        🛏 🛳 CTV ✕ D

RESTAURANT

MASTORIS RESTAURANT DINER   **Lunch:** $7-$8   **Dinner:** $10-$25   Phone: 609/298-4650
             Location: At n jct US 206 & US 130; I-295, exit 56 (US 130); NJ Tpk, exit 7 (US 206), 3 mi n. 144 Rt 130
American   08505. **Hours:** 5 am-1 am, Fri & Sat-2 am. Closed: 12/25. **Features:** carryout; cocktails & lounge. Casual
             family eatery offering exceptional value. Well prepared large amounts of food. Bakery on premises. NJ
favorite for generations. **Cards:** AE, DI, DS, MC, VI.   ✕

BRIDGEPORT—400

LODGING

HOLIDAY INN SELECT   Rates Subject to Change   Phone: 609/467-3322
◆◆◆   All Year   2P/1B: $99- 119 2P/2B: $99- 119
Motor Inn   **Location:** I-295 exit 10, 0.4 mi e. I-295 at Center Square Rd 08014 (PO Box 304). Fax: 609/467-3031.
             Terms: Sr. discount; no pets. **Facility:** 149 rooms. 6 suites $139-$179; rates for up to 4 persons. 12 whirlpool
rms, extra charge; 4 stories; interior corridors. **Dining:** Restaurant; 6:30 am-10 pm; $6-$20. **All Rooms:** free & pay movies.
Cards: AE, CB, DI, DS, JCB, MC, VI.   🛳 🅼 CTV 🛋 ✕ 🌀 D S

BROOKLAWN—1,800   (See map p. 368; index p. 366)

LODGING

DAYS INN   1P: $54- 79 2P/1B: $59- 84 2P/2B: $59- 84 XP: $5   [156]
[AAA] [SAVE] All Year [CP]   F12
◆◆◆   **Location:** I-295 exit 23, 2.5 mi n on SR 130; I-76 eastbound exit 1D, 1 mi s, westbound exit 1C, 1 mi s. 801
Motel   Rt 130 08030. Fax: 609/456-1413. **Terms:** Weekly/monthly rates; no pets. **Facility:** 115 rooms. Ground floor
             rooms with drive-up entry. 3 stories; exterior corridors; playground. **Services:** Fee: coin laundry.
             All Rooms: free movies. **Some Rooms:** microwaves, refrigerators. **Cards:** AE, CB, DI, DS, JCB, MC, VI.
See ad p 370)   🛳 🅼 🐾 CTV ✕ D S

BURLINGTON—9,800   (See map p. 368; index p. 366)

RESTAURANT

CAFE GALLERY Historical   **Lunch:** $6-$10   **Dinner:** $14-$20   Phone: 609/386-6150   [151]
[AAA]   **Location:** Downtown; 1 mi n of jct US 130; 6 mi nw of NJ Tpk, exit 5; 3 mi nw of I-295, exit 47B. 219 High
              St (SR 541) 08016. **Hours:** 11:30 am-3:30 & 5-10 pm, Fri & Sat-11 pm, Sun 11:30 am-3 & 5-10 pm. Closed
◆◆◆   major holidays. **Reservations:** suggested; Fri & Sat. **Features:** casual dress; health conscious menu items;
Regional   cocktails & lounge; street parking; a la carte. Casually elegant dining on charming, historic street. Art work on
French   display throughout; Al fresco terrace. Near shore of Delaware River. Outstanding Sunday buffet brunch.
              Cards: AE, CB, DI, MC, VI.   ✕

CHERRY HILL—69,300   (See map p. 368; index p. 366)

LODGINGS

DAYS INN   Phone: 609/663-0100
🛑 SAVE   All Year [CP]   1P: $60   2P/1B: $65   2P/2B: $65   XP: $5
◆   Location: I-295 exit 34B, 4 mi w on SR 70 to Cuthbert Blvd to SR 38, just ne. 525 Cuthbert Blvd (Rt
Motel   08002. Fax: 609/663-6449. Terms: Reserv deposit, 15 day notice; weekly rates; no pets. Facility: 50 ro
           Traditional style motel guest rooms. Updated guest rooms located in 2nd building close to the back. 2 whirl
           rms, extra charge. Handling fee imposed; 2 stories; exterior corridors. Dining: Restaurant nea
All Rooms: free movies. Some Rooms: 2 efficiencies, no utensils, refrigerators. Fee: VCR's. Cards: AE, CB, DI, DS,
VI. Special Amenities: Free breakfast.   CTV ✕

FOUR POINTS-CHERRY HILL BY ITT SHERATON   Rates Subject to Change   Phone: 609/428-2300
◆◆◆   All Year   1P: $89- 129   2P/1B: $99- 149   2P/2B: $99- 149 XP: $10
Motor Inn Location: I-295 exit 34B, just w. 1450 SR 70E 08034. Fax: 609/354-7662. Terms: No pets. Facility:
           rooms. 4 stories; interior corridors. Dining: Restaurant; 6:30 am-11 pm, Sat & Sun from 7 am; $7-
All Rooms: free & pay movies. Cards: AE, CB, DI, DS, MC, VI.   ◎ ⦿ CTV ✕ ⦿ D

HILTON AT CHERRY HILL   Rates Subject to Change   Phone: 609/665-6666
◆◆◆   All Year   1P: $119- 199   2P/1B: $129- 209   2P/2B: $129- 209 XP: $10
Hotel   Location: On SR 70 at Cuthbert; I-295 S, exit 34B; 4 mi w. 2349 W Marlton Pike 08002. Fax: 609/662-3
           Terms: No pets. Facility: 408 rooms. 14 stories; interior corridors. Dining: Restaurant; 6:30 am-11
$12-$25. All Rooms: free & pay movies. Cards: AE, CB, DI, DS, JCB, MC, VI. (See color ad p 18 & p 357)
                                                                           ◎ CTV 🚭 ✕ ⦿ D

HOLIDAY INN-CHERRY HILL   Rates Subject to Change   Phone: 609/663-5300
◆◆   All Year   1P: $89   2P/1B: $89   2P/2B: $89   XP: $10
Motor Inn Location: I-295 exit 34B, 2.5 mi w; opposite Garden State Race Track. Rt 70 & Sayer Ave 08
           Fax: 609/662-2913. Terms: Sr. discount; pets. Facility: 186 rooms. 6 stories; interior corric
Dining: Restaurant, coffee shop; 6 am-10 pm, Sat & Sun from 7 am. Coffee shop open for breakfast only; $7-
All Rooms: free & pay movies. Cards: AE, CB, DI, DS, JCB, MC, VI.   🐾 ◎ ◎ CTV ✕ ⦿ D

HOWARD JOHNSON EXPRESS INN & CONFERENCE CENTER   Phone: 609/317-1900
🛑 SAVE   All Year [CP]   1P: $65- 105   2P/1B: $65- 105 2P/2B: $65- 105
           Location: I-295, exit 34B, 4 mi w on SR 70; from Philadelphia via Ben Franklin Bridge, 2.5 mi via SR 30
◆◆   SR 70E. 2389 W Marlton Pike 08002. Fax: 609/317-0800. Terms: Weekly/monthly rates; package plans
Motor Inn pets. Facility: 100 rooms. 15 minutes from Philadelphia airport. Rates for up to 4 persons. 5 whirlpool
           extra charge; 2 stories; exterior corridors. Dining & Entertainment: Restaurant; 6:30 am-midnight; $10-
cocktails/lounge. Services: valet laundry. All Rooms: free movies, refrigerators. Some Rooms: 2 kitchens, microwa
Cards: AE, DI, DS, MC, VI. Special Amenities: Early check-in/late check-out and free breakfast.
                                                                           ◎ 🚭 CTV ✕

RESIDENCE INN BY MARRIOTT   Rates Subject to Change   Phone: 609/429-6111
◆◆◆   5/1-10/31 [CP]   1P: $128   2P/1B: $128   2P/2B: $131
Apartment 11/1-11/30 & 2/1-4/30 [CP] 1P: $116 2P/1B: $116   2P/2B: $117
Motel   12/1-1/31 [CP]   1P: $106   2P/1B: $106   2P/2B: $109
           Location: I-295 exit 34A, just e to Marlkress Rd jughandle, then back to Old Cuthbert Rd, just n. 1821
Cuthbert Rd 08034. Fax: 609/429-0345. Terms: Pets, $100 extra charge. Facility: 96 rooms. Handling fee imposed; 2 sto
exterior corridors. All Rooms: kitchens, free movies. Cards: AE, CB, DI, DS, MC, VI.   🐾 ◎ CTV ✕ ⦿

RESTAURANTS

ANDREOTTI'S VIENNESE CAFE &
PASTRY SHOP   Lunch: $6-$12   Dinner: $12-$20   Phone: 609/795-0172
🛑   Location: I-295 exit 34B, 0.5 mi w on SR 70, in Pine Tree Plaza Shopping Center. 1442 Rt 70 08
           Hours: 9 am-11 pm, Fri & Sat-2 am. Closed: 11/26 & 12/25. Reservations: suggested; weeke
◆◆   Features: casual dress; early bird specials; health conscious menu items; carryout; cocktails & lou
Continental Charming cafe/bakery feturing creative entrees, homemade soup & dessert. Expresso/cappuccino. S
           wines by the glass. Healthy Mediterranean influence. Cards: AE, DI, MC, VI.

CAFFE LAMBERTI   Lunch: $9-$13   Dinner: $13-$18   Phone: 609/663-1747
◆◆   Location: I-295 exit 34B, 2.5 mi w; across from Garden State Park. 2011 Rt 70W 08002. Hours: 1
Italian   am-10 pm, Sun 4 pm-9 pm. Closed major holidays. Reservations: suggested. Features: casual dr
           cocktails; a la carte. Casually elegant dining rooms featuring creative Italian & continental cuisine. Pat
season. Cards: AE, DI, DS, MC, VI.

LA CAMPAGNE   Lunch: $10-$13   Dinner: $17-$29   Phone: 609/429-7647
🛑   Location: 2 mi sw of Rt 70 & I-295. 312 Kresson Rd 08034. Hours: 11:30 am-2:30 & 5-9 pm, Sat &
           from 5 pm. Closed: 1/1, 12/25, Mon. Features: a la carte, also prix fixe. South of France dining experie
◆◆◆   Circa 1840 farm house with brick hearths, antiques, Oriental rugs & fresh flowers. Upscale cas
French   Cards: AE, DI, MC, VI.

SIRI'S THAI FRENCH CUISINE   Lunch: $7-$11   Dinner: $9-$25   Phone: 609/663-6781
◆◆   Location: Track Town Shopping Center (opposite Garden State Park). 2117-2119 Rt 70 W 08
Ethnic   Hours: 11:30 am-10 pm, Fri & Sat-11 pm, Sun 3 pm-10 pm. Closed: 1/1 & 11/26. Reservations: requ
           weekends. Features: health conscious menu items; a la carte. Upscale casual. Lunch specials include e
soup or appetizer with entree. Cards: AE, MC, VI.

MAPLE SHADE—19,200   (See map p. 368; index p. 366)

LODGING

RODEWAY INN   Phone: 609/235-3200
🛑 SAVE   5/1-12/31   1P: $52   2P/1B: $62   2P/2B: $62
           1/1-4/30   1P: $50   2P/1B: $50   2P/2B: $50
◆   Location: I-295 exit 36B, 1.5 mi nw; NJ Tpk exit 4, 2 mi nw. 2840 Rt 73 N 08052. Fax: 609/235-6
Motel   Terms: Reserv deposit; weekly rates; no pets. Facility: 50 rooms. Typical motel style guest rooms; all
           modern decor. Drive up entrances at each guest room. 1 story; exterior corridors. Dining: Restau
nearby. All Rooms: free & pay movies, combo or shower baths. Some Rooms: microwaves, refrigerators, whirlpe
Cards: AE, CB, DI, DS, MC, VI. Special Amenities: Free breakfast and free local telephone calls.
                                                                                          CTV ✕

MEDFORD—1,900   (See map p. 368; index p. 366)

RESTAURANT

BEAU RIVAGE RESTAURANT   **Lunch:** $7-$13   **Dinner:** $16-$32   **Phone:** 609/983-1999   (170)
◆◆◆   **Location:** From jct of SR 70 & 73 1 mi s to Marlton Pkwy (CR 544), 4 mi e to Taunton Blvd (CR 623), 1 mi
French   n; 0.3 mi s of jct Taunton Blvd & Tuckerton Rd. 128 Taunton Blvd 08055. **Hours:** 11:30 am-2:30 & 5:30-9:30
pm, Sat from 5:30 pm, Sun 4 pm-8 pm. Closed: 12/25, 1/1, Mon & last 2 weeks of Aug.
Reservations: required. **Features:** semi-formal attire; cocktails; a la carte. Fine dining in a setting of understated elegance.
Varied menu features daily specials. Emphasis on French country dining. **Cards:** AE, DI, MC, VI.

MOUNT HOLLY—10,600   (See map p. 368; index p. 366)

LODGINGS

BEST WESTERN BURLINGTON INN   Guaranteed Rates   **Phone:** 609/261-3800   (151)
ⓐⓐ   All Year   1P: $65- 79 2P/1B: $69- 84 2P/2B: $74- 84 XP: $8   F12
◆◆◆   **Location:** NJ Tpk, exit 5, just n on CR 541. Box 2020 Rt 541, RD 1 08060. Fax: 609/267-0958. **Terms:** Sr.
Motel   discount; small pets only, $5 extra charge. **Facility:** 62 rooms. 2 stories; interior corridors. **Cards:** AE, CB,
DI, DS, MC, VI. *(See color ad p 35 & p 389)*

HOWARD JOHNSON MOTOR LODGE   Rates Subject to Change   **Phone:** 609/267-6550   (150)
◆◆   All Year   1P: $55- 90 2P/1B: $58- 90 2P/2B: $70- 90 XP: $7   F18
Motor Inn   **Location:** NJ Tpk, exit 5, just n on CR 541. 08060 (PO Box 73). Fax: 609/267-2575. **Terms:** Sr. discount;
pets. **Facility:** 90 rooms. 2 stories; interior/exterior corridors. **Dining:** Restaurant; 6 am-11 pm; $7-$15.
All Rooms: free movies. **Cards:** AE, CB, DI, DS, MC, VI.

RESTAURANT

ROBIN'S NEST   **Lunch:** $6-$8   **Dinner:** $10-$17   **Phone:** 609/261-6149   (145)
◆◆   **Location:** Downtown. 2-4 Washington St 08060. **Hours:** 10 am-3 pm, Wed-Sat to 9 pm, Sun-2 pm. Closed
American   major holidays. **Reservations:** accepted. **Features:** Sunday brunch; carryout; cocktails & lounge; street
parking; a la carte. Quaintly decorated dining rooms. Homemade desserts. Retail dessert outlet. Lighted lot
parking avail. **Cards:** AE, MC, VI.

MOUNT LAUREL—30,300   (See map p. 368; index p. 366)

LODGINGS

COURTYARD BY MARRIOTT   Rates Subject to Change   **Phone:** 609/273-4400   (135)
◆◆◆   Sun-Thurs   1P: $109 2P/1B: $109 2P/2B: $109
Motel   Fri & Sat   1P: $79 2P/1B: $79 2P/2B: $89
Location: NJ Tpk, exit 4, just nw on SR 73 to Fellowship Rd, just s; I-295, exit 36A, just se on SR 73 to
Fellowship Rd, just s. 1000 Century Pkwy 08054. Fax: 609/273-2889. **Terms:** No pets. **Facility:** 151 rooms. 4 stories; interior
corridors. **Dining:** Coffee shop; 6:30-10 am, Sat & Sun 7 am-noon. **All Rooms:** free & pay movies. **Cards:** AE, CB, DI, DS,
JCB, MC, VI. *(See color ad below)*

(See map p. 368)

DOUBLETREE GUEST SUITES HOTEL Guaranteed Rates Phone: 609/778-8999 **146**
◆◆◆ All Year [BP] 1P: $129 2P/1B: $144 2P/2B: $144 XP: $15 F18
Suite Hotel **Location:** NJ Tpk exit 4, just nw to Fellowship Rd just n; I-295 exit 36A, just se on SR 73 to Fellowship Rd, just n. 515 Fellowship Rd N 08054. Fax: 609/778-9720. **Terms:** Sr. discount; no pets. **Facility:** 204 rooms. 3 stories; interior corridors. **Dining:** Restaurant; 6:30 am-10:30 pm, Sat 6:30 am-11:30 & 5-10 pm, Sun 6:30 am-11:30 am; $10-$17. **Cards:** AE, CB, DI, DS, MC, VI. [icons]

HAMPTON INN MT LAUREL Guaranteed Rates Phone: 609/778-5535 **144**
◆◆◆ All Year [CP] 1P: $81 2P/1B: $81 2P/2B: $81
Motel **Location:** NJ Tpk exit 4, 1 mi se on SR 73 (behind Chili's); I-295 exit 36A, 2 mi se on SR 73. 4000 Crawford Place 08054. Fax: 609/778-0377. **Terms:** No pets. **Facility:** 127 rooms. Rates up to 4 persons; 4 stories; interior corridors. **All Rooms:** free & pay movies. **Cards:** AE, CB, DI, DS, JCB, MC. [icons]

MCINTOSH INN OF MOUNT LAUREL Rates Subject to Change Phone: 609/234-7194 **141**
◆◆ All Year [CP] 1P: $43- 53 2P/1B: $49- 59 2P/2B: $63 XP: $6 F18
Motel **Location:** NJ Tpk exit 4, just se on SR 73; I-295 exit 36A, 0.8 mi se on SR 73. 1132 Rt 73 08054. Fax: 609/231-8516. **Terms:** Sr. discount; no pets. **Facility:** 93 rooms. 2 stories; exterior corridors. **All Rooms:** free movies. **Cards:** AE, CB, DI, MC, VI. *(See color ad p 220, p 353 & p 234)*
Roll in showers. [icons]

MT LAUREL FAIRFIELD INN BY MARRIOTT Phone: 609/642-0600
Motel Under construction; **Location:** 350 Century Pkwy 08054. **Facility:** 118 rooms. Scheduled to open March 1998.

QUALITY INN Rates Subject to Change Phone: 609/235-7400 **140**
◆◆ All Year 1P: $49- 89 2P/1B: $49- 89 2P/2B: $49- 89 XP: $10 F18
Motor Inn **Location:** I-295, exit 36A, just s to Fellowship Rd; NJ Tpk, exit 4, just n. 550 Fellowship Rd 08054. Fax: 609/778-9729. **Terms:** Sr. discount; no pets. **Facility:** 148 rooms. 2 stories; exterior corridors. **Dining:** Restaurant; 7 am-10 pm; $11-$22. **All Rooms:** free movies. **Cards:** AE, CB, DI, DS, JCB, MC, VI. *(See ad p 391)* [icons]

RADISSON HOTEL Rates Subject to Change Phone: 609/234-7300 **134**
◆◆◆ All Year 1P: $119 2P/1B: $119 2P/2B: $119 XP: $15 F17
Hotel **Location:** NJ Tpk exit 4, ne corner; I-295 exit 36A, just se. 915 Rt 73 08054. Fax: 609/802-3912. **Terms:** Sr. discount; no pets. **Facility:** 283 rooms. 10 stories; interior corridors. **Dining:** Restaurant; 6:30 am-11 pm; $12-$17. **All Rooms:** free & pay movies. **Cards:** AE, CB, DI, DS, JCB, MC, VI.
Roll in showers. [icons]

RED CARPET INN Phone: 609/235-5610 **142**
(AAA) [SAVE] All Year 1P: $44- 48 2P/1B: $46- 50 2P/2B: $50- 55 XP: $2 F16
◆ **Location:** NJ Tpk exit 4, just se; I-295 exit 36A, 0.8 mi se. 1104 SR 73S 08054. Fax: 609/235-6713. **Terms:** Weekly/monthly rates; no pets. **Facility:** 71 rooms. Basic budget oriented property offering large guest rooms. 2 stories; exterior corridors. **Dining:** Restaurant nearby. **All Rooms:** free movies. **Cards:** AE, DS, MC, VI. **Special Amenities:** Early check-in/late check-out and preferred room (subject to availability with advanced reservations). [icons]

RED ROOF INN Rates Subject to Change Phone: 609/234-5589 **138**
◆◆ All Year 1P: $46- 52 2P/1B: $56- 63 2P/2B: $50- 57 XP: $10 F18
Motel **Location:** NJ Tpk, exit 4, just nw on SR 73 to Fellowship Rd just s; I-295, exit 36A, just se on SR 73 to Fellowship Rd, just s. 603 Fellowship Rd 08054. Fax: 609/234-4063. **Terms:** Small pets only. **Facility:** 108 rooms. 2 stories; exterior corridors. **All Rooms:** free & pay movies. **Cards:** AE, CB, DI, DS, MC, VI. [icons]

SUMMERFIELD SUITES HOTEL Rates Subject to Change Phone: 609/222-1313 **143**
◆◆◆ All Year 1P: $90- 129 2P/1B: $90- 129 2P/2B: $130- 160
Suite Motel **Location:** I-295, exit 36A, Rt 73 S 1.5 mi; NJ Tpk exit 4, 1 mi on Rt 73 S. 3000 Crawford Pl 08054. Fax: 609/222-1919. **Terms:** Check-in 4 pm; pets, $100-$150 extra charge. **Facility:** 116 rooms. Larger rooms avail for up to 6 persons; 3 stories; interior/exterior corridors. **All Rooms:** kitchens. **Cards:** AE, CB, DI, DS, JCB, MC, VI.
Roll in showers. [icons]

SUPER 8 MOTEL Rates Subject to Change Phone: 609/802-2800 **137**
Motel All Year 1P: $39- 79 2P/1B: $39- 79 2P/2B: $39- 79 XP: $10 F18
Under major renovation; **Location:** I-295, exit 36A, just s to Fellowship Rd e; NJ Tpk exit 4, just n to Fellowship Rd e. 554 Fellowship Rd 08054. Fax: 609/234-6051. **Terms:** No pets. **Facility:** 98 rooms. Scheduled to open fall 1997; 2 stories; interior/exterior corridors. **All Rooms:** free movies. **Some Rooms:** 4 kitchens. **Cards:** AE, DI, DS, MC, VI. [icons]

TRACK & TURF MOTEL Guaranteed Rates Phone: 609/235-6500 **136**
(AAA) All Year 1P: $34- 38 2P/1B: $34- 38 2P/2B: $41- 45 XP: $4 F12
◆ **Location:** NJ Tpk exit 4, 0.8 mi nw; I-295 exit 36B, just nw. 809 SR 73 08054. Fax: 609/235-7624. **Terms:** Reserv deposit; **Facility:** 30 rooms. 1 story; exterior corridors. **All Rooms:** free movies. **Cards:** AE, CB, DI, DS, MC, VI. [icons]
Motel

TRAVELODGE HOTEL AND CONFERENCE CENTER Phone: 609/234-7000 **139**
(AAA) [SAVE] All Year 1P: $69 2P/1B: $69 2P/2B: $79 XP: $5 F12
◆◆ **Location:** NJ Tpk, exit 4, I-295, exit 36A, 0.5 mi se on SR 73 08054. Fax: 609/235-3909. **Terms:** Reserv deposit; monthly rates; small pets only, $25 extra charge. **Facility:** 229 rooms. Comfortable guest rooms offering, good accommodations for those on a budget. 4 suites, $150-$250; 9 stories; interior corridors; saunas, whirlpool. **Dining & Entertainment:** Restaurant; 7-11 am, Sat & Sun 6:30-10 am, 11:30-2 & 5-10 pm; $12-$18; cocktails/lounge. **Services:** valet laundry. **All Rooms:** coffeemakers, free & pay movies. **Cards:** AE, CB, DI, DS, JCB, MC, VI. **Special Amenities:** Free local telephone calls. [icons]

(See map p. 368)

RESTAURANT

SAGE DINER   **Lunch:** $5-$9   **Dinner:** $7-$11   **Phone:** 609/727-0770   140
◆
American
MC, VI.
Location: NJ Tpk, exit 4 just se, 1-295 exit 36A, 1 mi se. 1170 Rt 73 08054. **Hours:** 6 am-1 am, Fri & Sat-24 hours. **Reservations:** accepted. **Features:** children's menu; carryout. A local favorite for large variety of homecooked offerings. Inviting casual ambience with some art deco touches. Own desserts. **Cards:** AE, ⊗

PEMBERTON—1,400

LODGING

ISAAC HILLIARD HOUSE BED & BREAKFAST   Rates Subject to Change   **Phone:** 609/894-0756
◆◆◆   Fri-Sun [BP]   1P: $60- 120   2P/1B: $70- 130   XP: $20
Historic Bed Mon-Thurs [BP]   1P: $45- 105   2P/1B: $55- 115   XP: $20
& Breakfast   **Location:** Town Center. 31 Hanover St 08068. **Terms:** Age restrictions may apply; reserv deposit, 10 day notice; no pets. **Facility:** 4 rooms. Handling fee imposed; 2 stories; interior corridors; smoke free premises.
Cards: AE, MC, VI.   🏊 CTV ⊗ D

PENNS GROVE—5,200

LODGING

WELLESLEY INNS & SUITES   **Phone:** 609/299-3800
ⒶⒶⒶ SAVE   All Year [CP]   1P: $65   2P/1B: $70   2P/2B: $75   XP: $10   F18
◆◆◆   **Location:** 1 mi e of Delaware Memorial Bridge; jct US 40 & NJ Tpk exit 1; off I-295, exit 2B. 517 S
Motel   Pennsville-Auburn Rd 08069. Fax: 609/299-6982. **Terms:** Reserv deposit; small pets only, $25 dep req. **Facility:** 140 rooms. Breakfast served in attractive poolside atrium. Up-to-date rooms. 2 stories; interior corridors; pool table. **Dining:** Restaurant nearby. **Services:** Fee: coin laundry. **All Rooms:** coffeemakers, free & pay movies, refrigerators. **Some Rooms:** microwaves. **Cards:** AE, CB, DI, DS, MC, VI. **Special Amenities: Free breakfast and free local telephone calls.** (See color ad opposite inside back cover)   🐾 🛏 🆓 🍴 ⊗ D

RUNNEMEDE—9,000   (See map p. 368; index p. 366)

LODGINGS

COMFORT INN   **Phone:** 609/939-6700   116
ⒶⒶⒶ SAVE   All Year [CP]   1P: $60- 90   2P/1B: $60- 95 2P/2B: $60- 95 XP: $5   F18
◆◆◆   **Location:** 0.3 mi se on SR 168; from NJ Tpk exit 3, just c on 9th Ave, or 1 mi se of I-295, exit 28. 101 9th
Motel   Ave 08078. Fax: 609/939-6700. **Terms:** No pets. **Facility:** 42 rooms. Very contemporary rooms. Coffee/cappuccino machine in lobby. 6 suites $75-$95, 2 whirlpool rms, $100-$175; 2 stories; interior corridors. **Dining:** Restaurant nearby. **Services:** valet laundry. **All Rooms:** free movies. **Some Rooms:** refrigerators. Fee: microwaves. **Cards:** AE, CB, DI, DS, JCB. **Special Amenities: Early check-in/late check-out and free local telephone calls.**   🍴 🛏 CTV ⊗ 🈷 D

HOLIDAY INN-RUNNEMEDE   **Phone:** 609/939-4200   115
ⒶⒶⒶ SAVE   All Year   1P: $79   2P/1B: $89   2P/2B: $89   XP: $10   F18
◆◆◆   **Location:** NJ Tpk exit 3, 0.3 mi se to 9th Ave just e; I-295 exit 28, 1.3 mi se to 9th Ave. 109 9th Ave 08078.
Motor Inn   Fax: 609/939-3761. **Terms:** Package plans; pets, $50 dep req. **Facility:** 174 rooms. 7 stories; interior corridors. **Dining & Entertainment:** Restaurant; 6:30 am-9:30 & 6-10 pm, Sat & Sun from 7 am-11 & 6-10 pm; $10-$18; cocktails/lounge. **All Rooms:** free & pay movies. **Some Rooms:** Fee: refrigerators. **Cards:** AE, DI, DS, MC, VI. **Special Amenities: Early check-in/late check-out and preferred room (subject to availability with advanced reservations).**   🛏 🏊 🆓 CTV ⊗ D

THOROFARE—1,900

LODGING

BEST WESTERN WEST DEPTFORD   **Phone:** 609/848-4111
ⒶⒶⒶ SAVE   Sun-Thurs   1P: $69   2P/1B: $79   2P/2B: $69   XP: $5   F18
◆◆◆   Fri & Sat   1P: $65   2P/1B: $74   2P/2B: $65   XP: $5   F18
Motor Inn   **Location:** I-295 exit 20, just e. 101 Grove Rd 08086. Fax: 609/845-8977. **Terms:** Weekly/monthly rates; no pets. **Facility:** 100 rooms. Attractively furnished traditional motel rooms. 2 stories; interior corridors. **Dining & Entertainment:** Restaurant; 6:30 am-2 & 5-9 pm, Fri-10 pm, Sat 6:30 am-11 & 5-10 pm, Sun 6:30 am-11 am; $8-$20; cocktails/lounge. **Services:** Fee: coin laundry. **All Rooms:** free movies. **Some Rooms:** Fee: refrigerators. **Cards:** AE, CB, DI, DS, MC, VI. **Special Amenities: Free room upgrade (subject to availability with advanced reservations).**   🏊 🆓 🛏 CTV ⊗ D

VOORHEES—24,600   (See map p. 368; index p. 366)

LODGING

HAMPTON INN   Guaranteed Rates   **Phone:** 609/346-4500   160
◆◆◆   All Year [CP]   1P: $91- 98   2P/1B: $91- 98 2P/2B: $91- 98
Motel   **Location:** I-295, exit 32; 2.3 mi e on Haddonfield-Berlin Rd, s on White Horse Rd, 0.3 mi to Laurel Oak Rd in Voorhees Corporate Center. 121 Laurel Oak Rd 08043. Fax: 609/346-2402. **Terms:** Pets. **Facility:** 120 rooms. Rates for up to 4 persons; 4 stories; interior corridors. **All Rooms:** free & pay movies. **Cards:** AE, CB, DI, DS, MC, VI.   🐾 🏊 CTV ⊗ 🈷 D S

RESTAURANTS

MAMA VENTURA'S   **Lunch:** $7-$9   **Dinner:** $12-$22   **Phone:** 609/767-7400   148
◆◆   **Location:** 4 mi s of SR 70. 178 SR 73 08043. **Hours:** 11:30 am-3 & 4-10 pm, Fri-11 pm, Sat 4 pm-11 pm,
Continental Sun 3 pm-10 pm. Closed: 12/25. **Reservations:** suggested; weekends. **Features:** children's menu; early bird specials; cocktails & lounge; a la carte. Window seating overlooking waterfall garden. Variety of seafood. Terrace dining in season. **Cards:** AE, CB, DI, DS, MC, VI.

SOMSAK-THAI CUISINE   **Lunch:** $6-$8   **Dinner:** $8-$18   **Phone:** 609/782-1771   149
◆◆   **Location:** I-295, exit 32; 2.3 mi e to White Horse Rd, 0.5 mi s in Echo Shoppes. 200 White Horse Rd
Ethnic   08841. **Hours:** 11 am-10 pm. Closed major holidays & Sun. **Features:** carryout; a la carte. Authentic Thai cuisine in snug, pleasant storefront. Gracious service. Homemade ice cream. 3 course lunch specials. Smoke free premises. **Cards:** AE, DI, DS, MC, VI.   ⊗

WINSLOW—800

LODGING

KNIGHTS INN   **Phone:** 609/561-6200
🔺🔺🔺 [SAVE]   Fri & Sat 6/15-9/5   1P: $55- 70   2P/1B: $55- 70 2P/2B: $55- 70
               5/1-6/14, Sun-Thurs 6/15-9/5
◆◆   & 9/6-4/30   1P: $40- 55   2P/1B: $40- 55 2P/2B: $40- 55
Motel   **Location:** Atlantic City Expwy, exit 31 westbound or exit 33 eastbound, just nw. 530 Rt 73 08095 (PO Box
nearby. 189). Fax: 609/567-9340. **Terms:** Pets. **Facility:** 45 rooms. 2 stories; exterior corridors. **Dining:** Restaurant
nearby. **All Rooms:** free movies. **Some Rooms:** coffeemakers, microwaves, radios, refrigerators, whirlpools. **Cards:** AE,
CB, DI, DS, MC, VI. **Special Amenities:** Early check-in/late check-out and free local telephone calls.

(🛏) (CTV) (✕) (D)

PHILIPSBURG—3,000

LODGINGS

HARBOR INN   Rates Subject to Change   **Phone:** 814/342-0250
◆◆   All Year   1P: $48- 54 2P/1B: $59   2P/2B: $54- 59 XP: $5   F18
Motor Inn **Location:** At jct US 322 & SR 53N. (PO Box 145, 16866). Fax: 814/342-6103. **Terms:** Sr. discount; small
          pets only. **Facility:** 65 rooms. 2 stories; interior corridors. **Dining:** Restaurant; 6 am-10 pm; $10-$17.
Cards: AE, DI, DS, MC, VI.

(🛏) (CTV) (✕) (D)

MAIN LINER MOTEL   Rates Subject to Change   **Phone:** 814/342-2004
🔺🔺🔺   All Year   1P: $31- 35 2P/1B: $35- 41 2P/2B: $39   XP: $6   F10
          Location: 1 mi w of jct SR 53N. US 322 16866 (RD 3, Box 115). **Terms:** Sr. discount; reserv deposit, 5 day
◆   notice; small pets only, $6 extra charge. **Facility:** 21 rooms. Handling fee imposed; 1 story; exterior corridors.
Motel   **Cards:** AE, DS, MC, VI.

(🛏) (CTV) (✕) (D)

PINE GROVE—3,700

LODGINGS

COMFORT INN   Rates Subject to Change   **Phone:** 717/345-8031
◆◆   5/1-11/30 [CP]   1P: $50- 75 2P/1B: $55- 80 2P/2B: $55- 80 XP: $6   F18
Motel   12/1-4/30 [CP]   1P: $45- 65 2P/1B: $50- 70 2P/2B: $50- 70 XP: $6   F18
          Location: US 443 at I-81, exit 31 17963 (PO Box 327). Fax: 717/345-2308. **Terms:** Sr. discount; pets, $15
extra charge. **Facility:** 68 rooms. 3 stories; interior corridors. **Cards:** AE, CB, DI, DS, JCB, MC, VI.

(🛏) (⤴) (CTV) (♠) (✕) (♦) (D) (S)

ECONO LODGE   **Phone:** 717/345-4099
🔺🔺🔺 [SAVE] 5/1-9/30   1P: $40- 60 2P/1B: $45- 65 2P/2B: $45- 65 XP: $5   F18
          10/1-4/30   1P: $35- 45 2P/1B: $40- 50 2P/2B: $40- 50 XP: $5   F18
◆◆   **Location:** I-81 exit 31, just e on SR 443. (RD 5, Box 15, 17963). Fax: 717/345-4984. **Terms:** Pets, $5 extra
Motel   charge. **Facility:** 51 rooms. Whirlpool rm, extra charge; 2 stories; interior/exterior corridors.
          Dining: Restaurant nearby. **All Rooms:** free movies. **Some Rooms:** Fee: VCR's. **Cards:** AE, DI, DS, MC,
VI.

(🛏) (CTV) (✕) (D)

PINE GROVE MILLS—1,100

RESTAURANT

THE OLD OAK TAVERN   **Lunch:** $4-$6   **Dinner:** $7-$15   **Phone:** 814/238-5898
◆   **Location:** At s jct of SR 26 & 45, on SR 26. 101 E Pine Grove Rd 16868. **Hours:** 11:30 am-9 pm, Fri &
American Sat-10 pm. Closed major holidays, Sun & Mon. **Reservations:** suggested. **Features:** casual dress; children's
like ambience. **Cards:** AE, DS, MC, VI.

PIPERSVILLE—see Philadelphia & Vicinity p. 385.

Pittsburgh & Vicinity

PITTSBURGH—369,900   (See map p. 396; index p. 396)

To help you more easily locate accommodations in the Greater Pittsburgh area, the following two indexes and maps show lodgings and restaurants in multiple cities. Listings
for these establishments are found under the heading for the city in which they are located. The Pittsburgh area map comprises: Allison Park, Bethel Park, Blawnox, Bloomfield, Bridgeville, Coraopolis, Crafton, Gibsonia, Green Tree, Harmarville, Heidelberg,
Monroeville, New Kensington, Oakdale, Oakmont, Pittsburgh, Pleasant Hills, Sewickley,
Shadyside, Turtle Creek, Warrendale, West Mifflin and Wexford.

Airport Accommodations
Listings for these establishments are found under the heading for the city in which they are located.

PITTSBURGH

Clarion Royce Hotel Pittsburgh Airport, 6.5 mi e of airport/CORAOPOLIS
Courtyard by Marriott, 6 mi e of airport/CORAOPOLIS
🔺🔺🔺🔺 **Embassy Suites-Pittsburgh International Airport, 6 mi e of airport/CORAOPOLIS**
Hampton Inn Hotel Airport, 6.5 mi n of airport/CORAOPOLIS
🔺🔺🔺 **Holiday Inn-Pittsburgh Airport, 6.5 mi n of airport/CORAOPOLIS**
La Quinta Inn-Airport, 6.5 mi n of airport/CORAOPOLIS
🔺🔺🔺 **Motel 6 Airport - 1285, 6.5 mi e of airport/CORAOPOLIS**

Pittsburgh Airport Marriott, 1.3 mi se of airport/CORAOPOLIS
Red Roof Inn Pittsburgh Airport, 6.5 mi n of airport/CORAOPOLIS
Red Roof Inn South Airport, 9 mi e of airport via SR 60S/PITTSBURGH
Wyndham Garden Hotel-Pittsburgh Airport, 6 mi se of airport/CORAOPOLIS

Index of Establishments on the DOWNTOWN PITTSBURGH ACCOMMODATIONS Spotting Map

The Priory-A City Inn **1**
Pittsburgh Hilton & Towers.................... **2**
Doubletree Hotel Pittsburgh................. **3**
Pittsburgh Marriott City Center **4**
Ramada Plaza Suites & Conference Center **5**
Sheraton Hotel Station Square **7**

RESTAURANTS
Penn Brewery Restaurant **1**
Top of The Triangle **2**
The Terrace Room.......................... **3**
Max's Allegheny Tavern **4**
Grand Concourse Restaurant **5**
Tequila Junction **6**

Cheese Cellar Restaurant **7**
The Common Pleas........................ **8**
Cafe Victoria **9**
Froggy's................................ **10**
Harry G's............................... **11**
Jake's Above the Square **12**
Kiku's of Japan **13**
Piccolo Piccolo.......................... **16**
Primanti Bros **17**
Sesame Inn **18**
Seventh Street Grille...................... **19**
Sushi Kim **21**
The Carlton **22**

LODGINGS

DOUBLETREE HOTEL PITTSBURGH   Rates Subject to Change   Phone: 412/281-3700   **3**
Sun-Thurs   1P: $130
Hotel   Fri & Sat   1P: $99
Location: At Liberty Center, adjacent to convention center. 1000 Penn Ave 15222. Fax: 412/227-4500
Terms: Reserv deposit; pets. **Facility:** 618 rooms. 26 stories; interior corridors. Fee: parking. **Dining:** 2
restaurants; 6:30 am-1 am. **All Rooms:** free & pay movies. **Some Rooms:** 6 kitchens. **Cards:** AE, CB, DI
DS, MC, VI. *(See ad p 397)*

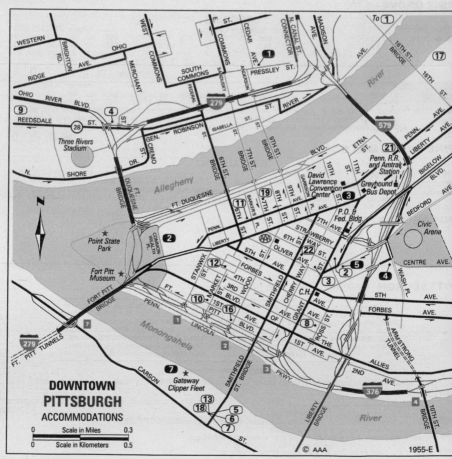

DOWNTOWN
PITTSBURGH
ACCOMMODATIONS

Scale in Miles   0   0.3
Scale in Kilometers   0   0.5

© AAA   1955-E

(See map p. 396)

PITTSBURGH MARRIOTT CITY CENTER   Rates Subject to Change   **Phone:** 412/471-4000   **4**
◆◆◆   Sun-Thurs 5/1-10/31   1P: $169   2P/1B: $169   2P/2B: $169
Hotel   11/1-3/31   1P: $139   2P/1B: $139   2P/2B: $139
    4/1-4/30   1P: $125   2P/1B: $125   2P/2B: $125
    Fri & Sat 5/1-10/31   1P: $84   2P/1B: $84   2P/2B: $84
Location: On Center Ave, just e of Crosstown Blvd, opposite Civic Arena. 112 Washington Pl 15219. Fax: 412/281-4797.
Terms: No pets. **Facility;** 401 rooms, 21 stories; interior corridors. Fee; parking. **Dining:** Dining room; 6:30 am-11 pm;
$10-$22. **All Rooms:** free & pay movies. **Cards:** AE, CB, DI, DS, JCB, MC, VI.   Roll in showers.

PITTSBURGH HILTON & TOWERS   Rates Subject to Change   **Phone:** 412/391-4600   **2**
◆◆◆   All Year   1P: $119- 264   2P/1B: $119- 264   2P/2B: $119- 264   XP: $25   F
Hotel   **Location:** In Gateway Center on Commonwealth, opposite Point State Park. Gateway Center 15222.
Fax: 412/594-5161. **Terms:** Small pets only. **Facility:** 712 rooms. 24 stories; interior corridors. Fee: parking.
Dining: Dining room, restaurant; 6:30 am-11:30 pm; $8-$28. **All Rooms:** free & pay movies. **Cards:** AE, CB, DI, DS, JCB,
MC, VI. *(See color ad p 18)*

(See map p. 396)

THE PRIORY-A CITY INN
Rates Subject to Change
Phone: 412/231-3338　❶
Mon-Thurs [CP]　　1P: $68- 110　2P/1B: $110- 125　　　　　　　XP: $12　F7
Fri-Sun [CP]　　　　1P: $100　　2P/1B: $100　　　　　　　　　　　XP: $12　F7
◆◆◆ **Location:** Exit 13 off I-279N, exit 15 off I 279S; w 3 blks on E Ohio St to Cedar, s 3 blks to Pressley. 614
Historic Bed Pressley St 15212. Fax: 412/231-4838. **Terms:** Reserv deposit; no pets. **Facility:** 24 rooms. 3 stories, no el-
& Breakfast evator; interior corridors. **Cards:** AE, CB, DI, DS, MC, VI. *(See color ad below)*　ECTV D S

RAMADA PLAZA SUITES & CONFERENCE CENTER　Rates Subject to Change　Phone: 412/281-5800　❺
◆◆　　All Year [CP]　　1P: $95- 109　2P/1B:　$95- 109　2P/2B:　$95- 109　XP: $10　F18
Suite Hotel **Location:** Jct of Bigelow & 6th sts, just n of Grant St. One Bigelow Square 15219. Fax: 412/281-8467.
Terms: No pets. **Facility:** 311 rooms. 20 stories; interior corridors. **Dining:** Dining room; 6:30 am-midnight;
Fri-1 am, Sat & Sun 7 am-1 am; $10-$17. **All Rooms:** Fee: movies. **Some Rooms:** 271 kitchens. **Cards:** AE, CB, DI, DS,
MC, VI.　　　　　　　　　　　　　　　　　　　　　　　Roll in showers.　🐦 CTV ✕ ⚅ D S

SHERATON HOTEL STATION SQUARE　Guaranteed Rates　Phone: 412/261-2000　❼
◆◆◆ All Year　　　　1P: $151- 170　2P/1B: $166- 185　2P/2B: $166- 185　XP: $15　F18
Hotel **Location:** South end of Smithfield St Bridge, I-376, Grant St exit. 7 Station Square Dr 15219.
Fax: 412/261-2932. **Terms:** Sr. discount; no pets. **Facility:** 292 rooms. 15 stories; interior corridors.
Dining: Restaurant; 6 am-midnight; $18-$29. **All Rooms:** free & pay movies. **Cards:** AE, CB, DI, DS, MC, VI.
　　　　　　　　　　　　　　　　　　　　　　　　　　　　　🐦 CTV ✕ D S

RESTAURANTS

CAFE VICTORIA　　Lunch: $4-$9　　Dinner: $14-$34　　Phone: 412/323-8881　❾
AAA SAVE **Location:** Jct Allegheny. 946 Western Ave 15233. **Hours:** 11:30 am-3 & 5:30-9 pm, Sun 10:30 am-2 pm.
◆ Closed major holidays. **Reservations:** suggested. **Features:** casual dress; Sunday brunch; health conscious
American menu; beer & wine only. Contemporary American cuisine served with authentic Victorian charm in a restored
mansion. Many of the Victorian antiques are for sale. There's a charming garden for outdoor dining. Coffee,
tea & dessert served between lunch & dinner. **Cards:** AE, CB, DI, DS, MC, VI. **Special Value:** 20%
discount on the price of any entree, excluding beverages, tax and gratuity.　　　　　　　　✕

THE CARLTON　　　　　　　　　　　　　　　　　　　　　　Phone: 412/391-4099　㉒
◆◆◆ **Location:** Center. One Mellon Bank Ctr-2nd level 15219. **Hours:** 11:30 am-3 & 5-10 pm, Sat-11 pm. Closed
Nouvelle major holidays & Sun. **Reservations:** accepted. **Features:** casual dress; children's menu; health conscious
American menu; cocktails & lounge. Sophisticated & comfortable decor. Traditional menu of steak, chops, seafood &
pasta. Sour dough rustic bread a signature item. **Cards:** AE, CB, DI, DS, MC, VI.　　　　✕

CHEESE CELLAR RESTAURANT　　Lunch: $6-$11　　Dinner: $7-$13　　Phone: 412/471-3355　❼
◆◆ **Location:** At Station Square, Smithfield & Carson sts. 25 Freight House Shops 15219. **Hours:** 11:30
American am-midnight, Fri & Sat-1 am, Sun 10:30 am-11 pm. Closed: 11/26 & 12/25. **Features:** casual dress;
children's menu; health conscious menu items; carryout; cocktails & lounge; fee for parking. Varied menu,
standard selections. **Cards:** AE, DI, DS, MC, VI.　　　　　　　　　　　　　　　　　✕

THE COMMON PLEAS　　Lunch: $8-$10　　Dinner: $16-$24　　Phone: 412/281-5140　❽
◆◆◆ **Location:** Jct 4th Ave near courthouse. 310 Ross St 15219. **Hours:** 11:30 am-2:30 pm & 5-10 pm, Sat from
Northern 5 pm. Closed major holidays & Sun. **Reservations:** accepted. **Features:** casual dress; cocktails & lounge.
Italian Political Italian with a court house theme. The gracious ambience, dark panelling, white linen & perfect
lighting attract many from the legal & political set. **Cards:** AE, DI, MC, VI.　　　　　　✕

FROGGY'S　　　Lunch: $6-$10　　Dinner: $12-$25　　Phone: 412/471-3764　❿
◆◆ **Location:** Jct Blvd of the Allies. 100 Market St 15222. **Hours:** 11 am-11 pm, Sat-1 pm. Closed major
Traditional holidays & Sun. **Reservations:** suggested. **Features:** casual dress; Sunday brunch; carryout; cocktails &
American lounge; entertainment. Live entertainment Wed-Sat. American steak, burgers, seafood & salad. Bar,
restaurant & roof-top patio. **Cards:** AE, DI, MC, VI.　　　　　　　　　　　　　　　✕

GRAND CONCOURSE RESTAURANT　Historical　Lunch: $6-$15　Dinner: $17-$25　Phone: 412/261-1717　❺
◆◆◆ **Location:** S end of Smithfield St Bridge, Grant St exit from I-376, in Pittsburgh & Lake Erie Railroad
Seafood Terminal Bldg. 1 Station Square 15219. **Hours:** 11:30 am-2:30 & 4:30-10 pm, Sat 4:30 pm-11 pm, Sun 10
am-2:30 & 4:30-10 pm. Closed: 1/1 & 12/25. **Reservations:** suggested. **Features:** casual dress; Sunday
brunch; children's menu; early bird specials; cocktails & lounge; entertainment; fee for parking; a la carte. Impressive dining
rooms in restored 1901 railroad terminal. Baroque styling typical of transition between Victorian & Edwardian eras. Seafood
featured. **Cards:** AE, CB, DI, DS, MC, VI.　　　　　　　　　　　　　　　　　　　✕

(See map p. 396)

HARRY G'S   Lunch: $8-$11   Dinner: $22-$29   Phone: 412/642-6677   ⑪
◆◆
Northern
Italian
Location: Between 6th & 7th sts. 613 Penn Ave 15221. Hours: 11 am-10 pm, Fri-midnight, Sat 4 pm-midnight, Sun 4 pm-9 pm. Closed major holidays. Reservations: suggested. Features: casual dress; cocktails & lounge; entertainment. Eclectic Italian cuisine from peasant to elegant. Pasta, veal, beef, seafood, lamb & chicken entrees. Live piano music nightly. Cards: AE, DI, MC, VI.   ⊠

JAKE'S ABOVE THE SQUARE   Lunch: $9-$16   Dinner: $19-$28   Phone: 412/338-0900   ⑫
◆◆◆
American
Location: Jct Market Square, downtown. 430 Market St 15222. Hours: 11 am-2 & 5-10 pm, Sat 5 pm-11 pm. Closed major holidays & Sun. Reservations: suggested. Features: casual dress; cocktails & lounge; a la carte. Modern American, globally influenced cuisine. On the 2nd level above Jenny Lee Bakery overlooking Market Square. Stylish & comfortable decor with seasonally changing menu. Cards: AE, CB, DI, DS, MC, VI.   ⊠

KIKU'S OF JAPAN   Lunch: $9-$12   Dinner: $15-$20   Phone: 412/765-3200   ⑬
◆◆
Ethnic
Location: Jct W Carson St. Shops at Station Square 15219. Hours: 11:30 am-2 & 5-10:30 pm, Fri-11:30 pm, Sat noon-11:30 pm, Sun noon-10 pm. Closed: 1/1, 11/26 & 12/25. Reservations: suggested. Features: casual dress; carryout; cocktails & lounge. Japanese Sushi bar & table seating. Extensive menu of authentic Japanese dishes in English & also in Japanese. Cards: AE, DI, DS, MC, VI.   ⊠

MAX'S ALLEGHENY TAVERN   Dinner: $6-$15   Phone: 412/231-1899   ④
◆
German
Location: 0.8 mi ne Three Rivers Stadium. 537 Suismon St 15212. Hours: 11 am-11 pm; Fri & Sat-midnight & Sun 9:30 am-10 pm. Closed major holidays. Features: casual dress; children's menu; carryout; cocktails & lounge. Enjoy German food in a restored 1903 hotel of old Dutchtown (North Side); Many elements of original bar & dining areas remain. Cards: AE, CB, DI, DS, MC, VI.   ⊠

PENN BREWERY RESTAURANT   Historical   Lunch: $7-$9   Dinner: $9-$16   Phone: 412/237-9402   ①
◆◆
German
Location: Just ne of 16th St bridge. 800 Vinial St 15212. Hours: 11 am-10 pm, Fri & Sat-11 pm. Closed major holidays & Sun. Features: casual dress; children's menu; carryout; cocktails & lounge. Restored 19th century German brewing complex. Cards: AE, DS, MC, VI.

PICCOLO PICCOLO   Lunch: $8-$12   Dinner: $12-$28   Phone: 412/261-7234   ⑯
AAA
◆◆
Traditional
Italian
Location: Jct Fort Pitt Blvd. One Wood St 15222. Hours: 11:30 am-3:30 & 5-10 pm, Fri-11 pm, Sat 5 pm-11 pm. Closed major holidays & Sun. Reservations: suggested. Features: casual dress; carryout; cocktails & lounge; fee for parking. Great variety of traditionally made Roman & Southern Italian cuisine. Family run with many of the desserts imported directly from Milan. Cards: AE, CB, DI, DS, MC, VI.   ⊠

PRIMANTI BROS   Lunch: $4-$4   Dinner: $4-$4   Phone: 412/263-2142   ⑰
◆
American
Location: Jct Smallman St. 46 18th St 15203. Hours: 24 hours. Closed: 12/25. Features: casual dress; cocktails & lounge; entertainment. Unique sandwich menu; deli sandwiches on Italian bread with cole slaw as a condiment. Cards: AE, DI, MC, VI.   ⊠

SESAME INN   Lunch: $5-$7   Dinner: $12-$15   Phone: 412/281-8282   ⑱
◆
Chinese
Location: Jct McKnight Rd. 711 Browns Ln 15222. Hours: 11:30 am-10 pm, Fri & Sat-11 pm, Sun noon-9 pm. Closed: 7/4, 11/26 & 12/25. Reservations: suggested. Features: casual dress; carryout; cocktails & lounge. Quality, pleasant decor, service & ambience with a good selection of popular Szechwan & Hunan dishes. Cards: AE, DI, DS, MC, VI.

SEVENTH STREET GRILLE   Phone: 412/338-0303   ⑲
AAA
◆
South
American
Location: 130 7th St 15222. Hours: 11:30 am-9 pm, Fri & Sat-11 pm, Sun noon-8 pm. Reservations: suggested. Features: casual dress; carryout; cocktails. Gorgeous clubby atmosphere. Caters to the lunch crowd, the pre-theater & after-show trade. Great selection of salad, soup, sandwiches, hamburgers, pasta, chicken, steak & seafood.   ⊠

SUSHI KIM   Lunch: $6-$9   Dinner: $8-$14   Phone: 412/281-9956   ㉑
◆
Ethnic
Location: Jct 13th St. 1241 Penn Ave 15222. Hours: 11:30 am-10 pm, Fri & Sat-11 pm, Sun noon-9 pm. Closed: Mon. Features: casual dress; carryout; wine only. Korean cuisine & Sushi. Nice selection of cooked & raw fish. Cards: AE, DS, MC, VI.

TEQUILA JUNCTION   Lunch: $5-$10   Dinner: $5-$10   Phone: 412/261-3265   ⑥
◆
Mexican
Location: Station Square Shops, Carson & Smithfield sts. 31 Station Sq 15219. Hours: 11:30 am-10 pm, Fri & Sat-midnight, Sun noon-9 pm. Closed major holidays. Features: casual dress; children's menu; carryout; cocktails & lounge; fee for parking. Southwestern decor, located on balcony, overlooking mall. Cards: AE, DI, DS, MC, VI.   ⊠

THE TERRACE ROOM   Lunch: $8-$13   Dinner: $17-$29   Phone: 412/281-7100   ③
◆◆
Continental
Location: Opposite Mellon Square, between Oliver St & 6th Ave; in The Westin William Penn. 530 William Penn Pl 15219. Hours: 6:30 am-10:30 pm. Reservations: suggested. Features: Sunday brunch; children's menu; health conscious menu items; cocktails & lounge; fee for parking. A fine dining experience. American cuisine also featured. Cards: AE, DI, DS, MC, VI.   ⊠

TOP OF THE TRIANGLE   Lunch: $6-$14   Dinner: $16-$35   Phone: 412/471-4100   ②
◆◆◆
American
Location: On 62nd floor of USX Tower. 600 Grant St 15219. Hours: 11:30 am-3 & 5:30-10 pm, Sat noon-3 & 5:30-10:30 pm, Sun 4 pm-9 pm. Closed: 5/26, 9/1 & 12/25. Reservations: suggested. Features: dressy casual; children's menu; cocktails & lounge; fee for parking. Panoramic outstanding city view. Cards: AE, CB, DI, DS, MC, VI.   ⊠

GREATER PITTSBURGH   (See map p. 401; index below)

Index of Establishments on the PITTSBURGH ACCOMMODATIONS Spotting Map

OAKDALE
Comfort Inn-Pittsburgh Airport.................. 18

CORAOPOLIS
Wyndham Garden Hotel-Pittsburgh Airport....... 20
Courtyard by Marriott........................... 21
Pittsburgh Airport Marriott...................... 22
La Quinta Inn-Airport........................... 23
Hampton Inn Hotel Airport...................... 24
Red Roof Inn Pittsburgh Airport 25
Embassy Suites-Pittsburgh International
  Airport...................................... 26
Clarion Royce Hotel Pittsburgh Airport 27
Motel 6 Airport - 1285......................... 28
Holiday Inn-Pittsburgh Airport................. 29

RESTAURANTS
Hyeholde Restaurant............................ 25
Clark's 26

CRAFTON
Days Inn....................................... 30

GREATER PITTSBURGH
ClubHouse Inn & Suites......................... 33
Red Roof Inn South Airport 34
Days Inn Pittsburgh 35
Holiday Inn Pittsburgh-McKnight Road....... 36

RESTAURANTS
Le Mont Restaurant............................ 29
Gullifty's...................................... 30
Pasta Piatto 31
Khalil's II. 32
Red Bull Steakhouse........................... 33
Abruzzi's...................................... 34
Amel's Restaurant 35
Armstrong's.................................... 36
Long Necker's.................................. 37
Jimmy Tsang's Chinese Restaurant............. 38
Bachri's 40
Baum Vivant 41
Cafe Allegro................................... 42
The Cafe at The Frick Art & Historical Center ... 43
Cafe Giorgio 44
Cafe Giovanni.................................. 45
City Grill...................................... 46
Crewsers...................................... 47
Davio 48
DeLuca's...................................... 49
Elbow Room 50
Harris Grill-A Cafe 52
Hot Licks...................................... 53
Hot Lick's..................................... 54
Kaya.. 55
La Feria 56
La Filipiniana.................................. 57
Le Pommier.................................... 58
Mallorca...................................... 59
The New Dumpling House 60
Palio 61
Papparazzi Italian Restorante 62
Pittsburgh Deli Company 64
Pittsburgh Steak Company 65
The Redwood 66
Shootz Cafe 67
Sushi Too..................................... 68
Suzie's 69
Tai Pei 70
Union Grill 71
Ya Fei.. 72

GREEN TREE
Holiday Inn-Pittsburgh Central (Green Tree)... 44
Pittsburgh Green Tree Marriott 45
Best Western-Parkway Center Inn 46
Hampton Inn Hotel Green Tree................. 49
Hawthorn Suites................................ 50

RESTAURANT
Piccolo Mondo 75

BRIDGEVILLE
Knights Inn-Pittsburgh/Bridgeville 55

RESTAURANT
Peters Place 80

WARRENDALE
Super 8 Motel-Cranberry 57
Holiday Inn Express............................ 58
Fairfield Inn 59
Hampton Inn Cranberry 60
Red Roof Inn-Cranberry 61
Sheraton Inn-Pittsburgh North................. 63

RESTAURANT
Tremont House................................. 85

MONROEVILLE
Radisson Hotel Pittsburgh 69
Harley Hotel 70
Wm Penn Motel 71
Holiday Inn 73
Days Inn-Monroeville.......................... 74
Red Roof Inn-Monroeville...................... 76

SEWICKLEY
The Sewickley Country Inn 78

NEW KENSINGTON
Days Inn of New Kensington 82

WEXFORD
Econo Lodge-Pittsburgh North 87

RESTAURANTS
Stone Mansion Restaurant...................... 90
Max Planks 93

BLAWNOX
Holiday Inn Hotel & Suites-RIDC Park.......... 92

OAKMONT
The Inn at Oakmont 101

HARMARVILLE
Valley Motel 105

GIBSONIA
Comfort Inn Gibsonia 109

RESTAURANT
The Pines Tavern 98

WEST MIFFLIN
Hampton Inn 111

BETHEL PARK
Holiday Inn Pittsburgh South.................. 114

RESTAURANT
The Roxy Cafe................................. 100

SHADYSIDE
Appletree Bed & Breakfast..................... 119

RESTAURANT
China Palace.................................. 105

PLEASANT HILLS
Howard Johnson - Pittsburgh South.......... 123

HEIDELBERG
RESTAURANT
Wright's Seafood Inn.......................... 110

ALLISON PARK
RESTAURANT
The Tuscan Inn 115

TURTLE CREEK
RESTAURANT
Pat's Place................................... 119

BLOOMFIELD
RESTAURANTS
El Dolce Cafe 123
Tessaro's..................................... 124

(See map below)

LODGINGS

CLUBHOUSE INN & SUITES   Rates Subject to Change   Phone: 412/788-8400   🔢33
◆◆◆   Sun-Thurs [BP]   1P: $85   2P/1B: $95   2P/2B: $95   XP: $10   F16
Motel   Fri & Sat [BP]   1P: $69   2P/1B: $69   2P/2B: $69   XP: $5   F16
    Location: Pkwy w to Moon Run exit, 0.3 mi w. 5311 Campbells Run Rd 15205. Fax: 412/788-2577.
Terms: No pets. **Facility:** 152 rooms. 3 stories; interior corridors. **All Rooms:** free movies. **Cards:** AE, DI, DS, MC, VI.
(See color ad below)   Roll in showers. 📶 ✈ 📺 ✕ D

(See map p. 401)

DAYS INN PITTSBURGH   Phone: 412/531-8900 ㉟
All Year [CP]   1P: $55- 60   2P/1B: $55- 60 2P/2B: $55- 60 XP: $5   F14
Location: 3.5 mi s on US 19. 1150 Banksville Rd 15216. Fax: 412/531-7630. Terms: Weekly/monthly rates,
in winter; weekend rates avail; no pets. Facility: 70 rooms. 2 stories; interior/exterior corridors. Dining &
Motor Inn   Entertainment: Dining room; 11:30 am-2:30 & 5-10:30 pm; $7-$13; cocktails/lounge. Services: area
DS, MC, VI. transportation, within 5 mi. All Rooms: free movies. Some Rooms: radios, whirlpools. Cards: AE, CB, DI,
DS, MC, VI. Special Amenities: Early check-in/late check-out and free breakfast.

HOLIDAY INN PITTSBURGH-MCKNIGHT ROAD   Phone: 412/366-5200 ㊱
All Year [BP]   1P: $89- 129 2P/1B: $89- 129 2P/2B: $89- 129 XP: $10   F18
Location: 7 mi n; adjacent to North Hills Village Mall, enter at n end of plaza by the appliance store. 4859
McKnight Rd 15237. Fax: 412/366-5682. Terms: Monthly rates; package plans; pets. Facility: 147 rooms. 7
Motor Inn   stories; interior corridors. Dining: Dining room; 6:30 am-10 pm, Sun from 7 am; $7-$18; cocktails. Services:
Fee: coin laundry. All Rooms: coffeemakers, free & pay movies. Some Rooms: whirlpools.
Fee: microwaves, refrigerators. Cards: AE, CB, DI, DS, JCB, MC, VI. Special Amenities: Free newspaper and free room
upgrade (subject to availability with advanced reservations).

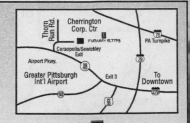

(See map p. 401)

RED ROOF INN SOUTH AIRPORT   Rates Subject to Change   **Phone:** 412/787-7870   **34**
◆◆   5/1-10/31   1P: $46- 66   2P/1B: $54- 74   2P/2B: $57- 77   XP: $8   F18
Motel   11/1-4/30   1P: $42- 62   2P/1B: $50- 70   2P/2B: $52- 62   XP: $8   F18
     Location: On SR 60, just e of jct US 22 & 30; 3.5 mi w of I-79, Moon Run exit. 6404 Steubenville Pike
15205.   **Fax:** 412/787-8392.   **Terms:** Small pets only.   **Facility:** 120 rooms. 2 stories; interior/exterior corridors.
All Rooms: free movies. **Cards:** AE, CB, DI, DS, MC, VI.   Roll in showers.   🛏 ♿ ⛻ ✕ 🛁 Ⓓ

RESTAURANTS

ABRUZZI'S   **Phone:** 412/431-4511   **34**
◆   **Location:** Southside jct Carson St. 52 S 10th St 15203. **Hours:** 11:30 am-10 pm, Sat-11 pm, Sun 4 pm-9
Traditional   pm. Closed major holidays. **Reservations:** accepted. **Features:** casual dress; carryout; cocktails & lounge.
Italian   Extensive menu including chicken, veal, beef, lamb, seafood, occasionally game & large variety of pasta.
     Cards: AE, CB, DI, DS, MC, VI.   ✕

AMEL'S RESTAURANT   **Phone:** 412/563-3466   **35**
◆◆   **Location:** Jct Sussex Rd. 435 McNeilly Rd 15226. **Hours:** 11:30 am-midnight, Sun 3 pm-10 pm. Closed
Ethnic   major holidays. **Reservations:** suggested. **Features:** casual dress; children's menu; early bird specials;
     health conscious menu; carryout; cocktails & lounge. Middle Eastern cuisine, including Italy, Spain, Greece,
Lebanon & Morocco; also American. Seafood focus. **Cards:** AE, DS, MC, VI.   ✕

ARMSTRONG'S   **Lunch:** $3-$7   **Dinner:** $2-$11   **Phone:** 412/341-9460   **36**
◆   **Location:** In Galleria. Galleria Washington Rd 15228. **Hours:** 11 am-11 pm, Sun noon-8 pm. Closed major
American   holidays. **Features:** casual dress; carryout; beer & wine only. Good home-cooked soup, salad, sandwiches,
     pasta & pizza plus veal, chicken, steak & seafood entrees. Popular & busy restaurant with large patio.   ✕

BACHRI'S   **Phone:** 412/343-2213   **40**
◆   **Location:** Rt 88S & jct Castle Shannon Blvd left on Willow Ave. 3821 Willow Ave 15234. **Hours:** 4 pm-9:30
Ethnic   pm, Fri & Sat-10:30 pm. Closed major holidays, Sun & Mon. **Reservations:** suggested. **Features:** casual
     dress; carryout. Authentic Indonesian & Middle Eastern cuisine. **Cards:** CB, DI, DS, MC, VI.   ✕

BAUM VIVANT   **Dinner:** $15-$25   **Phone:** 412/682-2620   **41**
◆◆   **Location:** In Shadyside, parallel to Centre Ave. 5102 Baum Blvd 15224. **Hours:** 5:30 pm-10 pm, Sat-11 pm.
Ethnic   Closed major holidays & Sun. **Reservations:** suggested. **Features:** casual dress; health conscious menu
     items; cocktails. Portuguese, French, Northern Italian & Californian cuisine. **Cards:** AE, CB, DI, DS, MC, VI.
                                                     ✕

CAFE ALLEGRO   **Dinner:** $18-$28   **Phone:** 412/481-7788   **42**
◆◆◆   **Location:** Jct Carson St. 51 S 12th St 15203. **Hours:** 5 pm to closing. Closed major holidays.
French   **Reservations:** suggested. **Features:** casual dress; cocktails & lounge. French & Italian Riviera style cooking
     using fresh ingredients & impeccable preparation. Menu based upon the availability of fresh foods in season.
Friendly European style dinning. **Cards:** AE, DI, MC, VI.   ✕

THE CAFE AT THE FRICK ART & HISTORICAL CENTER   **Lunch:** $4-$9   **Phone:** 412/371-0600   **43**
◆   **Location:** I-376, exit 9, Edgewood/Swissvale, Edgewood exit to Braddock Ave, 1.3 mi nw to Penn Ave, 0.3
Nouvelle   mi w to Homewood, just s to Circle. 7227 Reynolds St 15208. **Hours:** 11 am-5:30 pm, Sun noon-6 pm.
American   Closed major holidays & Mon. **Features:** casual dress; health conscious menu. Gourmet lunches, high tea &
     homemade pastry served in a garden setting with panoramic view of the estate. Smoke free premises.
Cards: DS, MC, VI.   ✕

CAFE GIORGIO   **Lunch:** $5-$8   **Dinner:** $13-$27   **Phone:** 412/833-7000   **44**
◆◆   **Location:** Jct Fort Couch Rd. 24 Donati Rd 15241. **Hours:** 11:30 am-2 & 5-10 pm, Mon & Sat from 5 pm.
Regional   Closed major holidays & Sun. **Reservations:** suggested. **Features:** casual dress; children's menu; cocktails
American   & lounge. American regional & International cuisine styles with the chef's own inventions. Seafood &
     flatbread specialties. Comfortable relaxed atmosphere. Smoke free premises. **Cards:** AE, MC, VI.   ✕

CAFE GIOVANNI   **Lunch:** $11-$20   **Dinner:** $11-$20   **Phone:** 412/481-6662   **45**
◆◆   **Location:** Across from Birmingham Bridge. 2302 E Carson St 15203. **Hours:** 11 am-3 & 4:30-10 pm, Fri-11
Traditional   pm, Sat 4:30 pm-11 pm, Sun-9 pm. Closed major holidays. **Reservations:** accepted; 6 or more.
Italian   **Features:** casual dress; cocktails & lounge; entertainment. Specialty veal, fresh pasta & homemade
     sausage. Chef/owner frequently uses old family recipes. **Cards:** AE, CB, DI, DS, MC, VI.   ✕

CITY GRILL   **Lunch:** $5-$6   **Dinner:** $8-$9   **Phone:** 412/481-6868   **46**
◆◆   **Location:** Between 19th & 20th sts. 2019 E Carson St 15203. **Hours:** 11 am-10 pm, Fri & Sat-11 pm, Sun
American   4:30 pm-10 pm. Closed major holidays. **Features:** casual dress; carryout; cocktails. Hardwood grill cooking
     featuring chicken, fish, burgers & ribs. Large portions & great salads. **Cards:** AE, MC, VI.   ✕

CREWSERS   **Phone:** 412/281-3679   **47**
◆◆   **Location:** Jct 15th in the Boardwalk Entertainment Complex. 1501 Smallman St 15222. **Hours:** 11 am-11
Steak and   pm, Sat-midnight, Sun-9 pm. Closed: 12/25. **Reservations:** accepted. **Features:** casual dress; Sunday
Seafood   brunch; children's menu; health conscious menu; carryout; cocktails. Constructed on barges anchored in the
     Allegheny River. Exciting view of Pittsburgh's skyline, the river & bridges. Outdoor deck dining avail in
summer. **Cards:** AE, MC, VI.   ✕

DAVIO   **Lunch:** $4-$11   **Dinner:** $13-$40   **Phone:** 412/531-7422   **48**
◆◆◆   **Location:** Jct Crosby Ave. 2100 Broadway Ave 15216. **Hours:** 11:30 am-2:30 & 4-11 pm, Sat 4 pm-1 pm,
Regional   Sun 4 am-9 am. Closed major holidays. **Reservations:** required. **Features:** casual dress; carryout. Great
American   ambience & excellent service. Intriguing appetizers, pasta & entrees to white pizza & oven-baked Sicilian
     sandwiches.   ✕

DELUCA'S   **Lunch:** $5-$6   **Phone:** 412/566-2195   **49**
◆   **Location:** Jct 21st St. 2015 Penn Ave 15222. **Hours:** 6 am-3 pm, Sun from 7 am. Closed: 1/1, 11/26, &
American   12/25. **Features:** casual dress. Family run, 60 year-old diner in The Strip. Excellent pancakes, French toast,
     ham & eggs with home fries, omelets & fritattas. Large portions.   ✕

(See map p. 401)

ELBOW ROOM
◆
American
Lunch: $4-$6   **Dinner:** $7-$10   **Phone:** 412/441-5222   ⑤⓪
Location: Jct Maryland Ave & Summerlea St. 5744 Ellsworth Ave 15232. **Hours:** 11 am-1:30 am, Fri & Sat-2 am, Sun-1 am. Closed major holidays. **Reservations:** accepted. **Features:** casual dress; Sunday brunch; children's menu; carryout; cocktails & lounge. Neighborhood bar, three dinning rooms & an outdoor, backyard style patio. Butcher paper-topped tables, crayons & Kiddie Korner menu. Dinner entrees of chicken, fish & steak. **Cards:** CB, DI, DS, MC, VI.

GULLIFTY'S
◆◆
American
Lunch: $5-$10   **Dinner:** $10-$18   **Phone:** 412/521-8222   ③⓪
Location: Just s of Forbes Ave, 1 mi n of I-376, Squirrel Hill exit. 1922 Murray Ave 15217. **Hours:** 11 am-midnight, Fri & Sat-1 am, Sun 10 am-midnight. Closed: 12/25. **Features:** casual dress; Sunday brunch; children's menu; health conscious menu items; carryout; cocktails & lounge; street parking. Voted as best desserts in Pittsburgh for last 14 years. **Cards:** AE, DI, DS, MC, VI.

HARRIS GRILL-A CAFE
◆
Greek
Dinner: $7-$10   **Phone:** 412/363-0833   ⑤②
Location: Between Maryland & Summerlea aves. 5747 Ellsworth Ave 15232. **Hours:** 5 pm-11 pm, summer 11 am-midnight. Closed: 12/25. **Features:** casual dress; cocktails & lounge. Friendly place with regular clientele. In the summer huge sunflowers surround the patio. Serving authentic Greek cuisine for over 35 years. **Cards:** AE, DS, MC, VI.

HOT LICKS
◆◆◆
Southwest
American
Lunch: $5-$8   **Dinner:** $6-$15   **Phone:** 412/341-7427   ⑤③
Location: The Galleria. 1500 Washington Rd 15228. **Hours:** 11:30 am-11 pm, Fri & Sat-midnight, Sun noon-10 pm. Closed major holidays. **Reservations:** accepted. **Features:** casual dress; children's menu; carryout; cocktails. Huge portions. Nachos, mesquite-grilled ribs, chicken & burgers. Outdoor patio. **Cards:** AE, CB, DI, DS, MC, VI.

HOT LICK'S
◆
Southwest
American
Lunch: $5-$7   **Dinner:** $6-$15   **Phone:** 412/683-2583   ⑤④
Location: Jct S Nagley. 5520 Walnut St 15232. **Hours:** 11:30 am-11 pm, Fri & Sat-midnight, Sun noon-10 pm. Closed major holidays. **Reservations:** accepted. **Features:** casual dress; children's menu; carryout; cocktails. Huge portions. Nachos, mesquite-grilled ribs, chicken & burgers. **Cards:** AE, CB, DI, DS, MC, VI.

JIMMY TSANG'S CHINESE RESTAURANT
◆◆
Chinese
Lunch: $5-$6   **Dinner:** $7-$15   **Phone:** 412/661-4226   ③⑧
Location: Jct Centre & Negley aves, just n of 5th Ave. 5700 Centre Ave 15206. **Hours:** 11:30 am-10 pm, Fri & Sat-11 pm, Sun 3:30 pm-9 pm. Closed: 7/4 & 11/26. **Reservations:** suggested; for 5 or more. **Features:** casual dress; early bird specials; carryout; cocktails; a la carte. A variety of Oriental cuisine including Mandarin, Szechuan, Cantonese, Hunan & Korean. **Cards:** AE, DS, MC, VI.

KAYA
◆◆
Regional
Ethnic
Phone: 412/261-6565   ⑤⑤
Location: In The Strip. 2000 Smallman St 15222. **Hours:** 11 am-11 pm, Sat-midnight. Closed major holidays. **Features:** casual dress; carryout; cocktails & lounge. Caribbean cuisine featuring charismatic chili, exotic roots & spices, low fat cooking techniques & vegetarian selections. **Cards:** AE, DS, MC, VI.

KHALIL'S II
ⓐⓐⓐ
◆◆
Ethnic
Dinner: $8-$14   **Phone:** 412/683-4757   ③②
Location: 0.8 mi n of Carnegie-Mellon University, at jct Millvale & Baum. 4757 Baum Blvd 15213. **Hours:** 4:00-10:30 pm. Closed major holidays & Mon. **Reservations:** suggested. **Features:** casual dress; cocktails. Eastern Mediterranean cuisine in Middle Eastern atmosphere.

LA FERIA
◆
South
American
Lunch: $8-$10   **Dinner:** $10-$15   **Phone:** 412/682-4501   ⑤⑥
Location: Between Ivy & Filbert sts. 5527 Walnut St 15232. **Hours:** 11 am-10 pm. Closed major holidays & Sun. **Features:** casual dress; health conscious menu; cocktails. 100% authentic Peruvian food served in small, serene, 2nd-floor restaurant with Latin American clothing & crafts shop in front. Always a daily meat & vegetarian special. **Cards:** AE, MC, VI.

LA FILIPINIANA
◆
Ethnic
Dinner: $10-$20   **Phone:** 412/781-8724   ⑤⑦
Location: Lawrenceville area. 5321 Butler St 15201. **Hours:** 5 pm-10 pm Fri & Sat only. **Reservations:** suggested. **Features:** semi-formal attire; children's menu; health conscious menu items; carryout. Philippine cuisine using natural ingredients & healthy cooking by chef/owner. Authentic Kare-kare, Morcon, Shanghai & Sotanghon. Courteous & efficient service. **Cards:** AE, MC, VI.

LE MONT RESTAURANT
ⓐⓐⓐ
◆◆◆◆
American
Dinner: $17-$40   **Phone:** 412/431-3100   ②⑨
Location: Atop Mt Washington, adjacent to the Duquesne incline. 1114 Grandview Ave 15211. **Hours:** 5 pm-11 pm, Fri & Sat-midnight, Sun 4 pm-10 pm. Closed major holidays. **Reservations:** suggested. **Features:** semi-formal attire; health conscious menu items; cocktails & lounge; fee for valet parking; a la carte. Continental decor. Panoramic view of downtown area. **Cards:** AE, DI, DS, JCB, MC, VI.

LE POMMIER
◆◆◆
Provincial
French
Dinner: $16-$26   **Phone:** 412/431-1901   ⑤⑧
Location: Jct 21st St. 2401 E Carson St 15203. **Hours:** 5:30 pm-9:30 pm, Fri & Sat-10:30 pm. Closed major holidays, Sun & Mon. **Reservations:** suggested. **Features:** casual dress; cocktails & lounge; a la carte. European atmosphere with sophisticated & intimate dining scattered throughout a number of small rooms on 2 floors. Chef/owner. **Cards:** AE, DI, DS, MC, VI.

LONG NECKER'S
◆◆
Seafood
Lunch: $6-$10   **Dinner:** $8-$18   **Phone:** 412/366-5200   ③⑦
Location: 7 mi n, adjacent to North Hills Village Mall, enter at n end of plaza by appliance store. 4859 McKnight Rd 15237. **Hours:** 6:30 am-10 pm. **Reservations:** suggested. **Features:** casual dress; Sunday brunch; children's menu; early bird specials; senior's menu; carryout; salad bar; cocktails. Seafood buffet on Fri. **Cards:** AE, CB, DI, DS, JCB, MC, VI.

MALLORCA
◆◆
Continental
Lunch: $7-$11   **Dinner:** $12-$24   **Phone:** 412/488-1818   ⑤⑨
Location: Jct 23rd St. 2228 E Carson St 15203. **Hours:** 11:30 am-10:30 pm, Sat-11:30 pm, Sun noon-10 pm. **Reservations:** suggested. **Features:** casual dress; cocktails & lounge. European atmosphere with outside patio in summer. Fish & shellfish dominate along with steak, goat & suckling pig. Polished service. **Cards:** AE, DI, DS, MC, VI.

(See map p. 401)

THE NEW DUMPLING HOUSE   **Lunch:** $5-$8   **Dinner:** $10-$20   **Phone:** 412/422-4178   60
◆◆
Chinese   **Location:** Between Phillips & Douglas sts. 2138 Murray Ave 15217. **Hours:** 11 am-10 pm, Sat-11 pm. **Closed:** 11/26. **Reservations:** accepted. **Features:** casual dress; carryout; cocktails & lounge. Elegantly decorated with sophisticated service & lovely presentations. Emphasis on authentic Szechuan & Hunan dishes. **Cards:** AE, DI, DS, MC, VI.   ✕

PALIO   **Dinner:** $20-$28   **Phone:** 412/531-8211   61
◆
Northern
Italian   **Location:** Beechview area jct Crosby Ave. 2056 Broadway St 15216. **Hours:** 4 pm-10 pm, Fri & Sat-11 pm, Sun-9 pm. Closed major holidays. **Reservations:** suggested. **Features:** casual dress; cocktails. Colorful chef/owner presents simple, direct flavors, grilled & roasted meat, seafood, Tuscan & Emilian pasta, pizza & focaccia sandwiches. Inviting trattoria with marble tables & distressed walls. **Cards:** AE, MC, VI.

PAPPARAZZI ITALIAN RESTORANTE   **Lunch:** $5-$9   **Dinner:** $9-$17   **Phone:** 412/488-0800   62
◆
Northern
Italian   **Location:** Jct 1st St. 2100 E Carson St 15203. **Hours:** 11 am-10 pm, Thurs-Sat to 11 pm, Sun 5 pm-11 pm. Closed major holidays. **Reservations:** required; weekends. **Features:** casual dress; cocktails & lounge; entertainment. Huge portions of pasta, veal, seafood & gourmet pizza. Fresh bread baked on premise. Live Jazz Thurs-Sun. **Cards:** AE, CB, DI, DS, JCB, MC, VI.   ✕

PASTA PIATTO   **Lunch:** $5-$10   **Dinner:** $9-$22   **Phone:** 412/621-5547   31
ⒶⒶⒶ
◆◆
Northern
Italian   **Location:** 5 mi e on 5th Ave, just n on S Aiken, just e on Walnut-Shadyside District. 736 Bellefonte St 15232. **Hours:** 11:30 am-3 & 4:30-10 pm, Wed & Thurs-10:30 pm, Fri & Sat-11 pm, Sun 4-9 pm. Closed major holidays. **Features:** casual dress; children's menu; carryout; cocktails & lounge; fee for parking. A variety of pasta made fresh on premises. Very popular. **Cards:** AE, MC, VI.   ✕

PITTSBURGH DELI COMPANY   **Lunch:** $6-$8   **Dinner:** $6-$8   **Phone:** 412/682-3354   64
ⒶⒶⒶ
◆
American   **Location:** Between Walnut & Ellesworth St. 728 Copeland St 15232. **Hours:** 11 am-8 pm. Closed: 11/26 & 12/25. **Features:** casual dress; health conscious menu items; carryout; cocktails & lounge. 80 different import, domestic & microbrewery beers avail. Create your oun singles from 13 deli delights. 10 kinds of bread & eight cheeses or a jaw stretcher gourmet sandwich. Great selection. Smoke free premises. **Cards:** AE, DI, DS, MC, VI.   ✕

PITTSBURGH STEAK COMPANY   **Phone:** 412/381-5505   65
◆
American   **Location:** South Side. 1924 E Carson St 15203. **Hours:** 11 am-midnight, Fri & Sat-1 am, Sun 4 pm-11 pm. Closed major holidays. **Features:** casual dress; cocktails & lounge. Neighborhood feel with large portions of steak, chicken, fish, chops & pasta. **Cards:** AE, CB, DI, DS, MC, VI.   ✕

RED BULL STEAKHOUSE   **Lunch:** $6-$10   **Dinner:** $13-$24   **Phone:** 412/787-2855   33
◆◆
American   **Location:** 7 mi w on I-279, US 22 & 30 exit, just n on SR 60, then e. 5205 Campbells Run Rd 15205. **Hours:** 11 am-11 pm, Fri-midnight, Sat 4 pm-midnight, Sun 4 pm-9 pm. Closed major holidays. **Features:** casual dress; children's menu; salad bar; cocktails & lounge. Traditional casual dining with prime rib featured. **Cards:** AE, CB, DI, DS, MC, VI.

THE REDWOOD   **Dinner:** $17-$28   **Phone:** 724/379-6540   66
◆◆
Continental   **Location:** Jct 1st St. 87 Castner Ave 15033. **Hours:** 6 pm-9 pm, Sat 5 pm-9:30 pm. Closed: 4/7, 11/26, 12/24, 12/25, Sun & Mon. **Reservations:** suggested. **Features:** casual dress; cocktails & lounge. Unique style with personable & accommodating service. **Cards:** AE, MC, VI.

SHOOTZ CAFE   **Phone:** 412/488-3820   67
◆
American   **Location:** South of city, jct Birmingham bridge. 2305 E Carson St 32746. **Hours:** 11:30 am-2 am, Sun-1 am. Closed major holidays. **Reservations:** accepted. **Features:** casual dress; health conscious menu; carryout; cocktails & lounge; entertainment. Housed in a renovated 1906 schoolhouse featuring fish, steak chops & pasta.   ✕

SUSHI TOO   **Phone:** 412/687-8744   68
◆
Ethnic   **Location:** East of downtown, jct Aiken Ave. 5432 Walnut St 15232. **Hours:** 11:30 am-3 & 5-10 pm, Fri-11 pm, Sat 11:30 am-11:30 pm, Sun 1 pm-9 pm. Closed: 11/26. **Reservations:** accepted. **Features:** casual dress; carryout; cocktails & lounge. Broad variety of Japanese dishes ranging from sushi to tempura. **Cards:** AE, DI, DS, MC, VI.   ✕

SUZIE'S   **Lunch:** $5-$8   **Dinner:** $10-$15   **Phone:** 412/422-8066   69
◆
Greek   **Location:** Jct Forbes Ave. 1704 Shady Ave 15217. **Hours:** 11:30 am-10 pm, Fri 11:30 am-9 pm. Closed major holidays. **Reservations:** accepted. **Features:** casual dress; Sunday brunch; early bird specials; health conscious menu; cocktails. Serious Greek food, including grape leaves, tarama, moussaka, spanakopita & honey-soaked dessert. **Cards:** AE, DI, DS, MC, VI.   ✕

TAI PEI   **Lunch:** $6-$8   **Dinner:** $10-$20   **Phone:** 412/683-2332   70
◆◆
Chinese   **Location:** Jct Ivy St. 5528 Walnut St 15232. **Hours:** 11:30 am-10 pm, Fri & Sat-11 pm, Sun 11:30 am-9:30 pm. **Reservations:** accepted. **Features:** casual dress; carryout; cocktails & lounge. Traditional & authentic Szechaun dishes including spicy chicken dumpling, ruby shrimp & tea smoked duck. Dim sum featured. **Cards:** AE, DI, DS, MC, VI.   ✕

UNION GRILL   **Phone:** 412/681-8620   71
◆◆
American   **Location:** Jct Forbes Ave. 413 S Craig St 15213. **Hours:** 11:30 am-10 pm, Fri & Sat-11 pm. Closed major holidays & Sun. **Reservations:** accepted. **Features:** casual dress; carryout; cocktails & lounge. Honest American food focuses on simple grilling & smoking. Large portions. Sandwiches, salad, soup, fish, chicken & vegetarian options. **Cards:** AE, DI, DS, MC, VI.   ✕

YA FEI   **Phone:** 412/788-9388   72
◆◆
Chinese   **Location:** West in Robinson Town Center. 1980 Park Manor Blvd 15205. **Hours:** 11 am-10 pm, Sun-9:30 pm. Closed major holidays. **Reservations:** suggested. **Features:** casual dress; Sunday brunch; health conscious menu; carryout; cocktails & lounge. Pacific Rim cooking & Chineese/California style dishes. **Cards:** AE, CB, DI, DS, MC, VI.   ✕

The Pittsburgh Vicinity

ALLISON PARK—5,600   (See map p. 401; index p. 400)

RESTAURANT

THE TUSCAN INN   **Dinner:** $8-$22   **Phone:** 412/486-7696   [115]
◆◆
Northern
Italian
Location: 2 mi s of I-76 exit 4 on SR 8, 0.3 mi w. 2684 Wildwood Rd 15101. **Hours:** 4 pm-10 pm, Fri & Sat-11 pm, Sun-9 pm. Closed major holidays & Mon. **Reservations:** suggested; for 6 or more. **Features:** casual dress; carryout; cocktails & lounge. Unpretentious & casual with a European feel. Wood-fired brick oven yielding fresh hearth-baked pizza & Tuscan bread. **Cards:** AE, DI, DS, MC, VI.   ⊠

BEAVER—5,000

RESTAURANT

THE WOODEN ANGEL   **Lunch:** $8-$13   **Dinner:** $12-$25   **Phone:** 724/774-7880
◆◆
American
Location: In West Bridgewater, from jct SR 68 (at w end of bridge), 0.5 mi n on SR 51, 0.3 mi w under the underpass & up the hill. Sharon Rd & Leopard Ln 15009. **Hours:** 11:30 am-11 pm, Sat from 5 pm. Closed major holidays, Sun & Mon. **Reservations:** suggested. **Features:** casual dress; children's menu; carryout; cocktails & lounge. Candlelight atmosphere. Extensive American wine list. Also family-style dining room. **Cards:** AE, DI, DS, MC, VI.   ⊠

BEAVER FALLS—10,700

LODGINGS

BEAVER VALLEY MOTEL   **Phone:** 724/843-0630
(AAA) [SAVE]
◆◆
Motel
| | All Year | 1P: $44 | 2P/1B: $52 | 2P/2B: $60 | XP: $5 | F18 |

Location: On SR 18, 0.5 mi n of Tpk exit 2. SR 18 15010 (7257 Big Beaver Blvd). Fax: 724/843-1610. **Terms:** Reserv deposit; weekly rates; no pets. **Facility:** 27 rooms. 1 story; exterior corridors. **All Rooms:** free movies, refrigerators, combo or shower baths. **Some Rooms:** 4 efficiencies, utensil deposit. **Cards:** AE, CB, DI, DS, MC, VI. **Special Amenities:** Free local telephone calls and free room upgrade (subject to availability with advanced reservations).   [CTV] ⊠ [D]

HOLIDAY INN   Rates Subject to Change   **Phone:** 724/846-3700
◆◆◆
Motor Inn
| 11/1-4/30 | 1P: $79- 99 | 2P/1B: $79- 89 | 2P/2B: $79- 89 |
| 5/1-10/31 | 1P: $84- 89 | 2P/1B: $84- 89 | 2P/2B: $84- 89 |

Location: On SR 18, 0.3 mi n of I-76 exit 2. SR 18 15010 (PO Box 696). Fax: 724/846-3700. **Terms:** Pets. **Facility:** 156 rooms. 3 stories; interior corridors. **Dining:** Dining room; 6:30 am-2 & 5-10 pm, Sat & Sun from 7 am; $10-$20. **All Rooms:** free movies. **Cards:** AE, CB, DI, DS, MC, VI.   🛏 🛄 [ECTV] ⊠ [D]

LARK MOTEL   **Phone:** 724/846-6507
(AAA) [SAVE]
◆◆
Motel
| 5/1-10/31 | 1P: $42 | 2P/1B: $48 | 2P/2B: $54 | XP: $7 |
| 11/1-4/30 | 1P: $36 | 2P/1B: $45 | 2P/2B: $48 | XP: $7 |

Location: SR 18, 0.5 mi n of tpk, exit 2. SR 18 15010. **Terms:** Weekly rates; no pets. **Facility:** 12 rooms. Well-maintained property. 1 story; exterior corridors. **All Rooms:** refrigerators. **Cards:** AE, DS, MC, VI. **Special Amenities:** Free local telephone calls and free room upgrade (subject to availability with advanced reservations).   [ECTV] ⊠ [D]

RESTAURANT

GIUSEPPE'S ITALIAN RESTAURANT   **Lunch:** $5-$8   **Dinner:** $9-$18   **Phone:** 724/843-5656
(AAA)

◆◆
Italian
Location: Just s on SR 18 off tpk exit 2. Rt 18, Box 852 15010. **Hours:** 11 am-11 pm, Sun-10 pm. Closed: 1/1, 11/26 & 12/25. **Features:** casual dress; carryout; cocktails & lounge; a la carte. Casual dining; also featuring steak, seafood & daily specials. Homemade bread, soup & sauce. **Cards:** AE, DI, DS, MC, VI.   ⊠

BETHEL PARK—33,800   (See map p. 401; index p. 400)

LODGING

HOLIDAY INN PITTSBURGH SOUTH   Guaranteed Rates   **Phone:** 412/833-5300   [114]
◆◆◆
Motor Inn
| All Year | 1P: $79 | 2P/1B: $79 | 2P/2B: $79 | XP: $10 | F19 |

Location: 1 mi n on US 19, opposite South Hills Village Mall. 164 Ft Couch Rd 15241. Fax: 412/831-8539. **Terms:** Small pets only. **Facility:** 210 rooms. 2-7 stories; interior corridors. **Dining:** Dining room; 6:30 am-11 pm; $9-$17. **All Rooms:** free & pay movies. **Cards:** AE, CB, DI, DS, JCB, MC, VI.   🛏 🛄 ♿ [CTV] ⊠ [D] [S]

RESTAURANT

THE ROXY CAFE   **Lunch:** $6-$9   **Dinner:** $10-$18   **Phone:** 412/854-2400   [100]
◆◆
American
Location: 1 mi n on US 19. South Hills Village Mall 15102. **Hours:** 11 am-10 pm, Fri & Sat-11 pm, Sun 10 am-9 pm. Closed: 11/26, 12/25. **Reservations:** suggested. **Features:** casual dress; Sunday brunch; children's menu; health conscious menu; carryout; cocktails. Creative cuisine. **Cards:** AE, DI, DS, MC, VI.   ⊠

BLAWNOX—1,600   (See map p. 401; index p. 400)

LODGING

HOLIDAY INN HOTEL & SUITES-RIDC PARK   Rates Subject to Change   **Phone:** 412/963-0600   [92]
◆◆
Motor Inn
| All Year | 1P: $82- 150 | 2P/1B: $82- 150 | 2P/2B: $82- 150 | XP: $10 | F17 |

Location: Off SR 28, RIDC, exit 10; 3.3 mi s of I-76, exit 5. 180 Gamma Dr 15238. Fax: 412/963-7852. **Terms:** Sr. discount; no pets. **Facility:** 223 rooms. 2 stories; interior corridors. **Dining:** Dining room; 6 am-2:30 & 4:30-10 pm, Sat & Sun from 7 am; $11-$17. **All Rooms:** free & pay movies. **Some Rooms:** 32 kitchens. **Cards:** AE, DI, DS, MC, VI.   🛄 ♿ [ECTV] ⊠ [D]

BLOOMFIELD   (See map p. 401; index p. 400)

RESTAURANTS

EL DOLCE CAFE   **Lunch:** $4-$6   **Dinner:** $4-$6   **Phone:** 412/681-5225   [123]
◆
American
Location: Jct Taylor St. 4525 Liberty Ave 15224. **Hours:** 8 am-11 am, Fri & Sat-noon. Closed major holidays & Sun. **Features:** casual dress; health conscious menu items; carryout. Breakfast items, homemade daily soups, antipasto, tortellini & garden salads. **Cards:** AE, DI, DS, MC, VI.   ⊠

(See map p. 401)

TESSARO'S
◆◆
American

	Lunch: $8-$10	Dinner: $12-$15	Phone: 412/682-6809	124

Location: Jct Taylor St. 4601 Liberty Ave 15224. **Hours:** 11 am-midnight. Closed major holidays & Sun. **Features:** casual dress; carryout; cocktails & lounge. Open-flame hardwood grill. Serious chops, steak, chicken, salad & fish. **Cards:** AE, DI, DS, MC, VI.

BRADDOCK HILLS—2,000

LODGING

HOLIDAY INN PARKWAY EAST
◆◆◆
Motor Inn

Phone: 412/247-2700

	Rates Subject to Change				
11/1-4/30	1P: $99- 129	2P/1B: $99- 129	2P/2B: $99- 129
5/1-10/31	1P: $99- 119	2P/1B: $99- 119	2P/2B: $99- 119

Location: 0.3 mi n of I-376, exit 11, SR 8. 915 Brinton Rd 15221. Fax: 412/371-9619. **Terms:** Sr. discount; pets. **Facility:** 180 rooms. 11 stories; interior corridors. **Dining:** Restaurant; 6:30 am-10 pm; $12-$20. **All Rooms:** free & pay movies. **Cards:** AE, CB, DI, DS, JCB, MC.

BRIDGEVILLE—5,400   (See map p. 401; index p. 400)

LODGING

KNIGHTS INN-PITTSBURGH/BRIDGEVILLE
AAA SAVE
◆◆
Motel

Phone: 412/221-8110 55

	All Year	1P: $45	2P/1B: $51	2P/2B: $51	XP: $6	F18

Location: At jct I-79 & SR 50, exit 11. 111 Hickory Grade Rd 15017. Fax: 412/257-1020. **Terms:** Weekly rates; pets. **Facility:** 104 rooms. 11 efficiencies, $43; 1 story; exterior corridors; small pool. **All Rooms:** free movies, combo or shower baths. **Some Rooms:** coffeemakers. Fee: microwaves, refrigerators, VCR's. **Cards:** AE, CB, DI, DS, MC, VI. **Special Amenities:** Free local telephone calls and preferred room (subject to availability with advanced reservations). Roll in showers.

RESTAURANT

PETERS PLACE
◆◆
American

	Lunch: $6-$11	Dinner: $11-$24	Phone: 412/221-5000	80

Location: From I-79, Kirwin Heights exit 12, then 0.3 mi w on US 50. 1199 Washington Pike 15017. **Hours:** 11 am-10 pm, Fri & Sat-midnight, Sun-8:30 pm. Closed major holidays. **Reservations:** suggested; weekends. **Features:** casual dress; early bird specials; carryout; cocktails & lounge. Specializing in seafood & veal dishes. **Cards:** AE, DI, DS, MC, VI.

BUTLER—15,700

LODGINGS

COMFORT INN
◆◆◆
Motel

Phone: 724/287-7177

	Rates Subject to Change				
All Year [CP]	1P: $49- 59	2P/1B: $65	2P/2B: $55	XP: $6	F18

Location: 4 mi s on SR 8. 1 Comfort Ln 16001. Fax: 724/287-4197. **Terms:** Sr. discount; no pets. **Facility:** 70 rooms. 3 stories; interior corridors. **All Rooms:** free movies. **Cards:** AE, CB, DI, DS, MC, VI. Roll in showers.

CONLEY RESORT INN

◆

Resort Motor Inn

MC, VI.

All Year [BP]
Rates Subject to Change
Phone: 724/586-7711
1P: $62- 65　2P/1B:　$99　　2P/2B:　$84- 99　XP: $10　　F18
Location: 8 mi s on SR 8; 10 mi n on SR 8 from Tpk, exit 4. 740 Pittsburgh Rd 16001. Fax: 724/586-2944.
Terms: Reserv deposit, 30 day notice; no pets. **Facility:** 56 rooms. 3 stories, no elevator; interior/exterior corridors. **Dining:** Restaurant; 7 am-11 pm; $8-$10. **Some Rooms:** 10 efficiencies. **Cards:** AE, CB, DI, DS, MC, VI.

DAYS INN

◆◆

Motor Inn

Rates Subject to Change
Phone: 724/287-6761
6/1-8/31　　　　　1P: $49- 79　2P/1B:　$49- 89　2P/2B:　$49- 89　XP: $6　　F17
5/1-5/31 & 9/1-4/30　1P: $45- 75　2P/1B:　$45- 79　2P/2B:　$45- 79　XP: $6　　F17
Location: 2 mi s on SR 8. 139 Pittsburgh Rd 16001. Fax: 724/287-4307. **Terms:** Sr. discount; small pets only, $25 dep req. **Facility:** 139 rooms. 2 stories; interior/exterior corridors. **Dining:** Dining room; 6 am-1:30 & 5-10 pm, Sat 7 am-noon & 5-10 pm, Sun 7 am-9 pm; $6-$17. **All Rooms:** free movies. **Cards:** AE, CB, DI, DS, MC, VI.
(See color ad p 407)

FAIRFIELD INN BY MARRIOTT

◆◆◆

Motor

Rates Subject to Change
Phone: 724/283-0009
6/1-9/30 [CP]　　1P: $67　　2P/1B:　$72　　　2P/2B:　$72
5/1-5/31 & 10/1-4/30 [CP]　1P: $52　　2P/1B:　$64　　　2P/2B:　$64
Location: Just sw of jct US 8 & SR 422. 200 Fairfield Lane 16001. Fax: 724/283-1045. **Terms:** No pets.
Facility: 64 rooms. 4 whirlpool rms, extra charge; 3 stories; interior corridors. **All Rooms:** free movies. **Cards:** AE, CB, DI, DS, MC, VI.
Roll in showers.

SUPER 8 MOTEL

◆◆

Motel

All Year [CP]
Rates Subject to Change
Phone: 724/287-8888
1P: $41　　2P/1B:　$46　　　2P/2B:　$46　　XP: $4　　F12
Location: 2 mi s on SR 8. 138 Pittsburgh/Rt 8 16001. Fax: 724/287-8888. **Terms:** Sr. discount; pets, $5 extra charge, $20 dep req. **Facility:** 66 rooms. 3 stories, no elevator; interior corridors. **All Rooms:** free & pay movies. **Cards:** AE, CB, DI, DS, MC, VI.

CORAOPOLIS—6,700　(See map p. 401; index p. 400)

LODGINGS

CLARION ROYCE HOTEL PITTSBURGH AIRPORT

◆◆◆

Motor Inn

All Year
Rates Subject to Change
Phone: 412/262-2400　　**27**
1P: $79- 135　2P/1B:　$79- 135　2P/2B:　$79- 135
Location: Business Rt 60 at Coraopolis/Sewickley exit on Thorn Run Rd exit. 1160 Thorn Run Rd Ext 15108. Fax: 412/264-9373. **Terms:** Sr. discount; no pets. **Facility:** 193 rooms. 9 stories; interior corridors.
Dining: Dining room; 6 am-10 pm; $10-$23. **All Rooms:** free & pay movies. **Cards:** AE, CB, DI, DS, JCB, MC, VI.
Roll in showers.

COURTYARD BY MARRIOTT

◆◆◆

Motor Inn

Rates Subject to Change
Phone: 412/264-5000　　**21**
Sun-Thurs　　　　1P: $104　　2P/1B:　$104　　2P/2B:　$104
Fri & Sat 5/1-11/27 &
4/19-4/30　　　　1P: $64　　2P/1B:　$64　　2P/2B:　$69
Fri & Sat 11/28-4/18　1P: $59　　2P/1B:　$59　　2P/2B:　$59
Location: Business Rt 60 at Coraopolis/Sewickley exit. 450 Cherrington Pkwy 15108. Fax: 412/264-7979. **Terms:** No pets.
Facility: 148 rooms. 2-3 stories; interior corridors. **Dining:** Restaurant; 6:30 am-10:30 & 6-10:30 pm; Fri-10:30 am; Sat & Sun 7-11:30 am; $8-$13. **All Rooms:** free & pay movies. **Cards:** AE, CB, DI, DS, MC, VI. *(See color ad p 397)*

EMBASSY SUITES-PITTSBURGH INTERNATIONAL AIRPORT

(AAA) (SAVE)

◆◆◆

Suite Hotel

Rates Subject to Change
Phone: 412/269-9070　　**26**
Mon-Thurs [BP]　　1P: $149　　2P/1B:　$159　　2P/2B:　$159　　XP: $15　　F15
Fri-Sun [BP]　　　1P: $119　　2P/1B:　$129　　2P/2B:　$129　　XP: $15　　F15
Location: From SR 60 Coraopolis/Sewickley exit, just e to Cherrington Pkwy. 550 Cherrington Pkwy 15108.
Fax: 412/262-4119. **Terms:** Reserv deposit; weekly/monthly rates; package plans; pets. **Facility:** 223 rooms.
Beautiful atrium landscaping with running stream, waterfall & live trout. Very attractive country theme & furnishing throughout. 2-line phones. 5 stories; interior corridors; sauna, whirlpool. **Dining & Entertainment:** Restaurant; 6:30 am-midnight; $7-$24; cocktails/lounge. **Services:** complimentary evening beverages; valet laundry.
All Rooms: coffeemakers, microwaves, free & pay movies, refrigerators, combo or shower baths, VCR's. **Cards:** AE, CB, DI, DS, JCB, MC, VI. **Special Amenities:** Free breakfast and free newspaper. *(See ad p 402)*
Roll in showers.

HAMPTON INN HOTEL AIRPORT

◆◆◆

Motel

VI.

All Year [CP]
Rates Subject to Change
Phone: 412/264-0020　　**24**
1P: $64　　2P/1B:　$74　　2P/2B:　$74
Location: 1 mi n of Business Rt 60. 1420 Beers School Rd 15108. Fax: 412/264-3220. **Terms:** Small pets only. **Facility:** 127 rooms. 5 stories; interior corridors. **All Rooms:** free movies. **Cards:** AE, CB, DI, DS, MC, VI.

HOLIDAY INN-PITTSBURGH AIRPORT

(AAA) (SAVE)

◆◆◆

Hotel

All Year
Rates Subject to Change
Phone: 412/262-3600　　**29**
1P: $119- 139　2P/1B:　$119- 139　2P/2B:　$119- 139
Location: 1 mi n of Business Rt 60. 1406 Beers School Rd 15108. Fax: 412/262-6221. **Terms:** Package plans; pets. **Facility:** 257 rooms. 11 stories; interior corridors; whirlpool. **Dining & Entertainment:** Dining room; 6 am-11 pm, Sun from 7 am; $14-$20; cocktails/lounge. **Services:** area transportation, within 5 mi. Fee: coin laundry. **All Rooms:** free & pay movies. **Some Rooms:** coffeemakers. **Cards:** AE, CB, DI, DS, JCB, MC, VI. **Special Amenities:** Early check-in/late check-out and free newspaper.

LA QUINTA INN-AIRPORT

◆◆◆

Motel

DI, DS, JCB, MC, VI.

All Year [CP]
Rates Subject to Change
Phone: 412/269-0400　　**23**
1P: $58- 64　2P/1B:　$58- 64　2P/2B:　$58　　XP: $7　　F18
Location: 1 mi n of Business Rt 60. 1433 Beers School Rd 15108-2509. Fax: 412/269-9258. **Terms:** Small pets only. **Facility:** 127 rooms. 3 stories; interior corridors. **All Rooms:** free & pay movies. **Cards:** AE, CB, DI, DS, JCB, MC, VI.

(See map p. 401)

MOTEL 6 AIRPORT - 1285 Guaranteed Rates Phone: 412/269-0990 **28**
All Year 1P: $39 2P/1B: $49 2P/2B: $49 XP: $6 F17
Location: Business Rt 60 to Coraopolis/Sewickley exit to Thorn Run Rd. 1170 Thorn Run Rd Ext 15108.
Fax: 412/269-0462. **Terms:** Sr. discount; small pets only. **Facility:** 95 rooms. 2 stories; interior corridors.
Motel **All Rooms:** free movies. **Cards:** AE, CB, DI, DS, MC, VI. 🛏️ ➡️ 📺 ✕ Ⓓ

PITTSBURGH AIRPORT MARRIOTT Rates Subject to Change Phone: 412/788-8800 **22**
Sun-Thurs 1P: $149 2P/1B: $164 2P/2B: $164
Hotel Fri & Sat 1P: $72 2P/1B: $72 2P/2B: $99
Location: SR 60 at Montour Run exit. 100 Aten Rd 15108. Fax: 412/788-0743. **Terms:** Small pets only.
Facility: 314 rooms. 15 stories; interior corridors. **Dining:** Dining room; 6 am-11 pm; $15-$24. **All Rooms:** free & pay
movies. **Cards:** AE, CB, DI, MC, VI. 🛏️ 🏊 ➡️ 📺 ✕ 🏌️ Ⓓ Ⓢ

RED ROOF INN PITTSBURGH AIRPORT Rates Subject to Change Phone: 412/264-5678 **25**
5/1-9/26 1P: $48- 59 2P/1B: $54- 67 2P/2B: $62- 67 XP: $7 F18
Motel 9/27-12/19 & 3/31-4/30 1P: $45- 56 2P/1B: $51- 63 2P/2B: $59- 64 XP: $7 F18
12/20-3/30 1P: $42- 53 2P/1B: $48- 60 2P/2B: $56- 61 XP: $7 F18
Location: 1 mi n of Business Rt 60. 1454 Beers School Rd 15108. Fax: 412/264-8034. **Terms:** Small pets only. **Facility:** 119
rooms. 3 stories; exterior corridors. **All Rooms:** free & pay movies. **Cards:** AE, CB, DI, DS, MC, VI. 🛏️ ➡️ ✕ Ⓓ

WYNDHAM GARDEN HOTEL-PITTSBURGH AIRPORT Rates Subject to Change Phone: 724/695-0002 **20**
Mon-Thurs [BP] 1P: $188 2P/1B: $208 2P/2B: $208 XP: $10 F18
Motor Inn Fri-Sun [BP] 1P: $64 2P/1B: $64 2P/2B: $64 XP: $10 F18
Location: Business Rt 60 at Montour Run exit. 1 Wyndham Cir 15275-1000. Fax: 724/695-7262. **Terms:** Sr.
discount; small pets only, with advance notice. **Facility:** 140 rooms. 4 stories; interior corridors. **Dining:** Dining room; 6:30
am-10 pm, Sat & Sun from 7 am; $12-$22. **All Rooms:** free & pay movies. **Cards:** AE, CB, DI, DS, JCB, MC, VI.
(See color ad p 397) Roll in showers. 🛏️ 🏊 ➡️ 📺 ✕ 🏌️ Ⓓ Ⓢ

RESTAURANTS

CLARK'S Lunch: $5-$11 Dinner: $18-$28 Phone: 412/269-9100 **26**
Location: 1 mi n of Coraopolis/Sewickley exit off Business Rt 60. 333 Rouser Rd 15108. **Hours:** 11 am-10
American pm; Sat from 5 pm. Closed major holidays & Sun. **Reservations:** suggested. **Features:** casual dress;
cocktails & lounge. Attractive Old English pub lounge with atrium dining room. **Cards:** AE, DI, DS, MC, VI. ✕

HYEHOLDE RESTAURANT Lunch: $10-$16 Dinner: $16-$32 Phone: 412/264-3116 **25**
Location: Coraopolis Heights Rd at Beaver Grade Rd. 190 Hyeholde Dr 15108. **Hours:** 11:30 am-2 & 5-10
Continental pm, Sat from 5 pm. Closed major holidays & Sun. **Reservations:** suggested; preferred.
Features: semi-formal attire; cocktails; a la carte. Fine dining in French country setting. Authentic medieval
farmhouse re-creation provides old ambience. **Cards:** AE, DI, DS, MC, VI. ✕

CRAFTON—7,200 (See map p. 401; index p. 400)

LODGING

DAYS INN Rates Subject to Change Phone: 412/922-0120 **30**
All Year [CP] 1P: $38 2P/1B: $44 2P/2B: $52 XP: $6 F18
Motel **Location:** On SR 60, from I-79N, exit 16, from I-79S, exit 16B. 100 Kisow Dr 15205. Fax: 412/922-0125.
Terms: Pets, $5 extra charge. **Facility:** 116 rooms. 2 stories; exterior corridors. **All Rooms:** free movies.
Cards: AE, CB, DI, DS, JCB, MC, VI. 🛏️ 📺 ✕ 🏌️ Ⓓ

DELMONT—2,000

LODGING

SUPER 8 MOTEL Rates Subject to Change Phone: 724/468-4888
All Year 1P: $43 2P/1B: $49 2P/2B: $49 XP: $6 F12
Motel **Location:** On SR 66, just s of US 22. 180 Sheffield Dr 15626. Fax: 724/468-4888. **Terms:** Sr. discount; pets,
$5 extra charge. **Facility:** 46 rooms. 3 whirlpool rms, $88.88 for up to 2 persons; 2 stories; interior corridors;
designated smoking area. **All Rooms:** free movies. **Cards:** AE, CB, DI, DS, MC, VI. 🛏️ 📺 🔥 ✕ Ⓓ Ⓢ

RESTAURANT

LAMPLIGHTER RESTAURANT Lunch: $5-$7 Dinner: $9-$16 Phone: 724/468-4545
Location: On US 22, w of jct SR 66. 330 Rt 22 15626. **Hours:** 7 am-10:30 pm, Fri & Sat-11:30 pm,
Sun-8:30 pm. Closed major holidays. **Reservations:** suggested. **Features:** casual dress; Sunday brunch;
children's menu; early bird specials; cocktails & lounge; a la carte. Coffee shop & dining room. Homemade
American soup, bread & dessert. **Cards:** AE, CB, DI, DS, MC, VI. ✕

FOX CHAPEL—5,300

RESTAURANT

FRANCO'S RISTORANTE Lunch: $8-$14 Dinner: $14-$27 Phone: 412/782-5155
Location: Exit 8 off SR 28, 0.3 mi s on Fox Chapel Rd, in Fox Chapel Plaza. 1193 Freeport Rd 15238.
Italian **Hours:** 11:30 am-10 pm, Fri & Sat-11 pm, Sun 3 pm-9 pm. Closed major holidays.
Reservations: suggested. **Features:** casual dress; carryout; cocktails & lounge. Handsome & sophisticated
decor. Many menu entries & daily specials prepared with very accomplished hands. **Cards:** AE, DI, DS, MC, VI. ✕

GIBSONIA—3,500 (See map p. 401; index p. 400)

LODGING

COMFORT INN GIBSONIA Rates Subject to Change Phone: 724/444-8700 **109**
All Year [CP] 1P: $49 2P/1B: $55 2P/2B: $57 XP: $6 F18
Motel **Location:** Exit 4 off I-76 tpk, just n. 5137 Rt 8 15044. Fax: 724/444-8744. **Terms:** Sr. discount; pets, $100
dep req. **Facility:** 63 rooms. 3 stories; exterior corridors. **All Rooms:** free movies. **Cards:** AE, DI, DS, MC,
VI. 🛏️ 📺 ✕ Ⓓ Ⓢ

(See map p. 401)

RESTAURANT

THE PINES TAVERN   Lunch: $6-$10   Dinner: $15-$22   Phone: 724/625-3252   98
AAA   Location: W from jct Rt 8 & 910. 484 Bakerstown-Warrendale Rd 15044. Hours: 11:30 am-2:30 & 5-9 pm,
      Fri & Sat-10 pm. Closed major holidays & Sun. Reservations: suggested. Features: casual dress; children's
◆◆   menu; early bird specials; health conscious menu; carryout; cocktails & lounge. Local landmark since 1914.
Traditional   Specializing in seafood with an evolving menu consisting of variations on old standards. Fine selection of
American   dessert & coffee. Cards: MC, VI.   ☒

GREEN TREE—4,900   (See map p. 401; index p. 400)

LODGINGS

BEST WESTERN-PARKWAY CENTER INN   Phone: 412/922-7070   46
AAA SAVE   Sun-Thurs [CP]   1P: $64- 100 2P/1B: $73- 100 2P/2B: $87- 108 XP: $9   F12
           Fri & Sat [CP]   1P: $64- 78 2P/1B: $68- 78 2P/2B: $68- 78 XP: $9   F12
◆◆◆   Location: 0.5 mi nw of I-279, northbound exit 4 & Greentree Rd, southbound exit 5 & Parkway Center Dr.
Motel   875 Greentree Rd 15220. Fax: 412/922-4949. Terms: Monthly rates; no pets. Facility: 138 rooms. 8 stories;
        interior corridors; saunas, whirlpool. Dining: Restaurant nearby. Services: complimentary evening
beverages, 5 pm-7 pm. Fee: coin laundry. All Rooms: free movies. Some Rooms: coffeemakers, 44 efficiencies,
microwaves, refrigerators. Cards: AE, CB, DI, DS, MC, VI. Special Amenities: Free breakfast and free newspaper.

🛏 🍴 ⊞ 🖤 ⅏ ☒ D S

HAMPTON INN HOTEL GREEN TREE   Rates Subject to Change   Phone: 412/922-0100   49
◆◆◆   All Year [CP]   1P: $64   2P/1B: $73   2P/2B: $73
Motel   Location: I-279, US 22 & 30, exit 4, 1 mi nw via Mansfield Ave. 555 Trumbull Dr 15205. Fax: 412/921-7631.
        Terms: Small pets only. Facility: 133 rooms. 6 stories; interior corridors. All Rooms: free movies.
Cards: AE, DI, DS.   🛏 ⊞ ⅏ ☒ 🛇 D S

HAWTHORN SUITES   Guaranteed Rates   Phone: 412/279-6300   50
◆◆◆   All Year [CP]   1P: $119   2P/1B: $119   2P/2B: $149
Apartment   Location: I-279, US 22 & 30, exit 4; 1.5 mi nw via Mansfield Ave. 700 Mansfield Ave 15205.
Motel   Fax: 412/279-4993. Terms: Sr. discount; reserv deposit; pets, $50 extra charge. Facility: 151 rooms. 2 stories;
        exterior corridors. All Rooms: free movies. Cards: AE, CB, DI, DS, JCB, MC, VI.

🛏 🚲 ⊞ ⅏ ☒ 🛇 D

HOLIDAY INN-PITTSBURGH CENTRAL (GREEN TREE)   Phone: 412/922-8100   44
AAA SAVE   All Year   1P: $99- 139 2P/1B: $99- 139 2P/2B: $99- 139 XP: $10   F17
◆◆◆   Location: I-279, US 22 & 30, exit 4, 1 mi nw via Mansfield Ave. 401 Holiday Dr 15220. Fax: 412/922-6511.
Motor Inn   Terms: Monthly rates; BP avail; package plans; pets. Facility: 200 rooms. 4 stories; interior corridors.
Fee: racquet club privileges. Dining & Entertainment: Restaurant; 6:30 am-11 pm; $11-$17;
cocktails/lounge. Services: valet laundry; area transportation, within 5 mi. All Rooms: coffeemakers, free &
pay movies. Some Rooms: microwaves, refrigerators. Cards: AE, CB, DI, DS, MC, VI. Special Amenities: Free
newspaper and free room upgrade (subject to availability with advanced reservations). (See color ad below)

🛏 🚲 🍴 ⊞ ⅏ 📺 ☒ D

PITTSBURGH GREEN TREE MARRIOTT   Rates Subject to Change   Phone: 412/922-8400   45
◆◆◆   Sun-Thurs 5/1-11/14   1P: $129   2P/1B: $129   2P/2B: $129   XP: $15   F
Hotel   Sun-Thurs 11/15-4/30   1P: $119   2P/1B: $119   2P/2B: $119   XP: $15   F
        Fri & Sat   1P: $81   2P/1B: $81   2P/2B: $81   XP: $15   F
Location: I-279, US 22 & 30; exit 4, 1.1 mi nw via Mansfield Ave. 101 Marriott Dr 15205. Fax: 412/922-8981. Terms: Small
pets only. Facility: 467 rooms. 7 stories; interior corridors. Dining: Dining room, coffee shop; $16-$25. All Rooms: free &
pay movies. Cards: AE, CB, DI, DS, MC, VI.   🛏 🚲 🚲 ⊞ 📺 ⌂ ☒ 🛇 D S

RESTAURANT

PICCOLO MONDO   Lunch: $9-$11   Dinner: $15-$36   Phone: 412/922-0920   75
◆◆   Location: I-279, US 22 & 30 exit 4, 1.1 mi nw via Mansfield Ave, 0.5 mi n on Andersen Dr; in Foster Plaza
Northern   Building 7. 661 Andersen Dr 15220. Hours: 11:30 am-10 pm, Fri-11 pm, Sat 4 pm-11 pm. Closed major
Italian   holidays & Sun. Reservations: required; for 6 or more. Features: dressy casual; carryout; cocktails &
          lounge. Varied menu in a relaxing atmsophere. Cards: AE, DI, DS, MC, VI.   ☒

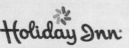

HARMARVILLE—1,200   (See map p. 401; index p. 400)

LODGING

VALLEY MOTEL   **Phone:** 412/828-7100   **105**
AAA **SAVE**   All Year   1P: $40- 50 2P/1B: $40- 50 2P/2B: $40- 50 XP: $6
◆   **Location:** Exit 5 off I-76 (PA Tpk), 1 mi s on Freeport Rd, exit 11 off SR 28. 2571 Freeport Rd 15238.
Motel   **Terms:** Reserv deposit, 7 day notice; weekly rates; no pets. **Facility:** 28 rooms. 1 story; exterior corridors.
All Rooms: free movies, combo or shower baths. **Some Rooms:** whirlpools. Fee: refrigerators. **Cards:** AE,
DS, MC, VI. **Special Amenities:** Early check-in/late check-out and preferred room (subject to
availability with advanced reservations).   **ECTV** **⊠** **D**

HEIDELBERG—3,800   (See map p. 401; index p. 400)

RESTAURANT

WRIGHT'S SEAFOOD INN   **Lunch:** $4-$12   **Dinner:** $14-$22   **Phone:** 412/279-7900   **110**
◆◆   **Location:** In Heidelberg, exit 12 off I-79, 1 mi e on Rt 50, just s on Collier & Washington sts. 1837
Seafood   Washington St 15106. **Hours:** 11 am-10 pm, Fri & Sat-11 pm, Sun 4 pm-9 pm. Closed major holidays.
Reservations: suggested. **Features:** casual dress; children's menu; early bird specials; senior's menu;
health conscious menu; carryout; cocktails & lounge; a la carte. Relaxed family dining. **Cards:** AE, DI, DS, MC, VI.   **⊠**

INDUSTRY—2,100

LODGING

WILLOWS INN   **Phone:** 724/643-4500
AAA **SAVE**   All Year   1P: $39- 45 2P/1B: $50   2P/2B: $44   XP: $5   F14
◆◆   **Location:** Midland exit off Rt 60, 4 mi w on SR 68. 1830 Beaver-Midland Rd 15052. Fax: 724/643-1765.
Motor Inn   **Terms:** No pets. **Facility:** 30 rooms. 2 stories; exterior corridors. **Dining:** Willows Inn Family Smorgasbord,
see separate listing. **Some Rooms:** microwaves, refrigerators, VCR's. **Cards:** AE, DS, MC, VI.
Special Amenities: Free local telephone calls.   **♿** **ECTV** **D**

RESTAURANT

WILLOWS INN FAMILY SMORGASBORD   **Phone:** 724/643-4500
◆◆   **Location:** Midland exit off Rt 60, 4 mi w on SR 68; in Willows Inn. 1830 Beaver-Midland Rd 15052.
American   **Hours:** 11:30 am-3 & 3:30-8:30 pm, Tues & Sat from 3:30 pm, Sun 10:30 am-6:30 pm. Closed: 1/1, 7/4,
12/25 & Mon. **Features:** Sunday brunch; senior's menu; salad bar; cocktails. Casual family atmosphere.
Cards: AE, DS, MC, VI.   **♿** **⊠**

MCMURRAY—4,100

RESTAURANT

THE CLASSROOM   **Lunch:** $7-$10   **Dinner:** $15-$25   **Phone:** 724/942-4878
AAA   **Location:** Jct Rt 19 South. 133 Camp Ln 15219. **Hours:** 11:30 am-2 & 5-10 pm, Sat from 5 pm. Closed
major holidays & Sun. **Reservations:** suggested. **Features:** casual dress; carryout; cocktails. Restored 1907
◆◆   1-room schoolhouse featuring homemade food prepared daily with fresh seasonal menu changes.
American   **Cards:** AE, DS, MC, VI.   **⊠**

MONESSEN—9,900

RESTAURANT

LUCCHESI'S   **Dinner:** $25-$30   **Phone:** 724/684-9889
◆◆   **Location:** Between 3rd & 4th sts. 372 Donner Ave 15062. **Hours:** 5 pm-9 pm. Closed major holidays, Sun &
Continental   Mon. **Reservations:** required. **Features:** casual dress; cocktails & lounge; a la carte. Personal attention by
chef/owner makes dining a nice experience. Entree options include seafood, veal, chicken, beef & pasta.
Cuisine centers on fresh, top-quality ingredients.

MONROEVILLE—29,100   (See map p. 401; index p. 400)

LODGINGS

DAYS INN-MONROEVILLE   Rates Subject to Change   **Phone:** 412/856-1610   **74**
◆◆   All Year   1P: $51- 66 2P/1B: $66- 76 2P/2B: $66- 76 XP: $6   F12
Motel   **Location:** Exit 6 off I-76 (PA Tpk), exit 16A off I-376; 1 mi s on SR 48. 2727 Mosside Blvd 15146.
Fax: 412/856-1628. **Terms:** Pets. **Facility:** 107 rooms. 2-3 stories; exterior corridors. **All Rooms:** free
movies. **Cards:** AE, CB, DI, DS, MC, VI.   **🛏** **CTV** **⊠** **D**

HAMPTON INN MONROEVILLE/PITTSBURGH   Rates Subject to Change   **Phone:** 412/380-4000
Motel   All Year [CP]   1P: $89   2P/1B: $99   2P/2B: $99
Too new to rate; **Location:** I-76 (PA Tpk) exit 6; I-376 exit 16A, 0.3 mi s on SR 48. 3000 Mosside Blvd
15146. Fax: 412/380-0185. **Terms:** Sr. discount; **Facility:** 140 rooms. Scheduled to open February 1998. **Cards:** AE, CB, DI,
DS, JCB, MC, VI.   **D**

HARLEY HOTEL   Rates Subject to Change   **Phone:** 412/244-1600   **70**
◆◆   All Year   1P: $111- 131 2P/1B: $131   2P/2B: $131   XP: $10   F18
Motor Inn   **Location:** 8 mi e on I-376 & US 22, exit 15. 699 Rodi Rd 15235. Fax: 412/829-2334. **Terms:** Sr. discount;
no pets. **Facility:** 152 rooms. 3 stories; interior corridors. **Dining:** Dining room; 6:30 am-2 & 5:30-10 pm, Fri
& Sat 6:30 am-11 pm, Sun 7 am-2 & 5:30-10 pm; $9-$20. **All Rooms:** Fee: movies. **Cards:** AE, CB, DI, DS, JCB, MC, VI.
(See ad p 402)   Roll in showers. **🛁** **🛁** **♿** **CTV** **⊠** **D**

HOLIDAY INN   Rates Subject to Change   **Phone:** 412/372-1022   **73**
◆◆◆   All Year   1P: $69- 139 2P/1B: $69- 139 2P/2B: $69- 139
Motor Inn   **Location:** Exit 6 off I-76 (PA Tpk), exit 16A off I-376; 0.4 mi s on SR 48. 2750 Mosside Blvd 15146.
Fax: 412/373-4065. **Terms:** Sr. discount; small pets only. **Facility:** 189 rooms. 4 stories; interior corridors.
Dining: Dining room; 6:30 am-10 pm; $10-$20. **All Rooms:** free & pay movies. **Cards:** AE, CB, DI, DS, JCB, MC, VI.
Roll in showers. **🛏** **🛁** **CTV** **⊠** **D**

(See map p. 401)

RADISSON HOTEL PITTSBURGH
Phone: 412/373-7300 69
(AAA) (SAVE)   All Year   1P: $89- 125   2P/1B: $89- 125   2P/2B: $89- 125   XP: $10   F18
◆◆◆   **Location:** Adj to Monroeville Mall; 2 mi w of I-76 tpk exit 6, on US 22. 101 Mall Blvd 15146.
Hotel   **Fax:** 412/373-1549. **Terms:** 15% service charge; package plans; no pets. **Facility:** 322 rooms. 7-14 stories; interior corridors; whirlpool. **Dining & Entertainment:** Dining room; 6:30 am-10 pm, Sat & Sun from 7 am; $9-$16; cocktails/lounge. **Services:** valet laundry; area transportation, area shopping. **All Rooms:** honor bars, coffeemakers, free & pay movies. **Some Rooms:** refrigerators, whirlpools. **Cards:** AE, CB, DI, DS, JCB, MC, VI.
Special Amenities: Early check-in/late check-out and free newspaper. *(See color ad p 394)*

RED ROOF INN-MONROEVILLE   Rates Subject to Change   Phone: 412/856-4738   76
◆◆   6/1-9/30   1P: $58- 73   2P/1B: $66- 82   2P/2B: $70- 85   XP: $7   F18
Motel   5/1-5/31, 10/1-12/31 &
   4/1-4/30   1P: $54- 69   2P/1B: $61- 77   2P/2B: $64- 79   XP: $7   F18
   1/1-3/31   1P: $51- 66   2P/1B: $58- 76   2P/2B: $61- 76   XP: $7   F18
Location: Exit 6 off I-76 (PA Tpk), exit 16A off I-376; 0.8 mi s on SR 48. 2729 Mosside Blvd 15146. **Fax:** 412/856-4758.
Terms: Small pets only. **Facility:** 117 rooms. 3 stories; exterior corridors. **All Rooms:** free movies. **Cards:** AE, CB, DI, DS, MC, VI.

WM PENN MOTEL   Phone: 412/373-0700   71
(AAA) (SAVE)   All Year   1P: $45- 53   2P/1B: $50- 54   2P/2B: $54- 58   XP: $5   F18
◆   **Location:** 0.3 mi w of tpk exit 6 on US 22 business route. 4139 Wm Penn Hwy 15146. **Fax:** 412/372-3814.
Motel   **Terms:** No pets. **Facility:** 22 rooms. Near 3 main traffic arteries, good location for budget minded. All rooms ground level, parking at door, downtown Pittsburgh 13 mi. 1 two-bedroom unit. 1 story; exterior corridors. **Dining:** Restaurant nearby. **All Rooms:** free movies, combo or shower baths. **Cards:** AE, CB, DI, MC, VI.
Special Amenities: Preferred room (subject to availability with advanced reservations).

MURRYSVILLE—17,000

RESTAURANT

SPADARO'S RESTAURANT   **Lunch:** $3-$7   **Dinner:** $7-$15   Phone: 724/327-5955
◆◆   **Location:** On US 22; just east of jct of SR 286. 4430 Wm Penn Hwy 15668. **Hours:** 11 am-10 pm, Fri &
Italian   Sat-11 pm, Sun 11 am-8 pm. Closed major holidays. **Reservations:** suggested; weekends. **Features:** casual dress; children's menu; health conscious menu items; carryout; cocktails & lounge. Italian & American cuisine. **Cards:** AE, CB, DI, DS, MC, VI.

NEW KENSINGTON—15,900   (See map p. 401; index p. 400)

LODGING

DAYS INN OF NEW KENSINGTON   Phone: 724/335-9171   82
(AAA) (SAVE)   All Year   1P: $50- 65   2P/1B: $60- 75   2P/2B: $60- 75   XP: $5   F18
◆◆   **Location:** On SR 366; 1.5 mi s of SR 28, exit 14; at s end of Tarentum Bridge. 300 Tarentum Bridge Rd
Motor Inn   15068. **Fax:** 724/335-6642. **Terms:** Pets. **Facility:** 111 rooms. 2 stories; interior corridors. **Dining:** Dining room; 7 am-2 & 5-9:30 pm, Sun 7 am-9 pm; $6-$14; cocktails. **Services:** Fee: coin laundry. **All Rooms:** free movies, safes. **Some Rooms:** Fee: microwaves, refrigerators. **Cards:** AE, CB, DI, DS, JCB, MC, VI.
Special Amenities: Early check-in/late check-out and free room upgrade (subject to availability with advanced reservations).

OAKDALE—1,800   (See map p. 401; index p. 400)

LODGING

COMFORT INN-PITTSBURGH AIRPORT   Rates Subject to Change   Phone: 412/787-2600   18
◆◆   All Year   1P: $53- 88   2P/1B: $58- 93   2P/2B: $58- 93   XP: $5   F18
Motor Inn   **Location:** On US 22 & 30, at jct SR 60; 4 mi w of I-279 & I-79. 7011 Old Steubenville Pike 15071.
Fax: 412/787-3590. **Terms:** Sr. discount; pets, $8 extra charge. **Facility:** 75 rooms. 2 stories; interior/exterior corridors. **Dining:** Restaurant; 11:30 am-10 pm, closed major holidays & Mon; $8-$17. **All Rooms:** free movies. **Cards:** AE, DI, DS, JCB, MC, VI. *(See color ad below)*

OAKLAND—1,500

LODGINGS

BEST WESTERN UNIVERSITY CENTER Rates Subject to Change **Phone:** 412/683-6100
◆◆ All Year 1P: $72- 90 2P/1B: $82- 100 2P/2B: $82- 100 XP: $8 F18
Motor Inn **Location:** Just w of jct Bates St. 3401 Blvd of the Allies 15213. Fax: 412/682-6115. **Terms:** Sr. discount; pets. **Facility:** 119 rooms. 9 stories; interior corridors. **Dining:** Restaurant; $6-$11. **All Rooms:** free movies.
Cards: AE, DI, DS, JCB, MC, VI.

HAMPTON INN-UNIVERSITY CENTER Rates Subject to Change **Phone:** 412/681-1000
◆◆◆ All Year [CP] 1P: $99 2P/1B: $109 2P/2B: $109
Motel **Location:** At jct Blvd of the Allies. 3315 Hamlet St 15213. Fax: 412/681-3022. **Terms:** Pets. **Facility:** 133 rooms. 8 stories; interior corridors. **All Rooms:** free movies. **Cards:** AE, CB, DI, DS, MC.

HOLIDAY INN SELECT AT UNIVERSITY CENTER **Phone:** 412/682-6200
(AAA) (SAVE) All Year 1P: $126 2P/1B: $126 2P/2B: $126
Location: Just nw of 5th Ave. 100 Lytton Ave 15213. Fax: 412/682-5745. **Terms:** Package plans; small pets only, $35 dep req. **Facility:** 251 rooms. 10 stories; interior corridors; luxury level rooms; sauna. Fee: parking.
◆◆◆ **Dining & Entertainment:** Restaurant; 6:30 am-11 pm; Sat & Sun from 7:30 am; $13-$20; cocktails/lounge.
Motor Inn **Services:** area transportation, within 5 mi. Fee: coin laundry. **All Rooms:** coffeemakers, free & pay movies, combo or shower baths. **Some Rooms:** refrigerators. **Cards:** AE, CB, DI, DS, JCB, MC, VI.

RESTAURANTS

ALI BABA **Phone:** 412/682-2829
◆ **Location:** 404 S Craig St 15213. **Hours:** 11:30 am-2:30 & 4-10 pm, Sat & Sun from 4 pm. Closed major
Ethnic holidays. **Reservations:** suggested. **Features:** casual dress; health conscious menu items; carryout; beer only. Small, unpretentious restaurant serving authentic Middle Eastern cuisine including lamb shanks, shish kebob, hummus & baba ghanouj. Many vegetarian options. **Cards:** AE, DI, MC, VI.

INDIA GARDEN **Phone:** 412/682-3000
(AAA) (SAVE) **Location:** 376 e to Forbes Ave exit, jct Bates St. 328 Atwood St 15213. **Hours:** 11:30 am-2:30 & 5-10 pm.
Reservations: suggested. **Features:** casual dress. North Indian cuisine with a speciality in Tandoori. Fine
◆◆ selection, natural & freshly prepared on premises, no additives. **Cards:** AE, DI, DS, MC, VI. **Special Value:**
Northern **20% discount on the price of any entree, excluding beverages, tax and gratuity.**
Ethnic

ORIENT KITCHEN Lunch: $4-$5 Dinner: $8-$12 **Phone:** 412/682-3311
◆ **Location:** Jct Bates St. 414 Semple St 15213. **Hours:** 11 am-1 am. Closed: Wed. **Features:** casual dress;
Chinese carryout. Small, unpretentious, specializing in Cantonese dishes, slow poached, steamed using light sauces to enhance fresh natural flavors. Featuring fresh fish, lobster & Pacific Northwest oysters.

THE SPICE ISLAND TEA HOUSE Lunch: $4-$6 Dinner: $5-$9 **Phone:** 412/687-8821
◆ **Location:** Jct Bates St. 253 Atwood St 15213. **Hours:** 11:30 am-9 pm, Fri & Sat-10 pm. Closed major
Ethnic holidays & Sun. **Features:** casual dress; carryout; cocktail lounge. Southeast Asian cuisine specializing in Burmese. Relaxing atmosphere with friendly service. Some of the fine fare produced are corn & shrimp fritters, Thai beef salad, Burmese barbeque chicken & Shan tribe hot & sour noodle soup. Smoke free premises. **Cards:** AE, DI, DS, MC, VI.

OAKMONT—7,000   (See map p. 401; index p. 400)

LODGING

THE INN AT OAKMONT Rates Subject to Change **Phone:** 412/828-0410 [101]
◆◆◆ All Year [BP] 1P: $100- 120 2P/1B: $130- 140 2P/2B: $130- 140 XP: $5
Bed & **Location:** 1 mi e on Hulton Rd, jct SR 909 & Hulton Rd. 15139 (PO Box 103). Fax: 412/828-1358.
Breakfast **Terms:** No pets. **Facility:** 8 rooms. 2 stories; interior corridors; smoke free premises. **Cards:** AE, DS, MC, VI.

PLEASANT HILLS—8,900   (See map p. 401; index p. 400)

LODGING

HOWARD JOHNSON - PITTSBURGH SOUTH Guaranteed Rates **Phone:** 412/884-6000 [123]
◆◆ All Year [BP] 1P: $69- 89 2P/1B: $79- 99 2P/2B: $79- 99 XP: $10 F18
Motel **Location:** 0.3 mi n of Lebanon Church Rd (Yellow Belt) on US 51. 5300 Clairton Blvd 15236.
Fax: 412/884-6000. **Terms:** Sr. discount; small pets only. **Facility:** 95 rooms. 2 stories; interior corridors.
Cards: AE, CB, DI, MC, VI.

SEWICKLEY—4,100   (See map p. 401; index p. 400)

LODGING

THE SEWICKLEY COUNTRY INN Rates Subject to Change **Phone:** 412/741-4300 [78]
◆ All Year [BP] 1P: $64- 70 2P/1B: $69- 80 2P/2B: $69- 80 XP: $10 F17
Motor Inn **Location:** 0.5 mi s on SR 65. 801 Ohio River Blvd 15143. Fax: 412/741-8893. **Terms:** Reserv deposit; small pets only. **Facility:** 149 rooms. 2 stories; interior/exterior corridors. **Dining:** Dining room; 6:30 am-10 pm, Sun-9 pm; $8-$18. **Cards:** AE, CB, DI, DS, MC, VI.

SHADYSIDE   (See map p. 401; index p. 400)

LODGING

APPLETREE BED & BREAKFAST Rates Subject to Change **Phone:** 412/661-0631 [119]
◆◆◆ Fri & Sat [BP] 1P: $99- 130 2P/1B: $99- 130 2P/2B: $99- 130 XP: $10
Bed & Sun-Thurs [BP] 1P: $89- 100 2P/1B: $89- 100 2P/2B: $89- 100 XP: $10
Breakfast **Location:** 0.3 mi n of 5th Ave. 703 S Negley Ave 15232. **Terms:** Sr. discount; no pets. **Facility:** 5 rooms. 3 stories, no elevator; interior corridors; smoke free premises. **Cards:** AE, DS, MC, VI.

(See map p. 401)

RESTAURANT

CHINA PALACE   Lunch: $5-$6   Dinner: $7-$13   Phone: 412/687-7423   105
◆
         Location: Between S Aiken & Bellefonte. 5440 Walnut St 15232. **Hours:** 11:30 am-10 pm, Fri & Sat-11 pm,
Chinese   Sun 2 pm-9 pm. Closed: 7/4, 9/1 & 11/26. **Features:** casual dress; carryout; cocktails & lounge. Good
         selection of fried & steamed dishes. **Cards:** AE, DI, DS, MC, VI.   ⊠

SPEERS

RESTAURANTS

THE BACK PORCH RESTAURANT   Historical   **Lunch:** $8-$10   **Dinner:** $14-$24   **Phone:** 724/483-4500
◆◆
         Location: Exit 17, I-70, located under exit bridge on river by marina. 114 Speers St 15012. **Hours:** 11:30
American am-10 pm, Fri-11 pm, Sat 5 pm-11 pm, Sun 4 pm-9 pm. Closed: 1/1, 12/24, 12/25 & Mon.
         Reservations: suggested; for dinner. **Features:** dressy casual; cocktails & lounge. Restored 1806 home.
Cards: AE, DI, DS, MC, VI.   ⊠

SNOOTERS WATERFRONT CAFE   **Lunch:** $6-$16   **Dinner:** $8-$16   **Phone:** 724/483-6000
◆◆
         Location: I-70, exit 17 e 0.3 mi under bridge near Marina. 119 River Rd 15012. **Hours:** 11:30 am-10 pm,
American 9/15-4/15 4 pm-10 pm. Closed: 12/25 & 1/1. **Reservations:** accepted. **Features:** casual dress; children's
         menu; carryout; cocktails & lounge. Casual dining with excellent scenic views of river & surrounding
countryside. **Cards:** AE, DS, MC, VI.   ⊠

SPRINGDALE—3,400

RESTAURANT

KLEINER DEUTSCHMANN   **Lunch:** $5-$8   **Dinner:** $10-$20   **Phone:** 724/274-5022
◆◆
         Location: Exit 5 off I-76 (PA Tpk), exit 11 off SR 28, 3 mi ne on Freeport Rd. 543 Pittsburgh St 15144.
German   **Hours:** 5 pm-10 pm. Closed major holidays, Sun & Mon. **Reservations:** suggested. **Features:** casual dress;
         cocktails. Victorian style bright pink house with a white polar bear standing outside makes this restaurant
easy to find. Large variety of wursts, schnitzels & spatzle. **Cards:** AE, MC, VI.   ⊠

TURTLE CREEK—6,600   (See map p. 401; index p. 400)

RESTAURANT

PAT'S PLACE   **Lunch:** $5-$10   **Dinner:** $9-$20   **Phone:** 412/823-9695   119
◆◆
         Location: From the Churchill exit 376, take 130 south to Turtle Creek, right off 130 to Monroeville Ave, left
Continental on to Airbrake Ave, at school. 1307 Airbrake Ave 15145. **Hours:** 11:30 am-10 pm, Sat 4 pm-11 pm, Sun 4
         pm-8 pm. Closed major holidays. **Reservations:** required. **Features:** early bird specials; carryout; cocktails &
lounge; entertainment. Popular with the locals. Italian/French cuisine well prepared & presented. Piano music Fri & Sun
evenings. **Cards:** AE, DI, DS, MC, VI.   ⊠

WARRENDALE—500   (See map p. 401; index p. 400)

LODGINGS

FAIRFIELD INN   **Phone:** 724/772-0600   59
Ⓐ Ⓢ   All Year [CP]   1P: $69   2P/1B: $79   2P/2B: $79   XP: $10   F18
◆◆◆   **Location:** I-76 exit 3, tpk 0.3 mi n on Rt 19; I-79 exit 25, 0.5 mi n on US 19. 30 St Francis Way 16066.
Motel   Fax: 724/772-6446. **Terms:** No pets. **Facility:** 105 rooms. Quiet setting. 3 stories; interior/exterior corridors.
         Services: valet laundry. **All Rooms:** free & pay movies. **Cards:** AE, CB, DI, DS, MC, VI.
         Special Amenities: Free breakfast and free local telephone calls.   ⊇ ⬚ CTV ⊠ ⬚ D S

HAMPTON INN CRANBERRY   Rates Subject to Change   **Phone:** 724/776-1000   60
◆◆◆   All Year [CP]   1P: $70- 75   2P/1B: $75   2P/2B: $85
Motel   **Location:** Tpk exit 3, 0.5 mi n on US 19, 0.3 mi w on Freedom Rd; exit 25 off I-79 1 mi n on US 19, 0.3 mi
         w on Freedom Rd; southbound I-79, exit 25; 0.5 mi w on Freedom Rd. 210 Executive Dr 16046.
Fax: 724/776-6699. **Terms:** Sr. discount; no pets. **Facility:** 117 rooms. 4 stories; interior corridors. **All Rooms:** free movies.
Cards: AE, CB, DI, DS, MC, VI.   ⊇ ECTV ⊠ ⬚ D S

HOLIDAY INN EXPRESS   Rates Subject to Change   **Phone:** 724/772-1000   58
◆◆◆   All Year [CP]   1P: $79   2P/1B: $89   2P/2B: $89
Motel   **Location:** Jct SR 19 & Tkpk. 20003 Route 19 16066. Fax: 724/772-9766. **Terms:** Sr. discount; pets.
         Facility: 102 rooms. 2 suites, $89-$119; 2 stories; interior corridors. **All Rooms:** free movies.
Some Rooms: 2 kitchens. **Cards:** AE, DI, DS, MC, VI.   ⛶ ECTV ⊠ D

RED ROOF INN-CRANBERRY   Rates Subject to Change   **Phone:** 724/776-5670   61
◆◆   5/1-9/30   1P: $49- 59   2P/1B: $55- 65 2P/2B: $59- 69 XP: $7   F18
Motel   4/1-4/30   1P: $45- 55   2P/1B: $50- 60 2P/2B: $55- 65 XP: $7   F18
         10/1-3/31   1P: $40- 50   2P/1B: $45- 55 2P/2B: $50- 60 XP: $7   F18
Location: I-76 & I-79 at SR 19. 20009 Rt 19 16066. Fax: 724/776-5687. **Terms:** Small pets only. **Facility:** 108 rooms. 2 stories; exterior corridors. **All Rooms:** free movies. **Cards:** AE, CB, DI, DS, MC, VI.   ⛶ CTV ⊠ ⬚ D

SHERATON INN-PITTSBURGH NORTH   Rates Subject to Change   **Phone:** 724/776-6900   63
◆◆◆   All Year [BP]   1P: $119   2P/1B: $119   2P/2B: $119   XP: $10   F18
Hotel   **Location:** I-79, exit 25 US 19N; tpk I-76, exit 3, 0.5 mi s on US 19. 910 Sheraton Dr 16046.
         Fax: 724/776-1115. **Terms:** Sr. discount; no pets. **Facility:** 191 rooms. 4 suites, $180; 5 stories; interior corri-
dors. **Dining:** Coffee shop; 6:30 am-11 pm, Sat & Sun from 7 am; $14-$25; also, Tremont House, see separate listing.
All Rooms: free & pay movies. **Cards:** AE, CB, DI, DS, JCB, MC, VI.   ⊇ ⊇ CTV ⊠ D S

SUPER 8 MOTEL-CRANBERRY   Rates Subject to Change   **Phone:** 724/776-9700   57
◆◆   All Year   1P: $53   2P/1B: $59   2P/2B: $53   XP: $6   F18
Motel   **Location:** Exit 25 off I-79, US 19N; Tpk I-76 exit 3, 0.5 mi s on US 19. 929 Sheraton Dr 16046.
         Fax: 724/776-4522. **Terms:** Sr. discount; no pets. **Facility:** 70 rooms. 3 stories; interior corridors.
All Rooms: free movies. **Some Rooms:** 5 efficiencies. **Cards:** AE, DI, DS, JCB, MC, VI.
                                               Roll in showers. ECTV ⊠ D S

(See map p. 401)

RESTAURANT

TREMONT HOUSE   **Lunch:** $6-$10   **Dinner:** $15-$23   **Phone:** 724/776-6900   85
◆◆◆   **Location:** I-79, exit 25 US 19N; tpk I-76, exit 3, 0.5 mi s on US 19; in Sheraton Inn-Pittsburgh North. 910
American   Sheraton Dr 16046. **Hours:** 6:30 am-11 pm, Sat from 7 am, Sun 7 am-10 pm. **Features:** dressy casual;
    Sunday brunch; children's menu; senior's menu; health conscious menu items; carryout; cocktails. Dining in
a relaxed atmosphere. **Cards:** AE, DI, DS, JCB, MC, VI.   🚫 ✕

WASHINGTON—15,900

LODGINGS

DAYS INN   **Phone:** 724/225-8500
(AAA) SAVE   All Year [CP]   1P: $44- 74   2P/1B: $54- 84   2P/2B: $54- 90   XP: $6   F18
◆◆   **Location:** On US 40; e of I-70, exit 4. 1370 W Chestnut St 15301. Fax: 724/222-7671. **Terms:** No pets.
Motel   **Facility:** 104 rooms. 2 stories; interior/exterior corridors. **Dining:** Restaurant nearby. **Services:** Fee: coin
    laundry. **All Rooms:** free movies. **Some Rooms:** coffeemakers. **Cards:** AE, CB, DI, DS, MC, VI.
    Special Amenities: Free local telephone calls and free newspaper.   🛰 🛁 🖥 ECTV ✕ D

HOLIDAY INN-MEADOW LANDS   Rates Subject to Change   **Phone:** 724/222-6200
◆◆◆   All Year   1P: $99- 129   2P/1B: $99- 129   2P/2B: $99- 129
Motor Inn   **Location:** Northbound I-79, exit 8B (Race Track Rd), 0.5 mi e; southbound I-79, exit 8 (Meadow Lands), 1.5
    mi e. 340 Race Track Rd 15301. Fax: 724/228-1977. **Terms:** Sr. discount; small pets only, $50 dep req.
Facility: 138 rooms. 2-bedroom suite with kitchen, $300-$399; 7 stories; interior corridors. **Dining:** Dining room; 6:30 am-2
& 5-10 pm, Fri-11 pm, Sat 7 am-2 & 5-11 pm, Sun from 7 am; $13-$20. **All Rooms:** free & pay movies. **Cards:** AE, CB, DI,
DS, JCB, MC. *(See ad below)*   Roll in showers.   🛏 🛰 🖥 ✕ D

LONGSTRETCH HARBOUR BED & BREAKFAST   Rates Subject to Change   **Phone:** 724/223-8283
◆   All Year [BP]   1P: $40- 60   2P/1B: $50- 75   2P/2B: $60- 75   XP: $15   D10
Historic Bed   **Location:** I-70 exit 9, 2.2 mi s on SR 519, 1 mi w on US 40. 951 National Pike E 15301. Fax: 724/223-8283.
& Breakfast   **Terms:** Sr. discount; reserv deposit, 3 day notice; pets, outside kennel. **Facility:** 5 rooms. 2 stories; interior
    corridors. **All Rooms:** free movies. **Cards:** AE, DS, MC, VI.   🛏 ECTV D

MOTEL 6 - 1283   Guaranteed Rates   **Phone:** 724/223-8040
(AAA)   All Year   1P: $40   2P/1B: $50   2P/2B: $50   XP: $6   F17
◆◆   **Location:** Off US 19; 0.5 mi s of I-70, exit 7A. 1283 Motel 6 Dr 15301. Fax: 724/228-6445. **Terms:** Sr.
Motel   discount; small pets only. **Facility:** 102 rooms. 1 story; exterior corridors. **All Rooms:** free movies.
    Cards: AE, CB, DI, DS, MC, VI.   Roll in showers. 🛏 CTV 🛗 ✕ D

RAMADA INN   Phone: 724/225-9750
(AAA) (SAVE)   5/1-10/31 [CP]   1P: $67- 76   2P/1B: $73- 82 2P/2B: $73- 82 XP: $8   F18
                11/1-4/30 [CP]   1P: $60- 66   2P/1B: $66- 72 2P/2B: $66- 72 XP: $8   F18
◆◆   **Location:** On US 40, 0.5 mi e of I-70, exit 4. 1170 W Chestnut St 15301 (PO Box 293). Fax: 724/223-2912.
Motor Inn   **Terms:** BP avail; package plans; no pets. **Facility:** 93 rooms. Attractive hilltop location. 2 stories;
               interior/exterior corridors. **Dining & Entertainment:** Dining room; 7 am-10 pm; dinner buffet Thurs $7.25, Sat
$9.95; lunch buffet Sun $7.95 with 10% senior discount; $7-$16; cocktails/lounge. **Some Rooms:** coffeemakers,
refrigerators. **Cards:** AE, CB, DI, MC, VI. **Special Amenities:** Early check-in/late check-out and free newspaper.

                                                                     (⊇) (📺) (✕) (D)

RED ROOF INN   Rates Subject to Change   Phone: 724/228-5750
◆◆   All Year   1P: $40- 51   2P/1B: $46- 57 2P/2B: $51- 62 XP: $5   F18
Motel   **Location:** On US 40; e of I-70, exit 4. 1399 W Chestnut St 15301. Fax: 724/228-5865. **Terms:** Small pets
               only. **Facility:** 110 rooms. 2 stories; interior/exterior corridors. **All Rooms:** free & pay movies. **Cards:** AE,
CB, DI, DS, MC, VI.   Roll in showers. (🛏) (CTV) (✕) (D)

WASHINGTON MOTOR INN   Phone: 724/222-6500
(AAA) (SAVE)   All Year [CP]   1P: $35- 60   2P/1B: $35- 60 2P/2B: $35- 60 XP: $6   F18
               Location: On US 40, e of I-70, exit 4. 1385 W Chestnut St 15301. Fax: 724/222-7671. **Terms:** No pets.
◆◆   **Facility:** 62 rooms. 1-2 stories; exterior corridors. **Dining:** Restaurant nearby. **Services:** valet laundry.
Motel   **All Rooms:** free movies. **Cards:** AE, CB, DI, DS, MC, VI.   (📺) (✕) (D)

RESTAURANTS

ANGELO'S RISTORANTE   **Lunch:** $5-$8   **Dinner:** $8-$22   Phone: 724/222-7120
(AAA)   **Location:** On US 40, 0.8 mi e of I-70, exit 4. 955 W Chestnut St 15301. **Hours:** 11 am-11 pm, Fri &
               Sat-midnight; 10/1-3/31 closes 1 hour earlier. **Closed:** Sun, 1/1, 11/26 & 12/25. **Reservations:** suggested.
◆◆   **Features:** casual dress; children's menu; health conscious menu items; carryout; cocktails & lounge. Good
Italian   wine selection. Diverse Italian & Novelle cuisine since 1939. Smoke free premises. **Cards:** AE, CB, DI, MC,
               VI.

CURINGA'S INN   **Lunch:** $6-$8   **Dinner:** $9-$19   Phone: 724/225-7747
◆◆   **Location:** 2 mi·n on US 19, from I-70, exit 7B. 1050 Washington Rd 15301. **Hours:** 11 am-10 pm, Fri-11
American   pm, Sat 4 pm-11 pm, Sun noon-8:30 pm. **Closed** major holidays. **Features:** casual dress; children's menu;
               early bird specials; carryout; cocktails & lounge. Old English atmosphere. Varied menu featuring beef,
chicken & seafood. **Cards:** AE, DI, DS, MC, VI.   (✕)

WEST MIFFLIN—23,600   (See map p. 401; index p. 400)

LODGING

HAMPTON INN   Rates Subject to Change   Phone: 412/650-1000   (111)
(AAA)   All Year [CP]   1P: $79- 94   2P/1B: $84- 99 2P/2B: $84- 99
               Location: 0.7 mi e of jct SR 51 & Lebanon Church Rd. (1550 Lebanon Church Rd, PITTSBURGH, 15236).
◆◆◆   Fax: 412/650-1001. **Terms:** Sr. discount; no pets. **Facility:** 70 rooms. 3 stories; interior corridors.
Motel   **All Rooms:** free movies. **Some Rooms:** 2 efficiencies. **Cards:** AE, CB, DI, DS, JCB, MC, VI.
                                                              Roll in showers. (⊇) (📺) (♿) (✕) (D) (S)

WEXFORD—1,100   (See map p. 401; index p. 400)

LODGING

ECONO LODGE-PITTSBURGH NORTH   Rates Subject to Change   Phone: 412/935-1000   (87)
◆◆   All Year   1P: $47- 65   2P/2B: $54- 62 XP: $5   F17
Motel   **Location:** 9 mi n, jct I-79, exit 22 & SR 910. 107 VIP Dr 15090. Fax: 412/935-6288. **Terms:** Sr. discount; no
               pets. **Facility:** 50 rooms. 2 stories; interior corridors. **All Rooms:** free movies. **Some Rooms:** kitchen.
Cards: AE, CB, DI, DS, JCB, MC, VI.   (CTV) (✕) (D)

RESTAURANTS

MAX PLANKS   Phone: 412/935-7550   (93)
◆◆   **Location:** Exit 22 off I-79, 2 mi e on SR 910, 1 mi s on US 19. One Wexford Sq 15090. **Hours:** 11 am-10
Regional   pm; Fri, Sat & Sun-midnight. **Closed:** 12/25. **Reservations:** accepted. **Features:** casual dress; Sunday
American   brunch; children's menu; health conscious menu; carryout; cocktails & lounge. Family orientated, grilled
               pizza, pasta, veal & chicken specialties. **Cards:** AE, DI, DS, MC, VI.   (✕)

STONE MANSION RESTAURANT   **Lunch:** $6-$10   **Dinner:** $18-$30   Phone: 412/934-3000   (90)
◆◆◆   **Location:** Jct SR 79 Wexford exit 22, PA Tpk exit 3. 1600 Stone Mountain Rd 16323. **Hours:** 11:45 am-3 &
Continental   4:30-10 pm, Fri & Sat-11 pm. **Closed** major holidays & Sun. **Reservations:** suggested; 6 or more.
               Features: casual dress; children's menu; health conscious menu items; carryout; cocktails & lounge;
entertainment; fee for valet parking; a la carte. Elegant dining with the feeling of old world luxury & ambience. **Cards:** AE,
CB, DI, DS, MC, VI.   (✕)

ZELIENOPLE—4,200

LODGING

THE INN ON GRANDVIEW   Guaranteed Rates   Phone: 724/452-0469
◆◆◆   All Year [BP]   1P: $85- 105 2P/1B: $85- 105 2P/2B: $85- 105
Historic Bed   **Location:** I-79 exit 27, 0.7 mi w on SR 68. 310 E Grandview Ave 16063. **Terms:** Check-in 4 pm; reserv
& Breakfast   deposit, 7 day notice; no pets. **Facility:** 4 rooms. Handling fee imposed; 2 stories; interior corridors; designated
               smoking area. **Cards:** DS, MC, VI.   (CTV) (✕) (D)

RESTAURANT

THE KAUFMAN HOUSE Historical   **Lunch:** $4-$8   **Dinner:** $9-$20   Phone: 724/452-8900
◆◆   **Location:** Rt 19N. 105 S Main St 16063. **Hours:** 7 am-9 pm, Fri & Sat-10 pm. **Closed** major holidays.
American   **Reservations:** suggested; weekends. **Features:** casual dress; children's menu; early bird specials; carryout;
               cocktails & lounge. In 1903 landmark building. Breakfast served in older diner-style coffee shop. **Cards:** AE,
CB, DI, MC, VI.   (✕)

PITTSTON—9,400   (See map p. 418; index below)

LODGING

KNIGHTS INN-SCRANTON/PITTSTON   Phone: 717/654-6020   [119]

⊕⊕ [SAVE] All Year   1P: $33- 36 2P/1B: $36- 41 2P/2B: $41- 46 XP: $5   F18
◆◆   **Location:** Just s on SR 315 from I-8, northbound exit 48, southbound exit 48A, & PA Tpk NE Extension exit
Motel   37. 310 SR 315 18640. Fax: 717/655-3767. **Terms:** Weekly rates; small pets only. **Facility:** 64 rooms. 6 effi-
           ciencies. Handling fee imposed; 1 story; exterior corridors. **Dining:** Restaurant nearby. **All Rooms:** free
           movies. **Some Rooms:** microwaves, radios, refrigerators, whirlpools. Fee: VCR's. **Cards:** AE, DI, DS, MC,
VI. **Special Amenities:** Free breakfast and free local telephone calls. *(See ad p 442)*   [🛒] [CTV] [✕] [D]

RESTAURANT

COOPER'S ON THE WATERFRONT   Lunch: $5-$8   Dinner: $12-$24   Phone: 717/654-6883   [62]
⊕⊕   **Location:** Center. 304 Kennedy Blvd 18640. **Hours:** 3:30 pm-11 pm; Fri 11 am-midnight; Sat 4 pm-midnight,
◆◆   Sun 10 am-11 pm. Closed major holidays. **Features:** casual dress; Sunday brunch; children's menu; early
Seafood   bird specials; carryout; cocktails & lounge. American Cajun, large variety of fresh seafood & meat entrees.
           Extensive beer menu from around the world. **Cards:** DS, MC, VI.   [✕]

PLEASANT HILLS—*see Pittsburgh & Vicinity p. 413.*

PLYMOUTH MEETING—*See Philadelphia & Vicinity p. 385.*

Pocono Mountains Area

POCONO MOUNTAINS

> To help you more easily locate accommodations in the Pocono Mountains area, the fol-
> lowing index and map show lodgings and restaurants in multiple cities. Listings for
> these establishments are found under the heading for the city in which they are located.
> The Pocono Mountains area map comprises: Archbald, Bartonsville, Bushkill, Ca-
> nadensis, Clarks Summit, Cresco, Dickson City, Drinker, Drums, Dunmore, Dupont, East
> Stroudsburg, Hamlin, Jermyn, Lakeville, Marshalls Creek, Moosic, Mount Pocono,
> Pittston, Scranton, Scotrun, Snydersville, Stroudsburg, Swiftwater, White Haven and
> Wilkes-Barre.

Index of Establishments on the POCONO MOUNTAINS & VICINITY ACCOMMODATIONS Spotting Map

DUNMORE
⊕⊕ Days Inn . . . . [1]
   Holiday Inn-Scranton East . . . . [3]
⊕⊕ Econo Lodge Scranton Northeast . . . . [4]

SCRANTON
⊕⊕ Comfort Suites . . . . [7]
   Hampton Inn-Scranton . . . . [8]
⊕⊕ Radisson Lackawanna Station
      Hotel Scranton . . . . [10]

RESTAURANTS
⊕⊕ Cooper's Seafood House & Ship's Pub . . . . [3]
⊕⊕ Farley's . . . . [4]
⊕⊕ Smiths Restaurant . . . . [5]
   Strazzeri's Restaurant . . . . [6]
⊕⊕ Carmen's . . . . [9]
   Tom & Jerry's Restaurant . . . . [10]

WILKES-BARRE
⊕⊕ Best Western East Mountain Inn . . . . [15]
⊕⊕ Best Western Genetti Hotel & Convention
      Center . . . . [16]
   Hampton Inn Wilkes-Barre at
      Cross Creek Pointe . . . . [19]
   Ramada Plaza Hotel . . . . [20]
   Red Roof Inn . . . . [21]
⊕⊕ Econo Lodge . . . . [23]
   The Woodlands Inn & Resort . . . . [25]

RESTAURANTS
⊕⊕ Peking Chef-East . . . . [18]
   Katana . . . . [19]
⊕⊕ Peking Chef . . . . [20]
   Pasta Lovers . . . . [21]

WHITE HAVEN
⊕⊕ Ramada Inn-Pocono . . . . [30]
⊕⊕ Days Inn & Suites . . . . [31]

RESTAURANTS
   Powerhouse Eatery . . . . [25]
   A Touch of Vanilla . . . . [26]

EAST STROUDSBURG
⊕⊕ Budget Motel . . . . [41]

   Super 8 Motel . . . . [42]
RESTAURANT
   Peppe's . . . . [35]

MOUNT POCONO
⊕⊕ Caesars Paradise Stream . . . . [44]
⊕⊕ Farmhouse Bed & Breakfast . . . . [45]
⊕⊕ Pocono Super 8 Motel . . . . [47]

RESTAURANT
⊕⊕ Hampton Court Inn Restaurant . . . . [40]

CRESCO
⊕⊕ Crescent Lodge . . . . [50]

RESTAURANTS
⊕⊕ Crescent Lodge . . . . [45]
⊕⊕ The Homestead Inn . . . . [46]

HAMLIN
⊕⊕ Comfort Inn . . . . [55]

RESTAURANT
⊕⊕ Twin Rocks Restaurant . . . . [48]

CANADENSIS
   Brookview Manor Bed & Breakfast . . . . [60]
⊕⊕ Hillside Lodge & Resort . . . . [61]

RESTAURANT
   Pump House Inn . . . . [50]

BUSHKILL
⊕⊕ Fernwood Resort and Country Club . . . . [65]

MOOSIC
⊕⊕ Days Inn-Montage . . . . [70]
   Courtyard by Marriott . . . . [71]

RESTAURANT
   Marvelous Muggs Restaurant & Pub . . . . [53]

BARTONSVILLE
   Holiday Inn . . . . [75]

DICKSON CITY
   Quality Hotel . . . . [85]

CLARKS SUMMIT
⊕⊕ Days Inn Scranton-North . . . . [92]

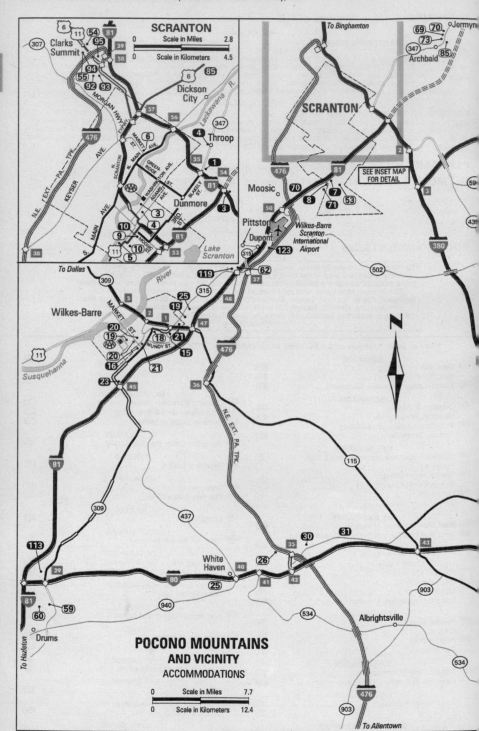

SCRANTON

Scale in Miles   2.8

Scale in Kilometers   4.5

POCONO MOUNTAINS
AND VICINITY
ACCOMMODATIONS

Scale in Miles   7.7

Scale in Kilometers   12.4

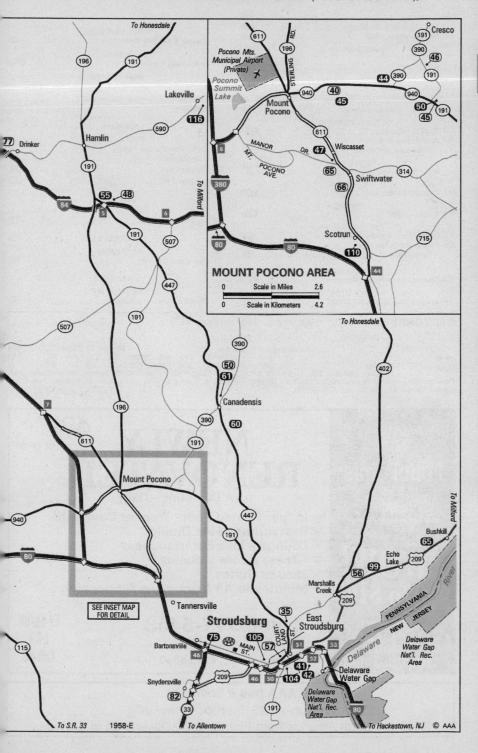

Travelodge 93
The Inn at Nichols Village 94
Ramada Plaza Hotel 95

RESTAURANTS
Ryah House 54
So-Journer.............................. 55

MARSHALLS CREEK
Caesars Pocono Palace 99

RESTAURANT
Tom X Inn Restaurant & Bar 56

STROUDSBURG
Days Inn-Poconos II 104
Four Points Sheraton
Stroudsburg-Pocono.................... 105

RESTAURANT
Sarah Street Grill 57

SCOTRUN
Caesars Brookdale 110

DRUMS
Econo Lodge............................... 113

RESTAURANTS
Countryside Family Restaurant.............. 59
Edgewood in the Pines
Restaurant 60

LAKEVILLE
Caesars Cove Haven Resort.................. 116

PITTSTON
Knights Inn-Scranton/Pittston 119

RESTAURANT
Cooper's On The Waterfront 62

DUPONT
Holiday Inn Express......................... 123

SWIFTWATER
RESTAURANTS
Brittania Country Inn & Restaurant.............. 65
Fanucci's 66

JERMYN
RESTAURANTS
Earl's Townhouse Family
Restaurant 69
Windsor Inn 70
Woodland Inn 73

DRINKER
RESTAURANT
My Brothers Place.......................... 77

SNYDERSVILLE
RESTAURANT
The Stone Bar Inn 82

ARCHBALD
RESTAURANT
Barrett's Family Restaurant 85

BARTONSVILLE—400   (See map p. 418; index p. 417)

LODGING

HOLIDAY INN ◆◆ Motor Inn

	Rates Subject to Change							75
5/1-11/1	1P: $72	2P/1B:	$79- 125	2P/2B:	$79- 125	XP:	$7	F19
11/2-4/30	1P: $62- 92	2P/1B:	$69- 99	2P/2B:	$69- 99	XP:	$7	F19

Phone: 717/424-6100

Location: I-80 exit 46B, just n. Rt 611 & I-80 18321. **Fax:** 717/421-4293. **Terms:** Sr. discount; pets. **Facility:** 151 rooms. 2 stories; interior corridors. **Dining:** Restaurant; 7 am-2 & 5-10 pm; $9-$16. **All Rooms:** free & pay movies. **Cards:** AE, CB, DI, DS, JCB, MC, VI.

BUSHKILL—5,500   (See map p. 418; index p. 417)

LODGING

FERNWOOD RESORT AND COUNTRY CLUB   Phone: 717/588-9500   65
All Year [MAP]   2P/1B: $198   2P/2B: $118- 198 XP: $8-30   F17
Location: 11 mi ne of I-80, exit 52. Rt 209 18324. **Fax:** 717/588-0403. **Terms:** Check-in 4 pm; reserv
deposit, 14 day notice; no pets. **Facility:** 177 rooms. Handling fee imposed; 2-3 stories; interior/exterior corri-
Resort Motor   dors. **Dining:** 2 restaurants; 6 am-midnight; 5/30-10/12 to 1 am; $9-$22. **Cards:** AE, CB, DI, DS, MC, VI.
Inn

CANADENSIS—1,200   (See map p. 418; index p. 417)

LODGINGS

BROOKVIEW MANOR BED & BREAKFAST   Rates Subject to Change   Phone: 717/595-2451   60
Fri & Sat [BP]   1P: $100- 140   2P/1B: $110- 150   XP: $20
Historic Bed   Sun-Thurs [BP]   1P: $90- 120   2P/1B: $100- 150   XP: $20
& Breakfast   **Location:** On SR 447, 1 mi s of jct SR 390. (RR 1 Box 365, 18325). **Fax:** 717/595-5065. **Terms:** Sr.
discount; age restrictions may apply; no pets. **Facility:** 9 rooms. 3 stories, no elevator; interior corridors; smoke
free premises. **Cards:** AE, DI, DS, MC, VI.

HILLSIDE LODGE & RESORT   Phone: 717/595-7551   61
All Year [MAP]   1P: $95   2P/1B: $144- 198 2P/2B: $144- 198 XP: $56   D17
Location: 1 mi n on SR 390. Rt 390 18325 (PO Box 268). **Fax:** 717/595-3050. **Terms:** Reserv deposit, 14
Resort   day notice; weekly rates; package plans; no pets. **Facility:** 33 rooms. Motel rooms, suites & 5 cottages with
Complex   living room & fireplace. Heart-shaped bathtub & 2-person whirlpool bath. Handling fee imposed; 1-2 stories;
interior/exterior corridors; miniature golf; 1 lighted tennis court; playground, basketball court, bocci court, horseshoes, shuffleboard, softball diamond, volleyball. **Dining & Entertainment:** Restaurant; 8:30 am-10 & 6-7:30
pm; cocktails/lounge. **Services:** Fee: coin laundry. **Recreation:** nature program, recreation program, social program,
summer day camp; ice skating, sledding. **All Rooms:** combo or shower baths. **Some Rooms:** coffeemakers, microwaves,
radios, refrigerators, VCR's, whirlpools. **Cards:** DS, MC, VI. **Special Amenities:** Free local telephone calls and preferred
room (subject to availability with advanced reservations). *(See color ad below)*

RESTAURANT

PUMP HOUSE INN   Country Inn   **Dinner:** $13-$25   Phone: 717/595-7501   50
Location: On SR 390, 1.5 mi n of jct SR 447. Skytop Rd 18325. **Hours:** 5 pm-9 pm, Sun 2:30 pm-8 pm.
Continental   **Closed:** 11/26, 12/25 & Mon 6/1-10/31. **Reservations:** suggested; weekends. **Features:** dressy casual;
cocktails & lounge. Intimate dining in circa 1842 former stagecoach inn. Menu features rack of lamb, salmon
with horseradish potato crust & daily specials. Smoke free premises. **Cards:** DI, MC, VI.

CRESCO—500   (See map p. 418; index p. 417)

LODGING

CRESCENT LODGE   Rates Subject to Change   Phone: 717/595-7486   50
Fri & Sat   2P/1B: $100- 295 2P/2B: $155   XP: $15
Sun-Thurs   2P/1B: $80- 295 2P/2B: $120   XP: $15
Country Inn   **Location:** 3 mi s on SR 191, at jct SR 940. Paradise Valley 18326. **Fax:** 717/595-3452. **Terms:** Reserv
deposit, 14 day notice; no pets. **Facility:** 30 rooms. 1-3 stories, no elevator; interior/exterior corridors.
Dining: Dining room, see separate listing. **Cards:** AE, CB, DI, DS, MC, VI. *(See color ad p 422)*

RESTAURANTS

CRESCENT LODGE   **Dinner:** $17-$25   Phone: 717/595-7486   45
Location: 3 mi s on SR 191, at jct SR 940; in Crescent Lodge. Paradise Valley 18326. **Hours:** 8 am-11 &
5:30-9 pm, Fri & Sat-10 pm. **Closed:** 12/25, Mon & Tues 11/1-4/30. **Reservations:** suggested.
Continental   **Features:** children's menu; cocktails & lounge. Attractive country decor; upscale casual atmosphere.
Cards: AE, CB, DI, DS, MC, VI. *(See color ad p 422)*

THE HOMESTEAD INN   **Dinner:** $14-$18   Phone: 717/595-3171   46
Location: 2.5 mi n of jct SR 390/191 following signs. Sandspring Dr 18326. **Hours:** 5 pm-9 pm, Sun from 4
pm. **Closed:** Mon 9/1-5/31. **Reservations:** suggested; in season. **Features:** casual dress; children's menu;
American   health conscious menu; carryout; cocktails & lounge. Fine dining in a relaxed country atmosphere.
Cards: AE, MC, VI. **Special Value:** 20% discount on the price of any entree, excluding beverages, tax
and gratuity.

ALWAYS ASK THE HOTEL OPERATOR ABOUT **HOTEL SURCHARGES ON LONG DISTANCE CALLS YOU PLACE FROM YOUR ROOM.** DOING SO COULD SAVE YOU AN UNPLEASANT SURPRISE AT CHECKOUT TIME.

EAST STROUDSBURG—8,800 (See map p. 418; index p. 417)

LODGINGS

BUDGET MOTEL ◆◆◆ Motor Inn
Rates Subject to Change
Phone: 717/424-5451   **41**

		1P:		2P/1B:			2P/2B:		
Fri-Sun		1P: $48-	52	2P/1B:	$55-	72	2P/2B:	$55-	72
Mon-Thurs		1P: $36-	46	2P/1B:	$39-	54	2P/2B:	$40-	54

Location: At jct I-80 exit 51, just se on Greentree Rd. I-80, exit 51 18301 (PO Box 216). Fax: 717/424-0389. **Terms:** Pets, $20 dep req. **Facility:** 115 rooms. Rates for up to 5 persons; 2-3 stories; interior/exterior corridors. **Dining:** Restaurant; 7 am-11 & 5-10 pm, Sun-9 pm; $8-$14. **Cards:** AE, DI, DS, MC, VI.
(See color ad p 422)   🛏 CTV ✕ D

SUPER 8 MOTEL ◆ Motel
Rates Subject to Change
Phone: 717/424-7411   **42**

		1P:		2P/1B:			2P/2B:			XP:	
6/1-10/31		1P: $56-	69	2P/1B:	$61-	71	2P/2B:	$65-	75	XP: $7	F12
5/1-5/31 & 4/1-4/30		1P: $49-	62	2P/1B:	$54-	64	2P/2B:	$59-	69	XP: $7	F12
11/1-3/31		1P: $46-	49	2P/1B:	$51-	61	2P/2B:	$56-	66	XP: $7	F12

Location: At jct I-80, exit 51, just se. 340 Green Tree Dr 18301. Fax: 717/424-7411. **Terms:** Pets, 1st floor, $25 extra charge. **Facility:** 57 rooms. 3 stories, no elevator; interior corridors. **All Rooms:** free movies. **Cards:** AE, CB, DI, DS, MC, VI.   🛏 CTV 👤 ✕ D

RESTAURANT

PEPPE'S ◆◆◆ Northern Italian
Dinner: $10-$24
Phone: 717/421-4460   **35**

Location: At jct Business Rt 209 & SR 447N, at the Eagle Valley Mall. Eagle Valley Mall 18360. **Hours:** 11:30 am-2:30 & 5:30-10 pm, Sat 4 pm-11 pm, Sun 3 pm-9 pm. Closed: 11/26, 12/25 & Easter. **Reservations:** suggested. **Features:** casual dress; children's menu; carryout; cocktails & lounge; a la carte. Roman arches, inviting atmosphere; tableside preparation. **Cards:** AE, CB, DI, DS, MC, VI.   ✕

HAMLIN—800 (See map p. 418; index p. 417)

LODGING

COMFORT INN 🆎 SAVE ◆◆◆ Motel
Phone: 717/689-4148   **55**

		1P:		2P/1B:			2P/2B:			XP:	
5/12-10/31 [CP]		1P: $59-	109	2P/1B:	$59-	109	2P/2B:	$59-	109	XP: $10	F18
5/1-5/11 & 11/1-4/30 [CP]		1P: $49-	69	2P/1B:	$49-	79	2P/2B:	$49-	79	XP: $10	F18

Location: I-84 exit 5, just n. SR 191 18436 (RD 5, LAKE ARIEL). Fax: 717/689-3043. **Terms:** Package plans; pets, $5 extra charge. **Facility:** 124 rooms. Immaculate rooms in Pocono Mountain area. 2 stories; interior corridors; sauna, whirlpool. **Dining & Entertainment:** Cocktail lounge; restaurant nearby. **Services:** Fee: coin laundry. **All Rooms:** Fee: movies. **Some Rooms:** refrigerators, whirlpools. **Cards:** AE, CB, DI, DS, JCB, MC, VI.   🛏 👤👤 CTV ✕ D

RESTAURANT

TWIN ROCKS RESTAURANT 🆎 ◆ American
Lunch: $2-$6
Dinner: $6-$13
Phone: 717/689-9112   **48**

Location: I-84 exit 5, just n. SR 191 18436. **Hours:** 24 hours. Closed: 12/25 & Sat 11 pm-Sun 7 am. **Features:** casual dress; children's menu. Family style dining. **Cards:** MC, VI.   ✕

HAWLEY—1,200

LODGINGS

FALLS PORT INN & RESTAURANT 🆎 SAVE ◆◆◆ Historic Country Inn
Phone: 717/226-2600

		2P/1B:			2P/2B:		
5/25-9/5 [CP]		2P/1B:	$75-	85	2P/2B:	$90-	95
5/1-5/24 & 9/6-4/30 [CP]		2P/1B:	$55-	65	2P/2B:	$65-	75

Location: At Main Ave (US 6) & Church St. 330 Main Ave 18428. **Terms:** Reserv deposit; 2 night min stay, weekends in season; small pets only. **Facility:** 9 rooms. Historic turn-of-the-century Inn. Quaint guestrooms furnished in period antiques. 3 stories, no elevator; interior corridors; off site parking only; exercise equipment; Lake Wallenpaupack nearby. **Dining & Entertainment:** Dining room; 11:30 am-10 pm, Sun 10:30 am-8:30 pm; $18-$28; cocktails/lounge; also, Falls Port Inn & Restaurant, see separate listing. **All Rooms:** no phones. **Some Rooms:** VCR's. **Cards:** AE, DS, MC, VI. **Special Amenities:** Free breakfast and free room upgrade (subject to availability with advanced reservations).   🛏 👤 CTV ✕ D

THE SETTLERS INN AT BINGHAM PARK 🆎 SAVE ◆◆◆ Historic Country Inn
Phone: 717/226-2993

		1P:		2P/1B:			2P/2B:			XP:	
7/1-10/31 [BP]		1P: $75-	90	2P/1B:	$95-	115	2P/2B:	$95-	115	XP: $15	F6
5/1-6/30 & 11/1-4/30 [BP]		1P: $70-	90	2P/1B:	$85-	110	2P/2B:	$90-	110	XP: $15	F6

Location: 0.3 mi w on US 6. 4 Main Ave 18428. Fax: 717/226-1874. **Terms:** Reserv deposit, 3 day notice; package plans; no pets. **Facility:** 18 rooms. 1927 Tudor Revival inn furnished with antiques. Across the street from the village park. 2 two-bedroom units. 3 stories, no elevator; interior corridors; horseshoes; tennis nearby. **Dining & Entertainment:** Cocktails/lounge; restaurant, see separate listing. **Recreation:** fishing. **All Rooms:** combo or shower baths. **Some Rooms:** coffeemakers, efficiency, refrigerators, VCR's, whirlpools. **Cards:** AE, DS, MC, VI.   👤 CTV ✕ D

RESTAURANTS

EHRHARDT'S LAKESIDE RESTAURANT 🆎 ◆◆ American
Lunch: $3-$8
Dinner: $10-$20
Phone: 717/226-2124

Location: 1 mi s of US Rt 6. SR 507 18428. **Hours:** 11 am-9 pm, Fri & Sat-11 pm, Sun 9 am-9 pm; 6/21-9/7 11 am-10 pm, Fri & Sat-11 pm, Sun 9 am-10 pm. Closed: 11/26 & 12/25. **Reservations:** suggested. **Features:** casual dress; children's menu; carryout; cocktails & lounge. Casual dining with scenic tranquil lakeside view. Breakfast buffet. **Cards:** AE, DS, MC, VI.

FALLS PORT INN & RESTAURANT Historical ◆◆◆ Continental
Lunch: $5-$10
Dinner: $14-$21
Phone: 717/226-2600

Location: At Main Ave (US 6) & Church St; in Falls Port Inn & Restaurant. 330 Main St 18428. **Hours:** 11:30 am-3 & 5:30-9 pm, Sun 10:30 am-3 & 5:30-8:30 pm. Closed: Tues, 12/25, & Mon 11/1-5/31. **Reservations:** suggested. **Features:** casual dress; Sunday brunch; children's menu; carryout; cocktails; street parking; a la carte. Fine dining in historic turn-of-the-century hotel. Tastefully decorated in period antiques. Only buffet served on Wed evenings. **Cards:** AE, DI, MC, VI.   ✕

THE SETTLERS INN AT BINGHAM PARK ◆◆◆ Regional American
Lunch: $6-$12
Dinner: $16-$26
Phone: 717/226-2993

Location: 0.3 mi w on US 6; in The Settlers Inn at Bingham Park. 4 Main Ave 18428. **Hours:** 11:30 am-2 & 5-9 pm, Fri & Sat-10 pm. Closed: 12/23-12/25. **Reservations:** suggested. **Features:** Sunday brunch; children's menu; health conscious menu items; carryout; cocktails & lounge; a la carte. Locally grown & produced ingredients, including fresh herbs from their own garden, served in classic Tudor manor style country inn; upscale casual atmosphere. Smoke free premises. **Cards:** AE, DS, MC, VI.   ✕

HONESDALE—5,000

LODGING

FIFE & DRUM MOTOR INN   Rates Subject to Change   **Phone: 717/253-1392**

(AAA)
◆
Motel

7/1-9/30	1P:	$35-	59	2P/1B:	$49-	79	2P/2B:	$59-	69	XP: $6	F10
5/1-6/30	1P:	$35-	49	2P/1B:	$43-	65	2P/2B:	$55		XP: $6	F10
10/1-4/30	1P:	$35-	46	2P/1B:	$43-	59	2P/2B:	$55		XP: $6	F10

Location: Just s on SR 191. 100 Terrace St 18431. **Fax:** 717/253-1716. **Terms:** Reserv deposit, 30 day notice; small pets only, $6 extra charge. **Facility:** 28 rooms. Handling fee imposed; 2 stories; exterior corridors.
Cards: AE, DI, DS, MC, VI.   [icons]

RESTAURANT

THE FIRESIDE   **Lunch:** $3-$8   **Dinner:** $9-$17   **Phone: 717/253-0141**

(AAA)
◆◆
American

Location: On SR 191, 4 mi n of US 6. 18431. **Hours:** 11 am-midnight. Closed: 1/1, 7/4, 12/25 & Mon. **Reservations:** accepted. **Features:** casual dress; children's menu; health conscious menu items; carryout; cocktails & lounge. Rustic country dining; some entertainment Sat & Sun. **Cards:** MC, VI.   [icon]

JIM THORPE—5,000

LODGINGS

THE HARRY PACKER MANSION   **Phone: 717/325-8566**

(AAA) (SAVE)
◆◆◆◆
Historic Bed
& Breakfast

All Year [BP]   1P: $75- 150   2P/1B: $75- 150

Location: Just n of downtown historic district off of US 209. Packer Hill 18229 (PO Box 458). **Terms:** Age restrictions may apply; check-in 5 pm; reserv deposit, 7 day notice; 2 night min stay, weekends; **Facility:** 12 rooms. 1874 Second Empire Italianate mansion; former home of industrial magnate. Lushly furnished in period antiques. Murder Mystery weekends held year round. 3 stories, no elevator; interior corridors; smoke free premises; mountain view. **Dining:** Restaurant nearby. **All Rooms:** no phones. **Special Amenities: Free local telephone calls and free room upgrade (subject to availability with advanced reservations).**   [icons]

THE INN AT JIM THORPE   Guaranteed Rates   **Phone: 717/325-2599**

(AAA)
◆◆◆
Historic
Country Inn

Fri & Sat [CP]	1P:	$65-	250	2P/1B:	$65-	110	2P/2B:	$90-	110	XP: $10	F6
Sun-Thurs [CP]	1P:	$49-	68	2P/1B:	$49-	68	2P/2B:	$68-	83	XP: $10	F6

Location: Downtown. 24 Broadway 18229. **Fax:** 717/325-9145. **Terms:** Reserv deposit, 3 day notice; 2 night min stay, most weekends; no pets. **Facility:** 29 rooms. 3 stories; interior corridors. **Dining:** Restaurant; 11:30 am-10 pm, Fri & Sat-11 pm; $9-$20. **All Rooms:** free movies. **Cards:** AE, DI, DS, MC, VI.   [icons]

RESTAURANT

J T'S STEAK & ALE HOUSE AT THE HOTEL SWITZERLAND   Historical   **Lunch:** $4-$6   **Dinner:** $7-$12   **Phone: 717/325-4563**

◆◆
American

Location: Off SR 209. 5 Hazard Square 18229. **Hours:** 11 am-9 pm, Fri & Sat-10 pm, Sun noon-9 pm. Closed: 12/25. **Reservations:** suggested. **Features:** casual dress; children's menu; carryout; cocktails & lounge; street parking. The oldest remaining structure from the early glory days of Hazard Square. Cozy Victorian atmosphere. **Cards:** MC, VI.   [icon]

LACKAWAXEN—600

LODGING

ROEBLING INN ON THE DELAWARE   Guaranteed Rates   **Phone: 717/685-7900**

◆◆
Historic Bed
& Breakfast

Fri-Sun 6/1-8/31 [BP]	1P:	$90-	100	2P/1B:	$95-	105	2P/2B:	$95- 105	XP: $5-10
Fri-Sun 5/1-5/31 & 9/1-4/30 [BP]	1P:	$80-	90	2P/1B:	$85-	95	2P/2B:	$85- 95	XP: $5-10
Mon-Thurs [BP]	1P:	$60-	70	2P/1B:	$65-	75	2P/2B:	$65- 75	XP: $5-10

Location: Center; just off SR 590. 155 Scenic Dr 18435 (PO Box 31). **Fax:** 717/685-1718. **Terms:** Reserv deposit, 7 day notice; 2 night min stay, weekends 5/1-10/31; no pets. **Facility:** 6 rooms. 2 stories; interior/exterior corridors. **Some Rooms:** efficiency. **Cards:** AE, DS, MC, VI.   [icons]

LAKEVILLE—500   (See map p. 418; index p. 417)

LODGING

CAESARS COVE HAVEN RESORT   **Phone: 717/226-4506**   [116]

(AAA) (SAVE)
◆◆◆
Resort
Complex

All Year [MAP]   2P/1B: $195- 325

Location: 7 mi w of jct US 6. SR 590 18438 (PO Box 40). **Fax:** 717/226-4697. **Terms:** Age restrictions may apply; reserv deposit, 5 day notice; package plans; no pets. **Facility:** 282 rooms. Spacious resort for couples only. Standard king size rooms, many with heart-shaped tub or whirlpool. Whirlpool suites & champagne tower suites. Units with mini indoor pool, steam bath & fireplace. Handling fee imposed; 1-4 stories; interior/exterior corridors; miniature golf, driving range; saunas, steamrooms, whirlpools; racquetball courts, 5 tennis courts (3 indoor, 1 lighted), handball; marina; archery, badminton, billiards, roller skating, volleyball, guest privileges at all Caesar's Pocono properties. **Dining & Entertainment:** Restaurant, cafeteria; 8:30 am-11 & 6-8 pm; $35-$40; cocktails/lounge entertainment, nightclub. **Services:** area transportation. Fee: coin laundry; massage. **Recreation:** recreation program, social program; swimming, fishing, paddleboats, sailboats, waterskiing, motorboat rides; ice skating, snowmobiling, tobogganing bicycles, hiking trails. **All Rooms:** refrigerators. **Some Rooms:** Fee: VCR's. **Cards:** AE, DI, DS, MC, VI. **Special Amenities: Free breakfast.** *(See color ad inside back cover)*   Roll in showers.   [icons]

MARSHALLS CREEK—100 (See map p. 418; index p. 417)

LODGING

CAESARS POCONO PALACE   **Phone: 717/588-6692** 99

🆎 SAVE   All Year [MAP]   2P/1B: $195- 365
◆◆◆◆   **Location:** 7 mi n of I-80, exit 52. Route 209 18335 (PO Box 1400). Fax: 717/588-0754. **Terms:** Age
Resort   restrictions may apply; reserv deposit, 14 day notice; package plans; no pets. **Facility:** 189 rooms. Couples
Complex   only resort. Variety of room types including lakeside chalets, whirlpool rooms & suites & champagne tower
suites. All units with fireplace, some with indoor mini pool. 1-2 stories; interior/exterior corridors; 9 holes golf,
miniature golf, driving range, golf pro on staff; beach, saunas, steamrooms, whirlpools; racquetball court, 2
tennis courts, badminton, indoor roller skating, indoor volleyball, recreation room; archery, billiards, bocci ball, horseshoes,
sand volleyball, shuffleboard. Fee: golf lessons. **Dining & Entertainment:** Dining room, cafeteria; 8:30 am-11 & 6-8 pm;
$35-$40; cocktails/lounge; entertainment, nightclub. **Services:** area transportation, within 8 mi. Fee: massage.
Recreation: nature program, recreation program, social program, guests may use facilities at Caesar's & other Pocono
properties; swimming, boating, fishing, paddleboats, waterskiing; cross country skiing, ice skating, snowmobiling; bicycles,
hiking trails. **All Rooms:** refrigerators. **Some Rooms:** Fee: VCR's. **Cards:** AE, DI, DS, MC, VI. **Special Amenities: Free
breakfast.** *(See color ad inside back cover)*   🛥️ 🛥️ 🍴 🛜 CTV 🏠 🎱 D

RESTAURANT

TOM X INN RESTAURANT & BAR   **Dinner:** $15-$24   **Phone: 717/223-8154** 56
◆◆   **Location:** I-80, exit 52, 5 mi n on US 209, 1 mi w on Sellersville Rd, then 0.5 mi s. Tom X Rd 18335.
American   **Hours:** 5 pm-10 pm. Closed: 11/26, 12/25 & Mon. **Reservations:** suggested; weekends. **Features:** casual
dress; children's menu; carryout; cocktails & lounge. Casual bustling atmosphere in circa 1940's former dude
ranch; menu features black peppercorn steak, hunter style chicken, barbeque ribs, swordfish & a variety of convenience
foods. **Cards:** AE, CB, DI, DS, MC, VI.   ✖️

MATAMORAS—1,900

LODGINGS

BEST WESTERN INN AT HUNT'S LANDING   **Phone: 717/491-2400**

🆎 SAVE	5/1-10/31 [CP]	1P:	$69- 99	2P/1B:	$77- 99	2P/2B:	$77- 99	XP:	$6	F12
	11/1-4/30 [CP]	1P:	$56- 66	2P/1B:	$64- 74	2P/2B:	$64- 74	XP:	$6	F12

◆◆◆   **Location:** At jct I-84 exit 11. 120 Rt 6 & 209 18336. Fax: 717/491-2422. **Terms:** Monthly rates; package
Motor Inn   plans; pets. **Facility:** 108 rooms. Borders Delaware River, spectacular views of Delaware Valley from some
rooms. Contemporary decor. 4 stories; interior corridors; mountain view; saunas; shuffleboard courts.
Dining & Entertainment: Restaurant; 6:30 am-9 pm, Fri & Sat-10 pm, Sat & Sun from 7 am; $8-$33; cocktails/lounge.
Services: Fee: coin laundry. **Recreation:** fishing. **All Rooms:** coffeemakers, free & pay movies. **Some Rooms:**
Fee: refrigerators, whirlpools. **Cards:** AE, CB, DI, DS, MC, VI. **Special Amenities: Free breakfast and free local
telephone calls.**   🐾 🛥️ 🍴 🛜 CTV ✖️ 🎱 D S

BLUE SPRUCE MOTEL   Rates Subject to Change   **Phone: 717/491-4969**

◆◆	5/1-10/31	1P:	$40- 55	2P/1B:	$50- 75	2P/2B:	$50- 75	XP:	$8	
Motel	11/1-4/30	1P:	$35- 45	2P/1B:	$40- 50	2P/2B:	$45- 55	XP:	$8	

Location: 0.5 mi sw of jct I-84, exit 11. 550 Rts 6 & 209 18336. Fax: 717/491-5113. **Terms:** Sr. discount; no
pets. **Facility:** 15 rooms. 1 story; exterior corridors. **Cards:** AE, DS, MC, VI.   CTV ✖️ D

MILFORD (PIKE COUNTY)—1,100

LODGINGS

BLACK WALNUT B & B COUNTRY INN   **Phone: 717/296-6322**

🆎 SAVE	Fri-Sun [BP]	1P:	$65- 100	2P/1B:	$65- 100		XP: $25	F10
	Mon-Thurs [BP]	1P:	$55- 90	2P/1B:	$50- 100		XP: $25	F10

◆◆   **Location:** From I-84 exit 10, 1 mi s on SR 6 & 1.4 mi ne on Fire Tower Rd, following signs. Rd 2, Box 9285
Bed &   Fire Tower Rd 18337. Fax: 717/296-7696. **Terms:** Reserv deposit; 2 night min stay, weekends 4/1-10/31; no
Breakfast   pets. **Facility:** 10 rooms. Centennial country home surrounded with wooded acreage. Rooms are small & intimate, all furnished with antiques. 3-bedroom cabin, $150-$450 for up to 6 persons; 3 stories; interior corridors;
whirlpool; petting zoo. **Dining & Entertainment:** Cocktail lounge. **Recreation:** boating, paddleboats, catch & release fishing;
cross country skiing, snowshoeing. **All Rooms:** no A/C, no phones. **Cards:** AE, MC, VI. **Special Amenities: Free breakfast
and free room upgrade (subject to availability with advanced reservations).**   🍴 ✖️ D

MILFORD MOTEL   Rates Subject to Change   **Phone: 717/296-6411**

🆎	Fri & Sat 5/1-10/31	1P:	$50	2P/1B:	$50	2P/2B:	$55	XP: $5
	Sun-Thurs 5/1-10/31	1P:	$40	2P/1B:	$42	2P/2B:	$46	XP: $9
◆	11/1-4/30	1P:	$36	2P/1B:	$40	2P/2B:	$44	XP: $6

Motel   **Location:** 0.7 mi e on SR 6E & SR 209N. (HC 77, Box 2, MILFORD, 18377). Fax: 717/296-8428.
Terms: Pets. **Facility:** 18 rooms. 1 story; exterior corridors. **Cards:** AE, DI, DS, MC, VI.
            🐾 🛥️ ECTV ✖️ D

MYER MOTEL   **Phone: 717/296-7223**

🆎 SAVE	5/1-10/31	1P:	$50- 83	2P/1B:	$50- 83	2P/2B:	$55- 83	XP: $7	F10
	11/1-4/30	1P:	$44- 66	2P/1B:	$44- 77	2P/2B:	$50- 77	XP: $7	F10

◆◆   **Location:** 0.5 mi ne on US 6 & 209. 18337 (RR 4, Box 8030, MILFORD). **Terms:** Reserv deposit; 4 night
Cottage   min stay, Kitchen unit; pets. **Facility:** 19 rooms. Spacious grounds, well maintained property. Country feeling.
Duplex cottages without kitchens. 1 kitchen, $20 extra charge. Handling fee imposed; 1 story; exterior corri-
dors. **Dining:** Restaurant nearby. **All Rooms:** refrigerators, combo or shower baths. **Some Rooms:** microwaves.
Cards: AE, CB, DI, DS, MC, VI. **Special Amenities: Free local telephone calls.**   🐾 CTV ✖️ D

PINE HILL FARM BED & BREAKFAST   Rates Subject to Change   **Phone: 717/296-7395**

◆◆◆	All Year [BP]	1P:	$85- 110	2P/1B:	$95- 120	XP: $25

Bed &   **Location:** I-84 exit 11, 2.5 mi s on Rt 209, 0.3 mi w on Cummins Hill Rd, 0.8 mi s. Pine Hill Farm Rd 18337
Breakfast   (PO Box 1001, MILFORD). Fax: 717/296-7395. **Terms:** Age restrictions may apply; 2 night min stay,
weekends 5/25-10/31; no pets. **Facility:** 5 rooms. Handling fee imposed; 2 stories; interior corridors; smoke
free premises. **Cards:** DS, MC, VI.   ✖️ D

RED CARPET INN-MILFORD   Phone: 717/296-9444

AAA SAVE

	6/1-10/31	1P: $65	2P/1B: $70	2P/2B: $75	XP: $5	F10
	5/1-5/31 & 3/1-4/30	1P: $55	2P/1B: $60	2P/2B: $65	XP: $5	F10
◆◆	11/1-2/28	1P: $55	2P/1B: $55	2P/2B: $60	XP: $5	F10

Motel   **Location:** Just s of I-84, exit 10. I-84 & Rt 6 18337 (RR 2, Box 9129, MILFORD). Fax: 717/296-4739.
Terms: Reserv deposit; pets, $5 extra charge. **Facility:** 26 rooms. Handling fee imposed; 2 stories; exterior
corridors. **Cards:** AE, DS, MC, VI.   [CTV] [X] [D]

TOURIST VILLAGE MOTEL   Rates Subject to Change   Phone: 717/491-4414

AAA

	Fri & Sat 5/1-11/1	1P: $38- 48	2P/1B: $58- 68	2P/2B: $63- 73	XP: $6
	Sun-Thurs 5/1-11/1	1P: $38- 48	2P/1B: $48- 58	2P/2B: $53- 63	XP: $6
◆	11/2-4/30	1P: $38	2P/1B: $38- 48	2P/2B: $43- 53	XP: $6

Motel   **Location:** 1 mi s of I-84, exit 11. US 6 & 209 18337 (PO Box 487, MILFORD). Fax: 717/491-4178.
Terms: Pets. **Facility:** 18 rooms. Handling fee imposed; 1 story; exterior corridors. **Some Rooms:** kitchen.
Cards: AE, DS, MC.   [CTV] [X] [D]

MOUNT POCONO—1,800   (See map p. 418; index p. 417)

LODGINGS

CAESARS PARADISE STREAM   Phone: 717/839-8881   [44]

AAA SAVE   All Year [MAP]   2P/1B: $220- 325

◆◆◆   **Location:** Just w of jct W SR 390. Route 940 18344 (Box 99). Fax: 717/839-1842. **Terms:** Age restrictions
Resort   may apply; reserv deposit, 5 day notice; package plans; no pets. **Facility:** 164 rooms. Couples only resort. Va-
Complex   riety of room types, including lakeside villas, whirlpool rooms & suites, Champagne Tower suites. Most units
with fireplace, some with indoor mini pool. Handling fee imposed; 1-4 stories, no elevator; exterior corridors;
miniature golf; beach, whirlpools; racquetball courts, 3 tennis courts; archery, bocci ball, sand volleyball,
shuffleboard, softball, guest priivileges at Caesar's & other Pocono properties. **Dining & Entertainment:** Dining room, coffee
shop; 8:30 am-11 & 6-8 pm; $35-$40; cocktails/lounge; entertainment, nightclub. **Services:** area transportation, within 8 mi.
Fee: coin laundry; massage. **Recreation:** recreation program, social program; boating, fishing, paddleboats; ice skating,
snowmobiling; bicycles, hiking trails. **All Rooms:** refrigerators, whirlpools. **Some Rooms:** VCR's. **Cards:** AE, DI, DS, MC,
VI. **Special Amenities:** Free breakfast. (See color ad inside back cover)   [symbols] [CTV] [symbols] [D]

FARMHOUSE BED & BREAKFAST   Rates Subject to Change   Phone: 717/839-0796   [45]

AAA   All Year [BP]   1P: $55- 75   2P/1B: $90- 110

◆◆   **Location:** 2.3 mi e on SR 940, 0.3 mi s. Grange Rd 18344 (HC 1, Box 6B). Fax: 717/839-0795. **Terms:** Age
Historic Bed   restrictions may apply; reserv deposit, 14 day notice; no pets. **Facility:** 5 rooms. 2 stories; exterior corridors;
& Breakfast   smoke free premises. **Some Rooms:** kitchen. **Cards:** DS, MC, VI.   [CTV] [X] [D]

POCONO SUPER 8 MOTEL   Phone: 717/839-7728   [47]

AAA SAVE

| | 5/27-9/5 | 1P: $58- 150 | 2P/1B: $62- 150 | 2P/2B: $69- 150 | XP: $10 | F12 |
| | 5/1-5/26 & 9/6-4/30 | 1P: $48- 135 | 2P/1B: $52- 135 | 2P/2B: $58- 135 | XP: $10 | F12 |

◆◆   **Location:** 1 mi s. SR 611 18344 (HCR 1, Box 115). Fax: 717/839-7728. **Terms:** Reserv deposit, 3 day
Motor Inn   notice; no pets. **Facility:** 38 rooms. 2-3 night min stay weekends in season. Handling fee imposed; 1 story;
exterior corridors. **All Rooms:** free movies. **Cards:** AE, CB, DI, DS, MC, VI.   [symbols] [CTV] [X] [D]

RESTAURANT

HAMPTON COURT INN RESTAURANT   **Dinner:** $15-$24   Phone: 717/839-2119   [40]

AAA SAVE   **Location:** 2 mi e of jct SR 940 & SR 611. Rt 940 E 18344. **Hours:** 5 pm-10 pm, Fri & Sat-11 pm. Closed:
11/26, 12/25 & Tues. **Reservations:** required; Sat. **Features:** casual dress; carryout; cocktails; minimum
◆◆◆   charge-$9. Century-old converted farm house. Quaint, intimate Henry VIII ambience. Featuring fresh seafood
Continental   & steak. Dessert made on premises. **Cards:** AE, CB, DI, MC, VI. **Special Value: 10% discount on the
price of any entree, excluding beverages, tax and gratuity.**   [X]

SCOTRUN—1,000   (See map p. 418; index p. 417)

LODGING

CAESARS BROOKDALE   Phone: 717/839-8844   [110]

AAA SAVE   All Year [MAP]   2P/1B: $195- 365   2P/2B: $195- 365   XP:$40-55   F4

◆◆◆   **Location:** From I-80, exit 44, 1 mi n on Rt 611, 1 mi w on Brookdale Rd. Rt 611 & Brookdale Rd 18355 (PO
Resort   Box 400). Fax: 717/839-2414. **Terms:** Reserv deposit, 14 day notice; weekly rates; package plans; no pets.
Complex   **Facility:** 127 rooms. Spacious, manicured grounds. Family & couples resort. Fireplace, whirlpool or champagne glass bathtub avail in a variety of room types. 1-2 stories; interior/exterior corridors; miniature golf;
beach, wading pool, whirlpools; 2 lighted tennis courts; playground, archery, ballfield, billiards & recreational
facilities at 3 nearby Caeser's resorts avail to guests. **Dining & Entertainment:** Dining room, coffee shop; 8:30 am-11 &
5:30-8 pm; $35-$40; health conscious menu; cocktails/lounge; entertainment, nightclub. **Services:** area transportation, within
10 mi. Fee: coin laundry. **Recreation:** children's program, nature trails, recreation program, social program, rollerskating,
volleyball; boating, fishing, paddleboats, sailboats; ice skating, snowmobiling, tobogganing; bicycles, hiking trails.
All Rooms: refrigerators. **Some Rooms:** radios, whirlpools. Fee: VCR's. **Cards:** AE, DI, DS, MC, VI. **Special Amenities:**
Free breakfast. (See color ad inside back cover)   [symbols] [CTV] [symbols] [D]

SNYDERSVILLE—100   (See map p. 418; index p. 417)

RESTAURANT

THE STONE BAR INN   **Dinner:** $9-$20   Phone: 717/992-6634   [82]

◆◆   **Location:** Center on US 209 business route. 18360. **Hours:** 5 pm-10 pm, Fri & Sat-11 pm, Sun from 4 pm.
American   Closed: 11/26, 12/25 & Mon. **Reservations:** suggested; weekends. **Features:** casual dress; children's menu;
health conscious menu; cocktails & lounge. Grand American tavern serving prime Angus beef, seafood &
native game. Fireside dining, intimate booths. Extensive beer & wine list. **Cards:** AE, DS, MC, VI.   [X]

STARLIGHT—100

LODGING

THE INN AT STARLIGHT LAKE   Guaranteed Rates   Phone: 717/798-2519

◆◆   All Year [MAP]   1P: $77- 93   2P/1B: $116- 154   2P/2B: $115- 140   XP: $54   D7

Historic   **Location:** Off SR 370, 1 mi n following signs. SR 4020 18461 (PO Box 27). Fax: 717/798-2672.
Country Inn   **Terms:** Reserv deposit, 14 day notice; no pets. **Facility:** 26 rooms. 1-3 stories, no elevator; interior/exterior
corridors. **Dining:** Restaurant; 8 am-10, noon-1:30 & 6-9 pm, Sun 8 am-2 & 3-8 pm; $10-$21.
All Rooms: no A/C. **Some Rooms:** kitchen. **Cards:** MC, VI.   [CTV] [X] [D]

STARRUCCA—200

LODGING

THE NETHERCOTT INN B&B   Rates Subject to Change   **Phone:** 717/727-2211
◆◆   All Year [BP]   1P: $80   2P/1B: $80   2P/2B: $105   XP: $15
Historic Bed   **Location:** Center. 1 Main St 18462 (PO Box 26). Fax: 717/727-3811. **Terms:** Sr. discount; reserv deposit, 7
& Breakfast   day notice; no pets. **Facility:** 5 rooms. Handling fee imposed; 3 stories, no elevator; interior corridors; designated smoking area. **Dining:** Breakfast served 8-9 am. **Cards:** AE, DS, MC, VI.   ⊠ D

STROUDSBURG—5,300   (See map p. 418; index p. 417)

LODGINGS

DAYS INN-POCONOS II   Rates Subject to Change   **Phone:** 717/424-1771   104
AAA   Fri-Sun   1P: $58- 99   2P/1B: $58- 99   2P/2B: $58- 99   XP: $10   F12
    Mon-Thurs   1P: $39- 58   2P/1B: $48- 69   2P/2B: $48- 69   XP: $10   F12
◆◆   **Location:** At I-80, exit 50. 100 Park Ave 18360. Fax: 717/424-1771. **Terms:** Sr. discount; reserv deposit; no
Motel   pets. **Facility:** 54 rooms. 2 stories; interior/exterior corridors. **All Rooms:** free movies. **Cards:** AE, DI, DS,
    MC, VI.   CTV ⊠ D

FOUR POINTS SHERATON STROUDSBURG-POCONO   **Phone:** 717/424-1930   105
AAA SAVE   Fri & Sat 5/1-11/1 [EP]   1P: $69- 89   2P/1B: $75- 95   2P/2B: $79- 119   XP: $9   F12
    Sun-Thurs 5/1-11/1 & Fri &
◆◆◆   Sat 11/2-4/30 [CP]   1P: $59- 79   2P/1B: $65- 85   2P/2B: $69- 109   XP: $9   F12
Motor Inn   Sun-Thurs 11/2-4/30 [CP]   1P: $49- 69   2P/1B: $55- 75   2P/2B: $59- 99   XP: $9   F12
Location: On US 209 business route, just n of I-80, exit 48. 1220 W Main St 18360. Fax: 717/424-5909.
Terms: Weekly/monthly rates; package plans; no pets. **Facility:** 134 rooms. 2 stories; interior/exterior corridors; miniature golf;
wading pool, sauna; game room. **Dining & Entertainment:** Restaurant; 6:30 am-2 & 5-10 pm, Sat & Sun from 7:30 am;
$9-$20; cocktails/lounge; entertainment. **Services:** valet laundry. **All Rooms:** free movies, combo or shower baths.
Some Rooms: whirlpools. Fee: refrigerators. **Cards:** AE, CB, DI, DS, MC, VI. **Special Amenities:** Early check-in/late
check-out and free local telephone calls. *(See color ad p 420)*   Roll in showers.   🌊 🍴 ♿ ECTV 🎮 D S

RESTAURANT

SARAH STREET GRILL   **Lunch:** $8-$16   **Dinner:** $8-$16   **Phone:** 717/424-9120   57
◆◆   **Location:** Center, between 5th & 6th sts at Quaker Plaza. 550 Quaker Alley 18360. **Hours:** 11 am-midnight,
American   Fri & Sat-1 pm. **Closed:** 4/7, 11/26 & 12/25. **Reservations:** suggested; Sat. **Features:** casual dress;
    children's menu; early bird specials; health conscious menu; carryout; cocktails & lounge; a la carte.
Specializing in their own marinated Del Monico steak, burger, pizza & vegetarian dishes. **Cards:** AE, MC, VI.   ⊠

SWIFTWATER—700   (See map p. 418; index p. 417)

RESTAURANTS

BRITTANIA COUNTRY INN & RESTAURANT   **Lunch:** $4-$7   **Dinner:** $10-$18   **Phone:** 717/839-7243   65
◆◆   **Location:** From I-80 exit 44, 3 mi nw on SR 611N; just w on SR 314, left at fork 1.2 mi. Upper Swiftwater
Ethnic   Rd 18370. **Hours:** 5 pm-10 pm, Sun 12:30 pm-3 & 5-10 pm, Thurs & Fri noon-2 pm, Sat noon-2 & 5-10 pm.
    Closed: 4/1-4/14. **Reservations:** suggested. **Features:** casual dress; Sunday brunch; children's menu;
health conscious menu; carryout; cocktails & lounge. Authentic British cuisine presented in country style. Warm & casual
ambience. Good selection of imported beer avail. Smoke free premises. **Cards:** AE, MC, VI.   ⊠

FANUCCI'S   **Dinner:** $12-$20   **Phone:** 717/839-7097   66
◆◆◆   **Location:** 2.8 mi n of I-80 exit 44. SR 611 18370. **Hours:** 4 pm-11 pm, Sat & Sun from noon. **Closed:** 12/24
Italian   & 12/25. **Reservations:** suggested. **Features:** casual dress; children's menu; early bird specials; carryout;
    cocktails & lounge; a la carte. Also American entrees. **Cards:** AE, CB, DI, DS, MC, VI.   ⊠

TANNERSVILLE—1,200

RESTAURANT

BARLEY CREEK BREWING COMPANY   **Lunch:** $6-$11   **Dinner:** $9-$22   **Phone:** 717/629-9399
◆   **Location:** I-80, exit 45, 1.5 mi w on Sullivan Trail. Camelback Rd & Sullivan Tr 18372. **Hours:** 11:30 am-11
American   pm, Fri & Sat-midnight. **Closed:** 12/25. **Features:** casual dress; children's menu; carryout; cocktail lounge;
beam" timber frame building; outdoor seasonal dining deck. **Cards:** AE, DS, MC, VI.   ♿ ⊠
beer only; a la carte. American & English pub cuisine served in a bustling microbrewery in a unique "post &

POINT PLEASANT—*see Philadelphia & Vicinity p. 385.*

POTTSTOWN—*See Philadelphia & Vicinity p. 385.*

PUNXSUTAWNEY—6,800

LODGINGS

COUNTRY VILLA MOTEL   Guaranteed Rates   **Phone:** 814/938-8330
◆   All Year   1P: $30- 34   2P/1B: $36- 40   2P/2B: $40- 44   XP: $4
Motor Inn   **Location:** 1.5 mi s on US 119. Rt 119 15767 (RD 8, Box 282). **Terms:** Reserv deposit, 7 day notice; pets,
    $4 extra charge. **Facility:** 27 rooms. 2 efficiencies, $60 for up to 4 persons; 2 stories; exterior corridors.
Dining: Restaurant; 6 am-9 pm, Sun 7:30 am-7:30 pm; $6-$16. **Cards:** AE, DS, MC, VI.   🍴 ECTV ⊠ D

PANTALL HOTEL   Rates Subject to Change   **Phone:** 814/938-6600
◆◆   All Year   1P: $50- 95   2P/1B: $58- 103   2P/2B: $58- 103   XP: $8   F5
Historic Hotel   **Location:** Downtown; on US 119 & SR 36. 135 E Mahoning St 15767. Fax: 814/938-8592. **Terms:** Pets.
    Facility: 57 rooms. 4 stories; interior corridors. Fee: parking. **Dining:** Dining room; 7 am-9 pm; $7-$14.
Cards: AE, DI, DS, MC, VI.   🍴 ECTV ⊠ D

QUAKERTOWN—*See Philadelphia & Vicinity p. 385.*

READING—78,400—*See also SHILLINGTON & WYOMISSING.*

LODGINGS

BEST WESTERN DUTCH COLONY INN & SUITES   Phone: 610/779-2345

5/1-11/30	1P:	$65-	80	2P/2B:	$70-	90 XP: $5	F18
12/1-4/30	1P:	$58-	73	2P/2B:	$63-	83 XP: $5	F18

Motor Inn **Location:** On US 422, 0.3 mi e of jct US 422 business route. 4635 Perkiomen Ave 19606.
Fax: 610/779-8348. **Terms:** Weekly rates; small pets only, $5 extra charge. **Facility:** 71 rooms. 2 two-bedroom
units. 2-3 stories; interior/exterior corridors; whirlpool; playground. **Dining & Entertainment:** Restaurant; 7
am-9:30 pm, Sun 7 am-1 pm; 1/1-3/30 7 am-9 pm, Mon & Sat from 8 am, Sun 8 am-1 pm; $7-$17; cocktails/lounge.
Services: Fee: coin laundry. **All Rooms:** free movies. **Some Rooms:** microwaves, refrigerators. Fee: VCR's. **Cards:** AE,
CB, DI, DS, MC, VI. **Special Amenities:** Early check-in/late check-out and free local telephone calls.

MAIL CALL: Check at your lodging's front desk;
you might have a surprise.

COMFORT INN Phone: 610/371-0500
AAA SAVE All Year [CP] 1P: $45- 115 2P/1B: $45- 115 2P/2B: $55- 115 XP: $5-10 F18
◆◆◆ **Location:** On US 222 business route (5th St); just s of Warren St Bypass. 5th St Hwy (2200 Stacy Dr,
Motel 19605). Fax: 610/478-9421. **Terms:** No pets. **Facility:** 60 rooms. Traditional motel rooms. 3 whirlpool rms,
extra charge; 2 stories; interior corridors. **Dining:** Restaurant nearby. **Services:** valet laundry.
All Rooms: free movies. **Some Rooms:** microwaves, refrigerators. Fee: VCR's. **Cards:** AE, CB, DI, DS,
JCB, MC, VI. **Special Amenities: Free breakfast and free local telephone calls.** *(See color ad p 428)*

RAMADA INN THE OUTLETS Rates Subject to Change Phone: 610/929-4741
◆◆◆ 5/1-12/31 1P: $89 2P/1B: $89 2P/2B: $89 XP: $10 F18
Motor Inn 1/1-4/30 1P: $79 2P/1B: $79 2P/2B: $79 XP: $10 F18
Location: US 222 business route (5th St); just s of Warren St bypass. 2545 N 5th St 19605.
Fax: 610/929-5237. **Terms:** Pets. **Facility:** 140 rooms. 2 stories; interior/exterior corridors. **Dining:** Dining room; 6:30
am-noon & 5-10 pm; $8-$17. **All Rooms:** free & pay movies. **Cards:** AE, DI, DS, MC, VI.

RESTAURANTS
ALPENHOF BAVARIAN RESTAURANT Lunch: $3-$5 Dinner: $8-$17 Phone: 610/373-1624
AAA **Location:** On SR 10, 1.3 mi s of jct US 222. 903 Morgantown Rd 19607. **Hours:** 11:30 am-2 & 5-8:30 pm,
◆ Sat 5 pm-9 pm, Sun 11:30 am-7 pm. **Closed:** 1/1, 12/25, 12/24 & Mon for dinner. **Reservations:** suggested;
German for dinner. **Features:** casual dress; children's menu; carryout; cocktails & lounge; a la carte. Bavarian
Gasthaus & bierstube decor. Varied menu. **Cards:** AE, MC, VI.

CRAB BARN Lunch: $8-$15 Dinner: $13-$26 Phone: 610/921-8922
◆◆ **Location:** 1.5 mi se of jct US 222 business route (5th St) & Warren St Bypass, Spring Valley Rd exit from
Seafood bypass. 2613 Hampden Blvd 19604. **Hours:** 11:30 am-2 & 4:30-9 pm, Fri-10 pm, Sat 3 pm-10 pm, Sun 3
pm-9 pm. **Closed:** 1/1, 11/26 & 12/25. **Features:** casual dress; children's menu; carryout; cocktails & lounge.
Casual dining amidst the nostalgia of a turn-of-the-19th century barn converted into what is reminiscent of a traditional
eastern shore crab house featuring seafood, ribs, chicken & steak. Seasonal dining deck. **Cards:** AE, MC, VI.

RIDGWAY—4,800

LODGING
THE ROYAL INN Phone: 814/773-3153
AAA SAVE All Year [CP] 1P: $39- 49 2P/1B: $42- 55 2P/2B: $45- 55 XP: $8 F12
◆◆ **Location:** 1 mi s on US 219. Boot Jack Rd (Rt 219) 15853. **Terms:** Pets. **Facility:** 45
Motor Inn rooms. Good variety of room types with some very spacious units. 2 stories; interior/exterior corridors.
Dining & Entertainment: Restaurant; 4:30 pm-9 pm; $5-$18; cocktails/lounge. **Services:** winter plug-ins.
All Rooms: free movies, combo or shower baths. **Some Rooms:** radios. Fee: refrigerators. **Cards:** AE, DI,
DS, MC, VI. **Special Amenities: Free local telephone calls.**

ROBESONIA—1,900

RESTAURANT
HEIDELBERG FAMILY RESTAURANT Lunch: $4-$8 Dinner: $6-$10 Phone: 610/693-5060
AAA **Location:** 1.5 mi w on US 422. US 422 19551. **Hours:** 6 am-8:30 pm. **Closed:** 1/1 & 12/25.
◆ **Reservations:** accepted. **Features:** casual dress; children's menu; carryout; salad bar. Pennsylvania Dutch
American specialties; homemade soup, bread, dessert & in-house bakery. Counter service. **Cards:** MC, VI.

RONKS—See Pennsylvania Dutch Country p. 349.

ST. DAVIDS—See Philadelphia & Vicinity p. 386.

ST. MARYS—5,500

LODGINGS
BEST WESTERN EXECUTIVE INN Phone: 814/834-0000
AAA SAVE All Year [CP] 1P: $53- 55 2P/1B: $53- 55 2P/2B: $55 XP: $7 F18
◆◆◆ **Location:** S end of town on SR 255. 1002 Earth Rd 15857. Fax: 814/834-1804. **Terms:** No pets. **Facility:** 57
Motel rooms. 3 stories; interior corridors; designated smoking area; small heated pool. **All Rooms:** coffeemakers.
Some Rooms: microwaves, whirlpools. Fee: refrigerators. **Cards:** AE, DI, DS, MC, VI. **Special Amenities:**
Early check-in/late check-out and free breakfast. Roll in showers.

OLD CHARM BED & BREAKFAST Guaranteed Rates Phone: 814/834-9429
◆◆ All Year [BP] 1P: $52 2P/1B: $52
Bed & **Location:** Just e of downtown on SR 120E. 444 Brussells St 15857. Fax: 814/834-9274. **Terms:** Reserv
Breakfast deposit; no pets. **Facility:** 6 rooms. 2 stories; interior/exterior corridors; designated smoking area.
All Rooms: free movies. **Cards:** AE, DS, MC, VI.

TOWNE HOUSE INN Phone: 814/781-1556
AAA SAVE All Year 1P: $52- 95 2P/1B: $59- 102 2P/2B: $59- 80 XP: $7 F18
◆◆◆ **Location:** Downtown; just n of "diamond" & jct of SR 255 & SR 120. 138 Center St 15857.
Historic Fax: 814/834-4449. **Terms:** No pets. **Facility:** 59 rooms. Conventional rooms & some handsomely appointed
Country Inn rooms in converted 1899 Victorian & Tudor house. Executive suites with whirlpool or fireplace, free continental
breakfast weekends; 3 stories, no elevator; interior/exterior corridors; designated smoking area.
Dining: Dining room; 6:30 am-2 & 5-9 pm, Sat from 5 pm; $9-$14; cocktails. **Services:** Fee: coin laundry.
All Rooms: coffeemakers, free movies, combo or shower baths. **Some Rooms:** 3 efficiencies, 2 kitchens, no utensils,
whirlpools. Fee: microwaves, refrigerators. **Cards:** AE, DI, DS, MC, VI. Roll in showers.

RESTAURANT
BAVARIAN INN Lunch: $4-$8 Dinner: $9-$15 Phone: 814/834-2161
◆◆ **Location:** Downtown. 33 S St. Marys St 15857. **Hours:** 7 am-10 pm, Sat from 4:30 pm. **Closed:** Sun &
German 12/25. **Features:** children's menu; carryout; salad bar; cocktails & lounge. Bavarian cuisine & decor. Some
American entrees including fresh seafood & steak. **Cards:** AE, MC, VI.

SAYRE—5,800

LODGING

GUTHRIE INN
Phone: 717/888-7711
🅐🅐🅐 SAVE   All Year   1P: $81- 88   2P/2B: $94- 97 XP: $10   F12
◆◆◆   **Location:** 1 mi n on SR 199, at jct NY SR 17 & PA SR 199, exit 61. 255 Spring St 18840.
Hotel   Fax: 717/888-0541. **Terms:** Weekly/monthly rates; package plans; pets, $15 extra charge. **Facility:** 99 rooms.
Victorian ambience. 4 stories; interior corridors; sauna, whirlpool; racquetball courts, 2 lighted tennis courts.
Fee: tanning booth. **Dining & Entertainment:** Restaurant; 6:30 am-9:30 pm, Sat 7 am-10 pm, Sun 7
am-7:30   pm; $9-$18;   cocktails/lounge.   **Services:**   valet   laundry;   area   transportation,   Guthrie   Clinic.
All Rooms: coffeemakers. **Some Rooms:** microwaves. Fee: refrigerators, VCR's. **Cards:** AE, CB, DI, DS, MC, VI.

SCENERY HILL—500

RESTAURANT

CENTURY INN DINING ROOM   Historical   **Lunch:** $7-$9   **Dinner:** $12-$27   **Phone:** 724/945-6600
◆◆◆   **Location:** Center, on US 40. US 40 15360. **Hours:** Open 5/1-12/30 & 3/14-4/30; noon-3 & 4:30-8 pm, Fri &
American   Sat-9 pm, Sun noon-3 & 3:30-7 pm. Closed: 12/25. **Reservations:** suggested. **Features:** casual dress;
children's menu; cocktails & lounge. Historic 1794 inn with dining room restored to period. Homemade bread,
soup & dessert. **Cards:** MC, VI.

SCHELLSBURG—200

LODGING

BEDFORD'S COVERED BRIDGE INN   Rates Subject to Change   **Phone:** 814/733-4093
◆◆◆   All Year [BP]   2P/1B: $65- 95 2P/2B: $95   XP: $15
Historic Bed   **Location:** Just w on US 30 from jct SR 96, 0.8 mi s on Mill St. RR 2, Box 196 15559. **Terms:** Age
& Breakfast   restrictions may apply; reserv deposit, 7 day notice; no pets. **Facility:** 7 rooms. 2 night min stay, weekends
2/1-2/28 & 10/1-10/31; 2 night min stay 2-bedroom house, $95 for up to 2 persons. Handling fee imposed; 2
stories; interior corridors; smoke free premises. **Some Rooms:** kitchen. **Cards:** AE, DS, MC, VI.

SCOTRUN—*See Pocono Mountains Area p. 426.*

SCRANTON—81,800   (See map p. 418; index p. 417)

LODGINGS

COMFORT SUITES
Phone: 717/347-1551   **7**
🅐🅐🅐 SAVE   All Year [CP]   1P: $78- 135   2P/1B: $83- 140 2P/2B: $83- 140 XP: $5   F18
◆◆◆   **Location:** I-81, exit 51. 44 Montage Mountain Rd 18505. Fax: 717/347-1511. **Terms:** Package plans, Skiing;
Suite Motel   no pets. **Facility:** 100 rooms. New facility with all suites including extra amenities in nice setting convenient to
interstate & Montage Mtn. 4 two-bedroom units. Tower Suite 4th floor has 2700 sq ft with l/r, d/r, kitchen & 2
br $375; 4 stories; interior corridors; mountain view; whirlpool; game room with game tables, billiards & arcade.
Dining: Restaurant nearby. **Services:** area transportation, 10 mi radius w/adv notice. Fee: coin laundry.
All Rooms: coffeemakers, microwaves, free movies, refrigerators, combo or shower baths. **Some Rooms:** 26 kitchens,
whirlpools. **Cards:** AE, CB, DI, DS, JCB, MC, VI. **Special Amenities: Free breakfast and free local telephone calls.**
Roll in showers.

HAMPTON INN-SCRANTON   Rates Subject to Change   **Phone:** 717/342-7002   **8**
◆◆◆   All Year [CP]   1P: $74- 79   2P/1B: $79- 84 2P/2B: $79- 84 XP: $5   F18
Motor Inn   **Location:** I-81, exit 51. 22 Montage Mountain Rd 18507. Fax: 717/342-7012. **Terms:** Sr. discount; no pets.
Facility: 129 rooms. 8 fireplace/whirlpool suites, $99-$150; 4 stories; interior corridors. **All Rooms:** free
movies. **Cards:** AE, CB, DI, DS, MC, VI.   Roll in showers.

(See map p. 418)

RADISSON LACKAWANNA STATION HOTEL SCRANTON   Phone: 717/342-8300   🔟
🅰🅰🅰 SAVE   All Year   1P: $89   2P/1B: $89   2P/2B: $89   XP: $10   F18
◆◆◆   **Location:** I-81 exit 53, at the confluence of Lackawanna Ave, Jefferson Ave & Spruce St. 700 Lackawanna
Historic Hotel   Ave 18503. Fax: 717/342-0380. **Terms:** Reserv deposit; monthly rates; no pets. **Facility:** 145 rooms. Elegant
public areas, very appealing & comfortable rooms. Historical downtown converted train station. 18 luxurious
suites, $139-$250. 4 whirlpool rms, extra charge. Handling fee imposed; 6 stories; interior corridors; sauna,
whirlpool; game room. **Dining & Entertainment:** Dining room, restaurant; 6:30 am-midnight; $16-$29; cocktails/lounge; Sun
brunch 10 am-2 pm; also, Carmen's, see separate listing; entertainment. **Services:** valet laundry; area transportation, within
2 mi; valet parking. **All Rooms:** coffeemakers, free & pay movies. **Some Rooms:** Fee: microwaves, refrigerators, VCR's.
Cards: AE, CB, DI, DS, JCB, MC, VI. **Special Amenities: Preferred room (subject to availability with advanced
reservations).** (See color ad p 431 & p 394)   🅂 🛬 🅂 CTV ✕ D S

RESTAURANTS

CARMEN'S   **Lunch:** $7-$13   **Dinner:** $16-$29   Phone: 717/342-8300   ⑨
🅰🅰🅰   **Location:** I-81 exit 53, at the confluence of Lackawanna Ave, Jefferson Ave & Spruce St; in Radisson
Lackawanna Station Hotel Scranton. 700 Lackawanna Ave 18503. **Hours:** 6:30 am-2:30 & 5-10 pm, Sun
◆◆◆   brunch 10 am-2 pm. **Reservations:** suggested. **Features:** dressy casual; Sunday brunch; early bird specials;
Continental   health conscious menu items; cocktails & lounge; entertainment; valet parking; also prix fixe. Fine dining in
an elegant atmosphere amid Italian marble & an authentic vaulted Tiffany glass ceiling. **Cards:** AE, CB, DI,
DS, JCB, MC, VI. (See color ad p 431)

COOPER'S SEAFOOD HOUSE & SHIP'S PUB   **Lunch:** $4-$8   **Dinner:** $9-$28   Phone: 717/346-6883   ③
🅰🅰🅰   **Location:** Center at Washington Ave & Pine St. 701 N Washington Ave 18509. **Hours:** 11 am-midnight, Fri &
Sat-1 am, Sun noon-11 pm. Closed major holidays. **Features:** casual dress; children's menu; carryout;
◆◆   cocktails & lounge; entertainment. New replica of turn-of-the-century sailing vessel serving a large variety of
Seafood   fresh seafood & meat entrees. Lite fare & music in ships pub. **Cards:** AE, DS, MC, VI.
(See color ad p 432)   ✕

FARLEY'S   **Lunch:** $7-$10   **Dinner:** $11-$24   Phone: 717/346-3000   ④
🅰🅰🅰   **Location:** Center; corner Adams Ave & Linden St (on Courthouse Square). 300 Adams Ave 18503.
Hours: 11 am-2 am. **Reservations:** suggested; weekends. **Features:** casual dress; cocktails & lounge;
◆◆   street parking. Pub atmosphere. Certified Angus beef, seafood, ribs, chicken & chops. Extensive beer
Steak and   selections. **Cards:** AE, DI, DS, MC, VI.   ✕
Seafood

SMITHS RESTAURANT   **Lunch:** $6-$13   **Dinner:** $7-$13   Phone: 717/961-9192   ⑤
🅰🅰🅰   **Location:** I-81 exit 51, w to US 11, 1.5 mi n. 1402 Cedar Ave 18505. **Hours:** 6 am-11 pm, Sat-8 pm. Closed
major holidays & Sun. **Reservations:** accepted. **Features:** casual dress; children's menu; health conscious
◆◆   menu; carryout; cocktails. Home cooking, family atmosphere. Family owned for 63 years.   ✕
American

STRAZZERI'S RESTAURANT   **Lunch:** $3-$5   **Dinner:** $4-$10   Phone: 717/961-8455   ⑥
◆   **Location:** I-81, exit 56 (Main Ave); 1.5 mi s. 1911 N Main Ave 18508. **Hours:** 11 am-9 pm. Closed major
Italian   holidays. **Reservations:** accepted. **Features:** casual dress; children's menu; carryout; cocktails & lounge.
Casual family atmosphere. Italian specialties.   ✕

TOM & JERRY'S RESTAURANT   **Lunch:** $3-$5   **Dinner:** $7-$14   Phone: 717/344-1771   🔟
◆   **Location:** At jct Pittston Ave & Birch St; from I-81, exit 51 to SR 11, 2 mi n. 731 Pittston Ave 18505.
American   **Hours:** 11 am-midnight. Closed major holidays. **Features:** casual dress; children's menu; carryout; cocktails.
Family oriented restaurant. Wall mounted cartoon characters will intrigue the children. **Cards:** AE, DS, MC,
VI.   ✕

SELINSGROVE—5,400

LODGING

COMFORT INN   Phone: 717/374-8880
🅰🅰🅰 SAVE   5/1-10/31 [CP]   1P: $60- 85   2P/1B: $70   2P/2B: $65- 90   XP: $5   F18
11/1-4/30 [CP]   1P: $45- 85   2P/1B: $55   2P/2B: $49- 85   XP: $5   F18
◆◆   **Location:** Just n of jct US 522. 710 S US Hwy 11 & 15 17870. Fax: 717/374-8880. **Terms:** Pets, $10 extra
Motel   charge. **Facility:** 62 rooms. 2 stories; interior corridors. **Dining & Entertainment:** Cocktail lounge.
All Rooms: free movies. **Some Rooms:** radios. **Cards:** AE, CB, DI, DS, MC, VI. **Special Amenities: Early
check-in/late check-out and free newspaper.**   🛏 🅂 ECTV ✕ D

SEWICKLEY—See Pittsburgh & Vicinity p. 413.

SHADYSIDE—See Pittsburgh & Vicinity p. 413.

SHAMOKIN DAM—1,700

LODGINGS

HAMPTON INN   Phone: 717/743-2223
(AAA) (SAVE)   All Year [CP]   1P: $59- 89 2P/1B: $69- 99 2P/2B: $69
◆◆◆   Location: On US 11 & 15, 1 mi s of jct SR 61. (3 Stettler Ave, SELINSGROVE, 17870). Fax: 717/743-5404.
Motel   Terms: Weekly/monthly rates; no pets. Facility: 76 rooms. Elegantly appointed guest rooms & public areas. 1
              whirlpool rm, $139; 3 stories; interior corridors; whirlpool. Services: Fee: coin laundry. All Rooms: free
              movies, combo or shower baths. Some Rooms: microwaves, refrigerators. Cards: AE, CB, DI, DS, MC, VI.
Special Amenities: Free breakfast and free local telephone calls.

Roll in showers. (symbols)

PHILLIPS MOTEL, INC   Rates Subject to Change   Phone: 717/743-3100
(AAA)   All Year   1P: $44- 50 2P/1B: $49- 60 2P/2B: $49- 64 XP: $5   D12
◆◆◆   Location: 0.5 mi s of jct SR 61. US Rts 11/15 & 11th Ave 17876 (PO Box 191). Fax: 717/743-4065.
Motel   Terms: Reserv deposit, 5 day notice; no pets. Facility: 47 rooms. 1 story; exterior corridors.
              All Rooms: free movies. Cards: AE, CB, DI, DS, MC, VI. (See color ad p 433)   (symbols)

RESTAURANT

TEDD'S LANDING   Lunch: $4-$10   Dinner: $10-$15   Phone: 717/743-1591
(AAA)   Location: 0.5 mi n at jct US 11 & 15. 17876. Hours: 11 am-10 pm, Sat 4 pm-11 pm, Sun 4 pm-9 pm.
              Closed major holidays. Reservations: accepted. Features: casual dress; carryout; cocktails & lounge.
◆◆   Rustic ambience, family operation. Fresh seafood specialty. Good river view. In-house baker & butcher.
American   Homemade bread, pastry & soup. Cafeteria style lunch avail. Cards: AE, DS, MC, VI.   (symbol)

SHARON—17,500

RESTAURANT

HOT ROD CAFE   Dinner: $8-$14   Phone: 724/981-3123
◆◆   Location: Downtown. 110 Connelly Blvd 16146. Hours: 4 pm-2 am & Sun 2 pm-2 am. Closed: Mon.
American   Features: casual dress; children's menu; carryout; cocktails & lounge; a la carte. Fresh seafood. Cards: AE,
              DI, DS, MC, VI.   (symbol)

SHARTLESVILLE—3,800

LODGING

DUTCH MOTEL   Phone: 610/488-1479
(AAA) (SAVE)   All Year   1P: $30- 35 2P/1B: $36- 41 2P/2B: $40- 45 XP: $7   F12
              Location: Nw of Shartlesville exit off I-78 & US 22 on Motel Rd. 19554 (PO Box 25). Terms: Reserv
◆   deposit; weekly rates; pets, $3 extra charge, small dogs only. Facility: 14 rooms. 1 story; exterior corridors.
Motel   Dining: Restaurant nearby. All Rooms: free movies, combo or shower baths. Cards: AE, DS, MC, VI.
              Special Amenities: Free local telephone calls and preferred room (subject to availability with
advanced reservations).   (symbols)

SHILLINGTON—5,000—See also READING.

LODGING

DAYS INN   Rates Subject to Change   Phone: 610/777-7888
◆◆   All Year [CP]   1P: $62   2P/1B: $68   2P/2B: $68   XP: $5   F18
Motel   Location: 5 mi s of US 422 & US 222 business route exit. 2299 Lancaster Pike 19607. Fax: 610/777-5138.
              Terms: Sr. discount; no pets. Facility: 142 rooms. 4 stories; interior corridors. All Rooms: free movies.
Cards: AE, CB, DI, DS, MC, VI.   (symbols)

SHIPPENSBURG—5,300

LODGINGS

AMERIHOST INN-SHIPPENSBURG   Phone: 717/532-5200
(AAA) (SAVE)   All Year [CP]   2P/1B: $64- 74 2P/2B: $59- 69
◆◆◆   Location: I-81, exit 10, 0.5 mi w on SR 174. 125 Walnut Bottom Rd 17257. Fax: 717/532-7148.
Motel   Terms: Package plans; no pets. Facility: 60 rooms. Modern rooms; appealing pool & patio area. 2 whirlpool
              rms, $110-$125. Rates for up to 4 persons; 2 stories; interior corridors; sauna, whirlpool.
              All Rooms: coffeemakers, free & pay movies, combo or shower baths. Fee: safes.
Some Rooms: microwaves, refrigerators. Cards: AE, CB, DI, DS, JCB, MC, VI. Special Amenities: Free breakfast and
free newspaper. (See ad p 254)   Roll in showers. (symbols)

SHIPPEN PLACE HOTEL   Phone: 717/532-4141
(AAA) (SAVE)   All Year   1P: $58- 80 2P/1B: $58- 80 2P/2B: $58- 80 XP: $5   F13
◆◆◆   Location: I-81 exit 10, 1.5 mi w on SR 174 then 0.8 mi s on US 11; just n jct SR 696. 32 E King St 17257.
Motor Inn   Fax: 717/532-5142. Terms: Weekly/monthly rates; MAP avail; no pets. Facility: 57 rooms. Upscale property
              with a rich, traditional flair. Some rooms with separate sitting room. Convenient in-town location. 5 whirlpool
              rms, extra charge; 4 stories; interior corridors. Dining & Entertainment: Restaurant; 6:30 am-11 pm;
$10-$15; cocktails/lounge. Services: valet laundry. All Rooms: coffeemakers, free movies, combo or shower baths.
Some Rooms: refrigerators. Cards: AE, CB, DI, DS, JCB, MC, VI. Special Amenities: Free local telephone calls and
free room upgrade (subject to availability with advanced reservations).   Roll in showers. (symbols)

RESTAURANT

BELLA NAPOLI   Lunch: $7-$17   Dinner: $7-$17   Phone: 717/530-8959
◆◆   Location: I-81, exit 10, 1.5 mi w on SR 174, then 1 mi s on US 11; just s jct SR 696. 105 W King St 17257.
Italian   Hours: 11 am-10 pm, Sun-9 pm. Closed major holidays. Reservations: suggested; weekends.
              Features: casual dress; children's menu; carryout; cocktails. Wide variety of traditional favorites, also
featuring veal, seafood & gourmet pizzas. Cheerful, cozy atmosphere. Cards: AE, DS, MC, VI.   (symbol)

SLIPPERY ROCK—3,000

LODGINGS

APPLEBUTTER INN Guaranteed Rates Phone: 724/794-1844
◆◆◆ Fri & Sat [BP] 1P: $75- 105 2P/1B: $95- 125 2P/2B: $125 XP: $10-15
Historic Bed Sun-Thurs [BP] 1P: $59- 79 2P/1B: $79- 99 2P/2B: $99 XP: $10-15
& Breakfast **Location:** Jct Rt 108 & 173, 1 mi s on Rt 173. 666 Centreville Pike 16057. Fax: 724/794-3319.
Terms: Reserv deposit, 7 day notice; $10 service charge; no pets. **Facility:** 11 rooms. Closed 11/26 & 12/25.
Handling fee imposed; 2 stories; interior corridors; smoke free premises. **All Rooms:** free movies. **Cards:** AE, MC, VI.

CTV ⊠ D S

EVENING STAR MOTEL Rates Subject to Change Phone: 724/794-3211
◆ All Year 1P: $38 2P/1B: $42 2P/2B: $42 XP: $3 F12
Motel **Location:** On SR 108; 0.5 mi e off I-79, exit 30. 16057 (RD 3, Box 380A). **Terms:** Reserv deposit; pets, $5
dep req. **Facility:** 18 rooms. Handling fee imposed; 1 story; exterior corridors. **Cards:** AE, DS, MC, VI.

🛏 CTV D

RESTAURANT

WOLF CREEK SCHOOL CAFE **Lunch:** $5-$8 **Dinner:** $8-$14 Phone: 724/794-1899
◆◆ **Location:** Jct Rt 108 & 173, 1 mi s on Rt 173. 664 Centreville Pike 16057. **Hours:** 11 am-8 pm, Fri & Sat-9
American pm. Closed major holidays & Mon. **Reservations:** suggested. **Features:** casual dress; children's menu;
carryout. Relaxing dining room in an original 1 room schoolhouse with creative menu items. **Cards:** MC, VI.

♿ ⊠

SMOKETOWN—*See Pennsylvania Dutch Country p. 350.*

SNYDERSVILLE—*See Pocono Mountains Area p. 426.*

SOMERSET—*See Laurel Highlands p. 315.*

SOUTH WILLIAMSPORT—6,500—*See also WILLIAMSPORT.*

LODGINGS

KINGS INN Phone: 717/322-4707
(AAA) SAVE 5/1-12/1 & 4/1-4/30 [CP] 1P: $32- 45 2P/1B: $39- 49 2P/2B: $39- 52 XP: $5 F12
  12/2-3/31 [CP] 1P: $29- 39 2P/1B: $34- 39 2P/2B: $36- 42 XP: $5 F12
◆◆ **Location:** 0.9 mi s on US 15. 590 Montgomery Pike 17701. Fax: 717/322-0946. **Terms:** Reserv deposit;
Motor Inn weekly/monthly rates, 12/1-3/31; pets dep req. **Facility:** 48 rooms. Close to Little League Baseball Museum &
stadium. Some units without writing surface. 1-2 stories; interior/exterior corridors. **Dining:** Kings Inn-St.
Regis Room, see separate listing. **All Rooms:** combo or shower baths. **Cards:** AE, DI, DS, MC, VI. **Special Amenities:**
Early check-in/late check-out and free room upgrade (subject to availability with advanced reservations).

🛏 🐾 ECTV ⊠ D

QUALITY INN WILLIAMSPORT Rates Subject to Change Phone: 717/323-9801
◆◆ All Year 1P: $52- 62 2P/1B: $58- 68 2P/2B: $58- 68 XP: $6 F18
Motor Inn **Location:** 0.8 mi s on US 15. 234 Montgomery Pike 17701. Fax: 717/322-5231. **Terms:** Sr. discount; no
pets. **Facility:** 117 rooms. 2 stories; interior corridors. **Dining:** Restaurant; 6:30 am-10:30 & 5-9 pm; $7-$14.
All Rooms: free movies. **Cards:** AE, CB, DI, DS, JCB, MC, VI. *(See ad p 446)*

🛎 ECTV ⊠ D

RIDGEMONT MOTEL Guaranteed Rates Phone: 717/321-5300
(AAA) All Year 2P/1B: $33 2P/2B: $37 XP: $1-2
◆◆ **Location:** 1.2 mi s on US 15. Montgomery Pike 17701 (RD 4, Box 536, WILLIAMSPORT). **Terms:** Age
Motel restrictions may apply; small pets only. **Facility:** 8 rooms. 1 story; exterior corridors. **All Rooms:** free
movies. **Cards:** DS, MC, VI.

🛏 ECTV ⊠ D

RESTAURANT

KINGS INN-ST. REGIS ROOM **Dinner:** $6-$22 Phone: 717/322-4707
◆◆◆ **Location:** 0.9 mi s on US 15; in Kings Inn. 590 Montgomery Pike 17701. **Hours:** 4:30 pm-10 pm, Fri &
American Sat-11 pm. Closed major holidays. **Reservations:** accepted. **Features:** casual dress; children's menu;
senior's menu; health conscious menu items; carryout; cocktails & lounge. Relaxed dining in elegant
surroundings. Also features Italian dishes. **Cards:** AE, CB, DI, DS, MC, VI. ⊠

SPEERS—*See Pittsburgh & Vicinity p. 414.*

SPRINGDALE—*See Pittsburgh & Vicinity p. 414.*

SPRINGFIELD (DELAWARE COUNTY)—*See Philadelphia & Vicinity p. 386.*

SPRING MILLS—500

RESTAURANT

THE HUMMINGBIRD ROOM Historical **Dinner:** $18-$24 Phone: 814/422-9025
◆◆◆ **Location:** 1.1 mi e. Rt 45 16875. **Hours:** 5 pm-10 pm. Closed: 1/1, 4/7, 11/26, 12/25, Mon & Tues.
Continental **Reservations:** suggested. **Features:** dressy casual; health conscious menu items; a la carte, also prix fixe.
Former Gothic revival 1847 home, in rural location. Several dining rooms decorated to reflect the original
home. Innovative cuisine. Owner chef. Smoke free premises. **Cards:** DS, MC, VI. ⊠

STAHLSTOWN—*See Laurel Highlands p. 318.*

STARLIGHT—*See Pocono Mountains Area p. 426.*

STARRUCCA—*See Pocono Mountains Area p. 427.*

STATE COLLEGE—38,900

LODGINGS

THE ATHERTON HOTEL   Phone: 814/231-2100
(AAA) [SAVE]   All Year   1P: $105   2P/1B: $115   2P/2B: $105   XP: $10   F12
◆◆   **Location:** Downtown, on US 322 business route, between north & southbound SR 26. 125 S Atherton St
Hotel   16801. Fax: 814/237-1130. **Terms:** Weekly rates; package plans; no pets. **Facility:** 149 rooms. Close to Penn
                State campus. 10 whirlpool rms, $160-$180; 7 stories; interior corridors. **Dining & Entertainment:**
                Restaurant; 6:30 am-2 & 5-10 pm, Sat & Sun from 7 am; $16-$20; cocktails/lounge. **Services:** valet laundry;
area transportation, within 6 mi. **All Rooms:** free & pay movies. **Some Rooms:** coffeemakers, refrigerators, whirlpools.
Cards: AE, CB, DI, DS, MC, VI. **Special Amenities: Free newspaper.** *(See ad below)*   [icons]

AUTOPORT MOTEL   Phone: 814/237-7666
(AAA) [SAVE]   5/1-10/31 & 3/1-4/30   1P: $64- 74 2P/1B: $69- 89 2P/2B: $69- 89 XP: $5   F16
◆◆   11/1-2/28   1P: $59- 69 2P/1B: $65- 75 2P/2B: $65- 75 XP: $5   F16
Motor Inn   **Location:** On US 322 business route, 1.4 mi e of jct SR 26. 1405 S Atherton St 16801. Fax: 814/237-7456.
                Terms: Check-in 4 pm; monthly rates; package plans; small pets only, $5 extra charge. **Facility:** 86 rooms.
                Traditional motel rooms & a few cottage-style units. Landscaped pool area under tall pines. 1 two-bedroom
unit. Handling fee imposed; 1-2 stories; interior/exterior corridors. **Dining & Entertainment:** Restaurant, coffee shop; 6
am-midnight; outdoor dining in season; $12-$18; cocktails/lounge. **Services:** Fee: coin laundry. **All Rooms:** coffeemakers,
free movies, combo or shower baths. **Some Rooms:** 14 efficiencies, microwaves, refrigerators. Fee: VCR's. **Cards:** AE, CB,
DI, DS, MC, VI. **Special Amenities: Early check-in/late check-out and free local telephone calls.**   [icons]

BEST WESTERN STATE COLLEGE INN   Phone: 814/237-8005
(AAA) [SAVE]   5/1-11/30 & 3/1-4/30 [CP] 1P: $64- 90 2P/1B: $70- 90 2P/2B: $70- 90 XP: $5   F
◆◆   12/1-2/28 [CP]   1P: $49- 85 2P/1B: $49- 85 2P/2B: $49- 85 XP: $5   F
Motel   **Location:** On US 322 business route, 1.6 mi e of jct SR 26. 1663 S Atherton St 16801. Fax: 814/238-8805.
                Terms: Weekly/monthly rates; small pets only. **Facility:** 139 rooms. 3 whirlpool suites, $125; rate for up to 4
persons; 3-4 stories; interior corridors; sauna, whirlpool. Fee: in-room video games. **Dining:** Restaurant
nearby. **Services:** valet laundry. **All Rooms:** free & pay movies. **Some Rooms:** coffeemakers, 18 efficiencies, no utensils,
microwaves, refrigerators, whirlpools. **Cards:** AE, DI, DS, MC, VI. **Special Amenities: Free breakfast and free newspaper.**   [icons]

BREWMEISTER'S BED & BREAKFAST MOTEL   Rates Subject to Change   Phone: 814/238-0015
◆   All Year [CP]   1P: $34- 40 2P/1B: $42- 49 2P/2B: $42- 49 XP: $7   F12
Motel   **Location:** On SR 26, 2.6 mi s of jct US 322 business route. 2070 Cato Ave 16801. Fax: 814/238-0035.
                Terms: Pets, $7 fee, in 1 designated room. **Facility:** 16 rooms. 1 story; exterior corridors. **Cards:** AE, DI,
DS, MC, VI.   [icons]

CARNEGIE HOUSE   Phone: 814/234-2424
(AAA) [SAVE]   All Year [CP]   1P: $125- 175 2P/1B: $125- 175 2P/2B: $125- 175 XP: $25   D10
◆◆◆◆   **Location:** 0.8 mi ne of jct US 322; Toftress exit, 4 mi w of jct SR 26. 100 Cricklewood Dr 16803.
Country Inn   Fax: 814/231-1299. **Terms:** Age restrictions may apply; reserv deposit, 14 day notice; package plans; no
                pets. **Facility:** 22 rooms. Contemporary style inn with Scottish country house warmth. Individually decorated
                rooms. 2 suites on 3rd floor. Gracious hospitality. 2 suites, $275; 2 stories; interior corridors; smoke free prem-
ises. **Dining & Entertainment:** Dining room; Prix-fixe menu avail; 11:30 am-1:30 & 6-8:30 pm; closed Sun & 12/25;
$15-$30; cocktails/lounge; Dinner by reservation only. **Services:** valet laundry; area transportation, to Penn State Campus.
Some Rooms: honor bars, microwaves, refrigerators, VCR's. **Cards:** AE, MC, VI. **Special Amenities: Free breakfast and
free room upgrade (subject to availability with advanced reservations).**   [icons]

COURTYARD BY MARRIOTT   Rates Subject to Change   Phone: 814/238-1881
◆◆◆   All Year   1P: $86- 115 2P/1B: $86- 110 2P/2B: $86- 115
Motel   **Location:** On US 322 business route, 1.5 mi e of jct SR 26. 1730 University Dr 16801. Fax: 814/238-3108.
                Terms: No pets. **Facility:** 78 rooms. Whirlpool rm, $105-$115; 3 stories; interior corridors. **Dining:** Coffee
shop; 6:30-10 am, Sat & Sun 7-11 am. **All Rooms:** free & pay movies. **Cards:** AE, CB, DI, DS, MC, VI.
                                                                            Roll in showers.   [icons]

DAYS INN PENN STATE
◆◆ All Year
Hotel
Rates Subject to Change
1P: $55- 165   2P/1B: $65- 175 2P/2B: $65- 175 XP: $10   F17
Phone: 814-238-8454

Location: Downtown; just e of SR 26 northbound, 0.4 mi n of jct US 322 business route. 240 S Pugh St 16801. Fax: 814/234-3377. **Terms:** Sr. discount; small pets only, $8 extra charge. **Facility:** 184 rooms. 5-6 stories; interior corridors. **Dining:** Restaurant; 6:30 am-10 pm, Sun from 7 am; $8-$16. **All Rooms:** Fee: movies. **Cards:** AE, CB, DI, DS, JCB, MC, VI. *(See color ad below)*

HAMPTON INN
◆◆◆ All Year [OP]
Motel
Rates Subject to Change
1P: $59- 70   2P/1B: $00- 00 2P/2B: $00- 00
Phone: 814/231-1590

Location: On SR 26, 0.7 mi s of jct US 322. 1101 E College Ave 16801. Fax: 814/238-7320. **Terms:** No pets. **Facility:** 121 rooms. 3 stories; interior corridors. **All Rooms:** free & pay movies. **Cards:** AE, CB, DI, DS, MC, VI.

THE NITTANY LION INN
◆◆◆ All Year
Historic Hotel
Rates Subject to Change
1P: $85- 115   2P/1B: $95- 125 2P/2B: $95- 125 XP: $10
Phone: 814/865-8500

Location: On US 322 business route; 0.5 mi w of jct SR 26, on Penn State campus. 200 W Park Ave 16803-3598. Fax: 814/865-8501. **Terms:** No pets. **Facility:** 237 rooms. 3 stories; interior corridors. **Dining:** Restaurant; 6:45-11 am, 11:30-2 & 5:30-9 pm, Sun-8 pm; $13-$20. **All Rooms:** free & pay movies. **Cards:** AE, CB, DI, DS, MC, VI. *(See color ad p 438)*   Roll in showers.

RAMADA INN - STATE COLLEGE   Rates Subject to Change   **Phone:** 814/238-3001
◆◆   All Year   1P: $72   2P/1B: $79   2P/2B: $79   XP: $10   F18
Motor Inn   **Location:** On US 322 business route, 1.4 mi e of jct SR 26. 1450 S Atherton St 16801. Fax: 814/237-1345.
    Terms: Small pets only. **Facility:** 288 rooms. 2 stories; exterior corridors. **Dining:** Restaurant; 7 am-2 & 5-10
pm; $8-$20. **All Rooms:** free movies. **Cards:** AE, CB, DI, DS, MC, VI. *(See ad below)*   🛏️ 🍽️ 📺 ✕ Ⓓ

RODEWAY INN   **Phone:** 814/238-6783
🆎 💾   All Year   1P: $39- 54   2P/1B: $44- 54   2P/2B: $49- 69   XP: $5   F16
    Location: On US 322 business route, 0.8 mi w of jct SR 26. 1040 N Atherton St 16803. Fax: 814/238-4519.
◆◆   **Terms:** No pets. **Facility:** 29 rooms. Close to Penn State campus. Variety of well-maintained comfortable
Motel   rooms. 2 stories; interior/exterior corridors. **Dining:** Restaurant nearby. **All Rooms:** free movies, combo or
    shower baths. **Some Rooms:** refrigerators. **Cards:** AE, CB, DI, DS, JCB, MC, VI. **Special Amenities:** Early
check-in/late check-out and free local telephone calls.   📺 ✕ Ⓓ

SLEEP INN   Rates Subject to Change   **Phone:** 814/235-1020
◆◆   All Year [CP]   1P: $49- 130   2P/1B: $49- 130   2P/2B: $49- 130   XP: $10   F18
Motel   **Location:** On US 332 business route, 1 mi w of jct SR 26. 111 Village Dr 16803. Fax: 814/235-1388.
    Terms: Sr. discount; no pets. **Facility:** 101 rooms. 3 stories; interior corridors. **All Rooms:** free movies.
Cards: AE, CB, DI, DS, MC, VI.   Roll in showers. 📺 🛇 ✕ Ⓓ Ⓢ

RESTAURANTS

MARIO & LUIGI'S ITALIAN RESTAURANT   **Dinner:** $6-$14   **Phone:** 814/237-0374
◆◆   **Location:** In town between College & Beaver sts. 112 S Garner St 16801. **Hours:** 5 pm-10 pm, Sat noon-11
Italian   pm, Sun noon-10 pm. Closed: 11/26 & 12/25. **Features:** casual dress; children's menu; health conscious
    menu items; carryout; cocktails; street parking. Fresh house pasta. Veal, chicken & seafood specialties.
Woodburning ovens & rotisserie in view. Close to Penn State Campus. **Cards:** AE, DI, DS, MC, VI.   ✕

THE TAVERN RESTAURANT   **Dinner:** $6-$14   **Phone:** 814/238-6116
◆◆   **Location:** On SR 26 (southbound), 5 blks n of US 322 business route. 220 E College Ave 16805. **Hours:** 5
American   pm-10:30 pm, Sun-8:30 pm. Closed major holidays. **Features:** casual dress; children's menu; health
    conscious menu items; cocktails & lounge; street parking. Serving the area since 1948. Photographs & prints
of Penn State & Pennsylvania's history. Close to Penn State campus. **Cards:** AE, CB, DI, DS, MC, VI.   ✕

ZIMM'S FAMILY RESTAURANT   **Lunch:** $5-$7   **Dinner:** $6-$10   **Phone:** 814/234-2447
◆   **Location:** From jct US 322 & SR 26; 1.5 mi n on SR 26. 2541 E College Ave 16801. **Hours:** 11 am-9 pm,
American   Sun 10:30 am-8 pm. Closed major holidays. **Features:** casual dress; children's menu; carryout; salad bar.
    All-you-can eat daily specials. **Cards:** AE, CB, DI, DS, MC, VI.   ✕

STRASBURG—*See Pennsylvania Dutch Country p. 350.*

STROUDSBURG—*See Pocono Mountains Area p. 427.*

SUNBURY—11,600

RESTAURANT

THE AUGUSTA HOUSE FAMILY RESTAURANT   **Lunch:** $3-$7   **Dinner:** $6-$10   **Phone:** 717/286-9979
◆◆   **Location:** Just s at corner of 2nd & Walnut sts. 212 Walnut St 17801. **Hours:** 7 am-8 pm, Sun 11 am-2 pm.
American   Closed major holidays. **Reservations:** accepted; Fri-Sun. **Features:** casual dress; children's menu; senior's menu; carryout. Family style, homemade soup & dessert. Attractive foyer & dining room.   ⊠

SWIFTWATER—*See Pocono Mountains Area p. 427.*

TANNERSVILLE—*See Pocono Mountains Area p. 427.*

TREVOSE—*See Philadelphia & Vicinity p. 386.*

TROY

LODGING

GOLDEN OAK INN BED & BREAKFAST   Rates Subject to Change   **Phone:** 717/297-4315
◆◆◆   All Year [BP]   1P: $55- 65   2P/1B: $55- 65   2P/2B: $55- 65
Historic Bed   **Location:** W jct Rts 6 & 14, just s on Rt 14. 196 Canton St 16947. **Terms:** Sr. discount; age restrictions may
& Breakfast   apply; reserv deposit, 7 day notice; no pets. **Facility:** 4 rooms. 2 stories; interior corridors; smoke free premises. **Dining:** Gourmet breakfast 7 am-9 am. **All Rooms:** no A/C. **Cards:** DS, MC, VI.   CTV ⊠ D

TUNKHANNOCK (WYOMING COUNTY)

LODGING

SHARPE'S HOUSE BED & BREAKFAST   Rates Subject to Change   **Phone:** 717/836-4900
◆◆   All Year [CP]   1P: $50   2P/1B: $60- 70
Historic Bed   **Location:** From jct SR 29, 3.8 mi w on US 6, 1 mi n. 259 Bartron Rd 18657 (PO Box L, TUNKHANNOCK).
& Breakfast   Fax: 717/836-6107. **Terms:** Age restrictions may apply; check-in 4 pm; reserv deposit, 10 day notice; no pets. **Facility:** 2 rooms. Handling fee imposed; 2 stories; interior corridors; smoke free premises. **Dining:** Breakfast served 7-9 am. **Cards:** AE, MC, VI.   ⊠ D

TURTLE CREEK—*See Pittsburgh & Vicinity p. 414.*

ULSTER—300

RESTAURANT

BISHOP'S FAMILY RESTAURANT   **Lunch:** $3-$6   **Dinner:** $3-$9   **Phone:** 717/358-9999
◆   **Location:** Rt 220, just s. Main St 18850. **Hours:** 5:30 am-8 pm, Sat from 6 am, Sun from 7 am. Closed:
American   11/26 & 12/25. **Reservations:** accepted. **Features:** casual dress; health conscious menu items; carryout. Popular local family dining establishment offering good value & almost always busy.   ⊠

UNIONTOWN—*See Laurel Highlands p. 318.*

WARMINSTER—*See Philadelphia & Vicinity p. 387.*

WARREN—11,100

LODGINGS

HOLIDAY INN OF WARREN   **Phone:** 814/726-3000
AAA SAVE   5/15-10/31   1P: $64- 67   2P/1B: $70- 73   2P/2B: $70- 73   XP: $6   F12
   11/1-4/30   1P: $55- 60   2P/1B: $61- 66   2P/2B: $61- 66   XP: $6   F12
◆◆◆   **Location:** 1.5 mi w on US 6; at Ludlow St exit. 210 Ludlow St 16365. Fax: 814/726-3720. **Terms:** Small pets
Motor Inn   only, with signed waiver. **Facility:** 110 rooms. 4 stories; interior corridors; sauna; game room. **Dining & Entertainment:** Dining room; 6:30 am-2 & 5-9 pm, Fri-10 pm, Sat 7:30 am-2 & 5-10 pm, Sun 8 am-2 & 5-8 pm; $8-$17; cocktails/lounge. **Services:** valet laundry. **All Rooms:** coffeemakers, free movies. **Some Rooms:** microwaves. **Fee:** refrigerators. **Cards:** AE, CB, DI, DS, MC, VI. **Special Amenities:** Free local telephone calls.
   🛏 🏊 🐾 ECTV ⊠ D

WARREN SUPER 8 MOTEL   Rates Subject to Change   **Phone:** 814/723-8881
◆◆   5/15-10/31 [CP]   1P: $48   2P/1B: $52   2P/2B: $52   XP: $10-15   F
Motel   5/1-5/14 [CP]   1P: $40   2P/1B: $46   2P/2B: $46   XP: $10-15   F
   11/1-4/30 [CP]   1P: $45   2P/1B: $49   2P/2B: $45   XP: $10-15   F
Location: 1.5 mi w on US 6, at Ludlow St exit. 204 Struthers St 16365. Fax: 814/723-8881. **Terms:** Sr. discount; small pets only, $25 dep req. **Facility:** 56 rooms. 3 stories; interior/exterior corridors. **All Rooms:** Fee: movies. **Cards:** AE, CB, DI, DS, JCB, MC, VI.   🛏 CTV ⊠ D S

WARRENDALE—*See Pittsburgh & Vicinity p. 414.*

WASHINGTON—*See Pittsburgh & Vicinity p. 415.*

WASHINGTON CROSSING—*See Philadelphia & Vicinity p. 387.*

WATSONTOWN—200

LODGING

ALOHA MOTEL   Guaranteed Rates   **Phone:** 717/538-5979
AAA   All Year   1P: $50   2P/1B: $50   2P/2B: $60   XP: $5   F5
◆◆   **Location:** I-80, exit 30N, n on Rt 15 to Watsontown exit; from Rt 405, just w. 16 W Brimmer Ave 17777.
Motel   Fax: 717/538-2081. **Terms:** Sr. discount; reserv deposit, 7 day notice; pets. **Facility:** 8 rooms. 1 story; exterior corridors. **All Rooms:** efficiencies. **Cards:** AE, DS, MC, VI.   🛏 CTV D

WAYNE—*See Philadelphia & Vicinity p. 387.*

WAYNESBORO—10,000

LODGING

BEST WESTERN WAYNESBORO Rates Subject to Change **Phone:** 717/762-9113
◆◆ All Year [BP] 1P: $53 2P/1B: $58 2P/2B: $62 XP: $5 F12
Motel **Location:** 0.5 mi w on SR 16. 239 W Main St 17268. **Fax:** 717/762-9113. **Terms:** Sr. discount; reserv deposit; pets, $5 extra charge, in designated rooms. **Facility:** 52 rooms. 2 whirlpool rms, $75; Fri-Sun $95, rates for up to 2 persons; 2 stories; exterior corridors. **Dining:** Coffee shop; 6:30 am-10, Sat & Sun 7 am-11 am. **Cards:** AE, CB, DI, DS, MC.

🛏 ECTV ⊗ D

WAYNESBURG—4,300

LODGINGS

ECONO LODGE **Phone:** 724/627-5544
(AAA) (SAVE) All Year 1P: $40- 59 2P/1B: $44- 63 2P/2B: $44- 69 XP: $5 F17
◆◆ **Location:** Jct I-79, exit 3 & SR 21. 350 Miller Ln 15370. **Fax:** 724/627-5544. **Terms:** Pets. **Facility:** 60 rooms.
Motel 2 stories; exterior corridors. **All Rooms:** free movies. **Some Rooms:** coffeemakers, microwaves, refrigerators. **Cards:** AE, DI, DS, JCB, MC, VI. **Special Amenities: Free local telephone calls.**

🛏 ECTV ⊗ D

SUPER 8 MOTEL Rates Subject to Change **Phone:** 724/627-8880
◆◆ All Year [CP] 1P: $41- 51 2P/1B: $46- 56 2P/2B: $46- 56 XP: $5 F12
Motel **Location:** Jct I-79 exit 3 & SR 21. 80 Miller Ln 15370. **Fax:** 724/627-8880. **Terms:** Sr. discount; pets. **Facility:** 56 rooms. 3 stories; interior corridors. **All Rooms:** free movies. **Cards:** AE, DI, DS, MC, VI.

🛏 ECTV ⊗ 🐾 D S

WELLSBORO—3,400

LODGINGS

CANYON MOTEL Rates Subject to Change **Phone:** 717/724-1681
(AAA) All Year 1P: $28- 35 2P/1B: $35- 49 2P/2B: $38- 49 XP: $5 F12
◆◆◆ **Location:** Just e on US 6 & SR 660. 18 East Ave 16901. **Fax:** 717/724-5202. **Terms:** Reserv deposit; pets, in smoking rooms. **Facility:** 28 rooms. 1 story; exterior corridors. **Cards:** AE, CB, DI, DS, MC, VI.
Motel

🛏 🛜 CTV ⊗ D

COLTON POINT MOTEL **Phone:** 717/724-2155
(AAA) (SAVE) All Year 2P/1B: $40 2P/2B: $45 XP: $5 F12
◆ **Location:** 13 mi w on US 6 from jct Rt 287. 16901 (RD 4, Box 138). **Fax:** 717/724-6424. **Terms:** Reserv
Motel deposit, 7 day notice; weekly rates; MAP avail; package plans; no pets. **Facility:** 14 rooms. Quiet, rural location. 1 story; exterior corridors; boat dock; playground. **Dining:** Restaurant, coffee shop; 8-10 am. **Recreation:** nature trails; fishing; downhill skiing, snowmobiling. **All Rooms:** free movies, shower baths, no A/C, no phones. **Cards:** DS, MC, VI. **Special Amenities:** Early check-in/late check-out and preferred room (subject to availability with advanced reservations).

CTV ⊗ D

PENN WELLS LODGE Rates Subject to Change **Phone:** 717/724-3463
(AAA) 5/1-1/1 1P: $53- 61 2P/2B: $59- 69 XP: $5 F18
  1/2-4/30 1P: $30- 52 2P/2B: $39- 60 XP: $5 F18
◆◆ **Location:** Just n on US 6 & SR 287. 4 Main St 16901. **Fax:** 717/724-2270. **Terms:** No pets. **Facility:** 55 rooms.
Motel 2 stories; interior/exterior corridors. **Cards:** AE, CB, DI, DS, MC, VI.

🛜 CTV ⊗ D

SHERWOOD MOTEL Rates Subject to Change **Phone:** 717/724-3424
(AAA) 5/1-12/15 [CP] 1P: $28- 35 2P/1B: $40- 55 2P/2B: $45- 56 XP: $5 D12
  12/16-4/30 [CP] 1P: $25- 35 2P/1B: $35- 49 2P/2B: $39- 51 XP: $5 D12
◆◆◆ **Location:** Just n on US 6 & SR 287. 2 Main St 16901. **Fax:** 717/724-5658. **Terms:** Reserv deposit; no pets.
Motel **Facility:** 32 rooms. 2 stories; exterior corridors. **All Rooms:** free movies. **Cards:** AE, DI, DS, MC, VI.

🛜 CTV ⊗ D

RESTAURANTS

COACH STOP INN Lunch: $3-$5 Dinner: $7-$18 **Phone:** 717/724-5361
(AAA) **Location:** 10 mi w on US 6 from jct Rt 287. Rt 6 16901. **Hours:** 11 am-9 pm, Fri & Sat-10 pm, Sun-8 pm.
◆ Closed: 12/24-12/26. **Reservations:** suggested. **Features:** children's menu; carryout; salad bar; cocktails & lounge. Rural location, casual atmosphere. **Cards:** DS, MC, VI.
American ⊗

HARLAND'S FAMILY STYLE RESTAURANT Lunch: $3-$10 Dinner: $3-$10 **Phone:** 717/724-3311
(AAA) **Location:** Just e of Main St. 17 Pearl St 16901. **Hours:** 6 am-10 pm, Fri & Sat-midnight. Closed: 1/1, 11/26
◆ & 12/25. **Features:** children's menu; early bird specials; health conscious menu items; carryout; salad bar.
American Fresh fish & special menu on Fri. Homemade soup & pie. **Cards:** MC, VI. ⊗

THE LOG CABIN Lunch: $4-$6 Dinner: $7-$17 **Phone:** 814/435-8808
(AAA) **Location:** 13 mi w on US 6. Rt 6 16901. **Hours:** 4:30 pm-9 pm, Fri-10 pm, Sat 11:30 am-10 pm, Sun 11:30
◆◆ am-9 pm. Closed: 12/24 & 12/25. **Reservations:** suggested; Fri & Sat. **Features:** dressy casual; children's menu; health conscious menu items; carryout; salad bar; cocktails & lounge. Casual dining in an older log
Steakhouse cabin decorated with hunting trophies. Steak & seafood dishes. Fresh trout is a specialty. Soup & salad bar. Sunday menu-all specials $5.95-$6.95. **Cards:** DS, MC, VI. ⊗

PENN WELLS DINING ROOM Lunch: $3-$11 Dinner: $7-$17 **Phone:** 717/724-2111
(AAA) **Location:** On SR 660 s of US 6; in Penn Wells Hotel. 62 Main St 16901. **Hours:** 7-11 am, 11:30-1:30 & 5-9
◆◆ pm, Sun 7 am-9 pm. Closed: 12/25. **Reservations:** suggested; summer & wkends. **Features:** casual dress; Sunday brunch; children's menu; carryout; salad bar; cocktails & lounge. Inviting dining room with traditional
American decor. Varied dinner menu. Smorgasbord Sat for dinner. **Cards:** AE, CB, DI, DS, MC, VI. ⊗

THE STEAK HOUSE Dinner: $7-$18 **Phone:** 717/724-9092
(AAA) **Location:** Center. 29 Main St 16901. **Hours:** 5 pm-9 pm. Closed: 11/26, 12/25 & Sun.
◆ **Reservations:** suggested. **Features:** children's menu; carryout; cocktails & lounge; a la carte. Well-prepared dishes in casual family restaurant. Generous portions, plain presentation. Country inn decor. Homemade pie
Steakhouse & soup, fresh roast turkey dinners. **Cards:** AE, CB, DI, DS, MC, VI. ⊗

WEST CHESTER—*See Philadelphia & Vicinity p. 388.*

WEST HAZLETON—4,100

LODGINGS

COMFORT INN-WEST HAZLETON   Rates Subject to Change   **Phone: 717/455-9300**
◆◆◆   5/1-10/31 [CP]   1P: $65- 95 2P/1B: $72- 95 2P/2B: $73- 95 XP: $8   F18
Motel   11/1-4/30 [CP]   1P: $65- 80 2P/1B: $75- 80 2P/2B: $76- 80 XP: $8   F18
      Location: 0.3 mi se of I-81, exit 41; 3.8 mi se of I-80, exit 38. SR 93 & Kiwanis Blvd 18201 (RR 1, Box 301, HAZLETON). Fax: 717/455-8720. **Terms:** Sr. discount; pets. **Facility:** 119 rooms. 3 stories; interior corridors. **Dining:** Coffee shop; 5 pm-10 pm; $3-$8. **All Rooms:** free movies. **Cards:** AE, CB, DI, DS, JCB, MC, VI.   🛏 CTV ⊠ 🐾 D S

FOREST HILL INN   **Phone: 717/459-2730**
AAA SAVE   All Year   1P: $47   2P/1B: $52   2P/2B: $52   XP: $5   F12
      Location: On SR 93, 0.3 mi se of I-81, exit 41; 3.8 mi se of I-80, exit 38. Rt 93 18201 (RD 1, Box 262,
◆◆◆   HAZLETON). **Terms:** Reserv deposit; pets. **Facility:** 40 rooms. 2 stories; exterior corridors. **Cards:** AE, CB,
Motel   DI, DS, MC, VI. *(See color ad p 300)*   🛏 CTV ⊠ D

HAMPTON INN   Rates Subject to Change   **Phone: 717/454-3449**
◆◆◆   All Year [CP]   1P: $71- 89 2P/1B: $71- 89 2P/2B: $71- 89
Motel   **Location:** Jct I-81, exit 41 & SR 93; on SR 93 3.5 mi se of I-80, exit 38. I-81 & Hwy 93 18201 (RR 1, Box
273A, HAZLETON). Fax: 717/454-3396. **Terms:** Pets. **Facility:** 123 rooms. 3 stories; interior corridors.
All Rooms: free movies. **Cards:** AE, CB, DI, DS, MC, VI.   Roll in showers. 🛏 🛆 CTV 👤 ⊠ 🐾 D S

RESTAURANT

TOP OF THE 80'S RESTAURANT   **Lunch:** $6-$15   **Dinner:** $14-$26   **Phone: 717/454-8795**
◆◆◆   **Location:** Jct I-81, exit 41 & SR 93; on SR 93 3.5 mi se of I-80, exit 38. I-81 & SR 93 18201. **Hours:** 11:30
American   am-11 pm. Closed: 12/25. **Reservations:** suggested. **Features:** casual dress; children's menu; health conscious menu; carryout; cocktails & lounge; entertainment. Casually elegant mountaintop dining with beautiful scenic view of Conyngham Valley; menu features steak, crab cakes & creatively prepared daily specials.
Cards: AE, CB, DI, DS, MC, VI.   ♿ ⊠

WEST LAWN

RESTAURANT

AUSTIN'S RESTAURANT   **Lunch:** $12-$24   **Dinner:** $12-$24   **Phone: 610/678-5500**
◆◆   **Location:** From Bern Rd exit off US 422 in Wyomissing, 1.7 mi w on Bern Rd, 0.5 mi s on Van Reed Rd.
Steakhouse   1101 Snyder Rd 19609. **Hours:** 11 am-10 pm, Fri & Sat-11 pm. Closed: 1/1, 11/26 & 12/25.
      Features: casual dress; Sunday brunch; children's menu; carryout; cocktails & lounge. Casual dining in contemporary bustling atmosphere with open kitchen. Menu features steak, seafood, ribs, chicken, pasta & bountiful salads.
Cards: AE, MC, VI.   ⊠

WEST MIDDLESEX—1,000

LODGINGS

RADISSON HOTEL SHARON   Rates Subject to Change   **Phone: 724/528-2501**
◆◆◆   All Year   1P: $75   2P/1B: $75   2P/2B: $75   XP: $8   F18
Motor Inn   **Location:** On SR 18, s of I-80 exit 1N. Rt 18 & I-80 16159 (PO Box 596). Fax: 724/528-2306. **Terms:** Sr. discount; 16% service charge; small pets only. **Facility:** 153 rooms. 3 stories; interior corridors. **Dining:** Dining room; 6:30 am-2 & 5-10 pm; $12-$20. **All Rooms:** Fee: movies. **Cards:** AE, CB, DI, DS, JCB, MC, VI.
(See color ad p 394)   🛏 🚤 ECTV ⊠ D S

SHENANGO VALLEY COMFORT INN   Rates Subject to Change   **Phone: 724/342-7200**
◆◆   5/1-9/30 [CP]   1P: $55   2P/1B: $65   2P/2B: $70   XP: $5   F16
Motel   10/1-4/30 [CP]   1P: $50   2P/1B: $55   2P/2B: $60   XP: $5   F16
   Location: N on SR 18 at jct I-80, exit 1N. Rt 18 & Wilson Rd 16159. Fax: 724/342-7213. **Terms:** Reserv deposit; small pets only, $10 extra charge. **Facility:** 61 rooms. 3 whirlpool rms, extra charge; 2 stories; interior corridors. **All Rooms:** free movies. **Cards:** AE, DS, JCB, MC, VI.
     🛏 🚤 ⊠ D

WEST MIFFLIN—*See Pittsburgh & Vicinity p. 416.*

WEXFORD—*See Pittsburgh & Vicinity p. 416.*

WHITE HAVEN—1,100   (See map p. 418; index p. 417)

LODGINGS

DAYS INN & SUITES   **Phone: 717/443-0391**   🔳
AAA SAVE   All Year [CP]   1P: $55- 149   2P/1B: $65- 169   2P/2B: $75- 169   XP: $10   F12
   Location: I-80 exit 42 & PA tpk (I-476) exit 35, 2.8 mi e on SR 940. HCR 1, Box 35 18661.
◆◆   Fax: 717/443-7542. **Terms:** Package plans; weekend rates avail; pets, $5 extra charge. **Facility:** 40 rooms.
Motel   Spacious units. 2 stories; exterior corridors. **All Rooms:** coffeemakers, efficiencies, free movies, refrigerators, combo or shower baths. Fee: safes. **Some Rooms:** whirlpools. Fee: VCR's. **Cards:** AE, CB, DI, DS, JCB, MC, VI. **Special Amenities: Free breakfast and preferred room (subject to availability with advanced reservations).**
     🛏 CTV ⊠ D

RAMADA INN-POCONO   **Phone: 717/443-8471**   🔳
AAA SAVE   Fri & Sat   1P: $70- 175   2P/1B: $80- 175   2P/2B: $80- 175   XP: $10   F18
   Sun-Thurs   1P: $54- 150   2P/1B: $59- 150   2P/2B: $59- 150   XP: $10   F18
◆◆◆   **Location:** On SR 940, 0.5 mi e of I-80, exit 42 & tpk exit 35. (Rt 940, PO Box 809, LAKE HARMONY,
Motor Inn   18624). Fax: 717/443-0326. **Terms:** MAP avail; package plans; pets, $50 dep req. **Facility:** 137 rooms. 4 stories; interior corridors; sauna; game room. Fee: miniature golf. **Dining & Entertainment:** 2 restaurants; 7 am-2 & 5-10 pm, Fri & Sat-10:30 pm; $10-$18; cocktails/lounge. **Services:** guest laundry. **All Rooms:** free movies, safes. **Some Rooms:** coffeemakers, refrigerators, whirlpools. Fee: VCR's. **Cards:** AE, CB, DI, DS, JCB, MC.
     🛏 🚤 🍴 CTV ⊠ 🐾 D

RESTAURANTS

A TOUCH OF VANILLA   **Dinner: $16-$24**   **Phone: 717/443-8411**   🔳
◆◆◆   **Location:** On SR 940, at jct I-80 exit 42 & PA tpk (I-476) exit 35; in Mountain Laurel Resort. 18661.
American   **Hours:** 6 pm-9 pm, Fri & Sat-10 pm. Closed: Sun. **Reservations:** required. **Features:** dressy casual; children's menu; cocktails & lounge; a la carte, also prix fixe. Intimate, artful atmosphere. **Cards:** AE, DI, DS, MC, VI.
     ⊠

POWERHOUSE EATERY   **Lunch: $6-$15**   **Dinner: $15-$32**   **Phone: 717/443-4480**   🔳
◆◆   **Location:** 0.3 mi w of I-80, exit 40. Powerhouse Rd 18661. **Hours:** 4 pm-10 pm, Sun noon-10 pm. Closed:
American   12/24 & 12/25. **Reservations:** suggested; weekends. **Features:** casual dress; carryout; cocktails & lounge. Italian-American cuisine served in a turn-of-the-century power plant. **Cards:** AE, DS, MC, VI.
     ⊠

WILKES-BARRE—47,500   (See map p. 418; index p. 417)

LODGINGS

BEST WESTERN EAST MOUNTAIN INN   **Phone: 717/822-1011**   🔳
AAA SAVE   All Year   1P: $89- 119   2P/1B: $89- 129   2P/2B: $89- 129   XP: $5   F12
   Location: I-81 exit 47A, 0.5 mi se on SR 115. 2400 East End Blvd 18702. Fax: 717/822-6072.
◆◆◆   **Terms:** Weekly/monthly rates; no pets. **Facility:** 156 rooms. On mountain top with view of the valley & city. At-
Hotel   tractive public areas. 7 stories; interior corridors; sauna; whirlpool; playground. **Dining & Entertainment:** 2 restaurants; 6 am-11 pm; $8-$22; cocktails/lounge; entertainment. **Services:** area transportation, downtown. Fee: coin laundry. **All Rooms:** free & pay movies, VCR's. **Some Rooms:** coffeemakers, microwaves, refrigerators. **Cards:** AE, CB, DI, DS, JCB, MC, VI. *(See ad p 443)*
     🚤 🍴 🔧 🏊 CTV ⊠ D S

(See map p. 418)

BEST WESTERN GENETTI HOTEL & CONVENTION CENTER   **Phone:** 717/823-6152   16
All Year   1P: $59- 79   2P/1B: $69- 89 2P/2B: $69- 89 XP: $5   F16
Location: At Market & Washington sts. 77 E Market St 18701. **Fax:** 717/820-8502. **Terms:** Pets, $25 dep
req. **Facility:** 72 rooms. 5 stories; interior corridors. **Dining:** Restaurant; 7 am-2 & 5-9 pm; $7-$15.
Hotel   **All Rooms:** Fee: movies. **Cards:** AE, DI, DS, MC, VI. *(See color ad below)*

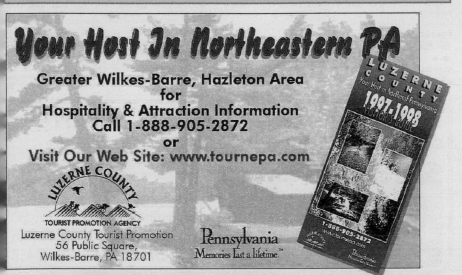

(See map p. 418)

ECONO LODGE   Phone: 717/823-0600 [23]
(AAA) (SAVE)   Fri & Sat [CP]   1P: $47   2P/1B: $53   2P/2B: $57   XP: $6   F18
◆◆   Sun-Thurs [CP]   1P: $43   2P/1B: $49   2P/2B: $53   XP: $6   F18
Motel   **Location:** On SR 309 business route at I-81 exit 45 southbound, exit 45B northbound. 1075 Wilkes-Barre Township Blvd 18702. Fax: 717/823-3294. **Terms:** Reserv deposit; weekly/monthly rates; no pets. **Facility:** 104 rooms. Immaculate, attractive rooms. 3 stories; interior corridors. **Dining:** Restaurant nearby. **Services:** Fee: coin laundry. **Some Rooms:** Fee: microwaves, refrigerators. **Cards:** AE, CB, DI, DS, MC, VI. **Special Amenities:** Free local telephone calls and free room upgrade (subject to availability with advanced reservations). *(See color ad below)*   (⌗) (CTV) (✕) (D) (S)

HAMPTON INN WILKES-BARRE AT CROSS CREEK POINTE   Rates Subject to Change   Phone: 717/825-3838 [19]
◆◆◆   All Year [CP]   1P: $60- 80   2P/1B: $68- 80   2P/2B: $68- 80
Motel   **Location:** 0.3 mi n of jct I-81, exit 47B. 1063 Hwy 315 18702. Fax: 717/825-8775. **Terms:** Sr. discount; small pets only. **Facility:** 122 rooms. 5 stories; interior corridors. **All Rooms:** free movies. **Cards:** AE, CB, DI, DS, MC, VI.   (☞) (CTV) (♠) (✕) (D) (S)

RAMADA PLAZA HOTEL   Guaranteed Rates   Phone: 717/824-7100 [20]
◆◆◆   All Year   1P: $69- 76   2P/1B: $74- 81   2P/2B: $74- 81   XP: $5   F18
Hotel   **Location:** SR 309, exit 2, s to city center, right to Public Square. 20 Public Square 18701. Fax: 717/823-5599. **Terms:** Sr. discount; no pets. **Facility:** 177 rooms. 8 stories; interior corridors. **Dining:** Dining room, restaurant; 6:30 am-11 pm; $9-$25. **All Rooms:** Fee: movies. **Cards:** AE, CB, DI, DS, JCB, MC, VI.   (✈) (CTV) (✕) (D) (S)

RED ROOF INN   Rates Subject to Change   Phone: 717/829-6422 [21]
◆◆   6/1-10/31   1P: $45- 62   2P/1B: $53- 70   2P/2B: $60- 75   XP: $7   F18
Motel   5/1-5/31 & 11/1-4/30   1P: $43- 60   2P/1B: $49- 66   2P/2B: $56- 73   XP: $7   F18
Location: At jct SR 115, 0.7 mi w of I-81, exit 47B, exit 1 on to SR 315. 1035 Hwy 315 18702. Fax: 717/820-7887. **Terms:** Small pets only. **Facility:** 115 rooms. 3 stories; exterior corridors. **All Rooms:** free movies. **Cards:** AE, CB, DI, DS, MC, VI.   (☞) (CTV) (✕) (D)

THE WOODLANDS INN & RESORT   Rates Subject to Change   Phone: 717/824-9831 [25]
◆◆◆   All Year   1P: $74- 119   2P/1B: $84- 139   2P/2B: $84- 139   XP: $10   F12
Motor Inn   **Location:** I-81 exit 47B onto SR 309 to exit 1, 0.3 mi n. 1073 Hwy 315 18702. Fax: 717/824-8865. **Terms:** No pets. **Facility:** 180 rooms. 2-9 stories; interior corridors. **Dining:** Restaurant; 6 am-11 pm, Sun 8 am-9 pm; $12-$25. **All Rooms:** free movies. **Some Rooms:** 25 kitchens. **Cards:** AE, CB, DI, DS, MC, VI.   (🏊) (🏊) (✈) (CTV) (✕) (D)

RESTAURANTS

KATANA   Lunch: $6-$12   Dinner: $12-$28   Phone: 717/825-9080 [19]
◆◆   **Location:** In Mid Town Village Shopping Plaza, just off Public Square. 41 S Main St 18701. **Hours:** 11:30 am-2:30 & 5-9:30 pm, Fri-10 pm, Sat 5 pm-10 pm, Sun 5-9 pm. Closed major holidays.
Ethnic   **Reservations:** suggested. **Features:** casual dress; children's menu; health conscious menu items; carryout cocktails & lounge; fee for parking. A Japanese Hibachi dining experience with sushi bar; weekday specials avail. **Cards:** AE, MC, VI.   (✕)

PASTA LOVERS   Lunch: $4-$6   Dinner: $6-$15   Phone: 717/821-0800 [21]
◆◆   **Location:** I-81 exit 46, 1.3 mi n on SR 309 business route. 410 Wilkes-Barre Township Blvd 18702. **Hours:** 11:30 am-9:30 pm, Fri & Sat-10:30 pm, Sun-9 pm. Closed major holidays. **Reservations:** suggested
Italian   for 5 or more. **Features:** casual dress; children's menu; early bird specials; health conscious menu items; carryout; cocktails & lounge; a la carte. Fine pasta, casual Italian garden atmosphere. **Cards:** AE, DI, MC, VI.   (✕)

PEKING CHEF   Lunch: $5-$6   Dinner: $8-$15   Phone: 717/825-0977 [20]
(AAA) (SAVE)   **Location:** Center. 15 Public Square 18701. **Hours:** 11:30 am-9:30 pm, Fri & Sat-10:30 pm. Closed: 11/26 & 12/25. **Reservations:** suggested. **Features:** casual dress; children's menu; carryout; cocktails & lounge.
◆◆   House specialties include seafood supreme, three flavor chicken, spicy garlic chicken, shrimp double delight
Chinese   steak-que & steamed vegetables. Free on street parking in front of restaurant after 6 pm or in rear all day. **Cards:** AE, DI, MC, VI. **Special Value:** 10% discount on the price of any entree, excluding beverages tax and gratuity.   (✕)

(See map p. 418)

PEKING CHEF-EAST   Lunch: $5-$9   Dinner: $9-$20   **Phone:** 717/824-1136   ⑱
Location: On Business Rt 309, 0.5 mi s of jct with SR 115. Wyoming Valley Mall 18702. **Hours:** 11 am-9 pm, Fri & Sat-10 pm, Sun noon-8 pm. Closed: 11/26 & 12/25. **Reservations:** suggested. **Features:** casual dress; children's menu; carryout; cocktails & lounge. House specials include seafood supreme, 3 flavor chicken, spicy garlic chicken, shrimp double delight, steak-que & steamed vegetables. **Cards:** AE, DI, MC, VI. **Special Value:** 10% discount on the price of any entree, excluding beverages, tax and gratuity. ✕
Chinese

WILLIAMSPORT—31,900—*See also SOUTH WILLIAMSPORT.*

LODGINGS

GENETTI HOTEL & SUITES   **Phone:** 717/326-6600
All Year   1P: $30- 80   2P/1B: $45- 95   2P/2B: $45- 95   XP: $6-10   F12
Location: Downtown, at W Fourth & William sts. 200 W Fourth St 17701. Fax: 717/326-5006.
Terms: Reserv deposit; monthly rates; package plans; pets. **Facility:** 200 rooms. 1922 landmark hotel. A few poolside rooms with outside entrance. 5 two-bedroom units. 10 stories; interior corridors; sauna. **Dining & Entertainment:** Restaurant; 7-10:30 am, 11:30-2 & 5-10 pm, Sun 7 am-2 pm; also 5 pm-9 pm in season; $9-$16; cocktails/lounge. **Services:** Fee: coin laundry. **All Rooms:** free movies, combo or shower baths. **Some Rooms:** 5 kitchens, whirlpools. Fee: microwaves, refrigerators, VCR's. **Cards:** AE, DI, DS, MC, VI. **Special Amenities:** Early check-in/late check-out and preferred room (subject to availability with advanced reservations).
(See color ad below)

HAMPTON INN WILLIAMSPORT   **Phone:** 717/323-6190
Motel   Under construction; **Location:** Downtown; jct 180, 220 & Rt 15. 160 Via Bella Dr 17701. **Facility:** 110 rooms. Scheduled to open April 1998.

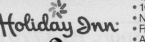

HOLIDAY INN-WILLIAMSPORT   Rates Subject to Change   **Phone:** 717/326-1981
◆◆   All Year   1P: $69   2P/2B: $69- 79 XP: $10   F18
Motor Inn   **Location:** Jct I-180 & US 220, Faxon St exit; just e on Third St eastbound, 1 mi w of Third St exit westbound. 1840 E Third St 17701. Fax: 717/323-9590. **Terms:** Sr. discount; small pets only. **Facility:** 160 rooms. 2 stories; exterior corridors. **Dining:** Restaurant; 6:30 am-1:30 am; $10-$15. **All Rooms:** free & pay movies. **Cards:** AE, CB, DI, DS, JCB, MC, VI. (See color ad p 445)

THE REIGHARD HOUSE   Guaranteed Rates   **Phone:** 717/326-3593
ⒶⒶⒶ   All Year [BP]   1P: $58- 68 2P/1B: $68- 78 2P/2B: $68- 78 XP: $25
◆◆◆   **Location:** Jct I-180 & US 220, Faxon St exit, 0.3 mi w. 1323 E Third St 17701. Fax: 717/323-4734.
Bed &   **Terms:** Reserv deposit; no pets. **Facility:** 6 rooms. 2 stories; interior corridors; designated smoking area.
Breakfast   **All Rooms:** free movies. **Cards:** AE, CB, DI, DS, MC, VI.

SHERATON INN   **Phone:** 717/327-8231
ⒶⒶⒶ ⓈⒶⓋⒺ   All Year   1P: $104   2P/1B: $114   2P/2B: $114 XP: $10   F17
◆◆◆   **Location:** Downtown, at jct US 220 & SR 15S. 100 Pine St 17701. Fax: 717/322-2957. **Terms:** Package plans; pets. **Facility:** 148 rooms. 2 whirlpool rms, extra charge; 5 stories; interior corridors. Fee: in-room
Hotel   video games. **Dining & Entertainment:** Restaurant; 6:30 am-2 & 5-10 pm; $12-$18; cocktails/lounge; entertainment. **Services:** valet laundry; area transportation, to hospitals & bus center. **All Rooms:** coffeemakers, free & pay movies. **Some Rooms:** microwaves, refrigerators. Fee: VCR's. **Cards:** AE, CB, DI, DS, MC, VI. **Special Amenities: Free local telephone calls and free newspaper.** (See color ad below)

RESTAURANTS

CHARLIE'S CABOOSE   **Dinner:** $10-$21   **Phone:** 717/327-9128
◆◆   **Location:** Downtown. Just n on Market St, just w on Little League Blvd. 500 Pine St 17701. **Hours:** 5 pm-10
American   pm. Closed major holidays & Sun. **Features:** casual dress; children's menu; health conscious menu items; cocktails. Dine in train cars set up inside building. Featuring steak, seafood & pasta. **Cards:** AE, MC, VI.

LEJEUNE CHEF   **Lunch:** $10-$17   **Dinner:** $17-$30   **Phone:** 717/327-4776
ⒶⒶⒶ   **Location:** On the Pennsylvania College of Technology campus. I-80 & US 220, Maynard St exit; n to W
◆◆◆   Third St, w to Park St. One College Ave 17701. **Hours:** 11:30 am-1:30 & 5:30-8 pm, Sat from 5:30 pm, Sun
Continental   11:30 am-1:30 pm; 5/15-8/15 Mon-Thurs 11:30 am-1:30, Wed-Sat 5:30 pm-8 pm, no Sun brunch. Closed major holidays. **Reservations:** suggested. **Features:** dressy casual; Sunday brunch; health conscious menu; beer & wine only; a la carte. Fine dining in teaching-learning environment. Classical cuisine also featured. Prix-fixe during academic year. Student chefs & staff. Extensive wine list. 15% service charge. Smoke free premises. **Cards:** AE, DS, MC, VI.

THE PETER HERDIC HOUSE Historical   **Dinner:** $9-$20   **Phone:** 717/322-0165
◆◆◆   **Location:** Downtown; w of Market St, between Elmira & Center sts. 407 W Fourth St 17701. **Hours:** 5
Continental   pm-9:30 pm. Closed major holidays & Sun. **Reservations:** accepted. **Features:** casual dress; health
    conscious menu items; carryout; cocktails & lounge; valet parking. In restored 1854 Heritage Victorian
mansion. Intimate dining rooms with nice table appointments. Ample selection of well prepared entrees. **Cards:** AE, MC, VI.
☒

PHILIPPE'S BISTRO   **Lunch:** $4-$10   **Dinner:** $10-$18   **Phone:** 717/326-6432
◆◆   **Location:** Downtown; between W 3rd & 4th sts, facing the county courthouse. 326 Court St 17701.
French   **Hours:** 11 am-2 & 5-9 pm, Sat 5 pm-10 pm, Sun 10 am-2 pm. Closed major holidays, 12/25 & Mon.
    Reservations: suggested. **Features:** casual dress; Sunday brunch; health conscious menu items; carryout;
cocktails; street parking; a la carte. Small, intimate bistro serving the cuisine of southern France plus a few pasta dishes.
Owner/chef. **Cards:** AE, DS, MC, VI.
☒

THOMAS LIGHTFOOTE INN   **Lunch:** $5-$7   **Dinner:** $11-$24   **Phone:** 717/326-6396
◆◆◆   **Location:** 5 mi w on I-180, Reach Rd exit, 1 mi s. 2887 S Reach Rd 17701. **Hours:** 11 am-2 & 5-9 pm, Fri
American   & Sat until 10 pm. Closed: 1/1, Sun, Mon & 12/23-12/26. **Reservations:** suggested. **Features:** casual dress;
    health conscious menu items; carryout; cocktails. 18th-century tavern. Imaginative variations of traditional
American cuisine. Working stone fireplace in dining rooms. Pub downstairs. Some continental entrees. Smoke free
premises. **Cards:** AE, DS, MC, VI.

TRIANGLE TAVERN   **Lunch:** $5-$11   **Dinner:** $5-$11   **Phone:** 717/322-9945
◆   **Location:** Just e of I-180 & US 220N, Faxon Rd exit. Between E Third & Washington Blvd. 308 Shiffler Ave
Italian   17701. **Hours:** 11 am-10 pm, Fri & Sat-11 pm. Closed: 11/26, 12/25 & Easter. **Features:** casual dress;
    children's menu; carryout; cocktails. Family owned since 1956. Unpretentious dining room. Also American
dishes & pizza. **Cards:** MC, VI.
☒

WILLOW GROVE—*See Philadelphia & Vicinity p. 388.*

WILLOW STREET—*See Pennsylvania Dutch Country p. 351.*

WINDBER—*See Laurel Highlands p. 319.*

WIND GAP—2,700

LODGING

TRAVEL INN OF WIND GAP   **Phone:** 610/863-4146

		1P:		2P/1B:		2P/2B:		XP:		
AAA SAVE	6/1-10/31	1P:	$60	2P/1B:	$65	2P/2B:	$70	XP:	$5	F10
	5/1-5/31 & 3/1-4/30	1P:	$50	2P/1B:	$55	2P/2B:	$60	XP:	$5	F10
◆◆	11/1-2/28	1P:	$45	2P/1B:	$50	2P/2B:	$55	XP:	$5	F10

Motel   **Location:** On SR 512, e of jct SR 33, Bath exit. 499 E Moorestown Rd 18091. Fax: 610/863-8951.
Terms: Reserv deposit; weekly rates; pets; $5 extra charge. **Facility:** 35 rooms. Rather small guest rooms with
vintage appointments; well maintained property. Handling fee imposed; 1 story; exterior corridors. **Dining:** Restaurant
nearby. **All Rooms:** free movies, combo or shower baths. **Some Rooms:** Fee: refrigerators. **Cards:** AE, DS, MC, VI.
**Special Amenities: Early check-in/late check-out and free room upgrade (subject to availability with advanced
reservations).** 🛏 CTV ☒ D

WOMELSDORF—2,300

RESTAURANT

THE STOUCH TAVERN 1785 Historical   **Lunch:** $5-$10   **Dinner:** $12-$20   **Phone:** 610/589-4577
◆◆◆   **Location:** Center. 138 W High St 19567. **Hours:** 11:30 am-2 & 5-9 pm, Fri-9:30 pm, Sat 5 pm-9:30 pm, Sun
American   noon-6:30 pm. Closed: 5/30, 9/1, Tues, 1/1-1/6 & 7/4-7/9. **Reservations:** suggested; weekends.
    Features: casual dress; children's menu; early bird specials; cocktails & lounge. Pleasant colonial
atmosphere. Hearty portions. Lunch buffet. Smoke free premises. **Cards:** AE, CB, DI, DS, MC, VI.
☒

WORMLEYSBURG—2,800   (See map p. 292; index p. 291)

RESTAURANT

CATALANO'S   **Lunch:** $5-$18   **Dinner:** $9-$32   **Phone:** 717/763-7905 ㉕
◆◆   **Location:** I-83, exit 22; 0.5 mi nw on 3rd St, 0.3 mi ne on Market St. 461 S Front St 17043. **Hours:** 11:30
Italian   am-10 pm, Sat from noon. Closed major holidays & Sun. **Reservations:** suggested. **Features:** casual dress;
    cocktails & lounge. Dining room & lounge views overlooking Susquehanna River & downtown; featuring
Italian & American cuisine. **Cards:** AE, DI, DS, MC, VI.
☒

WRIGHTSTOWN—*See Philadelphia & Vicinity p. 388.*

WRIGHTSVILLE—2,400

RESTAURANT

ACCOMAC INN Historical   **Dinner:** $16-$30   **Phone:** 717/252-1521
◆◆◆   **Location:** 1.5 mi n of Wrightsville exit off US 30, follow signs. S River Dr 17368. **Hours:** 5:30 pm-9:30 pm,
French   Sun 11 am-2:30 & 4-8:30 pm. Closed: 1/1 & 12/25. **Reservations:** suggested. **Features:** semi-formal attire;
    Sunday brunch; children's menu; health conscious menu items; cocktails & lounge; a la carte. A renowned
converted 18th-century inn & ferry crossing on the Susquehanna River. Champagne Sun brunch. Smoke free premises.
Cards: AE, MC, VI.
☒

WYOMISSING—7,300—*See also READING.*

LODGINGS

COUNTRY INN & SUITES BY CARLSON, WYOMISSING   **Phone:** 610/373-4444
AAA SAVE   All Year [CP]   1P: $65- 99   2P/1B: $75- 140   2P/2B: $75- 125   XP: $6
    Location: 1 mi s of US 422, Park Rd exit. 405 N Park Rd 19610. Fax: 610/373-4186. **Terms:** Monthly rates;
◆◆◆   package plans; no pets. **Facility:** 104 rooms. 3 stories; interior corridors; whirlpool; Gameroom.
Motel   **Dining:** Restaurant nearby. **Services:** Fee: coin laundry. **All Rooms:** coffeemakers, free movies, combo or
shower baths. **Some Rooms:** microwaves, refrigerators, whirlpools. **Cards:** AE, CB, DI, DS, JCB, MC, VI.
Special Amenities: Free breakfast and free newspaper. *(See color ad p 428)*
    Roll in showers. 📶 🈯 🛏 CTV ☒ 🕹 D

ECONO LODGE Phone: 610/378-5105
(AAA) (SAVE)   5/1-12/5 & 3/15-4/30 [CP]   1P: $49- 89   2P/1B: $49- 89   2P/2B: $49- 89   XP: $5   F18
◆◆   12/6-3/14 [CP]   1P: $45- 59   2P/1B: $45- 59   2P/2B: $45- 59   XP: $5   F18
Motel   **Location:** Just off US 422, Papermill Rd exit. 635 Spring St 19610. Fax: 610/373-3181. **Terms:** Weekly/monthly rates; small pets only, $5 extra charge. **Facility:** 84 rooms. 2 whirlpool rms, extra charge; 4 stories; interior corridors. **Dining:** Restaurant nearby. **Services:** Fee: coin laundry. **All Rooms:** free movies, combo or shower baths. Fee: VCR. **Some Rooms:** microwaves, refrigerators. **Cards:** AE, CB, DI, DS, JCB, MC, VI. **Special Amenities:** Free breakfast and free local telephone calls.   (🛏) (🍴) (📶) (CTV) (✕) (D)

HAMPTON INN   Rates Subject to Change   Phone: 610/374-8100
◆◆◆   All Year [CP]   1P: $69- 89   2P/1B: $73- 89   2P/2B: $69- 89   XP: $8   F18
Motel   **Location:** Papermill Rd exit off US 422, opposite Berkshire Mall. 1800 Papermill Rd 19610. Fax: 610/374-2076. **Terms:** No pets. **Facility:** 125 rooms. 5 stories; interior corridors. **All Rooms:** free movies. **Cards:** AE, CB, DI, DS, MC, VI.   (➔) (CTV) (✕) (📶) (D) (S)

THE INN AT READING   Rates Subject to Change   Phone: 610/372-7811
◆◆◆   All Year   1P: $89- 129   2P/1B: $89- 129   2P/2B: $89- 129   XP: $10   F18
Motor Inn   **Location:** 0.5 mi w on US 422, Park Rd exit. 1040 Park Rd 19610. Fax: 610/372-4545. **Terms:** Sr. discount; small pets only, $25 dep req. **Facility:** 248 rooms. Weekend rates for up to 4 persons; 13 rooms with exercycle; 2 stories; interior corridors. **Dining:** Dining room; 6:30 am-10 pm, Fri & Sat 7 am-11 pm, Sun 7 am-9 pm; $14-$30. **All Rooms:** free & pay movies. **Cards:** AE, DI, DS, MC, VI. *(See color ad p 428)*   (🛏) (🍴) (➔) (CTV) (✕) (📶) (D) (S)

SHERATON BERKSHIRE HOTEL   Rates Subject to Change   Phone: 610/376-3811
◆◆◆   All Year   1P: $113- 170   2P/1B: $152- 180   2P/2B: $123   XP: $10   F18
Hotel   **Location:** From US 422, exit Papermill Rd, opposite Berkshire Mall. 1741 W Papermill Rd 19610. Fax: 610/375-7562. **Terms:** Sr. discount; pets. **Facility:** 255 rooms. 2-4 stories; interior corridors. **Dining:** Dining room, restaurant; 6:30 am-10 pm; $9-$20. **All Rooms:** free & pay movies. **Cards:** AE, CB, DI, DS, JCB, MC, VI.   (🛏) (➔) (➔) (CTV) (✕) (📶) (D) (S)

WELLESLEY INN   Phone: 610/374-1500
(AAA) (SAVE)   5/1-11/30 & 4/1-4/30 [CP]   1P: $54- 110   2P/1B: $54- 110   2P/2B: $59- 110   XP: $5   F18
◆◆◆   12/1-3/31 [CP]   1P: $44- 89   2P/1B: $44- 89   2P/2B: $55- 89   XP: $5   F18
Motel   **Location:** US 422W, Papermill Rd exit, right at first stop light, 2 blks. 910 Woodland Ave 19610. Fax: 610/374-2554. **Terms:** Weekly rates; pets, $5 extra charge. **Facility:** 104 rooms. 4 stories; interior corridors; in-room video games. **Dining:** Restaurant nearby. **Services:** valet laundry. **All Rooms:** coffeemakers, free & pay movies. **Some Rooms:** microwaves, refrigerators. **Cards:** AE, CB, DI, DS, JCB, MC, VI. **Special Amenities:** Early check-in/late check-out and free local telephone calls. *(See color ad opposite inside back cover)*   (🛏) (🍴) (ECTV) (🔒) (✕) (📶) (D) (S)

WYSOX—500

LODGING

COMFORT INN   Rates Subject to Change   Phone: 717/265-5691
◆◆◆   All Year [CP]   1P: $74- 99   2P/1B: $81- 106   2P/2B: $69- 76   XP: $7   F18
Motel   **Location:** Center. US 6 18854 (RR 6, Box 6167A, TOWANDA, 18848). Fax: 717/265-2375. **Terms:** Sr. discount; pets. **Facility:** 51 rooms. 3 stories; interior corridors. **All Rooms:** free movies. **Cards:** AE, CB, DI, DS, JCB, MC, VI.   (🛏) (➔) (CTV) (🔒) (✕) (D) (S)

YORK—42,200

LODGINGS

BARNHART'S HOSPITALITY INN   Phone: 717/755-2806
(AAA) (SAVE)   All Year [CP]   1P: $35- 55   2P/1B: $40- 55   2P/2B: $42- 55   XP: $6   F12
◆◆   **Location:** I-83, exit 8 northbound, exit 8E southbound, 1.5 mi e on SR 462. 3021 E Market St 17402. Fax: 717/757-5475. **Terms:** Reserv deposit; weekly rates, in winter; no pets. **Facility:** 22 rooms. Up-to-date budget lodgings. 1 story; exterior corridors; basketball. **Dining:** Restaurant nearby. **Services:** winter plug-ins. Fee: coin laundry. **All Rooms:** free movies, refrigerators, combo or shower baths. **Some Rooms:** efficiency, microwaves. **Cards:** AE, CB, DI, DS, MC, VI. **Special Amenities:** Free breakfast and free local telephone calls. *(See color ad below)*   (ECTV) (✕) (D)

BEST WESTERN-WESTGATE   Rates Subject to Change   Phone: 717/767-6931
◆◆   All Year [CP]   1P: $59- 71   2P/1B: $69- 81   2P/2B: $69- 81   XP: $5   F18
Motel   **Location:** I-83 northbound, exit 9W, 2 mi w on US 30 then just n; I-83 southbound, exit 10, 0.5 mi s on SR 181, 1.7 mi w on US 30, just n. 1415 Kenneth Rd 17404. Fax: 717/767-6938. **Terms:** Sr. discount; no pets. **Facility:** 105 rooms. 3 stories; interior corridors. **All Rooms:** free movies. **Cards:** AE, DI, DS, MC, VI.   (➔) (ECTV) (✕) (D) (S)

BUDGET HOST INN SPIRIT OF 76   Rates Subject to Change   Phone: 717/755-1068
🔵   All Year   1P: $32- 38   2P/1B: $35- 40   2P/2B: $38- 50   XP: $4   F12
◆◆   **Location:** I-83, exit 7, just e on SR 124. 1162 Haines Rd 17402. Fax: 717/757-5571. **Terms:** No pets.
Motel   **Facility:** 40 rooms. 2 stories; exterior corridors. **Cards:** AE, DI, DS, MC, VI. *(See color ad p 254)*
    ⬛ ⊠ Ⓓ

THE CHATEAU MOTEL   Phone: 717/757-1714
🔵 SAVE   All Year   1P: $35- 39   2P/1B: $39- 43   2P/2B: $43- 47   XP: $4   F12
◆◆   **Location:** I-83, exit 8 northbound, 8E southbound; 3 mi e on SR 462. 3951 E Market St 17402.
Motel   **Terms:** Reserv deposit, 3 day notice; weekly rates, in winter; no pets. **Facility:** 12 rooms. 2-bedroom unit
$59-$69 for up to 3 persons. Handling fee imposed; 1 story; exterior corridors. **All Rooms:** free movies,
refrigerators, combo or shower baths. **Some Rooms:** microwaves. **Cards:** AE, DS, MC, VI.
**Special Amenities: Free local telephone calls and free room upgrade (subject to availability with advanced
reservations).**   ⬛ ⊠ Ⓓ

CLARION RESORT-THE INN AT HERITAGE HILLS   Rates Subject to Change   Phone: 717/755-0123
◆◆◆   All Year   1P: $89- 109   2P/1B: $96- 116   2P/2B: $96- 116   XP: $7   F18
Resort Hotel   **Location:** I-83 exit 7, 1 mi e on SR 124. 2700 Mount Rose Ave 17402. **Terms:** No pets.
Facility: 104 rooms. Presidential suite $395, rate for up to 4 persons; 13 whirlpool rms, extra charge; 5 stories;
interior corridors. **Dining:** Windows on the Green, see separate listing. **All Rooms:** free & pay movies. **Cards:** AE, CB, DI,
DS, MC, VI.   Roll in showers. ⬛ ⊠ Ⓓ Ⓢ

COMFORT INN & SUITES   Rates Subject to Change   Phone: 717/741-1000
◆◆◆   All Year [CP]   1P: $67- 85   2P/1B: $69- 87   2P/2B: $69- 87   XP: $8   F18
Motel   **Location:** I-83, exit 4, just w on SR 182. 140 Leader Heights Rd 17403. Fax: 717/741-5923. **Terms:** Sr.
discount; no pets. **Facility:** 136 rooms. 10 whirlpool rms, extra charge; 5 stories; interior corridors.
All Rooms: free movies. **Cards:** AE, CB, DI, DS, JCB, MC, VI.   Roll in showers. ⬛ ⊠ Ⓓ Ⓢ

DAYS INN CONFERENCE CENTER   Phone: 717/843-9971
🔵 SAVE   5/1-10/31 & 4/1-4/30 [CP]   1P: $69- 89   2P/1B: $69- 89   2P/2B: $69- 89   XP: $10   F12
   11/1-3/31 [CP]   1P: $49- 78   2P/1B: $49- 78   2P/2B: $62- 82   XP: $10   F12
◆◆   **Location:** I-83, exit 9E, just e on US 30. 222 Arsenal Rd 17402. Fax: 717/843-1806. **Terms:** Package plans;
Motel   small pets only, $10 dep req. **Facility:** 124 rooms. In busy commercial district. 2 stories; interior corridors.
Dining & Entertainment: Cocktail lounge; restaurant nearby. **Services:** Fee: coin laundry.
All Rooms: coffeemakers, free movies. **Some Rooms:** 2 efficiencies, microwaves, refrigerators. **Cards:** AE, DI, DS, MC, VI.
**Special Amenities: Free local telephone calls and preferred room (subject to availability with advanced
reservations).**   🛏 ➰ ⊕ ⬛ ⊠ Ⓓ

HAMPTON INN   Rates Subject to Change   Phone: 717/840-1500
◆◆◆   3/1-4/30 [CP]   1P: $84- 88   2P/1B: $96   2P/2B: $92
Motel   5/1-2/28 [CP]   1P: $79- 83   2P/1B: $91   2P/2B: $87
Location: I-83, exit 9E, 3 mi e on US 30 then just n on SR 24. 1550 Mt Zion Rd 17402. Fax: 717/840-1567.
Terms: No pets. **Facility:** 144 rooms. Rates for up to 4 persons; 5 stories; interior corridors. **All Rooms:** free movies.
Cards: AE, CB, DI, DS, MC, VI.   ➰ ⬛ ⊠ 🐾 Ⓓ Ⓢ

HOLIDAY INN EAST MARKET   Rates Subject to Change   Phone: 717/755-1966
◆◆◆   All Year   1P: $69- 75   2P/1B: $69- 75   2P/2B: $69- 75   XP: $10   F18
Motor Inn   **Location:** I-83 exit 8 northbound, 8E southbound, 1 mi e on SR 462. 2600 E Market St 17402.
Fax: 717/755-6936. **Terms:** Sr. discount; small pets only. **Facility:** 120 rooms. 2 stories; exterior corridors.
Dining: Restaurant; 6 am-2 & 5:30-10 pm, Sat & Sun from 7 am; $8-$17. **All Rooms:** free & pay movies. **Cards:** AE, CB,
DI, DS, JCB, MC, VI. *(See color ad below)*   🛏 ➰ ⊕ ⬛ ⊠ Ⓓ

HOLIDAY INN HOLIDOME & CONFERENCE CENTER   Rates Subject to Change   Phone: 717/846-9500
◆◆◆   All Year   1P: $89- 98   2P/1B: $89- 98   2P/2B: $89- 98   XP: $10   F18
Motor Inn   **Location:** I-83 northbound, exit 9W, 2.5 mi w on US 30, just n on SR 74; I-83 southbound, exit 10, 0.5 mi s
on SR 181, 2.2 mi w on US 30, just n. 2000 Loucks Rd 17404. Fax: 717/764-5038. **Terms:** Sr. discount;
pets, in designated rooms. **Facility:** 181 rooms. 2 stories; interior corridors. **Dining:** Restaurant; 6:30 am-2 & 4:30-10 pm;
$10-$19. **All Rooms:** free movies. **Cards:** AE, CB, DI, DS, JCB, MC, VI.   🛏 ➰ ➰ ⬛ ⊠ Ⓓ

HOLIDAY INN YORK I-83 & RT 30   Rates Subject to Change   Phone: 717/845-5671
◆◆◆   5/1-11/30 & 2/1-4/30   1P: $62   2P/1B: $62   2P/2B: $62
Motor Inn   12/1-1/31   1P: $49   2P/1B: $49   2P/2B: $49
Location: I-83, exit 9E, just e on US 30. 334 Arsenal Rd 17402. Fax: 717/845-1898. **Terms:** Sr. discount; no
pets. **Facility:** 100 rooms. Rates for up to 4 persons; 2 stories; exterior corridors. **Dining:** Restaurant; 6 am-2 & 5-10 pm,
Sat & Sun from 7 am; $8-$17. **All Rooms:** free & pay movies. **Cards:** AE, CB, DI, DS, JCB, MC, VI. *(See color ad below)*
    ➰ ⬛ ⊠ Ⓓ

RED ROOF INN
◆◆   Rates Subject to Change   Phone: 717/843-8181
Motel   5/1-11/30   1P: $37- 60 2P/1B: $45- 68 2P/2B: $47- 70 XP: $8   F18
         12/1-4/30   1P: $33- 56 2P/1B: $41- 64 2P/2B: $43- 66 XP: $6   F18
         Location: I-83, exit 9E, just e on US 30. 323 Arsenal Rd 17402. Fax: 717/843-8175. **Terms:** Small pets only.
Facility: 103 rooms. 3 stories; exterior corridors. **All Rooms:** free movies. **Cards:** AE, CB, DI, DS, MC, VI.

SUPER 8 MOTEL
◆◆   Rates Subject to Change   Phone: 717/852-8686
Motel   5/1-10/31 & 4/1-4/30   1P: $45- 49 2P/1B: $51   2P/2B: $55   XP: $5   F12
         11/1-3/31   1P: $42- 45 2P/1B: $48   2P/2B: $52   XP: $5   F12
         Location: I-83 northbound, exit 9W, 0.3 mi w on US 30; I-83 southbound, exit 10, 0.5 mi s on SR 181 to US
30. 40 Arsenal Rd 17404. Fax: 717/852-8686. **Terms:** Small pets only, $25 dep req. **Facility:** 94 rooms. 3 stories; interior cor-
ridors. **All Rooms:** free movies. **Cards:** AE, CB, DI, DS, MC, VI.

YORKTOWNE HOTEL
(AAA) (SAVE)   All Year   Phone: 717/848-1111
                1P: $52- 89 2P/1B: $59- 96 2P/2B: $78- 96 XP: $7   F18
         Location: On SR 462 eastbound & I-83 business route, just e of square. 48 E Market St 17401.
         Fax: 717/854-7678. **Terms:** Monthly rates; package plans; no pets. **Facility:** 161 rooms. 1925 National Historic
Historic Hotel Landmark Hotel, city center location. Some rooms very compact. 7 whirlpool rms, $125, rate for up to 2 per-
sons; 11 stories; interior corridors. **Dining & Entertainment:** Restaurant; 6:30 am-10 pm, Sun-noon;
$12-$19; cocktail lounge; The Commonwealth Room. **Services:** valet laundry; area transportation, within 10 mi; valet
parking. **All Rooms:** coffeemakers, free movies, combo or shower baths. **Some Rooms:** 8 efficiencies, microwaves,
refrigerators, phones. **Cards:** AE, DI, DS, MC, VI. **Special Amenities:** Early check-in/late check-out.

RESTAURANTS

THE COMMONWEALTH ROOM Historical   **Dinner:** $15-$24   Phone: 717/848-1111
◆◆◆   **Location:** On SR 462 eastbound & I-83 business route, just e of square; in Yorktowne Hotel. 48 E Market St
Continental 17401. **Hours:** 5:30 pm-9:30 pm. Closed major holidays. **Reservations:** suggested. **Features:** dressy
casual; children's menu; cocktails; street parking & valet parking; a la carte, also prix fixe. Comfortably
elegant dining room in historic downtown hotel. **Cards:** AE, CB, DI, DS, MC, VI.

FINLEY'S AMERICAN RESTAURANT   **Lunch:** $6-$8   **Dinner:** $8-$14   Phone: 717/755-1027
◆   **Location:** 0.8 mi e on SR 462 from jct I-83, exit 8E southbound; exit 8 northbound, just s on Haines Rd, 0.5
American mi e on Eastern Blvd. 2650 Eastern Blvd 17402. **Hours:** 11 am-10 pm, Fri & Sat-11 pm. Closed: 11/26 &
         12/25. **Features:** casual dress; children's menu; carryout. Casual family dining. Seasonally updated
specialties. Also chicken & rib entrees. **Cards:** AE, DI, DS, MC, VI.

ISAAC'S RESTAURANT & DELI   **Lunch:** $5-$7   **Dinner:** $5-$7   Phone: 717/751-0515
◆   **Location:** I-83, exit 9E, 3 mi e on US 30 then just n on SR 24; in Village at Meadowbrook shopping center.
American 2960 Whiteford Rd 17402. **Hours:** 10 am-9 pm, Fri & Sat-10 pm, Sun 11 am-9 pm. Closed major holidays.
         Features: casual dress; children's menu; carryout; a la carte. Pretzel sandwiches, pita pizzas & a wide
variety of healthful light fare. BYOB encouraged. **Cards:** AE, DS, MC, VI.

THE LEFT BANK RESTAURANT & BAR   **Lunch:** $6-$8   **Dinner:** $15-$24   Phone: 717/843-8010
◆◆◆   **Location:** On I-83 business route, just n of SR 462/74. 120 N George St 17401. **Hours:** 11 am-9 pm, Fri &
American Sat-10 pm. Closed major holidays & Sun. **Features:** dressy casual; cocktails & lounge; street parking. Chic
         bistro with very stylish presentation of popular favorites, including seafood, steak & lamb. Organic
vegetables, bread baked on premises featured. **Cards:** AE, MC, VI.

MR. BILL'S QUARTERDECK SEAFOOD
RESTAURANT & LOUNGE   **Lunch:** $5-$10   **Dinner:** $13-$23   Phone: 717/741-0872
(AAA)   **Location:** I-83, exit 4, just e on SR 182. 2600 Keyway Dr 17402. **Hours:** 11:30 am-10 pm, Fri & Sat-10:30
         pm, Sun-9 pm. **Reservations:** suggested. **Features:** casual dress; early bird specials; carryout; cocktails &
◆◆   lounge. Relaxed dining with nautical theme. Prime rib also featured. Raw bar. Outdoor deck in season.
Seafood **Cards:** AE, CB, DI, DS, MC.

ROOSEVELT TAVERN   **Lunch:** $4-$10   **Dinner:** $12-$23   Phone: 717/854-7725
◆◆◆   **Location:** 0.5 mi w on SR 462 & SR 74. 400 W Philadelphia St 17404. **Hours:** 11:30 am-9 pm, Fri &
American Sat-9:30 pm, Sun-7 pm. Closed major holidays. **Reservations:** suggested. **Features:** casual dress; Sunday
         brunch; children's menu; carryout; cocktails & lounge. Leisure dining in a casual atmosphere. **Cards:** AE, DI,
DS, MC, VI.

RUTTER'S FAMILY RESTAURANTS   **Lunch:** $5-$7   **Dinner:** $6-$8   Phone: 717/755-6616
◆   **Location:** I-83, exit 9E, 3 mi e on US 30 to SR 24, then just n. 1440 Mt. Zion Rd 17402. **Hours:** 5 am-10
American pm, Fri & Sat-11 pm, Sun 7 am-10 pm. Closed: 12/25. **Features:** casual dress; Sunday brunch; children's
         menu; health conscious menu; carryout; salad bar. Wholesome fare, family atmosphere. Lunch buffet
Mon-Fri 11 am-2 pm; weekend breakfast buffets. **Cards:** DS, MC, VI.

WINDOWS ON THE GREEN   **Lunch:** $6-$11   **Dinner:** $10-$24   Phone: 717/755-0123
◆◆◆   **Location:** I-83 exit 7, 1 mi w on SR 124; in Clarion Resort-The Inn at Heritage Hills. 2700 Mount Rose Ave
Continental 17402. **Hours:** 6 am-11 pm, Fri & Sat-midnight. **Reservations:** suggested; dinner. **Features:** dressy casual;
         Sunday brunch; carryout; cocktails & lounge. Stylish location overlooking pretty golf course & excellent fresh
fare prepared with a wide range of influences. Some dinner entrees avail in half portions. **Cards:** AE, CB, DI, DS, MC, VI.

ZELIENOPLE—See Pittsburgh & Vicinity p. 416.

For Your Information

Three handy sections to help make your vacation planning easier.

AAA CLUBS AND BRANCH OFFICES

Need a sheet map or Triptik map? Run out of travelers checks? Want the latest update on local road conditions? All this information and more awaits you at more than 1,000 AAA and CAA clubs and offices across the United States and Canada—a boon for travelers in an unfamiliar state, province or city. Each listing provides the office address, phone number and hours of service.

TEMPERATURE CHART

Knowing what clothes to pack for a trip can make the difference between pleasant vacationing and unpleasant surprises. Use the temperature chart to help determine your on-the-road wardrobe. The chart, found in each TourBook, lists average monthly maximum and minimum temperatures for representative cities.

DRIVING DISTANCES MAP

For safety's sake, it makes sense to take regular breaks while driving on the open road. The driving distances map is a quick and useful reference for trip planning—from a 1-day excursion to a cross-country jaunt. It provides both the mileage and the average driving time (excluding stops) between towns and cities located throughout a state or province.

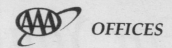 *OFFICES*

Cities with main offices are listed in **BOLD TYPE** and toll-free member service numbers in *ITALIC TYPE*
All are closed Saturdays, Sundays and holidays unless otherwise indicated.

The type of service provided is designated below the name of the city where the office is located:

    Auto travel services, including books/maps, marked maps and on-demand Triptik maps ✛
    Auto travel services, including books/maps, marked maps, but no on-demand Triptik maps ●
    Provides books/maps only. No marked maps or on-demand Triptik maps available ■
    Travel agency services ▲

NEW JERSEY

BRIDGEWATER—AAA Central-West Jersey, 500 Commons Way, 08807. Mon-Fri 9-6, Sat 9-4. (908) 722-2202, *(800) 374-9806.*✛▲

CAPE MAY COURT HOUSE—AAA Mid-Atlantic, 1200 US Rt 9 S, 08210. Mon-Fri 8:45-6, Sat 8:45-1. (609) 465-3033.✛▲

EDISON—AAA Central-West Jersey, 561 US Rt 1, 08817. Mon-Fri 9-6, Sat 9-4. (732) 985-9000.✛▲

ENGLISHTOWN—AAA Central-West Jersey, 318 Rt 9 at Union Hill Rd, 07726. Mon-Fri 9-6, Sat 9-4. (732) 972-3100, *(800) 374-9806.*✛▲

FAIR LAWN—AAA North Jersey, 23-16 Broadway, 07410. Mon-Fri 8:30-6, Mon 8:30-8, Fri 8:30-5, Sat 9-3. (201) 703-2000.✛▲

FLEMINGTON—AAA Central-West Jersey, 245 Rt 202 S Suite 1, 08822. Mon-Fri 9-6, Sat 9-4. (908) 782-3500, *(800) 374-9806.*✛▲

FLORHAM PARK—New Jersey Automobile Club, 1 Hanover Rd, 07932-1888. Mon-Fri 9-5, Mon & Wed 9-8, Sat 9-5. (973) 377-7200.✛▲

HAMILTON—AAA Central-West Jersey, 3 AAA Dr, 08691. Mon-Fri 9-6, Wed 9-7:30, Sat 9-4. (609) 890-2220, *(800) 374-9806.*✛▲

MILLVILLE—AAA South Jersey, 2277 N Second St, 08332. Mon-Fri 8:45-5, Wed 8:45-8, Sat 9-1. (609) 825-1212.✛▲

MOUNT LAUREL—AAA Central-West Jersey, 127 Ark Rd, 08054. Mon-Fri 9-6, Sat 9-4. (609) 778-8800.✛▲

NEWTON—AAA Central-West Jersey, 65 Newton Sparta Rd, 07860. Mon-Fri 9-6, Sat 9-4. (973) 383-5400.✛▲

NORTHFIELD—AAA Mid-Atlantic, 901 Tilton Rd, 08225. Mon-Fri 8:45-6, Sat 8:45-1. (609) 646-6000.✛▲

OCEAN—AAA Central-West Jersey, Rt 35 & Sunset Ave, 07712. Mon-Fri 9-6, Sat 9-4. (732) 918-0550.✛▲

ORADELL—AAA North Jersey, 505 Kinderkamack Rd, 07649. Mon-Fri 8:30-6, Thu 8:30-8, Fri 8:30-5, Sat 9-3. (201) 261-7900.✛▲

PHILLIPSBURG—AAA Central-West Jersey, 432 Memorial Pky, 08865. Mon-Fri 9-6, Sat 9-4. (908) 859-2177.✛▲

RANDOLPH—New Jersey Automobile Club, 711 Rt 10 E, 07869. Mon-Fri 9-5, Mon & Tue 9-8, Sat 9-5. (973) 361-0900.✛▲

SALEM—AAA South Jersey, 223 E Broadway Suite 105, 08079. Mon-Fri 8:45-5. (609) 935-8525.●▲

SECAUCUS—AAA North Jersey, 40C Meadowland Pky, 07094. Mon-Fri 8:30-6, Wed 8:30-8, Fri 8:30-5, Sat 9-3. (201) 902-1393.✛▲

SEWELL—AAA South Jersey, 508 Hurffville/Cross Keys Rd, 08080. Mon-Fri 8:45-5, Wed 8:45-8, Sat 8:45-1. (609) 589-6900.✛▲

SKILLMAN—AAA Central-West Jersey, 1378 Rt 206, 08558. Mon-Fri 9-6, Sat 9-4. (609) 683-4400.✛▲

SOUTH ORANGE—New Jersey Automobile Club, 136 S Orange Ave, 07079. Mon-Fri 9-5:30. (973) 763-4800.▲

SPRINGFIELD—New Jersey Automobile Club, 24 Echo Plz, 07081. Mon-Fri 9-5, Mon & Thu 9-8, Sat 9-5. (973) 467-2651.✛▲

TOMS RIVER—AAA Central-West Jersey, 864 Rt 37 W, 08755. Mon-Fri 9-6, Sat 9-4. (732) 244-6800.✛▲

VERONA—New Jersey Automobile Club, 155 Pompton Ave, 07044. Mon-Fri 9-5, Mon & Thu 9-8, Sat 9-5. (973) 857-5900.✛▲

VOORHEES—AAA South Jersey, 700 Laurel Oak Rd, 08043. Mon-Fri 8:45-5, Thu 8:45-8, Sat 9-3. (609) 783-4222.✛▲

WAYNE—AAA North Jersey, 418 Hamburg Tpke, 07470. Mon-Fri 8:30-6, Tue 8:30-8, Fri 8:30-5, Sat 9-3. (973) 956-2200.✛▲

PENNSYLVANIA

ALLENTOWN—AAA Lehigh Valley, 1020 Hamilton St, 18101-1085. Mon-Fri 9-5, Thu 9-8, Sat 9-12. (610) 434-5141.✛▲

ALLENTOWN—AAA Lehigh Valley, 4743 Tilghman St, 18104. Mon-Fri 9-6, Tue & Wed & Thu 9-8, Sat 10-5. (610) 336-9620.●▲

ALTOONA—AAA Blair County, 1634 Valley View Blvd, 16602. Mon-Fri 9-5, Sat 9-12. (814) 946-1277.✛▲

AMBRIDGE—AAA West Penn/West Virginia, 1236 Merchant St, 15003. Mon-Fri 9-5, Sat 10-2. (724) 266-5944.✛▲

BEDFORD—AAA Southern Pennsylvania, 317 S Richard St, 15522. Mon-Fri 9-5, Fri 9-7, Sat 9-12. (814) 623-5196, *(800) 222-1469.*●▲

BELLE VERNON—AAA West Penn/West Virginia, RD 2 Rt 201, 15012-0627. Mon-Fri 9-5, Sat 10-2. (724) 929-3310.✛▲

BETHLEHEM—AAA Lehigh Valley, 1520 Stefko Blvd, 18017-6296. Mon-Fri 9-5, Tue 9-8, Sat 9-12. (610) 867-7502.✛▲

BLOOMSBURG—AAA Mid-Atlantic, 460 Central Rd, 17815. Mon-Fri 8-5. (717) 784-3380.✛▲

BRADFORD—McKean County Motor Club, 587 South Ave, 16701. Mon-Fri 8:30-5, Fri 8:30-7. (814) 368-3113, *(800) 223-9562.*✛▲

BROOKVILLE—AAA West Penn/West Virginia, 195 Main St, 15825. Mon-Fri 8:30-5. (814) 849-5381, *(800) 522-9968.*✛▲

BUTLER—AAA West Penn/West Virginia, 138 Clearview Cir, 16001. Mon-Fri 9-5:30, Sat 9-12:30. (724) 287-2713.✛▲

CAMP HILL—AAA Central Penn Automobile Club, 3433 Trindle Rd, 17011. Mon-Fri 9-5, Sat 9-12. (717) 761-6811.✛▲

CARBONDALE—AAA Northeast Penn, 18 S Main St, 18407. Mon-Fri 9-5, Sat 9-12. (717) 282-1390.✛▲

CARLISLE—AAA Central Penn Automobile Club, 701C South West St, 17013-4117. Mon-Fri 9-5, Sat 9-12. (717) 243-1844.✛▲

CHAMBERSBURG—AAA Southern Pennsylvania, 230 Lincoln Way E, 17201. Mon-Fri 9-5, Fri 9-7, Sat 9-12. (717) 264-4191, *(800) 222-1469.*●▲

CORRY—AAA Erie County, 637 N Center St, 16407. Mon-Fri 9-5, Mon 9-7. (814) 665-3955.✛▲

COUDERSPORT—AAA North Central PA, 107 S Main St, 16915. Mon-Fri 8:30-5. (814) 274-8470.✛▲

CRANBERRY TOWNSHIP—AAA West Penn/West Virginia, 3 Landmark N 20395 Rt 19, 16066. Mon-Fri 10-6, Sat 10-2. (724) 772-1122.✛▲

DALLAS—AAA Mid-Atlantic, 309/415 Dallas Plz Bldg 4, 18612. Mon-Fri 8-5. (717) 675-8282.✛▲

DANVILLE—AAA Mid-Atlantic, 246 Walnut St Rt 11, 17821. Mon-Fri 8-5. (717) 275-1142.✛▲

DUBOIS—AAA Southern Pennsylvania, DuBois Mall, 15801. Mon-Fri 9-5, Fri & Sat 9-7. (814) 371-7001, *(800) 222-1469.*●▲

EASTON—**AAA Northampton County, 3914** Hecktown Rd, 18045. Mon-Fri 9-5, Tue 11-8, Sat 9-1. (610) 258-2371.✛▲

ERIE—**AAA Erie County,** 420 W 6th St, 16507. Mon-Fri 9-5, Mon 9-7. (814) 455-7538.✛▲

GETTYSBURG—AAA Central Penn Automobile Club, 1275 York Rd, 17325. Mon-Fri 9-5, Sat 9-12. (717) 334-1155.✛▲

GIRARD—AAA Erie County, 511 E Main St, 16417. Mon-Fri 9-5, Mon 9-7. (814) 774-9695.✛

GREENSBURG—AAA West Penn/West Virginia, 100 N Maple Ave, 15601-0458. Mon-Fri 9-5, Sat 10-2. (724) 834-8300.✛▲

GREENVILLE—AAA West Penn/West Virginia, 311 Main St, 16125. Mon-Fri 8:30-5. (724) 588-4300.✛▲

GROVE CITY—AAA West Penn/West Virginia, 112 Blair St, 16127. Mon-Fri 8:30-5. (724) 458-8930.●▲

HANOVER—AAA Southern Pennsylvania, Carlisle St, 17331. Mon-Fri 9-5, Fri 9-7, Sat 9-5. (717) 637-2400, *(800) 222-1469.*●▲

HARRISBURG—**AAA Central Penn Automobile Club,** 2023 Market St, 17103. Mon-Fri 9-5, Sat 9-12. (717) 236-4021, *(800) 717-4222.*✛▲

HARRISBURG—AAA Central Penn Automobile Club, 2301 Paxton Church Rd, 17110. Mon-Fri 9-5, Sat 9-12. (717) 657-2244.✛▲

HAVERFORD—AAA Mid-Atlantic, 394 W Lancaster Ave, 19041. Mon-Fri 8:45-5, Wed 8:45-8, Sat 8:45-1. (610) 649-9000.✛▲

HAZLETON—AAA Mid-Atlantic, 93 Airport Rd Suite I, 18201-6408. Mon-Fri 8:30-5, Wed 8:30-7, Sat 8:30-1. (717) 454-6658.✛▲

HERMITAGE—AAA West Penn/West Virginia, 1749 E State St, 16148. Mon-Fri 8:30-5. (724) 981-9141.✛▲

HERSHEY—AAA Central Penn Automobile Club, 11 Briarcrest Sq, 17033. Mon-Fri 9-5, Sat 9-12. (717) 533-3381.✛▲

HONESDALE—AAA Northeast Penn, 602 Church St, 18431. Mon-Fri 9-5, Sat 9-12. (717) 253-0160.✛▲

HUNTINGDON—AAA Central Penn Automobile Club, 608 Washington St, 16652. Mon-Fri 9-5, Sat 9-12. (814) 643-1030.✛▲

INDIANA—AAA West Penn/West Virginia, 1169 Wayne Ave, 15701-3549. Mon-Fri 8:30-5, Thu 8:30-7. (724) 349-4193.✛▲

JOHNSTOWN—AAA Southern Pennsylvania, 500 Galleria Dr, 15904. Mon-Fri 9-9, Tue & Thu & Sat 9-5. (814) 269-3641, *(800) 222-1469.*●▲

KITTANNING—AAA West Penn/West Virginia, 250 S Jefferson St, 16201. Mon-Fri 8:30-5, Sat 8:30-12. (724) 543-1924.✛▲

LANCASTER—**AAA Lancaster County,** 804 Estelle Dr, 17601-2121. Mon-Fri 8-5, Wed 10-7, Sat 8-12. (717) 298-6900.●▲

LANCASTER—AAA Lancaster County, 34 N Prince St, 17603-3866. Mon-Fri 8-5, Sat 8-12. (717) 397-4444.✛▲

LANGHORNE—AAA Mid-Atlantic, 584 Middletown Blvd A100, 19047. Mon-Fri 8:45-5, Wed 8:45-8, Sat 8:45-1. (215) 702-0700.✛▲

LANSDALE—AAA East Penn, 157 S Broad St, 19446-2036. Mon-Fri 9-5:30, Wed 9-6:30. (215) 855-8600.✛▲

LEBANON—AAA Central Penn Automobile Club, 984 Isabel Dr, 17042-7483. Mon-Fri 9-5, Sat 9-12. (717) 273-8533.✛▲

LEWISBURG—AAA Susquehanna Valley, 530 1/2 N Derr Dr, 17837. Mon-Fri 9-5, Closed 12-1. (717) 524-7455.●

LEWISTOWN—AAA Central Penn Automobile Club, 33 N Brown St, 17044. Mon-Fri 9-5, Sat 9-12. (717) 242-2221.✛▲

LITITZ—AAA Lancaster County, 120 W Airport Rd #B, 17543-9259. Mon-Fri 8-5, Sat 8-12. (717) 560-8706.●▲

LOCK HAVEN—AAA Southern Pennsylvania, 12 Oriole Rd, 17745. Mon-Fri 9-5, Fri 9-7, Sat 9-12. (717) 748-2405, *(800) 222-1469.*●▲

LOWER BURRELL—AAA West Penn/West Virginia, 2503 Leechburg Rd, 15068. Mon-Fri 9-5. (724) 339-4440.✛▲

MEADVILLE—AAA West Penn/West Virginia, 19023 Park Ave Plz, 16335. Mon-Fri 8:30-5. (814) 724-2247.✛▲

MONTROSE—AAA Northeast Penn, 61 Church St #102, 18801. Mon-Fri 9-5. (717) 278-1552.●▲

NEW CASTLE—AAA West Penn/West Virginia, 40 East St, 16101. Mon-Fri 9-5, Sat 10-2. (412) 658-8551.✛▲

NORTH EAST—AAA Erie County, 61 W Main St, 16428. Mon-Fri 9-5, Mon 9-7. (814) 725-3503.✛

ORWIGSBURG—AAA Schuylkill County, 340 S Liberty St, 17961. Mon-Fri 8:30-5. (717) 366-4991.●▲

PHILADELPHIA—**AAA Mid-Atlantic,** 2040 Market St, 19103. Mon-Fri 8-6. (215) 864-5000.✛▲

PHILADELPHIA—AAA Mid-Atlantic, Bustleton Ave & Levick St, 19149. Mon-Fri 8:45-5, Wed 8:45-8, Sat 8:45-1. (215) 289-6100.✛▲

PITTSBURGH—**AAA West Penn/West Virginia,** 5900 Baum Blvd, 15206-3854. Mon-Fri 8:30-5, Sat 10-2. (412) 363-5100, *(800) 441-5008.*✛▲

PITTSBURGH—AAA West Penn/West Virginia, 160 Fort Couch Rd, 15241. Mon-Fri 10-8, Sat 10-5. (412) 833-5203.✛▲

PITTSBURGH—AAA West Penn/West Virginia, 538 Smithfield St, 15222. Mon-Fri 8:30-5. (412) 338-4300.✛▲

PITTSBURGH—AAA West Penn/West Virginia, 201 Penn Center Blvd, 15235-5435. Mon-Fri 9-8, Sat 9-5. (412) 824-9990.✛▲

PITTSBURGH—AAA West Penn/West Virginia, 4790 McKnight Rd, 15237. Mon-Fri 9-8, Sat 9-5. (412) 367-7600.✛▲

PLYMOUTH MEETNG—AAA Mid-Atlantic, 505 W Germantown Pike, 19462. Mon-Fri 8:45-5, Wed 8:45-8, Sat 8:45-1. (610) 825-4001.✛▲

POTTSTOWN—**AAA East Penn,** 95 S Hanover St, 19464-5447. Mon-Fri 9-5:30, Wed 9-6:30. (610) 323-6300, *(800) 564-0300.*✛▲

POTTSVILLE—**AAA Schuylkill County,** 340 S Center St, 17901. Mon-Fri 8:30-5, Sat 9-12. (717) 622-4991.✛▲

RENO—AAA West Penn/West Virginia, Allegheny Ave, 16343. Mon-Fri 8:30-5. (814) 676-6551.✛▲

ROCHESTER—AAA West Penn/West Virginia, 300 Adams St, 15074. Mon-Fri 9-5, Sat 10-2. (724) 775-8000.✛▲

ST MARYS—AAA West Penn/West Virginia, 50 S St Marys St, 15857. Mon-Fri 8:30-5. (814) 834-7838.✛▲

SCRANTON—**AAA Northeast Penn,** 1035 N Washington Ave, 18509. Mon-Fri 8-5, Sat 8-5. (717) 348-2511, *(800) 982-4306.*✛▲

SHIPPENSBURG—AAA Southern Pennsylvania, Walnut Bottom Rd, 17257. Mon-Fri 9-5, Fri 9-7, Sat 9-12. (717) 532-6500, *(800) 222-1469.*●▲

SOMERSET—AAA West Penn/West Virginia, 110 N Center Ave, 15501. Mon-Fri 8:30-5, Fri 8:30-8. (814) 443-6526.✛▲

SOUTH WILLIAMSPORT—**AAA North Central PA,** 1 E 6th Ave, 17701. Mon-Fri 8:30-5, Mon 8:30-9. (717) 323-8431.✛▲

SPRINGFIELD—AAA Mid-Atlantic, 943 W Sproul Rd, 19064. Mon-Fri 8:45-5, Wed 8:45-8, Sat 8:45-1. (610) 544-3000.✛▲

STATE COLLEGE—AAA Southern Pennsylvania, 200 Shiloh Rd, 16801. Mon-Fri 9-5, Sat 9-5. (814) 237-0305, *(800) 222-1469.*●▲

STROUDSBURG—AAA Northeast Penn, Rt 611 RR7, 18360. Mon-Fri 9-5, Sat 9-12. (717) 421-2500.✛▲

SUNBURY—AAA Susquehanna Valley, 1001 Market St, 17801. Mon-Fri 9-5. (717) 286-4507.✛▲

TAMAQUA—AAA Schuylkill County, 202 E Broad St, 18252. Mon-Fri 8:30-5, Sat 9-12. (717) 668-1003.●▲

TOWANDA—AAA Northeast Penn, 515 Main St, 18848. Mon-Fri 9-5, Sat 9-12. (717) 265-6122.✛

TUNKHANNOCK—AAA Northeast Penn, 25 E Tioga St, 18657. Mon-Fri 9-5, Sat 9-12. (717) 836-5104.●▲

UNIONTOWN—AAA West Penn/West Virginia, 111 W Main St, 15401. Mon-Fri 8:30-5, Fri 8:30-8. (724) 438-8575.✛▲

WARREN—AAA West Penn/West Virginia, 1419 Market St Ext, 16365. Mon-Fri 9-5. (814) 723-6660.✛▲

WARRINGTON—AAA Mid-Atlantic, 1635 Easton Road, 18976. Mon-Fri 8:45-5, Wed 8:45-8, Sat 8:45-1. (215) 343-2660.✛▲

WASHINGTON—AAA West Penn/West Virginia, 196 Murtland Ave, 15301. Mon-Fri 8:30-5, Sat 8:30-12. (724) 222-3800.✛▲

WAYNESBORO—AAA Southern Pennsylvania, 2021 E Main St, 17268. Mon-Fri 9-5. (717) 762-9101, *(800) 222-1469.*●▲

WAYNESBURG—AAA West Penn/West Virginia, 89 S Washington St, 15370. Mon-Fri 9:30-5:30. (724) 627-3434.✛▲

WELLSBORO—AAA North Central PA, Queen St & Water St, 16901. Mon-Fri 8:30-5. (717) 724-4134.✛▲

WEST CHESTER—AAA Mid-Atlantic, 844 Paoli Pike, 19380. Mon-Fri 8:45-5, Wed 8:45-8, Sat 8:45-1. (610) 696-8100.✛▲

WEST MIFFLIN—AAA West Penn/West Virginia, 2070 Lebanon Church Rd, 15122-2432. Mon-Fri 10-8, Sat 10-5. (412) 655-6100.✛▲

WEST PITTSTON—AAA Mid-Atlantic, 200 Wyoming Ave, 18643. Mon-Fri 9-5:30. (717) 883-2582.✛▲

WHITE OAK—AAA West Penn/West Virginia, 2001 Lincoln Way, 15131. Mon-Fri 10-6, Sat 10-2. (412) 675-3400.✛▲

WILKES-BARRE—AAA Mid-Atlantic, 100 Hazle St, 18702. Mon-Fri 8-5. (717) 824-2444, *(800) 222-2410.*✛▲

WYOMISSING—AAA Reading-Berks, 920 Van Reed Rd, 19610. Mon-Fri 9-5, Wed 9-7, Sat 9-12. (610) 374-4531.✛▲

YORK—AAA Southern Pennsylvania, 118 E Market St, 17401. Mon-Fri 9-5. (717) 845-7676, *(800) 222-1469.*✛▲

YORK—AAA Southern Pennsylvania, 2512 Eastern Blvd, 17402. Mon-Fri 9-9, Tue & Thu & Sat 9-5. (717) 751-0514, *(800) 222-1469.*●▲

ZELIENOPLE—AAA West Penn/West Virginia, 200 S Main St, 16063. Mon-Fri 8:45-5, Sat 8:45-12:30. (724) 452-5504.✛▲

Temperature Averages - Maximum/Minimum
From the records of the National Weather Service

	JAN.	FEB.	MAR.	APR.	MAY	JUNE	JULY	AUG.	SEPT.	OCT.	NOV.	DEC.
NEW JERSEY												
Atlantic City	43	43	50	60	71	79	84	82	76	67	56	45
	27	26	32	42	52	61	66	65	58	48	38	28
Newark	40	41	49	61	72	81	86	84	77	66	54	42
	25	25	32	42	52	61	67	65	58	47	37	27
PENNSYLVANIA												
Allentown	37	38	47	61	72	81	85	83	76	65	51	39
	21	20	28	38	49	58	63	61	54	43	33	23
Erie	34	34	42	55	66	76	80	79	72	61	48	37
	21	19	26	36	47	57	62	61	55	44	34	25
Harrisburg	39	40	49	62	73	82	86	84	77	66	52	41
	25	25	32	42	52	61	65	64	56	46	36	26
Philadelphia	40	42	50	63	73	82	86	84	77	67	54	42
	24	25	32	41	52	60	65	64	56	45	35	26
Pittsburgh	37	38	46	60	71	80	83	82	76	64	50	43
	21	21	27	38	48	57	61	60	53	42	32	27
Reading...............	39	41	49	62	73	82	86	84	77	67	53	41
	26	26	33	43	53	63	67	66	58	48	38	28
Scranton..............	33	34	43	56	68	76	81	78	70	60	46	35
	21	20	28	38	49	58	62	60	53	42	33	23

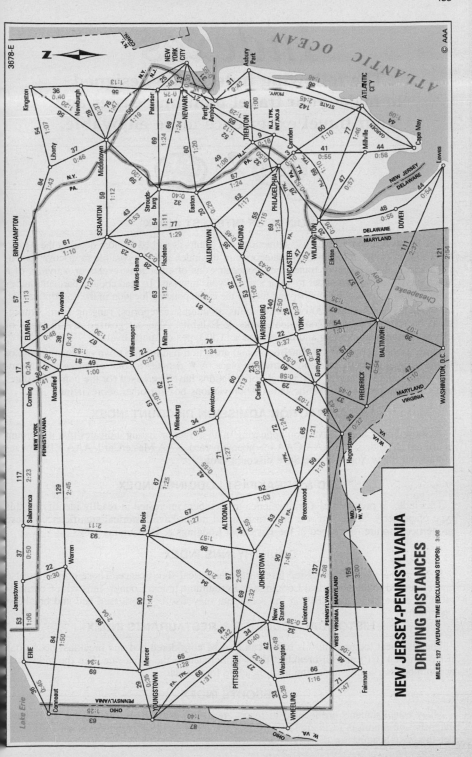

NEW JERSEY-PENNSYLVANIA
DRIVING DISTANCES

MILES: 137   AVERAGE TIME (EXCLUDING STOPS): 3:08

3678-E

© AAA

Indexes

The following indexes are designed
to make your travel planning easier and
your travel experience more enjoyable.

POINTS OF INTEREST INDEX

The Points of Interest Index lists attractions and events described in more detail in the Attractions section of the TourBook. The categories of the index make it possible to discover potential vacation destinations or routes with concentrations of attractions, events or activities of a specific type—making it easier to tailor a trip to your interests. To read about a particular index entry, simply note its page number and turn to the corresponding location in the descriptive text.

AAA/CAA uses nearly 200 specific points of interest categories, ranging from Amusement & Theme Parks to Zoological Parks & Exhibits. Also categorized are 15 types of events, 13 types of exhibits and collections and 10 types of sports events.

Index entries appear in the TourBook as an attraction listing, as a town or place listing, or in the general text of a referenced town or place. A ★ denotes a point of interest of unusually high quality. Standard U.S. postal abbreviations have been used for the names of states and Canadian provinces. See the Index Abbreviations box for other abbreviations used.

SAVE ATTRACTION ADMISSION DISCOUNT INDEX

A Show Your Card & Save icon appearing in an attraction listing indicates that a discount is offered to holders of a AAA/CAA membership card, AAA MasterCard, AAA VISA or international Show Your Card & Save discount card.

BED & BREAKFAST LODGINGS INDEX

This index is provided as a convenience to members interested in readily identifying this type of property. Some bed and breakfasts listed might have historical significance. Those properties also are referenced in the Historical Lodgings & Restaurants Index.

COUNTRY INNS INDEX

Some of the country inns listed might have historical significance. Those properties also are referenced in the Historical Lodgings & Restaurants Index. Country inns with Continental [CP] or Full breakfast [BP] in the room rate may also be considered bed and breakfast operations.

HISTORICAL LODGINGS & RESTAURANTS INDEX

The historical lodgings in this index can also be considered bed and breakfast operations if Continental [CP] or Full breakfast [BP] is included in the room rate. See the individual accommodation listing under the town heading for details.

RESORTS INDEX

Many establishments are located in resort areas; however, the resorts in this index have extensive on-premises recreational facilities. See the individual accommodation listing under the town heading for details.

POINTS OF INTEREST INDEX

AMUSEMENT & THEME PARKS
BLAND'S PARK.....................................TYRONE, PA 157
CASINO PIER AND WATER WORKS... SEASIDE HEIGHTS, NJ 48
THE CHALLENGE CENTER...................CANONSBURG, PA 144
CLEMENTON AMUSEMENT PARK & SPLASH WORLD
    WATER PARK ....CLEMENTON, NJ 131
★DORNEY PARK AND WILDWATER
    KINGDOM ....ALLENTOWN, PA 63
DUTCH WONDERLAND FAMILY FUN
    PARK ....LANCASTER, PA 102
★HERSHEYPARK ....HERSHEY, PA 86
★HOOTIN' HOLLER ....LIGONIER, PA 93
IDLEWILD PARK ....LIGONIER, PA 93
JUMPIN' JUNGLE ....LIGONIER, PA 93
KENNYWOOD PARK..................................PITTSBURGH, PA 139
★KNOEBELS AMUSEMENT RESORT ....ELYSBURG, PA 74
KOZIAR'S CHRISTMAS VILLAGE ....BERNVILLE, PA 66
LAKEMONT PARK......................................ALTOONA, PA 65
MARINER'S LANDING AND RAGING WATERS WATER
    PARK..WILDWOOD, NJ 51
MISTER ROGERS' NEIGHBORHOOD OF
    MAKE-BELIEVE...................................LIGONIER, PA 93
PLAYLAND ....OCEAN CITY, NJ 42
SANDCASTLE...PITTSBURGH, PA 140
SESAME PLACE.......................................LANGHORNE, PA 126
SHAWNEE PLACE PLAY AND
    WATER PARK ....SHAWNEE ON DELAWARE, PA 149
SIX FLAGS GREAT ADVENTURE ....JACKSON, NJ 35
STORY BOOK FOREST ....LIGONIER, PA 93
WALDAMEER PARK & WATER WORLD...............ERIE, PA 75
WILD WEST CITY ....NETCONG, NJ 40
WONDERLAND PIER ....OCEAN CITY, NJ 42

AMPHITHEATERS
MANN CENTER FOR THE PERFORMING
    ARTS ....PHILADELPHIA, PA 111
OPEN-AIR THEATRE ....KENNETT SQUARE, PA 126

ANTIQUES
RENNINGERS ANTIQUE & FARMERS
    MARKET...KUTZTOWN, PA 91
ROLLER MILLS EAST ....LEWISBURG, PA 92
ROLLER MILLS MARKETPLACE ....LEWISBURG, PA 92

AQUARIUMS
JENKINSON'S AQUARIUM ..... POINT PLEASANT BEACH, NJ 44
MARINE MAMMAL STRANDING CENTER.... BRIGANTINE, NJ 23
THOMAS H. KEAN NEW JERSEY STATE AQUARIUM AT
    CAMDEN ....CAMDEN, NJ 131

ARBORETUMS
FRELINGHUYSEN ARBORETUM............ MORRISTOWN, NJ 39
GEORGE WASHINGTON MEMORIAL
    ARBORETUM .... TRENTON, NJ 48
HORTICULTURE CENTER .... PHILADELPHIA, PA 111
INDIAN STEPS MUSEUM ....AIRVILLE, PA 62
MORRIS ARBORETUM OF THE UNIVERSITY OF
    PENNSYLVANIA............................ PHILADELPHIA, PA 115
THE TYLER ARBORETUM ....MEDIA, PA 127
WASHINGTON CROSSING SP......................TRENTON, NJ 48

ART GALLERIES
ALLENTOWN ART MUSEUM.......................ALLENTOWN, PA 63
THE ANDY WARHOL MUSEUM ....PITTSBURGH, PA 136
ART ASSOCIATION OF HARRISBURG ......HARRISBURG, PA 84
THE ART MUSEUM....................................PRINCETON, NJ 45
ATLANTIC CITY ART CENTER AND HISTORICAL
    MUSEUM ....ATLANTIC CITY, NJ 20
THE BARNES FOUNDATION.............. PHILADELPHIA, PA 110
BERMAN MUSEUM OF ART.............COLLEGEVILLE, PA 124
★BRANDYWINE RIVER MUSEUM .... CHADDS FORD, PA 124
★THE CARNEGIE ....PITTSBURGH, PA 136
THE CARNEGIE MUSEUM OF ART ....PITTSBURGH, PA 137
CENTER GALLERY ....LEWISBURG, PA 92
CHIMNEYS GALLERY 444, LTD......................HERSHEY, PA 86
ERIE ART MUSEUM...ERIE, PA 74
FRICK ART MUSEUM ....PITTSBURGH, PA 139
HOYT INSTITUTE OF FINE ARTS ....NEW CASTLE, PA 96
HUNTERDON ART CENTER ....CLINTON, NJ 28
INSTITUTE OF CONTEMPORARY ART ... PHILADELPHIA, PA 117
JAMES A. MICHENER ART MUSEUM .....DOYLESTOWN, PA 124
THE JANE VOORHEES ZIMMERLI
    ART MUSEUM.......................NEW BRUNSWICK, NJ 42
JUNIATA COLLEGE...............................HUNTINGDON, PA 88
THE KEMERER MUSEUM OF DECORATIVE
    ARTS ....BETHLEHEM, PA 67
THE MAIN MUSEUM................................... TRENTON, NJ 48
MONTCLAIR ART MUSEUM ....MONTCLAIR, NJ 38
THE MORRIS MUSEUM.............................MORRISTOWN, NJ 40
MUSEUM OF AMERICAN ART OF THE PENNSYLVANIA
    ACADEMY OF THE FINE ARTS .... PHILADELPHIA, PA 116
NATIONAL PORTRAIT GALLERY .... PHILADELPHIA, PA 115
NEWARK MUSEUM ....NEWARK, NJ 41
THE OLD JAIL CENTER ..........................WILLIAMSPORT, PA 160
PALMER MUSEUM OF ART...............STATE COLLEGE, PA 156
PAUL ROBESON CENTER............................NEWARK, NJ 41
★PHILADELPHIA MUSEUM OF ART ..... PHILADELPHIA, PA 111
PITTSBURGH CENTER FOR THE ARTS....... PITTSBURGH, PA 139
RODIN MUSEUM .................................PHILADELPHIA, PA 112
SCHOOL GALLERY OF THE PENNSYLVANIA ACADEMY OF
    THE FINE ARTS .... PHILADELPHIA, PA 117
★SECOND BANK OF UNITED STATES ... PHILADELPHIA, PA 115
SORDONI ART GALLERY ....WILKES-BARRE, PA 160
SOUTHERN ALLEGHENIES MUSEUM OF ART ....LORETTO, PA 94
TROUT ART GALLERY .... CARLISLE, PA 70
WESTMORELAND MUSEUM OF AMERICAN
    ART...GREENSBURG, PA 82
THE WHARTON ESHERICK STUDIO ....PAOLI, PA 128
WOODMERE ART MUSEUM .... PHILADELPHIA, PA 117

ARTS & CRAFTS
ARTS FESTIVAL ....JOHNSTOWN, PA 89
HUNTERDON ART CENTER ....CLINTON, NJ 28
INDIAN SUMMER ART SHOW............ATLANTIC CITY, NJ 23
★LANDIS VALLEY MUSEUM ....LANCASTER, PA 102
MAGIC TOWN OF GETTYSBURG ....GETTYSBURG, PA 78
MILL BRIDGE VILLAGE ....LANCASTER, PA 103
THE NOYES MUSEUM OF ART.....................OCEANVILLE, NJ 24
OCEAN CITY ARTS CENTER.....................OCEAN CITY, NJ 42
OLD BEDFORD VILLAGE ....BEDFORD, PA 66
THE PEOPLE'S PLACE ....INTERCOURSE, PA 101
THE PEOPLE'S PLACE QUILT MUSEUM... INTERCOURSE, PA 101
PETERS VALLEY........... DELAWARE WATER GAP NRA, PA 147
PLAIN AND FANCY FARM ....BIRD-IN-HAND, PA 99

INDEX ABBREVIATIONS

NB............................	national battlefield	NR............................	national river
NBP.....................	national battlefield park	NS............................	national seashore
NC............................	national cemetery	NWR.....................	national wildlife refuge
NF............................	national forest	PHP...................	provincial historic(al) park
NHM.........	national historic(al) monument	PHS...................	provincial historic(al) site
NHP.................	national historic(al) park	PP............................	provincial park
NHS.................	national historic(al) site	SF............................	state forest
NL............................	national lakeshore	SHM...............	state historic(al) monument
NME.....................	national memorial	SHP.................	state historic(al) park
NMO.....................	national monument	SHS.................	state historic(al) site
NMP.....................	national military park	SME.................	state memorial
NP............................	national park	SP............................	state park
NRA.................	national recreation area	SRA.................	state recreation area

RENFREW MUSEUM AND PARK.......... WAYNESBORO, PA 159
SHADYSIDE SUMMER ARTS FESTIVAL ..... PITTSBURGH, PA 143
THE WHARTON ESHERICK STUDIO .... PAOLI, PA 128
★WHEATON VILLAGE..............................MILLVILLE, NJ 38

ATOMIC ENERGY INSTALLATIONS & NUCLEAR PLANTS
LIMERICK ENERGY INFORMATION CENTER... LIMERICK, PA 126
SUSQUEHANNA ENERGY INFORMATION CENTER AND
  RIVERLANDS.. BERWICK, PA 67
THREE MILE ISLAND VISITORS CENTER.... MIDDLETOWN, PA 95

AUDITORIUMS
CIVIC ARENA .... PITTSBURGH, PA 138
CONVENTION HALL .... ASBURY PARK, NJ 18
GREAT AUDITORIUM........................ OCEAN GROVE, NJ 42

BATTLEFIELDS
BRANDYWINE BATTLEFIELD PARK ...... CHADDS FORD, PA 123
BUSHY RUN BATTLEFIELD SHS ....JEANNETTE, PA 144
★FORT NECESSITY NB..................................PA 76
★GETTYSBURG NMP....................................PA 80
JUMONVILLE GLEN ....FORT NECESSITY NB, PA 76
MONMOUTH BATTLEFIELD SP .... FREEHOLD, NJ 31
PRINCETON BATTLEFIELD SP................. PRINCETON, NJ 45
RED BANK BATTLEFIELD PARK .... WOODBURY, NJ 132
WASHINGTON CROSSING SP. .... TRENTON, NJ 48

BATTLE RE-ENACTMENTS
BATTLE OF GERMANTOWN................ PHILADELPHIA, PA 122
CROSSING OF THE DELAWARE ... WASHINGTON CROSSING
                                     HISTORIC PARK, PA 129

BIRTHPLACES
ALFRED JOYCE KILMER...............NEW BRUNSWICK, NJ 42
BUCHANAN'S BIRTHPLACE SP .... MERCERSBURG, PA 94
CAPT. JAMES LAWRENCE HOUSE.......BURLINGTON, NJ 131
DANIEL BOONE HOMESTEAD .... BAUMSTOWN, PA 65
GEN. ANTHONY WAYNE .... PAOLI, PA 128
GEN. FRANK ROSS MCCOY.................. LEWISTOWN, PA 92
GEN. GEORGE C. MARSHALL .... UNIONTOWN, PA 157
GROVER CLEVELAND BIRTHPLACE SHS.......CALDWELL, NJ 26
HENRY CLAY FRICK........................... SCOTTDALE, PA 153
JACK PALANCE .... HAZLETON, PA 85
JAMES FENIMORE COOPER HOUSE...BURLINGTON, NJ 131
JIMMY STEWART..................................INDIANA, PA 88
ROBERT FULTON ....QUARRYVILLE, PA 104

BOARDWALKS
BOARDWALK .... ATLANTIC CITY, NJ 19
SEASIDE HEIGHTS ....NJ 45

BRIDGES
DELAWARE AQUEDUCT ... UPPER DELAWARE SCENIC AND
                             RECREATIONAL RIVER, PA 158
KINZUA BRIDGE SP .... MOUNT JEWETT, PA 95
STONE ARCH BRIDGE .... LEWISTOWN, PA 92

BRIDGES, COVERED
BUCKS COUNTY ....PA 123
WERTZ'S BRIDGE .... READING, PA 152

BUILDINGS, MASONIC
THE MASONIC HOMES................... ELIZABETHTOWN, PA 100
★MASONIC TEMPLE......................... PHILADELPHIA, PA 115

BUILDINGS, OFFICE
UNITED STATES CUSTOM HOUSE........ PHILADELPHIA, PA 117

BUILDINGS, PUBLIC; CAPITOL; CITY HALL
CITY HALL .... NEWARK, NJ 41
CITY HALL .... PHILADELPHIA, PA 110
OLD CITY HALL .... PHILADELPHIA, PA 114
★STATE CAPITOL............................ HARRISBURG, PA 85
STATE HOUSE .... TRENTON, NJ 48
UNITED STATES MINT .... PHILADELPHIA, PA 117

CANALS
CANAL BOAT RIDES ....EASTON, PA 73
DELAWARE CANAL......................BUCKS COUNTY, PA 123

CANYONS
GRAND CANYON OF PENNSYLVANIA ..... WELLSBORO, PA 159
LEWISTOWN NARROWS .... LEWISTOWN, PA 92

CARILLONS
MERCERSBURG ACADEMY...............MERCERSBURG, PA 95
WASHINGTON MEMORIAL
  NATIONAL CARILLON ....VALLEY FORGE NHP, PA 129

CARROUSELS
CAROUSEL WORLD...........................LAHASKA, PA 126
★DORNEY PARK AND WILDWATER
  KINGDOM ....ALLENTOWN, PA 63

MARINER'S LANDING AND RAGING WATERS WATER
  THEME PARK.................................WILDWOOD, NJ 51

CAVES
CRYSTAL CAVE ....KUTZTOWN, PA 91
INDIAN CAVERNS .... SPRUCE CREEK, PA 155
INDIAN ECHO CAVERNS .... HERSHEY, PA 87
LAUREL CAVERNS.......................UNIONTOWN, PA 157
LINCOLN CAVERNS ....HUNTINGDON, PA 88
LOST RIVER CAVERNS AND THE GILMAN
  MUSEUM ....HELLERTOWN, PA 85
★PENN'S CAVE ....CENTRE HALL, PA 70
WOODWARD CAVE ....WOODWARD, PA 161

CEMETERIES
THE AVENUE OF 444 FLAGS ....HERMITAGE, PA 85
CHRIST CHURCH BURIAL GROUND ...... PHILADELPHIA, PA 110
FINNS POINT NC ....SALEM, NJ 132
★GETTYSBURG NC........................ GETTYSBURG NMP, PA 80
GRANDVIEW CEMETERY .... JOHNSTOWN, PA 90
HARLEIGH CEMETERY........................CAMDEN, NJ 131
LAUREL HILL CEMETERY..................... PHILADELPHIA, PA 111
PIONEER CEMETERY............................ FRANKLIN, PA 76

CHILDREN'S ATTRACTIONS
BLAND'S PARK.......................................TYRONE, PA 157
CAMELBACK ALPINE SLIDE AND
  WATERSLIDE .... TANNERSVILLE, PA 150
CHILDREN'S DISCOVERY WORKSHOP .... WILLIAMSPORT, PA 160
CLAWS 'N' PAWS WILD ANIMAL PARK..........HAMLIN, PA 148
CLEMENTON AMUSEMENT PARK & SPLASH WORLD
  WATER PARK .... CLEMENTON, NJ 131
CLYDE PEELING'S REPTILAND ....ALLENWOOD, PA 64
THE CRAYOLA FACTORY ....EASTON, PA 73
DAFFIN'S CANDIES CHOCOLATE KINGDOM ... SHARON, PA 154
★DORNEY PARK AND WILDWATER
  KINGDOM ....ALLENTOWN, PA 63
DUTCH WONDERLAND FAMILY FUN
  PARK.................................... LANCASTER, PA 102
ERIE ZOO ....ERIE, PA 75
EXPERIENCE CHILDREN'S MUSEUM ....ERIE, PA 75
HANDS-ON HOUSE, CHILDREN'S MUSEUM OF
  LANCASTER.................................... LANCASTER, PA 102
★HERSHEYPARK .... HERSHEY, PA 86
HOOTIN' HOLLER .... LIGONIER, PA 93
IDLEWILD PARK .... LIGONIER, PA 93
IMAGINE THAT!!! .... EAST HANOVER, NJ 28
JUMPIN' JUNGLE .... LIGONIER, PA 93
KENNYWOOD PARK........................... PITTSBURGH, PA 139
KNOEBELS AMUSEMENT RESORT ....ELYSBURG, PA 74
KOZIAR'S CHRISTMAS VILLAGE .... BERNVILLE, PA 66
KRAYNAK'S SANTA'S CHRISTMASLAND AND EASTER
  BUNNY LANE..................................HERMITAGE, PA 85
LAKEMONT PARK....................................ALTOONA, PA 65
LAND OF MAKE BELIEVE .... HOPE, NJ 34
LIVING TREASURES ANIMAL PARK ......NEW CASTLE, PA 96
LUCY THE MARGATE ELEPHANT.........MARGATE CITY, NJ 23
MARINER'S LANDING AND RAGING WATERS WATER
  THEME PARK.................................WILDWOOD, NJ 51
MISTER ROGERS' NEIGHBORHOOD OF
  MAKE-BELIEVE .... LIGONIER, PA 93
NEW JERSEY CHILDREN'S MUSEUM.........PARAMUS, NJ 43
PITTSBURGH CHILDREN'S MUSEUM...... PITTSBURGH, PA 139
★PITTSBURGH ZOO........................... PITTSBURGH, PA 139
PLEASE TOUCH MUSEUM .... PHILADELPHIA, PA 116
RAGING WATERS..............................WILDWOOD, NJ 51
SANDCASTLE...................................PITTSBURGH, PA 140
SESAME PLACE ....LANGHORNE, PA 126
SHAWNEE PLACE PLAY AND
  WATER PARK...............SHAWNEE ON DELAWARE, PA 149
STORY BOOK FOREST .... LIGONIER, PA 93
STORYBOOK LAND .... PLEASANTVILLE, NJ 24
WALDAMEER PARK & WATER WORLD................ERIE, PA 75
WILD WEST CITY ....NETCONG, NJ 40
ZOOLOGICAL GARDENS .... PHILADELPHIA, PA 112

CHURCHES, CATHEDRALS & BASILICAS
BASILICA OF THE SACRED HEART OF
  JESUS .... MCSHERRYSTOWN, PA 94
BINDNAGLES EVANGELICAL LUTHERAN
  CHURCH...PALMYRA, PA 98
BRYN ATHYN CATHEDRAL .... BRYN ATHYN, PA 122
CATHOLIC CATHEDRAL OF THE SACRED
  HEART ....NEWARK, NJ 41
★CHRIST CHURCH .... PHILADELPHIA, PA 110
CHURCH OF THE FALLING SPRING.... CHAMBERSBURG, PA 71
CHURCH ON THE GREEN ....HACKENSACK, NJ 32
FIRST PRESBYTERIAN CHURCH .... CARLISLE, PA 69
GLORIA DEI (OLD SWEDES') CHURCH... PHILADELPHIA, PA 113
OLD ST. JOSEPH'S CHURCH .... PHILADELPHIA, PA 116
OLD ST. MARY'S CHURCH ....BURLINGTON, NJ 131
OLD ST. MARY'S CHURCH .... PHILADELPHIA, PA 116
PAXTON PRESBYTERIAN CHURCH......... HARRISBURG, PA 83
ST. GEORGE'S UNITED METHODIST
  CHURCH.................................. PHILADELPHIA, PA 114
ST. MARK'S EPISCOPAL CHURCH ....JIM THORPE, PA 149
ST. PETER'S CHURCH .... PHILADELPHIA, PA 116

ALEM LUTHERAN CHURCH ....LEBANON, PA   91
ABOR UNITED CHURCH OF CHRIST ....LEBANON, PA   91
RINITY LUTHERAN CHURCH..................LANCASTER, PA   103
NITARIAN CHURCH ....MEADVILLE, PA   94

CHURCHES-CHAPELS
OLUMBUS CHAPEL AND BOAL MANSION
   MUSEUM .... BOALSBURG, PA   68
REEDOMS FOUNDATION AT
   VALLEY FORGE ....VALLEY FORGE, PA   128
EINZ MEMORIAL CHAPEL ....PITTSBURGH, PA   139
HE UNIVERSITY CHAPEL....................PRINCETON, NJ   45
ASHINGTON MEMORIAL
   CHAPEL................................VALLEY FORGE NHP, PA   129

CHURCHES-MEETING HOUSES
RIENDS MEETING HOUSE ....BURLINGTON, NJ   131
RIENDS MEETING HOUSE ....PLAINFIELD, NJ   44

CHURCHES-SHRINES
HE BLUE ARMY SHRINE OF THE IMMACULATE HEART OF
   MARY..WASHINGTON, NJ   49
ATIONAL SHRINE OF OUR LADY OF
   CZESTOCHOWA ....DOYLESTOWN, PA   125
ATIONAL SHRINE OF ST. JOHN
   NEUMANN .... PHILADELPHIA, PA   116
ACRED HEART SHRINE.........................HAZLETON, PA   85

CHURCHES-TEMPLES & SYNAGOGUES
MASONIC TEMPLE.........................PHILADELPHIA, PA   115
ENNONITE INFORMATION CENTER AND HEBREW
   TABERNACLE REPRODUCTION ....LANCASTER, PA   103
RI VENKATESWARA TEMPLE ....MONROEVILLE, PA   144

CONVENTS & MONASTERIES
PHRATA CLOISTER ....EPHRATA, PA   100

COURTHOUSES
EFFERSON COUNTY COURTHOUSE ....BROOKVILLE, PA   68
EHIGH COUNTY HISTORICAL SOCIETY ...ALLENTOWN, PA   64
UZERNE COUNTY COURT HOUSE ...... WILKES-BARRE, PA   160
ENANGO COUNTY COURTHOUSE ....FRANKLIN, PA   76

CULTURAL CENTERS & CIVIC CENTERS
VIC ARENA ....PITTSBURGH, PA   138
ID-ATLANTIC CENTER FOR THE ARTS.......CAPE MAY, NJ   27
NEW JERSEY STATE MUSEUM................TRENTON, NJ   48
CEAN CITY ARTS CENTER....................OCEAN CITY, NJ   42
CEAN CITY HISTORICAL MUSEUM...........OCEAN CITY, NJ   42
TTSBURGH CENTER FOR THE ARTS....... PITTSBURGH, PA   139

AMS
NZUA DAM ....ALLEGHENY NF, PA   62
NZUA DAM ....WARREN, PA   158
HIKELLAMY MARINA & FABRIDAM.........SUNBURY, PA   156

EVENTS-GENERAL
NTIQUE AND CLASSIC CAR AUCTION AND FLEA
   MARKET......................................ATLANTIC CITY, NJ   23
RCHERY CLASSIC ....ATLANTIC CITY, NJ   23
ACK HISTORY MONTH................. PHILADELPHIA, PA   121
HE BOOK AND THE COOK .... PHILADELPHIA, PA   121
HINESE NEW YEAR .... PHILADELPHIA, PA   120
ASTER PROMENADE .... PHILADELPHIA, PA   121
ARM ANIMAL FROLIC......................STROUDSBURG, PA   150
ANT TINKERTOY EXTRAVAGANZA ... PHILADELPHIA, PA   122
MBALAYA JAM........................... PHILADELPHIA, PA   121
LD TIME CHRISTMAS ....JIM THORPE, PA   148
DDLER'S VILLAGE ....LAHASKA, PA   126
TTENHOUSE SQUARE FINE ARTS
   ANNUAL .... PHILADELPHIA, PA   121
TTENHOUSE SQUARE FLOWER
   MARKET................................... PHILADELPHIA, PA   121
PER SUNDAY .... PHILADELPHIA, PA   121
LBORGSMASSOAFTON .... PHILADELPHIA, PA   121
ORLD'S LARGEST GARDEN PARTY .... PHILADELPHIA, PA   121
JLETIDE OBSERVANCE ....BETHLEHEM, PA   67

EVENTS-CARNIVAL & CIRCUSES
MBO SHRINE CIRCUS ....HARRISBURG, PA   84

EVENTS-EXPOSITIONS
NTIQUES AND COLLECTIBLES
   EXPOSITION .... ATLANTIC CITY, NJ   23

EVENTS-FAIRS
EVON HORSE SHOW AND COUNTRY
   FAIR .... PHILADELPHIA, PA   121
REAT ALLENTOWN FAIR......................ALLENTOWN, PA   63
REAT BEDFORD COUNTY FAIR ....BEDFORD, PA   66
AD HOUSE SQUARE CRAFTS FAIR..... PHILADELPHIA, PA   121
NNSYLVANIA RENAISSANCE FAIRE........MANHEIM, PA   104

EVENTS-FESTIVALS
RICAMERICAS FESTIVAL................. PHILADELPHIA, PA   121
PLEFEST CELEBRATION ....FRANKLIN, PA   77

ARTS FESTIVAL .... JOHNSTOWN, PA   89
BACH FESTIVAL .... BETHLEHEM, PA   67
CELTIC CLASSIC HIGHLAND GAMES AND
   FESTIVAL .... BETHLEHEM, PA   67
DUCKS UNLIMITED FESTIVAL................. LINESVILLE, PA   93
FALL FOLIAGE FESTIVAL......................BEDFORD, PA   66
FOLK FESTIVAL .... PITTSBURGH, PA   143
HARBORFEST.............................. ATLANTIC CITY, NJ   23
HARVEST FESTIVAL ....STROUDSBURG, PA   150
HOSS'S KEYSTONE COUNTRY FESTIVAL ....ALTOONA, PA   64
INTERNATIONAL THEATER FESTIVAL FOR
   CHILDREN.................................. PHILADELPHIA, PA   121
JOHNSTOWN FOLKFEST .... JOHNSTOWN, PA   89
LABOR DAY WEEKEND FESTIVAL......... ATLANTIC CITY, NJ   23
LUCIA FEST AND JULMARKNAD .... PHILADELPHIA, PA   122
MEMORIAL DAY FESTIVAL .... BOALSBURG, PA   68
MUSIKFEST .... BETHLEHEM, PA   67
NEW JERSEY FRESH SEAFOOD
   FESTIVAL .... ATLANTIC CITY, NJ   23
NEW JERSEY SHAKESPEARE FESTIVAL............MADISON, NJ   37
OKTOBERFEST .... PITTSBURGH, PA   143
PENNSYLVANIA GERMAN FESTIVAL .... KUTZTOWN, PA   90
PHILADELPHIA FOLK FESTIVAL .... PHILADELPHIA, PA   121
SHADYSIDE SUMMER ARTS FESTIVAL ..... PITTSBURGH, PA   143
THE SOUTH STREET SEVEN ARTS
   FESTIVAL .... PHILADELPHIA, PA   122
SUNOCO WELCOME AMERICA!.......... PHILADELPHIA, PA   121
THREE RIVERS ARTS FESTIVAL.............. PITTSBURGH, PA   143
YO! PHILADELPHIA FESTIVAL .... PHILADELPHIA, PA   122

EVENTS-PAGEANTS, PARADES, DAYS
ATLANTIC CITY CHRISTMAS PARADE... ATLANTIC CITY, NJ   23
COLUMBUS DAY PARADE................. PHILADELPHIA, PA   122
COMMUNITY HERITAGE DAYS.............WATERFORD, PA   159
ELFRETH'S ALLEY FETE DAYS........... PHILADELPHIA, PA   121
GROUNDHOG DAY ......................PUNXSUTAWNEY, PA   151
GROVE CITY STRAWBERRY DAYS .... GROVE CITY, PA   82
MISS AMERICA PAGEANT .... ATLANTIC CITY, NJ   23
MUMMERS PARADE.......................... PHILADELPHIA, PA   120
PHILADELPHIA THANKSGIVING DAY
   PARADE .... PHILADELPHIA, PA   122
PULASKI DAY PARADE..................... PHILADELPHIA, PA   122
ST. PATRICK'S DAY PARADE .... PHILADELPHIA, PA   121
VON STEUBEN DAY PARADE .... PHILADELPHIA, PA   122

EVENTS-REGATTAS
DAD VAIL REGATTA .... PHILADELPHIA, PA   121
PITTSBURGH THREE RIVERS REGATTA..... PITTSBURGH, PA   143

EVENTS-SHOWS
ATLANTIC CITY BOAT SHOW .... ATLANTIC CITY, NJ   23
AUTO SHOW..................................... HARRISBURG, PA   84
DEVON HORSE SHOW AND COUNTRY
   FAIR .... PHILADELPHIA, PA   121
EASTERN SPORTSMAN SHOW .... HARRISBURG, PA   84
HARVEST SHOW................................ PHILADELPHIA, PA   122
INDIAN SUMMER ART SHOW............. ATLANTIC CITY, NJ   23
MUMMERS STRING BAND SHOW OF
   SHOWS .... PHILADELPHIA, PA   121
NATIONAL BOARDWALK PROFESSIONAL ART
   SHOW....................................... ATLANTIC CITY, NJ   23
PENN'S LANDING IN-WATER BOAT
   SHOW....................................... PHILADELPHIA, PA   122
PENNSYLVANIA FARM SHOW .... HARRISBURG, PA   84
PENNSYLVANIA NATIONAL HORSE
   SHOW....................................... HARRISBURG, PA   84
PHILADELPHIA ANTIQUES SHOW .... PHILADELPHIA, PA   121
THE PHILADELPHIA BOAT SHOW .... PHILADELPHIA, PA   120
PHILADELPHIA CRAFTS SHOW .... PHILADELPHIA, PA   122
PHILADELPHIA FLOWER SHOW .... PHILADELPHIA, PA   121
PHILADELPHIA HOME SHOW .... PHILADELPHIA, PA   121
PHILADELPHIA INTERNATIONAL AUTO
   SHOW....................................... PHILADELPHIA, PA   120
RENNINGERS ANTIQUE & FARMERS
   MARKET...................................... KUTZTOWN, PA   91

EVENTS-SPORTS
CELTIC CLASSIC HIGHLAND GAMES AND
   FESTIVAL .... BETHLEHEM, PA   67

EXHIBITS & COLLECTIONS-GENERAL
AGRICULTURE AND INDUSTRIAL MUSEUM OF YORK
   COUNTY ....YORK, PA   161
AMERICAN CHRISTMAS MUSEUM........ CHADDS FORD, PA   123
AMERICAN LABOR MUSEUM/BOTTO HOUSE NATIONAL
   LANDMARK ....HALEDON, NJ   33
AMISH COUNTRY HOMESTEAD...........BIRD-IN-HAND, PA   99
ANTHRACITE MUSEUM COMPLEX............SCRANTON, PA   153
APPLETREE FARM...................MOUNT POCONO, PA   149
BAINBRIDGE HOUSE ....PRINCETON, NJ   44
★THE CARNEGIE MUSEUM OF NATURAL
   HISTORY .... PITTSBURGH, PA   137
★CATHEDRAL OF LEARNING .... PITTSBURGH, PA   138
DINGMANS FALLS
   VISITOR CENTER .... DELAWARE WATER GAP NRA, PA   147
EVERHART MUSEUM ....SCRANTON, PA   154
FORT LEE HISTORIC PARK.....................FORT LEE, NJ   30

FOUNDERS HALL.................................. HERSHEY, PA   86
FREEDOMS FOUNDATION AT
  VALLEY FORGE ....VALLEY FORGE, PA 128
GROUNDS FOR SCULPTURE .... HAMILTON, NJ   33
★HERSHEY'S CHOCOLATE WORLD............. HERSHEY, PA   87
HISTORIC SPEEDWELL........................ MORRISTOWN, NJ   39
HOUDINI TOUR AND SHOW .... SCRANTON, PA 154
HUNTERDON HISTORICAL MUSEUM............. CLINTON, NJ   28
THE JIMMY STEWART MUSEUM................. INDIANA, PA   89
JOCKEY HOLLOW ....MORRISTOWN NHP, NJ   40
JOHNSTOWN FLOOD NME .... JOHNSTOWN, PA   90
KITTATINNY POINT
  VISITOR CENTER........ DELAWARE WATER GAP NRA, PA 147
KRAYNAK'S SANTA'S CHRISTMASLAND AND EASTER
  BUNNY LANE......................................HERMITAGE, PA   85
LABORATORY COMPLEX .... WEST ORANGE, NJ   50
LEHIGHTON MODEL TRAIN DISPLAY.......... LEHIGHTON, PA 149
LIMERICK ENERGY INFORMATION CENTER... LIMERICK, PA 126
THE LINCOLN TRAIN MUSEUM .... GETTYSBURG, PA   78
LOST RIVER CAVERNS AND THE GILMAN
  MUSEUM..HELLERTOWN, PA   85
MAGIC TOWN OF GETTYSBURG .... GETTYSBURG, PA   78
THE MAIN MUSEUM... TRENTON, NJ   48
MCFADDEN RAILROAD MUSEUM .... MERCERSBURG, PA   95
MEMORIAL BUILDING............... WASHINGTON CROSSING
                                        HISTORIC PARK, PA 130
MONMOUTH BATTLEFIELD SP .... FREEHOLD, NJ   31
MORAVIAN MUSEUM OF BETHLEHEM .... BETHLEHEM, PA   67
THE MORRIS MUSEUM...................... MORRISTOWN, NJ   40
NATURAL HISTORY MUSEUM .... PRINCETON, NJ   45
NEW JERSEY MUSEUM OF
  AGRICULTURE............................NEW BRUNSWICK, NJ   42
OCEAN CITY HISTORICAL MUSEUM...........OCEAN CITY, NJ   42
PEIRCE-DU-PONT HOUSE ....KENNETT SQUARE, PA 125
PITTSBURGH CHILDREN'S MUSEUM .... PITTSBURGH, PA 139
STEVENS INSTITUTE OF TECHNOLOGY .... HOBOKEN, NJ   33
STRAWBERRY HILL NATURE CENTER AND
  PRESERVE .... FAIRFIELD, PA   75
THOMAS NEWCOMEN LIBRARY AND
  MUSEUM... EXTON, PA 125
TOWNSHIP OF LEBANON MUSEUM........... HAMPTON, NJ   33
TWIN LIGHTS SHS .... HIGHLANDS, NJ   33
U.S. ARMY COMMUNICATIONS-ELECTRONICS
  MUSEUM......................... FORT MONMOUTH, NJ   31
WASHINGTON CROSSING SP...................... TRENTON, NJ   48
WORLD OF SCOUTING MUSEUM ....VALLEY FORGE NHP, PA 129
ZANE GREY MUSEUM .... LACKAWAXEN, PA 149

EXHIBITS & COLLECTIONS-ANIMALS & BIRDS

HAWK MOUNTAIN SANCTUARY .... ECKVILLE, PA   73
JAMES A. MCFAUL ENVIRONMENTAL CENTER OF BERGEN
  COUNTY..WYCKOFF, NJ   51
MIDDLE CREEK WILDLIFE MANAGEMENT
  AREA.......................... KLEINFELTERSVILLE, PA   90
THE MORRIS MUSEUM...................... MORRISTOWN, NJ   40
MUDDY RUN INFORMATION CENTER ..... HOLTWOOD, PA 100
THE NATIONAL AVIARY .... PITTSBURGH, PA 139
PYMATUNING VISITOR CENTER .... LINESVILLE, PA   93
THOMAS H. KEAN NEW JERSEY STATE AQUARIUM AT
  CAMDEN .... CAMDEN, NJ 131
TRAILSIDE NATURE AND SCIENCE
  CENTER .... MOUNTAINSIDE, NJ   40

EXHIBITS & COLLECTIONS-AVIATION

AIR HERITAGE MUSEUM .... BEAVER FALLS, PA 144
AVIATION HALL OF FAME & MUSEUM OF NEW
  JERSEY .... TETERBORO, NJ   47
MID-ATLANTIC AIR MUSEUM .... READING, PA 152

EXHIBITS & COLLECTIONS-CIVIL WAR HISTORY

CIVIL WAR LIBRARY AND MUSEUM..... PHILADELPHIA, PA 110
CONFEDERATE STATES ARMORY AND
  MUSEUM.. GETTYSBURG, PA   77
CYCLORAMA CENTER .... GETTYSBURG NMP, PA   82
GETTYSBURG MUSEUM OF THE
  CIVIL WAR .... GETTYSBURG NMP, PA   82
LEE'S HEADQUARTERS AND MUSEUM ... GETTYSBURG, PA   78
SOLDIERS NATIONAL MUSEUM............ GETTYSBURG, PA   78

EXHIBITS & COLLECTIONS-CLOCKS

COLGATE CLOCK............................JERSEY CITY, NJ   36
HARMONY MUSEUM .... HARMONY, PA 144
★WATCH AND CLOCK MUSEUM OF THE NATIONAL
  ASSOCIATION OF WATCH AND CLOCK COLLECTORS
  INC... COLUMBIA, PA 100

EXHIBITS & COLLECTIONS-DOLLS & TOYS

CHOO CHOO BARN, TRAINTOWN, U.S.A...STRASBURG, PA 105
FRANKLIN MINT MUSEUM .... MEDIA, PA 127
MARY MERRITT DOLL MUSEUM............... READING, PA 152
MERCER COUNTY HISTORICAL MUSEUM ....MERCER, PA   94
THE NATIONAL TOY TRAIN MUSEUM ...... STRASBURG, PA 105

EXHIBITS & COLLECTIONS-HISTORICAL

AFRO-AMERICAN HISTORICAL AND CULTURAL
  MUSEUM .... PHILADELPHIA, PA 10
AGRICULTURE MUSEUM ....YORK, PA 16
ALLEGHENY PORTAGE RAILROAD NHS ...... CRESSON, PA   7
ALTOONA RAILROADERS MEMORIAL
  MUSEUM...................................... ALTOONA, PA   6
AMERICAN SWEDISH HISTORICAL
  MUSEUM .... PHILADELPHIA, PA 10
ASA PACKER MANSION.....................JIM THORPE, PA 14
THE ATHENAEUM OF PHILADELPHIA... PHILADELPHIA, PA 10
ATLANTIC CITY ART CENTER AND HISTORICAL
  MUSEUM .... ATLANTIC CITY, NJ   2
ATLANTIC COUNTY HISTORICAL SOCIETY LIBRARY AND
  MUSEUM .... SOMERS POINT, NJ   2
ATWATER KENT MUSEUM—THE PHILADELPHIA HISTORY
  MUSEUM .... PHILADELPHIA, PA 11
AVIATION HALL OF FAME & MUSEUM OF NEW
  JERSEY...................................... TETERBORO, NJ   4
B. FREE FRANKLIN POST OFFICE AND
  MUSEUM .... PHILADELPHIA, PA 11
THE BALCH INSTITUTE FOR ETHNIC
  STUDIES .... PHILADELPHIA, PA 11
BALDWIN-REYNOLDS HOUSE .... MEADVILLE, PA   9
BEAVER FALLS HISTORICAL SOCIETY AND
  MUSEUM....................................BEAVER FALLS, PA 14
BERKS COUNTY HERITAGE CENTER .... READING, PA 15
BERMAN MUSEUM OF ART ............COLLEGEVILLE, PA 12
BESSEMER COURT AT STATION SQUARE .... PITTSBURGH, PA 13
BETSY ROSS HOUSE .... PHILADELPHIA, PA 11
BISHOP WHITE HOUSE .... PHILADELPHIA, PA 11
BONHAM HOUSE ....YORK, PA 16
BRANDYWINE BATTLEFIELD PARK ...... CHADDS FORD, PA 12
BURLINGTON COUNTY HISTORICAL SOCIETY
  COMPLEX ....BURLINGTON, NJ 13
CAMDEN COUNTY HISTORICAL SOCIETY ...... CAMDEN, NJ 13
THE CANAL MUSEUM.........................GREENVILLE, PA   8
CANDY AMERICANA MUSEUM AND CANDY
  OUTLET..LITITZ, PA 10
★THE CARNEGIE MUSEUM OF NATURAL
  HISTORY .... PITTSBURGH, PA 13
★CARNEGIE SCIENCE CENTER .... PITTSBURGH, PA 13
CARPENTERS' HALL........................ PHILADELPHIA, PA 13
CHESTER COUNTY
  HISTORICAL SOCIETY .... WEST CHESTER, PA 13
CIVIL WAR LIBRARY AND MUSEUM..... PHILADELPHIA, PA 11
★CLAYTON .... PITTSBURGH, PA 13
THE COLLEGE OF PHYSICIANS OF
  PHILADELPHIA .... PHILADELPHIA, PA 11
COLUMBUS CHAPEL AND BOAL MANSION
  MUSEUM .... BOALSBURG, PA   9
THE COMPASS INN MUSEUM .... LAUGHLINTOWN, PA
CORNWALL IRON FURNACE .... CORNWALL, PA   7
CUMBERLAND COUNTY HISTORICAL SOCIETY LIBRARY
  AND MUSEUM .... CARLISLE, PA
DANIEL BOONE HOMESTEAD .... BAUMSTOWN, PA   6
DONEGAL MILLS PLANTATION .... MOUNT JOY, PA 10
DORFLINGER GLASS MUSEUM .... WHITE MILLS, PA 15
★DRAKE WELL MUSEUM........................ TITUSVILLE, PA 15
DREXEL COLLECTION......................... PHILADELPHIA, PA 1
ECKLEY MINERS' VILLAGE .... HAZLETON, PA   8
EDGAR ALLAN POE NHS..................... PHILADELPHIA, PA 1
★EISENHOWER NHS .... GETTYSBURG, PA
ERIE HISTORICAL MUSEUM ....ERIE, PA
ERIE HISTORY CENTER ....ERIE, PA
FARM MUSEUM (BRADFORD COUNTY HERITAGE
  ASSOCIATION) ....TROY, PA 15
FIRE MUSEUM .... HARRISBURG, PA   8
FIREMAN'S HALL—NATIONAL FIRE HOUSE AND MUSEUM
  OF PHILADELPHIA .... PHILADELPHIA, PA 1
FONTHILL MUSEUM ....DOYLESTOWN, PA 1
FORT BEDFORD MUSEUM .... BEDFORD, PA
FORT HANCOCK MUSEUM ....GATEWAY NRA, NJ
FORT HUNTER MANSION AND PARK ..... HARRISBURG, PA
FORT LIGONIER ....LIGONIER, PA
★FORT NECESSITY NB...PA
★FORT PITT MUSEUM .... PITTSBURGH, PA 1
★FRANKLIN INSTITUTE SCIENCE
  MUSEUM .... PHILADELPHIA, PA 1
FRANKLIN MINT MUSEUM .... MEDIA, PA 1
FREE LIBRARY OF PHILADELPHIA ...... PHILADELPHIA, PA 1
FRENCH AZILUM .... TOWANDA, PA 1
THE FRICK ART & HISTORICAL CENTER .... PITTSBURGH, PA 1
GEORGE F. BOYER HISTORICAL MUSEUM ... WILDWOOD, NJ
GERMANTOWN HISTORICAL SOCIETY ..... PHILADELPHIA, PA 1
GREATER HAZLETON HISTORICAL SOCIETY
  MUSEUM .... HAZLETON, PA 1
GREENE COUNTY HISTORICAL
  MUSEUM .... WAYNESBURG, PA 1
GREENVILLE RAILROAD MUSEUM...........GREENVILLE, PA
GREY TOWERS .... MILFORD, PA 1
HANS HERR HOUSE .... LANCASTER, PA
HARMONY MUSEUM .... HARMONY, PA 1
HEISEY MUSEUM .... LOCK HAVEN, PA
HERITAGE CENTER MUSEUM OF LANCASTER
  COUNTY .... LANCASTER, PA 1
HERITAGE MAP MUSEUM ....LITITZ, PA 1
★HERSHEY MUSEUM............................. HERSHEY, PA

HISTORIC FALLSINGTON .... FALLSINGTON, PA 125
HISTORIC HANNA'S TOWN...................GREENSBURG, PA 82
HISTORIC ROCK FORD PLANTATION .... LANCASTER, PA 102
HISTORIC MANSION .... CAPE MAY COURT HOUSE, NJ 27
HISTORICAL MUSEUM AND
  LIBRARY.............................MORRISTOWN NHP, NJ 40
HISTORICAL SOCIETY OF BERKS COUNTY..... READING, PA 152
HISTORICAL SOCIETY OF
  PENNSYLVANIA.......................... PHILADELPHIA, PA 113
★HISTORICAL SOCIETY OF YORK COUNTY ....YORK, PA 162
HOGE-OSMER HOUSE .... FRANKLIN, PA 76
HOUDINI TOUR AND SHOW .... SCRANTON, PA 154
★INDEPENDENCE HALL .... PHILADELPHIA, PA 114
★INDEPENDENCE NHP .... PHILADELPHIA, PA 113
INDEPENDENCE SEAPORT MUSEUM ..... PHILADELPHIA, PA 115
INDIAN KING TAVERN HOUSE
  MUSEUM ....HADDONFIELD, NJ 132
INDUSTRIAL MUSEUM ....YORK, PA 162
JAMES FENIMORE COOPER HOUSE ......BURLINGTON, NJ 131
JEFFERSON COUNTY HISTORICAL AND GENEALOGICAL
  SOCIETY ....BROOKVILLE, PA 69
THE JIMMY STEWART MUSEUM ....INDIANA, PA 89
JOHANNES MUELLER HOUSE...................LITITZ, PA 104
JOHN HARRIS/SIMON CAMERON
  MANSION .... HARRISBURG, PA 84
JOHNSTOWN FLOOD MUSEUM .... JOHNSTOWN, PA 90
JOSEPH PRIESTLEY HOUSE .... NORTHUMBERLAND, PA 96
LAKE SHORE RAILWAY MUSEUM ....NORTH EAST, PA 96
LANCASTER COUNTY HISTORICAL
  SOCIETY .... LANCASTER, PA 102
LANCASTER NEWSPAPERS NEWSEUM ...... LANCASTER, PA 102
LANDIS VALLEY MUSEUM .... LANCASTER, PA 102
LEE'S HEADQUARTERS AND MUSEUM ... GETTYSBURG, PA 78
LEHIGH COUNTY HISTORICAL SOCIETY ..... ALLENTOWN, PA 64
LEMOYNE HOUSE .... WASHINGTON, PA 145
LIBERTY BELL PAVILION .... PHILADELPHIA, PA 114
LINCOLN ROOM MUSEUM .... GETTYSBURG, PA 78
THE LINCOLN TRAIN MUSEUM .... GETTYSBURG, PA 78
LITTLE LEAGUE BASEBALL MUSEUM ... WILLIAMSPORT, PA 161
LYCOMING COUNTY HISTORICAL
  MUSEUM .... WILLIAMSPORT, PA 161
MENNONITE INFORMATION CENTER AND HEBREW
  TABERNACLE REPRODUCTION ..... LANCASTER, PA 103
MERCER COUNTY HISTORICAL MUSEUM ......MERCER, PA 94
MERCER MUSEUM ....DOYLESTOWN, PA 124
MERRITT'S MUSEUM OF CHILDHOOD .... READING, PA 152
MIFFLIN COUNTY HISTORICAL SOCIETY MUSEUM AND
  LIBRARY .... LEWISTOWN, PA 92
MONMOUTH COUNTY HISTORICAL ASSOCIATION
  MUSEUM AND LIBRARY ....FREEHOLD, NJ 31
MUMMERS MUSEUM .... PHILADELPHIA, PA 115
MUSEUM OF EARLY TRADES AND CRAFTS ... MADISON, NJ 37
MUTTER MUSEUM .... PHILADELPHIA, PA 110
NAIL MILL MUSEUM .... BRIDGETON, NJ 26
NATIONAL ARCHIVES PHILADELPHIA
  BRANCH .... PHILADELPHIA, PA 116
THE NATIONAL CANAL MUSEUM ....EASTON, PA 73
NATIONAL MUSEUM OF AMERICAN JEWISH
  HISTORY .... PHILADELPHIA, PA 116
NATIONAL PARK
  VISITOR CENTER .... GETTYSBURG NMP, PA 82
NEW HALL MILITARY MUSEUM .... PHILADELPHIA, PA 114
NEW JERSEY HISTORICAL SOCIETY .... NEWARK, NJ 41
NORTH MUSEUM OF NATURAL HISTORY AND
  SCIENCE .... LANCASTER, PA 103
OLD BARRACKS MUSEUM .... TRENTON, NJ 48
THE OLD JAIL .... CHAMBERSBURG, PA 71
PACKWOOD HOUSE MUSEUM .... LEWISBURG, PA 92
THE PEARL S. BUCK HOUSE ....PERKASIE, PA 128
PELLETIER LIBRARY .... MEADVILLE, PA 94
PENN STATE ROOM UNIVERSITY
  ARCHIVES ....STATE COLLEGE, PA 156
PENN-BRAD OIL MUSEUM ....BRADFORD, PA 68
PENNSBURY MANOR .... MORRISVILLE, PA 127
PENNSYLVANIA ANTHRACITE HERITAGE
  MUSEUM .... SCRANTON, PA 153
PENNSYLVANIA LUMBER MUSEUM ..... COUDERSPORT, PA 72
THE PEOPLE'S PLACE .... INTERCOURSE, PA 101
THE PEOPLE'S PLACE QUILT MUSEUM ... INTERCOURSE, PA 101
PETER WENTZ FARMSTEAD ....CENTER POINT, PA 123
THOLE CITY ....PLUMER, PA 145
THE PRESBYTERIAN HISTORICAL
  SOCIETY .... PHILADELPHIA, PA 116
QUIET VALLEY LIVING HISTORICAL
  FARM .... STROUDSBURG, PA 150
ROADSIDE AMERICA .... SHARTLESVILLE, PA 155
ROGERS MILL (PATERSON MUSEUM) ... PATERSON, NJ 43
SENATOR JOHN HEINZ PITTSBURGH REGIONAL HISTORY
  CENTER .... PITTSBURGH, PA 140
SLIFER HOUSE MUSEUM ....LEWISBURG, PA 92
SOLDIERS AND SAILORS MEMORIAL
  HALL .... PITTSBURGH, PA 140
SOMERSET HISTORICAL CENTER ...... SOMERSET, PA 155
SPRINGS MUSEUM .... SPRINGS, PA 155
STATE MUSEUM OF PENNSYLVANIA ... HARRISBURG, PA 85
STEPHEN FOSTER MEMORIAL .... PITTSBURGH, PA 141
TOY MUSEUM AND HAUCK MEMORIAL
  LIBRARY................................LEBANON, PA 91

STRASBURG COUNTRY STORE AND
  CREAMERY ....STRASBURG, PA 105
THADDEUS KOSCIUSZKO NME .... PHILADELPHIA, PA 115
THADDEUS STEVENS' BLACKSMITH
  SHOP................................. FAYETTEVILLE, PA 76
TWO RIVERS LANDING AND THE DELAWARE AND LEHIGH
  NATIONAL HERITAGE CORRIDOR VISITOR
  CENTER...............................EASTON, PA 73
VALLEY FORGE HISTORICAL SOCIETY
  MUSEUM..........................VALLEY FORGE NHP, PA 129
VINELAND HISTORICAL AND ANTIQUARIAN
  SOCIETY .... VINELAND, NJ 49
THE WAGNER MUSEUM .... IVYLAND, PA 125
WARREN COUNTY HISTORICAL SOCIETY ......WARREN, PA 158
WAYNE COUNTY HISTORICAL SOCIETY
  MUSEUM .... HONESDALE, PA 148
WAYNESBOROUGH .... PAOLI, PA 128
WELLER CENTER FOR HEALTH EDUCATION ....EASTON, PA 73
WEST OVERTON MUSEUMS.................. SCOTTDALE, PA 153
★WHEATLAND .... LANCASTER, PA 103
WRIGHT'S FERRY MANSION .... COLUMBIA, PA 100
WYOMING HISTORICAL AND GEOLOGICAL
  SOCIETY .... WILKES-BARRE, PA 160

EXHIBITS & COLLECTIONS-INDIAN

★HERSHEY MUSEUM............................. HERSHEY, PA 86
INDIAN STEPS MUSEUM ....AIRVILLE, PA 62
THE MAIN MUSEUM .... TRENTON, NJ 48
MERCER COUNTY HISTORICAL MUSEUM ......MERCER, PA 94
THE MORRIS MUSEUM .... MORRISTOWN, NJ 40
POCONO INDIAN MUSEUM ....BUSHKILL, PA 147
ROGERS MILL (PATERSON MUSEUM) ..... PATERSON, NJ 43
WOODRUFF INDIAN MUSEUM .... BRIDGETON, NJ 26

EXHIBITS & COLLECTIONS-MUSIC

DEBENCE'S ANTIQUE MUSIC WORLD .... FRANKLIN, PA 77
LE PETIT MUSEUM OF MUSICAL BOXES ......MARIETTA, PA 104
MARIO LANZA INSTITUTE AND
  MUSEUM .... PHILADELPHIA, PA 115
MUMMERS MUSEUM .... PHILADELPHIA, PA 115
RUTGERS INSTITUTE OF JAZZ STUDIES........ NEWARK, NJ 41

EXHIBITS & COLLECTIONS-SCIENCE

ACADEMY OF NATURAL SCIENCES....... PHILADELPHIA, PA 108
BOWMAN HILL
  WILDFLOWER PRESERVE........ WASHINGTON CROSSING
                                   HISTORIC PARK, PA 129
★THE CARNEGIE MUSEUM OF NATURAL
  HISTORY .... PITTSBURGH, PA 137
★CARNEGIE SCIENCE CENTER .... PITTSBURGH, PA 138
THE COLLEGE OF PHYSICIANS OF
  PHILADELPHIA .... PHILADELPHIA, PA 110
FELS PLANETARIUM .... PHILADELPHIA, PA 113
★FRANKLIN INSTITUTE SCIENCE
  MUSEUM .... PHILADELPHIA, PA 113
★LIBERTY SCIENCE CENTER............... JERSEY CITY, NJ 36
MANDELL CENTER .... PHILADELPHIA, PA 113
THE MORRIS MUSEUM .... MORRISTOWN, NJ 40
MUDDY RUN INFORMATION CENTER ..... HOLTWOOD, PA 100
MUSEUM OF SCIENTIFIC DISCOVERY ... HARRISBURG, PA 84
NEW JERSEY MUSEUM OF
  AGRICULTURE .... NEW BRUNSWICK, NJ 42
PITTSBURGH CHILDREN'S MUSEUM ...... PITTSBURGH, PA 139
PLEASE TOUCH MUSEUM .... PHILADELPHIA, PA 116
READING PUBLIC MUSEUM .... READING, PA 152
TUTTLEMAN OMNIVERSE THEATER...... PHILADELPHIA, PA 113
★THE UNIVERSITY OF PENNSYLVANIA MUSEUM OF
  ARCHAEOLOGY AND
  ANTHROPOLOGY .... PHILADELPHIA, PA 117
VENANGO MUSEUM OF ART, SCIENCE AND
  INDUSTRY............................. OIL CITY, PA 98

EXHIBITS & COLLECTIONS-VEHICLES

BOYERTOWN MUSEUM OF HISTORIC
  VEHICLES........................... BOYERTOWN, PA 68
★CLAYTON .... PITTSBURGH, PA 138
THE FRICK ART & HISTORICAL CENTER... PITTSBURGH, PA 138
GAST CLASSIC MOTORCARS EXHIBIT ......STRASBURG, PA 105
GREENVILLE RAILROAD MUSEUM.........GREENVILLE, PA 82
GRICE CLEARFIELD COMMUNITY
  MUSEUM .... CLEARFIELD, PA 71
JEM CLASSIC CAR MUSEUM ....ANDREAS, PA 65
RAILROAD MUSEUM OF PENNSYLVANIA ....STRASBURG, PA 105
RODNEY C. GOTT MUSEUM ....YORK, PA 162
SPACE FARMS ZOO AND MUSEUM........ BEEMERVILLE, NJ 25
STEAMTOWN NHS............................. SCRANTON, PA 154
SWIGART MUSEUM .... HUNTINGDON, PA 88

EXHIBITS & COLLECTIONS-WARS

AIR HERITAGE MUSEUM ....BEAVER FALLS, PA 144
CONFEDERATE STATES ARMORY AND
  MUSEUM .... GETTYSBURG, PA 77
NATIONAL ARCHIVES PHILADELPHIA
  BRANCH............................. PHILADELPHIA, PA 116
★NATIONAL PARK
  VISITOR CENTER.................... GETTYSBURG NMP, PA 82
PENNSYLVANIA MILITARY MUSEUM ...... BOALSBURG, PA 68

SOLDIERS AND SAILORS MEMORIAL
HALL .... PITTSBURGH, PA 140
SOLDIERS NATIONAL MUSEUM .... GETTYSBURG, PA   78

EXHIBITS & COLLECTIONS-WEAPONS
ARDEC MUSEUM ....PICATINNY ARSENAL, NJ   43
CONFEDERATE STATES ARMORY AND
MUSEUM.................................. GETTYSBURG, PA   77
FORBES ROAD GUN MUSEUM................... LIGONIER, PA   92
HISTORICAL MUSEUM AND
LIBRARY...............................MORRISTOWN NHP, NJ   40
SAMUEL COLT HERITAGE MUSEUM ... GETTYSBURG, PA   78
SOLDIERS AND SAILORS MEMORIAL
HALL .... PITTSBURGH, PA 140

FARMS
THE AMISH FARM AND HOUSE .... LANCASTER, PA 101
APPLETREE FARM ....MOUNT POCONO, PA 149
BURNSIDE PLANTATION .... BETHLEHEM, PA   67
CROOK FARM.....................................BRADFORD, PA   68
FOSTERFIELDS LIVING HISTORICAL
FARM .... MORRISTOWN, NJ   39
HOWELL LIVING HISTORY FARM .... LAMBERTVILLE, NJ   37
★LANDIS VALLEY MUSEUM .... LANCASTER, PA 102
LEAMING'S RUN GARDENS AND
COLONIAL FARM .... CAPE MAY COURT HOUSE, NJ   27
PENNSBURY MANOR........................ MORRISVILLE, PA 127
PETER WENTZ FARMSTEAD .... CENTER POINT, PA 123
PLAIN AND FANCY FARM ....BIRD-IN-HAND, PA   99
★QUIET VALLEY LIVING HISTORICAL
FARM ....STROUDSBURG, PA 150
ROUND HILL EXHIBIT FARM .... ELIZABETH, PA 144
SLATEFORD FARMHOUSE .... DELAWARE WATER GAP
NRA, PA 147
SPRINGTON MANOR FARM .... DOWNINGTOWN, PA 124
WALNUT ACRES ORGANIC FARMS ....PENNS CREEK, PA   98

FISH HATCHERIES
LIL'LE'HI TROUT NURSERY ....ALLENTOWN, PA   64
REYNOLDSDALE FISH CULTURAL STATION ...BEDFORD, PA   66

FORESTS
RUTGERS DISPLAY GARDENS AND
HELYAR WOODS ....NEW BRUNSWICK, NJ   42
WILLIAM L. HUTCHESON
MEMORIAL FOREST..................NEW BRUNSWICK, NJ   42

FORESTS, NATIONAL; STATE
ALLEGHENY NF..PA   62
FORBES SF .... THE LAUREL HIGHLANDS, PA   91

FORTS & MILITARY INSTALLATIONS
CARLISLE BARRACKS .... CARLISLE, PA   70
FORT HANCOCK..........................GATEWAY NRA, NJ   32
FORT LIGONIER.................................... LIGONIER, PA   92
FORT MIFFLIN................................ PHILADELPHIA, PA 112
FORT MONMOUTH ....NJ   31
★FORT NECESSITY NB...................................PA   76
FORT PITT BLOCKHOUSE .... PITTSBURGH, PA 140
FORT ROBERDEAU .... ALTOONA, PA   65

FOSSILS
EARTH AND MINERAL SCIENCES
MUSEUM...............................STATE COLLEGE, PA 156
GEOLOGY MUSEUM....................NEW BRUNSWICK, NJ   42
TRAILSIDE NATURE AND SCIENCE
CENTER .... MOUNTAINSIDE, NJ   40

FOUNTAINS
BARE MEMORIAL FOUNTAIN......... ROARING SPRING, PA 152
FIREWORKS AND FOUNTAINS........KENNETT SQUARE, PA 125
★LONGWOOD GARDENS ....KENNETT SQUARE, PA 125
MEMORIAL FOUNTAIN .... CHAMBERSBURG, PA   70
★POINT SP.................................... PITTSBURGH, PA 140

FURNACES
CORNWALL IRON FURNACE .... CORNWALL, PA   71
CURTIN VILLAGE .... MILESBURG, PA   95
HOPEWELL FURNACE NHS ....PA   87
SCRANTON IRON FURNACES ....SCRANTON, PA 153

GAPS & PASSES
CONEMAUGH GAP .... JOHNSTOWN, PA   89
DELAWARE WATER GAP ....MOUNT POCONO, PA 149
DELAWARE WATER GAP NRA...............................PA 147

GARDENS
BLUE BIRD GARDENS.............................SUNBURY, PA 156
BOWMAN HILL
WILDFLOWER PRESERVE......... WASHINGTON CROSSING
HISTORIC PARK, PA 129
★BRANDYWINE RIVER MUSEUM .... CHADDS FORD, PA 124
CHANTICLEER ....WAYNE, PA 130
CHATFIELD MEMORIAL GARDEN ....ELIZABETH, NJ   28
DUKE GARDENS................................ SOMERVILLE, NJ   46
★FAIRMOUNT PARK .... PHILADELPHIA, PA 111

FREEDOMS FOUNDATION AT
VALLEY FORGE ....VALLEY FORGE, PA   12
GLENDENNING ROCK GARDEN .... PHILADELPHIA, PA   11
HEREFORD INLET LIGHTHOUSE ....WILDWOOD, NJ   5
HERSHEY GARDENS .... HERSHEY, PA   8
HISTORIC BARTRAM'S GARDEN... PHILADELPHIA, PA   11
HORTICULTURAL HALL GARDENS .... PHILADELPHIA, PA   11
HORTICULTURE CENTER .... PHILADELPHIA, PA   11
JAPANESE HOUSE AND GARDEN .... PHILADELPHIA, PA   11
LEAMING'S RUN GARDENS AND
COLONIAL FARM .... CAPE MAY COURT HOUSE, NJ   2
LEMOYNE HISTORIC GARDEN ....WASHINGTON, PA   14
LEONARD J. BUCK GARDEN .... FAR HILLS, NJ   2
★LONGWOOD GARDENS ....KENNETT SQUARE, PA   12
THE MASONIC HOMES .... ELIZABETHTOWN, PA   10
MORRIS ARBORETUM OF THE UNIVERSITY OF
PENNSYLVANIA..................... PHILADELPHIA, PA   11
MOUNTAINSIDE PARK .... MONTCLAIR, NJ   3
NEW JERSEY STATE BOTANICAL
GARDENS .... RINGWOOD, NJ   4
OLD ECONOMY VILLAGE ....AMBRIDGE, PA   14
OLD-FASHIONED ROSE GARDEN..........ALLENTOWN, PA   6
PENNSYLVANIA HORTICULTURAL
SOCIETY .... PHILADELPHIA, PA   11
★PHIPPS CONSERVATORY .... PITTSBURGH, PA   14
POWEL HOUSE .... PHILADELPHIA, PA   11
RIVERFRONT PARK .... HARRISBURG, PA   8
RODEF SHALOM BIBLICAL BOTANICAL
GARDEN............................... PITTSBURGH, PA   14
RUTGERS DISPLAY GARDENS AND
HELYAR WOODS .... NEW BRUNSWICK, NJ   4
STONEHEDGE GARDENS.............. SOUTH TAMAQUA, PA   15
TERHUNE MEMORIAL PARK ....WAYNE, NJ   4
THE TYLER ARBORETUM .... MEDIA, PA   4
WARINANCO PARK ....ELIZABETH, NJ   2
WORLD'S LARGEST GARDEN PARTY .... PHILADELPHIA, PA   12

GRAVES & TOMBS
ARTHUR ST. CLAIR ....GREENSBURG, PA   8
BENJAMIN FRANKLIN .... PHILADELPHIA, PA   11
BLESSED KATHARINE DREXEL SHRINE ...... BENSALEM, PA   12
FRIENDSHIP HILL NHS .... POINT MARION, PA   15
GEN. EDWARD BRADDOCK ....FORT NECESSITY NB, PA   7
GRAVE OF GEN. JOHN A. SUTTER ....LITITZ, PA   10
JOHN HARRIS JR................................. HARRISBURG, PA   8
JOHN PALM .... PALMYRA, PA   9
MOLLY PITCHER .... CARLISLE, PA   6
NATIONAL SHRINE OF ST. JOHN
NEUMANN......................... PHILADELPHIA, PA   11
REV. JOHN ELDER .... HARRISBURG, PA   8
THOMAS ALVA EDISON .... WEST ORANGE, NJ   3
WALT WHITMAN .... CAMDEN, NJ   1
WILLIAM MACLAY .... HARRISBURG, PA

HALLS OF FAME
AVIATION HALL OF FAME & MUSEUM OF NEW
JERSEY .... TETERBORO, NJ   4
BOB HOFFMAN WEIGHTLIFTING
HALL OF FAME...................................YORK, PA   1
PENN STATE FOOTBALL
HALL OF FAME.........................STATE COLLEGE, PA   1

HISTORIC BUILDINGS & HOUSES
ALEX CRAWFORD HOYT MANSION ....NEW CASTLE, PA   4
ALEXANDER GRANT HOUSE ....SALEM, NJ   1
THE AMISH FARM AND HOUSE .... LANCASTER, PA   1
THE AMISH VILLAGE ....STRASBURG, PA   1
AMOS JUDSON HOUSE ....WATERFORD, PA   1
ANN WHITALL .... WOODBURY, NJ   1
ASA PACKER MANSION ....JIM THORPE, PA   1
B. FREE FRANKLIN POST OFFICE AND
MUSEUM .... PHILADELPHIA, PA   1
BAINBRIDGE HOUSE .... PRINCETON, NJ
BAKER MANSION .... ALTOONA, PA
BALDWIN-REYNOLDS HOUSE .... MEADVILLE, PA
BALLANTINE HOUSE.............................. NEWARK, NJ   1
BARD-HOW HOUSE........................BURLINGTON, NJ   1
BERKS COUNTY HERITAGE CENTER .... READING, PA   1
BETSY ROSS HOUSE .... PHILADELPHIA, PA   1
BISHOP WHITE HOUSE .... PHILADELPHIA, PA   1
BOBB LOG HOUSE ....YORK, PA   1
BONHAM HOUSE ....YORK, PA   1
BONNELL HOUSE.............................. ELIZABETH, NJ
BOXWOOD HALL SHS .... ELIZABETH, NJ
BRANDYWINE BATTLEFIELD PARK .... CHADDS FORD, PA   1
BREEZEDALE ....INDIANA, PA
BRINTON HOUSE .... WEST CHESTER, PA   1
BUBE'S BREWERY .... MOUNT JOY, PA   1
BURLINGTON COUNTY HISTORICAL SOCIETY
COMPLEX ....BURLINGTON, NJ   1
CALEB PUSEY HOUSE .... CHESTER, PA   1
CAMDEN COUNTY HISTORICAL SOCIETY ...... CAMDEN, NJ   1
CAPT. JAMES LAWRENCE HOUSE.........BURLINGTON, NJ   1
CARPENTERS' HALL .... PHILADELPHIA, PA   1
CEDAR GROVE........................... PHILADELPHIA, PA   1
CENTENNIAL COTTAGE .... OCEAN GROVE, NJ

CENTRAL RAILROAD OF NEW JERSEY
  TERMINAL .... JERSEY CITY, NJ 36
CHURCH OF THE FALLING SPRING.... CHAMBERSBURG, PA 71
*CLAYTON .... PITTSBURGH, PA 138
CLIVEDEN .... PHILADELPHIA, PA 110
COLUMBUS CHAPEL AND BOAL MANSION
  MUSEUM .... BOALSBURG, PA 68
THE COMPASS INN MUSEUM.......... LAUGHLINTOWN, PA 91
*CONGRESS HALL .... PHILADELPHIA, PA 114
CONRAD WEISER HOMESTEAD .... WOMELSDORF, PA 161
CRAIG HOUSE............................... FREEHOLD, NJ 31
CROOK FARM................................. BRADFORD, PA 68
CURTIN VILLAGE .... MILESBURG, PA 95
DANIEL BOONE HOMESTEAD .... BAUMSTOWN, PA 65
DAVID BRADFORD HOUSE .... WASHINGTON, PA 145
DECLARATION (GRAFF) HOUSE .... PHILADELPHIA, PA 114
DESHLER-MORRIS HOUSE .... PHILADELPHIA, PA 114
DEY MANSION.................................... WAYNE, NJ 49
DONEGAL MILLS PLANTATION............. MOUNT JOY, PA 104
EAGLE HOTEL................................. WATERFORD, PA 159
EDGAR ALLAN POE HOUSE .... PHILADELPHIA, PA 111
EIGHTEENTH-CENTURY INDUSTRIAL
  AREA .... BETHLEHEM, PA 67
*EISENHOWER NHS .... GETTYSBURG, PA 77
EMLEN PHYSICK ESTATE .... CAPE MAY, NJ 26
EPHRATA CLOISTER .... EPHRATA, PA 100
ERIE HISTORY CENTER .... ERIE, PA 75
ESPY HOUSE...................................... BEDFORD, PA 66
FAIRMOUNT PARK HISTORIC HOUSES .... PHILADELPHIA, PA 112
*FALLINGWATER .... OHIOPYLE, PA 97
THE FERRY HOUSE .... TRENTON, NJ 48
FIREMAN'S HALL—NATIONAL FIRE HOUSE AND MUSEUM
  OF PHILADELPHIA....................... PHILADELPHIA, PA 112
F.M. KIRBY CENTER FOR THE PERFORMING
  ARTS .... WILKES-BARRE, PA 160
FONTHILL MUSEUM .... DOYLESTOWN, PA 124
FORT PITT BLOCKHOUSE .... PITTSBURGH, PA 140
FOSTERFIELDS LIVING HISTORICAL
  FARM .... MORRISTOWN, NJ 39
FRANK BUCHMAN HOUSE .... ALLENTOWN, PA 62
FRANKLIN COURT .... PHILADELPHIA, PA 114
FRENCH AZILUM .... TOWANDA, PA 157
THE FRICK ART & HISTORICAL CENTER .... PITTSBURGH, PA 138
FRIEND'S SCHOOL............................ BURLINGTON, NJ 131
FRIENDSHIP HILL NHS .... POINT MARION, PA 150
GENERAL HORATIO GATES HOUSE............. YORK, PA 162
GEORGE TAYLOR HOUSE.................... ALLENTOWN, PA 62
GERMANTOWN HISTORICAL SOCIETY .. PHILADELPHIA, PA 113
GIBBON HOUSE .... GREENWICH, NJ 32
GLENMONT .... WEST ORANGE, NJ 50
GLORIA DEI (OLD SWEDES') CHURCH... PHILADELPHIA, PA 113
*GOLDEN PLOUGH TAVERN .... YORK, PA 162
GOLF HOUSE—U.S. GOLF ASSOCIATION ...... FAR HILLS, NJ 29
GRAEME PARK .... HORSHAM, PA 125
GREY TOWERS .... MILFORD, PA 149
GROVER CLEVELAND BIRTHPLACE SHS...... CALDWELL, NJ 26
GRUNDY MUSEUM .... BRISTOL, PA 122
HANCOCK HOUSE .... SALEM, NJ 132
HANS HERR HOUSE .... LANCASTER, PA 102
HARRITON HOUSE .... BRYN MAWR, PA 122
HARRY PACKER MANSION .... JIM THORPE, PA 148
*HARTWOOD .... PITTSBURGH, PA 139
HEISEY MUSEUM .... LOCK HAVEN, PA 94
HERITAGE CENTER MUSEUM OF LANCASTER
  COUNTY...................................... LANCASTER, PA 102
HISTORIC BARTRAM'S GARDEN...... PHILADELPHIA, PA 113
HISTORIC FALLSINGTON .... FALLSINGTON, PA 125
HISTORIC ROCK FORD PLANTATION........ LANCASTER, PA 102
HOGE-OSMER HOUSE .... FRANKLIN, PA 76
HOLMES-HENRICKSON HOUSE.................. HOLMDEL, NJ 34
HOPE LODGE .... FORT WASHINGTON, PA 125
HOPEWELL FURNACE NHS .... PA 87
HOWELL LIVING HISTORY FARM .... LAMBERTVILLE, NJ 37
HUNTER HOUSE .... SUNBURY, PA 156
HUNTER-LAWRENCE HOUSE.................. WOODBURY, NJ 132
*INDEPENDENCE HALL.................... PHILADELPHIA, PA 114
*INDEPENDENCE NHP .... PHILADELPHIA, PA 113
INDIAN KING TAVERN HOUSE
  MUSEUM.................................. HADDONFIELD, NJ 132
JAMES A. MICHENER ART MUSEUM .... DOYLESTOWN, PA 124
JAMES FENIMORE COOPER HOUSE .. BURLINGTON, NJ 131
JAPANESE HOUSE AND GARDEN .... PHILADELPHIA, PA 111
JEFFERSON COUNTY COURTHOUSE.... BROOKVILLE, PA 68
JEFFERSON COUNTY HISTORICAL AND GENEALOGICAL
  SOCIETY .... BROOKVILLE, PA 69
JENNIE WADE HOUSE AND
  OLDE TOWN................................. GETTYSBURG, PA 78
JOHANNES MUELLER HOUSE....................... LITITZ, PA 104
JOHN CHADS HOUSE .... CHADDS FORD, PA 123
JOHN HARRIS/SIMON CAMERON
  MANSION .... HARRISBURG, PA 84
JOHN HOSKINS HOUSE ....BURLINGTON, NJ 131
JOHN SEBASTIAN GOUNDIE HOUSE .... BETHLEHEM, PA 67
JOHN SUTTON HALL............................... INDIANA, PA 88
JOSEPH PRIESTLEY HOUSE ..... NORTHUMBERLAND, PA 96
KENNYWOOD PARK .... PITTSBURGH, PA 139
*KENTUCK KNOB .... CHALK HILL, PA 70
KUSER FARM MANSION AND PARK.......... HAMILTON, NJ 33

LABORATORY COMPLEX .... WEST ORANGE, NJ 50
LACKAWANNA STATION .... SCRANTON, PA 153
LAUREL HILL .... Philadelphia, PA 112
LEADER'S HOME .... AMBRIDGE, PA 144
LEE'S HEADQUARTERS AND MUSEUM ... GETTYSBURG, PA 78
LEMON HILL................................. PHILADELPHIA, PA 112
LEMOYNE HOUSE............................. WASHINGTON, PA 145
LIBERTY HALL.................................. ELIZABETH, NJ 28
LINCOLN ROOM MUSEUM .... GETTYSBURG, PA 78
LITITZ MORAVIAN ARCHIVES AND MUSEUM ...... LITITZ, PA 103
LITTLE RED SCHOOLHOUSE.......... FLORHAM PARK, NJ 29
MARLIN OPERA HOUSE........................ BROOKVILLE, PA 68
MARLPIT HALL .... MIDDLETOWN, NJ 38
MARY RITNER'S BOARDING HOUSE.. CHAMBERSBURG, PA 71
McCONKEY FERRY INN ... WASHINGTON CROSSING
  HISTORIC PARK, PA 130
McCOY HOUSE .... LEWISTOWN, PA 92
MEADOWCROFT MUSEUM OF RURAL LIFE..... AVELLA, PA 65
MILL GROVE, THE AUDUBON WILDLIFE
  SANCTUARY .... AUDUBON, PA 122
MILLIONAIRES' ROW .... WILLIAMSPORT, PA 160
MORAVIAN HISTORICAL SOCIETY'S MUSEUM AND
  RESEARCH LIBRARY........................... NAZARETH, PA 95
MORAVIAN MUSEUM OF BETHLEHEM .... BETHLEHEM, PA 67
MORAVIAN POTTERY AND TILE
  WORKS....................................... DOYLESTOWN, PA 125
MOUNT PLEASANT .... PHILADELPHIA, PA 112
MOUNT WASHINGTON TAVERN...FORT NECESSITY NB, PA 76
NATHAN DENISON HOUSE.................... FORTY FORT, PA 76
NATHANIEL DRAKE............................. PLAINFIELD, NJ 44
NELSON HOUSE .... TRENTON, NJ 48
NEMACOLIN CASTLE .... BROWNSVILLE, PA 69
NEW HALL MILITARY MUSEUM.......... PHILADELPHIA, PA 114
NEWLIN MILL PARK .... CONCORDVILLE, PA 124
OLD BEDFORD VILLAGE .... BEDFORD, PA 66
OLD CITY HALL .... PHILADELPHIA, PA 114
OLD DUTCH PARSONAGE SHS............... SOMERVILLE, NJ 46
OLD ECONOMY VILLAGE....................... AMBRIDGE, PA 143
THE OLD JAIL .... CHAMBERSBURG, PA 71
OLD MAIN .... STATE COLLEGE, PA 156
OLD STONE HOUSE .... SLIPPERY ROCK, PA 155
PACKWOOD HOUSE MUSEUM .... LEWISBURG, PA 92
PAGODA .... READING, PA 151
PARRY MANSION MUSEUM .... NEW HOPE, PA 127
PASTOR'S STUDY AND ACADEMY............. HERSHEY, PA 87
THE PEARL S. BUCK HOUSE .... PERKASIE, PA 128
PEIRCE-DU-PONT HOUSE .... KENNETT SQUARE, PA 125
PENN SQUARE .... READING, PA 151
PENNSBURY MANOR .... MORRISVILLE, PA 127
PETER WENTZ FARMSTEAD .... CENTER POINT, PA 123
PETERS VALLEY.......... DELAWARE WATER GAP NRA, PA 147
PINK HOUSE.................................... CAPE MAY, NJ 26
POTTSGROVE MANOR .... POTTSTOWN, PA 128
POWEL HOUSE .... PHILADELPHIA, PA 116
REVELL HOUSE .... BURLINGTON, NJ 131
RINGWOOD MANOR .... RINGWOOD, NJ 45
ROCKINGHAM SHS .... PRINCETON, NJ 45
SCHOOL GALLERY OF THE PENNSYLVANIA ACADEMY OF
  THE FINE ARTS .... PHILADELPHIA, PA 117
SEARIGHTS TOLLHOUSE .... UNIONTOWN, PA 157
SLIFER HOUSE MUSEUM .... LEWISBURG, PA 92
SMITHVILLE MANSION .... MOUNT HOLLY, NJ 132
SOLDIER HUTS .... MORRISTOWN NHP, NJ 40
SOMERS MANSION .... SOMERS POINT, NJ 24
SOMERSET HISTORICAL CENTER .... SOMERSET, PA 155
SPRINGS MUSEUM .... SPRINGS, PA 155
STENTON MANSION .... PHILADELPHIA, PA 117
STEUBEN HOUSE SHS (ACKERMAN-ZABRISKIE-STEUBEN
  HOUSE)...................................... RIVER EDGE, NJ 45
STRASBURG COUNTRY STORE AND
  CREAMERY .... STRASBURG, PA 105
STRAWBERRY MANSION .... PHILADELPHIA, PA 112
STROUD MANSION .... STROUDSBURG, PA 150
STURGIS PRETZEL HOUSE......................... LITITZ, PA 104
SUN INN .... BETHLEHEM, PA 67
SUNNYBANK .... WAYNE, NJ 49
SUTTON-DITZ HOUSE MUSEUM & LIBRARY .... CLARION, PA 71
SWEETBRIAR MANSION .... PHILADELPHIA, PA 112
*TARA .... CLARK, PA 71
TAYLOR HOUSE ...... WASHINGTON CROSSING
  HISTORIC PARK, PA 130
THADDEUS KOSCIUSZKO NME........... PHILADELPHIA, PA 115
THADDEUS STEVENS' BLACKSMITH
  SHOP .... FAYETTEVILLE, PA 76
THE THOMAS CLARKE HOUSE .... PRINCETON, NJ 45
THOMAS MASSEY HOUSE.................... BROOMALL, PA 122
THOMPSON-NEELY HOUSE .... WASHINGTON CROSSING
  HISTORIC PARK, PA 129
TODD HOUSE .... PHILADELPHIA, PA 115
TOWNSHIP OF LEBANON MUSEUM .... HAMPTON, NJ 33
TROUT HALL .... ALLENTOWN, PA 64
TROXELL-STECKEL HOUSE................... ALLENTOWN, PA 62
TWOMBLY MANSION .... FLORHAM PARK, NJ 29
*VALLEY FORGE NHP.. PA 128
VOLLENDAM WINDMILL .... FLEMINGTON, NJ 29
WALLACE HOUSE SHS............................ SOMERVILLE, NJ 46
WARREN COUNTY HISTORICAL SOCIETY ...... WARREN, PA 158
*WASHINGTON CROSSING HISTORIC PARK.............. PA 129

WASHINGTON'S
   HEADQUARTERS ....VALLEY FORGE NHP, PA 129
WASHINGTON'S HEADQUARTERS (FORD
   MANSION) ....MORRISTOWN NHP, NJ 40
WAYNESBOROUGH .... PAOLI, PA 128
WEAVERTOWN ONE-ROOM
   SCHOOLHOUSE ....BIRD-IN-HAND, PA 99
WEST OVERTON MUSEUMS...................SCOTTDALE, PA 153
★WHEATLAND ....LANCASTER, PA 103
WICK HOUSE....................................MORRISTOWN NHP, NJ 40
THE WILLIAM TRENT HOUSE ....TRENTON, NJ 48
WOODFORD MANSION .... PHILADELPHIA, PA 112
WRIGHT'S FERRY MANSION ....COLUMBIA, PA 100
YORK COUNTY COLONIAL COURT HOUSE ....YORK, PA 162

HISTORIC DOCUMENTS, MANUSCRIPTS & RARE BOOKS
FREE LIBRARY OF PHILADELPHIA........ PHILADELPHIA, PA 113
HISTORICAL SOCIETY OF
   PENNSYLVANIA .... PHILADELPHIA, PA 113
NATIONAL ARCHIVES PHILADELPHIA
   BRANCH .... PHILADELPHIA, PA 116
NEW JERSEY HISTORICAL SOCIETY............. NEWARK, NJ 41
★STATE MUSEUM OF PENNSYLVANIA ... HARRISBURG, PA 85

HISTORIC SITES
ALLEGHENY PORTAGE RAILROAD NHS .... CRESSON, PA 72
BOXWOOD HALL SHS.............................ELIZABETH, NJ 28
BUSHY RUN BATTLEFIELD SHS ....JEANNETTE, PA 144
CARL. E. STOTZ FIELD .... WILLIAMSPORT, PA 160
EDGAR ALLAN POE NHS....................... PHILADELPHIA, PA 111
★EDISON NHS .... WEST ORANGE, NJ 50
★EISENHOWER NHS .... GETTYSBURG, PA 77
FORT LEE HISTORIC PARK ....FORT LEE, NJ 30
FORT MOTT SP...SALEM, NJ 132
FORT NONSENSE ....MORRISTOWN NHP, NJ 40
FRIENDSHIP HILL NHS .... POINT MARION, PA 150
GROVER CLEVELAND BIRTHPLACE SHS.......CALDWELL, NJ 26
HISTORIC HANNA'S TOWN.......................GREENSBURG, PA 82
HISTORIC RITTENHOUSETOWN .... PHILADELPHIA, PA 111
HOPEWELL FURNACE NHS .... PA 87
★INDEPENDENCE NHP .... PHILADELPHIA, PA 113
JOCKEY HOLLOW.........................MORRISTOWN NHP, NJ 40
JOHN BROWN TANNERY .... MEADVILLE, PA 94
★LIBERTY BELL PAVILION .... PHILADELPHIA, PA 114
LIBERTY BELL SHRINE MUSEUM ....ALLENTOWN, PA 64
★MORRISTOWN NHP ....NJ 40
OLD DUTCH PARSONAGE SHS.............. SOMERVILLE, NJ 46
PENN'S LANDING.............................. PHILADELPHIA, PA 116
PITHOLE CITY ....PLUMER, PA 145
ROCKINGHAM SHS ....PRINCETON, NJ 45
SLATEFORD
   FARMHOUSE .... DELAWARE WATER GAP NRA, PA 147
STEAMTOWN NHS ....SCRANTON, PA 154
STEUBEN HOUSE SHS (ACKERMAN-ZABRISKIE-STEUBEN
   HOUSE) .... RIVER EDGE, NJ 45
TWIN LIGHTS SHS .... HIGHLANDS, NJ 33
★VALLEY FORGE NHP..PA 128
WALLACE HOUSE SHS........................... SOMERVILLE, NJ 46
★WASHINGTON CROSSING HISTORIC PARK.............PA 129
WASHINGTON CROSSING SP.....................TRENTON, NJ 48

HORSE FARMS
HANOVER SHOE FARMS........................HANOVER, PA 83
LAND OF LITTLE HORSES ....GETTYSBURG, PA 78

INDUSTRIAL TOURS
ANDERSON BAKERY COMPANY ....LANCASTER, PA 102
BENZEL'S PRETZEL FACTORY ....ALTOONA, PA 64
DAFFIN'S CANDIES CHOCOLATE KINGDOM... SHARON, PA 154
HARLEY-DAVIDSON ASSEMBLY PLANT ....YORK, PA 162
HERR'S SNACK FOODS ....NOTTINGHAM, PA 127
HISTORIC RENAULT WINERY ....EGG HARBOR CITY, NJ 23
MARTIN GUITAR COMPANY ....NAZARETH, PA 95
MCCLINTOCK WELL NO. 1.............................OIL CITY, PA 98
SELTZER'S LEBANON BOLOGNA CO. INC. ..... PALMYRA, PA 98
STRAUB BREWERY .... ST. MARYS, PA 153
THREE MILE ISLAND VISITORS CENTER..... MIDDLETOWN, PA 95
UTZ POTATO CHIPS..................................HANOVER, PA 83
WALNUT ACRES ORGANIC FARMS ....PENNS CREEK, PA 98
WENDELL AUGUST FORGE ....GROVE CITY, PA 82
YUENGLING BREWERY..........................POTTSVILLE, PA 151

ISLANDS
LONG BEACH ISLAND ....BARNEGAT LIGHT, NJ 24

JAILS
FORT HANCOCK MUSEUM ....GATEWAY NRA, NJ 32
THE OLD JAIL ......................................CHAMBERSBURG, PA 71
THE OLD JAIL CENTER......................... WILLIAMSPORT, PA 160

LAKES, PONDS & RESERVOIRS
ALLEGHENY RESERVOIR .... ALLEGHENY NF, PA 62
CONNEAUT LAKE ....CONNEAUT LAKE, PA 71
PYMATUNING RESERVOIR .... LINESVILLE, PA 93
RAYSTOWN LAKE ....HUNTINGDON, PA 87

LIBRARIES
ATLANTIC COUNTY HISTORICAL SOCIETY LIBRARY AND
   MUSEUM.. SOMERS POINT, NJ 24
THE BALCH INSTITUTE FOR ETHNIC
   STUDIES .... PHILADELPHIA, PA 110
C. EVERETT KOOP COMMUNITY HEALTH INFORMATION
   CENTER .... PHILADELPHIA, PA 110
THE CARNEGIE LIBRARY OF PITTSBURGH ...PITTSBURGH, PA 137
CHESTER COUNTY HISTORICAL
   SOCIETY .... WEST CHESTER, PA 130
CIVIL WAR LIBRARY AND MUSEUM..... PHILADELPHIA, PA 110
CUMBERLAND COUNTY HISTORICAL SOCIETY LIBRARY
   AND MUSEUM .... CARLISLE, PA 70
FREE LIBRARY OF PHILADELPHIA........ PHILADELPHIA, PA 113
GOLF HOUSE—U.S. GOLF ASSOCIATION ......FAR HILLS, NJ 29
HISTORICAL MUSEUM AND
   LIBRARY..................................MORRISTOWN NHP, NJ 40
JUNIATA COLLEGE.............................HUNTINGDON, PA 88
MIFFLIN COUNTY HISTORICAL SOCIETY MUSEUM AND
   LIBRARY... LEWISTOWN, PA 92
MONMOUTH COUNTY HISTORICAL ASSOCIATION
   MUSEUM AND LIBRARY ....FREEHOLD, NJ 31
MORAVIAN HISTORICAL SOCIETY'S MUSEUM AND
   RESEARCH LIBRARY ....NAZARETH, PA 95
NEW JERSEY HISTORICAL SOCIETY .... NEWARK, NJ 41
NEWARK PUBLIC LIBRARY .... NEWARK, NJ 41
PELLETIER LIBRARY .... MEADVILLE, PA 94
PENN STATE ROOM UNIVERSITY
   ARCHIVES .... STATE COLLEGE, PA 156
ROSENBACH MUSEUM AND LIBRARY..... PHILADELPHIA, PA 117
SPRUANCE LIBRARY ....DOYLESTOWN, PA 125
STOY MUSEUM AND HAUCK MEMORIAL
   LIBRARY...LEBANON, PA 91
WARREN COUNTY HISTORICAL SOCIETY ......WARREN, PA 158
WASHINGTON AND JEFFERSON COLLEGE MEMORIAL
   LIBRARY..WASHINGTON, PA 145

LIGHTHOUSES
BARNEGAT LIGHTHOUSE................BARNEGAT LIGHT, NJ 24
CAPE MAY POINT LIGHTHOUSE ....CAPE MAY, NJ 26
HEREFORD INLET LIGHTHOUSE ....WILDWOOD, NJ 51
SANDY HOOK LIGHTHOUSE ....GATEWAY NRA, NJ 32
TWIN LIGHTS SHS .... HIGHLANDS, NJ 33

MAPS
HERITAGE MAP MUSEUM....................................LITITZ, PA 104

MARINE ATTRACTIONS
MARINE MAMMAL STRANDING CENTER.... BRIGANTINE, NJ 23

MARKETS
BIRD-IN-HAND FARMER'S MARKET ....LANCASTER, PA 102
THE BROAD STREET MARKET ....HARRISBURG, PA 84
CENTRAL MARKET ....LANCASTER, PA 102
CENTRAL MARKET HOUSE ....YORK, PA 161
FARMERS' MARKET..YORK, PA 161
FARMER'S MARKET OF LIMERICK ....LIMERICK, PA 126
FARMERS' MARKETS ....LANCASTER, PA 102
GREEN DRAGON AUCTION MARKET............EPHRATA, PA 100
ITALIAN MARKET .... PHILADELPHIA, PA 120
MARKET HOUSE .... MEADVILLE, PA 94
MEADOWBROOK MARKET ....LANCASTER, PA 102
MILL BRIDGE VILLAGE ....LANCASTER, PA 103
NEW EASTERN MARKET ....YORK, PA 161
READING TERMINAL MARKET .... PHILADELPHIA, PA 120

MEMORIALS
THE AVENUE OF 444 FLAGS ....HERMITAGE, PA 85
★ETERNAL LIGHT PEACE
   MEMORIAL .... GETTYSBURG NMP, PA 80
★FRANKLIN INSTITUTE SCIENCE
   MUSEUM .... PHILADELPHIA, PA 113
JIM THORPE MEMORIAL ....JIM THORPE, PA 148
JOHNSTOWN FLOOD NME ....JOHNSTOWN, PA 90
MEMORIAL FLAGSTAFF............ WASHINGTON CROSSING
                                          HISTORIC PARK, PA 129
MEMORIAL FOUNTAIN ...............CHAMBERSBURG, PA 70
NATIONAL MEMORIAL ARCH ......VALLEY FORGE NHP, PA 129
NORTH CAROLINA....................... GETTYSBURG NMP, PA 80
RIVERFRONT PARK ....HARRISBURG, PA 84
STEPHEN FOSTER MEMORIAL .... PITTSBURGH, PA 141
TERHUNE MEMORIAL PARK ....WAYNE, NJ 49
VIRGINIA .... GETTYSBURG NMP, PA 80

MILLS
★BRANDYWINE RIVER MUSEUM .... CHADDS FORD, PA 124
CLINTON .... NJ 28
COOPER GRISTMILL.......................................CHESTER, NJ 28
HAINES MILL MUSEUM ....ALLENTOWN, PA 62
MILL BRIDGE VILLAGE ....LANCASTER, PA 103
NEWLIN MILL PARK .........................CONCORDVILLE, PA 124
OLD RED MILL .... CLINTON, NJ 28
THOMPSON'S GRIST MILL .... WASHINGTON CROSSING
                                          HISTORIC PARK, PA 129
THE UPPER MILL .... MILFORD, PA 149
VOLANT...PA 159

MINES & MINERALS

CAPE MAY DIAMONDS...........................CAPE MAY, NJ 26
CORNWALL ORE BANKS......................CORNWALL, PA 71
EARTH AND MINERAL SCIENCES
  MUSEUM...........................STATE COLLEGE, PA 156
FRANKLIN MINERAL MUSEUM..............FRANKLIN, NJ 31
LACKAWANNA COAL MINE TOUR...........SCRANTON, PA 154
MUSEUM OF ANTHRACITE MINING...........ASHLAND, PA 65
PIONEER TUNNEL COAL MINE AND STEAM TRAIN
  RIDE..................................ASHLAND, PA 65
SELDOM SEEN INC......................ST. BONIFACE, PA 152
STERLING HILL MINE & MUSEUM........OGDENSBURG, NJ 43
TOUR-ED MINE & MUSEUM..................TARENTUM, PA 144

MONUMENTS-GENERAL

DAVID ZEISBERGER......................COUDERSPORT, PA 72
FREEDOMS FOUNDATION AT
  VALLEY FORGE.....................VALLEY FORGE, PA 128
HENRY CLAY MONUMENT..................POTTSVILLE, PA 150
HIGH WATER MARK................. GETTYSBURG NMP, PA 80
JIM THORPE...............................CARLISLE, PA 69
SOLDIERS AND SAILORS MONUMENT..........EASTON, PA 73
WYOMING MASSACRE ....WYOMING, PA 161

MONUMENTS, NATIONAL; STATE

SOLDIERS' NMO ....GETTYSBURG NMP, PA 80
★STATUE OF LIBERTY NMO ....JERSEY CITY, NJ 36

MOUNTAINS

FIRST MOUNTAIN ....MONTCLAIR, NJ 38
MOUNT DAVIS.........THE LAUREL HIGHLANDS, PA 91
MOUNT MITCHILL ....HIGHLANDS, NJ 33
POCONO KNOB ....MOUNT POCONO, PA 149

MURALS & MOSAICS

LAND GRANT FRESCOES..................STATE COLLEGE, PA 156

MUSEUMS

AFRO-AMERICAN HISTORICAL AND CULTURAL
  MUSEUM..........................PHILADELPHIA, PA 108
AGRICULTURE AND INDUSTRIAL MUSEUM OF YORK
  COUNTY...................................YORK, PA 161
AGRICULTURE MUSEUM ....YORK, PA 162
AIR HERITAGE MUSEUM................BEAVER FALLS, PA 144
ALLENTOWN ART MUSEUM ....ALLENTOWN, PA 63
ALTOONA RAILROADERS MEMORIAL
  MUSEUM.................................ALTOONA, PA 64
AMERICAN CHRISTMAS MUSEUM .... CHADDS FORD, PA 123
AMERICAN FREEDOM MUSEUM ....HERMITAGE, PA 85
AMERICAN LABOR MUSEUM/BOTTO HOUSE NATIONAL
  LANDMARK.............................HALEDON, NJ 33
AMERICAN MUSEUM OF IMMIGRATION ....JERSEY CITY, NJ 36
AMERICAN SWEDISH HISTORICAL
  MUSEUM...........................PHILADELPHIA, PA 108
AMISH WORLD MUSEUM ....INTERCOURSE, PA 101
THE ANDY WARHOL MUSEUM ....PITTSBURGH, PA 136
ANTHRACITE MUSEUM COMPLEX...........SCRANTON, PA 153
ARDEC MUSEUM ....PICATINNY ARSENAL, NJ 43
THE ATHENEUM OF PHILADELPHIA... PHILADELPHIA, PA 108
ATLANTIC CITY ART CENTER AND HISTORICAL
  MUSEUM.........................ATLANTIC CITY, NJ 20
ATLANTIC COUNTY HISTORICAL SOCIETY LIBRARY AND
  MUSEUM..........................SOMERS POINT, NJ 24
ATWATER KENT MUSEUM—THE PHILADELPHIA HISTORY
  MUSEUM..........................PHILADELPHIA, PA 110
AVIATION HALL OF FAME & MUSEUM OF NEW
  JERSEY ....TETERBORO, NJ 47
B. FREE FRANKLIN POST OFFICE AND
  MUSEUM..........................PHILADELPHIA, PA 113
BAINBRIDGE HOUSE......................PRINCETON, NJ 44
THE BALCH INSTITUTE FOR ETHNIC
  STUDIES ........................PHILADELPHIA, PA 110
BARNEGAT BAY DECOY AND BAYMEN'S
  MUSEUM..............................TUCKERTON, NJ 49
BEAVER FALLS HISTORICAL SOCIETY AND
  MUSEUM.........................BEAVER FALLS, PA 144
BERGEN MUSEUM OF ART AND SCIENCE....PARAMUS, NJ 43
BERMAN MUSEUM OF ART...........COLLEGEVILLE, PA 124
BESSEMER COURT AT STATION SQUARE.. PITTSBURGH, PA 136
BONHAM HOUSE ....YORK, PA 162
BOYERTOWN MUSEUM OF HISTORIC
  VEHICLES.............................BOYERTOWN, PA 68
★BRANDYWINE RIVER MUSEUM ....CHADDS FORD, PA 124
BRIDGETON CITY PARK ....BRIDGETON, NJ 26
BURLINGTON COUNTY HISTORICAL SOCIETY
  COMPLEX.............................BURLINGTON, NJ 131
CAMDEN COUNTY HISTORICAL SOCIETY ......CAMDEN, NJ 131
THE CANAL MUSEUM ....GREENVILLE, PA 82
CANDY AMERICANA MUSEUM AND CANDY
  OUTLET...................................LITITZ, PA 103
★THE CARNEGIE ....PITTSBURGH, PA 136
THE CARNEGIE MUSEUM OF ART ....PITTSBURGH, PA 137
★THE CARNEGIE MUSEUM OF NATURAL
  HISTORY ....PITTSBURGH, PA 137
CAROUSEL WORLD ....LAHASKA, PA 126
CHESTER COUNTY HISTORICAL
  SOCIETY..........................WEST CHESTER, PA 130

CHILDREN'S DISCOVERY WORKSHOP .... WILLIAMSPORT, PA 160
CIVIL WAR LIBRARY AND MUSEUM..... PHILADELPHIA, PA 110
CLAUSSVILLE SCHOOL ....ALLENTOWN, PA 62
★CLAYTON ....PITTSBURGH, PA 138
THE COLLEGE OF PHYSICIANS OF
  PHILADELPHIA .....................PHILADELPHIA, PA 110
THE COMPASS INN MUSEUM.......... LAUGHLINTOWN, PA 91
CONFEDERATE STATES ARMORY AND
  MUSEUM...........................GETTYSBURG, PA 77
CUMBERLAND COUNTY HISTORICAL SOCIETY LIBRARY
  AND MUSEUM ....CARLISLE, PA 70
DEBENCE'S ANTIQUE MUSIC WORLD ....FRANKLIN, PA 77
DORFLINGER GLASS MUSEUM .... WHITE MILLS, PA 150
★DRAKE WELL MUSEUM.................TITUSVILLE, PA 156
DREXEL COLLECTION ................PHILADELPHIA, PA 111
DUNCAN MILLER GLASS MUSEUM ....WASHINGTON, PA 145
EARTH AND MINERAL SCIENCES
  MUSEUM...........................STATE COLLEGE, PA 156
ELFRETH'S ALLEY .....................PHILADELPHIA, PA 111
ELLARSLIE—THE TRENTON CITY MUSEUM ... TRENTON, NJ 48
ERIE ART MUSEUM ....ERIE, PA 74
ERIE HISTORICAL MUSEUM ....ERIE, PA 75
EVERHART MUSEUM ....SCRANTON, PA 154
EXPERIENCE CHILDREN'S MUSEUM ....ERIE, PA 75
FARM MUSEUM (BRADFORD COUNTY HERITAGE
  ASSOCIATION) ....TROY, PA 157
FIRE MUSEUM ....HARRISBURG, PA 83
FIREMAN'S HALL—NATIONAL FIRE HOUSE AND MUSEUM
  OF PHILADELPHIA...................PHILADELPHIA, PA 112
FONTHILL MUSEUM ....DOYLESTOWN, PA 124
FORBES ROAD GUN MUSEUM..............LIGONIER, PA 92
FORT BEDFORD MUSEUM ....BEDFORD, PA 66
FORT HANCOCK MUSEUM ....GATEWAY NRA, NJ 32
FORT HUNTER MANSION AND PARK ..... HARRISBURG, PA 84
FORT LEBOEUF MUSEUM.................WATERFORD, PA 158
FORT LIGONIER ....LIGONIER, PA 92
★FORT PITT MUSEUM ....PITTSBURGH, PA 140
FRANKLIN COURT ...................PHILADELPHIA, PA 114
★FRANKLIN INSTITUTE SCIENCE
  MUSEUM...........................PHILADELPHIA, PA 113
FRANKLIN MINERAL MUSEUM ....FRANKLIN, NJ 31
FRANKLIN MINT MUSEUM ....MEDIA, PA 127
THE FRICK ART & HISTORICAL CENTER .... PITTSBURGH, PA 138
FRICK ART MUSEUM ....PITTSBURGH, PA 139
FROST ENTOMOLOGICAL MUSEUM....STATE COLLEGE, PA 156
GARDNER'S CANDY MUSEUM ....TYRONE, PA 157
GAST CLASSIC MOTORCARS EXHIBIT ....STRASBURG, PA 105
GEOLOGY MUSEUM ....NEW BRUNSWICK, NJ 42
GEORGE F. BOYER HISTORICAL MUSEUM ... WILDWOOD, NJ 51
GERMANTOWN HISTORICAL SOCIETY .. PHILADELPHIA, PA 113
GETTYSBURG MUSEUM OF THE
  CIVIL WAR ....GETTYSBURG NMP, PA 82
GOLF HOUSE—U.S. GOLF ASSOCIATION ...... FAR HILLS, NJ 29
GREATER HAZLETON HISTORICAL SOCIETY
  MUSEUM..............................HAZLETON, PA 85
GREENE COUNTY HISTORICAL
  MUSEUM...........................WAYNESBURG, PA 159
GREENVILLE RAILROAD MUSEUM...........GREENVILLE, PA 82
GRICE CLEARFIELD COMMUNITY
  MUSEUM...........................CLEARFIELD, PA 71
HAINES MILL MUSEUM ....ALLENTOWN, PA 62
HANDS-ON HOUSE, CHILDREN'S MUSEUM OF
  LANCASTER...........................LANCASTER, PA 102
HANS HERR HOUSE ....LANCASTER, PA 102
HARMONY MUSEUM ....HARMONY, PA 144
HEISEY MUSEUM.......................LOCK HAVEN, PA 94
HERITAGE CENTER MUSEUM OF LANCASTER
  COUNTY..............................LANCASTER, PA 102
HERITAGE MAP MUSEUM....................LITITZ, PA 104
★HERSHEY MUSEUM ....HERSHEY, PA 86
HESSIAN POWDER MAGAZINE MUSEUM ..... CARLISLE, PA 70
HISTORIC RITTENHOUSETOWN .... PHILADELPHIA, PA 111
HISTORIC ROCK FORD PLANTATION ....LANCASTER, PA 102
HISTORICAL MUSEUM ..... CAPE MAY COURT HOUSE, NJ 27
HISTORICAL MUSEUM AND
  LIBRARY.........................MORRISTOWN NHP, NJ 40
HISTORICAL SOCIETY OF BERKS COUNTY..... READING, PA 152
HISTORICAL SOCIETY OF
  PENNSYLVANIA .....................PHILADELPHIA, PA 113
★HISTORICAL SOCIETY OF YORK COUNTY ....YORK, PA 162
HORSESHOE CURVE NATIONAL HISTORIC
  LANDMARK.............................ALTOONA, PA 65
HOUDINI TOUR AND SHOW ....SCRANTON, PA 154
HUNTERDON HISTORICAL MUSEUM ....CLINTON, NJ 28
INDEPENDENCE SEAPORT MUSEUM ... PHILADELPHIA, PA 115
INDIAN KING TAVERN HOUSE
  MUSEUM...........................HADDONFIELD, NJ 132
INDIAN STEPS MUSEUM ....AIRVILLE, PA 62
INDUSTRIAL MUSEUM ....YORK, PA 162
JAMES A. MICHENER ART MUSEUM .....DOYLESTOWN, PA 124
JEFFERSON COUNTY HISTORICAL AND GENEALOGICAL
  SOCIETY.............................BROOKVILLE, PA 69
JEM CLASSIC CAR MUSEUM ....ANDREAS, PA 65
THE JIMMY STEWART MUSEUM..................INDIANA, PA 89
JOHANNES MUELLER HOUSE.................LITITZ, PA 104
★JOHNSTOWN FLOOD MUSEUM...........JOHNSTOWN, PA 90
THE KEMERER MUSEUM OF DECORATIVE
  ARTS ....BETHLEHEM, PA 67

LAKE SHORE RAILWAY MUSEUM ....NORTH EAST, PA   96
LANCASTER COUNTY HISTORICAL
  SOCIETY .... LANCASTER, PA 102
LANCASTER NEWSPAPERS NEWSEUM...... LANCASTER, PA 102
★LANDIS VALLEY MUSEUM .... LANCASTER, PA 102
LE PETIT MUSEUM OF MUSICAL BOXES......MARIETTA, PA 104
LEE'S HEADQUARTERS AND MUSEUM ... GETTYSBURG, PA   78
LEHIGH COUNTY HISTORICAL SOCIETY ......ALLENTOWN, PA   64
LEHIGHTON MODEL TRAIN DISPLAY........ LEHIGHTON, PA 149
LIBERTY BELL SHRINE MUSEUM ....ALLENTOWN, PA   64
★LIBERTY SCIENCE CENTER..................... JERSEY CITY, NJ   36
LINCOLN ROOM MUSEUM .... GETTYSBURG, PA   78
THE LINCOLN TRAIN MUSEUM .... GETTYSBURG, PA   78
LITTLE LEAGUE BASEBALL MUSEUM ... WILLIAMSPORT, PA 161
LITTLE RED SCHOOLHOUSE .... FLORHAM PARK, NJ   29
LOCK RIDGE FURNACE MUSEUM ....ALLENTOWN, PA   62
LONG BEACH ISLAND HISTORICAL
  MUSEUM...................................BEACH HAVEN, NJ   25
LOST RIVER CAVERNS AND THE GILMAN
  MUSEUM .... HELLERTOWN, PA   85
LYCOMING COUNTY HISTORICAL
  MUSEUM .... WILLIAMSPORT, PA 161
THE MAIN MUSEUM................................ TRENTON, NJ   48
MARIO LANZA INSTITUTE AND
  MUSEUM .... PHILADELPHIA, PA 115
MARTIN GUITAR COMPANY.................NAZARETH, PA   95
MARY MERRITT DOLL MUSEUM .... READING, PA 152
★MASONIC TEMPLE .... PHILADELPHIA, PA 115
MCCOY HOUSE ....LEWISTOWN, PA   92
MCFADDEN RAILROAD MUSEUM ....MERCERSBURG, PA   95
MERCER COUNTY HISTORICAL MUSEUM ......MERCER, PA   94
MERCER MUSEUM ....DOYLESTOWN, PA 124
MERRITT'S MUSEUM OF CHILDHOOD .... READING, PA 152
MID-ATLANTIC AIR MUSEUM .... READING, PA 152
MIFFLIN COUNTY HISTORICAL SOCIETY MUSEUM AND
  LIBRARY.................................. LEWISTOWN, PA   92
MILL GROVE, THE AUDUBON WILDLIFE
  SANCTUARY .... AUDUBON, PA 122
MONMOUTH COUNTY HISTORICAL ASSOCIATION
  MUSEUM AND LIBRARY .... FREEHOLD, NJ   31
MORAVIAN HISTORICAL SOCIETY'S MUSEUM AND
  RESEARCH LIBRARY.......................NAZARETH, PA   95
MORAVIAN MUSEUM OF BETHLEHEM ... BETHLEHEM, PA   67
THE MORRIS MUSEUM......................MORRISTOWN, NJ   40
MUMMERS MUSEUM .... PHILADELPHIA, PA 115
MUSEUM OF AMERICAN GLASS .... MILLVILLE, NJ   38
MUSEUM OF ANTHRACITE MINING.........ASHLAND, PA   65
MUSEUM OF EARLY TRADES AND CRAFTS ...MADISON, NJ   37
MUSEUM OF SCIENTIFIC DISCOVERY ... HARRISBURG, PA   84
MUTTER MUSEUM .... PHILADELPHIA, PA 110
NAIL MILL MUSEUM .... BRIDGETON, NJ   26
THE NATIONAL CANAL MUSEUM ....EASTON, PA   73
NATIONAL CIVIL WAR WAX MUSEUM ... GETTYSBURG, PA   78
NATIONAL MUSEUM OF AMERICAN JEWISH
  HISTORY .... PHILADELPHIA, PA 116
NATIONAL PORTRAIT GALLERY.......... PHILADELPHIA, PA 115
THE NATIONAL TOY TRAIN MUSEUM ...... STRASBURG, PA 105
NATURAL HISTORY MUSEUM ....PRINCETON, NJ   45
NELSON HOUSE .... TRENTON, NJ   48
NEW HALL MILITARY MUSEUM.......... PHILADELPHIA, PA 114
NEW JERSEY CHILDREN'S MUSEUM..........PARAMUS, NJ   43
NEW JERSEY MUSEUM OF
  AGRICULTURE.......................... NEW BRUNSWICK, NJ   42
★NEW JERSEY STATE MUSEUM .... TRENTON, NJ   48
NEW SWEDEN FARMSTEAD MUSEUM...... BRIDGETON, NJ   26
NEWARK MUSEUM ....NEWARK, NJ   41
NORTH MUSEUM OF NATURAL HISTORY AND
  SCIENCE .... LANCASTER, PA 103
THE NOYES MUSEUM OF ART.................OCEANVILLE, NJ   24
OCEAN CITY HISTORICAL MUSEUM ...... OCEAN CITY, NJ   42
★OLD BARRACKS MUSEUM .... TRENTON, NJ   48
OMAR N. BRADLEY MUSEUM .... CARLISLE, PA   70
PACKWOOD HOUSE MUSEUM..............LEWISBURG, PA   92
PALMER MUSEUM OF ART.............. STATE COLLEGE, PA 156
PARRY MANSION MUSEUM .... NEW HOPE, PA 127
PENN-BRAD OIL MUSEUM ....BRADFORD, PA   68
PENNSYLVANIA ANTHRACITE HERITAGE
  MUSEUM....................................SCRANTON, PA 153
PENNSYLVANIA LUMBER MUSEUM ..... COUDERSPORT, PA   72
PENNSYLVANIA MILITARY MUSEUM ...... BOALSBURG, PA   68
PENNSYLVANIA TROLLEY MUSEUM ...... WASHINGTON, PA 145
THE PEOPLE'S PLACE .... INTERCOURSE, PA 101
THE PEOPLE'S PLACE QUILT MUSEUM... INTERCOURSE, PA 101
★PHILADELPHIA MUSEUM OF ART ...... PHILADELPHIA, PA 111
PHILLIPS MUSHROOM MUSEUM......KENNETT SQUARE, PA 126
PITTSBURGH CHILDREN'S MUSEUM ...... PITTSBURGH, PA 139
PLEASE TOUCH MUSEUM .... PHILADELPHIA, PA 116
POCONO INDIAN MUSEUM......................BUSHKILL, PA 147
POLISH AMERICAN CULTURAL CENTER
  MUSEUM .... PHILADELPHIA, PA 116
THE PRESBYTERIAN HISTORICAL
  SOCIETY .... PHILADELPHIA, PA 116
RAILROAD MUSEUM OF PENNSYLVANIA ....STRASBURG, PA 105
READING PUBLIC MUSEUM .... READING, PA 152
RENFREW MUSEUM AND PARK............WAYNESBORO, PA 159
ROCKHILL TROLLEY MUSEUM..... ROCKHILL FURNACE, PA 152
RODIN MUSEUM .... PHILADELPHIA, PA 112
RODNEY C. GOTT MUSEUM ....YORK, PA 162

ROGERS MILL (PATERSON MUSEUM) .... PATERSON, NJ   43
ROSENBACH MUSEUM AND LIBRARY..... PHILADELPHIA, PA 117
SAMUEL COLT HERITAGE MUSEUM....... GETTYSBURG, PA   78
SAYLOR CEMENT MUSEUM..................ALLENTOWN, PA   62
SENATOR JOHN HEINZ PITTSBURGH REGIONAL HISTORY
  CENTER .... PITTSBURGH, PA 140
SLIFER HOUSE MUSEUM.......................LEWISBURG, PA   92
SOLDIERS AND SAILORS MEMORIAL
  HALL.. PITTSBURGH, PA 140
SOLDIERS NATIONAL MUSEUM .... GETTYSBURG, PA   78
SOUTHERN ALLEGHENIES
  MUSEUM OF ART .... LORETTO, PA   94
SPACE FARMS ZOO AND MUSEUM........ BEEMERVILLE, NJ   25
SPRINGS MUSEUM .... SPRINGS, PA 155
★STATE MUSEUM OF PENNSYLVANIA ... HARRISBURG, PA   85
STEAMTOWN NHS ....SCRANTON, PA 154
STEPHEN FOSTER MEMORIAL .... PITTSBURGH, PA 141
STERLING HILL MINE & MUSEUM .... OGDENSBURG, NJ   43
STEUBEN HOUSE SHS (ACKERMAN-ZABRISKIE-STEUBEN
  HOUSE)..................................... RIVER EDGE, NJ   45
STOY MUSEUM AND HAUCK MEMORIAL
  LIBRARY....................................LEBANON, PA   91
SUBMARINE USS LING NEW JERSEY NAVAL
  MUSEUM..................................HACKENSACK, NJ   32
SUTTON-DITZ HOUSE MUSEUM & LIBRARY ....CLARION, PA   71
SWIGART MUSEUM ....HUNTINGDON, PA   88
THOMAS A. EDISON MEMORIAL TOWER AND
  MUSEUM .... MENLO PARK, NJ   38
THOMAS NEWCOMEN LIBRARY AND
  MUSEUM .... EXTON, PA 125
TOUR-ED MINE & MUSEUM .... TARENTUM, PA 144
TOWNSHIP OF LEBANON MUSEUM ....HAMPTON, NJ   33
TRAILSIDE NATURE AND SCIENCE
  CENTER .... MOUNTAINSIDE, NJ   40
TWIN LIGHTS SHS .... HIGHLANDS, NJ   33
UNIVERSITY MUSEUM ....INDIANA, PA   88
★THE UNIVERSITY OF PENNSYLVANIA
  MUSEUM OF ARCHAEOLOGY AND
  ANTHROPOLOGY .... PHILADELPHIA, PA 117
U.S. ARMY COMMUNICATIONS-ELECTRONICS
  MUSEUM.......................... FORT MONMOUTH, NJ   31
VALLEY FORGE HISTORICAL SOCIETY
  MUSEUM.........................VALLEY FORGE NHP, PA 129
VENANGO MUSEUM OF ART, SCIENCE AND
  INDUSTRY .... OIL CITY, PA   98
VINELAND HISTORICAL AND ANTIQUARIAN
  SOCIETY .... VINELAND, NJ   49
THE WAGNER MUSEUM............................. IVYLAND, PA 125
WARREN COUNTY HISTORICAL SOCIETY ......WARREN, PA 158
WASHINGTON CROSSING SP....................... TRENTON, NJ   48
★WATCH AND CLOCK MUSEUM OF THE NATIONAL
  ASSOCIATION OF WATCH AND CLOCK COLLECTORS
  INC..COLUMBIA, PA 100
WAYNE COUNTY HISTORICAL SOCIETY
  MUSEUM .... HONESDALE, PA 148
WELLER CENTER FOR HEALTH EDUCATION ....EASTON, PA   73
WEST OVERTON MUSEUMS........................SCOTTDALE, PA 153
WESTMORELAND MUSEUM OF AMERICAN
  ART..GREENSBURG, PA   82
THE WETLANDS INSTITUTE .... STONE HARBOR, NJ   46
WOODMERE ART MUSEUM .... PHILADELPHIA, PA 117
WOODRUFF INDIAN MUSEUM .... BRIDGETON, NJ   26
WORLD OF SCOUTING MUSEUM ..... VALLEY FORGE NHP, PA 129
WYOMING HISTORICAL AND GEOLOGICAL
  SOCIETY .... WILKES-BARRE, PA 160
ZANE GREY MUSEUM .... LACKAWAXEN, PA 149

MUSIC EVENTS

BACH FESTIVAL..................................... BETHLEHEM, PA   67
MELLON JAZZ FESTIVAL........................ PITTSBURGH, PA 143
MUSIC PIER ....OCEAN CITY, NJ   42
MUSIKFEST .... BETHLEHEM, PA   67
PECO ENERGY JAZZ WEEKEND........... PHILADELPHIA, PA 121
SHADYSIDE SUMMER ARTS FESTIVAL ..... PITTSBURGH, PA 143

MUSIC HALLS & OPERA HOUSES

CARNEGIE MUSIC HALL............................ PITTSBURGH, PA 136
HEINZ HALL .... PITTSBURGH, PA 139
MARLIN OPERA HOUSE.........................BROOKVILLE, PA   68
SYMPHONY HALL................................... NEWARK, NJ   41

MYTHICAL PERSONS & ANIMALS

"STRETCH" GARRISON ....MILLVILLE, NJ   38

NATIONALITIES & ETHNIC AREAS

THE BALCH INSTITUTE FOR ETHNIC
  STUDIES .... PHILADELPHIA, PA 110

NATURE CENTERS

BEECHWOOD FARMS NATURE RESERVE ....PITTSBURGH, PA 136
COOPER ENVIRONMENTAL CENTER ....TOMS RIVER, NJ   47
JACOBSBURG ENVIRONMENTAL EDUCATION
  CENTER .... NAZARETH, PA   95
JAMES A. MCFAUL ENVIRONMENTAL CENTER OF BERGEN
  COUNTY.......................................WYCKOFF, NJ   51
JENNINGS ENVIRONMENTAL EDUCATION
  CENTER .... SLIPPERY ROCK, PA 155

MONTOUR PRESERVE .... DANVILLE, PA 72
OWL HAVEN .... FREEHOLD, NJ 31
PRESQUE ISLE SP .... ERIE, PA 75
SOMERSET COUNTY PARK COMMISSION'S
  ENVIRONMENTAL EDUCATION
  CENTER .... BASKING RIDGE, NJ 25
STRAWBERRY HILL NATURE CENTER AND
  PRESERVE .... FAIRFIELD, PA 75
TRAILSIDE NATURE AND SCIENCE
  CENTER .... MOUNTAINSIDE, NJ 40
THE WETLANDS INSTITUTE .... STONE HARBOR, NJ 46

NATURE TRAILS

ALLEGHENY NF...PA 62
ALLEGHENY PORTAGE RAILROAD NHS .... CRESSON, PA 72
BEAR RUN NATURE RESERVE .... OHIOPYLE, PA 97
BEECHWOOD FARMS NATURE RESERVE ... PITTSBURGH, PA 136
BERKS COUNTY HERITAGE CENTER .... READING, PA 152
BOWMAN HILL WILDFLOWER PRESERVE .... WASHINGTON
                          CROSSING HISTORIC PARK, PA 129
BUSHKILL FALLS .... BUSHKILL, PA 146
*CAPE MAY COUNTY PARK
  AND ZOO .... CAPE MAY COURT HOUSE, NJ 27
CAPITAL AREA GREENBELT .... HARRISBURG, PA 84
CITY ISLAND .... HARRISBURG, PA 83
COOK FOREST SP................................. COOKSBURG, PA 71
CROOK FARM .... BRADFORD, PA 68
THE DORFLINGER-SUYDAM
  WILDLIFE SANCTUARY .... WHITE MILLS, PA 150
*DRAKE WELL MUSEUM .... TITUSVILLE, PA 156
EDWIN B. FORSYTHE NWR .... OCEANVILLE, NJ 23
*FAIRMOUNT PARK .... PHILADELPHIA, PA 111
FORT HUNTER MANSION AND PARK ..... HARRISBURG, PA 84
FORT ROBERDEAU .... ALTOONA, PA 65
FRENCH AZILUM .... TOWANDA, PA 157
FRIENDSHIP HILL NHS .... POINT MARION, PA 150
GHOST TOWN TRAIL .... INDIANA, PA 88
GREAT SWAMP NWR .... BASKING RIDGE, NJ 24
GREENE COUNTY HISTORICAL
  MUSEUM .... WAYNESBURG, PA 159
INDIAN STEPS MUSEUM .... AIRVILLE, PA 62
LAUREL HIGHLANDS TRAIL .... DONEGAL, PA 72
LINCOLN CAVERNS .... HUNTINGDON, PA 88
MIDDLE CREEK WILDLIFE MANAGEMENT
  AREA.................................... KLEINFELTERSVILLE, PA 90
MILL GROVE, THE AUDUBON WILDLIFE
  SANCTUARY .... AUDUBON, PA 122
MONTOUR PRESERVE .... DANVILLE, PA 72
NEWLIN MILL PARK .... CONCORDVILLE, PA 124
PYMATUNING VISITOR CENTER .... LINESVILLE, PA 93
RENFREW MUSEUM AND PARK........... WAYNESBORO, PA 159
RICKETTS GLEN SP .... RED ROCK, PA 152
RUTGERS DISPLAY GARDENS AND
  HELYAR WOODS .... NEW BRUNSWICK, NJ 42
SCHENLEY PARK .... PITTSBURGH, PA 140
SOMERSET COUNTY PARK COMMISSION'S
  ENVIRONMENTAL EDUCATION
  CENTER .... BASKING RIDGE, NJ 25
SPRINGTON MANOR FARM .... DOWNINGTOWN, PA 124
STRAWBERRY HILL NATURE CENTER AND
  PRESERVE .... FAIRFIELD, PA 75
SUSQUEHANNA ENERGY INFORMATION CENTER AND
  RIVERLANDS.. BERWICK, PA 67
TREXLER-LEHIGH COUNTY GAME
  PRESERVE................................. SCHNECKSVILLE, PA 153
THE TYLER ARBORETUM .... MEDIA, PA 127
VALLEY FORGE NHP...PA 128
THE WETLANDS INSTITUTE .... STONE HARBOR, NJ 46

NAUTICAL TOURS

AZELA OF PHILADELPHIA .... PHILADELPHIA, PA 116
JUPITER TUGBOAT .... PHILADELPHIA, PA 116
RECONSTRUCTION OF THE US BRIG NIAGARA...ERIE, PA 75
SS BECUNA .... PHILADELPHIA, PA 115
SS OLYMPIA .... PHILADELPHIA, PA 115
SS REQUIN .... PITTSBURGH, PA 138

OBSERVATORIES

ALLEGHENY OBSERVATORY................. PITTSBURGH, PA 136

PAINTINGS

PICKETT'S CHARGE .... GETTYSBURG NMP, PA 82
POLISH AMERICAN CULTURAL CENTER
  MUSEUM .... PHILADELPHIA, PA 116
"THE BATTLE OF GETTYSBURG: PICKETT'S
  CHARGE" .... HARRISBURG, PA 85
"WASHINGTON CROSSING THE
  DELAWARE" .... WASHINGTON CROSSING
                                    HISTORIC PARK, PA 130

PARKS, CITY; STATE; PROVINCIAL

ALLAIRE SP .... FARMINGDALE, NJ 29
BARNEGAT LIGHTHOUSE SP .... BARNEGAT LIGHT, NJ 24
BRANCH BROOK PARK .... NEWARK, NJ 41
BRANDYWINE BATTLEFIELD PARK ...... CHADDS FORD, PA 123
BRIDGETON CITY PARK....................... BRIDGETON, NJ 26
BUCCLEUCH PARK .... NEW BRUNSWICK, NJ 41

BUCHANAN'S BIRTHPLACE SP .... MERCERSBURG, PA 94
BUCKTAIL SP .... EMPORIUM, PA 74
BUSHY RUN BATTLEFIELD SHS .... JEANNETTE, PA 144
CADWALADER PARK .... TRENTON, NJ 47
CALEDONIA SP .... FAYETTEVILLE, PA 76
CAPE MAY POINT SP .... CAPE MAY, NJ 26
CATTUS ISLAND COUNTY PARK .... TOMS RIVER, NJ 47
CITY ISLAND .... HARRISBURG, PA 83
COOK FOREST SP................................. COOKSBURG, PA 71
ERIE ZOO .... ERIE, PA 75
*FAIRMOUNT PARK .... PHILADELPHIA, PA 111
FORT LEE HISTORIC PARK .... FORT LEE, NJ 30
FORT MOTT SP...................................... SALEM, NJ 132
FRANCES SLOCUM SP .... WILKES-BARRE, PA 160
HICKORY RUN SP....................... WHITE HAVEN, PA 159
HISTORIC BARTRAM'S GARDEN....... PHILADELPHIA, PA 113
HOPATCONG SP.................................. STANHOPE, NJ 46
HUDDY PARK .... TOMS RIVER, NJ 47
ITALIAN LAKE PARK .... HARRISBURG, PA 84
KINZUA BRIDGE SP .... MOUNT JEWETT, PA 95
LACKAWANNA SP .... SCRANTON, PA 153
LIBERTY SP .... JERSEY CITY, NJ 36
LITITZ SPRINGS PARK.............................. LITITZ, PA 104
MAUCH CHUNK LAKE PARK............. JIM THORPE, PA 148
MAX M. BROWN MEMORIAL PARK .... WILLIAMSPORT, PA 160
MONMOUTH BATTLEFIELD SP .... FREEHOLD, NJ 31
MOUNTAINSIDE PARK .... MONTCLAIR, NJ 38
NEWLIN MILL PARK .... CONCORDVILLE, PA 124
OHIOPYLE SP...................................... OHIOPYLE, PA 96
PARVIN SP .... VINELAND, NJ 49
*POINT SP.. PITTSBURGH, PA 140
PRESQUE ISLE SP .... ERIE, PA 75
PYMATUNING SP .... LINESVILLE, PA 93
RED BANK BATTLEFIELD PARK .... WOODBURY, NJ 132
RENFREW MUSEUM AND PARK........... WAYNESBORO, PA 159
RESERVOIR PARK .... HARRISBURG, PA 84
RICKETTS GLEN SP .... RED ROCK, PA 152
RINGWOOD SP .... RINGWOOD, NJ 45
RIVER COMMON .... WILKES-BARRE, PA 160
RIVERFRONT PARK................................ HARRISBURG, PA 84
ROUND VALLEY .... CLINTON, NJ 28
SCHENLEY PARK .... PITTSBURGH, PA 140
SEVEN PRESIDENTS PARK .... LONG BRANCH, NJ 37
SPRUCE RUN .... CLINTON, NJ 28
TERHUNE MEMORIAL PARK .... WAYNE, NJ 49
TURKEY SWAMP COUNTY PARK .... FREEHOLD, NJ 31
VETERANS' PARK................................. HAMILTON, NJ 33
WARINANCO PARK .... ELIZABETH, NJ 28
*WASHINGTON CROSSING HISTORIC PARK.............PA 129
WASHINGTON CROSSING SP.................. TRENTON, NJ 48
WINDING RIVER PARK .... TOMS RIVER, NJ 47

PARKS, NATIONAL

DELAWARE WATER GAP NRA...........................PA 147
*FORT NECESSITY NB.....................................PA 76
GATEWAY NRA ....NJ 31
*GETTYSBURG NMP ....PA 80
INDEPENDENCE NHP .... PHILADELPHIA, PA 113
*MORRISTOWN NHP ....NJ 40
UPPER DELAWARE SCENIC AND
  RECREATIONAL RIVER.....................................PA 157
*VALLEY FORGE NHP.......................................PA 128

PENINSULAS

PAULUS HOOK .... JERSEY CITY, NJ 36

PIERS

MUSIC PIER..................................... OCEAN CITY, NJ 42
WONDERLAND PIER .... OCEAN CITY, NJ 42

PLANETARIUMS

*CARNEGIE SCIENCE CENTER .... PITTSBURGH, PA 138
ERIE PLANETARIUM .... ERIE, PA 75
FELS PLANETARIUM .... PHILADELPHIA, PA 113
HENRY BUHL JR. PLANETARIUM AND
  OBSERVATORY .... PITTSBURGH, PA 138
NEWARK MUSEUM .... NEWARK, NJ 41
NORTH MUSEUM OF NATURAL HISTORY AND
  SCIENCE .... LANCASTER, PA 103
THE PLANETARIUM .... TRENTON, NJ 48
READING PUBLIC MUSEUM .... READING, PA 152
ROBERT J. NOVINS PLANETARIUM ...... TOMS RIVER, NJ 47
*STATE MUSEUM OF PENNSYLVANIA ... HARRISBURG, PA 85
TRAILSIDE NATURE AND SCIENCE
  CENTER .... MOUNTAINSIDE, NJ 40

PLAYS, DRAMAS & MUSICALS

MEDIEVAL TIMES DINNER AND
  TOURNAMENT................................ LYNDHURST, NJ 37
"MR. LINCOLN RETURNS TO
  GETTYSBURG" .... GETTYSBURG, PA 77

RACETRACKS-AUTO

NAZARETH SPEEDWAY .... NAZARETH, PA 95
POCONO RACEWAY..................... MOUNT POCONO, PA 149

RACETRACKS-HORSE
ATLANTIC CITY RACE COURSE .... ATLANTIC CITY, NJ   22
DELAWARE PARK .... PHILADELPHIA, PA   119
FREEHOLD RACEWAY .... FREEHOLD, NJ   31
GARDEN SP .... PHILADELPHIA, PA   119
LADBROKE AT THE MEADOWS .... PITTSBURGH, PA   142
MEADOWLANDS RACETRACK ....HACKENSACK, NJ   32
MONMOUTH PARK .... LONG BRANCH, NJ   37
MOUNTAINEER PARK .... PITTSBURGH, PA   142
PHILADELPHIA PARK .... PHILADELPHIA, PA   119
POCONO DOWNS .... WILKES-BARRE, PA   160

RAILROADS
BELLEFONTE HISTORIC RAILROAD .... MILESBURG, PA   95
THE BLACK RIVER & WESTERN
    RAILROAD .... FLEMINGTON, NJ   29
EAST BROAD TOP RAILROAD...... ROCKHILL FURNACE, PA   152
KNOX KANE RAILROAD .... MOUNT JEWETT, PA   95
NEW HOPE & IVYLAND RAIL ROAD .... NEW HOPE, PA   127
OIL CREEK AND TITUSVILLE RAILROAD .... OIL CITY, PA   98
OIL CREEK AND TITUSVILLE RAILROAD ...... TITUSVILLE, PA   157
PINE CREEK RAILROAD .... FARMINGDALE, NJ   29
PIONEER TUNNEL COAL MINE AND STEAM TRAIN
    RIDE ....ASHLAND, PA   65
STRASBURG RAIL ROAD CO.................... STRASBURG, PA   105
WHITE DEER STATION .... LEWISBURG, PA   92

RAILROADS-LOCOMOTIVES & CARS
ALTOONA RAILROADERS MEMORIAL
    MUSEUM .... ALTOONA, PA   64
BESSEMER COURT AT STATION SQUARE ....PITTSBURGH, PA   136
H.O. SCALE MODEL TRAIN DISPLAY ....JIM THORPE, PA   148
HORSESHOE CURVE NATIONAL HISTORIC
    LANDMARK .... ALTOONA, PA   65
LAKE SHORE RAILWAY MUSEUM ....NORTH EAST, PA   96
OIL CREEK AND TITUSVILLE RAILROAD ...... TITUSVILLE, PA   157
RAILROAD MUSEUM OF PENNSYLVANIA ...STRASBURG, PA   105
ROCKHILL TROLLEY MUSEUM..... ROCKHILL FURNACE, PA   152
STEAMTOWN NHS .... SCRANTON, PA   154
STOURBRIDGE LION .... HONESDALE, PA   148
STRASBURG RAIL ROAD CO.................... STRASBURG, PA   105

RAILWAYS & SKI LIFTS, CABLE; COG;
INCLINE; NARROW GAUGE
DUQUESNE INCLINE .... PITTSBURGH, PA   138
EAST BROAD TOP RAILROAD...... ROCKHILL FURNACE, PA   152
HORSESHOE CURVE NATIONAL HISTORIC
    LANDMARK .... ALTOONA, PA   65
INCLINED PLANE .... JOHNSTOWN, PA   90
MONONGAHELA INCLINE .... PITTSBURGH, PA   139
PENNSYLVANIA TROLLEY MUSEUM ...WASHINGTON, PA   145
PINE CREEK RAILROAD .... FARMINGDALE, NJ   29

RECREATION-SUMMER ACTIVITIES
ALLEGHENY NF...PA   62
ASBURY PARK .... NJ   18
ATLANTIC CITY .... ATLANTIC CITY, NJ   19
BARNEGAT LIGHT .... NJ   24
BEAR RUN NATURE RESERVE................... OHIOPYLE, PA   97
BUCKS COUNTY RIVER COUNTRY .... POINT PLEASANT, PA   128
BUSHKILL FALLS .... BUSHKILL, PA   146
CAPE MAY .... NJ   26
CAPITAL AREA GREENBELT .... HARRISBURG, PA   84
THE CHALLENGE CENTER.................... CANONSBURG, PA   144
CITY ISLAND .... HARRISBURG, PA   83
CONNEAUT LAKE DECK HOCKEY.....CONNEAUT LAKE, PA   71
COOK FOREST SP............................ COOKSBURG, PA   71
DELAWARE WATER GAP NRA........................PA   147
FISHERMAN'S PARADISE .... BELLEFONTE, PA   66
GATEWAY NRA .... NJ   31
GRAND CANYON OF PENNSYLVANIA ..... WELLSBORO, PA   159
HUNTINGDON ....PA   87
IDLEWILD PARK .... LIGONIER, PA   93
JIM THORPE RIVER ADVENTURES ....JIM THORPE, PA   148
THE LAUREL HIGHLANDS...PA   91
LAUREL HIGHLANDS RIVER TOURS............OHIOPYLE, PA   97
LEHIGH RAFTING RENTALS....................WHITE HAVEN, PA   159
LONG BRANCH .... NJ   37
MAUCH CHUNK LAKE PARK ....JIM THORPE, PA   148
MONTAGE SKI AND SUMMER RECREATION
    AREA .... SCRANTON, PA   154
MONTOUR PRESERVE .... DANVILLE, PA   72
MUDDY RUN INFORMATION CENTER ..... HOLTWOOD, PA   100
NORTHBROOK CANOE CO. .... WEST CHESTER, PA   130
OCEAN CITY .... NJ   42
OCEAN GROVE .... NJ   42
POCONO ADVENTURES STABLES .....MOUNT POCONO, PA   149
POCONO WHITEWATER RAFTING...........JIM THORPE, PA   149
PRESQUE ISLE SP .... ERIE, PA   75
PYMATUNING RESERVOIR .... LINESVILLE, PA   93
RAGING WATERS .... WILDWOOD, PA   51
RICKETTS GLEN SP .... RED ROCK, PA   152
RINGWOOD SP .... RINGWOOD, NJ   45
SCHENLEY PARK .... PITTSBURGH, PA   140
SOUTH PARK .... PITTSBURGH, PA   141
SUSQUEHANNA ENERGY INFORMATION CENTER AND
    RIVERLANDS .... BERWICK, PA   67

UPPER DELAWARE SCENIC AND
    RECREATIONAL RIVER......................................PA   157
WHITE HAVEN..PA   159
WILDWOOD...NJ   50

RECREATION-WINTER ACTIVITIES
ALLEGHENY NF...PA   62
BEAR RUN NATURE RESERVE................... OHIOPYLE, PA   97
BOYCE PARK .... PITTSBURGH, PA   142
CAPITAL AREA GREENBELT .... HARRISBURG, PA   84
THE CHALLENGE CENTER.................... CANONSBURG, PA   144
COOK FOREST SP............................ COOKSBURG, PA   71
THE LAUREL HIGHLANDS...PA   91
MONTAGE SKI AND SUMMER RECREATION
    AREA .... SCRANTON, PA   154
MONTOUR PRESERVE .... DANVILLE, PA   72
RICKETTS GLEN SP .... RED ROCK, PA   152
SCHENLEY PARK .... PITTSBURGH, PA   140
SOUTH PARK .... PITTSBURGH, PA   141
SUSQUEHANNA ENERGY INFORMATION CENTER AND
    RIVERLANDS .... BERWICK, PA   67
VERNON VALLEY GREAT GORGE ....VERNON, NJ   49
WHITE HAVEN..PA   159

RELIGIOUS COLONIES
HARMONY ....PA   144
OLD ECONOMY VILLAGE .... AMBRIDGE, PA   143

RESEARCH ORGANIZATIONS
IACOCCA INSTITUTE .... BETHLEHEM, PA   67

RESTORED VILLAGES & SETTLEMENTS
ALLAIRE SP .... FARMINGDALE, NJ   29
THE AMISH VILLAGE .... STRASBURG, PA   105
BATSTO HISTORIC VILLAGE .... BATSTO, NJ   136
CURTIN VILLAGE .... MILESBURG, PA   95
ECKLEY MINERS' VILLAGE .... HAZLETON, PA   89
EIGHTEENTH-CENTURY INDUSTRIAL
    AREA .... BETHLEHEM, PA   67
FRENCH AZILUM .... TOWANDA, PA   157
HISTORIC COLD SPRING VILLAGE ....CAPE MAY, NJ   27
HISTORIC FALLSINGTON .... FALLSINGTON, PA   127
HISTORIC HANNA'S TOWN ....GREENSBURG, PA   84
HISTORIC SPEEDWELL .... MORRISTOWN, NJ   37
HOPEWELL FURNACE NHS ....PA   87
HUNTERDON HISTORICAL MUSEUM .... CLINTON, NJ   29
MEADOWCROFT MUSEUM OF RURAL LIFE ... AVELLA, PA   67
MILL BRIDGE VILLAGE .... LANCASTER, PA   105
MILLBROOK VILLAGE ... DELAWARE WATER GAP NRA, PA   147
OLD BEDFORD VILLAGE .... BEDFORD, PA   67
OLD ECONOMY VILLAGE .... AMBRIDGE, PA   143
WATERLOO VILLAGE................................STANHOPE, NJ   45
★WHEATON VILLAGE........................MILLVILLE, PA   37

RIVERS
UPPER DELAWARE SCENIC AND
    RECREATIONAL RIVER....................................PA   157

ROCKS
★DEVIL'S DEN .... GETTYSBURG NMP, PA   87
WYOMING HISTORICAL AND GEOLOGICAL
    SOCIETY .... WILKES-BARRE, PA   160

SCENIC DRIVES
I-80 ....STANHOPE, NJ   45
OCEAN BOULEVARD .... HIGHLANDS, NJ   37
PALISADES INTERSTATE PARKWAY ....FORT LEE, NJ   37
PENNSYLVANIA TURNPIKE (I-70/76)..............THE LAUREL
    HIGHLANDS, PA   91

SCHOOL BUILDINGS
BENTLEY HALL.................................. MEADVILLE, PA   95
★CATHEDRAL OF LEARNING .... PITTSBURGH, PA   137
FOUNDERS HALL .... HERSHEY, PA   85
NASSAU HALL .... PRINCETON, NJ   45
OLD MAIN ....STATE COLLEGE, PA   159
OLD QUEENS ....NEW BRUNSWICK, NJ   45
STEPHEN FOSTER MEMORIAL .... PITTSBURGH, PA   140
WEAVERTOWN ONE-ROOM
    SCHOOLHOUSE ....BIRD-IN-HAND, PA   95

SCHOOLS
CARLISLE INDIAN SCHOOL .... CARLISLE, PA   67
LINDEN HALL......................................LITITZ, PA   105
MILTON S. HERSHEY MEDICAL CENTER .... HERSHEY, PA   85
PENNSYLVANIA FIRE SCHOOL................. LEWISTOWN, PA   95
SEEING EYE HEADQUARTERS............... MORRISTOWN, NJ   37
SETON HALL LAW SCHOOL ....NEWARK, NJ   45

SCHOOLS-ACADEMIES
ACADEMY OF NATURAL SCIENCES....... PHILADELPHIA, PA   105
MERCERSBURG ACADEMY................. MERCERSBURG, PA   95
MUSEUM OF AMERICAN ART OF THE PENNSYLVANIA
    ACADEMY OF THE FINE ARTS .... PHILADELPHIA, PA   115
NAZARETH HALL .... NAZARETH, PA   95
STATE POLICE ACADEMY .... HERSHEY, PA   85

SCHOOLS-COLLEGES & UNIVERSITIES

ALLEGHENY COLLEGE.... MEADVILLE, PA 94
BUCKNELL UNIVERSITY.... LEWISBURG, PA 92
COLLEGE OF AGRICULTURAL SCIENCES.... STATE COLLEGE, PA 156
COLLEGE OF ST. ELIZABETH.... FLORHAM PARK, NJ 29
DICKINSON COLLEGE.... CARLISLE, PA 69
DREW UNIVERSITY.... MADISON, NJ 37
DREXEL UNIVERSITY.... PHILADELPHIA, PA 107
ESSEX COUNTY COLLEGE.... NEWARK, NJ 41
FAIRLEIGH DICKINSON UNIVERSITY.... FLORHAM PARK, NJ 29
FAIRLEIGH DICKINSON UNIVERSITY.... MADISON, NJ 37
INDIANA UNIVERSITY OF PENNSYLVANIA.... INDIANA, PA 88
JUNIATA COLLEGE.... HUNTINGDON, PA 88
KUTZTOWN STATE UNIVERSITY.... KUTZTOWN, PA 90
LAFAYETTE COLLEGE.... EASTON, PA 73
LASALLE UNIVERSITY.... PHILADELPHIA, PA 107
LEHIGH UNIVERSITY.... BETHLEHEM, PA 67
MORAVIAN COLLEGE.... BETHLEHEM, PA 67
ON THE CAMPUS OF WILKES UNIVERSITY.... WILKES-BARRE, PA 160
PENNSYLVANIA STATE UNIVERSITY.... STATE COLLEGE, PA 155
PRINCETON UNIVERSITY.... PRINCETON, NJ 44
RUTGERS UNIVERSITY.... NEW BRUNSWICK, NJ 42
RUTGERS UNIVERSITY AT NEWARK.... NEWARK, NJ 41
ST. JOSEPH'S UNIVERSITY.... PHILADELPHIA, PA 107
SLIPPERY ROCK UNIVERSITY.... SLIPPERY ROCK, PA 155
SWARTHMORE COLLEGE.... PHILADELPHIA, PA 107
TEMPLE UNIVERSITY.... PHILADELPHIA, PA 107
UNIVERSITY OF MEDICINE AND DENTISTRY OF NEW JERSEY.... NEWARK, NJ 41
UNIVERSITY OF PENNSYLVANIA.... PHILADELPHIA, PA 117
U.S. ARMY WAR COLLEGE.... CARLISLE, PA 69
VILLANOVA UNIVERSITY.... PHILADELPHIA, PA 107
WAYNESBURG COLLEGE.... WAYNESBURG, PA 159

SCHOOLS-INSTITUTES

INSTITUTE FOR ADVANCED STUDY.... PRINCETON, NJ 44
NEW JERSEY INSTITUTE OF TECHNOLOGY.... NEWARK, NJ 41
RUTGERS INSTITUTE OF JAZZ STUDIES.... NEWARK, NJ 41
STEVENS INSTITUTE OF TECHNOLOGY.... HOBOKEN, NJ 33

SELF-GUIDING TOURS

ALLENTOWN.... PA 62
BEDFORD.... PA 66
BELLEFONTE.... PA 66
BETHLEHEM.... PA 67
BROOKVILLE.... PA 68
CAPE MAY.... NJ 26
CCINC. AUTO TAPE TOURS.... GETTYSBURG NMP, PA 80
CCINC. AUTO TAPE TOURS.... LANCASTER, PA 102
CHAMBERSBURG.... PA 70
EASTON.... PA 72
EDWIN B. FORSYTHE NWR.... OCEANVILLE, NJ 23
FRANKLIN.... PA 76
GETTYSBURG.... PA 77
HOPE.... NJ 34
KUSER FARM MANSION AND PARK.... HAMILTON, NJ 33
LEHIGH RAFTING RENTALS.... WHITE HAVEN, PA 159
LEWISBURG.... PA 92
LITITZ.... PA 103
LOCK HAVEN.... PA 93
PATERSON.... NJ 43
PRINCETON.... NJ 44
TALK-A-WALK.... PHILADELPHIA, PA 119
YORK.... PA 161

SHIPS & BOATS

GAZELA OF PHILADELPHIA.... PHILADELPHIA, PA 116
JUPITER TUGBOAT.... PHILADELPHIA, PA 116
A RECONSTRUCTION OF THE US BRIG NIAGARA.... ERIE, PA 75
SUBMARINE USS LING NEW JERSEY NAVAL MUSEUM.... HACKENSACK, NJ 32
USS BECUNA.... PHILADELPHIA, PA 115
USS OLYMPIA.... PHILADELPHIA, PA 115
USS REQUIN.... PITTSBURGH, PA 138
THE WORKSHOP ON THE WATER.... PHILADELPHIA, PA 115

SHOPS, FIRMS & STORES

AMERICA'S FIRST CHRISTMAS STORE.... SMETHPORT, PA 155
ARCADE SHOPS AT FIFTH AVENUE PLACE.... PITTSBURGH, PA 142
ATLANTIC AVENUE.... ATLANTIC CITY, NJ 22
THE BARNS AT POTTERS RUN LANDING.... VOLANT, PA 158
BERKSHIRE MALL.... READING, PA 151
BIRD-IN-HAND FARMER'S MARKET.... LANCASTER, PA 102
BLAIR WAREHOUSE.... ERIE, PA 74
BOURSE.... PHILADELPHIA, PA 119
THE BROAD STREET MARKET.... HARRISBURG, PA 84
BROOKPARK FARM.... LEWISBURG, PA 92
CAMP HILL MALL.... HARRISBURG, PA 84
CAPITAL CITY.... HARRISBURG, PA 84
CENTRAL MARKET.... LANCASTER, PA 102
CENTRAL MARKET HOUSE.... YORK, PA 161
CENTRAL SQUARE SHOPPING CENTER.... ATLANTIC CITY, NJ 22
CENTURY III MALL.... PITTSBURGH, PA 142
CHARLES CHIPS OUTLET STORE.... LANCASTER, PA 101
CHINA TOWN MALL.... PHILADELPHIA, PA 120
COHANSEY CROSSING.... BRIDGETON, NJ 26
COLONIAL PARK.... HARRISBURG, PA 84
COUNTRY CUPBOARD.... LEWISBURG, PA 92
COURT AND PLAZA AT KING OF PRUSSIA.... PHILADELPHIA, PA 120
COVENTRY MALL.... POTTSTOWN, PA 128
CROSS KEYS VILLAGE.... INTERCOURSE, PA 101
THE CROSSINGS.... POCONO MOUNTAINS AREA, PA 146
DANSK FACTORY OUTLET.... LANCASTER, PA 101
DESIDERATA FARM MALL.... LINESVILLE, PA 93
DESIGNERS PLACE.... READING, PA 151
DOWNTOWN.... EASTON, PA 73
DUTCH NECK VILLAGE.... BRIDGETON, NJ 26
EAST PROSPECT FACTORY OUTLET.... YORK, PA 161
EPHRATA.... PA 100
FAIRGROUND SQUARE.... READING, PA 151
FARMERS' MARKET.... YORK, PA 161
FARMER'S MARKET OF LIMERICK.... LIMERICK, PA 126
FARMERS' MARKETS.... LANCASTER, PA 102
FRANKLIN MILLS.... PHILADELPHIA, PA 120
THE GALLERIA.... PITTSBURGH, PA 143
THE GALLERIA.... YORK, PA 161
GARDNER'S CANDY MUSEUM.... TYRONE, PA 157
GOLDEN TRIANGLE.... PITTSBURGH, PA 142
GORDON'S ALLEY.... ATLANTIC CITY, NJ 22
GREENGATE MALL.... GREENSBURG, PA 82
GROVE CITY FACTORY SHOPS.... GROVE CITY, PA 82
HAMILTON MALL.... ATLANTIC CITY, NJ 22
HAMILTON WATCH AND CLOCK SHOPPE.... LANCASTER, PA 101
HARRISBURG EAST.... HARRISBURG, PA 84
HEAD HOUSE SQUARE.... PHILADELPHIA, PA 113
HERSHEY FOODS CORP.... HERSHEY, PA 86
HOLLY BEACH STATION.... WILDWOOD, NJ 50
ITALIAN MARKET.... PHILADELPHIA, PA 120
JOHNSTOWN GALLERIA.... JOHNSTOWN, PA 90
KEYSTONE CENTER.... ERIE, PA 74
KLINE VILLAGE SHOPPING CENTER.... HARRISBURG, PA 84
KOZIAR'S CHRISTMAS VILLAGE.... BERNVILLE, PA 66
L.E. SMITH GLASS CO..... MOUNT PLEASANT, PA 95
LEHIGH VALLEY MALL.... ALLENTOWN, PA 63
LIBERTY PLACE.... PHILADELPHIA, PA 120
LIBERTY VILLAGE.... FLEMINGTON, NJ 29
LOGAN VALLEY MALL.... ALTOONA, PA 64
LYCOMING MALL.... WILLIAMSPORT, PA 160
THE MALL AT STEAMTOWN.... SCRANTON, PA 153
MANUFACTURERS OUTLET MALL (MOM).... READING, PA 151
MARKET PLACE EAST.... PHILADELPHIA, PA 120
MARKET SQUARE.... PITTSBURGH, PA 142
MCINTYRE SQUARE.... PITTSBURGH, PA 142
MEADOWBROOK MARKET.... LANCASTER, PA 102
MEADOWBROOK VILLAGE.... YORK, PA 161
MILLCREEK MALL.... ERIE, PA 74
MILLSTREAM DESIGNER FACTORY SHOPS.... LANCASTER, PA 101
MONROEVILLE MALL.... PITTSBURGH, PA 143
NEW EASTERN MARKET.... YORK, PA 161
NEW SHORE MALL.... ATLANTIC CITY, NJ 22
NORTH HILLS VILLAGE.... PITTSBURGH, PA 142
NORTHWAY MALL.... PITTSBURGH, PA 142
OAKLAND.... PITTSBURGH, PA 143
OCEAN ONE.... ATLANTIC CITY, NJ 22
OLD COUNTRY STORE.... INTERCOURSE, PA 101
THE OLD JAIL CENTER.... WILLIAMSPORT, PA 160
OLD TOLLGATE VILLAGE.... YORK, PA 161
OLD VILLAGE STORE.... BIRD-IN-HAND, PA 99
THE OUTLETS ON HIESTERS LANE.... READING, PA 151
OXFORD CENTRE.... PITTSBURGH, PA 142
OXFORD VALLEY MALL.... LANGHORNE, PA 126
PEDDLER'S VILLAGE.... LAHASKA, PA 126
PLAIN AND FANCY FARM.... BIRD-IN-HAND, PA 99
PLYMOUTH MEETING MALL.... PHILADELPHIA, PA 120
POCONO OUTLET COMPLEX.... POCONO MOUNTAINS AREA, PA 146
PPG PLACE.... PITTSBURGH, PA 142
READING OUTLET CENTER.... READING, PA 151
READING STATION.... READING, PA 151
RENNINGERS ANTIQUE & FARMERS MARKET.... KUTZTOWN, PA 91
REYERS.... SHARON, PA 154
ROCKVALE SQUARE FACTORY OUTLET VILLAGE.... LANCASTER, PA 101
ROLLER MILLS EAST.... LEWISBURG, PA 92
ROLLER MILLS MARKETPLACE.... LEWISBURG, PA 92
ROSS PARK MALL.... PITTSBURGH, PA 142
SCALP AVENUE.... JOHNSTOWN, PA 90
SCHUYLKILL MALL.... POTTSVILLE, PA 150
SEWICKLEY.... PITTSBURGH, PA 142
SHADYSIDE.... PITTSBURGH, PA 143
SHOPS AT BELLEVUE.... PHILADELPHIA, PA 120
SHOPS AT STATION SQUARE.... PITTSBURGH, PA 142
SKIPPACK VILLAGE.... CENTER POINT, PA 123
SOUTH HILLS VILLAGE.... PITTSBURGH, PA 142
SQUIRREL HILL.... PITTSBURGH, PA 143
STRAWBERRY SQUARE.... HARRISBURG, PA 84
THE STRIP.... PITTSBURGH, PA 142
STURGIS PRETZEL HOUSE.... LITITZ, PA 104
SUSQUEHANNA VALLEY MALL.... SUNBURY, PA 156
TOTES FACTORY STORE.... LANCASTER, PA 101

TOWNE OF HISTORIC SMITHVILLE........ ATLANTIC CITY, NJ   22
UPTOWN PLAZA .... HARRISBURG, PA   84
VF FACTORY OUTLET .... READING, PA   151
VIEWMONT MALL .... SCRANTON, PA   153
VILLAGE OF BOALSBURG................... BOALSBURG, PA   68
VILLAGE SQUARE .... PITTSBURGH, PA   143
VOLANT...PA   158
VOLANT MILL...................................... VOLANT, PA   158
WAYNE TOWN CENTER.............................WAYNE, NJ   49
WEST MANCHESTER MALL.........................YORK, PA   161
WESTMORELAND MALL ....GREENSBURG, PA   82
WHITEHALL MALL ....ALLENTOWN, PA   63
WHITEHALL SQUARE MALL ....ALLENTOWN, PA   63
WILLOW BROOK ....WAYNE, NJ   49
THE WINNER ....SHARON, PA   154
WYOMING VALLEY MALL........... WILKES-BARRE, PA   160
YORK MALL MERCHANTS......................YORK, PA   161

SIGHTSEEING TOURS

ABE'S BUGGY RIDES..........................BIRD-IN-HAND, PA   99
AMISH COUNTRY TOURS..................... LANCASTER, PA   101
ATLANTIC CITY .... ATLANTIC CITY, NJ   19
ATLANTIC CITY FAMOUS
   ROLLING CHAIR CO. .... ATLANTIC CITY, NJ   21
CCINC. AUTO TAPE TOURS........... GETTYSBURG NMP, PA   80
CCINC. AUTO TAPE TOURS............... LANCASTER, PA   102
THE CULTURAL PITTSBURGH TOUR ....PITTSBURGH, PA   141
EAST BROAD TOP RAILROAD...... ROCKHILL FURNACE, PA   152
★FAIRMOUNT PARK .... PHILADELPHIA, PA   111
GETTYSBURG BATTLEFIELD TOURS... GETTYSBURG, PA   77
★GETTYSBURG NMP..................................PA   80
GRAY LINE .... PITTSBURGH, PA   141
HERDIC TROLLEY TOUR................ WILLIAMSPORT, PA   160
HISTORIC CONESTOGA CARRIAGE RIDES.....STRASBURG, PA   105
THE HISTORIC PITTSBURGH TOUR .... PITTSBURGH, PA   141
HISTORICAL SOCIETY OF PRINCETON...PRINCETON, NJ   44
LANCASTER WALKING TOUR................. LANCASTER, PA   102
MENNONITE INFORMATION CENTER AND HEBREW
   TABERNACLE REPRODUCTION .... LANCASTER, PA   103
NEW HOPE & IVYLAND RAIL ROAD ...... NEW HOPE, PA   127
★PENN'S CAVE ....CENTRE HALL, PA   70
PITTSBURGH AND ITS RIVERS TOUR....... PITTSBURGH, PA   141
PRINCETON ....NJ   44
STEAMTOWN NHS .... SCRANTON, PA   154
STOURBRIDGE LINE RAIL EXCURSIONS ... HONESDALE, PA   148
TALK-A-WALK .... PHILADELPHIA, PA   119

SIGHTSEEING TOURS-BOATS

CANAL BOAT RIDES ....EASTON, PA   73
CAPE MAY COUNTY DINNER CRUISE ....WILDWOOD, NJ   50
CAPTAIN SCHUMANN'S BOAT RIDES ....WILDWOOD, NJ   50
CAPTAIN SINN'S SIGHTSEEING CENTER.....WILDWOOD, NJ   51
DELTA LADY SIGHTSEEING CRUISES ....WILDWOOD, NJ   51
★GATEWAY CLIPPER FLEET................ PITTSBURGH, PA   141
HIAWATHA RIVERBOAT TOURS .... WILLIAMSPORT, PA   160
PRIDE OF THE SUSQUEHANNA .... HARRISBURG, PA   84
RIVER LADY CRUISE AND DINNER BOAT...TOMS RIVER, NJ   47
SANDY HOOK LADY .... JERSEY CITY, NJ   36
THE SCHOONER YANKEE ....CAPE MAY, NJ   27
SEVEN POINTS CRUISES .... HUNTINGDON, PA   88
SILVER BULLET SPEEDBOAT ....WILDWOOD, NJ   51
SPIRIT OF NEW JERSEY ....WEEHAWKEN, NJ   50
THE SPIRIT OF PHILADELPHIA .... PHILADELPHIA, PA   118

SIGHTSEEING TOURS-HOUSE & GARDEN

CHRISTMAS TOURS OF HISTORIC
   HOUSES .... PHILADELPHIA, PA 122
ELFRETH'S ALLEY FETE DAYS............. PHILADELPHIA, PA   121
PHILADELPHIA OPEN HOUSE .... PHILADELPHIA, PA   121

SIGHTSEEING TOURS-RAFTING/
CANOEING

JIM THORPE RIVER ADVENTURES ....JIM THORPE, PA   148
LAUREL HIGHLANDS RIVER TOURS............OHIOPYLE, PA   97
MOUNTAIN STREAMS & TRAILS
   OUTFITTERS ....OHIOPYLE, PA   97
POCONO WHITEWATER RAFTING ....JIM THORPE, PA   149
WHITE WATER ADVENTURERS INC...........OHIOPYLE, PA   97
WHITEWATER CHALLENGERS
   RAFT TOURS....................WHITE HAVEN, PA   159
WILDERNESS VOYAGEURS ....OHIOPYLE, PA   97

SOUND & LIGHT PRESENTATIONS

CYCLORAMA CENTER .... GETTYSBURG NMP, PA   82
★OLD BARRACKS MUSEUM .... TRENTON, NJ   48
YORK COUNTY COLONIAL COURT HOUSE ....YORK, PA   162

SPORTS ARENAS

CIVIC ARENA .... PITTSBURGH, PA   138
CONTINENTAL AIRLINES ARENA...........HACKENSACK, NJ   32
CORESTATES COMPLEX .... PHILADELPHIA, PA   111
GIANTS STADIUM ....HACKENSACK, NJ   32
HERSHEYPARK ARENA..............................HERSHEY, PA   86
LACKAWANNA COUNTY STADIUM ....SCRANTON, PA   153
MEADOWLANDS SPORTS COMPLEX ......HACKENSACK, NJ   32
VETERANS SPORT STADIUM .... PHILADELPHIA, PA   119

SPORTS EVENTS-FOOTBALL

ARMY-NAVY FOOTBALL CLASSIC .... PHILADELPHIA, PA   122

SPORTS EVENTS-GENERAL

AMERICA'S GOLD CUP .... PHILADELPHIA, PA   122
CRICKET... PHILADELPHIA, PA   119
LITTLE LEAGUE WORLD SERIES.......... WILLIAMSPORT, PA   160
PENN RELAYS .... PHILADELPHIA, PA   121
PITTSBURGH MARATHON .... PITTSBURGH, PA   143
POLO .... PHILADELPHIA, PA   119
U.S. INDOOR TENNIS
   CHAMPIONSHIPS.......................... PHILADELPHIA, PA   121

SPORTS EVENTS-WATER SPORTS

HARBORFEST................................ ATLANTIC CITY, NJ   23

SPRINGS

BIG SPRING .... BELLEFONTE, PA   66

STATUES

BENJAMIN FRANKLIN .... PHILADELPHIA, PA   113
HENRY CLAY MONUMENT.................... POTTSVILLE, PA   150
JIMMY STEWART............................INDIANA, PA   88
JOHN B. PUTNAM JR. MEMORIAL
   COLLECTION.........................PRINCETON, NJ   44
JOHN F. KENNEDY .... NEWARK, NJ   41
LAFAYETTE ....EASTON, PA   73
NORTH CAROLINA .... GETTYSBURG NMP, PA   80
★STATE CAPITOL .... HARRISBURG, PA   85
★STATUE OF LIBERTY NMO .... JERSEY CITY, NJ   36
VIRGINIA .... GETTYSBURG NMP, PA   80
WARS OF AMERICA ....NEWARK, NJ   41

STREETS, PLAZAS, SQUARES, CITY
AREAS

E. JERSEY STREET ....ELIZABETH, NJ   28
EIGHTEENTH-CENTURY INDUSTRIAL
   AREA .... BETHLEHEM, PA   67
ELFRETH'S ALLEY........................... PHILADELPHIA, PA   111
FRANKLIN COURT .... PHILADELPHIA, PA   114
GORDON'S ALLEY .... ATLANTIC CITY, NJ   22
GREAT FALLS/S.U.M. HISTORIC DISTRICT......PATERSON, NJ   43
HEAD HOUSE SQUARE....................... PHILADELPHIA, PA   113
JAMES STREET COMMONS.........................NEWARK, NJ   41
PENN SQUARE .... READING, PA   151
PENN'S LANDING............................ PHILADELPHIA, PA   116
SOCIETY HILL .... PHILADELPHIA, PA   106

SWAMPS

GREAT SWAMP BASIN .... BASKING RIDGE, NJ   25

THEATERS

ALLENBERRY PLAYHOUSE .... CARLISLE, PA   70
THE AMISH EXPERI ENCE THEATRE ......BIRD-IN-HAND, PA   99
BUCKS COUNTY PLAYHOUSE................... NEW HOPE, PA   127
GETTYSBURG BATTLE THEATRE .... GETTYSBURG, PA   77
HEDGEROW THEATRE .... MEDIA, PA   127
MANN CENTER FOR THE PERFORMING
   ARTS .... PHILADELPHIA, PA   111
OPEN AIR THEATRE.............................. TRENTON, NJ   48
OPEN-AIR THEATRE ....KENNETT SQUARE, PA   126
PAPER MILL PLAYHOUSE ....MILLBURN, NJ   38
THE PEOPLE'S PLACE .... INTERCOURSE, PA   101
"THE CONFLICT" .... GETTYSBURG, PA   77
TOTEM POLE PLAYHOUSE .... FAYETTEVILLE, PA   76
TUTTLEMAN OMNIVERSE THEATER ...... PHILADELPHIA, PA   113

TOWERS

BOWMAN'S HILL TOWER.......... WASHINGTON CROSSING
                                     HISTORIC PARK, PA   129
NATIONAL TOWER ....GETTYSBURG, PA   78
SOMERSET COUNTY PARK COMMISSION'S
   ENVIRONMENTAL EDUCATION
   CENTER.. BASKING RIDGE, NJ   25
THOMAS A. EDISON MEMORIAL TOWER AND
   MUSEUM.. MENLO PARK, NJ   38

TREES

FRIENDS BURYING GROUND.........................SALEM, NJ   132

TUNNELS

UNION CANAL TUNNEL............................LEBANON, PA   9

VIEWS

BARNEGAT LIGHTHOUSE.............BARNEGAT LIGHT, NJ   24
THE BATONA TRAIL ....NJ   14
DUQUESNE INCLINE .... PITTSBURGH, PA   13
EAGLE ROCK RESERVATION .... WEST ORANGE, NJ   5
GRAND CANYON OF PENNSYLVANIA ..... WELLSBORO, PA   15
KINZUA BRIDGE SP .... MOUNT JEWETT, PA   9
LIBERTY SP .... JERSEY CITY, NJ   3
MONONGAHELA INCLINE .... PITTSBURGH, PA   13
MOUNT DAVIS .... THE LAUREL HIGHLANDS, PA   9
NATIONAL TOWER ....GETTYSBURG, PA   7
PAGODA .... READING, PA   15

POCONO KNOB ....MOUNT POCONO, PA 149
WOPSONONOCK TABLELAND..................ALTOONA, PA 65

VISITOR CENTERS
ALLAIRE SP .... FARMINGDALE, NJ 29
BATSTO HISTORIC VILLAGE .... BATSTO, NJ 130
BRANDYWINE BATTLEFIELD PARK ...... CHADDS FORD, PA 123
BRANDYWINE VALLEY TOURIST INFORMATION
  CENTER.............................LONGWOOD, PA 126
BUSHKILL VISITOR
  CENTER .... DELAWARE WATER GAP NRA, PA 147
CAPE MAY...NJ 26
CAPE MAY COURT HOUSE ....NJ 27
★CLAYTON..............................PITTSBURGH, PA 138
CORNWALL IRON FURNACE .... CORNWALL, PA 71
DELAWARE WATER GAP NRA..........................PA 147
★EDISON NHS .... WEST ORANGE, NJ 50
FORT LEE HISTORIC PARK ....FORT LEE, NJ 30
THE FRICK ART & HISTORICAL CENTER .... PITTSBURGH, PA 138
GETTYSBURG ....PA 77
HAWK MOUNTAIN SANCTUARY .... ECKVILLE, PA 73
★HERSHEY'S CHOCOLATE WORLD............ HERSHEY, PA 87
HOPEWELL FURNACE NHS ....PA 87
JOSEPH PRIESTLEY HOUSE .... NORTHUMBERLAND, PA 96
LEONARD J. BUCK GARDEN .... FAR HILLS, NJ 29
LIMERICK ENERGY INFORMATION CENTER... LIMERICK, PA 126
MEMORIAL BUILDING.............. WASHINGTON CROSSING
                               HISTORIC PARK, PA 130
MENNONITE INFORMATION CENTER AND HEBREW
  TABERNACLE REPRODUCTION .... LANCASTER, PA 103
MIDDLE CREEK WILDLIFE MANAGEMENT
  AREA .... KLEINFELTERSVILLE, PA 90
MONMOUTH BATTLEFIELD SP .... FREEHOLD, NJ 31
★MORRISTOWN NHP ....NJ 40
★NATIONAL PARK VISITOR
  CENTER.......................... GETTYSBURG NMP, PA 82
PATERSON ....NJ 43
PITHOLE CITY ....PLUMER, PA 145
PYMATUNING VISITOR CENTER............... LINESVILLE, PA 93
STRASBURG ....PA 104
THREE MILE ISLAND VISITORS CENTER.... MIDDLETOWN, PA 95
TWO RIVERS LANDING AND THE DELAWARE AND LEHIGH
  NATIONAL HERITAGE CORRIDOR VISITOR
  CENTER...............................EASTON, PA 73
★VALLEY FORGE NHP...............................PA 128
VISITOR INFORMATION CENTER .... LANCASTER, PA 101
WASHINGTON CROSSING SP....................TRENTON, NJ 48

VISITOR INFORMATION
ALLENTOWN......................................PA 62
ALTOONA ....PA 64
ASBURY PARK ....NJ 18
BARNEGAT LIGHT ....NJ 24
BEDFORD ....PA 66
BELLEFONTE ....PA 66
BERWICK ....PA 66
BETHLEHEM ....PA 67
BOALSBURG ....PA 68
BRADFORD ....PA 68
BRIDGETON ....NJ 25
BROOKVILLE ....PA 68
BUCKS COUNTY ....PA 123
BURLINGTON ....NJ 130
CARLISLE ....PA 69
CHADDS FORD....................................PA 123
CHAMBERSBURG ....PA 70
COLUMBIA ....PA 100
CONNEAUT LAKE ....PA 71
COUDERSPORT ....PA 72
DOYLESTOWN ....PA 124
EASTON ....PA 72
ELIZABETH ....NJ 28
EPHRATA ....PA 100
ERIE ....PA 74
FORT LEE ....NJ 30
FRANKLIN.......................................PA 76
FREEHOLD ....NJ 31
GETTYSBURG ....PA 77
GREENSBURG ....PA 82
HACKENSACK ....NJ 32
HANOVER ....PA 83
HARRISBURG ....PA 83
HAZLETON ....PA 85
HERSHEY..PA 86
HONESDALE ....PA 148
HUNTINGDON ....PA 87
INDIANA ....PA 88
JACKSON ....NJ 35
JERSEY CITY ....NJ 36
JIM THORPE ....PA 148
JOHNSTOWN......................................PA 89
LANCASTER ....PA 101
THE LAUREL HIGHLANDS ....PA 91
LEBANON ....PA 91
LEWISBURG ....PA 92
LEWISTOWN ....PA 92
LOCK HAVEN ....PA 93
LONG BRANCH ....NJ 37

LONGWOOD.......................................PA 126
MADISON ....NJ 37
MANHEIM ....PA 104
MEADVILLE ....PA 94
MEDIA ....PA 127
MERCER ....PA 94
MIDDLETOWN ....NJ 38
MILLBURN ....NJ 38
MILLVILLE ....NJ 38
MONTCLAIR ....NJ 38
MORRISTOWN ....NJ 39
NAZARETH ....PA 95
NEW BRUNSWICK ....NJ 41
NEWARK ....NJ 41
OCEAN CITY ....NJ 42
OCEAN GROVE ....NJ 42
OHIOPYLE ....PA 96
OIL CITY ....PA 98
PATERSON ....NJ 43
PLAINFIELD ....NJ 44
POINT PLEASANT BEACH ....NJ 44
POTTSTOWN ....PA 128
POTTSVILLE ....PA 150
PRINCETON ....NJ 44
PUNXSUTAWNEY ....PA 151
READING..PA 151
RINGWOOD ....NJ 45
ST. MARYS......................................PA 153
SALEM ....NJ 132
SCRANTON ....PA 153
SHARON ....PA 154
SOMERVILLE ....NJ 46
STATE COLLEGE ....PA 155
STROUDSBURG ....PA 150
SUNBURY ....PA 156
TITUSVILLE ....PA 156
TOMS RIVER ....NJ 47
TOWANDA ....PA 157
TRENTON ....NJ 47
UNIONTOWN ....PA 157
VALLEY FORGE ....PA 128
VINELAND ....NJ 49
WASHINGTON ....PA 145
WAYNE ....NJ 49
WAYNESBORO ....PA 159
WAYNESBURG ....PA 159
WELLSBORO ....PA 159
WEST CHESTER ....PA 130
WILDWOOD ....NJ 50
WILKES-BARRE ....PA 160
WILLIAMSPORT ....PA 160
WOODBURY ....NJ 132
YORK ....PA 161

WALKING TOURS
ALLENTOWN......................................PA 62
BEDFORD ....PA 66
BELLEFONTE ....PA 66
BETHLEHEM ....PA 67
BROOKVILLE ....PA 68
CAPE MAY.......................................NJ 26
CHAMBERSBURG ....PA 70
EASTON ....PA 72
FRANKLIN.......................................PA 76
GETTYSBURG ....PA 77
★GETTYSBURG NMP................................PA 80
HISTORICAL SOCIETY OF PRINCETON........ PRINCETON, NJ 44
HOPE ....NJ 34
KUSER FARM MANSION AND PARK......... HAMILTON, NJ 33
LANCASTER WALKING TOUR................ LANCASTER, PA 102
LEWISBURG ....PA 92
LITITZ...PA 103
LOCK HAVEN ....PA 93
PATERSON ....NJ 43
PITHOLE CITY ....PLUMER, PA 145
PRINCETON ....NJ 44
STERLING HILL MINE & MUSEUM......... OGDENSBURG, NJ 43
TALK-A-WALK .... PHILADELPHIA, PA 119
UNIVERSITY OF PENNSYLVANIA......... PHILADELPHIA, PA 117
YORK ....PA 161

WATERFALLS
BUSHKILL FALLS......................BUSHKILL, PA 146
GREAT FALLS OF THE PASSAIC RIVER........ PATERSON, NJ 43
OHIOPYLE SP. .... OHIOPYLE, PA 96
RICKETTS GLEN SP ....RED ROCK, PA 152

WATER PARKS
BLAND'S PARK........................TYRONE, PA 157
CAMELBACK ALPINE SLIDE AND
  WATERSLIDE .... TANNERSVILLE, PA 150
CASINO PIER AND WATER WORKS... SEASIDE HEIGHTS, NJ 46
CLEMENTON AMUSEMENT PARK & SPLASH WORLD
  WATER PARK .... CLEMENTON, NJ 131
★DORNEY PARK AND WILDWATER
  KINGDOM .... ALLENTOWN, PA 63
RAGING WATERS....................WILDWOOD, NJ 51

SANDCASTLE.................................... PITTSBURGH, PA 140
SHAWNEE PLACE PLAY AND
  WATER PARK ....SHAWNEE ON DELAWARE, PA 149
WALDAMEER PARK & WATER WORLD...............ERIE, PA   75

WAX MUSEUMS
HALL OF PRESIDENTS .... GETTYSBURG, PA   78
NATIONAL CIVIL WAR WAX MUSEUM ...... GETTYSBURG, PA   78
WAX MUSEUM OF LANCASTER COUNTY
  HISTORY .... LANCASTER, PA 103

WILDERNESS AREAS
ALLEGHENY ISLANDS WILDERNESS .... ALLEGHENY NF, PA   62
HEART'S CONTENT.......................... ALLEGHENY NF, PA   62
HICKORY CREEK WILDERNESS .... ALLEGHENY NF, PA   62

WILDLIFE SANCTUARIES
BEECHWOOD FARMS NATURE RESERVE ....PITTSBURGH, PA 136
THE DORFLINGER-SUYDAM
  WILDLIFE SANCTUARY .... WHITE MILLS, PA 150
EDWIN B. FORSYTHE NWR ....OCEANVILLE, NJ   23
GREAT SWAMP NWR.................... BASKING RIDGE, NJ   24
HAWK MOUNTAIN SANCTUARY ....ECKVILLE, PA   73
JAMAICA BAY WILDLIFE REFUGE........GATEWAY NRA, NJ   32
JAMES A. MCFAUL ENVIRONMENTAL CENTER OF BERGEN
  COUNTY ....WYCKOFF, NJ   51
JOCKEY HOLLOW....................MORRISTOWN NHP, NJ   40
MARINE MAMMAL STRANDING CENTER.... BRIGANTINE, NJ   23
MILL GROVE, THE AUDUBON WILDLIFE
  SANCTUARY.. AUDUBON, PA 122
★PENN'S CAVE ....CENTRE HALL, PA   70
PRESQUE ISLE SP ....ERIE, PA   75
PROSPERTOWN LAKE ....JACKSON, NJ   35
SANDY HOOK UNIT ....GATEWAY NRA, NJ   32
SUSQUEHANNA ENERGY INFORMATION CENTER AND
  RIVERLANDS................................... BERWICK, PA   67
TREXLER-LEHIGH COUNTY GAME
  PRESERVE ................................SCHNECKSVILLE, PA 153
THE WETLANDS INSTITUTE .... STONE HARBOR, NJ   46

WINERIES
BUCKINGHAM VALLEY VINEYARDS AND
  WINERY ....BUCKINGHAM, PA 122

CLOVER HILL VINEYARDS &
  WINERY...ALLENTOWN, PA   64
CONNEAUT CELLARS WINERY..........CONNEAUT LAKE, PA   71
GLADES PIKE WINERY.........................LAVANSVILLE, PA   91
HISTORIC RENAULT WINERY ....EGG HARBOR CITY, NJ   23
LANCASTER COUNTY WINERY .... LANCASTER, PA 103
NISSLEY WINERY AND VINEYARDS............MARIETTA, PA 104
SAND CASTLE WINERY................................ERWINNA, PA   75

ZOOLOGICAL PARKS & EXHIBITS
BRIDGETON CITY PARK..................... BRIDGETON, NJ   26
★CAPE MAY COUNTY PARK
  AND ZOO .... CAPE MAY COURT HOUSE, NJ   27
CLAWS 'N' PAWS WILD
  ANIMAL PARK ....HAMLIN, PA 148
CLYDE PEELING'S REPTILAND .... ALLENWOOD, PA   64
COHANZICK ZOO .... BRIDGETON, NJ   26
ELMWOOD PARK ZOO .... NORRISTOWN, PA 127
ERIE ZOO ....ERIE, PA   75
LIVING TREASURES ANIMAL PARK ....NEW CASTLE, PA   96
THE NATIONAL AVIARY .... PITTSBURGH, PA 139
★PITTSBURGH ZOO........................... PITTSBURGH, PA 139
POPCORN PARK ZOO .... FORKED RIVER, NJ   30
PYMATUNING DEER PARK .... JAMESTOWN, PA   89
SPACE FARMS ZOO AND
  MUSEUM .... BEEMERVILLE, NJ   25
TREXLER-LEHIGH COUNTY GAME
  PRESERVE ................................SCHNECKSVILLE, PA 153
TURTLE BACK ZOO .... WEST ORANGE, NJ   50
ZOOAMERICA NORTH AMERICAN WILDLIFE
  PARK.. HERSHEY, PA   86
ZOOLOGICAL GARDENS .... PHILADELPHIA, PA 112

ZOOLOGICAL PARKS & EXHIBITS-CHILDREN'S ZOOS
ELMWOOD PARK ZOO....................... NORRISTOWN, PA 127
ERIE ZOO ....ERIE, PA   75
LAKE TOBIAS WILDLIFE PARK ....HALIFAX, PA   82
★PITTSBURGH ZOO......................... PITTSBURGH, PA 139
PYMATUNING DEER PARK .... JAMESTOWN, PA   89
ZOOLOGICAL GARDENS .... PHILADELPHIA, PA 112

SAVE ATTRACTION ADMISSION DISCOUNT INDEX

NEW JERSEY
BUSHY RUN BATTLEFIELD SHS .... JEANNETTE 144
CARNEGIE SCIENCE CENTER ....PITTSBURGH 138
DAVID BRADFORD HOUSE...................... WASHINGTON 145
FORT PITT MUSEUM ....PITTSBURGH 140
HARMONY MUSEUM ....HARMONY 144
LAND OF MAKE-BELIEVE ....HOPE   34
LIBERTY SCIENCE CENTER .... JERSEY CITY   36
THE NOYES MUSEUM OF ART....................OCEANVILLE   24
OLD ECONOMY VILLAGE...........................AMBRIDGE 143
ROBERT J. NOVINS PLANETARIUM ....TOMS RIVER   47
SIX FLAGS GREAT ADVENTURE ....JACKSON   35
STERLING HILL MINE & MUSEUM .... OGDENSBURG   43
SUBMARINE USS LING NEW JERSEY NAVAL
  MUSEUM ....HACKENSACK   32
THE WILLIAM TRENT HOUSE .... TRENTON   48

PENNSYLVANIA
ALTOONA RAILROADERS MEMORIAL
  MUSEUM ....ALTOONA   64
AMERICAN CHRISTMAS MUSEUM..........CHADDS FORD 123
AMERICAN SWEDISH HISTORICAL
  MUSEUM ....PHILADELPHIA 108
BAKER MANSION ....ALTOONA   64
BOYERTOWN MUSEUM OF HISTORIC
  VEHICLES...BOYERTOWN   68
BRANDYWINE BATTLEFIELD PARK ....CHADDS FORD 123
CHESTER COUNTY HISTORICAL
  SOCIETY .... WEST CHESTER 130
CHILDREN'S DISCOVERY WORKSHOP ......WILLIAMSPORT 160
CHOO CHOO BARN, TRAINTOWN, U.S.A....... STRASBURG 105
CLIVEDEN ....PHILADELPHIA 110
THE COMPASS INN MUSEUM.......LAUGHLINTOWN   91
CONFEDERATE STATES ARMORY AND
  MUSEUM ....GETTYSBURG   77
CONRAD WEISER HOMESTEAD ....WOMELSDORF 161
CORNWALL IRON FURNACE ....CORNWALL   71
DANIEL BOONE HOMESTEAD ....BAUMSTOWN   65
DRAKE WELL MUSEUM ....TITUSVILLE 156
ECKLEY MINERS' VILLAGE ....HAZLETON   85
EPHRATA CLOISTER ....EPHRATA 100
FARM MUSEUM (BRADFORD COUNTY HERITAGE
  ASSOCIATION) ....TROY 157
FORT BEDFORD MUSEUM .... BEDFORD   66
FORT HUNTER MANSION AND PARK ....HARRISBURG   84
FRANKLIN INSTITUTE SCIENCE
  MUSEUM ....PHILADELPHIA 113
GRAEME PARK ....HORSHAM 125

HERSHEY GARDENS ....HERSHEY   86
HERSHEY MUSEUM ....HERSHEY   86
HISTORIC ROCK FORD PLANTATION ....LANCASTER 102
HISTORICAL SOCIETY OF BERKS COUNTY.........READING 152
H.O. SCALE MODEL TRAIN DISPLAY .... JIM THORPE 148
HOPE LODGE..FORT WASHINGTON 125
INDIAN CAVERNS ....SPRUCE CREEK 155
JAMES A. MICHENER ART MUSEUM ...... DOYLESTOWN 124
JOHN HARRIS/SIMON CAMERON
  MANSION ....HARRISBURG   84
JOHNSTOWN FLOOD MUSEUM ....JOHNSTOWN   90
JOSEPH PRIESTLEY HOUSE ........NORTHUMBERLAND   96
LAND OF LITTLE HORSES ....GETTYSBURG   78
LANDIS VALLEY MUSEUM........................LANCASTER 102
LAUREL CAVERNS ....UNIONTOWN 157
LEHIGHTON MODEL TRAIN DISPLAY .... LEHIGHTON 149
LINCOLN CAVERNS ....HUNTINGDON   88
LINCOLN ROOM MUSEUM.....................GETTYSBURG   78
LITTLE LEAGUE BASEBALL MUSEUM.......WILLIAMSPORT 161
LYCOMING COUNTY HISTORICAL
  MUSEUM ....WILLIAMSPORT 161
MAGIC TOWN OF GETTYSBURG ....GETTYSBURG   78
MEADOWCROFT MUSEUM OF RURAL LIFE........AVELLA   65
MERCER MUSEUM ....DOYLESTOWN 124
MORAVIAN POTTERY AND TILE WORKS... DOYLESTOWN 125
MUMMERS MUSEUM .............................PHILADELPHIA 115
MUSEUM OF ANTHRACITE MINING ....ASHLAND   65
NATIONAL CIVIL WAR WAX MUSEUM ......GETTYSBURG   78
NATIONAL TOWER ....GETTYSBURG   78
THE NATIONAL TOY TRAIN MUSEUM .... STRASBURG 105
OIL CREEK AND TITUSVILLE RAILROAD ....TITUSVILLE 157
PARRY MANSION MUSEUM ....NEW HOPE 127
PENNSBURY MANOR...............................MORRISVILLE 127
PENNSYLVANIA ANTHRACITE HERITAGE
  MUSEUM ....SCRANTON 153
PENNSYLVANIA LUMBER MUSEUM .... COUDERSPORT   72
PENNSYLVANIA MILITARY MUSEUM ....BOALSBURG   88
PLEASE TOUCH MUSEUM .......................PHILADELPHIA 116
QUIET VALLEY LIVING
  HISTORICAL FARM .... STROUDSBURG 150
RAILROAD MUSEUM OF PENNSYLVANIA........ STRASBURG 105
A RECONSTRUCTION OF THE US BRIG NIAGARA...... ERIE   75
ROSENBACH MUSEUM AND LIBRARY .... PHILADELPHIA 117
SESAME PLACE .... LANGHORNE 126
SOMERSET HISTORICAL CENTER .... SOMERSET 153
STOURBRIDGE LINE RAIL EXCURSIONS ... HONESDALE 148
SWIGART MUSEUM ....HUNTINGDON   88
THE WHARTON ESHERICK STUDIO ....PAOLI 128
WHITEWATER CHALLENGERS
  RAFT TOURS.................................... WHITE HAVEN 159

BED & BREAKFAST LODGINGS INDEX

Some bed and breakfasts listed below might have historical significance. Those properties are also referenced in the Historical index. The indication that continental [CP] or full breakfast [BP] is included in the room rate reflects whether a property is a Bed-and-Breakfast facility.

NEW JERSEY

ACCOMMODATIONS

ABBOTT HOUSE BED & BREAKFAST	MAYS LANDING	182
AMBER STREET INN	BEACH HAVEN	184
ATLANTIC VIEW INN	AVON BY THE SEA	183
BAY HEAD GABLES	BAY HEAD	184
CABBAGE ROSE INN	FLEMINGTON	196
CANDLELIGHT INN	NORTH WILDWOOD	214
CASHELMARA BED & BREAKFAST INN	AVON BY THE SEA	184
CASTLE BY THE SEA	OCEAN CITY	215
CHIMNEY HILL BED & BREAKFAST	LAMBERTVILLE	200
COLVMNS BY THE SEA	CAPE MAY	187
CONOVERS BAY HEAD INN	BAY HEAD	184
CROSSED KEYS B&B	ANDOVER	171
DOWN THE SHORE BED & BREAKFAST	BELMAR	185
GINGERBREAD HOUSE	CAPE MAY	187
HAMILTON HOUSE INN	SPRING LAKE	228
HOLLY THORN HOUSE	WHITE HOUSE STATION	235
HUNTERDON HOUSE	FRENCHTOWN	197
ISAAC HILLIARD HOUSE BED & BREAKFAST	PEMBERTON	393
JERICA HILL-A BED & BREAKFAST INN	FLEMINGTON	196
LA MAISON	SPRING LAKE	229
MANOR HOUSE	CAPE MAY	187
NORMANDY INN	SPRING LAKE	229
NORTHWOOD INN	OCEAN CITY	216
SCARBOROUGH INN	OCEAN CITY	216
SEACREST BY THE SEA	SPRING LAKE	229
SERENDIPITY BED & BREAKFAST	OCEAN CITY	216
THE ABBEY BED & BREAKFAST	CAPE MAY	186
THE BRASS BED INN	CAPE MAY	187
THE INN AT THE SHORE	BELMAR	185
THE INN ON OCEAN	CAPE MAY	187
THE MAINSTAY	CAPE MAY	187
THE OCEAN HOUSE	SPRING LAKE	229
THE QUEEN VICTORIA	CAPE MAY	188
THE SOUTHERN MANSION	CAPE MAY	189
THE WHISTLING SWAN INN	STANHOPE	230
THE WOODEN DUCK BED & BREAKFAST	NEWTON	213
VICTORIAN LACE INN	CAPE MAY	189
WHITE DOVE COTTAGE	CAPE MAY	189

PENNSYLVANIA

ACCOMMODATIONS

9 PARTNERS INN BED & BREAKFAST	HARFORD	291
AARON BURR HOUSE INN & CONFERENCE CENTER	NEW HOPE	383
ADAMSTOWN INN	ADAMSTOWN	330
APPLEBUTTER INN	SLIPPERY ROCK	435
APPLEFORD INN	GETTYSBURG	283
APPLETREE BED & BREAKFAST	SHADYSIDE	413
AUSTRALIAN WALKABOUT INN B&B	LAMPETER	334
BALADERRY INN AT GETTYSBURG	GETTYSBURG	283
BED & BREAKFAST-THE MANOR	LAMPETER	334
BEDFORD'S COVERED BRIDGE INN	SCHELLSBURG	430
BEECHMONT INN	HANOVER	290
BLACK WALNUT B & B COUNTRY INN	MILFORD	425
BLUE BERRY MOUNTAIN INN	BLAKESLEE	262
BOXWOOD INN	AKRON	330
BROOKVIEW MANOR BED & BREAKFAST	CANADENSIS	421
CHARBERT FARM BED AND BREAKFAST	INDIANA	309
CLASSIC VICTORIAN BED & BREAKFAST	NAZARETH	326
CLEARVIEW FARM BED & BREAKFAST	CLAY	332
COCALICO CREEK BED & BREAKFAST	DENVER	332
CORNERSTONE INN BED & BREAKFAST	LANDENBERG	381
DAY LILY INN BED & BREAKFAST	CORRY	274
FARM FORTUNE BED & BREAKFAST	NEW CUMBERLAND	327

FARMHOUSE BED & BREAKFAST	MOUNT POCONO	426
FRANKENFIELD FARM BED & BREAKFAST	OTTSVILLE	384
GARDENS OF EDEN BED & BREAKFAST	LANCASTER	342
GOLDEN OAK INN BED & BREAKFAST	TROY	439
GRAPE ARBOR INN BED & BREAKFAST	NORTH EAST	328
HILLSIDE FARM B & B	MOUNT JOY	348
HISTORIC SMITHTON COUNTRY INN	EPHRATA	333
HOLLILEIF BED & BREAKFAST	WRIGHTSTOWN	388
INN TO THE WOODS BED & BREAKFAST	WASHINGTON CROSSING	387
INNE AT WATSON'S CHOICE	UNIONTOWN	318
INTERCOURSE VILLAGE BED & BREAKFAST SUITES	INTERCOURSE	334
JAMES GETTYS HOTEL	GETTYSBURG	288
LEIBERT GAP MANOR BED & BREAKFAST	EMMAUS	278
LIGHTFARM	KINTNERSVILLE	380
LONGSTRETCH HARBOUR BED & BREAKFAST	WASHINGTON	415
LYNNROSE BED & BREAKFAST	GROVE CITY	290
MEHARD MANOR BED & BREAKFAST	MERCER	324
MOUNTAIN VIEW BED & BREAKFAST	DONEGAL	311
O'FLAHERTY'S DINGELDEIN HOUSE BED & BREAKFAST	LANCASTER	345
OLD CHARM BED & BREAKFAST	ST. MARYS	429
OREGON BED & BREAKFAST	LANCASTER	345
PHEASANT FIELD BED & BREAKFAST	CARLISLE	268
PINE HILL FARM BED & BREAKFAST	MILFORD	425
PINEAPPLE HILL BED & BREAKFAST	NEW HOPE	384
PONDA-ROWLAND BED & BREAKFAST	DALLAS	274
QUILL HAVEN COUNTRY INN	SOMERSET	317
QUO VADIS BED & BREAKFAST	FRANKLIN	282
RIDGE HOUSE	MONTROSE	325
ROEBLING INN ON THE DELAWARE	LACKAWAXEN	424
SCARLETT HOUSE	KENNETT SQUARE	378
SHADY LANE BED & BREAKFAST	EAGLES MERE	277
SHARPE'S HOUSE BED & BREAKFAST	TUNKHANNOCK	439
SHEARER ELEGANCE BED & BREAKFAST	LINFIELD	381
SHIPPEN WAY INN	PHILADELPHIA	361
SHULTZ VICTORIAN MANSION B & B	CHAMBERSBURG	271
SNOW GOOSE INN	GROVE CITY	290
SPENCER HOUSE BED & BREAKFAST	ERIE	280
STRASBURG VILLAGE INN	STRASBURG	351
SWATARA CREEK INN	ANNVILLE	257
SWISS WOODS BED & BREAKFAST	LITITZ	348
TATTERSALL INN	POINT PLEASANT	385
TEN-ELEVEN CLINTON	PHILADELPHIA	361
THE APPLE BIN INN	WILLOW STREET	351
THE BARNYARD INN	ADAMSTOWN	330
THE BRAFFERTON INN	GETTYSBURG	283
THE BUCKSVILLE HOUSE	KINTNERSVILLE	380
THE FOX & HOUND BED & BREAKFAST OF NEW HOPE	NEW HOPE	383
THE GASLIGHT INN	GETTYSBURG	286
THE HARRY PACKER MANSION	JIM THORPE	424
THE INN AT GEORGIAN PLACE	SOMERSET	316
THE INN AT OAKMONT	OAKMONT	413
THE INN ON GRANDVIEW	ZELIENOPLE	416
THE KING'S COTTAGE	LANCASTER	343
THE MANSION INN	NEW HOPE	383
THE NETHERCOTT INN B&B	STARRUCCA	427
THE PRIORY-A CITY INN	PITTSBURGH	398
THE RED POPPY BED & BREAKFAST	BENTON	260
THE REIGHARD HOUSE	WILLIAMSPORT	446
THE THOMAS BOND HOUSE	PHILADELPHIA	361
THE VICTORIAN PEACOCK BED & BREAKFAST	PIPERSVILLE	385
THE WEDGWOOD INN	NEW HOPE	384
TWIN TURRETS INN	BOYERTOWN	263
VILLAGE INN OF BIRD-IN-HAND	BIRD-IN-HAND	331
WAYNEBROOK INN	HONEY BROOK	378
WEST RIDGE GUEST HOUSE	ELIZABETHTOWN	333
WHIPPLE TREE INN & FARM	EMLENTON	278
WYDNOR HALL INN	BETHLEHEM	261

All information in this TourBook is accurate at press time.
Changes may occur between publications.
Be sure to use the latest edition for the most recent information.

COUNTRY INNS INDEX

Some of the following country inns can also be considered as bed-and-breakfast operations. The indication that continental [CP] or full breakfast [BP] is included in the room rate reflects whether a property is a Bed-and-Breakfast facility.

NEW JERSEY

ACCOMMODATIONS

CARROLL VILLA BED & BREAKFAST ....CAPE MAY 187
GRENVILLE HOTEL ....BAY HEAD 184
THE BERNARDS INN .........................BERNARDSVILLE 185
THE CHATEAU ....SPRING LAKE 228
THE DOCTORS INN AT KINGS
 GRANT .... CAPE MAY COURT HOUSE 191
THE HEWITT WELLINGTON HOTEL ....SPRING LAKE 228

RESTAURANT

INN AT MILLRACE POND ....HOPE 199

PENNSYLVANIA

ACCOMMODATIONS

1740 HOUSE.............................LUMBERVILLE 382
CAMERON ESTATE INN ....MOUNT JOY 348
CARNEGIE HOUSE.........................STATE COLLEGE 436
CASHTOWN INN..............................CASHTOWN 269
CRESCENT LODGE...................................CRESCO 421
CRESTMONT INN ....EAGLES MERE 277
DULING-KURTZ HOUSE & COUNTRY INN ....EXTON 377
FAIRVILLE INN ....FAIRVILLE 377
FALLS PORT INN & RESTAURANT ....HAWLEY 423

GENERAL SUTTER INN.............................LITITZ 348
GETTYSTOWN INN BED & BREAKFAST ....GETTYSBURG 286
GLASBERN ....FOGELSVILLE 281
GLENDORN-A LODGE IN THE COUNTRY ....BRADFORD 263
GOLDEN PHEASANT INN ....ERWINNA 281
HERR TAVERN & PUBLICK HOUSE ....GETTYSBURG 287
HICKORY BRIDGE FARM BED & BREAKFAST ....ORRTANNA 329
HISTORIC STRASBURG INN ....STRASBURG 351
INN AT FELICITA..............................HARRISBURG 297
TARA-A COUNTRY INN ....CLARK 271
THE BRICK HOTEL.................................NEWTOWN 384
THE INN AT JIM THORPE ....JIM THORPE 424
THE INN AT NEW BERLIN ....NEW BERLIN 327
THE INN AT STARLIGHT LAKE ....STARLIGHT 426
THE INN AT THE ALTLAND HOUSE .... ABBOTTSTOWN 254
THE INN AT TURKEY HILL ....BLOOMSBURG 262
THE MERCERSBURG INN .... MERCERSBURG 324
THE NOON-COLLINS INN .... EBENSBURG 277
THE SETTLERS INN AT BINGHAM PARK ....HAWLEY 423
TOWNE HOUSE INN ....ST. MARYS 429
YE OLDE TEMPERANCE HOUSE ....NEWTOWN 384

RESTAURANTS

CENTRE BRIDGE INN.............................NEW HOPE 384
COVENTRY FORGE INN RESTAURANT ....COVENTRYVILLE 376
GABRIEL'S RESTAURANT ....NEW BERLIN 327
GOLDEN PHEASANT INN ....ERWINNA 281
PUMP HOUSE INN...............................CANADENSIS 421
RAILROAD HOUSE RESTAURANT ....MARIETTA 348

HISTORICAL LODGINGS & RESTAURANTS INDEX

Some of the following historical lodgings can also be considered as bed-and-breakfast operations. The indication that continental [CP] or full breakfast [BP] is included in the room rate reflects whether a property is a Bed-and-Breakfast facility.

NEW JERSEY

ACCOMMODATIONS

ABBOTT HOUSE BED & BREAKFAST....... MAYS LANDING 182
AMBER STREET INN..............................BEACH HAVEN 184
CABBAGE ROSE INN ....FLEMINGTON 196
CANDLELIGHT INN.....................NORTH WILDWOOD 214
CARROLL VILLA BED & BREAKFAST ....CAPE MAY 187
CASTLE BY THE SEA ....OCEAN CITY 215
CHIMNEY HILL BED & BREAKFAST .........LAMBERTVILLE 200
COLVMNS BY THE SEA..............................CAPE MAY 187
CONOVERS BAY HEAD INN ....BAY HEAD 184
CROSSED KEYS B&B ....ANDOVER 171
GINGERBREAD HOUSE ....CAPE MAY 187
GRENVILLE HOTEL ....BAY HEAD 184
HOLLY THORN HOUSE .... WHITE HOUSE STATION 235
HUNTERDON HOUSE ....FRENCHTOWN 197
ISAAC HILLIARD HOUSE BED & BREAKFAST....PEMBERTON 393
JERICA HILL-A BED & BREAKFAST INN........ FLEMINGTON 196
LA MAISON...................................SPRING LAKE 229
LAMBERTVILLE HOUSE-A NATIONAL HISTORIC
 INN ...............................LAMBERTVILLE 200
MANOR HOUSE ....CAPE MAY 187
MOLLY PITCHER INN ....RED BANK 222
NORMANDY INN ....SPRING LAKE 229
NORTHWOOD INN ....OCEAN CITY 216
QUEENS HOTEL ....CAPE MAY 188
SCARBOROUGH INN ....OCEAN CITY 216
SEACREST BY THE SEA ....SPRING LAKE 229
SERENDIPITY BED & BREAKFAST.................OCEAN CITY 216
THE ABBEY BED & BREAKFAST ....CAPE MAY 186
THE BERNARDS INN .........................BERNARDSVILLE 185
THE BRASS BED INN ....CAPE MAY 187
THE CHATEAU ....SPRING LAKE 228
THE DOCTORS INN AT
 KINGS GRANT.................. CAPE MAY COURT HOUSE 191
THE HEWITT WELLINGTON HOTEL ....SPRING LAKE 228
THE INN AT THE SHORE ....BELMAR 185
THE INN ON OCEAN ....CAPE MAY 190
THE MADISON HOUSE HOTEL ... ATLANTIC CITY 177
THE OCEAN HOUSE.................................SPRING LAKE 229
THE QUEEN VICTORIA ....CAPE MAY 188
THE SOUTHERN MANSION ....CAPE MAY 189
VICTORIAN LACE INN.................................CAPE MAY 189
WHITE DOVE COTTAGE.................................CAPE MAY 189

RESTAURANTS

410 BANK STREET...............................CAPE MAY 190
BRADBURY'S FINE DINING ..... CAPE MAY COURT HOUSE 191
CAFE GALLERY ....BURLINGTON 389
CLAUDE'S HO-HO-KUS INN ....HO-HO-KUS 198
FRESCOS ....CAPE MAY 190
GRENVILLE BY THE SEA..............................BAY HEAD 184
HIGHLAWN PAVILION...................... WEST ORANGE 234
KROGH'S RESTAURANT ....SPARTA 227
MERION INN ....CAPE MAY 190
STAGE HOUSE INN...........................SCOTCH PLAINS 224
STONY HILL INN ....HACKENSACK 197
THE BERNARDS INN .... BERNARDSVILLE 185
THE BLACK HORSE INN & PUB ....MENDHAM 203
THE FRENCHTOWN INN...........................FRENCHTOWN 197
THE FROG AND THE PEACH................NEW BRUNSWICK 213
THE GRAIN HOUSE AT THE
 OLDE MILL INN .... BASKING RIDGE 184
THE LAMBERTVILLE STATION .... LAMBERTVILLE 200
THE MAD BATTER RESTAURANT ....CAPE MAY 190
THE WASHINGTON INN...............................CAPE MAY 190

PENNSYLVANIA

ACCOMMODATIONS

9 PARTNERS INN BED & BREAKFAST..............HARFORD 291
AARON BURR HOUSE INN &
 CONFERENCE CENTER...........................NEW HOPE 383
ADAMSTOWN INN ....ADAMSTOWN 330
APPLEBUTTER INN ....SLIPPERY ROCK 435
APPLEFORD INN ....GETTYSBURG 283
AUSTRALIAN WALKABOUT INN B&B ....LAMPETER 334
BALADERRY INN AT GETTYSBURG ....GETTYSBURG 283
BEDFORD'S COVERED BRIDGE INN ....SCHELLSBURG 430
BEECHMONT INN ....HANOVER 290
BEST WESTERN GETTYSBURG HOTEL EST.
 1797.......................GETTYSBURG 283
BEST WESTERN INDEPENDENCE
 PARK INN ...................................PHILADELPHIA 353
BOXWOOD INN ....AKRON 330
BROOKVIEW MANOR BED & BREAKFAST....CANADENSIS 421
CAMERON ESTATE INN ....MOUNT JOY 348
CASHTOWN INN ....CASHTOWN 269
CHESTNUT HILL HOTEL .... GREATER PHILADELPHIA 367

HISTORICAL LODGINGS & RESTAURANTS (CONT'D)

CLASSIC VICTORIAN BED & BREAKFAST.........NAZARETH 326
CLEARVIEW FARM BED & BREAKFAST.................CLAY 332
COCALICO CREEK BED & BREAKFAST............ DENVER 332
CORNERSTONE INN BED & BREAKFAST ..... LANDENBERG 381
CRESTMONT INN ....EAGLES MERE 277
FALLS PORT INN & RESTAURANT .... HAWLEY 423
FARM FORTUNE BED &
  BREAKFAST .... NEW CUMBERLAND 327
FARMHOUSE BED & BREAKFAST .... MOUNT POCONO 426
FRANKENFIELD FARM BED & BREAKFAST .... OTTSVILLE 384
GARDENS OF EDEN BED & BREAKFAST ....LANCASTER 342
GENERAL SUTTER INN.................................LITITZ 348
GENETTI HOTEL & SUITES ...... WILLIAMSPORT 445
GETTYSTOWN INN BED & BREAKFAST ....GETTYSBURG 286
GLENDORN-A LODGE IN THE COUNTRY ....BRADFORD 263
GOLDEN OAK INN BED & BREAKFAST.................TROY 439
GOLDEN PHEASANT INN ....ERWINNA 281
HERR FARM & PUBLICK HOUSE ....GETTYSBURG 287
HISTORIC SMITHTON COUNTRY INN...........EPHRATA 333
HOLLILEIF BED & BREAKFAST ....WRIGHTSTOWN 388
INNE AT WATSON'S CHOICE....................UNIONTOWN 318
JAMES GETTYS HOTEL ....GETTYSBURG 288
LIGHTFARM ....................................KINTNERSVILLE 380
LONGSTRETCH HARBOUR BED &
  BREAKFAST .... WASHINGTON 415
MEHARD MANOR BED & BREAKFAST .... MERCER 324
MOUNTAIN VIEW BED & BREAKFAST ....DONEGAL 311
O'FLAHERTY'S DINGELDEIN HOUSE BED &
  BREAKFAST ....LANCASTER 345
OREGON BED & BREAKFAST......................LANCASTER 345
PANTALL HOTEL .... PUNXSUTAWNEY 427
PARK HYATT PHILADELPHIA AT THE
  BELLEVUE .... PHILADELPHIA 360
PENN'S VIEW HOTEL ..........................PHILADELPHIA 360
PHEASANT FIELD BED & BREAKFAST .... CARLISLE 268
PINEAPPLE HILL BED & BREAKFAST ....NEW HOPE 384
QUILL HAVEN COUNTRY INN.....................SOMERSET 317
RADISSON LACKAWANNA STATION HOTEL
  SCRANTON .... SCRANTON 433
RIDGE HOUSE ....MONTROSE 325
ROEBLING INN ON THE DELAWARE........LACKAWAXEN 424
SCARLETT HOUSE .... KENNETT SQUARE 378
SHARPE'S HOUSE BED & BREAKFAST ....TUNKHANNOCK 439
SHEARER ELEGANCE BED & BREAKFAST...........LINFIELD 381
SHIPPEN WAY INN ..............................PHILADELPHIA 361
SHULTZ VICTORIAN MANSION B & B .. CHAMBERSBURG 271
STRASBURG VILLAGE INN ....STRASBURG 351
SWATARA CREEK INN..............................ANNVILLE 257
TARA-A COUNTRY INN ....CLARK 271
TATTERSALL INN ....POINT PLEASANT 385
TEN-ELEVEN CLINTON............................PHILADELPHIA 361
THE BARNYARD INN ....ADAMSTOWN 330
THE BRAFFERTON INN ....GETTYSBURG 283
THE BRICK HOTEL ....NEWTOWN 384
THE BUCKSVILLE HOUSE ....................KINTNERSVILLE 380
THE FOX & HOUND BED & BREAKFAST OF NEW
  HOPE..NEW HOPE 383
THE GASLIGHT INN ....GETTYSBURG 286
THE HARRY PACKER MANSION .... JIM THORPE 424
THE INN AT GEORGIAN PLACE ....SOMERSET 316
THE INN AT JIM THORPE .... JIM THORPE 424
THE INN AT NEW BERLIN......................NEW BERLIN 327
THE INN AT STARLIGHT LAKE ....STARLIGHT 426
THE INN AT THE ALTLAND HOUSE .... ABBOTTSTOWN 254
THE INN ON GRANDVIEW......................ZELIENOPLE 416
THE KING'S COTTAGE ....LANCASTER 343
THE MANSION INN ....NEW HOPE 383
THE MERCERSBURG INN ....MERCERSBURG 324
THE NETHERCOTT INN B&B .... STARRUCCA 427
THE NITTANY LION INN .... STATE COLLEGE 437
THE NOON-COLLINS INN ....EBENSBURG 277

THE PRIORY-A CITY INN ....PITTSBURGH 398
THE RED POPPY BED & BREAKFAST ....BENTON 260
THE SETTLERS INN AT BINGHAM PARK .... HAWLEY 423
THE THOMAS BOND HOUSE................ PHILADELPHIA 361
THE WEDGWOOD INN ....NEW HOPE 384
TOWNE HOUSE INN ....ST. MARYS 429
TWIN TURRETS INN .... BOYERTOWN 263
VILLAGE INN OF BIRD-IN-HAND ..... BIRD-IN-HAND 331
WALNUT ST INN ..................................PHILADELPHIA 361
WAYNEBROOK INN .... HONEY BROOK 378
WYDNOR HALL INN ....BETHLEHEM 261
YE OLDE TEMPERANCE HOUSE .... NEWTOWN 384
YORKTOWNE HOTEL................................. YORK 450

RESTAURANTS

ACCOMAC INN ................................WRIGHTSVILLE 447
ALBERTO'S NEWTOWN SQUIRE.....NEWTOWN SQUARE 384
ALEXANDER DOBBIN DINING ROOMS
  IN THE DOBBIN HOUSE TAVERN ....GETTYSBURG 288
ALFRED'S VICTORIAN RESTAURANT .... MIDDLETOWN 324
ALOIS RESTAURANT ....MOUNT JOY 348
BLUE BELL INN ....BLUE BELL 375
BOILING SPRINGS TAVERN ....BOILING SPRINGS 263
BOOKBINDER'S OLD ORIGINAL .... PHILADELPHIA 362
CAB FRYE'S TAVERN................................... PALM 385
CALIFORNIA CAFE ....CARLISLE 269
CAMERON ESTATE INN RESTAURANT ....MOUNT JOY 348
CENTURY INN DINING ROOM ....SCENERY HILL 430
CHADDS FORD INN RESTAURANT ....CHADDS FORD 376
CHEZ GERARD ....HOPWOOD 313
CIBOULETTE .... PHILADELPHIA 362
D & S BRASSERIE ....LANCASTER 347
DEUX CHEMINEES .... PHILADELPHIA 363
DILWORTHTOWN INN .... WEST CHESTER 388
DISALVO'S STATION RESTAURANT ....LATROBE 313
DUFFY'S BOALSBURG TAVERN ....BOALSBURG 262
FALLS PORT INN & RESTAURANT ....HAWLEY 423
FARNSWORTH HOUSE ....GETTYSBURG 288
FOUNDER'S...PHILADELPHIA 363
GRAND CONCOURSE RESTAURANT ....PITTSBURGH 398
HAYDN ZUG'S .... EAST PETERSBURG 333
HICKORY BRIDGE FARM RESTAURANT.........ORRTANNA 329
J T'S STEAK & ALE HOUSE AT THE
  HOTEL SWITZERLAND ....JIM THORPE 424
JAMES BUCHANAN PUB &
  RESTAURANT ....MERCERSBURG 324
JOSEPHINE'S CAFE & RESTAURANT ....MARIETTA 348
KENNEDY SUPPLEE MANSION
  RESTAURANT .... KING OF PRUSSIA 380
MOUNTAIN VIEW INN .... GREENSBURG 312
PENN BREWERY RESTAURANT ....PITTSBURGH 399
RISTORANTE PANORAMA......................... PHILADELPHIA 365
SPRINGHOUSE TAVERN AT THE DOBBIN
  HOUSE..GETTYSBURG 289
THE ALTLAND HOUSE .... ABBOTTSTOWN 254
THE BACK PORCH RESTAURANT...................SPEERS 414
THE BARN RESTAURANT .... MOUNT PLEASANT 326
THE CATACOMBS ....MOUNT JOY 349
THE COMMONWEALTH ROOM .... YORK 450
THE HERR TAVERN & PUBLICK HOUSE ......GETTYSBURG 288
THE HISTORIC FAIRFIELD INN....................FAIRFIELD 281
THE HUMMINGBIRD ROOM ....SPRING MILLS 435
THE KAUFMAN HOUSE .... ZELIENOPLE 416
THE PETER HERDIC HOUSE.................WILLIAMSPORT 447
THE STONE HOUSE RESTAURANT ....CHALK HILL 311
THE STOUCH TAVERN 1785..................WOMELSDORF 447
THE SUN INN ....BETHLEHEM 261
THE TAVERN ....NEW WILMINGTON 328
TIMBERS ....MERCER 324
WAHTNEY'S INN ....EPHRATA 333

RESORTS INDEX

Many establishments are located in resort areas; however, the following places have extensive on-premises recreational facilities:

NEW JERSEY

ACCOMMODATIONS

MARRIOTT'S SEAVIEW RESORT .... ABSECON 181
THE GREAT GORGE RESORT ....VERNON 232

PENNSYLVANIA

ACCOMMODATIONS

CAESARS BROOKDALE................................ SCOTRUN 426
CAESARS COVE HAVEN RESORT .... LAKEVILLE 424

CAESARS PARADISE STREAM............. MOUNT POCONO 426
CAESARS POCONO PALACE.............. MARSHALLS CREEK 425
CLARION RESORT-THE INN AT HERITAGE HILLS ..... YORK 449
CONLEY RESORT INN..................................BUTLER 408
FERNWOOD RESORT AND
  COUNTRY CLUB ....BUSHKILL 421
HILLSIDE LODGE & RESORT .... CANADENSIS 421
HOLIDAY INN LANCASTER HOST HOTEL & CONFERENCE
  CENTER...LANCASTER 343
THE HERSHEY LODGE & CONVENTION
  CENTER ....HERSHEY 304
THE HOTEL HERSHEY ....HERSHEY 306
WILLOW VALLEY FAMILY RESORT & CONFERENCE
  CENTER...LANCASTER 345

476

When you pick up a AAA TourBook®, be alert for the establishments that display a bright red AAA logo beside their listing. These establishments place a high value on the patronage they receive from AAA members. They are telling you they're willing to go the extra mile to get your business. Some even offer special amenities designed just for you.

And don't forget to look for the

establishments that display the familiar icon to receive discounts.

So, when you turn to the AAA TourBook to make your travel plans, be on the look out for the establishments that will give you the special treatment you deserve.

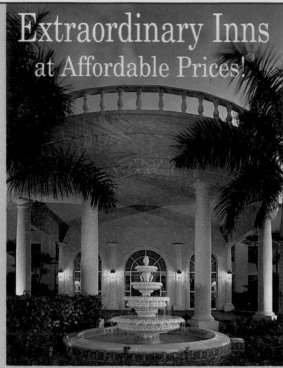